EXAMINATION GUI

HBJ CONSUMER MATHE

HBJ Consumer Mathematics is designed for high sc in a consumer mathematics course. The program is based on the latest results of research into the teaching/learning process. A problem-solving approach is used in the presentation of skills, concepts, and strategies. The textbook makes provision for students who exhibit deficiencies with essential computational skills.

CONSUMER CONCEPTS AND SKILLS

STRATEGY LESSONS

APPLICATIONS

Although the focus of the lessons in the textbook is on applications to consumer situations, the "Math In" and "Math And" Lessons illustrate additional applications of the concepts, skills, and strategies to career- and consumer-related areas (p. M-4).

DECISION MAKING

Each of Chapters 3-14 culminates with a *Consumer's Choice* lesson that is an application of the chapter content to a consumer situation that has more than one solution. Having students explore choices before making a decision simulates real-world problem solving (p. M-5).

REVIEW – MAINTENANCE – TESTING

TEACHING SUPPORT MATERIALS

Page M-1 contains a brief description of the ancillary publications that accompany the textbook. Pages M-8 through M-11 present a more detailed description, both verbally and pictorially, of these support materials. The *Overview* on pages M-12 through M-15 describes the philosophy, pedagogy, and major issues of a course in consumer mathematics and how these issues are attended to in the program.

HBJ Harcourt Brace Jovanovich, Inc.
School Department

Teacher's Edition

HBJ Consumer Mathematics

Sheldon Erickson
Russell F. Jacobs
Penny Coyne McAdoo

HBJ
Harcourt Brace Jovanovich, Publishers
Orlando San Diego Chicago Dallas

We do not include a Teacher's Edition automatically with each shipment of a classroom set of textbooks. We prefer to send a Teacher's Edition only when it is requested by the teacher or administrator concerned or by one of our representatives. A Teacher's Edition can easily be mislaid when it arrives as part of a shipment delivered to a school stockroom and since it contains answer materials, we want to be sure that it is sent directly to the person who will use it or to someone concerned with the use or selection of textbooks.

If your class assignment changes and you no longer are using or examining this Teacher's Edition, you may wish to pass it on to a teacher who has use for it.

CONTENTS

Requests for permission to make copies of any part of the work should be mailed to:
Permissions, Harcourt Brace Jovanovich, Publishers, Orlando, Florida 32887

Printed in the United States of America ISBN 0-15-353021-9

DESCRIPTION OF THE PROGRAM

Overview

Pages M-2 through M-7 describe, both verbally and pictorially, the features of the student textbook. The ancillary publications are described on pages M-8 through M-11. The *Overview: HBJ Consumer Mathematics* on pages M-12 through M-15 deals with the major issues of a course in consumer mathematics and with how these issues are attended to in the program.

Consumer Activities Workbook

This 160-page paperback contains both additional practice and enrichment. The related concrete materials are also included. It is accompanied by an annotated *Teacher's Edition.* See page M-8.

Visuals

The *Interactive Overhead Transparencies* is a boxed-set of 48 overhead transparencies that also includes a copying master version of each transparency. See page M-8.

Test Booklet

This self-cover publication contains perforated pages of the following components: *Chapter Tests: Form A, Chapter Tests: Form B,* and *Cumulative Tests.* See page M-9. The answers for these tests appear in the *Teacher's ResourceBank*™.

NOTE: The *Teacher's ResourceBank*™ contains two *Quizzes* for each chapter, as well as a copying master version of the *Test Booklet.* See page M-9.

Teacher's ResourceBank™

This 3-ring binder consists of four separate publications: *Testing Program Copying Masters, Consumer Activities Copying Masters with Answer Key, Interactive Overhead Transparencies Copying Masters,* and *Computer Activities Copying Masters with Answer Key.* Tabbed dividers, a sheet of tabs, and a sampler of the *Interactive OverheadTransparencies* are also included. See page M-9.

Annotated Teacher's Edition

The numerous aids that are provided in the margin of the annotated textbook pages are described on page M-10. The textbook page, which is reduced approximately eleven percent, contains the answers to the exercises. Answers that cannot be annotated are listed under *Additional Answers* in the margin. The *Overview* for each chapter appears on the chapter opening page along with teaching suggestions titled *Using the Page.*

Teacher's Manual

The *Lesson Resources* chart (see page M-10) contains references to the suggested activities that appear in the *Teaching Resources* on pages M-16 through M-49. (See page M-11.) This is followed by a *Pacing Chart* on page M-50. A list of suggested professional references and resources for supplementary instructional materials follows on pages M-51 through M-59.

The Lesson

The **Check Your Skills** review skills and concepts that are used in the lesson. Additional practice is provided in Appendix A. (See page M-7.)

The situation that is described on the chapter opening page is explored in each lesson of the chapter.

Tina Chavez is shopping for a new car. She sees this sticker in the window of a car she likes.

JETSTREAM ZX		BASE PRICE $7890
C/C	OPTIONS DESCRIPTION	List Price
H51	Air Conditioning	740.20
D34	Automatic transmission	460.00
G11	Tinted glass	94.80
M25	AM/FM Stereo with Cassette deck	412.50
R36	Power brakes	116.00
014	DESTINATION CHARGE	312.30

1. How much is the **destination** or **delivery charge?**

The sum of the base price, the cost of the optional equipment, and the destination charge is called the **sticker price.**

EXAMPLE 1 Find the sticker price of the Jetstream ZX.

Base Price	+	Cost of Optional Equipment	+	Destination Charge	=	Sticker Price
$7890	+	$1823.50	+	$312.30	=	**$10,025.80**

Tina knows that **sales tax** must be added to the sticker price. The state in which she lives has a sales tax rate of 6%.

2. Will 6% of $10,000 be closer to $600 or to $700?

EXAMPLE 2 Find the total cost of the Jetstream ZX.

[1] Find the amount of sales tax.

6% of $10,025.80 = 0.06 × $10,025.80
= $601.548, or **$601.55** *Rounded to the nearest cent*

[2] Find the total cost.

$10,025.80 + $601.55 = **$10,627.35** *Sticker Price + Sales Tax = Total Cost*

3. How close is the amount of sales tax in Example 2 to the estimate in Exercise 2?

126 CHAPTER 6

The questions asked in the lesson along with those provided in the Teacher's Edition (see page M-10) reflect a pedagogical approach that is concerned with understanding and not simply rote learning.

CHECK YOUR SKILLS

Estimate to determine whether the answer is reasonable.

1. $512 + $676 + $103 = $1191
2. $892 + $754 + $204 = $2050
3. $8476.39 − $3435.79 = $5040.60
4. $7506.34 − $6126.57 = $2609.77
5. $4000 − $3964.16 = $135.68
6. $7000 − $4909.82 = $2090.18

Write each decimal as a percent.

7. 6%
8. 8%
9. 4%
10. 5%
11. 9%
12. 10%

Estimate.

13. Is 9% of $20,000 closer to $1...

The **guided practice** provided by Exercises 1-3 and the non-verbal applications (Exercises 4-9 and 12-17) help to determine how well the students comprehend the concepts and skills.

or to $3500.

EXERCISES

Complete. Choose your answers from the box at the right.

1. Air conditioning and tinted glass are examples of __?__ on a new car.
2. The fee for delivering a car is called the __?__.
3. Sticker Price = __?__ + Cost of Optional Equipment + Destination Charge

base price
optional equipment
destination charge
sticker price
total cost

For Exercises 4–9, find the sticker price of each car.

	Base Price	Total Options	Destination Charge		Base Price	Total Options	Destination Charge
4.	$7950	$1430	$238.50	7.	$8342	$1619	$187.75
5.			$287.50	8.	$9998	$1735.40	

The remaining exercises provide **independent practice** on the concepts and skills.

The cost of certain optional equipment is listed below. Use these costs for Exercises 18–23.

Air Conditioning $765	AM/FM Radio $395
Automatic Transmission $675	Power Steering $290
Electric Sunroof $530	Cruise Control $200

18. Tina's cousin John wants an automatic transmission, an AM/FM radio, and power steering for his new car. Which is the best estimate of the total cost of these options?
a. $1100 b. $1250
c. $1400 d. $1500

19. Corinne wants air conditioning, cruise control, and an electric sunroof for her new car. Which is the best estimate of the total cost of these options?
a. $1400 b. $1500
c. $1600 d. $1700

20. Robert can afford to spend no more than $8000 on a new car. The car he likes has a base price of $7160 and a destination charge of $283.50. Can Robert afford air conditioning? Explain.

21. Jose is buying a car that has a base price of $9878. He wants air conditioning and power steering. The destination charge is $315.85, and the sales tax rate is 5%. Find the total cost of the car.

22. The base price of a car is $8975.

Strategy Lessons

The approach to problem solving used in the program is an application of George Polya's four-step method: **Understand, Plan, Solve,** and **Look Back** (Check).

Strategy: MAKING A MODEL

Tony wants to fence in as large a rectangular pen as possible for his dog. His father told him to use the thirty feet of fencing stored in the garage.

1. Will Tony find the perimeter or the area of the pen?
2. What must Tony find before he can determine the area of the pen?

EXAMPLE What will be the dimensions of the pen?

READ What are the facts?
The pen will be a rectangle.
The perimeter of the pen will be 30 feet.

PLAN Use graph paper to draw possible rectangles having a perimeter 30.

Think: $2\ell + 2w = 30$
$\ell + w = 15$ ◀ *One length + one width equals half the perimeter.*

SOLVE Complete the table to find the rectangle with the greatest area.

Width (ft)	Length (ft)	Perimeter (ft) $2\ell + 2w = P$	Area (ft²) $\ell \times w = A$
1	14	2 + 28 = 30	1 × 14 = 14
2	?	4 + 26 = 30	2 × 13 = 26
3	12	?	3 × ? = 36
4	?	8 + 22 = 30	?
?	10	?	5 × 10 = 50
6	9	12 + 18 = 30	?
?	8	?	7 × 8 = 56 ◀ *Greatest area: 56 ft²*

The pen with the greatest area is 7 feet wide and 8 feet long.

CHECK Did you use the facts correctly in the problem?
Is the answer reasonable?

Strategy: INTERPRETING INFORMATION

Food manufacturers often introduce new products on television commercials. Time for television commercials is usually sold in 10-second, 30-second, and 60-second intervals as follows.

Cost of 10-second commercial = $\frac{1}{2}$ × Cost of 30-second commercial
Cost of 60-second commercial = 2 × Cost of 30-second commercial

EXAMPLE The marketing manager of Ings Foods, Inc. plans to use television commercials to advertise three new soft drinks. The list at the right shows the number and length of the commercials, the showing times, and the rates for day and prime time advertising. What is the total cost?

READ What are the facts? Refer to the table.

PLAN To find the total cost, first answer these "hidden questions."
What is the cost of the 30-second commercials?
What is the cost of the 10-second commercials?

EXERCISES

1. Draw three different rectangles having a perimeter of 12 units.
   a. Find the area of each rectangle.
   b. Which rectangle has the greatest area?
2. Draw 3 different rectangles having an area of 16 square units.
   a. Find the perimeter of each rectangle.
   b. Which rectangle has the smallest perimeter?
3. Sarah plans to buy edging for the perimeter of a rectangular flower garden. The garden will have an area of 12 square yards. What are the width and length of the garden that will need the least amount of edging?

4. A vacant lot has an area of 100 square meters. It will cost the owner $15 per meter to fence in the lot. What is the least amount the owner can expect to pay for the fencing?
5. The Chung family plans to enclose 60 square feet of their back yard with a fence. What should be the length and width of the enclosed area if they want the shape to be as close to a square as possible?

For Exercises 6–9, choose a strategy from the box at the right that you can use to solve each problem.
a. Name the strategy.
b. Solve the problem.

Solving a simpler problem
Guess and check
Using estimation
More than one step

6. John is buying wallpaper and paint for his den. The total cost of both is $150. The paper costs four times as much as the paint. Find the cost of the wallpaper.
7. The perimeter of a storage room is 15.4 meters. The walls are 2.9 meters high. You compute the total area of the four walls to be 33.6 square meters. Is your answer reasonable?
8. For the first five months of the year, Alma's average electric bill was $87.40. For the next seven months, her average electric bill was $73.00. Find her average monthly electric bill for the year.
9. Roy spent $13,000 remodeling three rooms in his home. The cost of remodeling the living room was half the cost of remodeling the kitchen. The cost of remodeling the den was one-fourth the cost of remodeling the living room. How much did it cost to remodel the living room?

Selecting and Matching Strategies
Prior-taught strategies are maintained in an ongoing fashion. Students are asked to choose a strategy for solving each problem.

Applications

These lessons are applications of the skills and concepts presented in the chapter and of the strategies presented in prior chapters.

Math in/Math and
The **Math in** and **Math and** lessons illustrate applications of the content to career areas, as well as to everyday life.

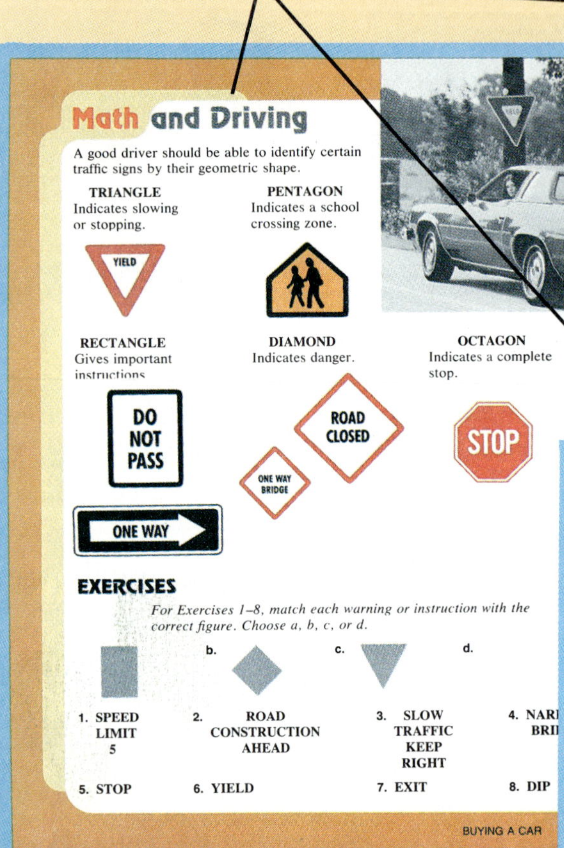

Math and Driving

A good driver should be able to identify certain traffic signs by their geometric shape.

TRIANGLE
Indicates slowing or stopping.

PENTAGON
Indicates a school crossing zone.

RECTANGLE
Gives important instructions.

DIAMOND
Indicates danger.

OCTAGON
Indicates a complete stop.

EXERCISES

For Exercises 1–8, match each warning or instruction with the correct figure. Choose a, b, c, or d.

b. c. d.

1. SPEED LIMIT 5
2. ROAD CONSTRUCTION AHEAD
3. SLOW TRAFFIC KEEP RIGHT
4. NARI BRI
5. STOP
6. YIELD
7. EXIT
8. DIP

BUYING A CAR

Math and Making Change

Susan Wiggins works at the Greenville Food Mart as a cashier. The cash register computes how much change she needs to give to each customer. Then Susan uses this rule to count out the change.

Use as few bills and as few coins as possible.

EXERCISES

Choose the best way to make change. Choose a, b, or c.

1. 

   a. Three $1-billls, 2 dimes, 1 nickel
   b. Three $1-bills, 1 quarter
   c. Two $1-bills, 5 quarters

2. 0.68 TOTAL CHANGE SUBTOTAL
   a. Two quarters, 1 dime, 1 nickel, three pennies
   b. Six dimes, 8 pennies
   c. One quarter, 4 dimes, 3 pennies

3. 6.46 TOTAL CHANGE SUBTOTAL
   a. Six $1-bills, 1 quarter, 2 dimes, 1 penny
   b. Six $1-bills, 4 dimes, 1 nickel, 1 penny
   c. One $5-bill, one $1-bill, 1 quarter,

4. 

   a. Seven quarters, 4 pennies
   b. One $1-bill, 3 quarters, 4 pennies
   c. One $1-bill, 2 quarters, 2 dimes, 9 pennies

Job Application

To apply for a job, you usually need to complete a job application. The application asks you to provide personal information, educational background, employment experience, and *references*. **References** are persons who will vouch for your character and ability.

The school librarian helped Stuart find a book about applying for a job. The book included a sample application.

EXERCISES

For Exercises 1–8, use the sample application on page 59.

1. For what job is Stuart applying?
2. What high school did Stuart attend?
3. What were Stuart's duties as a draftsman at Kelly Architectural Designs?
4. What skill does Stuart have which may help him get the job?
5. Use the information below to determine what should be written in each of the blanks labeled **A–G** on the job application.

   Stuart earned an associate's degree in architectural drafting from Parkland Vocational School located in Springfield, Illinois. He attended Parkland from August, 1986 to May, 1988.
6. Use the information below to determine what should be written in each of the blanks labeled **H–O** on the job application.

   Stuart worked as a drafting assistant at Dalton and Associates from January to August of 1986 for $4.10 per hour. His duties included running blueprints and checking them for accuracy. His supervisor was Dave Sheldon, a draftsman.
7. Why did Stuart list his job at Kelly Architectural Designs before his job at Dalton and Associates?
8. Why is it a good idea to ask for permission before listing someone as a reference?

PROJECT
a. List three businesses in your community that provide jobs for young people.
b. Pick up a job application from one of these businesses. Complete the application as if you were applying for a job.

58 CHAPTER 3

Projects
Many of these special application lessons contain **projects** that direct the student to activities outside the textbook.

Consumer's Choice

Each of the **Consumer's Choice** lessons is designed to provide material for discussion, to provide the opportunity to share ideas, and to help students recognize that there can be more than one solution to a given situation.

Each of Chapters 3-14 contains a Consumer's Choice. Each of these situational lessons presents a problem that relates directly to the focus of the chapter.

Comparing the Choices exercises are included with most lessons. These exercises are concerned with collecting facts about each listed choice.

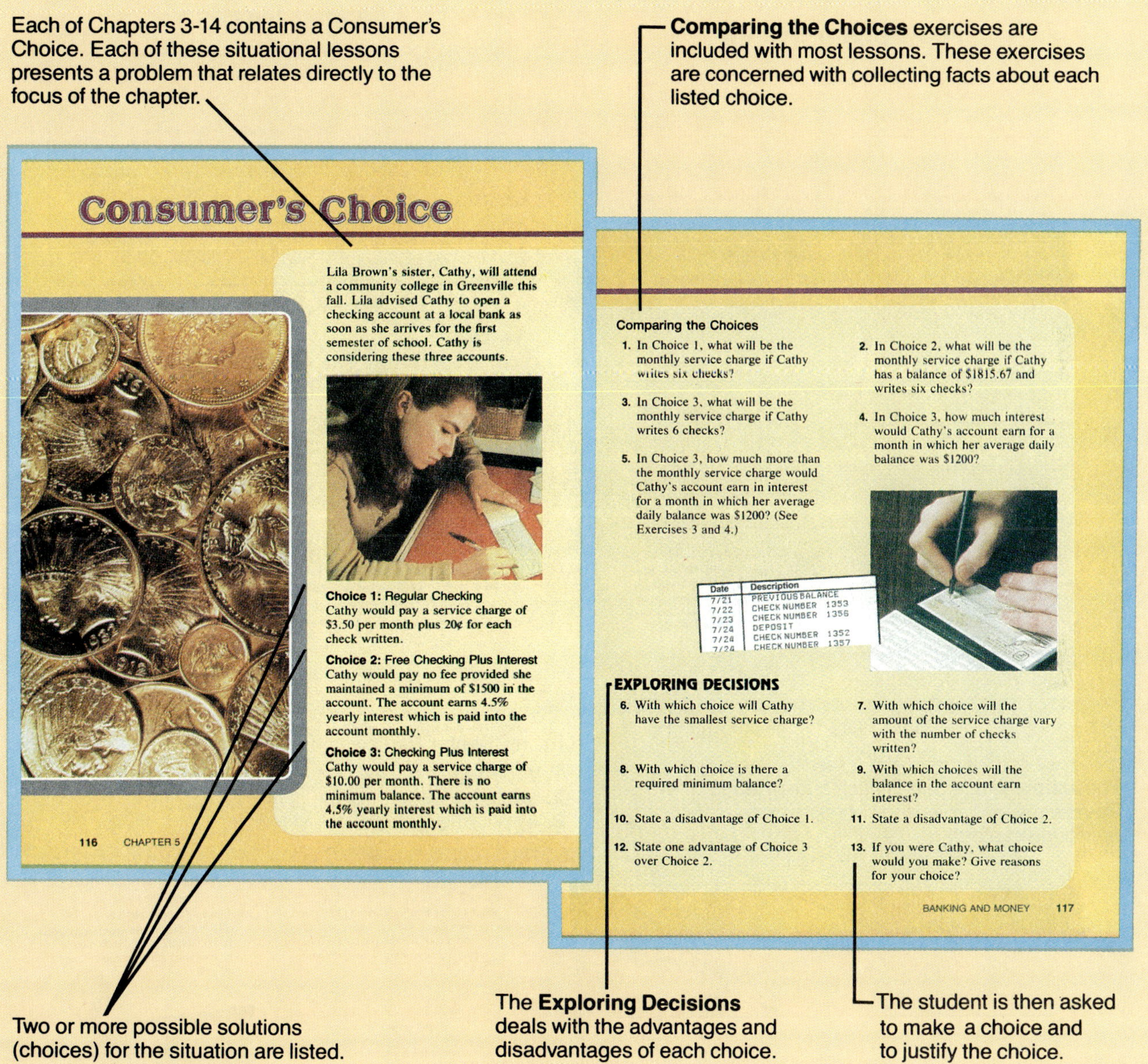

Consumer's Choice

Lila Brown's sister, Cathy, will attend a community college in Greenville this fall. Lila advised Cathy to open a checking account at a local bank as soon as she arrives for the first semester of school. Cathy is considering these three accounts.

Choice 1: Regular Checking
Cathy would pay a service charge of $3.50 per month plus 20¢ for each check written.

Choice 2: Free Checking Plus Interest
Cathy would pay no fee provided she maintained a minimum of $1500 in the account. The account earns 4.5% yearly interest which is paid into the account monthly.

Choice 3: Checking Plus Interest
Cathy would pay a service charge of $10.00 per month. There is no minimum balance. The account earns 4.5% yearly interest which is paid into the account monthly.

116 CHAPTER 5

Comparing the Choices

1. In Choice 1, what will be the monthly service charge if Cathy writes six checks?
2. In Choice 2, what will be the monthly service charge if Cathy has a balance of $1815.67 and writes six checks?
3. In Choice 3, what will be the monthly service charge if Cathy writes 6 checks?
4. In Choice 3, how much interest would Cathy's account earn for a month in which her average daily balance was $1200?
5. In Choice 3, how much more than the monthly service charge would Cathy's account earn in interest for a month in which her average daily balance was $1200? (See Exercises 3 and 4.)

EXPLORING DECISIONS

6. With which choice will Cathy have the smallest service charge?
7. With which choice will the amount of the service charge vary with the number of checks written?
8. With which choice is there a required minimum balance?
9. With which choices will the balance in the account earn interest?
10. State a disadvantage of Choice 1.
11. State a disadvantage of Choice 2.
12. State one advantage of Choice 3 over Choice 2.
13. If you were Cathy, what choice would you make? Give reasons for your choice?

BANKING AND MONEY 117

Two or more possible solutions (choices) for the situation are listed.

The **Exploring Decisions** deals with the advantages and disadvantages of each choice.

The student is then asked to make a choice and to justify the choice.

Review and Testing

Each set of exercises in the **Mid-Chapter Review** is referenced to the related pages in the chapter.

Each **Chapter Summary** consists of a listing of the important ideas that were presented in the chapter.

Mid-Chapter Review

For Exercises 1–4, find the amount of federal income tax withheld for a single wage earner. Use the table on page 70. (Pages 70–71)

	Weekly Gross Pay	Number of Exemptions
1.	$347	0
2.	$300	2

	Hours Worked Per Week	Hourly Pay	Number of Exemptions
3.	34	$9.20	2
4.	40	$6.96	1

5. Danny Curtis earned $14,482 as a delivery person last year. He also received $126.35 in interest from a savings account. Find his adjusted gross income. (Pages 72–73)

6. Laura Berryman, a single wage earner, has deductions that total $2367. Could she choose to itemize deductions? Refer to the table on page 72. (Pages 72–73)

For Exercises 7–8, find the amount of the refund or the balance due. (Pages 75–77)

7. Federal tax withheld: $2356
   Tax owed: $2792

8. Federal tax withheld: $3752
   Tax owed: $3569

MAINTENANCE

The bar graph at the right shows the number of books sold at Ted's Book Store over a six-month period. Use this graph for Exercises 9–10.

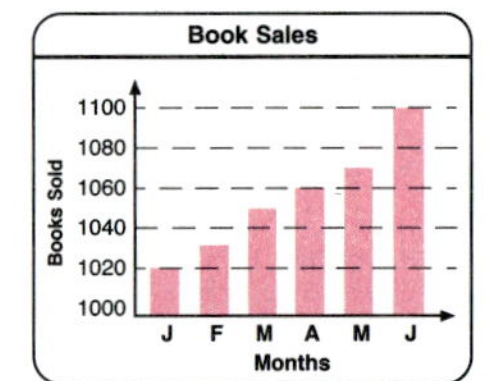

9. How many more books were sold in June than in May? (Pages 2–3)

10. Find the average number of books sold for the six months. (Pages 2–3, 10–11)

11. From a batch of light bulbs, fifty are chosen at random. Two of the fifty are found to be defective. What is the probability that a light bulb randomly chosen from the batch will be defective? (Pages 30–31)

12. Tom Baker works as a welder for $10.50 per hour. He is paid time and a half for all hours worked over 40. One week Tom worked 45 hours. Find Tom's total earnings for the week. (Pages 42–44)

78 CHAPTER 4

Chapter Summary

IMPORTANT IDEAS

1. Employees are often paid time and a half for overtime.
2. **Base Pay + Overtime Pay = Total Pay**
3. Salespersons are often paid commissions for selling a product or service.
4. **Total Sales × Rate of Commission = Commission**
5. **Net Pay = Gross Pay − Total Deductions**
6. Social Security tax is deducted from wages to provide benefits for retired workers and for disabled people and their dependents.
7. Social security benefits provide income for retired workers, for persons who become disabled, and for certain dependents of workers who die. Benefits also supplement medical costs for persons covered by Medicare.

Chapter Review

Part 1: VOCABULARY

For Exercises 1–5, choose from the box at the right the word(s) that complete(s) each statement.

1. Pay earned for working extra hours is called __?__. (Page 42)
2. When a salesperson's pay includes a percent of total sales, the amount received is called __?__. (Page 45)
3. Total earnings for a pay period is __?__. (Page 48)
4. After taxes and personal deductions are subtracted from a person's gross pay, the remaining amount is the __?__. (Page 48)
5. FICA taxes are also called __?__ taxes. (Page 48)

deductions
social security
overtime pay
net pay
taxes
gross pay
commission

MAKING MONEY 63

The **Maintenance** part of each **Mid-Chapter Review** reviews skills and concepts from previous chapters.

Each **Chapter Review** consists of
1. **Vocabulary** review
2. **Skills** review
3. **Applications** review

Note the help reference.

Part 2: SKILLS

For Exercises 6–9, find the total weekly ... paid for all hours worked over 40. (Pages 42–44)

	Hourly Pay Rate	Hours Worked	Weekly Pay
6.	$4.75	37	?
7.	$6.50	42	?

	Hourly Pay Rate	Hours Worked	Weekly Pay
8.	$8.30	46	?
9.	$7.28	32	?

For Exercises 10–15, complete each table. (Pages 45–50)

	Sales	Rate of Commission	Commission
10.	$63,500	6%	?
11.	$42,870	12%	?

	Salary	Sales	Rate of Commission	Total Earnings
12.	$325	$5680	$2\frac{1}{2}$ %	?
13.	$480	$3000	3%	?

Part 3: APPLICATIONS

23. Deanne Pendry earns $12.50 per hour for a 40-hour week with time and a half for overtime. Find her pay for a 46-hour week. (Pages 42–44)

24. Laura Yancey sold a house for $83,500. Her commission was $5\frac{1}{2}$% of the selling price. How much commission did she earn? (Pages 45–47)

25. As a computer salesperson, Kendall Davis receives a salary of $17,200 per year plus a commission of 2% on sales. Find the total earnings for a year in which his total sales amounted to $652,000. (Pages 45–47)

26. Valerie receives a 9% commission as an automobile dealer. Her total sales for a week were $39,825. Estimate the commission. (Pages 45–47)

Review and Testing

The **Cumulative Maintenance** that appears at the end of each chapter (except Chapter 1) is in a multiple-choice format.

The **Chapter Test** that follows each Chapter Review will help to prepare students for the formal Chapter Tests that are included in the *Teacher's ResourceBank*.™ See page M-9.

CHAPTER TEST

For Exercises 1–2, use the table to find the amount of federal tax withheld.

	Gross Pay	Number of Exemptions	Federal Tax
1.	$298	2	?
2.	$310	0	?

Wages		Number of exemptions claimed		
At least	But less than	0	1	2
		Amount of tax to be withheld		
$270	$280	$38	$33	$27
280	290	40	34	29
290	300	41	36	30
300	310	43	37	32
310	320	44	39	33

3. Stuart Palmer earned $11,487 last year. He received $2956.70 in tips and $94.57 in interest on a savings account. Find his adjusted gross income.

4. Julio Cortez received $15,840 in wages last year. He also received a bonus equivalent to 3% of his salary. Find his adjusted gross income.

Determine the amount of the refund or the balance due.

5. Federal tax withheld: $3196
   Tax owed: $2957

6. Federal tax withheld: $1857
   Tax owed: $1903

For Exercises 7–9, use the table at the right to find the federal income tax due.

	Taxable Income	Filing Status
7.	$15,089	Single
8.	$15,158	Head of a household
9.	$15,100	Married filing jointly

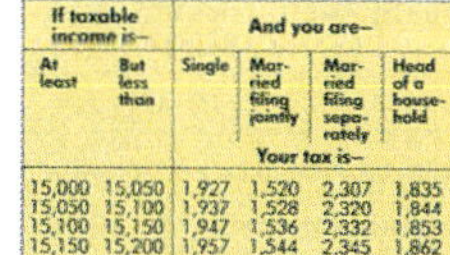

If taxable income is—		And you are—			
At least	But less than	Single	Married filing jointly	Married filing separately	Head of a household
		Your tax is—			
15,000	15,050	1,927	1,520	2,307	1,835
15,050	15,100	1,937	1,528	2,320	1,844
15,100	15,150	1,947	1,536	2,332	1,853
15,150	15,200	1,957	1,544	2,345	1,862

10. Ellen White claims 3 exemptions. Her adjusted gross income was $16,482 last year. Her deductions were $2397 for interest and $309.64 for contributions. Find the taxable income.

Write A if an exact answer ... good enough. Give a reason

12. Checking the amount of total deductions on income tax returns

92 CHAPTER 4

Cumulative Maintenance: Chapters 1–5

Choose the correct answer. Choose a, b, c, or d.

1. Find the net deposit.

		Dollars	Cents
CASH			
CHECKS	1	51	15
List	2	481	29
Each	3		
Check	4		
SUBTOTAL		?	
Less Cash Rec'd		25	00
NET DEPOSIT		?	

a. $557.44 b. $507.44
c. $532.44 d. $405.14

2. Yvonne Egbert sold a house for $121,000. Her commission was $6\frac{1}{2}$% of the selling price. How much did Yvonne earn?

a. $7865 b. $786,500
c. $78,650 d. $786.50

3. Steven Enright deposited $1500 in an account that pays 6% interest compounded quarterly. Use the compound interest table below to find the new balance after 1 year.

Total Interest	Interest Rate Per Period

4. Karen Cook's bank statement shows a balance of $319.45. She has an outstanding check for $89.75 and an outstanding deposit for $100.00. What should her adjusted check register balance be?

a. $309.20 b. $509.20
c. $329.70 d. $379.70

5. On which day were twice as many cars sold as were sold on Wednesday?

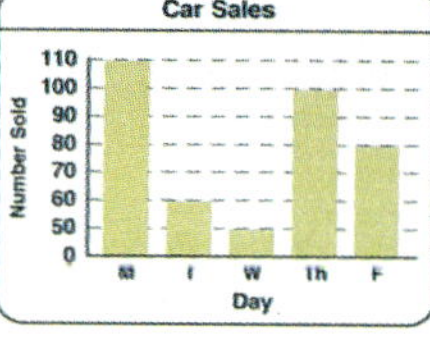

a. Monday b. Friday
c. Tuesday d. Thursday

...n apartment complex offers a new ...nant the choice of three different ...lors of carpet and two different ...allpaper designs. How many ...ssible combinations can the tenant ...oose?

b. 6
d. 5

BANKING AND MONEY 123

Rounding and Estimation

Recall the symbol ≈ means "is approximately equal to."

EXAMPLE Estimate each answer.

a. 5.89 + 3.12 **b.** 794 − 418 **c.** 59 × 71 **d.** 207.5 ÷ 28.4

Solutions:

a. Round each number to the nearest whole number.
Think: $5.89 + 3.12 \approx 6 + 3 = \mathbf{9}$

b. Round each number to the nearest hundred.
Think: $794 - 418 \approx 800 - 400 = \mathbf{400}$

c. Round each number to the nearest ten.
Think: $59 \times 71 \approx 60 \times 70 = \mathbf{4200}$

d. Round each number to the nearest ten.
Think: $207.5 \div 28.4 \approx 210 \div 30 = \mathbf{7}$

PRACTICE *Choose the best estimate. Choose a, b, or c.*

		a.	b.	c.
1.	438 + 21	430 + 20	440 + 20	440 + 30
2.	10.2 − 7.8	10 − 8	11 − 8	10 − 7
3.	22 × 49	30 × 40	30 × 50	20 × 50
4.	3.8 × 10.1	4 × 10	4 × 11	3 × 10
5.	321 ÷ 83	330 ÷ 80	320 ÷ 80	330 ÷ 90
6.	60.3 ÷ 29.8	61 ÷ 20	70 ÷ 30	60 ÷ 30

Choose the best estimate. Choose a, b, c, or d.

		a.	b.	c.	d.
7.	39 + 572	640	620	610	600
8.	14.8 + 6.75	25	22	20	18
9.	397 − 241	180	170	150	160
10.	10.3 × 28.9	500	400	300	200
11.	78 ÷ 19	2	3	5	4
12.	19.9 ÷ 1.8	15	10	5	20

380 APPENDIX A

Appendix A: Additional Practice
Pages 366-422 contain additional practice with examples as a supplement to the *Check Your Skills.* (See page M-2.)

A reference to the use of the Appendix is included as an annotation in the Teacher's Edition.

Consumer's Activities Workbook

This 160-page publication provides additional exercises and examples for each skill and strategy lesson. **Enrichment** pages are also included to extend many of the textbook lessons. See page M-11.

Each overhead transparency and each Consumer Activities Worksheet is referenced to the related textbook pages.

LIABILITY INSURANCE (Pages 135–136)

35

The table below shows sample rates for liability insurance.

Liability Insurance: Drivers 17 Years Old or Less	
Coverage	*Basic Rate*
50/100/50	$238
100/300/50	$286
250/500/50	$302

Yearly Premiums	
With Grade Average of B+ or Better	*With Grade Average Lower Than B+*
Male Basic rate × 2.16	Male Basic rate × 2.7
Female Basic rate × 1.5	Female Basic rate × 1.65

Example: Christa is 17 years old and has an A average. Find the yearly premium for liability coverage of 50/100/50.

Solution:
1. Find the rate in the table for 50/100/50 coverage. — 50/100/50 $238
2. Find the rate for a female with an A average. — Basic Rate × 1.5
3. Basic rate × 1.5 = Yearly Premium
   $238 × 1.5 = **$357**

For Exercises 1–6, use the table to compute the yearly premium.

	Coverage	*Grades of B+ or higher*	*Male/Female*	*Premium*
1.	50/100/50	Yes	Female	$357
2.	250/500/50	No	Male	$815.40
3.	100/300/50	Yes	Male	$617.76
4.	250/500/50	No	Female	$498.30
5.	50/100/50	No	Female	$392.70
6.	100/300/50	No	Male	$772.20

7. Scott Jones is 17 years old and has an A average. Find his yearly premium for 100/300/50 liability insurance coverage. **7.** $617.76

W-73

Interactive Overhead Transparencies

This boxed-set of 48 overhead transparencies also includes a copying master version for those who wish to have students work at their desks as a transparency is being shown.

38 Credit Card Statement — Page 290

Last date on which purchases are added to bill — *Last date for payments*

ACCOUNT NUMBER	BILLING DATE	DUE DATE	For bill inquiry, call (816) 430-9724
594 89 157	7–7–88	8–3–88	

DATE	STORE	REFERENCE NO.	DESCRIPTION	AMOUNT OF PURCHASE	PAYMENTS, AND CREDITS
6/19	841	379832	GARDEN SHOP	138.65	
6/30		508662	PAYMENT THANK YOU		50.00

PREVIOUS BALANCE	PAYMENTS AND CREDITS	FINANCE CHARGE BALANCE	FINANCE CHARGE	NEW BALANCE	MINIMUM PAYMENT DUE
286.44	50.00				40.00

FINANCE CHARGE IS COMPUTED AT A MONTHLY RATE (PERIODIC RATE) of 1.5% Annual percentage rate: 18%

To avoid FINANCE CHARGE next month, payment of New Balance must reach us by Due Date shown above.

Amount subject to finance charge this month.

Find the finance charge balance, the finance charge, and the new balance.

1. **Finance Charge Balance = Previous Balance − Payments**

2. **Finance Charge = Finance Charge Balance × Monthly Rate**

3. **New Balance = Finance Charge Balance + Finance Charge + Purchases**

HBJ CONSUMER MATHEMATICS

Reteaching/Alternate Teaching Strategy

The transparencies can be used when presenting the related lesson in the textbook, as an alternate teaching strategy, or for reteaching the lesson. See page M-9.

Teacher's ResourceBank™

A copying-master version of the *Consumer Activities Workbook* and the *Interactive Overhead Transparencies* is included in the *Teacher's ResourceBank*.™ See page M-9.

Teacher's ResourceBank™

This 3-ring binder consists of four separate publications and tabbed dividers.

1. *Testing Program Copying Masters*
- **a.** Quizzes (two per chapter)
- **b.** Chapter Tests: Form A
- **c.** Chapter Tests: Form B
- **d.** Cumulative Tests
- **e.** Answer Key

2. *Consumer Activities* Copying Masters *with Answer Key.* (See page M-8.)

3. *Interactive Overhead Transparencies Copying Masters* (See p. M-8.)

NOTE: The vinyl sleeve contains a sampler of the *Interactive Overhead Transparencies.*

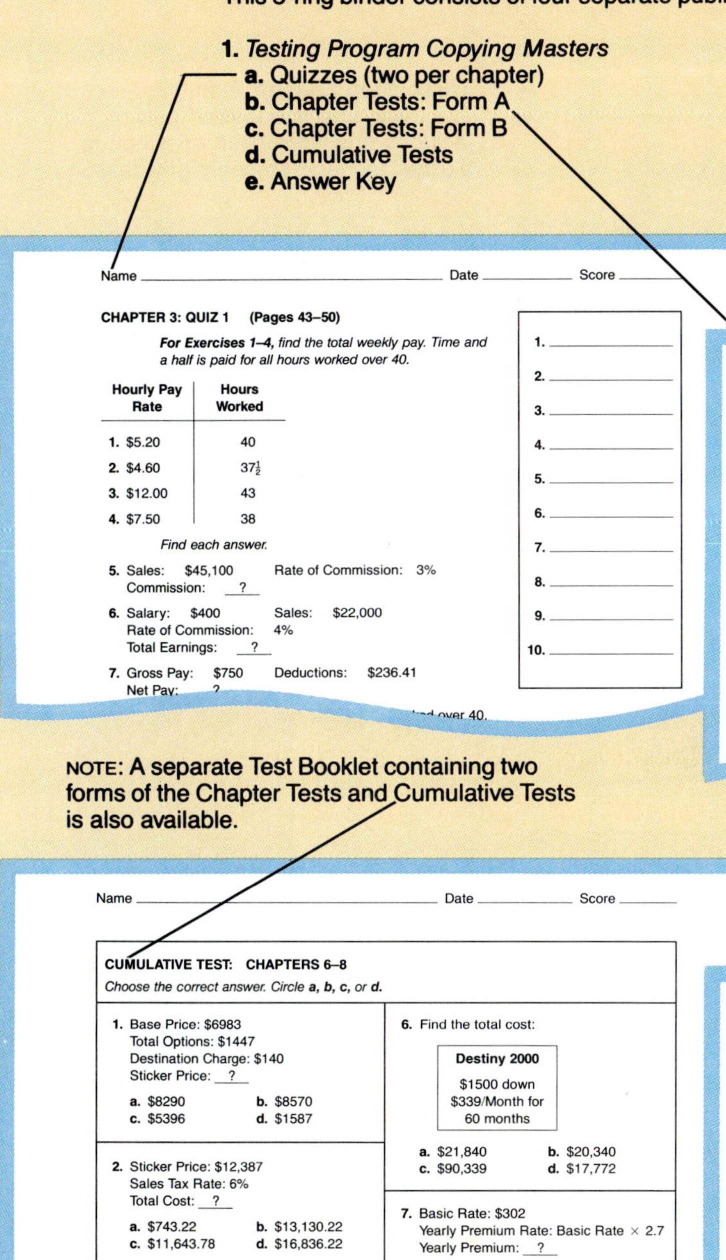

Name ______________ Date ________ Score ________

CHAPTER 3: QUIZ 1 (Pages 43–50)

For Exercises 1–4, *find the total weekly pay. Time and a half is paid for all hours worked over 40.*

	Hourly Pay Rate	Hours Worked
1.	$5.20	40
2.	$4.60	$37\frac{1}{2}$
3.	$12.00	43
4.	$7.50	38

Find each answer.

5. Sales: $45,100 Rate of Commission: 3%
Commission: ___?___

6. Salary: $400 Sales: $22,000
Rate of Commission: 4%
Total Earnings: ___?___

7. Gross Pay: $750 Deductions: $236.41
Net Pay: ?

1. ______
2. ______
3. ______
4. ______
5. ______
6. ______
7. ______
8. ______
9. ______
10. ______

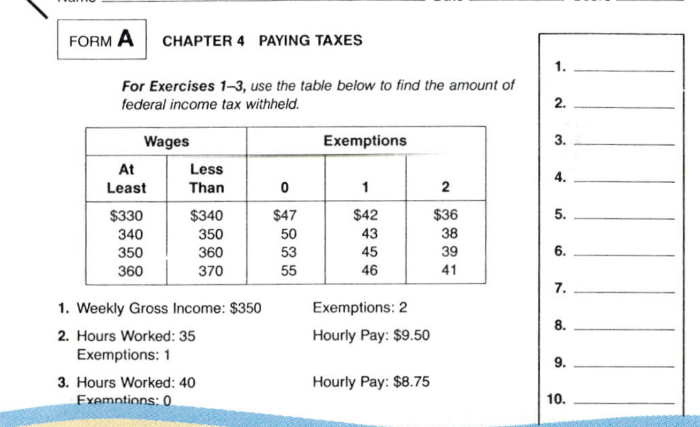

Name ______________ Date ________ Score ________

FORM **A** CHAPTER 4 PAYING TAXES

For Exercises 1–3, *use the table below to find the amount of federal income tax withheld.*

Wages		Exemptions		
At Least	Less Than	0	1	2
$330	$340	$47	$42	$36
340	350	50	43	38
350	360	53	45	39
360	370	55	46	41

1. Weekly Gross Income: $350 Exemptions: 2

2. Hours Worked: 35 Hourly Pay: $9.50
Exemptions: 1

3. Hours Worked: 40 Hourly Pay: $8.75
Exemptions: 0

1. ______
2. ______
3. ______
4. ______
5. ______
6. ______
7. ______
8. ______
9. ______
10. ______

NOTE: A separate Test Booklet containing two forms of the Chapter Tests and Cumulative Tests is also available.

Name ______________ Date ________ Score ________

CUMULATIVE TEST: CHAPTERS 6–8

Choose the correct answer. Circle ***a, b, c,*** *or* ***d.***

1. Base Price: $6983
Total Options: $1447
Destination Charge: $140
Sticker Price: ___?___

a. $8290 **b.** $8570
c. $5396 **d.** $1587

2. Sticker Price: $12,387
Sales Tax Rate: 6%
Total Cost: ___?___

a. $743.22 **b.** $13,130.22
c. $11,643.78 **d.** $16,836.22

3. Tony Balboni wants to buy a car that has a base price of $11,486. He has selected options that cost $1775. The destination charge is $259. Tony learned that the dealer pays 88% of the base price and 75% of the cost of options.

6. Find the total cost:

Destiny 2000
$1500 down
$339/Month for
60 months

a. $21,840 **b.** $20,340
c. $90,339 **d.** $17,772

7. Basic Rate: $302
Yearly Premium Rate: Basic Rate × 2.7
Yearly Premium: ___?___

a. $513.40 **b.** $310.15
c. $815.40 **d.** $8154

8. Diane Mason was in an accident in which she was at fault. The repair bill for her car was $869.75. Her collision policy had a $200 deductible. How much did the insurance company ...

4. *Computer Activities Copying Masters with Answer Key*

NOTE: No knowledge of the computer is assumed. Teaching suggestions are included for each activity.

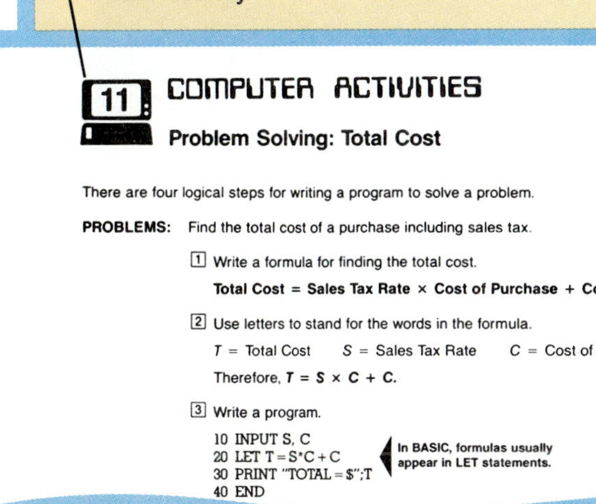

11 COMPUTER ACTIVITIES

Problem Solving: Total Cost

There are four logical steps for writing a program to solve a problem.

PROBLEMS: Find the total cost of a purchase including sales tax.

1. Write a formula for finding the total cost.

   Total Cost = Sales Tax Rate × Cost of Purchase + Cost of Purchase

2. Use letters to stand for the words in the formula.

   T = Total Cost S = Sales Tax Rate C = Cost of Purchase

   Therefore, $T = S \times C + C$.

3. Write a program.

```
10 INPUT S, C
20 LET T=S*C+C
30 PRINT "TOTAL=$";T
40 END
```

In BASIC, formulas usually appear in LET statements.

Annotated Teacher's Edition

Lesson Resources
The supplementary material that is available for the lesson is listed.

Maintenance
These exercises help to keep alive prior-taught skills and concepts.

Three-Step Lesson Plan
The **Teaching the lesson** portion includes questions (with answers) to aid the teacher in presenting the lesson.

Lesson Resources

Maintenance: See below.
Reteaching/Alternate Teaching Strategy: p. M-27 (Visual 14)
Practice: p. M-27
Enrichment: p. M-27
Concrete Materials: Activity Worksheet 27A (pages W-57 and W-58), Visual 14
Visual 14

Objectives

Student will

1. solve multi-step problems that involve completing check stubs for a checking account.
2. solve multi-step problems that involve completing check registers for a checking account.

Maintenance

Perform the indicated operations.

1. 8.09 + 13.47 + 5.86 ANS. 27.42
2. 302.4 − 275.9 ANS: 26.5
3. 1.8 × 40.3 ANS: 72.54
4. 21.5 ÷ 2.5 ANS: 8.6
5. Gary has tax deductions of $119.35 and personal deductions of $10.75. His gross pay is $487.20. Find his net pay. ANS: $357.10

1 Lesson Focus

Motivation: Ask students to focus on the check stubs in the lesson. Have students make a generalization by looking at the completed check stub: Deposits are _?_ (added) to the balance forward on a check stub, and the amount of the check written is _?_ (subtracted) from the total of the check stub.

Purpose: Point out that check registers and check stubs are necessary to keep accurate records of deposits made and checks written.

100

STRATEGY: USING "HIDDEN QUESTIONS" TO SOLVE A M

Check Stubs and Check

After opening their checking account, stubs to keep a record of deposits ma stubs also show the **balance,** or amou

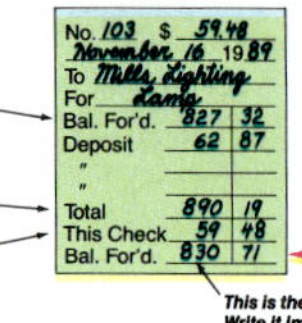

Balance brought forward from the previous check stub

Balance For'd + Deposits

Subtract from the total.

This is the Write it imm

1. What was the amount of check numb
2. To whom was check number 103 pay
3. What was the balance brought forwar number 102? $827.32
4. After writing check number 103, what account? $830.71

Many people use a **check register** rath

EXAMPLE

On December 1, Jana Cochran, a neig $362.19 in her checking account. On I for groceries at Top Market. She paid number 296. On December 10, Jana d account. Complete the check register.

100 CHAPTER 5

CHECK YOUR SKILLS

ESTIMATION/MENTAL MATH: Ex. 1–6

Estimate to determine whether the answer is reasonable. Answer Yes *or* No.

1. $554.69 + $226.85 = $781.54 Yes
2. $9.60 + $19.45 = $29.05 Yes
3. $118.40 − $72.60 = $34.50 No
4. $326.41 − $46.08 = $280.83 Yes
5. $346.15 + $39.60 = $408.21 No
6. $44.72 + $514.03 = $583.91 No

EXERCISES

Complete. Choose the answer from the box at the right.

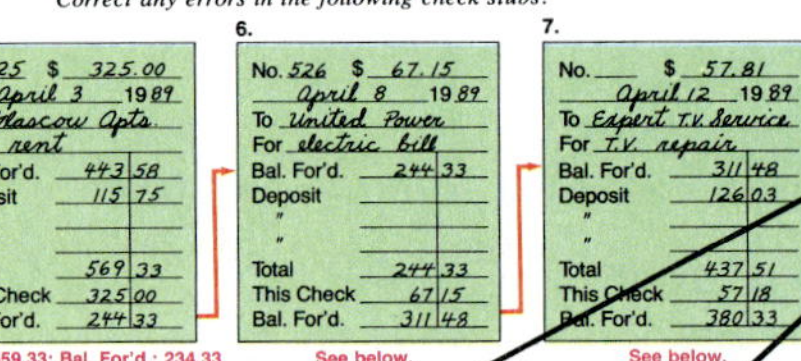

1. The amount of money in an account is called the _?_. balance
2. Total = Balance Brought Forward + _?_ deposits
3. New Balance Brought Forward = Total − _?_ check amount
4. You can use a check register to record _?_ and check amounts. deposits

Correct any errors in the following check stubs.

Total: 559.33; Bal. For'd.: 234.33 — See below. — See below.

For Exercises 8–9, copy a check stub shown on page 100. Use the information to complete the stub.

8. On November 26, the Browns had $963.95 in their checking account. Ron then made a deposit of $75.00. He also wrote check number 119 for $43.58 to Maddux Department Store for curtains. Bal. For'd. is $995.37
9. On December 10, the Browns' checking account showed a balance of $501.13. Lila then deposited checks for $35.72 and $51.69. She also wrote check number 123 for $76.79 to Lincoln Gas Company for the gas bill. Bal. For'd. is $511.75.

6. Bal. For'd.: 234.33; Total: 234.33; Bal. For'd.: 167.18
7. Bal. For'd.: 167.18; Total: 293.21; This Check: 57.81; Bal. For'd.: 236.03

BANKING AND MONEY 101

2 Teaching the Lesson

Have students read the opening paragraph. Then direct the students' attention to the check stubs on page 100 and have them answer questions 1–4. Give a more detailed explanation of the check stubs if it seems necessary. Focus students' attention on the check register on page 101. These questions could be asked.

1. What was the balance of the checking account before check 296 was written? ($362.19)
2. To whom was check 296 payable? (Top Market)
3. What transaction occured on 12/10? (A deposit of $143.85 was made.)
4. Why are the transactions of 12/2 and 12/10 written in different columns? (On a check register, different columns are used for payments and deposits.)

3 Close

Summary: Ask students to explain in their own words the importance of keeping accurate records for a checking account.

Evaluation
Guided Practice: Ex. 1–5
Independent Practice: Ex. 6, 8–15

Extension

Organize students in groups and have each group make a list of at least five errors that might occur when completing a check stub or register.

Problem-Solving Skills

Solving a multi-step problem (Ex. 8–9, 13)
Working backwards (Ex. 12–13)
Using logical reasoning (Ex. 14)

Critical Thinking

You may wish to have students work in small groups to solve this problem or you may wish to work with the class.
Ex. 15

101

Guided Practice and Independent Practice
The exercises designed for guided practice and independent practice are clearly identified.

Extension
Suggestions for extension and projects are included where appropriate.

Problem-Solving Skills
This item identifies the problem-solving skills that are used to solve the indicated problems.

Critical Thinking
The exercises that relate to improving higher level thinking skills are identified for the teacher.

Teaching Resources

The *Teaching Resources* portion of the *Teacher's Manual* (see pages M-16–M-49) includes teaching suggestions and references to copying master that are included in the *Teacher's ResourceBank*.™

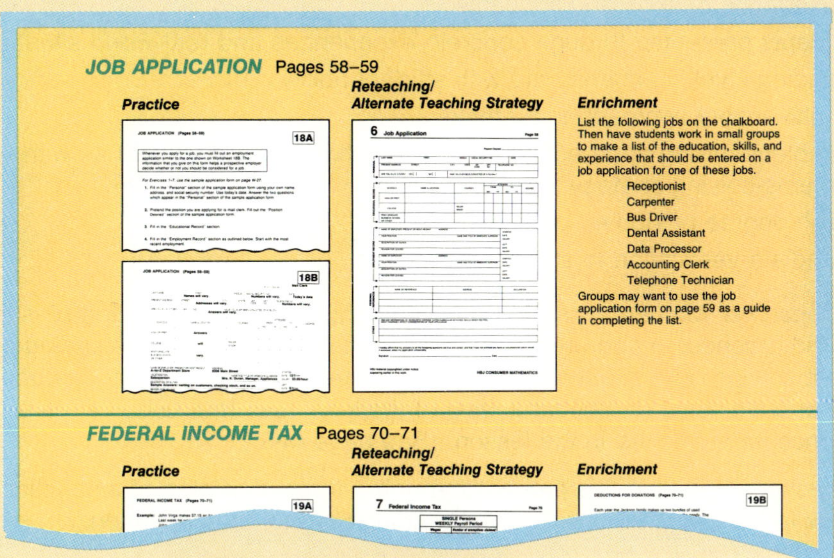

JOB APPLICATION Pages 58–59

Practice	Reteaching/ Alternate Teaching Strategy	Enrichment
18A, 18B	6 Job Application	List the following jobs on the chalkboard. Then have students work in small groups to make a list of the education, skills, and experience that should be entered on a job application for one of these jobs. Receptionist, Carpenter, Bus Driver, Dental Assistant, Data Processor, Accounting Clerk, Telephone Technician. Groups may want to use the job application form on page 59 as a guide in completing the list.

FEDERAL INCOME TAX Pages 70–71

Practice	Reteaching/ Alternate Teaching Strategy	Enrichment
19A	7 Federal Income Tax	19B

Enrichment: Student Textbook
In addition to the suggestions for enrichment included in the *Teaching Resources,* each chapter contains an Enrichment lesson. The term *Enrichment* only appears in the Teacher's Edition for these lessons.

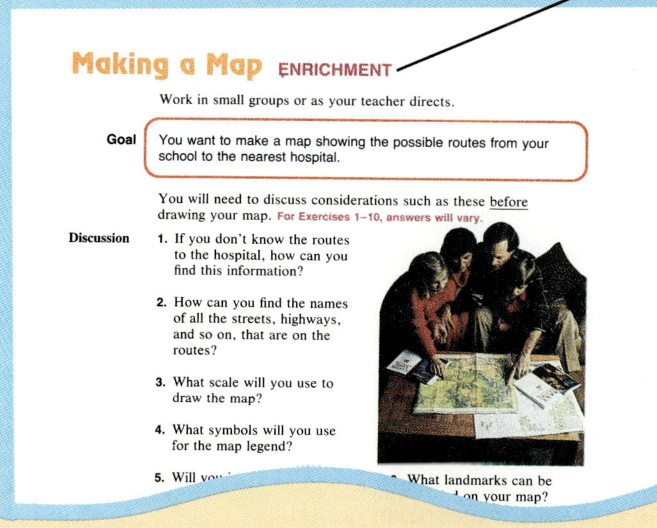

Making a Map ENRICHMENT

Work in small groups or as your teacher directs.

Goal You want to make a map showing the possible routes from your school to the nearest hospital.

You will need to discuss considerations such as these before drawing your map. For Exercises 1–10, answers will vary.

Discussion

1. If you don't know the routes to the hospital, how can you find this information?
2. How can you find the names of all the streets, highways, and so on, that are on the routes?
3. What scale will you use to draw the map?
4. What symbols will you use for the map legend?

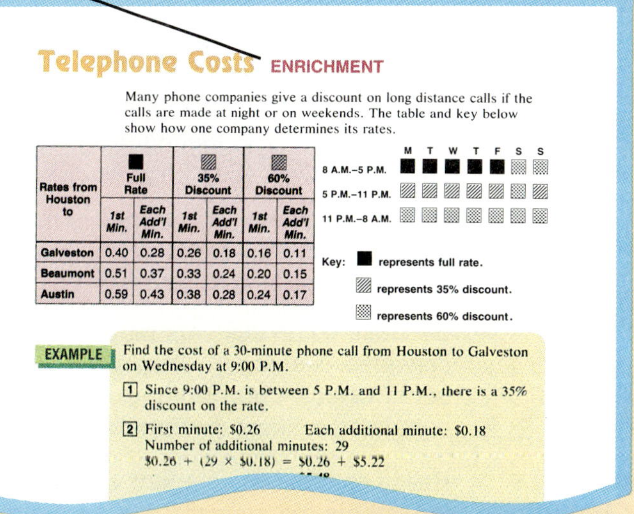

Telephone Costs ENRICHMENT

Many phone companies give a discount on long distance calls if the calls are made at night or on weekends. The table and key below show how one company determines its rates.

Rates from Houston to	Full Rate 1st Min.	Full Rate Each Add'l Min.	35% Discount 1st Min.	35% Discount Each Add'l Min.	60% Discount 1st Min.	60% Discount Each Add'l Min.
Galveston	0.40	0.28	0.26	0.18	0.16	0.11
Beaumont	0.51	0.37	0.33	0.24	0.20	0.15
Austin	0.59	0.43	0.38	0.28	0.24	0.17

Key: ■ represents full rate.
▨ represents 35% discount.
▨ represents 60% discount.

EXAMPLE Find the cost of a 30-minute phone call from Houston to Galveston on Wednesday at 9:00 P.M.

1. Since 9:00 P.M. is between 5 P.M. and 11 P.M., there is a 35% discount on the rate.
2. First minute: $0.26 Each additional minute: $0.18
Number of additional minutes: 29
$\$0.26 + (29 \times \$0.18) = \$0.26 + \$5.22$

OVERVIEW: HBJ CONSUMER MATHEMATICS

Philosophy

HBJ Consumer Mathematics is organized around the latest results of research into the teaching/learning process. Investigations reveal that students learn more efficiently and retain longer when the following elements are present in daily classroom instruction.

- Maintenance of skills and concepts
- Concepts presented through concrete experiences and real-world situations
- A reading level commensurate with student ability
- A multisensory approach to learning
- A problem-solving approach in the presentation of skills as well as with problems-solving strategy lessons
- A high degree of student participation
- Immediate verification to student responses

Pedagogy

HBJ Consumer Mathematics places less emphasis on memorization of isolated facts and procedures and greater emphasis on conceptual understanding and problem solving. The questions that appear with each lesson in the textbook are aimed at developing an understanding of the key ideas that underlie the skills and concepts presented in the lesson. (See page M-2.)

The teacher is aided in this process through a three-step plan of instruction that appears in the margin of the *Teacher's Edition* of the related lesson:

Focus **Teaching the Lesson** **Close**

The *Teaching the Lesson* portion includes questions (with answers) that the teacher can use in strengthening this problem-solving process approach to instruction. These questions can be used to provide informal assessment on a daily basis. (See page M-10.)

Exercises

The heart of a mathematics textbook is the exercises. In *HBJ Consumer Mathematics,* the first set of exercises for most lessons is concerned with new terms and expressions presented in the lesson. In these exercises, the student is asked to select the term or expression that best completes each sentence. This completion-type format has proven to be very successful because it places the emphasis on understanding. These exercises form the cornerstone for guided practice. (See page M-2)

In *HBJ Consumer Mathematics,* the Exercises for a typical lesson consist of a variety of different types which measure the student's understanding of underlying skills and concepts.

Because some students may be deficient in the prerequisite skills for the consumer lessons in Chapters 3–14, most lessons in these chapters contain a set of **Check Your Skills** exercises. (See page M-2.) These exercises are correlated to the **Additional Practice** that is included in *Appendix A.*

Estimation/ Mental Math

Estimation lessons present various strategies that are then maintained throughout the program. Mental math strategies and exercises are, in general, integrated with the work on estimation.

Critical Thinking

The Exercises for most lessons also contain problems that encourage students to think. Because these critical thinking exercises are clearly identified in the *Teacher's Edition,* the teacher may choose to deal with them as a classroom activity and not assign them for homework. (See page M-10.)

Cooperative Learning

The exercises that deal with critical thinking lend themselves well to **cooperative learning groups.** Recent studies suggest that cooperative learning promotes greater achievement. The basis elements of cooperative learning are:

- Positive interdependence and desire to succeed together
- Face-to-face interaction with peers
- Appropriate use of interpersonal and small-group skills
- Individual accountability

In a small group (about four students), each student has an opportunity to speak, ask questions, and discuss problems with other students. Concepts that some students have difficulty in comprehending in a traditional classroom setting are often clarified by the members of the group. In establishing cooperative learning groups, you may wish initially to select each member of the group in a random fashion. As you become more familiar with your students, you will be in a position to "balance" each group. It is important that each member of the group has a specific responsibility, such as recorder, chairperson, and the like. Each student's role and responsibility should also change each time this mode of instruction is used.

HBJ Consumer Mathematics contains numerous opportunities for structuring cooperative learning groups:

- Critical Thinking exercises
- Problem-Solving Strategy lessons
- Projects
- Situational lessons
- Enrichment
- Math In and Math And lessons
- Consumer's Choice

The *Teacher's Edition* also contains suggested extension activities and projects that lend themselves to this approach to instruction.

For more information, use the two titles outlined by Johnson and Johnson listed on page M-74.

Problem Solving

The plan provided for solving problems in *HBJ Consumer Mathematics* is modeled after the steps recommended by the late George Polya.

Polya's Steps in Problem Solving

1. Understanding the problem (**Read**)
2. Devising a plan (**Plan**)
3. Carrying out the plan (**Solve**)
4. Looking back (**Check**)

A list of the problem-solving strategies used in the text is shown on the next page.

Problem Solving Strategies

Choosing computation methods	Predicting
Finding a pattern	Selecting and matching
Guess and check	Solving a simpler problem
Interpreting graphs	Using a map
Interpreting information	Using a drawing
Making a map	Using estimation
Making a model	Using formulas
More than one step	Using mental computation
Organizing data	Using patterns

The **Teaching the Lesson** step for strategy lessons provides a guided trace of the problem-solving process for the Example in the lesson or for one of the problems in the Exercises. This trace contains questions (with answers) that are designed to illustrate the application of the Polya approach.

Concrete Materials

Research has shown that students can move toward the abstract representation of a concept when they have internalized the concept through the use of concrete materials. The content of a viable course in consumer mathematics provides a natural setting for the use of concrete materials. *HBJ Consumer Mathematics* provides two types of concrete materials.

The *Teacher's ResourceBank™* includes a copying master version of the **Consumer's Activities Workbook** that contains the essential hands-on material, such as deposit slips, check registers, utility bills, invoice forms, and so on. (See page M-8.)

The *Teacher's ResourceBank™* also contains a copying master version of the *Interactive Overhead Transparencies.* Providing each student with a copy of the transparency being presented allows the student to be an active participant when this visual mode of instruction is used either in conjunction with the related textbook lesson or as an alternate teaching strategy. (See page M-8.)

Situational Lessons

Each chapter opener presents a situation that relates directly to the lessons that will then explore the situation presented in the chapter opener. Teaching suggestions are included in the *Teacher's Edition.*

Each of Chapters 3–14 contains a **Consumer's Choice** lesson that presents a situation with more than one solution. Having students explore these choices before making a decision is a simulation of real-world problem solving (See page M-5.)

Lesson Resources

A **Lesson Resource chart** is included in the *Teacher's Edition* for each skill and strategy lesson. This chart lists all the materials that are provided in the *Teacher's Edition* and in the *Teacher's ResourceBank™* for these lessons. (See page M-10.)

Maintenance

In addition to the **Chapter Summary, Chapter Review,** and **Chapter Test** for each chapter, a list of those "tools" designed to maintain skills, concepts, and strategies in a mixed practice setting is given on the next page.

Check Your Skills (See page M-2.)
Mid-Chapter Review/Maintenance (See page M-6.)
Selecting and Matching Strategies (See page M-3.)
Cumulative Maintenance (See page M-7.)
Maintenance in Teacher's Edition (See page M-10.)

Assessment

The program provides a variety of ways for assessing students' learning. The questions included within each lesson coupled with the questions included in the **Teaching the Lesson** in the *Teacher's Edition* provide an effective method for assessing students' learning on a daily basis.

The *Interactive Overhead Transparencies Copying Masters* in the *Teacher's ResourceBank*™ provide a second method of assessment. (See page M-8.)

The **Close** step in the three–step lesson plan and the exercises that are identified for guided practice provide an excellent strategy for assessing students' learning.

The *Testing Program Copying Masters* in the *Teacher's ResourceBank*™ provide a complete method for assessing achievement. (See page M-9.)

Other situations that can be used for assessing students' understanding of problem solving strategies are included in the textbook. Most of the strategy lessons include a set of problems that ask the student to **select and match** strategies to given situations. (See page M-3.)

Technology

The use of the calculator has been integrated into the program as a problem solving tool. To further assist the student with the use of the calculator, a calculator manual is included in the back of the student textbook.

The *Computer Activities Copying Masters* in the *Teacher's ResourceBank*™ provide a resource of computer activities that do not assume any background or knowledge of the computer.

Enrichment/ Extension

Each chapter in the textbook culminates with an **Enrichment** lesson or activity. (See page M-11). In addition, suggestions for enrichment for a given lesson are included in the **Lesson Resource Chart.**

Projects that direct students to activities outside the textbook are included in each chapter. Additional suggestions for extension are included in the *Teacher's Edition.*

TEACHING RESOURCES

The *Teaching Resources* on pages M-16 through M-49 contain suggestions for practice, reteaching/alternate teaching strategies, and enrichment for most lessons. The worksheets that are suggested for practice and enrichment are included in the *Consumer Activities Copying Masters with Answer Key* section of the *Teacher's ResourceBank*™. The visuals that are suggested for the reteaching/alternate teaching strategies appear in the *Interactive Overhead Transparencies Copying Masters* section of the *Teacher's ResourceBank*™.

BAR GRAPHS AND THE CONSUMER Pages 2–3

Practice

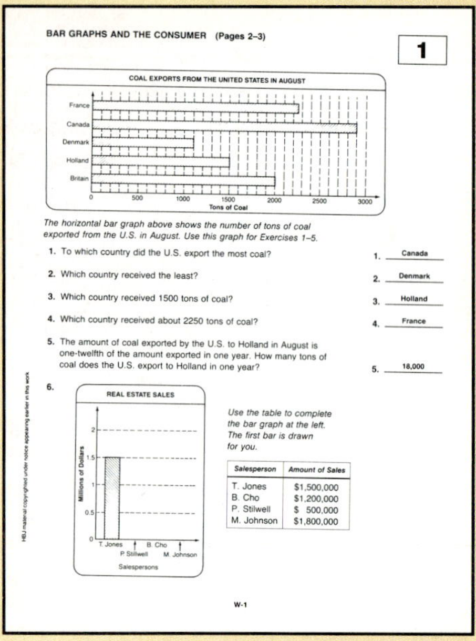

BAR GRAPHS AND THE CONSUMER (Pages 2–3) **1**

COAL EXPORTS FROM THE UNITED STATES IN AUGUST

France, Canada, Denmark, Holland, Britain

0 500 1000 1500 2000 2500 3000
Tons of Coal

The horizontal bar graph above shows the number of tons of coal exported from the U.S. in August. Use this graph for Exercises 1–5.

1. To which country did the U.S. export the most coal? 1. Canada
2. Which country received the least? 2. Denmark
3. Which country received 1500 tons of coal? 3. Holland
4. Which country received about 2250 tons of coal? 4. France
5. The amount of coal exported by the U.S. to Holland in August is one-twelfth of the amount exported in one year. How many tons of coal does the U.S. export to Holland in one year? 5. 18,000
6. REAL ESTATE SALES

Use the table to complete the bar graph at the left. The first bar is drawn for you.

Salesperson	Amount of Sales
T. Jones	$1,500,000
B. Cho	$1,200,000
P. Stilwell	$ 500,000
M. Johnson	$1,800,000

Millions of Dollars; Salespersons

W-1

HBJ material copyrighted under notice appearing earlier in this work

Reteaching/ Alternate Teaching Strategy

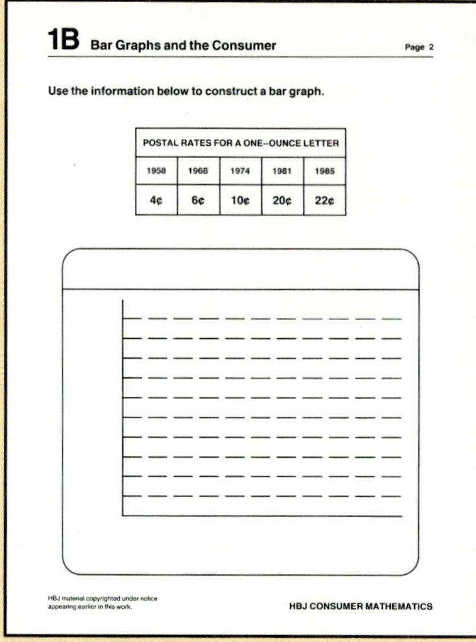

1B Bar Graphs and the Consumer — Page 2

Use the information below to construct a bar graph.

POSTAL RATES FOR A ONE-OUNCE LETTER				
1958	1968	1974	1981	1985
4¢	6¢	10¢	20¢	22¢

HBJ material copyrighted under notice appearing earlier in this work.

HBJ CONSUMER MATHEMATICS

Enrichment

Materials: graph paper, reference books

Let students use almanacs or other reference books to find the distance in miles (nearest million) from the sun to each of these planets.

Mercury — Jupiter
Earth — Uranus
Mars

Then have them make a bar graph to show this data. Tell them that they can include other planets if they wish. Remind them to choose an appropriate scale.

(**Ans:** Mercury: **36,** Earth: **93,** Mars: **142,** Jupiter: **484,** Uranus: **1781**)

LINE GRAPHS AND THE CONSUMER Pages 4–5

Practice

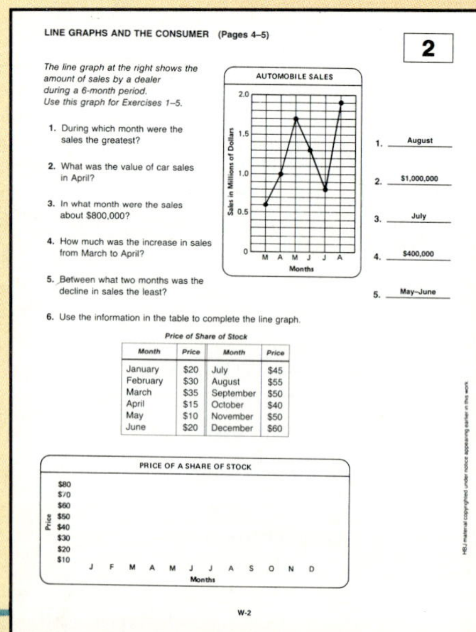

LINE GRAPHS AND THE CONSUMER (Pages 4–5) **2**

The line graph at the right shows the amount of sales by a dealer during a 6-month period. Use this graph for Exercises 1–5.

AUTOMOBILE SALES

Sales in Millions of Dollars; Months: M A M J J A

1. During which month were the sales the greatest? 1. August
2. What was the value of car sales in April? 2. $1,000,000
3. In what month were the sales about $800,000? 3. July
4. How much was the increase in sales from March to April? 4. $400,000
5. Between what two months was the decline in sales the least? 5. May–June
6. Use the information in the table to complete the line graph.

Price of Share of Stock

Month	Price	Month	Price
January	$20	July	$45
February	$30	August	$55
March	$35	September	$50
April	$15	October	$40
May	$10	November	$50
June	$20	December	$60

PRICE OF A SHARE OF STOCK

Price: $80 $70 $60 $50 $40 $30 $20 $10
Months: J F M A M J J A S O N D

W-2

HBJ material copyrighted under notice appearing earlier in this work

Reteaching/ Alternate Teaching Strategy

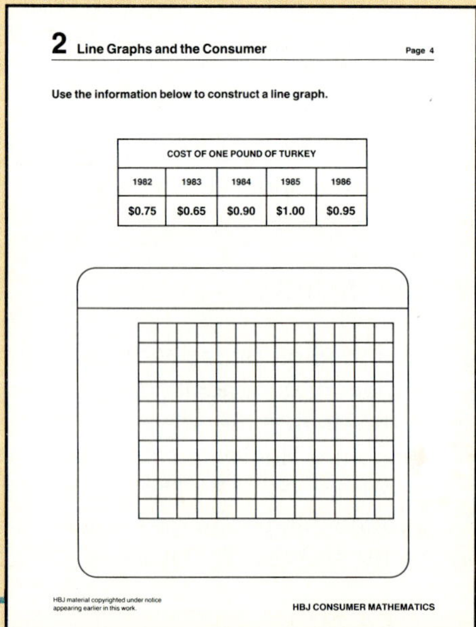

2 Line Graphs and the Consumer — Page 4

Use the information below to construct a line graph.

COST OF ONE POUND OF TURKEY				
1982	1983	1984	1985	1986
$0.75	$0.65	$0.90	$1.00	$0.95

HBJ material copyrighted under notice appearing earlier in this work.

HBJ CONSUMER MATHEMATICS

Enrichment

Materials: local newspapers

Have students record the average temperature, the high temperature, and the low temperature in their town every day for a week. At the end of the week, have students make a line graph showing those temperatures for each day. Ask some of the following questions. On which day was the average temperature the highest? On which day was it the lowest? What was the high temperature for the week? What was the low temperature for the week?

CIRCLE GRAPHS AND THE CONSUMER Pages 6–7

Practice

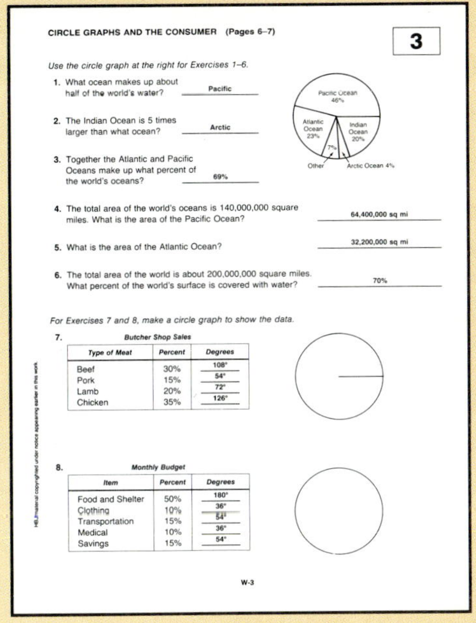

CIRCLE GRAPHS AND THE CONSUMER (Pages 6–7) **3**

Use the circle graph at the right for Exercises 1–6.

1. What ocean makes up about half of the world's water? Pacific
2. The Indian Ocean is 5 times larger than what ocean? Arctic
3. Together the Atlantic and Pacific Oceans make up what percent of the world's oceans? 69%
4. The total area of the world's oceans is 140,000,000 square miles. What is the area of the Pacific Ocean? 64,400,000 sq mi
5. What is the area of the Atlantic Ocean? 32,200,000 sq mi
6. The total area of the world is about 200,000,000 square miles. What percent of the world's surface is covered with water? 70%

Pacific Ocean 46%
Atlantic Ocean 23%
Indian Ocean 20%
7%
Other
Arctic Ocean 4%

For Exercises 7 and 8, make a circle graph to show the data.

7. *Butcher Shop Sales*

Type of Meat	Percent	Degrees
Beef	30%	108°
Pork	15%	54°
Lamb	20%	72°
Chicken	35%	126°

8. *Monthly Budget*

Item	Percent	Degrees
Food and Shelter	50%	180°
Clothing	10%	36°
Transportation	15%	54°
Medical	10%	36°
Savings	15%	54°

W-3

Reteaching/ Alternate Teaching Strategy

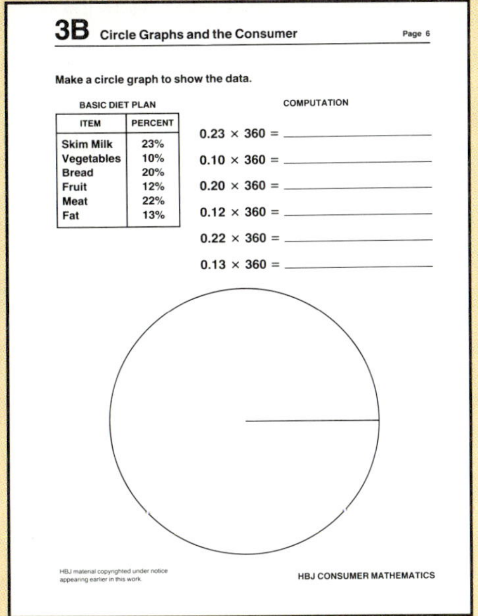

3B Circle Graphs and the Consumer Page 6

Make a circle graph to show the data.

BASIC DIET PLAN

ITEM	PERCENT
Skim Milk	23%
Vegetables	10%
Bread	20%
Fruit	12%
Meat	22%
Fat	13%

COMPUTATION

$0.23 \times 360 =$ ______
$0.10 \times 360 =$ ______
$0.20 \times 360 =$ ______
$0.12 \times 360 =$ ______
$0.22 \times 360 =$ ______
$0.13 \times 360 =$ ______

HBJ CONSUMER MATHEMATICS

Enrichment

Have students work in pairs to conduct an investigation. Instruct them to stand at a window by a fairly busy street and note the colors of the cars that pass by. They can keep a record of 100 cars that are blue, white, red, green or yellow. Demonstrate the use of tally marks if needed.

Have students convert their figures into percents. In a follow-up discussion, encourage students to share their results. Work together to create a circle graph.

THE MEAN AND THE MODE Pages 10–11

Practice

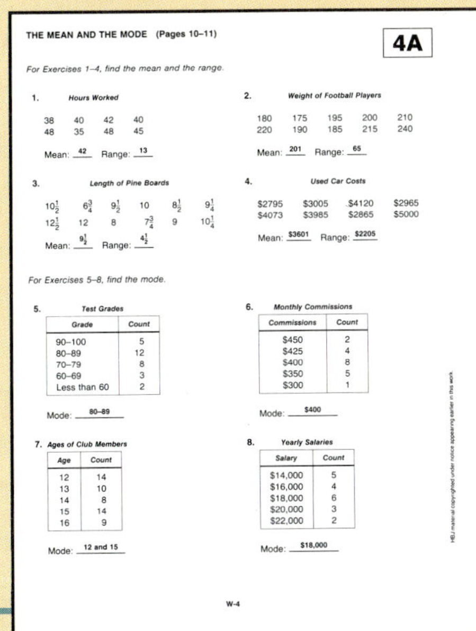

THE MEAN AND THE MODE (Pages 10–11) **4A**

For Exercises 1–4, find the mean and the range.

1. *Hours Worked*

38 40 42 40
48 35 48 45

Mean: 42 Range: 13

2. *Weight of Football Players*

180 175 195 200 210
220 190 185 215 240

Mean: 201 Range: 65

3. *Length of Pine Boards*

$10\frac{1}{2}$ $6\frac{3}{4}$ $9\frac{1}{2}$ 10 $8\frac{1}{2}$ $9\frac{1}{4}$
$12\frac{1}{2}$ 12 8 $7\frac{3}{4}$ 9 $10\frac{1}{4}$

Mean: $9\frac{1}{2}$ Range: $4\frac{1}{2}$

4. *Used Car Costs*

$2795 $3005 $4120 $2965
$4073 $3985 $2865 $5000

Mean: $3601 Range: $2205

For Exercises 5–8, find the mode.

5. *Test Grades*

Grade	Count
90–100	5
80–89	12
70–79	8
60–69	3
Less than 60	2

Mode: 80–89

6. *Monthly Commissions*

Commissions	Count
$450	2
$425	4
$400	8
$350	5
$300	1

Mode: $400

7. *Ages of Club Members*

Age	Count
12	14
13	10
14	8
15	14
16	9

Mode: 12 and 15

8. *Yearly Salaries*

Salary	Count
$14,000	5
$16,000	4
$18,000	6
$20,000	3
$22,000	2

Mode: $18,000

W-4

Reteaching/ Alternate Teaching Strategy

MATERIALS: 10 index cards for each pair of students

Write each score on an index card: 1, 2, 2, 3, 4, 4, 4, 5, 5, and 6. Shuffle the cards and deal them all out to two players. Each player finds the range of his or her scores and records that number. Reshuffle the cards and deal them out again. This time each player finds the mode of his or her scores and records that number. Repeat the procedure again, this time having the students find the mean of the scores.

The winner is the player with the higher total of the 3 results.

Enrichment

Have students match each list of numbers with the mean.

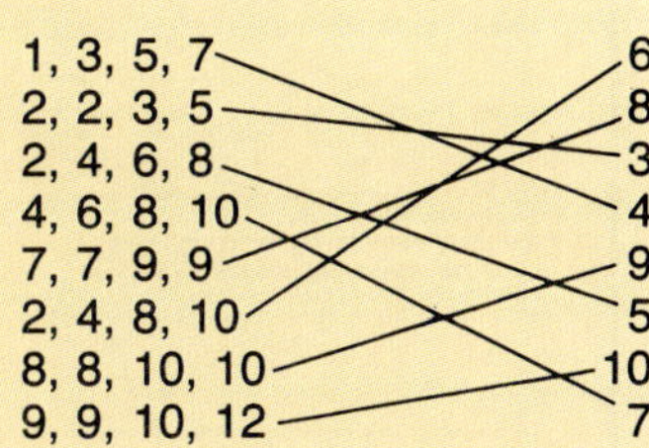

THE MEDIAN Pages 12–13

Practice

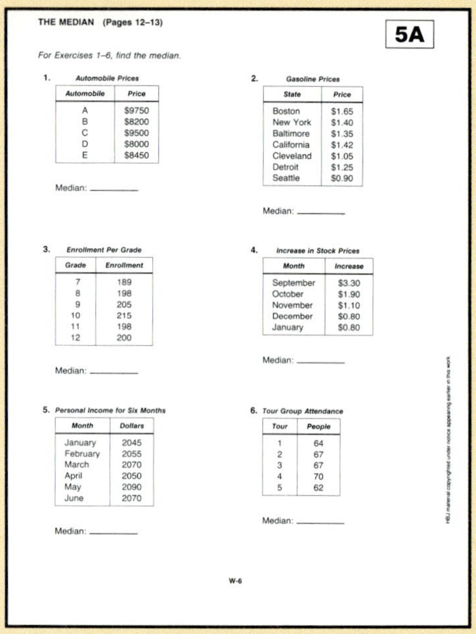

THE MEDIAN (Pages 12–13) **5A**

For Exercises 1–6, find the median.

1. *Automobile Prices*

Automobile	Price
A	$9750
B	$8200
C	$9500
D	$8000
E	$8450

Median: ________

2. *Gasoline Prices*

State	Price
Boston	$1.65
New York	$1.40
Baltimore	$1.35
California	$1.42
Cleveland	$1.05
Detroit	$1.25
Seattle	$0.90

Median: ________

3. *Enrollment Per Grade*

Grade	Enrollment
7	189
8	198
9	205
10	215
11	198
12	200

Median: ________

4. *Increase in Stock Prices*

Month	Increase
September	$3.30
October	$1.90
November	$1.10
December	$0.80
January	$0.80

Median: ________

5. *Personal Income for Six Months*

Month	Dollars
January	2045
February	2055
March	2070
April	2050
May	2090
June	2070

Median: ________

6. *Tour Group Attendance*

Tour	People
1	64
2	67
3	67
4	70
5	62

Median: ________

W-6

Reteaching/ Alternate Teaching Strategy

Have students match each list of numbers with the median.

28, 35, 38, 45, 50 — 38
25, 27, 29, 34 — 28
30, 35, 40 — 35
15, 17, 19, 22, 25, 26, 32 — 22
18, 23, 27, 35 — 25
43, 49, 51, 55, 56 — 51
32, 48, 49, 53, 55, 58, 60 — 53
45, 47, 53, 62 — 50

Enrichment

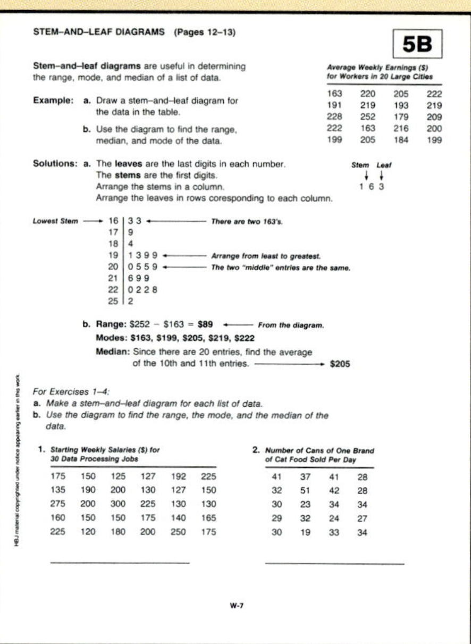

STEM-AND-LEAF DIAGRAMS (Pages 12–13) **5B**

Stem-and-leaf diagrams are useful in determining the range, mode, and median of a list of data.

Average Weekly Earnings ($) for Workers in 20 Large Cities

163	220	205	222
191	219	193	219
228	252	179	209
222	163	216	200
199	205	184	199

Example: a. Draw a stem-and-leaf diagram for the data in the table.

b. Use the diagram to find the range, median, and mode of the data.

Solutions: a. The **leaves** are the last digits in each number. The **stems** are the first digits. Arrange the stems in a column. Arrange the leaves in rows coresponding to each column.

Stem Leaf: 16 3

Lowest Stem → 16 | 3 3 ← *There are two 163's.*
17 | 9
18 | 4
19 | 1 3 9 9 ← *Arrange from least to greatest.*
20 | 0 5 5 9 ← *The two "middle" entries are the same.*
21 | 6 9 9
22 | 0 2 2 8
25 | 2

b. **Range:** $252 − $163 = **$89** ← *From the diagram.*
Modes: $163, $199, $205, $219, $222
Median: Since there are 20 entries, find the average of the 10th and 11th entries. → **$205**

For Exercises 1–4:
a. *Make a stem-and-leaf diagram for each list of data.*
b. *Use the diagram to find the range, the mode, and the median of the data.*

1. *Starting Weekly Salaries ($) for 30 Data Processing Jobs*

175	150	125	127	192	225
135	190	200	130	127	150
275	200	300	225	130	130
160	150	150	175	140	165
225	120	180	200	250	175

2. *Number of Cans of One Brand of Cat Food Sold Per Day*

41	37	41	28
32	51	42	28
30	23	34	34
29	32	24	27
30	19	33	34

W-7

TREE DIAGRAMS/THE COUNTING PRINCIPLE Pages 22–23

Practice

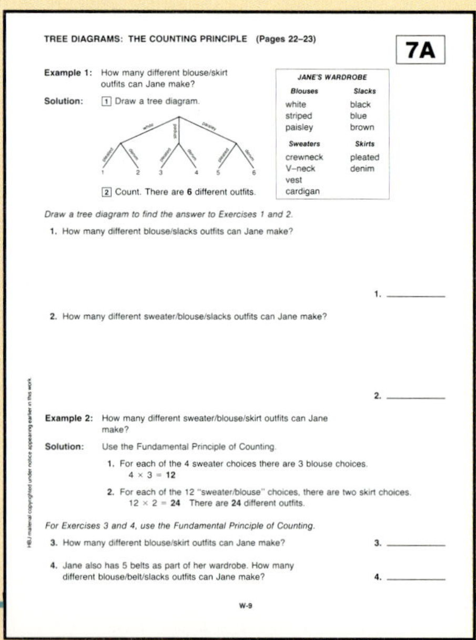

TREE DIAGRAMS: THE COUNTING PRINCIPLE (Pages 22–23) **7A**

Example 1: How many different blouse/skirt outfits can Jane make?

Solution: [1] Draw a tree diagram.

[2] Count. There are **6** different outfits.

JANE'S WARDROBE

Blouses	*Slacks*
white	black
striped	blue
paisley	brown
Sweaters	***Skirts***
crewneck	pleated
V-neck	denim
vest	
cardigan	

Draw a tree diagram to find the answer to Exercises 1 and 2.

1. How many different blouse/slacks outfits can Jane make? 1. ________

2. How many different sweater/blouse/slacks outfits can Jane make? 2. ________

Example 2: How many different sweater/blouse/skirt outfits can Jane make?

Solution: Use the Fundamental Principle of Counting.

1. For each of the 4 sweater choices there are 3 blouse choices. $4 \times 3 = \mathbf{12}$

2. For each of the 12 "sweater/blouse" choices, there are two skirt choices. $12 \times 2 = \mathbf{24}$ There are **24** different outfits.

For Exercises 3 and 4, use the Fundamental Principle of Counting.

3. How many different blouse/skirt outfits can Jane make? 3. ________

4. Jane also has 5 belts as part of her wardrobe. How many different blouse/belt/slacks outfits can Jane make? 4. ________

W-9

Reteaching/ Alternate Teaching Strategy

A number cube and a coin are tossed. Complete the tree diagram to find the number of different possible combinations.

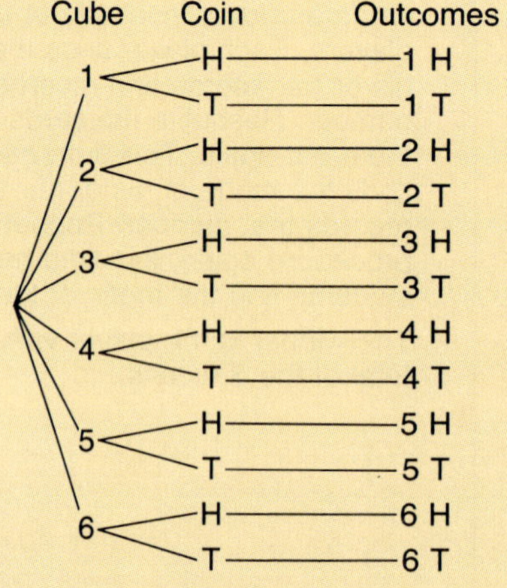

Enrichment

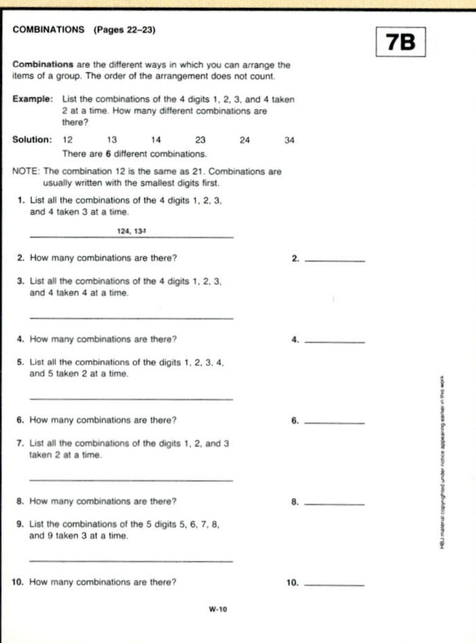

COMBINATIONS (Pages 22–23) **7B**

Combinations are the different ways in which you can arrange the items of a group. The order of the arrangement does not count.

Example: List the combinations of the 4 digits 1, 2, 3, and 4 taken 2 at a time. How many different combinations are there?

Solution: 12 13 14 23 24 34
There are **6** different combinations.

NOTE: The combination 12 is the same as 21. Combinations are usually written with the smallest digits first.

1. List all the combinations of the 4 digits 1, 2, 3, and 4 taken 3 at a time.
124, 134
2. How many combinations are there? 2. ________
3. List all the combinations of the 4 digits 1, 2, 3, and 4 taken 4 at a time.
4. How many combinations are there? 4. ________
5. List all the combinations of the digits 1, 2, 3, 4, and 5 taken 2 at a time.
6. How many combinations are there? 6. ________
7. List all the combinations of the digits 1, 2, and 3 taken 2 at a time.
8. How many combinations are there? 8. ________
9. List the combinations of the 5 digits 5, 6, 7, 8, and 9 taken 3 at a time.
10. How many combinations are there? 10. ________

W-10

PERMUTATIONS Pages 24–25

Practice

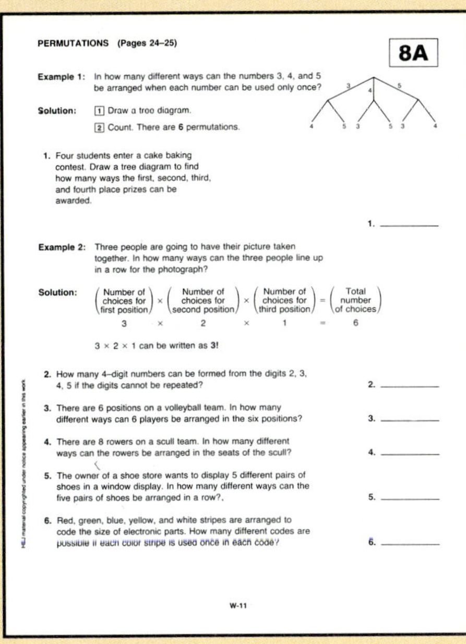

PERMUTATIONS (Pages 24–25)

8A

Example 1: In how many different ways can the numbers 3, 4, and 5 be arranged when each number can be used only once?

Solution: [1] Draw a tree diagram.

[2] Count. There are **6** permutations.

1. Four students enter a cake baking contest. Draw a tree diagram to find how many ways the first, second, third, and fourth place prizes can be awarded. 1. ______

Example 2: Three people are going to have their picture taken together. In how many ways can the three people line up in a row for the photograph?

Solution: (Number of choices for first position) × (Number of choices for second position) × (Number of choices for third position) = (Total number of choices)

3 × 2 × 1 = 6

3 × 2 × 1 can be written as **3!**

2. How many 4–digit numbers can be formed from the digits 2, 3, 4, 5 if the digits cannot be repeated? 2. ______
3. There are 6 positions on a volleyball team. In how many different ways can 6 players be arranged in the six positions? 3. ______
4. There are 8 rowers on a scull team. In how many different ways can the rowers be arranged in the seats of the scull? 4. ______
5. The owner of a shoe store wants to display 5 different pairs of shoes in a window display. In how many different ways can the five pairs of shoes be arranged in a row?. 5. ______
6. Red, green, blue, yellow, and white stripes are arranged to code the size of electronic parts. How many different codes are possible if each color stripe is used once in each code? 6. ______

W-11

Reteaching/ Alternate Teaching Strategy

Have students draw pictures to solve the following problems. Have them check by multiplying.

Three people line up at the teacher's desk for help. In how many different ways can they line up? **(ANS: 6)**

Four students want to sit in the 4 chairs at the front of the classroom. In how many different ways can they be seated? **(ANS: 24)**

Two people want to use the same piece of chalk at the chalkboard. In how many different orders can they use the chalk? **(ANS: 2)**

Enrichment

PERMUTATIONS (Pages 24–25)

8B

Permutations can be found using the following formula:

$_nP_r = \frac{n!}{(n-r)!}$ — n represents the number of objects. r represents the number taken at a time.

Example: Find the number of possible permutations of 4 letters taken 2 at a time.

Solution: $_4P_2 = \frac{4!}{(4-2)!} = \frac{4!}{2!} = \frac{4 \times 3 \times \overset{1}{2} \times 1}{\underset{1}{2} \times 1} = 12$

Use the formula to find the number of permutations for Exercises 1–5. Show the entire calculation.

1. $_5P_2$ ______
2. $_7P_4$ ______
3. $_6P_2$ ______
4. $_6P_3$ ______
5. $_{10}P_2$ ______

Five people get on a bus. There are 4 empty seats. In how many ways can 4 of the 5 people arrange themselves in the 4 seats?

6. Write the formula for the number of permutations. 6. ______
7. Solve the formula. Show the entire calculation.

$_5P_4 = \frac{5!}{(5-4)!} = \frac{5!}{1!} = \frac{5 \times 4 \times 3 \times 2 \times 1}{1} = 120$

A group of 6 men are on a bowling team. In how many ways can 4 of the 6 men arrange themselves for a tournament?

8. Write the formula for the number of permutations. 8. ______
9. Solve the formula. Show the entire calculation.

W-12

PROBABILITY Pages 26–27

Practice

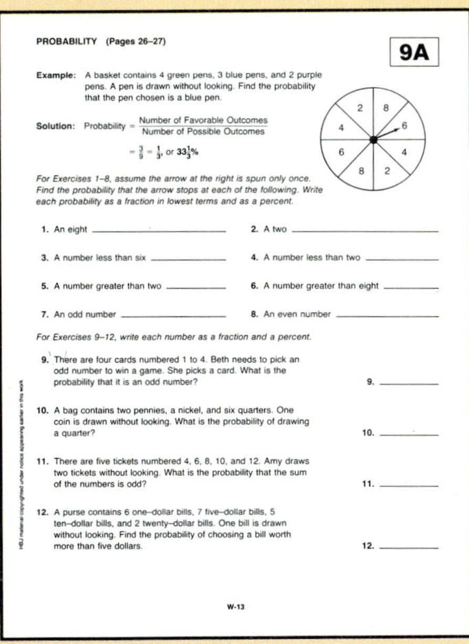

PROBABILITY (Pages 26–27)

9A

Example: A basket contains 4 green pens, 3 blue pens, and 2 purple pens. A pen is drawn without looking. Find the probability that the pen chosen is a blue pen.

Solution: Probability = $\frac{\text{Number of Favorable Outcomes}}{\text{Number of Possible Outcomes}}$

$= \frac{3}{9} = \frac{1}{3}$, or $33\frac{1}{3}\%$

For Exercises 1–8, assume the arrow at the right is spun only once. Find the probability that the arrow stops at each of the following. Write each probability as a fraction in lowest terms and as a percent.

1. An eight ______
2. A two ______
3. A number less than six ______
4. A number less than two ______
5. A number greater than two ______
6. A number greater than eight ______
7. An odd number ______
8. An even number ______

For Exercises 9–12, write each number as a fraction and a percent.

9. There are four cards numbered 1 to 4. Beth needs to pick an odd number to win a game. She picks a card. What is the probability that it is an odd number? 9. ______
10. A bag contains two pennies, a nickel, and six quarters. One coin is drawn without looking. What is the probability of drawing a quarter? 10. ______
11. There are five tickets numbered 4, 6, 8, 10, and 12. Amy draws two tickets without looking. What is the probability that the sum of the numbers is odd? 11. ______
12. A purse contains 6 one–dollar bills, 7 five–dollar bills, 5 ten–dollar bills, and 2 twenty–dollar bills. One bill is drawn without looking. Find the probability of choosing a bill worth more than five dollars. 12. ______

W-13

Reteaching/ Alternate Teaching Strategy

Materials: 1 white, 3 red, 4 blue, 2 yellow marbles; 1 jar for each group of 5 students

Have students work in groups of five. They should determine the probability of each of the following events.

- picking a red marble **(ANS: $\frac{3}{10}$)**
- picking a blue marble **(ANS: $\frac{2}{5}$)**
- picking a marble that is not white **(ANS: $\frac{9}{10}$)**
- picking a marble that is not blue **(ANS: $\frac{3}{5}$)**

Then students should pick marbles from their jars and record the results. Each student can have two turns. How closely do the results match the probabilities?

Enrichment

CONDITIONAL PROBABILITY (Pages 26–27)

9B

When performing a probability experiment, conditions are sometimes changed so that some information concerning the outcome is known. This is known as **conditional probability.**

Example: What is the probability that a die will land on a 2 if you know it will land on a number less than or equal to 3?

Solution: Possible Outcomes: **3 2 1**
Thus, (P)2 = $\frac{1}{3}$

For Exercises 1–10, use the cards below to find the conditional probability.

Blue 1	Blue 2	Blue 3	Green 1	Green 2	Red 1	Red 2	Red 1	Red 3	Red 3

1. What is the probability of a 1 if you know the card is not green? 1. ______
2. What is the probability of a 3 if you know the card is not blue? 2. ______
3. What is the probability of a 2 if you know the card is not red? 3. ______
4. What is the probability of a 1 if you know the card is not red? 4. ______
5. What is the probability of a 3 if you know the card is not red? 5. ______
6. What is the probability of a 2 if you know the card is not green? 6. ______
7. What is the probability of a red card if you know the card is not a 1? 7. ______
8. What is the probability of a blue card if you know the card is not a 2? 8. ______
9. What is the probability of a green card if you know the card is not a 2? 9. ______
10. What is the probability of a red card if you know the card is not a 3? 10. ______

W-14

WHAT ARE THE ODDS? Pages 32–33

Practice

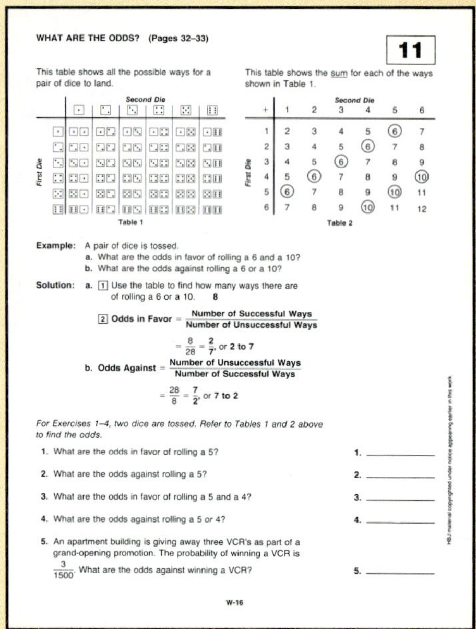

WHAT ARE THE ODDS? (Pages 32–33) **11**

This table shows all the possible ways for a pair of dice to land.

First Die \ Second Die	⚀	⚁	⚂	⚃	⚄	⚅
⚀	⚀⚀	⚀⚁	⚀⚂	⚀⚃	⚀⚄	⚀⚅
⚁	⚁⚀	⚁⚁	⚁⚂	⚁⚃	⚁⚄	⚁⚅
⚂	⚂⚀	⚂⚁	⚂⚂	⚂⚃	⚂⚄	⚂⚅
⚃	⚃⚀	⚃⚁	⚃⚂	⚃⚃	⚃⚄	⚃⚅
⚄	⚄⚀	⚄⚁	⚄⚂	⚄⚃	⚄⚄	⚄⚅
⚅	⚅⚀	⚅⚁	⚅⚂	⚅⚃	⚅⚄	⚅⚅

Table 1

This table shows the sum for each of the ways shown in Table 1.

+ (First Die \ Second Die)	1	2	3	4	5	6
1	2	3	4	5	(6)	7
2	3	4	5	(6)	7	8
3	4	5	(6)	7	8	9
4	5	(6)	7	8	9	(10)
5	(6)	7	8	9	(10)	11
6	7	8	9	(10)	11	12

Table 2

Example: A pair of dice is tossed.
a. What are the odds in favor of rolling a 6 and a 10?
b. What are the odds against rolling a 6 or a 10?

Solution: a. [1] Use the table to find how many ways there are of rolling a 6 or a 10. **8**

[2] Odds in Favor $= \frac{\text{Number of Successful Ways}}{\text{Number of Unsuccessful Ways}}$

$= \frac{8}{28} = \frac{2}{7}$, or **2 to 7**

b. Odds Against $= \frac{\text{Number of Unsuccessful Ways}}{\text{Number of Successful Ways}}$

$= \frac{28}{8} = \frac{7}{2}$, or **7 to 2**

For Exercises 1–4, two dice are tossed. Refer to Tables 1 and 2 above to find the odds.

1. What are the odds in favor of rolling a 5? 1. ______
2. What are the odds against rolling a 5? 2. ______
3. What are the odds in favor of rolling a 5 and a 4? 3. ______
4. What are the odds against rolling a 5 *or* 4? 4. ______
5. An apartment building is giving away three VCR's as part of a grand-opening promotion. The probability of winning a VCR is $\frac{3}{1500}$. What are the odds against winning a VCR? 5. ______

W-16

Reteaching/ Alternate Teaching Strategy

A reteaching lesson can be structured for this topic by having students supply the concrete materials. These concrete materials then would be the basis for the lesson.

Have each student bring to class a milk bottle cap. Number the bottle caps 1 through the total number of caps.

Then have students pick one cap at random from a box. Next, have the student calculate the odds of picking a second cap at random with a higher number and one with a lower number.

Enrichment

The line graph shows the probability that two persons in a group will have the same birthday.
Have students use the graph and calculate the odds for a birthday match in your class. Then record all birthdays on the chalkboard to see if a match does occur.

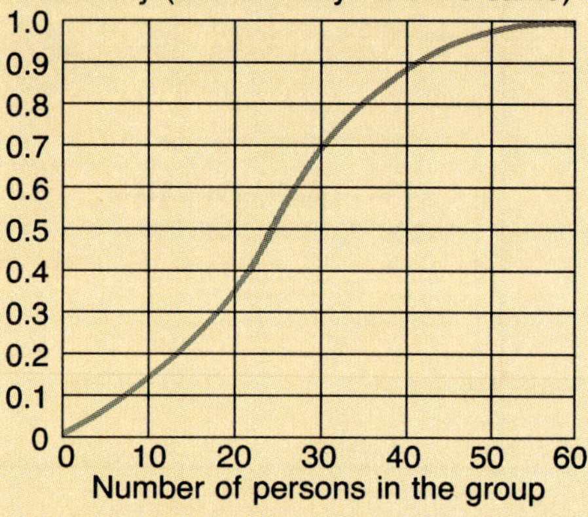

HOURLY WAGES Pages 42–44

Practice

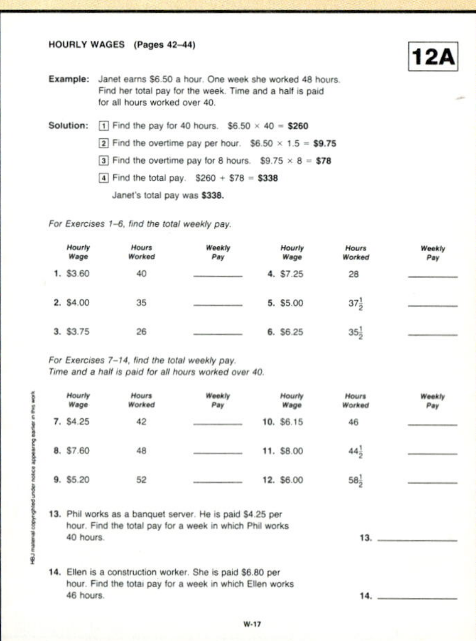

HOURLY WAGES (Pages 42–44) **12A**

Example: Janet earns $6.50 a hour. One week she worked 48 hours. Find her total pay for the week. Time and a half is paid for all hours worked over 40.

Solution: [1] Find the pay for 40 hours. $6.50 × 40 = **$260**
[2] Find the overtime pay per hour. $6.50 × 1.5 = **$9.75**
[3] Find the overtime pay for 8 hours. $9.75 × 8 = **$78**
[4] Find the total pay. $260 + $78 = **$338**
Janet's total pay was **$338.**

For Exercises 1–6, find the total weekly pay.

	Hourly Wage	Hours Worked	Weekly Pay		Hourly Wage	Hours Worked	Weekly Pay
1.	$3.60	40	______	4.	$7.25	28	______
2.	$4.00	35	______	5.	$5.00	$37\frac{1}{2}$	______
3.	$3.75	26	______	6.	$6.25	$35\frac{1}{2}$	______

For Exercises 7–14, find the total weekly pay. Time and a half is paid for all hours worked over 40.

	Hourly Wage	Hours Worked	Weekly Pay		Hourly Wage	Hours Worked	Weekly Pay
7.	$4.25	42	______	10.	$6.15	46	______
8.	$7.60	48	______	11.	$8.00	$44\frac{1}{2}$	______
9.	$5.20	52	______	12.	$6.00	$58\frac{1}{2}$	______

13. Phil works as a banquet server. He is paid $4.25 per hour. Find the total pay for a week in which Phil works 40 hours. 13. ______
14. Ellen is a construction worker. She is paid $6.80 per hour. Find the totai pay for a week in which Ellen works 46 hours. 14. ______

W-17

Reteaching/ Alternate Teaching Strategy

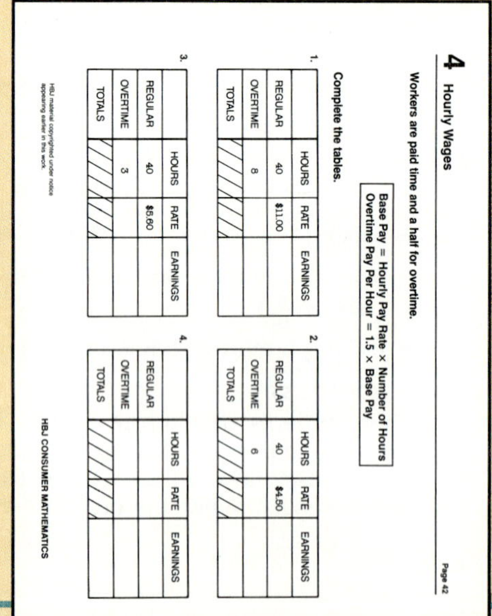

4 Hourly Wages

Workers are paid time and a half for overtime.

Base Pay = Hourly Pay Rate × Number of Hours
Overtime Pay Per Hour = 1.5 × Base Pay

Complete the tables.

1.

	HOURS	RATE	EARNINGS
REGULAR	40	$11.00	
OVERTIME	8		
TOTALS			

2.

	HOURS	RATE	EARNINGS
REGULAR	40	$4.80	
OVERTIME	6		
TOTALS			

3.

	HOURS	RATE	EARNINGS
REGULAR	40	$5.60	
OVERTIME	3		
TOTALS			

4.

	HOURS	RATE	EARNINGS
REGULAR			
OVERTIME			
TOTALS			

HBJ CONSUMER MATHEMATICS

Page 42

Enrichment

TIME CARDS (Pages 42–44) **12B**

Complete each time card to find the GROSS PAY. Time and a half is paid for all hours worked over 40 hours. The first time card is begun for you.

1.

DAYS	IN	OUT	IN	OUT	DAILY TOTALS
1	7:00	12:00	1:00	3:30	7.5
2	7:00	1:00	2:00	5:00	9
3	7:30	12:30	1:30	5:30	9
4	7:00	1:00	3:00	5:00	8
5	7:00	12:00	1:00	3:30	7.5

REGULAR	OVERTIME	RATE	GROSS PAY
40	1	$7.50	$311.25

2.

DAYS	IN	OUT	IN	OUT	DAILY TOTALS
1	8:00	12:00	1:00	3:30	6.5
2	8:30	12:30	1:00	3:30	6.5
3	8:00	1:00	2:00	4:00	7
4	8:30	1:00	1:30	5:00	8
5	8:00	12:00	1:00	4:00	7

REGULAR	OVERTIME	RATE	GROSS PAY
35	0	$11.40	$399.00

3.

DAYS	IN	OUT	IN	OUT	DAILY TOTALS
1	9:00	12:00	1:00	8:00	10
2	9:00	12:30	1:30	7:00	9
3	9:00	1:00	2:00	6:30	8.5
4	7:30	11:30	12:30	6:30	10
5	8:00	1:00	2:00	6:00	9

REGULAR	OVERTIME	RATE	GROSS PAY
40	6.5	$6.00	$298.50

4.

DAYS	IN	OUT	IN	OUT	DAILY TOTALS
1	8:30	12:00	1:00	5:30	8
2	9:00	12:00	2:00	7:00	8
3	9:00	12:30	1:30	6:30	8.5
4	7:45	1:00	1:30	6:15	10
5	8:15	12:15	1:15	5:15	8

REGULAR	OVERTIME	RATE	GROSS PAY
40	2.5	$4.60	$201.25

5.

DAYS	IN	OUT	IN	OUT	DAILY TOTALS
1	8:00	12:00	1:00	4:30	7.5
2	8:30	12:30	2:00	5:00	7
3	8:30	12:30	1:30	5:00	7.5
4	8:00	12:00	1:00	4:00	7
5	9:00	1:30	–	–	4.5

REGULAR	OVERTIME	RATE	GROSS PAY
33.5	0	$12.00	$402.00

6.

DAYS	IN	OUT	IN	OUT	DAILY TOTALS
1	8:00	12:00	1:00	5:00	8.5
2	8:00	11:30	1:00	6:00	8.5
3	8:30	12:30	1:30	6:30	9
4	8:00	12:30	1:30	6:00	9
5	8:00	12:30	1:30	6:00	9

REGULAR	OVERTIME	RATE	GROSS PAY
40	4	$3.80	$174.80

W-18

COMMISSION Pages 45–47

Practice

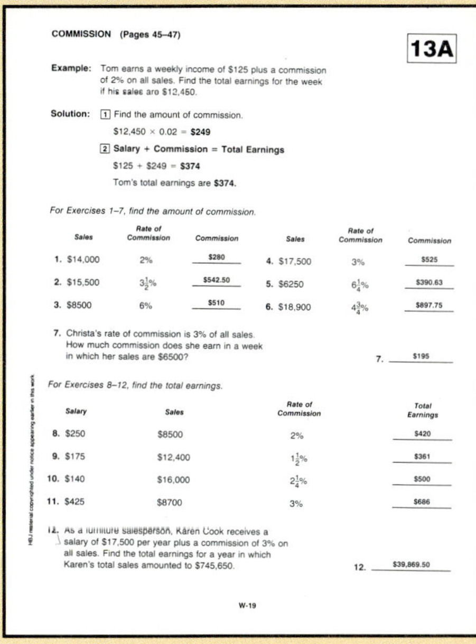

COMMISSION (Pages 45–47)

13A

Example: Tom earns a weekly income of $125 plus a commission of 2% on all sales. Find the total earnings for the week if his sales are $12,450.

Solution: [1] Find the amount of commission.

$12,450 × 0.02 = **$249**

[2] **Salary + Commission = Total Earnings**

$125 + $249 = **$374**

Tom's total earnings are **$374.**

For Exercises 1–7, find the amount of commission.

	Sales	Rate of Commission	Commission		Sales	Rate of Commission	Commission
1.	$14,000	2%	$280	4.	$17,500	3%	$525
2.	$15,500	$3\frac{1}{2}$%	$542.50	5.	$6250	$6\frac{1}{4}$%	$390.63
3.	$8500	6%	$510	6.	$18,900	$4\frac{3}{4}$%	$897.75

7. Christa's rate of commission is 3% of all sales. How much commission does she earn in a week in which her sales are $6500? 7. $195

For Exercises 8–12, find the total earnings.

	Salary	Sales	Rate of Commission	Total Earnings
8.	$250	$8500	2%	$420
9.	$175	$12,400	$1\frac{1}{2}$%	$361
10.	$140	$16,000	$2\frac{1}{4}$%	$500
11.	$425	$8700	3%	$686

12. As a furniture salesperson, Karen Cook receives a salary of $17,500 per year plus a commission of 3% on all sales. Find the total earnings for a year in which Karen's total sales amounted to $745,650. 12. $39,869.50

W-19

Reteaching/ Alternate Teaching Strategy

A reteaching lesson can be structured for this topic by having students supply the concrete materials. These concrete materials then would be the basis for the lesson.

Have students bring to class several advertisements for sales positions listed in newspaper classifieds. The advertisements should include options for earnings by straight commission or a salary and commission option.

These advertisements then become a source bank of real world problems that you can use for presenting the lesson.

Enrichment

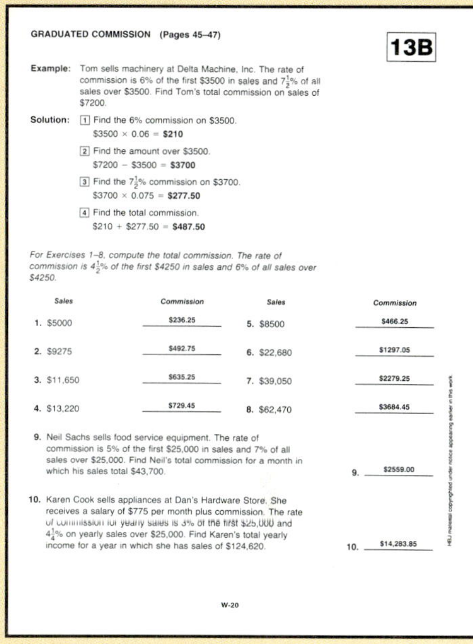

GRADUATED COMMISSION (Pages 45–47)

13B

Example: Tom sells machinery at Delta Machine, Inc. The rate of commission is 6% of the first $3500 in sales and $7\frac{1}{2}$% of all sales over $3500. Find Tom's total commission on sales of $7200.

Solution: [1] Find the 6% commission on $3500.
$3500 × 0.06 = **$210**

[2] Find the amount over $3500.
$7200 − $3500 = **$3700**

[3] Find the $7\frac{1}{2}$% commission on $3700.
$3700 × 0.075 = **$277.50**

[4] Find the total commission.
$210 + $277.50 = **$487.50**

For Exercises 1–8, compute the total commission. The rate of commission is $4\frac{1}{2}$% of the first $4250 in sales and 6% of all sales over $4250.

	Sales	Commission		Sales	Commission
1.	$5000	$236.25	5.	$8500	$466.25
2.	$9275	$492.75	6.	$22,680	$1297.05
3.	$11,650	$635.25	7.	$39,050	$2279.25
4.	$13,220	$729.45	8.	$62,470	$3684.45

9. Neil Sachs sells food service equipment. The rate of commission is 5% of the first $25,000 in sales and 7% of all sales over $25,000. Find Neil's total commission for a month in which his sales total $43,700. 9. $2559.00

10. Karen Cook sells appliances at Dan's Hardware Store. She receives a salary of $775 per month plus commission. The rate of commission for yearly sales is 3% of the first $25,000 and $4\frac{1}{4}$% on yearly sales over $25,000. Find Karen's total yearly income for a year in which she has sales of $124,620. 10. $14,283.85

W-20

DEDUCTIONS AND NET PAY Pages 48–50

Practice

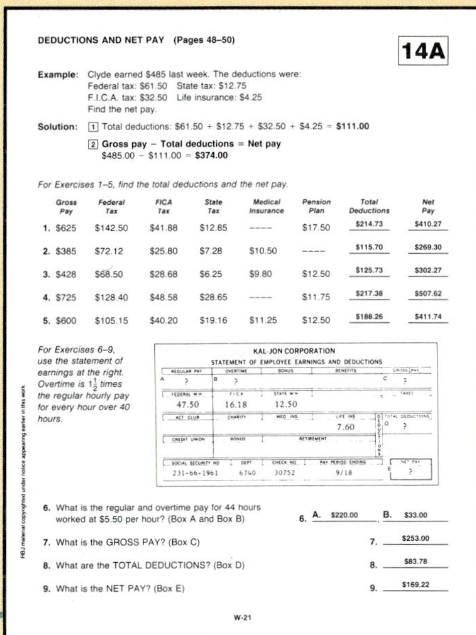

DEDUCTIONS AND NET PAY (Pages 48–50)

14A

Example: Clyde earned $485 last week. The deductions were:
Federal tax: $61.50 State tax: $12.75
F.I.C.A. tax: $32.50 Life insurance: $4.25
Find the net pay.

Solution: [1] Total deductions: $61.50 + $12.75 + $32.50 + $4.25 = **$111.00**

[2] **Gross pay − Total deductions = Net pay**
$485.00 − $111.00 = **$374.00**

For Exercises 1–5, find the total deductions and the net pay.

	Gross Pay	Federal Tax	FICA Tax	State Tax	Medical Insurance	Pension Plan	Total Deductions	Net Pay
1.	$625	$142.50	$41.88	$12.85	----	$17.50	$214.73	$410.27
2.	$385	$72.12	$25.80	$7.28	$10.50	----	$115.70	$269.30
3.	$428	$68.50	$28.68	$6.25	$9.80	$12.50	$125.73	$302.27
4.	$725	$128.40	$48.58	$28.65	----	$11.75	$217.38	$507.62
5.	$600	$105.15	$40.20	$19.16	$11.25	$12.50	$188.26	$411.74

For Exercises 6–9, use the statement of earnings at the right. Overtime is $1\frac{1}{2}$ times the regular hourly pay for every hour over 40 hours.

KAL-JON CORPORATION
STATEMENT OF EMPLOYEE EARNINGS AND DEDUCTIONS

REGULAR PAY	OVERTIME	BONUS	BENEFITS	GROSS PAY
A ?	B ?			C ?

FEDERAL W.H.	FICA	STATE W.H.		TAXES
47.50	16.18	12.50		

ACT. CLUB	CHARITY	MED. INS.	LIFE INS.	TOTAL DEDUCTIONS
			7.60	D ?

CREDIT UNION	BONUS	RETIREMENT

SOCIAL SECURITY NO.	DEPT	CHECK NO.	PAY PERIOD ENDING	NET PAY
231-66-1961	6740	30752	9/18	E ?

6. What is the regular and overtime pay for 44 hours worked at $5.50 per hour? (Box A and Box B) 6. A. $220.00, B. $33.00

7. What is the GROSS PAY? (Box C) 7. $253.00

8. What are the TOTAL DEDUCTIONS? (Box D) 8. $83.78

9. What is the NET PAY? (Box E) 9. $169.22

W-21

Reteaching/ Alternate Teaching Strategy

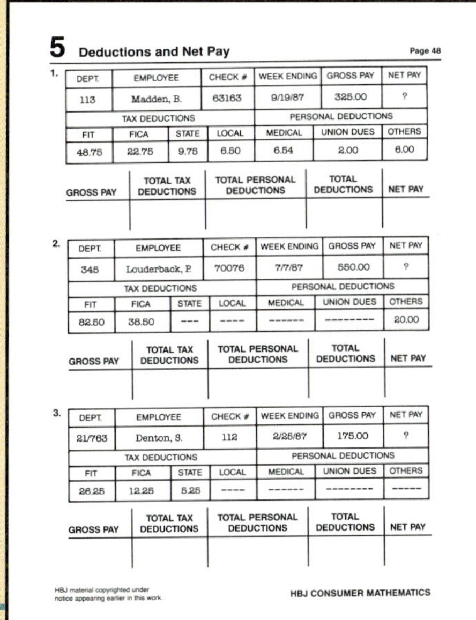

5 Deductions and Net Pay Page 48

1.

DEPT.	EMPLOYEE	CHECK #	WEEK ENDING	GROSS PAY	NET PAY
113	Madden, B.	63163	9/19/87	325.00	?

FIT	FICA	STATE	LOCAL	MEDICAL	UNION DUES	OTHERS
TAX DEDUCTIONS				PERSONAL DEDUCTIONS		
48.75	22.75	9.75	6.50	6.54	2.00	6.00

GROSS PAY	TOTAL TAX DEDUCTIONS	TOTAL PERSONAL DEDUCTIONS	TOTAL DEDUCTIONS	NET PAY

2.

DEPT.	EMPLOYEE	CHECK #	WEEK ENDING	GROSS PAY	NET PAY
345	Louderback, P.	70076	7/7/87	550.00	?

FIT	FICA	STATE	LOCAL	MEDICAL	UNION DUES	OTHERS
TAX DEDUCTIONS				PERSONAL DEDUCTIONS		
82.50	38.50	---	----	------	--------	20.00

GROSS PAY	TOTAL TAX DEDUCTIONS	TOTAL PERSONAL DEDUCTIONS	TOTAL DEDUCTIONS	NET PAY

3.

DEPT.	EMPLOYEE	CHECK #	WEEK ENDING	GROSS PAY	NET PAY
21/763	Denton, S.	112	2/25/87	175.00	?

FIT	FICA	STATE	LOCAL	MEDICAL	UNION DUES	OTHERS
TAX DEDUCTIONS				PERSONAL DEDUCTIONS		
26.25	12.25	5.25	----	------	--------	-----

GROSS PAY	TOTAL TAX DEDUCTIONS	TOTAL PERSONAL DEDUCTIONS	TOTAL DEDUCTIONS	NET PAY

HBJ CONSUMER MATHEMATICS

Enrichment

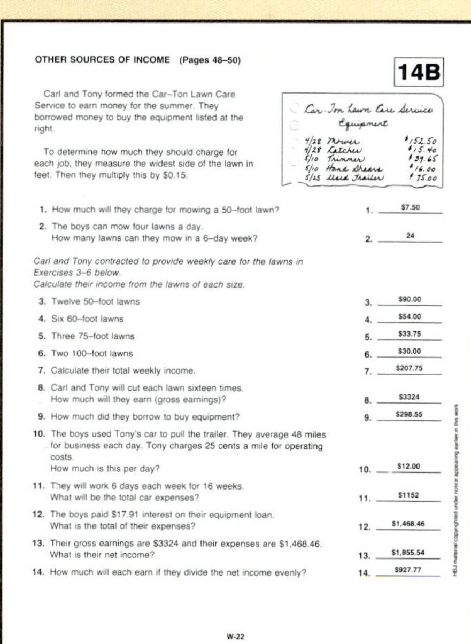

OTHER SOURCES OF INCOME (Pages 48–50)

14B

Carl and Tony formed the Car–Ton Lawn Care Service to earn money for the summer. They borrowed money to buy the equipment listed at the right.

To determine how much they should charge for each job, they measure the widest side of the lawn in feet. Then they multiply this by $0.15.

Car-Ton Lawn Care Service
Equipment

4/28	Mower	$152.50
4/28	Catcher	$15.40
5/10	Trimmer	$39.65
5/10	Hand Shears	$16.00
5/25	Used Trailer	$75.00

1. How much will they charge for mowing a 50–foot lawn? 1. $7.50
2. The boys can mow four lawns a day. How many lawns can they mow in a 6–day week? 2. 24

Carl and Tony contracted to provide weekly care for the lawns in Exercises 3–6 below. Calculate their income from the lawns of each size.

3. Twelve 50–foot lawns 3. $90.00
4. Six 60–foot lawns 4. $54.00
5. Three 75–foot lawns 5. $33.75
6. Two 100–foot lawns 6. $30.00
7. Calculate their total weekly income. 7. $207.75
8. Carl and Tony will cut each lawn sixteen times. How much will they earn (gross earnings)? 8. $3324
9. How much did they borrow to buy equipment? 9. $298.55
10. The boys used Tony's car to pull the trailer. They average 48 miles for business each day. Tony charges 25 cents a mile for operating costs. How much is this per day? 10. $12.00
11. They will work 6 days each week for 16 weeks. What will be the total car expenses? 11. $1152
12. The boys paid $17.91 interest on their equipment loan. What is the total of their expenses? 12. $1,468.46
13. Their gross earnings are $3324 and their expenses are $1,468.46. What is their net income? 13. $1,855.54
14. How much will each earn if they divide the net income evenly? 14. $927.77

W-22

SOCIAL SECURITY TAXES Pages 54–55

Practice

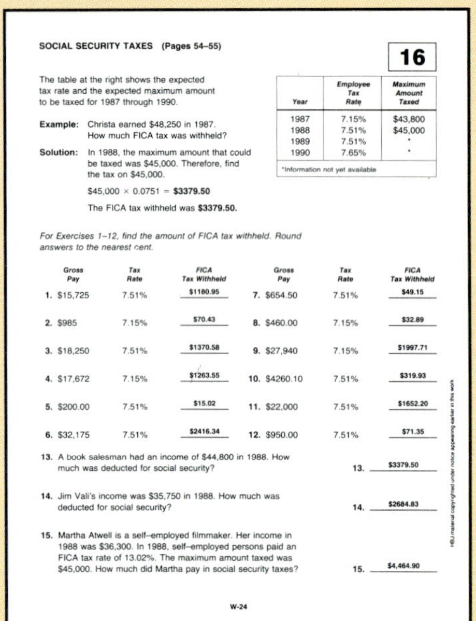

SOCIAL SECURITY TAXES (Pages 54–55)

16

The table at the right shows the expected tax rate and the expected maximum amount to be taxed for 1987 through 1990.

Year	*Employee Tax Rate*	*Maximum Amount Taxed*
1987	7.15%	$43,800
1988	7.51%	$45,000
1989	7.51%	*
1990	7.65%	*

*Information not yet available

Example: Christa earned $48,250 in 1987. How much FICA tax was withheld?

Solution: In 1988, the maximum amount that could be taxed was $45,000. Therefore, find the tax on $45,000.

$45,000 × 0.0751 = **$3379.50**

The FICA tax withheld was **$3379.50.**

For Exercises 1–12, find the amount of FICA tax withheld. Round answers to the nearest cent.

	Gross Pay	*Tax Rate*	*FICA Tax Withheld*		*Gross Pay*	*Tax Rate*	*FICA Tax Withheld*
1.	$15,725	7.51%	$1180.95	**7.**	$654.50	7.51%	$49.15
2.	$985	7.15%	$70.43	**8.**	$460.00	7.15%	$32.89
3.	$18,250	7.51%	$1370.58	**9.**	$27,940	7.15%	$1997.71
4.	$17,672	7.15%	$1263.55	**10.**	$4260.10	7.51%	$319.93
5.	$200.00	7.51%	$15.02	**11.**	$22,000	7.51%	$1652.20
6.	$32,175	7.51%	$2416.34	**12.**	$950.00	7.51%	$71.35

13. A book salesman had an income of $44,800 in 1988. How much was deducted for social security? **13.** $3379.50

14. Jim Vali's income was $35,750 in 1988. How much was deducted for social security? **14.** $2684.83

15. Martha Atwell is a self-employed filmmaker. Her income in 1988 was $36,300. In 1988, self-employed persons paid an FICA tax rate of 13.02%. The maximum amount taxed was $45,000. How much did Martha pay in social security taxes? **15.** $4,464.90

W-24

Reteaching/ Alternate Teaching Strategy

A reteaching lesson can be structured for this topic by having students supply the concrete materials. These concrete materials then would be the basis for the lesson.

Have students bring to class articles about changes in the social security taxes. You may wish to suggest such sources as newspapers, magazines, The World Almanac, and other library reference books.

These articles then become a source bank of real world problems that you can use for presenting the lesson.

Enrichment

In 1987, the withholdings for social security were 7.15% of earnings up to a maximum of $43,800. Have students use this table to find:

a. the FICA tax paid by persons earning each amount.

b. what percent of **total earnings** persons earning each amount paid. Round each percent to the nearest hundredth.

Earnings		
$40,000	**a. $286.00**	**b. 7.15%**
$50,000	**a. $3131.70**	**b. 6.26%**
$60,000	**a. $3131.70**	**b. 5.22%**
$70,000	**a. $3131.70**	**b. 4.47%**
$80,000	**a. $3131.70**	**b. 3.91%**
$100,000	**a. $3131.70**	**b. 3.13%**

Ask students to calculate the amount that must be earned for a total social security tax withholding of exactly 1% of the annual income.

SOCIAL SECURITY BENEFITS Pages 56–57

Practice

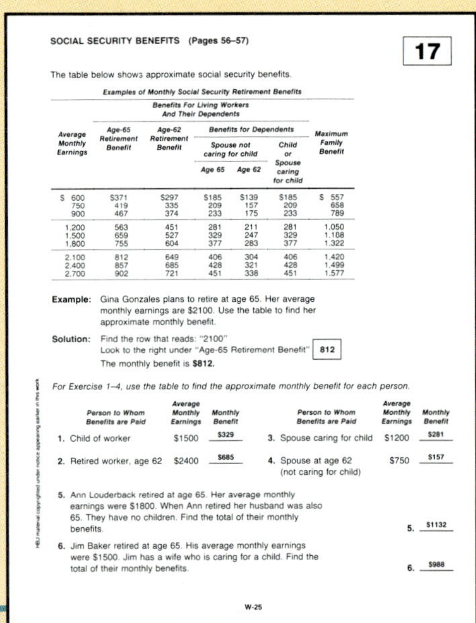

SOCIAL SECURITY BENEFITS (Pages 56–57)

17

The table below shows approximate social security benefits.

Examples of Monthly Social Security Retirement Benefits

Average Monthly Earnings	*Benefits For Living Workers And Their Dependents*					*Maximum Family Benefit*
	Age-65 Retirement Benefit	*Age-62 Retirement Benefit*	*Benefits for Dependents*			
			Spouse not caring for child		*Child or Spouse caring for child*	
			Age 65	*Age 62*		
$ 600	$371	$297	$185	$139	$185	$ 557
750	419	335	209	157	209	658
900	467	374	233	175	233	789
1.200	563	451	281	211	281	1.050
1.500	659	527	329	247	329	1.188
1.800	755	604	377	283	377	1.322
2.100	812	649	406	304	406	1.420
2.400	857	685	428	321	428	1.499
2.700	902	721	451	338	451	1.577

Example: Gina Gonzales plans to retire at age 65. Her average monthly earnings are $2100. Use the table to find her approximate monthly benefit.

Solution: Find the row that reads: "2100"
Look to the right under "Age-65 Retirement Benefit" **812**
The monthly benefit is **$812.**

For Exercise 1–4, use the table to find the approximate monthly benefit for each person.

	Person to Whom Benefits are Paid	*Average Monthly Earnings*	*Monthly Benefit*		*Person to Whom Benefits are Paid*	*Average Monthly Earnings*	*Monthly Benefit*
1.	Child of worker	$1500	$329	**3.**	Spouse caring for child	$1200	$281
2.	Retired worker, age 62	$2400	$685	**4.**	Spouse at age 62 (not caring for child)	$750	$157

5. Ann Louderback retired at age 65. Her average monthly earnings were $1800. When Ann retired her husband was also 65. They have no children. Find the total of their monthly benefits. **5.** $1132

6. Jim Baker retired at age 65. His average monthly earnings were $1500. Jim has a wife who is caring for a child. Find the total of their monthly benefits. **6.** $988

W-25

Reteaching/ Alternate Teaching Strategy

A reteaching lesson can be structured for this topic by having students supply the concrete materials. These concrete materials then would be the basis for the lesson.

Have students bring to class news and information excerpts about social security programs that provide benefits to persons other than the worker. Among those included are children, the worker's spouse, and the disabled.

These excerpts then become a source bank of real world problems that you can use for presenting the lesson.

Enrichment

Two persons have average monthly earnings of $1500. One retires at age 62 and the other retires at age 65. Challenge students to use the table on page 56 to find the monthly benefits for each and determine the age when both have received the same total amount of benefits.

You may wish to construct a double line graph (see below) to show total benefits for each year.

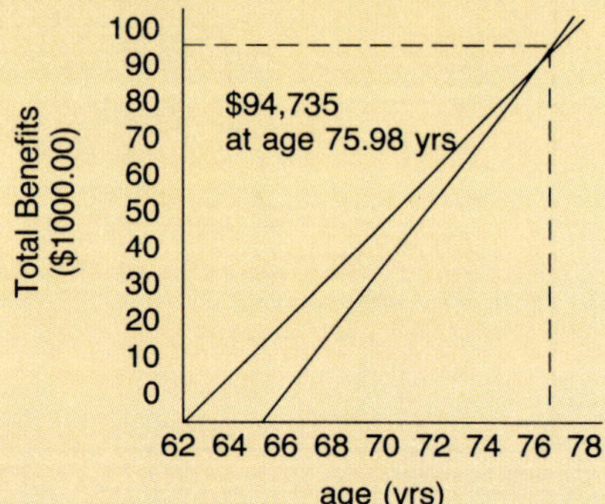

JOB APPLICATION Pages 58–59

Practice

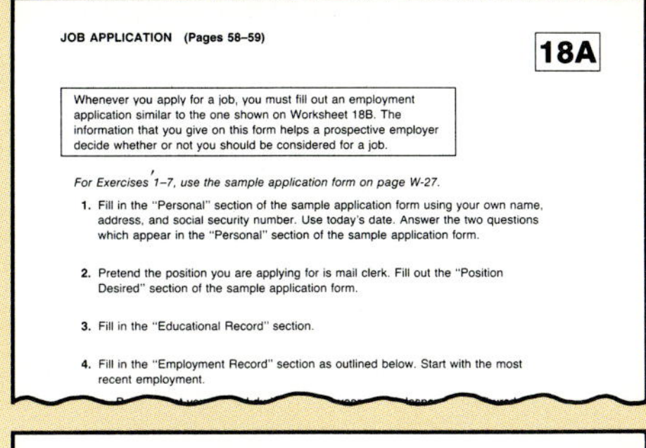

JOB APPLICATION (Pages 58–59) **18A**

Whenever you apply for a job, you must fill out an employment application similar to the one shown on Worksheet 18B. The information that you give on this form helps a prospective employer decide whether or not you should be considered for a job.

For Exercises 1–7, use the sample application form on page W-27.

1. Fill in the "Personal" section of the sample application form using your own name, address, and social security number. Use today's date. Answer the two questions which appear in the "Personal" section of the sample application form.
2. Pretend the position you are applying for is mail clerk. Fill out the "Position Desired" section of the sample application form.
3. Fill in the "Educational Record" section.
4. Fill in the "Employment Record" section as outlined below. Start with the most recent employment.

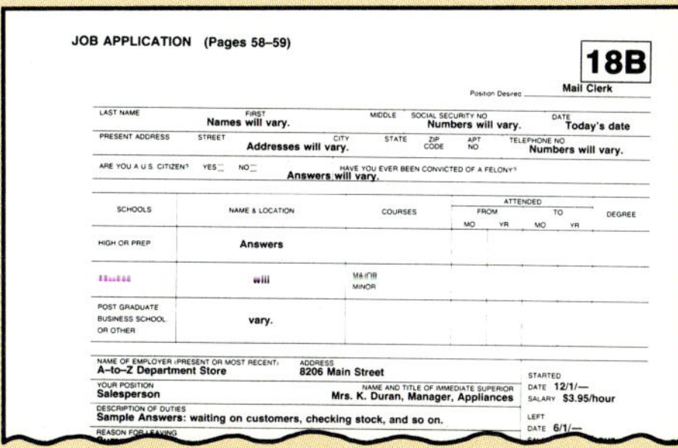

JOB APPLICATION (Pages 58–59) **18B**

Position Desired **Mail Clerk**

LAST NAME / FIRST **Names will vary.** MIDDLE / SOCIAL SECURITY NO **Numbers will vary.** DATE **Today's date**

PRESENT ADDRESS STREET / CITY **Addresses will vary.** STATE ZIP CODE APT NO TELEPHONE NO **Numbers will vary.**

ARE YOU A U.S. CITIZEN? YES ☐ NO ☐ HAVE YOU EVER BEEN CONVICTED OF A FELONY? **Answers will vary.**

SCHOOLS	NAME & LOCATION	COURSES	ATTENDED FROM MO YR	TO MO YR	DEGREE
HIGH OR PREP	**Answers**				
[illegible]	**will**	MAJOR MINOR			
POST GRADUATE BUSINESS SCHOOL OR OTHER	**vary.**				

NAME OF EMPLOYER (PRESENT OR MOST RECENT) **A-to-Z Department Store** ADDRESS **8206 Main Street**

YOUR POSITION **Salesperson** NAME AND TITLE OF IMMEDIATE SUPERIOR **Mrs. K. Duran, Manager, Appliances**

STARTED DATE **12/1/—** SALARY **$3.95/hour**

DESCRIPTION OF DUTIES **Sample Answers: waiting on customers, checking stock, and so on.**

LEFT DATE **6/1/—**

REASON FOR LEAVING

Reteaching/ Alternate Teaching Strategy

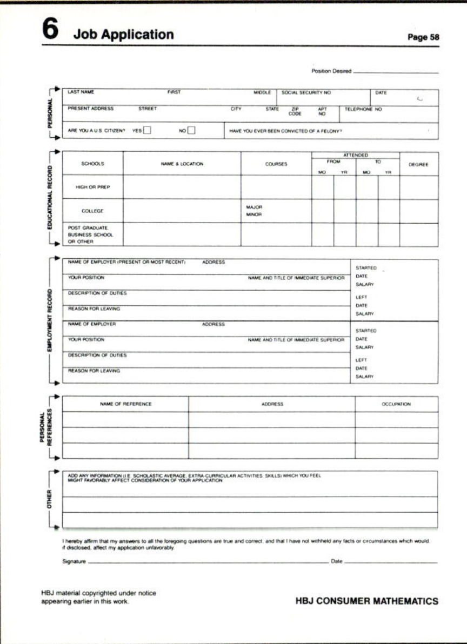

6 Job Application Page 58

Position Desired ______

PERSONAL: LAST NAME / FIRST / MIDDLE / SOCIAL SECURITY NO / DATE; PRESENT ADDRESS / STREET / CITY / STATE / ZIP CODE / APT NO / TELEPHONE NO; ARE YOU A U.S. CITIZEN? YES ☐ NO ☐ / HAVE YOU EVER BEEN CONVICTED OF A FELONY?

EDUCATIONAL RECORD:

SCHOOLS	NAME & LOCATION	COURSES	ATTENDED FROM MO YR	TO MO YR	DEGREE
HIGH OR PREP					
COLLEGE		MAJOR MINOR			
POST GRADUATE BUSINESS SCHOOL OR OTHER					

EMPLOYMENT RECORD: NAME OF EMPLOYER (PRESENT OR MOST RECENT) / ADDRESS; YOUR POSITION / NAME AND TITLE OF IMMEDIATE SUPERIOR; DESCRIPTION OF DUTIES; REASON FOR LEAVING; STARTED DATE SALARY; LEFT DATE SALARY; NAME OF EMPLOYER / ADDRESS; YOUR POSITION / NAME AND TITLE OF IMMEDIATE SUPERIOR; DESCRIPTION OF DUTIES; REASON FOR LEAVING; STARTED DATE SALARY; LEFT DATE SALARY

PERSONAL REFERENCES:

NAME OF REFERENCE	ADDRESS	OCCUPATION

OTHER: ADD ANY INFORMATION (I.E. SCHOLASTIC AVERAGE, EXTRA-CURRICULAR ACTIVITIES, SKILLS) WHICH YOU FEEL MIGHT FAVORABLY AFFECT CONSIDERATION OF YOUR APPLICATION

I hereby affirm that my answers to all the foregoing questions are true and correct, and that I have not withheld any facts or circumstances which would, if disclosed, affect my application unfavorably.

Signature ______ Date ______

HBJ CONSUMER MATHEMATICS

Enrichment

List the following jobs on the chalkboard. Then have students work in small groups to make a list of the education, skills, and experience that should be entered on a job application for one of these jobs.

- Receptionist
- Carpenter
- Bus Driver
- Dental Assistant
- Data Processor
- Accounting Clerk
- Telephone Technician

Groups may want to use the job application form on page 59 as a guide in completing the list.

FEDERAL INCOME TAX Pages 70–71

Practice

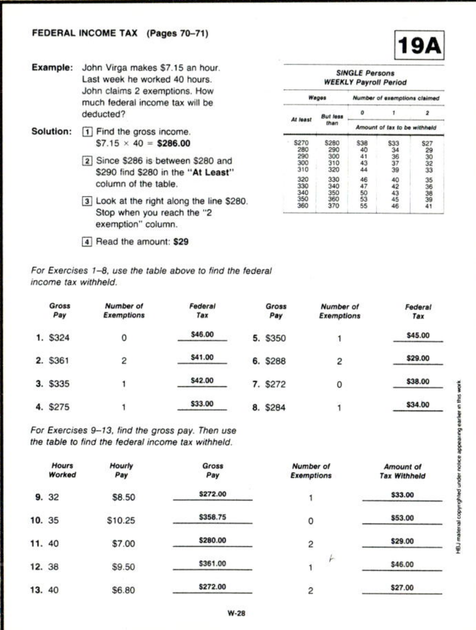

FEDERAL INCOME TAX (Pages 70–71) **19A**

Example: John Virga makes $7.15 an hour. Last week he worked 40 hours. John claims 2 exemptions. How much federal income tax will be deducted?

Solution:
1. Find the gross income. $7.15 × 40 = **$286.00**
2. Since $286 is between $280 and $290 find $280 in the **"At Least"** column of the table.
3. Look at the right along the line $280. Stop when you reach the "2 exemption" column.
4. Read the amount: **$29**

SINGLE Persons WEEKLY Payroll Period

Wages: At least	Wages: But less than	0	1	2
		Amount of tax to be withheld		
$270	$280	$38	$33	$27
280	290	40	34	29
290	300	41	36	30
300	310	43	37	32
310	320	44	39	33
320	330	46	40	35
330	340	47	42	36
340	350	50	43	38
350	360	53	45	39
360	370	55	46	41

For Exercises 1–8, use the table above to find the federal income tax withheld.

	Gross Pay	Number of Exemptions	Federal Tax
1.	$324	0	$46.00
2.	$361	2	$41.00
3.	$335	1	$42.00
4.	$275	1	$33.00
5.	$350	1	$45.00
6.	$288	2	$29.00
7.	$272	0	$38.00
8.	$284	1	$34.00

For Exercises 9–13, find the gross pay. Then use the table to find the federal income tax withheld.

	Hours Worked	Hourly Pay	Gross Pay	Number of Exemptions	Amount of Tax Withheld
9.	32	$8.50	$272.00	1	$33.00
10.	35	$10.25	$358.75	0	$53.00
11.	40	$7.00	$280.00	2	$29.00
12.	38	$9.50	$361.00	1	$46.00
13.	40	$6.80	$272.00	2	$27.00

W-28

Reteaching/ Alternate Teaching Strategy

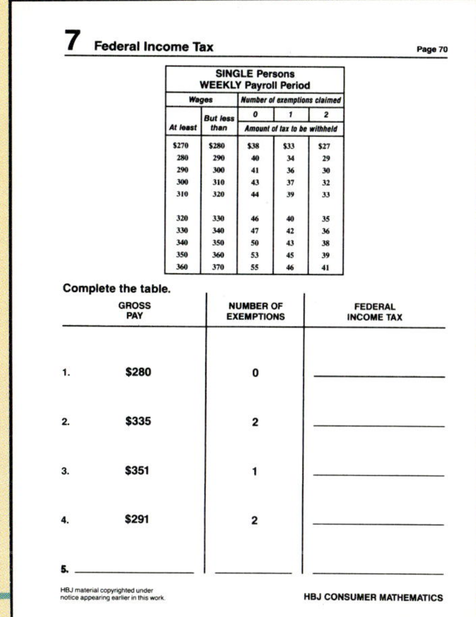

7 Federal Income Tax Page 70

SINGLE Persons WEEKLY Payroll Period

Wages: At least	Wages: But less than	0	1	2
		Amount of tax to be withheld		
$270	$280	$38	$33	$27
280	290	40	34	29
290	300	41	36	30
300	310	43	37	32
310	320	44	39	33
320	330	46	40	35
330	340	47	42	36
340	350	50	43	38
350	360	53	45	39
360	370	55	46	41

Complete the table.

	GROSS PAY	NUMBER OF EXEMPTIONS	FEDERAL INCOME TAX
1.	$280	0	
2.	$335	2	
3.	$351	1	
4.	$291	2	
5.			

HBJ CONSUMER MATHEMATICS

Enrichment

DEDUCTIONS FOR DONATIONS (Pages 70–71) **19B**

Each year the Jackson family makes up two bundles of used clothing that they donate to the Salvation Army for the needy. The value of such donations may be used as a deduction on income tax.

In Exercises 1–2, find the total value of each bundle.

1. Bundle 1		2. Bundle 2	
2 men's suits at $15.00	$30.00	1 jacket at $3.00	$3.00
3 dresses at $17.00	$51.00	4 play suits at $1.50	$6.00
2 jackets at $3.50	$7.00	5 dresses at $2.75	$13.75
4 pairs shoes at $4.25	$17.00	1 raincoat at $4.75	$4.75
3 sweaters at $2.50	$7.50	2 snow suits at $7.50	$15.00
2 pairs slacks at $3.50	$7.00	3 winter coats at $13.00	$39.00
TOTAL	$119.50	TOTAL	$81.50

The amount a person saves on such a deduction depends on the "tax bracket."

Example: Mr. Jackson is in the 28% tax bracket. Thus, he will save 28% of the total value of the clothing he donates.

Problem: Last year he donated $80.00 worth of clothing. How much did he save on taxes?

Solution: $80 × 28% = $80 × .28 = **$22.40**

3. Compute the tax savings on Bundle 1 if the tax bracket is 15%. 3. $17.93
4. Compute the tax savings on Bundle 1 if the tax bracket is 28%. 4. $33.46
5. Compute the tax savings on Bundle 2 if the tax bracket is 15%. 5. $12.23
6. Compute the tax savings on Bundle 2 if the tax bracket is 28%. 6. $22.82
7. Sylvia Green is in the 15% tax bracket. She donated $97 worth of clothing to the needy. What is the tax saving? 7. $14.55

W-29

ADJUSTED GROSS INCOME AND DEDUCTIONS Pages 72–73

Practice

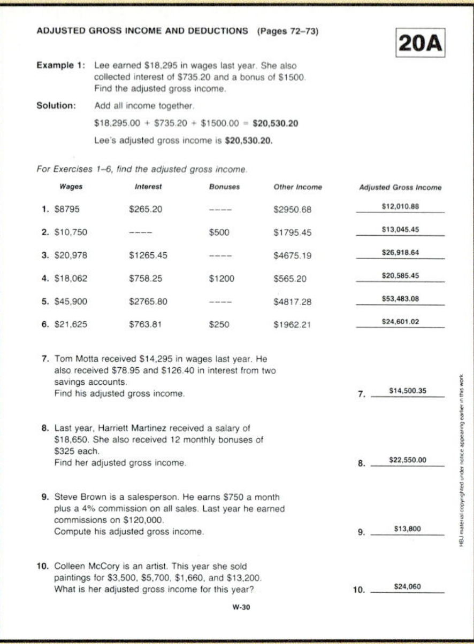

ADJUSTED GROSS INCOME AND DEDUCTIONS (Pages 72–73) **20A**

Example 1: Lee earned $18,295 in wages last year. She also collected interest of $735.20 and a bonus of $1500. Find the adjusted gross income.

Solution: Add all income together.

$18,295.00 + $735.20 + $1500.00 = **$20,530.20**

Lee's adjusted gross income is **$20,530.20.**

For Exercises 1–6, find the adjusted gross income.

	Wages	Interest	Bonuses	Other Income	Adjusted Gross Income
1.	$8795	$265.20	----	$2950.68	$12,010.88
2.	$10,750	----	$500	$1795.45	$13,045.45
3.	$20,978	$1265.45	----	$4675.19	$26,918.64
4.	$18,062	$758.25	$1200	$565.20	$20,585.45
5.	$45,900	$2765.80	----	$4817.28	$53,483.08
6.	$21,625	$763.81	$250	$1962.21	$24,601.02

7. Tom Motta received $14,295 in wages last year. He also received $78.95 and $126.40 in interest from two savings accounts. Find his adjusted gross income. 7. $14,500.35

8. Last year, Harriett Martinez received a salary of $18,650. She also received 12 monthly bonuses of $325 each. Find her adjusted gross income. 8. $22,550.00

9. Steve Brown is a salesperson. He earns $750 a month plus a 4% commission on all sales. Last year he earned commissions on $120,000. Compute his adjusted gross income. 9. $13,800

10. Colleen McCory is an artist. This year she sold paintings for $3,500, $5,700, $1,660, and $13,200. What is her adjusted gross income for this year? 10. $24,060

W-30

Reteaching/ Alternate Teaching Strategy

A reteaching lesson can be structured for this topic by having students supply the concrete materials. These concrete materials then would be the basis for the lesson.

Have students write the following on an index card:

- Wages between $10,000 and $25,000
- Interest, $100 to $500
- Five deductions with name and the amount for each
- A taxpayer filing status as shown in the table on page 72

These index cards then become a source bank of problems that you can use for presenting the lesson.

Enrichment

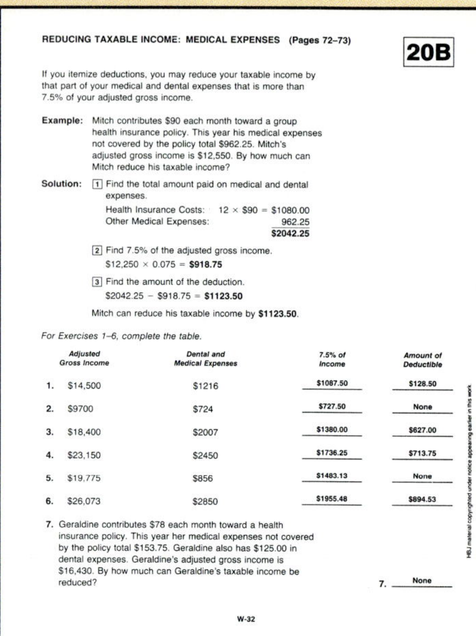

REDUCING TAXABLE INCOME: MEDICAL EXPENSES (Pages 72–73) **20B**

If you itemize deductions, you may reduce your taxable income by that part of your medical and dental expenses that is more than 7.5% of your adjusted gross income.

Example: Mitch contributes $90 each month toward a group health insurance policy. This year his medical expenses not covered by the policy total $962.25. Mitch's adjusted gross income is $12,550. By how much can Mitch reduce his taxable income?

Solution: [1] Find the total amount paid on medical and dental expenses.

Health Insurance Costs: 12 × $90 = $1080.00
Other Medical Expenses: 962.25
$2042.25

[2] Find 7.5% of the adjusted gross income.
$12,250 × 0.075 = **$918.75**

[3] Find the amount of the deduction.
$2042.25 − $918.75 = **$1123.50**

Mitch can reduce his taxable income by **$1123.50.**

For Exercises 1–6, complete the table.

	Adjusted Gross Income	Dental and Medical Expenses	7.5% of Income	Amount of Deductible
1.	$14,500	$1216	$1087.50	$128.50
2.	$9700	$724	$727.50	None
3.	$18,400	$2007	$1380.00	$627.00
4.	$23,150	$2450	$1736.25	$713.75
5.	$19,775	$856	$1483.13	None
6.	$26,073	$2850	$1955.48	$894.53

7. Geraldine contributes $78 each month toward a health insurance policy. This year her medical expenses not covered by the policy total $153.75. Geraldine also has $125.00 in dental expenses. Geraldine's adjusted gross income is $16,430. By how much can Geraldine's taxable income be reduced? 7. None

W-32

FORM 1040EZ-THE SHORT FORM Pages 75–77

Practice

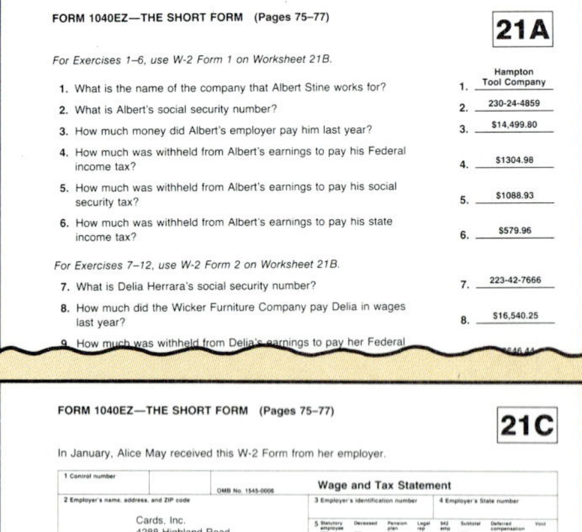

FORM 1040EZ—THE SHORT FORM (Pages 75–77) **21A**

For Exercises 1–6, use W-2 Form 1 on Worksheet 21B.

1. What is the name of the company that Albert Stine works for? 1. Hampton Tool Company
2. What is Albert's social security number? 2. 230-24-4859
3. How much money did Albert's employer pay him last year? 3. $14,499.80
4. How much was withheld from Albert's earnings to pay his Federal income tax? 4. $1304.98
5. How much was withheld from Albert's earnings to pay his social security tax? 5. $1088.93
6. How much was withheld from Albert's earnings to pay his state income tax? 6. $579.96

For Exercises 7–12, use W-2 Form 2 on Worksheet 21B.

7. What is Delia Herrara's social security number? 7. 223-42-7666
8. How much did the Wicker Furniture Company pay Delia in wages last year? 8. $16,540.25
9. How much was withheld from Delia's earnings to pay her Federal

FORM 1040EZ—THE SHORT FORM (Pages 75–77) **21C**

In January, Alice May received this W-2 Form from her employer.

1 Control number		OMB No. 1545-0008	Wage and Tax Statement
2 Employer's name, address, and ZIP code: Cards, Inc., 4288 Highland Road, Eckart, LA 70737		3 Employer's identification number	4 Employer's State number
		5 Statutory employee, Deceased, Pension plan, Legal rep, 942 emp, Subtotal, Deferred compensation, Void	
		6 Allocated tips	7 Advance EIC payment
8 Employee's social security number: 469-32-2648	9 Federal income tax withheld: $3130.15	10 Wages, tips, other compensation: $19,622.45	11 Social security tax withheld: $1473.65
12 Employee's name, address, and ZIP code: Alice B. May, 24 Lakewood Drive, Eckart, LA 70737		13 Social security wages: $19,622.45	14 Social security tips
		16	16a Fringe benefits incl in Box 10
		17 State income tax: $451.32 / 20 Local income tax	18 State wages, tips, etc.: $19,622.45 / 21 Local wages, tips, etc. / 19 Name of State: LA / 22 Name of locality

For Exercises 1–8, refer to Alice's W-2 Form and the information below to complete Form 1040EZ on Worksheet 21D.

1. Print Alice's name and address in the appropriate box.

Reteaching/ Alternate Teaching Strategy

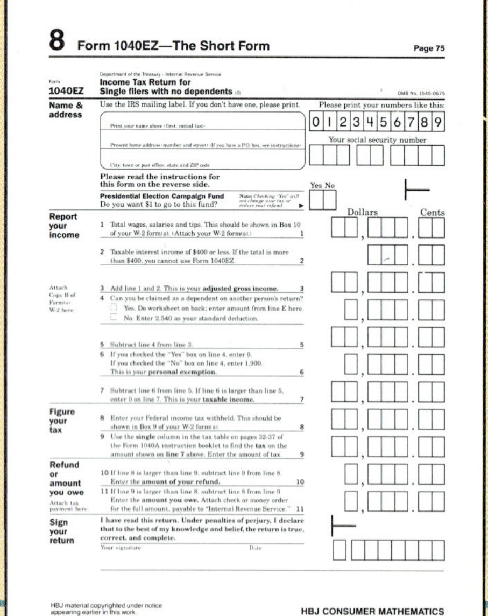

8 Form 1040EZ—The Short Form Page 75

Form 1040EZ — Department of the Treasury - Internal Revenue Service — **Income Tax Return for Single filers with no dependents** (0) — OMB No. 1545-0675

Name & address — Use the IRS mailing label. If you don't have one, please print. Please print your numbers like this: 0 1 2 3 4 5 6 7 8 9

Print your name above (first, initial, last)

Present home address (number and street) (If you have a P.O. box, see instructions)

City, town or post office, state and ZIP code

Your social security number

Please read the instructions for this form on the reverse side.

Presidential Election Campaign Fund — Do you want $1 to go to this fund? Note: Checking "Yes" will not change your tax or reduce your refund. Yes No

Dollars Cents

Report your income

1 Total wages, salaries and tips. This should be shown in Box 10 of your W-2 form(s). (Attach your W-2 form(s).) 1

2 Taxable interest income of $400 or less. If the total is more than $400, you cannot use Form 1040EZ. 2

Attach Copy B of Form(s) W-2 here

3 Add line 1 and 2. This is your **adjusted gross income.** 3

4 Can you be claimed as a dependent on another person's return?
Yes. Do worksheet on back; enter amount from line E here.
No. Enter 2,540 as your standard deduction.

5 Subtract line 4 from line 3. 5

6 If you checked the "Yes" box on line 4, enter 0. If you checked the "No" box on line 4, enter 1,900. This is your **personal exemption.** 6

7 Subtract line 6 from line 5. If line 6 is larger than line 5, enter 0 on line 7. This is your **taxable income.** 7

Figure your tax

8 Enter your Federal income tax withheld. This should be shown in Box 9 of your W-2 form(s). 8

9 Use the **single** column in the tax table on pages 32-37 of the Form 1040A instruction booklet to find the **tax** on the amount shown on **line 7** above. Enter the amount of tax. 9

Refund or amount you owe — Attach tax payment here

10 If line 8 is larger than line 9, subtract line 9 from line 8. Enter the **amount of your refund.** 10

11 If line 9 is larger than line 8, subtract line 8 from line 9. Enter the **amount you owe.** Attach check or money order for the full amount, payable to "Internal Revenue Service." 11

Sign your return — **I have read this return. Under penalties of perjury, I declare that to the best of my knowledge and belief, the return is true, correct, and complete.**

Your signature Date

 HBJ CONSUMER MATHEMATICS

Enrichment

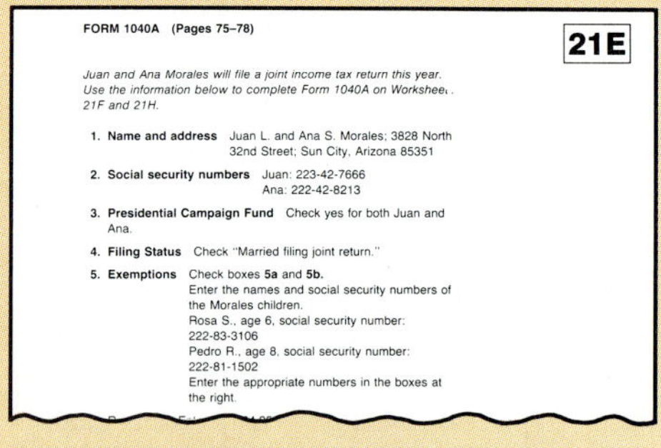

FORM 1040A (Pages 75–78) **21E**

Juan and Ana Morales will file a joint income tax return this year. Use the information below to complete Form 1040A on Worksheet 21F and 21H.

1. **Name and address** Juan L. and Ana S. Morales; 3828 North 32nd Street; Sun City, Arizona 85351
2. **Social security numbers** Juan: 223-42-7666 Ana: 222-42-8213
3. **Presidential Campaign Fund** Check yes for both Juan and Ana.
4. **Filing Status** Check "Married filing joint return."
5. **Exemptions** Check boxes **5a** and **5b.** Enter the names and social security numbers of the Morales children. Rosa S., age 6, social security number: 222-83-3106 Pedro R., age 8, social security number: 222-81-1502 Enter the appropriate numbers in the boxes at the right.

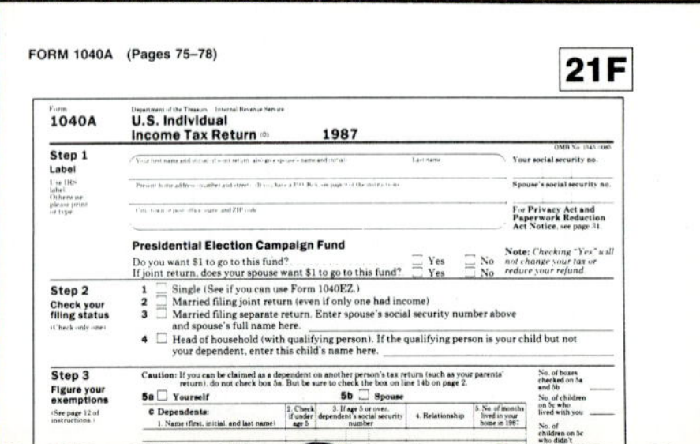

FORM 1040A (Pages 75–78) **21F**

Form 1040A — Department of the Treasury - Internal Revenue Service — **U.S. Individual Income Tax Return** (0) **1987**

Step 1 Label — Your social security no. / Spouse's social security no. / For Privacy Act and Paperwork Reduction Act Notice, see page 31.

Presidential Election Campaign Fund
Do you want $1 to go to this fund? Yes No
If joint return, does your spouse want $1 to go to this fund? Yes No
Note: Checking "Yes" will not change your tax or reduce your refund.

Step 2 Check your filing status (Check only one)
1 Single (See if you can use Form 1040EZ.)
2 Married filing joint return (even if only one had income)
3 Married filing separate return. Enter spouse's social security number above and spouse's full name here.
4 Head of household (with qualifying person). If the qualifying person is your child but not your dependent, enter this child's name here.

Step 3 Figure your exemptions (See page 12 of instructions.)
Caution: If you can be claimed as a dependent on another person's tax return (such as your parents' return), do not check box 5a. But be sure to check the box on line 14b on page 2.
5a Yourself 5b Spouse
c Dependents: 1. Name (first, initial, and last name) | 2. Check if under age 5 | 3. If age 5 or over, dependent's social security number | 4. Relationship | 5. No. of months lived in your home in 1987
No. of boxes checked on 5a and 5b / No. of children on 5c who lived with you / No. of children on 5c who didn't live with you

TAXABLE INCOME AND TAX TABLES Pages 80–81

Practice

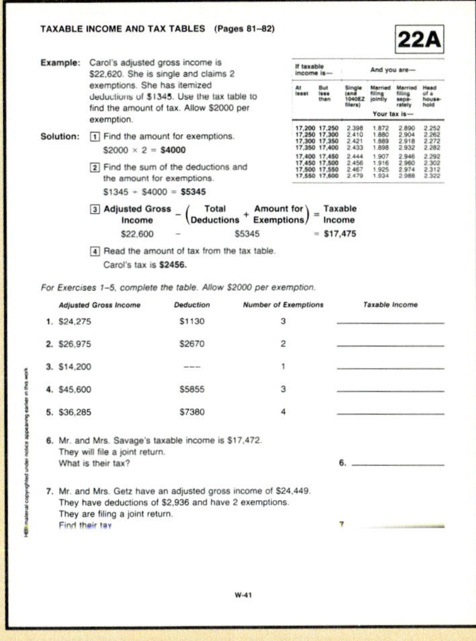

TAXABLE INCOME AND TAX TABLES (Pages 81–82) **22A**

Example: Carol's adjusted gross income is $22,620. She is single and claims 2 exemptions. She has itemized deductions of $1345. Use the tax table to find the amount of tax. Allow $2000 per exemption.

If taxable income is—		And you are—			
At least	But less than	Single (and 1040EZ filers)	Married filing jointly	Married filing separately	Head of a household
		Your tax is—			
17,200	17,250	2,398	1,872	2,890	2,252
17,250	17,300	2,410	1,880	2,904	2,262
17,300	17,350	2,421	1,889	2,918	2,272
17,350	17,400	2,433	1,898	2,932	2,282
17,400	17,450	2,444	1,907	2,946	2,292
17,450	17,500	2,456	1,916	2,960	2,302
17,500	17,550	2,467	1,925	2,974	2,312
17,550	17,600	2,479	1,934	2,988	2,322

Solution:
1. Find the amount for exemptions.
   $2000 × 2 = **$4000**
2. Find the sum of the deductions and the amount for exemptions.
   $1345 + $4000 = **$5345**
3. **Adjusted Gross Income − (Total Deductions + Amount for Exemptions) = Taxable Income**
   $22,600 − $5345 = **$17,475**
4. Read the amount of tax from the tax table.
   Carol's tax is **$2456.**

For Exercises 1–5, complete the table. Allow $2000 per exemption.

	Adjusted Gross Income	*Deduction*	*Number of Exemptions*	*Taxable Income*
1.	$24,275	$1130	3	________
2.	$26,975	$2670	2	________
3.	$14,200	---	1	________
4.	$45,600	$5855	3	________
5.	$36,285	$7380	4	________

6. Mr. and Mrs. Savage's taxable income is $17,472. They will file a joint return. What is their tax? 6. ________

7. Mr. and Mrs. Getz have an adjusted gross income of $24,449. They have deductions of $2,936 and have 2 exemptions. They are filing a joint return. Find their tax 7. ________

W-41

Reteaching/ Alternate Teaching Strategy

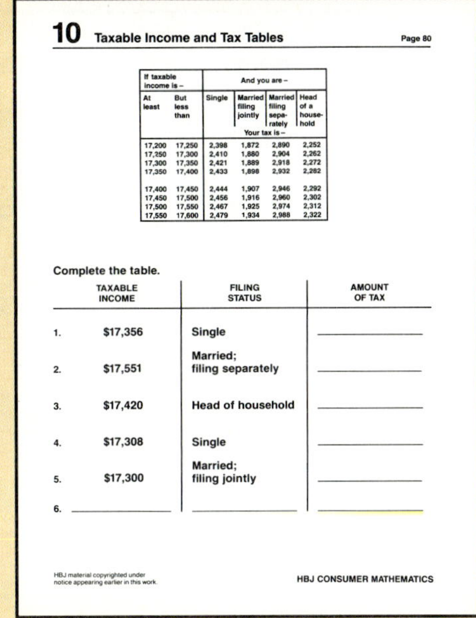

10 Taxable Income and Tax Tables — Page 80

If taxable income is –		And you are –			
At least	But less than	Single	Married filing jointly	Married filing separately	Head of a household
		Your tax is –			
17,200	17,250	2,398	1,872	2,890	2,252
17,250	17,300	2,410	1,880	2,904	2,262
17,300	17,350	2,421	1,889	2,918	2,272
17,350	17,400	2,433	1,898	2,932	2,282
17,400	17,450	2,444	1,907	2,946	2,292
17,450	17,500	2,456	1,916	2,960	2,302
17,500	17,550	2,467	1,925	2,974	2,312
17,550	17,600	2,479	1,934	2,988	2,322

Complete the table.

	TAXABLE INCOME	FILING STATUS	AMOUNT OF TAX
1.	$17,356	Single	________
2.	$17,551	Married; filing separately	________
3.	$17,420	Head of household	________
4.	$17,308	Single	________
5.	$17,300	Married; filing jointly	________
6.	________	________	________

HBJ CONSUMER MATHEMATICS

Enrichment

Worksheets 22B through 22I show students how to complete Schedules A and B and Form 1040.

STATE AND CITY INCOME TAXES Pages 82–83

Practice

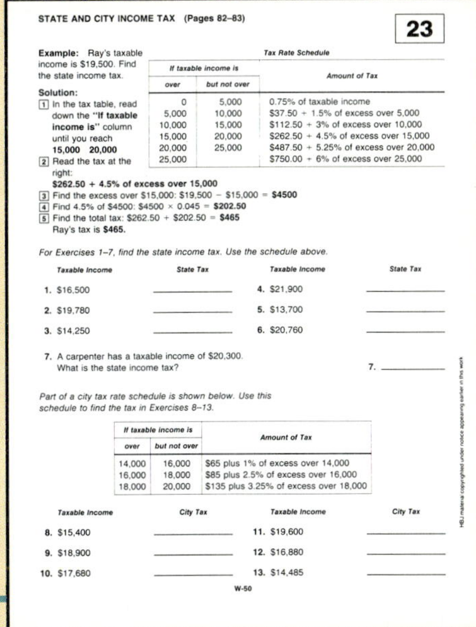

STATE AND CITY INCOME TAX (Pages 82–83) **23**

Example: Ray's taxable income is $19,500. Find the state income tax.

Tax Rate Schedule

If taxable income is over	*but not over*	*Amount of Tax*
0	5,000	0.75% of taxable income
5,000	10,000	$37.50 + 1.5% of excess over 5,000
10,000	15,000	$112.50 + 3% of excess over 10,000
15,000	20,000	$262.50 + 4.5% of excess over 15,000
20,000	25,000	$487.50 + 5.25% of excess over 20,000
25,000		$750.00 + 6% of excess over 25,000

Solution:
1. In the tax table, read down the "**If taxable income is**" column until you reach **15,000 20,000**
2. Read the tax at the right:
   $262.50 + 4.5% of excess over 15,000
3. Find the excess over $15,000: $19,500 − $15,000 = **$4500**
4. Find 4.5% of $4500: $4500 × 0.045 = **$202.50**
5. Find the total tax: $262.50 + $202.50 = **$465**
   Ray's tax is **$465.**

For Exercises 1–7, find the state income tax. Use the schedule above.

Taxable Income	*State Tax*	*Taxable Income*	*State Tax*
1. $16,500	________	4. $21,900	________
2. $19,780	________	5. $13,700	________
3. $14,250	________	6. $20,760	________

7. A carpenter has a taxable income of $20,300. What is the state income tax? 7. ________

Part of a city tax rate schedule is shown below. Use this schedule to find the tax in Exercises 8–13.

If taxable income is over	*but not over*	*Amount of Tax*
14,000	16,000	$65 plus 1% of excess over 14,000
16,000	18,000	$85 plus 2.5% of excess over 16,000
18,000	20,000	$135 plus 3.25% of excess over 18,000

Taxable Income	*City Tax*	*Taxable Income*	*City Tax*
8. $15,400	________	11. $19,600	________
9. $18,900	________	12. $16,880	________
10. $17,680	________	13. $14,485	________

W-50

Reteaching/ Alternate Teaching Strategy

11 State and City Income Taxes — Page 82

Tax Rate Schedule		
If taxable income is		
over	*but not over*	*Amount of Tax*
0	5,000	0.75% of taxable income
5,000	10,000	$37.50 + 1.5% of excess over 5,000
10,000	15,000	$112.50 + 3% of excess over 10,000
15,000	20,000	$262.50 + 4.5% of excess over 15,000
20,000	25,000	$487.50 + 5.25% of excess over 20,000
25,000		$750.00 + 6% of excess over 25,000

Find the amount of tax.

Taxable income:

1. **Amount of tax from the table:** ________ **plus** ________ **of excess over** ________
2. **Find the excess over the base tax amount.**
   ____
3. **Write and solve the percent equation.**
   ____
4. **Find the total tax.**
   ____

HBJ CONSUMER MATHEMATICS

Enrichment

Have students use the tax rate tables on page 82 and page 83 to find solutions to the following.

Ron Gilbert paid $262.50 state income tax. How much did he have to pay in city tax? **(ANS: $75)**

Susan Starr calculated that her city tax bill for this year is $85. Use the table to find her state income tax on the same taxable income. $307.50

DEPOSIT SLIPS Pages 96–97

Practice

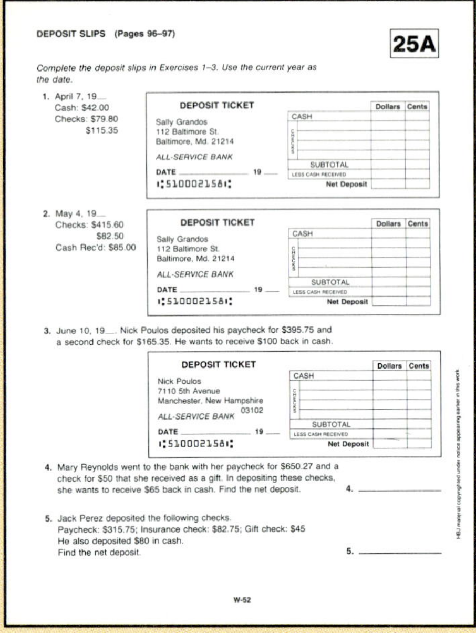

DEPOSIT SLIPS (Pages 96–97) **25A**

Complete the deposit slips in Exercises 1–3. Use the current year as the date.

1. April 7, 19__
   Cash: $42.00
   Checks: $79.80
   $115.35

DEPOSIT TICKET — Sally Grandos, 112 Baltimore St, Baltimore, Md. 21214 — ALL-SERVICE BANK — DATE ______ 19 __ — CASH / SUBTOTAL / LESS CASH RECEIVED / Net Deposit — Dollars | Cents

2. May 4, 19__
   Checks: $415.60
   $82.50
   Cash Rec'd: $85.00

DEPOSIT TICKET — Sally Grandos, 112 Baltimore St, Baltimore, Md. 21214 — ALL-SERVICE BANK — DATE ______ 19 __ — CASH / SUBTOTAL / LESS CASH RECEIVED / Net Deposit — Dollars | Cents

3. June 10, 19__. Nick Poulos deposited his paycheck for $395.75 and a second check for $165.35. He wants to receive $100 back in cash.

DEPOSIT TICKET — Nick Poulos, 7110 5th Avenue, Manchester, New Hampshire 03102 — ALL-SERVICE BANK — DATE ______ 19 __ — CASH / SUBTOTAL / LESS CASH RECEIVED / Net Deposit — Dollars | Cents

4. Mary Reynolds went to the bank with her paycheck for $650.27 and a check for $50 that she received as a gift. In depositing these checks, she wants to receive $65 back in cash. Find the net deposit. 4. ______

5. Jack Perez deposited the following checks.
   Paycheck: $315.75; Insurance check: $82.75; Gift check: $45
   He also deposited $80 in cash.
   Find the net deposit. 5. ______

Reteaching/ Alternate Teaching Strategy

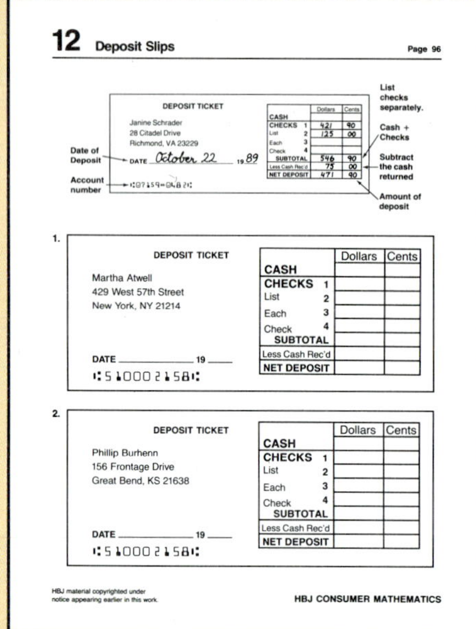

12 Deposit Slips — Page 96

DEPOSIT TICKET — Janine Schrader, 28 Citadel Drive, Richmond, VA 23229 — DATE October 22 19 89

	Dollars	Cents
CASH		
CHECKS 1	421	90
List 2	125	00
Each 3		
Check 4		
SUBTOTAL	546	90
Less Cash Rec'd	75	00
NET DEPOSIT	471	90

1. DEPOSIT TICKET — Martha Atwell, 429 West 57th Street, New York, NY 21214 — DATE ______ 19 ____

	Dollars	Cents
CASH		
CHECKS 1		
List 2		
Each 3		
Check 4		
SUBTOTAL		
Less Cash Rec'd		
NET DEPOSIT		

2. DEPOSIT TICKET — Phillip Burhenn, 156 Frontage Drive, Great Bend, KS 21638 — DATE ______ 19 ____

	Dollars	Cents
CASH		
CHECKS 1		
List 2		
Each 3		
Check 4		
SUBTOTAL		
Less Cash Rec'd		
NET DEPOSIT		

Enrichment

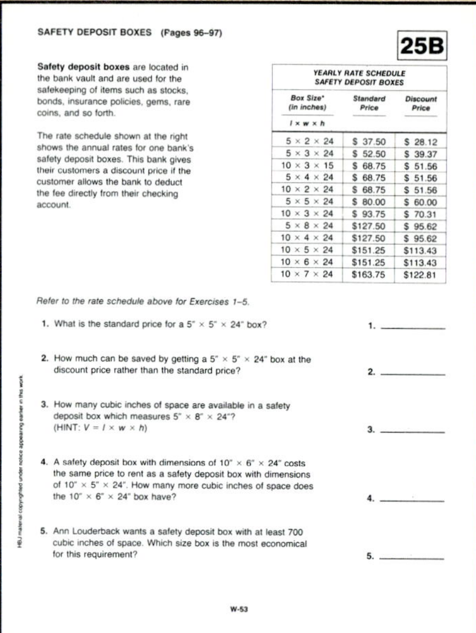

SAFETY DEPOSIT BOXES (Pages 96–97) **25B**

Safety deposit boxes are located in the bank vault and are used for the safekeeping of items such as stocks, bonds, insurance policies, gems, rare coins, and so forth.

The rate schedule shown at the right shows the annual rates for one bank's safety deposit boxes. This bank gives their customers a discount price if the customer allows the bank to deduct the fee directly from their checking account.

YEARLY RATE SCHEDULE SAFETY DEPOSIT BOXES		
Box Size* (in inches) $l \times w \times h$	**Standard Price**	**Discount Price**
5 × 2 × 24	$ 37.50	$ 28.12
5 × 3 × 24	$ 52.50	$ 39.37
10 × 3 × 15	$ 68.75	$ 51.56
5 × 4 × 24	$ 68.75	$ 51.56
10 × 2 × 24	$ 68.75	$ 51.56
5 × 5 × 24	$ 80.00	$ 60.00
10 × 3 × 24	$ 93.75	$ 70.31
5 × 8 × 24	$127.50	$ 95.62
10 × 4 × 24	$127.50	$ 95.62
10 × 5 × 24	$151.25	$113.43
10 × 6 × 24	$151.25	$113.43
10 × 7 × 24	$163.75	$122.81

Refer to the rate schedule above for Exercises 1–5.

1. What is the standard price for a 5" × 5" × 24" box? 1. ______
2. How much can be saved by getting a 5" × 5" × 24" box at the discount price rather than the standard price? 2. ______
3. How many cubic inches of space are available in a safety deposit box which measures 5" × 8" × 24"? (HINT: $V = l \times w \times h$) 3. ______
4. A safety deposit box with dimensions of 10" × 6" × 24" costs the same price to rent as a safety deposit box with dimensions of 10" × 5" × 24". How many more cubic inches of space does the 10" × 6" × 24" box have? 4. ______
5. Ann Louderback wants a safety deposit box with at least 700 cubic inches of space. Which size box is the most economical for this requirement? 5. ______

WRITING CHECKS Pages 98–99

Practice

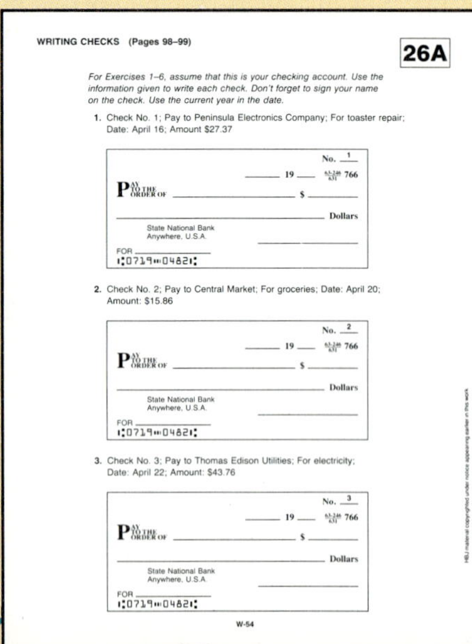

WRITING CHECKS (Pages 98–99) **26A**

For Exercises 1–6, assume that this is your checking account. Use the information given to write each check. Don't forget to sign your name on the check. Use the current year in the date.

1. Check No. 1; Pay to Peninsula Electronics Company; For toaster repair; Date: April 16; Amount $27.37

No. 1 — 19 __ — 63-246/631 766 — PAY TO THE ORDER OF ______ $ ____ — Dollars — State National Bank, Anywhere, U.S.A. — FOR ______

2. Check No. 2; Pay to Central Market; For groceries; Date: April 20; Amount: $15.86

No. 2 — 19 __ — 63-246/631 766 — PAY TO THE ORDER OF ______ $ ____ — Dollars — State National Bank, Anywhere, U.S.A. — FOR ______

3. Check No. 3; Pay to Thomas Edison Utilities; For electricity; Date: April 22; Amount: $43.76

No. 3 — 19 __ — 63-246/631 766 — PAY TO THE ORDER OF ______ $ ____ — Dollars — State National Bank, Anywhere, U.S.A. — FOR ______

Reteaching/ Alternate Teaching Strategy

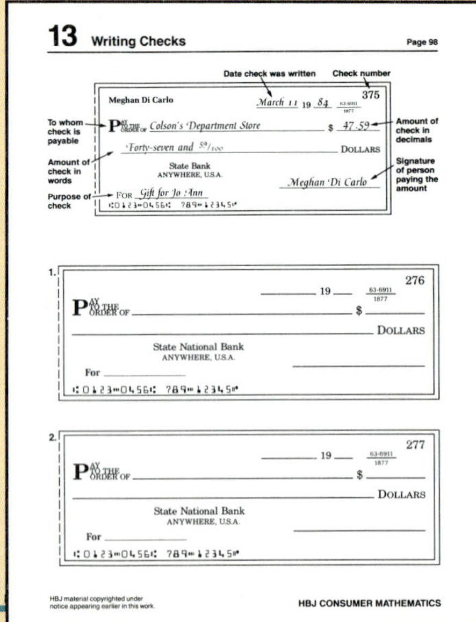

13 Writing Checks — Page 98

Meghan Di Carlo — March 11 19 84 — 375 — PAY TO THE ORDER OF Colson's Department Store $ 47.59 — Forty-seven and 59/100 DOLLARS — State Bank, ANYWHERE, U.S.A. — FOR Gift for Jo Ann — Meghan Di Carlo

1. 276 — 19 __ — 63-6911/1877 — PAY TO THE ORDER OF ______ $ ____ — DOLLARS — State National Bank, ANYWHERE, U.S.A. — For ______

2. 277 — 19 __ — 63-6911/1877 — PAY TO THE ORDER OF ______ $ ____ — DOLLARS — State National Bank, ANYWHERE, U.S.A. — For ______

Enrichment

CASHIER'S CHECKS (Pages 98–99) **26B**

A cashier's check is a bank's own check issued in exchange for money. The fee for a cashier's check is usually $1.75.

Cashier's Check — THE FIRST NATIONAL BANK — 70-6/227 — No. 182399 — PURCHASER ______ DATE ______ — PAY TO THE ORDER OF ______ $ ______ — First National Bank — $59 AND 51 CTS — AUTHORIZED BANK PERSONNEL

Refer to the sample cashier's check above to complete Exercises 1–5.

1. Who issued this cashier's check? 1. ______
2. Who purchased this cashier's check? 2. ______
3. On what date was this cashier's check written? 3. ______
4. How much money did the purchaser need to give the bank for this cashier's check? 4. ______
5. To whom is the cashier's check made payable? 5. ______
6. Jill Bradley wants to pay Dellwood Auto Supply $78.24. Complete the cashier's check below using today's date. Sign your name as the authorized bank personnel.

Cashier's Check — THE FIRST NATIONAL BANK — 70-6/227 — No. 182731 — PURCHASER ______ DATE ______ — PAY TO THE ORDER OF ______ $ ______ — First National Bank — $78 AND 24 CTS — AUTHORIZED BANK PERSONNEL

CHECK STUBS AND CHECK REGISTERS Pages 100–102

Practice

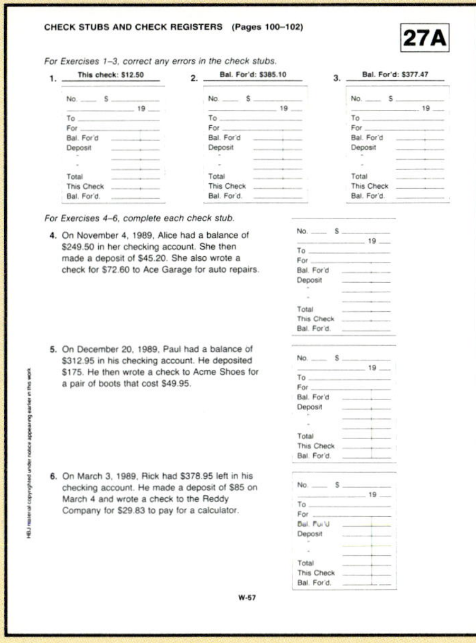
CHECK STUBS AND CHECK REGISTERS (Pages 100–102) **27A**

For Exercises 1–3, correct any errors in the check stubs.

1. This check: $12.50
2. Bal. For'd: $385.10
3. Bal. For'd: $377.47

For Exercises 4–6, complete each check stub.

4. On November 4, 1989, Alice had a balance of $249.50 in her checking account. She then made a deposit of $45.20. She also wrote a check for $72.60 to Ace Garage for auto repairs.
5. On December 20, 1989, Paul had a balance of $312.95 in his checking account. He deposited $175. He then wrote a check to Acme Shoes for a pair of boots that cost $49.95.
6. On March 3, 1989, Rick had $378.95 left in his checking account. He made a deposit of $85 on March 4 and wrote a check to the Reddy Company for $29.83 to pay for a calculator.

W-57

Reteaching/ Alternate Teaching Strategy

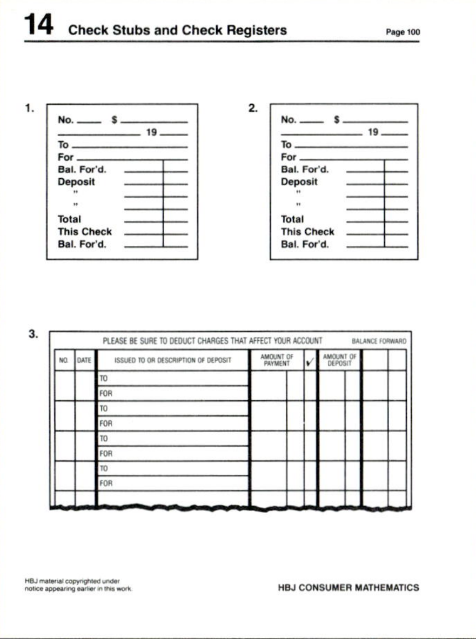
14 Check Stubs and Check Registers Page 100

1. No. ____ $ ____ 19 ____ To For Bal. For'd. Deposit " " Total This Check Bal. For'd.
2. No. ____ $ ____ 19 ____ To For Bal. For'd. Deposit " " Total This Check Bal. For'd.
3. PLEASE BE SURE TO DEDUCT CHARGES THAT AFFECT YOUR ACCOUNT — BALANCE FORWARD

NO.	DATE	ISSUED TO OR DESCRIPTION OF DEPOSIT	AMOUNT OF PAYMENT	✓	AMOUNT OF DEPOSIT
		TO			
		FOR			
		TO			
		FOR			
		TO			
		FOR			
		TO			
		FOR			

HBJ material copyrighted under notice appearing earlier in this work. HBJ CONSUMER MATHEMATICS

Enrichment

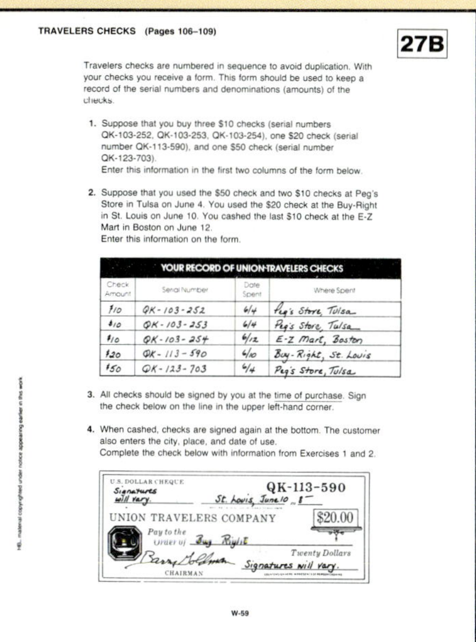
TRAVELERS CHECKS (Pages 106–109) **27B**

Travelers checks are numbered in sequence to avoid duplication. With your checks you receive a form. This form should be used to keep a record of the serial numbers and denominations (amounts) of the checks.

1. Suppose that you buy three $10 checks (serial numbers QK-103-252, QK-103-253, QK-103-254), one $20 check (serial number QK-113-590), and one $50 check (serial number QK-123-703). Enter this information in the first two columns of the form below.
2. Suppose that you used the $50 check and two $10 checks at Peg's Store in Tulsa on June 4. You used the $20 check at the Buy-Right in St. Louis on June 10. You cashed the last $10 check at the E-Z Mart in Boston on June 12. Enter this information on the form.

YOUR RECORD OF UNION TRAVELERS CHECKS

Check Amount	Serial Number	Date Spent	Where Spent
$10	QK-103-252	6/4	Peg's Store, Tulsa
$10	QK-103-253	6/4	Peg's Store, Tulsa
$10	QK-103-254	6/12	E-Z Mart, Boston
$20	QK-113-590	6/10	Buy-Right, St. Louis
$50	QK-123-703	6/4	Peg's Store, Tulsa

3. All checks should be signed by you at the time of purchase. Sign the check below on the line in the upper left-hand corner.
4. When cashed, checks are signed again at the bottom. The customer also enters the city, place, and date of use. Complete the check below with information from Exercises 1 and 2.

U.S. DOLLAR CHEQUE QK-113-590 Signatures will vary. St. Louis, June 10 UNION TRAVELERS COMPANY $20.00 Pay to the order of Buy-Right Twenty Dollars Signatures will vary. CHAIRMAN

W-59

RECONCILING A BANK STATEMENT Pages 106–109

Practice

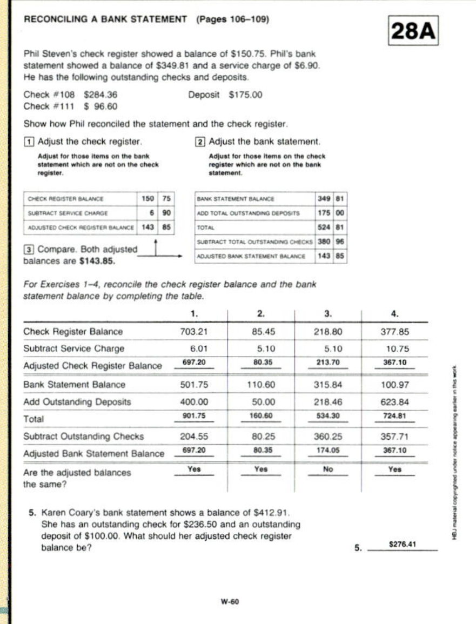
RECONCILING A BANK STATEMENT (Pages 106–109) **28A**

Phil Steven's check register showed a balance of $150.75. Phil's bank statement showed a balance of $349.81 and a service charge of $6.90. He has the following outstanding checks and deposits.

Check #108 $284.36 Deposit $175.00
Check #111 $ 96.60

Show how Phil reconciled the statement and the check register.

[1] Adjust the check register. **Adjust for those items on the bank statement which are not on the check register.**

CHECK REGISTER BALANCE	150	75
SUBTRACT SERVICE CHARGE	6	90
ADJUSTED CHECK REGISTER BALANCE	143	85

[2] Adjust the bank statement. **Adjust for those items on the check register which are not on the bank statement.**

BANK STATEMENT BALANCE	349	81
ADD TOTAL OUTSTANDING DEPOSITS	175	00
TOTAL	524	81
SUBTRACT TOTAL OUTSTANDING CHECKS	380	96
ADJUSTED BANK STATEMENT BALANCE	143	85

[3] Compare. Both adjusted balances are **$143.85.**

For Exercises 1–4, reconcile the check register balance and the bank statement balance by completing the table.

	1.	2.	3.	4.
Check Register Balance	703.21	85.45	218.80	377.85
Subtract Service Charge	6.01	5.10	5.10	10.75
Adjusted Check Register Balance	697.20	80.35	213.70	367.10
Bank Statement Balance	501.75	110.60	315.84	100.97
Add Outstanding Deposits	400.00	50.00	218.46	623.84
Total	901.75	160.60	534.30	724.81
Subtract Outstanding Checks	204.55	80.25	360.25	357.71
Adjusted Bank Statement Balance	697.20	80.35	174.05	367.10
Are the adjusted balances the same?	Yes	Yes	No	Yes

5. Karen Coary's bank statement shows a balance of $412.91. She has an outstanding check for $236.50 and an outstanding deposit of $100.00. What should her adjusted check register balance be? 5. $276.41

HBJ material copyrighted under notice appearing earlier in this work.

W-60

Reteaching/ Alternate Teaching Strategy

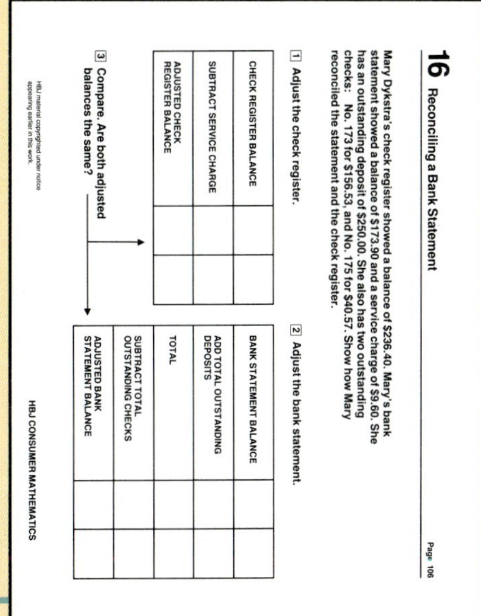
16 Reconciling a Bank Statement Page 106

Mary Dykstra's check register showed a balance of $236.40. Mary's bank statement showed a balance of $173.90 and a service charge of $9.60. She has an outstanding deposit of $250.00. She also has two outstanding checks: No. 173 for $156.53, and No. 175 for $40.57. Show how Mary reconciled the statement and the check register.

[1] Adjust the check register.

CHECK REGISTER BALANCE	
SUBTRACT SERVICE CHARGE	
ADJUSTED CHECK REGISTER BALANCE	

[2] Adjust the bank statement.

BANK STATEMENT BALANCE	
ADD TOTAL OUTSTANDING DEPOSITS	
TOTAL	
SUBTRACT TOTAL OUTSTANDING CHECKS	
ADJUSTED BANK STATEMENT BALANCE	

[3] Compare. Are both adjusted balances the same? ____

HBJ material copyrighted under notice appearing earlier in this work. HBJ CONSUMER MATHEMATICS

Enrichment

MAKING FUNDS AVAILABLE (Pages 106–109) **28B**

Banks must make funds available within a specified period of time. The chart below gives the number of business days required for a check to clear in a New York City bank.

MAKING FUNDS AVAILABLE FOR PERSONAL ACCOUNTS	
CHECKS	****Number of Business Days Required to Clear***
$100 or less Any check drawn on a bank in the U.S.	1
Over $100–$2,500 Checks drawn on this bank	1
U.S. Treasury checks/N.Y. Government checks	1
Checks drawn on other N.Y. City Banks	2
Checks drawn on N.Y. State Banks	3
Checks drawn on banks in the other 49 states and in the District of Columbia	6

*Business days exclude Saturday and Sunday

Example: Mr. Quinn lives in New York. He deposits a check for $200 drawn on a New York State bank on Monday, June 3. When will the funds be available to Mr. Quinn?

Solution: Deposit: **Monday, June 3**
Days to Clear: **3** (Tuesday Wednesday Thursday)
Funds Available: **Friday, June 7**

Refer to the chart above to complete Exercises 1–6. Assume all the accounts are New York City bank accounts.

1. Which days of the week are business days? 1. ____
2. Betty deposits a check for $75. The check was drawn on a bank in Florida. How many business days are required for the check to clear? 2. ____
3. Jim deposits a check for $150 sent to him drawn on another New York City bank on Monday, May 5. When will the funds be available to him? 3. ____
4. Pat deposits a check for $500 sent to her drawn on a bank in Kansas on Tuesday, April 10. When will the funds be available to her? 4. ____
5. Don receives a check for $2,000 from his cousin in the District of Columbia. He deposits it in his bank account on Wednesday, September 4. When will the funds be available to him? 5. ____

W-61

INTEREST Pages 110–111

Practice

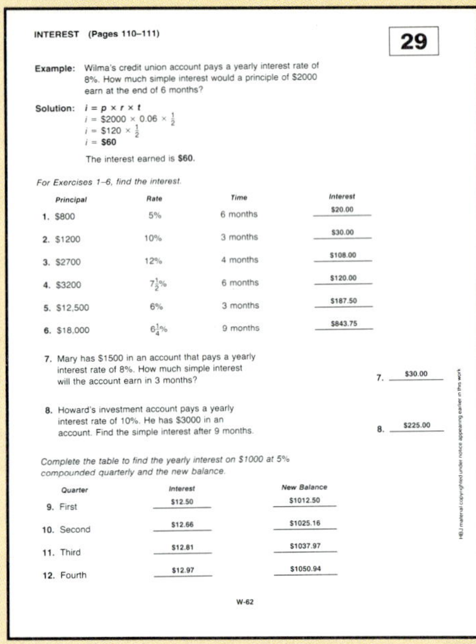

INTEREST (Pages 110–111) **29**

Example: Wilma's credit union account pays a yearly interest rate of 8%. How much simple interest would a principle of $2000 earn at the end of 6 months?

Solution: $i = p \times r \times t$
$i = \$2000 \times 0.06 \times \frac{1}{2}$
$i = \$120 \times \frac{1}{2}$
$i =$ **$60**

The interest earned is **$60.**

For Exercises 1–6, find the interest.

	Principal	Rate	Time	Interest
1.	$800	5%	6 months	$20.00
2.	$1200	10%	3 months	$30.00
3.	$2700	12%	4 months	$108.00
4.	$3200	$7\frac{1}{2}$%	6 months	$120.00
5.	$12,500	6%	3 months	$187.50
6.	$18,000	$6\frac{1}{4}$%	9 months	$843.75

7. Mary has $1500 in an account that pays a yearly interest rate of 8%. How much simple interest will the account earn in 3 months? 7. $30.00

8. Howard's investment account pays a yearly interest rate of 10%. He has $3000 in an account. Find the simple interest after 9 months. 8. $225.00

Complete the table to find the yearly interest on $1000 at 5% compounded quarterly and the new balance.

	Quarter	Interest	New Balance
9.	First	$12.50	$1012.50
10.	Second	$12.66	$1025.16
11.	Third	$12.81	$1037.97
12.	Fourth	$12.97	$1050.94

W-62

Reteaching/ Alternate Teaching Strategy

17 Interest Page 110

Problem: Find the interest on a principal of $1500 left on deposit for one year at $5\frac{3}{4}$% compounded quarterly.

$i = p \times r \times t$ — i = interest; p = principal; r = rate; t = time in years

[1] First quarter: ____________

New balance: ____________

[2] Second quarter: ____________

New balance: ____________

[3] Third quarter: ____________

New balance: ____________

[4] Fourth quarter: ____________

New balance: ____________

Interest for one year: ____________

HBJ CONSUMER MATHEMATICS

Enrichment

MATERIALS: 13 index cards
Write the following on separate cards.

p: $500 $1,000 $2,000 $5,000

r: 12.5% per year 1.5% per month
16% per year 2% per month

t: 1 year, 2 years, 6 months, 3 months

Have pairs of students take turns computing the amount of interest on each kind of card. Then ask: "Given the same amount of principal and time, which rate would be best to borrow money?" Which rate would be best if you had the money in a savings account?"

COMPOUND INTEREST Pages 112–113

Practice

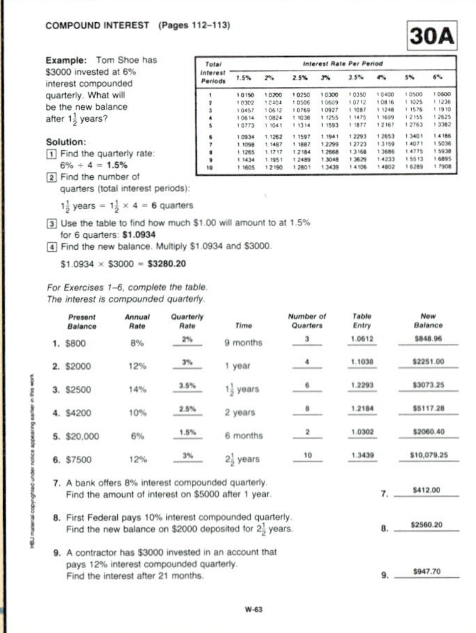

COMPOUND INTEREST (Pages 112–113) **30A**

Example: Tom Shoe has $3000 invested at 6% interest compounded quarterly. What will be the new balance after $1\frac{1}{2}$ years?

Total Interest Periods	Interest Rate Per Period 1.5%	2%	2.5%	3%	3.5%	4%	5%	6%
1	1.0150	1.0200	1.0250	1.0300	1.0350	1.0400	1.0500	1.0600
2	1.0302	1.0404	1.0506	1.0609	1.0712	1.0816	1.1025	1.1236
3	1.0457	1.0612	1.0769	1.0927	1.1087	1.1248	1.1576	1.1910
4	1.0614	1.0824	1.1038	1.1255	1.1475	1.1699	1.2155	1.2625
5	1.0773	1.1041	1.1314	1.1593	1.1877	1.2167	1.2763	1.3382
6	1.0934	1.1262	1.1597	1.1941	1.2293	1.2653	1.3401	1.4186
7	1.1098	1.1487	1.1887	1.2299	1.2723	1.3159	1.4071	1.5036
8	1.1265	1.1717	1.2184	1.2668	1.3168	1.3686	1.4775	1.5938
9	1.1434	1.1951	1.2489	1.3048	1.3629	1.4233	1.5513	1.6895
10	1.1605	1.2190	1.2801	1.3439	1.4106	1.4802	1.6289	1.7908

Solution:

[1] Find the quarterly rate:
6% ÷ 4 = **1.5%**

[2] Find the number of quarters (total interest periods):
$1\frac{1}{2}$ years = $1\frac{1}{2} \times 4$ = **6** quarters

[3] Use the table to find how much $1.00 will amount to at 1.5% for 6 quarters: **$1.0934**

[4] Find the new balance. Multiply $1.0934 and $3000.
$1.0934 × $3000 = **$3280.20**

For Exercises 1–6, complete the table. The interest is compounded quarterly.

	Present Balance	Annual Rate	Quarterly Rate	Time	Number of Quarters	Table Entry	New Balance
1.	$800	8%	2%	9 months	3	1.0612	$848.96
2.	$2000	12%	3%	1 year	4	1.1038	$2251.00
3.	$2500	14%	3.5%	$1\frac{1}{2}$ years	6	1.2293	$3073.25
4.	$4200	10%	2.5%	2 years	8	1.2184	$5117.28
5.	$20,000	6%	1.5%	6 months	2	1.0302	$2060.40
6.	$7500	12%	3%	$2\frac{1}{2}$ years	10	1.3439	$10,079.25

7. A bank offers 8% interest compounded quarterly. Find the amount of interest on $5000 after 1 year. 7. $412.00

8. First Federal pays 10% interest compounded quarterly. Find the new balance on $2000 deposited for $2\frac{1}{2}$ years. 8. $2560.20

9. A contractor has $3000 invested in an account that pays 12% interest compounded quarterly. Find the interest after 21 months. 9. $947.70

W-63

Reteaching/ Alternate Teaching Strategy

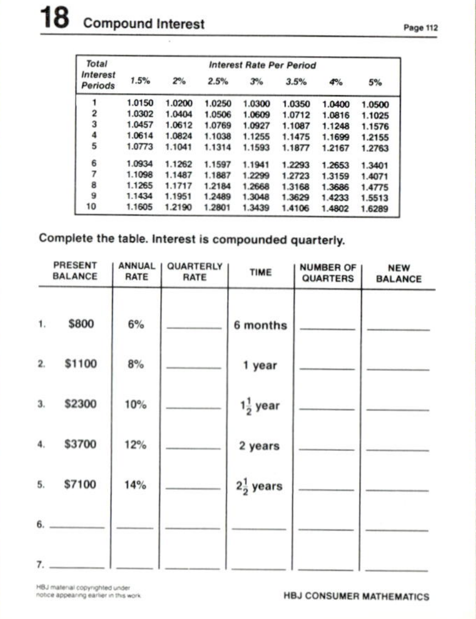

18 Compound Interest Page 112

Total Interest Periods	Interest Rate Per Period 1.5%	2%	2.5%	3%	3.5%	4%	5%
1	1.0150	1.0200	1.0250	1.0300	1.0350	1.0400	1.0500
2	1.0302	1.0404	1.0506	1.0609	1.0712	1.0816	1.1025
3	1.0457	1.0612	1.0769	1.0927	1.1087	1.1248	1.1576
4	1.0614	1.0824	1.1038	1.1255	1.1475	1.1699	1.2155
5	1.0773	1.1041	1.1314	1.1593	1.1877	1.2167	1.2763
6	1.0934	1.1262	1.1597	1.1941	1.2293	1.2653	1.3401
7	1.1098	1.1487	1.1887	1.2299	1.2723	1.3159	1.4071
8	1.1265	1.1717	1.2184	1.2668	1.3168	1.3686	1.4775
9	1.1434	1.1951	1.2489	1.3048	1.3629	1.4233	1.5513
10	1.1605	1.2190	1.2801	1.3439	1.4106	1.4802	1.6289

Complete the table. Interest is compounded quarterly.

	PRESENT BALANCE	ANNUAL RATE	QUARTERLY RATE	TIME	NUMBER OF QUARTERS	NEW BALANCE
1.	$800	6%		6 months		
2.	$1100	8%		1 year		
3.	$2300	10%		$1\frac{1}{2}$ year		
4.	$3700	12%		2 years		
5.	$7100	14%		$2\frac{1}{2}$ years		
6.						
7.						

HBJ CONSUMER MATHEMATICS

Enrichment

SAVING AND COMPOUND INTEREST (Pages 112–113) **30B**

The table below shows the monthly savings needed to obtain a given amount in 5 years at $5\frac{1}{4}$% compounded daily. Use this table to answer Exercises 1–11.

Amount Needed	Monthly Savings
$1,000	$14.35
$5,000	$71.75
$10,000	$143.50
$15,000	$215.25
$20,000	$287.00

Mr. and Mrs. Ramirez plan to buy a house in five years. They need a down payment of $10,000.

1. How much must they save each month? 1. $143.50
2. How much will this amount to in one year? 2. $1722
3. Mr. Ramirez has a yearly income of $15,563. To the nearest percent, what percent of his annual income must they save? 3. 11%
4. Mrs. Ramirez has a yearly income of $10,630. What is their total income? 4. $26,193
5. To the nearest percent, what percent of their total income must they save? 5. 7%

The Smith family will need $15,000 in five years for education expenses.

6. How much must they save each month at $5\frac{1}{4}$% compounded continuously? 6. $215.25
7. How much will the Smiths contribute to the savings plan over one year? 7. $2583
8. How much will they contribute to the savings plan over five years? 8. $12,915
9. At the end of five years, what will be the total interest earned by this savings plan? 9. $2085

The Smith family members have the following yearly incomes.

Mr. Smith: $23,500 Mrs. Smith: $13,200
Dan Smith: $1650 Marge Smith: $1740

10. What is their total yearly income? 10. $40,090
11. What percent of their total yearly income must the Smith family save each year to reach their goal? 11. 6%

W-64

STICKER PRICE Pages 126–128

Practice

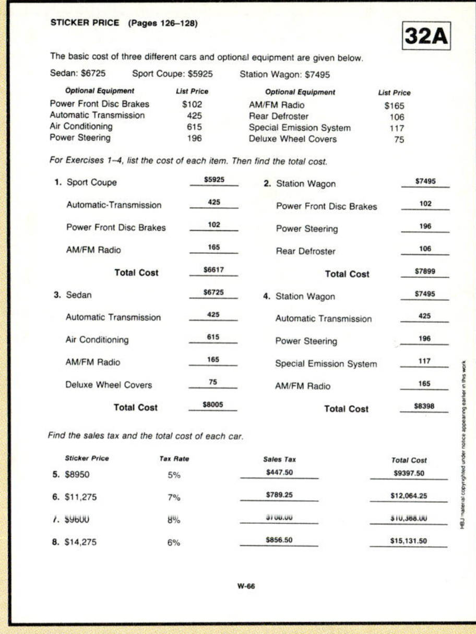

STICKER PRICE (Pages 126–128) **32A**

The basic cost of three different cars and optional equipment are given below.

Sedan: $6725 Sport Coupe: $5925 Station Wagon: $7495

Optional Equipment	List Price	Optional Equipment	List Price
Power Front Disc Brakes	$102	AM/FM Radio	$165
Automatic Transmission	425	Rear Defroster	106
Air Conditioning	615	Special Emission System	117
Power Steering	196	Deluxe Wheel Covers	75

For Exercises 1–4, list the cost of each item. Then find the total cost.

1. Sport Coupe $5925
   Automatic Transmission 425
   Power Front Disc Brakes 102
   AM/FM Radio 165
   Total Cost $6617
2. Station Wagon $7495
   Power Front Disc Brakes 102
   Power Steering 196
   Rear Defroster 106
   Total Cost $7899
3. Sedan $6725
   Automatic Transmission 425
   Air Conditioning 615
   AM/FM Radio 165
   Deluxe Wheel Covers 75
   Total Cost $8005
4. Station Wagon $7495
   Automatic Transmission 425
   Power Steering 196
   Special Emission System 117
   AM/FM Radio 165
   Total Cost $8398

Find the sales tax and the total cost of each car.

	Sticker Price	Tax Rate	Sales Tax	Total Cost
5.	$8950	5%	$447.50	$9397.50
6.	$11,275	7%	$789.25	$12,064.25
7.	$9600	8%	$768.00	$10,368.00
8.	$14,275	6%	$856.50	$15,131.50

W-66

Reteaching/ Alternate Teaching Strategy

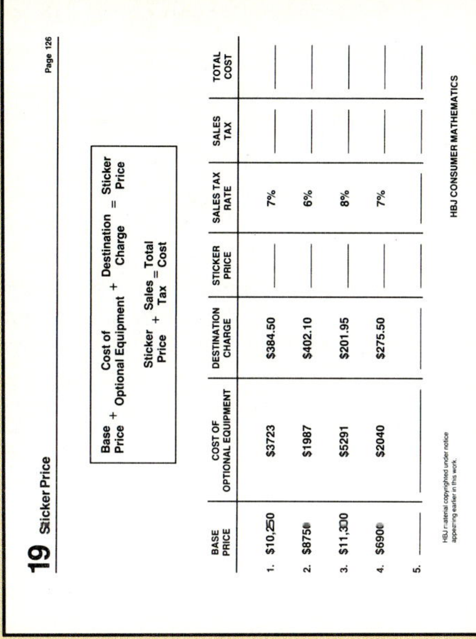

Page 126

19 Sticker Price

Base Price + Cost of Optional Equipment + Destination Charge = Sticker Price

Sticker Price + Sales Tax = Total Cost

	BASE PRICE	COST OF OPTIONAL EQUIPMENT	DESTINATION CHARGE	STICKER PRICE	SALES TAX RATE	SALES TAX	TOTAL COST
1.	$10,250	$3723	$384.50		7%		
2.	$8750	$1987	$402.10		6%		
3.	$11,300	$5291	$201.95		8%		
4.	$6900	$2040	$275.50		7%		
5.							

HBJ CONSUMER MATHEMATICS

Enrichment

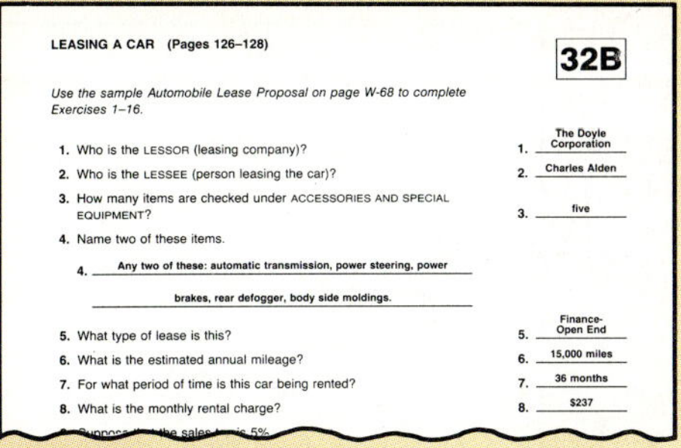

LEASING A CAR (Pages 126–128) **32B**

Use the sample Automobile Lease Proposal on page W-68 to complete Exercises 1–16.

1. Who is the LESSOR (leasing company)? 1. The Doyle Corporation
2. Who is the LESSEE (person leasing the car)? 2. Charles Alden
3. How many items are checked under ACCESSORIES AND SPECIAL EQUIPMENT? 3. five
4. Name two of these items.
   4. Any two of these: automatic transmission, power steering, power brakes, rear defogger, body side moldings.
5. What type of lease is this? 5. Finance-Open End
6. What is the estimated annual mileage? 6. 15,000 miles
7. For what period of time is this car being rented? 7. 36 months
8. What is the monthly rental charge? 8. $237

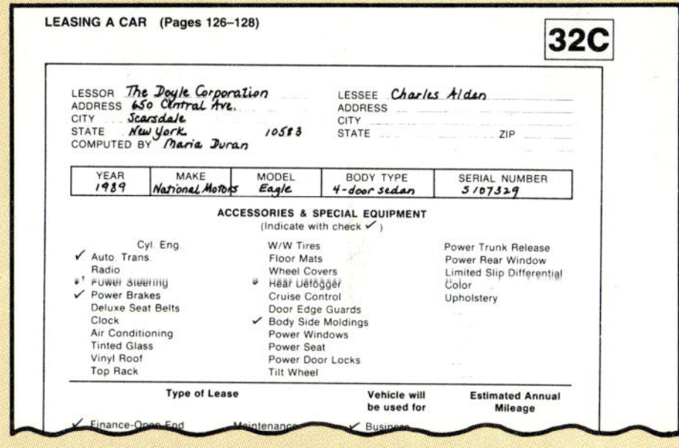

LEASING A CAR (Pages 126–128) **32C**

LESSOR The Doyle Corporation
ADDRESS 650 Central Ave.
CITY Scarsdale
STATE New York 10583
COMPUTED BY Maria Duran

LESSEE Charles Alden
ADDRESS
CITY
STATE ZIP

YEAR	MAKE	MODEL	BODY TYPE	SERIAL NUMBER
1989	National Motors	Eagle	4-door sedan	5107329

ACCESSORIES & SPECIAL EQUIPMENT
(Indicate with check ✓)

Cyl. Eng.
✓ Auto. Trans.
Radio
✓ Power Steering
✓ Power Brakes
Deluxe Seat Belts
Clock
Air Conditioning
Tinted Glass
Vinyl Roof
Top Rack

W/W Tires
Floor Mats
Wheel Covers
✓ Rear Defogger
Cruise Control
Door Edge Guards
✓ Body Side Moldings
Power Windows
Power Seat
Power Door Locks
Tilt Wheel

Power Trunk Release
Power Rear Window
Limited Slip Differential
Color
Upholstery

Type of Lease | Vehicle will be used for | Estimated Annual Mileage

✓ Finance-Open End Maintenance ✓ Business

MAKING A DEAL Pages 130–131

Practice

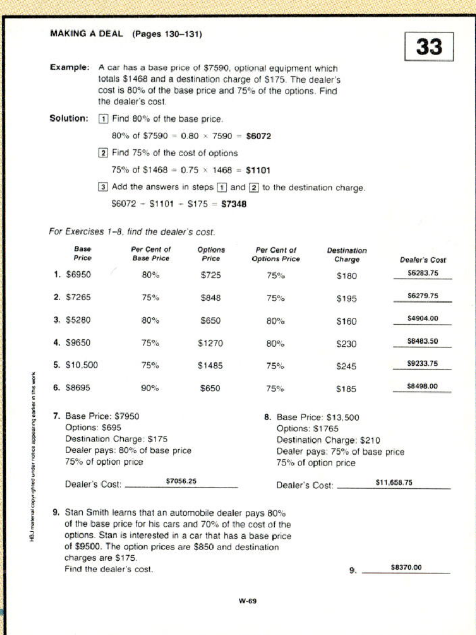

MAKING A DEAL (Pages 130–131) **33**

Example: A car has a base price of $7590, optional equipment which totals $1468 and a destination charge of $175. The dealer's cost is 80% of the base price and 75% of the options. Find the dealer's cost.

Solution: [1] Find 80% of the base price.

80% of $7590 = 0.80 × 7590 = **$6072**

[2] Find 75% of the cost of options

75% of $1468 = 0.75 × 1468 = **$1101**

[3] Add the answers in steps [1] and [2] to the destination charge.

$6072 + $1101 + $175 = **$7348**

For Exercises 1–8, find the dealer's cost.

	Base Price	Per Cent of Base Price	Options Price	Per Cent of Options Price	Destination Charge	Dealer's Cost
1.	$6950	80%	$725	75%	$180	$6283.75
2.	$7265	75%	$848	75%	$195	$6279.75
3.	$5280	80%	$650	80%	$160	$4904.00
4.	$9650	75%	$1270	80%	$230	$8483.50
5.	$10,500	75%	$1485	75%	$245	$9233.75
6.	$8695	90%	$650	75%	$185	$8498.00

7. Base Price: $7950
   Options: $695
   Destination Charge: $175
   Dealer pays: 80% of base price
   75% of option price
   Dealer's Cost: $7056.25
8. Base Price: $13,500
   Options: $1765
   Destination Charge: $210
   Dealer pays: 75% of base price
   75% of option price
   Dealer's Cost: $11,658.75
9. Stan Smith learns that an automobile dealer pays 80% of the base price for his cars and 70% of the cost of the options. Stan is interested in a car that has a base price of $9500. The option prices are $850 and destination charges are $175.
   Find the dealer's cost. 9. $8370.00

W-69

Reteaching/ Alternate Teaching Strategy

Write a base price and the cost of the options for a new car on one index card for each student.

Have each student draw a card and calculate the dealer's cost if the dealer pays 85% of base price and 75% of cost of options. Then have the students make an offer that will give the dealer a 7% proft on the sale.

You may wish to have two students exchange cards and check the other's calculations.

Enrichment

Have the students use this information to solve the exercises that follow.

The dealer pays destination charge, 85% of the base price, and 75% of the cost of options

The dealers cost is $10,531.00. The cost of options is $1,484.00 and the base price is $10,860.00. What is the destination charge**? (ANS: $187.00)**

The dealer wants to make a 7% profit on all cars. He sells a car for $12,770. The cost of options is $2472, the destination charge is $240, and the base price is $11,780. Find the dealer's cost. Did he receive a 7% profit? **(ANS: $107; No)**

FINANCING A CAR Pages 132–133

Practice

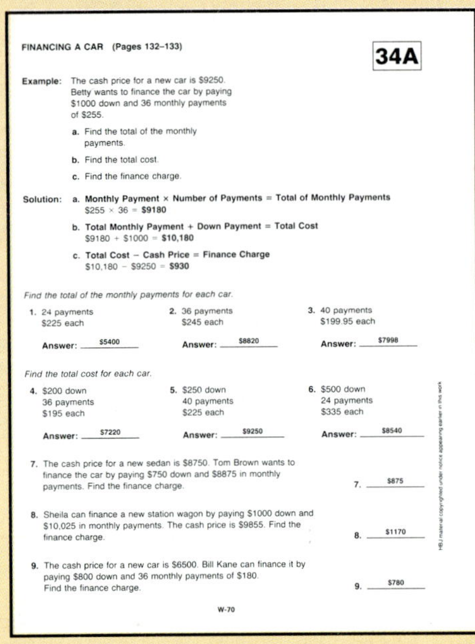

FINANCING A CAR (Pages 132–133) **34A**

Example: The cash price for a new car is $9250. Betty wants to finance the car by paying $1000 down and 36 monthly payments of $255.

a. Find the total of the monthly payments.

b. Find the total cost.

c. Find the finance charge.

Solution: a. **Monthly Payment × Number of Payments = Total of Monthly Payments**
$255 × 36 = **$9180**

b. **Total Monthly Payment + Down Payment = Total Cost**
$9180 + $1000 = **$10,180**

c. **Total Cost − Cash Price = Finance Charge**
$10,180 − $9250 = **$930**

Find the total of the monthly payments for each car.

1. 24 payments, $225 each — Answer: $5400
2. 36 payments, $245 each — Answer: $8820
3. 40 payments, $199.95 each — Answer: $7998

Find the total cost for each car.

4. $200 down, 36 payments, $195 each — Answer: $7220
5. $250 down, 40 payments, $225 each — Answer: $9250
6. $500 down, 24 payments, $335 each — Answer: $8540

7. The cash price for a new sedan is $8750. Tom Brown wants to finance the car by paying $750 down and $8875 in monthly payments. Find the finance charge. — 7. $875

8. Sheila can finance a new station wagon by paying $1000 down and $10,025 in monthly payments. The cash price is $9855. Find the finance charge. — 8. $1170

9. The cash price for a new car is $6500. Bill Kane can finance it by paying $800 down and 36 monthly payments of $180. Find the finance charge. — 9. $780

W-70

Reteaching/ Alternate Teaching Strategy

A reteaching lesson can be structured for this topic by having students supply the concrete materials. These concrete materials then would be the basis for the lesson.

Have each student bring to class one newspaper advertisement in which the sales price, down payment, and monthly payment are named.

These advertisements then become a source bank of real world problems that you can use for presenting the lesson.

Enrichment

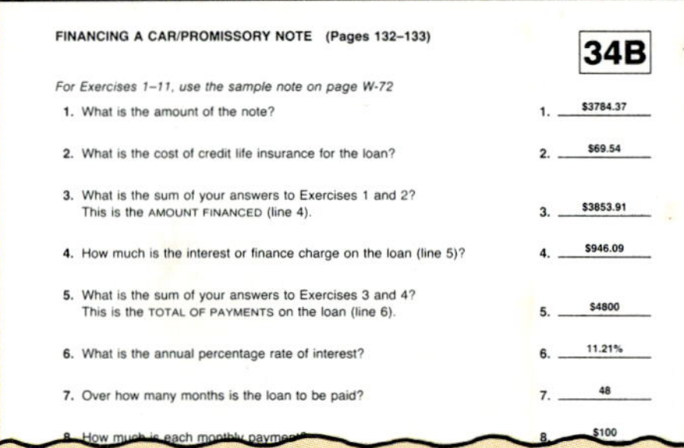

FINANCING A CAR/PROMISSORY NOTE (Pages 132–133) **34B**

For Exercises 1–11, use the sample note on page W-72

1. What is the amount of the note? — 1. $3784.37
2. What is the cost of credit life insurance for the loan? — 2. $69.54
3. What is the sum of your answers to Exercises 1 and 2? This is the AMOUNT FINANCED (line 4). — 3. $3853.91
4. How much is the interest or finance charge on the loan (line 5)? — 4. $946.09
5. What is the sum of your answers to Exercises 3 and 4? This is the TOTAL OF PAYMENTS on the loan (line 6). — 5. $4800
6. What is the annual percentage rate of interest? — 6. 11.21%
7. Over how many months is the loan to be paid? — 7. 48
8. How much is each monthly payment? — 8. $100

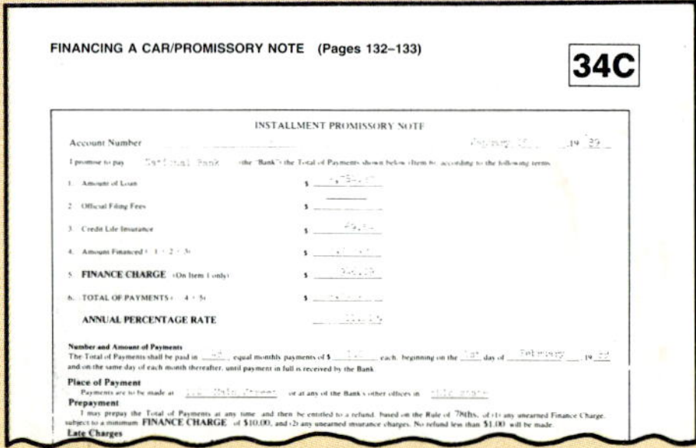

FINANCING A CAR/PROMISSORY NOTE (Pages 132–133) **34C**

INSTALLMENT PROMISSORY NOTE

Account Number

1. Amount of Loan $
2. Official Filing Fees $
3. Credit Life Insurance $
4. Amount Financed $
5. FINANCE CHARGE $
6. TOTAL OF PAYMENTS $

ANNUAL PERCENTAGE RATE

Number and Amount of Payments

Place of Payment

Prepayment

Late Charges

LIABILITY INSURANCE Pages 135–136

Practice

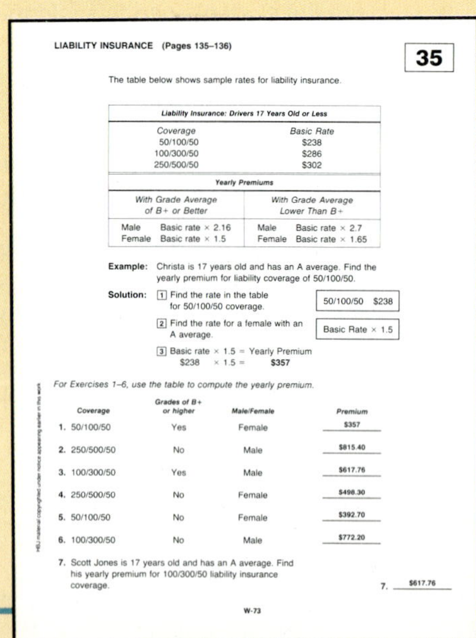

LIABILITY INSURANCE (Pages 135–136) **35**

The table below shows sample rates for liability insurance.

Liability Insurance: Drivers 17 Years Old or Less	
Coverage	*Basic Rate*
50/100/50	$238
100/300/50	$286
250/500/50	$302

Yearly Premiums	
With Grade Average of B+ or Better	*With Grade Average Lower Than B+*
Male Basic rate × 2.16	Male Basic rate × 2.7
Female Basic rate × 1.5	Female Basic rate × 1.65

Example: Christa is 17 years old and has an A average. Find the yearly premium for liability coverage of 50/100/50.

Solution: [1] Find the rate in the table for 50/100/50 coverage. — 50/100/50 $238

[2] Find the rate for a female with an A average. — Basic Rate × 1.5

[3] Basic rate × 1.5 = Yearly Premium
$238 × 1.5 = **$357**

For Exercises 1–6, use the table to compute the yearly premium.

	Coverage	Grades of B+ or higher	Male/Female	Premium
1.	50/100/50	Yes	Female	$357
2.	250/500/50	No	Male	$815.40
3.	100/300/50	Yes	Male	$617.76
4.	250/500/50	No	Female	$498.30
5.	50/100/50	No	Female	$392.70
6.	100/300/50	No	Male	$772.20

7. Scott Jones is 17 years old and has an A average. Find his yearly premium for 100/300/50 liability insurance coverage. — 7. $617.76

W-73

Reteaching/ Alternate Teaching Strategy

Use the insurance rate table on page 135 or make a similar table. Write each level of coverage (three) and each driver category (four) on index cards.

Then have each student draw a card from each pack and use the table to find the annual premium for that combination of driver catagory and liability coverage.

You may wish to use two tables and ask students to find the savings possible if they can use the better rates when calculating the premium.

Enrichment

Have students interview an insurance agent to learn the conditions that result in higher or lower premium rates for liability insurance, conditions like those given in the table on page 135. Some examples are:

- safe driving record
- low mileage use of car
- multiple cars insured
- weight/horsepower of car

Ask students to learn, also, how one can arrive at the schedule for coverage that will provide sufficient liability protection at the most reasonable cost.

COLLISION/COMPREHENSIVE INSURANCE Pages 137–138

Practice

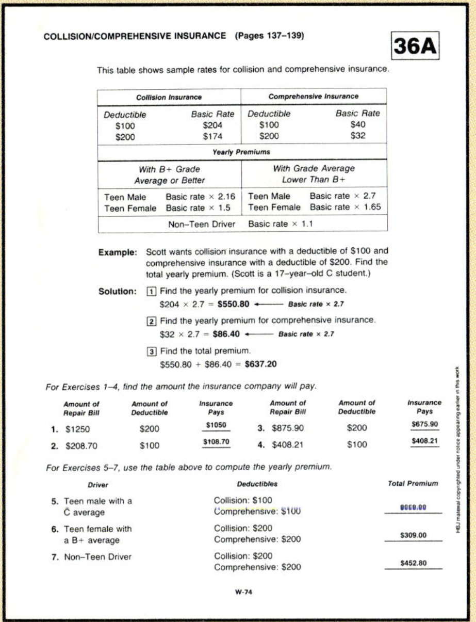

COLLISION/COMPREHENSIVE INSURANCE (Pages 137–139) **36A**

This table shows sample rates for collision and comprehensive insurance.

Collision Insurance		*Comprehensive Insurance*	
Deductible	*Basic Rate*	*Deductible*	*Basic Rate*
$100	$204	$100	$40
$200	$174	$200	$32
Yearly Premiums			
With B+ Grade Average or Better		*With Grade Average Lower Than B+*	
Teen Male	Basic rate × 2.16	Teen Male	Basic rate × 2.7
Teen Female	Basic rate × 1.5	Teen Female	Basic rate × 1.65
Non–Teen Driver	Basic rate × 1.1		

Example: Scott wants collision insurance with a deductible of $100 and comprehensive insurance with a deductible of $200. Find the total yearly premium. (Scott is a 17–year–old C student.)

Solution:
1. Find the yearly premium for collision insurance.
   $204 × 2.7 = **$550.80** ← ***Basic rate × 2.7***
2. Find the yearly premium for comprehensive insurance.
   $32 × 2.7 = **$86.40** ← ***Basic rate × 2.7***
3. Find the total premium.
   $550.80 + $86.40 = **$637.20**

For Exercises 1–4, find the amount the insurance company will pay.

	Amount of Repair Bill	Amount of Deductible	Insurance Pays		Amount of Repair Bill	Amount of Deductible	Insurance Pays
1.	$1250	$200	$1050	3.	$875.90	$200	$675.90
2.	$208.70	$100	$108.70	4.	$408.21	$100	$408.21

For Exercises 5–7, use the table above to compute the yearly premium.

	Driver	Deductibles	Total Premium
5.	Teen male with a C average	Collision: $100 Comprehensive: $100	[illegible]
6.	Teen female with a B+ average	Collision: $200 Comprehensive: $200	$309.00
7.	Non–Teen Driver	Collision: $200 Comprehensive: $200	$452.80

W-74

Reteaching/ Alternate Teaching Strategy

Use the insurance rate table on page 137. Then mark 12 index cards with the four possible choices of insurance and deductibles and 10 index cards with the five possible driver catagories.

Have each student write a repair or loss amount on a sheet of paper. Then have them draw a card from each stack to find the insurance rate and the amount of the claim that will be paid by the insurance company after the deductible is subtracted from the total bill.

Enrichment

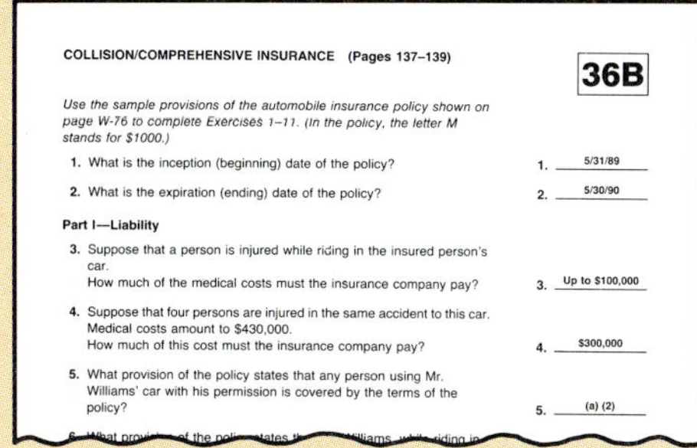

COLLISION/COMPREHENSIVE INSURANCE (Pages 137–139) **36B**

Use the sample provisions of the automobile insurance policy shown on page W-76 to complete Exercises 1–11. (In the policy, the letter M stands for $1000.)

1. What is the inception (beginning) date of the policy? 1. 5/31/89
2. What is the expiration (ending) date of the policy? 2. 5/30/90

Part I—Liability

3. Suppose that a person is injured while riding in the insured person's car. How much of the medical costs must the insurance company pay? 3. Up to $100,000
4. Suppose that four persons are injured in the same accident to this car. Medical costs amount to $430,000. How much of this cost must the insurance company pay? 4. $300,000
5. What provision of the policy states that any person using Mr. Williams' car with his permission is covered by the terms of the policy? 5. (a) (2)

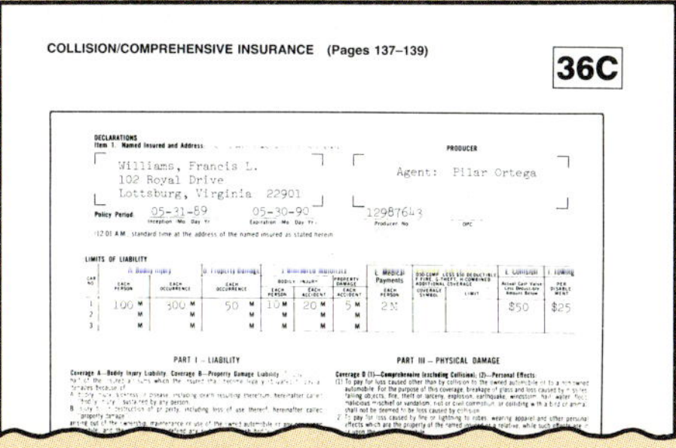

COLLISION/COMPREHENSIVE INSURANCE (Pages 137–139) **36C**

MAINTENANCE COSTS Pages 152–154

Practice

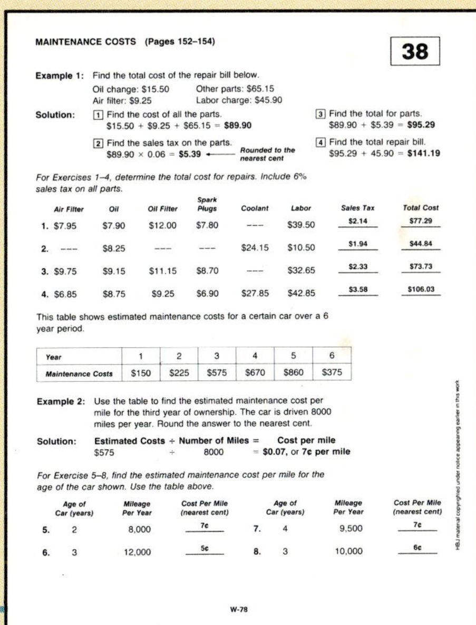

MAINTENANCE COSTS (Pages 152–154) **38**

Example 1: Find the total cost of the repair bill below.
Oil change: $15.50 Other parts: $65.15
Air filter: $9.25 Labor charge: $45.90

Solution:
1. Find the cost of all the parts.
   $15.50 + $9.25 + $65.15 = **$89.90**
2. Find the sales tax on the parts.
   $89.90 × 0.06 = **$5.39** ← ***Rounded to the nearest cent***
3. Find the total for parts.
   $89.90 + $5.39 = **$95.29**
4. Find the total repair bill.
   $95.29 + 45.90 = **$141.19**

For Exercises 1–4, determine the total cost for repairs. Include 6% sales tax on all parts.

	Air Filter	Oil	Oil Filter	Spark Plugs	Coolant	Labor	Sales Tax	Total Cost
1.	$7.95	$7.90	$12.00	$7.80	---	$39.50	$2.14	$77.29
2.	---	$8.25	---	---	$24.15	$10.50	$1.94	$44.84
3.	$9.75	$9.15	$11.15	$8.70	---	$32.65	$2.33	$73.73
4.	$6.85	$8.75	$9.25	$6.90	$27.85	$42.85	$3.58	$106.03

This table shows estimated maintenance costs for a certain car over a 6 year period.

Year	1	2	3	4	5	6
Maintenance Costs	$150	$225	$575	$670	$860	$375

Example 2: Use the table to find the estimated maintenance cost per mile for the third year of ownership. The car is driven 8000 miles per year. Round the answer to the nearest cent.

Solution: **Estimated Costs ÷ Number of Miles = Cost per mile**
$575 ÷ 8000 = **$0.07,** or **7¢ per mile**

For Exercise 5–8, find the estimated maintenance cost per mile for the age of the car shown. Use the table above.

	Age of Car (years)	Mileage Per Year	Cost Per Mile (nearest cent)		Age of Car (years)	Mileage Per Year	Cost Per Mile (nearest cent)
5.	2	8,000	7¢	7.	4	9,500	7¢
6.	3	12,000	5¢	8.	3	10,000	6¢

W-78

Reteaching/ Alternate Teaching Strategy

A reteaching lesson can be structured for this topic by having students supply the concrete materials. These concrete materials then would be the basis for the lesson.

Have students bring to class several advertisements which include prices for parts and labor for an automobile maintenance/repair job. Use these prices to find the greatest and least cost for a selected job, such as a 6-cyclinder tune-up or brake repair.

Enrichment

Explain to students that some auto maintenance depends only on the number of miles driven. Then post the following list or distribute one copy to each student.

Item	Cost	Miles
4 tires	$200.00	30,000
Oil Change	18.60	3,000
Air Filter	6.00	15,000
Spark Plugs (set)	20.00	30,000
Battery	75.00	50,000
Repair Brakes	65.00	50,000
Align front end	26.50	15,000
Wiper blades	6.50	40,000

Have students find the cost per mile of each item, to the nearest $0.001, and the total per mile for all items, to the nearest $0.01. **(ANS: $0.007, $0.006, $0.000, $0.001, $0.002, $0.001, $0.002, $0.000,** total per mile: **$0.02)**

DEPRECIATION Pages 156–158

Practice

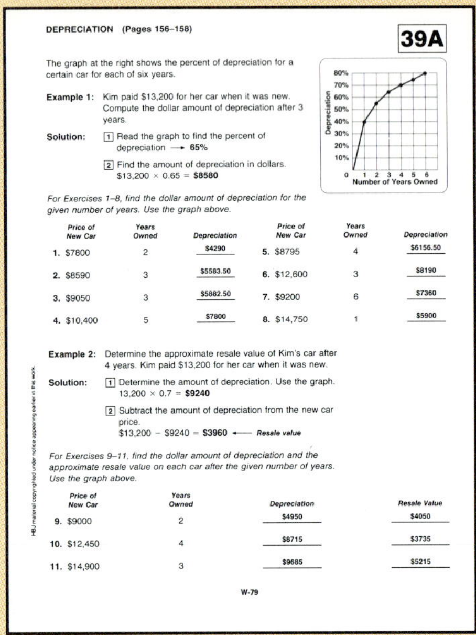

DEPRECIATION (Pages 156–158) **39A**

The graph at the right shows the percent of depreciation for a certain car for each of six years.

Example 1: Kim paid $13,200 for her car when it was new. Compute the dollar amount of depreciation after 3 years.

Solution: [1] Read the graph to find the percent of depreciation → **65%**

[2] Find the amount of depreciation in dollars. $13,200 × 0.65 = **$8580**

For Exercises 1–8, find the dollar amount of depreciation for the given number of years. Use the graph above.

	Price of New Car	Years Owned	Depreciation		Price of New Car	Years Owned	Depreciation
1.	$7800	2	$4290	5.	$8795	4	$6156.50
2.	$8590	3	$5583.50	6.	$12,600	3	$8190
3.	$9050	3	$5882.50	7.	$9200	6	$7360
4.	$10,400	5	$7800	8.	$14,750	1	$5900

Example 2: Determine the approximate resale value of Kim's car after 4 years. Kim paid $13,200 for her car when it was new.

Solution: [1] Determine the amount of depreciation. Use the graph. 13,200 × 0.7 = **$9240**

[2] Subtract the amount of depreciation from the new car price. $13,200 − $9240 = **$3960** ← *Resale value*

For Exercises 9–11, find the dollar amount of depreciation and the approximate resale value on each car after the given number of years. Use the graph above.

	Price of New Car	Years Owned	Depreciation	Resale Value
9.	$9000	2	$4950	$4050
10.	$12,450	4	$8715	$3735
11.	$14,900	3	$9685	$5215

W-79

Reteaching/ Alternate Teaching Strategy

A reteaching lesson can be structured for this topic by having students supply the concrete materials. These concrete materials then would be the basis for the lesson.

Have students bring to class several newspaper and magazine advertisements for both new and used cars. Match the similar car makes and models to find the new and depreciated prices.

Then have students use these prices to find the amount of depreciation and the percent depreciation for several car models.

You may wish to find the rate of depreciation for boats or small trucks if there is evident student interest.

Enrichment

DEPRECIATION TABLE (Pages 156–158) **39B**

The table below gives estimates for the amount of the annual depreciation of a certain car over a ten-year period.

Year	Amount of Depreciation	Year	Amount of Depreciation
First	$1282	Sixth	$323
Second	$ 789	Seventh	$308
Third	$ 661	Eighth	$308
Fourth	$ 492	Ninth	$307
Fifth	$ 359	Tenth	$292

1. For which year was the estimated amount of depreciation the most? 1. First
2. For which year was the estimated amount of depreciation the least? 2. Tenth

In Exercises 3–8, find the total estimated amount of depreciation.

3. First two years $2071 | 4. First three years $2732
5. First five years $3583 | 6. Last two years $599
7. Last three years $907 | 8. Last five years $1538
9. Find the total estimated amount of depreciation over the ten year period. 9. $5121

Use the estimates in the table to find the average yearly depreciation for these time periods.

10. First three years $910.67 | 11. Last three years $302.33
12. Use the estimates in the table to find the average yearly depreciation over the ten year period. 12. $512.10

Suppose that this car was driven 10,000 miles each year. Compute each amount of depreciation per mile. Give your answer to the nearest cent.

13. For the first year 13¢ | 14. For the fifth year 4¢

Suppose that this car was driven 16,000 kilometers each year. Compute the amount of depreciation per kilometer. Give your answer to the nearest cent.

15. For the first year 8¢ | 16. For the third year 4¢
17. For the fifth year 2¢ | 18. For the sixth year 2¢
19. For the ninth year 2¢ | 20. For the tenth year 2¢

W-80

GASOLINE COSTS Pages 160–162

Practice

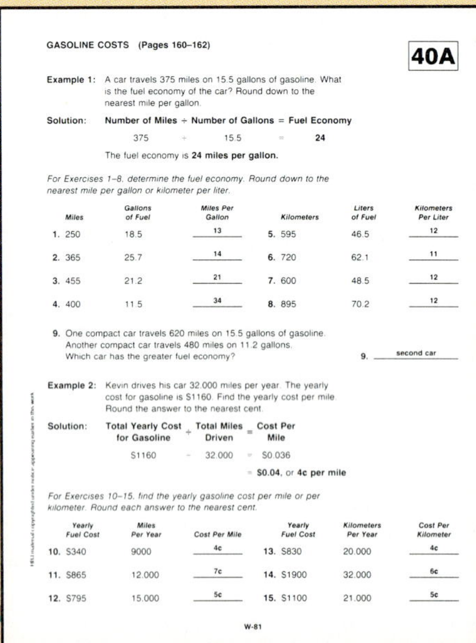

GASOLINE COSTS (Pages 160–162) **40A**

Example 1: A car travels 375 miles on 15.5 gallons of gasoline. What is the fuel economy of the car? Round down to the nearest mile per gallon.

Solution: **Number of Miles ÷ Number of Gallons = Fuel Economy**

375 ÷ 15.5 = **24**

The fuel economy is **24 miles per gallon.**

For Exercises 1–8, determine the fuel economy. Round down to the nearest mile per gallon or kilometer per liter.

	Miles	Gallons of Fuel	Miles Per Gallon		Kilometers	Liters of Fuel	Kilometers Per Liter
1.	250	18.5	13	5.	595	46.5	12
2.	365	25.7	14	6.	720	62.1	11
3.	455	21.2	21	7.	600	48.5	12
4.	400	11.5	34	8.	895	70.2	12

9. One compact car travels 620 miles on 15.5 gallons of gasoline. Another compact car travels 480 miles on 11.2 gallons. Which car has the greater fuel economy? 9. second car

Example 2: Kevin drives his car 32,000 miles per year. The yearly cost for gasoline is $1160. Find the yearly cost per mile. Round the answer to the nearest cent.

Solution: **Total Yearly Cost for Gasoline ÷ Total Miles Driven = Cost Per Mile**

$1160 ÷ 32,000 = $0.036

= **$0.04**, or **4¢ per mile**

For Exercises 10–15, find the yearly gasoline cost per mile or per kilometer. Round each answer to the nearest cent.

	Yearly Fuel Cost	Miles Per Year	Cost Per Mile		Yearly Fuel Cost	Kilometers Per Year	Cost Per Kilometer
10.	$340	9000	4¢	13.	$830	20,000	4¢
11.	$865	12,000	7¢	14.	$1900	32,000	6¢
12.	$795	15,000	5¢	15.	$1100	21,000	5¢

W-81

Reteaching/ Alternate Teaching Strategy

A reteaching lesson can be structured for this topic by having students supply the concrete materials. These concrete materials then would be the basis for the lesson.

Have students bring to class any statements about the miles-per-gallon economy of all kinds of automobiles, trucks, and recreational vehicles. List the vehicles in order from best to worst economy rating.

Then have students find the cost of the round trip to a selected city at the current price per gallon of gasoline for each vehicle.

Enrichment

REDUCING GASOLINE COSTS (Pages 160–162) **40B**

Here are some ways of increasing fuel efficiency.

- Keep engine tuned.
- Drive within speed limits.
- No sudden stopping or starting.
- Avoid prolonged idling.
- Keep proper tire pressure.

Beth estimates that she will use 600 gallons of gasoline this year.

1. Find the total amount Beth will spend on gasoline at $1.17 per gallon. 1. $702
2. Beth can save 20% of this cost by having her car properly tuned. How much money can Beth save? 2. $14.04

Six minutes of idling will use as much gasoline as driving a car one mile at 30 miles per hour.

3. Bill left his car idling for 12 minutes. How far could Bill have driven at a speed of 30 miles per hour and still use the same amount of gasoline? 3. 2 miles

For every 4 gallons of gasoline used driving at a speed of 30 miles per hour, it would take 5 gallons of gasoline to cover the same distance driving at a speed of 50 miles per hour.

4. Andy used 20 gallons of gasoline on a trip in which he drove at a speed of 50 miles per hour. How many gallons of gasoline would Andy have used driving at a speed of 30 miles per hour? 4. 16 gallons
5. If gasoline costs Andy $1.24 per gallon, how much money could Andy have saved on his trip by traveling at a speed of 30 miles per hour rather than at a speed of 50 miles per hour? 5. $4.96
6. Andy used 32 gallons of gasoline on a trip by driving at 30 miles per hour. How many more gallons would he have used by driving at 50 miles per hour? 6. 8

W-82

YEARLY DRIVING COSTS Pages 163–165

Practice

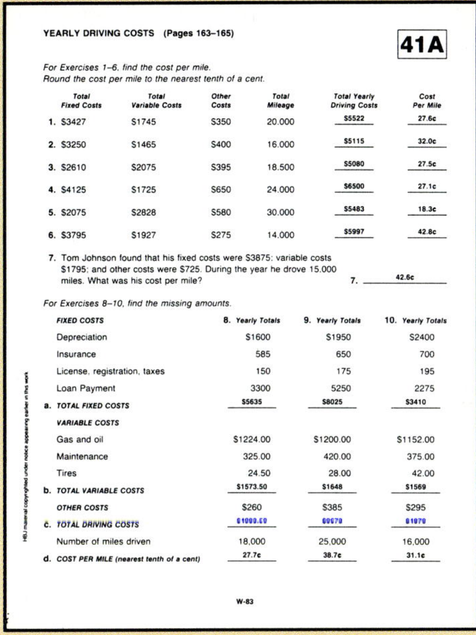

YEARLY DRIVING COSTS (Pages 163–165)

41A

For Exercises 1–6, find the cost per mile.
Round the cost per mile to the nearest tenth of a cent.

	Total Fixed Costs	Total Variable Costs	Other Costs	Total Mileage	Total Yearly Driving Costs	Cost Per Mile
1.	$3427	$1745	$350	20.000	$5522	27.6¢
2.	$3250	$1465	$400	16.000	$5115	32.0¢
3.	$2610	$2075	$395	18.500	$5080	27.5¢
4.	$4125	$1725	$650	24.000	$6500	27.1¢
5.	$2075	$2828	$580	30.000	$5483	18.3¢
6.	$3795	$1927	$275	14.000	$5997	42.8¢

7. Tom Johnson found that his fixed costs were $3875: variable costs $1795; and other costs were $725. During the year he drove 15.000 miles. What was his cost per mile? 7. 42.6¢

For Exercises 8–10, find the missing amounts.

		8. Yearly Totals	9. Yearly Totals	10. Yearly Totals
	FIXED COSTS			
	Depreciation	$1600	$1950	$2400
	Insurance	585	650	700
	License, registration, taxes	150	175	195
	Loan Payment	3300	5250	2275
a.	*TOTAL FIXED COSTS*	$5635	$8025	$3410
	VARIABLE COSTS			
	Gas and oil	$1224.00	$1200.00	$1152.00
	Maintenance	325.00	420.00	375.00
	Tires	24.50	28.00	42.00
b.	*TOTAL VARIABLE COSTS*	$1573.50	$1648	$1569
	OTHER COSTS	$260	$385	$295
c.	*TOTAL DRIVING COSTS*	[illegible]	[illegible]	[illegible]
	Number of miles driven	18,000	25,000	16,000
d.	*COST PER MILE (nearest tenth of a cent)*	27.7¢	38.7¢	31.1¢

W-83

Reteaching/ Alternate Teaching Strategy

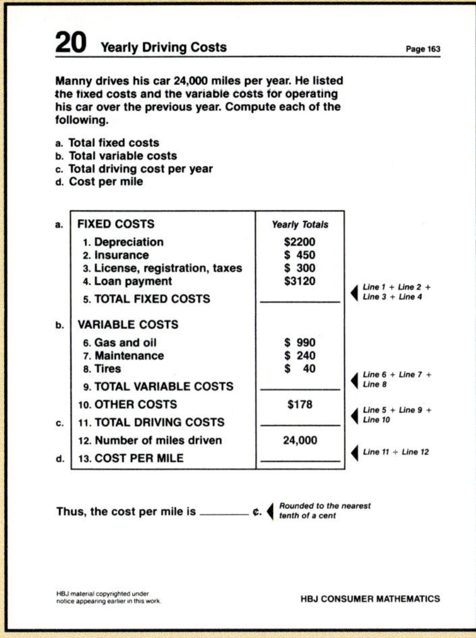

20 Yearly Driving Costs Page 163

Manny drives his car 24,000 miles per year. He listed the fixed costs and the variable costs for operating his car over the previous year. Compute each of the following.

a. Total fixed costs
b. Total variable costs
c. Total driving cost per year
d. Cost per mile

		Yearly Totals	
a.	FIXED COSTS		
	1. Depreciation	$2200	
	2. Insurance	$ 450	
	3. License, registration, taxes	$ 300	
	4. Loan payment	$3120	
	5. TOTAL FIXED COSTS		◀ Line 1 + Line 2 + Line 3 + Line 4
b.	VARIABLE COSTS		
	6. Gas and oil	$ 990	
	7. Maintenance	$ 240	
	8. Tires	$ 40	
	9. TOTAL VARIABLE COSTS		◀ Line 6 + Line 7 + Line 8
	10. OTHER COSTS	$178	
c.	11. TOTAL DRIVING COSTS		◀ Line 5 + Line 9 + Line 10
	12. Number of miles driven	24,000	
d.	13. COST PER MILE		◀ Line 11 ÷ Line 12

Thus, the cost per mile is ________ ¢. ◀ Rounded to the nearest tenth of a cent

HBJ CONSUMER MATHEMATICS

Enrichment

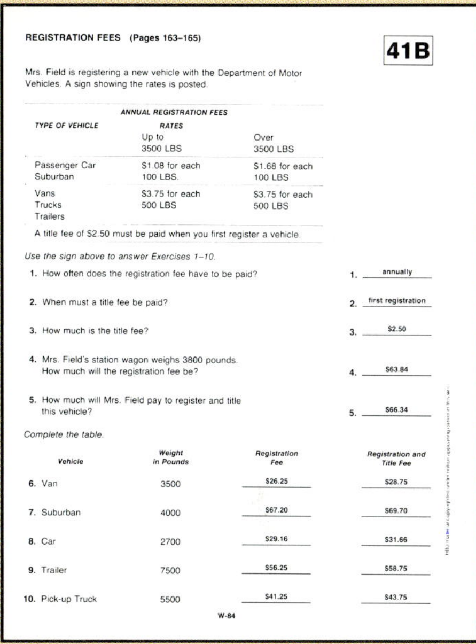

REGISTRATION FEES (Pages 163–165)

41B

Mrs. Field is registering a new vehicle with the Department of Motor Vehicles. A sign showing the rates is posted.

TYPE OF VEHICLE	*ANNUAL REGISTRATION FEES* *RATES* Up to 3500 LBS	Over 3500 LBS
Passenger Car Suburban	$1.08 for each 100 LBS.	$1.68 for each 100 LBS
Vans Trucks Trailers	$3.75 for each 500 LBS	$3.75 for each 500 LBS

A title fee of $2.50 must be paid when you first register a vehicle.

Use the sign above to answer Exercises 1–10.

1. How often does the registration fee have to be paid? 1. annually
2. When must a title fee be paid? 2. first registration
3. How much is the title fee? 3. $2.50
4. Mrs. Field's station wagon weighs 3800 pounds. How much will the registration fee be? 4. $63.84
5. How much will Mrs. Field pay to register and title this vehicle? 5. $66.34

Complete the table.

Vehicle	*Weight in Pounds*	*Registration Fee*	*Registration and Title Fee*
6. Van	3500	$26.25	$28.75
7. Suburban	4000	$67.20	$69.70
8. Car	2700	$29.16	$31.66
9. Trailer	7500	$56.25	$58.75
10. Pick-up Truck	5500	$41.25	$43.75

W-84

COMPARING TRAVEL COSTS: AUTO AND BUS Pages 178–179

Practice

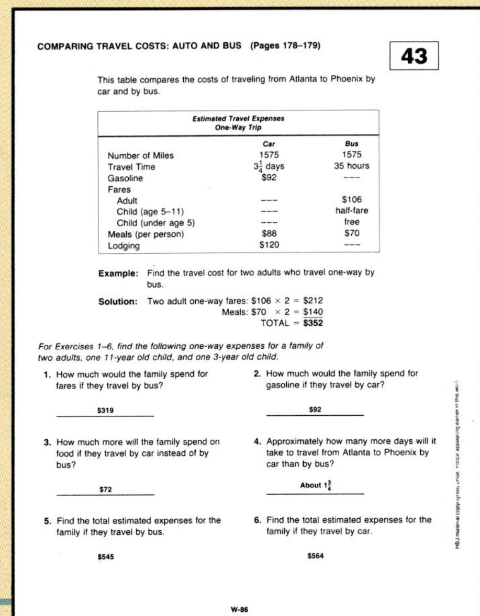

COMPARING TRAVEL COSTS: AUTO AND BUS (Pages 178–179)

43

This table compares the costs of traveling from Atlanta to Phoenix by car and by bus.

Estimated Travel Expenses One-Way Trip

	Car	*Bus*
Number of Miles	1575	1575
Travel Time	$3\frac{1}{4}$ days	35 hours
Gasoline	$92	---
Fares		
Adult	---	$106
Child (age 5–11)	---	half-fare
Child (under age 5)	---	free
Meals (per person)	$88	$70
Lodging	$120	---

Example: Find the travel cost for two adults who travel one-way by bus.

Solution: Two adult one-way fares: $106 × 2 = $212
Meals: $70 × 2 = $140
TOTAL = **$352**

For Exercises 1–6, find the following one-way expenses for a family of two adults, one 11-year old child, and one 3-year old child.

1. How much would the family spend for fares if they travel by bus? $319
2. How much would the family spend for gasoline if they travel by car? $92
3. How much more will the family spend on food if they travel by car instead of by bus? $72
4. Approximately how many more days will it take to travel from Atlanta to Phoenix by car than by bus? About $1\frac{3}{4}$
5. Find the total estimated expenses for the family if they travel by bus. $545
6. Find the total estimated expenses for the family if they travel by car. $564

W-86

Reteaching/ Alternate Teaching Strategy

A reteaching lesson can be structured for this topic by having students supply the concrete materials. These concrete materials then would be the basis for the lesson.

Have students bring to class a local bus company rate schedule along with any special excursion rates currently available in your area. For car expense, you may wish to obtain the operating cost per mile suggested by an auto club or car rental agency.

These rate/cost figures then become a source bank of real world problems that you can use for presenting the lesson.

Enrichment

Obtain, or have students obtain, bus route and fare schedules. Then have students work in small groups to plan a trip to a selected city. Plans for the trip should include driving expenses, cost of meals and lodging, and any restricted bus fare specials that are available.

Have each group choose a preferred way to travel and give reasons for their choice.

COMPARING TRAVEL COSTS: PLANE AND TRAIN Pages 180–181

Practice

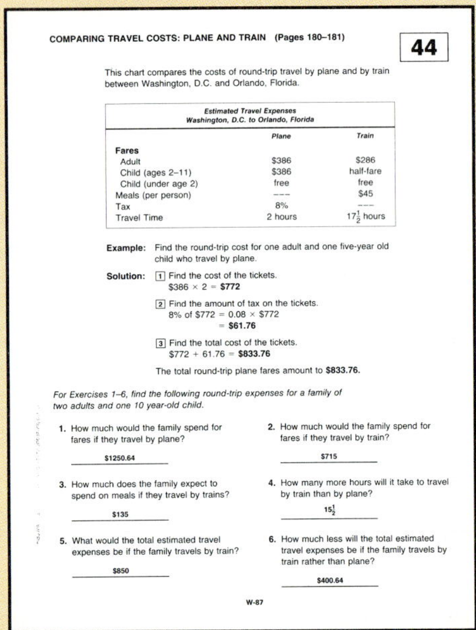

COMPARING TRAVEL COSTS: PLANE AND TRAIN (Pages 180–181) **44**

This chart compares the costs of round-trip travel by plane and by train between Washington, D.C. and Orlando, Florida.

Estimated Travel Expenses
Washington, D.C. to Orlando, Florida

	Plane	*Train*
Fares		
Adult	\$386	\$286
Child (ages 2–11)	\$386	half-fare
Child (under age 2)	free	free
Meals (per person)	---	\$45
Tax	8%	---
Travel Time	2 hours	$17\frac{1}{2}$ hours

Example: Find the round-trip cost for one adult and one five-year old child who travel by plane.

Solution: [1] Find the cost of the tickets.
\$386 × 2 = **\$772**

[2] Find the amount of tax on the tickets.
8% of \$772 = 0.08 × \$772
= **\$61.76**

[3] Find the total cost of the tickets.
\$772 + 61.76 = **\$833.76**

The total round-trip plane fares amount to **\$833.76.**

For Exercises 1–6, find the following round-trip expenses for a family of two adults and one 10 year-old child.

1. How much would the family spend for fares if they travel by plane? **\$1250.64**
2. How much would the family spend for fares if they travel by train? **\$715**
3. How much does the family expect to spend on meals if they travel by trains? **\$135**
4. How many more hours will it take to travel by train than by plane? **$15\frac{1}{2}$**
5. What would the total estimated travel expenses be if the family travels by train? **\$850**
6. How much less will the total estimated travel expenses be if the family travels by train rather than plane? **\$400.64**

W-87

Reteaching/ Alternate Teaching Strategy

A reteaching lesson can be structured for this topic by having students supply the concrete materials. These concrete materials then would be the basis for the lesson.

Have one group of students bring to class plane fares and trip schedules. Have another group obtain the same for trains. Each group should be encouraged to find special trip fares that represent significant savings.

These fare and trip schedules then become a source bank of real world problems that you can use for presenting the lesson.

Enrichment

Have students work in small groups to plan one trip of more than 1000 miles and another trip of less than 200 miles. Have the groups plan travel on locally available train and plane accomodations.

Then have the groups find totals and calculate the cost per mile for each kind of travel for each trip. Total costs should include commuting to and from airports and savings resulting from use of fare specials for each trip.

You may wish to have each group compare their costs per mile with other groups.

RENTING A CAR Pages 184–186

Practice

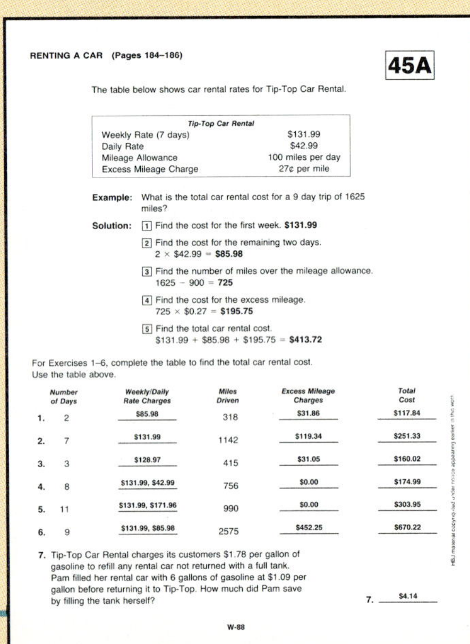

RENTING A CAR (Pages 184–186) **45A**

The table below shows car rental rates for Tip-Top Car Rental.

Tip-Top Car Rental	
Weekly Rate (7 days)	\$131.99
Daily Rate	\$42.99
Mileage Allowance	100 miles per day
Excess Mileage Charge	27¢ per mile

Example: What is the total car rental cost for a 9 day trip of 1625 miles?

Solution: [1] Find the cost for the first week. **\$131.99**

[2] Find the cost for the remaining two days.
2 × \$42.99 = **\$85.98**

[3] Find the number of miles over the mileage allowance.
1625 − 900 = **725**

[4] Find the cost for the excess mileage.
725 × \$0.27 = **\$195.75**

[5] Find the total car rental cost.
\$131.99 + \$85.98 + \$195.75 = **\$413.72**

For Exercises 1–6, complete the table to find the total car rental cost. Use the table above.

	Number of Days	*Weekly/Daily Rate Charges*	*Miles Driven*	*Excess Mileage Charges*	*Total Cost*
1.	2	\$85.98	318	\$31.86	\$117.84
2.	7	\$131.99	1142	\$119.34	\$251.33
3.	3	\$128.97	415	\$31.05	\$160.02
4.	8	\$131.99, \$42.99	756	\$0.00	\$174.99
5.	11	\$131.99, \$171.96	990	\$0.00	\$303.95
6.	9	\$131.99, \$85.98	2575	\$452.25	\$670.22

7. Tip-Top Car Rental charges its customers \$1.78 per gallon of gasoline to refill any rental car not returned with a full tank. Pam filled her rental car with 6 gallons of gasoline at \$1.09 per gallon before returning it to Tip-Top. How much did Pam save by filling the tank herself? 7. **\$4.14**

HBJ material copyrighted under notice appearing earlier in this work.

W-88

Reteaching/ Alternate Teaching Strategy

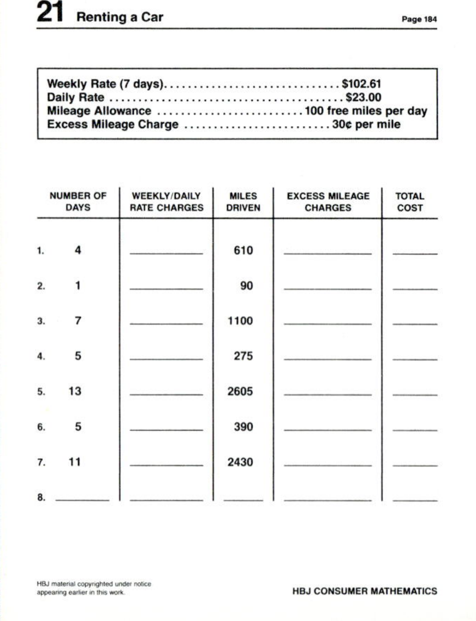

21 Renting a Car Page 184

Weekly Rate (7 days) \$102.61
Daily Rate \$23.00
Mileage Allowance .... 100 free miles per day
Excess Mileage Charge .... 30¢ per mile

	NUMBER OF DAYS	WEEKLY/DAILY RATE CHARGES	MILES DRIVEN	EXCESS MILEAGE CHARGES	TOTAL COST
1.	4	_____	610	_____	_____
2.	1	_____	90	_____	_____
3.	7	_____	1100	_____	_____
4.	5	_____	275	_____	_____
5.	13	_____	2605	_____	_____
6.	5	_____	390	_____	_____
7.	11	_____	2430	_____	_____
8.	_____	_____	_____	_____	_____

HBJ material copyrighted under notice appearing earlier in this work.

HBJ CONSUMER MATHEMATICS

Enrichment

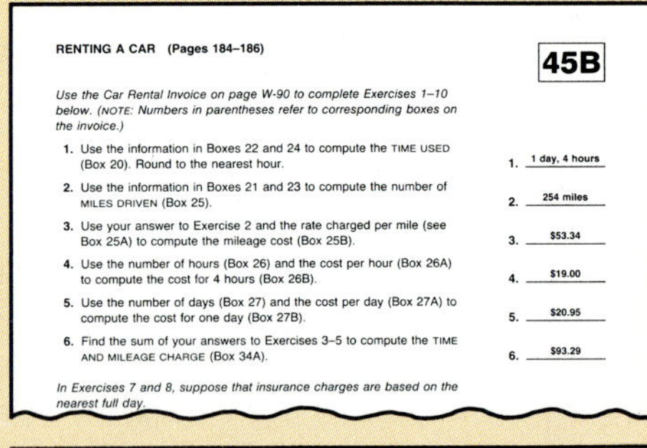

RENTING A CAR (Pages 184–186) **45B**

Use the Car Rental Invoice on page W-90 to complete Exercises 1–10 below. (NOTE: Numbers in parentheses refer to corresponding boxes on the invoice.)

1. Use the information in Boxes 22 and 24 to compute the TIME USED (Box 20). Round to the nearest hour. 1. **1 day, 4 hours**
2. Use the information in Boxes 21 and 23 to compute the number of MILES DRIVEN (Box 25). 2. **254 miles**
3. Use your answer to Exercise 2 and the rate charged per mile (see Box 25A) to compute the mileage cost (Box 25B). 3. **\$53.34**
4. Use the number of hours (Box 26) and the cost per hour (Box 26A) to compute the cost for 4 hours (Box 26B). 4. **\$19.00**
5. Use the number of days (Box 27) and the cost per day (Box 27A) to compute the cost for one day (Box 27B). 5. **\$20.95**
6. Find the sum of your answers to Exercises 3–5 to compute the TIME AND MILEAGE CHARGE (Box 34A). 6. **\$93.29**

In Exercises 7 and 8, suppose that insurance charges are based on the nearest full day.

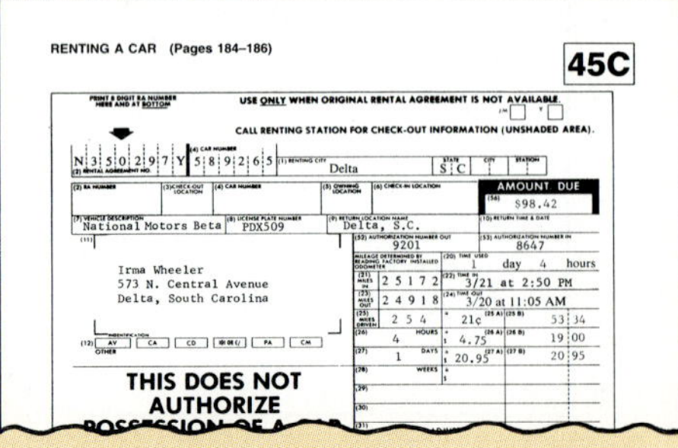

RENTING A CAR (Pages 184–186) **45C**

USE ONLY WHEN ORIGINAL RENTAL AGREEMENT IS NOT AVAILABLE.

CALL RENTING STATION FOR CHECK-OUT INFORMATION (UNSHADED AREA).

(2) Rental Agreement No.: N 3 5 0 2 9 7 Y
(4) Car Number: 5 8 9 2 6 5
(1) Renting City: Delta State: S C

AMOUNT DUE (56): \$98.42

(7) Vehicle Description: National Motors Beta
(8) License Plate Number: PDX509
(9) Return Location Name: Delta, S.C.

(52) Authorization Number Out: 9201
(53) Authorization Number In: 8647

Irma Wheeler
573 N. Central Avenue
Delta, South Carolina

(20) Time Used: 1 day 4 hours
(21) Miles In: 2 5 1 7 2 (22) Time In: 3/21 at 2:50 PM
(23) Miles Out: 2 4 9 1 8 (24) Time Out: 3/20 at 11:05 AM
(25) Miles Driven: 2 5 4 @ 21¢ (25 B) 53.34
(26) 4 Hours @ \$4.75 (26 B) 19.00
(27) 1 Days @ \$20.95 (27 B) 20.95
(28) Weeks

THIS DOES NOT AUTHORIZE POSSESSION OF A CAR

NUTRITION LABELS Pages 200–202

Practice

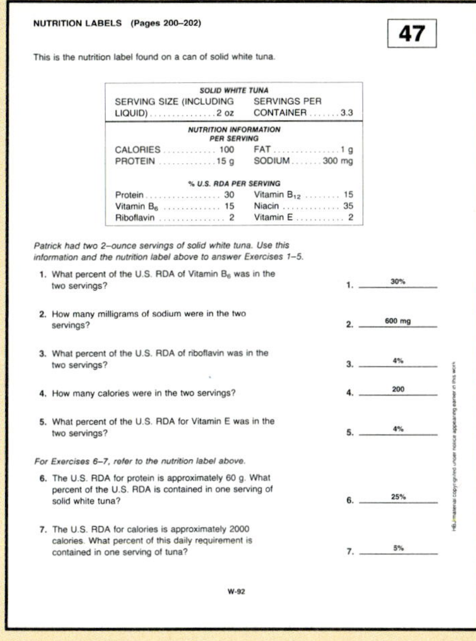

NUTRITION LABELS (Pages 200–202) **47**

This is the nutrition label found on a can of solid white tuna.

SOLID WHITE TUNA

SERVING SIZE (INCLUDING LIQUID) .... 2 oz — SERVINGS PER CONTAINER 3.3

NUTRITION INFORMATION PER SERVING

CALORIES	100	FAT	1 g
PROTEIN	15 g	SODIUM	300 mg

% U.S. RDA PER SERVING

Protein	30	Vitamin B_{12}	15
Vitamin B_6	15	Niacin	35
Riboflavin	2	Vitamin E	2

Patrick had two 2–ounce servings of solid white tuna. Use this information and the nutrition label above to answer Exercises 1–5.

1. What percent of the U.S. RDA of Vitamin B_6 was in the two servings? 1. 30%
2. How many milligrams of sodium were in the two servings? 2. 600 mg
3. What percent of the U.S. RDA of riboflavin was in the two servings? 3. 4%
4. How many calories were in the two servings? 4. 200
5. What percent of the U.S. RDA for Vitamin E was in the two servings? 5. 4%

For Exercises 6–7, refer to the nutrition label above.

6. The U.S. RDA for protein is approximately 60 g. What percent of the U.S. RDA is contained in one serving of solid white tuna? 6. 25%
7. The U.S. RDA for calories is approximately 2000 calories. What percent of this daily requirement is contained in one serving of tuna? 7. 5%

W-92

Reteaching/ Alternate Teaching Strategy

23 Nutrition Labels — Page 200

STEWED TOMATOES

Net Weight .... $14\frac{1}{2}$ oz

NUTRITION INFORMATION—PER $\frac{1}{2}$-CUP SERVING

SERVINGS PER CAN APPROX. 4

CALORIES	35	CARBOHYDRATE	8 g
PROTEIN	1 g	FAT	0 g
		SODIUM	360 mg

% U.S. RDA PER SERVING

VITAMIN A	10	NIACIN	2
VITAMIN C	30	CALCIUM	2

1. What percent of the U.S. RDA for calcium is contained in one serving of stewed tomatoes?
2. How much protein would there be in two servings of stewed tomatoes?
3. The U.S. RDA for calcium for adults is approximately 800 grams. How many grams of calcium are supplied by one serving of stewed tomatoes?
4. There are 18 milligrams of Vitamin C in one serving of stewed tomatoes. What is the approximate total U.S. RDA for Vitamin C?

HBJ CONSUMER MATHEMATICS

Enrichment

Have students work in small groups to prepare a list of questions for a professional who is responsible to plan and prepare nutritious menus.

Then prepare a questionaire that could be presented to the cafeteria manager, a hospital nutritionist, or the home economics teacher.

You may wish to have students compile the responses on the chalkboard for comparison and discussion.

COMPARING COSTS: UNIT PRICE Pages 203–205

Practice

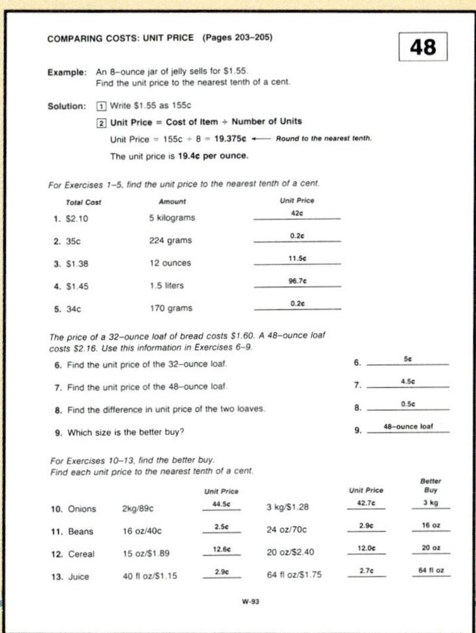

COMPARING COSTS: UNIT PRICE (Pages 203–205) **48**

Example: An 8–ounce jar of jelly sells for $1.55. Find the unit price to the nearest tenth of a cent.

Solution: [1] Write $1.55 as 155c

[2] **Unit Price = Cost of Item ÷ Number of Units**

Unit Price = 155c ÷ 8 = **19.375c** ← *Round to the nearest tenth.*

The unit price is **19.4c per ounce.**

For Exercises 1–5, find the unit price to the nearest tenth of a cent.

	Total Cost	Amount	Unit Price
1.	$2.10	5 kilograms	42c
2.	35c	224 grams	0.2c
3.	$1.38	12 ounces	11.5c
4.	$1.45	1.5 liters	96.7c
5.	34c	170 grams	0.2c

The price of a 32–ounce loaf of bread costs $1.60. A 48–ounce loaf costs $2.16. Use this information in Exercises 6–9.

6. Find the unit price of the 32–ounce loaf. 6. 5c
7. Find the unit price of the 48–ounce loaf. 7. 4.5c
8. Find the difference in unit price of the two loaves. 8. 0.5c
9. Which size is the better buy? 9. 48–ounce loaf

For Exercises 10–13, find the better buy. Find each unit price to the nearest tenth of a cent.

			Unit Price		Unit Price	Better Buy
10.	Onions	2kg/89c	44.5c	3 kg/$1.28	42.7c	3 kg
11.	Beans	16 oz/40c	2.5c	24 oz/70c	2.9c	16 oz
12.	Cereal	15 oz/$1.89	12.6c	20 oz/$2.40	12.0c	20 oz
13.	Juice	40 fl oz/$1.15	2.9c	64 fl oz/$1.75	2.7c	64 fl oz

W-93

Reteaching/ Alternate Teaching Strategy

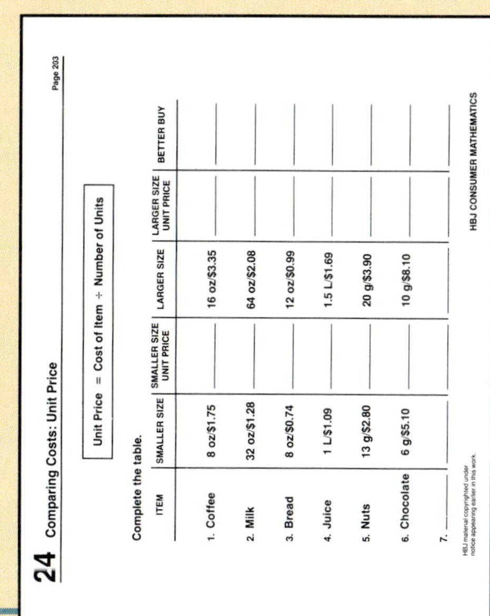

24 Comparing Costs: Unit Price — Page 203

Unit Price = Cost of Item ÷ Number of Units

Complete the table.

ITEM	SMALLER SIZE	SMALLER SIZE UNIT PRICE	LARGER SIZE	LARGER SIZE UNIT PRICE	BETTER BUY
1. Coffee	8 oz/$1.75		16 oz/$3.35		
2. Milk	32 oz/$1.28		64 oz/$2.08		
3. Bread	8 oz/$0.74		12 oz/$0.99		
4. Juice	1 L/$1.09		1.5 L/$1.69		
5. Nuts	13 g/$2.80		20 g/$3.90		
6. Chocolate	6 g/$5.10		10 g/$8.10		
7.					

HBJ CONSUMER MATHEMATICS

Enrichment

Another method of finding the best buy compares the price of the same number (or weight) of objects.

Example: 5 bars for 99¢
3 bars for 60¢

Find the cost of 3 × 5 or 15 bars of each by multiplying each price by the number of items in the competing price:

5 bars for 99¢ 3 × $.99 = $2.97

3 bars for 60¢ 5 × $0.60 = $3.00

Each price is for 15 bars, so 5 for 99¢ is a better buy.

SAVING MONEY: COUPONS Pages 206–207

Practice

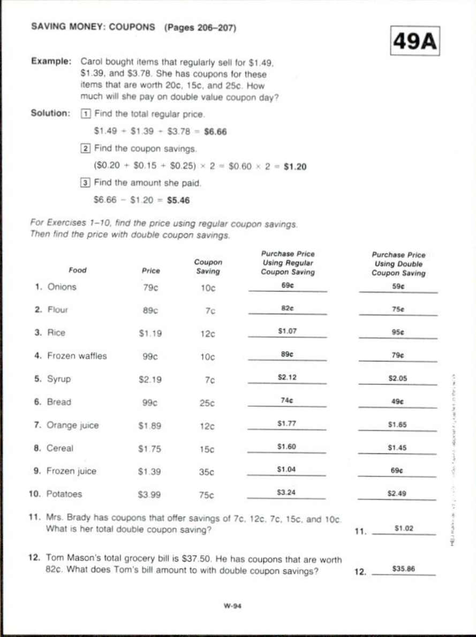

SAVING MONEY: COUPONS (Pages 206–207) **49A**

Example: Carol bought items that regularly sell for $1.49, $1.39, and $3.78. She has coupons for these items that are worth 20¢, 15¢, and 25¢. How much will she pay on double value coupon day?

Solution: 1 Find the total regular price.
$1.49 + $1.39 + $3.78 = **$6.66**
2 Find the coupon savings.
($0.20 + $0.15 + $0.25) × 2 = $0.60 × 2 = **$1.20**
3 Find the amount she paid.
$6.66 − $1.20 = **$5.46**

For Exercises 1–10, find the price using regular coupon savings. Then find the price with double coupon savings.

	Food	Price	Coupon Saving	Purchase Price Using Regular Coupon Saving	Purchase Price Using Double Coupon Saving
1.	Onions	79¢	10¢	69¢	59¢
2.	Flour	89¢	7¢	82¢	75¢
3.	Rice	$1.19	12¢	$1.07	95¢
4.	Frozen waffles	99¢	10¢	89¢	79¢
5.	Syrup	$2.19	7¢	$2.12	$2.05
6.	Bread	99¢	25¢	74¢	49¢
7.	Orange juice	$1.89	12¢	$1.77	$1.65
8.	Cereal	$1.75	15¢	$1.60	$1.45
9.	Frozen juice	$1.39	35¢	$1.04	69¢
10.	Potatoes	$3.99	75¢	$3.24	$2.49

11. Mrs. Brady has coupons that offer savings of 7¢, 12¢, 7¢, 15¢, and 10¢. What is her total double coupon saving? 11. $1.02

12. Tom Mason's total grocery bill is $37.50. He has coupons that are worth 82¢. What does Tom's bill amount to with double coupon savings? 12. $35.86

W-94

Reteaching/ Alternate Teaching Strategy

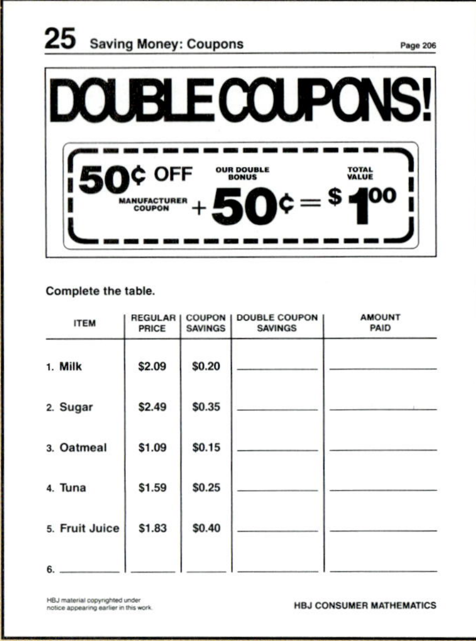

25 Saving Money: Coupons Page 206

Complete the table.

ITEM	REGULAR PRICE	COUPON SAVINGS	DOUBLE COUPON SAVINGS	AMOUNT PAID
1. Milk	$2.09	$0.20		
2. Sugar	$2.49	$0.35		
3. Oatmeal	$1.09	$0.15		
4. Tuna	$1.59	$0.25		
5. Fruit Juice	$1.83	$0.40		
6.				

 HBJ CONSUMER MATHEMATICS

Enrichment

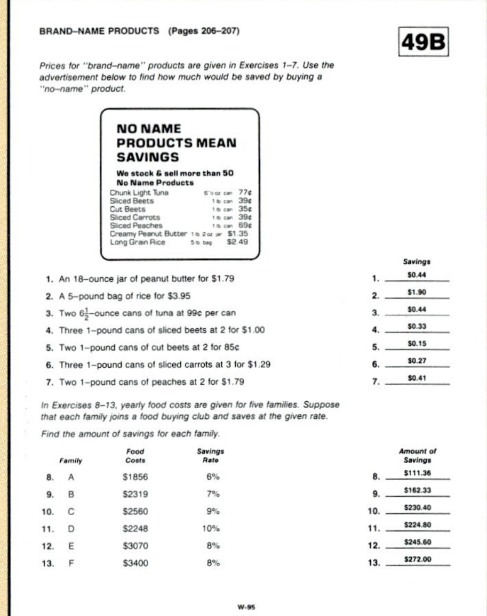

BRAND–NAME PRODUCTS (Pages 206–207) **49B**

Prices for "brand–name" products are given in Exercises 1–7. Use the advertisement below to find how much would be saved by buying a "no–name" product.

		Savings
1.	An 18–ounce jar of peanut butter for $1.79	1. $0.44
2.	A 5–pound bag of rice for $3.95	2. $1.90
3.	Two $6\frac{1}{2}$–ounce cans of tuna at 99¢ per can	3. $0.44
4.	Three 1–pound cans of sliced beets at 2 for $1.00	4. $0.33
5.	Two 1–pound cans of cut beets at 2 for 85¢	5. $0.15
6.	Three 1–pound cans of sliced carrots at 3 for $1.29	6. $0.27
7.	Two 1–pound cans of peaches at 2 for $1.79	7. $0.41

In Exercises 8–13, yearly food costs are given for five families. Suppose that each family joins a food buying club and saves at the given rate.

Find the amount of savings for each family.

	Family	Food Costs	Savings Rate	Amount of Savings
8.	A	$1856	6%	8. $111.36
9.	B	$2319	7%	9. $162.33
10.	C	$2560	9%	10. $230.40
11.	D	$2248	10%	11. $224.80
12.	E	$3070	8%	12. $245.60
13.	F	$3400	8%	13. $272.00

W-95

COST PER SERVING Pages 210–212

Practice

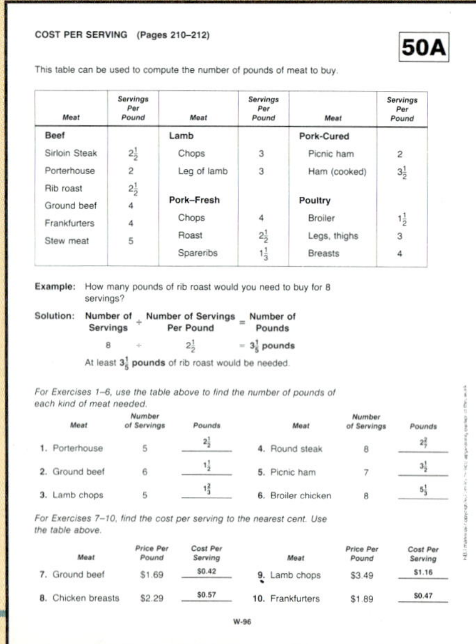

COST PER SERVING (Pages 210–212) **50A**

This table can be used to compute the number of pounds of meat to buy.

Meat	Servings Per Pound	Meat	Servings Per Pound	Meat	Servings Per Pound
Beef		**Lamb**		**Pork-Cured**	
Sirloin Steak	$2\frac{1}{2}$	Chops	3	Picnic ham	2
Porterhouse	2	Leg of lamb	3	Ham (cooked)	$3\frac{1}{2}$
Rib roast	$2\frac{1}{2}$	**Pork–Fresh**		**Poultry**	
Ground beef	4	Chops	4	Broiler	$1\frac{1}{2}$
Frankfurters	4	Roast	$2\frac{1}{2}$	Legs, thighs	3
Stew meat	5	Spareribs	$1\frac{1}{3}$	Breasts	4

Example: How many pounds of rib roast would you need to buy for 8 servings?

Solution: Number of Servings ÷ Number of Servings Per Pound = Number of Pounds
8 ÷ $2\frac{1}{2}$ = $3\frac{1}{5}$ **pounds**
At least $3\frac{1}{5}$ **pounds** of rib roast would be needed.

For Exercises 1–6, use the table above to find the number of pounds of each kind of meat needed.

	Meat	Number of Servings	Pounds		Meat	Number of Servings	Pounds
1.	Porterhouse	5	$2\frac{1}{2}$	4.	Round steak	8	$2\frac{2}{3}$
2.	Ground beef	6	$1\frac{1}{2}$	5.	Picnic ham	7	$3\frac{1}{2}$
3.	Lamb chops	5	$1\frac{2}{3}$	6.	Broiler chicken	8	$5\frac{1}{3}$

For Exercises 7–10, find the cost per serving to the nearest cent. Use the table above.

	Meat	Price Per Pound	Cost Per Serving		Meat	Price Per Pound	Cost Per Serving
7.	Ground beef	$1.69	$0.42	9.	Lamb chops	$3.49	$1.16
8.	Chicken breasts	$2.29	$0.57	10.	Frankfurters	$1.89	$0.47

W-96

Reteaching/ Alternate Teaching Strategy

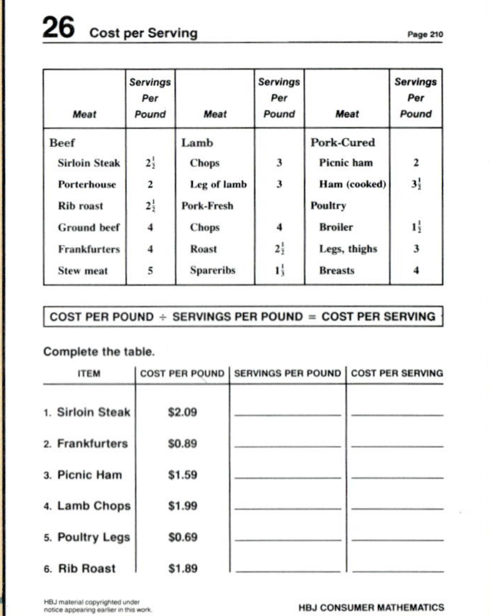

26 Cost per Serving Page 210

Meat	Servings Per Pound	Meat	Servings Per Pound	Meat	Servings Per Pound
Beef		**Lamb**		**Pork-Cured**	
Sirloin Steak	$2\frac{1}{4}$	Chops	3	Picnic ham	2
Porterhouse	2	Leg of lamb	3	Ham (cooked)	$3\frac{1}{3}$
Rib roast	$2\frac{1}{4}$	**Pork-Fresh**		**Poultry**	
Ground beef	4	Chops	4	Broiler	$1\frac{1}{2}$
Frankfurters	4	Roast	$2\frac{1}{2}$	Legs, thighs	3
Stew meat	5	Spareribs	$1\frac{1}{3}$	Breasts	4

COST PER POUND ÷ SERVINGS PER POUND = COST PER SERVING

Complete the table.

ITEM	COST PER POUND	SERVINGS PER POUND	COST PER SERVING
1. Sirloin Steak	$2.09		
2. Frankfurters	$0.89		
3. Picnic Ham	$1.59		
4. Lamb Chops	$1.99		
5. Poultry Legs	$0.69		
6. Rib Roast	$1.89		

 HBJ CONSUMER MATHEMATICS

Enrichment

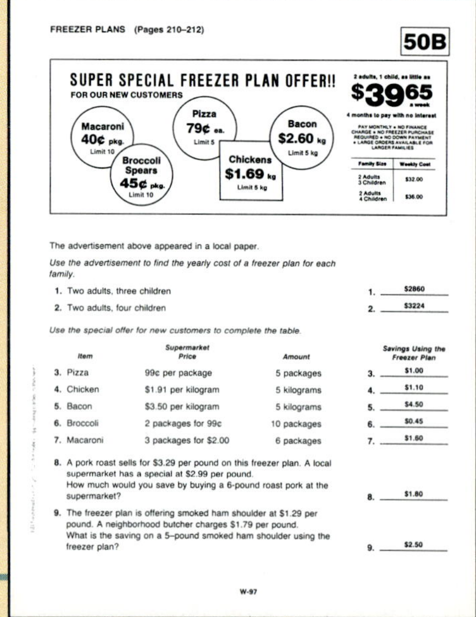

FREEZER PLANS (Pages 210–212) **50B**

The advertisement above appeared in a local paper.

Use the advertisement to find the yearly cost of a freezer plan for each family.

1. Two adults, three children 1. $2860
2. Two adults, four children 2. $3224

Use the special offer for new customers to complete the table.

	Item	Supermarket Price	Amount	Savings Using the Freezer Plan
3.	Pizza	99¢ per package	5 packages	3. $1.00
4.	Chicken	$1.91 per kilogram	5 kilograms	4. $1.10
5.	Bacon	$3.50 per kilogram	5 kilograms	5. $4.50
6.	Broccoli	2 packages for 99¢	10 packages	6. $0.45
7.	Macaroni	3 packages for $2.00	6 packages	7. $1.60

8. A pork roast sells for $3.29 per pound on this freezer plan. A local supermarket has a special at $2.99 per pound. How much would you save by buying a 6-pound roast pork at the supermarket? 8. $1.80

9. The freezer plan is offering smoked ham shoulder at $1.29 per pound. A neighborhood butcher charges $1.79 per pound. What is the saving on a 5-pound smoked ham shoulder using the freezer plan? 9. $2.50

W-97

DINING OUT Pages 213–215

Practice

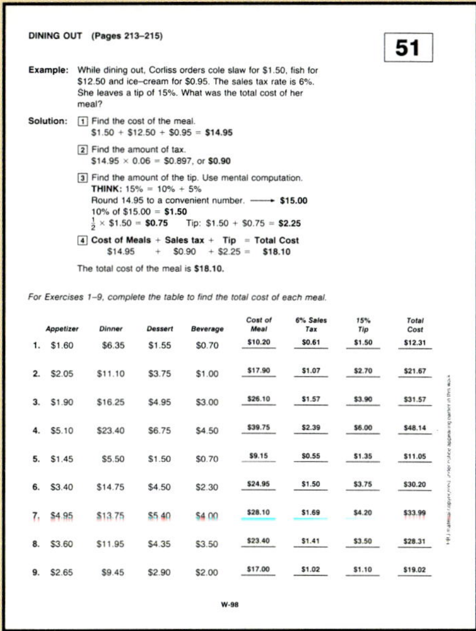

DINING OUT (Pages 213–215) **51**

Example: While dining out, Corliss orders cole slaw for \$1.50, fish for \$12.50 and ice–cream for \$0.95. The sales tax rate is 6%. She leaves a tip of 15%. What was the total cost of her meal?

Solution: [1] Find the cost of the meal.
\$1.50 + \$12.50 + \$0.95 = **\$14.95**

[2] Find the amount of tax.
\$14.95 × 0.06 = \$0.897, or **\$0.90**

[3] Find the amount of the tip. Use mental computation.
THINK: 15% = 10% + 5%
Round 14.95 to a convenient number. ⟶ **\$15.00**
10% of \$15.00 = **\$1.50**
$\frac{1}{2}$ × \$1.50 = **\$0.75** Tip: \$1.50 + \$0.75 = **\$2.25**

[4] **Cost of Meals + Sales tax + Tip = Total Cost**
\$14.95 + \$0.90 + \$2.25 = **\$18.10**

The total cost of the meal is **\$18.10.**

For Exercises 1–9, complete the table to find the total cost of each meal.

	Appetizer	Dinner	Dessert	Beverage	Cost of Meal	6% Sales Tax	15% Tip	Total Cost
1.	\$1.60	\$6.35	\$1.55	\$0.70	\$10.20	\$0.61	\$1.50	\$12.31
2.	\$2.05	\$11.10	\$3.75	\$1.00	\$17.90	\$1.07	\$2.70	\$21.67
3.	\$1.90	\$16.25	\$4.95	\$3.00	\$26.10	\$1.57	\$3.90	\$31.57
4.	\$5.10	\$23.40	\$6.75	\$4.50	\$39.75	\$2.39	\$6.00	\$48.14
5.	\$1.45	\$5.50	\$1.50	\$0.70	\$9.15	\$0.55	\$1.35	\$11.05
6.	\$3.40	\$14.75	\$4.50	\$2.30	\$24.95	\$1.50	\$3.75	\$30.20
7.	\$4.95	\$13.75	\$5.40	\$4.00	\$28.10	\$1.69	\$4.20	\$33.99
8.	\$3.60	\$11.95	\$4.35	\$3.50	\$23.40	\$1.41	\$3.50	\$28.31
9.	\$2.65	\$9.45	\$2.90	\$2.00	\$17.00	\$1.02	\$1.10	\$19.02

W-98

Reteaching Alternate Teaching Strategy

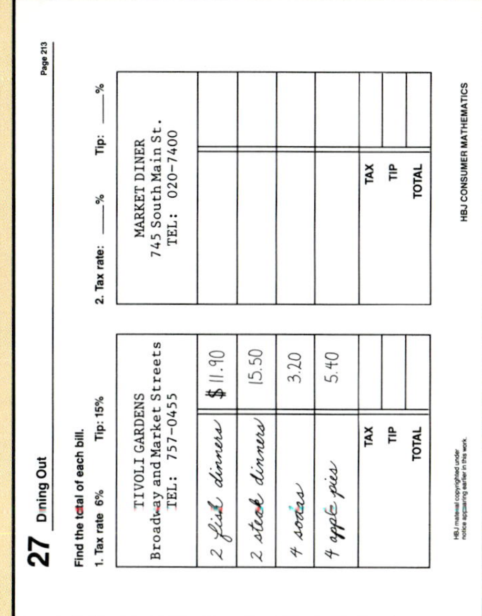

27 Dining Out

Page 213

Find the total of each bill.

1. Tax rate 6% Tip: 15%

TIVOLI GARDENS
Broadway and Market Streets
TEL: 757-0455

2 fish dinners	\$11.90
2 steak dinners	15.50
4 sodas	3.20
4 apple pies	5.40
TAX	
TIP	
TOTAL	

2. Tax rate: ____% Tip: ____%

MARKET DINER
745 South Main St.
TEL: 020-7400

TAX	
TIP	
TOTAL	

HBJ CONSUMER MATHEMATICS

Enrichment

Distribute a menu to each student on which all prices have been omitted. Then have students select any meal and calculate what they think is the total bill, including 6% tax and a tip.

Finally, reveal the actual price of all items and have students calculate a bill using actual menu prices.

You may wish to make a tally of students who guessed prices too high and too low.

RENTING Pages 230–231

Practice

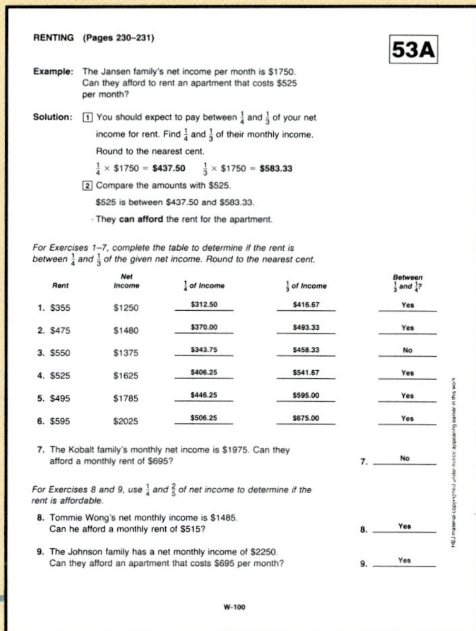

RENTING (Pages 230–231) **53A**

Example: The Jansen family's net income per month is \$1750. Can they afford to rent an apartment that costs \$525 per month?

Solution: [1] You should expect to pay between $\frac{1}{4}$ and $\frac{1}{3}$ of your net income for rent. Find $\frac{1}{4}$ and $\frac{1}{3}$ of their monthly income.
Round to the nearest cent.
$\frac{1}{4}$ × \$1750 = **\$437.50** $\frac{1}{3}$ × \$1750 = **\$583.33**

[2] Compare the amounts with \$525.
\$525 is between \$437.50 and \$583.33.
They **can afford** the rent for the apartment.

For Exercises 1–7, complete the table to determine if the rent is between $\frac{1}{4}$ and $\frac{1}{3}$ of the given net income. Round to the nearest cent.

	Rent	Net Income	$\frac{1}{4}$ of Income	$\frac{1}{3}$ of Income	Between $\frac{1}{3}$ and $\frac{1}{4}$?
1.	\$355	\$1250	\$312.50	\$416.67	Yes
2.	\$475	\$1480	\$370.00	\$493.33	Yes
3.	\$550	\$1375	\$343.75	\$458.33	No
4.	\$525	\$1625	\$406.25	\$541.67	Yes
5.	\$495	\$1785	\$446.25	\$595.00	Yes
6.	\$595	\$2025	\$506.25	\$675.00	Yes

7. The Kobalt family's monthly net income is \$1975. Can they afford a monthly rent of \$695? 7. No

For Exercises 8 and 9, use $\frac{1}{4}$ and $\frac{2}{5}$ of net income to determine if the rent is affordable.

8. Tommie Wong's net monthly income is \$1485. Can he afford a monthly rent of \$515? 8. Yes

9. The Johnson family has a net monthly income of \$2250. Can they afford an apartment that costs \$695 per month? 9. Yes

W-100

Reteaching Alternate Teaching Strategy

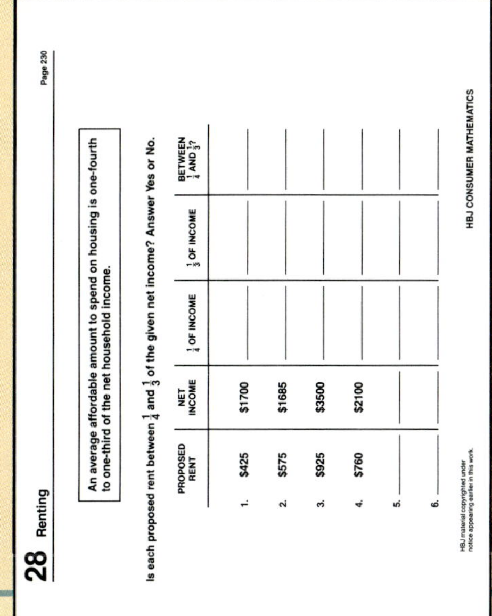

28 Renting

Page 230

An average affordable amount to spend on housing is one-fourth to one-third of the net household income.

Is each proposed rent between $\frac{1}{4}$ and $\frac{1}{3}$ of the given net income? Answer Yes or No.

	PROPOSED RENT	NET INCOME	$\frac{1}{4}$ OF INCOME	$\frac{1}{3}$ OF INCOME	BETWEEN $\frac{1}{4}$ AND $\frac{1}{3}$?
1.	\$425	\$1700			
2.	\$575	\$1685			
3.	\$925	\$3500			
4.	\$760	\$2100			
5.					
6.					

HBJ CONSUMER MATHEMATICS

Enrichment

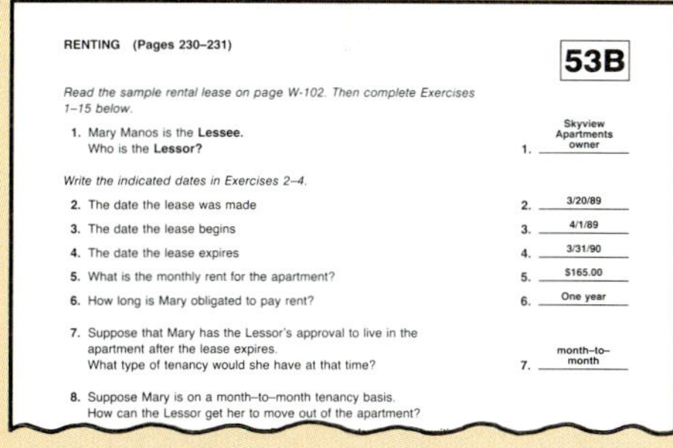

RENTING (Pages 230–231) **53B**

Read the sample rental lease on page W-102. Then complete Exercises 1–15 below.

1. Mary Manos is the **Lessee.** Who is the **Lessor?** 1. Skyview Apartments owner

Write the indicated dates in Exercises 2–4.

2. The date the lease was made 2. 3/20/89
3. The date the lease begins 3. 4/1/89
4. The date the lease expires 4. 3/31/90
5. What is the monthly rent for the apartment? 5. \$165.00
6. How long is Mary obligated to pay rent? 6. One year
7. Suppose that Mary has the Lessor's approval to live in the apartment after the lease expires. What type of tenancy would she have at that time? 7. month–to–month
8. Suppose Mary is on a month–to–month tenancy basis. How can the Lessor get her to move out of the apartment?

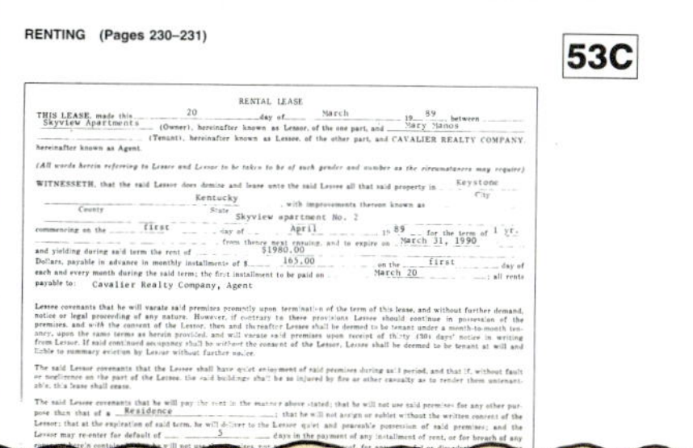

RENTING (Pages 230–231) **53C**

RENTAL LEASE

THIS LEASE, made this 20 day of March 19 89 between Skyview Apartments (Owner), hereinafter known as Lessor, of the one part, and Mary Manos (Tenant), hereinafter known as Lessee, of the other part, and CAVALIER REALTY COMPANY, hereinafter known as Agent.

(All words herein referring to Lessee and Lessor to be taken to be of such gender and number as the circumstances may require)

WITNESSETH, that the said Lessor does demise and lease unto the said Lessee all that said property in Keystone (City), Kentucky (County, State), with improvements thereon known as Skyview apartment No. 2 commencing on the first day of April 19 89 for the term of 1 yr. from thence next ensuing, and to expire on March 31, 1990 and yielding during said term the rent of \$1980.00 Dollars, payable in advance in monthly installments of \$ 165.00 on the first day of each and every month during the said term; the first installment to be paid on March 20; all rents payable to: Cavalier Realty Company, Agent

Lessee covenants that he will vacate said premises promptly upon termination of the term of this lease, and without further demand, notice or legal proceeding of any nature. However, if contrary to these provisions Lessee should continue in possession of the premises, and with the consent of the Lessor, then and thereafter Lessee shall be deemed to be tenant under a month-to-month tenancy, upon the same terms as herein provided, and will vacate said premises upon receipt of thirty (30) days' notice in writing from Lessor. If said continued occupancy shall be without the consent of the Lessor, Lessee shall be deemed to be tenant at will and liable to summary eviction by Lessor without further notice.

The said Lessor covenants that the Lessee shall have quiet enjoyment of said premises during said period, and that if, without fault or negligence on the part of the Lessee, the said buildings shall be so injured by fire or other casualty as to render them untenantable, this lease shall cease.

The said Lessee covenants that he will pay the rent in the manner above stated; that he will not use said premises for any other purpose than that of a Residence; that he will not assign or sublet without the written consent of the Lessor; that at the expiration of said term, he will deliver to the Lessor quiet and peaceable possession of said premises; and the Lessor may re-enter for default of 5 days in the payment of any installment of rent, or for breach of any

MORTGAGE LOANS Pages 232–234

Practice

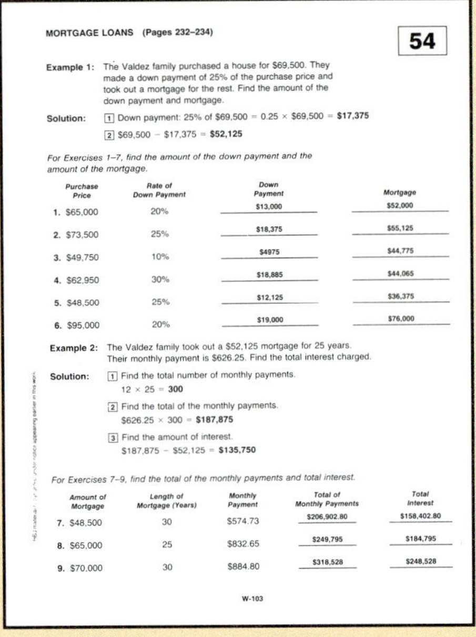

MORTGAGE LOANS (Pages 232–234) **54**

Example 1: The Valdez family purchased a house for $69,500. They made a down payment of 25% of the purchase price and took out a mortgage for the rest. Find the amount of the down payment and mortgage.

Solution: [1] Down payment: 25% of $69,500 = 0.25 × $69,500 = **$17,375**

[2] $69,500 − $17,375 = **$52,125**

For Exercises 1–7, find the amount of the down payment and the amount of the mortgage.

	Purchase Price	Rate of Down Payment	Down Payment	Mortgage
1.	$65,000	20%	$13,000	$52,000
2.	$73,500	25%	$18,375	$55,125
3.	$49,750	10%	$4975	$44,775
4.	$62,950	30%	$18,885	$44,065
5.	$48,500	25%	$12,125	$36,375
6.	$95,000	20%	$19,000	$76,000

Example 2: The Valdez family took out a $52,125 mortgage for 25 years. Their monthly payment is $626.25. Find the total interest charged.

Solution: [1] Find the total number of monthly payments.
12 × 25 = **300**

[2] Find the total of the monthly payments.
$626.25 × 300 = **$187,875**

[3] Find the amount of interest.
$187,875 − $52,125 = **$135,750**

For Exercises 7–9, find the total of the monthly payments and total interest.

	Amount of Mortgage	Length of Mortgage (Years)	Monthly Payment	Total of Monthly Payments	Total Interest
7.	$48,500	30	$574.73	$206,902.80	$158,402.80
8.	$65,000	25	$832.65	$249,795	$184,795
9.	$70,000	30	$884.80	$318,528	$248,528

W-103

Reteaching
Alternate Teaching Strategy

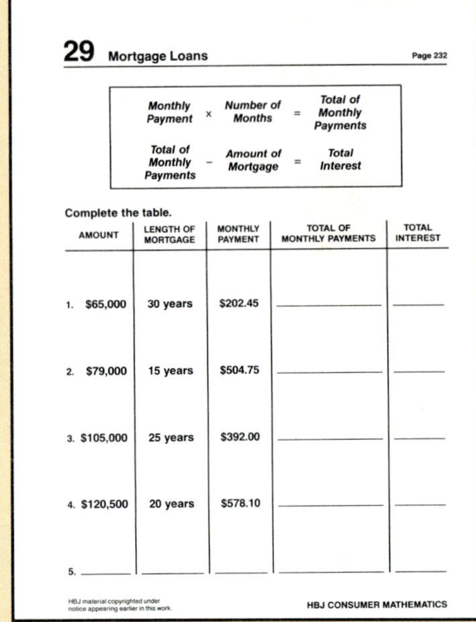

29 Mortgage Loans — Page 232

Monthly Payment	×	Number of Months	=	Total of Monthly Payments
Total of Monthly Payments	−	Amount of Mortgage	=	Total Interest

Complete the table.

	AMOUNT	LENGTH OF MORTGAGE	MONTHLY PAYMENT	TOTAL OF MONTHLY PAYMENTS	TOTAL INTEREST
1.	$65,000	30 years	$202.45		
2.	$79,000	15 years	$504.75		
3.	$105,000	25 years	$392.00		
4.	$120,500	20 years	$578.10		
5.					

HBJ material copyrighted under notice appearing earlier in this work. HBJ CONSUMER MATHEMATICS

Enrichment

Most lenders charge **points** for origination of mortgage loans. Points are a one–time charge of 1% of the amount borrowed. Have students find the origination charge (points) for these two mortgages. The sale price of the home is $103,000.

Down Payment	15%	10%
Years of Mtg.	15	30
Points charge	2.75	3.25
Amount of Loan	? **($87,550)**	? **($92,700)**
Origination Fee	? **(2407.63)**	? **($3012.75)**

Which mortgage has the lower fee? **(ANS: The first)**

How much lower? **(ANS: $605.12)**

MONTHLY MORTGAGE PAYMENTS Pages 235–237

Practice

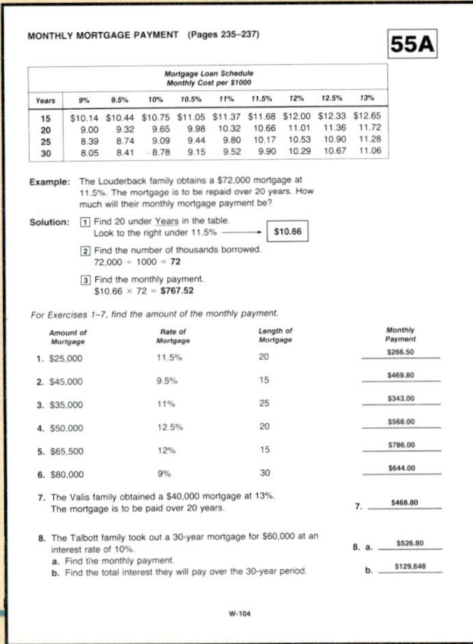

MONTHLY MORTGAGE PAYMENT (Pages 235–237) **55A**

Mortgage Loan Schedule
Monthly Cost per $1000

Years	9%	9.5%	10%	10.5%	11%	11.5%	12%	12.5%	13%
15	$10.14	$10.44	$10.75	$11.05	$11.37	$11.68	$12.00	$12.33	$12.65
20	9.00	9.32	9.65	9.98	10.32	10.66	11.01	11.36	11.72
25	8.39	8.74	9.09	9.44	9.80	10.17	10.53	10.90	11.28
30	8.05	8.41	8.78	9.15	9.52	9.90	10.29	10.67	11.06

Example: The Louderback family obtains a $72,000 mortgage at 11.5%. The mortgage is to be repaid over 20 years. How much will their monthly mortgage payment be?

Solution: [1] Find 20 under Years in the table. Look to the right under 11.5% ⟶ **$10.66**

[2] Find the number of thousands borrowed.
72,000 ÷ 1000 = **72**

[3] Find the monthly payment.
$10.66 × 72 = **$767.52**

For Exercises 1–7, find the amount of the monthly payment.

	Amount of Mortgage	Rate of Mortgage	Length of Mortgage	Monthly Payment
1.	$25,000	11.5%	20	$266.50
2.	$45,000	9.5%	15	$469.80
3.	$35,000	11%	25	$343.00
4.	$50,000	12.5%	20	$568.00
5.	$65,500	12%	15	$786.00
6.	$80,000	9%	30	$644.00

7. The Valis family obtained a $40,000 mortgage at 13%. The mortgage is to be paid over 20 years. — 7. $468.80

8. The Talbott family took out a 30-year mortgage for $60,000 at an interest rate of 10%.
   a. Find the monthly payment. — 8. a. $526.80
   b. Find the total interest they will pay over the 30-year period. — b. $129,648

W-104

Reteaching
Alternate Teaching Strategy

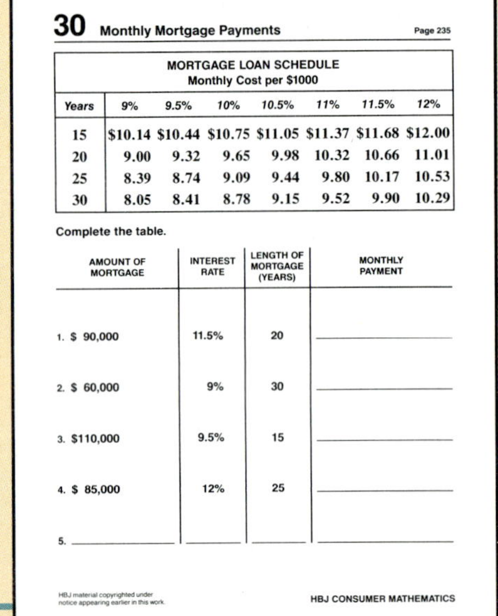

30 Monthly Mortgage Payments — Page 235

MORTGAGE LOAN SCHEDULE
Monthly Cost per $1000

Years	9%	9.5%	10%	10.5%	11%	11.5%	12%
15	$10.14	$10.44	$10.75	$11.05	$11.37	$11.68	$12.00
20	9.00	9.32	9.65	9.98	10.32	10.66	11.01
25	8.39	8.74	9.09	9.44	9.80	10.17	10.53
30	8.05	8.41	8.78	9.15	9.52	9.90	10.29

Complete the table.

	AMOUNT OF MORTGAGE	INTEREST RATE	LENGTH OF MORTGAGE (YEARS)	MONTHLY PAYMENT
1.	$ 90,000	11.5%	20	
2.	$ 60,000	9%	30	
3.	$110,000	9.5%	15	
4.	$ 85,000	12%	25	
5.				

HBJ material copyrighted under notice appearing earlier in this work. HBJ CONSUMER MATHEMATICS

Enrichment

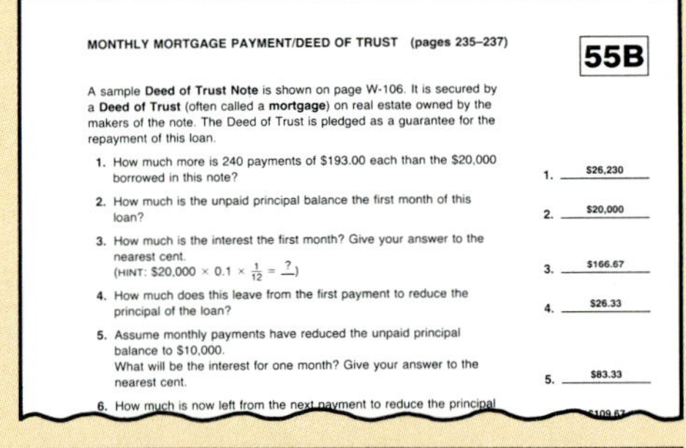

MONTHLY MORTGAGE PAYMENT/DEED OF TRUST (pages 235–237) **55B**

A sample **Deed of Trust Note** is shown on page W-106. It is secured by a **Deed of Trust** (often called a **mortgage**) on real estate owned by the makers of the note. The Deed of Trust is pledged as a guarantee for the repayment of this loan.

1. How much more is 240 payments of $193.00 each than the $20,000 borrowed in this note? — 1. $26,230
2. How much is the unpaid principal balance the first month of this loan? — 2. $20,000
3. How much is the interest the first month? Give your answer to the nearest cent. (HINT: $20,000 × 0.1 × $\frac{1}{12}$ = ?) — 3. $166.67
4. How much does this leave from the first payment to reduce the principal of the loan? — 4. $26.33
5. Assume monthly payments have reduced the unpaid principal balance to $10,000. What will be the interest for one month? Give your answer to the nearest cent. — 5. $83.33
6. How much is now left from the next payment to reduce the principal

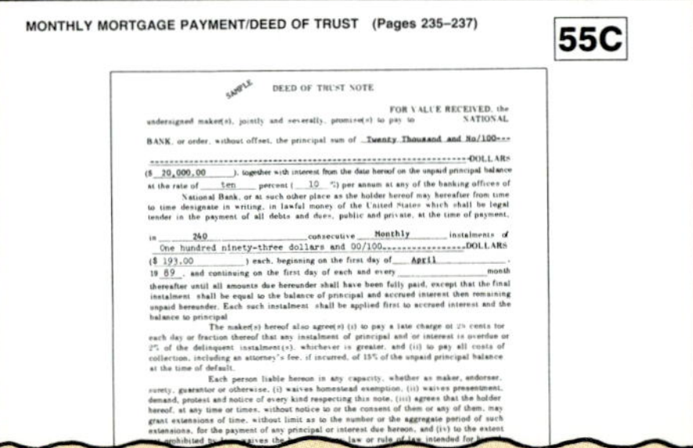

MONTHLY MORTGAGE PAYMENT/DEED OF TRUST (Pages 235–237) **55C**

SAMPLE DEED OF TRUST NOTE

FOR VALUE RECEIVED, the undersigned maker(s), jointly and severally, promise(s) to pay to NATIONAL BANK, or order, without offset, the principal sum of Twenty Thousand and No/100------------DOLLARS ($ 20,000.00), together with interest from the date hereof on the unpaid principal balance at the rate of ten percent (10 %) per annum at any of the banking offices of National Bank, or at such other place as the holder hereof may hereafter from time to time designate in writing, in lawful money of the United States which shall be legal tender in the payment of all debts and dues, public and private, at the time of payment, in 240 consecutive Monthly instalments of One hundred ninety-three dollars and 00/100------DOLLARS ($ 193.00) each, beginning on the first day of April, 19 89, and continuing on the first day of each and every month thereafter until all amounts due hereunder shall have been fully paid, except that the final instalment shall be equal to the balance of principal and accrued interest then remaining unpaid hereunder. Each such instalment shall be applied first to accrued interest and the balance to principal.

The maker(s) hereof also agree(s) (i) to pay a late charge of 25 cents for each day or fraction thereof that any instalment of principal and/or interest is overdue or 2% of the delinquent instalment(s), whichever is greater, and (ii) to pay all costs of collection, including an attorney's fee, if incurred, of 15% of the unpaid principal balance at the time of default.

Each person liable hereon in any capacity, whether as maker, endorser, surety, guarantor or otherwise, (i) waives homestead exemption, (ii) waives presentment, demand, protest and notice of every kind respecting this note, (iii) agrees that the holder hereof, at any time or times, without notice to or the consent of them or any of them, may grant extensions of time, without limit as to the number or the aggregate period of such extensions, for the payment of any principal or interest due hereon, and (iv) to the extent

HOMEOWNER'S INSURANCE Pages 240–242

Practice

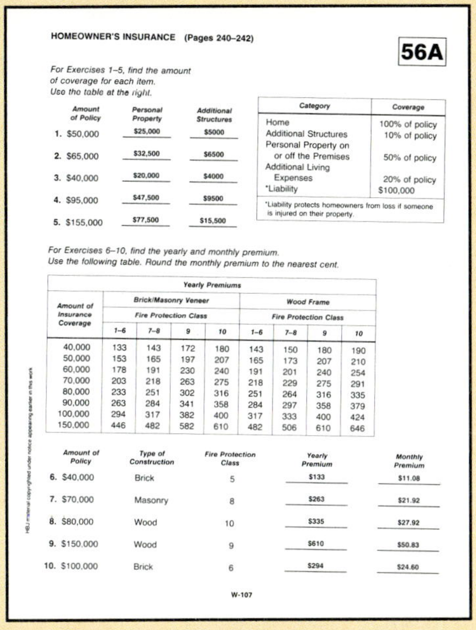

HOMEOWNER'S INSURANCE (Pages 240–242)

56A

For Exercises 1–5, find the amount of coverage for each item. Use the table at the right.

	Amount of Policy	Personal Property	Additional Structures
1.	$50,000	$25,000	$5000
2.	$65,000	$32,500	$6500
3.	$40,000	$20,000	$4000
4.	$95,000	$47,500	$9500
5.	$155,000	$77,500	$15,500

Category	Coverage
Home	100% of policy
Additional Structures	10% of policy
Personal Property on or off the Premises	50% of policy
Additional Living Expenses	20% of policy
*Liability	$100,000

*Liability protects homeowners from loss if someone is injured on their property.

For Exercises 6–10, find the yearly and monthly premium. Use the following table. Round the monthly premium to the nearest cent.

Yearly Premiums								
Amount of Insurance Coverage	Brick/Masonry Veneer				Wood Frame			
	Fire Protection Class				Fire Protection Class			
	1–6	7–8	9	10	1–6	7–8	9	10
40,000	133	143	172	180	143	150	180	190
50,000	153	165	197	207	165	173	207	210
60,000	178	191	230	240	191	201	240	254
70,000	203	218	263	275	218	229	275	291
80,000	233	251	302	316	251	264	316	335
90,000	263	284	341	358	284	297	358	379
100,000	294	317	382	400	317	333	400	424
150,000	446	482	582	610	482	506	610	646

	Amount of Policy	Type of Construction	Fire Protection Class	Yearly Premium	Monthly Premium
6.	$40,000	Brick	5	$133	$11.08
7.	$70,000	Masonry	8	$263	$21.92
8.	$80,000	Wood	10	$335	$27.92
9.	$150,000	Wood	9	$610	$50.83
10.	$100,000	Brick	6	$294	$24.60

W-107

Reteaching
Alternate Teaching Strategy

Visuals 31 and 32 show students how to compute the amount of coverage and the monthly premium for homeowner's insurance.

Enrichment

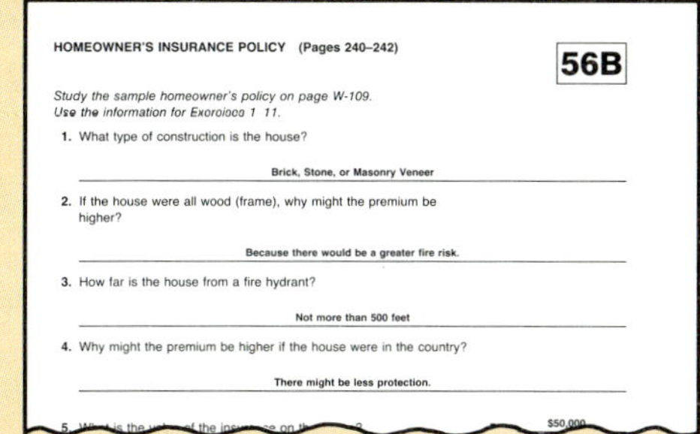

HOMEOWNER'S INSURANCE POLICY (Pages 240–242)

56B

Study the sample homeowner's policy on page W-109. Use the information for Exercises 1 11.

1. What type of construction is the house?

   Brick, Stone, or Masonry Veneer

2. If the house were all wood (frame), why might the premium be higher?

   Because there would be a greater fire risk.

3. How far is the house from a fire hydrant?

   Not more than 500 feet

4. Why might the premium be higher if the house were in the country?

   There might be less protection.

$50,000

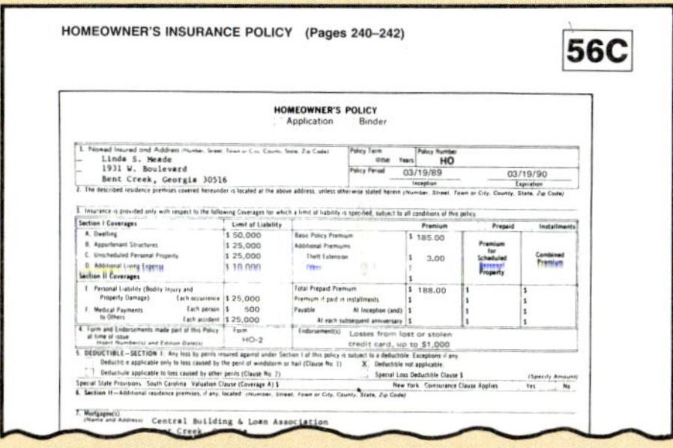

HOMEOWNER'S INSURANCE POLICY (Pages 240–242)

56C

HOMEOWNER'S POLICY

Application Binder

PROPERTY TAXES Pages 245–247

Practice

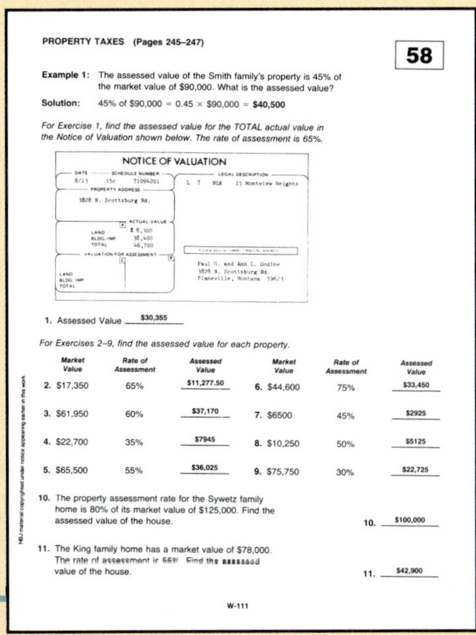

PROPERTY TAXES (Pages 245–247)

58

Example 1: The assessed value of the Smith family's property is 45% of the market value of $90,000. What is the assessed value?

Solution: 45% of $90,000 = 0.45 × $90,000 = **$40,500**

For Exercise 1, find the assessed value for the TOTAL actual value in the Notice of Valuation shown below. The rate of assessment is 65%.

NOTICE OF VALUATION

DATE 8/13 — SCHEDULE NUMBER 15c 71094201 — LEGAL DESCRIPTION L 7 BLK 15 Montview Heights

PROPERTY ADDRESS 3828 N. Scottsburg Rd.

ACTUAL VALUE [A]
LAND $ 8,300
BLDG./IMP. 38,400
TOTAL 46,700

VALUATION FOR ASSESSMENT [B] [C]
LAND
BLDG./IMP.
TOTAL

Paul G. and Ann L. Godine
3828 N. Scottsburg Rd.
Planeville, Montana 59623

1. Assessed Value **$30,355**

For Exercises 2–9, find the assessed value for each property.

	Market Value	Rate of Assessment	Assessed Value		Market Value	Rate of Assessment	Assessed Value
2.	$17,350	65%	$11,277.50	6.	$44,600	75%	$33,450
3.	$61,950	60%	$37,170	7.	$6500	45%	$2925
4.	$22,700	35%	$7945	8.	$10,250	50%	$5125
5.	$65,500	55%	$36,025	9.	$75,750	30%	$22,725

10. The property assessment rate for the Sywetz family home is 80% of its market value of $125,000. Find the assessed value of the house. 10. **$100,000**

11. The King family home has a market value of $78,000. The rate of assessment is 55%. Find the assessed value of the house. 11. **$42,900**

W-111

Reteaching
Alternate Teaching Strategy

Materials: One index card for each student

Mark each card as a taxpayer record card with the following:

A taxpayer name

A real estate market value

A rate of assessment

At tax rate (per $100)

Have each student select a taxpayer card at random. Then have them show all work and find the assessed value and property tax for the selected taxpayer.

You may wish to have students select more taxpayer cards as time permits.

Enrichment

Explain to students that **mills** and **millage** are terms sometimes used to express tax rates in newspapers and on tax forms. One mill is $\frac{1}{10}$ of a cent; A one-mill tax rate is $\frac{1}{10}$ of a cent per dollar of assessed value, or $1 per $1000.

Have students complete the table and solve the exercise.
(Answers given in bold–face type)

–Tax Rate–		
Per Dollar	Per $100	Per $1000
3 mills	$0.30	$3.00
6.5 mills	$0.65	**$6.50**
14 mills	$1.40	**$14.00**
3.8 mills	**$0.38**	**$3.80**

Find the tax on $43,760 assessed value. The tax rate is 7.4 mills. You save 2% for early payment. **(ANS: $317.35)**

HEATING AND COOLING COSTS Pages 258–260

Practice

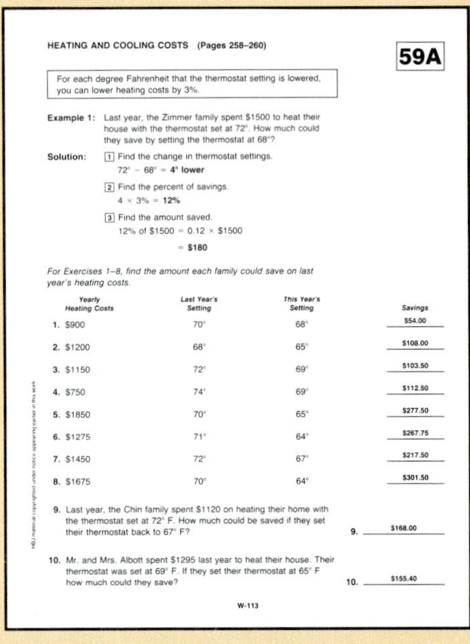

HEATING AND COOLING COSTS (Pages 258–260) **59A**

For each degree Fahrenheit that the thermostat setting is lowered, you can lower heating costs by 3%.

Example 1: Last year, the Zimmer family spent $1500 to heat their house with the thermostat set at 72°. How much could they save by setting the thermostat at 68°?

Solution: [1] Find the change in thermostat settings.
72° − 68° = **4° lower**
[2] Find the percent of savings.
4 × 3% = **12%**
[3] Find the amount saved.
12% of $1500 = 0.12 × $1500
= **$180**

For Exercises 1–8, find the amount each family could save on last year's heating costs.

	Yearly Heating Costs	Last Year's Setting	This Year's Setting	Savings
1.	$900	70°	68°	$54.00
2.	$1200	68°	65°	$108.00
3.	$1150	72°	69°	$103.50
4.	$750	74°	69°	$112.50
5.	$1850	70°	65°	$277.50
6.	$1275	71°	64°	$267.75
7.	$1450	72°	67°	$217.50
8.	$1675	70°	64°	$301.50

9. Last year, the Chin family spent $1120 on heating their home with the thermostat set at 72° F. How much could be saved if they set their thermostat back to 67° F? 9. $168.00

10. Mr. and Mrs. Albott spent $1295 last year to heat their house. Their thermostat was set at 69° F. If they set their thermostat at 65° F how much could they save? 10. $155.40

W-113

Reteaching
Alternate Teaching Strategy

A reteaching lesson can be structured for this topic by having students supply the concrete materials. These concrete materials then would be the basis for the lesson.

Have students bring to class sales literature for heating and cooling equipment available in your locality. Challenge them to learn the meanings of terms or phrases used in these materials to express a quality or efficiency of the product.

This sales literature then becomes a source bank of real world problems that you can use for presenting the lesson.

Enrichment

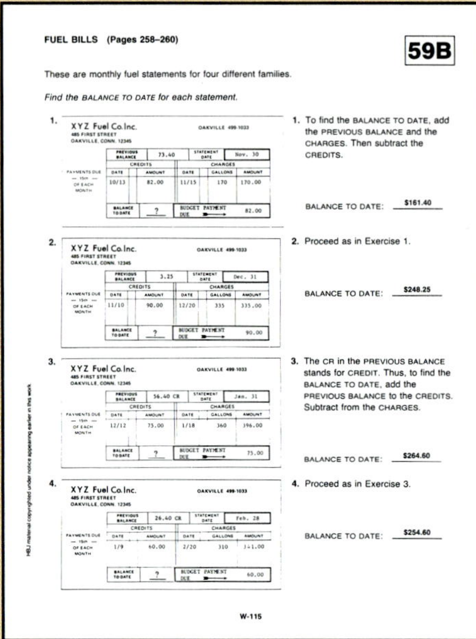

FUEL BILLS (Pages 258–260) **59B**

These are monthly fuel statements for four different families.

Find the BALANCE TO DATE for each statement.

1. XYZ Fuel Co. Inc. — Previous balance 73.40; Statement date Nov. 30; Credits 10/13 82.00; Charges 11/15 170 170.00; Balance to date ?; Budget payment due 82.00

1. To find the BALANCE TO DATE, add the PREVIOUS BALANCE and the CHARGES. Then subtract the CREDITS.
BALANCE TO DATE: $161.40

2. XYZ Fuel Co. Inc. — Previous balance 3.25; Statement date Dec. 31; Credits 11/10 90.00; Charges 12/20 335 335.00; Balance to date ?; Budget payment due 90.00

2. Proceed as in Exercise 1.
BALANCE TO DATE: $248.25

3. XYZ Fuel Co. Inc. — Previous balance 56.40 CR; Statement date Jan. 31; Credits 12/12 75.00; Charges 1/18 360 396.00; Balance to date ?; Budget payment due 75.00

3. The CR in the PREVIOUS BALANCE stands for CREDIT. Thus, to find the BALANCE TO DATE, add the PREVIOUS BALANCE to the CREDITS. Subtract from the CHARGES.
BALANCE TO DATE: $264.60

4. XYZ Fuel Co. Inc. — Previous balance 26.40 CR; Statement date Feb. 28; Credits 1/9 60.00; Charges 2/20 310 341.00; Balance to date ?; Budget payment due 60.00

4. Proceed as in Exercise 3.
BALANCE TO DATE: $254.60

W-115

COST OF OPERATING APPLIANCES Pages 262–263

Practice

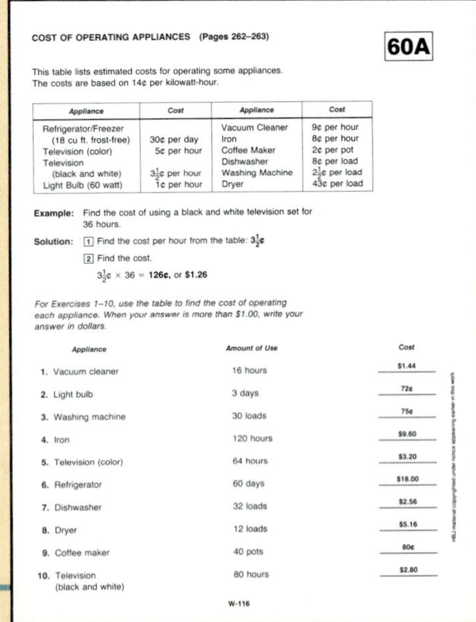

COST OF OPERATING APPLIANCES (Pages 262–263) **60A**

This table lists estimated costs for operating some appliances. The costs are based on 14¢ per kilowatt-hour.

Appliance	Cost	Appliance	Cost
Refrigerator/Freezer (18 cu ft. frost-free)	30¢ per day	Vacuum Cleaner	9¢ per hour
Television (color)	5¢ per hour	Iron	8¢ per hour
Television (black and white)	$3\frac{1}{2}$¢ per hour	Coffee Maker	2¢ per pot
Light Bulb (60 watt)	1¢ per hour	Dishwasher	8¢ per load
		Washing Machine	$2\frac{1}{2}$¢ per load
		Dryer	43¢ per load

Example: Find the cost of using a black and white television set for 36 hours.

Solution: [1] Find the cost per hour from the table: $3\frac{1}{2}$¢
[2] Find the cost.
$3\frac{1}{2}$¢ × 36 = **126¢, or $1.26**

For Exercises 1–10, use the table to find the cost of operating each appliance. When your answer is more than $1.00, write your answer in dollars.

	Appliance	Amount of Use	Cost
1.	Vacuum cleaner	16 hours	$1.44
2.	Light bulb	3 days	72¢
3.	Washing machine	30 loads	75¢
4.	Iron	120 hours	$9.60
5.	Television (color)	64 hours	$3.20
6.	Refrigerator	60 days	$18.00
7.	Dishwasher	32 loads	$2.56
8.	Dryer	12 loads	$5.16
9.	Coffee maker	40 pots	80¢
10.	Television (black and white)	80 hours	$2.80

W-116

Reteaching
Alternate Teaching Strategy

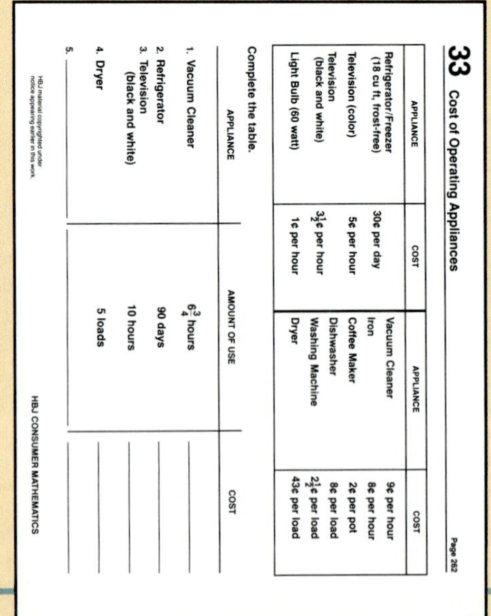

33 Cost of Operating Appliances — Page 262

APPLIANCE	COST	APPLIANCE	COST
Refrigerator/Freezer (18 cu ft. frost-free)	30¢ per day	Vacuum Cleaner	9¢ per hour
Television (color)	5¢ per hour	Iron	8¢ per hour
Television (black and white)	$3\frac{1}{2}$¢ per hour	Coffee Maker	2¢ per pot
Light Bulb (60 watt)	1¢ per hour	Dishwasher	8¢ per load
		Washing Machine	$2\frac{1}{2}$¢ per load
		Dryer	43¢ per load

Complete the table.

	APPLIANCE	AMOUNT OF USE	COST
1.	Vacuum Cleaner	$6\frac{3}{4}$ hours	
2.	Refrigerator	90 days	
3.	Television (black and white)	10 hours	
4.	Dryer	5 loads	
5.			

HBJ CONSUMER MATHEMATICS

Enrichment

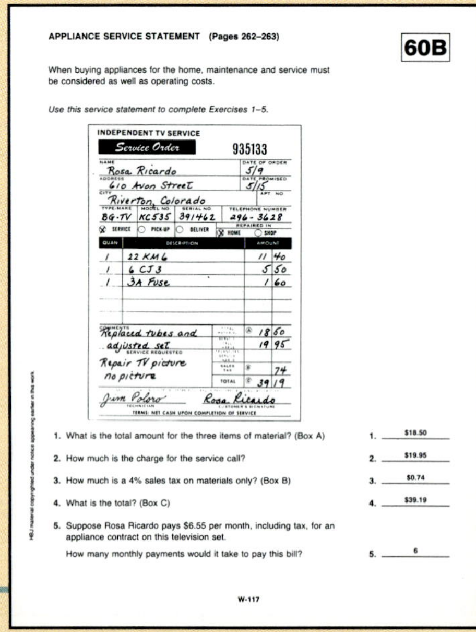

APPLIANCE SERVICE STATEMENT (Pages 262–263) **60B**

When buying appliances for the home, maintenance and service must be considered as well as operating costs.

Use this service statement to complete Exercises 1–5.

INDEPENDENT TV SERVICE
Service Order 935133
Name: Rosa Ricardo — Date of order: 5/9
Address: 610 Avon Street — Date promised: 5/15
City: Riverton, Colorado
Type/Make: BG-TV; Model no.: KC535; Serial no.: 391462; Telephone number: 296-3628

QUAN	DESCRIPTION	AMOUNT
1	22 KM6	11.40
1	6 CJ3	5.50
1	3A Fuse	1.60

Replaced tubes and adjusted set — (A) 18.60; 19.95
Service requested: Repair TV picture no picture — Sales tax (B) .74; Total (C) 39.19
Jim Poloro (Technician) — Rosa Ricardo (Customer's signature)
TERMS: NET CASH UPON COMPLETION OF SERVICE

1. What is the total amount for the three items of material? (Box A) 1. $18.50
2. How much is the charge for the service call? 2. $19.95
3. How much is a 4% sales tax on materials only? (Box B) 3. $0.74
4. What is the total? (Box C) 4. $39.19
5. Suppose Rosa Ricardo pays $6.55 per month, including tax, for an appliance contract on this television set. How many monthly payments would it take to pay this bill? 5. 6

W-117

READING METERS Pages 264–265

Practice

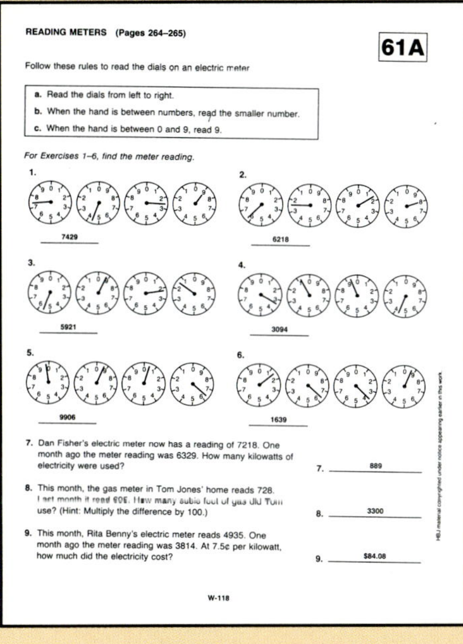

READING METERS (Pages 264–265)

61A

Follow these rules to read the dials on an electric meter

a. Read the dials from left to right.
b. When the hand is between numbers, read the smaller number.
c. When the hand is between 0 and 9, read 9.

For Exercises 1–6, find the meter reading.

1. 7429
2. 6218
3. 5921
4. 3094
5. 9906
6. 1639

7. Dan Fisher's electric meter now has a reading of 7218. One month ago the meter reading was 6329. How many kilowatts of electricity were used? 7. 889

8. This month, the gas meter in Tom Jones' home reads 728. Last month it read 695. How many cubic feet of gas did Tom use? (Hint: Multiply the difference by 100.) 8. 3300

9. This month, Rita Benny's electric meter reads 4935. One month ago the meter reading was 3814. At 7.5¢ per kilowatt, how much did the electricity cost? 9. $84.08

W-118

Reteaching/ Alternate Teaching Strategy

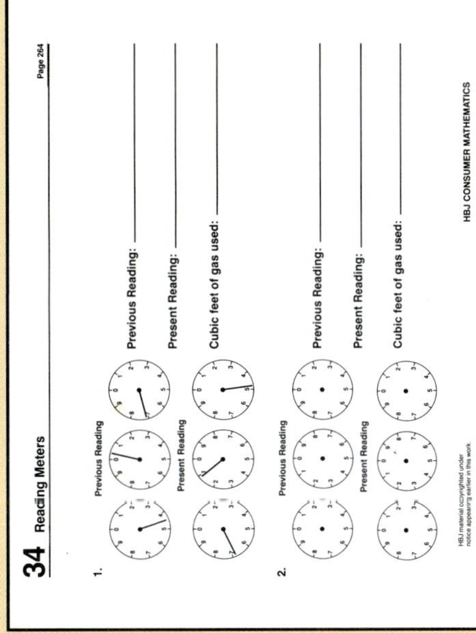

34 Reading Meters

Page 264

1. Previous Reading: ___
Present Reading: ___
Cubic feet of gas used: ___

Previous Reading | Present Reading

2. Previous Reading: ___
Present Reading: ___
Cubic feet of gas used: ___

Previous Reading | Present Reading

HBJ CONSUMER MATHEMATICS

Enrichment

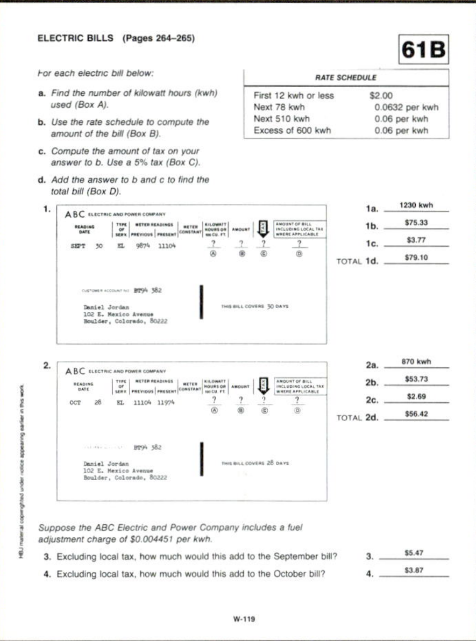

ELECTRIC BILLS (Pages 264–265)

61B

For each electric bill below:

a. *Find the number of kilowatt hours (kwh) used (Box A).*
b. *Use the rate schedule to compute the amount of the bill (Box B).*
c. *Compute the amount of tax on your answer to b. Use a 5% tax (Box C).*
d. *Add the answer to b and c to find the total bill (Box D).*

RATE SCHEDULE	
First 12 kwh or less	$2.00
Next 78 kwh	0.0632 per kwh
Next 510 kwh	0.06 per kwh
Excess of 600 kwh	0.06 per kwh

1. ABC ELECTRIC AND POWER COMPANY

READING DATE		TYPE OF SERV.	METER READINGS PREVIOUS	PRESENT	METER CONSTANT	KILOWATT HOURS OR 100 CU. FT.	AMOUNT	TAX	AMOUNT OF BILL INCLUDING LOCAL TAX WHERE APPLICABLE
SEPT	30	EL	9874	11104		? Ⓐ	? Ⓑ	? Ⓒ	? Ⓓ

CUSTOMER ACCOUNT NO. BT94 382
Daniel Jordan
102 E. Mexico Avenue
Boulder, Colorado, 80222

THIS BILL COVERS 30 DAYS

1a. 1230 kwh
1b. $75.33
1c. $3.77
TOTAL 1d. $79.10

2. ABC ELECTRIC AND POWER COMPANY

READING DATE		TYPE OF SERV.	METER READINGS PREVIOUS	PRESENT	METER CONSTANT	KILOWATT HOURS OR 100 CU. FT.	AMOUNT	TAX	AMOUNT OF BILL INCLUDING LOCAL TAX WHERE APPLICABLE
OCT	28	EL	11104	11974		? Ⓐ	? Ⓑ	? Ⓒ	? Ⓓ

BT94 382
Daniel Jordan
102 E. Mexico Avenue
Boulder, Colorado, 80222

THIS BILL COVERS 28 DAYS

2a. 870 kwh
2b. $53.73
2c. $2.69
TOTAL 2d. $56.42

Suppose the ABC Electric and Power Company includes a fuel adjustment charge of $0.004451 per kwh.

3. Excluding local tax, how much would this add to the September bill? 3. $5.47
4. Excluding local tax, how much would this add to the October bill? 4. $3.87

W-119

WALLPAPERING AND ESTIMATION Pages 268–269

Practice

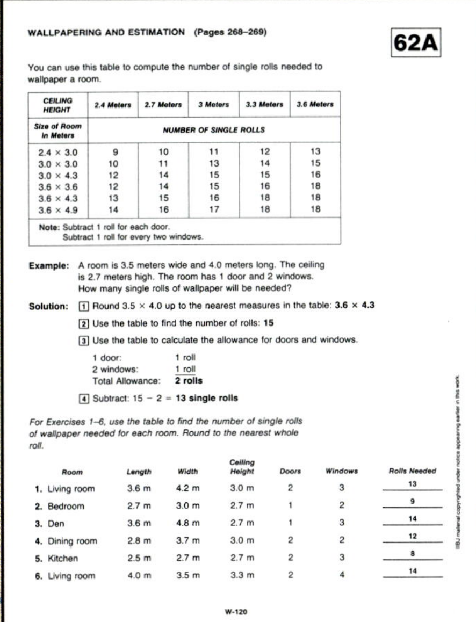

WALLPAPERING AND ESTIMATION (Pages 268–269)

62A

You can use this table to compute the number of single rolls needed to wallpaper a room.

CEILING HEIGHT	2.4 Meters	2.7 Meters	3 Meters	3.3 Meters	3.6 Meters
Size of Room in Meters	NUMBER OF SINGLE ROLLS				
2.4 × 3.0	9	10	11	12	13
3.0 × 3.0	10	11	13	14	15
3.0 × 4.3	12	14	15	15	16
3.6 × 3.6	12	14	15	16	18
3.6 × 4.3	13	15	16	18	18
3.6 × 4.9	14	16	17	18	18

Note: Subtract 1 roll for each door.
Subtract 1 roll for every two windows.

Example: A room is 3.5 meters wide and 4.0 meters long. The ceiling is 2.7 meters high. The room has 1 door and 2 windows. How many single rolls of wallpaper will be needed?

Solution:
[1] Round 3.5 × 4.0 up to the nearest measures in the table: **3.6 × 4.3**
[2] Use the table to find the number of rolls: **15**
[3] Use the table to calculate the allowance for doors and windows.

1 door: 1 roll
2 windows: 1 roll
Total Allowance: **2 rolls**

[4] Subtract: 15 − 2 = **13 single rolls**

For Exercises 1–6, use the table to find the number of single rolls of wallpaper needed for each room. Round to the nearest whole roll.

Room	Length	Width	Ceiling Height	Doors	Windows	Rolls Needed
1. Living room	3.6 m	4.2 m	3.0 m	2	3	13
2. Bedroom	2.7 m	3.0 m	2.7 m	1	2	9
3. Den	3.6 m	4.8 m	2.7 m	1	3	14
4. Dining room	2.8 m	3.7 m	3.0 m	2	2	12
5. Kitchen	2.5 m	2.7 m	2.7 m	2	3	8
6. Living room	4.0 m	3.5 m	3.3 m	2	4	14

W-120

Reteaching/ Alternate Teaching Strategy

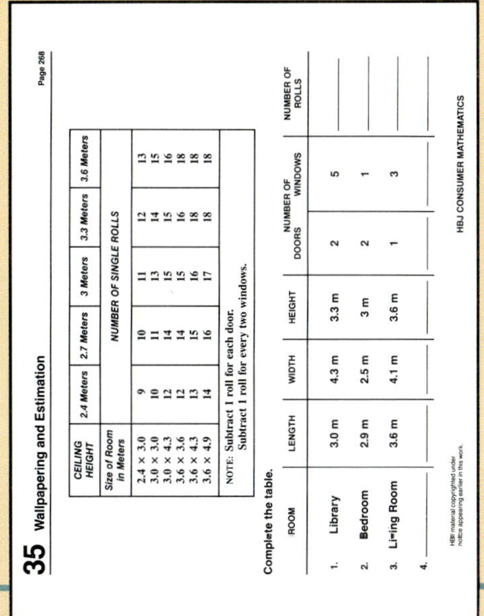

35 Wallpapering and Estimation

Page 268

CEILING HEIGHT	2.4 Meters	2.7 Meters	3 Meters	3.3 Meters	3.6 Meters
Size of Room in Meters	NUMBER OF SINGLE ROLLS				
2.4 × 3.0	9	10	11	12	13
3.0 × 3.0	10	11	13	14	15
3.0 × 4.3	12	14	15	15	16
3.6 × 3.6	12	14	15	16	18
3.6 × 4.3	13	15	16	18	18
3.6 × 4.9	14	16	17	18	18

NOTE: Subtract 1 roll for each door.
Subtract 1 roll for every two windows.

Complete the table.

ROOM	LENGTH	WIDTH	HEIGHT	NUMBER OF DOORS	NUMBER OF WINDOWS	NUMBER OF ROLLS
1. Library	3.0 m	4.3 m	3.3 m	2	5	
2. Bedroom	2.9 m	2.5 m	3 m	2	1	
3. Living Room	3.6 m	4.1 m	3.6 m	1	3	
4.						

HBJ CONSUMER MATHEMATICS

Enrichment

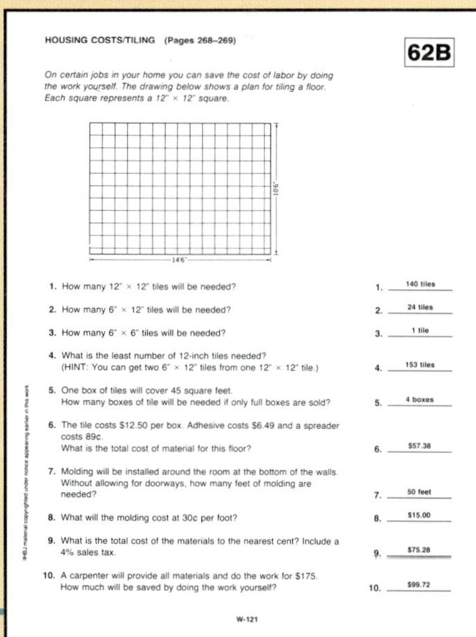

HOUSING COSTS/TILING (Pages 268–269)

62B

On certain jobs in your home you can save the cost of labor by doing the work yourself. The drawing below shows a plan for tiling a floor. Each square represents a 12" × 12" square.

1. How many 12" × 12" tiles will be needed? 1. 140 tiles
2. How many 6" × 12" tiles will be needed? 2. 24 tiles
3. How many 6" × 6" tiles will be needed? 3. 1 tile
4. What is the least number of 12-inch tiles needed? (HINT: You can get two 6" × 12" tiles from one 12" × 12" tile.) 4. 153 tiles
5. One box of tiles will cover 45 square feet. How many boxes of tile will be needed if only full boxes are sold? 5. 4 boxes
6. The tile costs $12.50 per box. Adhesive costs $6.49 and a spreader costs 89¢. What is the total cost of material for this floor? 6. $57.38
7. Molding will be installed around the room at the bottom of the walls. Without allowing for doorways, how many feet of molding are needed? 7. 50 feet
8. What will the molding cost at 30¢ per foot? 8. $15.00
9. What is the total cost of the materials to the nearest cent? Include a 4% sales tax. 9. $75.28
10. A carpenter will provide all materials and do the work for $175. How much will be saved by doing the work yourself? 10. $99.72

W-121

PAINTING AND ESTIMATION Pages 270–271

Practice

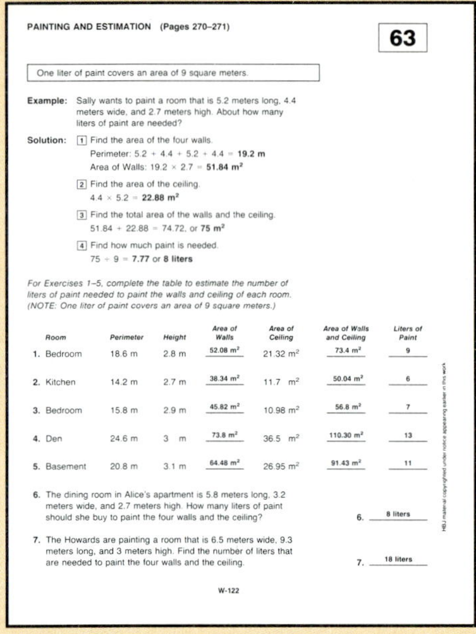

PAINTING AND ESTIMATION (Pages 270–271)

63

One liter of paint covers an area of 9 square meters.

Example: Sally wants to paint a room that is 5.2 meters long, 4.4 meters wide, and 2.7 meters high. About how many liters of paint are needed?

Solution: [1] Find the area of the four walls.
Perimeter: 5.2 + 4.4 + 5.2 + 4.4 = **19.2 m**
Area of Walls: 19.2 × 2.7 = **51.84 m²**

[2] Find the area of the ceiling.
4.4 × 5.2 = **22.88 m²**

[3] Find the total area of the walls and the ceiling.
51.84 + 22.88 = 74.72, or **75 m²**

[4] Find how much paint is needed.
75 ÷ 9 = **7.77** or **8 liters**

For Exercises 1–5, complete the table to estimate the number of liters of paint needed to paint the walls and ceiling of each room. (NOTE: One liter of paint covers an area of 9 square meters.)

Room	Perimeter	Height	Area of Walls	Area of Ceiling	Area of Walls and Ceiling	Liters of Paint
1. Bedroom	18.6 m	2.8 m	52.08 m²	21.32 m²	73.4 m²	9
2. Kitchen	14.2 m	2.7 m	38.34 m²	11.7 m²	50.04 m²	6
3. Bedroom	15.8 m	2.9 m	45.82 m²	10.98 m²	56.8 m²	7
4. Den	24.6 m	3 m	73.8 m²	36.5 m²	110.30 m²	13
5. Basement	20.8 m	3.1 m	64.48 m²	26.95 m²	91.43 m²	11

6. The dining room in Alice's apartment is 5.8 meters long, 3.2 meters wide, and 2.7 meters high. How many liters of paint should she buy to paint the four walls and the ceiling? 6. **8 liters**

7. The Howards are painting a room that is 6.5 meters wide, 9.3 meters long, and 3 meters high. Find the number of liters that are needed to paint the four walls and the ceiling. 7. **18 liters**

W-122

Reteaching/ Alternate Teaching Strategy

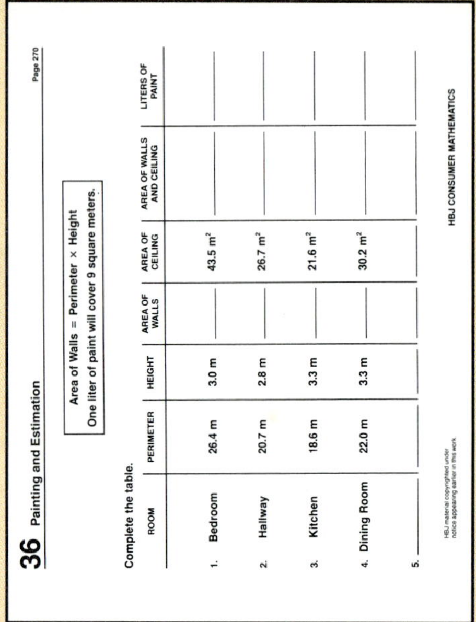

36 Painting and Estimation Page 270

Area of Walls = Perimeter × Height
One liter of paint will cover 9 square meters.

Complete the table.

ROOM	PERIMETER	HEIGHT	AREA OF WALLS	AREA OF CEILING	AREA OF WALLS AND CEILING	LITERS OF PAINT
1. Bedroom	26.4 m	3.0 m		43.5 m²		
2. Hallway	20.7 m	2.8 m		26.7 m²		
3. Kitchen	18.6 m	3.3 m		21.6 m²		
4. Dining Room	22.0 m	3.3 m		30.2 m²		
5.						

HBJ CONSUMER MATHEMATICS

Enrichment

Have students prepare a painter's estimate for walls and ceilings of one room. A liter of ceiling paint costs $5.79 and covers 9 square meters. A liter of wall paint costs $3.98 and covers 8 square meters. The painter's labor charge is $5 per liter plus $7 extra for each additional color used.

The room is 3.6 meters long, 3.0 meters wide, and 2.6 meters high. We wish to have blue walls and a white ceiling. **(ANS: $73.48)**

DISCOUNT Pages 284–285

Practice

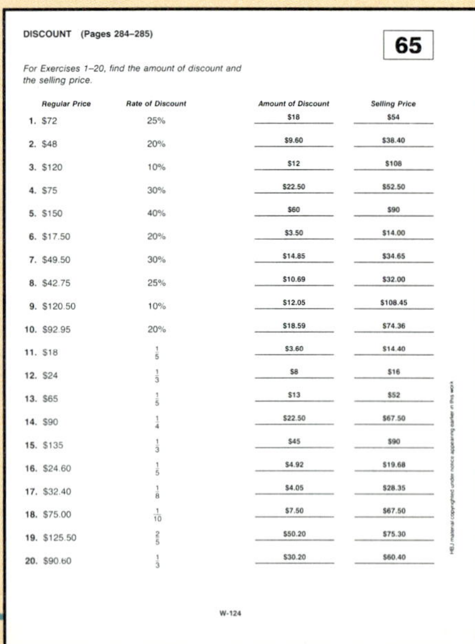

DISCOUNT (Pages 284–285)

65

For Exercises 1–20, find the amount of discount and the selling price.

Regular Price	Rate of Discount	Amount of Discount	Selling Price
1. $72	25%	$18	$54
2. $48	20%	$9.60	$38.40
3. $120	10%	$12	$108
4. $75	30%	$22.50	$52.50
5. $150	40%	$60	$90
6. $17.50	20%	$3.50	$14.00
7. $49.50	30%	$14.85	$34.65
8. $42.75	25%	$10.69	$32.00
9. $120.50	10%	$12.05	$108.45
10. $92.95	20%	$18.59	$74.36
11. $18	$\frac{1}{5}$	$3.60	$14.40
12. $24	$\frac{1}{3}$	$8	$16
13. $65	$\frac{1}{5}$	$13	$52
14. $90	$\frac{1}{4}$	$22.50	$67.50
15. $135	$\frac{1}{3}$	$45	$90
16. $24.60	$\frac{1}{5}$	$4.92	$19.68
17. $32.40	$\frac{1}{8}$	$4.05	$28.35
18. $75.00	$\frac{1}{10}$	$7.50	$67.50
19. $125.50	$\frac{2}{5}$	$50.20	$75.30
20. $90.60	$\frac{1}{3}$	$30.20	$60.40

W-124

Reteaching Alternate Teaching Strategy

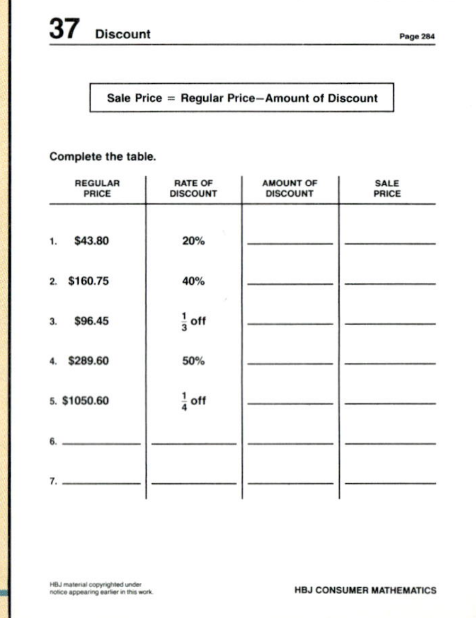

37 Discount Page 284

Sale Price = Regular Price−Amount of Discount

Complete the table.

REGULAR PRICE	RATE OF DISCOUNT	AMOUNT OF DISCOUNT	SALE PRICE
1. $43.80	20%		
2. $160.75	40%		
3. $96.45	$\frac{1}{3}$ off		
4. $289.60	50%		
5. $1050.60	$\frac{1}{4}$ off		
6.			
7.			

HBJ CONSUMER MATHEMATICS

Enrichment

Sometimes a business will give more than one discount for paying promptly or for buying a large quantity. Two or more discounts are called successive discounts. Find the sale price of a $450 T.V. with successive discounts of 20% and 5%

$450 \times .20 = 90 \quad 360 \times .05 = 18$
$450 - 90 = 360 \quad 360 - 18 = 342$

The sale price is $342.
Find the sale price for these purchases and successive discounts.

$120;	10% and 5%;	**ANS: $102.60**
$180;	12% and 8%;	**$145.73**
$640;	15% and 10%;	**$489.60**
$1600;	$12\frac{1}{2}$% and 10%;	**$1260.00**

BUYING BY MAIL Pages 286–287

Practice

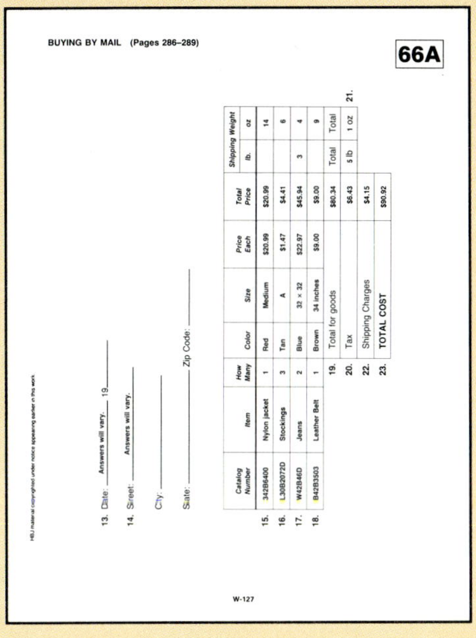

BUYING BY MAIL (Pages 286–289)

66A

13. Date: Answers will vary. 19___

14. Street: Answers will vary.

City: ______

State: ______ Zip Code: ______

	Catalog Number	Item	How Many	Color	Size	Price Each	Total Price	Shipping Weight lb.	Shipping Weight oz
15.	342B6400	Nylon jacket	1	Red	Medium	$20.99	$20.99		14
16.	L30B2072D	Stockings	3	Tan	A	$1.47	$4.41		6
17.	W42B46D	Jeans	2	Blue	32 × 32	$22.97	$45.94	3	4
18.	B42B3503	Leather Belt	1	Brown	34 inches	$9.00	$9.00		9
19.	Total for goods						$80.34	Total	Total
20.	Tax						$6.43	5 lb	1 oz
22.	Shipping Charges						$4.15	21.	
23.	TOTAL COST						$90.92		

HBJ material copyrighted under notice appearing earlier in this work.

W-127

Reteaching
Alternate Teaching Strategy

Use the form on page W-127 and Exercises 13–23 on page W-126 of the Teacher's ResourceBank™.

Enrichment

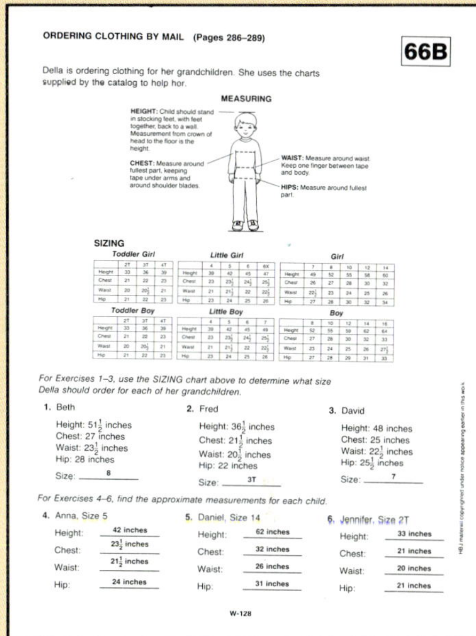

ORDERING CLOTHING BY MAIL (Pages 286–289)

66B

Della is ordering clothing for her grandchildren. She uses the charts supplied by the catalog to help her.

MEASURING

SIZING

Toddler Girl

	2T	3T	4T
Height	33	36	39
Chest	21	22	23
Waist	20	$20\frac{1}{2}$	21
Hip	21	22	23

Little Girl

	4	5	6	6X
Height	39	42	45	47
Chest	23	$23\frac{1}{2}$	$24\frac{1}{2}$	$25\frac{1}{2}$
Waist	21	$21\frac{1}{2}$	22	$22\frac{1}{2}$
Hip	23	24	25	26

Girl

	7	8	10	12	14
Height	49	52	55	58	60
Chest	26	27	28	30	32
Waist	$22\frac{1}{2}$	23	24	25	26
Hip	27	28	30	32	34

Toddler Boy

	2T	3T	4T
Height	33	36	39
Chest	21	22	23
Waist	20	$20\frac{1}{2}$	21
Hip	21	22	23

Little Boy

	4	5	6	7
Height	39	42	45	49
Chest	23	$23\frac{1}{2}$	$24\frac{1}{2}$	$25\frac{1}{2}$
Waist	21	$21\frac{1}{2}$	22	$22\frac{1}{2}$
Hip	23	24	25	26

Boy

	8	10	12	14	16
Height	52	55	59	62	64
Chest	27	28	30	32	33
Waist	23	24	25	26	$27\frac{1}{2}$
Hip	27	28	29	31	33

For Exercises 1–3, use the SIZING chart above to determine what size Della should order for each of her grandchildren.

1. Beth
   Height: $51\frac{1}{2}$ inches
   Chest: 27 inches
   Waist: $23\frac{1}{2}$ inches
   Hip: 28 inches
   Size: 8

2. Fred
   Height: $36\frac{1}{2}$ inches
   Chest: $21\frac{1}{2}$ inches
   Waist: $20\frac{1}{2}$ inches
   Hip: 22 inches
   Size: 3T

3. David
   Height: 48 inches
   Chest: 25 inches
   Waist: $22\frac{1}{2}$ inches
   Hip: $25\frac{1}{2}$ inches
   Size: 7

For Exercises 4–6, find the approximate measurements for each child.

4. Anna, Size 5
   Height: 42 inches
   Chest: $23\frac{1}{2}$ inches
   Waist: $21\frac{1}{2}$ inches
   Hip: 24 inches

5. Daniel, Size 14
   Height: 62 inches
   Chest: 32 inches
   Waist: 26 inches
   Hip: 31 inches

6. Jennifer, Size 2T
   Height: 33 inches
   Chest: 21 inches
   Waist: 20 inches
   Hip: 21 inches

HBJ material copyrighted under notice appearing earlier in this work.

W-128

CREDIT CARD STATEMENT Pages 290–292

Practice

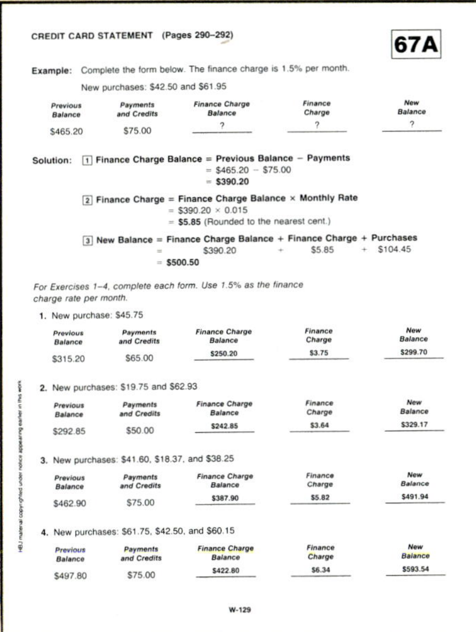

CREDIT CARD STATEMENT (Pages 290–292)

67A

Example: Complete the form below. The finance charge is 1.5% per month.

New purchases: $42.50 and $61.95

Previous Balance	Payments and Credits	Finance Charge Balance	Finance Charge	New Balance
$465.20	$75.00	?	?	?

Solution: [1] **Finance Charge Balance = Previous Balance − Payments**
= $465.20 − $75.00
= **$390.20**

[2] **Finance Charge = Finance Charge Balance × Monthly Rate**
= $390.20 × 0.015
= **$5.85** (Rounded to the nearest cent.)

[3] **New Balance = Finance Charge Balance + Finance Charge + Purchases**
= $390.20 + $5.85 + $104.45
= **$500.50**

For Exercises 1–4, complete each form. Use 1.5% as the finance charge rate per month.

1. New purchase: $45.75

Previous Balance	Payments and Credits	Finance Charge Balance	Finance Charge	New Balance
$315.20	$65.00	$250.20	$3.75	$299.70

2. New purchases: $19.75 and $62.93

Previous Balance	Payments and Credits	Finance Charge Balance	Finance Charge	New Balance
$292.85	$50.00	$242.85	$3.64	$329.17

3. New purchases: $41.60, $18.37, and $38.25

Previous Balance	Payments and Credits	Finance Charge Balance	Finance Charge	New Balance
$462.90	$75.00	$387.90	$5.82	$491.94

4. New purchases: $61.75, $42.50, and $60.15

Previous Balance	Payments and Credits	Finance Charge Balance	Finance Charge	New Balance
$497.80	$75.00	$422.80	$6.34	$593.54

HBJ material copyrighted under notice appearing earlier in this work.

W-129

Reteaching
Alternate Teaching Strategy

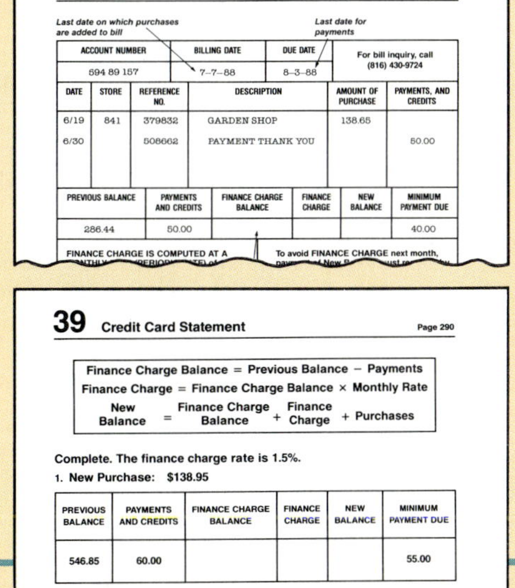

38 Credit Card Statement — Page 290

ACCOUNT NUMBER	BILLING DATE	DUE DATE	For bill inquiry, call (816) 430-9724
594 89 157	7–7–88	8–3–88	

DATE	STORE	REFERENCE NO.	DESCRIPTION	AMOUNT OF PURCHASE	PAYMENTS, AND CREDITS
6/19	841	379832	GARDEN SHOP	138.65	
6/30		508662	PAYMENT THANK YOU		50.00

PREVIOUS BALANCE	PAYMENTS AND CREDITS	FINANCE CHARGE BALANCE	FINANCE CHARGE	NEW BALANCE	MINIMUM PAYMENT DUE
286.44	50.00				40.00

FINANCE CHARGE IS COMPUTED AT A ... To avoid FINANCE CHARGE next month, ...

39 Credit Card Statement — Page 290

Finance Charge Balance = Previous Balance − Payments
Finance Charge = Finance Charge Balance × Monthly Rate
New Balance = Finance Charge Balance + Finance Charge + Purchases

Complete. The finance charge rate is 1.5%.

1. New Purchase: $138.95

PREVIOUS BALANCE	PAYMENTS AND CREDITS	FINANCE CHARGE BALANCE	FINANCE CHARGE	NEW BALANCE	MINIMUM PAYMENT DUE
546.85	60.00				55.00

Enrichment

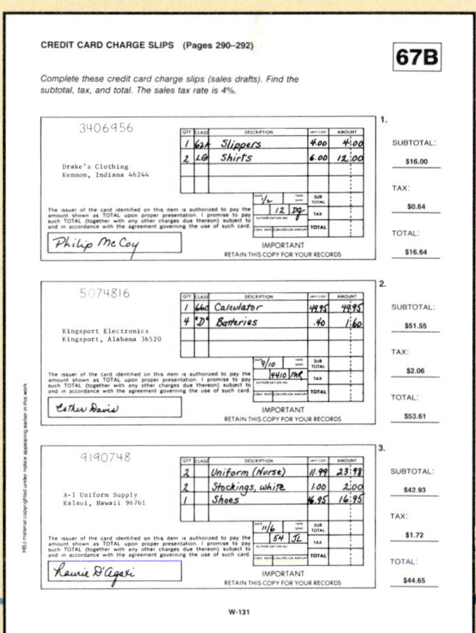

CREDIT CARD CHARGE SLIPS (Pages 290–292)

67B

Complete these credit card charge slips (sales drafts). Find the subtotal, tax, and total. The sales tax rate is 4%.

1. 3406956 — Drake's Clothing, Kennon, Indiana 46244

QTY	CLASS	DESCRIPTION	UNIT COST	AMOUNT
1	62A	Slippers	4.00	4.00
2	LG	Shirts	6.00	12.00

Date 1/2; Authorization 12 DG; Signed: Philip McCoy

SUBTOTAL: $16.00
TAX: $0.64
TOTAL: $16.64

2. 5074816 — Kingsport Electronics, Kingsport, Alabama 36520

QTY	CLASS	DESCRIPTION	UNIT COST	AMOUNT
1	66C	Calculator	49.95	49.95
4	"D"	Batteries	.40	1.60

Date 9/10; Authorization 4410 MR; Signed: Esther David

SUBTOTAL: $51.55
TAX: $2.06
TOTAL: $53.61

3. 9190748 — A-1 Uniform Supply, Kalaui, Hawaii 96761

QTY	CLASS	DESCRIPTION	UNIT COST	AMOUNT
2		Uniform (Nurse)	11.99	23.98
2		Stockings, white	1.00	2.00
1		Shoes	16.95	16.95

Date 11/6; Authorization 54 JL; Signed: Laurie D'Agati

SUBTOTAL: $42.93
TAX: $1.72
TOTAL: $44.65

The issuer of the card identified on this item is authorized to pay the amount shown as TOTAL upon proper presentation. I promise to pay such TOTAL (together with any other charges due thereon) subject to and in accordance with the agreement governing the use of such card.

IMPORTANT
RETAIN THIS COPY FOR YOUR RECORDS

HBJ material copyrighted under notice appearing earlier in this work.

W-131

CREDIT CARD: MINIMUM PAYMENTS Pages 295–296

Practice

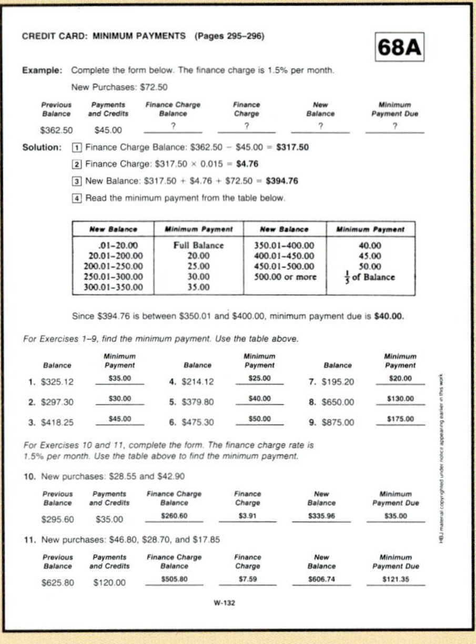

CREDIT CARD: MINIMUM PAYMENTS (Pages 295–296)

68A

Example: Complete the form below. The finance charge is 1.5% per month.

New Purchases: $72.50

Previous Balance	Payments and Credits	Finance Charge Balance	Finance Charge	New Balance	Minimum Payment Due
$362.50	$45.00	?	?	?	?

Solution: [1] Finance Charge Balance: $362.50 − $45.00 = **$317.50**

[2] Finance Charge: $317.50 × 0.015 = **$4.76**

[3] New Balance: $317.50 + $4.76 + $72.50 = **$394.76**

[4] Read the minimum payment from the table below.

New Balance	Minimum Payment	New Balance	Minimum Payment
.01–20.00	Full Balance	350.01–400.00	40.00
20.01–200.00	20.00	400.01–450.00	45.00
200.01–250.00	25.00	450.01–500.00	50.00
250.01–300.00	30.00	500.00 or more	$\frac{1}{3}$ of Balance
300.01–350.00	35.00		

Since $394.76 is between $350.01 and $400.00, minimum payment due is **$40.00.**

For Exercises 1–9, find the minimum payment. Use the table above.

	Balance	Minimum Payment		Balance	Minimum Payment		Balance	Minimum Payment
1.	$325.12	$35.00	4.	$214.12	$25.00	7.	$195.20	$20.00
2.	$297.30	$30.00	5.	$379.80	$40.00	8.	$650.00	$130.00
3.	$418.25	$45.00	6.	$475.30	$50.00	9.	$875.00	$175.00

For Exercises 10 and 11, complete the form. The finance charge rate is 1.5% per month. Use the table above to find the minimum payment.

10. New purchases: $28.55 and $42.90

Previous Balance	Payments and Credits	Finance Charge Balance	Finance Charge	New Balance	Minimum Payment Due
$295.60	$35.00	$260.60	$3.91	$335.96	$35.00

11. New purchases: $46.80, $28.70, and $17.85

Previous Balance	Payments and Credits	Finance Charge Balance	Finance Charge	New Balance	Minimum Payment Due
$625.80	$120.00	$505.80	$7.59	$606.74	$121.35

W-132

Reteaching/ Alternate Teaching Strategy

Use the credit card statement and Exercises 12–21 on page W-133 of the Teacher's ResourceBank™.

Enrichment

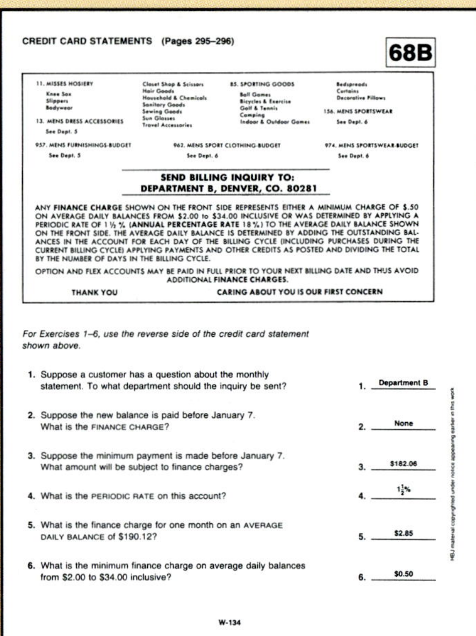

CREDIT CARD STATEMENTS (Pages 295–296)

68B

11. MISSES HOSIERY
Knee Sox
Slippers
Bodywear

13. MENS DRESS ACCESSORIES
See Dept. 5

Closet Shop & Scissors
Hair Goods
Household & Chemicals
Sanitary Goods
Sewing Goods
Sun Glasses
Travel Accessories

85. SPORTING GOODS
Ball Games
Bicycles & Exercise
Golf & Tennis
Camping
Indoor & Outdoor Games

Bedspreads
Curtains
Decorative Pillows

156. MENS SPORTSWEAR
See Dept. 6

957. MENS FURNISHINGS-BUDGET
See Dept. 5

962. MENS SPORT CLOTHING-BUDGET
See Dept. 6

974. MENS SPORTSWEAR-BUDGET
See Dept. 6

SEND BILLING INQUIRY TO:
DEPARTMENT B, DENVER, CO. 80281

ANY **FINANCE CHARGE** SHOWN ON THE FRONT SIDE REPRESENTS EITHER A MINIMUM CHARGE OF $.50 ON AVERAGE DAILY BALANCES FROM $2.00 to $34.00 INCLUSIVE OR WAS DETERMINED BY APPLYING A PERIODIC RATE OF 1½ % (**ANNUAL PERCENTAGE RATE** 18 %) TO THE AVERAGE DAILY BALANCE SHOWN ON THE FRONT SIDE. THE AVERAGE DAILY BALANCE IS DETERMINED BY ADDING THE OUTSTANDING BALANCES IN THE ACCOUNT FOR EACH DAY OF THE BILLING CYCLE (INCLUDING PURCHASES DURING THE CURRENT BILLING CYCLE) APPLYING PAYMENTS AND OTHER CREDITS AS POSTED AND DIVIDING THE TOTAL BY THE NUMBER OF DAYS IN THE BILLING CYCLE.

OPTION AND FLEX ACCOUNTS MAY BE PAID IN FULL PRIOR TO YOUR NEXT BILLING DATE AND THUS AVOID ADDITIONAL **FINANCE CHARGES.**

THANK YOU — CARING ABOUT YOU IS OUR FIRST CONCERN

For Exercises 1–6, use the reverse side of the credit card statement shown above.

1. Suppose a customer has a question about the monthly statement. To what department should the inquiry be sent? — 1. Department B
2. Suppose the new balance is paid before January 7. What is the FINANCE CHARGE? — 2. None
3. Suppose the minimum payment is made before January 7. What amount will be subject to finance charges? — 3. $182.06
4. What is the PERIODIC RATE on this account? — 4. $1\frac{1}{2}$%
5. What is the finance charge for one month on an AVERAGE DAILY BALANCE of $190.12? — 5. $2.85
6. What is the minimum finance charge on average daily balances from $2.00 to $34.00 inclusive? — 6. $0.50

W-134

INSTALLMENT LOANS Pages 297–299

Practice

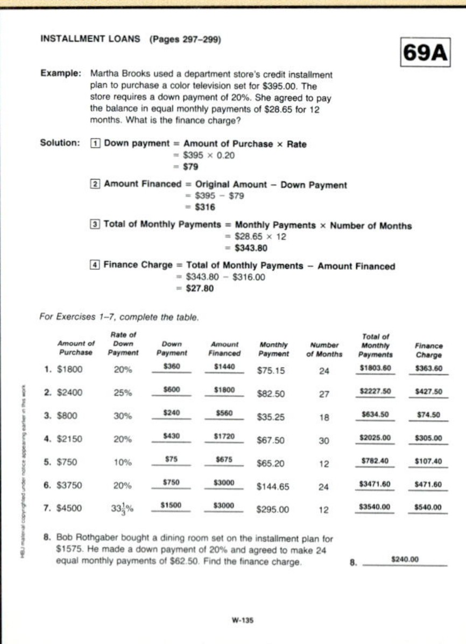

INSTALLMENT LOANS (Pages 297–299)

69A

Example: Martha Brooks used a department store's credit installment plan to purchase a color television set for $395.00. The store requires a down payment of 20%. She agreed to pay the balance in equal monthly payments of $28.65 for 12 months. What is the finance charge?

Solution: [1] **Down payment = Amount of Purchase × Rate**
= $395 × 0.20
= **$79**

[2] **Amount Financed = Original Amount − Down Payment**
= $395 − $79
= **$316**

[3] **Total of Monthly Payments = Monthly Payments × Number of Months**
= $28.65 × 12
= **$343.80**

[4] **Finance Charge = Total of Monthly Payments − Amount Financed**
= $343.80 − $316.00
= **$27.80**

For Exercises 1–7, complete the table.

	Amount of Purchase	Rate of Down Payment	Down Payment	Amount Financed	Monthly Payment	Number of Months	Total of Monthly Payments	Finance Charge
1.	$1800	20%	$360	$1440	$75.15	24	$1803.60	$363.60
2.	$2400	25%	$600	$1800	$82.50	27	$2227.50	$427.50
3.	$800	30%	$240	$560	$35.25	18	$634.50	$74.50
4.	$2150	20%	$430	$1720	$67.50	30	$2025.00	$305.00
5.	$750	10%	$75	$675	$65.20	12	$782.40	$107.40
6.	$3750	20%	$750	$3000	$144.65	24	$3471.60	$471.60
7.	$4500	$33\frac{1}{3}$%	$1500	$3000	$295.00	12	$3540.00	$540.00

8. Bob Rothgaber bought a dining room set on the installment plan for $1575. He made a down payment of 20% and agreed to make 24 equal monthly payments of $62.50. Find the finance charge. — 8. $240.00

W-135

Reteaching/ Alternate Teaching Strategy

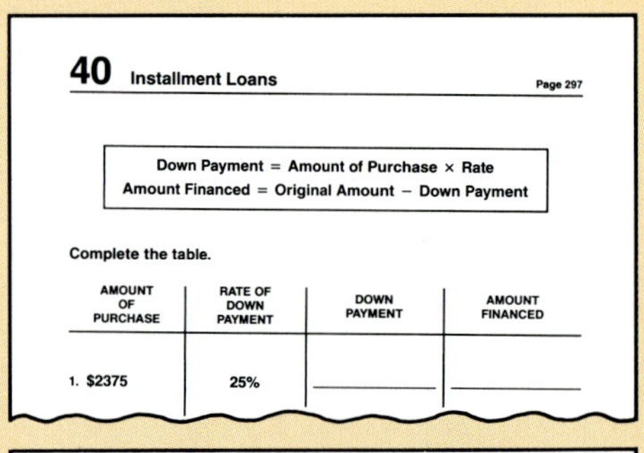

40 Installment Loans — Page 297

Down Payment = Amount of Purchase × Rate
Amount Financed = Original Amount − Down Payment

Complete the table.

AMOUNT OF PURCHASE	RATE OF DOWN PAYMENT	DOWN PAYMENT	AMOUNT FINANCED
1. $2375	25%		

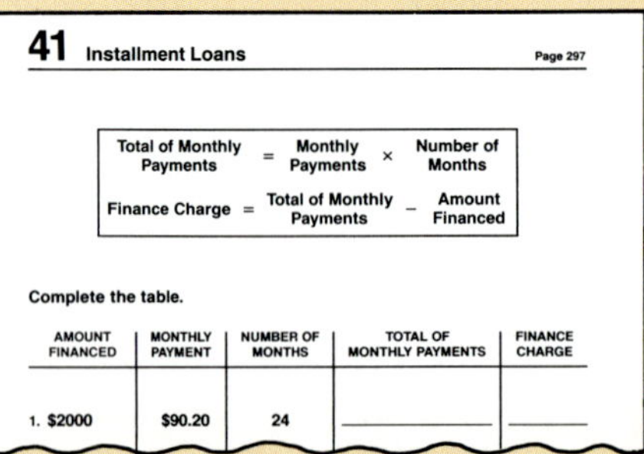

41 Installment Loans — Page 297

Total of Monthly Payments = Monthly Payments × Number of Months
Finance Charge = Total of Monthly Payments − Amount Financed

Complete the table.

AMOUNT FINANCED	MONTHLY PAYMENT	NUMBER OF MONTHS	TOTAL OF MONTHLY PAYMENTS	FINANCE CHARGE
1. $2000	$90.20	24		

Enrichment

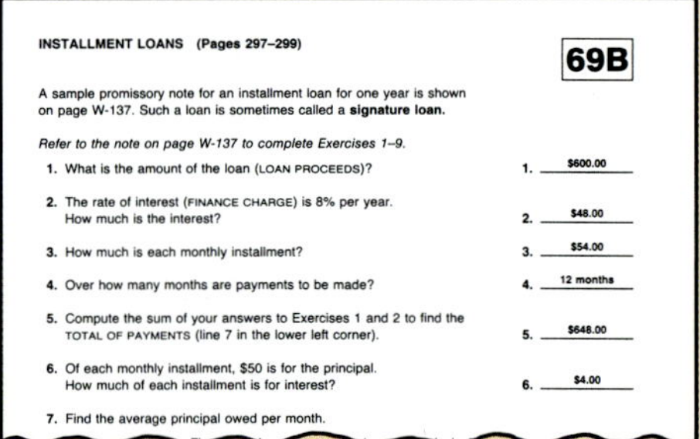

INSTALLMENT LOANS (Pages 297–299)

69B

A sample promissory note for an installment loan for one year is shown on page W-137. Such a loan is sometimes called a **signature loan.**

Refer to the note on page W-137 to complete Exercises 1–9.

1. What is the amount of the loan (LOAN PROCEEDS)? — 1. $600.00
2. The rate of interest (FINANCE CHARGE) is 8% per year. How much is the interest? — 2. $48.00
3. How much is each monthly installment? — 3. $54.00
4. Over how many months are payments to be made? — 4. 12 months
5. Compute the sum of your answers to Exercises 1 and 2 to find the TOTAL OF PAYMENTS (line 7 in the lower left corner). — 5. $648.00
6. Of each monthly installment, $50 is for the principal. How much of each installment is for interest? — 6. $4.00
7. Find the average principal owed per month.

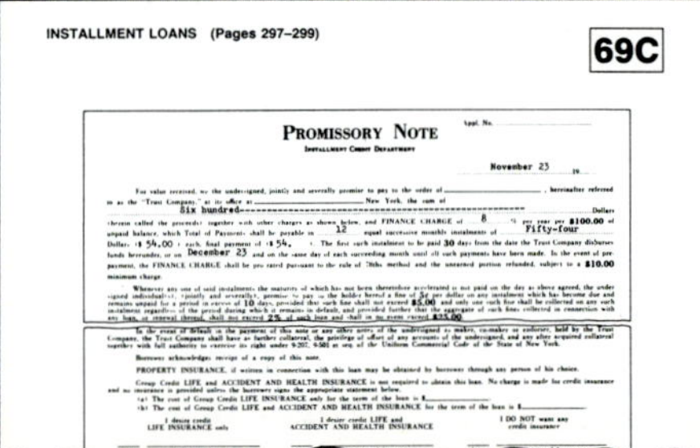

INSTALLMENT LOANS (Pages 297–299)

69C

PROMISSORY NOTE
Installment Credit Department

Appl. No.

November 23, 19

For value received, we the undersigned, jointly and severally promise to pay to the order of ________, hereinafter referred to as the "Trust Company," at its office at ________ New York, the sum of Six hundred———— Dollars (herein called the proceeds) together with other charges as shown below, and FINANCE CHARGE of 8 % per year per $100.00 of unpaid balance, which Total of Payments shall be payable in 12 equal successive monthly instalments of Fifty-four Dollars ($ 54.00) each, final payment of ($ 54.). The first such instalment to be paid 30 days from the date the Trust Company disburses funds hereunder, or on December 23 and on the same day of each succeeding month until all such payments have been made. In the event of prepayment, the FINANCE CHARGE shall be pro rated pursuant to the rule of 78ths method and the unearned portion refunded, subject to a $10.00 minimum charge.

Whenever any one of said instalments the maturity of which has not been theretofore accelerated is not paid on the day as above agreed, the undersigned individual(s), jointly and severally, promise to pay to the holder hereof a fine of 5¢ per dollar on any instalment which has become due and remains unpaid for a period in excess of 10 days, provided that such fine shall not exceed $5.00 and only one such fine shall be collected on any such instalment regardless of the period during which it remains in default, and provided further that the aggregate of such fines collected in connection with any loan, or renewal thereof, shall not exceed 2% of such loan and shall in no event exceed $25.00.

In the event of default in the payment of this note or any other notes of the undersigned as maker, co-maker or endorser, held by the Trust Company, the Trust Company shall have as further collateral, the privilege of offset of any accounts of the undersigned, and any after acquired collateral together with full authority to exercise its right under 9-207, 9-501 et seq. of the Uniform Commercial Code of the State of New York.

Borrower acknowledges receipt of a copy of this note.

PROPERTY INSURANCE, if written in connection with this loan may be obtained by borrower through any person of his choice.

Group Credit LIFE and ACCIDENT AND HEALTH INSURANCE is not required to obtain this loan. No charge is made for credit insurance and no insurance is provided unless the borrower signs the appropriate statement below.

(a) The cost of Group Credit LIFE INSURANCE only for the term of the loan is $________.
(b) The cost of Group Credit LIFE and ACCIDENT AND HEALTH INSURANCE for the term of the loan is $________.

I desire credit LIFE INSURANCE only — I desire credit LIFE and ACCIDENT AND HEALTH INSURANCE — I DO NOT want any credit insurance

date — signature of borrower — date — signature of borrower — date — signature of borrower

LIFE INSURANCE: TERM AND WHOLE LIFE Pages 312–314

Practice

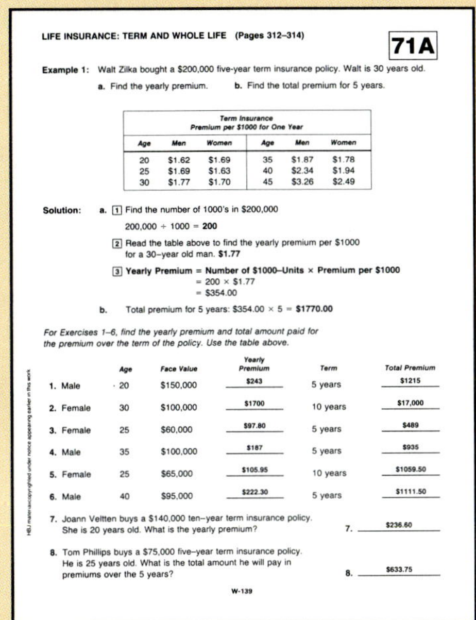

LIFE INSURANCE: TERM AND WHOLE LIFE (Pages 312–314) **71A**

Example 1: Walt Zilka bought a $200,000 five-year term insurance policy. Walt is 30 years old.

a. Find the yearly premium. b. Find the total premium for 5 years.

Term Insurance Premium per $1000 for One Year					
Age	**Men**	**Women**	**Age**	**Men**	**Women**
20	$1.62	$1.69	35	$1.87	$1.78
25	$1.69	$1.63	40	$2.34	$1.94
30	$1.77	$1.70	45	$3.26	$2.49

Solution: a. [1] Find the number of 1000's in $200,000

200,000 ÷ 1000 = **200**

[2] Read the table above to find the yearly premium per $1000 for a 30–year old man. **$1.77**

[3] **Yearly Premium = Number of $1000–Units × Premium per $1000**
= 200 × $1.77
= $354.00

b. Total premium for 5 years: $354.00 × 5 = **$1770.00**

For Exercises 1–6, find the yearly premium and total amount paid for the premium over the term of the policy. Use the table above.

	Age	Face Value	Yearly Premium	Term	Total Premium
1. Male	20	$150,000	$243	5 years	$1215
2. Female	30	$100,000	$1700	10 years	$17,000
3. Female	25	$60,000	$97.80	5 years	$489
4. Male	35	$100,000	$187	5 years	$935
5. Female	25	$65,000	$105.95	10 years	$1059.50
6. Male	40	$95,000	$222.30	5 years	$1111.50

7. Joann Veltten buys a $140,000 ten–year term insurance policy. She is 20 years old. What is the yearly premium? 7. $236.60

8. Tom Phillips buys a $75,000 five–year term insurance policy. He is 25 years old. What is the total amount he will pay in premiums over the 5 years? 8. $633.75

W-139

Reteaching/ Alternate Teaching Strategy

Make a line graph showing the 5 year term insurance yearly premium per $1000. Use the table on page 312 or a similar table obtained from an insurance company. Identify a line as premiums for women and a line as premiums for men. The graph can then be used as an alternate source for rates you can use in presenting the lesson.

You may wish to explain that graphs are useful only when comparing rates, that tables are used by representatives of insurance companies who quote and sell insurance.

Enrichment

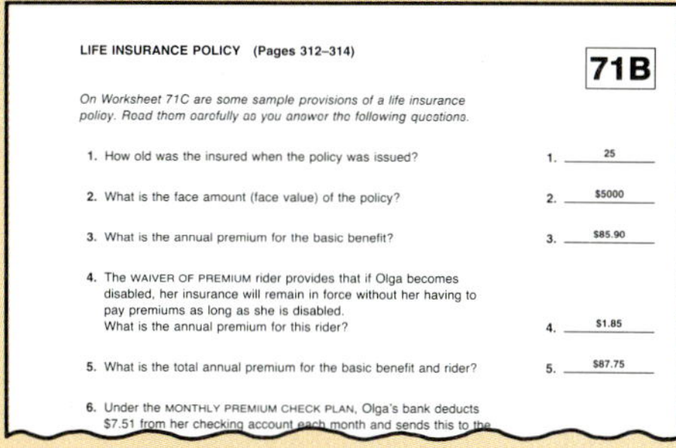

LIFE INSURANCE POLICY (Pages 312–314) **71B**

On Worksheet 71C are some sample provisions of a life insurance policy. Read them carefully as you answer the following questions.

1. How old was the insured when the policy was issued? 1. 25
2. What is the face amount (face value) of the policy? 2. $5000
3. What is the annual premium for the basic benefit? 3. $85.90
4. The WAIVER OF PREMIUM rider provides that if Olga becomes disabled, her insurance will remain in force without her having to pay premiums as long as she is disabled. What is the annual premium for this rider? 4. $1.85
5. What is the total annual premium for the basic benefit and rider? 5. $87.75
6. Under the MONTHLY PREMIUM CHECK PLAN, Olga's bank deducts $7.51 from her checking account each month and sends this to the

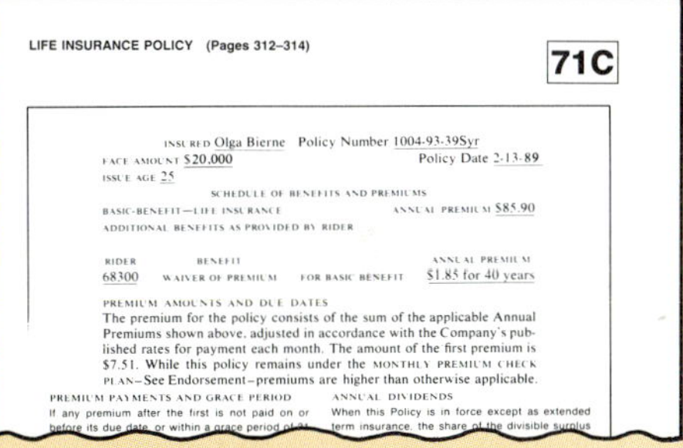

LIFE INSURANCE POLICY (Pages 312–314) **71C**

INSURED Olga Bierne Policy Number 1004-93-39Syr
FACE AMOUNT $20,000 Policy Date 2-13-89
ISSUE AGE 25
SCHEDULE OF BENEFITS AND PREMIUMS
BASIC BENEFIT—LIFE INSURANCE ANNUAL PREMIUM $85.90
ADDITIONAL BENEFITS AS PROVIDED BY RIDER
RIDER 68300 BENEFIT WAIVER OF PREMIUM FOR BASIC BENEFIT ANNUAL PREMIUM $1.85 for 40 years
PREMIUM AMOUNTS AND DUE DATES
The premium for the policy consists of the sum of the applicable Annual Premiums shown above, adjusted in accordance with the Company's published rates for payment each month. The amount of the first premium is $7.51. While this policy remains under the MONTHLY PREMIUM CHECK PLAN—See Endorsement—premiums are higher than otherwise applicable.
PREMIUM PAYMENTS AND GRACE PERIOD
If any premium after the first is not paid on or before its due date or within a grace period
ANNUAL DIVIDENDS
When this Policy is in force except as extended term insurance, the share of the divisible surplus

UNIVERSAL LIFE INSURANCE Pages 315–317

Practice

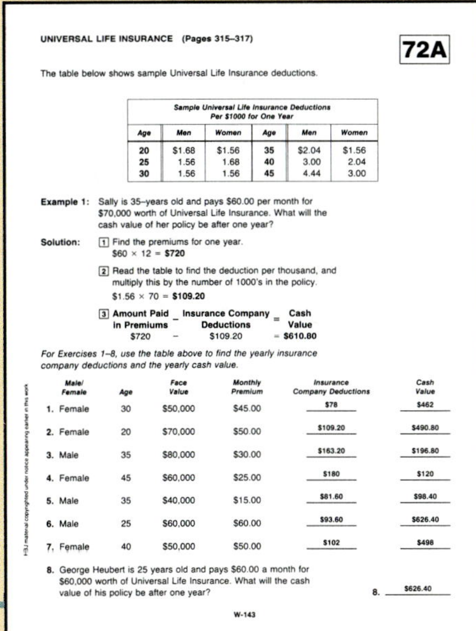

UNIVERSAL LIFE INSURANCE (Pages 315–317) **72A**

The table below shows sample Universal Life Insurance deductions.

Sample Universal Life Insurance Deductions Per $1000 for One Year					
Age	**Men**	**Women**	**Age**	**Men**	**Women**
20	$1.68	$1.56	35	$2.04	$1.56
25	1.56	1.68	40	3.00	2.04
30	1.56	1.56	45	4.44	3.00

Example 1: Sally is 35–years old and pays $60.00 per month for $70,000 worth of Universal Life Insurance. What will the cash value of her policy be after one year?

Solution: [1] Find the premiums for one year.
$60 × 12 = **$720**

[2] Read the table to find the deduction per thousand, and multiply this by the number of 1000's in the policy.
$1.56 × 70 = **$109.20**

[3] **Amount Paid in Premiums − Insurance Company Deductions = Cash Value**
$720 − $109.20 = **$610.80**

For Exercises 1–8, use the table above to find the yearly insurance company deductions and the yearly cash value.

	Male/ Female	Age	Face Value	Monthly Premium	Insurance Company Deductions	Cash Value
1.	Female	30	$50,000	$45.00	$78	$462
2.	Female	20	$70,000	$50.00	$109.20	$490.80
3.	Male	35	$80,000	$30.00	$163.20	$196.80
4.	Female	45	$60,000	$25.00	$180	$120
5.	Male	35	$40,000	$15.00	$81.60	$98.40
6.	Male	25	$60,000	$60.00	$93.60	$626.40
7.	Female	40	$50,000	$50.00	$102	$498

8. George Heubert is 25 years old and pays $60.00 a month for $60,000 worth of Universal Life Insurance. What will the cash value of his policy be after one year? 8. $626.40

W-143

Reteaching/ Alternate Teaching Strategy

You can use the Investment Multiple Table on page 316 as a pattern for making a Total Cash Value Table as shown below. Remember to supply students with a yearly cash value with which to work the problem.

Number of Years	Total Cash Value Yearly Cash Value = $_____		
	5%	7.5%	10%
1			
4			
5			
10			

This table can be used to present the lesson by an alternate method.

Enrichment

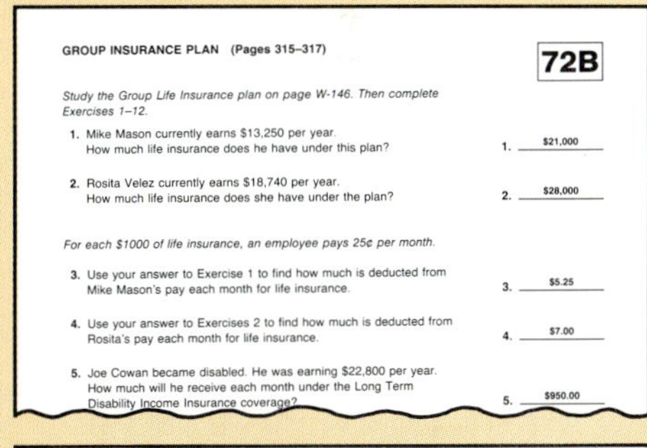

GROUP INSURANCE PLAN (Pages 315–317) **72B**

Study the Group Life Insurance plan on page W-146. Then complete Exercises 1–12.

1. Mike Mason currently earns $13,250 per year. How much life insurance does he have under this plan? 1. $21,000
2. Rosita Velez currently earns $18,740 per year. How much life insurance does she have under the plan? 2. $28,000

For each $1000 of life insurance, an employee pays 25¢ per month.

3. Use your answer to Exercise 1 to find how much is deducted from Mike Mason's pay each month for life insurance. 3. $5.25
4. Use your answer to Exercises 2 to find how much is deducted from Rosita's pay each month for life insurance. 4. $7.00
5. Joe Cowan became disabled. He was earning $22,800 per year. How much will he receive each month under the Long Term Disability Income Insurance coverage? 5. $950.00

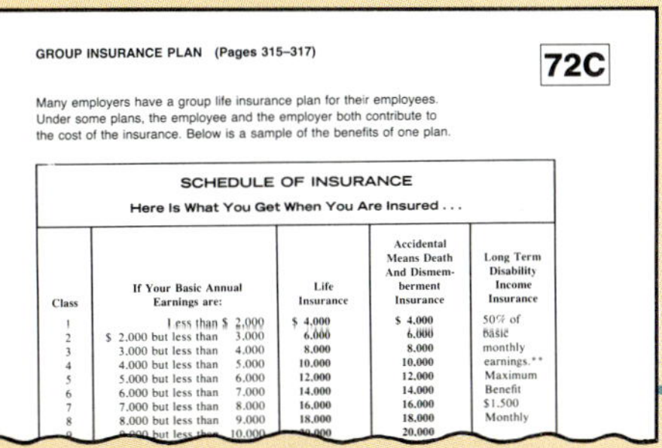

GROUP INSURANCE PLAN (Pages 315–317) **72C**

Many employers have a group life insurance plan for their employees. Under some plans, the employee and the employer both contribute to the cost of the insurance. Below is a sample of the benefits of one plan.

SCHEDULE OF INSURANCE
Here Is What You Get When You Are Insured . . .

Class	If Your Basic Annual Earnings are:	Life Insurance	Accidental Means Death And Dismemberment Insurance	Long Term Disability Income Insurance
1	Less than $ 2,000	$ 4,000	$ 4,000	50% of basic monthly earnings.** Maximum Benefit $1,500 Monthly
2	$ 2,000 but less than 3,000	6,000	6,000	
3	3,000 but less than 4,000	8,000	8,000	
4	4,000 but less than 5,000	10,000	10,000	
5	5,000 but less than 6,000	12,000	12,000	
6	6,000 but less than 7,000	14,000	14,000	
7	7,000 but less than 8,000	16,000	16,000	
8	8,000 but less than 9,000	18,000	18,000	
9	9,000 but less than 10,000	[illegible]	20,000	

CERTIFICATES OF DEPOSIT Pages 318–319

Practice

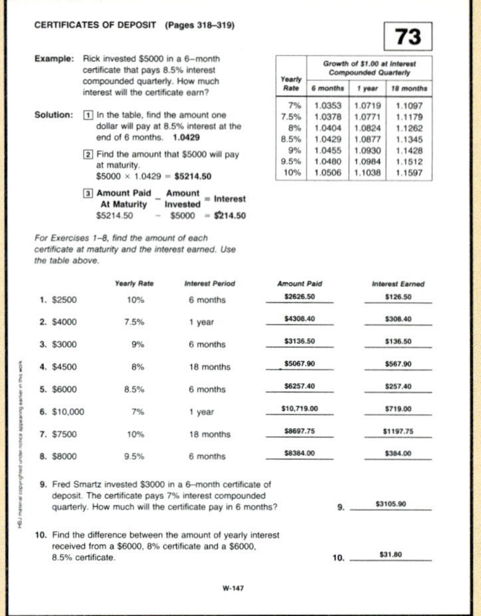

CERTIFICATES OF DEPOSIT (Pages 318–319)

73

Example: Rick invested \$5000 in a 6–month certificate that pays 8.5% interest compounded quarterly. How much interest will the certificate earn?

Yearly Rate	Growth of \$1.00 at Interest Compounded Quarterly		
	6 months	1 year	18 months
7%	1.0353	1.0719	1.1097
7.5%	1.0378	1.0771	1.1179
8%	1.0404	1.0824	1.1262
8.5%	1.0429	1.0877	1.1345
9%	1.0455	1.0930	1.1428
9.5%	1.0480	1.0984	1.1512
10%	1.0506	1.1038	1.1597

Solution: [1] In the table, find the amount one dollar will pay at 8.5% interest at the end of 6 months. **1.0429**

[2] Find the amount that \$5000 will pay at maturity.
\$5000 × 1.0429 = **\$5214.50**

[3] **Amount Paid At Maturity** − **Amount Invested** = **Interest**
\$5214.50 − \$5000 = **\$214.50**

For Exercises 1–8, find the amount of each certificate at maturity and the interest earned. Use the table above.

	Yearly Rate	Interest Period	Amount Paid	Interest Earned
1. \$2500	10%	6 months	\$2626.50	\$126.50
2. \$4000	7.5%	1 year	\$4308.40	\$308.40
3. \$3000	9%	6 months	\$3136.50	\$136.50
4. \$4500	8%	18 months	\$5067.90	\$567.90
5. \$6000	8.5%	6 months	\$6257.40	\$257.40
6. \$10,000	7%	1 year	\$10,719.00	\$719.00
7. \$7500	10%	18 months	\$8697.75	\$1197.75
8. \$8000	9.5%	6 months	\$8384.00	\$384.00

9. Fred Smartz invested \$3000 in a 6–month certificate of deposit. The certificate pays 7% interest compounded quarterly. How much will the certificate pay in 6 months? 9. \$3105.90

10. Find the difference between the amount of yearly interest received from a \$6000, 8% certificate and a \$6000, 8.5% certificate. 10. \$31.80

W-147

Reteaching/ Alternate Teaching Strategy

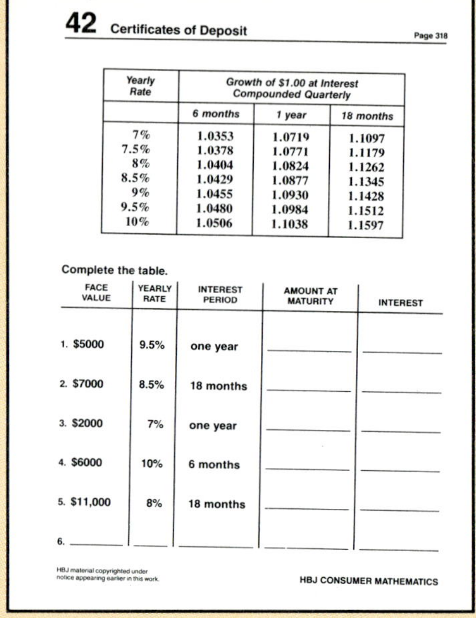

42 Certificates of Deposit Page 318

Yearly Rate	Growth of \$1.00 at Interest Compounded Quarterly		
	6 months	1 year	18 months
7%	1.0353	1.0719	1.1097
7.5%	1.0378	1.0771	1.1179
8%	1.0404	1.0824	1.1262
8.5%	1.0429	1.0877	1.1345
9%	1.0455	1.0930	1.1428
9.5%	1.0480	1.0984	1.1512
10%	1.0506	1.1038	1.1597

Complete the table.

FACE VALUE	YEARLY RATE	INTEREST PERIOD	AMOUNT AT MATURITY	INTEREST
1. \$5000	9.5%	one year		
2. \$7000	8.5%	18 months		
3. \$2000	7%	one year		
4. \$6000	10%	6 months		
5. \$11,000	8%	18 months		
6.				

HBJ CONSUMER MATHEMATICS

Enrichment

Challenge students with this problem.

Sue Ellington invested \$8,000 in Certificates of Deposit (CDs). She could buy one \$8,000 CD, but she chose to buy four \$2,000 CDs with terms of 3 months, 6 months, 9 months, and 12 months. When each CD matures, Sue plans to replace it with a 12 month CD.

What are some advantages and disadvantages of Sue's plan for investing? **(ANS: Advantages: She receives interest income every 3 months, and can avoid early withdrawal penalty if she needs cash.)**

BUYING AND SELLING STOCK Pages 321–323

Practice

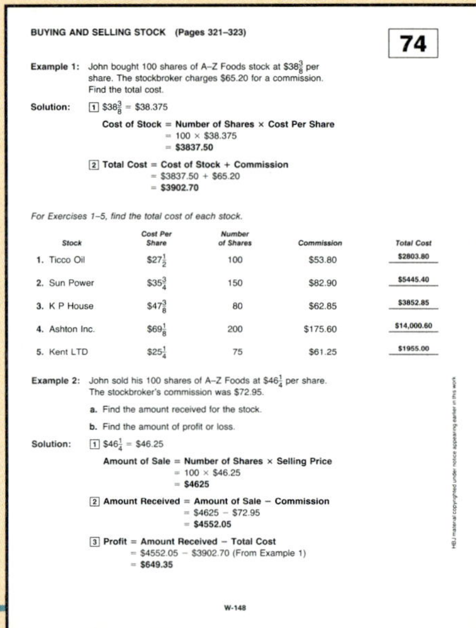

BUYING AND SELLING STOCK (Pages 321–323)

74

Example 1: John bought 100 shares of A–Z Foods stock at $\$38\frac{3}{8}$ per share. The stockbroker charges \$65.20 for a commission. Find the total cost.

Solution: [1] $\$38\frac{3}{8} = \$38.375$

Cost of Stock = Number of Shares × Cost Per Share
= 100 × \$38.375
= **\$3837.50**

[2] **Total Cost = Cost of Stock + Commission**
= \$3837.50 + \$65.20
= **\$3902.70**

For Exercises 1–5, find the total cost of each stock.

Stock	Cost Per Share	Number of Shares	Commission	Total Cost
1. Ticco Oil	$\$27\frac{1}{2}$	100	\$53.80	\$2803.80
2. Sun Power	$\$35\frac{3}{4}$	150	\$82.90	\$5445.40
3. K P House	$\$47\frac{3}{8}$	80	\$62.85	\$3852.85
4. Ashton Inc.	$\$69\frac{1}{8}$	200	\$175.60	\$14,000.60
5. Kent LTD	$\$25\frac{1}{4}$	75	\$61.25	\$1955.00

Example 2: John sold his 100 shares of A–Z Foods at $\$46\frac{1}{4}$ per share. The stockbroker's commission was \$72.95.

a. Find the amount received for the stock.

b. Find the amount of profit or loss.

Solution: [1] $\$46\frac{1}{4} = \$46.25$

Amount of Sale = Number of Shares × Selling Price
= 100 × \$46.25
= **\$4625**

[2] **Amount Received = Amount of Sale − Commission**
= \$4625 − \$72.95
= **\$4552.05**

[3] **Profit = Amount Received − Total Cost**
= \$4552.05 − \$3902.70 (From Example 1)
= **\$649.35**

W-148

Reteaching/ Alternate Teaching Strategy

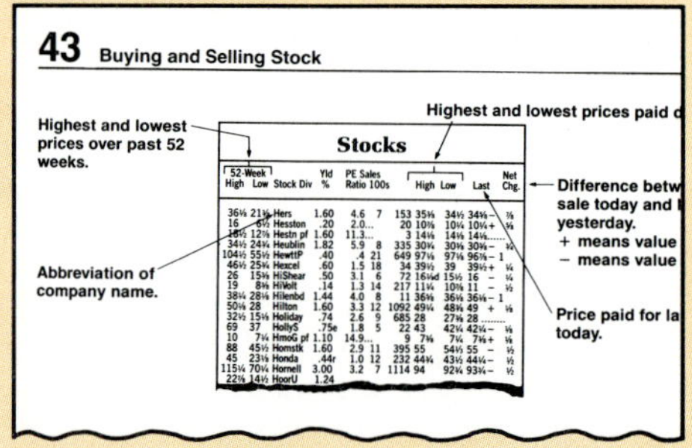

44 Buying and Selling Stock

Cost of Stock = Number of Shares × Cost Per Share
Total Cost = Cost of Stock + Commission

Complete the table.

STOCK	COST PER SHARE	NUMBER OF SHARES	COMMISSION	COST OF STOCK
1. DeltaAir	$\$36\frac{1}{8}$	200	\$95.50	
2. Disney	$\$108\frac{1}{2}$	75	\$125.50	

Enrichment

Materials: Two newspaper stock listings from the library, with dates about one month apart

Post the early stock listing on the bulletin board. Then assign each student a \$2,000 account with which to buy shares of any ONE selected stock. Next, post the later listing by which students "sell" their stock at the new value and calculate the individual gains or losses.

Students may wish to form investing teams and compete for best performance status.

DIVIDENDS/ANNUAL YIELD Pages 324–325

Practice

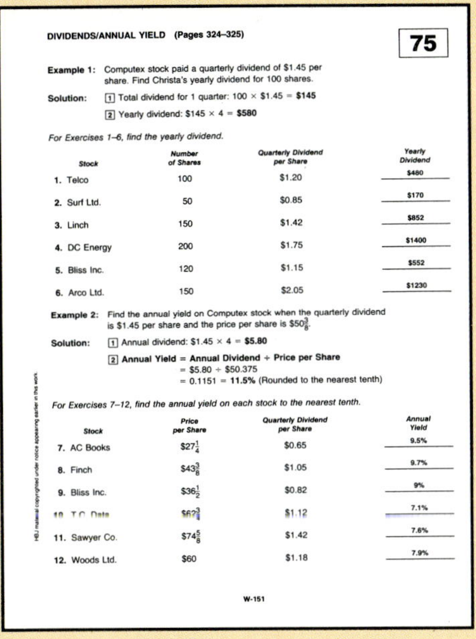

DIVIDENDS/ANNUAL YIELD (Pages 324–325)

75

Example 1: Computex stock paid a quarterly dividend of $1.45 per share. Find Christa's yearly dividend for 100 shares.

Solution: [1] Total dividend for 1 quarter: 100 × $1.45 = **$145**

[2] Yearly dividend: $145 × 4 = **$580**

For Exercises 1–6, find the yearly dividend.

Stock	Number of Shares	Quarterly Dividend per Share	Yearly Dividend
1. Telco	100	$1.20	$480
2. Surf Ltd.	50	$0.85	$170
3. Linch	150	$1.42	$852
4. DC Energy	200	$1.75	$1400
5. Bliss Inc.	120	$1.15	$552
6. Arco Ltd.	150	$2.05	$1230

Example 2: Find the annual yield on Computex stock when the quarterly dividend is $1.45 per share and the price per share is 50\frac{3}{8}$.

Solution: [1] Annual dividend: $1.45 × 4 = **$5.80**

[2] **Annual Yield = Annual Dividend ÷ Price per Share**
= $5.80 ÷ $50.375
= 0.1151 = **11.5%** (Rounded to the nearest tenth)

For Exercises 7–12, find the annual yield on each stock to the nearest tenth.

Stock	Price per Share	Quarterly Dividend per Share	Annual Yield
7. AC Books	27\frac{1}{4}$	$0.65	9.5%
8. Finch	43\frac{3}{8}$	$1.05	9.7%
9. Bliss Inc.	36\frac{1}{2}$	$0.82	9%
10. T.C. Data	62\frac{3}{4}$	$1.12	7.1%
11. Sawyer Co.	74\frac{5}{8}$	$1.42	7.6%
12. Woods Ltd.	$60	$1.18	7.9%

W-151

Reteaching/ Alternate Teaching Strategy

Distribute one copy of the following table of stock listings to each student. Then have students use the entries in the first four columns to find required values and insert the entries in the last three columns as shown below.

Stock	Number of Shares	Price per Share	Quarterly Dividend per Share
Epcon	70	18$\frac{1}{4}$	$0.38
TechInc	160	33$\frac{1}{2}$	$0.82
XZZ	100	42$\frac{3}{8}$	$1.09
NeCo	140	65$\frac{1}{4}$	$1.26

(Continuation of table)

Yearly Dividend per Share	Total Yearly Dividend	Annual Yield
? **$1.52**	? **$106.40**	? **8.3%**
? **$3.28**	? **$524.80**	? **9.8%**
? **$4.36**	? **$436.00**	? **10.3%**
? **$5.04**	? **$705.60**	? **7.7%**

Enrichment

Challenge students to find the best annual yield with these exercises.

1. Find the annual yield of each stock.
2. "Purchase" 100 shares of each stock. Find the total cost of all the shares. **(ANS: $22,437.50)**
3. Find the total yearly dividend of the 3 best shares. **(ANS: $3.30)**
4. Find the total yearly dividend of the 3 worst shares. **(ANS: $4.87)**
5. Find the average annual yield for the 3 best stocks and for the 3 worst stocks. **(ANS: 7.1%; 2.9%)**

Stock	Price	Yearly Div.	**ANS:** Annual Yield
ABC	27$\frac{1}{4}$	$1.83	**6.7%**
RTR	39$\frac{1}{2}$	$1.37	**3.5%**
PNC	11$\frac{3}{4}$	$0.81	**6.9%**
OLn	8$\frac{3}{8}$	$0.66	**7.7%**
VoE	63$\frac{1}{4}$	$1.97	**3.1%**
LOS	74	$1.53	**2.1%**

BONDS Pages 326–328

Practice

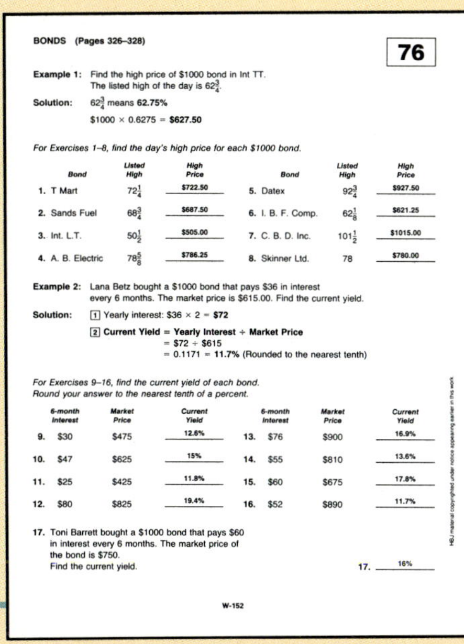

BONDS (Pages 326–328)

76

Example 1: Find the high price of $1000 bond in Int TT. The listed high of the day is 62$\frac{3}{4}$.

Solution: 62$\frac{3}{4}$ means **62.75%**

$1000 × 0.6275 = **$627.50**

For Exercises 1–8, find the day's high price for each $1000 bond.

Bond	Listed High	High Price	Bond	Listed High	High Price
1. T Mart	72$\frac{1}{4}$	$722.50	5. Datex	92$\frac{3}{4}$	$927.50
2. Sands Fuel	68$\frac{3}{4}$	$687.50	6. I. B. F. Comp.	62$\frac{1}{8}$	$621.25
3. Int. L.T.	50$\frac{1}{2}$	$505.00	7. C. B. D. Inc.	101$\frac{1}{2}$	$1015.00
4. A. B. Electric	78$\frac{5}{8}$	$786.25	8. Skinner Ltd.	78	$780.00

Example 2: Lana Betz bought a $1000 bond that pays $36 in interest every 6 months. The market price is $615.00. Find the current yield.

Solution: [1] Yearly interest: $36 × 2 = **$72**

[2] **Current Yield = Yearly Interest ÷ Market Price**
= $72 ÷ $615
= 0.1171 = **11.7%** (Rounded to the nearest tenth)

For Exercises 9–16, find the current yield of each bond. Round your answer to the nearest tenth of a percent.

	6-month Interest	Market Price	Current Yield		6-month Interest	Market Price	Current Yield
9.	$30	$475	12.6%	13.	$76	$900	16.9%
10.	$47	$625	15%	14.	$55	$810	13.6%
11.	$25	$425	11.8%	15.	$60	$675	17.8%
12.	$80	$825	19.4%	16.	$52	$890	11.7%

17. Toni Barrett bought a $1000 bond that pays $60 in interest every 6 months. The market price of the bond is $750. Find the current yield. 17. 16%

W-152

Reteaching/ Alternate Teaching Strategy

Distribute one copy of the following table of bond listings to each student. Then have students use the values in the first four columns to find the required values and insert the entries in the last three columns as shown below.

Bond	Last Listed	Face Value	6-Month Interest
GXTO	88$\frac{1}{2}$	$1000	$53
AirCo	92$\frac{1}{4}$	$1000	$64
IcInc	76	$5000	$187
SanP	108	$5000	$213

(Continuation of table)

Market Price	Yearly Interest	Current Yield
? **$885**	? **$106**	? **12.0%**
? **$928**	? **$128**	? **13.8%**
? **$3800**	? **$374**	? **9.8%**
? **$5400**	? **$426**	? **7.9%**

Enrichment

Have students make a verbal or a written report on one or more of the topics listed below. Sources of information may be the libraries, local newspapers, or experts in banks and brokerage firms.

- Government Savings Bonds
- Municipal tax free Bonds
- Industrial Bonds
- The bond rating, how it is determined and what it means.
- Zero Coupon Bonds

You may wish to have students work in small groups when they elect to make a verbal report.

PREPARING A BUDGET Pages 342–343

Practice

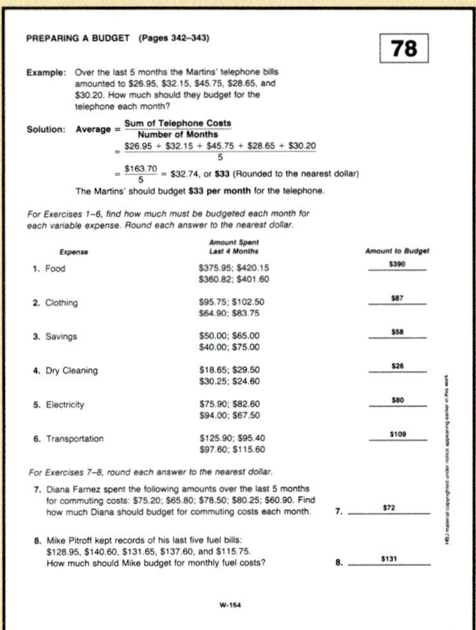

PREPARING A BUDGET (Pages 342–343)

78

Example: Over the last 5 months the Martins' telephone bills amounted to \$26.95, \$32.15, \$45.75, \$28.65, and \$30.20. How much should they budget for the telephone each month?

Solution: $\text{Average} = \frac{\text{Sum of Telephone Costs}}{\text{Number of Months}}$

$= \frac{\$26.95 + \$32.15 + \$45.75 + \$28.65 + \$30.20}{5}$

$= \frac{\$163.70}{5} = \$32.74$, or **\$33** (Rounded to the nearest dollar)

The Martins' should budget **\$33 per month** for the telephone.

For Exercises 1–6, find how much must be budgeted each month for each variable expense. Round each answer to the nearest dollar.

Expense	Amount Spent Last 4 Months	Amount to Budget
1. Food	\$375.95; \$420.15 \$360.82; \$401.60	\$390
2. Clothing	\$95.75; \$102.50 \$64.90; \$83.75	\$87
3. Savings	\$50.00; \$65.00 \$40.00; \$75.00	\$58
4. Dry Cleaning	\$18.65; \$29.50 \$30.25; \$24.60	\$26
5. Electricity	\$75.90; \$82.60 \$94.00; \$67.50	\$80
6. Transportation	\$125.90; \$95.40 \$97.60; \$115.60	\$109

For Exercises 7–8, round each answer to the nearest dollar.

7. Diana Farnez spent the following amounts over the last 5 months for commuting costs: \$75.20; \$65.80; \$78.50; \$80.25; \$60.90. Find how much Diana should budget for commuting costs each month. 7. \$72

8. Mike Pitroff kept records of his last five fuel bills: \$128.95, \$140.60, \$131.65, \$137.60, and \$115.75. How much should Mike budget for monthly fuel costs? 8. \$131

W-154

Reteaching/ Alternate Teaching Strategy

Have students use the table below to find the amount a family should budget for each payment with monthly income of \$1840. Round each payment to the nearest dollar. Then have students find the percent of the total budget that is allowed for each listed item. Round to the nearest tenth of a percent.

Family Budget: \$1840 monthly income

Payment	JAN/ MAR	APR/ JUN	Avg./ Month	% of Income
Mortgage	\$1617	\$1617	_____	_____
Food	\$826	\$913	_____	_____
Utilities	\$462	\$458	_____	_____
Auto	\$873	\$873	_____	_____
Insurance	\$438	\$438	_____	_____
Clothing	\$185	\$268	_____	_____
Recreation	\$243	\$156	_____	_____
Savings	\$435	\$430	_____	_____
Other	\$411	\$367	_____	_____

(**ANS:** Mortgage: **\$539, 29.3%;** Food: **\$290, 15.8%;** Utilities: **\$168, 9.1%;** Auto: **\$291, 15.8%;** Insurance: **\$146, 7.9%;** Clothing: **\$76, 4.1%;** Recreation: **\$67, 3.6%;** Savings: **\$144, 7.8%** Other: **\$130, 7.1%**)

Enrichment

Have students fill in the time budget form below as accurately as they can estimate the amount of time spent for each entry.

Then explain that the first step in the preparation of a budget is to learn what we have done in the past. Next have them record the time they spend on the same items for 24 hours and compare those records with the estimated times entered earlier.

Item	Time
Sleeping	
Eating	
Watching Movies/TV	
Working	
Recreation	
Grooming	
Traveling	
Doing Chores	

AVERAGE SPENDING Pages 344–346

Practice

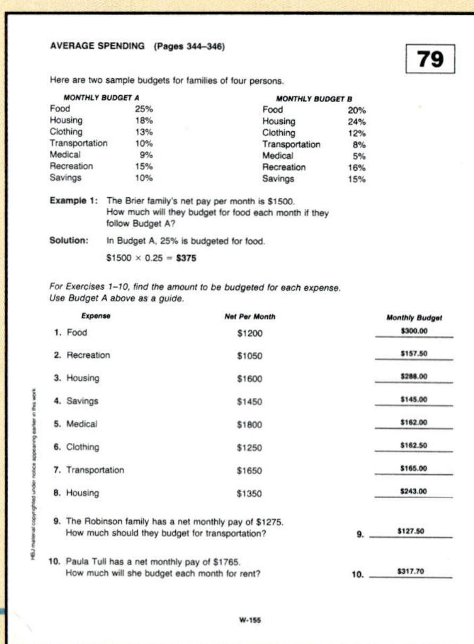

AVERAGE SPENDING (Pages 344–346)

79

Here are two sample budgets for families of four persons.

MONTHLY BUDGET A		MONTHLY BUDGET B	
Food	25%	Food	20%
Housing	18%	Housing	24%
Clothing	13%	Clothing	12%
Transportation	10%	Transportation	8%
Medical	9%	Medical	5%
Recreation	15%	Recreation	16%
Savings	10%	Savings	15%

Example 1: The Brier family's net pay per month is \$1500. How much will they budget for food each month if they follow Budget A?

Solution: In Budget A, 25% is budgeted for food.

$\$1500 \times 0.25 = \mathbf{\$375}$

For Exercises 1–10, find the amount to be budgeted for each expense. Use Budget A above as a guide.

Expense	Net Per Month	Monthly Budget
1. Food	\$1200	\$300.00
2. Recreation	\$1050	\$157.50
3. Housing	\$1600	\$288.00
4. Savings	\$1450	\$145.00
5. Medical	\$1800	\$162.00
6. Clothing	\$1250	\$162.50
7. Transportation	\$1650	\$165.00
8. Housing	\$1350	\$243.00

9. The Robinson family has a net monthly pay of \$1275. How much should they budget for transportation? 9. \$127.50

10. Paula Tull has a net monthly pay of \$1765. How much will she budget each month for rent? 10. \$317.70

W-155

Reteaching/ Alternate Teaching Strategy

Visuals 45 and 46 deal with two sample standard budgets.

Enrichment

Remind students that a budget is a plan for better management of our money.

Then ask them how we should prepare for such unplanned expenses as a major car repair or need to replace a refrigerator that fails.

You may wish to have students make a list of suggestions for a solution and evaluate each suggestion by group discussion.

HEALTH INSURANCE Pages 348–350

Practice

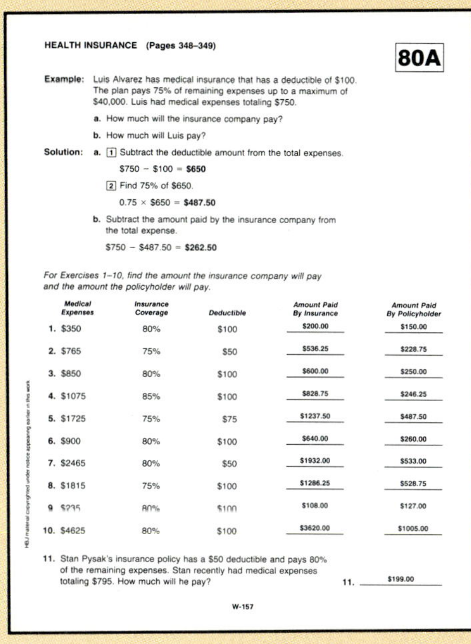

HEALTH INSURANCE (Pages 348–349)

80A

Example: Luis Alvarez has medical insurance that has a deductible of $100. The plan pays 75% of remaining expenses up to a maximum of $40,000. Luis had medical expenses totaling $750.

a. How much will the insurance company pay?

b. How much will Luis pay?

Solution: a. [1] Subtract the deductible amount from the total expenses.

$750 − $100 = **$650**

[2] Find 75% of $650.

0.75 × $650 = **$487.50**

b. Subtract the amount paid by the insurance company from the total expense.

$750 − $487.50 = **$262.50**

For Exercises 1–10, find the amount the insurance company will pay and the amount the policyholder will pay.

	Medical Expenses	Insurance Coverage	Deductible	Amount Paid By Insurance	Amount Paid By Policyholder
1.	$350	80%	$100	$200.00	$150.00
2.	$765	75%	$50	$536.25	$228.75
3.	$850	80%	$100	$600.00	$250.00
4.	$1075	85%	$100	$828.75	$246.25
5.	$1725	75%	$75	$1237.50	$487.50
6.	$900	80%	$100	$640.00	$260.00
7.	$2465	80%	$50	$1932.00	$533.00
8.	$1815	75%	$100	$1286.25	$528.75
9.	$235	80%	$100	$108.00	$127.00
10.	$4625	80%	$100	$3620.00	$1005.00

11. Stan Pysak's insurance policy has a $50 deductible and pays 80% of the remaining expenses. Stan recently had medical expenses totaling $795. How much will he pay? 11. $199.00

W-157

Reteaching/ Alternate Teaching Strategy

A reteaching lesson can be structured for this topic by having students supply the concrete materials. These concrete materials then would be the basis for the lesson.

Have students bring to class advertisements for primary health care plans and supplemental health insurance.

These advertisements then become a source bank of real world problems that you can use for presenting the lesson.

Enrichment

HEALTH INSURANCE (Pages 348–349)

80B

A sample medical statement is shown below.

EXPLANATION OF MEDICAL BENEFITS

SERVICES WERE PROVIDED BY	WHEN FROM MO. DAY	WHEN TO MO. DAY YR.	CHARGES SUBMITTED	CHARGES ALLOWED
DPB PVT CLINIC		09 14	17.00	13.50
DPB PVT CLINIC		09 14	26.50	18.30
DPB PVT CLINIC		09 14	15.00	9.10
DPB PVT CLINIC		09 21	10.00	9.10
DPB PVT CLINIC		10 02	17.50	15.40
DPB PVT CLINIC		10 03	63.00	63.00
DPB PVT CLINIC		10 03	175.00	175.00
		TOTALS	324.00	303.40

Total Allowed Charges subject to the $50 Deductible & 20% Coinsurance	303.40	
This Went Toward the $50 Deductible	.00	
Allowed Charges Over the Deductible insurance pays 80%.	303.40	
TOTAL MEDICAL PAYMENT		

1. The insurance company will pay 80% of the ALLOWED CHARGES OVER THE DEDUCTIBLE. How much will the insurance company pay? 1. $242.72

2. The total of the CHARGES SUBMITTED is $324.00. How much will the patient pay? 2. $81.28

The additional charges for the hospital room and related charges amounted to $1348.70. The insurance company will pay 80% of this amount. Use this information in Exercises 4 and 5.

3. How much will the insurance company pay? 3. $1078.96

4. How much will the patient pay? 4. $269.74

5. How much of the total cost of this operation (see Exercises 2 and 4) was paid by the patient? 5. $351.02

6. How much of the total cost (see Exercises 1 and 3) was paid by the insurance company? 6. $1321.68

W-158

ADJUSTING A BUDGET Pages 352–353

Practice

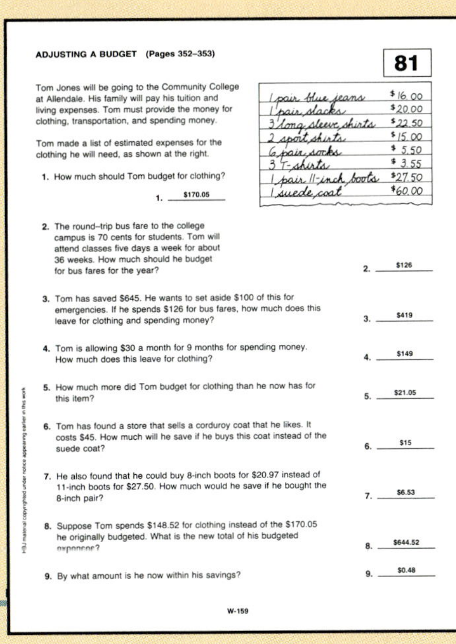

ADJUSTING A BUDGET (Pages 352–353)

81

Tom Jones will be going to the Community College at Allendale. His family will pay his tuition and living expenses. Tom must provide the money for clothing, transportation, and spending money.

Tom made a list of estimated expenses for the clothing he will need, as shown at the right.

1 pair blue jeans	$16.00
1 pair slacks	$20.00
3 long sleeve shirts	$22.50
2 sport shirts	$15.00
6 pair socks	$5.50
3 T-shirts	$3.55
1 pair 11-inch boots	$27.50
1 suede coat	$60.00

1. How much should Tom budget for clothing? 1. $170.05

2. The round–trip bus fare to the college campus is 70 cents for students. Tom will attend classes five days a week for about 36 weeks. How much should he budget for bus fares for the year? 2. $126

3. Tom has saved $645. He wants to set aside $100 of this for emergencies. If he spends $126 for bus fares, how much does this leave for clothing and spending money? 3. $419

4. Tom is allowing $30 a month for 9 months for spending money. How much does this leave for clothing? 4. $149

5. How much more did Tom budget for clothing than he now has for this item? 5. $21.05

6. Tom has found a store that sells a corduroy coat that he likes. It costs $45. How much will he save if he buys this coat instead of the suede coat? 6. $15

7. He also found that he could buy 8-inch boots for $20.97 instead of 11-inch boots for $27.50. How much would he save if he bought the 8-inch pair? 7. $6.53

8. Suppose Tom spends $148.52 for clothing instead of the $170.05 he originally budgeted. What is the new total of his budgeted expenses? 8. $644.52

9. By what amount is he now within his savings? 9. $0.48

W-159

Reteaching/ Alternate Teaching Strategy

Use the present monthly budget in the table on page 352 to solve the following.

Explain to students that we must reduce the total monthly expenses by 10% of the present budget. Then have students reduce three items in the budget to accomplish this reduction. Also have students state how much each item is reduced and the percent it is reduced.

Enrichment

Distribute to each student a copy of the following budget for a family with annual income of $22,000.

Mortgage	$575.00
Food	345.00
Utilities	142.00
Car Payment	212.00
Insurance	112.00
Clothing	80.00
Recreation	67.00
Miscellaneous	145.00
Savings	122.00

Then have students work in small groups to revise the budget when the annual income is **(a)** reduced to $18,600; **(b)** increased to $26,000.
Answers will vary.

PACING CHART

Overview

The following pacing chart shows one possible way to provide for individual differences in assigning the year's work. The number of days indicated for each chapter includes days for reviewing and testing.

Each chapter contains lessons that are optional. The lessons are clearly identified as such in the *Teacher's Manual.* The use of these lessons, the *Appendices,* and the supplementary publications that are included in the *Teacher's ResourceBank*™ (see page M-5) may affect the number of days spent on each chapter. Thus, the pacing chart should be used as a guideline only.

PACING CHART

CHAPTER		PAGES	BASIC	AVERAGE	ENRICHED
1	The Consumer and Statistics	1-20	**12 days**	**11 days**	**11 days**
2	The Consumer and Probability	21-40	**10 days**	**10 days**	**10 days**
3	Making Money	41-68	**13 days**	**12 days**	**12 days**
4	Paying Taxes	69-94	**12 days**	**13 days**	**13 days**
5	Banking and Money	95-124	**14 days**	**14 days**	**14 days**
6	Buying a Car	125-150	**12 days**	**12 days**	**12 days**
7	Owning a Car	151-176	**12 days**	**12 days**	**12 days**
8	Other Ways to Travel	177-198	**10 days**	**10 days**	**10 days**
9	Buying Foods	199-228	**12 days**	**12 days**	**12 days**
10	Housing	229-256	**12 days**	**12 days**	**12 days**
11	Housing Costs	257-282	**13 days**	**13 days**	**13 days**
12	Buying Goods	283-310	**13 days**	**13 days**	**13 days**
13	Investing Money	311-340	**14 days**	**14 days**	**14 days**
14	Budgeting Money	341-364	**11 days**	**12 days**	**12 days**
	TOTAL		**170 days**	**170 days**	**170 days**

REFERENCES AND RESOURCES

The following pages list both general and chapter-by-chapter references and resources for *HBJ Consumer Mathematics.* General references and resources include books and articles on topics such as problem solving and group learning as well as on curriculum and teaching suggestions from educators and national educational organizations. Software listings include items related to curriculum areas which students find troublesome as well as to consumer-related topics.

The chapter-by-chapter listings contain both readings and software related to each chapter topic. Software listings are intended only as suggestions of products which teachers may wish to review and evaluate with respect to their usefulness and relevancy to specific classroom needs.

GENERAL REFERENCES AND RESOURCES

Consumer Information Center-E
P. O. Box 100
Pueblo, CO 81002

Consumer Information Catalog

Dale Seymour Publications
P. O. Box 10888
Palo Alto, CA 94303

How to Solve It
George Polya

Interaction Book Company
7208 Cornelin Drive
Edina, Minnesota 55435

Circles of Learning: Cooperation in the Classroom (Revised)
Johnson and Johnson

National Council of Teachers of Mathematics
1906 Association Drive
Reston, Virginia 22091

1985 NCTM Yearbook
1983 NCTM Yearbook
1980 NCTM Yearbook
1979 NCTM Yearbook

P.O. Box 2480
Boulder, CO 80322

Consumer Reports

Prentice Hall, Inc.
Englewood Cliffs, NJ 07632

Joining Together: Group Theory and Skills
Johnson and Johnson

Subscription Center/Customer Service
Editors Park, MD 20782

Changing Times

Software

Educational Activities, Inc.
P. O. Box 392
Freeport, NY 11520

Math for Everyday Living

Media Materials, Inc.
2936 Remington Avenue
Baltimore, MD 21211

Percents

Science Research Associates
155 North Washer Drive
Chicago, IL 60606

Math Strategies: Estimation
Math Strategies: Problem Solving

Sunburst Communications
Room D 7575, 39 Washington Avenue
Pleasantville, NY 10570-9971

Explorer Metros: A Metric Adventure
Survival Math Simulations
Four simulations providing practice in using math as an analytical tool for everyday life situations.

Chapter 1: The Consumer and Statistics

Dale Seymour Publications
P. O. Box 10888
Palo Alto, CA 94303

Developing Skills with Tables and Graphs
Exploring Data

National Council of Teachers of Mathematics
1906 Association Drive
Reston, VA 22091

1983 NCTM Yearbook
1982 NCTM Yearbook
1981 NCTM Yearbook

Woodrow Wilson National Fellowship Foundation
Princeton, NJ 08542

Focus on Statistics

Software

Sunburst Communications
Room D 7575, 39 Washington Avenue
Pleasantville, NY 10370-9971

Interpreting Graphs

Chapter 2: The Consumer and Probability

Creative Publications
5005 West 110th Street
Oak Lawn, IL 60453

What are My Chances Book B

National Council of Teachers of Mathematics
1906 Association Drive
Reston, VA 22091

1983 NCTM Yearbook
1982 NCTM Yearbook
1981 NCTM Yearbook

Chapter 3: Making Money

Consumer Information Center-D
P. O. Box 100
Pueblo, CO 81002

Merchandising Your Job Talents
Resumes, Application Forms, Cover Letters, and Interviews

CUNA International, Inc.
P. O. Box 431
Madison, WI 53701

Managing Your Money

Superintendent of Documents
U.S. Government Printing Office
Washington, D.C. 10016

Social Security Handbook

U.S. Department of Health & Human Services
Social Security Administration
(nearest regional office)

Social Security for Young Families
Your Social Security

Chapter 3: Making Money (continued)

Software

Sunburst Communications
Room D 7575, 39 Washington Avenue
Pleasantville, NY 10570-9971

The Whatsit Corporation
Business calculations, wages, banking, taxes

Chapter 4: Paying Taxes

Public Affairs Pamphlets
381 Park Avenue South
New York, NY 10016

The Taxes We Pay

U.S. Treasury Department
Internal Revenue Service
(nearest IRS Office)

Explanation of the Tax Reform Act of 1986 for Individuals

SOFTWARE

Sunburst Communications
Room D 7575, 39 Washington Avenue
Pleasantville, NY 10570-9971

The Whatsit Corporation
Business calculations, wages, banking, taxes

Chapter 5: Banking and Money

American Banker's Association
Banking Education Committee
1120 Connecticut Avenue, N.W.
Washington, D.C. 20036

Using Bank Services

Federal Reserve Bank of New York
Publications Section
33 Liberty Street
New York, NY 10045

The Story of Money
The Story of Banks
The Story of Checks and Electronic Payments
The Story of Inflation
The Story of Consumer Credit

Federal Reserve Bank of Minneapolis
Office of Public Information
250 Marquette Avenue
Minneapolis, MN 55480

Money, Banking and the Federal Reserve Building
You're the Banker Simulation Game

Household Finance Corporation
Money Management Institute
2700 Sanders Road
Prospect Heights, IL 60070

Your Savings and Investment Dollar

Chapter 5: Paying Taxes (continued)

SOFTWARE

Sunburst Communications
Room D 7575, 39 Washington Avenue
Pleasantville, NY 10570-9971

The Whatsit Corporation
Business calculations, wages, banking, taxes

The Learning Seed
330 Telser Road
Lake Zurich, IL 60047

How to Handle a Checking Account

Chapter 6: Buying a Car

Consumer Information Center-D
P. O. Box 100
Pueblo, CO 81002

Buying a Used Car

Cost of Owning and Operating Autos and Vans

Ford Motor Company
Dearborn, MI 48121

Car Buying Made Easier

Household Finance Corporation
Money Management Institute
2700 Sanders Road
Prospect Heights, IL 60070

Your Automobile Dollar

Liberty Mutual
P. O. Box 777CT
Boston, MA 02116

30 Questions You May Ask About Your Personal Automobile Insurance

The Traveler's Office of Consumer Info.
One Tower Square
Hartford, CT 06115

No-fault Insurance

Plain Talk About Auto Insurance

Chapter 7: Owning a Car

Consumer Information Center-D
P. O. Box 100
Pueblo, CO 81002

A Consumer's Guide to Vehicle Leasing

Cost of Owning and Operating Autos and Vans

Technical Information Center
Department of Energy
P. O. Box 62
Oak Ridge, TN 37830

Gas Mileage Guide

How to Save Gasoline and Money

Chapter 8: Other Ways to Travel

Consumer Information Center-D
P. O. Box 100
Pueblo, CO 91002

Fly Rights

Guide and Map to the National Parks

Household Finance Corporation
Money Management Institute
2700 Sanders Road
Prospect Heights, IL 60070

Your Recreation Dollar

Money Management Institute
Household Financial Services
2700 Sanders Road
Prospect Heights, IL 60080

Your Travel Dollar

MPO 442
Jersey City, NJ 07302

AETC Travel Planner

Passenger Service and Communication Group
National Railroad Passenger Corporation
400 N. Capitol Street, N.W.
Washington, DC 20001

(For passenger service information on AMTRAK)

Chapter 9: Food

Appliance Information Service
Whirlpool Corporation
Benton Harbor, MI 49022

Adventures in Basic Cooking

Consumer Information Center-E
P. O. Box 100
Pueblo, CO 81002

Consumers' Guide to Food Labels

Food Additives

Making Food Dollars Count

Meat and Poultry Labels Wrap it Up

Nutritive Value of Foods

Same Facts and Myths about Vitamins

Your Money's Worth in Foods

U.S.D.A.F. S/S RM 1165-S
Washington, D.C. 20250

The Safe Food Book: Your Kitchen Guide

SOFTWARE

The Learning Seed
330 Telser Road
Lake Zurich, IL 60047

The Grocery Games

Understanding Food Labels

Chapter 10: Housing

Consumer Information Center-E
P. O. Box 100
Pueblo, CO 81002

Consumer Handbook on Adjustable Rate Mortgages

The Mortgage Money Guide Settlement Costs

Public Information Department
Federal Reserve Bank of New York
33 Liberty Street
New York, NY 10045

The Arithmetic of Interest Rates

Real Estate Center
Publications Room
Texas A and M University
College Station, TX 77843-2115

Analyzing Your Housing Costs

Determining How Much Your Family Can Spend for a House

Home Buyers Checklist

Home Buyers Guide

Rental Property

Superintendent of Documents
U.S. Government Printing Office
Washington, D.C. 20402

Selecting and Financing a Home

Home and Garden Bulletin Number 182

Chapter 11: Housing Costs

Consumer Information Center
Household Finance Corporation
Pueblo, CO 81002

Carpets and Rugs

Enterprise for Education

Teaching About Energy, Part 1

Money Management Institute
2700 Sanders Road
Prospect Heights, IL 60070

Your Equipment Dollar

Your Home Furnishings Dollar

Your Housing Dollar

Chapter 12: Buying Goods

Bank Holders of America
333 Pennsylvania Avenue
Washington, D.C. 20003

How to Choose a Credit Card

Consumer Information Catalog
Center E, P. O. Box 100
Pueblo, CO 81002

Buying and Borrowing: Cash in on the Facts

Choosing a Credit Card

Consumer Credit Handbook

Fair Credit Reporting Act

Chapter 13: Investing Money

Consumer Information Catalog
Center E, P. O. Box 100
Pueblo, CO 81002

A Consumer's Guide to Life Insurance
Financial Tools Used in Money Management
Investors' Bill of Rights
What Every Investor Should Know
What is a Mutual Fund?

Chapter 14: Budgeting Money

Consumer Information Catalog
Consumer Information Center-E
P. O. Box 100
Pueblo, CO 81002

Managing Your Personal Finances
The Principles for Managing Your Finances (Part 1)

Genesis Press
P. O. Box 678, CT
Tusken, GA 30085

Is Your Spending Spontaneous or Compulsive?

Health Insurance Institute
1850 K Street, N.W.
Washington, D.C. 20006

New Group Health Insurance

TEACHER'S NOTES

TEACHER'S NOTES

TEACHER'S NOTES

HBJ

Consumer Mathematics

Sheldon Erickson
Russell F. Jacobs
Penny Coyne McAdoo

HBJ
Harcourt Brace Jovanovich, Publishers
Orlando San Diego Chicago Dallas

About the Authors

Sheldon Erickson
Mathematics Teacher
Edison Computech High School
Fresno, California

Russell F. Jacobs
Formerly Mathematics Supervisor for
the Phoenix Union High School District
Phoenix, Arizona

Penny Coyne McAdoo
Mathematics Consultant
Education Service Center, Region 10
Richardson, Texas

Editorial Advisors

Elizabeth Cozby Chandler
Mathematics Consultant
Richardson Independent School District
Richardson, Texas

Hilde Howden
District Mathematics Coordinator
Albuquerque Public Schools
Albuquerque, New Mexico

Mary E. Shepherd Lester
Director of Mathematics
Dallas Independent School District
Dallas, Texas

Terry E. Parks, Ph.D.
K-12 Director of Mathematics and
Computer Education
Shawnee Mission Public Schools
Shawnee Mission, Kansas

Dian Perkins
Mathematics Department Chairperson
Franklin Simpson High School
Franklin, Kentucky

Printed in the United States of America

ISBN 0-15-353020-0

CONTENTS

CHAPTER 5 BANKING AND MONEY 95

UNIT III TRANSPORTATION COSTS

CHAPTER 6 BUYING A CAR 125

CHAPTER 7 OWNING A CAR 151

CHAPTER 8 OTHER WAYS TO TRAVEL 177

UNIT IV LIVING COSTS

CHAPTER 13 INVESTING MONEY 311

CHAPTER 14 BUDGETING MONEY 341

The Consumer and Statistics

In everyday life situations, consumers make decisions based on the data they hear and see on television, listen to on the radio, and read in newspapers and magazines. Understanding how the data is organized helps consumers to interpret the data.

- How are bar graphs, line graphs, and circle graphs used to organize data?
- How can the mean, median, and mode be used to interpret data?
- How can the mean, median, and mode be used in consumer decision-making?

Chapter 1: The Consumer and Statistics

Overview

The focus of this chapter is on the role of statistics in real-life consumer situations. You may wish to have students look through newspapers and magazines and bring to class examples of bar graphs, line graphs, and circle graphs that display consumer-related information.

Although all lessons in this chapter involve problem-solving, the strategy lesson on pages 14–15 presents a **situational lesson** in which students are asked to interpret information and make consumer-related decisions regarding the appropriate use of the mean, median, and mode.

Finally, the *Enrichment* lesson on page 16 shows students how to make a histogram to represent data.

Using This Page

Have students read the introductory paragraph and questions. Have them list possible solutions to the problems presented. After completing the chapter, have students review their suggested solutions, comparing them with those presented in the lessons. You may wish to have students suggest other possible problems resulting from the situation described on this page and to discuss possible solutions.

You may wish to organize the class into small groups to complete the situational activity described in this *Using the Page*.

Lesson Resources

Maintenance: See below.
Reteaching/Alternate Teaching Strategy: p. M-16 (Visual 1B)
Practice: p. M-16
Enrichment: p. M-16
Visual 1B

Objectives

Student will

1. read a bar graph and use the information to solve problems.
2. use information in a table to complete a bar graph.

Maintenance

Perform the indicated operations.

1. 184 + 217 ANS: 401
2. 323 − 247 ANS: 76
3. 23.45 + 321.5 ANS: 344.95
4. 5.35 − 4.48 ANS: 0.87
5. You buy a candy bar for $0.50, a magazine for $1.25 and are charged $0.11 tax. How much change should you get from $2.00? ANS: $0.14

1 Lesson Focus

Motivation: Ask students to list who they think is willing to pay more for "full service" gas.

Purpose: This lesson shows students how to interpret information presented by bar graphs.

2 Teaching the Lesson

Have students read the first paragraph and discuss question 1. Then focus students' attention on the bar graph in the lesson. Ask these questions.

1. What group used self-service the least? (Less than $15,000)
2. What percent of this group used self-service? (70–75%)

Bar Graphs and the Consumer

You can save at least a dime per gallon of gasoline if you use the "self-service" pumps instead of the "full-service" pumps.

1. Who do you think is more likely to use self-service, a person who earns less than $15,000 a year or a person who earns more than $75,000 a year? **Answers will vary.**

This ***bar graph*** shows the results of a survey of 805 people. The people surveyed were asked:

"Do you use *self-service* or *full-service*?"

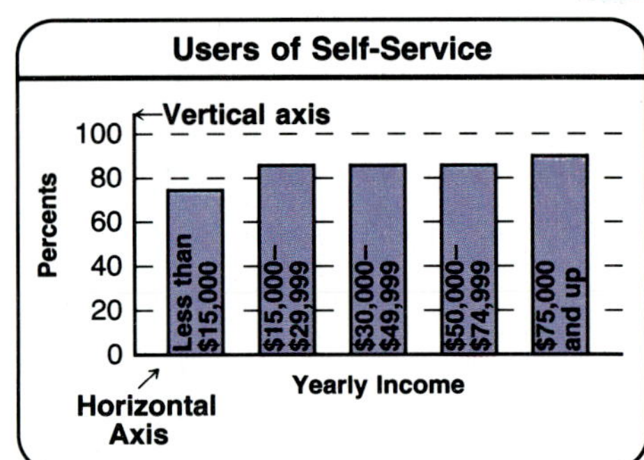

The **horizontal axis** shows the yearly income of the people surveyed. The **vertical axis** shows the percent of each income level group that uses self-service. You use the **scale** on the vertical axis to read what percent of each income group uses self-service.

2. Does your answer to Exercise 1 agree with the results of the survey? **Answers will vary.**
3. What conclusion can you draw from the graph regarding yearly income and the use of self-service? **The higher the income, the more likely the person is to use self-service.**

EXERCISES

For Exercises 1–5, refer to the graph at the right.

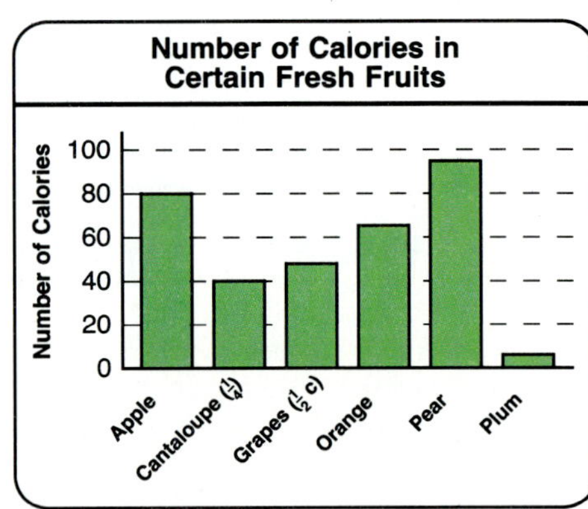

1. How many calories are there in a whole cantaloupe? **160 calories**
2. Which fruit has the most calories? **Cantaloupe**
3. About how many more calories are there in an apple than in $\frac{1}{2}$ cup of grapes? **About 30 more calories**
4. About how many plums would you have to eat to equal the number of calories in an apple? **About 16 plums**
5. You want your daily diet to have 120 calories in fruit. Use the graph to list two different ways to do this. **Answers will vary.**

This multiple-bar graph compares the prices of four items over a ten-year period.

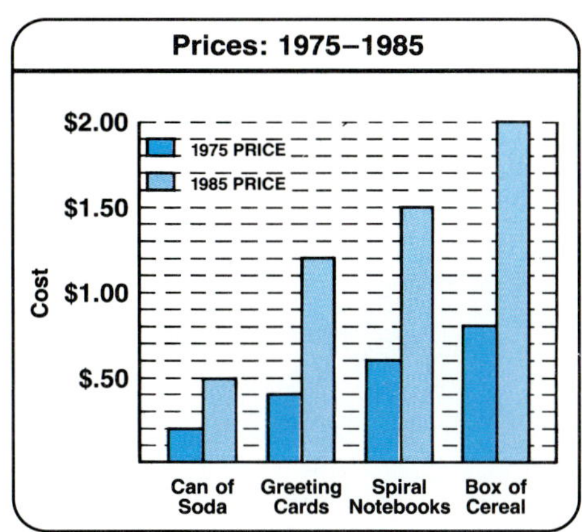

6. Which item increased the most in price from 1975 to 1985? **Box of cereal**

7. How much more did 5 spiral notebooks cost in 1985 than in 1975? **$4.50 more**

8. How much more change would you have received from a $5-bill if you bought 3 greeting cards in 1975 than if you bought them in 1985? **$2.40 more**

9. What was the percent of increase in the cost of a can of soda from 1975 to 1985? **150%**

10. What was the percent of increase in the cost of a box of cereal from 1975 to 1985? **150%**

For Exercises 11–12, use the tables to complete the bar graphs. The first bar is drawn for you.

11.

State	*Millions of Kilograms of Honey Produced*
California	10
Florida	11
Minnesota	5.75
Texas	4.5
Wisconsin	4

Honey Production

CA
FL
MN
TX
WI
0 2 4 6 8 10 12
Millions of Killograms

12.

Food	*Minutes of Running to Use Calories*
Large apple	5
Ham, 2 slices	9
Pork chop	16
Hamburger	18

Running To Use Calories

20
15
10
5
0
Minutes
Apple Ham Pork Chop Hamburger

3. What group used self-service the most? (More than $75,000)

4. What percent of this group used self-service? (85–90%)

Have students discuss questions 2 and 3 in the lesson. Encourage them to make inferences from the information provided by the graph.

3 Close

Summary: Ask a student to explain why a bar graph is a good way to show information.

Evaluation
Guided Practice: Ex. 2–10 even
Independent Practice: Ex. 1–9 odd, 11, 12

Extension

Have students take a simple survey of the class, voting on a favorite movie, television show, or musical group. Have them display the data in a bar graph.

Problem-Solving Skills

Reading a graph (Ex. 1–10)
Solving a multi-step problem (Ex. 8)
Reading a table (Ex. 11, 12)
Completing a graph (Ex. 11, 12)

Critical Thinking

You may wish to have students work in small groups to solve this problem or you may wish to work with the class.

Question 3 (in Lesson)

Lesson Resources

Maintenance: See below.
Reteaching/Alternate Teaching Strategy: p. M-16 (Visual 2)
Practice: p. M-16
Enrichment: p. M-16
Visual 2

Objectives

Student will

1. read a line graph and use the information to solve problems.
2. use information in a table to make a line graph.

Maintenance

Multiply.

1. 4 × 2415 ANS: 9660
2. 24 × 630.50 ANS: 15,132
3. 16 × 2.5 ANS: 40
4. 32 × $1\frac{1}{2}$ ANS: 48
5. Bill sold 18 stereos in his first month on the job. His goal for the next month is to sell two and one half times as many stereos. How many stereos will he need to sell to make his goal? ANS: 45

1 Lesson Focus

Motivation: Ask a student to tell the difference in the way a line graph looks as opposed to a bar graph.

Purpose: This lesson shows students how to interpret information presented by line graphs.

2 Teaching the Lesson

Focus students' attention on the graph on page 4. Discuss questions 1–4 in the lesson. Extend the questioning by asking these questions.

1. What is the general trend of CD sales? (Upward or greater)
2. What year did not follow this trend? (1983)

Line Graphs and the Consumer

The **double line graph** below shows CD (compact disc) and cassette sales of the Silverbeam Rock Group over a seven-year period.

A line graph shows changes and relationships over a period of time.

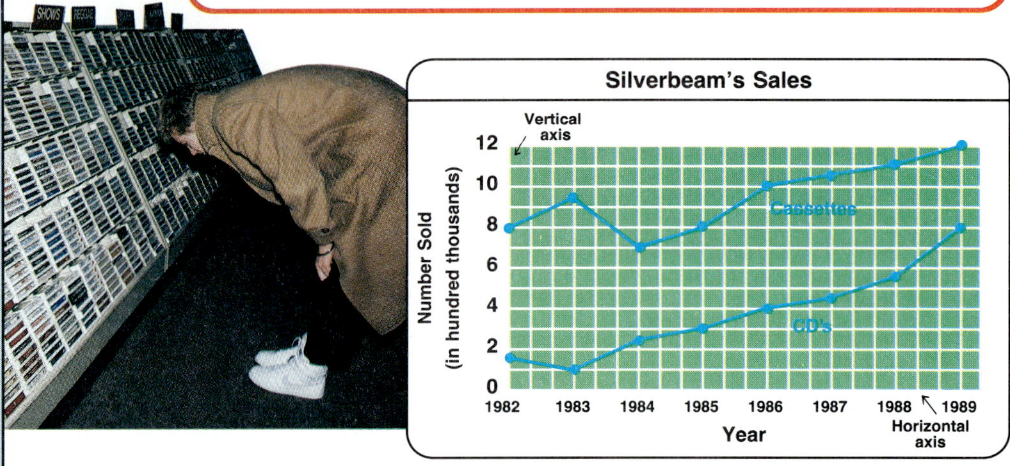

1. What information is given on the horizontal axis? Year
2. What information is given on the vertical axis? Number Sold (in hundred thousands)
3. Estimate the total of cassettes and CD's sold in 1982. 950,000
4. In what year were $2\frac{1}{2}$ times as many cassettes sold as CD's? 1986

EXERCISES

For Exercises 1–4, refer to the graph above.

1. In what year were five hundred thousand more cassettes sold than CD's? 1985
2. Between which two years did the sales of Silverbeam's CD's increase the most? 1988 and 1989
3. Use the graph to estimate the group's cassette sales in 1990. Give a reason for your answer. About 1,300,000 cassettes
4. If the trend for 1988–1989 continues, will sales of cassettes or of CD's increase the most from 1989 to 1990? sales of CD's

This line graph shows the total monthly sales for Company A (solid line) and Company B (dashed line).

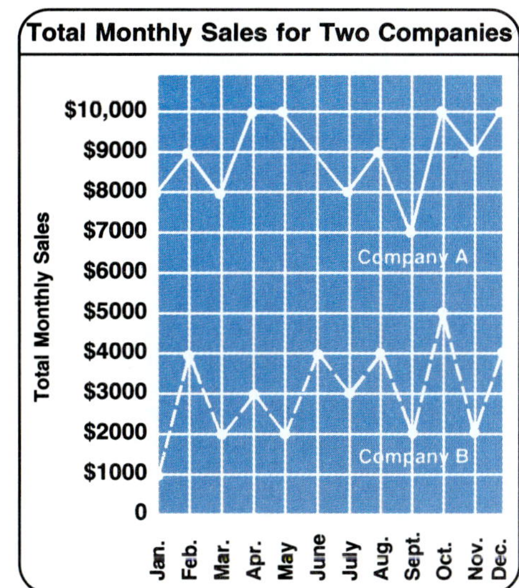

5. For which month were Company B's sales the highest? **October**

6. For what period did Company A's earnings remain unchanged? **April to May**

7. What were Company B's total earnings for the year? **$36,000**

8. How much higher were sales by Company A than by Company B for the first 6 months of the year? **$38,000 higher**

9. Between which two months did Company A have the greatest increase in earnings? **September and October**

10. What was the total combined income for both companies from September through December? **$49,000**

11. Use the table to complete the line graph below.

Televisions in the U.S.

Year	Number in Millions
1965	80
1970	85
1975	120
1980	180
1985	200

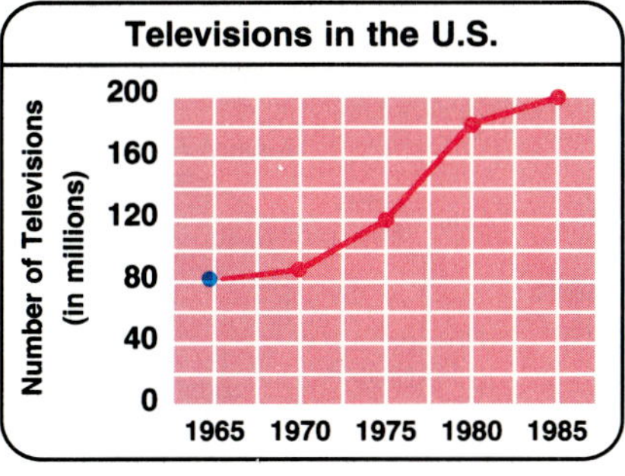

12. Use the table and the instructions below to draw a line graph.

Sales of Camping Equipment

Month	Amount
January	$2000
February	$2500
March	$4000
April	$8000
May	$12,000
June	$12,000

a. Draw and label a horizontal axis to show the months.
b. Draw and label a vertical axis.
c. Find the lines for January and $2000. Draw a dot at the point where they meet.
d. Locate the points for the other years and amounts. Connect the points with a line.
e. Write a title for the graph.

3. What might have caused this drop in sales? (Answers will vary.)

4. What would you expect to happen to CD sales in 1990? (Increase)

3 Close

Summary: Have students discuss the difference between bar graphs and line graphs and when they think one would be more appropriate than the other.

Evaluation
Guided Practice: Ex. 2–10 even
Independent Practice: Ex. 1–9 odd, 11, 12

Extension

Have a student volunteer do sit-ups for 2 minutes while other students record how many sit-ups are done in each 20-second time period. Have students make a line graph to show the information.

Problem-Solving Skills

Reading a graph (Ex. 1–10)
Solving a multi-step problem (Ex. 8)
Reading a table (Ex. 11, 12)
Completing a graph (Ex. 11)
Making a graph (Ex. 12)

Additional Answers

12.

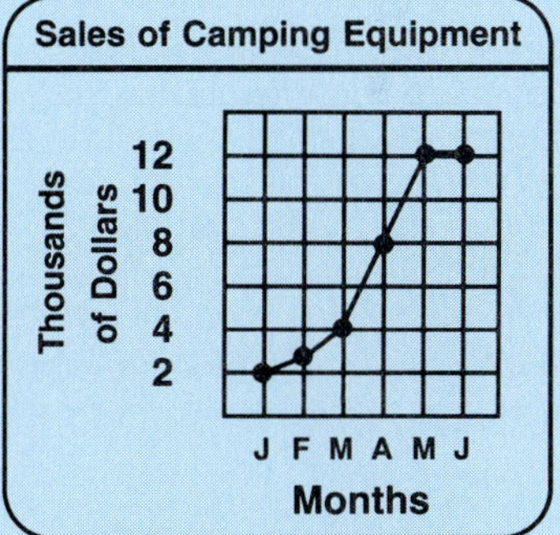

Estimation Ex. 3

Lesson Resources

Maintenance: See below.
Reteaching/Alternate Teaching Strategy: p. M-17 (Visual 3B)
Practice: p. M-17
Enrichment: p. M-17
Visual 3B

Objectives

Student will

1. read a circle graph and use the information to solve problems.
2. use information in a table to make a circle graph.

Maintenance

Write each percent as a decimal.

1. 27% ANS: 0.27
2. 9% ANS 0.09

Multiply.

3. 0.25×360 ANS: 90
4. $\frac{1}{3} \times 360$ ANS: 120
5. Jane saves 15% of her weekly salary of $250. How much will she save in a year? ANS: $1950

1 Lesson Focus

Motivation: Show students examples of circle graphs that you have taken from newspapers or magazines. Ask students to tell what they think are the differences between the circle graphs and bar graphs or line graphs.

Purpose: This lesson will show students that circle graphs are used to show the parts of a whole.

STRATEGY: USING "HIDDEN QUESTIONS" TO SOLVE A MULTI-STEP PROBLEM

Circle Graphs and the Consumer

You use a **circle graph** when you want to show the parts of a whole. Recall that there are **360°** in a circle.

The job of an advertising agency is to influence what consumers will buy. This table shows where one agency spent its money for advertising and the percent spent in each area.

Advertising Expenses

Type	Percent
Television/Radio	30
Direct Mail	27
Newspapers/Mag.	23
Other	20

EXAMPLE Make a circle graph of this data.

1 Write a decimal for each percent.

$30\% = 0.3$ $27\% = 0.27$ $23\% = 0.23$ $20\% = 0.2$

2 Multiply each decimal by 360°.

$0.3 \times 360 = 108°$
$0.27 \times 360 = 97.2$, or $97°$
$0.23 \times 360 = 82.8$, or $83°$
$0.2 \times 360 = 72°$

3 Use a protractor to draw the circle graph.

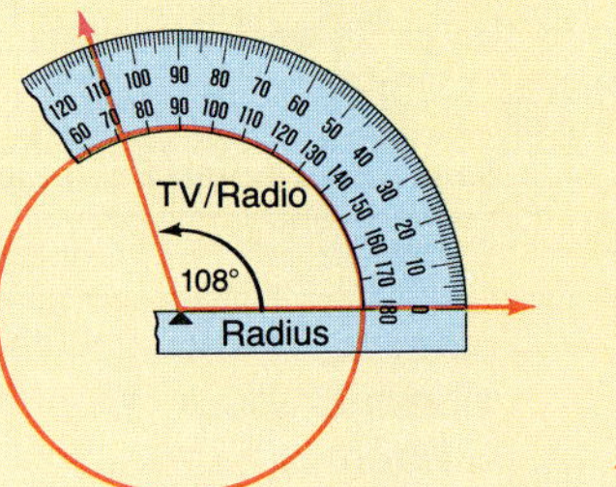

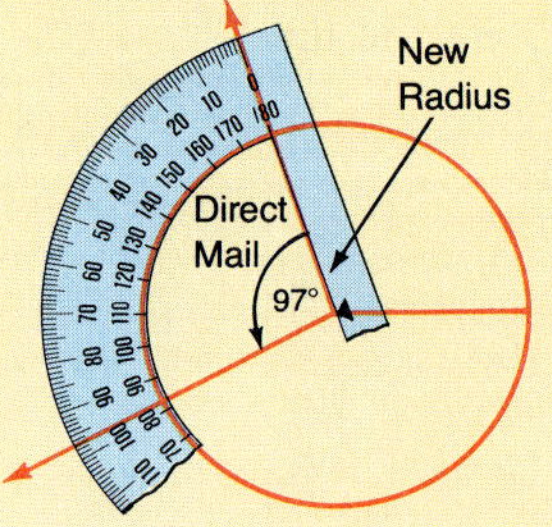

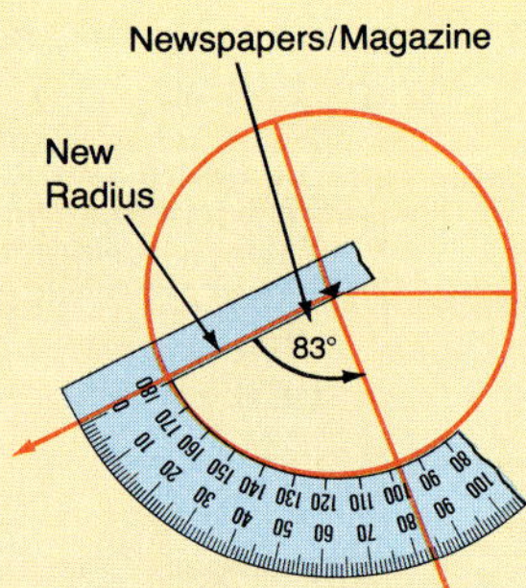

Draw a radius. Place the protractor on the radius. Draw an angle of 108° for *TV/Radio*.

Place the protractor on the "new" radius. Draw an angle of 97° for *Direct Mail*.

Place the protractor on the "new" radius. Draw an angle of 72° for *Newspapers/Magazines*.

The remaining angle represents *Other*.

This figure represents the complete graph. Write the title of the graph as well as the title of each part with its percent.

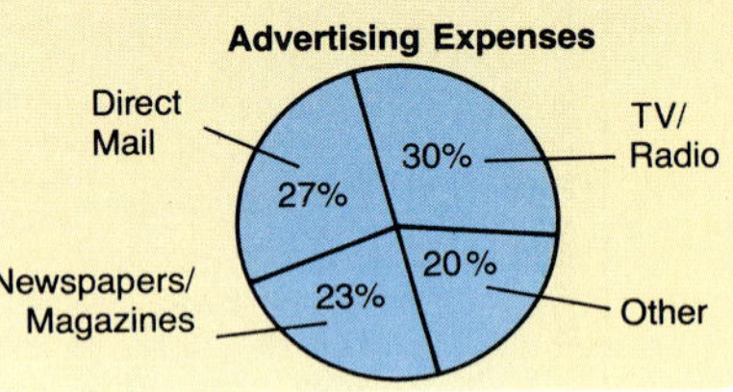

EXERCISES

1. What is the total percent of all the parts in a circle graph? 100%

2. What is the total number of degrees in a circle? 360°

How many degrees does each of these represent in a circle graph?

3. 10% 36°
4. 5% 18°
5. $\frac{2}{5}$ 144°
6. $\frac{1}{3}$ 120°
7. 65% 234°
8. 70% 252°

Refer to the circle graph at the right for Exercises 9–13.

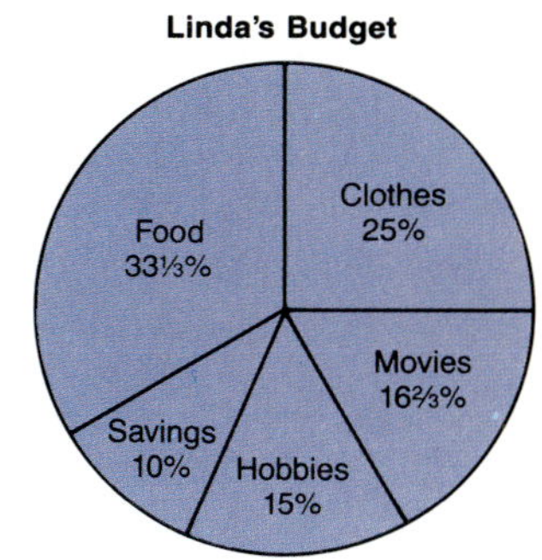

9. For which item does Linda budget the most money? Food

10. On which two items added together does Linda budget 40% of her money? Clothes and Hobbies

11. On which two items added together does Linda budget $\frac{1}{2}$ of her money? Food and Movies

12. Suppose that Linda earned $80 last week. How much of this amount is budgeted for clothes? $20

13. In a week for which Linda's earnings are $90, how much is budgeted for savings? $9

For Exercises 14–17, make a circle graph to show the data.

14. ***Monthly Budget***

Item	Percent	
Food and Shelter	45	162°
Clothing	5	18°
Medical	10	36°
Gasoline	10	36°
Miscellaneous	30	108°

15. ***A Disc Jockey's Hour***

Activity	Percent	
Music	50	180°
Commercials	13	47°
Sports	10	36°
Chatter	7	25°
News and Weather	20	72°

16. ***Car Expenses***

Item	Percent	
Gas and Oil	25	90°
Insurance	20	72°
Repairs	$13\frac{1}{3}$	48°
Fees (licenses, tolls, etc.)	$8\frac{1}{3}$	30°
Payments	$33\frac{1}{3}$	120°

17. ***Town Budget***

Item	Percent	
Education	45	162°
Highways	20	72°
Parks	15	54°
Health	10	36°
Library	5	18°
Administration	5	18°

2 Teaching the Lesson

Have a student volunteer read the first two paragraphs. Then focus students' attention on the table and ask these questions.

1. On what type of advertising did they spend the most? (Television/Radio)
2. On what type of advertising did they spend the least? (Other)
3. What was the difference in spending in these two categories? (10%)

Explain to students that circle graphs are used to illustrate how something is divided. Then work through the Example with the students.

3 Close

Summary: Have students list the steps for making a circle graph.

Evaluation

Guided Practice: Ex. 2–10 even, 14
Independent Practice: Ex. 1–11 odd, 12, 13, 15–17

Extension

Have students take a simple survey of the class, voting on a favorite movie, television show, or musical group. Have them display the information in a circle graph. They will need to be able to convert their raw data into percents.

Problem-Solving Skills

Reading a graph (Ex. 9–13)
Reading a table (Ex. 14–17)
Making a graph (Ex. 14–17)

Additional Answers

See page 19 for the graphs of Exercises 14 and 16.

Objective

Student will

1. review the skills, concepts, and applications in the first part of Chapter 1.
2. maintain key skills and concepts previously taught.

Using the Page

Exercises 1–4 provide an informal assessment of the student's mastery of the major skills and concepts presented in the first half of Chapter 1. Each item is referenced to the related pages where the particular item was presented. These exercises parallel the quiz provided in the *Teacher's ResourceBank.*™

A quiz covering the second half of the chapter is also provided in the *Teacher's ResourceBank.*™

Exercises 5–8 maintain skills and concepts previously taught.

Additional Answers

4. Distribution of Commercial Fishing

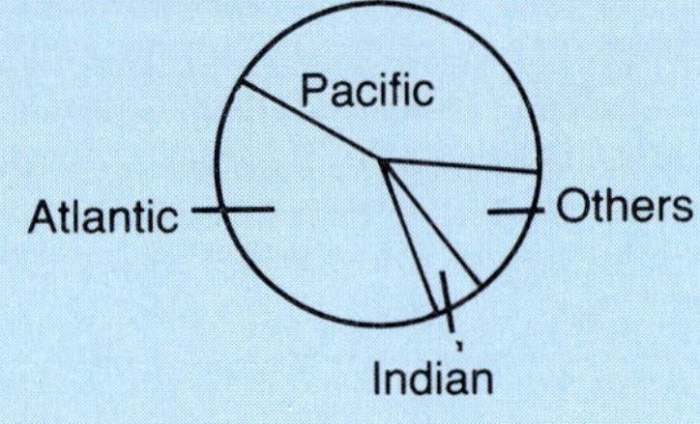

Mid-Chapter Review

The bar graph at the right shows the approximate yearly amount of food consumed by the average person. Use this graph for Exercises 1–2. (Pages 2–3)

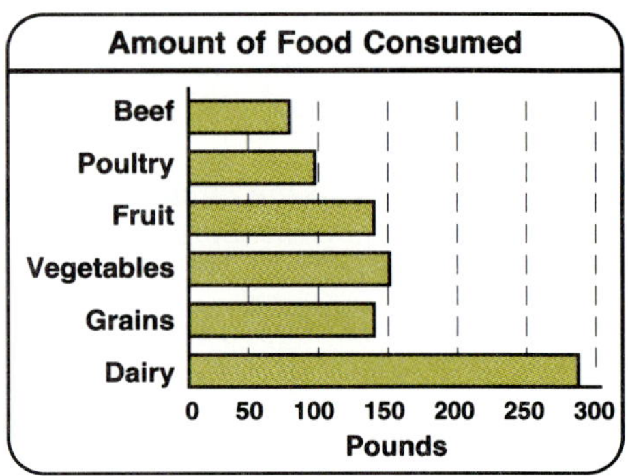

1. Estimate the total amount of fruits and vegetables consumed by an average person each year. **About 290 pounds**
2. About how many more pounds of poultry than beef are consumed by an average person each year? **About 20 pounds more**
3. Use the table below to draw a line graph. (Pages 4–5)

Car Sales for Six Months

Month	J	F	M	A	M	J
Number of Cars	50	75	110	150	225	250

4. Use the table below to draw a circle graph. (Pages 6–7)

Distribution of Commercial Fishing

Body of Water	*Percent*	
Pacific Ocean	43	155°
Atlantic Ocean	39	140°
Indian Ocean	5	18°
Others	13	47°

MAINTENANCE

The pictograph below shows the number of billions of dollars spent on certain items in one year in the United States.

Items	Dollars Spent
Cosmetics	$ $ $ $ $ $ $ $ $ $ ½$
Pet Food	$ $ $ $ $ $
Textbooks	$ ½$
	Key: $ = 1 billion dollars

5. How much money is spent on pet food? **6 billion dollars**
6. How much money is spent on textbooks? **1.5 billion dollars**
7. *Complete:* The amount spent on pet food is _?_ times the amount spent on textbooks. **4**
8. How much more is spent on cosmetics than on pet food? **4.5 billion dollars**

Math in Advertising

What colors appear most often on cracker boxes? Why are most cracker boxes similar in shape?

Manufacturers answer these questions by taking a *sample*. For example, a manufacturer might ask people in supermarkets in different parts of the country to select which of three different cracker boxes they prefer. The design and colors for new products are based on the results of this sampling.

> A **sample** is a group chosen to represent a larger group, called the **population.**

In order for the sample to represent the population, the sample must be sufficiently large and chosen at random; that is, completely by chance.

EXERCISES

Does the sample represent the population? Give a reason.

No; sample is not sufficiently large.

1. This advertisement is based on a sample of 20 dentists.

Four out of every five dentists recommend Long's!

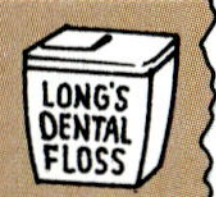

No; sample is not random.

2. This advertisement is based on a survey of 100 people living in the same neighborhood.

Latest Survey Results! 90% for Suds Plus!

3. A survey is taken of people entering an athletic shoe store to determine how many people in the city are joggers. No; sample is not random.

4. To estimate how many people over 65 live in a city, people are interviewed at random in the city's business district and asked to give their ages. No; sample is not random.

Objective

Student will determine whether a sample represents a population.

Overview

This page is an extension of the skills and ideas presented in the previous lessons of this chapter. Since the content presented on this page is not included in the Chapter Review or Chapter Test, its use is optional.

Using the Pages

You may wish to have students work this lesson in small groups or you may wish to work with the class. Using it with the class, focus students' attention on the art of the cereal boxes. Have a student read the first two paragraphs and the definition of a sample. Make sure students understand what is meant by "sufficiently large" and "chosen at random." Discuss Exercise 1 with the class and assign Exercises 2–4 as independent practice. Then ask for volunteers to discuss their answers.

Problem-Solving Skills

Interpreting Information (Ex. 1–4)

Lesson Resources

Maintenance: See below.
Reteaching/Alternate Teaching Strategy: p. M-17
Practice: p. M-17
Enrichment: p. M-17

Objectives

Student will

1. use a formula to find the mean or average of a list of measures.
2. find the range and mode of a list of measures.

Maintenance

Perform the indicated operations.

1. 230 + 243 + 217 + 241 ANS: 931
2. 221.3 + 134.34 + 198 ANS: 553.64
3. 184 ÷ 8 ANS: 23
4. 319.5 ÷ 9 ANS: 35.5
5. Albert made $325, $228, $305, and $290, respectively, during 4 weeks last year. Find the average amount he made each week. ANS: $287

1 Lesson Focus

Motivation: Ask students to discuss how they would determine their grade if they had a record of their test scores.

Purpose: This lesson introduces students to two measures of central tendency, the mean and the mode.

2 Teaching the Lesson

Focus students' attention on the table of vacation expenses. Ask these questions.

1. What was the most that the Corleys spent in a day? ($210)
2. What is the least that the Corleys spent in a day? ($125)

The Mean and the Mode

The Corley family kept a record of expenses during their recent 7-day vacation. Now they would like to find the **mean,** or average, amount spent per day.

$$\text{Mean} = \frac{\text{Sum of Items}}{\text{Number of Items}}$$

EXAMPLE What is the mean amount spent per day by the Corley family?

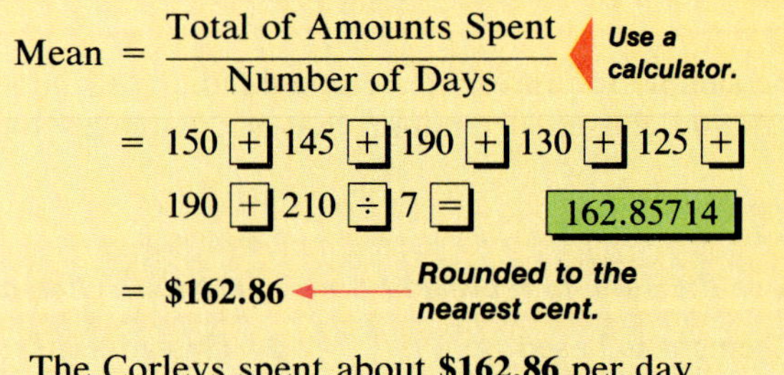

$$\text{Mean} = \frac{\text{Total of Amounts Spent}}{\text{Number of Days}}$$ ◄ *Use a calculator.*

= 150 [+] 145 [+] 190 [+] 130 [+] 125 [+] 190 [+] 210 [÷] 7 [=] 162.85714

= **$162.86** ◄— *Rounded to the nearest cent.*

The Corleys spent about **$162.86** per day.

1. Did the Corleys spend $162.86 every day? No
2. On how many days did they spend less than the average amount? 4
3. On how many days did they spend more than the average amount? 3

In a list of numbers, the **range** is the difference between the greatest and smallest numbers.

4. What is the range of the amounts the Corleys spent on vacation? $85

In a list of data, the **mode** is the item that occurs most often. It is possible to have more than one mode, or no mode.

5. What is the mode of the amounts the Corleys spent per day? $190

EXERCISES

Complete. Choose your answers from the box at the right.

1. In a listing of data, the __?__ is the item that occurs most often. **mode**
2. Another word for mean is __?__. **average**
3. To find the mean of a list of five numbers, first __?__ the numbers. Then divide by __?__. **add, 5**
4. For the numbers 1, 1, 3, 3, 6, 6, 6, 6, the mode is __?__. **6**
5. The mean of the list of numbers in Exercise 4 is __?__. **4**

1
3
4
5
6
add
average
mean
mode

For Exercises 6–9, find the mean and the range.

6. ***Prices for Six Cars***

\$11,500	\$8680	\$7954
\$10,900	\$7850	\$6840

Mean: \$8954; Range: \$4660

7. ***Salaries of Five Employees***

\$18,000	\$19,500	\$21,300
\$22,900	\$27,800	

Mean: \$21,900; Range: \$9800

8. ***Number of Hours Worked in a Day by Twelve Adults***

$7\frac{1}{2}$	8	$7\frac{1}{2}$	$8\frac{1}{2}$	7	$8\frac{1}{2}$
6	$7\frac{1}{2}$	8	$6\frac{1}{2}$	6	9

Mean: $7\frac{1}{2}$; Range: 3

9. ***Costs per Month at Eight Day Camps***

\$258	\$260	\$285	\$325
\$300	\$295	\$240	\$275

Mean: \$279.75; Range: \$85

For Exercises 10–11, find the mode.

10. ***Weekly Salaries of Twenty Secretaries*** **\$200**

Salary	Count
\$100	1
\$150	3
\$200	8
\$250	5
\$300	2
\$350	1

11. ***Customers at a Newsstand***

Hours	Count
6–8 A.M.	30
8–10 A.M.	41
10–12 A.M.	25
12–2 P.M.	13
2–4 P.M.	26
4–6 P.M.	49

4–6 P.M.

3. What is the difference between the two amounts in questions 1 and 2? (\$85)
4. There is a big difference in what the Corleys spent each day. How would you estimate about how much the Corleys could expect to spend each day? (Answers will vary.)

Have students discuss their strategies to answer question 4 above. Then explain that in mathematics, this estimation is done in several ways: mean, median, and mode. Work through the Example to show students how to determine the mean. Then have students answer questions 1–3 in the lesson. Discuss the definitions of range and mode and have students answer questions 4 and 5.

3 Close

Summary: Have students explain how to find the mean, mode, and range for a list of data.

Evaluation
Guided Practice: Ex. 1–5
Independent Practice: Ex. 6–11

Extension

Have students measure and record their heights on a chart. Have them determine the mean, mode, and range of the heights.

Problem-Solving Skills

Interpreting data (Ex. 6–11)
Using a formula (Ex. 6–11)
Reading a table (Ex. 10, 11)

Lesson Resources

Maintenance: See below.
Reteaching/Alternate Teaching Strategy: p. M-18
Practice: p. M-18
Enrichment: p. M-18

Objectives

Student will

1. find the median for an odd number of measures.
2. find the median for an even number of measures.

Maintenance

Arrange the numbers from least to greatest.

1. 5.67 4.89, 6.78, 5.72, 5.06
   ANS: 4.89, 5.06, 5.67, 5.72, 6.78
2. $2\frac{1}{2}$, $2\frac{3}{4}$, $2\frac{1}{8}$, $2\frac{7}{8}$, $2\frac{5}{8}$
   ANS: $2\frac{1}{8}$, $2\frac{1}{2}$, $2\frac{5}{8}$, $2\frac{3}{4}$, $2\frac{7}{8}$
3. Add: 432 + 419 ANS: 851
4. Divide: 725 ÷ 2 ANS: 362.5
5. Robert bought 2 pairs of pants at $24.50 each and a jacket for $57.50. Which cost more, the 2 pairs of pants, or the jacket? How much more? ANS: Jacket; $8.50

1 Lesson Focus

Motivation: Have 7 student volunteers come to the front of the room. Ask students to suggest how they might find the middle height of this group of students. (Arrange from shortest to tallest, choose the middle student)

Purpose: This lesson shows that the median is another way of determining the central tendency of a set of numbers.

The Median

Ramon and Delia Ortega would like to buy a cabin in the mountains. The signs show the costs of five cabins that interest them.

1. How can you organize the costs to find the "middle" cost? **Least to greatest or greatest to least**
2. What is the "middle" cost" **$49,000**
3. How many costs are greater than the "middle" cost? **2**
4. How many costs are less than the "middle" cost? **2**

In a list of numbers organized from least to greatest (or from greatest to least), the **median** is the middle number. When a list has two middle numbers, the median is the mean of these two numbers.

Suppose that the Ortegas also looked at a cabin that costs $49,800.

5. Which two costs will now be the "middle" costs? **$49,000 and $49,500**
6. What is the mean of these two "middle" costs? **$49,250**
7. What is the new median cost? **$49,250**
8. Is the new median one of the actual costs? **No**

EXERCISES

Complete. Choose your answers from the box at the right.

greater than
less than
mean
median
middle
one half

1. In a list of nine numbers arranged in order, the median is the ? number. **middle**
2. In a list of ten numbers arranged in order, the median is the ? of the two ? numbers. **mean, middle**
3. In a list of eight numbers arranged in order, exactly ? are greater than or equal to the median and exactly ? are less than or equal to the median. **one half, one half**
4. In a list of 11 numbers arranged in order, there are as many numbers ? the median as there are ? the median. **greater than, less than**

For Exercises 5–12, find the median.

5. **Rent per Square Foot for Five Apartments** **43¢**

40¢	43¢	46¢	42¢	48¢

6. **Costs of Six Different Brands of Toothpaste (5 oz)**

$1.39	$1.43	$1.40
$1.45	$1.48	$1.45

$1.44

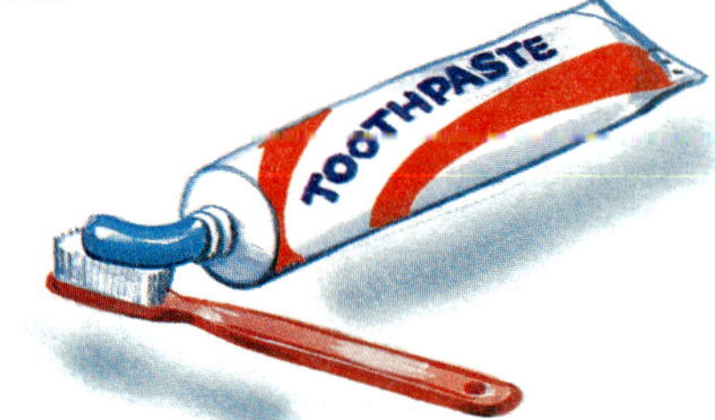

7. **Costs of One Model of Personal Computer**

$4416	$4000	$3400
$2500	$2350	$1802

$2950

8. **Price of One Share of Stock for Ten Days**

$7\frac{1}{8}$	$7\frac{1}{4}$	$7\frac{5}{8}$	$7\frac{3}{4}$	$7\frac{3}{8}$
$6\frac{7}{8}$	7	7	$7\frac{1}{4}$	$7\frac{1}{2}$

$7\frac{1}{4}$

9. **Prices of Several VCR's**

$650	$512	$499
$460	$312	$209

$479.50

10. **Population in Seven Small Towns**

4620 5794 6300 3725
4350 6347 5481 **5481**

11. **Net Income Per Farm**

State	Farm Income
Georgia	$3700
Nebraska	$7017
Oregon	$4268
S. Dakota	$11,367
Vermont	$8412
Wisconsin	$12,105

$7714.50

12. **Summer Costs for Appliances**

Appliance	Cents per Hour
Color Television	5.1
Fan	2.1
Iron	8.1
Room Air Conditioner	18.4
Vacumn cleaner	10.0

8.1

2 Teaching the Lesson

Have a group of students (5–15) tell what time they got up this morning and record the times on the board. Ask the students to arrange the times in order from earliest to latest. Then ask what they would consider as the typical time of getting-up for this group. They may suggest a range, a mode, and, reluctantly, a mean. Encourage them to consider the middle number as a typical time. Explain that the middle by rank is called the median. Work through questions 1–8 in the lesson with the students.

3 Close

Summary: Have students explain in their own words how to find the median of a group of numbers.

Evaluation
Guided Practice: Ex. 1–4
Independent Practice: Ex. 5–12

Extension

Have student choose 15 houses at random out of the newspaper classified ads and record the price of each. Have them find the mean and the median price. Have them discuss which appears to be a better measure of central tendency.

Problem-Solving Skills

Using a table (Ex. 5–12)
Using a formula (Ex. 6, 7, 9, 11)

Lesson Resources

Maintenance: See below.
Reteaching/Alternate Teaching Strategy: See the margin on page 15.
Practice: Activity Worksheet 6
Enrichment: See the enrichment topic "Histograms" on page 16.

Objectives

Student will

1. solve word problems that involve the mean, median, and mode.
2. determine which average, the mean, the median, or the mode, is the most appropriate for a given situation.

Maintenance

Use the following list of numbers for problem 1–4.

68, 79, 96, 83, 82, 80, 79

1. Find the range. ANS: 28
2. Find the mode. ANS: 79
3. Find the mean. ANS: 81
4. Find the median. ANS: 80
5. Bill makes $5.00, $8.50. and $7.50 for the three lawns he cuts. What is the average amount that he makes per lawn? ANS: $7.00

1 Lesson Focus

Motivation: Have students discuss the differences in finding the mean, the median, and the mode.

Purpose: This lesson allows students an opportunity to apply each of the different measures of central tendency in appropriate ways.

Strategy: INTERPRETING INFORMATION

You are the manager of a store. You make many decisions each day. To make the decisions, you must first ask questions such as the following.

"Which of these should I use, the mean, the median, or the mode?"

The following exercises will help to see how this problem-solving process works.

EXERCISES

Problem: *During what hours of the day will I need part-time employees?*

Knowing the average number (mean) of customers for each hour will help to solve this problem. This table shows the averages.

Hours	*Customers*
9:00–10:00	10
10:00–11:00	22
11:00–12:00	25
12:00–1:00	27
1:00–2:00	30
2:00–3:00	40
3:00–4:00	35
4:00–5:00	45
5:00–6:00	53

1. Over what 5-hour period does the store have the greatest number of customers? 1:00–6:00
2. During what hour does the mode occur? 5:00–6:00
3. Suppose that you decide to hire part-time help from 4:00 P.M. to 6:00 P.M. Why is this a reasonable decision? The greatest number of customers are in the store during these hours.
4. What is the mean number of customers per hour coming into the store? Round your answer to the nearest whole number. 32 customers
5. Would the answer to Exercise 4 justify hiring part-time help from 2:00 to 6:00? Explain. Yes; the number of customers is above the mean during these hours.

Problem: *How many employees should I have on duty for each hour?*

You want one employee on duty for every 10 customers in a given hour.

6. Complete this chart. The first two are done for you.

Customers	1–10	11–20	21–30	31–40	41–50	51–60
Employees	1	2	? 3	? 4	? 5	? 6

7. In the following chart, why are 3 employees needed from 10–11?
The store had more than 20 customers.

Hours	9–10	10–11	11–12	12–1	1–2	2–3	3–4	4–5	5–6
Customers	10	22	25	27	30	40	35	45	53
Employees	1	3	? 3	? 3	? 3	? 4	? 4	? 5	? 6

8. Use your answers to Exercise 6 to complete the chart above.

9. You have decided to hire no more than three full-time employees. During which hours will you need part-time help? **2–6**

10. How many part-time employees will you need during each of these hours? **2–3: 1; 3–4: 1; 4–5: 2; 5–6: 3**

Problem: *How do our salaries compare with those of employees at other stores?*

This table shows the yearly salaries for you and your employees.

Yearly Salaries	
Manager	$40,000
Assistant	$25,000
Clerk	$12,500
Clerk	$12,000
Clerk	$11,500
Clerk	$10,000

11. What is the mean yearly salary? **$18,500**

12. Is the mean yearly salary greater or less than most of the salaries? **Greater**

13. What is the median yearly salary? **$12,250**

14. Are most of the salaries closer to the mean yearly salary or the median yearly salary? **Closer to the median yearly salary.**

15. Which average, the mean yearly salary or the median yearly salary, better represents most of the yearly salaries? Why? **Median yearly salary; it is closer to most of the salaries.**

2 Teaching the Lesson

Have a volunteer read the opening paragraph. Before the students work the exercises for each problem:

1. Have them discuss the steps they might use to solve the Problem.
2. Have them decide how they might gather the information they need to solve the Problem.

3 Close

Summary: Have students review the Problems and the exercises. Ask these questions.

1. In which Problem was it appropriate to find the mode? (The second Problem)
2. In which Problem was it appropriate to find the mean? (The first Problem)
3. In which Problem was it appropriate to find the median? (The third Problem)

Evaluation
Guided Practice: Ex. 1–5
Independent Practice: Ex. 6–15

Critical Thinking

Ex. 3, 5, 14, 15

Alternate Teaching Strategy

You may wish to have students work in small groups to complete the exercises. Have them discuss their ideas for each exercise and record a group consensus for each.

NOTE: A quiz covering the second half of the chapter is provided in the *Teacher's ResourceBank™*.

Objectives

Student will

1. read a histogram and use the information to solve problems.
2. use a frequency table to make a histogram.

Overview

This topic is optional. The word "Enrichment" that appears to the right of the title in this Teacher's Edition does not appear in the student textbook. Therefore, this material is not included in the Chapter Review and Chapter Test.

Using the Page

You may wish to have students work this Enrichment in small groups or you may wish to work with the class.

Problem-Solving Skills

Reading a graph (Ex. 1–6)
Using a table (Ex. 7)
Making a graph (Ex. 7)

Histograms ENRICHMENT

Another way to organize data is to use a *histogram*. A **histogram** is a special kind of bar graph that shows the number of occurrences, or **frequency**, of groups of data arranged in intervals.

EXAMPLE A used car dealer wanted an estimate of the prices paid for certain used cars. This data is shown in a frequency table that shows the prices paid for 30 cars. Draw a histogram to show the data.

Price Interval (hundreds of dollars)	*Count*	*Frequency*
26–30	𝍸 II	7
31–35	I	1
36–40	III	3
41–45	𝍸 I	6
46–50	IIII	4
51–55	IIII	4
56–60	II	2
61–65	I	1
66–70	II	2

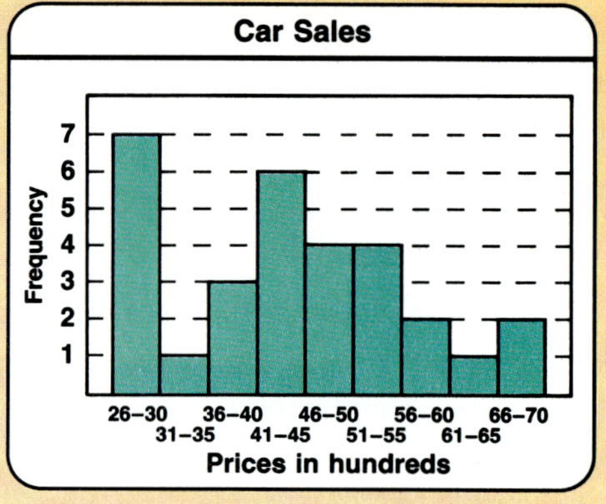

EXERCISES

Refer to the histogram for Exercises 1–6.

1. How many cars sold for \$6100 or more? 3
2. How many cars sold for \$5100 or more? 9
3. How many cars sold for \$3500 or less? 8
4. In which price ranges were the least number of cars sold? \$3100–\$3500 and \$6100–\$6500
5. What fraction of the cars were sold for \$5600 or more? $\frac{1}{6}$
6. Explain this statement: "About half the cars sell in a price range of \$3600 to \$5500." 17 of the 30 cars sold were in this price range.
7. The frequency table at the right shows the speeds of cars passing a point on a highway over a 20-minute period. Make a histogram to show the data.
See the Answers to Selected Exercises.

Interval (miles per hour)	*Frequency*
40–45	5
46–50	25
51–55	30
56–60	130

The Chapter Summary contains a listing of the procedures that are related to the skills and concepts presented in the chapter. An example that illustrates each procedure appears at the right of each procedure. This listing is intended to assist the student with the Chapter Review that follows.

Chapter Summary

IMPORTANT IDEAS

1. To read a bar graph:

[1] Look for the number scale on one of the axes.

[2] Use the scale to interpret the graph.

1.

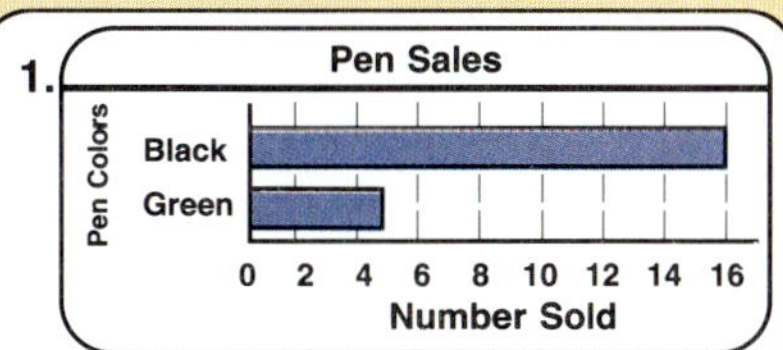

Sixteen black pens were sold.

2. To read a line graph:

[1] Find the given number or time on one axis.

[2] Use the second axis to find the unknown number or time.

2.

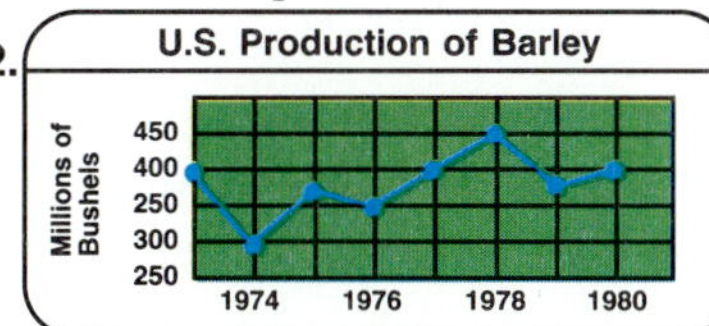

In 1974, barley production dropped to 300 million bushels.

3. To draw a circle graph:

[1] Write a decimal for each percent.

[2] Multiply the decimal by 360°. Round your answer to the nearest degree.

[3] Use a protractor to draw the graph.

3. Vacation Destinations:
New York City: 37%
37% = 0.37;
$0.37 \times 360° \approx 133°$

Vacation Destinations

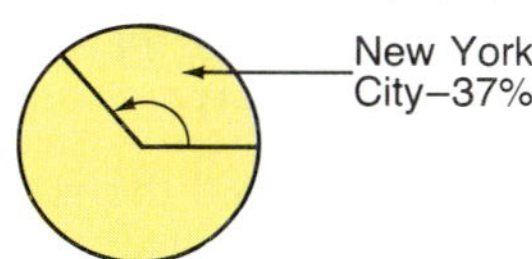

4. To find the mean, use this formula.

$$\text{Mean} = \frac{\text{Sum of Items}}{\text{Number of Items}}$$

4. Find the mean: 6, 8, 10, 18, 16

$$\text{Mean} = \frac{6 + 8 + 10 + 18 + 16}{5} = \mathbf{11.6}$$

5. To find the mode of a list of data, identify the item that occurs most often.

5. Find the mode:
1, 3, 4, 7, 7, 3, 3, 5
The mode is **3.**

6. To find the median:

[1] Arrange the data in order.

[2] **a.** For an odd number of items, the median is the middle measure listed.

b. For an even number of items, the median is the mean of the two middle measures.

6. a. Find the median:
1, 5, 7, 8, 9, 10, 12
The median is **8.**

b. Find the median:
2, 3, 4, 5, 7, 8, 15, 20

$\frac{5 + 7}{2} = \mathbf{6}$ ← *Median*

Objective

To review the important terms, skills, problem solving, and applications presented in Chapter 1.

Overview

The Chapter Review is structured in two parts. Part 1 is a review of the important terms that were introduced in the chapter. Part 2 reviews the skills, the problem-solving strategies, and applications that were presented in the chapter. Each item in the Chapter Review is referenced to the related pages where the concept, skill, or application was presented.

Using the Pages

You may wish to assign this Chapter Review for homework or treat it as a class review prior to administering the formal Chapter Test. In doing this, it is suggested that you only use the even- or odd-numbered exercises. You can then use the remaining exercises as a bank for use later.

Chapter Review

Part 1: VOCABULARY

For Exercises 1–6, choose from the box at the right the word or number that completes each statement.

median
360
width
length
number
change
mode
mean
270

1. On a bar graph, the length of the bar represents a __?__. (Page 2) number
2. Line graphs show the amount of __?__ over a period of time. (Page 4) change
3. A circle contains __?__ degrees. (Page 6) 360
4. The average obtained by dividing the sum of the measures by the number of measures is the __?__. (Page 10) mean
5. In a group of measures, the one that occurs most often is the __?__. (Page 10) mode
6. In a listing of data, the middle measure is the __?__. (Page 12) median

Part 2: SKILLS AND APPLICATIONS

The vertical bar graph at the right shows the number of bushels of corn produced in a certain year in the Midwest. (Pages 2–3)

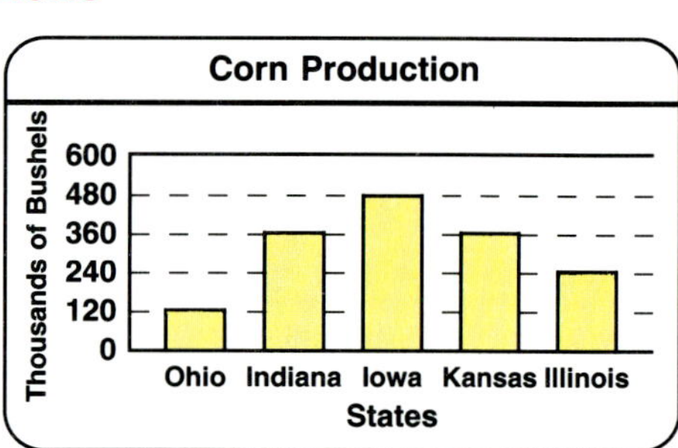

7. Which state produced the most corn? Iowa
8. Which state produced the least corn? Ohio
9. Which states produced the same number of bushels of corn? Indiana and Kansas
10. Use this information to complete the bar graph. (Pages 2–3)

Calories Per 100 Grams of 5 Shellfish

Shellfish	Calories
Clams	50
Lobsters	82
Crabs	120
Mussels	73
Scallops	62

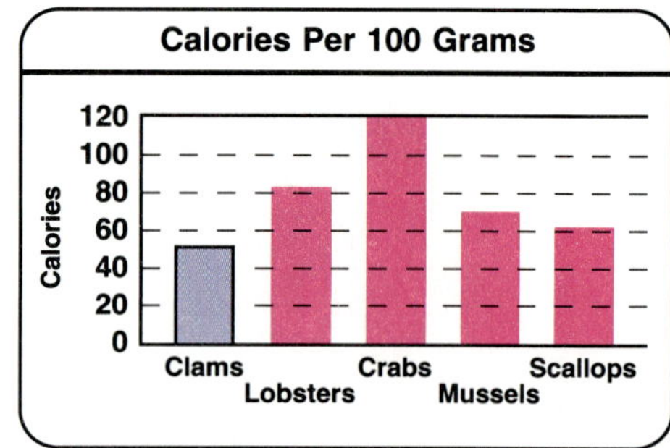

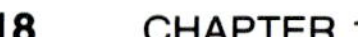

Use the line graph for Exercises 11–14. (Pages 4–5)

11. In which year was the price for wheat the greatest? **1981**

12. Between which two years did the price increase the most? **1977 and 1979**

13. About how much more did a farmer receive for a bushel of wheat in 1983 than in 1977? **About $1 more**

14. About how much did a farmer receive for 100 bushels of wheat in 1985? **About $310**

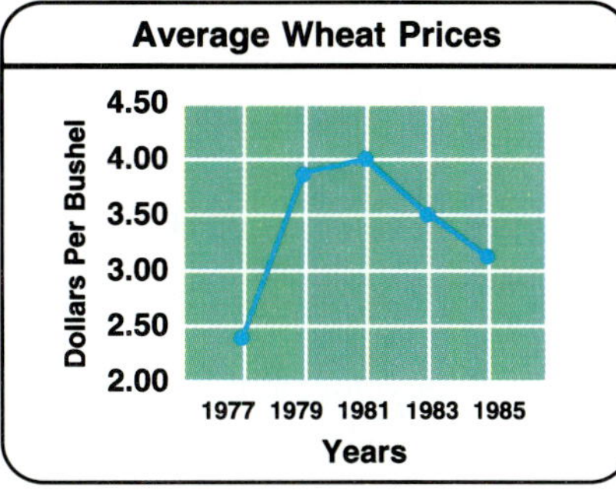

15. Use this information to complete the line graph at the right. (Pages 4–5)

Television Advertising Expenditures

Year	Billions of Dollars
1970	3.6
1975	5.3
1980	11.4
1985	20.8

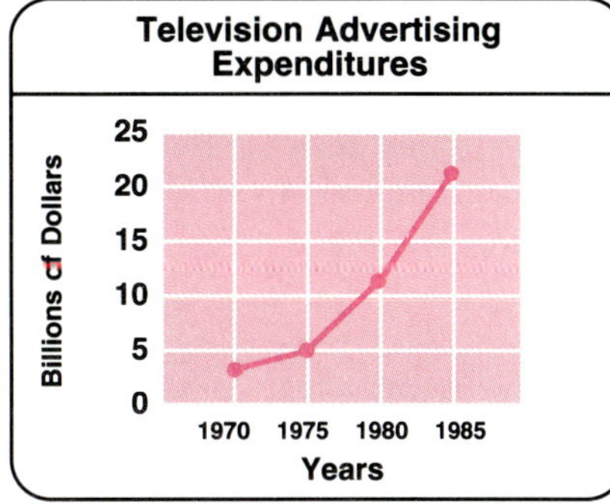

16. Use the table below to make a circle graph. (Pages 6–7)

Average Daily Sales at a Service Station

Item	Unleaded Fuel	Regular Fuel	Premium Fuel	Oil	Miscellaneous
Per Cent	42%	20%	18%	5%	15%
	151°	72°	65°	18°	54°

For Exercises 17–18, find the mean and the mode. (*Pages 10–11*)

17. ***Weekly Wages of Eight Workers***

$125	$180	$250	$310
$225	$210	$270	$320

Mean: $236.25; Mode: None

18. ***Yearly Salaries for Five Employees***

$40,000 $25,000 $12,500
$12,500 $12,000

Mean: $20,400; Mode: $12,500

For Exercises 19–20, find the median. (Pages 12–13)

19. ***Cost of Eight Different Brands of Cereal (64 oz)***

$2.49	$1.71	$1.99	$3.09
$2.42	$1.83	$2.52	$2.12

$2.27

20. ***Cost of Seven Different American Automobiles***

$9400 $8788 $13,200 $10,990
$11,100 $15,474 $10,300

$10,900

Additional Answers, page 7

14. Monthly Budget

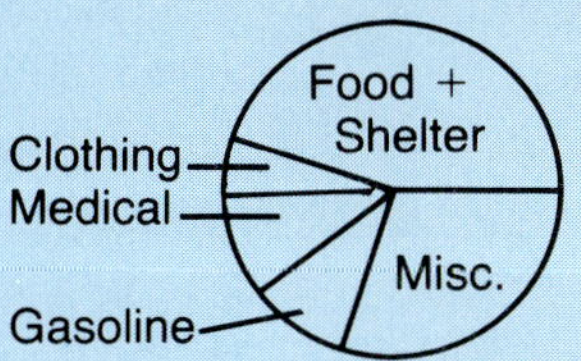

16. Car Expenses

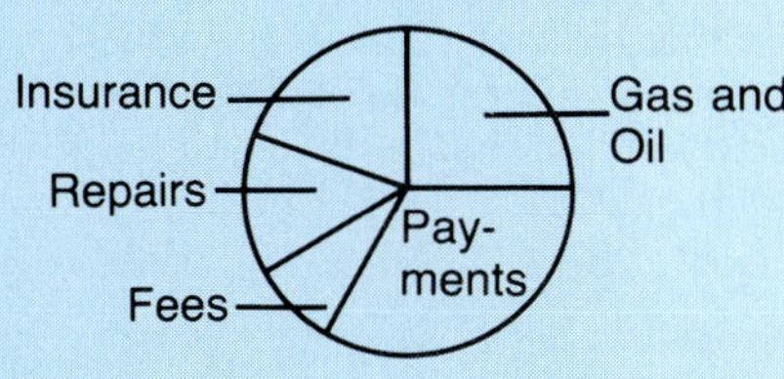

Additional Answers Chapter Review

16. Average Daily Sales

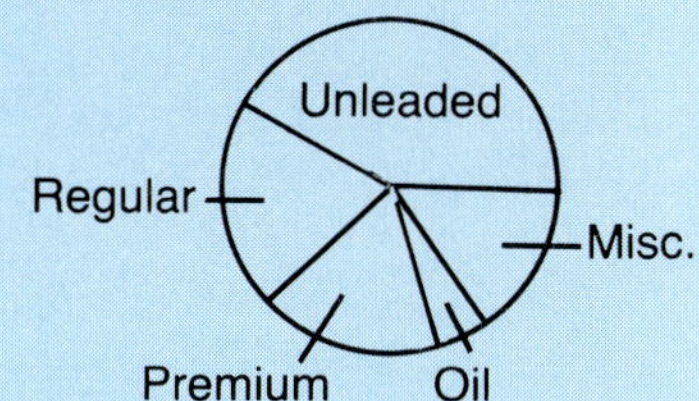

Objective

To informally assess students' mastering of the major skills, concepts, problem solving, and applications presented in Chapter 1.

Using the Page

After completing the Chapter Review with the class, you may wish to use this Chapter Test as an informal assessment. This Chapter Test parallels the formal chapter tests (Form A and Form B) provided in the *Teacher's ResourceBank.*™

Chapter Test

The bar graph at the right shows the average prices of houses in five developments. Use the graph for Exercises 1–3.

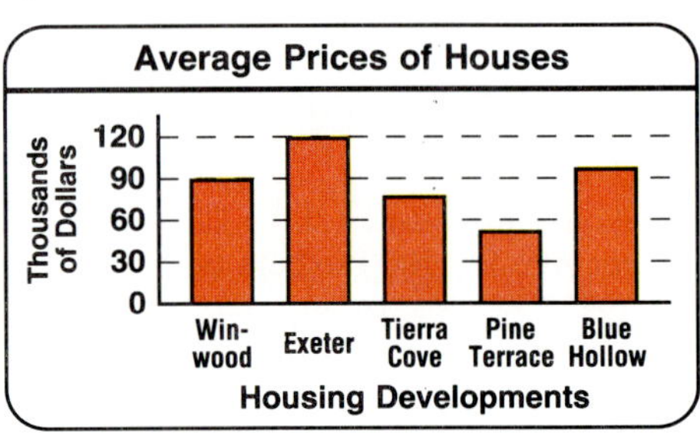

1. Which developments contain houses with an average price of more than $90,000? **Exeter and Blue Hollow**
2. Which development has the lowest average price for a house? **Pine Terrace**
3. How much greater is the average price for a house in Exeter than in Winwood? **$30,000**

This line graph shows the total monthly sales for Company X (solid line) and Company Y (dashed line).

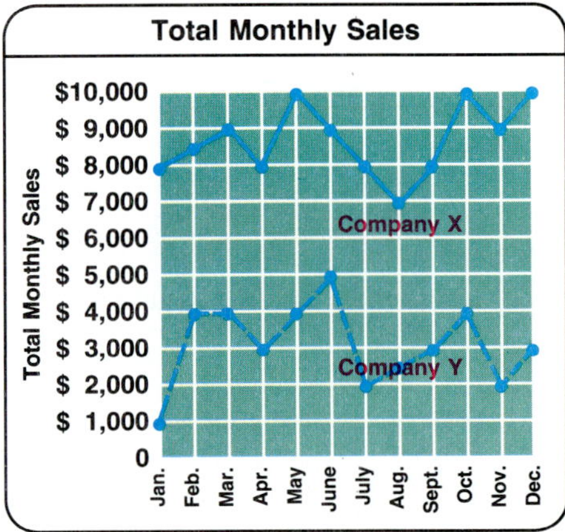

4. Between which three months did Company X have the greatest decrease in sales? **June, July, and August**
5. During which month did Company Y have the greatest increase in sales? **February**
6. Which company had greater sales in July than in January? How much greater? **Company Y; $1000**
7. Use the table below to make a circle graph.

Advertising Budget

Item	Newspaper	TV	Radio	Other
Percent	15%	60%	20%	5%
	54°	**216°**	**72°**	**18°**

8. Find the mean and the mode.

Prices of Eight Books

$13.38 $ 8.95 $10.00 $8.50
$12.50 $10.80 $ 7.00 $8.95

Mean: $10.01; Mode: $8.95

9. Find the median.

Automobile Prices

$13,495 $25,215 $9944
$11,679 $12,555

$12,555

10. Which average, the mean or median, better represents the automobile prices in Exercise 9? Give a reason for your answer.
Median; the mean is higher than four of the five prices.

The Consumer and Probability

Consumers often make decisions based on probability. For example, when a weather forecaster says that there is an 80% chance of rain, many people decide to carry an umbrella to work or to go shopping. **Probability** is concerned with how likely it is that a certain event will happen.

- How can a tree diagram be used to show the number of ways in which an event can happen?
- How can the manager of a hot dog stand use probability to predict how many hot dogs will be needed at the next high school football game?

Chapter 2: The Consumer and Probability

Overview

The focus of Chapters 2 is on the use of counting methods and probability to predict solutions to problems in consumer-related situations. Thus, the strategy lesson on pages 30–31 provides a model for using emphirical data to solve problems. The lesson on odds provides another view of probability as well as another way of expressing it. Finally, the *Enrichment* lesson on page 34 introduces the topic of random numbers which may be expanded by further research on its relation to sampling techniques.

Using This Page

Have students read the introductory paragraph and questions. Have them list possible solutions to the problems presented. After completing the chapter, have students review their suggested solutions, comparing them with those presented in the lessons. You may wish to have students suggest other possible problems resulting from the situation described on this page and to discuss possible solutions.

You may wish to organize the class into small groups to complete the situational activity described in this *Using the Page.*

Lesson Resources

Maintenance: See below.
Reteaching/Alternate Teaching Strategy: p. M-18
Practice: p. M-18
Enrichment: p. M-18

Objectives

Student will

1. use a tree diagram to determine the number of choices.
2. use the fundamental counting principle to determine the number of choices.

Maintenance

Multiply.

1. $4 \times 3 \times 5$ ANS: 60
2. $7 \times 3 \times 4$ ANS: 84
3. $2 \times 2 \times 2 \times 2 \times 2$ ANS: 32
4. $5 \times 5 \times 5 \times 5$ ANS: 625
5. Robert had 5 books. Every book had 20 pages. Every page had 30 lines. How many lines are there in all five books? ANS: 3000

1 Lesson Focus

Motivation: Ask students to discuss how they would determine how many different outfits they could make if they had 4 sweaters and 2 pairs of jeans.

Purpose: This lesson shows students how to determine the number of combinations they can get when they know the possible alternatives of each selection.

Tree Diagrams: THE COUNTING PRINCIPLE

All consumers want to save money. At a Mix and Match sale you buy 4 different sweaters and 2 different pairs of jeans. By mixing and matching, you can have more outfits to wear without having to buy more clothes.

PROBLEM How many different outfits can you make?

There is more than one way to solve this problem.

MAKING A MODEL: TREE DIAGRAM

1 Begin the tree diagram with a branch for each sweater.

2 Draw the "jeans" branches. There are 2 jeans branches for each "sweater" branch.

3 **Count.** There are **8** different outfits.

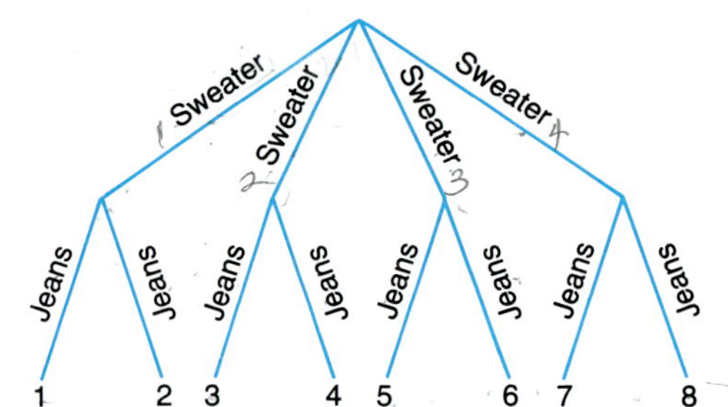

The tree diagram suggests a second way to solve the problem.

COMPUTATION: THE FUNDAMENTAL COUNTING PRINCIPLE

In the tree diagram, you can see that for each of the 4 sweaters you can choose from two pairs of jeans. Thus, $4 \times 2 = 8$.

This illustrates the **Fundamental Principle of Counting.**

If there are r choices for the way one thing can be done and s choices for the way another thing can be done, then together they may be done in $r \times s$ different ways.

The rule can be extended to include more choices.

EXAMPLE In how many different ways can you order lunch?

SANDWICHES	SALADS
Tuna	Potato
Chicken	Spinach
Roast Beef	Fruit

BEVERAGES
Milk • Cocoa • Juice

READ What are the facts?
3 sandwiches, 3 salads, 3 beverages

PLAN Use the Fundamental Principle of Counting.

SOLVE **Think:** For each of the 3 sandwiches, there are 3 salad choices. Thus, $3 \times 3 = \mathbf{9}$.

For each "sandwich/salad" choice, there are 3 beverage choices.

There are $9 \times 3 =$ **27 different ways** to order lunch.

CHECK Draw a tree diagram to show that there are 27 ways.

EXERCISES

For Exercises 1–2, copy and complete the tree diagram to find the total number of choices.

1. Bertrum's Rice sells white rice, Cajun rice, and brown rice. Each is available in a 16-ounce box and a 24-ounce box. How many different choices of rice are there?

white, Cajun, brown
16-oz box, 24-oz box, 16-oz box, 24-oz box, 16-oz box, 24-oz box
6 choices

2. A bakery bakes French and Italian breads in 8-inch, 12-inch, and 14-inch loaves. Both regular and garlic are available in each size. How many different choices of bread are there?

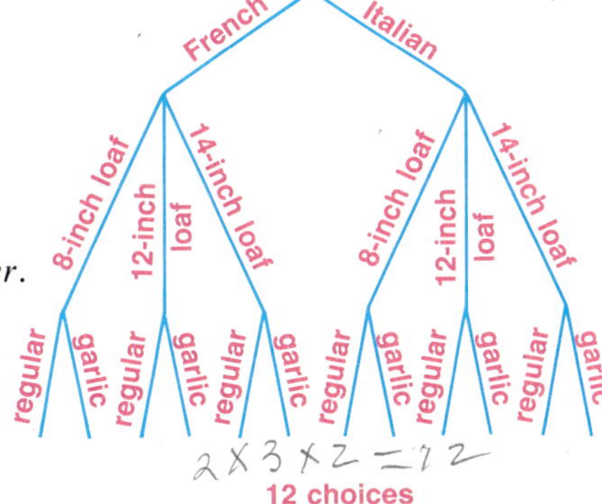

Solve. Use the method you prefer.

3. A deli serves 4 kinds of sandwiches, 2 kinds of salad, and 3 beverages. You want to order a sandwich, a salad, and a beverage. How many different choices are there? 24 choices

4. From 3 different exterior colors, 3 different interior colors, and 2 wheel styles for a car, you choose one of each. How many different choices do you have? 18 choices

5. Daybreak Dairy bottles whole, skim, and 2% lowfat milk in pints, quarts, half gallons, and gallons. How many different choices of bottled milk are there? 12 choices

6. An outfit includes a pair of pants, a shirt, and a sweater. How many different outfits can you make from 2 pairs of pants, 3 shirts and 2 sweaters? 12 outfits

7. You are shopping for a stereo system. You can choose from 5 amplifiers, 3 compact disc players, and 4 pairs of speakers. How many different systems can you buy? 60 systems

2 Teaching the Lesson

Prior to having students look at the lesson, have them discuss the Motivation section above. Then have a volunteer read the first paragraph. Focus students' attention on the tree diagram and ask questions such as these.

1. How does the tree diagram show that there are four choices of sweaters? (4 branches)
2. How does the tree diagram show that there are two choices of jeans? (2 branches from each sweater)
3. How does the tree diagram show how many outfits there are? (8 ends)

Then have a student read the paragraph above the box and the information in the box. Ask these questions.

4. How many sweaters can you choose? (4)
5. How many jeans can you choose? (2)
6. What could you do with 4 and 2 to find out there are 8 outfits? (Mulitply; $4 \times 2 = 8$)

Have students work through the Example.

3 Close

Summary: Have students discuss when it would be more useful to use a tree diagram and when it would be more useful to use the counting principle. (The tree diagram is more useful when the choices have to be named and not just counted.)

Evaluation
Guided Practice: Ex. 1, 2
Independent Practice: Ex. 3–7

Problem-Solving Skills

Making a model (Ex. 1–7)

Lesson Resources

Maintenance: See below.
Reteaching/Alternate Teaching Strategy: p. M-19
Practice: p. M-19
Enrichment: p. M-19

Objectives

Student will

1. use a tree diagram to find the number of permutations.
2. use factorials to find the number of permutations.

Maintenance

Perform the indicated operations.

1. 5 × 4 × 3 × 2 × 1 ANS: 120
2. 10 × 9 × 8 × 7 ANS: 5040
3. 1 + 2 + 3 + 4 + 5 + 6 + 7 ANS: 28
4. 31 + 32 + 33 + 34 + 35 + 36 ANS: 201
5. Joan is going to double the distance she runs each day for 7 days. The first day she runs 100 yards. How far will she run on the seventh day? ANS: 6400 yards

1 Lesson Focus

Motivation: Place 3 chairs at the front of the room and have three students sit in the chairs. Have a student write down the arrangement on the chalkboard. Then have students suggest other arrangements.

Purpose: This lesson teaches students how to find the number of ways that members of a group can be arranged.

Permutations

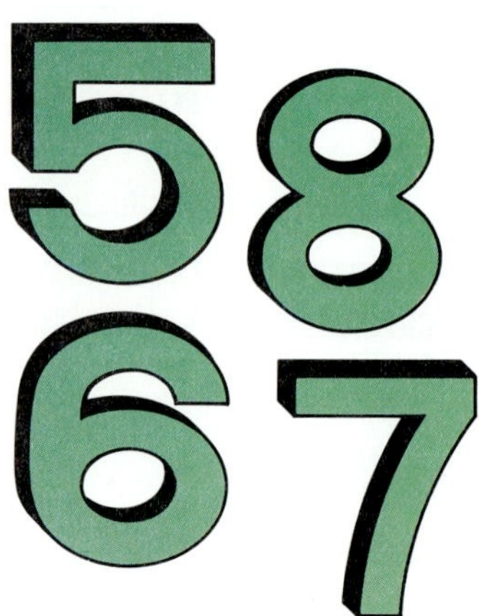

You are the manager of a grocery store. You want to set up a four-digit code system for the vegetables you sell. The digits you will use are 5, 6, 7, and 8. Each digit can be used only once in the code. For example, the code 8576 could mean yellow onions.

PROBLEM How many vegetables will you be able to code?

Here is another way to state the problem.

"In how many different ways can the digits 5, 6, 7, and 8 be arranged?"

There is more than one way to solve this problem.

USING A TREE DIAGRAM

1 **First digit:** There are 4 choices. Draw a branch for each digit.

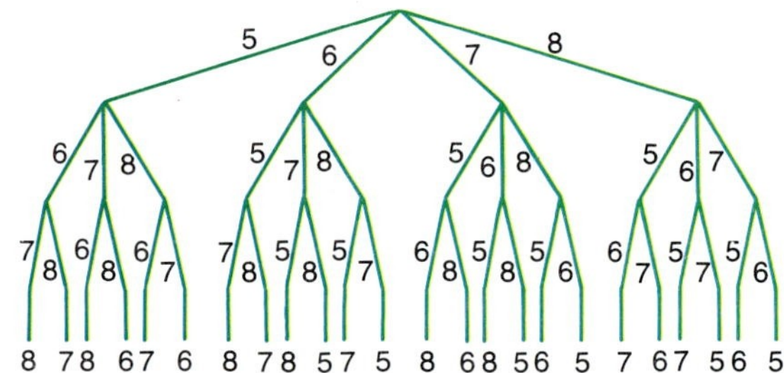

2 **Second digit:** There are 3 choices for each first digit. Draw 3 branches for each first-digit branch.

3 **Third digit:** There are 2 choices for each second digit. Draw 2 branches for each second-digit branch.

4 **Count.** You can code **24 vegetables** because there are 24 different arrangements, or *permutations* of four digits when each digit can be used only once.

> **Permutations** are the different ways that the members of a group can be arranged.

The tree diagram suggests a shorter way to solve this problem.

COMPUTATION: FACTORIALS

Think: (Number of choices for first digit) × (Number of choices for second digit) × (Number of choices for third digit) × (Number of choices for fourth digit) = (Total number of choices)

4 × 3 × 2 × 1 = **24**

A shortcut way to write this product is to use the **factorial symbol.**

4 × 3 × 2 × 1 can be written as **4!** *Read 4! as 4 factorial.*

1. Use the factorial symbol to show in how many different ways 9 people could choose 9 seats. 9! ways

2. Use a calculator to find 9! 362,880

EXERCISES

Draw a tree diagram to find the number of permutations.

1. Three people sit in a row of three chairs. 6 ways

2. Four people sit in a row of four chairs. 24 ways

For Exercises 3–4, find the number of permutations.

3. Carole, Gwen, Larry, Sergio, and Carlos attend a student council meeting. There are 5 unoccupied seats in the auditorium. In how many different ways can they choose the 5 seats? 120 ways

4. A shuttle bus seats 6 people. In how many different ways can 6 people choose 6 seats? 720 ways

Complete the table. Use a calculator.

	Number of Chairs in a Row	Number of People to Sit in the Chairs	Number of Arrangements
5.	10	10	? 3,628,800
6.	11	11	? 39,916,800
7.	12	12	? 479,001,600
8.	13	13	? 6,227,020,800

Draw a tree diagram to find the number of permutations.

9. How many 4-digit numbers can be formed from the digits 1, 2, 3, and 4 if the digits cannot be repeated? 24 numbers

10. How many 6-digit numbers can be formed from the digits 2, 3, 4, 5, 6, and 7 if the digits cannot be repeated? 720 numbers

2 Teaching the Lesson

Have a student volunteer read the first paragraph and the Problem. Focus students' attention on the tree diagram and ask these questions.

1. How many choices are there for the first digit? (4)
2. How many choices are there for the second digit? (3)
3. How many choices are there for the third digit? (2)
4. Why are there fewer choices each time? (Some numbers have already been chosen.)

Have students work through the Problem. Make sure they understand the meaning of permutation before going on. Have students work through the factorial example step by step.

3 Close

Summary: Have students discuss when they would want to use the tree diagram and when they would like to use the factorial method.

Evaluation
Guided Practice: Ex. 1, 2
Independent Practice: Ex. 3–10

Extension

Have students determine the number of possible arrangements for 52 playing cards.

Problem-Solving Skills

Drawing a diagram (Ex. 1, 2, 11, 12)
Completing a table (Ex. 7–10)

Lesson Resources

Maintenance: See below.
Reteaching/Alternate Teaching Strategy: p. M-19
Practice: p. M-19
Enrichment: p. M-19

Objective

Maintenance

Reduce to lowest terms.

1. $\frac{12}{18}$ ANS: $\frac{2}{3}$
2. $\frac{10}{25}$ ANS: $\frac{2}{5}$

Multiply.

3. $\frac{2}{5} \times \frac{5}{7}$ ANS: $\frac{10}{35}$, or $\frac{2}{7}$
4. $\frac{3}{14} \times \frac{4}{9}$ ANS: $\frac{12}{126}$, or $\frac{2}{21}$
5. Ten students earned an A on a test. There are 30 students in the class. What fraction of the class did not earn A's? ANS: $\frac{20}{30}$, or $\frac{2}{3}$

1 Lesson Focus

Motivation: Ask a student to tell how many times a coin will probably land on heads if it is tossed 10 times. Then have another student toss a coin 10 times and record the results.

Purpose: This lesson teaches the student to understand probability as a ratio comparing the successful ways of something happening to the possible ways of something happening.

2 Teaching the Lesson

Have a volunteer read the introductory section. Discuss statements 1, 2, and 3. Then focus students' attention on the spinner in Example 1 and ask these questions.

1. On how many possible numbers can the spinner land? (6)

Probability

Three events are listed below. Write 1 if the event is certain to happen. Write 0 if you think it is impossible.

1. The sun will rise in the east. 1
2. The sun will set in the west. 1
3. The sun will rise in the north. 0

The chances that an event will happen is a number between 0 and 1. For example, the chance or *probability* of tossing a coin and getting "heads" is "1 out of 2" which equals $\frac{1}{2}$, or 50%.

4. What is the probability of getting "tails?" $\frac{1}{2}$, or 50%

EXAMPLE 1 The arrow on this spinner is spun once. What is the probability of getting a 7?

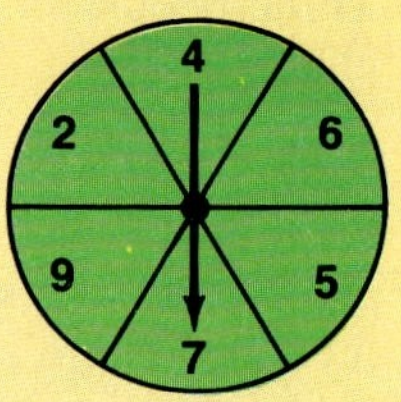

Think: There are 6 ways for the arrow to land.

In this case, landing on 7 is "successful."

$P(7) = \frac{1}{6}$ *P(7) means the "probability of landing on 7."*

This suggests the **probability ratio.**

$$\textbf{Probability ratio} = \frac{\textbf{Number of Successful Ways}}{\textbf{Number of Possible Ways}}$$

The possible ways in which an event can occur is called the **sample space.** In Example 1, the numbers 2, 4, 5, 6, 7, and 9 form the sample space.

EXAMPLE 2 In the event for Example 1, what is the probability of landing on an even number?

Think: The even numbers are 2, 4, and 6. So there are three successful ways.

$P(\text{Even Number}) = \frac{3}{6}$ ← *Number of Successful Ways* / *Number of Possible Ways*

$= \frac{1}{2}$, or **50%**

EXERCISES

For Exercises 1–3, write "1" if the event is certain to happen. Write "0" if you think it is impossible.

1. You will roll a 7 on a single die. **0**
2. It will snow in Atlanta, Georgia in August. **0**
3. A 2-headed coin will come up heads when tossed. **1**

The spinner at the right is spun once. Find each probability. Write each probability as:
a. *a fraction in lowest terms.* **b.** *a percent.*

4. Spinning a three **a.** $\frac{1}{8}$ **b.** $12\frac{1}{2}\%$
5. Spinning a one **a.** $\frac{1}{8}$ **b.** $12\frac{1}{2}\%$
6. Spinning an even number **a.** $\frac{1}{2}$ **b.** 50%
7. Spinning an odd number **a.** $\frac{1}{2}$ **b.** 50%
8. Spinning a number less than three **a.** $\frac{1}{4}$ **b.** 25%
9. Spinning a number greater than five **a.** $\frac{3}{8}$ **b.** $37\frac{1}{2}\%$

A coin purse contains four pennies, a nickel, three dimes, and two quarters. One coin is drawn without looking. Find each probability. Write each probability as:
a. a fraction in lowest terms **b.** a percent

10. Drawing a nickel **a.** $\frac{1}{10}$ **b.** 10%
11. Drawing a dime **a.** $\frac{3}{10}$ **b.** 30%
12. Drawing a penny **a.** $\frac{2}{5}$ **b.** 40%
13. Drawing a quarter **a.** $\frac{1}{5}$ **b.** 20%
14. Drawing a coin worth less than 25¢ **a.** $\frac{4}{5}$ **b.** 80%
15. Drawing a coin worth more than 25¢ **a.** $\frac{0}{10}$ **b.** 0%
16. There are six cards numbered 1 to 6. Jerry needs to pick an even number to win a game. He picks a card. What is the probability that it is an even number? **$\frac{1}{2}$, or 50%**
17. There are 125 plastic containers in a machine. Eight contain prizes. The rest are empty. What is the probability of getting a prize? **$\frac{8}{125}$, or $6\frac{2}{5}\%$**
18. There are four tickets numbered 2, 4, 6, and 8. Tim draws two tickets without looking. What is the probability that the sum of the numbers is even? **$\frac{1}{1}$, or 100%**
19. A box contains 15 chips, 3 white, 7 blue, and 5 green. You pick one without looking. What is the probability that it is not green? **$\frac{2}{3}$, or $66\frac{2}{3}\%$**
20. One match box contains clips, another contains erasers, and a third contains stamps. The boxes are not labeled. Nick chooses one box. What is the probability that the box does not contain clips? **$\frac{2}{3}$, or $66\frac{2}{3}\%$**
21. There are 8 red socks and 6 blue socks in a drawer. Without looking, you pick a sock. What is the difference between the probability of picking a red sock and the probability of picking a blue sock? **$\frac{1}{7}$, or $14\frac{2}{7}\%$**

2. If you win by getting a 7, how many possible ways are there for you to win? (1)
3. What is the ratio that compares the possible ways of winning to the total possible outcomes? ($\frac{1}{6}$)

Work through Example 1. Make sure students understand the meaning of the probability ratio before going on to Example 2.

Exercise 18 provides an opportunity for students to apply inductive reasoning. Ask students to discuss how they might prove that the probability of getting an even sum is 1 without doing the problem. (All possible outcomes are even since the sum of any two even numbers is even.)

3 Close

Summary: Have students explain how to find the probability of an event.

Evaluation
Guided Practice: Ex. 2–14 even
Independent Practice: Ex. 1–15 odd, 16–21

Extension

Have students find the following probabilities.

You have a standard deck of 52 playing cards.

1. What is the probability of drawing a red card? ($\frac{26}{52}$, or $\frac{1}{2}$)
2. What is the probability of drawing an ace? ($\frac{4}{52}$, or $\frac{1}{13}$)
3. What is the probability of drawing a face card? ($\frac{12}{52}$, or $\frac{3}{13}$)

Objective

Student will

1. review the skills, concepts, and applications in the first part of Chapter 2.
2. maintain key skills and concepts taught in Chapter 1.

Using the Page

Exercises 1–10 provide an informal assessment of the student's mastery of the major skills and concepts presented in the first half of Chapter 2. Each item is referenced to the related pages where the particular item was presented. These exercises parallel the quiz provided in the *Teacher's ResourceBank.*™

A quiz covering the second half of the chapter is also provided in the *Teacher's ResourceBank.*™

Exercises 11–24 maintain skills and concepts taught in Chapter 1.

Mid-Chapter Review

Solve. Use the method you prefer. (Pages 22–23)

1. Ed needs to buy a sweater. Two styles are on sale, a pullover and a cardigan. Each style is available in four colors,—blue, red, yellow, and green. How many choices does Ed have? **8 choices**
2. Rosa can order a cheese, a roast beef, or a tuna sandwich on whole wheat, white, or rye bread. How many choices of sandwiches does Rosa have? **9 choices**
3. On their way home, Ed and his friends had dinner at a cafe. They could choose from 3 appetizers, 6 entrees, and 4 desserts. How many three-course dinner choices were available? **72 choices**
4. A new motorcycle is available in four different models and in 5 different colors. How many different choices for motorcycles are there? **20 choices**

Find the number of permutations. (Pages 24–25)

5. In how many different ways can 4 people at a diner choose 4 stools at the counter? **24 ways**
6. How many 6-digit numbers can be formed from the digits 0, 2, 4, 6, 8, and 9, if the digits cannot be repeated? **720 ways**

A deck of cards contains 8 blue cards, 6 yellow cards, 8 green cards, and 2 red cards. The cards are shuffled and one card is drawn. Find each probability. Write each probability as:

a. *a fraction in lowest terms* **b.** *a percent.* (Pages 26–27)

7. Drawing a yellow card **a. $\frac{1}{4}$ b. 25%**
8. Drawing a green card **a. $\frac{1}{3}$ b. $33\frac{1}{3}$%**
9. Drawing a red card **a. $\frac{1}{12}$ b. $8\frac{1}{3}$%**
10. Drawing a purple card **a. $\frac{0}{24}$ b. 0%**

MAINTENANCE

Find the mean, median, and mode. (Pages 10–13)

11. 2, 4, 8, 7, 4, 9, 1 **Mean: 5; Median: 4; Mode: 4**
12. 10, 15, 13, 21, 18, 15, 15, 21 **Mean: 16; Median: 15; Mode: 15**
13. 102, 115, 85, 94 **Mean: 99; Median: 98; Mode: None**
14. 22, 22, 22, 25, 34 **Mean: 25; Median: 22; Mode: 22**
15. 16, 12, 18, 4 **Mean: 12.5; Median: 14; Mode: None**
16. 42, 42, 18, 25, 21 **Mean: 29.6; Median: 25; Mode: 42**
17. 8, 10, 7, 7, 6, 2, 9 **Mean: 7; Median: 7; Mode: 7**
18. 104, 121, 118, 118, 99, 100 **Mean: 110; Median: 111; Mode: 118**

Write each fraction in lowest terms. (Page 382)

19. $\frac{15}{25}$ **$\frac{3}{5}$**
20. $\frac{32}{48}$ **$\frac{2}{3}$**
21. $\frac{25}{30}$ **$\frac{5}{6}$**
22. $\frac{12}{21}$ **$\frac{4}{7}$**
23. $\frac{22}{33}$ **$\frac{2}{3}$**
24. $\frac{36}{54}$ **$\frac{2}{3}$**

Math and Large Populations

This frequency table shows the results of tossing 10 pennies all at once. This was done 100 times. Because this experiment was done 100 times, you can read the probability as a percent from the Frequency column. In this experiment, the **frequency** is the number of times each number of heads was obtained. Thus, the probability of tossing 5 heads is

25 out of 100 or **25%.**

Number of heads per toss	Tally	Frequency
0	I	1
1	II	2
2	IIII	4
3	~~IIII~~ ~~IIII~~ II	12
4	~~IIII~~ ~~IIII~~ ~~IIII~~ ~~IIII~~	20
5	~~IIII~~ ~~IIII~~ ~~IIII~~ ~~IIII~~ ~~IIII~~	25
6	~~IIII~~ ~~IIII~~ ~~IIII~~ III	18
7	~~IIII~~ ~~IIII~~ I	11
8	IIII	4
9	II	2
10	I	1

This is a graph of the results of this experiment. The *bell-shaped* curve is called a **normal curve.**

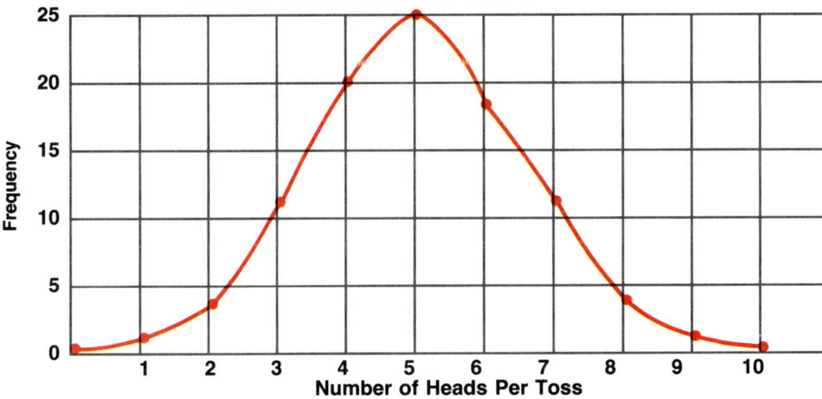

If you surveyed a large number of people regarding height, weight, or waist size, the graph of the data would be like a normal curve.

PROJECTS

A. Perform the coin–tossing experiment 100 times. Place the 10 coins in a cup and then "dump" the coins. Record the results in a frequency distribution table. Graph the results. Is it a normal curve? **Answers will vary.**

B. Prepare a frequency-distribution table of the heights of all the students in your class. Then graph the results. Although the number of students is not a large population, compare your graph with the normal curve. **Answers will vary.**

Objective

Student will compare the graph of experimental data to the graph of a normal curve.

Overview

This page is an extension of the skills and ideas presented in the previous lessons of this chapter. Since the content presented on this page is not included in the Chapter Review or Chapter Test, its use is optional.

Using the Pages

You may wish to have students work this lesson in small groups or you may wish to work with the class. Using it with the class, focus students' attention on the frequency table while one student reads the first paragraph. Then focus students' attention on the graph of the normal curve and discuss its shape.

You may want students to do Project A in pairs, with one tossing and one recording. For Project B, you may want to put a frequency-distribution table on the chalkboard and have students record their heights on the chart. Then have everyone make a record of the data and make a graph.

Problem-Solving Skills

Gathering information (Projects A and B)
Making a table (Projects A and B)
Making a graph (Projects A and B)
Interpreting information (Projects A and B)

Lesson Resources

Maintenance: See below.
Reteaching/Alternate Teaching Strategy: See the margin on page 31.
Practice: Activity Worksheet 10
Enrichment: See the enrichment topic "Sampling and Random Numbers" on page 34.

Objectives

Student will

1. use a sample to determine the probability of an event.
2. use probability to make predictions.

Maintenance

Write each fraction as a percent.

1. $\frac{21}{42}$ ANS: 50%
2. $\frac{25}{40}$ ANS: 62.5%

Multiply.

3. 0.37×400 ANS: 148
4. 0.58×350 ANS: 203
5. There are 2500 students at Walker High School. Twenty-five percent of the students walk to school and 35% of the students ride the bus. How many students do not walk or ride the bus? ANS: 1000

1 Lesson Focus

Motivation: Have the students discuss how they might decide on how many hot dogs to buy for a concession stand at a football game where 2000 people are expected to attend.

Purpose: This lesson will show students how to use a survey to predict the likely outcomes and how to use that information in planning.

Strategy: PREDICTING

You are the manager of a fast-food stand at the high school stadium. You expect to serve about 2000 customers at the next game. You sell only hot dogs, hamburgers, and pizza by the slice.

PROBLEM Should you order the same amount of each item?

It is impossible to find out what food each of the 2000 customers prefer. So you take a poll of 200 students. This is your **sample.**

Poll Question: Which food do you prefer?

Hot dogs Hamburgers Pizza

You collect the data and organize it in a table.

	Hot dog	Hamburgers	Pizza
Seniors	12	20	18
Juniors	9	28	13
Sophomores	10	25	15
Freshman	13	17	20
Totals	44	90	66

1. Find the probability that a customer will choose each of the following. Write the probability as a fraction in lowest terms.
   a. Hot dog $\frac{11}{50}$ b. Hamburger $\frac{9}{20}$ c. Pizza $\frac{33}{100}$

$$P(\text{hot dog}) = \frac{11}{50}, \text{ or } 50\overline{)11.00} = 0.22 = \mathbf{22\%}$$

P(hot dog) means the "probability of choosing a hot dog."

2. Express P(hamburger) and P(pizza) as percents. 45% 33%

EXAMPLE How much should you order of each food?

Think: Since 22% of the students polled prefer hot dogs,
22% of $2000 = 0.22 \times 2000 = \mathbf{440}$ ← 400 hot dogs
Similarly,
45% of $2000 = 0.45 \times 2000 = \mathbf{900}$ ← 900 hamburgers
33% of $2000 = 0.33 \times 2000 = \mathbf{660}$ ← 660 slices of pizza

Selecting the sample is the key for making predictions.

3. If you ran out of hotdogs before the game was half over, what would this tell you about your sample? It did not truly represent the food preferences of the customers at the game.

The information collected in a survey is called **empirical data.** The probability you arrive at by using this data is called **empirical probability.**

EXERCISES

The Gulfview City Commission plans to improve the streets around the public beach, the zoo, the theme park, and the wildlife sanctuary. The commissioners have $15,000,000 to spend.

The commissioners decide to base the amount spent for each attraction on the attraction's popularity. They poll 2000 residents to find their favorite attraction.

1. Write a poll question to determine the public's favorite attraction. **Answers will vary.**

The table below shows the results of the poll.

Favorite Local Attraction

Attraction	Number of People
Public beach	800
Zoo	280
Theme park	700
Wildlife sanctuary	220

For Exercises 2–5, find the probability of a resident's choosing each of the following as a favorite attraction.

a. *Write the probability as a fraction in lowest terms.*

b. *Write the probability as a percent.*

2. Public beach **a.** $\frac{2}{5}$ **b. 40%**
3. Zoo **a.** $\frac{7}{50}$ **b. 14%**
4. Theme park **a.** $\frac{7}{20}$ **b. 35%**
5. Wildlife sanctuary **a.** $\frac{11}{100}$ **b. 11%**

For Exercises 6–9, use your answers to Exercises 2–5 to determine how much of the $15,000,000 the city should spend on each project.

6. Public beach **$6,000,000**
7. Zoo **$2,100,000**
8. Theme park **$5,250,000**
9. Wildlife sanctuary **$1,650,000**

10. The table at the right shows attendance at each attraction during the month following the completion of the projects. Do the attendance figures agree with the predicted popularity of each attraction? If not, how do the attendance figures differ? **No; Public beach: 15%, Zoo: 20%, Theme park: 45%, Wildlife sanctuary: 20%**

Attraction	Attendance
Public beach	105,000
Zoo	140,000
Theme park	315,000
Wildlife sanctuary	140,000
TOTAL	700,000

2 Teaching the Lesson

Have a volunteer read the introductory paragraph and the Problem. Focus students' attention on the table and ask questions such as these.

1. What can you expect to be the most popular item at the concession stand? (Hamburgers)
2. What fraction of the students surveyed preferred hamburgers? ($\frac{90}{200}$, or $\frac{9}{20}$)
3. What percent of the students preferred hamburgers? (45%)
4. If you planned on buying 1000 items for the concession stand, how many would be hamburgers? (450)

Work through the Example with the students. Emphasize that probability is a prediction tool. It does not guarantee that an event will happen.

3 Close

Summary: Have students look at the question "Which food do you prefer?" Have students discuss if this survey will help them know how much food to buy or only the proportions.

Evaluation
Guided Practice: Ex. 1, 2
Independent Practice: Ex. 3–10

Problem-Solving Skills

Reading a table (Ex. 2–5, 10)
Interpreting information (Ex. 6–9)

Critical Thinking

Question 3 (in Lesson)

Alternate Teaching Strategy

You may wish to have the students work this lesson in small groups. Direct them to discuss the Problem and Example on page 30 and to answer questions 1–3 in the lesson. They should discuss their ideas for the answers for Exercises 1–10 and record the group consensus for each.

Lesson Resources

Maintenance: See below.
Reteaching/Alternate Teaching Strategy: p. M-20
Practice: p. M-20
Enrichment: p. M-20

Objectives

Student will

1. Find the odds in favor of an event.
2. Find the odds against an event.

Maintenance

1. Subtract: 3456 − 353 ANS: 3103
2. Subtract: 8987 − 7909 ANS: 1078
3. Find 48% of 75. ANS: 36
4. Find 70% of 50. ANS: 35
5. Robert earns $1560 each month. He saves 15% of this amount. How much will he save in 6 months? ANS: $1404

1 Lesson Focus

Motivation: Have students discuss what they think the odds tell you about a game of chance.

Purpose: This lesson will show students the difference between odds and probability.

2 Teaching the Lesson

Focus students' attention on the first table. Ask these questions.

1. How does the probability column differ from the odds column? (Answers will vary.)
2. What does the numerator in the probability tell you? (Favorable outcomes)
3. What does the denominator in the probability tell you? (Total possible outcomes)

What Are the Odds?

Every time you shop at Perkin's Grocery, you get a game card. The instructions on the back of the card include the probability of winning and the odds for winning.

As the table shows, there are 115 successful ways out of 100,000 possible ways of winning a camera.

	Probability	Odds
New Car	$\frac{1}{1,000,000}$	1 to 999,999
Color TV	$\frac{19}{500,000}$	19 to 499,981
Stereo	$\frac{23}{250,000}$	23 to 249,977
Camera	$\frac{115}{100,000}$	115 to 99,885

1. How many ways are there of not winning a camera? **99,885 ways**

To find the odds in favor of winning, you use this ratio.

$$\text{Odds in Favor} = \frac{\text{Number of Successful Ways}}{\text{Number of Unsuccessful Ways}}$$

Odds in favor of winning a camera $= \frac{115}{99,885}$, or **115 to 99,885.**

Since the odds in favor of winning a camera are 115 to 99,885, the odds against winning a camera are **99,885 to 115.**

PROBLEM A pair of dice are tossed. What are the odds in favor of rolling a 7 or an 11?

This table shows all the possible ways for a pair of dice to land.

First Die \ Second Die	⚀	⚁	⚂	⚃	⚄	⚅
⚀	⚀⚀	⚀⚁	⚀⚂	⚀⚃	⚀⚄	⚀⚅
⚁	⚁⚀	⚁⚁	⚁⚂	⚁⚃	⚁⚄	⚁⚅
⚂	⚂⚀	⚂⚁	⚂⚂	⚂⚃	⚂⚄	⚂⚅
⚃	⚃⚀	⚃⚁	⚃⚂	⚃⚃	⚃⚄	⚃⚅
⚄	⚄⚀	⚄⚁	⚄⚂	⚄⚃	⚄⚄	⚄⚅
⚅	⚅⚀	⚅⚁	⚅⚂	⚅⚃	⚅⚄	⚅⚅

Table 1

This table shows the sum for each of the ways show in Table 1.

+ (First Die \ Second Die)	1	2	3	4	5	6
1	2	3	4	5	6	(7)
2	3	4	5	6	(7)	8
3	4	5	6	(7)	8	9
4	5	6	(7)	8	9	10
5	6	(7)	8	9	10	(11)
6	(7)	8	9	10	(11)	12

Table 2

2. What is the total number of possible sums in Table 2? **36**
3. How many ways are there of rolling a 7 or an 11? **8**

4. How many ways are there of not rolling a 7 or an 11? 28

Thus, the odds in favor of rolling a 7 or an 11 $= \frac{8}{28} = \frac{2}{7}$, or **2 to 7.**

5. What are the odds against rolling a 7 or an 11? 7 to 2

EXERCISES

For Exercises 1–4, refer to the table at the top of page 32 to find the odds.

1. What are the odds in favor of winning a new car? 1 to 999,999
2. What are the odds against winning a new car? 999,999 to 1
3. What are the odds in favor of winning a stereo? 23 to 249,977
4. What are the odds against winning a stereo? 249,977 to 23

Bill and Maria are playing the board game Big Bucks. Part of the rules require them to draw from a stack of cards every time they land on a certain space. Complete the table by finding the odds in favor and the odds against drawing each type of card.

	Card	Probability	Odds in Favor	Odds Against
5.	Payday	$\frac{1}{6}$	? 1 to 5	? 5 to 1
6.	Advance 3 places	$\frac{2}{9}$	? 2 to 7	? 7 to 2
7.	Collect $3500.	$\frac{1}{8}$	? 1 to 7	? 7 to 1
8.	Pay a $2000 fine.	$\frac{7}{36}$	? 7 to 29	? 29 to 7
9.	Go backward 5 places.	$\frac{7}{24}$	? 7 to 17	? 17 to 7

For Exercises 10–19, two dice are tossed. Refer to Tables 1 and 2 on page 32 to find the odds.

10. What are the odds in favor of rolling a 2? 1 to 35
11. What are the odds against rolling a 2? 35 to 1
12. What are the odds in favor of rolling a 10? 1 to 11
13. What are the odds against rolling a 10? 11 to 1
14. What are the odds in favor of rolling a 3 or an 11? 1 to 8
15. What are the odds against rolling a 3 or 11? 8 to 1
16. What are the odds in favor of rolling a 6 or a 7? 11 to 25
17. What are the odds against rolling a 6 or a 7? 25 to 11
18. What are the odds in favor of rolling a 2 or a 12? 1 to 17
19. What are the odds against rolling a 4 or an 8? 7 to 2

4. How could you use the probability column to determine the odds column? (First number is the numerator, second number is the difference between the numerator and the denominator.)

Have a student answer question 1 in the lesson. Point out the difference in the ratio for odds and the ratio for probability shown on page 26. Then work through the Problem, having students answer questions 2–5.

3 *Close*

Summary: Have students discuss and list the differences and similarities of odds and probability.

Evaluation
Guided Practice: Ex. 1–4
Independent Practice: Ex. 5–19

Problem-Solving Skills

Reading a table (Ex. 1–4, 10–19)
Completing a table (Ex. 5–9)

NOTE: A quiz covering the second half of the chapter is provided in the *Teacher's ResourceBank™*.

Objective

Student will

1. use a table of random numbers to solve problems.
2. use a spinner to make a table of random numbers.

Overview

This topic is optional. The word "Enrichment" that appears to the right of the title in this Teacher's Edition does not appear in the student textbook. Therefore, this material is not included in the Chapter Review and Chapter Test.

Using the Page

You may wish to have students work this Enrichment in small groups or you may wish to work with the class.

Problem-Solving Skills

Making a list (Ex. 1)
Reading a table (Ex. 1, 2)
Making a table (Ex. 3)
Interpreting information (Ex. 4)

Sampling and Random Numbers ENRICHMENT

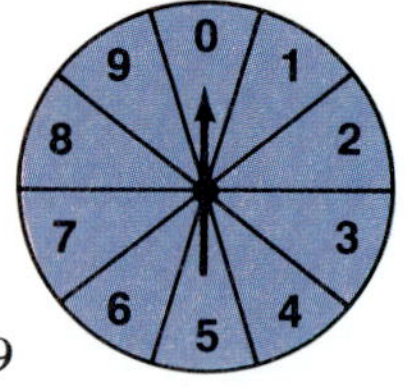

Using *random numbers* is a popular method for selecting a sample. **Random numbers** are the digits

0, 1, 2, 3, 4, 5, 6, 7, 8, 9

that are arranged so that each digit occurs about the same number of times.

A table of random numbers can be made by using a spinner. After each spin, write down the digit on which the arrow lands.

EXAMPLE There are 300 freshmen in your high school. You plan to poll 30 students.

[1] Assign a number 1 to 300 to each student. Use 001 for 1, 002 for 2, and so on up to 300.

[2] Look at the first 3 digits only of each number in Column 1. Write the 3 digits when they name a number from 1 to 300. For example, the first 3 digits in Column 1 are 779. Ignore these. The first 3 digits you will write are in Line 6: **289**

[3] Read down the columns until you have chosen 30 numbers.

Here are the first fifteen.

289	071	070	296	069
094	023	293	007	143
103	010	024	053	127

Table of Random Numbers

LINE \ COL.	I	II	III	IV
1	77921	06907	11008	42751
2	99562	72905	56420	69994
3	96301	91977	05463	07972
4	89579	14342	63661	10281
5	85475	36857	53342	53988
6	28918	69578	88231	33276
7	63553	40961	48235	03427
8	09429	93969	52636	92737
9	10365	61129	87529	85689
10	07119	97336	71048	08178
11	51085	12765	51821	51259
12	02368	21382	52404	60268
13	01011	54092	33362	94904
14	52162	53916	46369	58586
15	07056	97628	33787	09998
16	48663	91245	85828	12346
17	54164	58492	22421	74103
18	32639	32363	05597	24200
19	29334	27001	87637	87308
20	02488	33062	28834	07351
21	81525	72295	04839	96423
22	29676	20591	68086	26432
23	00742	57392	39064	66432
24	05366	04213	25669	26422
25	91921	26418	64117	94305

EXERCISES

1. Complete the list of 30 numbers. **213, 270, 205, 042, 264, 110, 054, 224, 055, 288, 048, 256, 079, 102, 034**
2. Each of the 150 people at the awards dinner receives a number from 1 to 150. You plan to give away 15 prizes. Begin with Column II and list the 15 winning numbers. **069, 143, 127, 042, 110, 054, 055, 048, 079, 102, 034, 081, 099, 123, 073**
3. Use a spinner such as the one above to make a table of 100 random numbers. Each number is to have four digits. **Answers will vary.**
4. Count how many times each of the digits 0 through 9 occurs in your table. Is the number of times approximately the same for each digit? **Yes**

The Chapter Summary contains a listing of the procedures that are related to the skills and concepts presented in the chapter. An example that illustrates each procedure appears at the right of each procedure. This listing is intended to assist the student with the Chapter Review that follows.

Chapter Summary

IMPORTANT IDEAS

1. If there are r choices for the way one thing can be done and s choices for the way another thing can be done, then together they may be done in $r \times s$ different ways.

   1. A print shop sells 5 different sizes of paper. Each size is available in 4 colors. Total choices: $5 \times 4 =$ **20**

2. To find the total number of different ways that the members of a group can be arranged, find the product of the number of choices for the first item, the number of choices for the second item, and so on.

   2. There are 3 people and 3 different notebooks. There are $3 \times 2 \times 1$, or 6 different ways 3 people could be given **3 notebooks.**

3. To find the probability that an event will occur, use this ratio.

$$\frac{\textbf{Number of Successful Ways}}{\textbf{Number of Possible Ways}}$$

   3. A die is tossed. What is the probability of getting a 2? $P(2) = \frac{1}{6}$

4. To find the odds in favor of an event occurring, use this ratio.

$$\frac{\textbf{Number of Successful Ways}}{\textbf{Number of Unsuccessful Ways}}$$

   4. Two dice are rolled. What are the odds in favor of rolling a 5 or a 9? **Ans.:** $\frac{8}{28}$, or $\frac{2}{7}$

5. To find the odds against an event's occurring:

   [1] Write a fraction for the odds in favor of the event.

   [2] Write the reciprocal of the fraction.

   5. Odds in favor: $\frac{2}{5}$

      Odds against: $\frac{5}{2}$

Objective

To review the important terms, skills, problem solving, and applications presented in Chapter 2.

Overview

The Chapter Review is structured in two parts. Part 1 is a review of the important terms that were introduced in the chapter. Part 2 reviews the skills, the problem-solving strategies, and applications that were presented in the chapter. Each item in the Chapter Review is referenced to the related pages where the concept, skill, or application was presented.

Using the Pages

You may wish to assign this Chapter Review for homework to treat it as a class review prior to administering the formal Chapter Test. In doing this, it is suggested that you only use the even- or odd-numbered exercises. You can then use the remaining exercises as a bank for use later.

Chapter Review

Part 1: VOCABULARY

For Exercises 1–6, choose from the box at the right the word(s) that complete(s) each statement.

empirical
sample space
tree diagram
odds
statistics
probability
permutations

1. To find the number of choices, you can use a __?__. (Page 22) **tree diagram**
2. The different ways in which items can be arranged are called __?__. (Page 24) **permutations**
3. Dividing the number of successful ways by the number of possible ways gives the __?__. (Page 26) **probability**
4. The probability you arrive at by using information collected in a survey is called __?__ probability. (Page 31) **empirical**
5. The possible ways in which an event can occur is called the __?__. (Page 26) **sample space**
6. Dividing the number of successful ways by the number of unsuccessful ways gives the __?__ in favor of the event. (Page 32) **odds**

Part 2: SKILLS AND APPLICATIONS

For Exercises 7–8, draw a tree diagram. (Pages 22–23)

7. A snack bar sells 3 different snacks and 2 different beverages. How many different choices of a snack and beverage are there? **6 choices**
8. Clara can choose one of 3 car models in one of 4 colors. How many different choices are there? **12 choices**

For Exercises 9–10, use the Fundamental Principle of Counting. (Pages 22–23)

9. You can buy football T-shirts in red or white with the team logo of any one of the 28 National Football League teams. How many choices are there? **56 choices**
10. Judy's refrigerator contains a soft drink can, a bottle of juice, a carton of milk, and a jug of water. The cupboard contains 6 cups of different colors. How many choices for having a drink are there? **24 choices**

Find the number of permutations. (Pages 24–25)

11. Nine employees play on the company softball team. How many different ways are there to name the batting order? **362,880 ways**
12. A radio disc jockey will play 8 records in the next half hour. In how many different orders can the records be played? **40,320 orders**

These four cards were shuffled and placed face down. One card is drawn. Find each probability. Write each probability as:
a. *A fraction in lowest terms.*
b. *a percent.* (Pages 26–27)

13. Drawing the ace of spades **a.** $\frac{1}{4}$ **b.** 25%

14. Drawing the 10 of clubs **a.** $\frac{1}{4}$ **b.** 25%

15. Drawing an ace **a.** $\frac{1}{2}$ **b.** 50%

16. Drawing a black card **a.** $\frac{3}{4}$ **b.** 75%

17. Drawing a heart **a.** $\frac{0}{4}$ **b.** 0%

18. Not drawing an ace **a.** $\frac{1}{2}$ **b.** 50%

The table below shows the results of a survey of students at Middleton High School. Use this information for Exercises 19–22.

Lunch Preferences	
	Number of Students
Buy a hot lunch.	35
Buy a cold lunch.	90
Do not eat lunch.	5
Bring a bag lunch.	20
TOTAL	150

For Exercises 19–22, find each probability. Write the probability as a percent. (Pages 30–31)

19. A student will buy a hot lunch. $23\frac{1}{3}$%

20. A student will buy a cold lunch. 60%

21. A student does not eat lunch. $3\frac{1}{3}$%

22. A student brings a bag lunch. $13\frac{1}{3}$%

There are 1200 students at Middleton High School. For Exercises 23–26, use your answers to Exercises 19–22. (Pages 30–31)

23. How many students would you expect to buy a hot lunch? **About 280 students**

24. How many students would you expect to buy a cold lunch? **About 720 students**

25. How many students would you expect not to eat lunch? **About 40 students**

26. How many students would you expect to bring a bag lunch? **About 160 students**

For Exercises 27–30, two dice are tossed. Refer to Tables 1 and 2 on page 32 to find the odds. (Pages 32–33)

27. What are the odds in favor of rolling a 4? **1 to 11**

28. What are the odds against rolling a 4? **11 to 1**

29. What are the odds in favor of rolling a 5 or a 7? **5 to 13**

30. What are the odds against rolling a 5 or a 7? **13 to 5**

Objective

To informally assess students' mastering of the major skills, concepts, problem solving, and applications presented in Chapter 2.

Using the Page

After completing the Chapter Review with the class, you may wish to use this Chapter Test as an informal assessment. This Chapter Test parallels the formal chapter tests (Form A and Form B) provided in the *Teacher's ResourceBank.*™

Chapter Test

1. Iola has the choice of taking a one-week, two-week, or three-week vacation. She has the choice of going to the mountains to ski or to the shore to swim. How many choices does Iola have? **6 choices**

2. A restaurant serves 5 kinds of sandwiches, 3 kinds of salad, and 4 beverages. You want to order a sandwich, a salad, and a beverage. How many different choices are there? **60 choices**

3. In how many different ways can 5 people choose 5 seats? **120 ways**

4. In how many different ways can 7 people choose 7 seats? **5040 ways**

The spinner at the right is spun once. Find each probability. Write each probability as:
a. *a fraction in lowest terms.*
b. *a percent*

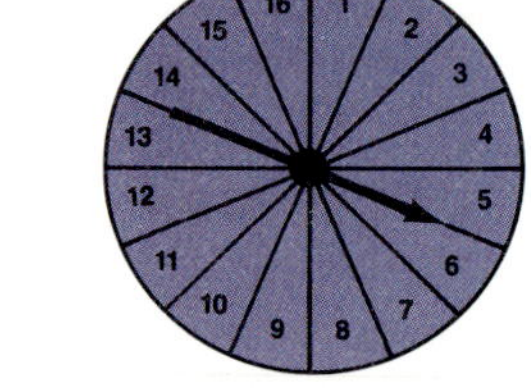

5. Spinning a 6 **a.** $\frac{1}{16}$ **b.** $6\frac{1}{4}\%$

6. Spinning an even number **a.** $\frac{1}{2}$ **b.** 50%

7. Spinning a number less than 7 **a.** $\frac{3}{8}$ **b.** $37\frac{1}{2}\%$

8. Spinning a number greater than 7 **a.** $\frac{9}{16}$ **b.** $56\frac{1}{4}\%$

The table at the right shows the results of a survey of students at a certain middle school. For Exercises 9–12, find the probability that a student will prefer each type of music. Write the probability as a percent.

Favorite Music	
Music	***Number of Students***
Rock	80
Country	60
Classical	20
Folk	40
TOTAL	200

9. Rock **40%**

10. Country **30%**

11. Classical **10%**

12. Folk **20%**

There are 1400 students at the middle school.

13. How many students would you expect to prefer rock music? **About 560 students**

14. How many students would you expect to prefer classical or folk music? **About 420 students**

Lucy is a contestant on a game show. To win a prize, she must choose one box from among 8 boxes. Three of the boxes contain a prize. The others are empty.

15. What are the odds in favor of her winning a prize? **3 to 5**

16. What are the odds against her winning a prize? **5 to 3**

Cumulative Maintenance Chapters 1–2

Choose the correct answer. Choose **a, b, c,** *or* **d.**

1. What is the total value of eighteen \$5-bills, five \$10-bills, and thirteen \$20-bills? b

a. \$160 **b.** \$400
c. \$350 **d.** \$360

2. The salaries of five workers are \$275, \$305, \$280, \$325 and \$315. What is the median salary? b

a. \$315 **b.** \$305
c. \$1525 **d.** \$300

3. What is the probability of rolling a 12 with a pair of dice? d

a. $\frac{1}{6}$ **b.** 12 **c.** 1 **d.** $\frac{1}{36}$

4. The graph below shows how June spends her income. On which item does she spend the least amount of money? c

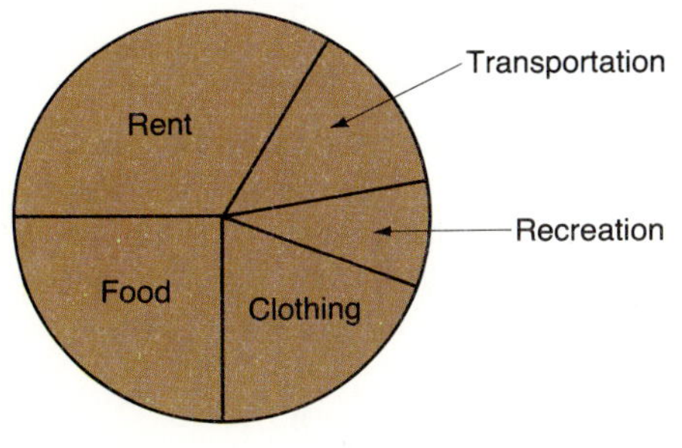

a. Rent **b.** Transportation
c. Recreation **d.** Clothing

5. During which month was the average temperature the highest? c

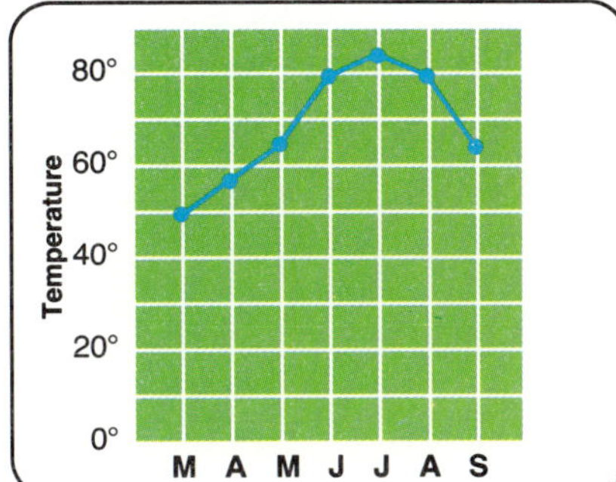

a. May **b.** June
c. July **d.** August

6. Write a per cent for $\frac{3}{4}$. d

a. 25% **b.** 65%
c. 12% **d.** 75%

7. Use the graph below to tell which product sold twice as well as product A. c

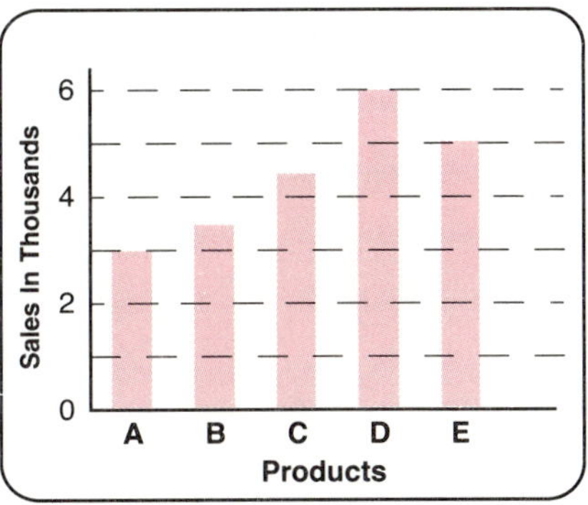

a. B **b.** C **c.** D **d.** E

Objective

To review the content presented in Chapters 1–2

Using the Pages

You may wish to use this Cumulative Maintenance as an informal assessment tool. These pages can be assigned for homework or they may be used as review in class.

NOTE: The *Teacher's ResourceBank*™ contains a Cumulative Test for Chapters 1–2. The Cumulative Test is presented in a standardized-test format.

8. Three football players have weights of 88 lb, 101 lb, and 90 lb. Find the mean. b

a. 90 **b.** 93
c. 279 **d.** 101

9. Add. Write your answer in lowest terms.

$\frac{3}{8} + \frac{1}{8} + \frac{5}{8}$ b

a. $\frac{7}{8}$ **b.** $1\frac{1}{8}$
b. $1\frac{1}{4}$ **d.** $\frac{11}{8}$

10. Find 15% of 80. a

a. 12 **b.** 120
c. 1.2 **d.** 1200

11. The circle graph below shows how one family spent its money while on vacation. How many degrees represent the section for "Gasoline"? d

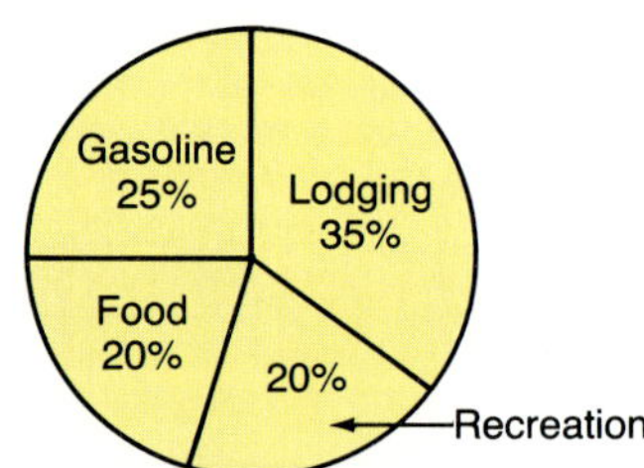

a. 45° **b.** 120° **c.** 180° **d.** 90°

12. What is the probability of getting a 3 on one spin in the game below? a

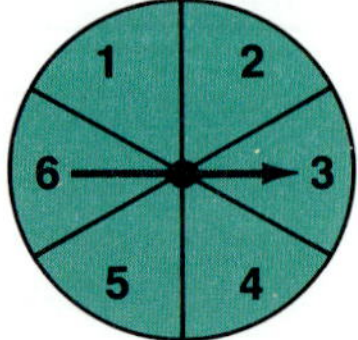

a. $\frac{1}{6}$ **b.** $\frac{1}{3}$ **c.** $\frac{1}{5}$ **d.** 1

13. What are the odds in favor of rolling a number greater than 4 on a single roll of one die? b

a. $\frac{1}{3}$ **b.** $\frac{1}{2}$ **c.** $\frac{1}{6}$ **d.** 2

14. Write a decimal for 58%. c

a. 5.8 **b.** 0.058
c. 0.58 **d.** 58.0

15. Juan's 5 test grades wre 90, 85, 80, 95 and 85. What was the mode? d

a. 435 **b.** 87
c. 90 **d.** 85

16. Ruth wrote the name of each month on a separate slip of paper and put them in a box. She chose one slip. What is the probability that it was November? b

a. $\frac{1}{7}$ **b.** $\frac{1}{12}$
c. 1 **d.** $\frac{11}{12}$

Making Money

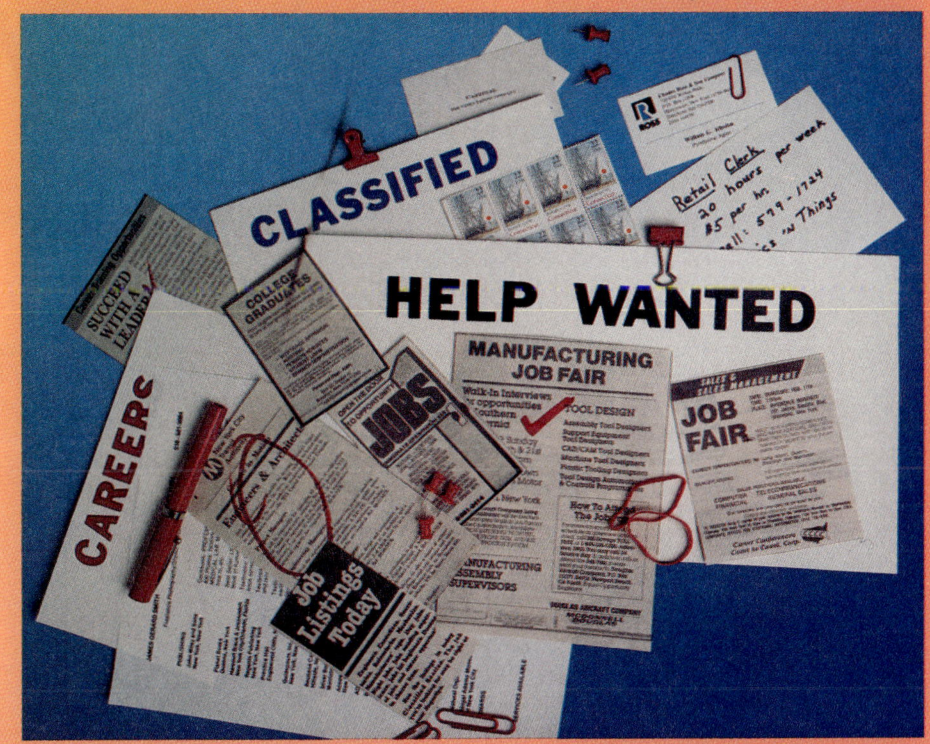

Bonnie Benedict and several of her friends are looking for their first jobs. Because they have no previous job experience, they have many questions to be answered before they can make sensible decisions about job opportunities and job offers.

- How much can they expect to earn per week, per month, and per year?
- For what kind of jobs can they expect to receive a commission?
- What is the difference between net pay and gross pay?
- What kinds of deductions are withheld from each paycheck?
- What is the FICA tax?

Chapter 3: Making Money

Overview

The focus of Chapter 3 is on the world of work,—deciding on a job, hourly wages, commission, deductions and net pay, and social security taxes and benefits. Because these topics are computation-oriented, the strategies of estimation and mental computation are presented as useful tools in determining the reasonableness of computational results. The *Consumer's Choice* on pages 60–61 presents a **situational lesson** in which students compare choices and make decisions in a real-life situation. Finally, a sample job application provides for student experience with concrete materials while an *Enrichment* lesson on fringe benefits gives students additional perspective on the world of work.

Using This Page

Have students read the introductory paragraph and questions. Have them list possible solutions to the problems presented. After completing the chapter, have students review their suggested solutions, comparing them with those presented in the lessons. You may wish to have students suggest other possible problems resulting from the situation described on this page and to discuss possible solutions.

You may wish to organize the class into small groups to complete the situational activity described on this *Using the Page.*

Lesson Resources

Maintenance: See below.
Reteaching/Alternate Teaching Strategy: p. M-20 (Visual 4)
Practice: p. M-20
Enrichment: p. M-20
Visual 4

Objectives

Student will

1. identify the important facts in classified "help wanted" ads.
2. solve one-step problems that involve weekly income.
3. solve multi-step problems that involve overtime pay.

Maintenance

1. Write $\frac{6}{8}$ in lowest terms. ANS: $\frac{3}{4}$
2. Round 32.435 to the nearest tenth. ANS: 32.4
3. Write 45% as a decimal. ANS: 0.45
4. Find the average. $412, $506, $395, $455 ANS: $442
5. A random drawing is made of the names of six girls and four boys in a class. One name is chosen. Find the probability that a girl's name is chosen. ANS: $\frac{3}{5}$

1 Lesson Focus

Motivation: Ask students to suggest some of the job conditions they would consider important when making a choice between job offers.

Purpose: This lesson shows students how to compute the total weekly income of a worker. It also reveals other factors besides income to consider when applying for a job.

Hourly Wages

Bonnie Benedict is looking for a job. She is interested in these three jobs that were advertised in the Daily Times.

1. Which job would pay the most per hour? **Delivery truck driver**
2. Which jobs might include some overtime? **Delivery truck driver, stock clerk**
3. On which job would Bonnie work fewer than 37 hours per week? **Hostess**
4. Besides the hourly wage and the amount of overtime, what other considerations might Bonnie have to think about? **benefits, uniforms**

Bonnie would receive $1\frac{1}{2}$, or 1.5 times the regular hourly rate when she works **overtime;** that is, when she works more than a 40 hour week. This rate is often called **time and a half.**

5. *Complete:*

   Regular pay per hour × ___?___ = Overtime pay per hour **1.5**

6. *Complete:*

   Total Pay = Pay for 40 hours + ___?___ **overtime pay**

EXAMPLE Suppose that Bonnie decides to take the job of stock clerk. Find her total pay for a 48-hour week.

READ What are the facts?

The job pays $6.60 per hour. Bonnie would receive 1.5 times the regular hourly rate for any hours she works over 40 hours.

PLAN To find her total pay, first answer these "hidden questions."

1. **What is the base pay for 40 hours?**
2. **What is the overtime pay per hour?**
3. **What is the overtime pay for 8 hours?**

SOLVE

[1] Find the pay for 40 hours.

$6.60 × 40 = **$264.00** ◀ *Base Pay*

[2] Find the overtime pay per hour.

$6.60 × 1.5 = **$9.90** ◀ *Overtime Pay Per Hour*

[3] Find the overtime pay for 8 hours.

$9.90 × 8 = **$79.20** ◀ *Overtime Pay*

[4] Now you can find the total weekly pay.

$264.00 + $79.20 = **$343.20** ◀ *Base Pay* + *Overtime Pay* = *Total Pay*

CHECK

Did you use all the facts correctly to solve the problem?

Bonnie's total pay for the week would be **$343.20.**

CHECK YOUR SKILLS

Multiply. For additional practice, see page 372.

1. $6.65 × 40 $266
2. $5.20 × $35\frac{1}{2}$ $184.60
3. $9.40 × $4\frac{1}{2}$ $42.30
4. $7.62 × 8 $60.96
5. $7.80 × $1\frac{1}{2}$ $11.70
6. $4.70 × 1.5 $7.05
7. $8.10 × 1.5 $12.15
8. $6.50 × $1\frac{1}{2}$ $9.75

Add or subtract as indicated. For additional practice, see page 368.

9. $123.60 + $62.70 $186.30
10. $236.15 + $47.35 $283.50
11. $173.96 + $59.49 $233.45

Divide. For additional practice, see page 377.

12. $79.20 ÷ $7.20 11
13. $91.20 ÷ $5.70 16
14. $77.40 ÷ $4.30 18
15. $62.10 ÷ $6.90 9

EXERCISES

Complete. Choose your answers from the box at the right.

Base pay
Base pay rate
Hours
Overtime hours
Overtime pay
Weekly pay

1. Base Pay = Hourly Pay Rate × Number of __?__ Hours
2. Overtime Pay Per Hour = 1.5 × __?__ Base Pay Rate
3. Total weekly pay = __?__ + overtime pay Base Pay
4. Total hours worked = 40 + Number of __?__ Overtime Hours
5. Overtime pay per hour × Number of overtime hours = __?__ Overtime Pay

[2] Teaching the Lesson

Direct the attention of students to the help wanted ads. Ask questions such as:

1. Where do you normally find ads like these? (In the classified section of a newspaper)
2. What are the most important facts in job ads? (Job title, location, pay scale, and how to apply)
3. What is meant by overtime? (Hours worked beyond what is normally expected, usually 40 hours per week)
4. What is meant by "good benefits?" (Health, hospitalization plans, vacation policies, etc.)
5. Who is benefited by "help wanted" ads besides the person who is looking for a job? (The prospective employer)

[3] Close

Summary: Explain what has been learned in this lesson: a. the use of classified ads to hunt for a job
b. computing the total weekly income of a job.

Evaluation

Guided Practice: Ex. 1–5, 7–13 odd
Independent Practice: Ex 6–12 even, 14–21

Extension

Have students write some help wanted ads which they think would be appealing to students their own age. Have them find the cost of ads in a local newspaper and compute the cost of each ad they write.

For Exercises 6–13, find the total weekly pay. Time and a half is paid for all hours worked over 40.

	Hourly Pay Rate	Hours Worked	Weekly Pay
6.	\$4.50	35	? \$157.50
7.	\$5.80	37	? \$214.60
8.	\$7.00	41	? \$290.50
9.	\$8.90	45	? \$422.75

	Hourly Pay Rate	Hours Worked	Weekly Pay
10.	\$6.40	$38\frac{1}{2}$	? \$246.40
11.	\$9.10	$25\frac{1}{2}$	? \$232.05
12.	\$10.20	46	? \$499.80
13.	\$ 8.40	$44\frac{1}{2}$	? \$392.70

For Exercises 14–17, refer to the advertisement for a delivery truck driver on page 42.

14. Suppose that Bonnie decides to become a delivery truck driver. Estimate how much she will be paid for a 40-hour week. **About \$280**

15. As a delivery truck driver, Bonnie will have to buy two uniforms at \$25 each. Estimate how many hours she will have to work to pay for the uniforms. **About 7 hours**

16. Bonnie will also have to spend about \$2.25 per week to get her driver's uniforms cleaned.

a. What will this cost for 50 weeks? **\$112.50**

b. About how many hours will she have to work to pay the cleaning costs for 50 weeks? **16 hours**

17. Delivery truck drivers sometimes get called to work on weekends. On Sundays or holidays, the worker earns **double time** (Base Pay Rate × 2). Suppose that Bonnie works a regular 40-hour week and 6 hours on a holiday. Find her total pay for that week. **\$358.80**

For Exercises 18–21, refer to the advertisements on page 42.

18. Suppose that Bonnie accepts the job as a restaurant hostess. How much will she earn for a 25-hour week? **\$162.50**

19. What is the least amount Bonnie could receive in tips as a hostess for a week (25 hours) in order for her total weekly pay to equal the total weekly pay (40 hours) of a stock clerk? **\$101.50**

20. Bonnie lives 3 miles from the business that needs a delivery truck driver, 10 miles from the warehouse, and 6 miles from the restaurant. At a cost of 25¢ per mile, how much would it cost her to travel back and forth to work per 5-day week for each job? **Driver: \$7.50; Clerk: \$25; Hostess: \$15**

21. a. List the advantages and disadvantages of each job Bonnie is considering. **See below.**

b. Which job would you choose if you were Bonnie Benedict? Give reasons for your choice. **Answers will var**

a. Advantages: Driver: highest hourly pay; Clerk: benefits; Hostess: No overtime
Disadvantages:
Driver: must buy own uniforms; Clerk: farthest distance to drive; Hostess: lowest hourly pay

Problem-Solving Skills

Reading an ad (Ex. 14–21)
Using estimation (Ex. 14, 15)
Solving a multi-step problem (Ex. 15, 17, 19, 20)
Making a comparison (Ex. 19, 20, 21a, 21b)

Critical Thinking

You may wish to have students work in small groups to solve these problems or you may wish to work with the class.

Question 4 (in Lesson); Ex. 21a and 21b

Estimation

Ex. 14–16

STRATEGY: USING A "HIDDEN QUESTION" TO SOLVE A MULTI-STEP PROBLEM

Commission

Bonnie's friend, Delores Sweeney, enjoys talking to people. Delores thinks that she would be good at a job involving selling. She has offers from two different companies. In both jobs, she will sell office products for a *commission*.

A **commission** is an amount of money paid for selling a product or service. The amount is based on a fixed percent of total sales, called the **rate of commission.** When the commission is the only pay received, it is called **straight commission.**

1. *Complete:* Amount of Commission = Total Sales × ___?___
   Rate of Commission
2. Total Sales: $54,000 Rate of Commission: 4% Commission: ___?___
   $2160

EXAMPLE 1

Delores was told that she could expect yearly sales of $750,000 if she works at United Office Products. How much would she be paid in straight commission for sales of $750,000?

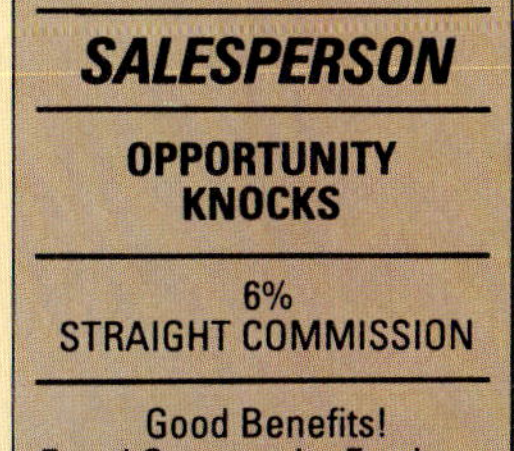

Total Sales	×	Rate of Commission	=	Commission
$750,000	×	0.06	=	**$45,000**

Delores can expect to earn **$45,000.**

3. How could Delores compute her expected monthly earnings at United Office Products? How much would this be per month?
   Divide her expected yearly earnings by 12; $3750.

EXAMPLE 2

The Imperial Pen Company told Delores that she could expect monthly sales of $75,000. How much can she expect to earn per month at Imperial Pen Company?

IMPERIAL PEN COMPANY
Good opportunity to earn high pay!
$800 per month + 4% commission on sales
Car provided. Will train. Call 305-391-0609 for appointment.

To find the total monthly earnings, first answer the "hidden question."

What is the amount of commission?

Lesson Resources

Maintenance: See below.
Reteaching/Alternate Teaching Strategy: p. M-21
Practice: p. M-21
Enrichment: p. M-21

Objectives

Student will

1. use a formula to find the amount of commission.
2. solve multi-step problems involving salary and commission.

Maintenance

Perform the indicated operations.

1. 2 lb 6 oz + 4 lb 10 oz ANS: 7 lb
2. $5200 × 0.5 ANS: $2600
3. $3\frac{1}{2} + 2\frac{1}{8}$ ANS: $5\frac{5}{8}$
4. 360.25 ÷ 12.5 ANS: 28.82
5. Parona Dairy sells whole milk, skim milk, and chocolate milk. Each type of milk is available in a quart, a half-gallon or a gallon container. How many different choices of milk are there? ANS: 9

1 Lesson Focus

Motivation: Ask students to name some types of occupations in which salaries are paid on a commission basis.

Purpose: In their future careers, some students may be paid on a commission basis. Thus, it is important for students to be able to compute and verify total earnings on a commission basis. Also, students may need to make a decision between accepting a salaried position, and one that pays on a commission basis.

2 Teaching the Lesson

As you discuss the two examples, direct students' attention to the ads describing the sales positions. Ask questions such as:

1. In Example 1, what two factors affect the amount of earnings? (Rate of commission and total sales)
2. In Example 2, what three factors affect the amount of earnings? (Rate of commission, total sales, salary)
3. Does either ad clarify whether or not expenses of the employee will be paid by the employer? Discuss. (Only the second ad indicates a car is provided. Applicant should clarify this before accepting a job.)

3 Close

Summary: Ask selected students what they have learned from the presentation of the lesson. Review the meanings of the new terms covered.

Evaluation
Guided Practice: Ex. 1–4, 6–14 even
Independent Practice: Ex. 5–13 odd, 15–20

Extension

Ask each student to write to the personnel department of a company to find out whether they pay on a commission or salary basis.

---

1 Find the amount of commission.

$75,000 × 0.04 = **$3000** ◀ *Total Sales × Rate of Commission = Commission*

2 Now you can find the total monthly earnings.

$3000 + $800 = **$3800** ◀ *Salary + Commission = Total Earnings*

4. What would be Delores' estimated earnings per year at Imperial Pen Company? $45,600
5. If you were Delores, which job would you take? Why? Answers will vary.

CHECK YOUR SKILLS

Write a decimal for each percent. For additional practice, see page 403.

1. 12% 0.12 2. 15% 0.15 3. 4% 0.04 4. 6% 0.06 5. $5\frac{1}{2}\%$ 0.055 6. $3\frac{1}{2}\%$ 0.035

Find each answer. For additional practice, see page 407.

7. 6% of $20,000 $1200 8. 16% of $24,600 $3936 9. $2\frac{1}{2}\%$ of $1200 $30 10. 5% of $100,000 $5000

Estimate each answer. For additional practice, see page 412. Estimates will vary.

11. $4\frac{1}{2}\%$ of $20,000 $1000 12. 5% of $79,900 $4000 13. $9\frac{1}{2}\%$ of $12,000 $1200 14. 9% of $69,000 $6300
15. 11% of $81,000 $8100 16. $5\frac{1}{2}\%$ of $100,000 $6000 17. $2\frac{1}{2}\%$ of $50,000 $1500 18. 8% of $91,000 $7200

EXERCISES

Complete. Choose your answers from the box at the right.

commission
rate of commission
salary
sales
straight commission

1. Commission is based on a fixed percent of the total _?_. sales
2. To find the amount of commission, multiply the total sales by the _?_. rate of commission
3. Doug works part time selling books. He receives a percent of the amount sold as his pay. This is called a _?_. straight commission
4. To find the total monthly income of a person not on straight commission, find the sum of the amount of commission and the monthly _?_. salary

For Exercises 5–8, find the amount of commission.

	Sales	Rate of Commission	Commission
5.	$15,000	3%	? $450
6.	$87,000	6%	? $5220
7.	$29,000	2%	? $580
8.	$10,500	5%	? $525

For Exercises 9–14, compute the total earnings.

	Salary	Sales	Rate of Commission	Total Earnings
9.	$580	$12,000	8%	? $1540
10.	$275	$20,000	3%	? $875
11.	$515	$15,200	4%	? $1123
12.	$420	$20,000	6%	? $1620
13.	$610	$100,000	2%	? $2610
14.	$580	$3000	15%	? $1030

15. Herb Gregg sold a house for $99,800. His commission was 5% of the selling price. Estimate how much commission he earned. **$5000**

16. As a salesperson, Joan Temple is paid a commission of $6\frac{1}{2}$%. Last year, she averaged sales of $86,000 per month. What was her average monthly commission? **$5590**

17. Carlos Lopez sells cars for a dealership. He receives a salary of $650 per month plus a commission of $1\frac{1}{2}$% on total sales. Find his total earnings for a month in which sales total $150,000. **$2900**

18. Ken Swift can choose to be paid for his work in either of these two ways.

a. By a straight commission of 5% on total sales

b. By a salary of $27,500 plus a commission of 2% on sales

On sales of $785,000, which choice will give Ken the greater total earnings? How much greater? **b; $3950**

19. Nell Larsen receives a yearly salary of $35,600. Next year, she will receive a salary of $20,000 plus a 3% commission on sales. What amount of sales will be needed next year for her earnings to equal this year's earnings? **$520,000**

20. If you were a salesperson, would you prefer to work for a salary only, a commission only, or a combination of salary and commission? Give reasons for your choice. **Answers will vary.**

Problem Solving Skills

Using estimation (Ex. 15)
Solving a multi-step problem (Ex. 17–19)
Making a comparison (Ex. 18–19)

Critical Thinking

You may wish to have students work in small groups to solve this problem or you may wish to work with the class.

Ex. 20

Estimation

Ex. 15

Lesson Resources

Maintenance: See below.
Reteaching/Alternate Teaching Strategy: p. M-21 (Visual 5)
Practice: p. M-21
Enrichment: p. M-21
Concrete Materials: Activity Worksheet 14A, and Visual 5
Visual 5

Objectives

Student will

1. identify the information on a statement of earnings.
2. solve multi-step problems that involve gross pay, deductions, and net pay.

Maintenance

1. Write $\frac{2}{6}$ in lowest terms. ANS: $\frac{1}{3}$
2. Add: \$28.13 + \$15.09 + \$247.88 ANS: \$291.10
3. Find 30% of 1200. ANS: 360
4. Write 1.5 as a percent. ANS: 150%
5. A coin purse contains 4 pennies, 3 nickels, and 2 dimes. One coin is chosen at random. What is the probability that the coin chosen is not a penny? ANS: $\frac{5}{9}$

1 Lesson Focus

Motivation: Ask students to name the different kinds of information found on a statement of earnings.

Purpose: This lesson shows students how to compute total deductions and net pay from a statement of earnings. This will help students check the accuracy of their earnings statements when they become wage-earners.

STRATEGY: USING A "HIDDEN QUESTION" TO SOLVE A MULTI-STEP PROBLEM

Deductions and Net Pay

Jeff Baker, a classmate of Bonnie's, found his job through the Quick Find Employment Agency. When he received his first weekly paycheck, he also received a statement of earnings.

DEPT.	EMPLOYEE		CHECK#	WEEK ENDING	GROSS PAY	NET PAY
14	Baker, J.		10-422	10/31/—	\$460.50	?
TAX DEDUCTIONS				PERSONAL DEDUCTIONS		
FIT	FICA	STATE	LOCAL	MEDICAL	LIFE INS.	MISC.
\$83.10	\$32.93	\$11.51	----	\$5.70	------	2.50

Gross pay is the total earnings for a pay period.

1. What was Jeff Baker's gross pay? \$460.50

Tax deductions show the amounts that are deducted (subtracted) from gross pay for taxes.

2. How much was deducted for **federal income taxes** (FIT)? \$83.10
3. How much was deducted for **social security taxes** (FICA or Federal Insurance Contribution Act)? \$32.93
4. How much was deducted for **state taxes?** \$11.51

Personal deductions include other items such as medical insurance which you have chosen to have subtracted from your gross pay.

5. How much was subtracted for personal deductions? \$8.20

Net pay, or **take-home pay,** is the amount left after the taxes and personal deductions are subtracted from gross pay.

6. *Complete:* Net Pay = __?__ − Total Deductions Gross Pay

EXAMPLE

What was Jeff Baker's net pay?

1 First find the total deductions.

Tax deductions: \$83.10 + \$32.93 + \$11.51 = \$127.54
Personal deductions: \$5.70 + \$2.50 = + 8.20
Total deductions: **\$135.74**

2 Now you can find the net pay.

\$460.50 − \$135.74 = **\$324.76** ◀ *Gross Pay* − *Total Deductions* = *Net Pay*

CHECK YOUR SKILLS

Add or subtract as indicated. For additional practice, see pages 368 and 369.

1. $4.69 + $73.62 + $143.52 **$221.83**
2. $39.46 + $69.81 + $93.27 **$202.54**
3. $34.08 + $102.87 + $45.49 + $52.92 **$235.36**
4. $157.83 + $44.53 + $26.15 + $7.92 **$236.43**
5. $225.00 − $136.64 **$88.36**
6. $510.00 − $173.50 **$336.50**
7. $358.40 − $73.74 **$284.66**
8. $279.80 − $62.91 **$216.89**
9. $463.54 − $102.60 **$360.94**
10. $558.26 − $134.15 **$424.11**

Multiply. For additional practice, see page 372.

11. $7.85 × 40 **$314**
12. $8.95 × 14 **$125.30**
13. $9.27 × 7 **$64.89**

EXERCISES

Complete.

1. Federal Insurance Contribution Act taxes are also called __?__ taxes. **social security**
2. Total income for a pay period is called __?__. **gross pay**
3. To find net pay, you __?__ the total deductions from gross pay. **subtract**
4. The amount in the box labeled FIT is for __?__ taxes. **federal income**

For Exercises 5–10, find the total deductions and the net pay.

	Gross Pay	Federal Tax	FICA Tax	State Tax	Medical Insurance	Pension Plan	Total Deductions	Net Pay
5.	$254	$19.46	$18.16	$2.92	—	$12.70	? **$53.24**	? **$200.76**
6.	$386	$33.78	$27.60	$5.07	$2.37	$30.88	? **$99.70**	? **$286.30**
7.	$214	$33.42	$15.30	$3.51	—	$10.70	? **$62.93**	? **$151.07**
8.	$336	$36.24	$24.02	$3.60	$1.89	$26.85	? **$92.60**	? **$243.40**
9.	$228	$25.52	$16.30	$2.45	$1.93	$11.40	? **$57.60**	? **$170.40**
10.	$410	$31.90	$29.32	$4.40	$2.04	$30.75	? **$98.41**	? **$311.59**

Find the missing amount on each statement of earnings.

11.

DEPT.	EMPLOYEE		CHECK#	WEEK ENDING	GROSS PAY	NET PAY
07	Schur, L.		54601	8/24/—	972.00	?
TAX DEDUCTIONS				PERSONAL DEDUCTIONS		
FIT	FICA	STATE	LOCAL	MEDICAL	LIFE INS.	MISC.
97.65	69.50	19.53	----	4.50	------	-----

$780.82

2 Teaching the Lesson

Focus the attention of students on the statement of earnings. Ask questions such as:

1. Why do you think employees receive a statement of earnings? (So they can make sure their earnings and deductions have been computed correctly)
2. What medical services might be covered by the medical deduction? (These could be items like health insurance, dental insurance, disability insurance, and so on.)
3. Why do you think there are no entries for Local Tax Deductions and for Life Insurance? (For this particular situation there is no local tax, and the employer apparently has no life insurance program.)
4. What services might be covered by Miscellaneous Deductions? (These could be items like union dues, supplemental pension plan contributions, credit union savings, and so forth.)
5. What is the length of the pay period? (One week)

3 Close

Summary: Have students recap the procedure for computing the net pay from a statement of earnings.

Evaluation
Guided Practice: Ex. 1–4, 5–9 odd
Independent Practice: 6–10 even, 11–20

Extension

Although these topics will be covered later in the course, have students find how the deductions for Federal Income Taxes, FICA Tax, and State Income Tax are computed.

Problem Solving Skills

Solving a multi-step problem (Ex. 12–13, 18–20)
Reading a chart (Ex. 12–13, 20)
Using estimation (Ex. 19)

Estimation Ex. 19

12.

DEPT.	EMPLOYEE	CHECK#		WEEK ENDING	GROSS PAY	NET PAY
A	Hadad, P.	8002349		1/16/—	?	794.61
TAX DEDUCTIONS				PERSONAL DEDUCTIONS		
FIT	FICA	STATE	LOCAL	MEDICAL	LIFE INS.	MISC.
89.83	70.07	17.97	----	5.25	------	2.25

$979.98

13.

DEPT.	EMPLOYEE	CHECK#		WEEK ENDING	GROSS PAY	NET PAY
15	Gilbo, R.	91166		3/31/—	390.00	314.96
TAX DEDUCTIONS				PERSONAL DEDUCTIONS		
FIT	FICA	STATE	LOCAL	MEDICAL	LIFE INS.	MISC.
35.18	?	7.04	----	4.93	------	-----

$27.89

For Exercises 14–17, estimate the net pay by rounding each deduction to the nearest ten dollars.

	Gross Pay	Federal Tax	FICA Tax	Personal Deductions	Estimated Net Pay
14.	$340	$ 31.70	$24.31	—	? $290
15.	$710	$119.90	$50.76	$9.00	? $530
16.	$350	$ 59.20	$26.46	$3.10	? $260
17.	$695	$ 72.19	$49.69	$7.85	? $565

Solve.

18. Clyde McCoy's monthly gross pay is $1172. Find Clyde's monthly net pay for these deductions.

Federal tax:	$275.80
State tax:	70.16
FICA:	77.94
Life insurance:	5.00

$743.10

19. Cheryl Hyde's weekly gross pay is $298.75. Total deductions are about 24% of her gross pay. Estimate the total deductions. $75

This statement of earnings shows the rate of pay per hour, the number of regular hours, the number of overtime hours, and the overtime rate of pay. Find the gross pay and net pay.

20.

DEPT.	NAME	CHECK #	DATE	REGULAR HOURS	HOURLY RATE	OVERTIME HOURS	OVERTIME RATE
53	Richards, T.	009821	031289	40	7.85	14	11.78
TAX DEDUCTIONS			PERSONAL DEDUCTIONS				
FEDERAL	FICA	STATE	MEDICAL	PENSION	MISC.	GROSS PAY	NET PAY
47.18	34.24	9.44	4.78	23.95	---	?	?

$478.92 $359.33

Mid-Chapter Review

For Exercises 1–3, find the total weekly pay. Time and a half is paid for all hours worked over 40. (Pages 42–44)

1. Hourly Pay Rate: \$6.90
   Hours Worked: 42 **\$296.70**
2. Hourly Pay Rate: \$9.10
   Hours Worked: 38 **\$345.80**
3. Linda Lewis is paid \$7.20 per hour as a receptionist. How much will she be paid for a 45-hour week? **\$342**
4. Brenda Collins earns a commission of $2\frac{1}{2}\%$ on all sales. Last week her sales totaled \$2200. Find how much commission Brenda earned last week. (Pages 45–47) **\$55**
5. Bill Scheffler earns a weekly salary of \$310 plus a commission of 2% on sales. Last week his sales totaled \$3150. Find his total earnings for the week. (Pages 45–47) **\$373**

For Exercises 6–7, complete the table. (Pages 48–50)

	Gross Pay	Federal Tax	FICA Tax	State Tax	Medical Insurance	Pension Plan	Total Deductions	Net Pay
6.	\$276	\$33.12	\$19.74	\$4.42	\$6.79	\$18.59	? **\$82.66**	? **\$193.34**
7.	\$450	\$54.00	\$32.18	\$7.20	\$5.25	\$27.16	? **\$125.79**	? **\$324.21**

MAINTENANCE

The line graph at the right shows the amount of steel the United States imported during the first six months of a recent year. Use this graph for Exercises 8–9. (Pages 4–5)

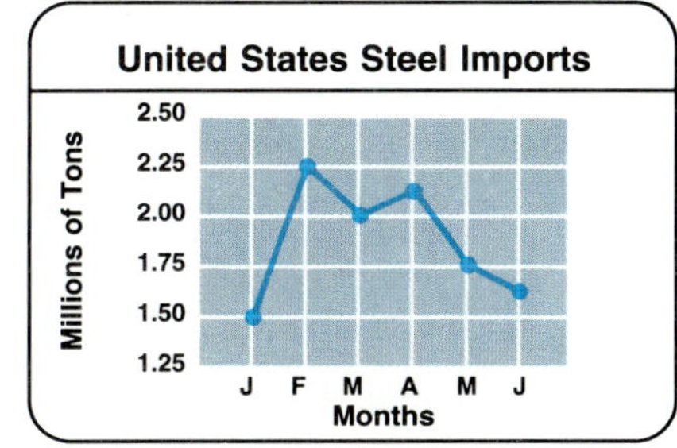

8. About how many millions of tons of steel were imported in May? **1.75 million**
9. Find the average amount of steel imported over the six months. **1.875 million tons**
10. A car dealer offers six different car models. Each model is available in 12 different colors. The dealer has one of each model and color in stock. How many cars does the dealer have? (Pages 22–23) **6 × 12, or 72 cars**
11. A weather forecaster predicts that there is a 40% chance of rain. Which is more likely, that it will rain or that it will not rain? (Pages 26–27) **It will not rain.**

Objective

Student will

1. review the skills, concepts, and applications in the first part of Chapter 3.
2. maintain key skills and concepts taught in Chapters 1–2.

Using the Page

Exercises 1–7 provide an informal assessment of the student's mastery of the major skills and concepts presented in the first half of Chapter 3. Each item is referenced to the related pages where the particular item was presented. These exercises parallel the quiz provided in the *Teacher's ResourceBank.*™

A quiz covering the second half of the chapter is also provided in the *Teacher's ResourceBank.*™

Exercises 8–11 maintain skills and concepts taught in Chapters 1 and 2.

Lesson Resources

Maintenance: See below.
Reteaching/Alternate Teaching Strategy p. M–79
Practice: Activity Worksheet 15
Enrichment: See the enrichment topic "Fringe Benefits" on page 62.

Objective

Student will use estimation to determine if answers are reasonable.

Maintenance

Round to the nearest whole number.

1. 534.69 ANS: 535
2. 87.48 ANS: 87

Round to the nearest 10.

3. 764.89 ANS: 760
4. 3768.10 ANS: 3770
5. Christopher bought items that cost $5.89, $8.19, and $3.72. How much change did he receive from $20.00? ANS: $2.20

1 *Lesson Focus*

Motivation: Write these numbers on the chalkboard: 879, 723, 590, 643, 787. Ask students to tell how they would estimate the sum of these numbers.

Purpose: This lesson shows students three methods of estimation. Estimation is an important skill that helps consumers determine whether the total cost of a bill is reasonable.

2 *Teaching the Lesson*

After presenting the Examples, select a problem to show how the strategy can be applied to other situations, such as in exercise 8.

Strategy: USING ESTIMATION

You can use estimation and mental computation to check whether an answer is reasonable.

EXAMPLE 1 You compute the cost of 8 place settings as $99.12. Is your answer reasonable?

Think: Use **front-end estimation.**

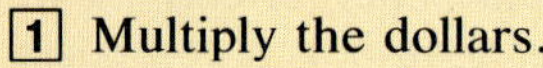

1 Multiply the dollars.	8 × $12 =	$96.00
2 Multiply the cents (rounded).	8 × $0.40 =	3.20
3 Add.		$99.20 ◀ *Estimate*

The estimate and the answer are close.

The answer is **reasonable.**

Sometimes you can use *compatible numbers* to estimate. **Compatible numbers** are numbers convenient to use, that is; they make the computation easier.

1. Which numbers are more compatible, 8)‾2500 or 8)‾2400? **8)‾2400**
2. Which numbers are more compatible, 18)‾3600 or 18)‾3800? **18)‾3600**

EXAMPLE 2 Joel Bates agreed to pay $3852 for a computer in 18 equal monthly payments. He computed the monthly payment to be $120.88. Is his answer reasonable?

Think: Use **compatible numbers.**
3852 is about 3600 and 3600 is divisible by 18.

Estimate: $18\overline{)3600}$ = 200 ◀ ***Monthly payment: About $200***

There is a difference of $79.12 between Joel's answer and the estimate.

The answer is **not reasonable. Joel should check his computation.**

Example 3 uses **clustering** (or grouping) and the idea of an "average" to estimate a sum.

EXAMPLE 3 Janine invited four friends to lunch. After estimating the total, she asked the cashier to check the computation. Is Janine right?

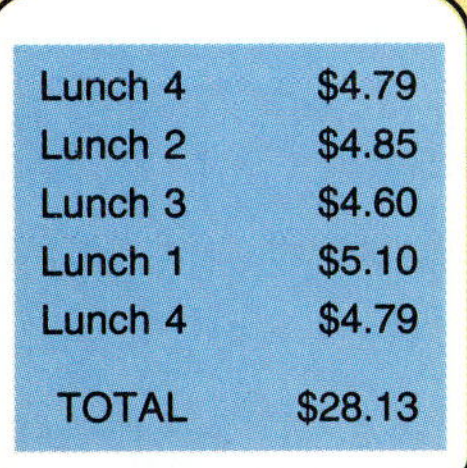

Lunch 4	$4.79
Lunch 2	$4.85
Lunch 3	$4.60
Lunch 1	$5.10
Lunch 4	$4.79
TOTAL	$28.13

Think: The numbers "cluster" around 5.
Average cost: $5.00

Estimate: $\$5.00 \times 5 = \$25$

The computation should be checked.

EXERCISES

Use estimation to check whether the answer is reasonable.
Estimates will vary: [Estimate]

1.

$4.19
0.98
1.39
0.29
2.74
TOTAL: $13.59

No; [$9.60]

2.

Entree No	Price
3	$ 9.50
2	10.20
3	9.50
1	11.05
TOTAL:	$40.25

Yes; [$40.00]

3.

HOUSE SALES
$63,950
$72,400
$91,800
$89,750
$88,900
TOTAL: $406,800

Yes; [$407,000]

Estimate to determine whether the answer is reasonable.

4. Jean bought 8 paint brushes at $4.29 each. She computed the total cost as $34.32. Yes; [$34.40]

5. Mark agreed to pay $513 for a refrigerator in 12 equal monthly payments. He calculated the payments to be $42.75. Yes; [$40.00]

6. Clark computed the average price of these six used cars to be $3108.

$31,060	$1785	$3400
$17,900	$3200	$3018

No; Prices do not cluster around $3100.

7. John has a job after school. He earned $19.80 on Monday, $21.60 on Tuesday, and $20.25 on Wednesday. He calculated his total earnings as $61.65. Yes; [$60.00]

8. A parking garage charges $3.25 for the first hour and $1.65 for each additional hour. Jill figures it will cost her $30 to park five hours. No; [$11]

1. **Ask:** What is the problem about? (How much it costs to park for 5 hours)
2. **Read** the problem to determine the FACTS. **Ask:** How much does it cost to park for the first hour? ($3.25) **Ask:** How much does it cost to park for each of the remaining hours? ($1.65)
3. **Plan** the solution. **Ask:** What method of estimation would be easiest to use in this situation? (Answers will vary. Have students give reasons for their choices.)
4. **Solve.** Have students do the estimation with the method of their choice to determine if Jill's solution is reasonable.
5. **Check** the answer by having students read the problem again to check the facts with their solution.

3 Close

Summary: Have students explain the three methods of estimation in their own words. Have them discuss when they think the use of one method is more appropriate than another.

Evaluation
Guided Practice: Ex. 1, 2
Independent Practice: Ex. 3–8

Problem-Solving Skills

Using estimation (Ex. 1–8)
Reading a table (Ex. 1–3)

Alternate Teaching Strategy

You may wish to have students work in groups of three to complete the exercises. One student should work the problem with front-end estimation, the second student with compatible numbers, and the third student with clustering. Then the group should discuss which method they think was the most appropriate. The students should take turns using the different methods of estimation.

Estimation Ex. 1–8

Mental Math Ex. 1–8

Lesson Resources

Maintenance: See below.
Reteaching/Alternate Teaching Strategy: p. M-22
Practice: p. M-22
Enrichment: p. M-22

Objective

Student will use a table to find the deductions for social security tax.

Maintenance

1. Add: $17 + $19 + $14 + $36 + $52 ANS: $138
2. Divide: $138 ÷ 5 ANS: $27.60
3. List in order from least to greatest: 32.764 316.53 3.999 41.63 85.421 ANS: 3.999, 32.764, 41.63, 85.421, 316.53
4. Multiply: $43,500 × 0.0751 ANS: $3266.85
5. At one store, the prices of five different volleyballs are $18, $25, $22, $21, and $28. Find the mean price. ANS: $22.80

1 Lesson Focus

Motivation: Ask students if they know any persons who are receiving social security benefits, perhaps a parent or grandparent.

Purpose: Students should be familiar with the Social Security program. It collects a large amount of a worker's earnings during a lifetime. A worker should know how the amount of social security is calculated.

Social Security Taxes

The social security (FICA) **withholdings** (deductions) on wages of employees and on the earnings of self-employed people are used to provide benefits for retired workers and for disabled people and their dependents.

There are two parts to the FICA tax.

a. The tax rate

b. The maximum amount of earnings that are taxed.

The table at the right shows the expected tax rate and the expected maximum amount to be taxed for 1987 through 1990. Employers must send the employee's tax amount and an equal matching amount to the federal government.

Year	Employee Tax Rate	Maximum Amount Taxed
1987	7.15%	$43,800
1988	7.51%	$45,000
1989	7.51%	*
1990	7.65%	*

*Information not yet available.

1. What was the FICA tax rate for employees in 1988? 7.51%
2. What is the expected FICA tax rate for 1990? 7.65%

EXAMPLE Evelyn Tomson, Bonnie's stepsister, works for Hubert Industries. Her gross earnings in 1988 were $46,160. How much was deducted for social security taxes?

Since the maximum amount that could be taxed in 1988 was $45,000, find the amount of tax on $45,000.

$45,000 × 0.0751 = **$3379.50** ◀ Amount Taxed × Tax Rate = Amount of Tax

Evelyn paid **$3379.50** for social security taxes in 1988.

3. How much did Hubert Industries pay in FICA taxes for its employee, Evelyn Tomson? $3379.50

CHECK YOUR SKILLS

Write a decimal for each percent. For additional practice, see page 403.

1. 8.9% 0.089 2. 5.4% 0.054 3. 9.25% 0.0925 4. 7.15% 0.0715 5. 7.65% 0.0765 6. 3.05% 0.0305

For additional practice, see page 407.

Find each answer. Round to the nearest cent when necessary.

7. 15% of $1800 $270 **8.** 12% of $819 $98.28 **9.** 15% of $437.63 $65.64

10. 7.15% of $1260 $90.09 **11.** 7.65% of $326 $24.94 **12.** 8.15% of $754.34 $61.48

Subtract. For additional practice, see page 367.

13. $46,000 − $43,500 $2500 **14.** $57,469 − $35,800 $21,669 **15.** $5000 − $3960 $1040

EXERCISES

Write true, T, or false, F, for each statement. When a statement is false, correct it.

1. FICA taxes are paid to the state government. F; federal government
2. Social security taxes are usually deducted regularly from an employee's paycheck. T
3. Only a certain amount of gross yearly earnings are subject to FICA taxes. T
4. The social security tax rate is the same every year. F; rate may change
5. A person having gross earnings of $43,000 in 1987 was required to pay FICA taxes on the entire amount. T

For Exercises 6–11, complete the table. Round answers to the nearest cent.

	Gross Pay	Tax Rate	FICA Tax Withheld
6.	$1500.00	7.15%	? $107.25
7.	$625.00	7.15%	? $44.69
8.	$1021.80	7.15%	? $73.06
9.	$895.80	7.51%	? $67.27
10.	$900.00	7.51%	? $67.59
11.	$25,430	7.65%	? $1945.40

12. A mechanic's gross pay was $230 for one week in 1988. How much was deducted for social security? $17.27

13. A worker had monthly earnings of $4350.00 in 1987. How much was withheld for social security in October, 1987? in November, 1987? in December 1987? $311.03; $21.44; 0 The maximum taxable amount was reached in November, so no tax was withheld in December.

In 1988, self-employed persons paid an FICA tax rate of 13.02%. The maximum contribution (amount paid) was $5859.

14. Henry Sims, a self-employed cabinetmaker, earned $28,400 in 1988. How much of his earnings did he pay for social security tax? $3697.68

15. As a self-employed person in 1988, Linda earned $47,000. How much did she pay in social security taxes? $5859

2 Teaching the Lesson

Have a student read the first three paragraphs of the lesson. Then direct the students' attention to the table. Ask the following questions.

1. Why do you think the employee tax rate increased from 1987 to 1988? (The tax rate is increased to keep up with the increase in cost of living.)
2. A person who earned $50,000 in 1988 would be taxed on what amount? ($45,000)

Have students answer questions 1 and 2. Then discuss the Example and question 3.

3 Close

Summary: Ask students to summarize how the amount of social security tax is computed.

Evaluation
Guided Practice: Ex 1–5, 7–11 odd
Independent Practice: Ex 6–10 even, 12–15

Extension

Ask students to find out about the history of the social security program, and the laws regarding social security.

Problem-Solving Skills

Reading a table (Ex. 12–13)
Interpreting information (Ex. 13, 15)
Solving a multi-step problem (Ex. 13, 15)

Lesson Resources

Maintenance: See below.
Reteaching/Alternate Teaching Strategy: p. M-22
Practice: p. M-22
Enrichment: See p. M-22

Objective

Student will read a table to find approximate social security benefits.

Maintenance

1. List in order from greatest to least: $17.50 $15.40 $80.60 $8.90
   ANS: $8.90, $15.40, $17.50, $80.60
2. Divide: 11 ÷ 2 ANS. 5.5
3. Add: 8 + 6 + 9 + 4 + 3 + 6
   ANS: 36
4. Round to the nearest cent: $273.96825
   ANS: $273.97
5. For six different temporary employment agencies, the pay per hour for a typist is $7, $6, $6, $5, $8, and $8.
   Find the median pay per hour.
   ANS: $6.50

1 Lesson Focus

Motivation: Ask students how much they think people getting social security benefits receive each month.

Purpose: Students should be aware of who is eligible to recieve social security benefits. This lesson will also show students that the amount of the benefit depends on the average monthly earnings.

Social Security Benefits

Social security provides these types of benefits.

Social Security Benefits

a. Retirement income
b. Benefits for the dependents (spouse and children) of a worker who dies
c. Income for persons who become disabled
d. Medical costs for persons covered by Medicare

The amount of social security benefits is based on the average monthly earnings on which social security taxes were paid. The table below shows some approximate benefits.

Examples of Monthly Social Security Retirement Benefits

Average Monthly Earnings	Benefits For Living Workers And Their Dependents					Maximum Family Benefit
	Age-65 Retirement Benefit	Age-62 Retirement Benefit	Benefits for Dependents			
			Spouse not caring for child		Child or Spouse caring for child	
			Age 65	Age 62		
$ 600	$371	$297	$185	$139	$185	$ 557
750	419	335	209	157	209	658
900	467	374	233	175	233	789
1,200	563	451	281	211	281	1,050
1,500	659	527	329	247	329	1,188
1,800	755	604	377	283	377	1,322
2,100	812	649	406	304	406	1,420
2,400	857	685	428	321	428	1,499
2,700	902	721	451	338	451	1,577

EXAMPLE Juana Martín plans to retire at age 62. Her average monthly earnings are $1500. Use the table to estimate the monthly benefits.

Find the row that reads: "1500."
Look to the right under "Age-62 Retirement Benefit." **527**

The monthly benefit is **$527.**

EXERCISES

For Exercises 1–3, find the approximate monthly benefit for each person. Use the table on page 56.

	Person to Whom Benefits are Paid	Average Monthly Earnings	Monthly Benefit
1.	Retired worker at age 65	$1200	? $563
2.	Spouse caring for child	$2400	? $428
3.	Spouse at age 62 (no child)	$750	? $157

For Exercises 4–6, find the total monthly benefits for each family. Use the table on page 56.

4. When Jason Le Mar retired, his family was eligible for the maximum family benefit. Jason's average monthly earnings were $1200. Find the monthly benefit. $1050

5. Lisa Chung is retiring. Her average monthly earnings are $1500. Both Lisa and her husband are 65 years old. Find the total of their monthly benefits.
   Retired worker at age 65: ? $659
   Spouse at age 65: ? $329
   Total: ? $988

6. Max Martinez retired at age 62. His average monthly earnings were $900. When Max retired, his wife was caring for a child. Find the total of their monthly benefits. $607

7. Evelyn Anderson retires at age 65. Her average monthly earnings are $750. How much does she receive in benefits per year? $5028

8. Eloise Crow is thinking about retiring. Her average monthly earnings are $1800. How much more will she receive in benefits per year if she retires at age 65 rather than at age 62? $1812

9. Ben Springer is thinking about retiring at age 65. His average monthly earnings are $2100. How much will he receive in benefits over 5 years? $48,720

10. Janine Freund receives a monthly benefit of $467.00. Next month a cost-of-living adjustment will increase this benefit by 8%. What will her new monthly benefit be? $504.36

2 Teaching the lesson

Direct students attention to the table on page 56. Ask questions such as:

1. On what is the amount of the social security benefit based? (Average monthly earnings)
2. What is meant by maximum family benefit? (The maximum amount that one family can receive in social security benefits)
3. What are the two ages of retirement shown on the table? (62 and 65)

3 Close

Summary: Ask students to summarize the two factors that determine the amount of a retired person's benefit.

Evaluation
Guided Practice: Ex. 1–3
Independent Practice: Ex. 4–10

Extension

Have students find information on the costs and benefits of Medicare.

Problem-Solving Skills

Reading a table (Ex. 4–19)
Solving a multi-step problem (Ex. 5–6, 8–9)
Making a comparison (Ex. 8)

Lesson Resources

Maintenance: See below.
Reteaching/Alternate Teaching Strategy: p. M-23 (Visual 6)
Practice: p. M-23
Enrichment: p. M-23
Concrete Materials: Activity Worksheet 18B, and Visual 6
Visual 6

Objectives

Student will

1. interpret a job application form.
2. complete the blanks on a job application form.

Maintenance

1. Write $\frac{8}{104}$ in lowest terms. ANS: $\frac{1}{13}$
2. Write $\frac{6}{10}$ in lowest terms. ANS: $\frac{3}{5}$
3. Write $\frac{1}{8}$ as a decimal. ANS: 0.125
4. Find 80% of 348. ANS: 278.4
5. There are 150 people in the audience of a game show. Eight people from the audience are chosen at random to appear on the show. What is the probability of being chosen to appear on the show? ANS: $\frac{4}{75}$

1 Lesson Focus

Motivation: Have students discuss why businesses require prospective employees to fill out job applications. Have students give reasons why job applications should be filled out accurately and completely.

Purpose: This lesson focuses on the importance of a job application and on the different types of information needed to complete a job application.

Job Application

To apply for a job, you usually need to complete a job application. The application asks you to provide personal information, educational background, employment experience, and *references*. **References** are persons who will vouch for your character and ability.

The school librarian helped Stuart find a book about applying for a job. The book included a sample application.

EXERCISES

For Exercises 1–8, use the sample application on page 59.

1. For what job is Stuart applying? **Draftsman**
2. What high school did Stuart attend? **Peoria High School**
3. What were Stuart's duties as a draftsman at Kelly Architectural Designs? **Preparation of construction prints, plan layouts, and elevations**
4. What skill does Stuart have which may help him get the job? **His experience in computer-assisted drafting.**
5. Use the information below to determine what should be written in each of the blanks labeled **A–G** on the job application.

   Stuart earned an associate's degree in architectural drafting from Parkland Vocational School located in Springfield, Illinois. He attended Parkland from August, 1986 to May, 1988. **See the job application on the following page.**
6. Use the information below to determine what should be written in each of the blanks labeled **H–O** on the job application.

   Stuart worked as a drafting assistant at Dalton and Associates from January to August of 1986 for $4.10 per hour. His duties included running blueprints and checking them for accuracy. His supervisor was Dave Sheldon, a draftsman. **See the job application on the following page.**
7. Why did Stuart list his job at Kelly Architectural Designs before his job at Dalton and Associates? **The most recent job is listed first.**
8. Why is it a good idea to ask for permission before listing someone as a reference? **It is courteous and wise to let them know they may be contacted by the employer.**

PROJECT

a. List three businesses in your community that provide jobs for young people.

b. Pick up a job application from one of these businesses. Complete the application as if you were applying for a job.

APPLICATION FOR EMPLOYMENT WITH McDONALD ARCHITECTURE

AN EQUAL OPPORTUNITY EMPLOYER POSITION DESIRED DRAFTSMAN

PERSONAL

LAST NAME	FIRST	MIDDLE	SOCIAL SECURITY NO.	DATE
JOHNSON	STUART	MARK	159-26-9735	4/15/1990

PRESENT ADDRESS STREET	CITY	STATE	ZIP CODE	APT. NO.	TELEPHONE NO.
1807 LORIMAR RD.	CHATHAM,	IL.	62629	—	217-483-0009

ARE YOU A U.S. CITIZEN? YES [✓] NO [ ] HAVE YOU EVER BEEN CONVICTED OF A FELONY? NO

EDUCATIONAL RECORD

SCHOOLS	NAME & LOCATION	COURSES	ATTENDED FROM MO.	FROM YR.	TO MO.	TO YR.	DEGREE
HIGH OR PREP	PEORIA HIGH SCHOOL 712 SCHOOL STREET PEORIA, IL. 61601	SCIENCE, MATH, ENG., DRAFTING, MECH. DRAWING	AUG	82	MAY	86	DIPLOMA
COLLEGE		MAJOR MINOR					
POST GRADUATE BUSINESS SCHOOL OR OTHER	Ⓐ PARKLAND VOCATIONAL SCHOOL SPRINGFIELD, ILLINOIS	Ⓑ ARCHITECTURAL DRAFTING	Ⓒ AUG.	Ⓓ 86	Ⓔ MAY	Ⓕ 88	Ⓖ ASSOC. DEGREE

EMPLOYMENT RECORD

NAME OF EMPLOYER (PRESENT OR MOST RECENT): KELLY ARCHITECTURAL DESIGNS
ADDRESS: 41 E. 7th ST. CHATHAM, IL 62629
YOUR POSITION: DRAFTSMAN
NAME AND TITLE OF IMMEDIATE SUPERIOR: GENE McKENZIE, ARCHITECT
DESCRIPTION OF DUTIES: PREPARE CONSTRUCTION PRINTS, PLAN LAYOUTS, ELEVATIONS
REASON FOR LEAVING: RELOCATION TO ANOTHER CITY
STARTED DATE: JUNE, 1988 SALARY: $16,800
LEFT DATE: MARCH, 1990 SALARY: $18,100

NAME OF EMPLOYER: Ⓗ DALTON AND ASSOCIATES
ADDRESS: 415 SEMORAN PEORIA, IL. 61601
YOUR POSITION: Ⓘ DRAFTING ASSISTANT
NAME AND TITLE OF IMMEDIATE SUPERIOR: Ⓙ DAVE SHELDON, DRAFTSMAN
DESCRIPTION OF DUTIES: Ⓚ RUNNING AND CHECKING BLUEPRINTS
REASON FOR LEAVING: TO ATTEND VOCATIONAL SCHOOL
STARTED DATE: Ⓛ JAN. 1986 SALARY: Ⓜ $4.10/HR
LEFT DATE: Ⓝ AUG. 1986 SALARY: Ⓞ $4.10/HR

PERSONAL REFERENCES

NAME OF REFERENCE	ADDRESS	OCCUPATION
JUAN HURTADO	1036 BOX RD. PEORIA, IL 61601	DRAFTSMAN
JEFF McLEOD	RT. 2 BOX 187 SPRINGFIELD, IL. 62701	TEACHER
PATRICIA GOODING	P.O. BOX 419, PEORIA, IL. 61601	ARCHITECT

OTHER

Add any information (i.e. scholastic average, extra-curricular activities, skills) which you feel might favorably affect consideration of your application.
COMPUTER-ASSISTED DRAFTING

I hereby affirm that my answers to all the foregoing questions are true and correct, and that I have not withheld any facts or circumstances which would, if disclosed, affect my application unfavorably.

Signature *Stuart M. Johnson* Date 4/15/1990

2 Teaching the Lesson

Direct students' attention to the application form. These questions, in addition to the ones in the text, may be useful.

1. If you were an employer, can you think of other information you would like to have from a job applicant? (Answers will vary.)
2. What are some other ways that employers can get information about prospective employees other than by a job application form? (By personal interview, by the applicant's own resume, through an employment firm, etc.)
   Point out the words "Equal Opportunity Employer" on the application. Explain that this appears on most job applications because of the Civil Rights Act of 1964 which forbids discrimination in employment because of race, color, religion, sex, or national origin.

3 Close

Summary: Summarize the important steps in filling out a job application. Emphasize the importance of being neat and accurate.

Evaluation
Guided Practice: Ex. 1–4
Independent Practice: Ex. 5–8

Extension

See the Project on page 58.

Problem-Solving Skills

Interpreting information (Ex. 1–8)
Completing a table (Ex. 1–8)

Critical Thinking

You may wish to have students work in small groups to solve this problem or you may wish to work with the class.

Ex. 8

NOTE: A quiz covering the second half of the chapter is provided in the *Teacher's ResourceBank™*.

Objectives

Students will

1. explore solutions to a variety of problems that emerge from this situational lesson.
2. explore solutions to job problems that have more than one solution.
3. make consumer decisions relevant to their teen-age world.

Situational Lesson

These two pages present a situational lesson as the framework from which a variety of problem situations emerge.

Teaching Strategies

This lesson lends itself to cooperative learning groups for the problem solving activities of comparing choices and exploring decisions. (See page M-13.)

However, these activities can also be carried out by the class as a whole or by individual students.

1 Lesson Focus

Motivation: Have students discuss different jobs that people their ages have and the advantages and disadvantages of each.

Purpose: This lesson will show students some of the things they will have to consider before they apply for a job.

2 Teaching the Lesson

Have a volunteer read the introductory paragraph. Then focus students' attention on the three advertisements and ask questions such as these.

1. Which job has the highest hourly wage? (Retail clerk)
2. Which job would allow you to work the most hours per day? (Delivery person)
3. How much would you earn each week as a delivery person? ($172)

Consumer's Choice

Sarah DuPont, Bonnie's best friend, wants to buy a used car for $2000. She has decided to get a summer job for 12 weeks to earn the money that she needs. She noticed these three job advertisements posted on the school bulletin board. (See the three ads at the left.)

COMPARING THE CHOICES

1. Which jobs require that Sarah works at least 30 hours per week? **Delivery person, Food server**
2. Will each job provide hourly earnings that will amount to $2000 by the end of the summer? Explain. **See the margin on page 61.**
3. Which jobs will provide earnings that will vary from week to week? Explain. **Food server; rental clerk; Tips and commissions will vary.**

EXPLORING DECISIONS

4. If Sarah chooses the job at the Country Inn, how much additional money must she earn in tips to make the $2000 she needs? **$1100**
5. How much must she average in tips per week? per day? **$91.67; $18.33**
6. Is it possible for Sarah to earn $16 in tips one day and still meet her average? Explain. **See the margin on page 61.**

7. If Sarah chooses the job as the retail clerk, how much additional money must she earn in commissions to have the $2000 she needs? $689.60

8. To earn $2000 altogether, how much merchandise does Sarah need to sell over the summer? $34,480 worth of merchandise

9. Is it possible for Sarah to earn more than the $2000 she needs if she works as a food server or as a retail clerk? Explain. See the margin.

No matter which job Sarah chooses, she will have to ride the bus back and forth to work. This will cost her 85¢ twice a day.

10. If Sarah takes the job at Finnegan's Market, how much will she spend on bus fares over the summer? $122.40

11. If Sarah takes the job at Finnegan's Market and pays for bus fare, will she still be able to earn the $2000 she needs? No

12. If Sarah takes the job at Country Inn, how much will it cost her to ride the bus each week? $8.50

13. How much less will Sarah's bus transportation cost over the summer if she accepts the job at Newman's Department Store instead of the job at Country Inn? $20.40

14. Besides salary and transportation costs, what other things might Sarah consider before choosing a job? Answers will vary.

15. Which job would you choose if you were Sarah? Why? Answers will vary.

4. What other things would you consider before deciding on which job to take? (Answers will vary.)

Then work through Exercises 1–3 with the students. Have students do Exercises 4–13 independently. Then you may wish to discuss Exercises 14 and 15 with the class.

3 Close

Summary: Have students discuss the advantages and disadvantages of having a job that might not pay the same amount each week.

Problem-Solving Skills

Using logical reasoning (Ex. 6)
Solving a multi-step problem (Ex. 8, 14, 15)

Critical Thinking

Ex. 6, 9, 16, 17

Project

Have students use the want ads in newpapers to find jobs that they might be able to get as summer employment. Have them determine how much they would make over the course of the summer, assuming that they must pay the cost of transportation.

Additional Answers

2. No; The food server and retail clerk jobs provide less than $2000. Tips and commission would have to provide the remaining amount.
6. Yes; On another day she will need to earn $2.33 more than the daily average.
9. Yes; She could exceed the amount needed in tips or commission.

Objective

Student will use a formula to solve multi-step problems that involve the fringe-benefit rate.

Overview

This topic is optional. The word "Enrichment" that appears to the right of the title in this Teacher's Edition does not appear in the student textbook. Therefore, this material is not included in the Chapter Review and Chapter Test.

Using the Page

You may wish to have students work this Enrichment in small groups or you may wish to work with the class.

Problem-Solving Skills

Solving a multi-step problem (Ex. 1–3)
Using a formula (Ex. 1–3)

Fringe Benefits ENRICHMENT

Employees at many companies receive **fringe benefits,** such as life insurance, disability insurance, pension plans, and so on, at little or no cost to the employee. Fringe benefits may be evaluated as a percent of the yearly gross pay.

Fringe-Benefit Rate = Fringe Benefits ÷ Gross Pay

EXAMPLE Marlene Johnson's employer pays yearly health insurance premiums of $882.60, and life insurance premiums of $630 for Marlene. The employer's social security contribution for Marlene is $1308.45. Marlene's yearly gross pay is $18,300. Find her fringe-benefit rate (nearest tenth of a percent).

[1] Find the total of fringe benefits.

$882.60 + $630 + $1308.45 = **$2821.05**

[2] Fringe-Benefit Rate = Fringe Benefits ÷ Gross Pay
= $2821.05 ÷ $18,300
= 0.1541557, or about **15.4%**

Fringe benefits amount to **15.4%** of Marlene's salary.

EXERCISES

1. Hiroshi's gross pay is $26,700. His fringe benefits include $1838.76 for health insurance, $500 for disability insurance, $1500 toward a pension plan, and a matching social security payment of $2005.17. What is his fringe-benefit rate? 21.9%

2. Sandy Jones' gross pay is $33,000. Her fringe benefits include $1919.40 for health insurance, $930 for life insurance, and a matching social security payment of $2478.30. What is her fringe-benefit rate? 16.1%

3. Maria's yearly gross pay is $48,000. Her employer matches her social security payment of 7.51% of $45,000. The company also pays an amount equal to $8\frac{1}{2}$% of Maria's yearly salary to a retirement plan. What is Maria's fringe-benefit rate? 15.5%

Chapter Summary

IMPORTANT IDEAS

1. Employees are often paid time and a half for overtime.
2. **Base Pay + Overtime Pay = Total Pay**
3. Salespersons are often paid commissions for selling a product or service.
4. **Total Sales × Rate of Commission = Commission**
5. **Net Pay = Gross Pay − Total Deductions**
6. Social Security tax is deducted from wages to provide benefits for retired workers and for disabled people and their dependents.
7. Social security benefits provide income for retired workers, for persons who become disabled, and for certain dependents of workers who die. Benefits also supplement medical costs for persons covered by Medicare.

Chapter Review

Part 1: VOCABULARY

For Exercises 1–5, choose from the box at the right the word(s) that complete(s) each statement.

deductions
social security
overtime pay
net pay
taxes
gross pay
commission

1. Pay earned for working extra hours is called ? . (Page 42) overtime pay
2. When a salesperson's pay includes a percent of total sales, the amount received is called ? . (Page 45) commission
3. Total earnings for a pay period is ? . (Page 48) gross pay
4. After taxes and personal deductions are subtracted from a person's gross pay, the remaining amount is the ? . (Page 48) net pay
5. FICA taxes are also called ? taxes. (Page 48) social security

Chapter Summary

The Chapter Summary contains a listing of the important ideas that were presented in the chapter. This listing is intended to assist the student with the Chapter Review that follows.

Objective

To review the important terms, skills, problem solving, and applications presented in Chapter 3.

Overview

The Chapter Review is structured in three parts. Part 1 is a review of the important terms that were introduced in the chapter. Part 2 reviews the skills that were presented in the chapter. Part 3 reviews the problem-solving strategies and applications that were presented in the chapter. Each item in the Chapter Review is referenced to the related pages where the concept, skill, or application was presented.

Using the Pages

You may wish to assign this Chapter Review for homework or treat it as a class review prior to administering the formal Chapter Test. In doing this, it is suggested that you only use the even- or odd-numbered exercises. You can then use the remaining exercises as a bank for use later.

Part 2: SKILLS

For Exercises 6–9, find the total weekly income. Time and a half is paid for all hours worked over 40. (Pages 42–44)

	Hourly Pay Rate	Hours Worked	Weekly Pay
6.	$4.75	37	? $175.75
7.	$6.50	42	? $279.50
8.	$8.30	46	? $406.70
9.	$7.28	32	? $232.96

For Exercises 10–15, complete each table. (Pages 45–50)

	Sales	Rate of Commission	Commission
10.	$63,500	6%	? $3810
11.	$42,870	12%	? $5144.40

	Salary	Sales	Rate of Commission	Total Earnings
12.	$325	$5680	$2\frac{1}{2}$ %	? $467
13.	$480	$3000	3%	? $570

	Gross Pay	Federal Tax	FICA Tax	State Tax	Medical Insurance	Pension Plan	Total Deductions	Net Pay
14.	$352	$30.81	$25.17	$5.02	$4.26	$25.62	? $90.88	? $261.12
15.	$289	$25.29	$20.67	$4.12	$5.05	$12.70	? $67.83	? $221.17

Find the net pay. (Pages 48–50)

16.

DEPT.	EMPLOYEE	CHECK#	WEEK ENDING	GROSS PAY	NET PAY
12	Richards, R	11352	5/03/—	390.00	?

TAX DEDUCTIONS				PERSONAL DEDUCTIONS		
FIT	FICA	STATE	LOCAL	MEDICAL	LIFE INS.	MISC.
35.18	27.89	7.04	----	4.93	------	-----

$314.96

For Exercises 17–20, find the amount of social security tax withheld. Round answers to the nearest cent. (Pages 54–55)

	Gross Pay	Tax Rate	FICA Tax Withheld
17.	$1250	7.15%	? $89.38
18.	$825	7.15%	? $58.99
19.	$1863	7.51%	? $139.91
20.	$2400	7.65%	? $183.60

Use the table on page 56 to complete this table. (Pages 56–57)

	Person to Whom Benefits are Paid	Average Monthly Earnings	Monthly Benefit
21.	Retired worker at age 62	$900	? $374
22.	Retired worker at age 65	$2100	? $812

Part 3: APPLICATIONS

23. Deanne Pendry earns $12.50 per hour for a 40-hour week with time and a half for overtime. Find her pay for a 46-hour week. (Pages 42–44) **$612.50**

24. Laura Yancey sold a house for $83,500. Her commission was $5\frac{1}{2}\%$ of the selling price. How much commission did she earn? (Pages 45–47) **$4592.50**

25. As a computer salesperson, Kendall Davis receives a salary of $17,200 per year plus a commission of 2% on sales. Find the total earnings for a year in which his total sales amounted to $652,000. (Pages 45–47) **$30,240**

26. Valerie receives a 9% commission as an automobile dealer. Her total sales for a week were $39,825. Estimate the commission. (Pages 45–47) **$4000**

27. Jeff Strossner earned $415 last week. His deductions were: federal tax-$51.88; social security tax-$29.67; state tax-$26.50. Find his net pay for last week. (Pages 48–50) **$306.95**

28. Louis Rodgers earned $250.00 last week. His total deductions are about 19% of his gross pay. Estimate his total deductions. (Pages 48–50) **$50**

For Exercises 29–30, use estimation to determine whether the answer is reasonable. Write Yes or No. Give a reason for your choice. (Pages 52–53) **Estimates and reasons may vary.**

29. In March, 0.1 inch, 0.89 inch, 0.07 inch, and 1.23 inches of rain fell. A weather forecaster reported that more than 4 inches of rain fell in March. **Estimate: 2.5 in; No**

30. Exactly 5980 feet of twine is wound in equal amounts on 29 spools. Hugh calculated that there were 20 feet of twine on each spool. **Estimate: 200; No**

31. Paula Ehren earned $1733 in January of 1988. The FICA tax rate was 7.51%. How much was withheld from her pay for FICA tax? (Pages 54–55) **$130.15**

32. A cost-of-living adjustment will increase a retiree's monthly benefit of $451 by 6%. What will the new benefit be? (Pages 56–57) **$478.06**

Objective

To informally assess students' mastering of the major skills, concepts, problem solving, and applications presented in Chapter 3.

Using the Page

After completing the Chapter Review with the class, you may wish to use this Chapter Test as an informal assessment. This Chapter Test parallels the formal chapter tests (Form A and Form B) provided in the *Teacher's ResourceBank.*™

Chapter Test

For Exercises 1–4, find the total weekly pay. Time and a half is paid for all hours worked over 40.

	Hourly Pay Rate	Hours Worked	Weekly Pay
1.	$8.45	40	? $338
2.	$6.60	42	? $283.80
3.	$7.20	47	? $363.60
4.	$5.42	36	? $195.12

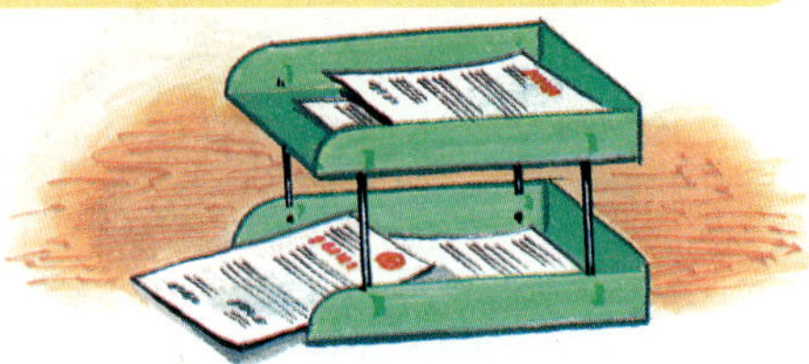

5. Mike Collins sells office supplies. He receives a salary of $1750 per month plus a commission of $3\frac{1}{2}\%$ on all sales. Last month his sales totaled $35,000. Find his total earnings for the month. **$2975**

For Exercises 6–7, complete each statement of earnings.

6.

DEPT.	EMPLOYEE		CHECK#	WEEK ENDING	GROSS PAY	NET PAY
07	Guinan, J.		54601	8/24/—	1240.63	?
TAX DEDUCTIONS				PERSONAL DEDUCTIONS		
FIT	FICA	STATE	LOCAL	MEDICAL	LIFE INS.	MISC.
156.00	88.71	49.63	----	5.15	------	-----

$941.14

7.

DEPT.	EMPLOYEE		CHECK#	WEEK ENDING	GROSS PAY	NET PAY
12	Neathery, D.		11352	5/03/—	?	865.90
TAX DEDUCTIONS				PERSONAL DEDUCTIONS		
FIT	FICA	STATE	LOCAL	MEDICAL	LIFE INS.	MISC.
144.32	81.68	46.16	----	4.32	------	-----

$1142.38

8. Lawrence's tax deductions are: federal tax-$97.50; FICA tax-$28.60; medical insurance-$12.70. Estimate the total tax deductions to the nearest ten dollars. **$140**

9. John Mays earned $47,300 in 1987. The FICA tax rate that year was 7.15% on a maximum of $43,800. Find the amount of tax John paid. **$3,131.70**

10. Corliss bought 5.8 pounds of steak at $3.95 per pound and 2.7 pounds of onions at $0.40 per pound. She computes the total bill to be $33.99. Estimate to determine whether her answer is reasonable. **Estimate: $25; Not reasonable**

11. Lem's total deductions from net pay are listed below.

Federal tax:	$51.40
State tax:	$10.06
FICA:	$29.30

He calculates his total deductions to be $90.76. Estimate to determine whether Lem's answer is reasonable. **Estimate: $90; Reasonable**

Cumulative Maintenance Chapters 1–3

Choose the correct answer. Choose **a, b, c,** *or* **d.**

1. The graph below shows the percent of each of four kinds of tissue in the human body. What percent of the body is not muscle tissue? c

Body Tissue

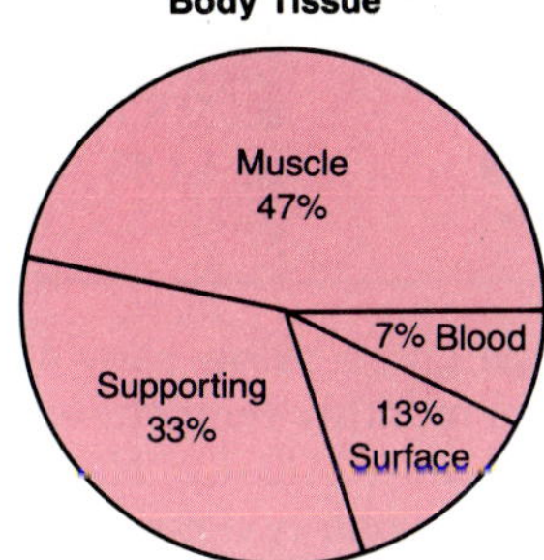

a. 33% **b.** 13% **c.** 53% **d.** 47%

2. Write 4% as a decimal. a

a. 0.04 **b.** 0.0004
c. 0.40 **d.** 0.004

3. Charlene earns \$8.20 per hour with time and half for all hours worked over 40. Find her earnings for a 43-hour week. c

a. \$352.60 **b.** \$36.90
c. \$364.90 **d.** \$354.90

4. There is an 80% chance of rain. What is the probability that it will not rain? b

a. $\frac{1}{20}$ **b.** $\frac{1}{5}$ **c.** $\frac{4}{5}$ **d.** $\frac{1}{80}$

5. Find $2\frac{1}{2}$% of \$1400. b

a. \$87.50 **b.** \$35.00
c. \$25.00 **d.** \$350.00

6. Karen Coleman's monthly income in 1987 was \$1445. The FICA tax rate was 7.15% on a maximum of \$43,800. Find the FICA tax withheld from her pay each month. a

a. \$103.32 **b.** \$3110.25
c. \$1033.18 **d.** \$101.59

7. The table below shows Kyle's earnings in tips for five months. Find his average monthly earnings in tips. d

Month	Tips
January	\$386.00
February	\$410.20
March	\$423.57
April	\$351.40
May	\$380.83

a. \$392.00 **b.** \$386.00
c. \$1952.00 **d.** \$390.40

8. Round 12,394 to the nearest thousand. c

a. 13,000 **b.** 12,400
c. 12,000 **d.** 10,000

Objective

To review the content presented in Chapters 1–3

Using the Pages

You may wish to use this Cumulative Maintenance as an informal assessment tool. These pages can be assigned for homework or they may be used as review in class.

9. Twelve unlabeled boxes of shoes are shipped to a shoe store. Six boxes contain size 9 shoes, two boxes contain size 8, and four boxes contain size 7. If a box is chosen at random, what is the probability that it contains size 7 shoes? d

a. $\frac{3}{4}$ **b.** $\frac{2}{3}$
c. $\frac{1}{2}$ **d.** $\frac{1}{3}$

10. Add: \$356 + \$24.15 + \$13.92 b

a. \$41.63 **b.** \$394.07
c. \$383.07 **d.** \$384.07

11. Larry Kopatz earned \$358 last week. His deductions were: federal tax-\$44.75; state tax-\$14.32; social security tax-\$25.60. Find Larry's net pay. a

a. \$273.33 **b.** \$84.67
c. \$442.67 **d.** \$274.67

12. A restaurant offers two different appetizers, four different main dishes, and three different desserts. How many combinations are possible? d

a. 9 **b.** 11 **c.** 14 **d.** 24

13. Write a fraction for 45%. d

a. $\frac{1}{45}$ **b.** $\frac{9}{11}$ **c.** $\frac{9}{25}$ **d.** $\frac{9}{20}$

14. Milton sold a house for \$87,500. His commission was 6% of the selling price. How much did he earn? b

a. \$6.00 **b.** \$5250
c. \$52,500 **d.** \$4820

15. Multiply: \$3.92 × 1.5 c

a. \$1.25 **b.** \$58.80
c. \$5.88 **d.** \$4.88

16. The line graph below shows the average monthly temperatures for a recent year in Albany, New York. Between which two months do temperatures increase the most? a

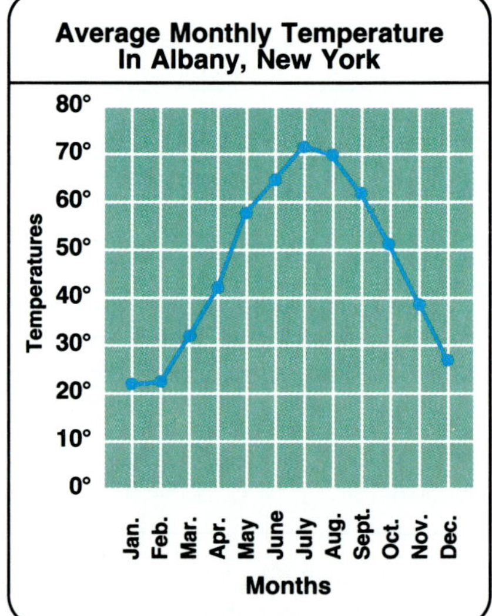

a. April and May **b.** May and June
c. Sept. and Oct. **d.** Feb. and Mar.

Paying Taxes

Sylvia Knox and her fellow employees at Century Printing Company are filing their income tax returns. Some of them have never filed a return, and they have many questions.

- How is the amount of income tax withheld from paychecks determined?
- What is the difference between gross pay and adjusted gross income?
- When may employees choose to itemize deductions?
- What is a W-2 Form?
- When are the tax return forms 1040EZ and 1040 used?
- How do deductions and exemptions affect taxable income?

Chapter 4: Paying Taxes

Overview

The focus of this chapter is on federal, state, and city income taxes. Since changes in tax laws occur frequently, you will want to obtain the most recent information before studying this chapter. A helpful source of information is the publication *Your Federal Income Tax* available from your local IRS office or from the Forms Distribution Center for your state.

Although all lessons in this chapter involve problem-solving, the strategy lesson on page 84–85 presents problem situations in which students first consider whether an exact answer or an estimate will provide an appropriate solution. Then they are asked to decide whether mental computation, a calculator, paper and pencil, or some combination of these would be the most efficient method of solution.

The *Consumer's Choice* on pages 86–87 presents a **situational lesson** in which students make consumer choices related to exemptions and income taxes. Finally, the *Enrichment* lesson on page 88 explores the topic of "hidden taxes."

Using This Page

Have students read the introductory paragraph and questions. Have them list possible solutions to the problems presented. After completing the chapter, have students review their suggested solutions, comparing them with those presented in the lessons. You may wish to have students suggest other possible problems resulting from the situation described on this page and to discuss possible solutions.

You may wish to organize the class into small groups to complete the situational activity described on this *Using the Page.*

Lesson Resources

Maintenance: See below.
Reteaching/Alternate Teaching Strategy: p. M-23 (Visual 7)
Practice: p. M-23
Enrichment: p. M-23
Concrete Materials: Visual 7
Visual 7

Objectives

Student will

1. compute weekly gross pay.
2. read a table to determine the amount of federal income tax to withhold.

Maintenance

1. Find 8% of $55,000. ANS: $4400
2. Multiply: 40 × $6.75. ANS: $270
3. Find 6% of $14.83. Round to two decimal places. ANS: $0.89
4. Martin had gross pay of $485.75. His deductions were $94.37. Find his net pay. ANS: $391.38
5. Sally earned a commission of 4% on sales of $28,000. Find her total income. ANS: $1120

1 Lesson Focus

Motivation: Ask students to tell how much federal income tax they think would be withheld from wages of $300 per week.

Purpose: This lesson is about federal income tax withholding. It is helpful for students to know that they have some control over the amount of tax that is withheld from their pay. It is also important for them to know that the correct amount is withheld.

2 Teaching the Lesson

Set the situation by having a student read the opening paragraph. Then direct students' attention to the table. Questions such as the following will help students learn how to use the table.

Federal Income Tax

Sylvia Knox is a payroll clerk for Century Printing Company. As part of her job, she determines the amount of federal income tax to **withhold**, or deduct, from each employee's paycheck.

Sylvia uses a table such as the one at the right to determine the amount of tax to be withheld.

Refer to the table to complete each of the following.

SINGLE Persons WEEKLY Payroll Period

Wages		Number of exemptions claimed		
At least	But less than	0	1	2
		Amount of tax to be withheld		
$270	$280	$38	$33	$27
280	290	40	34	29
290	300	41	36	30
300	310	43	37	32
310	320	44	39	33
320	330	46	40	35
330	340	47	42	36
340	350	50	43	38
350	360	53	45	39
360	370	55	46	41

1. Does "At least $300" include $300? Yes
2. Does "But less than $340" include $340? No

As a taxpayer, you can take one exemption for yourself and one exemption for each person dependent on you for support.

EXAMPLE Mark Wilkins is single and claims two exemptions. He works 40 hours per week at $8.65 per hour. How much federal income tax will be deducted from Mark's weekly gross pay?

1 Find the weekly gross pay.

$8.65 × 40 = **$346.00**

2 Since $346.00 is between $340 and $350, find $340 in the "At least" column of the table.

3 Read the amount withheld for two exemptions.

340	350	50	43	38

The amount of tax is **$38.00.**

3. How much tax will be withheld from Mark's pay over a year? $1976

CHECK YOUR SKILLS

Multiply. For additional practice, see page 372.

1. $8.60 × 40 $344
2. $7.46 × 32 $238.72
3. $9.85 × 38 $374.30
4. $6.20 × 35 $217
5. $5.25 × 6 $31.50
6. $12.10 × 37 $447.70
7. $7.45 × 4 $29.80
8. $3.35 × 40 $134

EXERCISES

Complete. Choose the answers from the box at the right.

expenses increases gross pay exemptions decreases remains the same

1. The amount of income tax withheld depends on ___?___ and the number of ___?___ claimed. **gross pay; exemptions**
2. Usually, as the number of exemptions increases, the amount of tax withheld ___?___. **decreases**
3. Usually, as gross pay increases, the amount of tax withheld ___?___. **increases**

For Exercises 4–7, use the table on page 70 to find the amount of federal income tax withheld.

4. Weekly gross pay: $295
   Exemptions claimed: 2 **$30**
5. Weekly gross pay: $330
   Exemptions claimed: 1 **$42**
6. Weekly gross pay: $362
   Exemptions claimed: 0 **$55**
7. Weekly gross pay: $312
   Exemptions claimed: 2 **$33**

For Exercises 8–11:

a. *Find the gross pay.*

b. *Use the table on page 70 to find the amount of federal income tax withheld.*

	Hours Worked	Hourly Pay	Gross Pay	Number of Exemptions	Amount of Tax Withheld
8.	37	$ 9.50	? **$351.50**	1	? **$45**
9.	40	$ 6.85	? **$274**	0	? **$38**
10.	35	$ 8.27	? **$289.45**	1	? **$34**
11.	32	$10.80	? **$345.60**	2	? **$38**

For Exercises 12–14, find the amount of federal income tax withheld. Use the table on page 70.

12. A typesetter has weekly gross earnings of $308. The typesetter is single and claims two exemptions. **$32**
13. A graphic artist worked 28 hours last week at $12.10 per hour. The artist is single and claims no exemptions. **$47**
14. Connie Fifer is paid $7.50 per hour plus time and a half for overtime. Last week she worked 42 hours. Connis is single and claims one exemption. **$40**
15. Gina Lucero claims one exemption. If she increases the number of her exemptions to three, will her weekly net pay increase or decrease? Explain. **Increase; as the number of exemptions increases, the amount of tax withheld decreases.**

1. What amount is withheld if wages are $275 and there are two exemptions? ($27)
2. What amount is withheld if wages are $319 and only one exemption is claimed? ($39)
3. What amount is withheld if wages are $350 and no exemptions are claimed? ($53)
4. For a given wage amount, how does the amount withheld change if the number of exemptions increases? (Decreases)

3 Close

Summary: Ask selected students to explain how to determine the amount of withholding.

Evaluation
Guided Practice: Ex. 1–3, Ex. 4–10 even
Independent Practice: Ex. 5–11 odd, 12–15

Extension

Show students some other parts of the withholding tables for different payroll periods and different categories of taxpayer such as married persons. Have them write and solve some problems based on the tables.
Have students find out what exemptions (withholding allowances) besides those for dependents are possible.

Problem Solving Skills

Reading a table (Ex. 12–15)
Solving a multi-step problem (Ex. 13–15)

Critical Thinking

You may wish to have students work in small groups to solve this problem or you may wish to work with the class.

Ex. 15

Lesson Resources

Maintenance: See below.
Reteaching/Alternate Teaching Strategy: p. M-24
Practice: p. M-24
Enrichment: p. M-24

Objectives

Student will

1. compute adjusted gross income.
2. read a table to determine whether or not deductions may be itemized.

Maintenance

1. Add: 98 + 1023 + 475 + 9
   ANS: 1605
2. Write in order from greatest to least: 14.019, 14.0019, 14.109, 14.009
   ANS: 14.109, 14.019, 14.009, 14.0019
3. Round to the nearest tenth.
   a. 8.44 b. 8.448 c. 8.451
   ANS: a. 8.4 b. 8.4 c. 8.5
4. Divide: 26.4 ÷ 3 ANS: 8.8
5. Three workers earn these hourly wages: $6.85, $7.90, $8.43. Find the mean hourly wage rounded to two decimal places. ANS: $7.73

1 Lesson Focus

Motivation: Ask students what the deadline is for most taxpayers to file an income tax return.

Purpose: All students will eventually be taxpayers. They should be familiar with the information that is needed to prepare an income tax return.

Adjusted Gross Income and Deductions

Sylvia is preparing her federal income tax return. She lists the different kinds of income that she received over the past year. The total of these amounts is her **adjusted gross income.**

Income
Wages: $16,942
Interest: $274
Commission: $800

EXAMPLE What is Sylvia's adjusted gross income?

$16,942 + $274 + $800 = **$18,016** ◀ *Add all income together.*

Sylvia's adjusted gross income is **$18,016.**

Sylvia knows that certain expenses, such as interest paid on mortgage loans, may be subtracted from adjusted gross income. Listing these expenses, or **deductions,** on a special tax form, Schedule A, is called **itemizing deductions.**

Some taxpayers do not choose to itemize deductions. Sylvia's deductions total $2156.40. She is single. To decide whether to itemize deductions, she consults this table.

You may choose to itemize deductions if you are:		
Married and filing jointly	**and**	your itemized deductions are more than $3760.
Single, or a head of household	**and**	your itemized deductions are more than $2540.

1. *Complete:* Single people may choose to itemize deductions if the deductions total more than __?__. $2540
2. May Sylvia choose to itemize deductions? No
3. *Complete:* Married persons who file jointly may choose to itemize deductions if the deductions total more than __?__. $3760

CHECK YOUR SKILLS

ESTIMATION/MENTAL MATH: Ex. 1–6

Estimate to determine whether the answer is reasonable.

For additional practice, see pages 52–53.

1. $17,412 + $136.95 = $17,548.95 Yes
2. $121.56 + $3415.26 = $3936.82 No
3. $34.75 + $127.80 = $152.55 No
4. $1432 + $59.72 = $1591.02 No
5. $126 × 12 = $1512 Yes
6. $963 × 12 = $10,006 No

EXERCISES

Complete. Choose the answer from the box at the right.

$2540
adjusted gross income
wages
total
itemizing deductions
interest
$3760

1. Adjusted gross income includes earnings such as ___?___ and ___?___. wages; interest
2. Listing deductions on a special tax form, Schedule A, is called ___?___. itemizing deductions
3. Itemizing deductions allows certain expenses to be subtracted from ___?___. adjusted gross income
4. A married person filing jointly may itemize deductions if the deductions total more than ___?___. $3760

For Exercises 5–8, find the adjusted gross income.

	Wages	Interest	Other Income	Adjusted Gross Income
5.	$16,400	$63.17	$413.29	? $16,876.46
6.	$12,730	$34.92	$786.71	? $13,551.63

	Wages	Interest	Other Income	Adjusted Gross Income
7.	$11,686	None	$ 965.59	? 7. $12,651.59
8.	$21,397	$392.69	$1416.02	? 8. $23,205.71

9. Mary Hannah earned $12,719.60 as a secretary last year. She also received a **bonus** (money in addition to usual wages) of $500. Find her adjusted gross income. $13,219.60

10. Greg Bell's gross pay last year was $20,280. He also received $710 in interest from a savings account. Estimate his adjusted gross income. $20,990

11. Jeff Taylor's monthly gross income last year was $965. He also received $86.13 and $92.59 in interest from two savings accounts. Find his adjusted gross income for the year. $11,758.72

For Exercises 12–17, use the table on page 72 to decide whether the deductions may be itemized.

	Filing Status	Total Deductions
12.	Married, filing jointly	$2516.72 No
13.	Single	$3278.81 Yes

	Filing Status	Total Deductions
14.	Single	$1715.64 No
15.	Married, filing jointly	$4162.79 Yes

16. Juan Garcias and his wife are filing a joint return. Their deductions total $3572.70. No

17. Florence Garner has deductions that total $2795.60. Florence is single. Yes

2 Teaching the Lesson

Direct students' attention to the table on page 72 showing Sylvia's earnings. Ask if they can name some other sources of income a taxpayer might have.
Explain that in preparing a tax form you must first list your total income. There may be adjustments you can make such as business expenses, moving expenses, and retirement account contributions. Subtracting these adjustments from the total income gives the adjusted gross income. In this lesson, adjustments are not considered.
Discuss the Example. Then explain the process of itemizing deductions. Explain that all taxpayers fit into one of the following three deduction categories:

1. deductions must be itemized
2. deductions may be itemized
3. deductions may not be itemized

3 Close

Summary: Conclude the lesson by asking students to summarize what has been learned about a. adjusted gross income and b. itemizing deductions.

Evaluation
Guided Practice: Ex. 1–4, 5, 7, 13, 15
Independent Practice: Ex. 6, 8–12, 14, 16–17

Extension

Have students use the instruction booklet for preparing Form 1040 to make a list of types of income that do not have to be reported on an income tax form. Also, have them list as many examples as possible of types of income that must be reported.

Problem-Solving Skills

Using estimation (Ex. 10)
Solving a multi-step problem (Ex. 11)
Reading a table (Ex. 16–17)

Estimation Ex. 10

Objective

Student will use a flowchart to determine whether income tax returns must be filed for dependents.

Overview

This page is an extension of the skills and ideas presented in the previous lessons of this chapter. Since the content presented on this page is not included in the Chapter Review or Chapter Test, its use is optional.

Using the Pages

You may wish to have students work this lesson in small groups or you may wish to work with the class. Using it with the class, have a student read the first two paragraphs. Then focus students' attention on the flowchart. Work through the flowchart step-by-step to show students how to determine whether Alex Griffin or Nancy Griffin will have to file a return. Have students work Exercises 1–4 as independent practice.

Problem-Solving Skills

Reading a chart (Ex. 1–4)
Making a comparison (Ex. 1–4)

Math and Income Tax

Alicia Sims is an income tax preparer. She is completing the tax return for Mr. Griffin. Mr. Griffin claims his 17-year-old son, Alex, and his 68-year-old mother, Nancy, as dependents. Alex Griffin earned $2350 this year from a part-time job, and Nancy Griffin received $1200 in interest.

Alicia Sims used the following flowchart to determine whether separate tax returns will have to be filed for Alex and Nancy Griffin.

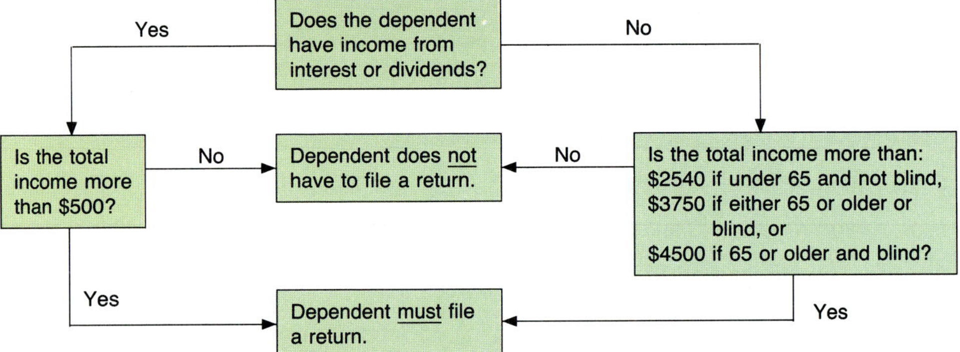

Since Alex Griffin's total income is less than $2540, a return **will not** have to be filed for him.

Since Nancy Griffin's total income from interest is more than $500, a return **must be** filed for her.

EXERCISES

Determine whether the following dependents will have to file a separate income tax return.

1. A 15-year-old who earned $120 in interest from a savings account **No**

2. A blind 35-year-old who earned $4700 from a part-time job **Yes**

3. A 65-year-old who earned $300 in interest from a savings account and $450 in dividends from an investment **Yes**

4. A 70-year-old who earned $1500 from one part-time job and $2020 from a second part-time job **No**

Form 1040EZ-The Short Form

In January, Sylvia receives this **W-2 form** from her employer, Century Printing Company. This is a **Wage and Tax Statement.**

1 Control number 32		OMB No. 1545-0008	WAGE AND TAX STATEMENT		
2 Employer's name, address, and ZIP code CENTURY PRINTING COMPANY 1726 MAIN STREET PHOENIX, AZ 85026		3 Employer's identification number 71-6038590		4 Employer's state I.D. number 71-6038590	
		5 Statutory employee ☐ Deceased ☐ Pension plan ☐ Legal rep. ☐ 942 emp. ☐ Subtotal ☐ Deferred compensation ☐ Void ☐			
		6 Allocated tips		7 Advance EIC payment	
8 Employee's social security number 478-12-4836	9 Federal income tax withheld 1627.00	10 Wages, tips, other compensation 17,742		11 Social security tax withheld 1268.55	
12 Employee's name, address, and ZIP code Sylvia R. Knox 19 Hastings Road Phoenix, AZ 85026		13 Social security wages 17,742		14 Social security tips	
		16		16a Fringe benefits incl. in Box 10	
		17 State income tax 185.38	18 State wages, tips, etc. 17,742	19 Name of state	
		20 Local income tax	21 Local wages, tips, etc.	22 Name of locality	

Form **W-2 Wage and Tax Statement 1987**
This information is being furnished to the Internal Revenue Service.
Copy B To be filed with employee's FEDERAL tax return
Dept. of the Treasury—IRS

1. What is Sylvia's social security number (Box 8)? **478-12-4836**
2. How much social security tax was withheld from Sylvia's pay (Box 11)? **$1268.55**
3. Which box shows how much federal income tax was withheld? **Box 9**
4. Which box shows Sylvia's gross earnings (wages, tips, and other compensation?) **Box 10**

Sylvia needs the information on the W-2 form to prepare her income tax return. Because Sylvia is single and has an adjusted gross income less than $20,000 she uses **Form 1040EZ,** the short form, to prepare her tax return. Sylvia does not itemize deductions.

The Exercises on page 76 will show you how to complete Form 1040EZ.

CHECK YOUR SKILLS

Add or subtract as indicated. **For additional practice, see pages 368 and 369.**

1. 3458.62 + 27.09 **3485.71**
2. 15,486.61 + 139.57 **15,626.18**
3. 8946.24 + 321.79 **9268.03**
4. 17,392.61 − 32.73 **17,359.88**
5. 5469.87 − 2451.50 **3018.37**
6. 3849.29 − 3572.45 **276.84**

Lesson Resources

Maintenance: See below.
Reteaching/Alternate Teaching Strategy: p. M-24 (Visual 8)
Practice: p. M-24
Enrichment: p. M-24
Concrete Materials: Activity Worksheets 21B, 21C, 21D, 21F, and 21H, Visual 8
Visual 8

Objectives

Student will

1. identify the information on a W-2 form.
2. complete an income tax return (Form 1040EZ).

Maintenance

Perform the indicated operations.

1. 23 × 309 Ans: 7107
2. $\frac{3}{4}$ × 264 Ans: 198
3. $25.06 + $39.59 + $109.78 Ans: $174.43
4. 192 ÷ 24 Ans: 8
5. Neil Sachs is a food service equipment salesman. He receives a salary of $600 per month plus a commission of $1\frac{3}{4}$% on total sales. Find Neil's earnings for a month in which his total sales equal $11,640. ANS: $803.70

1 Lesson Focus

Motivation: Ask students to explain why some taxpayers receive a tax refund.

Purpose: Most students will be responsible for filing tax returns some day. They should have knowledge of how to prepare a tax form.

2 *Teaching the Lesson*

Direct students' attention to the W-2 Wage and Tax Statement on page 75. Have the class answer questions 1–4 on this page. You may want to briefly discuss some of the blanks in the form that are not completed and determine why they do not apply here. Have a student read the paragraph following the questions.

3 *Close*

Summary: Review the meaning and purpose of the various entries in the W-2 Wage and Tax Statement.

Evaluation
Guided Practice: Ex. 1–13
Independent Practice: Ex. 14–21

Extension

Have students obtain information about the various tax reporting forms in use and what the conditions are for a taxpayer to use a particular form. Also, you may want them to research some of the penalties involved for violation of income tax regulations.

Problem-Solving Skills

Reading a table (Ex. 1–13, 20)
Interpreting information (Ex. 12–13)

Critical Thinking

You may wish to have students work in small groups to solve this problem or you may wish to work with the class.

Ex. 20

EXERCISES

For Exercises 1–13, refer to Form 1040EZ on page 77.

1. If Sylvia does not have an IRS mailing label, should she print or write her name and address? **print**
2. **Line 1:** From the W-2 form on page 75, find Sylvia's gross pay. **$17,742.00**
3. **Line 2:** What was Sylvia's income from interest? **$274.00**
4. **Line 3:** Add the amounts on lines 1 and 2 to find the adjusted gross income. **$18,016.00**
5. **Line 4:** Sylvia checks the "No" box. What amount should she enter for the standard deduction? **$2,540**
6. **Line 5:** Find the difference between lines 3 and 4. **$15,476.00**
7. **Line 6:** What is the amount of Sylvia's personal exemption? **$1900**
8. **Line 7:** Subtract line 6 from line 5 to find Sylvia's taxable income. What is Sylvia's taxable income? **$13,576.00**
9. **Line 8:** From the W-2 form, find the amount of federal income tax withheld. **$1627.00**
10. **Line 9:** What is the actual amount of tax on Sylvia's taxable income? **$1644**
11. **Lines 10 and 11:** Find the difference between lines 8 and 9. **$17**

If the amount on line 8 is greater than the amount on line 9, Sylvia will receive a ***refund.*** *The difference is entered on line 10. If the amount on line 9 is greater than the amount on line 8, Sylvia will* **owe money.** The difference is entered on line 11.

12. Will Sylvia receive a refund or owe money? **owe money**
13. On which line will Sylvia write the answer to Exercise 11? **Line 11**

For Exercises 14–19:
a. *Determine whether the taxpayer will receive a refund or owe money.*
b. *Find the amount to be refunded or the balance due.*

14. Tax withheld: $726
Tax owed: $813
a. owe money b. $87
15. Tax withheld: $879
Tax owed: $1086
a. owe money b. $207
16. Tax withheld: $1651
Tax owed: $1618
a. refund b. $33
17. Tax withheld: $1356
Tax owed: $978
a. refund b. $378
18. Tax withheld: $2658
Tax owed: $1809
a. refund b. $849
19. Tax withheld: $1246
Tax owed: $1762
a. owe money b. $516
20. Which will be greater on any taxpayer's return, the adjusted gross income or the taxable income? Explain. **Adjusted gross income; taxable income is found by subtracting from the adjusted gross income.**
21. Marla Cohen is married. She has two children. Can she use Form 1040EZ to prepare her income tax return? Explain. **No; Form 1040EZ is only for single persons with no dependents.**

Form **1040EZ**

Department of the Treasury - Internal Revenue Service

Income Tax Return for Single filers with no dependents (0)

OMB No. 1545-0675

Name & address

Use the IRS mailing label. If you don't have one, please print:

Print your name above (first, initial, last)

Present home address (number and street)

City, town, or post office, state and ZIP code

Please print your numbers like this.

0 1 2 3 4 5 6 7 8 9

Your social security number

4 7 8 | 1 2 | 4 8 3 6

Presidential Election Campaign Fund
Do you want $1 of your tax to go to this fund? ▸ Yes [X] No [ ]

		Dollars	Cents
Figure your tax	1 Total wages, salaries, and tips. This should be shown in Box 10 of your W-2 form(s). (Attach your W-2 form(s).) 1	??,???	??
	2 Taxable interest income of $400 or less. If the total is more than $400, you cannot use Form 1040EZ. 2	274	00
Attach Copy B of Form(s) W-2 here	3 Add line 1 and line 2. This is your **adjusted gross income.** 3	??,???	??
	Can you be claimed as a dependent on another person's return? 4 ☐ Yes. Do worksheet on back; enter amount from line E here. ☐ No. Enter 2,540 as your standard deduction. 4	?,???	??
	5 Subtract line 4 from line 3. 5	??,???	??
	If you checked the "Yes" box on line 4, enter 0. If you checked the "No" box on line 4, enter 1,900. 6 This is your **personal exemption.** 6	1,900	00
	7 Subtract line 6 from line 5. If line 6 is larger than line 5, enter 0 on line 7. This is your **taxable income.** 7	??,???	??
	8 Enter your Federal income tax withheld. This should be shown in Box 9 of your W-2 form(s). 8	??,???	??
	9 Use the **single** column in the tax table on pages 32–37 of the Form 1040A instruction booklet to find the **tax** on the amount shown on **line 7.** Enter the amount of tax. 9	1,644	00
Refund or amount you owe	10 If line 8 is larger than line 9, subtract line 9 from line 8. Enter the **amount of your refund.** 10	?,???	??
Attach tax payment here	11 If line 9 is larger than line 8, subtract line 8 from line 9. Enter the **amount you owe.** Attach check or money order for the full amount, payable to "Internal Revenue Service." 11	?,???	??

Sign your return

I have read this return. Under penalties of perjury, I declare that to the best of my knowledge and belief, the return is true, correct, and complete.

Your signature Date

For IRS Use Only—Please do not write in boxes below.

For Privacy Act and Paperwork Reduction Act Notice, see page 31. Form **1040EZ**

Objective

Student will

1. review the skills, concepts, and applications in the first part of Chapter 4.
2. maintain key skills and concepts taught in Chapters 1–3.

Using the Page

Exercises 1–8 provide an informal assessment of the student's mastery of the major skills and concepts presented in the first half of Chapter 4. Each item is referenced to the related pages where the particular item was presented. These exercises parallel the quiz provided in the *Teacher's ResourceBank.*™

A quiz covering the second half of the chapter is also provided in the *Teacher's ResourceBank.*™

Exercises 9–12 maintain skills and concepts taught in Chapters 1–3.

Mid-Chapter Review

For Exercises 1–4, find the amount of federal income tax withheld for a single wage earner. Use the table on page 70. (Pages 70–71)

	Weekly Gross Pay	Number of Exemptions
1.	$347	0 **$50**
2.	$300	2 **$32**

	Hours Worked Per Week	Hourly Pay	Number of Exemptions
3.	34	$9.20	2 **$33**
4.	40	$6.96	1 **$33**

5. Danny Curtis earned $14,482 as a delivery person last year. He also received $126.35 in interest from a savings account. Find his adjusted gross income. (Pages 72–73) **$14,608.35**

6. Laura Berryman, a single wage earner, has deductions that total $2367. Could she choose to itemize deductions? Refer to the table on page 72. (Pages 72–73) **No**

For Exercises 7–8, find the amount of the refund or the balance due. (Pages 75–77)

7. Federal tax withheld: $2356
   Tax owed: $2792
   $436 balance due

8. Federal tax withheld: $3752
   Tax owed: $3569
   $183 refund

MAINTENANCE

The bar graph at the right shows the number of books sold at Ted's Book Store over a six-month period. Use this graph for Exercises 9–10.

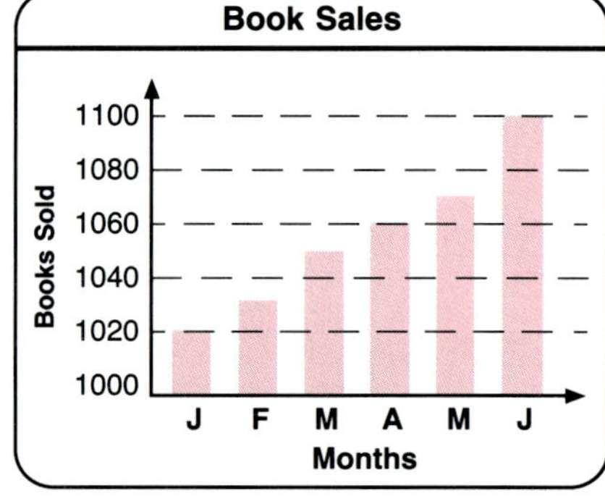

9. How many more books were sold in June than in May? (Pages 2–3) **30 books**

10. Find the average number of books sold for the six months. (Pages 2–3, 10–11) **1055 books**

11. From a batch of light bulbs, fifty are chosen at random. Two of the fifty are found to be defective. What is the probability that a light bulb randomly chosen from the batch will be defective? (Pages 30–31) $\frac{1}{25}$

12. Tom Baker works as a welder for $10.50 per hour. He is paid time and a half for all hours worked over 40. One week Tom worked 45 hours. Find Tom's total earnings for the week. (Pages 42–44) **$498.75**

Math and Sales Tax

Albert Ramirez is a sales clerk at Hobbes Hobby Shop. He uses a table similar to the one at the right to determine the amount of sales tax.

EXAMPLE What is the total cost for a purchase of $12.85?

READ What are the facts?
Amount of purchase: $12.85

PLAN First answer the "hidden question": **What is the amount of sales tax?**

SOLVE
1. Look at the "Amount of Sale" column in the table. Find the interval for $12.85.

12.75–12.91	**0.77**	◀ Tax

2. Amount of Purchase: $12.85
   Tax: + 0.77
   Total Cost: **$13.62**

CHECK Did you use the facts correctly in the solution? Is the answer reasonable?

EXERCISES

Find the sales tax on each purchase.

1. $7.59 $0.46
2. $3.55 $0.21
3. $10.28 $0.62
4. $9.96 $0.60
5. $15.05 $0.90
6. $8.72 $0.52

Find the total cost for each purchase.

7. $0.73 $0.77
8. $1.85 $1.96
9. $5.92 $6.28
10. $17.16 $18.19
11. $11.25 $11.93
12. $13.84 $14.67

Amount of Sale	Tax	Amount of Sale	Tax
0.00– 0.08	0.00	8.92– 9.08	0.54
0.09– 0.24	0.01	9.09– 9.24	0.55
0.25– 0.41	0.02	9.25– 9.41	0.56
0.42– 0.58	0.03	9.42– 9.58	0.57
0.59– 0.74	0.04	9.59– 9.74	0.58
0.75– 0.91	0.05	9.75– 9.91	0.59
0.92– 1.08	0.06	9.92–10.08	0.60
1.09– 1.24	0.07	10.09–10.24	0.61
1.25– 1.41	0.08	10.25–10.41	0.62
1.42– 1.58	0.09	10.42–10.58	0.63
1.59– 1.74	0.10	10.59–10.74	0.64
1.75– 1.91	0.11	10.75–10.91	0.65
1.92– 2.08	0.12	10.92–11.08	0.66
2.09– 2.24	0.13	11.09–11.24	0.67
2.25– 2.41	0.14	11.25–11.41	0.68
2.42– 2.58	0.15	11.42–11.58	0.69
2.59– 2.74	0.16	11.59–11.74	0.70
2.75– 2.91	0.17	11.75–11.91	0.71
2.92– 3.08	0.18	11.92–12.08	0.72
3.09– 3.24	0.19	12.09–12.24	0.73
3.25– 3.41	0.20	12.25–12.41	0.74
3.42– 3.58	0.21	12.42–12.58	0.75
3.59– 3.74	0.22	12.59–12.74	0.76
3.75– 3.91	0.23	12.75–12.91	0.77
3.92– 4.08	0.24	12.92–13.08	0.78
4.09– 4.24	0.25	13.09–13.24	0.79
4.25– 4.41	0.26	13.25–13.41	0.80
4.42– 4.58	0.27	13.42–13.58	0.81
4.59– 4.74	0.28	13.59–13.74	0.82
4.75– 4.91	0.29	13.75–13.91	0.83
4.92– 5.08	0.30	13.92–14.08	0.84
5.09– 5.24	0.31	14.09–14.24	0.85
5.25– 5.41	0.32	14.25–14.41	0.86
5.42– 5.58	0.33	14.42–14.58	0.87
5.59– 5.74	0.34	14.59–14.74	0.88
5.75– 5.91	0.35	14.75–14.91	0.89
5.92– 6.08	0.36	14.92–15.08	0.90
6.09– 6.24	0.37	15.09–15.24	0.91
6.25– 6.41	0.38	15.25–15.41	0.92
6.42– 6.58	0.39	15.42–15.58	0.93
6.59– 6.74	0.40	15.59–15.74	0.94
6.75– 6.91	0.41	15.75–15.91	0.95
6.92– 7.08	0.42	15.92–16.08	0.96
7.09– 7.24	0.43	16.09–16.24	0.97
7.25– 7.41	0.44	16.25–16.41	0.98
7.42– 7.58	0.45	16.42–16.58	0.99
7.59– 7.74	0.46	16.59–16.74	1.00
7.75– 7.91	0.47	16.75–16.91	1.01
7.92– 8.08	0.48	16.92–17.08	1.02
8.09– 8.24	0.49	17.09–17.24	1.03
8.25– 8.41	0.50	17.25–17.41	1.04
8.42– 8.58	0.51	17.42–17.58	1.05
8.59– 8.74	0.52	17.59–17.74	1.06
8.75– 8.91	0.53	17.75–17.91	1.07

Objective

Student will use a table to solve problems that involve sales tax.

Overview

This page is an extension of the skills and ideas presented in the previous lessons of this chapter. Since the content presented on this page is not included in the Chapter Review or Chapter Test, its use is optional.

Using the Pages

You may wish to have students work this lesson in small groups or you may wish to work with the class. Using it with the class, focus students' attention on the sales tax table. Ask questions such as these.

1. What is the tax on $1.45? ($0.09)
2. What is the tax on $16.60? ($1.00)

Then work though the Example. Assign Exercises 1–12 as independent practice.

You may want to use Visual 9 as you present this lesson.

Problem-Solving Skills

Using a table (Ex. 1–12)

Lesson Resources

Maintenance: See below.
Reteaching/Alternate Teaching Strategy: p. M-25 (Visual 10)
Practice: p. M-25
Enrichment: p. M-25
Concrete Materials: Activity Worksheets 22C, 22E, 22G, and 22I, and Visual 10
Visual 10

Objectives

Student will

1. use a formula involving order of operations to compute taxable income.
2. read a table to determine the amount of income tax given the taxable income.

Maintenance

Perform the indicated operations.

1. 40 × 8.50 ANS: 340
2. 8 × 12.75 ANS: 102
3. \$78.18 × 0.055 ANS: \$4.2999, or \$4.30
4. \$259.95 + \$809.17 − \$343.09 ANS: \$726.03
5. Mabel earns \$9.40 per hour for 40 hours. She works 8 overtime hours at one and one-half times the hourly rate. Find her total pay. ANS: \$488.80

1 Lesson Focus

Motivation: Direct students' attention to the formula for taxable income on page 80. Ask how the amount of taxable income would be found.

Purpose: This lesson covers two important parts of the task of preparing an income tax return. Most students will become taxpayers, and many will prepare the returns by themselves. They need to know how to make the basic tax computations and how to use a tax table.

STRATEGY: USING "HIDDEN QUESTIONS" TO SOLVE A MULTI-STEP PROBLEM

Taxable Income and Tax Tables

Sue Chambers, a graphic artist at Century Printing Company, is itemizing deductions this year.

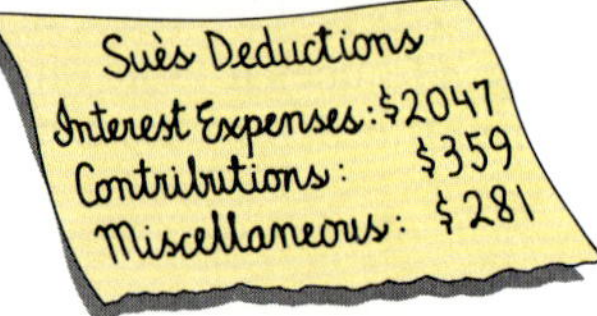

1. What is the total of Sue's deductions? \$2687

Because she is itemizing deductions on her tax returns in 1988, Sue uses **Form 1040,** the long form. To compute taxable income on this form, she uses this formula.

$$\textbf{Taxable Income} = \textbf{Adjusted Gross Income} - \left(\textbf{Total Deductions} + \textbf{Amount for Exemptions}\right)$$

EXAMPLE Sue's adjusted gross income is \$23,992. She claims herself and her mother as exemptions. Find her taxable income.

1 Find the amount for exemptions.

\$1900 × 2 = **\$3800** — *\$1900 is allowed for each exemption.*

2 Find the sum of the deductions and the amount for exemptions.

\$2687 + \$3800 = **\$6487**

3 Find the taxable income.

$$\textbf{Adjusted Gross Income} - \left(\textbf{Total Deductions} + \textbf{Amount for Exemptions}\right) = \textbf{Taxable Income}$$

$$\$23{,}992 - \$6487 = \mathbf{\$17{,}505}$$

Sue's taxable income is **\$17,505.**

Sue is single. To compute her tax, she uses a table such as the one at the right.

If taxable income is—		And you are—			
At least	But less than	Single	Married filing jointly	Married filing separately	Head of a household
		Your tax is—			
17,200	17,250	2,398	1,872	2,890	2,252
17,250	17,300	2,410	1,880	2,904	2,262
17,300	17,350	2,421	1,889	2,918	2,272
17,350	17,400	2,433	1,898	2,932	2,282
17,400	17,450	2,444	1,907	2,946	2,292
17,450	17,500	2,456	1,916	2,960	2,302
17,500	17,550	2,467	1,925	2,974	2,312
17,550	17,600	2,479	1,934	2,988	2,322

2. *Complete.* On the tax table, 17,505 is between 17,500 and _?_. 17,550
3. How much tax will Sue pay? \$2467
4. Which means the same as filing jointly?
   a. filing together?
   b. filing separately?
   a

CHECK YOUR SKILLS

For additional practice, see pages 366 and 367.

Find the answer. Do the work inside parentheses first.

1. $1826 + $396 + __?__ = $2679 $457
2. $37,692 − __?__ = $34,896 $2,796
3. $32,887 − ($4000 + $5327) = __?__ $23,560
4. $26,210 − ($1000 + $1645) = __?__ $23,565

EXERCISES

Complete. Choose your answers from the box below.

$1000
$1900
increases
amount for exemptions
1040
1040EZ
total deductions
decreases

1. If a taxpayer itemizes deductions, the taxpayer uses Form __?__ to file a tax return. 1040
2. Taxable Income = Adjusted Gross Income − (__?__ + __?__) total deductions; amount for exemptions
3. The amount allowed for each exemption is __?__. $1900
4. As the amount of itemized deductions increases, the amount of tax owed __?__. decreases

Complete the table. Allow $1900 for each exemption.

	Adjusted Gross Income	Deductions			Total Deductions	Exemptions	Taxable Income
		Interest	Contributions	Other			
5.	$22,298	$2196	$237	$319	? $2752	1	?
6.	$24,682	$3250	$365	$203	? $3818	1	?
7.	$19,365	$3659	$162	$179	? $4000	3	?
8.	$27,856	$3546	$259	$189	?	2	?

Taxable Income: 5. $17,646 6. $18,964 7. $9665 8. $20,062 Total Deductions 8. $3994

For Exercises 9–14, find the tax. Use the table on page 80.

	Taxable Income	Filing Status
9.	$17,281	Single $2410
10.	$17,450	Head of a household $2302

	Taxable Income	Filing Status
11.	$17,393	Married filing separately $2932
12.	$17,567	Married filing jointly $1934

13. Mr. and Mrs. Kelly are filing separately. Mr. Kelly has a taxable income of $17,316. Mrs. Kelly has a taxable income of $17,502. If they filed jointly, they would pay $5885 in taxes. How much less would they pay if they were filing jointly? $7

14. Mark Hulse is single. His taxable income last year was $17,489. Each month of last year, his employer withheld $207 from his pay for federal income tax. Is Mark entitled to a tax refund? Explain. Yes; his tax bill is $2456. Since his employer withheld $2484, Mark is entitled to a refund of $28.

2 Teaching the Lesson

You may want to show the class a Form 1040 so they can see that it is more extensive than Form 1040EZ. You may also want to name some of the other reasons, besides itemizing deductions, which require a taxpayer to use Form 1040.

Discuss the deductions listed in the table on page 80. Have students compute the total deductions. Then go over the Example carefully. Direct students' attention to the tax table on page 80. Have students answer questions 2, 3, and 4. Ask further questions about the table if students need more help.

3 Close

Summary: Ask one or more students to explain how to compute taxable income. Then ask them to explain how to use the tax table.

Evaluation

Guided Practice: Ex. 1–4, Ex. 6–12 evens

Independent Practice: Ex. 5–11 odds, 13–14

Extension

Provide students with portions of a tax table other than the one on page 80. Have them determine the tax based on various amounts of taxable income. You may also want to specify the filing status of the taxpayer.

Problem-Solving Skills

Solving a multi-step problem (Ex. 13–14)
Making a comparison (Ex. 13–14)
Reading a table (Ex. 13–14)

Lesson Resources

Maintenance: See below.
Reteaching/Alternate Teaching Strategy: p. M-25 (Visual 11)
Practice: p. M-25
Enrichment: p. M-25
Concrete Materials: Visual 11
Visual 11

Objectives

Student will use a table to solve multi-step problems involving state or city income tax.

Maintenance

1. Write 23% as a decimal. ANS: 0.23
2. Multiply: 0.25 × 360 ANS: 90
3. Find 2.5% of $1100. ANS: $27.50
4. Round 25.637 to the nearest hundredth. ANS: 25.64
5. Sausage sales represent 15% of a butcher's total sales for one day. How many degrees would 15% be on a circle graph? ANS: 54°

1 Lesson Focus

Motivation: Ask students whether their state and city collect income taxes.

Purpose: This lesson requires students to use a tax table to determine state income tax. Many students will be taxpayers, as adults, in a state or city where income taxes are collected. Also, the nature of the computation in this lesson will provide students with review of their computational skills.

STRATEGY: USING "HIDDEN QUESTIONS" TO SOLVE A MULTI-STEP PROBLEM

State and City Income Tax

Sue Chambers also pays a state income tax. The main difference between federal, state, and city income taxes is the tax rate. Sue uses the tax rate schedule below to compute her state income tax.

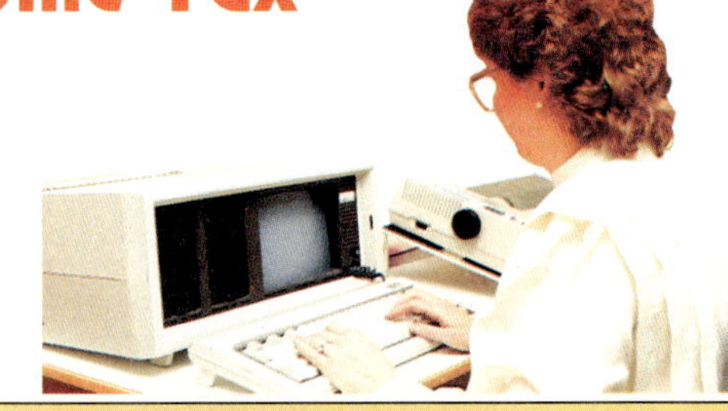

If taxable income is		*Amount of Tax*
over	***but not over***	
0	5,000	0.75% of taxable income
5,000	10,000	$37.50 + 1.5% of excess over 5,000
10,000	15,000	$112.50 + 3% of excess over 10,000
15,000	20,000	$262.50 + 4.5% of excess over 15,000
20,000	25,000	$487.50 + 5.25% of excess over 20,000
25,000		$750.00 + 6% of excess over 25,000

Sue had a taxable income of $17,505 last year.

1. *Complete:* On the tax rate schedule above, 17,505 is between 15,000 and __?__. 20,000
2. *Complete:* The tax rate for Sue is $262.50 plus __?__. 4.5% of excess over 15,000
3. For an income of $8500, what is the excess over $5000? $3500

EXAMPLE Find the amount of Sue's state income tax.

1 Find how much of Sue's taxable income exceeds $15,000.

$17,505 − $15,000 = **$2,505**

2 Find 4.5% of $2505. Round your answer to the nearest cent.

$2505 × 0.045 = **$112.73** — *On a calculator:* 2505 [×] 4.5 [%]

3 Now you can find the total tax.

$262.50 + $112.73 = **$375.23** — *$262.50 plus 4.5% of $2505*

Sue's state income tax is **$375.23.**

The tax rate schedule and procedure for computing city income tax is similar to that for state taxes.

CHECK YOUR SKILLS

Round each number to the nearest hundredth. For additional practice, see page 378.

1. 24.804 24.80 **2.** 24.809 24.81 **3.** 24.805 24.81 **4.** 9.155 9.16 **5.** 6.198 6.20 **6.** 3.006 3.01

Solve. Round each answer to the nearest cent. For additional practice, see page 407.

7. Find 3% of $1460. $43.80 **8.** Find 4.5% of $2645. $119.03 **9.** Find 5.25% of $1326. $69.62

EXERCISES

For Exercises 1–7, use the tax rate schedule on page 82.

	Taxable Income	State Tax		Taxable Income	State Tax		Taxable Income	State Tax
1.	$11,400	? $154.50	**3.**	$ 9,480	? $104.70	**5.**	$ 4,598	? $34.49
2.	$18,900	? $438	**4.**	$27,563	? $903.78	**6.**	$21,950	? $589.88

7. Gail Jansen, a photographer, had a taxable income of $21,490 last year. How much did she pay in state taxes? $565.73

8. Sue Doyle's taxable income last year was $18,500. Her state spends 35% of state taxes on education. What amount of Sue's money was spent on education? $147

Part of a city tax rate schedule is shown below. Use this schedule for Exercises 9–17.

If taxable income is		Amount of Tax
over	but not over	
14,000	16,000	$65 plus 1% of excess over 14,000
16,000	18,000	$85 plus 2.5% of excess over 16,000
18,000	20,000	$135 plus 3.25% of excess over 18,000

	Taxable Income	City Tax		Taxable Income	City Tax		Taxable Income	City Tax
9.	$16,000	? $85	**11.**	$17,690	? $127.25	**13.**	$18,650	? $156.13
10.	$15,400	? $79	**12.**	$14,800	? $73	**14.**	$19,486	? $183.30

15. Lloyd Jones had a taxable income of $15,486 last year. How much was his city income tax? $79.86

16. Celia Weaver's taxable income was $15,075 last year. Estimate how much she paid in city income tax. $75

17. Last year, Lori Bastian's taxable income was $16,780. Each month, $8.50 had been withheld from her pay for city income tax. Was enough money withheld? Explain. No, her city tax is $104.50. Since her employer withheld $8.50 × 12, or $102, Lori owes $2.50.

2 Teaching the Lesson

Direct students' attention to the tax table on page 82. Ask questions such as the following to prepare students for the Example.

1. How would you express 0.75% in the first line in order to multiply by the taxable income? (0.0075)
2. How would you express 4.5% in line 4 in order to multiply by the taxable income? (0.045)
3. If the taxable income is $18,000, what is the excess over $15,000? ($3000)
4. If the taxable income is $12,500, how would you compute the tax? ($112.50 + 3% of excess over $10,000)

Have students read the first paragraph of the lesson and then write their answers to questions 1, 2, and 3.
Then discuss the Example.

3 Close

Summary: Review the steps for using a state income tax table.

Evaluation
Guided Practice: Ex. 1–5 odd, 9–13 odd
Independent Practice: Ex. 2–6 even, 7–8, 10–14 even, 15–17

Extension

Have students obtain income tax tables for their state or city. Have each student compute the amount of tax for 5 different amounts of taxable income.

Problem-Solving Skills

Reading a table (Ex. 7–8, 15–17)
Solving a multi-step problem (Ex. 7–8, 15–17)
Using Estimation (Ex. 16)
Making a comparison (Ex. 17)

Estimation Ex. 16

Lesson Resources

Maintenance: See below.
Reteaching/Alternate Teaching Strategy: See the margin on page 85.
Practice: Activity Worksheet 24
Enrichment: See the enrichment topic "Hidden Taxes" on page 88.

Objectives

Student will

1. determine whether an exact answer is needed for a problem or whether an estimate is close enough.
2. decide whether to use mental computation, a calculator, or pencil and paper to solve a problem.

Maintenance

Use estimation to check if each answer is reasonable.

1. 47 + 32 + 85 = 164 ANS: Yes
2. 476.78 − 387.63 = 189.15 ANS: No
3. 425 × 8 = 2400 ANS: No
4. 1160 ÷ 9 = 128.89 ANS: Yes
5. Ingrid earned $7.50, $8.75, and $4.50. What are her total earnings? ANS: $20.75

1 Lesson Focus

Motivation: List the following amounts on the chalkboard: $1.98, $2.01, $1.55, $0.57, $3.21. Ask students to decide whether a person buying items with those prices should pay with a $5-bill, a $10-bill, or with both. Then ask them how they made their decision.
Purpose: This lesson will show students that there are times when estimating an answer will give them all the information they need. This lesson also shows that the method of computation that they choose can save them time when solving a problem.

Strategy: METHODS OF COMPUTATION

In everyday situations, you often have to consider whether you need an **exact answer** to a problem or whether **an estimate** will give an answer that is close enough. Then you have to decide whether to use **mental computation,** a **calculator, paper and pencil,** or some combination of these to solve the problem efficiently.

EXAMPLE Nona stopped at the supermarket on her way home from work. As she approached the checkout counter with her purchases, Nona thought: "I have only $20 in my wallet. Do I have enough money to pay for everything?"

1. Does Nona need to find the exact total or will an estimate be close enough? An estimate will be close enough.
2. Which would be the more efficient way for Nona to estimate the sum, use a calculator or use mental computation? Give a reason for your answer. Answers will vary.

Nona used **front-end estimation** and **clustering.**

[1] Add the dollars first.

$3 + $2 + $9 + $2 = $16

[2] Estimate the cents. → $0.49, 0.48 } ← About $1; 0.89, 0.19 } ← About $1

Estimate: $16 + $2 = **$18**

3. How close was Nona's estimate to the actual cost? 5¢ less than the actual cost
4. Did Nona have enough money to purchase all the items? Yes
5. Use front-end estimation to estimate each of the following.
   a. $1.29 + $5.69 + $0.99 + $1.45 + $3.58 $13.00
   b. $6.23 × 4 $25.00

EXERCISES

The manager of the Barlow High School baseball team updates a list of the batting averages of the team members after each game. He uses this formula to find the batting average. Then he writes each average as a decimal rounded to the nearest thousandth.

Player	Number of Hits	Times at Bat	Average
Steve	15	60	? .250
Brian	19	61	? .311
Gregg	17	59	? .288
Clarence	20	60	? .333
Fred	14	57	? .246
Frank	17	49	? .347
Phil	21	65	? .323
Julio	18	59	? .305
Sam	16	55	? .291

$$\textbf{Batting Average} = \frac{\textbf{Number of hits}}{\textbf{Times at bat}}$$

1. Should the manager compute an exact average or use an estimate? Why? **Exact average; batting averages need to be precise.**
2. To find the average before rounding, would it be more efficient to use a calculator or to use paper and pencil? Why? **Calculator; it is faster and more accurate.**
3. To round the quotients to the nearest thousandth, would it be more efficient to use paper and pencil or to use mental computation? Why? **Mental computation; it is faster.**

4. Find the average for each player. **See table.**
5. Rank the players according to batting average, from highest to lowest. **Frank, Clarence, Phil, Brian, Julio, Sam, Gregg, Steve, Fred**
6. What computation method did you use to arrange the rankings? Why? **Answers may vary.**

Mahala plans to make gingersnaps for her younger brother's birthday party. In order to have enough, she triples the recipe.

Ingredient	Single Batch	Triple Batch
Flour	$3\frac{3}{4}$ cups	?
Sugar	2 cups	?
Eggs	2	?
Molasses	$\frac{1}{2}$ cup	?
Oleo	$\frac{3}{4}$ cup	?
Soda	1 tsp	?
Cinnamon	$\frac{1}{2}$ tsp	?
Cloves	$\frac{1}{4}$ tsp	?

7. Should Mahala estimate the amount of each ingredient to triple the recipe? Why or why not? **No; recipes require exact amounts**
8. What computation method or methods would you use to triple the recipe? Give reasons for your answer. **Answers may vary.**
9. Find the amount needed for each ingredient when the recipe is tripled. **Flour, $11\frac{1}{4}$ c; Sugar, 6 c; Eggs, 6; Molasses, $1\frac{1}{2}$ c; Oleo, $2\frac{1}{4}$ c; Soda, 3 tsp; Cinnamon, $1\frac{1}{2}$ tsp; Cloves $\frac{3}{4}$ tsp**

2 Teaching the Lesson

Have a student volunteer read the introductory paragraph. Then work through the Example. Have students answer questions 1 and 2 as you come to them in the Example. Then have students answer questions 3 and 4. Before doing question 5, ask students to tell what Nona would do if her estimate had totaled $20. (Find the exact total)

3 Close

Summary: Have students name situations that need exact calculations and those where estimation is appropriate.

Evaluation
Guided Practice: Ex. 1–3, 7, 8
Independent Practice: Ex. 4–6, 9

Problem-Solving Skills

Reading a table (Ex. 1–5, 9)
Using a Formula (Ex. 4)
Making a comparison (Ex. 5)

Alternate Teaching Strategy

You may wish to have students work in small groups to complete the exercises. Have them discuss their ideas for each question and record the group consensus.

Mental Math
Ex. 3

Estimation
Ex. 1 and 7

NOTE: A quiz covering the second half of the chapter is provided in the *Teacher's ResourceBank™*.

Objectives

Students will

1. explore solutions to a variety of problems that emerge from this situational lesson.
2. explore solutions to exemption problems having more than one solution.

Situational Lesson

These two pages present a situational lesson as the framework from which a variety of problem situations emerge.

Teaching Strategies

This lesson lends itself to cooperative learning groups for the problem solving activities of comparing choices and exploring decisions. (See page M-13.)

However, these activities can also be carried out by the class as a whole or by individual students.

1 Lesson Focus

Motivation: Ask students if they think it is better to receive a tax refund or not to receive a tax refund.

Purpose: This lesson shows students that withholding and tax refunds do not mean less or more tax is paid, but reflect how the tax is paid.

2 Teaching the Lesson

Have a volunteer read the introductory paragraph. Then focus students' attention on the 4 choices. Ask questions such as these.

1. How does Choice 1 solve the problem?
2. How does Choice 2 solve the problem?
3. How does Choice 3 solve the problem?
4. How does Choice 4 solve the problem?

Consumer's Choice

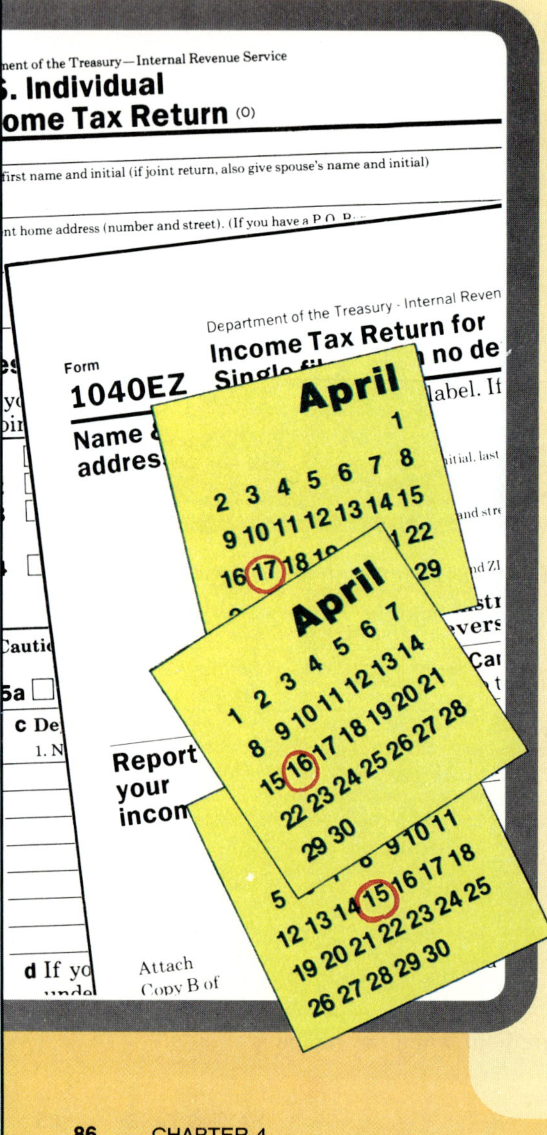

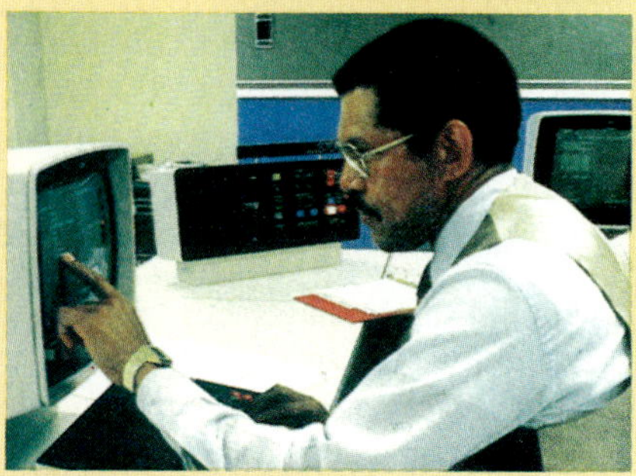

Bill Waters is a foreman at Century Printing Company. He is entitled to four exemptions which he claims on his Employee Withholding Certificate. When Bill filed his federal income tax return this year, he had to pay an additional $600 in taxes. So Bill is considering the following choices for next year.

Choice 1

Claim four exemptions as before. He would then deposit $50 a month in a savings account to cover additional taxes.

Choice 2

Claim four exemptions as before. He would then borrow money in April to pay any additional taxes.

Choice 3

Claim three exemptions. Then withholdings from paychecks would probably cover all of his income tax.

Choice 4

Claim one exemption. Then withholdings from paychecks would more than cover his income tax. Bill would also receive a refund.

Comparing the Choices

1. Which choice will give Bill the least amount of take-home pay? **Choice 4**

2. Which choice will make the most money available to Bill during the year? **Choice 2**

3. Which choice will result in Bill's paying out more than the amount of tax he owes? **Choice 4**

4. Which choices will probably require Bill to make changes in the way he presently spends his take-home pay? **Choices 1, 3, and 4**

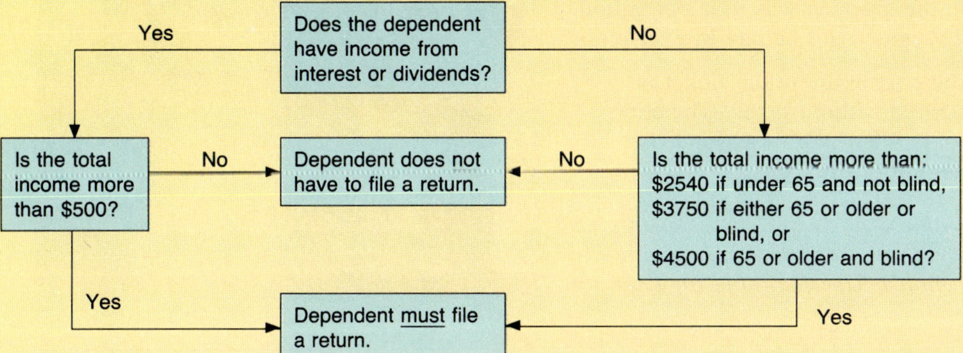

Exploring Decisions

5. Suppose that Bill selects Choice 1 and that he has to pay $520 in additional income taxes next year. Will the difference between the amount he has saved and the amount he has to pay out in additional taxes be exactly $80 or more than $80? Explain. **See the margin.**

6. State one advantage of Choice 1 over the other three choices. **See the margin.**

7. Suppose that Bill selects Choice 2. State one disadvantage to this choice. **See the margin.**

8. State one disadvantage to Choice 4. **See the margin.**

9. State one advantage to Choice 4. **See the margin.**

10. If you were Bill, what choice would you make? Why? **Answers will vary.**

Then have students work the exercises. You may wish to discuss Exercises 6–10 with the class.

3 Close

Summary: Have selected students explain how changing the number of exemptions changes the amount of withholding. Then have them explain how the amount of withholding may affect the tax refund.

Problem-Solving Skills

Making a comparison (Ex. 1–9)

Critical Thinking

Ex. 6–10

Additional Answers

5. More than $80; The amount in his savings account will be $50 × 12, or $600, plus the interest it earns during the 12 months.
6. One advantage: He would earn interest on the additional money needed for taxes. Answers will vary.
7. One disadvantage: He must pay interest on the loan. Answers will vary.
8. One disadvantage: His take-home pay would be less. Answers will vary.
9. One advantage: He would not owe any additional taxes. Answers will vary.

Objective

Student will

1. find the amount of excise tax.
2. use a table to find the amount of import duty.

Overview

This topic is optional. The word "Enrichment" that appears to the right of the title in this Teacher's Edition does not appear in the student textbook. Therefore, this material is not included in the Chapter Review and Chapter Test.

Using the Page

You may wish to have students work this Enrichment in small groups or you may wish to work with the class.

Problem-Solving Skills

Using a table (Ex. 3–6)
Solving a multi-step problem (Ex. 5, 6)

Hidden Taxes ENRICHMENT

Many taxes that consumers pay are **indirect taxes,** or "hidden taxes." These taxes are included in the price of items and services. They are passed on to the consumer in the form of higher prices.

Two of these "hidden taxes" are **excise tax** and **import duty.**

EXERCISES

1. Gregg filled up his car with 12 gallons of gasoline. The excise tax on the gasoline was 9.5¢ per gallon. How much did he pay in excise tax? $1.14
2. The cost of an airline ticket is $254.00 without taxes. The excise tax is 8% of the cost. Find the amount of the excise tax. $20.32

The table at the right shows examples of how some import duties may be determined. Use the table for Exercises 3–6.

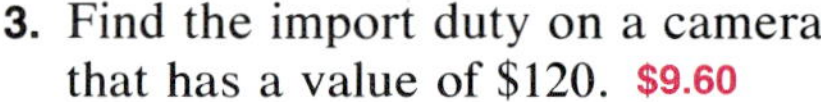

3. Find the import duty on a camera that has a value of $120. $9.60
4. Find the import duty on 140 pounds of chestnuts. $8.75
5. What is the import duty on a clock valued at $58.00? $11.28
6. Find the import duty on 200 pounds of dried mushrooms valued at 40¢ per pound. $16.00
7. The import duty on a gold necklace valued at $400 is 15% of the value.
   a. Find the import duty. $60.00
   b. To find the dealer's cost, the import duty is added to the value. What is the dealer's cost for the necklace? $460.00

Items	*Import Duty*
Cameras	8% of value
Clocks	$2 + 16% of value
Dried Mushrooms	4¢ per pound + 10% of value
Music boxes	8% of value
Toys	18% of value
Records	5% of value
Chestnuts	6.25¢ per pound

8. The selling price of the necklace in Exercise 7 is the sum of the dealer's cost, a $100 markup, and a $35 excise tax.
   a. What is the selling price? $595.00
   b. Find the total price of the necklace after a sales tax of 5% is added to the selling price. $624.75

Chapter Summary

IMPORTANT IDEAS

1. The amount of federal income tax withheld depends on gross pay and the number of exemptions claimed.
2. A W-2 Form provides information needed to prepare an income tax return.
3. Itemizing deductions allows certain expenses to be subtracted from adjusted gross income.
4. $$\text{Taxable Income} = \text{Adjusted Gross Income} - \left(\text{Total Deductions} + \text{Amount for Exemptions}\right)$$
5. The main difference between federal, state, and city income taxes is the tax rate.

Chapter Review

Part 1: VOCABULARY

For Exercises 1–5, choose from the box at the right the word(s) that complete(s) each statement.

exemptions
W-2 Form
taxable income
Form 1040
adjusted gross income
deduction

1. The sum of all income such as wages, tips, commission, and interest is called _?_. (Page 72) adjusted gross income
2. Persons dependent on a taxpayer for support can be listed on a tax return as _?_. (Page 70) exemptions
3. When you subtract the interest on a mortgage loan from adjusted gross income, it is called a _?_. (Page 72) deduction
4. The Wage and Tax Statement sent to each wage earner is called a _?_. (Page 75) W-2 Form
5. When deductions and exemptions are subtracted from adjusted gross income, the difference is called _?_. (Page 80) taxable income

Part 2: SKILLS

Find the amount of federal income tax withheld. Assume that the wage earner is single. Use the table on page 70. (Pages 70–71)

6. Weekly gross pay: $365
   Exemptions claimed: 1 $46
7. Weekly gross pay: $290
   Exemptions claimed: 0 $41

Chapter Summary

The Chapter Summary contains a listing of the important ideas that were presented in the chapter. This listing is intended to assist the student with the Chapter Review that follows.

Objective

To review the important terms, skills, problem solving, and applications presented in Chapter 4.

Overview

The Chapter Review is structured in three parts. Part 1 is a review of the important terms that were introduced in the chapter. Part 2 reviews the skills that were presented in the chapter. Part 3 reviews the problem-solving strategies and applications that were presented in the chapter. Each item in the Chapter Review is referenced to the related pages where the concept, skill, or application was presented.

Using the Pages

You may wish to assign this Chapter Review for homework or treat it as a class review prior to administering the formal Chapter Test. In doing this, it is suggested that you only use the even- or odd-numbered exercises. You can then use the remaining exercises as a bank for use later.

For Exercises 8–11, find the adjusted gross income. (Pages 72–73)

	Yearly Wages	Interest	Other Income
8.	$13,496	$34.96	$413.29 $13,944.25
9.	$19,587	None	$376.45 $19,963.45
10.	$24,630	$127.52	None $24,757.52
11.	$11,389	$206.86	$213.27 $11,809.13

For Exercises 12-15, decide whether deductions may be itemized. Refer to the table on page 72. (Pages 72–73)

	Filing Status	Total Deductions
12.	Married filing jointly	$3809 Yes
13.	Single	$2316 No
14.	Single	$3127 Yes
15.	Married filing jointly	$3751 No

For Exercises 16–17, find the amount of the refund or the balance due. (Pages 75–77)

16. Federal tax withheld: $1942
Tax owed: $2076 **balance due: $134**

17. Federal tax withheld: $2396
Tax owed: $2168 **refund: $228**

For Exercises 18–20, complete the table. (Pages 80–81)

	Adjusted Gross Income	Deductions			Total Deductions	Exemptions	Taxable Income
		Interest	Contributions	Other			
18.	$23,492	$3450	$462	—	? $3912	2	? 15,780
19.	$16,879	$2469	$209	$156	? $2834	1	? $12,145
20.	$27,761	$3113	—	$664	?	3	?

20. Taxable Income: $18,284; Total Deductions: $3777

For Exercises 21–24, find the federal income tax due. Use the tax table on page 80. (Pages 80–81)

	Taxable Income	Filing Status
21.	$17,356	Married filing separately $2932
22.	$17,502	Married filing jointly $1925
23.	$17,250	Single $2410
24.	$17,550	Head of a household $2322

For Exercises 25–28, find the state income tax due. Use the table on page 82. (Pages 82–83)

25. Taxable Income: $14,639 **$251.67**

26. Taxable Income: $19,350 **$458.25**

27. Taxable Income: $4,320 **$32.40**

28. Taxable Income: $29,492 **$1019.52**

Part 3: APPLICATIONS

29. Marie Power worked 40 hours last week at $7.20 per hour. Marie is single and claims two exemptions. Find the amount of federal income tax withheld from her pay. Use the table on page 70. (Pages 70–71) **$29**

30. Karen Schuler earned $21,236 as a salesperson last year. She also earned $2849.60 in commissions. Find her adjusted gross income. (Pages 72–73) **$24,085.60**

31. Saundra earned $19,996 in wages. She also received $688 in interest from a savings account. Estimate her adjusted gross income. (Pages 72–73) **$20,700**

32. Mr. and Mrs. Crowe are filing a joint return. Their deductions total $2946.50. Decide whether they may choose to itemize deductions. Refer to the table on page 72. (Pages 72–73) **No**

33. George Doerfler must pay $3649 in federal income tax this year. The amount of tax withheld from his pay was $3821. Find the amount of the refund or the balance due. (Pages 75–77) **refund: $172**

34. During one year, the federal tax withheld from Polly Ortiz' salary was $3001. Polly actually owed $2695 in taxes. Estimate the amount of Polly's refund. (Pages 75–77) **$300**

35. Jerry Brewer's adjusted gross income last year was $23,459. His deductions are: interest—$2346; contributions—$429; miscellaneous—$252. He claims one exemption. Find the taxable income. (Pages 80–81) **$18,532**

36. Anna Mendoza's taxable income was $24,346 last year. Find her state income tax. Use the tax rate schedule on page 82. (Pages 82–83) **$715.67**

37. Miranda is preparing her Federal income tax return. The amount of tax withheld from her yearly pay is $6912. The amount of tax due is $7005.

a. Should Miranda compute the actual amount owed or will an estimate be good enough? Why?

b. Would you use paper and pencil or a calculator to determine the amount owed? Give a reason for your answer. (Pages 84–85)

a. The actual amount is needed on an income tax return.
b. Answers may vary.

Objective

To informally assess students' mastering of the major skills, concepts, problem solving, and applications presented in Chapter 4.

Using the Page

After completing the Chapter Review with the class, you may wish to use this Chapter Test as an informal assessment. This Chapter Test parallels the formal chapter tests (Form A and Form B) provided in the *Teacher's ResourceBank.*™

CHAPTER TEST

For Exercises 1–2, use the table to find the amount of federal tax withheld.

	Gross Pay	Number of Exemptions	Federal Tax
1.	$298	2	? $30
2.	$310	0	? $44

Wages		Number of exemptions claimed		
At least	But less than	0	1	2
		Amount of tax to be withheld		
$270	$280	$38	$33	$27
280	290	40	34	29
290	300	41	36	30
300	310	43	37	32
310	320	44	39	33

3. Stuart Palmer earned $11,487 last year. He received $2956.70 in tips and $94.57 in interest on a savings account. Find his adjusted gross income. **$14,538.27**

4. Julio Cortez received $15,840 in wages last year. He also received a bonus equivalent to 3% of his salary. Find his adjusted gross income. **$16,315.20**

Determine the amount of the refund or the balance due.

5. Federal tax withheld: $3196
Tax owed: $2957
refund: $239

6. Federal tax withheld: $1857
Tax owed: $1903
balance due: $46

For Exercises 7–9, use the table at the right to find the federal income tax due.

	Taxable Income	Filing Status
7.	$15,089	Single **$1937**
8.	$15,158	Head of a household **$1862**
9.	$15,100	Married filing jointly **$1536**

If taxable income is—		And you are—			
At least	But less than	Single	Married filing jointly	Married filing separately	Head of a household
		Your tax is—			
15,000	15,050	1,927	1,520	2,307	1,835
15,050	15,100	1,937	1,528	2,320	1,844
15,100	15,150	1,947	1,536	2,332	1,853
15,150	15,200	1,957	1,544	2,345	1,862

10. Ellen White claims 3 exemptions. Her adjusted gross income was $16,482 last year. Her deductions were $2397 for interest and $309.64 for contributions. Find the taxable income. **$8075.36**

11. The tax on income over $22,000 in a certain state is as follows:

$400 plus 4% of excess over $22,000.

Tom Rothrock's taxable income is $22,860. Find his state income tax. **$434.40**

Write A if an exact answer is needed; write E if an estimate will be good enough. Give a reason for each answer.

12. Checking the amount of total deductions on income tax returns **E; an estimate is enough to determine whether the sum is reasonable.**

13. Finding the refund amount on a state income tax return **A; an exact answer is needed on income tax returns.**

Cumulative Maintenance Chapters 1–4

Choose the correct answer. Choose a, b, c, or d.

1. Write a fraction for 75%. c

   a. $\frac{1}{15}$ b. $\frac{2}{3}$
   c. $\frac{3}{4}$ d. $\frac{7}{5}$

2. Julie received $14,496 in wages last year. She also received $1072 in commission. Find the adjusted gross income. a

   a. $15,568 b. $13,424
   c. $15,468 d. $14,568

3. Use the graph below to tell how much higher the average temperature was in June than in February. d

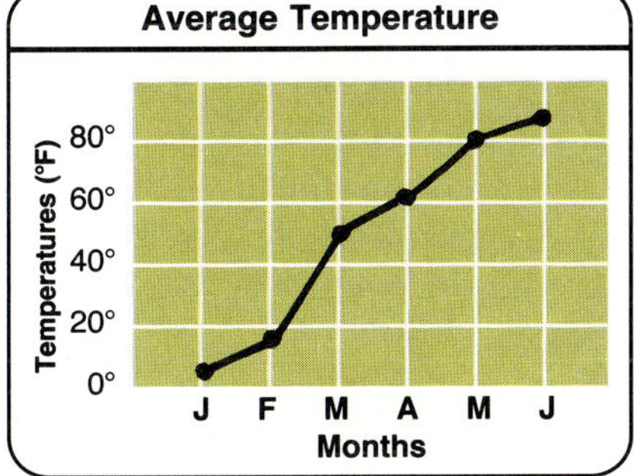

   a. 65° b. 80°
   c. 10° d. 70°

4. Divide 0.75 by 12. d

   a. 0.625 b. 62.5
   c. 6.25 d. 0.0625

5. Ten defective clocks were mistakenly shipped to a department store along with 60 working clocks. What is the probability that a clock randomly chosen from the shipment will be defective? c

   a. $\frac{1}{6}$ b. $\frac{1}{10}$
   c. $\frac{1}{7}$ d. $\frac{1}{70}$

6. Rose earns a weekly salary of $180 plus a 3% commission on sales. Find her total income for a week when her sales total $6500. a

   a. $375 b. $6680
   c. $2130 d. 365

7. Round to the nearest ten. b

   29,346

   a. 30,000 b. 29,350
   c. 29,340 d. 29,300

8. Susan's last five lunches cost $3.86, $4.50, $2.93, $5.60, and $3.21. What was the average cost of these lunches? d

   a. $5.03 b. $3.86
   c. $3.40 d. $4.02

Objective

To review the content presented in Chapters 1–4

Using the Pages

You may wish to use this Cumulative Maintenance as an informal assessment tool. These pages can be assigned for homework or they may be used as review in class.

9. There is a 60% chance of rain. What is the probability that it will *not* rain? b

a. $\frac{3}{5}$ **b.** $\frac{2}{5}$
c. $\frac{1}{40}$ **d.** $\frac{1}{60}$

10. Multiply: 42×0.83 b

a. 33.86 **b.** 34.86
c. 34.26 **d.** 3.486

11. The graph below shows how Mike budgets his weekly income of $360. What amount is budgeted for groceries each week? d

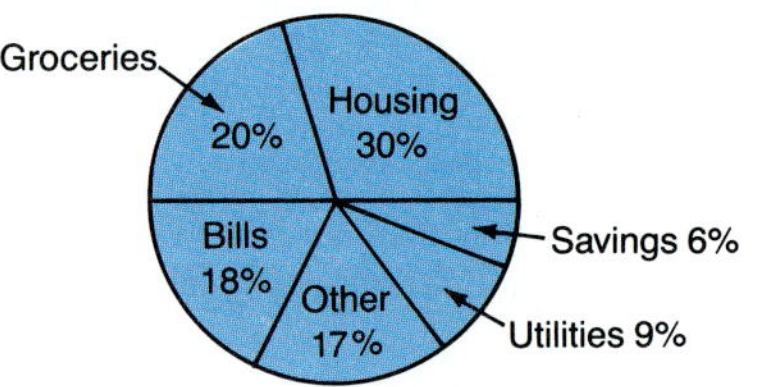

a. $20 **b.** $108
c. $62 **d.** $72

12. Write a decimal for 8%. b

a. 0.8 **b.** 0.08
c. 0.008 **d.** 0.0008

13. Tony Garavelli's net pay is $258.66. His deductions total $127.40. Find the gross pay. c

a. $375.06 **b.** $258.66
c. $386.06 **d.** $131.26

14. Add.

$2480 + $62.46 + $146.57 a

a. $2689.03 **b.** $233.83
c. $2688.03 **d.** $2688.93

15. Willis earns $7.20 per hour for a 40-hour week. He is paid time and a half for overtime. Find his earnings for working 46 hours one week. b

a. $358.80 **b.** $352.80
c. $496.80 **d.** $331.20

16. Kim Begaye's adjusted gross income last year was $20,936. Her deductions total $3694. She claims two exemptions. Find Kim's taxable income. c

a. $17,242 **b.** $24,630
c. $13,442 **d.** $15,242

17. Tom earns $347 each week and claims one exemption. Use the table below to find how much tax is withheld from his pay. b

Wages		Number of exemptions claimed		
		0	1	2
At least	But less than	Amount of tax to be withheld		
$320	$330	$46	$40	$35
330	340	47	42	36
340	350	50	43	38
350	360	53	45	39
360	370	55	46	41

a. $38 **b.** $43 **c.** $50 **d.** $42

Banking and Money

Lila and Ron Brown have just moved to Greenville where Lila has a new job. One of the first things they must decide is where to conduct their banking business. Their decision will be based on what kinds of accounts and services the various banks have to offer.

- What forms will they need for their joint checking account?
- How will they keep a record of deposits made and checks written?
- What interest rates can they expect the banks to pay on their checking and savings accounts?
- Will the interest paid on savings accounts be simple interest or compound interest paid at regular intervals?

Chapter 5: Banking and Money

Overview

The focus of Chapter 5 is on the basic tools of banking, — deposit slips, checks, check stubs, and check registers. The simple interest formula is presented and extended to show its relation to compound interest.

Although all lessons in this chapter involve problem-solving, the strategy lesson on pages 114–115 introduces students to the technique of using a simpler problem to arrive at solutions to more complex problems.

The *Consumer's Choice* on pages 116–117 presents a **situational lesson** in which students make consumer choices in a familiar, real–life situation related to opening a checking account. Finally, the *Enrichment* lesson on page 118 traces the transfer of funds from a consumer's bank account to a retailer's account.

Using This Page

Have students read the introductory paragraph and questions. Have them list possible solutions to the problems presented. After completing the chapter, have students review their suggested solutions, comparing them with those presented in the lessons. You may wish to have students suggest other possible problems resulting from the situation described on this page and to discuss possible solutions.

You may wish to organize the class into small groups to complete the situational activity described on this *Using the Page.*

Lesson Resources

Maintenance: See below.
Reteaching/Alternate Teaching Strategy: p. M-26 (Visual 12)
Practice: p. M-26
Enrichment: p. M-26
Concrete Materials: Activity Worksheet 25A, and Visual 12
Visual 12

Objective

Student will solve multi-step problems that involve completing deposit slips for a checking account.

Maintenance

1. Find 12% of 240. ANS: 28.8
2. Write $\frac{5}{8}$ as a percent. ANS: 62.5%
3. 66 is 12% of what number? ANS: 550
4. 80% of the senior class of 350 students attended the prom. How many did not attend? ANS: 70
5. Hank had $45 deducted from his pay. This was 10% of his total pay. What was his total pay? ANS: $450

1 Lesson Focus

Motivation: Ask students to name several banks in their town or neighborhood.

Purpose: Most students will eventually be bank customers. The ability to correctly complete a deposit slip is an important consumer skill.

2 Teaching the Lesson

Direct students' attention to the deposit slip on page 96. You may want to ask questions such as these in order to introduce the topic.

1. What is the name of the bank? (First Bank of Greenville)

STRATEGY: USING A "HIDDEN QUESTION" TO SOLVE A MULTI-STEP PROBLEM

Deposit Slips

Lila and Ron like to use checks to pay bills because it is safer and more convenient than using cash. Soon after the move to Greenville, they opened a new checking account at a local bank. To put money into their account, Lila and Ron complete a **deposit slip.**

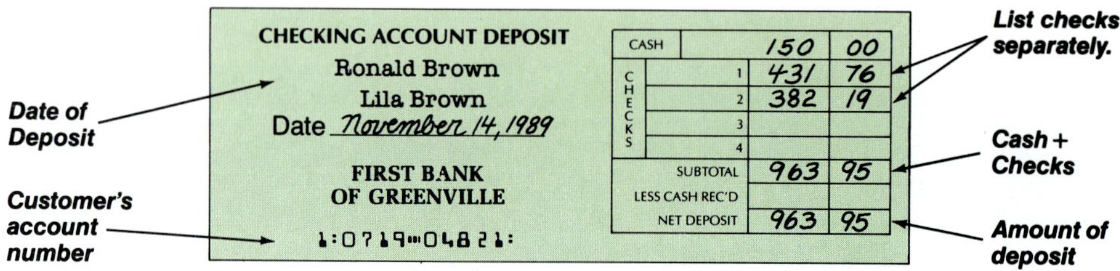
CHECKING ACCOUNT DEPOSIT
Ronald Brown
Lila Brown
Date November 14, 1989
FIRST BANK
OF GREENVILLE
⑆:0719⑈04821⑆:

CASH		150	00
CHECKS	1	431	76
	2	382	19
	3		
	4		
SUBTOTAL		963	95
LESS CASH REC'D			
NET DEPOSIT		963	95

1. How much cash did Lila and Ron deposit? $150.00
2. How many checks did Lila and Ron deposit? 2

EXAMPLE

Lila and Ron have checks of $352.60 and $340.15. They want to receive $80.00 in cash and deposit the rest in their checking account. Find the net deposit.

To find the net deposit, first answer the "hidden question."

What is the subtotal?

1 Add to find the subtotal.
$352.60 + $340.15 = **$692.75**

2 Now you can find the net deposit.
$692.75 − $80.00 = **$612.75** ◀ *Subtotal − Cash Received = Net Deposit*

The net deposit is **$612.75.**

3. If the subtotal is the same as the net deposit, how much cash is received? None

CHECK YOUR SKILLS

For additional practice, see page 374.

Estimate by rounding to the nearest ten.

1. 112.38 + 49.95 160
2. 209.15 + 182.79 390
3. 167.34 − 75 95
4. 48.89 − 14.65 35
5. 347.70 − 181.90 170
6. 308.65 + 48.24 360
7. 21 + 18.56 + 17.60 60
8. 17.36 + 108.40 − 41.20 90

EXERCISES

Complete. Choose the answer from the box at the right.

1. Amount of Cash + Amount of Checks = ? subtotal
2. On a deposit slip the amount which is actually being put into the account is called the ?. net deposit
3. Net Deposit = Subtotal − ? cash received

net deposit
checks
cash received
subtotal
account number

For Exercises 4–6, find the SUBTOTAL *and the* NET DEPOSIT.

4.

	Dollars	Cents
CASH	43	48
CHECKS 1	127	35
List 2		
Each 3		
Check 4		
SUBTOTAL	?	
▶ Less Cash Rec'd	0	
NET DEPOSIT	?	

Subtotal: 170.83;
Net Deposit: 170.83

5.

	Dollars	Cents
CASH		
CHECKS 1	87	19
List 2	248	46
Each 3		
Check 4		
SUBTOTAL	?	
▶ Less Cash Rec'd	50	00
NET DEPOSIT	?	

Subtotal: 335.65;
Net Deposit: 285.66

6.

	Dollars	Cents
CASH		
CHECKS 1	316	08
List 2	256	34
Each 3	93	27
Check 4		
SUBTOTAL	?	
▶ Less Cash Rec'd	72	50
NET DEPOSIT	?	

Subtotal: 665.69
Net Deposit: 593.19

For Exercises 7–9, correct any errors in the deposit slips shown.

7.

	Dollars	Cents
CASH	108	47
CHECKS 1	95	16
List 2		
Each 3		
Check 4		
SUBTOTAL	193	53
▶ Less Cash Rec'd	0	
NET DEPOSIT	193	53

Subtotal: 203.63; Net Deposit: 203.63

8.

	Dollars	Cents
CASH		
CHECKS 1	28	94
List 2	75	19
Each 3		
Check 4		
SUBTOTAL	104	13
▶ Less Cash Rec'd	50	00
NET DEPOSIT	154	13

Net Deposit: 54.13

9.

	Dollars	Cents
CASH		
CHECKS 1	118	24
List 2	239	07
Each 3		
Check 4		
SUBTOTAL	357	31
▶ Less Cash Rec'd	27	50
NET DEPOSIT	330	21

Net Deposit: 329.81

10. Ron Brown wants to deposit a check for $409.54 in his checking account. He also wants to deposit $135.76 in cash. What is the net deposit? $545.30
11. Lila Brown has a check for $309.83 and a check for $187.09. She wants to receive $75.00 in cash and deposit the rest in the checking account. Find the net deposit. $421.92
12. Lila deposits 4 ten-dollar bills, 7 five-dollar bills, 3 one-dollar bills, and a check for $37.13 in the checking account. Find the net deposit. $115.13
13. Lila has a gift check for $138.27. She also has $272.30 in cash. She deposits the check and half the cash in the checking account. Find the net deposit. $274.42

2. What is meant by "less cash received"? (If you do not want to deposit the entire subtotal, the amount that you want to receive must be subtracted from the subtotal.)
3. Why is the account number printed with "computer" numerals? (To speed up processing at the bank)

Point out that some deposit slips use the words "coin" and "currency" instead of "cash." Explain that currency is paper money.

Have a student read the first paragraph. Then have all students write their answers to questions 1 and 2. Discuss the Example and question 3 that follows.

3 Close

Summary: Review the possibilities that can occur in filling out a deposit slip. These depend on whether there is more than one item being deposited and whether cash is received by the depositor.

Evaluation
Guided Practice: Ex. 1–3, 5–9 odd
Independent Practice: 4–8 even, 10–13

Extension

Have students obtain samples of at least five different deposit slips from local banks. They should note any differences that exist in the information contained on them.

Problem-Solving Skills

Solving a multi-step problem (Ex. 11–13)

Critical Thinking

You may wish to have students work in small groups to solve this problem or you may wish to work with the class.

Question 3 (in Lesson)

Lesson Resources

Maintenance: See below.
Reteaching/Alternate Teaching Strategy: p. M-26 (Visual 13)
Practice: p. M-26
Enrichment: p. M-26
Concrete Materials: Activity Worksheet 26A (pages W–54 and W–55), Visual 13
Visual 13

Objectives

Student will

1. apply place value and the skill of writing a decimal in words to writing the amount of a check.
2. solve problems that involve writing and endorsing checks.

Maintenance

1. Write 3.8% as a decimal. ANS: 0.038
2. Multiply: 0.064 × 13,600 ANS: 870.40
3. Find 7% of 8300. ANS: 581
4. Write $\frac{3}{4}$% as a decimal. ANS: 0.0075
5. Jill Clark paid a city income tax of 2.4% of $12,500. Find the amount of tax Jim paid. ANS: $300

1 Lesson Focus

Motivation: Ask students to discuss the advantage of having a checking account and being able to write checks as opposed to paying cash.

Purpose: Students must learn how to write checks properly because banks will not process checks which have been filled in incorrectly.

2 Teaching the Lesson

Have students read the paragraph preceding the sample check on page 98. Then direct their attention to the check and have them write their answers for questions 1–4. The following additional questions may be helpful.

Writing Checks

Ron and Lila Brown decide to buy a refrigerator for their new home from their neighbor Jana Cochran. To pay for the refrigerator, Ron writes a check. This check directs the bank to deduct money from the Browns' checking account.

When there is not enough money in an account to cover the amount of a check, the account is **overdrawn.** The bank may not cash the check and impose a fine. Some banks may cash the check and consider the overdrawn amount as a loan on which interest is charged.

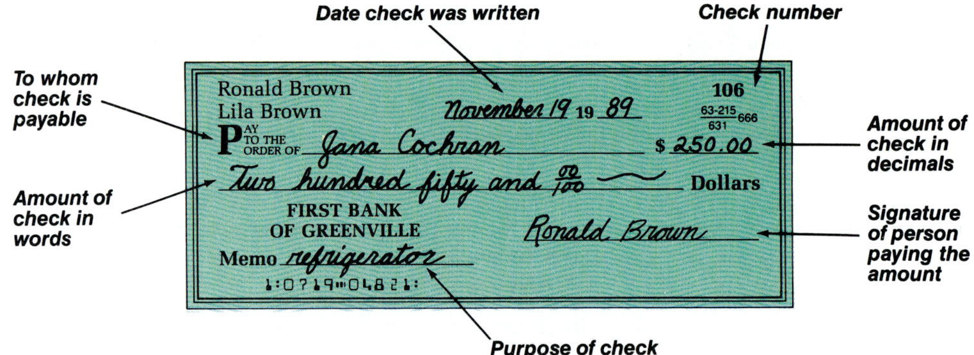

1. On what date did Ron write the check for the refrigerator? November 9, 1989
2. To whom is the check made payable? Jana Cochran
3. How much did the refrigerator cost? $250.00
4. Where did Ron indicate that the check was written to pay for a refrigerator? On the memo line

Jana can sign, or **endorse,** the back of the check in three ways.

To cash the check, Jana endorses it in this manner after she arrives at the bank.

This check can be deposited only in Jana's checking account or Jana's savings account.

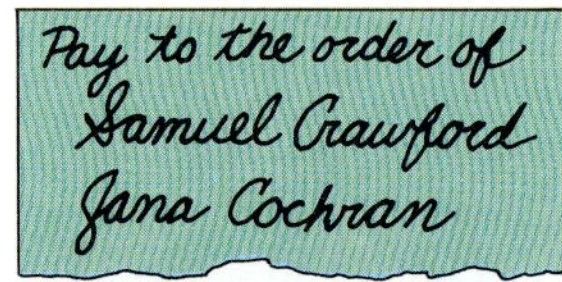

This check is signed over to Samuel Crawford. Both Jana and Samuel must endorse the check.

5. If Jana wishes to cash the check, why is it better for her to wait until she arrives at the bank to endorse it? If she endorsed the check before arriving at the bank and then lost it, anyone who finds the check could cash it.

EXERCISES

1. Three and 47/100 2. Eight and 19/100 3. Thirty-four and 21/100
4. Fifty-six and 99/100 5. Sixty-three and 00/100 6. One hundred two and 00/100

Write the amount in words as it would appear on a check.

1. $3.47 **2.** $8.19 **3.** $34.21 **4.** $56.99 **5.** $63.00

7. One hundred twenty-one and 14/100 8. Three hundred fifteen and 95/100

6. $102.00 **7.** $121.14 **8.** $315.95 **9.** $1540.51 **10.** $2611.69

9. One thousand five hundred forty and 51/100 10. Two thousand six hundred eleven and 69/100

11. Choose from the box at the right the item that should be written in each position (**a** through **g**) on the check.

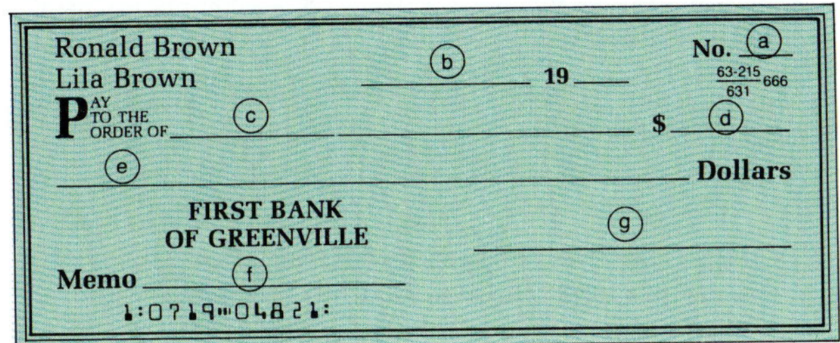

a	116
c	Parks' Home Center
g	Lila Brown
d	$16.70
f	curtain rods
b	November 28
e	Sixteen and $\frac{70}{100}$

For Exercises 12–15, refer to the checks shown below.

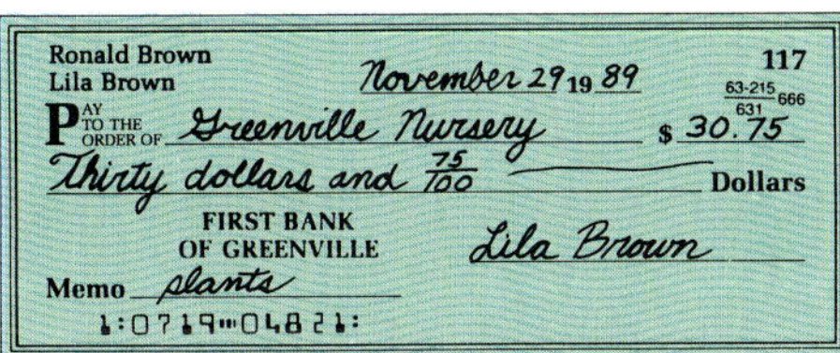

Ronald Brown
Lila Brown
118
December 1 19 89
63-215/631 666
PAY TO THE ORDER OF Dr. Mc Clung $ 65.67
Sixty five sixty-seven Dollars
FIRST BANK OF GREENVILLE
Memo yearly check up

12. What is the purpose of check 117? To pay for plants

13. When was check 117 written? November 29, 1989

14. Is the amount written correctly in words on check 118? If not, write it correctly. No. Sixty-five and $\frac{67}{100}$

15. What is missing on check 118? The signature

For Exercises 16–19, use the endorsements shown below.

a. Pay to the order of Lila Brown Jana Cochran

b.

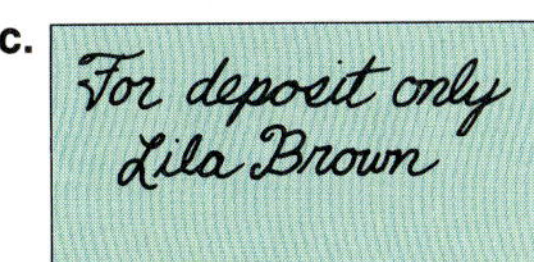

c. For deposit only Lila Brown

16. Which check is signed over to another person? a

17. Which check can be deposited only in Jana Cochran's account? b

18. Why are checks usually written with a pen rather than a pencil? The amount of the check could be changed if it is written in pencil.

19. Why is it not a good idea to sign a check and write in the amount at a later time? If the check is lost, anyone who finds it could fill in the amount.

1. Why do you think the check amount is written in words? (It serves as a verification of the amount written as a decimal.)
2. Which amount would the bank use as the correct one if the amount in decimals and the amount in words differ? (The amount in words because it usually takes more time and thought to write the amount in words)

Discuss the various ways to endorse a check as shown on page 98. Then have students discuss question 5.

3 Close

Summary: Review the procedure for writing a check by naming all the items that the check writer must complete.

Evaluation

Guided Practice: 2–10 evens, 11
Independent Practice: 9–11 odd, 12–19

Extension

Have students obtain information from at least three banks about their checking accounts. This would include the cost of writing checks, the cost of the check forms, any interest paid, and so forth. Students might also be interested in researching some of the types of violations of the law relating to check writing and some of the possible consequences.

Problem-Solving Skills

Reading a chart (Ex. 11–17)

Critical Thinking

You may wish to have students work in small groups to solve these problems or you may wish to work with the class.

Ex. 17, 18, Question 5 (in Lesson)

Lesson Resources

Maintenance: See below.
Reteaching/Alternate Teaching Strategy: p. M-27 (Visual 14)
Practice: p. M-27
Enrichment: p. M-27
Concrete Materials: Activity Worksheet 27A (pages W-57 and W-58), Visual 14
Visual 14

Objectives

Student will

1. solve multi-step problems that involve completing check stubs for a checking account.
2. solve multi-step problems that involve completing check registers for a checking account.

Maintenance

Perform the indicated operations.

1. 8.09 + 13.47 + 5.86 ANS. 27.42
2. 302.4 − 275.9 ANS: 26.5
3. 1.8 × 40.3 ANS: 72.54
4. 21.5 ÷ 2.5 ANS: 8.6
5. Gary has tax deductions of $119.35 and personal deductions of $10.75. His gross pay is $487.20. Find his net pay. ANS: $357.10

1 Lesson Focus

Motivation: Ask students to focus on the check stubs in the lesson. Have students make a generalization by looking at the completed check stub: Deposits are __?__ (added) to the balance forward on a check stub, and the amount of the check written is __?__ (subtracted) from the total of the check stub.

Purpose: Point out that check registers and check stubs are necessary to keep accurate records of deposits made and checks written.

STRATEGY: USING "HIDDEN QUESTIONS" TO SOLVE A MULTI-STEP PROBLEM

Check Stubs and Check Registers

After opening their checking account, Ron and Lila use the check stubs to keep a record of deposits made and checks written. The stubs also show the **balance,** or amount, in the account.

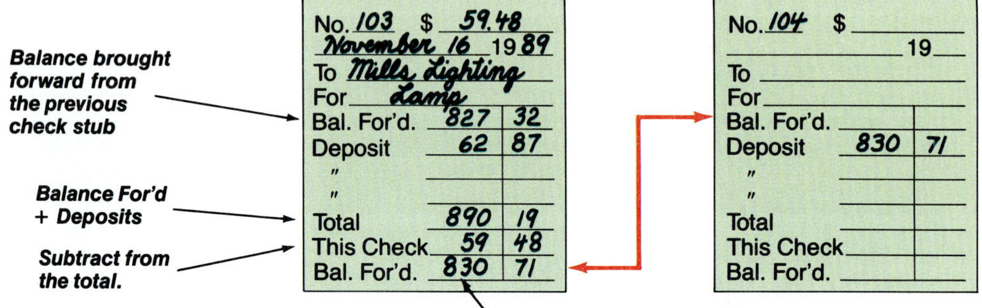

1. What was the amount of check number 103? **$59.48**
2. To whom was check number 103 payable? **Mills Lighting**
3. What was the balance brought forward from the stub of check number 102? **$827.32**
4. After writing check number 103, what is the new balance in the account? **$830.71**

Many people use a **check register** rather than check stubs.

EXAMPLE On December 1, Jana Cochran, a neighbor of the Browns, had $362.19 in her checking account. On December 2, she spent $55.43 for groceries at Top Market. She paid for the groceries with check number 296. On December 10, Jana deposited $143.85 in the account. Complete the check register.

PLEASE BE SURE TO **DEDUCT** CHARGES THAT AFFECT YOUR ACCOUNT

NO	DATE	ISSUED TO OR DESCRIPTION OF DEPOSIT	AMOUNT OF DEPOSIT	✓	AMOUNT OF PAYMENT	BALANCE FORWARD
						362 19
296	12/2	TO Top Market FOR groceries			55 43	306 76
	12/10	TO FOR	143 85			450 61
		TO				

Balance brought forward
Balance after subtracting amount of check
Balance after adding deposit

CHECK YOUR SKILLS

ESTIMATION/MENTAL MATH: Ex. 1–6

Estimate to determine whether the answer is reasonable. Answer Yes or No.

1. \$554.69 + \$226.85 = \$781.54 **Yes**
2. \$9.60 + \$19.45 = \$29.05 **Yes**
3. \$118.40 − \$72.60 = \$34.50 **No**
4. \$326.41 − \$46.08 = \$280.83 **Yes**
5. \$346.15 + \$39.60 = \$408.21 **No**
6. \$44.72 + \$514.03 = \$583.91 **No**

EXERCISES

Complete. Choose the answer from the box at the right.

deposits
check stub
check amount
balance
total

1. The amount of money in an account is called the _?_. **balance**
2. Total = Balance Brought Forward + _?_ **deposits**
3. New Balance Brought Forward = Total − _?_ **check amount**
4. You can use a check register to record _?_ and check amounts. **deposits**

Correct any errors in the following check stubs.

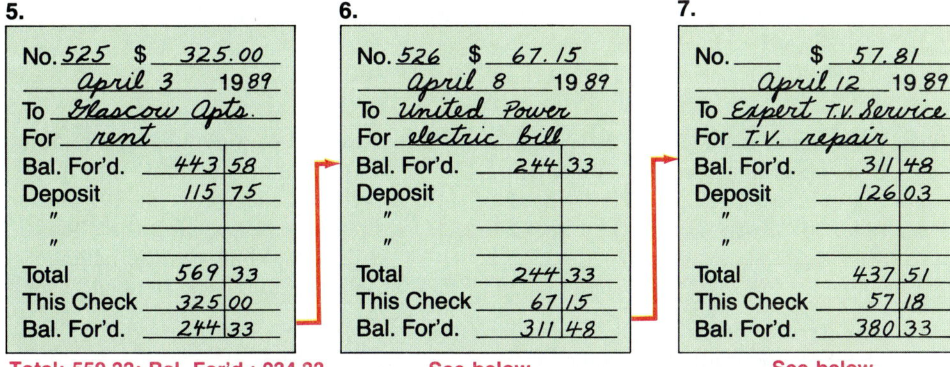
5. No. 525 \$ 325.00
April 3 1989
To Glascow Apts.
For rent
Bal. For'd. 443 58
Deposit 115 75
Total 569 33
This Check 325 00
Bal. For'd. 244 33

6. No. 526 \$ 67.15
April 8 1989
To United Power
For electric bill
Bal. For'd. 244 33
Total 244 33
This Check 67 15
Bal. For'd. 311 48

7. No. \$ 57.81
April 12 1989
To Expert T.V. Service
For T.V. repair
Bal. For'd. 311 48
Deposit 126 03
Total 437 51
This Check 57 18
Bal. For'd. 380 33

Total: 559.33; Bal. For'd.: 234.33 **See below.** **See below.**

For Exercises 8–9, copy a check stub shown on page 100. Use the information to complete the stub. **6. Bal. For'd.: 234.33; Total: 234.33; Bal. For'd.: 167.18**

8. On November 26, the Browns had \$963.95 in their checking account. Ron then made a deposit of \$75.00. He also wrote check number 119 for \$43.58 to Maddux Department Store for curtains. **Bal. For'd. is \$995.37**

9. On December 10, the Browns' checking account showed a balance of \$501.13. Lila then deposited checks for \$35.72 and \$51.69. She also wrote check number 123 for \$76.79 to Lincoln Gas Company for the gas bill. **Bal. For'd. is \$511.75.**

7. Bal. For'd.: 167.18; Total: 293.21; This Check: 57.81; Bal. For'd.: 236.03

2 Teaching the Lesson

Have students read the opening paragraph. Then direct the students' attention to the check stubs on page 100 and have them answer questions 1–4. Give a more detailed explanation of the check stubs if it seems necessary. Focus students' attention on the check register on page 101. These questions could be asked.

1. What was the balance of the checking account before check 296 was written? (\$362.19)
2. To whom was check 296 payable? (Top Market)
3. What transaction occured on 12/10? (A deposit of \$143.85 was made.)
4. Why are the transactions of 12/2 and 12/10 written in different columns? (On a check register, different columns are used for payments and deposits.)

3 Close

Summary: Ask students to explain in their own words the importance of keeping accurate records for a checking account.

Evaluation
Guided Practice: Ex. 1–5
Independent Practice: Ex. 6, 8–15

Extension

Organize students in groups and have each group make a list of at least five errors that might occur when completing a check stub or register.

Problem-Solving Skills

Solving a multi-step problem (Ex. 8–9, 13)
Working backwards (Ex. 12–13)
Using logical reasoning (Ex. 14)

Critical Thinking

You may wish to have students work in small groups to solve this problem or you may wish to work with the class.
Ex. 15

For Exercise 10–11, copy and complete each check register.

10.

PLEASE BE SURE TO **DEDUCT** CHARGES THAT AFFECT YOUR ACCOUNT								BALANCE FORWARD	
NO	DATE	ISSUED TO OR DESCRIPTION OF DEPOSIT	AMOUNT OF PAYMENT		✓	AMOUNT OF DEPOSIT		374	03
412	7/2	TO FOR	127	86				246	17
	7/5	TO FOR				176	35	?	
		TO							

422.52

11.

PLEASE BE SURE TO **DEDUCT** CHARGES THAT AFFECT YOUR ACCOUNT								BALANCE FORWARD	
NO	DATE	ISSUED TO OR DESCRIPTION OF DEPOSIT	AMOUNT OF PAYMENT		✓	AMOUNT OF DEPOSIT		213	92
209	10/21	TO FOR	21	89				192	03
210	10/23	TO FOR	6	57				?	
	10/23	TO FOR				85	16	?	
211	10/25	TO FOR	35	00				?	

185.46
270.62
235.62

12. Jana writes a check for $62.86. The balance in her account after writing the check is $129.56. What was the balance before writing the check? **$192.42**

13. Lila makes a deposit of $72.50 in the checking account. She then writes a check for $98.29. The balance after writing the check is $279.30. What was the balance before making the deposit? **$305.09**

14. The amount of the deposit is greater. The new balance is greater than the balance before the deposit.

14. The Browns have $279.82 in their checking account. Lila makes a deposit. Then Ron writes a check. The new balance brought forward is $300.00. Which is greater, the amount of the deposit or the amount of the check? Explain.

15. A check for $25.14 is mistakenly recorded as a deposit. By how much will the balance shown differ from the actual balance? **$50.28**

Mid-Chapter Review

Find the SUBTOTAL *and the* NET DEPOSIT. (Pages 96–97)
581.25; 506.25

1.

	Dollars	Cents
CASH		
CHECKS 1	148	65
List 2	72	60
Each 3	360	00
Check 4		
SUBTOTAL	?	
Less Cash Rec'd	75	00
NET DEPOSIT	?	

Find the TOTAL *and the* BALANCE FORWARD. (Pages 100–102)
523.19; 351.09

2.

No. 528 $ 172.10
April 16 19 89
To All City Insurance
For Car Insurance

Bal. For'd.	380	33
Deposit	142	86
"		
"		
Total	?	
This Check	172	10
Bal. For'd.	?	

For Exercises 3–6, use the information on this check. (Pages 98–99)

Ronald Brown
Lila Brown
May 4 19 89 101
63-215/631 666
PAY TO THE ORDER OF Riker's Automotive Shop $ 49.95
Forty - nine and 95/100 Dollars
FIRST BANK OF GREENVILLE
Memo new battery Ronald Brown
⑆:0719⑈0482⑆:

3. What is the amount of the check? $49.95
4. On what date was the check written? May 4, 1989
5. To whom is the check made payable? Riker's Automotive Shop
6. What is the purpose of the check? To pay for a new battery

MAINTENANCE

7. Cathy Whitehead is a record company executive. Her yearly salary is \$44,500. She also receives $1\frac{1}{2}\%$ of the company's profits. How much does she earn in a year in which profits were \$6,184,000? (Pages 45–47) $137,260

8. In preparation for her party, Matilda needs to go to three stores, the bakery, the card shop, and the grocery store. In how many different orders could Matilda arrange her shopping trip. (Pages 24–25) 3 × 2 × 1, or 6 ways

9. Sue Barker's grades on four tests were 72, 86, 69, and 83. She would like her mean score on five tests to be 80. What is lowest grade she can get on the fifth test? (Pages 10–11) 90

10. John Pruitt received $23,000 in wages last year. He also received $126.65 in interest from his savings account, and a $500 incentive bonus. Find John's adjusted gross income. (Pages 72–73) $23,626.65

Objective

Student will

1. review the skills, concepts and applications in the first part of Chapter 5.
2. maintain key skills and concepts taught in Chapters 1–4.

Using the Page

Exercises 1–6 provide an informal assessment of the student's mastery of the major skills and concepts presented in the first half of Chapter 5. Each item is referenced to the related pages where the particular item was presented. These exercises parallel the quiz provided in the *Teacher's ResourceBank.*™

A quiz covering the second half of the chapter is also provided in the *Teacher's ResourceBank.*™

Exercises 7–10 maintain skills and concepts taught in Chapters 1–4.

Objective

Student will apply the skills of addition, subtraction, and multiplication to solving multi-step problems that involve making change.

Overview

This page is an extension of the skills and ideas presented in the previous lessons of this chapter. Since the content presented on this page is not included in the Chapter Review or Chapter Test, its use is optional.

Using the Pages

You may wish to have students work this lesson in small groups or you may wish to work with the class. Using it with the class, have students read the first paragraph and the rule. Then ask student volunteers to answer Exercises 1–4. Work Exercise 6 with the class and assign Exercises 7–20 as independent practice.

You may want to use Visual 15 as you present this lesson.

Problem-Solving Skills

Completing a table (Ex. 6–12)
Solving a multi-step problem (Ex. 9–20)

Math and Making Change

Susan Wiggins works at the Greenville Food Mart as a cashier. The cash register computes how much change she needs to give to each customer. Then Susan uses this rule to count out the change.

Use as few bills and as few coins as possible.

EXERCISES

Choose the best way to make change. Choose a, b, or c.

1. 3.25 — TOTAL | CHANGE | SUBTOTAL   b

a. Three $1-billls, 2 dimes, 1 nickel
b. Three $1-bills, 1 quarter
c. Two $1-bills, 5 quarters

2. 0.68 — TOTAL | CHANGE | SUBTOTAL   a

a. Two quarters, 1 dime, 1 nickel, three pennies
b. Six dimes, 8 pennies
c. One quarter, 4 dimes, 3 pennies

3. 6.46 — TOTAL | CHANGE | SUBTOTAL   c

a. Six $1-bills, 1 quarter, 2 dimes, 1 penny
b. Six $1-bills, 4 dimes, 1 nickel, 1 penny
c. One $5-bill, one $1-bill, 1 quarter, 2 dimes, 1 penny

4. 1.79 — TOTAL | CHANGE | SUBTOTAL   b

a. Seven quarters, 4 pennies
b. One $1-bill, 3 quarters, 4 pennies
c. One $1-bill, 2 quarters, 2 dimes, 9 pennies

For Exercises 5–8, make a chart like the one below. Write the number of bills and coins in the boxes to show the best way to make change. The first one is done for you.

	Change Due	Change: Number of						
		$10-bills	$5-bills	$1-bills	Quarters	Dimes	Nickels	Pennies
5.	$3.22	None	None	3	None	2	None	2
6.	$2.36	? None	? None	? 2	? 1	? 1	? None	? 1
7.	$6.73	? None	? 1	? 1	? 2	? 2	? None	? 3
8.	$15.98	? 1	? 1	? None	? 3	? 2	? None	? 3

For Exercises 9–12, make a chart like the one below. First, find the change due. Then write the number of bills and coins in the boxes to show the best way to make change.

	Amount of Sale	Money Received	Change Due	Change: Number of						
				$10-bills	$5-bills	$1-bills	Quarters	Dimes	Nickels	Pennies
9.	$3.77	$10	? $6.23	? None	? 1	? 1	? None	? 2	? None	? 3
10.	$16.56	$20	? $3.44	? None	? None	? 3	? 1	? 1	? 1	? 4
11.	$8.09	$20	? $11.91	? 1	? None	? 1	? 3	? 1	? 1	? 1
12.	$28.35	$40	? $11.65	? 1	? None	? 1	? 2	? 1	? 1	? None

a. *Find the change due.*
b. *Give the best way to make change.*

13. Scott's total bill for groceries was $7.32. He gave the cashier a $10 bill. **$2.68; Two $1-bills, 2 quarters, 1 dime, 1 nickel, 3 pennies**

14. Lila's total bill for groceries was $12.76. She gave the cashier a $20-bill. **$7.24; One $5-bill, Two $1-bills, 2 dimes, 4 pennies**

15. Derrick's total bill for canned goods was $5.13. He gave the cashier a $20-bill. **$14.87; One $10-bill, four $1-bills, 3 quarters, 1 dime, 2 pennies**

16. Jerome bought a book for $5.98 and a card for $1.25. The sales tax was $0.43. He gave the cashier a $10-bill. **$2.34; Two $1-bills, 1 quarter, 1 nickel, 4 pennies**

17. Karen bought a plant for $7.85, a bag of fertilizer for $3.43, and a rake for $10.19. The sales tax was $1.07. She gave the cashier a $20-bill and a $5-bill. **$2.46; Two $1-bills, 1 quarter, 2 dimes, 1 penny**

18. Amy bought 2 records for $7.50 each and a compact disc for $14.40. The sales tax was $1.76. She gave the cashier a $50-bill. **See below.**

$13.00; One $10-bill, three $1-bills

19. Larry's total bill for groceries was $7.01. He gave the cashier a $20-bill and 1 penny.

20. Elsa's total bill for groceries was $25.37. She gave the cashier two $20-bills and 2 pennies. **$14.65; One $10-bill, four $1-bills, 2 quarters, 1 dime, 1 nickel**

18. $18.84; One $10-bill, one $5-bill, three $1-bills, 3 quarters, 1 nickel, 4 pennies

Lesson Resources

Maintenance: See below.
Reteaching/Alternate Teaching Strategy: p. M-27 (Visual 16)
Practice: p. M-27
Enrichment: p. M-27
Concrete Materials: Visual 16
Visual 16

Objective

Student will solve multi-step problems that involve reconciling a check register balance with a bank statement balance.

Maintenance

1. Write $\frac{1}{4}$ as a decimal. ANS: 0.25
2. Write 0.32 as a percent. ANS: 32%
3. Multiply: $\frac{2}{3} \times 36$ ANS: 24
4. Multiply: 0.35×40 ANS: 14
5. The probability of guessing the correct answer on a multiple-choice test question with five choices is $\frac{1}{5}$. About how many correct answers could you expect to get by guessing on a test of 50 questions? ANS: 10

1 Lesson Focus

Motivation: Ask students how they would know that their check records were correct if they had a checking account.

Purpose: Most students will have a checking account in the future. Understanding a bank statement and being able to reconcile a check register balance with a bank statement are important consumer skills.

STRATEGY: USING "HIDDEN QUESTIONS" TO SOLVE A MULTI-STEP PROBLEM

Reconciling a Bank Statement

Each month, the Browns receive a checking account statement from their bank. This statement includes a **service charge,** which is a fee banks charge for handling checking accounts. The service charge may be a fixed amount, or it may be based on the number of checks paid by the bank, or it may be a combination of these depending on bank policy.

The Browns also receive their canceled checks with their statement. **Canceled checks** are checks that the bank has paid.

Ronald Brown
Lila Brown
315 E. Pasco Drive
Greenville, TX 75401

FIRST BANK OF GREENVILLE

		ACCOUNT NUMBER	AS OF DATE	ACTIVITY ON THIS STATEMENT: DEPOSITS	ACTIVITY ON THIS STATEMENT: CHECKS
11	18	5119 4825	01/05/90	2	4

ENDING BALANCE ON PREVIOUS STATEMENT	+	DEPOSITS AND OTHER CREDITS	−	WITHDRAWALS AND FEES	=	BALANCE AS OF THIS STATEMENT DATE
376.09		997.60		593.28		780.41

DATE	DESCRIPTION	DEPOSITS	WITHDRAWALS	BALANCE
12/09	CHECK—224		45.00	331.09
12/13	DEPOSIT	530.92		862.01
12/15	CHECK—227		134.80	727.21
12/15	CHECK—225		375.00	352.21
12/21	DEPOSIT	466.68		818.89
12/29	CHECK—223		34.78	784.11
1/5	SERVICE CHARGE		3.70	780.41

1. What is Ron and Lila's checking account number? 5119 4825
2. How many deposits are shown on this statement? 2
3. How many canceled checks did the Browns receive with this statement? 4
4. What was the balance in the account at the end of the statement? $780.41

Some checks and deposits listed on the check register did not reach the bank in time to be recorded on the bank statement. These are called **outstanding checks** and **outstanding deposits.**

EXAMPLE Lila and Ron's check register showed a balance of $605.32. Lila compared each canceled check and deposit slip with her check register and bank statement to find the following outstanding checks and outstanding deposits.

Check #222: **$187.36** Check #226: **$32.60** Deposit: **$41.17**

Show how Lila **reconciled** the statement and the check register.

1 Adjust the check register.

Adjust for those items on the bank statement which are not on the check register.

CHECK REGISTER BALANCE	605	32
SUBTRACT SERVICE CHARGE	3	70
ADJUSTED CHECK REGISTER BALANCE	601	62

2 Adjust the bank statement.

Adjust for those items on the check register which are not on the bank statement.

BANK STATEMENT BALANCE	780	41
ADD TOTAL OUTSTANDING DEPOSITS	41	17
TOTAL	821	58
SUBTRACT TOTAL OUTSTANDING CHECKS	219	96
ADJUSTED BANK STATEMENT BALANCE	601	62

3 Compare. Both adjusted balances are $601.62.

CHECK YOUR SKILLS

Add or subtract as indicated. For additional practice, see pages 368–369.

1. $695.45 + $7.50 $702.95
2. $704.09 + $355.57 $1059.66
3. $220.98 + $429.81 $650.79
4. $433.69 − $218.84 $214.85
5. $745.50 − $619.90 $125.60
6. $685.72 + $108.33 + $16.49 $810.54
7. $807.65 + $201.95 + $313.58 $1323.18
8. $419.90 + $807.40 + $212.30 $1439.60

EXERCISES

Complete. Choose the answer from the box at the right.

multiplied by
added to
outstanding
balanced
canceled
subtracted from

1. Checks that are recorded in the check register but do not appear on the bank statement are called _?_ checks. outstanding
2. Checks that are recorded both on the check register and the bank statement are _?_ checks. canceled
3. To reconcile a bank statement and a check register, outstanding checks are _?_ the bank statement balance. subtracted from
4. To reconcile a bank statement and a check register, outstanding deposits are _?_ the bank statement balance. added to

2 Teaching the Lesson

Direct students' attention to the bank statement on page 106. Have a student read the opening paragraph. Then have students write the answers to questions 1–4. These additional questions may help students learn more about a bank statement.

1. What was the ending balance of the previous statement? ($376.09)
2. Why are deposits added to the previous balance? (Deposits are money put into the account.)
3. Why are checks that are written subtracted from the previous balance? (Check written are money taken out of the account.)
4. What fees might appear on a bank statement? (Service charge, charges for overdrawn checks, charges for new checks, etc.)

Then discuss the Example on page 107 which shows how to reconcile the bank statement and check register balance.

3 Close

Summary: Review the various elements of the bank statement and the steps in reconciling the balances.

Evaluation
Guided Practice: Ex. 1–4, 6, 8
Independent Practice: Ex. 5, 7, 9–18

Extension

Have each student make a list of errors that would cause the bank statement and the check register to not agree.

For Exercises 5–8, reconcile the check register balance and the bank statement balance by completing the table.

	5.	6.	7.	8.
Check Register Balance	611.49	264.51	358.95	270.86
Subtract Service Charge	2.80	4.20	9.09	7.10
Adjusted Check Register Balance	? 608.69	? 260.31	? 349.86	? 263.76
Bank Statement Balance	692.73	247.54	129.86	419.02
Add Outstanding Deposits	30.00	54.19	275.00	0.00
Total	? 722.73	? 301.73	? 404.86	? 419.02
Subtract Outstanding Checks	114.04	41.42	55.00	155.26
Adjusted Bank Statement Balance	? 608.69	? 260.31	? 349.86	? 263.76
Are the adjusted balances the same?	Yes ?	Yes ?	Yes ?	Yes ?

Problem-Solving Skills

Choosing the operation (Ex. 9–12)
Interpreting information (Ex. 9–16, 18)
Solving a multi-step problem (Ex. 10–13, 18)

9. The balance on Lila and Ron's bank statement is $216.02. They have an outstanding deposit of $125.00. What is their adjusted bank statement balance? **$341.02**

10. The Brown's bank statement shows their balance to be $186.84. They have outstanding checks for $15.89 and $34.56. What is the adjusted balance? **$136.39**

11. Jana's bank statement shows her balance to be $381.14. She has an outstanding check for $156.43 and an outstanding deposit for $80.00. What should her adjusted check register balance be? **$304.71**

12. The balance on Jana's bank statement is $164.89. She has outstanding checks of $54.23 and $14.87. She has an outstanding deposit of $99.53. What is her adjusted check register balance? **$195.32**

13. The service charge at Newton Memorial Trust is $3.00 per month plus 20¢ for each canceled check. The service charge at Newton Savings and Loan is a fixed fee of $7.00 per month.

a. At which bank will the service charge be less for a month in which eleven checks were canceled? **Newton Memorial Trust**

b. How much less is it? **$1.80**

For Exercises 14–19, use the information in the check register and the bank statement below.

PLEASE BE SURE TO **DEDUCT** CHARGES THAT AFFECT YOUR ACCOUNT — BALANCE FORWARD

NO	DATE	ISSUED TO OR DESCRIPTION OF DEPOSIT	AMOUNT OF PAYMENT	✓	AMOUNT OF DEPOSIT	BALANCE FORWARD
						256 14
101	5/14	TO County Electric FOR electricity	56 63			199 51
	5/17	TO FOR			700 00	899 51
102	5/17	TO Fabricland FOR cloth	12 71			886 80
103	5/17	TO Griener Foods FOR groceries	47 39			839 41
104	5/23	TO Belmont Apts FOR rent	410 00			429 41
	5/25	TO FOR			75 00	504 41
	5/26	TO service charge FOR				

DATE	DESCRIPTION	DEPOSITS	WITHDRAWALS	BALANCE
5/16	CHECK PAID—101		56.63	199.51
5/17	DEPOSIT	700.00		899.51
5/21	CHECK PAID—103		47.39	852.12
5/18	CHECK PAID—102		12.71	839.41
5/22	SERVICE CHARGE		5.90	833.51

14. How many checks are recorded in the check register? **4**

15. How many checks were paid by the bank? **3**

16. Which checks are outstanding? **Check 104**

17. Are there any outstanding deposits? **Yes; one**

18. Reconcile the bank statement and the check register. **The adjusted balances are $498.51.**

19. Why does the date for check number 101 in the check register differ from the date on the bank statement?

19. The check did not arrive at the bank until two days after it was written.

Critical Thinking

You may wish to have students work in small groups to solve this problem or you may wish to work with the class.

Ex. 19

Lesson Resources

Maintenance: See below.
Reteaching/Alternate Teaching Strategy: p. M-28 (Visual 17)
Practice: p. M-28
Enrichment: p. M-28
Visual 17

Objectives

Student will

1. use a formula to solve problems that involve simple interest.
2. solve multi-step problems that involve compound interest.

Maintenance

Perform the indicated operations.

1. $4.20 × 20 ANS: $84
2. $6.80 × 1.5 ANS: $10.20
3. $9.32 × 5 ANS: $46.60
4. $156.80 + $28.70 ANS: $185.50
5. Lisa Marlowe earns $6.50 per hour and receives time and half for hours worked over her regular 40 hours. She worked 44 hours last week. Find her total earnings. ANS: $299.00

1 Lesson Focus

Motivation: Ask students if they know the difference between simple interest and compound interest.

Purpose: Most students will be concerned about interest earnings when they become adult consumers. They should have a basic knowledge of how interest is computed.

2 Teaching the Lesson

Introduce the situation by having students read the first paragraph. Then introduce the interest formula by explaining what the letters represent in the formula. Explain that the rate should be expressed in decimal form, and the time must be expressed in years.

Interest

Ron and Lila Brown decide to open a savings account at First Bank of Greenville. The **principal,** or the amount of money deposited in their account, earns **interest.**

To find how much interest is earned, Lila uses the **simple interest** formula.

$$i = p \times r \times t$$

i = interest; p = principal; r = rate; t = time in years

EXAMPLE The Browns opened their savings account with a deposit of $2500. Their account pays a yearly interest rate of $5\frac{1}{4}\%$. How much simple interest is earned at the end of 3 months?

$$i = p \times r \times t$$

p = $2500; $r = 5\frac{1}{4}\% = 0.0525$; t = 3 months = $\frac{1}{4}$ year

$$i = \$2500 \times 0.0525 \times \frac{1}{4}$$

$$i = \$131.25 \times \frac{1}{4}$$

$$i = \$32.8125, \text{ or } \mathbf{\$32.81}$$

Rounded to the nearest cent

The simple interest earned after 3 months is **$32.81.**

You can use a calculator to find simple interest.

2500 [×] .0525 [÷] 4 [=] 32.8125 — $5\frac{1}{4}\% = 5.25\%$

Banks often pay interest at the end of each **quarter** (every 3 months or $\frac{1}{4}$ year). Both the original deposit <u>and</u> the interest are left in the account to earn interest. This is **compound interest paid quarterly.**

Quarter	Interest (to nearest cent) $i = p \times r \times t$	New balance
First	$2500 × 0.0525 × $\frac{1}{4}$ = $32.81	$2500 + $32.81 = $2532.81
Second	$2532.81 × 0.0525 × $\frac{1}{4}$ = $33.24	$2532.81 + $33.24 = $2566.05
Third	$2566.05 × 0.0525 × $\frac{1}{4}$ = $33.68	$2566.05 + $33.68 = $2599.73
Fourth	$2599.73 × 0.0525 × $\frac{1}{4}$ = $34.12	$2599.73 + $34.12 = **$2633.85**

1. What was the balance in the account after the first quarter? **$2532.81**

2. *Complete:* New Balance = Principal + __?__ **Interest**

3. Why was more interest earned during the second quarter than during the first quarter? **The second quarter balance (principal) was higher.**

4. What was the total amount of interest earned during the year? **$133.85**

5. Would you rather have money in an account that paid simple interest or compound interest? Why? **Compound interest; the balance increases faster.**

CHECK YOUR SKILLS

Write a decimal for each percent. **For additional practice, see page 403.**

1. 12% **0.12**
2. $6\frac{1}{4}$% **0.0625**
3. $8\frac{1}{2}$% **0.085**
4. $6\frac{3}{4}$% **0.0675**
5. 5% **0.05**
6. 6% **0.06**

Multiply. Round answers to the nearest cent. **For additional practice, see page 372.**

7. $800 × 0.0625 **$50**
8. $1200 × 0.12 **$144**
9. $18.40 × $\frac{3}{4}$ **$13.80**
10. $576 × $\frac{1}{2}$ **$288**

EXERCISES

For Exercises 1–6, find the simple interest.

	Principal	Rate	Time
1.	$600	10%	6 months **$30**
2.	$900	12%	4 months **$36**
3.	$2100	8%	3 months **$42**

	Principal	Rate	Time
4.	$3500	6%	6 months **$105**
5.	$12,600	$4\frac{1}{2}$%	4 months **$189**
6.	$15,200	$6\frac{1}{4}$%	3 months **$237.50**

7. Lila's friend has $800 in an account that pays a yearly interest rate of $4\frac{3}{4}$%. How much simple interest will the account earn in 6 months? **$19**

8. After 6 months, how much more simple interest will $1000 earn at an 8% interest rate than at a 6% interest rate? **$10**

For Exercises 9–12, complete the table to find the yearly interest on $4000 at 4% compounded quarterly.

Quarter	Interest	New Balance
9. First	? **$40**	? **$4040**
10. Second	? **$40.40**	? **$4080.40**
11. Third	? **$40.80**	? **$4121.20**
12. Fourth	? **$41.21**	? **$4162.41**

For Exercises 13–16, complete the table to find the yearly interest on $2700 at 5% compounded quarterly.

Quarter	Interest	New Balance
13. First	? **$33.75**	? **$2733.75**
14. Second	? **$34.17**	? **$2767.92**
15. Third	? **$34.60**	? **$2802.52**
16. Fourth	? **$35.03**	? **$2837.55**

Discuss the Example on page 110 in detail. You might explain that one-fourth year can also be expressed as the decimal 0.25. Ask students to compare the calculator method of using percent to the method shown in the Example.
The steps for computing the new balance when interest is compounded will have to be carefully explained. You may wish to use Visual 17 to develop the steps on an overhead projector so students will have a better understanding of the process.
Use questions 1–4 on page 111 as you develop these steps.

3 Close

Summary: Summarize the use of the interest formula by going through a single example with different data than for the Example on page 110. Ask one or more students to explain the difference between simple and compound interest. Have one or more students explain how compound interest can be computed.

Evaluation
Guided Practice: Ex. 1–3, 9–14
Independent Practice: Ex. 4–8, 11–16

Extension

Have students check with five banks or lending institutions to find out what their interest rates are on savings accounts. They should also find out how the interest is compounded (yearly, quarterly, daily, etc.).

Problem-Solving Skills

Using a formula (Ex. 1–16)
Solving a multi-step problem (Ex. 8–16)

Critical Thinking

You may wish to have students work in small groups to solve this problem or you may wish to work with the class.
Question 5 (in Lesson)

Lesson Resources

Maintenance: See below.
Reteaching/Alternate Teaching Strategy: p. M-28 (Visual 18)
Practice: p. M-28
Enrichment: p. M-28
Concrete Materials: Visual 18
Visual 18

Objective

Student will use a table to solve multi-step problems that involve compound interest.

Maintenance

Perform the indicated operations.

1. 38 + 4075 + 927 + 9 ANS: 5049
2. 5,564.25 − 5000 ANS: 564.25
3. 515 − 127 ANS: 388
4. 260 ÷ 40 ANS: 6.5
5. Sam Harris earned $102 one week for 8 hours of overtime work. His total pay for 48 hours was $442. Find his hourly rate for the first 40 hours. ANS: $8.50

1 Lesson Focus

Motivation: Give an example of an amount of $1000 invested at 6% for 10 years. The simple interest that would be earned is $600. If the interest is compounded quarterly, the earnings are about $814. This shows the power of compounding.

Purpose: Students, as future adult consumers, must be able to make intelligent decisions as investors.

2 Teaching the Lesson

Direct the students' attention to the interest table on page 112. Explain the purpose of the table. Then have students read the opening paragraphs and write the answer to question 1. The following questions may help the explanation of the Example.

STRATEGY: USING "HIDDEN QUESTIONS" TO SOLVE A MULTI-STEP PROBLEM

Compound Interest

Jana can use the compound interest table below to find how much each dollar in her savings account will amount to after a certain number of interest periods.

Total Interest Periods	Interest Rate Per Period									
	1.5%	2%	2.5	3%	3.5%	4%	5%	6%	7%	8%
1	1.0150	1.0200	1.0250	1.0300	1.0350	1.0400	1.0500	1.0600	1.0700	1.0800
2	1.0302	1.0404	1.0506	1.0609	1.0712	1.0816	1.1025	1.1236	1.1449	1.1664
3	1.0457	1.0612	1.0769	1.0927	1.1087	1.1248	1.1576	1.1910	1.2250	1.2597
4	1.0614	1.0824	1.1038	1.1255	1.1475	1.1699	1.2155	1.2625	1.3108	1.3605
5	1.0773	1.1041	1.1314	1.1593	1.1877	1.2167	1.2763	1.3382	1.4026	1.4693
6	1.0934	1.1262	1.1597	1.1941	1.2293	1.2653	1.3401	1.4186	1.5007	1.5869
7	1.1098	1.1487	1.1887	1.2299	1.2723	1.3159	1.4071	1.5036	1.6058	1.7138
8	1.1265	1.1717	1.2184	1.2668	1.3168	1.3686	1.4775	1.5938	1.7182	1.8059
9	1.1434	1.1951	1.2489	1.3048	1.3629	1.4233	1.5513	1.6895	1.8385	1.9990
10	1.1605	1.2190	1.2801	1.3439	1.4106	1.4802	1.6289	1.7908	1.9672	2.1589

1. How much will $1.00 amount to after 6 interest periods at an interest rate of 3.5% per period? $1.23

EXAMPLE

Jana Cochran's savings account pays 6% yearly interest compounded quarterly. She has $3000 in her account. What will her new balance be at the end of 2 years?

To find the new balance, first answer the "hidden questions."

What is the interest rate per quarter?

How many interest periods (quarters) are there in 2 years?

1 Find the interest rate per quarter.

6% ÷ 4 = **1.5%** ◀ *Yearly interest rate* ÷ *Number of interest periods per year*

2 Find the number of interest periods.

2 × 4 = **8** ◀ *Number of years* × *Number of interest periods per year*

3 Use the table to find how much $1.00 will amount to at 1.5% after 8 interest periods: **$1.1265**

4 Now you can find the new balance.

$1.1265 × $3000 = **$3379.50** ◀ *Balance at the end of 2 years*

2. How much interest did Jana's account earn in 2 years? $379.50

CHECK YOUR SKILLS

Multiply. For additional practice, see page 372.

1. 1000 × 1.0600 1060
2. 5000 × 1.3605 6802.5
3. 800 × 1.9672 1573.76
4. 7000 × 1.2625 8837.5
5. 3600 × 1.1597 4174.92
6. 2000 × 1.3401 2680.2
7. 900 × 1.0500 945
8. 5000 × 1.1262 5631

EXERCISES

Complete. Choose the answer from the box at the right.

1. When the yearly interest rate is 6%, the interest rate per quarter is _?_%. $1\frac{1}{2}$
2. Interest in one bank is compounded quarterly. This means that there are _?_ interest periods in $1\frac{1}{2}$ years. 6
3. New balance − Principal = _?_ interest
4. New balance = _?_ × Principal table entry

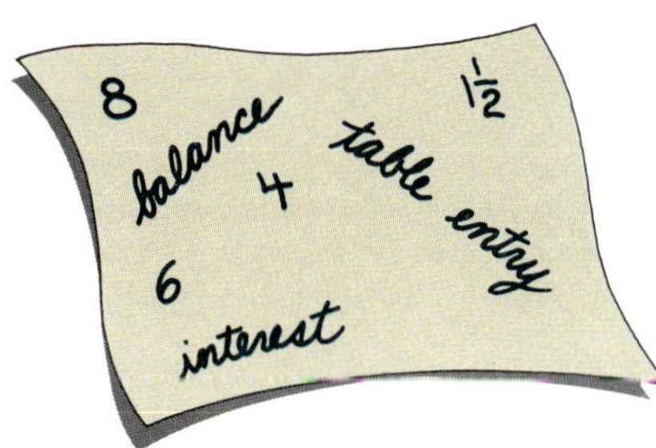

For Exercises 5–9, complete the table. Interest is compounded quarterly. Use the table on page 112.

	Present Balance	Annual Rate	Quarterly Rate	Time	Number of Quarters	Table Entry	New Balance
5.	$500	8%	? 2%	1 year	? 4	? 1.0824	? $541.20
6.	$900	12%	? 3%	6 months	? 2	? 1.0609	? $954.81
7.	$1800	10%	? 2.5%	$2\frac{1}{2}$ years	? 10	? 1.2801	? $2304.18
8.	$2400	6%	? 1.5%	2 years	? 8	? 1.1265	? $2703.60
9.	$12,600	14%	? 3.5%	18 months	? 6	? 1.2293	? $15,489.18

10. Lila's parents deposited $3600 in an account that paid 8% interest compounded quarterly. Find the new balance after 1 year. $3896.64

11. Ron's friend has $4200 in an investment account. The account pays 10% interest compounded quarterly. Find the amount of interest earned after 15 months. $551.88

12. The Browns invested $1000 for 2 years at 6% interest compounded quarterly. Jana invested $1000 for 2 years at 6% simple interest. How much more interest did the Browns earn than Jana? $6.50

13. After how many years will $1.00 invested at a yearly interest rate of 6% amount to $1.16 if interest is compounded quarterly? $2\frac{1}{2}$ years

1. How much would $100 amount to after 4 periods if the interest rate is 2.5% per period? ($110.38)
2. How much would $1 amount to after 4 periods if the *yearly* interest rate is 8%? ($1.0824, or $1.08)
3. What is the interest rate for each of 4 periods if the yearly rate is 7%? (1.75%)

Then discuss the Example in detail. A careful explanation will be necessary to understand it. An understanding of question 2 is also important.

3 Close

Summary: Summarize the use of the compound interest table on page 112 by reviewing the main steps of the Example.

Evaluation
Guided Practice: Ex. 1–4, 6, 8
Independent Practice: Ex. 5, 7, 10–13

Extension

Show students the following compound interest formula where A represents the balance after one year for a deposit of $1.

$$A = \left(1 + \frac{r}{n}\right)^n$$

r = yearly rate
n = number of compounding periods.

Show them how to work a problem using this formula and a calculator.

r [÷] n [+] 1 [x] [=] [=] etc.

(Press [=] once if $n = 2$, twice if $n = 3$, three times if $n = 4$, and so on.)

Problem-Solving Skills

Using a table (Ex. 5–13)
Solving a multi-step problem (Ex. 5–12)
Interpreting information (Ex. 10–13)
Making a comparison (Ex. 12)

Lesson Resources

Maintenance: See below.
Reteaching/Alternate Teaching Strategy: See the margin on page 115.
Practice: Activity Worksheet 31
Enrichment: See the enrichment topic "Computers and Banking" on page 118.

Objective

Student will use the strategy of solving a simpler problem to solve problems that involve prize money.

Maintenance

Multiply.

1. $\frac{1}{5} \times 200$ ANS: 40
2. $\frac{1}{10} \times 750$ ANS: 75
3. 300×50 ANS: 15,000
4. 37.5×200 ANS: 7500
5. There are 32 students in a math class. Of these students, $\frac{7}{8}$ passed a recent test. How many students did not pass the test? ANS: 4

1 *Lesson Focus*

Motivation: Ask students if they have ever won a prize in a contest or drawing.

Purpose: This lesson shows students that solving a simpler problem allows them to apply the understanding they have gained to a more complicated situation.

2 *Teaching the Lesson*

After presenting the Example, use the problem below to show how the strategy can be applied to other situations.

$9000 worth of prize money
Second Prize: $\frac{2}{3}$ of First Prize
Third Prize: $\frac{1}{2}$ of Second Prize
How much money for each prize?

Strategy: SOLVING A SIMPLER PROBLEM

The new First Bank is holding a drawing to celebrate its first anniversary. The four lucky winners share $33,000 according to the following rules.

RULES

Second Prize:	One-half of the first prize
Third Prize:	One-fourth of the second prize
Fourth Prize:	One-fifth of the third prize

EXAMPLE How much will each winner receive?

READ What are the facts?

The sum of the four prizes is $33,000.
The money will be shared according to the rules.

PLAN Solve a simpler problem; that is, use smaller numbers.

Assume the first prize is $100. Follow the rules to compute the other prizes.

SOLVE

First Prize:	$100.00	
Second Prize:	50.00	← *One half of $100*
Third Prize:	12.50	← *One fourth of $50*
Fourth Prize:	2.50	← *One fifth of $12.50*
Sum:	**$165.00**	

Now use the results to solve the problem.

Think: Compare $165 (the sum) with $33,000.

Since 33,000 ÷ 165 = 200, multiply each prize in the simpler problem by 200.

First Prize:	$20,000	← *200 × $100*
Second Prize:	10,000	← *200 × $50*
Third Prize:	2,500	← *200 × $12.50*
Fourth Prize:	500	← *200 × $2.50*
Sum:	**$33,000**	

CHECK Did you use all the facts correctly in solving the problem?

EXERCISES

Use the rules on page 114 for Exercises 1–8.

Compute the amount of each prize if the bank gives away $66,000.

1. First prize $40,000
2. Second prize $20,000
3. Third prize $5000
4. Fourth prize $1000

Compute the amount of each prize if the bank gives away $16,500.

5. First prize $10,000
6. Second prize $5000
7. Third prize $1250
8. Fourth prize $250

These are the rules that the bank used for the drawing to celebrate its second anniversary. Use these rules for Exercises 9–16.

Second Prize:	One-half of the first prize
Third Prize:	One-fourth of the first prize
Fourth Prize:	One-fifth of the first prize

9. The four winners will share $19,500. How much will each receive? $10,000; $5000; $2500; $2000
10. The four winners will share $39,000. How much will each receive? $20,000; $10,000; $5000; $4000
11. If the first prize is $30,000, what is the total prize money? $58,500
12. If the fourth prize is $8,000, what is the first prize? $40,000
13. If the third prize is $10,000, what is the second prize? $20,000
14. If the second prize is $25,000, what is the total prize money? $97,500

15. A number from 1 to 10,000 will be picked at random from a box. What is the probability that a "7" will be the first number drawn? $\frac{1}{10,000}$
16. In the drawing for Exercise 16, what are the odds that the first number drawn will be a "7"? $\frac{1}{9999}$
17. **Write your own problem** for a drawing that will have five prizes.

    Work with a partner (or with a small group, or as your teacher directs) to write the rules and to write at least one problem.

1. **Ask:** what is the problem about? (Finding the amount of each prize)
2. **Read** the problem to determine the FACTS. **Ask:** How much prize money is there? ($9000) **Ask:** How will the second and third prizes be determined? (Second: $\frac{2}{3}$ of first; third: $\frac{1}{2}$ of second)
3. **Plan** the solution. **Ask:** How would you make this a simpler problem? (Pick a small amount for first prize and determine the others from that.)
4. **Solve.** Have the students use $12 as first prize. **Ask:** What are the amounts for the second and third prizes? (Second: $8; third: $4) **Ask:** What was the total amount of money to be given away in the simpler problem? ($24) **Ask:** How does $9000 compare to $24? (9000 ÷ 24 = 375) **Ask:** Since each prize will be 375 times bigger than in the simpler problem, how much will be given away for each prize? (First: $4500; second: $3000; third: $1500)
5. **Check** the answer by having students read the problem again to check their facts with the solution. Ask: Does $4500 + $3000 + $1500 = $9000? (Yes)

3 *Close*

Summary: Have students discuss situations where solving a simpler problem could be used.

Evaluation
Guided Practice: Ex. 1–4
Independent Practice Ex. 5–16

Alternate Teaching Strategy

You may wish to have students work in small groups to complete the exercises. Have them discuss their ideas for each question and record the group concensus. Exercise 17 provides a group learning situation that can be used to give students more applications for using simpler problems.

NOTE: A quiz covering the second half of the chapter is provided in the *Teacher's ResourceBank™*.

Objectives

Students will

1. explore solutions to a variety of problems that emerge from this situational lesson.
2. explore solutions to checking account problems that have more than one solution.

Situational Lesson

These two pages present a situational lesson as the framework from which a variety of problem situations emerge.

Teaching Strategies

This lesson lends itself to cooperative learning groups for the problem solving activities of comparing choices and exploring decisions. (See page M-13.) However, these activities can also be carried out by the class as a whole or by individual students.

1 Lesson Focus

Motivation: Have students tell how much they think it costs to have a checking account.

Purpose: Students should understand that the cost of a checking account is paid by the user, either as a direct charge or as a reduced interest payment.

2 Teaching the Lesson

Have a volunteer read the introductory paragraphs. Then focus students' attention on the three choices. Ask these questions.

1. What are the costs of the checking account in Choice 1? ($3.50 per month plus 20¢ for each check written)
2. What is the minimum balance in Choice 2? ($1500)
3. If the bank invests your $1500 for a month at 8%, how much interest will the bank earn? ($\$1500 \times 0.08 \times \frac{1}{12} = \$10$)

Consumer's Choice

Lila Brown's sister, Cathy, will attend a community college in Greenville this fall. Lila advised Cathy to open a checking account at a local bank as soon as she arrives for the first semester of school. Cathy is considering these three accounts.

Choice 1: Regular Checking
Cathy would pay a service charge of $3.50 per month plus 20¢ for each check written.

Choice 2: Free Checking Plus Interest
Cathy would pay no fee provided she maintained a minimum of $1500 in the account. The account earns 4.5% yearly interest which is paid into the account monthly.

Choice 3: Checking Plus Interest
Cathy would pay a service charge of $10.00 per month. There is no minimum balance. The account earns 4.5% yearly interest which is paid into the account monthly.

Comparing the Choices

1. In Choice 1, what will be the monthly service charge if Cathy writes six checks? **$4.70**
2. In Choice 2, what will be the monthly service charge if Cathy has a balance of $1815.67 and writes six checks? **No service charge**
3. In Choice 3, what will be the monthly service charge if Cathy writes 6 checks? **$10.00**
4. In Choice 3, how much interest would Cathy's account earn for a month in which her average daily balance was $1200? **$54**
5. In Choice 3, how much more than the monthly service charge would Cathy's account earn in interest for a month in which her average daily balance was $1200? (See Exercises 3 and 4.) **$44 more**

Date	Description
7/21	PREVIOUS BALANCE
7/22	CHECK NUMBER 1353
7/23	CHECK NUMBER 1356
7/24	DEPOSIT
7/24	CHECK NUMBER 1352
7/24	CHECK NUMBER 1357

EXPLORING DECISIONS

6. With which choice will Cathy have the smallest service charge? **Choice 2**
7. With which choice will the amount of the service charge vary with the number of checks written? **Choice 1**
8. With which choice is there a required minimum balance? **Choice 2**
9. With which choices will the balance in the account earn interest? **Choices 2 and 3**
10. State a disadvantage of Choice 1.
11. State a disadvantage of Choice 2.
12. State one advantage of Choice 3 over Choice 2. **One advantage: there is no minimum balance. Answers will vary.**
13. If you were Cathy, what choice would you make? Give reasons for your choice? **Answers will vary.**

4. How much interest will the bank give you for your $1500 for one month in Choice 2? ($\$1500 \times 0.045 \times \frac{1}{12} = \$5.625$)
5. What is the service charge in Choice 3? ($10.00 per month)

Have students work individually on Exercises 1–9. Then discuss Exercises 10–13 with the class.

3 Close

Have a student explain the differences in the three types of bank accounts shown.

Problem-Solving Skills

Solving a multi-step problem (Ex. 1, 5)

Critical Thinking

Ex. 10–13

Project

Have students visit or call local banks to find the different types of checking accounts offered. Have them compare these to the ones described in the lesson and tell which of the accounts they would choose.

Additional Answers

10. One disadvantage: The account does not earn interest. Answers will vary.
11. One disadvantage: The minimum balance must be maintained. Answers will vary.

Objective

Student will learn how POS terminals transfer funds from a bank account to a retailer.

Overview

This topic is optional. The word "Enrichment" that appears to the right of the title in this Teacher's Edition does not appear in the student textbook. Therefore, this material is not included in the Chapter Review and Chapter Test.

Using the Page

You may wish to divide the class into small groups for this Enrichment. Have each student read the lesson and then assign the Project to each group. Have one person from each group report the group's findings to the class.

Computers and Banking ENRICHMENT

Point-of-sale (POS) terminals found in many retail stores and supermarkets are similar to cash registers. However, there are important differences. Each POS terminal is linked to a central computer system. Consumers will soon be able to make use of some POS terminals to transfer funds from their bank accounts to a retailer. Here's how it works!

1

A store clerk enters each purchase and the total cost into a POS terminal.

2

The customer uses a special "bank" card to input a personal identification number (ID) and authorize the purchase.

3

A central computer receives the information from the merchant plus the customer's ID and authorization. The computer sends the data to the customer's bank.

4

The customer's bank receives the data and confirms the transaction. The bank sends approval to the central computer.

5

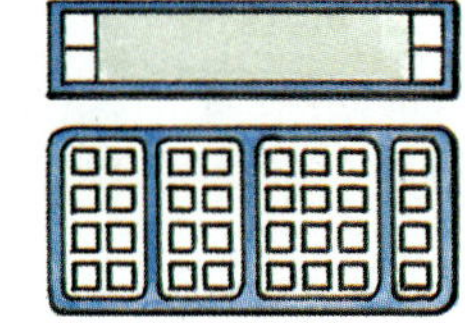

The central computer relays the approval to the merchant's POS terminal.

6

The sales clerk completes the approved transaction. The total purchase amount is subtracted from the customer's bank account and added to the merchant's account.

DATE OF TRANSACTION:
OCTOBER 25, 1989
THOMPSON CLOTHING N. 85
AMOUNT $415.50

The customer receives a receipt for the purchases and a POS receipt. The customer also receives a monthly bank statement showing all transactions.

PROJECT Find the names of businesses in your community that have POS terminals as described on this page. Report your findings to the class.

Chapter Summary

IMPORTANT IDEAS

1. To put money in a checking account, a person completes a deposit slip.
2. $\text{Net Deposit} = \text{Subtotal} - \text{Cash Received}$
3. You can use check stubs or a check register to record deposits and check amounts.
4. The back of a check is signed, or endorsed, by the person to whom the check is made payable.
5. To reconcile a bank statement, outstanding deposits are added to the bank statement balance. Outstanding checks are subtracted.
6. To find simple interest, use the formula $i = p \times r \times t$.
7. When an account earns compound interest, interest is paid both on the principal and interest previously earned.

Chapter Review

Part 1: VOCABULARY

For Exercises 1–5, choose from the box at the right the word(s) that complete(s) each statement.

principal balance canceled compound outstanding endorsed deposits rate

1. The amount of money in a checking account is called the _?_. (Page 100) **balance**
2. In order to deposit or cash a check, the back of the check must be _?_. (Page 98) **endorsed**
3. Checks that the bank has paid are called _?_ checks. **canceled** (Page 106)
4. In order to reconcile a bank statement and check register, _?_ checks are subtracted from the bank statement balance and outstanding _?_ are added to the bank statement balance. (Page 106) **outstanding; deposits**
5. _?_ interest is computed on the principal plus the interest previously earned. (Page 110) **compound**

Chapter Summary

The Chapter Summary contains a listing of the important ideas that were presented in the chapter. This listing is intended to assist the student with the Chapter Review that follows.

Objective

To review the important terms, skills, problem solving, and applications presented in Chapter 5.

Overview

The Chapter Review is structured in three parts. Part 1 is a review of the important terms that were introduced in the chapter. Part 2 reviews the skills that were presented in the chapter. Part 3 reviews the problem-solving strategies and applications that were presented in the chapter. Each item in the Chapter Review is referenced to the related pages where the concept, skill, or application was presented.

Using the Pages

You may wish to assign this Chapter Review for homework or treat it as a class review prior to administering the formal Chapter Test. In doing this, it is suggested that you only use the even- or odd-numbered exercises. You can then use the remaining exercises as a bank for use later.

Part 2: SKILLS

6. *Find the SUBTOTAL and the NET DEPOSIT.* (Pages 96–97)

	Dollars	Cents
CASH	200	00
CHECKS 1	87	70
List 2		
Each 3		
Check 4		
SUBTOTAL	?	
Less Cash Rec'd	0	
NET DEPOSIT	?	

287.70

287.70

7. *Complete this check stub.* (Pages 100–102)

No. 206 $ 26.75
April 30 19 89
To Greensville Post office
For mail box deposit

Bal. For'd.	418	25
Deposit	125	00
"		
"		
Total	?	
This Check	26	75
Bal. For'd.	?	

543.25

516.50

For Exercises 8–11, use the information on this check. (Pages 98–99)

June 4 19 89
PAY TO THE ORDER OF Sun Appliances $ 104.85
One hundred four and 35/100 Dollars
FIRST BANK OF GREENVILLE
Pamela Coalter
Memo ceiling fan
⑆:0719⑈0482⑆:

8. To whom is the check payable?
Sun Appliances

9. What is the number of the check?
313

10. What is the amount of the check?
$104.85

11. What is the purpose of the check?
To pay for a ceiling fan

For Exercises 12–16, write the amount in words as they would appear on a check. (Pages 98–99)

12. Six and 19/100 13. Twenty-one and 45/100 14. One hundred thirty-eight and 00/100

12. $6.19 **13.** $21.45 **14.** 138.00 **15.** $372.60 **16.** $1124.24

15. Three hundred seventy-two and 60/100 16. One thousand one hundred twenty-four and 24/100

For Exercises 17–22, find the simple interest. (Pages 110–111)

	Principal	Rate	Time
17.	$500	10%	3 months $12.50
18.	$750	$6\frac{1}{2}$%	4 months $16.25
19.	$1000	8%	6 months $40
20.	$1500	12%	4 months $60
21.	$2000	$5\frac{1}{2}$%	6 months $55
22.	$2500	4%	3 months $25

For Exercises 23–26, complete the table to find the yearly interest on $3000 at 5% compounded quarterly. (Pages 110–111)

	Quarter	Interest	New Balance
23.	First	? $37.50	? $3037.50
24.	Second	? $37.97	? $3075.47
25.	Third	? $38.44	? $3113.91
26.	Fourth	? $38.92	? $3152.83

Part 3: APPLICATIONS

27. Lila's tax refund check is for \$401.71. Ron's tax refund check is for \$378.83. The Browns want to deposit both these checks and receive \$100 back in cash. What is the net deposit? (Pages 96–97) **\$680.54**

28. On January 5, the Browns' checking account showed a balance of \$376.41. Ron then made a deposit of \$100.00. He also wrote a check for \$84.50. What is the new balance? (Pages 100–102) **\$391.91**

For Exercises 29–30, use the endorsements below. (Pages 98–99)

a.

b.

c.

Pay to the order of
Lila Brown
Jana Cochran

29. Which check is signed over to Lila Brown? **c**

30. Which check is Lila Brown cashing at the bank? **a**

31. The Browns' bank statement shows a balance of \$932.84. They have an outstanding deposit of \$200.00. They also have outstanding checks for \$63.54 and \$136.48. What should their check register balance be? (Pages 100–102) **\$932.82**

32. Jana's bank statement shows a balance of \$149.90. She has outstanding deposits of \$250.75 and \$310.86. She also has an outstanding check for \$685.45. What should her adjusted bank statement balance be? (Pages 100–102) **\$26.06**

33. Ron's brother has \$1100 in an account that pays a yearly interest rate of $6\frac{1}{2}\%$. How much simple interest will the account earn in 6 months? (Pages 110–111) **\$35.75**

34. Ron's sister has \$2000 in an account that pays a yearly interest rate of $5\frac{3}{4}\%$. How much simple interest will the account earn in 3 months? (Pages 110–111) **\$28.75**

For Exercises 35–36, use the table on page 112. (Pages 112–113)

35. Lila's uncle invested \$4500 in an account that pays 12% interest compounded quarterly. Find the interest earned after 1 year. **\$564.75**

36. Lila's nephew deposited \$2000 in an account that paid 6% interest compounded quarterly. Find the new balance after 2 years. **\$2253.00**

37. Three contest winners will share \$800. The third prize is one-half the second prize. The second prize is two-fifths the first prize. What is the first prize? (Pages 114–115) **\$500**

38. A total of \$24,000 is divided into three parts. The largest part is 3 times the smallest. The smallest is half the second part. How much is the smallest part? (Pages 114–115) **\$4000**

Objective

To informally assess students' mastering of the major skills, concepts, problem solving, and applications presented in Chapter 5.

Using the Page

After completing the Chapter Review with the class, you may wish to use this Chapter Test as an informal assessment. This Chapter Test parallels the formal chapter tests (Form A and Form B) provided in the *Teacher's ResourceBank.*™

Chapter Test

1. Lila and Ron have a check for \$401.88 and a check for \$201.90. They want to receive \$100 in cash and deposit the rest in their checking account. What is the net deposit? **\$503.78**

2. What are the two ways in which the dollar amount is written on a check? **In decimals and in words**

3. What is the memo line on a check used for? **To record the purpose of the check**

4. *Find the TOTAL and the BALANCE FORWARD.*

No. 169 \$ 110.90
January 11 19 89
To Lawn Care
For Lawn work

Bal. For'd.	79	61
Deposit	100	00
"		
"		
Total	?	
This Check	110	90
Bal. For'd.	?	

Total: **179.61**
Bal. For'd.: **68.71**

For Exercises 5–8, find the simple interest.

	Principal	Rate	Time
5.	\$600	6%	4 months **\$12**
6.	\$1200	$7\frac{1}{2}$%	9 months **\$67.50**
7.	\$1800	10%	6 months **\$90**
8.	\$800	8%	3 months **\$16**

9. The Browns' bank statement shows a balance of \$221.80. They have an outstanding check for \$215.40 and an outstanding deposit for \$100.00. What should their adjusted check register balance be? **\$106.40**

10. Ron Brown Sr. has \$1800 in an account that earns 10% interest compounded quarterly. Use the table on page 112 to find the amount of interest earned after 9 months. **\$138.42**

11. Raoul's investment account pays a yearly interest rate of 16%. He has \$960 in the account. Find the simple interest after 9 months. **\$115.20**

12. The four winners of a contest will share \$10,800 as follows.
Second prize: $\frac{1}{2}$ the first prize
Third prize: $\frac{1}{4}$ the second prize
Fourth prize: $\frac{1}{2}$ the third prize
How much will each receive? **\$6400; \$3200; \$800; \$400**

Cumulative Maintenance: Chapters 1–5

Choose the correct answer. Choose ***a, b, c,*** *or* ***d.***

1. Find the net deposit. b

	Dollars	Cents
CASH		
CHECKS 1	51	15
List 2	481	29
Each 3		
Check 4		
SUBTOTAL	?	
▶ Less Cash Rec'd	25	00
NET DEPOSIT	?	

a. \$557.44 **b.** \$507.44
c. \$532.44 **d.** \$405.14

2. Yvonne Egbert sold a house for \$121,000. Her commission was $6\frac{1}{2}\%$ of the selling price. How much did Yvonne earn? a

a. \$7865 **b.** \$786,500
c. \$78,650 **d.** \$786.50

3. Steven Enright deposited \$1500 in an account that pays 6% interest compounded quarterly. Use the compound interest table below to find the new balance after 1 year. c

Total Interest Periods	Interest Rate Per Period		
	1.5%	2%	2.5%
1	1.0150	1.0200	1.0250
2	1.0302	1.0404	1.0506
3	1.0457	1.0612	1.0769
4	1.0614	1.0824	1.1038

a. \$1568.55 **b.** \$1530.00
c. \$1592.10 **d.** \$1655.70

4. Karen Cook's bank statement shows a balance of \$319.45. She has an outstanding check for \$89.75 and an outstanding deposit for \$100.00. What should her adjusted check register balance be? c

a. \$309.20 **b.** \$509.20
c. \$329.70 **d.** \$379.70

5. On which day were twice as many cars sold as were sold on Wednesday? d

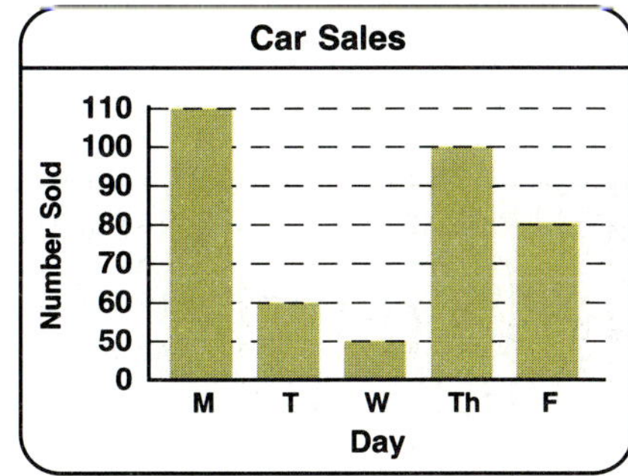

a. Monday **b.** Friday
c. Tuesday **d.** Thursday

6. An apartment complex offers a new tenant the choice of three different colors of carpet and two different wallpaper designs. How many possible combinations can the tenant choose? b

a. $\frac{2}{3}$ **b.** 6
c. $\frac{3}{2}$ **d.** 5

Objective

To review the content presented in Chapters 1–5

Using the Pages

You may wish to use this Cumulative Maintenance as an informal assessment tool. These pages can be assigned for homework or they may be used as review in class.

NOTE: The *Teacher's ResourceBank*™ contains a Cumulative Test for Chapters 3–5. The Cumulative Test is presented in a standardized-test format.

7. Write 0.06 as a percent. b

a. 60% **b.** 6%
c. 600% **d.** 66%

8. Kim Higgins earns $360 each week and claims one exemption. Use the table to find how much Federal Income Tax is withheld from her pay. c

Wages		*Number of exemptions claimed*		
At least	*But less than*	*0*	*1*	*2*
		Amount of tax to be withheld		
$320	$330	$46	$40	$35
330	340	47	42	36
340	350	50	43	38
350	360	53	45	39
360	370	55	46	41

a. $45 **b.** $55 **c.** $46 **d.** $41

9. Find the mean. b

Prices for Six Cars

$9875 $7651 $10,200
$8900 $9875 $11,651

a. $10,200 **b.** $9692
c. $7651 **d.** $9875

10. Multiply: $18,600 × 0.0705 a

a. $1311.30 **b.** $1301.30
c. $2411.40 **d.** $1031.40

11. Find the median. c

State Sales Tax Rates	
Florida	5.0
Nevada	5.75
Minnesota	6.0
Tennessee	5.5
Arizona	5.0

a. 5.45 **b.** 5.0
c. 5.5 **d.** 6.0

12. Find the balance forward. b

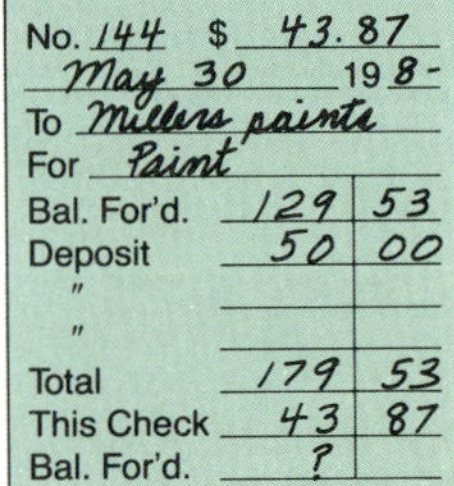

No. 144 $ 43.87
May 30 19 8-
To Millers paints
For Paint

Bal. For'd.	129	53
Deposit	50	00
"		
"		
Total	179	53
This Check	43	87
Bal. For'd.	?	

a. $402.90 **b.** $135.66
c. $126.93 **d.** $179.53

13. Add: $3\frac{1}{2} + 4\frac{2}{5}$ c

a. $7\frac{3}{7}$ **b.** $7\frac{3}{4}$
c. $7\frac{9}{10}$ **d.** 8

14. For which year are average car maintenance costs $400? c

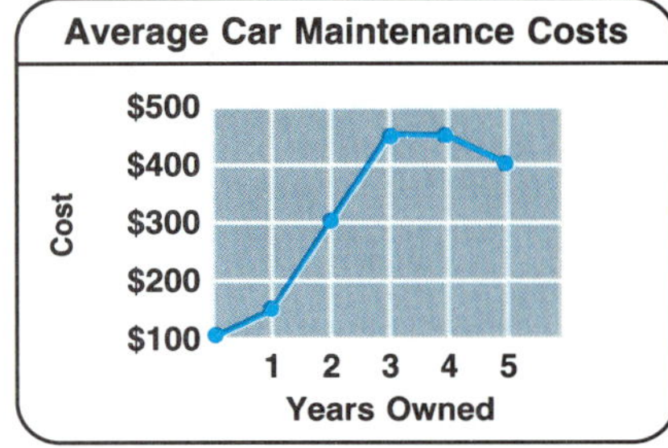

a. Third **b.** Second
c. Fifth **d.** Fourth

15. John Jacob's monthly gross pay is $1800. The deductions are federal tax-$321.60; state tax- $90.84 FICA tax-$89.60. What is John's monthly net pay? a

a. $1297.96 **b.** $1478.40
c. $502.04 **d.** $2302.04

Buying a Car

Tina Chavez wants to buy a new car. After she decides upon the make and model of the car, she will have many questions to answer.

- What are the different costs which comprise the total price of the car?
- Will the car dealer accept an offer that is below the sticker price?
- How will Tina finance her new car?
- How do the different types of car insurance protect car owners?
- How much will car insurance cost?

Chapter 6: Buying a Car

Overview

The focus of this chapter is on the costs connected with buying a car. Since prices vary from time to time and from community to community, you may wish to have students collect currect local data to round out their knowledge of costs in your area. Topics presented in Chapter 6 include sticker prices, making a deal, financing a car, and car insurance.

Although all lessons in this chapter involve problem-solving, the strategy lesson on pages 140–141 presents three strategies from which students are asked to select the most appropriate to apply in a given problem-solving situation. The *Consumer's Choice* on pages 142–143 presents a **situational lesson** in which students make consumer choices related to financing a car. Finally, the *Enrichment* lesson on page 144 introduces the topic of inflation and its effects on several consumer items such as medical care, automobile prices, housing, and so on.

Using This Page

Have students read the introductory paragraph and questions. Have them list possible solutions to the problems presented. After completing the chapter, have students review their suggested solutions, comparing them with those presented in the lessons. You may wish to have students suggest other possible problems resulting from the situation described on this page and to discuss possible solutions.

You may wish to organize the class into small groups to complete the situational activity described on this *Using the Page.*

Lesson Resources

Maintenance: See below.
Reteaching/Alternate Teaching Strategy: p. M-29
Practice: p. M-29
Enrichment: p. M-29
Concrete Materials: Activity Worksheet 32C
Visual 19

Objectives

Student will
1. find the sticker price of a car.
2. solve multi-step problems involving the total price of a car.

Maintenance

1. Add: 36 + 105 + 332 ANS: 473
2. Divide: 135 ÷ 3 ANS: 45
3. Round 3.426 to the nearest hundredth. ANS: 3.43
4. Write 125% as a decimal. ANS: 1.25
5. Find the mean for these hourly wage amounts. Round to two decimal places.
   $5.83 $6.95 $7.18   ANS: $6.65

1 Lesson Focus

Motivation: Ask students if they know what kinds of information are shown on the window sticker of a new car.

Purpose: As future consumers, students will be involved in purchasing a new car at some time. They should be familiar with the information that is on a window sticker.

STRATEGY: USING A "HIDDEN QUESTION" TO SOLVE A MULTI-STEP PROBLEM

Sticker Price

Tina Chavez is shopping for a new car. She sees this sticker in the window of a car she likes.

JETSTREAM ZX		BASE PRICE $7890
C/C	OPTIONS DESCRIPTION	List Price
H51	Air Conditioning	740.20
D34	Automatic transmission	460.00
G11	Tinted glass	94.80
M25	AM/FM Stereo with Cassette deck	412.50
R36	Power brakes	116.00
014	DESTINATION CHARGE	312.30

1. How much is the **destination** or **delivery charge?** $312.30

The sum of the base price, the cost of the optional equipment, and the destination charge is called the **sticker price.**

EXAMPLE 1 Find the sticker price of the Jetstream ZX.

Base Price	+	Cost of Optional Equipment	+	Destination Charge	=	Sticker Price
$7890	+	$1823.50	+	$312.30	=	**$10,025.80**

Tina knows that **sales tax** must be added to the sticker price. The state in which she lives has a sales tax rate of 6%.

2. Will 6% of $10,000 be closer to $600 or to $700? $600

EXAMPLE 2 Find the total cost of the Jetstream ZX.

1 Find the amount of sales tax.

6% of $10,025.80 = 0.06 × $10,025.80
= $601.548, or **$601.55** ◀ *Rounded to the nearest cent*

2 Find the total cost.

$10,025.80 + $601.55 = **$10,627.35** ◀ *Sticker Price + Sales Tax = Total Cost*

3. How close is the amount of sales tax in Example 2 to the estimate in Exercise 2? The sales tax is $1.55 higher than the estimate.

CHECK YOUR SKILLS

For additional practice, see pages 52–53.

Estimate to determine whether the answer is reasonable.

1. $512 + $676 + $103 = $1191 No
2. $892 + $754 + $204 = $2050 No
3. $8476.39 − $3435.79 = $5040.60 Yes
4. $7506.34 − $6126.57 = $2609.77 No
5. $4000 − $3964.16 = $135.68 No
6. $7000 − $4909.82 = $2090.18 Yes

Write each percent as a decimal. For additional practice, see page 405.

7. 6% 0.06
8. 8% 0.08
9. 4% 0.04
10. 5% 0.05
11. 9% 0.09
12. 10% 0.10, or 0.1

Estimate. For additional practice, see page 412.

13. Is 9% of $20,000 closer to $1000 or to $2000? $2000
14. Is 8% of $10,105 closer to $800 or to $1000? $800
15. Is 11% of $32,000 closer to $3000 or to $3500? $3500
16. Is 6% of $12,875 closer to $780 or to $880? $780

EXERCISES

Complete. Choose your answers from the box at the right.

base price
optional equipment
destination charge
sticker price
total cost

1. Air conditioning and tinted glass are examples of __?__ on a new car. optional equipment
2. The fee for delivering a car is called the __?__. destination charge
3. Sticker Price = __?__ (base price) + Cost of Optional Equipment + Destination Charge

For Exercises 4–9, find the sticker price of each car.

	Base Price	Total Options	Destination Charge
4.	$7950	$1430	$238.50 $9618.50
5.	$6580	$1090	$287.50 $7957.50
6.	$10,435	$1983	$148.25 $12,566.25

	Base Price	Total Options	Destination Charge
7.	$8342	$1619	$187.75 $10,148.75
8.	$9998	$1735.40	$319.20 $12,052.60
9.	$12,095	$1501.65	$264.15 $13,860.80

10. Linda is interested in buying a Cyclone 290X. The base price is $9261. The total cost of the options she wants is $2209, and the destination charge is $194.75. Find the sticker price. $11,664.75

11. Sometimes car manufacturers offer a **rebate** (discount) on the sticker price. The base price of a Neptune 400 is $7492. The options cost $1965, the destination charge is $234.50 and the rebate is $1000. Find the sticker price. $8,691.50

2 Teaching the Lesson

Direct the students' attention to the portion of a window sticker shown on page 126. Tell them to read the opening sentences. Then discuss question 1. Ask students if they can name other options that might be listed on window stickers. Discuss Example 1 which shows how to compute the sticker price. Then discuss Example 2 which shows how to compute the tax on the sticker price and then how to compute the total cost.

3 Close

Summary: Ask the following questions to summarize the lesson.

1. What various costs are included in the sticker price of a car? (Base price, options, destination charge)
2. How do you compute the sales tax on a car? (Sales tax rate x sticker price)
3. What is meant by the total cost? (Sticker price + sales tax)

Evaluation

Guided Practice: Ex. 1–3, 4–8 even, 12–16 even

Independent Practice: Ex. 5–9 odd, 10, 11, 13–17 odd, 18–23

Extension

Ask students to visit a new car dealer's lot and make a list of items that are shown on the window sticker of a car, including prices.

Problem-Solving Skills

Solving a multi-step problem (Ex. 12–17, 20–23)
Using estimation (Ex. 18, 19)
Working backward (Ex. 22, 23)

Estimation Ex. 18 and 19

For Exercises 12–17, complete the table.

	Sticker Price	Tax Rate	Sales Tax	Total Cost
12.	$8770	6%	? **$526.20**	? **$9296.20**
13.	$9420	5%	? **$471**	? **$9891**
14.	$7995	7%	? **$559.65**	? **$8554.65**

	Sticker Price	Tax Rate	Sales Tax	Total Cost
15.	$10,130	8%	? **$810.40**	? **$10,940.40**
16.	$12,785	6%	? **$767.10**	? **$13,552.10**
17.	$6942	7%	? **$485.94**	? **$7427.94**

The cost of certain optional equipment is listed below. Use these costs for Exercises 18–23.

Air Conditioning $765	AM/FM Radio $395
Automatic Transmission $675	Power Steering $290
Electric Sunroof $530	Cruise Control $200

18. Tina's cousin John wants an automatic transmission, an AM/FM radio, and power steering for his new car. Which is the best estimate of the total cost of these options? **c**

a. $1100 **b.** $1250
c. $1400 **d.** $1500

19. Corinne wants air conditioning, cruise control, and an electric sunroof for her new car. Which is the best estimate of the total cost of these options? **b**

a. $1400 **b.** $1500
c. $1600 **d.** $1700

20. Robert can afford to spend no more than $8000 on a new car. The car he likes has a base price of $7160 and a destination charge of $283.50. Can Robert afford air conditioning? Explain. **No; the sticker price would be $8208.50.**

21. Jose is buying a car that has a base price of $9878. He wants air conditioning and power steering. The destination charge is $315.85, and the sales tax rate is 5%. Find the total cost of the car. **$11,811.29**

22. The base price of a car is $8975, and the sticker price is $10,021.60. The sticker price includes an automatic transmission and cruise control. Find the destination charge. **$171.60**

23. A car has a base price of $8230 and a destination charge of $257.80. The sticker price is $9172.80. What optional equipment did the buyer purchase? **An AM/FM radio and power steering**

Math and Driving

A good driver should be able to identify certain traffic signs by their geometric shape.

TRIANGLE
Indicates slowing or stopping.

PENTAGON
Indicates a school crossing zone.

RECTANGLE
Gives important instructions.

DO NOT PASS

DIAMOND
Indicates danger.

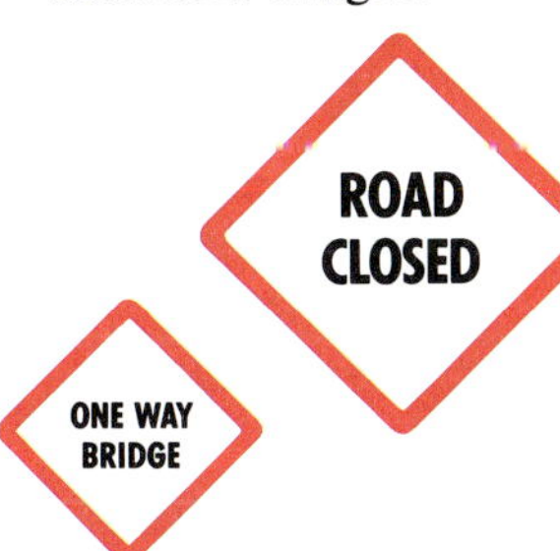

OCTAGON
Indicates a complete stop.

EXERCISES

For Exercises 1–8, match each warning or instruction with the correct figure. Choose a, b, c, or d.

a.

b. 

c. 

d. 

1. SPEED LIMIT 5 a
2. ROAD CONSTRUCTION AHEAD c
3. SLOW TRAFFIC KEEP RIGHT a
4. NARROW BRIDGE b
5. STOP d
6. YIELD c
7. EXIT a
8. DIP b

Objective

Student will apply the geometric skill of identifying polygons to automobile driving.

Overview

This page is an extension of the skills and ideas presented in the previous lessons of this chapter. Since the content presented on this page is not included in the Chapter Review or Chapter Test, its use is optional.

Using the Pages

You may wish to have students work this lesson in small groups or you may wish to work with the class. Using it with the class, discuss the 5 shapes of road signs. Ask students if they are familiar with all of the signs. Then assign Exercises 1–8 as independent practice.

Lesson Resources

Maintenance: See below.
Reteaching/Alternate Teaching Strategy: p. M-29
Practice: p. M-29
Enrichment: p. M-29

Objective

Student will solve multi-step problems involving the dealer's cost of a new car.

Maintenance

1. Write 35% as a decimal. ANS: 0.35
2. Multiply: 0.6 × 1500 ANS: 900
3. 5% of 120 is what number? ANS: 6
4. Round 351.123 to the nearest hundredth. ANS: 351.12
5. A consumer paid 3.4% of her taxable income of $15,286 in state income tax. How much was the tax? Round to the nearest dollar. ANS: $520

1 Lesson Focus

Motivation: Ask students if they have ever accompanied a parent or friend when they were negotiating with a car dealer for the purchase of a new car.

Purpose: Students should have some knowledge of the process of negotiating on the price of a new car. As future consumers, they should understand that this process is unique in the field of merchandising of consumer products.

2 Teaching the Lesson

Introduce the lesson by reviewing the formula for computing the sticker price. Then point out that information about a dealer's cost of a particular model of car is public information.
Direct the students' attention to the table showing the dealer's cost on page 130. Explain that these percents will vary depending on the model of car and other factors.

Making a Deal

The sticker price of the Jetstream ZX is $10,025.80. Tina knows that the price of a new car is often negotiable.

Base Price	+	**Cost of Optional Equipment**	+	**Destination Charge**	=	**Sticker Price**
$7890	+	$1823.50	+	$312.30	=	$10,025.80

Tina read in a consumer magazine that she should make an offer for the car that is below the sticker price and above the dealer's cost.

Dealer's Cost
Jetstream ZX

85% of Base Price
80% of Cost of Options
Destination Charge

1. Dealer's Cost = 85% of ? + 80% of ? + ?
Base Price   Cost of Options   Destination charge

EXAMPLE What is the dealer's cost for the Jetstream ZX?

Dealer's Cost = **85% of Base Price** + **80% of Cost of Options** + **Destination Charge**

= ($7890 × 0.85) + (1823.50 × 0.80) + $312.30 ◀ *Use a calculator.*

= $6706.50 + $1458.80 + $312.30

= **$8477.60** The dealer's cost is **$8477.60.**

2. Do you think the dealer will accept an offer of $8477.50 for the car? Explain. No; the dealer would not make a profit.

Tina offered the dealer $9000 for the car.

3. How much will Tina save if the dealer accepts the offer? $1025.80
4. How much profit will the dealer make by accepting the offer? $522.50

CHECK YOUR SKILLS

Find each answer. For additional practice, see page 407.

1. 85% of $9876 $8394.60
2. 72% of $12,370 $8906.40
3. 5% of $8315 $415.75

Find each answer. Do the work inside the parentheses first.

4. ($8608 × 0.85) + ($1434 × 0.80) $8464
5. ($6840 × 0.84) + ($2020 × 0.78) $7321.20
6. ($9250 × 0.85) + ($1084 × 0.75) $8675.50
7. ($7850 × 0.85) + ($2175 × 0.75) $8303.75

EXERCISES

For Exercises 1–6, find the dealer's cost.

	Base Price	Percent of Base Price	Cost of Options	Percent of Cost of Options	Destination Charge	Dealer's Cost
1.	$8608	85%	$1434	80%	$210.00	? $8674.00
2.	$9970	86%	$1585	75%	$194.00	? $9956.95
3.	$10,312	88%	$1775	82%	$148.50	? $10,678.56
4.	$6840	84%	$2020	78%	$256.25	? $7577.45

Use the information at the right for Exercises 5–6.

Base Price: $9250
Options: $1084
Destination Charge: $205
Dealer pays 85% of base price and 75% of cost of options.

5. Find the dealer's cost. **$8880.50**

6. The dealer wants to make a profit of at least $400 on the car. Find the lowest offer the dealer will accept. **$9280.50**

7. Sally George wants to buy a car that has a base price of $10,395. She has selected options that cost $1665. The destination charge is $148. Sally learned that the dealer pays 88% of the base price and 75% of the cost of options. Find the dealer's cost. **$10,544.35**

8. Frank Marek wants to buy a car that has a base price of $7850. The options he wants cost $2175, and the destination charge is $435. The dealer pays 80% of the base price and 70% of the cost of options. Frank offers $8750 for the car. If this offer is accepted, how much profit will the dealer make? **$512.50**

This advertisement appeared in today's paper. The "5% over invoice" means that the following formula is used to compute the selling price.

THROUGH
DEC. 31
ALL CARS
5%
OVER INVOICE

Selling price = Dealer's Cost + 5% of Dealer's Cost

Use the information in Exercises 9–10 to find the selling price of each car.

9. Base Price: $6900
Options: $1865
Destination Charge: $286
Dealer pays 87% of base price and 78% of cost of options. **$8130.89**

10. Base Price: $8920
Options: $1400
Destination Charge: $302
Dealer pays 85% of base price and 80% of cost of options. **$9454.20**

Discuss the Example on page 130 showing how to compute a dealer's cost. You may want to ask why there is no percent found for the destination charge. Discuss question 2. Then have students write their answers to questions 3 and 4.

3 Close

Summary: Ask selected students to summarize what they have learned in this lesson.

Evaluation
Guided Practice: Ex. 1, 3, 9
Independent Practice: Ex. 2, 4, 5–8, 10

Extension

You may want to obtain some current information on dealers' costs of various new car models. Then use this information to prepare a variety of problems for students to work. Here are some suggested sources of this information.

The Car Book, 1987 by Jack Gillis
Harper & Row Publishers, NY

1988 New Car Cost Guide
Automobile Invoice Service
San Jose, CA

Consumer Guide Magazine
Auto Series
Publications International, Ltd.
Skokie, IL

Problem-Solving Skills

Solving a multi-step problem (Ex. 1–5, 7–10)
Interpreting information (Ex. 5–10)
Choosing the operation (Ex. 6)

Critical Thinking

You may wish to have students work in small groups to solve this problem or you may wish to work with the class.

Question 2 (in Lesson)

Lesson Resources

Maintenance: See below.
Reteaching/Alternate Teaching Strategy: p. M-30
Practice: p. M-30
Enrichment: p. M-30
Concrete Materials: Activity Worksheet 34C

Objectives

Student will

1. solve problems involving the down payment for a new car.
2. solve multi-step problems that involve the finance charge.

Maintenance

1. Round 385 to the nearest ten. ANS: 390
2. Round $4582 to the nearest hundred dollars. ANS: $4600
3. Find 12.5% of $220. ANS: $27.50
4. Estimate the sum to the nearest dollar. $4.56 + $1.22 + $3.82 ANS: $10
5. A worker has the following payroll deductions.
   $62.24 $88.29 $12.59
   Which is the best estimate of the total deductions?
   a. $170 **b.** $150 **c.** $160
   ANS: $160

1 Lesson Focus

Motivation: Ask students if they have any estimate of how much more the purchase of a car actually costs by making monthly payments rather than paying cash.

Purpose. Students should have an appreciation of the extra costs involved when consumer items are purchased on credit.

Financing a Car

Tina agreed to buy the Jetstream ZX for $9000. In order to purchase the car the dealer explained that a 10% **down payment** is required. This means that 10% of the full price of the car must be paid at the time of purchase. Tina would then borrow the remainder of the purchase price and repay the loan in equal monthly payments of $186 for 60 months.

1. What is the amount of Tina's down payment? **$900**
2. How much will Tina's monthly payments total over 60 months? **$11,160**
3. *Complete:* Down Payment + ? = Total Cost **Total of Monthly Payments**

EXAMPLE 1 What will be the total cost of the car?

Down Payment	+	Total of Monthly Payments	=	Total Cost
$900	+	$11,160	=	$12,060

4. If Tina increases her down payment and keeps the same number of monthly payments, will the monthly payment amount remain the same? Explain. **No; she will be borrowing less money, so her payment will be less.**

The payments include a **finance charge,** which is the amount charged for borrowing the money.

EXAMPLE 2 Find the finance charge Tina is paying.

Total Cost	−	Cash Price	=	Finance Charge
$12,060	−	$9000	=	$3060

CHECK YOUR SKILLS

ESTIMATION/MENTAL MATH: Ex. 5–10

Solve. **For additional practice, see page 407.**

1. Find 12% of $9890. **$1186.80**
2. Find 8% of $10,450. **$836**
3. Find 9% of $8945. **$805.05**
4. Find 10% of $6670 **$667**

For additional practice, see pages 52–53.

Estimate to determine whether the answer is reasonable.

5. $186 × 60 = $11,160 **Yes**
6. $235 × 48 = $8240 **No**
7. $294 × 54 = $15,876 **Yes**
8. $324 × 60 = $19,440 **Yes**
9. $487 × 48 = $20,376 **No**
10. $187 × 54 = $7888 **No**

EXERCISES

Complete. Choose your answers from the box at the right.

amount borrowed
finance charge
cash price
down payment
total cost

1. Car dealers usually require a ? on the purchase of a car. **down payment**
2. Down Payment + Total of Monthly Payments = ? **Total Cost**
3. Interest paid for borrowing money is called a ?. **finance charge**
4. Total Cost = Finance Charge + ? **Cash Price**

For Exercises 5–13, find the indicated amount.

5. Cost of Car: $9465
   Down Payment: 10%
   Down payment: ?
   $946.50
6. Cost of Car: $8100
   Down Payment: 15%
   Down Payment: ?
   $1215
7. Cost of Car: $11,300
   Down Payment: 9%
   Down Payment: ?
   $1017
8. **Destiny**
   $1525 Down
   $192/Month for
   60 Months
   Total of Monthly Payments: ?
   $11,520
9. **Greyhound 480**
   $9700 Cash or
   15% Down and
   $217/Month for
   48 Months
   Finance Charge: ?
   $2171
10. **Cobra GL**
    $895 Down
    $295/Month for
    36 Months
    Total of Monthly Payments: ? **$10,620**
11. **Foxfire 55**
    $7800 Cash or
    20% Down and
    $142/Month for
    60 Months
    Finance Charge: ?
    $2280
12. **Venus 3000**
    $1775 Down
    $165/Month for
    60 Months
    Total Cost: ? **$11,675**
13. **Cheetah 150**
    $1480 Down
    $286/Month for
    36 Months
    Total Cost: ?
    $11,776
14. Linda is buying a car for $11,800. There is a 20% down payment. Linda has $2100 in her savings account. Is this enough for the down payment? Explain. **No; 20% of $11,800 is $2360.**
15. For which of these will the total of monthly payments be the greatest? **b**
    a. $285/month for 48 months
    b. $229/month for 60 months
    c. $376/month for 36 months
16. Rick can put $900 down on a new car and make 48 monthly payments of $221 each, or he can put $2000 down and make 36 monthly payments of $221 each. With which choice will the total cost for the car be less? **$2000 down and 36 monthly payments of $221 each.**
17. Louie is buying a new car for $6950. He is paying 12% down. He can make 48 monthly payments of $160 each or 60 monthly payments of $136 each. How much less will the finance charge be for the 48 monthly payments? **$480**

2 Teaching the Lesson

Have students read the opening paragraph and then find the answers to questions 1–3. The following question may create some discussion.
Why aren't the monthly payments determined by dividing the amount owed ($8100) by 60 months? (A finance charge must be included)
Discuss Example 1 which shows how to compute the total cost excluding sales tax, license fees, and other closing costs. Then discuss question 4. Example 2 can then be covered. It is important because it shows how to compute the finance charge on the purchase of a car.

3 Close

Summary: Ask selected students to summarize the methods for finding the total cost and the finance charge on the purchase of a new car.

Evaluation
Guided Practice: Ex. 1–4, 6–16 even
Independent Practice: Ex. 5–17 odd

Extension

Have students work some problems in finding the finance charge based on a given annual percentage rate and the amount to be financed. These rates are often shown in new car ads in newspapers.

Problem-Solving Skills

Choosing the operation (Ex. 8–13)
Solving a multi-step problem (Ex. 9, 11, 13, 16, 17, 20–23)
Making comparisons (Ex. 14–17)
Interpreting information (Ex. 14–17)

Critical Thinking

You may wish to have students work in small groups to solve this problem or you may wish to work with the class.

Question 4 (in Lesson)

Objective

Student will

1. review the skills, concepts, and applications in the first part of Chapter 6.
2. maintain key skills and concepts taught in Chapters 1, 3, 4, and 5.

Using the Page

Exercises 1–7 provide an informal assessment of the student's mastery of the major skills and concepts presented in the first half of Chapter 6. Each item is referenced to the related pages where the particular item was presented. These exercises parallel the quiz provided in the *Teacher's ResourceBank.*™

A quiz covering the second half of the chapter is also provided in the *Teacher's ResourceBank.*™

Exercises 8–11 maintain skills and concepts taught in Chapters 1, 3, 4, and 5.

Mid-Chapter Review

For Exercises 1–2, find the sticker price of each car. (Pages 126–128)

	Base Price	Total Options	Destination Charge
1.	\$5840	\$1426	\$221.65 **\$7487.65**
2.	\$10,600	\$1872	\$304.57 **\$12,776.57**

3. Kate wants to buy a Cheetah 250 with a base price of \$7680. The total cost of the options she wants is \$1421. The destination charge is \$279.50, and the sales tax rate is 4%. Find the total cost of the car. (Pages 126–128) **\$9755.72**

For Exercises 4–5, find the dealer's cost. (Pages 130–131)

	Base Price	Percent of Base Price	Cost of Options	Percent of Cost of Options	Destination Charge	Dealer's Cost
4.	\$9820	85%	\$1501	75%	\$196.00	? **\$9668.75**
5.	\$6460	88%	\$1276	80%	\$212.56	? **\$6918.16**

6. Lisa Beam is buying a new car. She is putting \$800 down and intends to pay \$212 per month for 48 months. Find the total cost of the car. (Pages 132–133) **\$10,976**

7. Tom Burton wants to buy a Wildcat ZT for \$8400. He will put 20% down and make 60 monthly payments of \$164 each. Find the finance charge. (Pages 132–133) **\$3120**

MAINTENANCE

8. Make a bar graph to show this data. (Pages 2–3)

Animal	Maximum Speed
Cheetah	110 km/hr
Rabbit	29 km/hr
Black Bear	40 km/hr
Horse	64 km/hr

9. As a salesman for an office supply company, Greg Skinner earns a yearly salary of \$14,500. He also receives a 3% commission on all sales. Find Greg's earnings for a year in which his sales total \$175,000. (Pages 45–47) **\$19,750**

10. Pam Myers opens a savings account with a deposit of \$1800. Her account pays a yearly interest rate of 6%. How much simple interest is earned after 3 months? (Pages 110–111) **\$27**

11. Art Enteman owes \$2467 in federal income tax this year. The amount of tax withheld from his pay was \$2156. What is the amount of the refund or the balance due? (Pages 75–77) **balance due: \$311**

STRATEGY: USING A "HIDDEN QUESTION" TO SOLVE A MULTI-STEP PROBLEM

Liability Insurance

The state in which Tina lives requires her to have **liability insurance** on her car. The insurance agent explains that liability insurance has two parts.

Bodily injury liability will protect Tina from financial loss if others are injured by her car.
Property damage liability will protect Tina from financial loss if her car damages someone else's property.

Tina learns that insurance companies show the limits of liability coverage in the special way shown below.

$50,000 maximum payment to any one person injured in an accident ▶ **50/100/25** ◀ *$25,000 maximum payment for property damaged in an accident*

$100,000 maximum payment to two or more persons injured in an accident

1. What does "maximum payment" mean? **The greatest amount that the insurance company will pay.**

Tina reads the table below to compute her **yearly premium,** or yearly cost, for liability insurance.

Liability Insurance: Drivers 17 Years Old or Less	
Coverage	*Basic Rate*
50/100/50	$238
100/300/50	$286
250/500/50	$302
Yearly Premiums	
With Grade Average of B+ or Better	*With Grade Average Lower Than B+*
Male Basic rate × 2.16	Male Basic rate × 2.7
Female Basic rate × 1.5	Female Basic rate × 1.65

2. How much greater is the basic rate for liability coverage of 100/300/50 than for liability coverage of 50/100/50? **$48**

Lesson Resources

Maintenance: See below.
Reteaching/Alternate Teaching Strategy: p. M-30
Practice: p. M-30
Enrichment: p. M-30

Objective

Student will use a table to find the cost of liability insurance.

Maintenance

1. Express $2\frac{3}{4}$ years as months. ANS: 33 months
2. Express 3 months as years. ANS: $\frac{1}{4}$ year, or 0.25 year
3. Write 6% as a decimal. ANS: 0.06
4. Multiply: 0.05 × 300 × 0.12 ANS: 1.8
5. Find the amount of interest on a loan of $200 for 9 months at a yearly rate of 8%. ANS: $12

1 Lesson Focus

Motivation: Ask students what factors affect the yearly premium or cost of automobile liability insurance for drivers.

Purpose: Some students may have a driver's license and other students expect to have one. They should be aware of ways to keep automobile insurance costs down—yet have adequate insurance coverage.

2 Teaching the Lesson

Select students to read the opening paragraph and the definitions of bodily injury liability and property damage liability. Then have a student read the material explaining the meaning of 10/100/25 coverage. Ask students to explain the meaning of these liability coverages.

15/30/10 50/100/15
100/300/25 250/500/50

Discuss question 1. Then direct the students' attention to the premium table on page 135. Discuss in detail the information that is provided in this table. Have students respond to question 2. Discuss the Example showing how to compute a yearly premium.

3 Close

Summary: Ask selected students to summarize what has been learned in this lesson. Ask one student to explain the two types of liability coverage. Ask another student to explain the meaning of 250/500/50. Ask a third student to tell how premiums are affected by school grades. Ask another student how to compute the yearly premium.

Evaluation
Guided Practice: Ex. 1–4, 6–10 even
Independent Practice: Ex. 5–9 odd, 11–14

Extension

Ask students to obtain information about the automobile liability insurance laws in your state including enforcement provisions and penalties for violations.

Problem-Solving Skills

Using a table (Ex. 5–14)
Interpreting information (Ex. 11–14)
Making comparisons (Ex. 13)
Solving a multi-step problem (Ex. 13, 14)

EXAMPLE Tina is 17 years old and has a C average. Find her yearly premium for liability coverage of 100/300/50.

1 Find the rate in the table for 100/300/50 coverage.

100/300/50	$286

2 Find the yearly premium.

Basic rate × **1.65** = **Yearly Premium**
$286 × 1.65 = **$471.90**

EXERCISES

Complete. Choose your answers from the box at the right.

$100,000
property damage
$50,000
$100
bodily injury
premius
liability

1. Liability insurance protects you from financial loss if others suffer _?_ or _?_ from your car. bodily injury; property damage
2. With liability coverage of 250/500/50, a maximum of $50,00 is paid for _?_. property damage
3. With liability coverage of 50/100/50, a maximum of _?_ is paid to two or more persons injured in an accident. $100,000
4. The amount a person pays each year for insurance is called a _?_. premium

Use the table on page 135 to find the yearly premium.

	Coverage	Grades of B+ or Higher?	Male/ Female
5.	50/100/50	Yes	Male $514.08
6.	250/500/50	Yes	Female $453
7.	250/500/50	No	Female $498.30

	Coverage	Grades of B+ or Higher?	Male/ Female
8.	50/100/50	No	Female $392.70
9.	100/300/50	Yes	Male $617.76
10.	100/300/50	No	Male $772.20

11. A 16-year-old boy has an **A** average. What is his yearly premium for 250/500/50 liability insurance coverage? $652.32
12. A 17-year-old girl has a **B** average. What is her yearly premium for 50/100/50 liability insurance coverage? $392.70
13. Patty Zelinka is a 17-year-old **C** student. Right now she has liability coverage of 50/100/50. How much more would she pay in yearly premiums if she increased her coverage to 250/500/50? $105.60
14. Dale Burkett is a 16-year-old student with a **C** average. He has liability coverage of 50/100/50. How much can he save in yearly premiums if he raises his grade average to a **B+**? $128.52

Collision/Comprehensive Insurance

The lending institution which financed the loan for Tina's car requires her to buy **collision insurance** to help pay for repairs if her car is damaged in an accident. Tina purchased insurance with a **deductible** of $200. This means that she will pay the first $200 of a repair bill. The insurance company will pay the rest.

EXAMPLE 1 Suppose Tina was involved in an accident in which she was at fault and the repair bill for her car was $943.85. How much would the insurance company pay?

$943.85 − $200.00 = **$743.85** ◀ *Repair Bill − Deductible = Amount Insurance Pays*

The insurance company will pay **$743.85.**

Another type of insurance Tina purchased was **comprehensive insurance.** This will protect from losses due to theft, fire, vandalism, and so on.

Collision Insurance		Comprehensive Insurance	
Deductible	*Basic Rate*	*Deductible*	*Basic Rate*
$100	$204	$100	$40
$200	$174	$200	$32
Yearly Premium			
With B+ Grade Average or Better		*With Grade Average Lower Than B+*	
Teen Male	Basic rate × 2.16	Teen Male	Basic rate × 2.7
Teen Female	Basic rate × 1.5	Teen Female	Basic rate × 1.65
Non–Teen Driver	Basic rate × 1.1		

1. Which has a higher premium, collision insurance or comprehensive insurance? **collision insurance**
2. As Tina gets older, will her insurance premiums remain the same? Explain. **No; when she turns 20 years old her premium will be only 1.1 times the basic rate rather than 1.65 times.**

Lesson Resources

Maintenance: See below.
Reteaching/Alternate Teaching Strategy: p. M-31
Practice: p. M-31
Enrichment: p. M-31
Concrete materials: Activity Worksheet 36C

Objectives

Student will

1. determine the amount of damage paid by collision insurance based on a deductible amount.
2. use a table to solve problems that involve collision/comprehensive insurance.

Maintenance

1. Add: $28.47 + $39.19 + $108.96 ANS: $176.62
2. Subtract: $302.14 − $185.79 ANS: $116.35
3. Write 5% as a decimal. ANS: 0.05
4. Multiply: 0.06 × 960 ANS: 57.6
5. Victor Ramos has 4% of his salary deducted for a savings plan. How much is deducted from his paycheck of $650? ANS: $26

1 Lesson Focus

Motivation: Ask students to tell what is meant by collision and comprehensive insurance.

Purpose: It is important for students to be informed about various kinds of automobile insurance. It has implications for them as future consumers because of the financial risks involved in owning and driving an automobile.

2 Teaching the Lesson

Ask a student to read the opening paragraph. Then discuss Example 1 showing the effect of the deductible amount on the cost of auto repairs to a consumer. Then direct students' attention to the definition of comprehensive insurance and the table on page 137 showing the premium rates for collision and comprehensive insurance. Have students answer questions 1 and 2. Then discuss Example 2.

3 Close

Summary: Summarize what the students should have learned in this lesson as follows.

1. Collision insurance covers the cost of damage to your own car in an accident.
2. The greater the deductible amount, the lower the premium.
3. Comprehensive insurance covers the cost of theft, fire, vandalism, glass breakage, and so on.

Evaluation
Guided Practice: Ex: 1–4, 6, 8, 12, 14
Independent Practice: Ex. 5–9 odd, 10, 11, 13, 15–20

Extension

Have students do some research to find answers to these questions.

1. What percent of car owners in your locality (City, county, or state) carry collision insurance?
2. What is the estimated annual cost of automobile accidents in your locality (City, county, or state)?
3. How much is spent yearly in your locality (City, county, or state) on automobile insurance premiums?

EXAMPLE 2 Tina wants collision insurance with a deductible of \$200 and comprehensive insurance with a deductible of \$100. Find the total yearly premium. (Tina is a 17-year-old **C** student.)

1 Find the yearly premium for collision insurance.

\$174 × 1.65 = **\$287.10** ◀ *Basic rate × 1.65*

2 Find the yearly premium for comprehensive insurance.

\$40 × 1.65 = **\$66.00** ◀ *Basic rate × 1.65*

3 Find the total premium.

\$287.10 + \$66.00 = **\$353.10**

CHECK YOUR SKILLS

Find each answer. For additional practice, see pages 372 and 376.

1. \$48 × 4.2 = ? \$201.60
2. \$154 × ? = \$377.30 2.45
3. \$50 × ? = \$187.50 3.75
4. \$52 × 1.65 = ? \$85.80
5. \$286 × 3.8 = ? \$1086.80
6. \$45 × ? = \$74.25 1.65

EXERCISES

Complete. Choose your answers from the box at the right.

comprehensive
increases
insured person
collision
decreases
insurance company
accident

1. If an insured car is damaged in an accident, ? insurance helps pay the repair bill. collision
2. A deductible of \$100 means the ? will pay the first \$100 in damages or loss. insured person
3. If an insured car is damaged in a flood, ? insurance helps pay the repair bill. comprehensive
4. As the amount of the deductible increases, the yearly premium ?. decreases

For Exercises 5–8, find the amount the insurance company will pay.

	Amount of Repair Bill	Amount of Deductible	Insurance Pays
5.	\$847.92	\$200	? \$647.92
6.	\$1094.35	\$250	? \$844.35
7.	\$1503.27	\$100	? \$1403.27
8.	\$213.40	\$300	? \$0

9. Phil Comeau was in an accident in which he was at fault. The repair bill for his car was $914.25. His collision policy had a $200 deductible. How much did the insurance company pay? $714.25

10. Suzy Kahn accidentally backed her car into a tree. The repair bill was $315.60. Suzy had collision insurance with a $100 deductible. How much will her insurance company pay? $215.60

Use the table on page 137 to find the yearly premiums for collision and comprehensive insurance.

	Driver	Collision Deductible	Yearly Premium
11.	Teen female with a **B+** average	$100	? $306
12.	Teen male with an **A** average	$200	? $375.84

	Driver	Comprehensive Deductible	Yearly Premium
13.	Teen male with a **C** average	$100	? $108
14.	Non-Teen Driver	$200	? $35.20

15. Paula Lowry is a teen driver with a **B** average. She has comprehensive insurance with a $100 deductible. Find her yearly premium. $66

16. Chin Yoshira's collision premium is $319.25. His comprehensive premium is $62.60. Estimate the total premium. About $380

17. Sean O'Grady is 30 years old. Compute his total yearly premium for collision and comprehensive insurance if the deductible on each is $100. $268.40

18. Diane Mallone is a 16-year-old **A** student. She has comprehensive insurance with a $200 deductible. By how much will her yearly premium increase if she changes to a $100 deductible? $12

19. Rosa Diaz is a teen driver with a **C** average. She has collision insurance with a deductible of $100. To save for her yearly insurance premium, Rosa wants to make 12 equal monthly deposits in her savings account. How much should she deposit in her savings account each month? $28.05

20. Marilyn Bennet is a 17-year-old **C** student. She has collision insurance with a $200 deductible and comprehensive insurance with a $100 deductible. Marilyn pays $\frac{1}{4}$ of her total yearly premium every three months, along with an additional handling charge of $2.10. How much does she actually pay for the total yearly premium? $361.50

Problem-Solving Skills

Choosing the operations (Ex. 5–20)
Using a table (Ex. 11–15, 17–20)
Solving a multi-step problem (Ex. 11–15, 17–20)
Interpreting information (Ex. 15–20)
Making an estimate (Ex. 16)
Making a comparison (Ex. 18)

Critical Thinking

You may wish to have students work in small groups to solve this problem or you may wish to work with the class. Question 2 (in Lesson)

Estimation

Ex. 16

Lesson Resources

Maintenance: See below.
Reteaching/Alternate Teaching Strategy
See the margin on page 141.
Practice: Activity Worksheet 37
Enrichment: See the enrichment topic "Inflation" on page 144.

Objectives

Student will

1. use the conditions in a problem and the guess and check strategy to solve the problem.
2. choose and apply an appropriate strategy to solve a problem.

Maintenance

Write the amounts in words as they would appear on a check.

1. \$53.85 ANS: Fifty-three and $\frac{85}{100}$
2. \$125.98 ANS: One hundred twenty-five and $\frac{98}{100}$
3. \$87.05 ANS: Eight-seven and $\frac{05}{100}$
4. Add: \$456.20 + \$182.15 ANS: \$638.35
5. On March 3, Joanne had a balance of \$325.40 in her checking account. She made a deposit of \$150.52 and wrote a check for \$92.18. Find her new balance. ANS: \$383.74

1 Lesson Focus

Motivation: Ask students how they would solve this problem.

Rob is three years older than John. The sum of their ages is 33. How old are they? (15 and 18)

Purpose: Guessing is a very common strategy for finding a solution. Students should understand that the checking part of the process is the most important step because of the information gained from it.

Strategy: GUESS AND CHECK

Sometimes you can solve a problem by identifying *conditions*. You use one condition to help you guess the answer. Then you use the other condition to check your guess.

Two new models are on display in the showroom. The sum of the prices of the two cars is \$22,500. They differ in price by \$1,500.

EXAMPLE What is the price of each car?

READ What are the facts?

Car A + Car B = \$22,500 ← *Call this Condition 1.*
Car A − Car B = \$ 1,500 ← *Call this Condition 2.*

PLAN
1 Start with Condition 1 and guess each price.
2 Use Condition 2 to check your guess.

SOLVE

	Guess 1	Guess 2
Car A:	\$12,500	\$12,000
Car B:	\$10,000	\$10,500
Sum:	\$22,500	\$22,500

CHECK \$12,500 − \$10,000 $\stackrel{?}{=}$ \$2,500 \$12,000 − \$10,500 $\stackrel{?}{=}$ \$1,500 Yes.

Since \$12,000 − \$10,000 = \$2,500, the prices are too far apart.
Thus, **Car A: \$12,000 Car B: \$10,500.**

1. Once you guess at a price for Car A, you do not need to guess at a price for Car B. Why? **The sum of the prices of the two cars is \$22,500.**

EXERCISES

For Exercises 1–4, use the two conditions and the guess and check strategy.

1. Sum of two whole numbers: 20
Difference of the numbers: 2
11 and 9

2. Sum of two whole numbers: 11
Product of the numbers: 30
6 and 5

3. Sum of two numbers: 14
Difference of the numbers: 3
$8\frac{1}{2}$ and $5\frac{1}{2}$

4. Item A + Item B = 12
Item A = 2 × Item B
Item A, 8; Item B, 4

Solve.

5. You need a spare tire. The Radial Star costs $6 less than the Radial Sun. The sum of the costs of the two tires is $96. What does each tire cost? **Radial Star, $45; Radial Sun, $51**

6. The two-day sale at Win Motors drew 200 people. Thirty more people showed up on the second day than on the first day. What was each day's attendance? **85; 115**

7. You decide to buy two optional items for your car. The cost of the two items is $120. One item costs twice as much as the other. What is the cost of each item? **$40; $80**

8. The 800-mile Grand Slam Auto Race is a two-part race. The length of the first part is $\frac{1}{3}$ the length of the second part. How long is the first part? **200 miles**

9. The odometer of your car read 166 miles when you left home. When you got to Tampa, it read 230 miles. You made one stop at a garage. The distance from your home to the garage is 12 miles more than the distance from the garage to Tampa. How far is it from the garage to Tampa? **26 miles**

For Exercises 10–11, choose a strategy from the box at the right that you can use to solve each problem.
a. *Name the strategy.*
b. *Solve the problem.*

Interpreting information
Solving a simpler problem
Predicting

10. A quality control technician at Acme Batteries tested 120 car batteries. Of these, 6 were defective. About how many defective batteries could you expect in a shipment of 12,000 batteries? **Predicting; 600**

11. These are the rules for the Gold M drawing.

The winners will share $37,000.
2nd Prize: $\frac{1}{5}$ of the first prize
3rd Prize: $\frac{1}{6}$ of the second prize

How much will each receive?
Solving a simpler problem; $30,000, $6000, $1000

2 Teaching the Lesson

After presenting the example, select a problem to show how the strategy can be applied to other situations, such as in Exercise 1.

1. **Ask:** What is the problem about? (Finding two whole numbers)
2. **Read** the problem to determine the FACTS. **Ask:** What are the facts of this problem? (Sum is 20 and the difference is 2)
3. **Plan** the solution. **Ask:** How will you find the numbers? (Guess the numbers and check to see if they meet the conditions.)
4. **Solve** the problem. **Ask:** What number do you think would work as the large number? (Answers will vary.) What would the smaller number have to be? (Answers will vary.)
5. **Check. Ask:** Do the numbers you guessed meet the two conditions of the problem? Have the students continue to guess and check until they get the correct answer.

3 Close

Summary: Have students discuss when guess and check would be a more appropriate strategy than solving a simpler problem. (Chapter 5)

Evaluation
Guided Practice: Ex. 1–4
Independent Practice: Ex. 5–11

Problem-Solving Skills

Predicting (Ex. 10)
Solving a simpler problem (Ex. 11)

Alternate Teaching Strategy

You may wish to have students work in small groups to complete the exercises. Have each student guess a solution and have the group check each solution. Then have them record their decision for the correct solution.

NOTE: A quiz covering the second half of the chapter is provided in the *Teacher's ResourceBank™*.

Objectives

Students will

1. explore solutions to a variety of problems that emerge from this situational lesson.
2. explore solutions to monthly payment problems that have more than one solution.

Situational Lesson

These two pages present a situational lesson as the framework from which a variety of problem situations emerge.

Teaching Strategies

This lesson lends itself to cooperative learning groups for the problem solving activities of comparing choices and exploring decisions. (See page M-13.)

However, these activities can also be carried out by the class as a whole or by individual students.

1 Lesson Focus

Motivation: Focus students' attention on the ad in the lesson. Have them discuss why they think a higher interest rate is charged for a longer payment period.

Purpose: This lesson shows students that although payments are lowered when they are stretched over a longer period, there are disadvantages to making that choice.

2 Teaching the Lesson

Focus students' attention on the advertisement and ask these questions.

1. What happens to the interest rate as the payment period gets longer? (Increases)
2. What happens to the monthly payment as the payment period gets longer? (Decreases)
3. What is 10% of $11,067? ($1106.70)

Have students read Choice 1 and Choice 2 and work Exercises 1–6. Then discuss Exercises 7–9 with the class.

Consumer's Choice

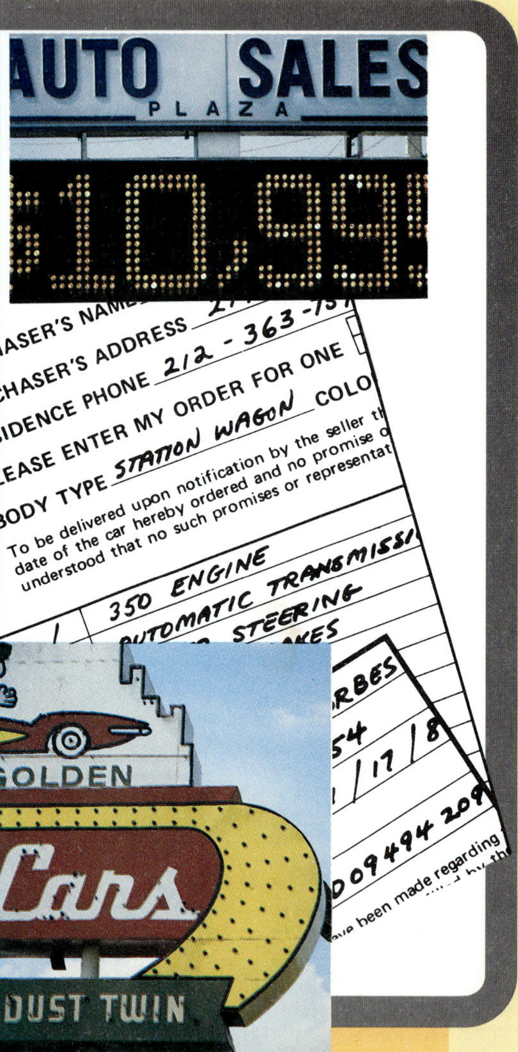

Teresa Martori is interested in buying the Moonbird GT. After reading the advertisement, Teresa began to think about how she could finance the car.

Moonbird GT		
Suggested Retail Price	**$11,067**	
Low Financing	**10% down**	
3.9%	$432.08 monthly for 24 months	
5.9%	$302.56 monthly for 36 months	
6.9%	$238.04 monthly for 48 months	
Amount financed does not include license, fees, taxes, or customer-selected service and insurance.		

Choice 1

Choose the dealer's financing at 3.9%, 5.9%, or 6.9%

Choice 2

Make a down payment. Borrow $9960 from her credit union at 6% yearly interest

Comparing the Choices

1. In Choice 1, what will be the amount of the down payment? $1106.70
2. In Choice 2, what will be the amount of the down payment? $1107

PACKING LIST (CUSTOMER'S COPY)

PACKING LIST

Grune & Stratton, Inc.

l returns to:

R
TARY

PAGE NO.
1

ACADEMY
E T GOODMAN
OOD & ARGYLE RDS
E PA 19003

Z5

*********EXAM COPY*********
89

*********EXAM COPY*********
89

* * * * * * * * * * * * * * *

PT

ECKER | OTHER SHP INSTRUCTIONS

583

0000001124

Holt, Rinehart and Winston, Inc.
W. B. Saunders Company
Saunders College Publishing
Dryden Press
Coronado Publishers, Inc.
Grune & Stratton, Inc.

7401 DOWDEN ROAD
ORLANDO, FL 32887

ADDRESS CORRECTION REQUESTED RETURN POSTAGE GUARANTEED

(SAMPLE NO. 90022-71615-001)
(SALES REP. 10-077)

TORAH ACADEMY
DR IONE T GOODMAN
WYNNEWOOD & ARGYLE RDS
ARDMORE PA

Z5 19003
RPS

Holt, Rinehart and Winston, Inc.
W. B. Saunders Company
Saunders College Publishing
Dryden Press
Coronado Publishers, Inc.
Grune & Stratton, Inc.

7401 DOWDEN ROAD
ORLANDO, FL 32887

ADDRESS CORRECTION REQUESTED RETURN POSTAGE GUARANTEED

(SAMPLE NO. 90022-71615-001)
(SALES REP. 10-077)

TORAH ACADEMY
DR IONE T GOODMAN
WYNNEWOOD & ARGYLE RDS
ARDMORE PA

Z5 19003
RPS

School titles cannot

College Publishing (Holt, Rinehart anc
authorization returns from booksellers c
following terms and conditions:

1. Returns must reach our wareho
Books received by us more thar

2. To receive credit at prices billed,
returned quantity, author, title, inv
the ISBN's for all titles. If you us

3. We reserve the right to impose a

4. Materials declared out-of-print a
May and November. Titles identi
available your order will be can
indicated. On those dates the b
extensions of the time limit for re

Last date titles will be sold
Date by which returns must reac

TERMS: Subject to change witho

DOMESTIC RETURNS POLICY

SCHOOL TITLES

returned without prior written authorization from our Regional Office which serves your state.

COLLEGE AND PROFESSIONAL TITLES

/inston, Dryden Press and Saunders College Publishing) and W.B. Saunders will accept without prior written l (100%) overstocked College Publishing and W.B. Saunders books in new and unmarked condition, subject to the

e within 18 months of their invoice date. Given this liberal time period we will not consider requests for extension. 3 months after their invoice date will be retained by us and no credit will be issued.

e return shipment must be accompanied by an invoice/packing list or customer packing list including for each title e number, invoice date, price and discount billed. It speeds processing if on your packing list you list your SAN and our own packing lists please make sure the information on the form is legible.

)% overstock returns limitation on booksellers whose returns are determined by us to be excessive.

not acceptable for return or credit. Out-of-print titles will be identified in our Complete List which is mailed to stores in as OSI (out-of-stock indefinitely) in the Complete List will be sold for a short period if stock is available. If no stock is led immediately and you will be so notified. Returns of these OSI titles must reach our warehouse by the dates ks are declared out of print and return of these OP titles will be retained by us and no credit will be issued. No ns can be granted.

	May list	November list
	June 15	December 15
'arehouse	September 1	March 1

otice.

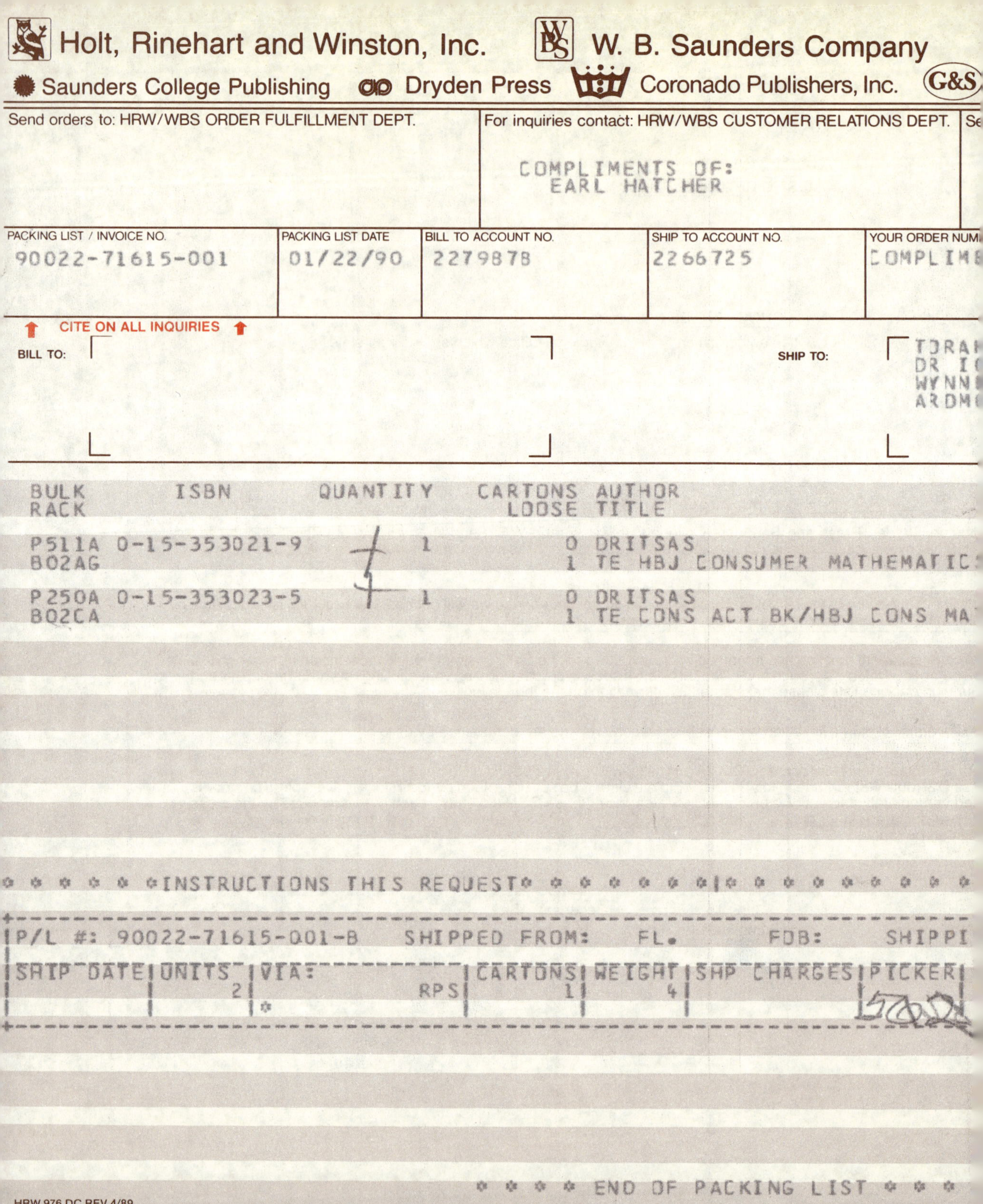

Holt, Rinehart and Winston, Inc. W. B. Saunders Company

Saunders College Publishing Dryden Press Coronado Publishers, Inc. G&S

Send orders to: HRW/WBS ORDER FULFILLMENT DEPT.

For inquiries contact: HRW/WBS CUSTOMER RELATIONS DEPT.

COMPLIMENTS OF:
EARL HATCHER

PACKING LIST / INVOICE NO.	PACKING LIST DATE	BILL TO ACCOUNT NO.	SHIP TO ACCOUNT NO.	YOUR ORDER NUM
90022-71615-001	01/22/90	2279878	2266725	COMPLIME

CITE ON ALL INQUIRIES

BILL TO:

SHIP TO:
TORA
DR I
WYNN
ARDM

BULK RACK	ISBN	QUANTITY	CARTONS LOOSE	AUTHOR TITLE
P511A B02AG	0-15-353021-9	1	0 1	DRITSAS TE HBJ CONSUMER MATHEMATIC
P250A B02CA	0-15-353023-5	1	0 1	DRITSAS TE CONS ACT BK/HBJ CONS MA

* * * * * *INSTRUCTIONS THIS REQUEST* * * * * * * * * * * * * * * * *

P/L #: 90022-71615-001-B SHIPPED FROM: FL. FOB: SHIPPI

SHIP DATE	UNITS	VIA:	CARTONS	WEIGHT	SHP CHARGES	PICKER
	2	RPS	1	4		

* * * * END OF PACKING LIST * * *

HRW 976 DC REV 4/89

The car dealer provided this table as part of the advertisement.

Annual Percentage Rate	Length of Contract	Amount Financed	Monthly Payment	Total Payment
3.9%	24 months	$9960.30	$432.08	$10,369.92
5.9%	36 months	$9960.30	$302.56	$10,892.16
6.9%	48 months	$9960.30	$238.04	$11,425.92

3. How much more is the total of monthly payments for the 5.9% rate than for the 3.9% rate? $522.24 more

4. How much more is the total of monthly payments for the 6.9% rate than for the 3.9% rate? $1056 more

The credit union provides this table to show the monthly payment on a loan of $9960 at 6% interest for 24 months, 36 months, and 48 months.

	24 months	36 months	48 months
Monthly Payment	$441.44	$303.00	$233.91
Total of Monthly Payments	? $10,594.56	? $10,908.00	? $11,227.68

5. Complete the table to find the total of monthly payments for each time period. See the table.

6. For the credit union loan, how much more is the total of monthly payments for the 48-month loan than for the 36-month loan? $319.68 more

EXPLORING DECISIONS

7. Which loan would allow Teresa to put more of her monthly income aside for savings?

8. For which loan would Teresa pay the least amount in finance charges?

9. Suppose you are Teresa. Which financing would you choose? Give reasons for your choice.

3 Close

Summary: Ask students to tell why many people choose to have low payments for a longer period of time instead of large payments for a shorter period of time.

Problem-Solving Skills

Completing a table (Ex. 5)
Interpreting information (Ex. 7–9)

Critical Thinking

Ex. 9

Project

Have students visit car dealers to find the payment plans that are available. Have them write a summary explaining the different plans and which one they would select.

Additional Answers

7. The 48-month loan at the credit union'

8. The 3.9% loan at the car dealer

9. Answers will vary.

Objective

Student will use a graph to solve multi-step problems that involve inflation.

Overview

This topic is optional. The word "Enrichment" that appears to the right of the title in this Teacher's Edition does not appear in the student textbook. Therefore, this material is not included in the Chapter Review and Chapter Test.

Using the Page

You may wish to have students work this Enrichment in small groups or you may wish to work with the class.

Problem-Solving Skills

Solving a multi-step problem (Ex. 1–3)
Using a graph (Ex. 1–3)

Inflation ENRICHMENT

George Hubert bought a new car last year. This year George's wife, Teresa, plans to buy the same model.

While reading the paper, Teresa saw this graph which shows the inflation rate for several consumer items over the past year. **Inflation** refers to increase in costs.

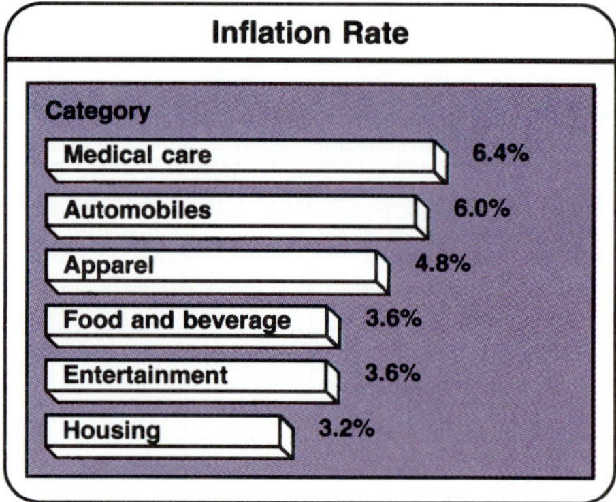

Teresa used the graph to estimate the cost of the car this year.

1. *Complete:* Because of inflation, automobile costs are up ___?___ over last year. **6.0%**

EXAMPLE Last year, a Turbo Sun Machine cost $10,500. Use the graph to estimate how much the car will cost this year.

[1] Read the graph to find the inflation rate. ⟶ **6%**

[2] Multiply last year's price by the inflation rate.

$10,500 × 0.06 = **$630** ◀ *Last Year's Price* × *Inflation Rate* = *Amount of Increase*

[3] Add the amount of increase to last year's price.

$10,500 + $630 = **$11,130** ◀ *Last Year's Price* + *Amount of Increase* = *This Year's Price*

The price of the car this year will be about **$11,130.**

EXERCISES

For Exercises 1–3, refer to the graph above.

1. A house was sold last year for $110,000. How much would the same house sell for this year? **$113,520**

2. Last year a family spent $140 per week for food. How much can they expect to spend per week for food this year? **$145.04**

3. Last year, a four-door Star-Quest cost $8200. This year the same car sells for $8707.40.
   a. According to the information of the graph, does the car cost more or less than you would expect? **More**
   b. How much more or less? **$15.40**

Chapter Summary

IMPORTANT IDEAS

1. Base Price + Cost of Optional Equipment + Destination Charge = Sticker Price
2. Dealers will usually accept a price offer for a car below the sticker price and above the dealer's cost.
3. Many car buyers put a down payment on a car. Then they make monthly payments on the unpaid balance.
4. Down Payment + Total of Monthly Payments = Total Cost of Car
5. Total Cost of Car − Cash Price of Car = Finance Charge
6. Liability insurance has two parts—bodily injury liability, and property damage liability.
7. Car buyers often buy collision and comprehensive insurance to protect themselves from financial loss if their own cars become damaged.
8. Most car insurance policies have a deductible amount that the car owner pays. The insurance company pays the rest.

Chapter Review

Part 1: VOCABULARY

collision
comprehensive
down payment
premium
deductible
finance charge
sticker price
liability

1. The amount of cash that a car buyer pays at the time of purchase is the ?. (Pages 132–133) down payment
2. The interest paid for borrowing money to buy a car is called a ?. (Pages 132–133) finance charge
3. If someone else's car is damaged by your car, ? insurance will protect you from financial loss. (Pages 135–136) liability
4. The amount a person pays each year for insurance is called a ?. (Pages 135–136) premium
5. If you are at fault in an accident, ? insurance will help pay for the repairs to your car. (Pages 137–139) collision

Chapter Summary

The Chapter Summary contains a listing of the important ideas that were presented in the chapter. This listing is intended to assist the student with the Chapter Review that follows.

Objective

To review the important terms, skills, problem solving, and applications presented in Chapter 6.

Overview

The Chapter Review is structured in three parts. Part 1 is a review of the important terms that were introduced in the chapter. Part 2 reviews the skills that were presented in the chapter. Part 3 reviews the problem-solving strategies and applications that were presented in the chapter. Each item in the Chapter Review is referenced to the related pages where the concept, skill, or application was presented.

Using the Pages

You may wish to assign this Chapter Review for homework or treat it as a class review prior to administering the formal Chapter Test. In doing this, it is suggested that you only use the even- or odd-numbered exercises. You can then use the remaining exercises as a bank for use later.

Part 2: SKILLS

For Exercises 6–7, complete the table. (Pages 126–128)

	Base Price	Total Options	Destination Charge	Sticker Price	Tax Rate	Sales Tax	Total Cost
6.	$6247	$940	$387.50	? $7574.50	4%	? $302.98	? $7877.48
7.	$9360	$1263	$209.80	? $10,832.80	5%	? $541.64	? $11,374.44

For Exercises 8–9, find the dealer's cost. (Pages 130–131)

	Base Price	Percent of Base Price	Cost of Options	Percent of Cost of Options	Destination Charge	Dealer's Cost
8.	$10,200	80%	$1260	75%	$189.13	? $9294.13
9.	$8475	88%	$1542	80%	$262.59	? $8954.19

Find the total cost of the car in each advertisement. (Pages 132–133)

10. **Jupiter 300**
$1800 Down and
$146/Month for
60 Months
$10,560

11. **Cobra XT**
$2100 Down and
$182/Month for
48 Months
$10,836

12. **Venus 1000**
$1500 Down and
$235/Month for
36 Months
$9960

Find the finance charge for the car in each advertisement. (Pages 132–133)

13. **Myriah 200**
$8320 Cash or
15% Down and
$209/Month for
48 Months
$2960

14. **Cheyenne 500**
$6400 Cash or
20% Down and
$182/Month for
36 Months
$1432

15. **Moondust ZT**
$11,650 Cash or
10% Down and
$222/Month for
60 Months
$2835

For Exercises 16–19, use the table on page 135 to find the yearly insurance premium for these teenage drivers. (Pages 135–136)

	Liability Coverage	Grades of B+ or Higher?	Male/ Female
16.	50/100/50	Yes	Male $514.08
17.	100/300/50	No	Male $772.20

	Liability Coverage	Grades of B+ or Higher?	Male/ Female
18.	100/300/50	No	Female $471.90
19.	250/500/50	Yes	Female $453

146 CHAPTER 6

For Exercises 20–23, find the amount an insurance company will pay for each accident. (Pages 137–139)

	Amount of Repair Bill	Amount of Deductible	Insurance Pays
20.	$846.17	$100	? $746.17
21.	$956.04	$200	? $756.04
22.	$1254.20	$50	? $1204.20
23.	$413.59	$250	? $163.59

Part 3: APPLICATIONS

24. Greg Jones is interested in a new car with a base price of $6792. The total cost of the options is $1650, and the destination charge is $223.50. Find the sticker price. (Pages 126–128) $8665.50

25. The base price of a new car is $9715. The total cost of the options on the car is $1826. The destination charge is $302.80, and the sales tax rate is 5%. Find the total cost of the car. (Pages 126–128) $12,435.99

26. Emily is buying a car that has a base price of $10,300. The options cost $1850, and the destination charge is $289. The dealer pays 85% of the base price and 80% of the cost of options. Find the dealer's cost. (Pages 130–131) $10,524

27. Nancy Pettigrew wants to buy a Venus 400 which sells for $8920. She wants to put 20% down and make 48 monthly payments of $227 each. Find the finance charge. (Pages 132–133) $3760

28. Bruce McCastlain can put $1800 down on a new car and make 60 monthly payments of $184 each. What will be the total cost of the car? (Pages 132–133) $12,840

29. A 17-year-old boy has a **C** average. Use the table on page 135 to find his yearly premium for 100/300/50 liability insurance coverage. (Pages 135–136) $772.20

30. Paul Kopatz was in an accident in which he was at fault. The repair bill for his car was $856.30. His collision insurance policy had a $200 deductible. How much did the insurance company pay? (Pages 137–139) $656.30

31. Connie Fifer is a 16-year old **B** student. She has comprehensive insurance with a $100 deductible. Use the table on page 137 to find how much Connie's yearly premium would decrease if she changed her coverage to $200 deductible. (Pages 137–139) $13.20

32. Two cars differ in price by $1200. The sum of their prices is $26,400. What is the cost of each car? (Pages 140–141) $13,800; $12,600

33. An AM/FM radio for a car costs $105 more than power steering. The total cost of these options is $680. How much does the radio cost? (Pages 140–141) $392.50

Objective

To informally assess students' mastering of the major skills, concepts, problem solving, and applications presented in Chapter 6.

Using the Page

After completing the Chapter Review with the class, you may wish to use this Chapter Test as an informal assessment. This Chapter Test parallels the formal chapter tests (Form A and Form B) provided in the *Teacher's ResourceBank.*™

Chapter Test

1. Theodore Chase wants to buy a new car with a base price of $10,150. The cost of the options he wants is $1352, and the destination charge is $315.47. Find the sticker price. **$11,817.47**

2. A car's base price is $6260. Optional equipment costs $1530. The destination charge is $193.50, and the sales tax rate is 6%. Find the total cost of the car. **$8462.51**

For Exercises 3–4, complete the table to find the dealer's cost.

	Base Price	Percent of Base Price	Cost of Options	Percent of Cost of Options	Destination Charge	Dealer's Cost
3.	$7460	80%	$1250	75%	$213.59	? **$7119.09**
4.	$9420	86%	$1684	80%	$287.96	? **$9736.36**

5. Angie Coleman wants to buy a Wildcat ZT. She can put $1200 down and make 48 monthly payments of $174 each. What will be the total cost of the car? **$9552**

6. Ed Corrigan is buying a new car which sells for $8540. He puts 15% down and intends to make 60 monthly payments of $166 each. Find the finance charge. **$2701**

For Exercises 7–8, use the table below.

Yearly Insurance Premiums for Drivers 17 Years Old or Less	
With B+ Grade Average or Better	*With Grade Average Lower Than B+*
Male Basic rate × 2.16 Female Basic rate × 1.5	Male Basic rate × 2.7 Female Basic rate × 1.65

7. Sam Klein is a 17-year-old student with an A average. The basic yearly rate for the liability insurance coverage that he has is $238. Find Sam's yearly premium. **$514.08**

8. Jane Straight is a 16-year-old C student. The basic yearly rate for the liability insurance that she has is $286. How much would Jane save in yearly premiums if she raised her average to a B+? **$42.90**

9. Dwayne Webb accidentally backed his car into a tree. The repair bill was $514.73. Dwayne had collision insurance with a $100 deductible. How much did his insurance company pay? **$414.73**

10. The base price of the TX 10 is $600 less than that of the PQ 12. The sum of the base prices is $20,000. What is the base price of the TX 10? **$9700**

Cumulative Maintenance Chapters 1–6

Choose the correct answer. Choose **a, b, c,** *or* **d.**

1. Greg Hinds earns $5.20 per hour, plus time and a half for all hours worked over 40. Find his earnings for a 44-hour week. b

   a. $228.80 b. $239.20
   c. $31.20 d. $343.20

2. Nancy McCloud wants to buy a Cobra ZL which has a base price of $12,300. The cost of the options she wants is $1392, and the destination charge is $226.34. Find the sticker price. b

   a. $34,326 b. $13,918.34
   c. $13,692 d. $13,818.34

3. Use the deposit slip below to find the net deposit. d

	Dollars	Cents
CASH		
CHECKS 1	56	39
List 2	114	62
Each 3		
Check 4		
TOTAL	171	01
▶ Less Cash Rec'd	35	00
NET DEPOSIT	?	

   a. $206.01 b. $377.02
   c. $146.01 d. $136.01

4. Find 12% of $11,650. a

   a. $1398 b. $1398.12
   c. $1387 d. $139,800

5. Rosalind's income in 1987 was $45,000. The FICA tax rate was 7.15% on a maximum of $43,500. How much FICA tax did Rosalind pay? c

   a. $3217.50 b. $31,102.50
   c. $3110.25 d. $3099.25

6. Find the finance charge for the car advertised below. a

Starfire 500
$7250 Cash or
20% Down and
$140/Month for
60 Months

   a. $2600 b. $1450
   c. $1150 d. $9850

7. Round 36,549 to the nearest thousand. d

   a. 36,000 b. 36,500
   c. 36,550 d. 37,000

8. Tom Burton must pay $2456 in federal income tax this year. The amount of tax withheld from his pay was $2613. Find the amount of the refund or the balance due. d

   a. Balance due: $257
   b. Refund: $257
   c. Balance due: $157
   d. Refund: $157

Objective

To review the content presented in Chapters 1–6

Using the Pages

You may wish to use this Cumulative Maintenance as an informal assessment tool. These pages can be assigned for homework or they may be used as review in class.

9. What percent of 800 is 160? a

a. 20%   b. 2%   c. 5%   d. 50%

10. A store clerk is trying to arrange four different music boxes side by side on a shelf. In how many ways can these music boxes be arranged? b

a. 4   b. 24   c. 12   d. 8

11. William Hovey's taxable income was $9200 last year. From a state income tax schedule, he finds that he must pay a tax of $38 + 1.5% of the excess taxable income over $5000. Find the amount of tax William must pay. c

a. $113   b. $668
c. $101   d. $63

12. Multiply: $356 × 2.45 d

a. $8.72   b. $861.20
c. $737.90   d. $872.20

13. The graph below shows how Anna Garcias budgets her monthly income. For which item is the most money budgeted? b

Transportation 10%
Food 25%
Savings 10%
Utilities 8%
Other 17%
Housing 30%

a. Utilities   b. Housing
c. Food   d. Savings

14. There are nine irons on a shelf. Two have green handles, three have red handles, and four have black handles. What is the probability that an iron chosen at random will have a black handle? b

a. $\frac{4}{5}$ b. $\frac{4}{9}$
c. $\frac{1}{4}$ d. $\frac{1}{9}$

15. Write a decimal for $8\frac{1}{2}$%. d

a. 8.05   b. 0.85
c. 8.5   d. 0.085

16. Dave opened his checking account with a deposit of $362.41. He then wrote a check to Hilton's Grocery for $56.93 and a check to Warehouse Jeans for $39.42. What was the new balance? a

a. $266.06   b. $96.35
c. $376.16   d. $458.76

17. Five people on a bowling league have bowling scores of 150, 164, 142, 178, and 158. Find the average of these scores. a

a. 158.4
b. 792
c. 158
d. 198

18. Multiply: $8.56 × $1\frac{1}{2}$ c

a. $128.40   b. $8.99
c. $12.84   d. $12.74

Owning a Car

Andy Hyde owns a three-year-old car. He heard that a good way to determine whether or not to buy a new car is to compare present yearly car expenses with the amount you would spend per year on a new car. So, Andy decided to compute the yearly operating costs for his car.

- How much is spent per year and per mile on maintenance costs?
- How much will the hidden expense of depreciation cost Andy when he tries to resell his car?
- How can Andy determine the car's fuel economy and yearly gasoline costs?
- How can Andy compute yearly driving costs per mile?

Chapter 7: Owning a Car

Overview

The focus of Chapter 7 is on operating costs for a car. It is important for teenagers to realize that, in addition to gasoline costs, repair and upkeep add considerably to car operating costs. A lesson on depreciation is included to make students aware of this "hidden" operating cost.

Although all lessons in this chapter involve problem-solving, the strategy lesson on pages 166–167 shows students how the use of frequency tables and histograms to organize data can facilitate consumer decision-making.

The *Consumer's Choice* on pages 168–169 presents a **situational lesson** in which students consider alternatives related to transportation needs and make choices in a familiar, real-life situation. Finally, the *Enrichment* lesson on page 170 explores one aspect of automobile maintenance, the effect of temperature on oil.

Using This Page

Have students read the introductory paragraph and questions. Have them list possible solutions to the problems presented. After completing the chapter, have students review their suggested solutions, comparing them with those presented in the lessons. You may wish to have students suggest other possible problems resulting from the situation described on this page and to discuss possible solutions.

You may wish to organize the class into small groups to complete the situational activity described on this *Using the Page.*

Lesson Resources

Maintenance: See below.
Reteaching/Alternate Teaching Strategy: p. M-31
Practice: p. M-31
Enrichment: p. M-31

Objectives

Student will

1. solve multi-step problems that involve automobile repair costs.
2. use a table and a formula to solve problems that involve maintenance costs per mile.

Maintenance

Perform the indicated operations.

1. $105.13 + $36.28 − $46.87 ANS: $94.54
2. $36.23 − $14.75 − $8.97 ANS: $12.51
3. $34.50 × 0.06 + $34.50 ANS: $36.57
4. $278.40 − ($25.88 + $65.92) ANS: $186.60
5. Juan pays 4.5% state income tax on taxable income of $13,580. How much state tax does he pay? ANS: $611.10

1 Lesson Focus

Motivation: Ask students to name some of the common repairs that are necessary to maintain a car.

Purpose: Maintenance costs on a car are often overlooked when considering the cost of owning and operating a car. Students should be aware of these costs and of what to expect in terms of maintenance expenses over a period of time.

2 Teaching the Lesson

Ask a student to read the opening paragraph. Then call students' attention to the repair bill on the same page. Ask students if they know how the labor charges are computed on a repair bill. Then have them answer questions 1 and 2.

STRATEGY: USING "HIDDEN QUESTIONS" TO SOLVE A MULTI-STEP PROBLEM

Maintenance Costs

Andy Hyde is examining his car repair bill. There are two separate costs for car repairs—the cost of parts and the cost of labor. The costs of upkeep and repair for a car are called **maintenance costs.**

A portion of Andy's repair bill is shown below.

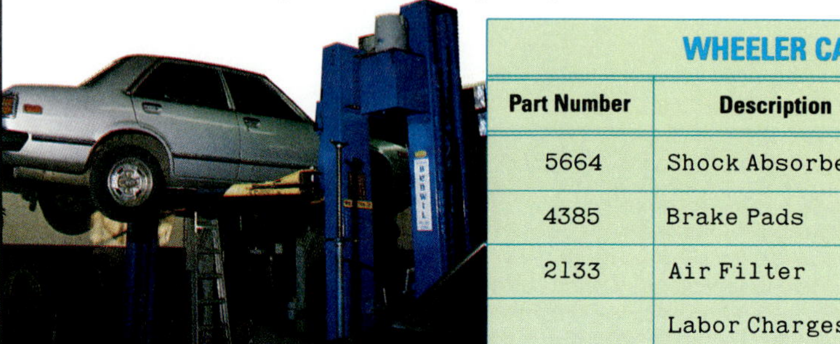

WHEELER CAR REPAIR

Part Number	Description	Quantity	Amount
5664	Shock Absorbers	2	$59.90
4385	Brake Pads	2	$46.90
2133	Air Filter	1	$12.30
	Labor Charges		$68.40

1. Estimate the total cost of the parts to the nearest ten dollars. $120
2. How much more will Andy pay for labor than for 2 shock absorbers? $8.50

The sales tax rate in Andy's state is 6%. Usually, sales tax is charged on parts but not on labor.

EXAMPLE 1 Find the total cost of Andy's repair bill.

1 Find the cost of all the parts.
$59.90 + $46.90 + $12.30 = **$119.10**

2 Find the sales tax on the parts.
6% of $119.10 = $119.10 × 0.06 = **$7.15** ◀ *Rounded to the nearest cent*

3 Find the total for parts.
$119.10 + $7.15 = **$126.25** ◀ *Cost of Parts* + *Sales Tax on Parts* = *Total for Parts*

4 Find the total repair bill.
$126.25 + $68.40 = **$194.65** ◀ *Total for Parts* + *Labor Charge* = *Total for Repairs*

Andy's total cost for repairs is **$194.65.**

Andy saw the chart on the next page in a consumer magazine. The chart shows the estimated maintenance costs over 6 years for the type of car that Andy owns.

Years Owned	1	2	3	4	5	6
Maintenance Costs	$100	$190	$480	$490	$1325	$960

3. For which year are the estimated maintenance costs the highest? Explain why this might happen. **The fifth year; answers will vary.**

4. For which year are the estimated maintenance costs less than the previous year? Explain why this might happen. **The sixth year; answers will vary.**

EXAMPLE 2 Use the chart to find Andy's estimated maintenance cost per mile for the fourth year of ownership. Andy drives 12,000 miles per year.

Estimated Costs ÷ **Number of Miles** = **Cost per Mile**

$490 ÷ 12,000 = $0.04 ◀ $12{,}000\overline{)490.0000}$ = 0.0408

= **4¢ per mile** (nearest cent)

5. Suppose Andy drove fewer than 12,000 miles per year. Would his estimated maintenance cost per mile be more or less than 4¢? **More than 4¢**
6. Suppose Andy drove 24,000 miles per year. Would his estimated maintenance cost per mile be doubled or divided in half? **Divided in half**

CHECK YOUR SKILLS

Write a decimal for each percent. For additional practice, see page 403.

1. 4% **0.04** **2.** 7% **0.07** **3.** 6% **0.06** **4.** 8% **0.08** **5.** 5% **0.05**

Round to the nearest hundredth. For additional practice, see page 378.

6. 19.349 **19.35** **7.** 12.3998 **12.40** **8.** 47.297 **47.30** **9.** 264.818 **264.82** **10.** 31.275 **31.28**

Divide. Round each answer to the nearest cent. For additional practice, see page 379.

11. $300 ÷ 20,000 **2¢** **12.** $490 ÷ 14,000 **4¢** **13.** $500 ÷ 21,000 **2¢** **14.** $644 ÷ 30,000 **2¢**

Find each answer. For additional practice, see page 407.

15. 6% of $815 **$48.90** **16.** 5% of $564.40 **$28.22** **17.** 7% of $119 **$8.33** **18.** 6% of $165.50 **$9.93**

Discuss Example 1 in detail, explaining that tax is usually applied only to the cost of parts. Then have students focus on the table of maintenance costs on page 153. Explain that these are estimated costs only and might vary considerably from one car to another. Discuss questions 3 and 4. Then go over Example 2 and discuss questions 5 and 6.

3 Close

Summary: Summarize what has been covered in the lesson by asking these questions.

1. What are the two main costs that are shown on a car repair bill? (Parts and labor)
2. What are the various steps involved in computing the cost of a car repair bill? (Find total cost of parts, sales tax on parts, total of parts and tax, total of parts and labor)
3. How can you estimate the maintenance cost per mile for a car? (Estimated costs ÷ number of miles)

Evaluation
Guided Practice: Ex. 1–4, 6, 8
Independent Practice: Ex. 5, 7, 9, 10–12

Extension

Make a list of automobile parts and have students obtain prices from at least three different parts suppliers. Suggest that one of the suppliers be a new car dealer. This extension of the lesson will help students see that prices of car parts do vary from one supplier to another.

Critical Thinking

You may wish to have students work in small groups to solve these problems or you may wish to work with the class. Questions 3 and 4 (in Lesson)

Problem-Solving Skills

Solving a multi-step problem (Ex. 5, 6, 10, 11)
Using a table (Ex. 7–10)
Interpreting information (Ex. 10–12)
Choosing the operation (Ex. 12)

Estimation Ex. 7–10 and 12

EXERCISES

Complete. Choose your answers from the box at the right.

labor
cost of the parts
sales tax rate
sales tax
maintenance costs
parts

1. Car repair costs are based on the cost of the ___?___ and the cost of the ___?___. parts; labor
2. To find the sales tax on parts, multiply the cost of the parts and the ___?___. sales tax rate
3. To find the total for parts, add the ___?___ and the amount of ___?___. cost of the parts; sales tax
4. The costs of upkeep and repair for a car are called ___?___. maintenance costs

For Exercises 5–6, use the auto parts price list at the right. Determine the total cost for repairs. Include 6% sales tax on all parts.

Auto Parts	
2 Shock absorbers	$73.00
1 Oil filter	$9.50
1 Air cleaner	$11.25
1 Fuel pump	$36.50
1 Carburetor tune-up kit	$36.50

5. Parts: 2 shock absorbers, 1 air cleaner, 1 oil filter
   Labor Charge: $38.00 $137.38
6. Parts: 1 carburetor tune-up kit, 1 fuel pump
   Labor Charge: $68.40 $145.78

For Exercises 7–10, find the estimated maintenance cost per mile for the age of the car shown. Use the table on page 153.

	Age (Years Owned)	Miles Per Year
7.	4	20,000 2¢
8.	5	25,000 5¢
9.	6	15,000 6¢

10. Find the estimated maintenance cost per mile for Andy's sixth year of car ownership. Andy drives his car the same number of miles in the sixth year as in the fourth year. (Example 2, page 153) 8¢

11. Tina paid $10.75 for 4 spark plugs and $49.75 for a muffler exhaust pipe. Other parts cost $61.50. The labor charge was $66.50. The sales tax rate is 7%. Find the total repair bill. $197.04

12. Chuck received a car repair bill which totaled $398.96. The total for parts was $346.75. Estimate the labor charges. d

    a. $100 **c.** $40 **b.** $60 **d.** $50

Math and Braking Distance

The ability of a motorist to stop quickly in an emergency depends on the vehicle's speed, brakes, and the conditions of the road.

The distance a car travels after the brakes have been applied and until the car stops completely is the **braking distance.** The graph at the right shows braking distances for cars on wet and dry asphalt roads.

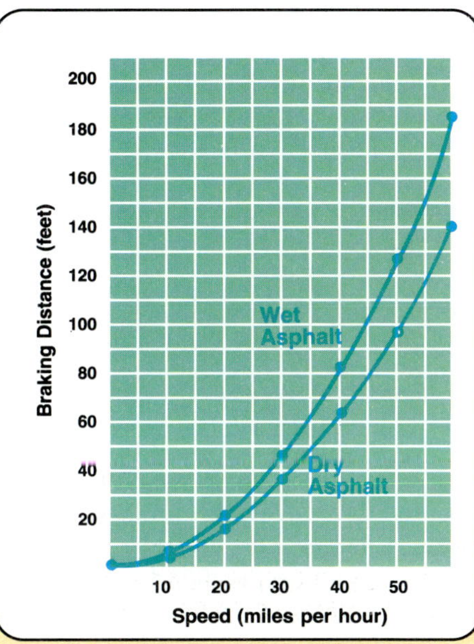

Karla Sands was driving 40 miles per hour on dry asphalt when she saw a branch lying on the road. Use the graph to estimate the braking distance.

1. Find the point on the graph for "Dry Asphalt" that corresponds to 40 miles per hour.

2. The approximate braking distance is **62 feet.**

EXERCISES

For Exercises 1–4, use the graph to estimate the braking distance.

1. A car traveling 30 miles per hour on wet asphalt **45 ft**
2. A car traveling 50 miles per hour on dry asphalt **97 ft**
3. A car traveling 25 miles per hour on dry asphalt **25 ft**
4. A car traveling 55 miles per hour on wet asphalt **150 ft**

For Exercises 5–8, use the graph to estimate the speed of each car.

5. Braking Distance: 50 feet
   Driving Surface: dry asphalt **35 mph**
6. Braking Distance: 100 feet
   Driving Surface: wet asphalt **44 mph**
7. Braking Distance: 130 feet
   Driving Surface: wet asphalt **51 mph**
8. Braking Distance: 10 feet
   Driving Surface: dry asphalt **16 mph**

Objective

Student will apply the skill of reading a graph to solving problems that involve braking distance.

Overview

This page is an extension of the skills and ideas presented in the previous lesson of this chapter. Since the content presented on this page is not included in the Chapter Review or Chapter Test, its use is optional.

Using the Pages

You may wish to have students work this lesson in small groups or you may wish to work with the class. Using it with the class, have a student read the first two paragraphs. Then focus students' attention on the graph and work through the Example. Use Exercises 1 and 5 as guided practice and Exercises 2–4 and 6–8 as independent practice.

Problem-Solving Skills

Reading a graph (Ex. 1–8)

Lesson Resources

Maintenance: See below.
Reteaching/Alternate Teaching Strategy: p. M-32
Practice: p. M-32
Enrichment: p. M-32

Objectives

Student will

1. use a table to find the amount of depreciation on a car.
2. use a table to solve multi-step problems involving depreciation and resale value.

Maintenance

Perform the indicated operations.

1. 1.5 × $8.36 ANS: $12.54
2. 0.15 × $25,840 ANS: $3876
3. $392.14 − $87.24 ANS: $304.90
4. $1435.26 + $124 ANS: $1559.26
5. Mildred has a balance of $345.18 in her checking account. She writes a check for $28.29 and makes a deposit of $108.45. Find the new balance. ANS: $425.34

1 Lesson Focus

Motivation: Ask students if they have any idea what percent of the value of a new car is lost after one year of driving it.

Purpose: Depreciation is one of the hidden costs of owning a car. Students, who will be future owners of cars, should know about depreciation in order to help them make wise consumer decisions.

2 Teaching the Lesson

Have students read the opening paragraph. Ask them what is meant by depreciation. Direct students' attention to the depreciation graph. Ask the following questions.

STRATEGY: USING A "HIDDEN QUESTION" TO SOLVE A MULTI-STEP PROBLEM

Depreciation

The decrease in value of a car due to age and usage is called **depreciation.**

To determine the dollar amount of depreciation, Andy Hyde uses the graph at the right. It shows the percent of depreciation for his car for each of 6 years.

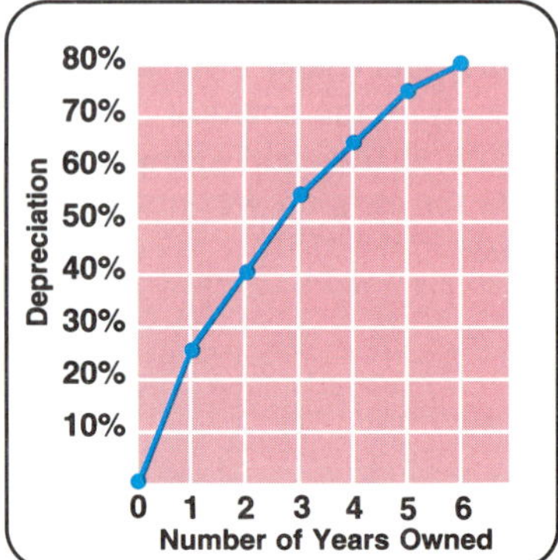

1. What is the total percent of depreciation for the 6 years? 80%
2. By what percent will the car depreciate from the beginning of the third year through the end of the fifth year? 35%

EXAMPLE 1 Andy paid $10,500 dollars for his car when it was new. Compute the amount of depreciation in dollars after 4 years.

1 Read the graph to find the percent of depreciation for the 4 years → **65%**

2 Find the amount of depreciation in dollars.
65% of $10,500 = $10,500 × 0.65
= **$6825** ← *Depreciation*

When you know the amount of depreciation in dollars, you can determine the approximate resale value of a car.

3. *Complete:* Cost of new car − _?_ = Resale value of car   Depreciation

EXAMPLE 2 Determine the approximate resale value of Andy's car after 5 years. Andy paid $10,500 for his car when it was new.

1 Determine the amount of depreciation. Use the graph.

75% of $10,500 = $10,500 × 0.75
= **$7875**

2 Subtract the amount of depreciation from the new car price.

$10,500 − $7875 = **$2625** ← *Resale Value*

4. If the approximate resale value of a car is 36% of the original price, what is the percent of depreciation? 64%

CHECK YOUR SKILLS

Write a decimal for each percent. For additional practice, see page 403.

1. 45% 0.45
2. 62% 0.62
3. 20% 0.20 or 0.2
4. 50% 0.50 or 0.5
5. 65% 0.65
6. 35% 0.35

Find each answer. For additional practice, see page 407.

7. 54% of 13,600 7344
8. 35% of 7425 2598.75
9. 3% of 30 0.9
10. 75% of 9745 7308.75
11. 20% of 11,000 2200
12. 8% of 12,685 1014.8
13. Which is greater, 80% of $9000 or 90% of $7000? 80% of $9000
14. Which is less, 20% of $7000 or 25% of $6000? 20% of $7000
15. Which is less, 70% of $6000 or 60% of $7000? They are equal.
16. Which is more, $33\frac{1}{3}$% of $600 or 30% of $7000? 30% of $7000
17. Which is more, 75% of $2000 or 80% of $1500? 75% of $2000
18. Which is less, 5% of $2000 or 4% of $3000? 5% of $2000

EXERCISES

Complete. Choose your answers from the box at the right.

percent
dollar amount
depreciation
resale value

1. The decrease in value of a car due to age and usage is called __?__. depreciation
2. If you know the percent of depreciation for a car and the new car price, you can calculate the __?__ of depreciation. dollar amount
3. Once you know the amount of depreciation, you can calculate the approximate __?__ of a car. resale value

For Exercises 4–12, find the dollar amount of depreciation for the given number of years. Refer to the graph on page 156.

	Price of New Car	Years		Price of New Car	Years		Price of New Car	Years
4.	$9800	1 $2450	7.	$6995	6 $5596	10.	$11,400	2 $4560
5.	$10,750	4 $6987.50	8.	$13,050	5 $9787.50	11.	$8975	4 $5833.75
6.	$5780	2 $2312	9.	$7360	3 $4048	12.	$7670	6 $6136

Explain that this graph applies to a specific car. Not all cars depreciate at the same rate. Ask these questions.

1. What percent of the value of the car is depreciated after one year? (25%)
2. What percent of the value of the car is depreciated after two years? (40%)
3. If the car costs $10,000 when new, how much did its value depreciate after two years? ($4000) What was its approximate resale value after two years? ($6000)
4. What percent of the value of the car is depreciated from year 1 to year 2? (15%)

Have students write answers to questions 1 and 2 on page 156. Then explain Example 1. Before discussing Example 2, have a student complete question 4 correctly. Then have all students write an answer to question 4.

3 Close

Summary: Ask students to explain in their own words how depreciation and resale value are related.

Evaluation

Guided Practice: Ex. 1–3, 4–16 even
Independent Practice: Ex. 5–17 odd, 18–21

Extension

Provide some depreciation percents in table form for students and have them draw graphs of the depreciations. A variation of this is to provide the new car value and resale values of a car at the end of each year. Students then can compute the depreciation percents and graph the data.

Problem-Solving Skills

Using a graph (Ex. 4–17)
Solving a multi-step problem (Ex. 13–17, 19, 21)
Interpreting information (Ex. 18–21)

Estimation

Ex. 18 and 19

For Exercises 13–17, complete the table below. Use the graph at the right to determine the dollar amount of depreciation for each of four years. Then find the approximate resale value after four years.

	Price of New Car	Depreciation after				Resale Value after 4 yrs
		1 yr	2 yrs	3 yrs	4 yrs	
13.	$11,600	? $2320	? $4060	? $5220	? $6380	? $5220
14.	$10,200	? $2040	? $3570	? $4590	? $5610	? $4590
15.	$9690	? $1938	? $3391.50	? $4360.50	? $5329.50	? $4360.50
16.	$14,000	? $2800	? $4900	? $6300	? $7700	? $6300
17.	$6950	? $1390	? $2432.50	? $3127.50	? $3822.50	? $3127.50

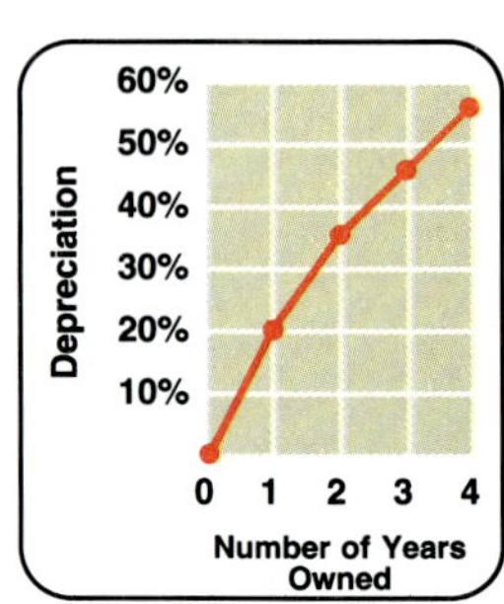

18. After 4 years a car which cost $7925 has depreciated 62%. Estimate the total dollar amount of depreciation. **About $4800**

19. After 3 years a car which cost $8950 has depreciated 33%. Estimate the resale value of the car. **About $6000**

20. A new car cost $12,600. It depreciates 24% its first year, 17% its second year, and 13% its third year.

a. Find the total percent of depreciation after 3 years. **54%**

b. Find the total dollar amount of depreciation after 3 years. **$6804**

21. Car rental agencies figure depreciation on their cars per month. One agency uses a monthly rate of 3% depreciation on cars which are less than two years old. Find the amount of depreciation on a 20-month-old car which originally sold for $8425. **$5055**

Mid-Chapter Review

For Exercises 1–2, use the auto parts price list below to determine the total for repairs. Include a 5% sales on all parts. (Pages 152–154)

Auto Parts	
4 Spark plugs	$4.75
2 Wheel cylinders	$9.00
1 Master cylinder	$53.75
2 Radiator hoses	$30.25

1. Parts: 4 Spark plugs, 1 master cylinder
Labor: $42.00 **$103.43**

2. Parts: 2 wheel cylinders, 1 master cylinder
Labor: $68.75 **$134.64**

3. Katey spent $465 on maintenance last year for her car. She drove her car 18,000 kilometers. Find her maintenance cost per kilometer. Round your answer to the nearest cent. (Pages 152–154) **3¢**

4. Ben spent $1260 on maintenance last year for his car. He drove his car 25,000 miles. Find his maintenance cost per mile. Round your answer to the nearest cent. (Pages 152–154) **5¢**

5. After 3 years, a car which cost $7386 has depreciated 45%. What is the total dollar amount of depreciation? (Pages 156–158) **$3323.70**

6. After 4 years, a car which cost $8475 has depreciated 60%. What is the approximate resale value of the car? (Pages 156–158) **$3390**

MAINTENANCE

7. Sue and Phyllis have part-time jobs. Sue works 25 hours per week for $9.80 per hour and Phyllis works 28 hours per week for $9.30 per hour. How much less than Phyllis does Sue earn per week? (Pages 42–44) **$15.40**

8. Find the total cost of the car below. Include a 6% sales tax.
Base Price: $8200
Optional Equipment: $1634.75
Destination Charge: $314.40
(Pages 126–128) **$10,758.10**

9. A certain type of sports car is available in 3 different models. Each model is available in 5 different colors. How many possible choices would you have if you decided to order the sports car? (Pages 22–25) **15**

10. John Whitehurst has $2100 in a savings account that pays a yearly interest rate of 5%. Use the formula $i = p \times r \times t$ to find how much simple interest the account will earn in 6 months. (Pages 110–111) **$52.50**

Objective

Student will

1. review the skills, concepts, and applications in the first part of Chapter 7.
2. maintain key skills and concepts taught in Chapters 2, 3, 5, and 6.

Using the Page

Exercises 1–6 provide an informal assessment of the student's mastery of the major skills and concepts presented in the first half of Chapter 7. Each item is referenced to the related pages where the particular item was presented. These exercises parallel the quiz provided in the *Teacher's ResourceBank.*™

A quiz covering the second half of the chapter is also provided in the *Teacher's ResourceBank.*™

Exercises 7–10 maintain skills and concepts taught in Chapters 2, 3, 5, and 6.

Lesson Resources

Maintenance: See below.
Reteaching/Alternate Teaching Strategy: p. M-32
Practice: p. M-32
Enrichment: p. M-32

Objectives

Student will

1. use a formula to find the fuel economy of a car.
2. use a formula to find the fuel cost per kilometer or per mile.

Maintenance

1. Round 125.46 to the nearest whole number.
   ANS: 125
2. Which is greater, 112 ÷ 12, or 150 ÷ 10?
   ANS: 150 ÷ 10
3. Subtract: 13,416 − 3160 ANS: 10,256
4. Multiply: 24 × 235 ANS: 5640
5. Chester Hanes buys a new car for $12,500. He pays $2000 down. What will his finance costs be if he makes 36 monthly payments of $375 each?
   ANS: $3000

1 Lesson Focus

Motivation: Ask students to suggest some good fuel economy figures in miles per gallon. Then ask them if they know some good comparable figures in kilometers per liter.

Purpose: Fuel economy is one consideration when buying a car although it may be more of an emotional issue than a cost concern. Nevertheless, students hear many references to fuel economy and they should know how to compute it. Also, it should be a concern of all citizens because of the necessity to conserve energy.

STRATEGY: USING A "HIDDEN QUESTION" TO SOLVE A MULTI-STEP PROBLEM

Gasoline Costs

Andy Hyde knows that **fuel economy** is an important consideration when buying a car. Fuel economy is expressed in **miles per gallon** or in **kilometers per liter**.

1. *Complete:* For Andy to determine the fuel economy of a car in miles per gallon, he must know the number of __?__ driven, and the number of __?__ of gasoline used. **miles; gallons**

2. Why is fuel economy important when buying a car? **Because a greater fuel economy means total yearly fuel costs will be lower.**

EXAMPLE 1 Andy is considering buying a new car. He looks at two cars. One car will travel 390 miles on 15.8 gallons of fuel; the other will travel 371 miles on 13.1 gallons of fuel. Which has the better fuel economy?

1 Find the fuel economy of the first car.

390 ÷ 15.8 = 24.68 ◀ *Number of Miles ÷ Number of Gallons = Fuel Economy*

= **24 miles per gallon** ◀ *Round down to the nearest mile per gallon.*

2 Find the fuel economy of the second car.

371 ÷ 13.1 = 28.32

= **28 miles per gallon** ◀ *Round down to the nearest mile per gallon.*

Since 28 > 24, the **second car** has the greater fuel economy.

3. Why is the fuel economy rounded <u>down</u> to the nearest mile per gallon? **To ensure that the motorist will not run out of gasoline.**

Every year Andy must calculate the cost per kilometer spent on gasoline for his work truck.

EXAMPLE 2 Andy knows that he drove 28,000 kilometers last year, and spent $924 for fuel. What was Andy's approximate fuel cost per kilometer last year?

Total Yearly Cost	÷	**Total Kilometers Driven**	=	**Cost per Kilometer**
$924	÷	28,000	=	0.033 ◀ *Round to the nearest cent.*
			=	**3¢ per kilometer**

CHECK YOUR SKILLS

Round to the nearest whole number. For additional practice, see page 378.

1. 28.3 28 **2.** 33.5 34 **3.** 39.9 40 **4.** 10.1 10 **5.** 12.7 13 **6.** 14.4 14

Divide. Round each answer to the nearest whole number. For additional practice, see page 378.

7. 489 ÷ 12.6 39 **8.** 935 ÷ 66.8 14 **9.** 500 ÷ 15.1 33 **10.** 400 ÷ 32.6 12

Round to the nearest hundredth. For additional practice, see page 378.

11. 0.0378 0.04 **12.** 0.0764 0.08 **13.** 0.0881 0.09 **14.** 0.0712 0.07 **15.** 0.0561 0.06 **16.** 0.0651 0.07

Divide. Round each answer to the nearest cent. For additional practice, see pages 376 and 378.

17. \$1214 ÷ 13,500 9¢ **18.** \$1508 ÷ 27,000 6¢ **19.** \$928 ÷ 14,000 7¢ **20.** \$2900 ÷ 51,000 6¢

EXERCISES

Complete. Choose your answers from the box at the right.

total yearly cost
miles
smaller
approximate
gallons
total kilometers driven
greater

1. The less fuel used per mile or per kilometer, the __?__ the fuel economy of the car. greater
2. Fuel Economy = Number of __?__ ÷ Number of __?__ miles; gallons
3. To find the cost per kilometer for fuel for one year, divide the __?__ by the __?__. total yearly cost; total kilometers driven
4. Since both fuel economy and cost per mile or per kilometer are rounded numbers, they are both __?__ figures. approximate

For Exercises 5–12, determine the fuel economy.

	Miles	Gallons of Fuel
5.	298	10.9 27
6.	400	14.1 28
7.	378	11.6 32
8.	311	12.2 25

	Kilometers	Liters of Fuel
9.	591	51.9 11
10.	617	60.6 10
11.	841	65.9 12
12.	200	13.8 14

2 Teaching the Lesson

To introduce the lesson, you might obtain a list of the fuel economy ratings of popular cars and read some of them to students. Ask them if they know whether such figures accurately reflect what the fuel economy actually is under ordinary driving conditions. Have students read the opening paragraph and then discuss questions 1 and 2. Then explain Example 1 and emphasize that the results are rounded down. Explain this technique as you discuss question 3. Ask students how Example 1 would be worked if the distance is expressed in kilometers and the amount of fuel in liters.

Then discuss Example 2 and ask how it would be computed if the distance is in miles. The question below may help to challenge students' thinking.

Would the amount spent in a year for fuel for a car be greater per kilometer than per mile or less per kilometer than per mile?

3 Close

Summary: Ask students how to compute the fuel economy of a car in both customary and metric units. Then ask how to find the cost of fuel per mile or per kilometer over a period of time.

Evaluation

Guided Practice: Ex. 1–4, 6–22 even
Independent Practice: Ex. 5–21 odd, 23–27

Extension

Have the students work in groups to find the city fuel economy and the highway fuel economy for 3 different cars. Then have the students give reasons why the two fuel economies are different.

Critical Thinking

You may wish to have students work in small groups to solve these problems or you may wish to work with the class.

Questions 2 and 3 (in Lesson)

Problem-Solving Skills

Interpreting information (Ex. 23–27)
Making comparisons (Ex. 23–27)
Solving a multi-step problem (Ex. 24–27)

Estimation Ex. 23

For Exercises 13–22:

a. *Find the yearly gasoline cost per kilometer or per mile.*

b. *Round answers to the nearest cent.*

	Yearly Fuel Cost	Kilometers Per Year
13.	$760	20,000 4¢
14.	$2400	32,000 8¢
15.	$2800	50,000 6¢
16.	$1480	20,000 7¢
17.	$1408	22,000 6¢

	Yearly Fuel Cost	Miles Per Year
18.	$1014	13,000 8¢
19.	$968	11,000 9¢
20.	$938	14,000 7¢
21.	$1207	17,000 7¢
22.	$780	15,000 5¢

23. Andy Hyde drives 40,000 miles per year. His yearly cost for gasoline is $3985. Estimate his yearly gasoline cost per mile. **About 10¢**

For Exercises 24–25, determine which has the greater fuel economy.

24. One mid-size car can travel 455 miles on 21.2 gallons of gasoline. Another mid-size car can travel 400 miles on 11.5 gallons of gasoline. **The second car**

25. One sports car travels 595 kilometers on 46.5 liters of fuel. Another sports car travels 600 kilometers on 48.5 liters of fuel. **The first car**

26. Two different models of the same car have fuel economy ratings of 32 miles per gallon and 27 miles per gallon. Based on a price of $1.09 per gallon and 17,280 miles driven each year, how much more will the yearly fuel cost be for one model than the other? **$109**

27. The fuel economy ratings of two new cars are listed as 28 miles per gallon and 22 miles per gallon. Based on a price of $1.05 per gallon and 15,400 miles driven, how much more will fuel cost for one car than for the other car? **$157.50**

STRATEGY: USING A "HIDDEN QUESTION" TO SOLVE A MULTI-STEP PROBLEM

Yearly Driving Costs

Andy Hyde keeps records of all his car expenses. He uses these records to compute the average cost per mile for owning and operating his car.

Andy groups the costs in three categories.

Fixed Costs: Costs which are not affected by the number of miles he drives
Variable Costs: Costs which increase as the number of miles increases
Other Costs

Andy's car costs during his fourth year of ownership are shown at the right.

Automobile Costs	
Fixed Costs	***Yearly Totals***
Depreciation	$945
Insurance	$1258
License and Taxes	$124
Loan Payment	$1931
Variable Costs	
Gas and Oil	$651
Maintenance	$380
Tires	$75
Other Costs	
Parking and Tolls	$148
Car Wash	$125

1. What is the total of the fixed costs? **$4258**
2. What is the total of the variable costs? **$1106**
3. Which costs are higher, the fixed costs or the variable costs? **fixed**
4. How much higher are they? **$3152**

EXAMPLE Compute Andy's average cost per mile for his fourth year of car ownership in which he drove 15,000 miles.

[1] **Total Fixed Costs** + **Total Variable Costs** + **Other Costs** = **Total Cost**

$4258 + $1106 + $273 = **$5637**

[2] Divide the total cost by the number of miles driven.

$5637 ÷ 15,000 = $0.3758

= **37.6¢** ◀ *Rounded to the nearest tenth of a cent*

The average cost per mile for the year is **37.6¢.**

5. Why is depreciation included as a yearly driving cost? **Because a car sold this year could have been sold for a higher price last year.**

Lesson Resources

Maintenance: See below.
Reteaching/Alternate Teaching Strategy: p. M-33 (Visual 20)
Practice: p. M-33
Enrichment: p. M-33
Visual 20

Objectives

Student will

1. identify car expenses as fixed or variable costs.
2. solve multi-step problems that involve yearly driving costs per mile.

Maintenance

Perform the indicated operations.

1. $\frac{2}{3} + \frac{3}{4}$ ANS: $1\frac{5}{12}$
2. $\frac{2}{3} \times \frac{3}{4}$ ANS: $\frac{1}{2}$
3. $\frac{3}{8} \times \$86.56$ ANS: $32.46
4. 15% of $14.60 ANS: $2.19
5. One compact car that cost $8245 when new retained 60% of its value after four years. What was its value after four years? ANS: $4947

[1] Lesson Focus

Motivation: Ask students to name as many different car expenses as they can.

Purpose: The expense of owning and operating an automobile is an item that must be included in consumer budget planning. Students, as future car owners, must realize that this cost is not an insignificant one.

[2] Teaching the Lesson

Have students read the opening paragraph and the definitions of the three types of car costs. Then have students write their answers to questions 1–4. Discuss the Example by whatever method best fits your instructional style. Then discuss question 5.

3 Close

Summary: Have students name as many of the car expenses in each category that they can. Ask selected students to explain the method for finding the cost per mile of car ownership.

Evaluation
Guided Practice: Ex. 1–4, 6–12 even
Independent Practice: Ex. 5–13 odd, 14–17

Extension

Obtain a copy of the publication Cost of Owning and Operating Automobiles and Vans available from the U. S. Department of Transportation. You can develop many activities based on the information in this publication. A worksheet is included that enables you to convert the costs to any locality.

Problem-Solving Skills

Solving a multi-step problem (Ex. 5–13, 17)
Interpreting information (Ex. 13–17)

Critical Thinking

You may wish to have students work in small groups to solve this problem or you may wish to work with the class.
Question 5 (in Lesson)

CHECK YOUR SKILLS

Round each number to the nearest hundredth.

1. 0.3758 0.38 **2.** 0.0522 0.05 **3.** 0.0555 0.06 **4.** 0.8109 0.81 **5.** 0.7253 0.73

Round each number to the nearest thousandth. For additional practice, see page 378.

6. 0.32961 0.330 **7.** 0.29991 0.300 **8.** 0.41652 0.417 **9.** 0.39652 0.397

Divide. Round each quotient to the nearest thousandth. For additional practice, see pages 376 and 378.

10. 7989 ÷ 25,000 0.320 **11.** 6993 ÷ 18,000 0.389 **12.** 6648 ÷ 15,000 0.443 **13.** 5621 ÷ 13,000 0.432

Multiply each amount by 100. Then write the amount in cents (nearest tenth). The first one is done for you.

14. $0.4768 = **47.7¢** **15.** $0.3917 39.2¢ **16.** $0.8582 85.8¢ **17.** $0.1005 10.1¢

18. $0.9246 92.5¢ **19.** $0.0688 6.9¢ **20.** $0.0455 4.6¢ **21.** $0.3992 39.9¢

EXERCISES

Complete. Choose your answers from the box at the right.

number of miles driven
fixed
variable

1. Costs which increase as the number of miles driven increase are called __?__ costs. variable
2. Costs which do not increase or decrease as the number of miles driven increase or decrease are called __?__ costs. fixed
3. For any given year, a consumer has more control over __?__ costs than over __?__ costs. variable; fixed
4. Average Cost Per Mile = Total Costs ÷ __?__ number of miles driven

Find the cost per mile (nearest tenth of a cent).

	Total Fixed Costs	Total Variable Costs	Other Costs	Total Mileage	Total Yearly Driving Costs	Cost Per Mile
5.	$3527	$1845	$450	20,000	? $5822	? 29.1¢
6.	$4250	$2465	$500	36,000	? $7215	? 20¢
7.	$2600	$2065	$385	18,500	? $5050	? 27.3¢
8.	$4000	$1600	$650	24,000	? $6250	? 26¢
9.	$2075	$3800	$680	30,000	? $6555	? 21.9¢
10.	$3895	$1827	$275	14,000	? $5997	? 42.8¢

For Exercises 11–13, find the missing amounts. Round the COST PER MILE to the nearest tenth of a cent.

	FIXED COSTS	11. Yearly Totals	12. Yearly Totals	13. Yearly Totals
	Depreciation	$2200	$2500	$ 900
	Insurance	$ 960	$ 690	$ 580
	License, registration, taxes	$ 440	$ 340	$ 410
	Loan Payment	$2700	$2340	$1340
a.	TOTAL FIXED COSTS	? $6300	? $5870	? $3230
	VARIABLE COSTS			
	Gas and oil	$1490	$ 850	$1200
	Maintenance	$ 498	$ 530	$1070
	Tires	$ 105	$ 40	$ 296
b.	TOTAL VARIABLE COSTS	? $2093	? $1420	? $2566
	OTHER COSTS	$ 400	$ 150	$ 180
c.	TOTAL DRIVING COSTS	? $8793	? $7440	? $5976
	Number of Miles Driven	20,000	15,000	24,000
d.	COST PER MILE	? 44.0¢	? 49.6¢	? 24.9¢

Martha Atwell bought a new car two years ago. She has driven it 14,000 miles. Her driving costs for the two years were $4700 for fixed costs, $2080 for variable costs, and $525 for other costs. Use this information for Exercises 14–16.

14. Find Martha's total driving costs over the two years. **$7305**

15. Find Martha's average driving costs per year. **$3652.50**

16. Find Martha's driving costs per mile for the two years to the nearest tenth of a cent. **52.2¢**

17. Kyle Ignacio uses his van for both business and personal driving. He divides his yearly driving costs in thirds, and charges two-thirds of the expenses to his business. Find Kyle's personal yearly driving costs for a year in which he spent $3580 for fixed costs, $1598.70 for variable costs, and $200 for other costs. **$1792.90**

Lesson Resources

Maintenance: See below.
Reteaching/Alternate Teaching Strategy: See the margin on page 167.
Practice: Activity Worksheet 42
Enrichment: See the enrichment topic "Automobile Maintenance" on page 170.

Objectives

Student will

1. use a list of data to make a frequency table and a histogram.
2. use the midpoints of intervals to find the mean.

Maintenance

Use the following list of numbers for problems 1–4.

35, 26, 33, 37, 33, 34, 33

1. Find the mean. ANS: 33
2. Find the mode. ANS: 33
3. Find the median. ANS: 33
4. Find the range. ANS: 11
5. Salvador has grades of 86, 93, and 91 on three tests. What is his average grade? ANS: 90

1 Lesson Focus

Motivation: Ask the students to discuss the following question.

How would you decide what is the most typical mileage for cars on the road?

Purpose: Students will learn to organize data to help them make decisions. They should learn that many times decisions are made from the information that is available, and that if they organize the data, they may find patterns.

Strategy: ORGANIZING DATA

Statisticians use tables, charts, and graphs to organize and display data. One way to organize data is to use a **frequency table.**

EXAMPLE: The highway mileage ratings in miles per gallon for forty compact cars are listed at the left below.

a. Make a frequency table for the data.

SOLUTION: Organize the data in intervals of 5 units.

Mileage Ratings (miles per gallon)

24	35	27	23	26	23	28	29
35	33	34	24	24	35	34	42
18	26	26	26	24	33	28	26
35	26	21	28	33	33	32	36
24	34	42	32	28	22	22	40

Frequency Table

Interval	Midpoint	Tally	Frequency
15–19	17	I	1
20–24	22	𝍸 𝍸	10
25–29	27	𝍸 𝍸 II	12
30–34	32	𝍸 IIII	9
35–39	37	𝍸	5
40–44	42	III	3

b. Use the midpoints of the intervals to compute the approximate mean of the data.

NOTE: In statistics, $\bar{x}$ (read: x bar) is used to represent the mean.

SOLUTION: $\bar{x} \approx \dfrac{1(17) + 10(22) + 12(27) + 9(32) + 5(37) + 3(42)}{40}$

17 [+] 220 [+] 324 [+] 288 [+]

185 [+] 126 [=] [÷] 40 [=] 29.

The mean, $\bar{x}$, is about **29.**

Thus, the mean highway mileage rating for the forty compact cars is **29 miles per gallon.**

c. Use the frequency table to draw a **histogram** for the data.

SOLUTION: The horizontal axis shows the gas mileage data.
The vertical axis shows the frequencies.
The interval midpoint is the center of each bar.

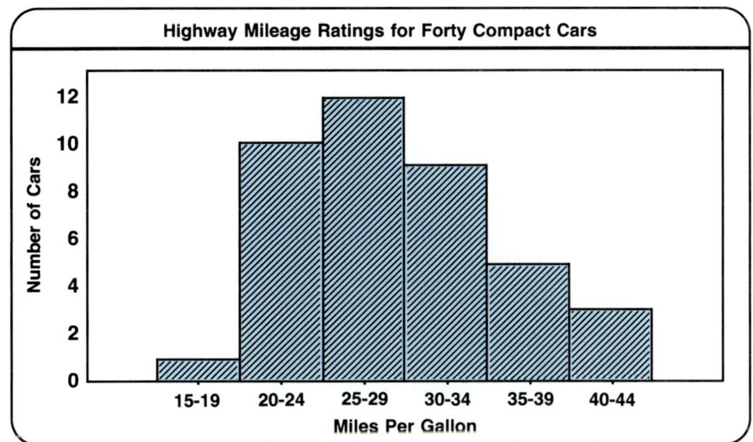

EXERCISES

For Exercises 1–2, make a frequency table using the suggested interval width. Then draw a histogram for the data.

1. ***Number of Customers at a Certain Gas Station Each Day***

226	211	256	227	250
214	191	196	234	243
203	229	190	238	235
245	236	259	217	228
223	219	234	243	231

Interval width: 10

See the Answers to Odd-Numbered Exercises.

2. ***Number of Tires Sold at Brook Tire Store Each Week***

48	53	41	69	69	51
59	57	64	63	59	42
54	50	62	68	44	46
63	57	59	54	49	47
72	60	57	58	64	48

Interval width: 5

See page 170.

3. Compute the mean of the data in Exercise 2 by using the midpoints of the intervals as values. **56**

4. In January, Roy's Used Cars sold 50 cars at a mean price of $5479. In February, Roy's Used Cars sold 50 years at a mean price of $5263. What was the mean price of cars sold during January and February? **$5371**

5. In July, Allied Car Sales sold 70 new cars at a mean price of $10,350. In August, 80 new cars were sold at a mean price of $9600. What was the mean price of new cars sold during the two-month period? **$9975**

2 Teaching the Lesson

Have a student read the first paragraph. Then work through part a of the Example. Ask: What is the first thing you should do with the list of data? (Put the numbers in order.) Explain that the frequency in the table is the sum of the tally marks. Then work through part b of the Example. Explain that they are multiplying the frequency by the midpoint of the interval and then dividing the sum by the total number of cars.

In part c, make sure students understand that each bar in the histogram is a graph of an interval.

3 Close

Summary: Have students discuss when organizing data would be an appropriate strategy for problem solving.

Evaluation
Guided Practice: Ex. 1
Independent Practice: Ex. 2–5

Problem-Solving Skills

Making a table (Ex. 1, 2)
Making a graph (Ex. 1, 2)
Using a table (Ex. 3)
Solving a multi-step problem (Ex. 3–5)

Alternate Teaching Strategy

You may wish to work through all the steps of the Example on the chalkboard or overhead projector. Show students how to organize the data in the frequency table step-by-step, how to find the mean, and how to set up the histogram. You may want to have student volunteers make the table and the histogram as you give them instructions. Then you may wish to have the students work in small groups to complete the exercises.

Additional Answers

See page 170 for the answer to Exercise 2.

NOTE: A quiz covering the second half of the chapter is provided in the *Teacher's ResourceBank™*.

Objectives

Students will

1. explore solutions to a variety of problems that emerge from this situational lesson.
2. explore solutions to problems that have more than one solution.
3. make consumer decisions relevant to their teen-age world.

Situational Lesson

These two pages present a situational lesson as the framework from which a variety of problem situations emerge.

Teaching Strategies

This lesson lends itself to cooperative learning groups for the problem solving activities of comparing choices and exploring decisions. (See page M-13.)

However, these activities can also be carried out by the class as a whole or by individual students.

1 Lesson Focus

Motivation: Have students discuss and list the different expenses they would have if they owned a car.

Purpose: As consumers, students will need to be aware of the variety of expenses related to transportation and will need to consider the possible choices.

2 Teaching the Lesson

Have a volunteer read the introductory paragraphs and the three choices. Then ask these questions.

1. How much does Adam save each week? ($30)
2. $45 per month is how much per week (4 weeks = 1 month)? ($11.25)
3. $105.99 per month would be how much per week (nearest cent)? ($26.50)

Consumer's Choice

Adam Dowd, a senior at Dedham High, drives to his part-time job in a five-year old car. The car is worth $1200 and needs $240 worth of repairs.

Adam earns $85 a week. He spends about $55 of this and saves the rest. He is trying to decide which of the following things to do.

Choice 1

Have the car repaired and pay for the repairs at the rate of $45 a month for 6 months.

Choice 2

Use the old car as a down payment on a two-year old car. Pay the balance at the rate of $105.99 per month for 24 months.

Choice 3

Sell his old car. Use city buses to travel to work. This will cost $1.00 for each round trip.

Comparing the Choices

1. In Choice 1, how much would Adam pay in all for the repairs? $270

2. In Choice 2, how much would Adam actually pay out for the two-year old car? $3743.76

3. Suppose that Adam travels 25 miles per day to work. He makes this round trip 6 days per week. Gasoline costs him $1.05 a gallon and the fuel economy of his old car is 16 miles per gallon. Find Adam's weekly cost for gasoline. About $19.69

4. The fuel economy of the two-year old car is 25 miles per gallon. How much less will Adam spend per week for gasoline if he buys the two-year old car? About $7.09 less

5. How much will it cost Adam to travel back and forth to work each week if he travels by bus? $6

6. Suppose Adam selects Choice 3. How many weeks of paying bus fares will it take to equal the total cost in Choice 1? 45 weeks

EXPLORING DECISIONS

7. Suppose that it takes Adam about 50 minutes to travel back and forth to work each day. The round trip by bus takes 1 hour and 20 minutes. How might this influence his decision?

8. State one advantage of Choice 1 over Choice 2. One advantage: the total cost is less. Answers will vary.

9. State one advantage of Choice 3 over Choices 1 and 2.

10. Suppose that Adam selects Choice 2. State one advantage and one disadvantage of this choice.

11. Suppose that Adam feels that he must save at least $20 a week. How will this affect his choices? It eliminates Choices 1 and 2.

12. Suppose that you are Adam. Which choice would you make? Give reasons for your answer. Answers will vary.

Have students work Exercises 1–6. Then discuss Exercises 7–12 with the class.

3 Close

Summary: Have students discuss the advantages and disadvantages of having an old car and not making payments and the advantages and disadvantages of having a newer car and making payments.

Problem-Solving Skills

Solving a multi-step problem (Ex. 3, 4)
Making comparisons (Ex. 4, 6)

Critical Thinking

Exercises 7–12

Project

Have students choose the car that they would like to own. Then have them find the price of the car, the amount of the average monthly payment they would have to make, the cost of insurance, the cost of an oil change and a tune-up, the cost of new tires, and the cost of gasoline for 10,000 miles of driving.

Additional Answers

7. He might not want to spend the additional 30 minutes traveling each way.
9. One advantage: It is the least expensive choice. Answers will vary.
10. One advantage: He would own a newer car.
One disadvantage: The monthly cost is greater.
Answers will vary.

Objective

Student will use a chart to solve problems that involve the temperature range of oil.

Overview

This topic is optional. The word "Enrichment" that appears to the right of the title in this Teacher's Edition does not appear in the student textbook. Therefore, this material is not included in the Chapter Review and Chapter Test.

Using the Page

You may wish to have students work this Enrichment in small groups or you may wish to work with the class.

Problem-Solving Skills

Reading a chart (Ex. 1–6)

Additional Answers, page 167

2.

Interval	Midpoint	Tally	Frequency
40–44	42	III	3
45–49	47	~~IIII~~	5
50–54	52	~~IIII~~	5
55–59	57	~~IIII~~ II	7
60–64	62	~~IIII~~ I	6
65–69	67	III	3
70–74	72	I	1

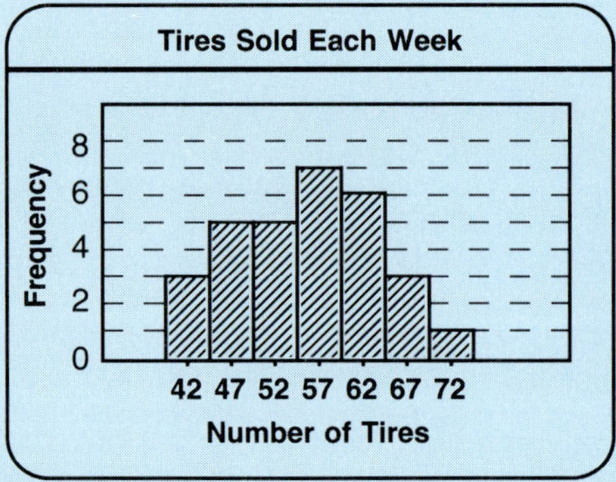

Automobile Maintenance ENRICHMENT

Consumer magazines suggest this rule for changing the oil in your car.

Change the oil every 3000 miles or every three months.

Some oils work well over a wide range of temperatures. These oils have code names such as **5W-20** or **10W-40.**

The chart below shows the temperature ranges for four different oils.

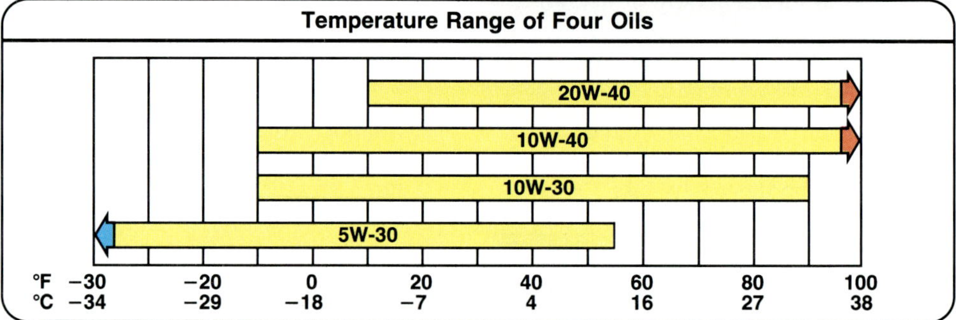

EXAMPLE Which oils can be used for temperatures between 0° F and 70° F?

Look at the chart. Find the bars that extend between 0° F and 70° F.

Either **10W-40** or **10W-30** will work.

EXERCISES

1. Which oil can be used only with temperatures above 10° F? 20W-40
2. Which oil can be used only in winter temperatures? 5W-30
3. Which oil can be used with temperatures below −29° C? 5W-30
4. Which oil can be used in temperatures from −10° F to over 100° F? 10W-40
5. How many degrees Fahrenheit are there between the highest and lowest temperatures in which Oil 10W-30 can be used? 100° F
6. How many degrees Celsius are there between the highest and lowest temperatures in which Oil 10W-30 can be used? 57° C

Chapter Summary

IMPORTANT IDEAS

1. The total cost of a car repair bill is computed by adding the cost of the parts, the sales tax on the parts, and the labor charges.
2. When you know the amount of depreciation of a car, you can determine the approximate resale value of the car.
3. $$\text{Fuel Economy} = \text{Number of Miles} \div \text{Number of Gallons} \text{ or } \left(\text{Number of Kilometers} \div \text{Number of Liters}\right)$$
4. When comparing the fuel economies of two cars, the car with the greater fuel economy gets more miles per gallon (or miles per liter).
5. Yearly driving costs consist of fixed costs, variable costs, and other costs.
6. $$\text{Average Yearly Driving Cost per Mile} = \text{Total Yearly Driving Costs} \div \text{Number of Miles Driven}$$

Chapter Review

Part 1: VOCABULARY

miles per gallon
variable
fixed
maintenance
depreciation
fuel economy

1. The costs of upkeep and repair for a car are called ? costs. (Page 152) **maintenance**
2. The decrease in value of a car due to age and usage is called ? . (Page 156) **depreciation**
3. The number of miles a car can travel on one gallon (or liter) of gasoline is refered to as its ? . (Page 160) **fuel economy**
4. Depreciation and loan payments are ? costs. (Page 163) **fixed**
5. Gas and maintenance are ? costs. (Page 163) **variable**

Part 2: SKILLS

For Exercises 6–7, find the total cost for repairs. The sales tax rate is 7%. Sales tax is charged on parts only. (Pages 152–154)

6. Total for Parts: $191.83
   Labor Charge: $73.90 **$279.16**
7. Total for Parts: $69.85
   Labor Charge: $31.08 **$105.82**

Chapter Summary

The Chapter Summary contains a listing of the important ideas that were presented in the chapter. This listing is intended to assist the student with the Chapter Review that follows.

Objective

To review the important terms, skills, problem solving, and applications presented in Chapter 7.

Overview

The Chapter Review is structured in three parts. Part 1 is a review of the important terms that were introduced in the chapter. Part 2 reviews the skills that were presented in the chapter. Part 3 reviews the problem-solving strategies and applications that were presented in the chapter. Each item in the Chapter Review is referenced to the related pages where the concept, skill, or application was presented.

Using the Pages

You may wish to assign this Chapter Review for homework or treat it as a class review prior to administering the formal Chapter Test. In doing this, it is suggested that you only use the even- or odd-numbered exercises. You can then use the remaining exercises as a bank for use later.

For Exercises 8–13, complete the tables. Refer to the graph on page 156. (Pages 156–158)

	Price of New Car	Years	Amount of Depreciation
8.	$9800	6	? **$7840**
9.	$11,650	4	? **$7572.50**
10.	$6400	1	? **$1600**

	Price of New Car	Years	Approximate Resale Value
11.	$8700	2	? **$5220**
12.	$12,340	5	? **$3085**
13.	$7841	3	? **$3528.45**

For Exercises 14–17, determine the fuel economy. (Pages 160–162)

	Miles	Gallons of Fuel
14.	487	15.2 **32**
15.	408	13.6 **30**
16.	237	10.9 **21**
17.	245	12.4 **19**

For Exercises 18–20, find the yearly gasoline cost per kilometer to the nearest cent. (Pages 160–162)

	Yearly Fuel Costs	Kilometers Per Year
18.	$615	15,000 **4¢**
19.	$1344	21,000 **6¢**
20.	$882	18,000 **5¢**

For Exercises 21–23, find the yearly driving cost per mile to the nearest tenth of a cent. (Pages 163–165)

	Total Fixed Costs	Total Variable Costs	Other Costs	Total Mileage	Total Yearly Driving Costs	Cost Per Mile
21.	$3940	$2772	$200	20,000	? **$6912**	? **34.6¢**
22.	$7600	$3596	$250	20,000	? **$11,446**	? **57.2¢**
23.	$3770	$1900	$442	25,000	? **$6112**	? **24.4¢**

Part 3: APPLICATIONS

24. Find the estimated maintenance cost per mile for a year in which \$1139 was spent on maintenance, and 17,000 miles were driven. (Pages 152–154) **6.7¢**

25. Linda received a car repair bill which listed the cost of parts as \$89.50 and the labor charge as \$32.60. Find the total cost of the bill including a 6% sales tax on the parts. (Pages 152–154) **\$127.47**

26. After 3 years, a car which cost \$9360 has depreciated 60%. What is the total dollar amount of depreciation? (Pages 156–158) **\$5616**

27. After 2 years, a car which cost \$7150 has depreciated 49%. What is the approximate resale value of the car? (Pages 156–158) **\$3646.50**

28. One car travels 344 miles on 13.2 gallons of gasoline. Another car travels 297 miles on 10.6 gallons of gasoline. Determine which car has the greater fuel economy. (Pages 160–162) **The second car**

29. Simone Telamaco, a business consultant, drives 36,000 kilometers per year. Last year he spent \$2700 on fuel. Find Simone's yearly gasoline cost per kilometer (nearest cent). (Pages 163–165) **8¢**

The yearly gasoline costs per mile for forty drivers are listed in the table at the right. (Pages 166–167)

Yearly Gasoline Costs Per Mile

3¢	6¢	10¢	8¢	4¢	12¢	8¢	9¢
9¢	10¢	13¢	11¢	10¢	11¢	11¢	14¢
7¢	10¢	8¢	6¢	14¢	11¢	11¢	13¢
9¢	13¢	5¢	9¢	6¢	8¢	12¢	6¢
7¢	10¢	12¢	9¢	13¢	10¢	9¢	14¢

30. Make a frequency table for the data. Use these intervals:

3¢–5¢	6¢–8¢	9¢–11¢	12¢–14¢
3	10	17	10

31. Use the frequency table to draw a histogram for the data. **See the Answers to Odd-Numbered Exercises.**

32. Use the midpoints of the intervals to compute the approximate mean of the data. **About 10¢ per mile**

Objective

To informally assess students' mastering of the major skills, concepts, problem solving, and applications presented in Chapter 7.

Using the Page

After completing the Chapter Review with the class, you may wish to use this Chapter Test as an informal assessment. This Chapter Test parallels the formal chapter tests (Form A and Form B) provided in the *Teacher's ResourceBank.*™

Additional Answers

12.

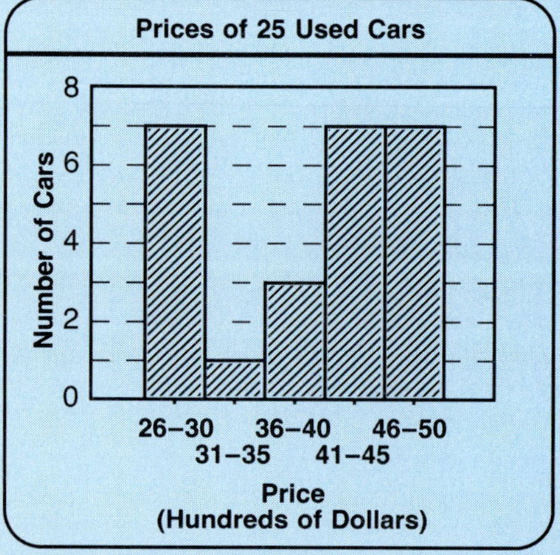

Chapter Test

1. Hisako paid $42.75 for a new battery for his car and $12.50 for a new oil filter. The labor charge was $21.50. There is a 5% sales tax on the parts. Find the total repair bill. $79.51

2. Sonia paid $24.75 for parts and $10.15 to have the tires rotated. Labor cost $29.80. Estimate the total cost before sales tax. c

   a. $60 **b.** $50 **c.** $65 **d.** $70

For Exercises 3–5, use the graph at the right. The new car price is $9360.

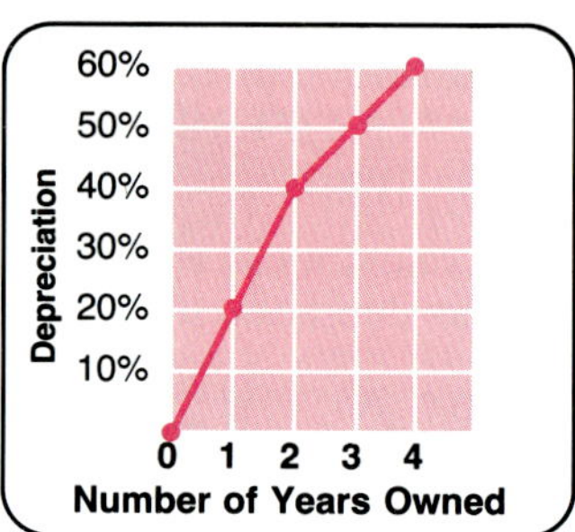

3. Find the dollar amount of depreciation after 2 years. $3744

4. Find the dollar amount of depreciation after 4 years. $5616

5. Find the approximate resale value of the car after 4 years. $3744

6. One sports car travels 496 kilometers on 47.6 liters of fuel. Another travels 888 kilometers on 68.8 liters of fuel. Which car has the greater fuel economy? second car

7. Carl drove his car 16,990 miles last year. The cost per mile for gas was $0.099. Estimate the cost for fuel for last year. c

   a. $1600 **b.** $1500 **c.** $1700 **d.** $1800

For Exercises 8–10, find the yearly driving cost per mile to the nearest tenth of a cent.

	Total Fixed Costs	Total Variable Costs	Other Costs	Total Mileage	Total Yearly Driving Costs	Cost Per Mile
8.	$4280	$2310	$550	15,000	? $7140	? 47.6¢
9.	$3990	$3124	$500	18,000	? $7614	? 42.3¢
10.	$4190	$1552	$450	16,000	? $6192	? 38.7¢

The table at the right shows the prices paid for 25 used cars.

Prices of 25 Used Cars

2700	2800	2800	2800	2800
2800	2800	3400	3700	3700
4100	4400	4400	4400	4400
4400	4400	4700	4700	4700
4700	4800	4800	4900	4900

11. Make a frequency table to show the data. Use these intervals (in hundreds of dollars).

   26–30 31–35 36–40 41–45 46–50
   7 1 2 7 8

12. Draw a histogram to show the data.

Cumulative Maintenance Chapters 1–7

Choose the correct answer. Choose **a, b, c,** *or* **d.**

1. A certain sports car can travel 387 miles on 12.9 gallons of gasoline. What is the car's fuel economy? d

   a. 31.5 **b.** 4,992.30 **c.** 29 **d.** 30

2. Between which years did the amount of depreciation increase 15%? b

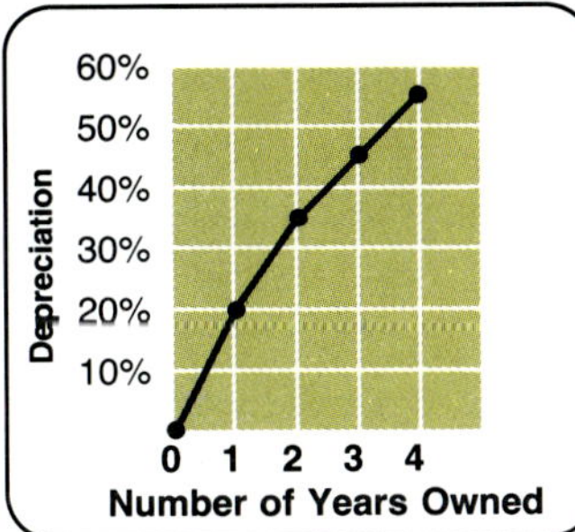

   a. 0 and 1 **b.** 1 and 2
   c. 2 and 3 **d.** 3 and 4

3. Find the dealer's cost. c

   Base Price: $8000
   Options: $888.00
   Destination Charge: $186.00
   Dealer Pays: 80% of base price and 70% of options price.

   a. $7259.20 **b.** $9074
   c. $7207.60 **d.** $6792.80

4. Barry's gross pay last week was $426.45. His net pay was $307.04. Find the total deductions. b

   a. $733.49 **b.** $119.41
   c. $121.41 **d.** $109.41

5. Casey had $3402 withheld from his pay for federal income tax. He owes only $2789. Estimate the refund. b

   a. $500 **b.** $600 **c.** $400 **d.** $800

6. In one year Susan has the following deductions. Find the total deductions.

   Medical: $450 Contributions: $475
   Interest: $650 Taxes: $1850 a

   a. $3425 **b.** $1857
   c. $3415 **d.** $3325

7. Add: $\frac{1}{4} + \frac{1}{3}$ d

   a. $\frac{2}{7}$ **b.** $\frac{2}{12}$ **c.** $\frac{3}{4}$ **d.** $\frac{7}{12}$

8. Use the graph below to tell which product sold twice as well as product A. c

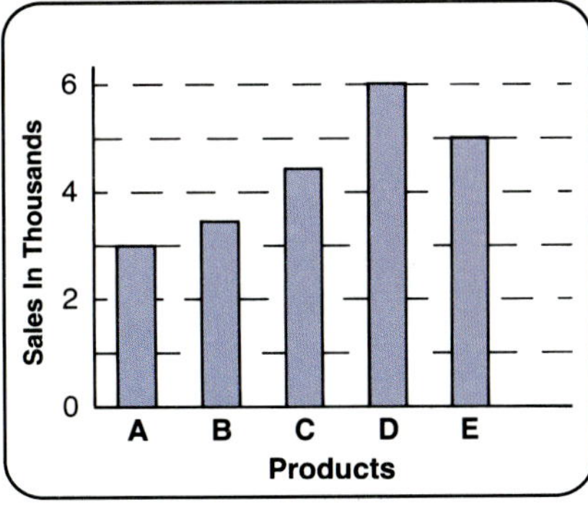

   a. B **b.** C **c.** D **d.** E

Objective

To review the content presented in Chapters 1–7

Using the Pages

You may wish to use this Cumulative Maintenance as an informal assessment tool. These pages can be assigned for homework or they may be used as review in class.

9. Jose has \$1500 in an account that pays a yearly interest rate of 8%. How much simple interest will the account earn in 9 months? c

a. \$120 b. \$60 c. \$90 d. \$30

10. Subtract: $\frac{3}{5} - \frac{1}{3}$ a

a. $\frac{4}{15}$ b. $\frac{2}{15}$ c. $\frac{2}{2}$ d. $\frac{4}{8}$

11. The amount of interest paid on a certain savings account is $6\frac{1}{2}\%$. Write a decimal for this percent. b

a. 6.5 b. 0.065
c. 0.65 d. 0.0065

12. Find the total cost of the car in the advertisement. c

Tornado '86
\$2000 Down
\$198 per month for
48 months

a. \$9504
b. \$7504
c. \$11,504
d. \$13,504

13. The cash price for a car is \$8800. George can buy the car by making a 25% down payment and paying \$7300 in monthly payments. Find the finance charge. c

a. \$2200 b. \$5100
c. \$700 d. \$1500

14. Divide: 12.788 ÷ 46 a

a. 0.278 b. 278
c. 2.78 d. 0.277

15. The bar graph below shows the results of a survey of 100 people who were asked: "Do you favor a national 55 mile-per-hour speed limit to promote energy conservation?"

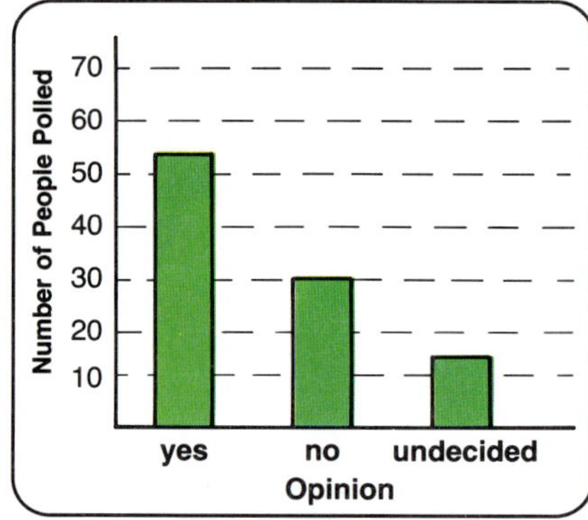

How many people were against the 55 mile-per-hour speed limit? a

a. 30 b. 110 c. 60 d. 55

16. A refrigerator contains 5 cans of diet cola and 2 cans of root beer. Denton chooses a can of soda at random. What are the chances that the soda he chooses is not a diet cola? d

a. $\frac{5}{2}$ b. $\frac{2}{5}$ c. $\frac{5}{7}$ d. $\frac{2}{7}$

17. Write a percent for $\frac{3}{4}$. d

a. 25% b. 65%
c. 12% d. 75%

18. The sticker price for a new car is \$10,500. The tax rate is 6%. Find the total cost. d

a. \$630 b. \$10,130
c. \$11,030 d. \$11,130

Other Ways To Travel

The Wilson family is planning a vacation trip to Colorado. They must decide whether to travel by car, bus, plane, or train.

- What travel expenses can they expect with each method of transportation?
- What advantages and disadvantages are there to each method of transportation?
- How much will it cost for them to rent a car after they arrive in Colorado?
- How can they use a map to help them compute distances and travel times?

Chapter 8: Other Ways to Travel

Overview

The focus of Chapter 8 is on comparing travel costs by plane, train, and car. Critical thinking questions in the Exercises ask students to list advantages and disadvantages for each mode of travel in order to make them aware that time, enjoyment, comfort, and so on, are also to be considered when selecting a method of travel.

The strategy lesson on using a map on pages 187–188 applies map-reading skills to solving problems related to travel. The *Consumer's Choice* on pages 190–191 presents a **situational lesson** in which students plan a vacation trip for a four-member family. Lastly, the *Enrichment* lesson on making a map provides an activity that can be a valuable learning experience for all students.

Using This Page

Have students read the introductory paragraph and questions. Have them list possible solutions to the problems presented. After completing the chapter, have students review their suggested solutions, comparing them with those presented in the lessons. You may wish to have students suggest other possible problems resulting from the siutation described on this page and to discuss possible solutions.

You may wish to organize the class into small groups to complete the situational activity described on this *Using the Page.*

Lesson Resources

Maintenance: See below.
Reteaching/Alternate Teaching Strategy: p. M-33
Practice: p. M-33
Enrichment: p. M-33

Objectives

Student will

1. solve multi-step problems which involve the estimated cost of gasoline for a trip.
2. use a table to solve multi-step problems that involve the cost of round-trip bus fares.

Maintenance

1. Add: \$380.20 + \$160.50 ANS: \$540.70
2. Express 6 months in years. ANS: $\frac{1}{2}$ year
3. Multiply and round to two decimal places. 0.0715 × \$351 ANS: \$25.10
4. Multiply: \$538.50 × $\frac{1}{2}$ ANS: \$269.25
5. Find the simple interest earned on a deposit of \$500 for 9 months at a yearly rate of 8%. ANS: \$30

[1] Lesson Focus

Motivation: Ask students if they think it would be more economical for a family of four to travel 2000 miles by car or by bus.

Purpose: This lesson illustrates some of the planning that is needed in preparing for a vacation trip. Students should learn some of the cost savings that can be effected by making choices in vacation travel.

STRATEGY: USING "HIDDEN QUESTIONS" TO SOLVE A MULTI-STEP PROBLEM

Comparing Travel Costs: AUTO AND BUS

Tom and Valerie Wilson are planning to take their children, 12-year-old Tami and 9-year-old Marshall, on a two-week vacation to Colorado. Their home in Boston is 1950 miles from Denver.

1. How many miles will the Wilsons travel on the round trip? 3900 miles

EXAMPLE 1 The Wilson family car averages 25 miles per gallon of gasoline. Valerie estimates that gasoline will cost \$1.05 per gallon. How much should the Wilsons expect to spend on gasoline if they travel to Denver and back by car?

[1] Find the number of gallons of gasoline needed.

3900 ÷ 25 = **156** ◀ *Miles Driven* ÷ *Miles Per Gallon of Gasoline* = *Gallons of Gasoline Needed*

[2] Find the estimated cost of the gasoline.

156 × \$1.05 = **\$163.80** ◀ *Total estimated cost*

Tom and Valerie want to compare the cost of traveling by car and the cost of traveling by bus. They collected this data.

2. How much is the round-trip fare for a 12-year-old child? \$238
3. How much is the round-trip fare for a 9-year-old child? \$119

*One-Way Bus Fare**	
Adult	\$119
Child (age 5–11)	half-fare
Child (under age 5)	free

*A one-way fare is one-half a round-trip fare.

EXAMPLE 2 How much will the Wilson family pay for round-trip bus fares from Boston to Denver?

[1] One-way fare for Marshall: $\frac{1}{2}$ × \$119 = **\$59.50**

[2] One-way fares for Valerie, Tom, and Tami: 3 × \$119 = **\$357**

[3] Total of the one-way fares: \$59.50 + \$357.00 = **\$416.50**

[4] Total round-trip fares: \$416.50 × 2 = **\$833**

CHECK YOUR SKILLS

Multiply or divide as indicated. For additional practice, see pages 370, 372, 375, and 389.

1. \$115 × 4 \$460	**2.** \$86 × 4 \$344	**3.** \$1.08 × 156 \$168.48	**4.** \$1.05 × 8 \$8.40
5. \$115 × $\frac{1}{2}$ \$57.50	**6.** \$221 × $\frac{1}{4}$ \$55.25	**7.** \$142 × $\frac{1}{4}$ \$35.50	**8.** \$187 × $\frac{1}{2}$ \$93.50
9. 300 ÷ 25 12	**10.** 2700 ÷ 15 180	**11.** 1800 ÷ 15 120	**12.** 900 ÷ 25 36

EXERCISES

The table at the right compares the costs of traveling from Boston to Denver by car and by bus.

Use this table for Exercises 1–6.

Estimated Travel Expenses for Round Trip

	Car	Bus
Gasoline	\$163.80	—
Fares	—	\$833
Meals	\$75 per person	\$40 per person
Lodging	\$300	None
Travel Time (one way)	$3\frac{1}{2}$ days	50 hours

1. Will the Wilsons spend more on food if they travel by car instead of by bus? **Yes**

2. How much more will the family spend on food if they travel by car instead of by bus? **About \$140 more**

3. Approximately how many more days will it take to travel from Boston to Denver by car than by bus? **About $1\frac{1}{2}$ days**

4. Find the total estimated expenses if the Wilsons travel by car. **\$763.80**

5. Find the total estimated expenses if the Wilsons travel by bus. **\$993**

6. If the Wilsons travel by car, they may decide to drive along a scenic route. This will add 300 miles to their round trip. Use the information in Example 1 on page 178 to find the additional gasoline cost. **\$12.60**

7. What are some advantages and disadvantages of traveling by car? **Answers will vary.**

8. What are some advantages and disadvantages of traveling by bus? **Answers will vary.**

2 Teaching the Lesson

Have students read the opening paragraph and answer question 1. Then discuss Example 1. Ask students to name other expenses that the Wilsons will have if they travel to Denver by car (Food, lodging, etc.). Have students read the paragraph following Example 1. Direct their attention to the table of bus fares and have them answer questions 2 and 3. Then discuss Example 2. Ask students whether the Wilsons will have the same additional expenses if they travel by bus as they will if they travel by car.

3 Close

Summary: Ask students to summarize these main skills of the lesson: 1) how to find the estimated cost of gasoline for a trip, and 2) how to find the bus fares for a family trip.

Evaluation
Guided Practice: Ex. 1, 3
Independent Practice: Ex. 2, 4–8

Extension

Have students find the cost of gasoline and bus fares for a round-trip between two cities other than Boston and Denver.

Problem-Solving Skills

Using a table (Ex. 1–5)
Making comparisons (Ex. 1–3)
Solving a multi-step problem (Ex. 2, 4–6)

Critical Thinking

You may wish to have students work in small groups to solve these problems or you may wish to work with the class.

Ex. 7 and 8

Estimation Ex. 4 and 5

Lesson Resources

Maintenance: See below.
Reteaching/Alternate Teaching Strategy: p. M-34
Practice: p. M-34
Enrichment: p. M-34

Objective

Student will use a table to solve multi-step problems that involve travel costs by plane and by train.

Maintenance

1. Divide: 300 ÷ 1250 ANS: 0.24
2. Express 0.26 as a percent. ANS: 26%
3. Express 0.0125 as a percent. ANS: 1.25%
4. 30 is what percent of 75? ANS: 40%
5. Sam Murphy paid $2250 in taxes on his income of $18,000. Find what percent of his income he paid in taxes. ANS: 12.5%

1 Lesson Focus

Motivation: Ask students which they think is more economical, traveling by plane or traveling by train. Also, ask if they have ever traveled by plane or by train.

Purpose: As adult consumers, students may have to make some decisions about methods of transportation. It is important that they be able to compare costs of various modes of transportation as well as know the advantages and disadvantages of the various modes.

STRATEGY: USING "HIDDEN QUESTIONS" TO SOLVE A MULTI-STEP PROBLEM

Comparing Travel Costs: PLANE AND TRAIN

Valerie and Tom Wilson consider traveling to Colorado by plane. A travel agent tells them that the round-trip plane fare from Boston to Denver is $287 per person plus an 8% tax.

EXAMPLE 1 Compute the total round-trip plane fare for the family.

1 Find the cost of four tickets.
$287 × 4 = **$1148**

2 Find the amount of tax.
8% of $1148 = 0.08 × $1148
= **$91.84**

3 Find the total cost of the tickets.
$1148.00 + $91.84 = **$1239.84** ◀ *Base Price* + *Amount of Tax* = *Total Cost*

The total round-trip plane fares amount to **$1239.84.**

1. What travel expenses will be eliminated if the Wilsons travel by plane rather than by car? **Gasoline, meals, and lodging**

The travel agent also gave the Wilsons cost figures for traveling by train.

EXAMPLE 2 Find the total round-trip train cost for the Wilson family.

Round-Trip Train Fare Boston to Denver	
Adult	$188
Child (age 2–11)	Half-fare
Child (under age 2)	free
Sleeper for 4	$724

1 Find the fare for 9-year-old Marshall.
$\frac{1}{2}$ × $188 = **$94**

2 Find the total fare for Tom, Valerie, and Tami.
3 × $188 = **$564**

3 Find the total transportation costs.
$94 + $564 + $724 = **$1382** ◀ *Total fare plus sleeping quarters.*

The total round-trip train cost is **$1382.**

2. What additional expenses might the Wilsons have if they travel by train rather than by plane? **meals**

CHECK YOUR SKILLS

Find the answer. For additional practice, see page 407.

1. 8% of \$183 **\$14.64** 2. 4% of \$326 **\$13.04** 3. 6% of \$415 **\$24.90** 4. 3% of \$219 **\$6.57**

Multiply. For additional practice, see pages 370 and 389.

5. \$95 × 3 **\$285** 6. \$356 × 4 **\$1424** 7. \$252 × 2 **\$504** 8. \$87 × 6 **\$522**

9. \$119 × $\frac{1}{2}$ **\$59.50** 10. \$327 × $\frac{1}{2}$ **\$163.50** 11. \$214 × $\frac{1}{2}$ **\$107** 12. \$496 × $\frac{1}{2}$ **\$248**

Add. For additional practice, see page 368.

13. \$126.42 + \$329.52 **\$455.94** 14. \$246 + \$137.16 **\$383.16** 15. \$352 + \$273.14 **\$625.14**

EXERCISES

For Exercises 1–4, find the total cost of each plane ticket.

	Base Price	Sales Tax	Amount of Tax	Total Cost
1.	\$290	8%	? **\$23.20**	? **\$313.20**
2.	\$360	8%	? **\$28.80**	? **\$388.80**
3.	\$256	8%	? **\$20.48**	? **\$276.48**
4.	\$178	8%	? **\$14.24**	? **\$192.24**

The table at the right compares the costs for the Wilson family to travel from Boston to Denver by plane and by train.

Estimated Travel Expenses for Round Trip

	Plane	Train
Fare	\$1239.84	\$1382
Meals	None	\$50 per person
Travel Time (one way)	$3\frac{1}{2}$ hours	48 hours

5. How much does the Wilson family expect to spend on meals if they travel by train? **\$200**

6. If the Wilsons travel by plane, how much less will their total estimated travel expenses be? **\$342.16**

7. How many more hours will it take to reach Denver if the Wilsons travel by train? **$44\frac{1}{2}$ hours**

8. What are the advantages and disadvantages of traveling by plane? **Answers will vary.**

9. What are the advantages and disadvantages of train travel? **Answers will vary.**

2 Teaching the Lesson

Have students read the opening paragraph. Then ask how a tax of 8% would be figured on the ticket price. Discuss Example 1. Have students answer question 1. Point out that the Wilsons will save on lodging expenses for the trip to and from Denver. However, they may have more lodging expenses in Denver since they will be there for a longer time. Then discuss Example 2 and question 2.

3 Close

Summary: Ask selected students to summarize what they have learned in this lesson.

Evaluation
Guided Practice: Ex. 2, 4
Independent Practice: Ex. 1, 3, 5–9

Extension

Have students find the cost of plane fares and train fares between two cities other than Boston and Denver. Students should contact airlines and train systems in order to determine the rates.

Problem-Solving Skills

Solving a multi-step problem (Ex. 1–4, 6)
Using a table (Ex. 5–9)
Making comparisons (Ex. 6, 7)

Critical Thinking

You may wish to have students work in small groups to solve these problems or you may wish to work with the class.

Ex. 8 and 9

Objective

Student will

1. review the skills, concepts, and applications in the first part of Chapter 8.
2. maintain key skills and concepts taught in Chapters 1 and 2.

Using the Page

Exercises 1–5 provide an informal assessment of the student's mastery of the major skills and concepts presented in the first half of Chapter 8. Each item is referenced to the related pages where the particular item was presented. These exercises parallel the quiz provided in the *Teacher's ResourceBank.*™

A quiz covering the second half of the chapter is also provided in the *Teacher's ResourceBank.*™

Exercises 6–9 maintain skills and concepts taught in Chapters 1 and 2.

Mid-Chapter Review

For Exercises 1–2, use the bus fare schedule at the right. (Pages 178–179)

One-Way Bus Fare*	
Adult	$209
Child (age 5–11)	half-fare
Child (under age 5)	free

*A one-way fare is one-half a round-trip fare.

1. How much is the round-trip fare for a 12-year old child? $418
2. How much is the total of fares for a family of two adults, one 12-year old child, and one five-year old child? $731.50

3. The cost per person for meals on a certain bus trip is $50. The cost per person for meals for the same trip by car is $85. How much more will a family of four pay for meals when traveling by car? (pages 178–179) $140

4. The travel time by plane between New York City and Orlando, Florida is 2 hours. The travel time by train is $22\frac{1}{2}$ hours. How many more hours will it take to travel by train than by plane? (Pages 180–181) $20\frac{1}{2}$ hours

5. **Trip:** New York to Orlando
Train Fare: $138 (one-way)
Plane Fare: $168 (one-way)

How much less is the round-trip fare by train than by plane? (Pages 180–181) $60

MAINTENANCE

6. Find the mean. (Pages 10–11)

Five Stock Prices				
$7\frac{1}{2}$	$7\frac{1}{4}$	$7\frac{3}{4}$	7	8

$7\frac{1}{2}$

7. A change purse contains 4 quarters, 3 dimes, 5 nickels, and 2 pennies. A coin is chosen at random. What is the probability that the coin chosen is not a nickel? (Pages 26–27) $\frac{9}{14}$

Refer to the bar graph at the right. (Pages 2–3)

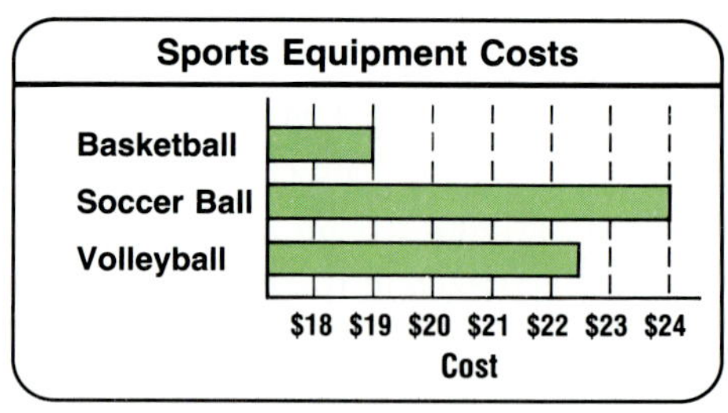

8. How much change would be given to a customer who bought a soccer ball and a basketball and paid for them with a $50.00 bill? $7.00
9. The price of a volleyball is expected to increase 10% over the next three years. How much will the volleyball cost in three years? $24.75

Math and Time Zones

Keith Brantley is a flight attendant for a major airline. In order to determine what time it is in a particular city, Keith has to know in which **time zone** the city is located.

The clocks below show that when it is 10:00 A.M. in the Pacific Time Zone, it is

11:00 A.M. Mountain time   12:00 Noon Central time
1:00 P.M. Eastern time

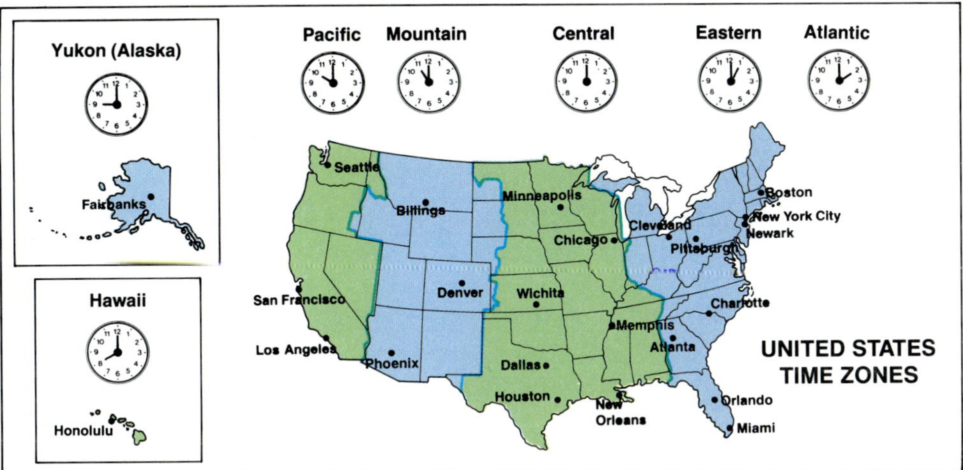

RULE Going from west to east, add one hour for each zone.
Going from east to west, subtract one hour for each zone.

EXERCISES

It is 3:00 P.M. in New Orleans. Find the time in each city.

1. Philadelphia 4:00 P.M.
2. Seattle 1:00 P.M.
3. Denver 2:00 P.M.
4. Honolulu 11:00 A.M.

It is 8:30 A.M. in Phoenix. Find the time in each city.

5. Los Angeles 7:30 A.M.
6. Memphis 9:30 A.M.
7. Fairbanks 6:30 A.M.
8. Miami 10:30 A.M.

9. A plane left Dallas at 7:00 P.M. A different plane left San Francisco at 6:00 P.M. Which plane left earlier? How much earlier? The plane leaving Dallas; 1 hr earlier

10. A plane left New York City at 9:30 A.M. (Eastern time) and arrived in Denver 4 hours later. At what time did it arrive (Mountain time)? 11:30 A.M.

Objective

Student will apply addition and subtraction skills and the skill of reading a map to problems that involve time zones.

Overview

This page is an extension of the skills and ideas presented in the previous lessons of this chapter. Since the content presented on this page is not included in the Chapter Review or Chapter Test, its use is optional.

Using the Pages

You may wish to have students work this lesson in small groups or you may wish to work with the class. Using it with the class, have a student read the information above the map. Then focus students' attention on the map. Ask them to tell what time it is in several cities, according to the clocks that are shown. Work Exercises 1 and 5 with the class and assign the remaining exercises as independent practice.

Problem-Solving Skills

Reading a chart (Ex. 1–10)

Lesson Resources

Maintenance: See below.
Reteaching/Alternate Teaching Strategy: p. M-34 (Visual 21)
Practice: p. M-34
Enrichment: p. M-34
Concrete Materials: Activity Worksheet 45C, and Visual 21
Visual 21

Objective

Student will use a table to solve multi-step problems that involve the costs of renting a car.

Maintenance

1. Multiply: 0.25×782 ANS: 195.5
2. Find 80% of 1250. ANS: 1000
3. Round $378.20 to the nearest $10. ANS: $380
4. Round $3595 to the nearest $100. ANS: $3600
5. Ruth Bass buys a new car for $13,290. She estimates that it will depreciate 18% in the first year. What will be the estimated value of the car after one year? Round the answer to the nearest $100. ANS: $10,900

1 Lesson Focus

Motivation: Ask students to name as many national car rental agencies as they can.

Purpose: This lesson emphasizes problems on computing car rental rates. As future consumers, students should learn that car rental rates differ from one company to another and from one locale to another.

STRATEGY: USING "HIDDEN QUESTIONS" TO SOLVE A MULTI-STEP PROBLEM

Renting a Car

If the Wilsons decide not to travel from Boston by car, they will rent a compact car to go sight-seeing after they arrive in Colorado. Z-T Car Rental Company will charge them this rate.

Weekly Rate (7 days)	$102.61
Daily Rate	$23.00
Mileage Allowance	100 free miles per day
Excess Mileage Charge	30¢ per mile

1. How much less does it cost to rent a car for 7 days at the weekly rate than at the daily rate? **$58.39**
2. How much more will it cost to drive 110 miles in one day than to drive 100 miles in one day? **$3**
3. Why do car rental companies charge persons an additional fee for excess mileage? **To help pay for the increased depreciation which results from the extra mileage.**

Tom and Valerie will pay a weekly rate for the first seven days they rent a car. They will pay a daily rate for any additional days.

EXAMPLE The Wilsons estimate that they will drive 1200 miles over a 10-day period. Find the total expected cost for car rental.

1 Find the cost for the first week. → **$102.61** ◀ *From the table above*

2 Find the cost for the remaining three days.

$3 \times \$23.00 = \mathbf{\$69.00}$

3 Find the number of miles over the free mileage allowance.

10 days × 100 miles per day = **1000 miles** ◀ *Mileage Allowance*

1200 − 1000 = **200** ◀ *Miles Driven − Mileage Allowance = Excess Mileage*

4 Find the cost for excess mileage.

$200 \times \$0.30 = \mathbf{\$60.00}$

5 Find the total expected cost.

$\$102.61 + \$69.00 + \$60.00 = \mathbf{\$231.61}$

The total expected cost is **$231.61.**

CHECK YOUR SKILLS

ESTIMATION/MENTAL MATH: Ex. 1–10

Estimate to determine whether the answer is reasonable. Answer Yes or No. For additional practice, see pages 52–53.

1. 34.8 × 3 = 8.4 No
2. 27.99 × 4 = 111.96 Yes
3. 1.08 × 45 = 48.6 Yes
4. 217.63 − 156 = 61 Yes
5. 196 − 126.43 = 51.57 No
6. 238.05 − 98.2 = 139.85 Yes
7. 305.16 + 76 + 5.16 = 386.32 Yes
8. 229.47 + 57.18 + 4 = 335.65 No
9. 7624.9 − 6376.9 = 1248 Yes
10. 12,605.3 − 10,597.8 = 2007.5 Yes

EXERCISES

Complete. Choose your answers from the box at the right.

1. The number of miles for which a rental car driver does not have to pay is called the __?__. mileage allowance
2. If Dave rents a car with a mileage allowance of 100 miles per day and drives 516 miles over 4 days, he must pay for __?__ miles. 116
3. Basic Rental Cost + Mileage Cost = __?__ Total Rental Cost
4. A car rental company offers both a weekly rate and a daily rate. If Valerie rents a car for 9 days, she will pay the daily rate for __?__ days. 2

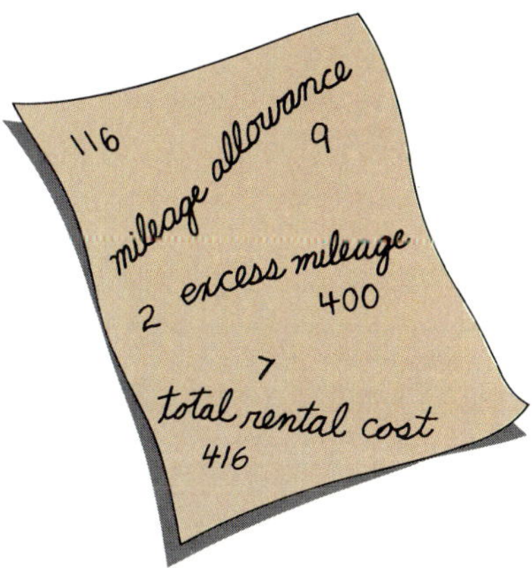

The table below shows car rental rates for two companies.

	Columbia Car Rental	Economy Car Rental
Weekly Rate (7 days)	$113	$87.99
Daily Rate	$35.99	$24.99
Mileage Allowance	unlimited mileage	100 free miles per day
Excess Mileage Charge	—	28¢ per mile

Complete the tables to find the total car rental cost.

Columbia Car Rental

	Number of Days	Miles Driven	Total Cost
5.	2	179	? $71.98
6.	8	1016	? $148.99

Economy Car Rental

	Number of Days	Miles Driven	Total Cost
7.	10	1426	? $282.24
8.	3	318	? $80.01

2 Teaching the Lesson

Focus students' attention on the opening paragraph and the rate table on page 184. Then discuss questions 1, 2, and 3 as well as the following questions.

1. What would determine whether you would pay the daily rate or the weekly rate? (The number of days you are renting the car)
2. What other charges might there be for a rental car besides the ones shown? (Insurance, tax, gasoline)

Then discuss the Example which shows how to find the total expected cost of renting a car.

3 Close

Summary: Ask selected students to explain the steps in finding the cost of renting a car.

Evaluation

Guided Practice: Ex. 1–4, 6, 8, 16, 18
Independent Practice: Ex. 5, 7, 9–15, 17, 19, 20

Extension

Have the students work in groups. Ask each group to contact several local car rental agencies to find the rates on optional insurance coverage available when renting a car.

Problem-Solving Skills

Using a table (Ex. 5–14)
Solving a multi-step problem (Ex. 5–18)
Interpreting information (Ex. 9–14, 19, 20)
Making a comparison (Ex. 11, 12)

9. Sally Randolph rented a car from Economy Car Rental and drove 1570 miles over 9 days. Find the total rental cost. **$325.57**

10. Kim Lanterman wants to rent a car from Columbia Car Rental for six days. How much will she save if the pays the weekly rate rather than the daily rate? **$102.94**

11. Bill Hinds wants to rent a car for one week and drive 900 miles. Will it cost less to rent a car from Columbia Car Rental or Economy Car Rental? How much less? **Columbia Car Rental; $30.99**

12. Lynn Alexander wants to rent a car for three days and drive 200 miles. Will it cost less to rent a car from Columbia Car Rental or Economy Car Rental? How much less? **Economy Car Rental; $33**

13. Pete Merrill rented a car from Economy Car Rental for an 8-day trip. The odometer (mileage meter) readings at the beginning and end of his trip were 6376.9 and 7624.9, respectively. How much did Pete pay for car rental? **$238.42**

14. Stuart Byers rented a car from Columbia Car Rental and drove a total of 1200 miles. The fuel economy of the car was 30 miles per gallon. He paid an average of $1.08 per gallon. Find the total cost of gasoline. **$43.20**

When you return a rental car, you can either fill the gas tank yourself or pay the rental company to fill it. For Exercises 15–18, find how much you will save by filling the tank yourself.

	Gallons of Fuel Needed	Consumer Fills Tank		Rental Company Fills Tank		Difference in Costs
		Cost Per Gallon	Total Cost	Cost Per Gallon	Total Cost	
15.	8.0	$0.959	? **$7.67**	$1.80	? **$14.40**	? **$6.73**
16.	10.5	$1.059	? **$11.12**	$1.65	? **$17.33**	? **$6.21**
17.	12.2	$1.109	? **$13.53**	$1.75	? **$21.35**	? **$7.82**
18.	6.8	$0.995	? **$6.77**	$1.70	? **$11.56**	? **$4.79**

19. Besides rental rates, what else should you consider when choosing a car rental company? **One consideration would be the convenience of the rental company's location.**

20. Explain why most car rental companies require that drivers have a major credit card. **In order to guarantee payment.**

Critical Thinking

You may wish to have students work in small groups to solve these problems or you may wish to work with the class.

Question 3 (in Lesson), Ex. 19, 20

Strategy: USING A MAP

To prepare for their vacation trip, the Wilsons study this Colorado road map. The **map legend** explains what the symbols mean.

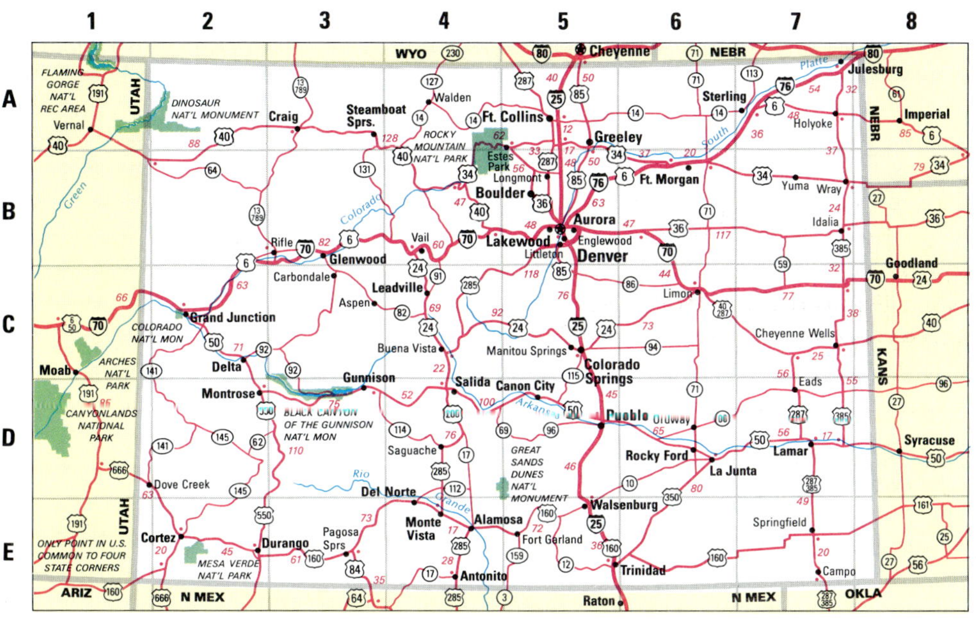

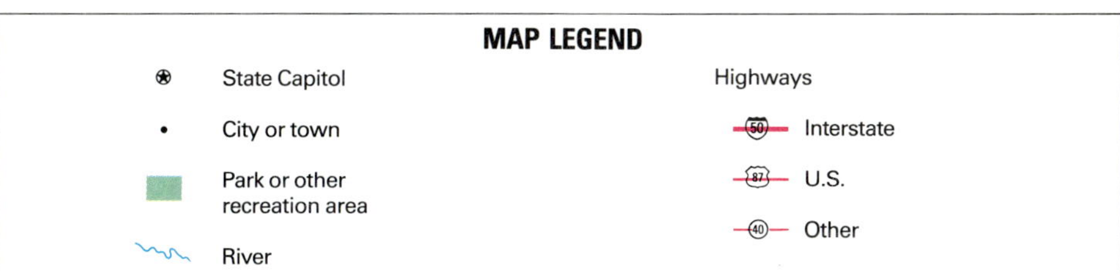

1. In what color are parks and other recreation areas shown? **green**
2. Why might the Wilsons prefer to drive on an interstate rather than on a county road? **It usually takes less time.**

Valerie Wilson notices the **grid** drawn on the map. Each square of the grid can be located by a **letter-number pair,** such as **A-1.**

3. In what square is Denver located? **B-5**
4. In what square is Colorado Springs located? **C-5**

Lesson Resources

Maintenance: See below.
Reteaching/Alternate Teaching Strategy: See the margin on page 188.
Practice: Activity Worksheet 46
Enrichment: You may wish to use the Project on page 189 or the enrichment topic "Making a Map" on page 192.
Concrete Materials: Visual 22
Visual 22

Objectives

Student will

1. use a map legent to identify symbols on a map.
2. use a letter-number pair to locate cities on a map.
3. use a map to solve problems that involve distance and travel time.

Maintenance

1. Add: 35 + 46 + 72 ANS: 153
2. Find 40% of 36. ANS: 14.4
3. Multiply: \$0.98 × 32 ANS: \$31.36
4. Divide: 455 ÷ 50 ANS: 9.1
5. Jerry drove his car 264 miles. The fuel economy of his car is 22 miles per gallon. The gasoline cost \$1.06 per gallon. What was his total cost for gasoline on the trip? ANS: \$12.72

1 Lesson Focus

Motivation: Have students discuss different ways they can find distances on road maps.

Purpose: There are numerous ways to determine mileage on a map. Students need to realize that problem solving can be approached in a number of different ways.

2 *Teaching the Lesson*

Have students read the introductory paragraph. Then focus students' attention on the map and have volunteers answer questions 1–5 in the lesson. Then ask these questions.

1. How could you use this map to determine the distance from the northern border of Colorado to the southern border? (Add the mileage on I-25; estimate the distance for each grid)
2. Estimate the distance from the northern border to the southern border. (About 275 miles)
3. If you traveled by private airplane at 150 miles per hour, how long would it take to cross the state from north to south? (1 hour, 50 minutes)

Then work through the Example with the class.

3 *Close*

Summary: Have students tell why it is important to be able to read a map.

Evaluation
Guided Practice: Ex. 2–10 even, 12
Independent Practice: Ex. 1–11 odd, 13–19

Alternate Teaching Strategy

After discussing the map and questions 1–5 in the lesson, you may wish to have students work in small groups to complete the exercises. Have them discuss their ideas for each exercise and record the group consensus.

On the map distances in miles between two points are written in red. The points are marked with red dots.

5. What is the distance from Denver to Colorado Springs along Interstate 25? **76 miles**

EXAMPLE

How long will it take the Wilsons to drive from Denver to Pueblo (D-5) on Interstate 25 at an average speed of 55 miles **per hour**?

1 Find the distance from Denver to Colorado Springs. → **76**

2 Find the distance from Colorado Springs to Pueblo. → **45**

3 Find the total distance.
$76 + 45 = \mathbf{121}$

4 Find the travel time.
$121 \div 55 = \mathbf{2.2}$ ◀ ***Distance ÷ Rate = Time***
The travel time will be **2.2 hours.**

CHECK YOUR SKILLS

Multiply or divide as indicated. **For additional practice, see pages 372 and 375.**

1. $1.08 × 42 **$45.36**
2. $1.06 × 39 **$41.34**
3. $1.03 × 26 **$26.78**
4. $1.05 × 36 **$37.80**
5. 182 ÷ 40 **4.55**
6. 110 ÷ 50 **2.2**
7. 242 ÷ 55 **4.4**
8. 321 ÷ 75 **4.28**

EXERCISES

For each item, write the letter of the symbol that corresponds to it.

1. State Capital **b**
2. Interstate **f**
3. City or town **a**
4. River **d**
5. U.S. Highway **c**

a. • b. ⊛
c. (40) d. ∼
e. ▬ f. (55)
g. -(15)-

For Exercises 6–11, refer to the map on page 187. In what square is each city located?

6. Boulder **B-5**
7. Ft. Morgan **B-6**
8. Montrose **D-2**
9. Leadville **C-4**
10. Walden **A-4**
11. Yuma **B-7**

For Exercises 12–20, refer to the map on page 187.

12. Stephanie Mellott wants to make a round trip from Buena Vista (C-4) to Monte Vista (E-4). She plans to travel on Highway 285. Estimate the number of miles Stephanie will travel during the round trip. **About 200 miles**

13. Jeff Copeland used Highway 160 to drive from Durango (E-2) to Monte Vista (E-4). He traveled at an average speed of 40 miles per hour. Find Jeff's travel time. **3.35 hours**

14. Randy Barckley ran out of gasoline 30 miles south of Pueblo (D-5) on Interstate 25. How far was Randy from Walsenburg (D-5)? **16 miles**

15. Carla Shannon used Interstate 25 to drive from Denver (B-5) to Walsenburg (D-5). The car's fuel economy was 35 miles per gallon. About how much did she spend on gasoline if it cost $1.09 per gallon? **About $5.20**

16. Debbie Cantrell left her home in Colorado Springs (C-5) and traveled 127 miles south on Interstate 25 to visit a friend. In what town did her friend live? **Trinidad**

17. Which is the shorter distance, traveling from Julesburg (A-7) to Denver (B-5) on Interstate 76, or traveling from Julesburg to Cheyenne Wells (C-7) on Highway 385? Explain.
Julesburg to Cheyenne Wells; It is 163 miles to Cheyenne Wells and 173 miles to Denver.

18. Diane Jones plans to travel from Denver (B-5) to Vail (B-4) on Interstate 70 at an average speed of 54 miles per hour. Diane leaves Denver at 11:00 A.M. At what time should she arrive in Vail? **1:00 P.M.**

19. Carlos Mendoza travels from Trinidad (E-6) to LaJunta (D-6) on Highway 350 and from LaJunta to Lamar (D-7) on Highway 50. He drives at an average speed of 50 miles per hour. To the nearest hour, how long does the trip take? **3 hours**

PROJECT

Plan a trip from Denver to Durango.

a. Identify the highways on which you will travel.

b. Find the distance between the two cities.

c. Suppose you plan to travel at an average speed of 40 miles per hour. How long will the trip take?

Problem-Solving Skills

Using estimation (Ex. 12)
Solving a multi-step problem (Ex. 13, 15, 17–19)
Making a comparison (Ex. 17)

Estimation Ex. 12

NOTE: A quiz covering the second half of the chapter is provided in the *Teacher's ResourceBank™*.

Objectives

Students will

1. explore solutions to a variety of problems that emerge from this situational lesson.
2. explore solutions to vacation planning problems having more than one solution.
3. make consumer decisions relevant to their teen-age world.

Situational Lesson

These two pages present a situational lesson as the framework from which a variety of problem situations emerge.

Teaching Strategies

This lesson lends itself to cooperative learning groups for the problem solving activities of comparing choices and exploring decisions. (See page M–13.)

However, this activity can also be carried out by individual students.

1 Lesson Focus

Motivation: Have students discuss where they have gone and would like to go on a family vacation. Have them discuss the expenses they would have on the trip.

Purpose: Students should know that there are many expenses involved when taking a vacation. This lesson shows them many of these expenses and how to estimate the total expenses.

2 Teaching the Lesson

Before doing this lesson in your class, you will want to gather travel materials including travel guides, maps, and motel directories. You may want to ask the students to bring these materials from home if they are available.

Have a volunteer read the opening paragraph and the specifications in the box. Ask these questions.

Consumer's Choice

Your family has agreed on the following details for a vacation trip. You have agreed to plan the trip for your four-member family.

a. The vacation will last two weeks (including travel time).

b. The family has decided to spend $1800 on the vacation.

c. The plan includes spending at least one full day in each of two major cities. It also includes visiting at least three tourist attractions (scenic areas, historical places, theme parks) on the trip.

d. Lodging plans include staying at medium-priced motels or camping out, or both.

e. The family will travel by car. The plan is to travel up to 12 hours a day when necessary. The family car has an average fuel economy of 25 miles per gallon. Gasoline costs an average of $1.02 per gallon.

EXPLORING DECISIONS

1. At what time of year will the family take the vacation?
2. What major cities will they visit?
3. What tourist attractions will the family enjoy?
4. Trace the round trip route on a map.
5. Estimate the distance the family plans to travel each day.
6. Estimate the total distance for the trip and the total cost for gasoline.
7. Make a chart similar to the one below. Use the chart to prepare an estimate of daily and total expenses for the trip.

CHART OF EXPENSES

Date	*Location*	*Scenic Sights Visited*	*Automobile Expenses*	*Lodging Expenses*	*Food Expenses*	*Recreation and Others*	*Daily Totals*
		Totals					

1. How would you find information on the tourist attractions you would like to visit? (Look at a map, use a travel guide, write to the city chamber of commerce)
2. How would you find out how much a medium price motel costs? (Look in the travel guide, motel directory, or write the city chamber or commerce)
3. If the family leaves on Sunday and returns on Sunday (2 weeks), how many days do they have to pay for a motel or camping? (14)
4. What major expense is not included in the list in the box? (Food)

From the material available, have each group or student decide on a specific vacation destination. Then have them work Exercises 1–7. If you do not have enough materials available, pick a destination and work with the class to decide on the costs they should use for attractions, lodging, food, and recreation.

3 Close

Summary: Have students discuss what difficult decisions they made in their planning and how they solved them.

Problem-Solving Skills

Using Estimation (Ex. 5–6)
Completing a table (Ex. 7)

Critical Thinking

This whole lesson deals with considering possibilities, making judgements, and determining outcomes.

Project

Have students visit and interview travel agents to find out what careers in travel are like. Students may also gather material for the lesson activity and compare their costs to the cost of tours offered by the agent.

Objective

Student will

1. Make decisions on how to make a map.
2. Make a map.

Overview

This topic is optional. The word "Enrichment" that appears to the right of the title in this Teacher's Edition does not appear in the student textbook. Therefore, this material is not included in the Chapter Review and Chapter Test.

Using the Page

You may wish to have students work this Enrichment in small groups or you may wish to work with the class.

Problem-Solving Skills

Making a map

Making a Map ENRICHMENT

Work in small groups or as your teacher directs.

Goal You want to make a map showing the possible routes from your school to the nearest hospital.

You will need to discuss considerations such as these before drawing your map. For Exercises 1–10, answers will vary.

Discussion

1. If you don't know the routes to the hospital, how can you find this information?
2. How can you find the names of all the streets, highways, and so on, that are on the routes?
3. What scale will you use to draw the map?
4. What symbols will you use for the map legend?

5. Will you include distances between points on your map?
6. What landmarks can be included on your map?

Use the map you made to answer these questions.

7. How can you use the map to determine the total number of miles each route covers?
8. How can you use the map to estimate how long a trip to the hospital would take via each route?
9. Which route covers the fewest miles?
10. With which route is the travel time the shortest?

PROJECT Make a map of the route you take home from school everyday. Include your name, address, and telephone number on the map. These maps can be given to friends who are coming to your home for the first time.

Chapter Summary

IMPORTANT IDEAS

1. **Miles Driven ÷ Miles Per Gallon of Gasoline = Gallons of Gasoline Needed**
2. **Base Price of Plane Fare + Amount of Tax = Total Cost of Plane Fare**
3. **Basic Car Rental Cost + Mileage Cost = Total Car Rental Cost**
4. Cities and towns can be located on a map by a letter-number pair, such as C-4.
5. **Distance ÷ Rate = Time**

Chapter Review

Part 1: VOCABULARY

For Exercises 1-4, choose from the box at the right the word(s) that complete(s) each statement.

map legend excess mileage letter-number mileage allowance round trip

1. Traveling from St. Louis to Seattle and back to St. Louis is an example of a __?__. (Page 178) **round trip**
2. Cities can be located on a map by a __?__ pair, such as A-3. (Page 187) **letter-number**
3. The number of miles for which a rental car driver does not have to pay is called the __?__. (Page 184) **mileage allowance**
4. The chart that explains what the symbols on a map mean is a __?__. (Page 187) **map legend**

Part 2: SKILLS

Find the total price of each plane ticket. (Pages 180–181)

	Base Price	Sales Tax	Amount of Tax	Total Cost
5.	$182	8%	? **$14.56**	? **$196.56**
6.	$279	8%	? **$22.32**	? **$301.32**

	Base Price	Sales Tax	Amount of Tax	Total Cost
7.	$324	8%	? **$25.92**	? **$349.92**
8.	$210	8%	? **$16.80**	? **$226.80**

Chapter Summary

The Chapter Summary contains a listing of the important ideas that were presented in the chapter. This listing is intended to assist the student with the Chapter Review that follows.

Objective

To review the important terms, skills, problem solving, and applications presented in Chapter 8.

Overview

The Chapter Review is structured in three parts. Part 1 is a review of the important terms that were introduced in the chapter. Part 2 reviews the skills that were presented in the chapter. Part 3 reviews the problem-solving strategies and applications that were presented in the chapter. Each item in the Chapter Review is referenced to the related pages where the concept, skill, or application was presented.

Using the Pages

You may wish to assign this Chapter Review for homework or treat it as a class review prior to administering the formal Chapter Test. In doing this, it is suggested that you only use the even- or odd-numbered exercises. You can then use the remaining exercises as a bank for use later.

For Exercises 9–12, use the table below to find the total car rental cost. (Pages 184–186)

Weekly Rate (7 days)	\$87.00
Daily Rate	\$22.99
Mileage Allowance	100 free miles per day
Excess Mileage Charge	24¢ per mile

	Number of Days	Miles Driven	Total Cost
9.	2	126	? \$52.22
10.	8	750	? \$109.99
11.	10	1260	? \$218.37
12.	3	627	? \$147.45

Part 3: APPLICATIONS

13. Mary Burtle is planning a 1480-mile trip. Her car's fuel economy is 25 miles per gallon, and Mary expects to pay an average of \$1.02 per gallon of gasoline. Will Mary's gasoline costs be closer to \$50 or to \$60? Explain. (Pages 178–179) **\$60; 1500 ÷ 25 = 60 and 60 × \$1 = \$60**

14. Rosalind and Juan Cortez are taking their 9-year-old son on a vacation. They estimate that their travel expenses will be \$70 for gasoline, \$65 per person for meals, and \$100 for lodging. Find the total estimated travel expenses. (Pages 178–179) **\$365**

15. A round-trip train fare from Boston to St. Louis is \$138. Children under age 12 pay half-fare. Find the total of the fares for two adults and two eight-year-old children. (Pages 180–181) **\$414**

16. The round-trip plane fare from Boston to Chicago is \$230 per person plus an 8% tax. How much are plane fares for a family of three? (Pages 180–181) **\$745.20**

For Exercises 17–18, use the table below to find the car rental cost. (Pages 184–186)

Weekly Rate (7 days)	\$105
Daily Rate	\$31.99
Mileage Allowance	100 free miles per day
Excess Mileage Charge	30¢ per mile

17. During her vacation, Ellen White rented a car and drove 567 miles over 3 days. Find the total rental cost. **\$176.07**

18. Ray Chapman wants to rent a car for 6 days and drive 580 miles. How much will he save if he pays the weekly rate rather than the daily rate? **\$86.94**

For Exercises 19–20, refer to the map on page 187. (Pages 187–189)

19. Which is the shorter distance, driving from Pueblo (D-5) to Lamar (D-7) on Highway 50 or driving from Pueblo to Gunnison (D-3) on Highway 50? Explain. **See below.**

20. Brian Doerfler used Highway 160 to drive from Walsenburg (D-5) to Monte Vista (E-4). He traveled at an average speed of 50 miles per hour. Find the travel time to the nearest hour. **About 2 hours**

19. Pueblo to Lamar; it is 152 miles to Gunnison, but only 121 miles to Lamar.

Objective

To informally assess student's mastering of the major skills, concepts, problem solving, and applications presented in Chapter 8.

Using the Page

After completing the Chapter Review with the class, you may wish to use this Chapter Test as an informal assessment. This Chapter Test parallels the formal chapter tests (Form A and Form B) provided in the *Teacher's ResourceBank.*™

Chapter Test

1. The one-way bus fare from Dallas to San Francisco is $119. Children between the ages of 5 and 12 qualify for half-fare. Find the total of the one-way fares for two adults and a 10-year old child. **$297.50**

2. On a recent 810-mile trip, Peter Kelly paid $1.06 per gallon of gasoline. His car's fuel economy was 36 miles per gallon. Find Peter's total gasoline cost on the trip. **$23.85**

3. The round-trip plane fare from Houston to Salt Lake City is $276 per person plus an 8% tax. What is the total of the plane fares for a family of five? **$1490.40**

4. If the Crawford family travels to Minnesota by plane, they estimate that they will pay $970 in plane fares. If they travel by bus, they estimate that they will pay $720 in bus fares and $200 for meals. With which method of transportation will the total estimated travel expenses be less? How much less? **Bus; $50**

For Exercises 5-8, use the table below to find the total car rental cost.

Weekly Rate (7 days)	$87.99
Daily Rate	$19
Mileage Allowance	100 free miles per day
Excess Mileage Charge	24¢ per mile

	Number of Days	Miles Driven	Total Cost
5.	3	267	? **$57**
6.	7	930	? **$143.19**
7.	8	1208	? **$204.91**
8.	9	715	? **$125.99**

9. Tim Huffaker traveled from a town located in Square A-7 on a map to a town located in Square D-7. In what direction did he travel? **South**

10. On a map, if you moved directly east from a point in Square C-2, would you be more likely to go through Square C-5 or Square D-2? **C-5**

Cumulative Maintenance Chapters 1–8

Choose the correct answer. Choose **a, b, c,** *or* **d.**

1. Find the total of the monthly payments for the car advertised below. **a**

Sungazer 500
$900 Down
$203/Month for
60 Months

a. $12,180 **b.** $12,780
c. $263 **d.** $11,280

2. A shipment of shoes contains 12 boxes of tennis shoes, 10 boxes of sandals, and 8 boxes of slippers. All boxes are the same size and shape. What is the probability that a box randomly chosen from the shipment contains sandals? **d**

a. $\frac{1}{10}$ **b.** $\frac{2}{3}$ **c.** $\frac{1}{4}$ **d.** $\frac{1}{3}$

3. Add: $4590 + $17.63 + $134.56 **c**

a. $198.09 **b.** $4732.19
c. $4742.19 **d.** $4842.19

4. Find the average price of these four automobiles. **c**

Automobile	*Price*
A	$7850
B	$8300
C	$9890
D	$5820

a. $31,860 **b.** $8075
c. $7965 **d.** $6372

5. Katie Dyer earns $7.20 per hour plus time and a half for all hours worked over 40. Find her gross earnings for a 46-hour week. **b**

a. $64.80 **b.** $352.80
c. $298.80 **d.** $496.80

6. Mr. and Mrs. Davenport file a joint income tax return. Their taxable income is $17,556. Use the table below to find the tax they owe. **a**

If taxable income is—		*And you are—*			
At Least	*But Less Than*	*Single*	*Married filing jointly*	*Married filing separately*	*Head of a household*
		Your tax is—			
17,200	17,250	2,398	1,872	2,890	2,252
17,250	17,300	2,410	1,880	2,904	2,262
17,300	17,350	2,421	1,889	2,918	2,272
17,350	17,400	2,433	1,898	2,932	2,282
17,400	17,450	2,444	1,907	2,946	2,292
17,450	17,500	2,456	1,916	2,960	2,302
17,500	17,550	2,467	1,925	2,974	2,312
17,550	17,600	2,479	1,934	2,988	2,322

a. $1934 **b.** $1925
c. $2988 **d.** $2479

7. Lloyd Jones writes a check for $75.14. After writing the check, the balance in his account is $315.26. What was the balance before writing the check? **b**

a. $240.12 **b.** $390.40
c. $380.30 **d.** $340.12

Objective

To review the content presented in Chapters 1–8

Using the Pages

You may wish to use this Cumulative Maintenance as an informal assessment tool. These pages can be assigned for homework or they may be used as review in class.

NOTE: The *Teacher's ResourceBank™* contains a Cumulative Test for Chapters 6–8. The Cumulative Test is presented in a standardized-test format.

8. Round 4562 to the nearest hundred. b

a. 5000 b. 4600
c. 4500 d. 4560

9. The round-trip plane fare from New York to Denver is $388 per person plus an 8% tax. How much are plane fares for a family of three? a

a. $1257.12 b. $419.04
c. $1257.92 d. $1258.26

10. A Myriah ZT travels 450 miles on 12.5 gallons of gasoline. What is the car's fuel economy? d

a. 427.5 miles per gallon
b. 3.6 miles per gallon
c. 37 miles per gallon
d. 36 miles per gallon

11. The graph below shows how the price of a share of stock changed over a 6-month period. By how much did the price increase from January to March? a

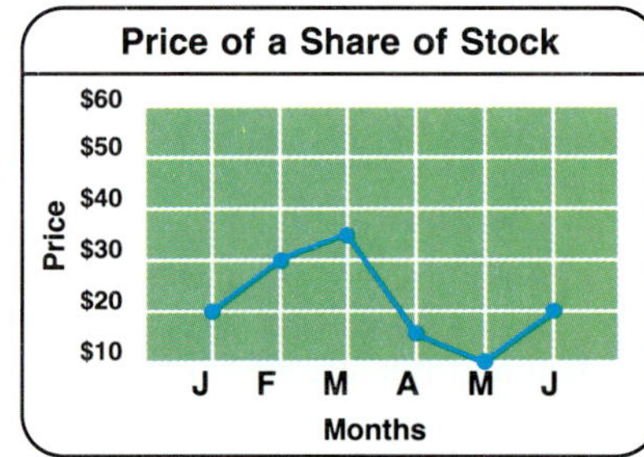

a. $15 b. $35
c. $20 d. $5

12. Find the net deposit. c

		Dollars	Cents
CASH			
CHECKS	1	24	75
List	2	193	63
Each	3		
Check	4		
SUBTOTAL		218	38
▶ Less Cash Rec'd		50	00
NET DEPOSIT		?	

a. $268.38 b. $486.76
c. $168.38 d. $248.38

13. Write 8% as a decimal. b

a. 0.8 b. 0.08
c. 0.008 d. 0.0008

14. When Kathy Marek had her car repaired, the parts cost $189.50, and the labor cost $85.00. Kathy paid a sales tax of 4% on the parts. Find the total repair bill. d

a. $274.54 b. $197.08
c. $285.48 d. $282.08

15. Carolyn Farrell's gross income last year was $17,653. She also received $78.96 and $121.50 in interest from two savings accounts. Find her adjusted gross income. d

a. $17,853.56 b. $17,452.54
c. $376.99 d. $17,853.46

16. Multiply: $4.80 × 1.5 a

a. $7.20 b. $28.80
c. $6.20 d. $72.00

Buying Foods

This year, the Brady family's food budget has to accommodate two additional teenagers. Gina Brady's niece, who is the same age as Susan Brady, has come to live with the family for a year. Phil Brady's cousin Mark will also live with the family while attending a local community college.

- How can the Bradys keep within their food budget while continuing to eat a balanced diet with foods essential for health and growth?
- How can the Bradys save money on food costs?
- What are the additional costs when Phil and Gina Brady decide to "dine out" with their two children and their houseguests?

Chapter 9: Food Costs

Overview

Chapter 9 deals with food costs and ways of saving money on food while maintaining good nutrition. Since food costs are constantly fluctuating, it may be a good idea to have students bring in food advertisements from supermarkets and other food markets in order to build an awareness of current food costs.

Although all lessons in this chapter involve problem-solving, the strategy lesson on pages 216–218 presents four strategies from which students are asked to select the most appropriate to apply in a given problem-solving situation. The *Consumer's Choice* on pages 220–221 presents a **situational lesson** in which students make consumer choices in a familiar, real-life situation. Finally, the *Enrichment* lesson on page 222 introduces the topic of price index which may be expanded into further research on the Consumer Food Index and the Consumer Price Index.

Have students read the introductory paragraph and questions. Have them list possible solutions to the problems presented. After completing the chapter, have students review their suggested solutions, comparing them with those presented in the lessons. You may wish to have students suggest other possible problems resulting from the situation described on this page and to discuss possible solutions.

You may wish to organize the class into small groups to complete the situational activity described on this *Using the Page.*

Lesson Resources

Maintenance: See below.
Reteaching/Alternate Teaching Strategy: p. M-35 (Visual 23)
Practice: p. M-35
Enrichment: p. M-35
Concrete Materials: Visual 23

Objectives

Students will

1. identify nutritional information on food labels.
2. use the information on food labels to solve problems related to nutrition.

Maintenance

1. Write a decimal for $\frac{3}{4}$. ANS: 0.75
2. Write a fraction for 60%. ANS: $\frac{60}{100} = \frac{3}{5}$
3. Add: $184.20 + $350 + $21.75 ANS: $555.95
4. Subtract: $872.50 − $322.85 ANS: $549.65
5. Peter deposits the following in his checking account: a paycheck for $324.80, a refund check for $150.00, and a gift check for $35.00. He wants to get $60.00 back in cash. Find his net deposit. ANS: $449.80

1 Lesson Focus

Motivation: Ask students to name the different kinds of information found on food labels.

Purpose: This lesson describes how to use food labels to determine the nutritional value of foods. This information can help students in their present and future roles as consumers to select foods that are good nutritional buys.

Nutrition Labels

Whenever she shops for food, Gina Brady scans the nutrition labels on food packages to help her select foods that are good "nutrition buys." She also notes the percent of the U. S. Recommended Daily Allowances (U.S. RDA) of protein and of important minerals and vitamins that one serving of each food contains.

SWEET PEAS

Net Weight.....1 lb 1 oz

NUTRITION INFORMATION—PER ¼-CUP SERVING
SERVINGS PER CAN APPROX. 4

CALORIES	60	CARBOHYDRATE	10 g
PROTEIN	3 g	FAT	0 g
		SODIUM	360 mg

% U.S. RDA PER SERVING

PROTEIN	4	NIACIN	4
VITAMIN A	8	CALCIUM	2
VITAMIN C	20	IRON	6
THIAMIN (VIT B_1)	6	PHOSPHORUS	4
RIBOFLAVIN (VIT B_2)	4	MAGNESIUM	4

WT. OF PEAS 10¼ OZ BEFORE ADDITION OF LIQUID NECESSARY FOR PROCESSING.

1. How many calories does each serving of sweet peas contain? **60 calories**
2. How many grams of protein does each serving contain? **3 grams**
3. What percent of the U.S. RDA of protein does one serving contain? **4%**
4. What percent represents the approximate total U.S. RDA for protein? **100%**

EXAMPLE

What is 100% of the U.S. RDA for protein?
Grams of protein per serving: **3** % of U.S. RDA per serving: **4**

Think: 4% of total U.S. RDA = 3

1% of total U.S. RDA = 3 ÷ 4 ◀ $4\overline{)3.00}$ = 0.75

100% of total U.S. RDA = 0.75 × 100

= **75**

So the total U.S. RDA for protein is about **75 grams.**

CHECK YOUR SKILLS

Complete. For additional practice, see page 372.

1. 0.15 × 100 = ? 15
2. 0.06 × 10 = ? 0.6
3. 0.32 × ? = 32 100
4. 0.625 × ? = 62.5 100
5. 0.372 × ? = 3.72 10
6. 0.05 × ? = 5 100

Solve. For additional practice, see pages 407 and 409.

7. 2 is what percent of 5? 40%
8. 9 is what percent of 15? 60%
9. Find 8% of 15. 1.2
10. Find 15% of 20. 3

Divide. For additional practice, see page 376.

11. 0.72 ÷ 4 0.18
12. 0.48 ÷ 4 0.12
13. 0.036 ÷ 4 0.009
14. 0.052 ÷ 4 0.013

EXERCISES

For Exercises 1–11, refer to the nutrition label at the right.

Complete this table.

	1 Serving of Cereal	1 Serving Plus $\frac{1}{2}$ Cup Milk
1. Calories	? 110	? 150
2. Fat	? g 0	? g 0
3. Carbohy–drates	? g 20	? g 26
4. Vitamin A	? % 25	? % 30
5. Vitamin D	? % 10	? % 25
6. Zinc	? % 25	? % 30
7. Copper	? % 6	? % 8

BREAKFAST CEREAL
NUTRITION INFORMATION PER SERVING
SERVING SIZE 1 OZ (28.4 g or about 1 cup)

	Per Serving of Cereal	With Skim Milk (½ cup)
CALORIES	110	150
PROTEIN	6 g	10 g
FAT	0 g	0 g
CARBOHYDRATE	20 g	26 g
POTASSIUM	50 mg	250 mg
% U.S. RDA PER SERVING		
PROTEIN	10	20
VITAMIN A	25	30
VITAMIN C	25	25
VITAMIN D	10	25
ZINC	25	30
COPPER	6	8

Charles had two one-ounce servings of cereal with skim milk for breakfast one morning. Use this information in Exercises 8–11.

8. What percent of the U.S. RDA of copper was in the two servings? 16%
9. How many milligrams of potassium were in the two servings? 500 milligrams
10. In the two servings, how many grams of protein came from the skim milk? 8 grams
11. What percent of the protein in the two servings came from the skim milk? 40%

2 Teaching the Lesson

Have a volunteer read the introductory paragraph. Then focus students' attention on the label and ask these questions.

1. What kind of information is given? (Nutrition)
2. What does "net weight" mean? (Weight of the contents of the cans)
3. How are the numbers for the U.S. RDA given? (As percents)
4. How many servings does the can contain? (Approximately 4)
5. What is the size of each serving? ($\frac{1}{4}$ cup)

Make sure students can find all the necessary information on the can before having them work on the Example.

3 Close

Summary: Have students discuss how the nutrition labels on food cans can help consumers to make better food choices.

Evaluation
Guided Practice: Ex. 2–10 even
Independent Practice: Ex. 1–11 odd, 12–20

Extension

Have students gather nutritional information from food cans. Have them rank the nutrients for each food in order from least to greatest. Then have them compare the RDA percents for each food.

Problem-Solving Skills

Reading a table (Ex. 1–17)
Solving a multi-step problem (Ex. 10, 11)
Choosing the operation (Ex. 10–17)
Interpreting information (Ex. 8–17)

For Exercises 12–15, refer to the nutrition label at the right.

12. There are 0.72 milligrams of iron in one serving of the salmon. What is the approximate U.S. RDA for iron? **18 milligrams**

13. There are 0.068 milligrams of riboflavin (vitamin B_2) in one serving of the salmon. What is the approximate U.S. RDA for riboflavin? **1.7 milligrams**

PINK SALMON

SERVING SIZE (INCLUDING LIQUID) .... 2 oz
SERVINGS PER CONTAINER 6

NUTRITION INFORMATION PER SERVING

CALORIES	60	FAT	2 g
PROTEIN	10 g	SODIUM	280 mg

% U.S. RDA PER SERVING

PROTEIN	20	IRON	4
THIAMINE	2	VITAMIN B_6	6
RIBOFLAVIN	4	VITAMIN B_{12}	15
NIACIN	15		

The approximate U.S. RDA for niacin is 20 milligrams. Use this information in Exercises 14–15.

14. What percent of the U.S. RDA for niacin is contained in one serving of the salmon? **15%**

15. How many milligrams of niacin are supplied by one serving of the salmon? **3 milligrams**

For Exercises 16–17, refer to the nutrition label at the right.

16. A diet low in sodium (salt) requires no more than 500 milligrams of sodium per day. What percent of this daily requirement is contained in one serving of asparagus? **71%**

17. A diet low in carbohydrates requires no more than 120 grams of carbohydrates per day. What percent of this daily requirement is contained in one serving of asparagus? **2.5%**

18. Is cost the only consideration when shopping for food? Explain. **No; nutrition is an important consideration.**

19. How can nutrition labels help the consumer determine which of two products may be the better buy? **See below.**

20. What does getting the "most for your money" mean when related to food shopping?

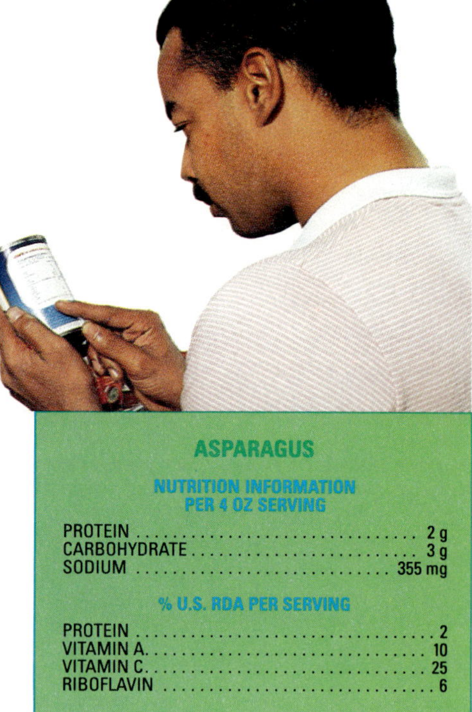

ASPARAGUS

NUTRITION INFORMATION PER 4 OZ SERVING

PROTEIN	2 g
CARBOHYDRATE	3 g
SODIUM	355 mg

% U.S. RDA PER SERVING

PROTEIN	2
VITAMIN A	10
VITAMIN C	25
RIBOFLAVIN	6

19. They help consumers compare the nutritional value of the products.
20. It means getting the best nutritional value for the money you spend.

Critical Thinking

You may wish to have students work in small groups to solve these problems or you may wish to work with the class.

Ex. 18–20

STRATEGY: USING "HIDDEN QUESTIONS" TO SOLVE A MULTI-STEP PROBLEM

Comparing Costs: UNIT PRICE

On their weekly shopping expedition for groceries, Gina and Phil compared the price of bell peppers at two different supermarkets.

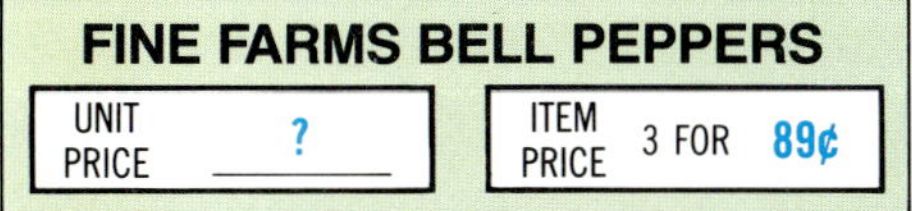

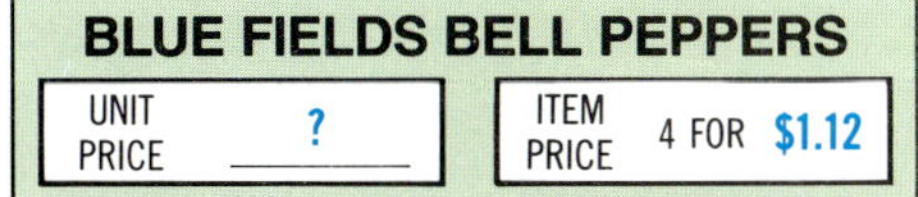

1. How would you find the price of *one* bell pepper at Fine Farms? **Divide 89¢ by 3.**
2. How would you find the price of *one* bell pepper at Blue Fields? **Divide $1.12 by 4.**
3. *Complete:* To compute the price of one bell pepper at either supermarket, divide the _?_ by the number of peppers. This is the price per _?_, or the unit price. **item price; unit**

Unit Price = Price of Item ÷ Number of Units

To find the better buy, Gina and Phil compared the unit prices of the peppers at both markets.

EXAMPLE Which is the better buy, bell peppers at 3 for 89¢ at Fine Farms or bell peppers at 4 for $1.12 at Blue Fields?

[1] Find the unit price at Fine Farms.

Unit price = 89 ÷ 3 = 29.66 ◀ *Round to the nearest tenth.*

= **29.7¢ per pepper**

[2] Find the unit price at Blue Fields.

Unit price = 112 ÷ 4 = 28.0 ◀ *$1.12 = 112¢*

= **28¢ per pepper**

[3] Compare the unit prices. ⟶ **28¢ < 29.7¢**

Since they have the lower unit price, the **peppers at Blue Fields** are the better buy.

When using unit price to determine the better buy, be sure that the *quality* of the products compared is the same.

Lesson Resources

Maintenance: See below.
Reteaching/Alternate Teaching Strategy: p. M-35 (Visual 24)
Practice: p. M-35
Enrichment: p. M-35
Visual 24

Objective

Student will use a formula to solve multi-step problems that involve unit price.

Maintenance

1. Multiply: $4.45 × 30 ANS: $133.50
2. Find 5% of $6500. ANS: $325.00
3. Multiply: $43,000 × 0.0715 ANS: $3074.50
4. Subtract: $550 − $129.25 ANS: $420.75
5. Clyde Jones earned $1558 one month. The deductions were: federal tax: $258.40, state tax: $54.20, F.I.C.A. tax: $103.61. Find his net pay. ANS: $1141.79

[1] Lesson Focus

Motivation: Have students discuss what things are often sold in groups of more than one and how these things are priced in the store.

Purpose: Students need to understand that to compare the price of two or more things, you need to compare the same amount. Students will see that the unit price allows you to make comparisons of equal amounts.

2 Teaching the Lesson

Focus students' attention on the advertisements and ask these questions.

1. What makes it hard to determine which peppers are a better deal? (Different amounts of units)
2. How could you make it easier to compare the prices? (Determine the cost of one pepper)

3 Close

Summary: Have students discuss why retailers might choose to give the item price rather than the unit price.

Evaluation
Guided Practice: Ex. 1–3, 4–20 even
Independent Practice: Ex. 5 21 odd, 22–23

Extension

Have students go to the grocery store and find the unit prices of two different brands of an item such as canned vegetables or canned fruit. Then discuss why there may be a difference in unit price. (Name brand that has higher advertising costs, better quality product, etc.)

CHECK YOUR SKILLS

Round to the nearest tenth. For additional practice, see page 378.

1. 3.46 **3.5** 2. 4.52 **4.5** 3. 6.97 **7.0** 4. 14.98 **15.0** 5. 23.53 **23.5**

Divide. Round each answer to the nearest tenth when necessary. For additional practice, see pages 375, 376, and 378.

6. 59 ÷ 5 **11.8** 7. 61 ÷ 25 **2.4** 8. 74 ÷ 16 **4.6** 9. 320 ÷ 18 **17.8** 10. 119 ÷ 600 **0.2**

11. 56 ÷ $\frac{1}{4}$ **224** 12. 28 ÷ $\frac{3}{4}$ **37.3** 13. 25 ÷ $\frac{4}{5}$ **31.3** 14. 64 ÷ $5\frac{1}{2}$ **11.6** 15. 14 ÷ $5\frac{1}{4}$ **2.7**

Compare. Write <, =, or >. For additional practice, see page 373.

16. 6.1 __?__ 6.12 **<** 17. 0.1 __?__ 0.01 **>** 18. 0.7 __?__ 0.09 **>** 19. 4.5 __?__ 4.50 **=**

Subtract. For additional practice, see page 369.

20. 15.9 − 12.3 **3.6** 21. 19.6 − 11.2 **8.4** 22. 39.6 − 14.8 **24.8** 23. 29.1 − 13.7 **15.4**

Complete. For additional practice, see page 413.

24. 1 gallon = __?__ quarts **4** 25. 1 liter = __?__ milliliters **1000**

EXERCISES

Complete the following.

1. The unit price of an item is its cost per __?__. **unit**
2. Unit price = Cost ÷ Number of __?__ **units**
3. When comparing to determine the better buy, be sure that the __?__ of the items compared is the same. **quality**

Find each unit price. Round answers to the nearest tenth of a cent.

4. ORANGE MARMALADE 2-lb jar 49¢ **24.5¢**
5. LAUNDRY DETERGENT 147-oz box $5.99 **4.1¢**
6. TEA BAGS 100/box $1.79 **1.8¢**

	Item	Quantity	Price
7.	Canned beans	16 oz	40¢ **2.5¢**
8.	Oranges	10	99¢ **9.9¢**
9.	Celery seed	45 g	$1.35 **3.0¢**

	Item	Quantity	Price
10.	Canned peaches	8 oz	42¢ **5.3¢**
11.	Ground mustard	50 g	$1.05 **2.1¢**
12.	Cucumbers	4	78¢ **19.5¢**

For Exercises 13–21, find the better buy.

13. Cottage Cheese

32-oz size

14. Vanilla Extract

118-mL size

15. Vegetable Oil

4-qt size

	Item	Smaller Quantity	Larger Quantity
16.	Flour	2 lb/59¢	5 lb/$1.08 **Larger**
17.	Cereal	226 g/$1.19	510 g/$2.15 **Larger**
18.	Oranges	3/55¢	6/$1.05 **Larger**

	Item	Smaller Quantity	Larger Quantity
19.	Tuna	$6\frac{1}{2}$ oz/88¢ **Smaller**	12 oz/$1.65
20.	Corn	6 ears/$1.25	10 ears/$1.89 **Larger**
21.	Juice	40 fl oz/$1.15	64 fl oz/$1.75 **Larger**

22. Two 6.5-ounce cans of tuna cost $1.00. Find the unit price. **7.7¢**

23. Swiss cheese is on sale at 89¢ for $\frac{1}{4}$ of a pound. Find the unit price. **$3.56**

24. Which is the better buy? **b**

a. 16-oz can of peaches for 70¢

b. 24-oz can of peaches for $1.00

25. Which is the better buy? **a**

a. Four grapefruit for $1.05

b. Six grapefruit for $1.65

26. John buys a 24-ounce box of cereal for $2.64 instead of a 12-ounce box for $1.89. How much does he save per ounce? **4.75¢**

27. Maria buys a 25-pound bag of dog food for $8.98 instead of a 10-pound bag of dog food for $5.32. How much does she save per pound? **17.28¢**

28. Which is the better buy, a two-liter bottle of soda for 98¢ or an 8-pack of the same brand for $2.29? Each can in the 8-pack contains 354 milliliters. **2-liter bottle**

29. Cucumbers are priced at 3 for 89¢. How much will one cost? **30¢**

30. Apples are priced at 3 for 50¢. How much will 7 apples cost? **$1.17**

31. Why do you think many items are priced in multiples such as 3 for 89¢? **To sell larger quantities of the items.**

32. Gina can buy a gallon of vegetable oil at Fine Farms for $2.98, or one quart of the same oil at Blue Fields for 78¢.

a. Give three reasons why Gina might prefer to buy the oil at Fine Farms. **Answers will vary.**

b. Give three reasons why Gina might prefer to buy the oil at Blue Fields. **Answers will vary.**

Problem-Solving Skills

Solving multi-step problems (Ex. 13–21, 24–28)

Critical Thinking

You may wish to have students work in small groups to solve these problems or you may wish to work with the class.

Ex. 31 and 32

Lesson Resources

Maintenance: See below.
Reteaching/Alternate Teaching Strategy: p. M-36 (Visual 25)
Practice: p. M-36
Enrichment: p. M-36
Visual 25

Objective

Student will solve problems that involve coupon savings on food costs.

Maintenance

1. Multiply: $4.50 × 20 ANS: $90
2. Add: $8194.79 + $286.50 + $44.41 ANS: $8525.70
3. Find 2% of 86. ANS: 1.72
4. Add $1.25 + $0.06 ANS: $1.31
5. Albert bought a loaf of bread for $0.98 and a magazine for $2.00. He paid a 6% sales tax on the magazine. What was his total bill? ANS: $3.10

1 Lesson Focus

Motivation: Ask students to discuss how they could use coupons to help them save money on food costs.

Purpose: Students should know that coupons can be a source of savings if they will take the time to gather, organize, and use them.

2 Teaching the Lesson

Focus students' attention on the coupons and ask these questions.

1. Where can you get coupons? (Newspapers, magazines, stores, manufacturers, etc.)
2. How do you use coupons? (Redeem them with the purchase of the item)
3. Why do producers offer these coupons? (To encourage people to buy the items)

Have students answer questions 1–5 in the lesson.

Saving Money: Coupons

The Bradys also save money on food costs by clipping discount coupons from newspapers and magazines. When doing their weekly shopping, Phil and Gina used these coupons from Fine Farms Supermarket.

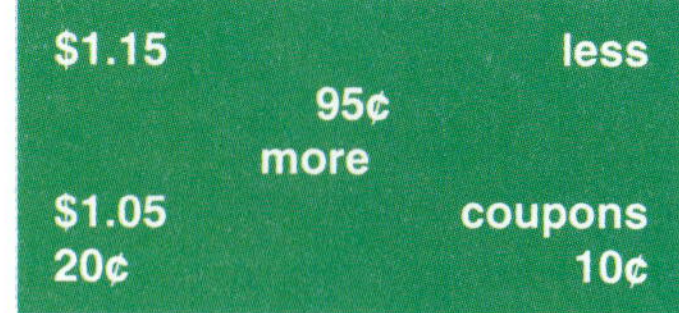

1. What is the total regular price of these items? $6.33
2. What is the total coupon savings? 85¢
3. What would the total coupon savings be on double coupon days? $1.70
4. How much would the Brady's pay for thc itcms on doublc coupon days? $4.63
5. *Complete:* Amount paid = Regular price − ? coupon savings

CHECK YOUR SKILLS

Perform the indicated operations. For additional practice, see pages 372, 369, and 368.

1. $0.35 × 2 $0.70
2. $1.04 × 4 $4.16
3. $1.17 × 46 $53.82
4. $0.98 × 52 $50.96
5. $1.12 − $0.35 $0.77
6. $1.35 − $0.42 $0.93
7. $3.56 − $1.15 $2.41
8. $5.14 − $1.89 $3.25
9. $0.55 + $1.15 + $0.60 $2.30
10. $1.12 + $0.72 + $0.48 $2.32

Divide. Round your answer to the nearest tenth. For additional practice, see pages 375 and 379.

11. 634 ÷ 30 21.1
12. 361 ÷ 40 9.0
13. 271 ÷ 28 9.7
14. 447 ÷ 18 24.8

EXERCISES

Complete. Choose your answers from the box at the right.

1. Shoppers who use ? pay ? than the regular price for an item. coupons; less
2. A jar of peanut butter that sells for ? will cost ? on double coupon days with a ?-off coupon. $1.15; 95¢; 10¢

$1.15		less
	95¢	
	more	
$1.05		coupons
20¢		10¢

For Exercises 3–10, first double the coupon savings. Then find the actual price.

	Item	Regular Price	Coupon Savings		Item	Regular Price	Coupon Savings
3.	Bread	$0.75	$0.15 **$0.45**	**7.**	Frankfurters	$1.20	$0.25 **$0.70**
4.	Corn syrup	$1.09	$0.20 **$0.69**	**8.**	Macaroni	$0.65	$0.12 **$0.41**
5.	Pie filling	$0.89	$0.10 **$0.69**	**9.**	Sugar	$2.20	$0.35 **$1.50**
6.	Detergent	$1.49	$0.16 **$1.17**	**10.**	Eggs	$0.99	$0.10 **$0.79**

Refer to these coupons for Exercises 11–15.

11. Gina bought tomato paste at a store offering double coupon savings. She paid 42¢ for it. What was the regular price? **72¢**

12. Find the price Stuart Palmer paid for two packages of paper plates and a can of pineapple juice when he used discount coupons. **$4.55**

13. How much would Stuart have paid at a store offering double discount savings? **$4.00**

14. A customer paid for a box of pancake mix, a can of pineapple juice, and 2 packages of paper plates with a $20-bill, receiving more than $14 in change. Did the customer use coupons? Explain.
Yes; the cost with coupons is $5.48 and without it is $6.18

15. Ricky has $5.00 in his pocket. Does he have enough money to buy 3 packages of paper plates with a discount coupon if the store is offering double discount savings?
No; the cost would be $5.10.

16. Phil Brady has a coupon for 30¢ off a 28-ounce jar of peanut butter selling for $2.71. He also has a coupon for 35¢ off a 40-ounce jar selling for $3.61. Which is the better buy? **40-ounce jar**

17. Phil and Gina Brady estimate that they save about $7.00 per week in food costs by using discount coupons.

a. About how much do they save in a year? **$364**

b. Should the time Phil and Gina spend in cutting out and organizing the coupons be taken into account when determining how much is saved per month and per year? Explain. **Answers will vary.**

3 Close

Summary: Have students discuss how they would organize themselves to make the most of coupon savings.

Evaluation
Guided Practice: Ex. 1, 2, 4–10 even
Independent Practice: Ex. 3–9 odd, 11–17

Problem-Solving Skills

Solving a multi-step problem (Ex. 3–12)
Making a comparison (Ex. 15, 16)

Critical Thinking

You may wish to have students work in small groups to solve this problem or you may wish to work with the class.

Ex. 17

Objective

Student will

1. review the skills, concepts, and applications in the first part of Chapter 9.
2. maintain key skills and concepts taught in Chapters 2, 3, 5, and 7.

Using the Page

Exercises 1–7 provide an informal assessment of the student's mastery of the major skills and concepts presented in the first half of Chapter 9. Each item is referenced to the related pages where the particular item was presented. These exercises parallel the quiz provided in the *Teacher's ResourceBank.*™

A quiz covering the second half of the chapter is also provided in the *Teacher's ResourceBank.*™

Exercises 8–11 maintain skills and concepts taught in Chapters 2, 3, 5, and 7.

Mid-Chapter Review

For Exercises 1–3, use the nutrition label. (Pages 200–202)

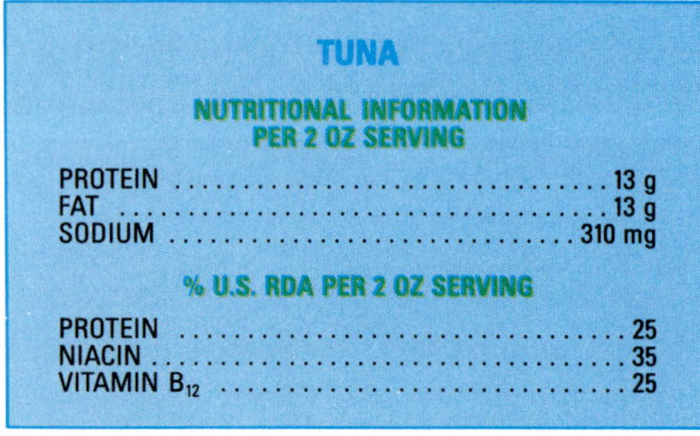

1. How many milligrams of sodium does one serving of tuna contain? **310 milligrams**
2. A diet low in fat requires no more than 50 grams of fat per day. What percent of this daily requirement is contained in one serving of tuna? **26%**
3. There are 7 milligrams of niacin in one serving of tuna. What is the approximate U.S. RDA for niacin? **20 milligrams**

Find the better buy. (Pages 203–205)

	Item	Smaller Quantity	Larger Quantity
4.	Apples	3/59¢	12/$1.99 **Larger**

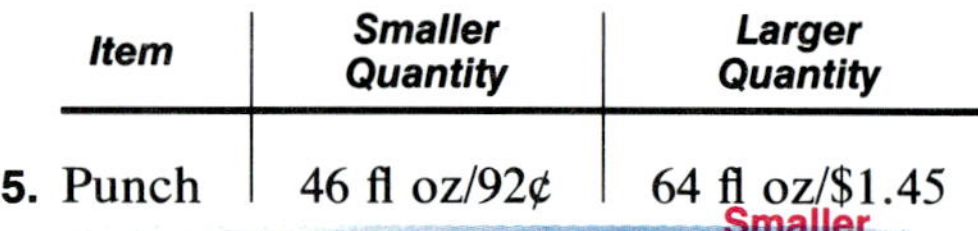

	Item	Smaller Quantity	Larger Quantity
5.	Punch	46 fl oz/92¢	64 fl oz/$1.45 **Smaller**

Refer to these coupons for Exercises 6–7. (Pages 206–207)

6. How much did Phil Brady pay for two boxes of cereal at a store offering double discount savings? **$3.88**
7. Gina has $3.00 in her purse. Does she have enough to buy three cans of corn and a box of cereal if she uses discount coupons? **No; the total would be $3.11.**

MAINTENANCE

8. There are four cans of green beans and two cans of corn on a shelf. One can is chosen without looking. What is the probability of choosing a can of corn? **$\frac{1}{3}$** (Pages 26–27)
9. Scott earns a weekly salary of $120 plus a 15% commission on sales. Find his total pay for a week in which his sales total $2400. **$480** (Pages 45–47)
10. Kathy has $1800 in a savings account that pays a yearly interest rate of 6%. How much simple interest will the account earn in four months? **$36** (Pages 110–111)
11. One car travels 450 miles on 17.3 gallons of fuel. Another car travels 360 miles on 12.9 gallons of fuel. Which car has the greater fuel economy? (Pages 160–162) **The car that travels 360 miles on 12.9 gallons.**

Math and Volume

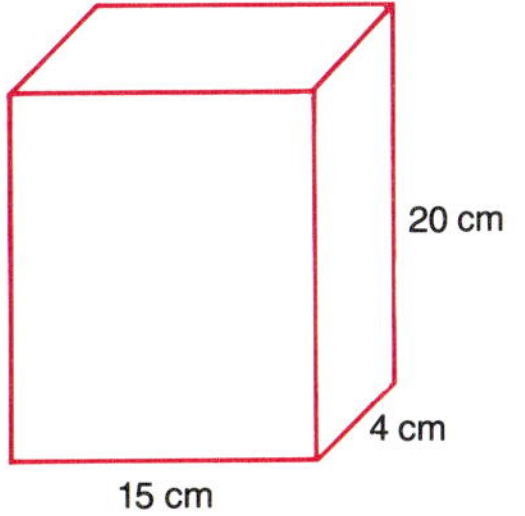

One of Clarence Bartow's responsibilities as a design engineer for the Healthco Cereal Company is to determine the size of cereal boxes.

Clarence designed a small cereal box that is 20 centimeters high, 4 centimeters wide, and 15 centimeters long. The volume of the small box is 1200 cubic centimeters. He wants to design a larger box having twice the volume, but the same length and height as the smaller box.

EXAMPLE

What will be the width of the larger box?

Volume $= l \times w \times h$

$$2(1200) = 15 \times w \times 20$$

$$2400 = 300w$$

$$\frac{2400}{300} = \frac{300w}{300}$$

$$8 = w$$

width: 8 centimeters

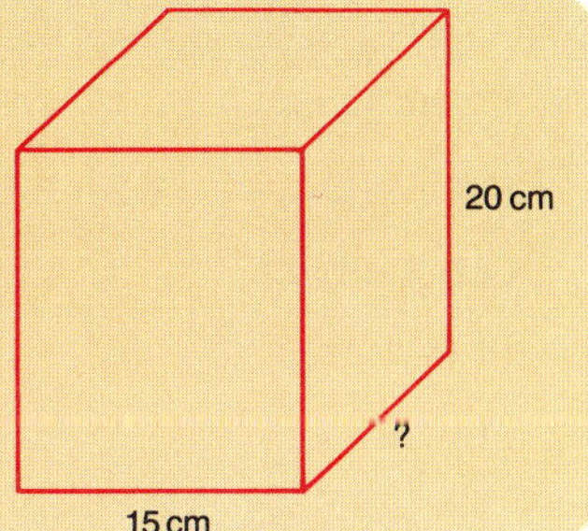

1. How many times as wide as the smaller box is the larger box? **2 times**
2. Suppose Clarence decides to double the volume of the smaller box and keep the same length and width. What will be the height of the larger box? **40 cm**
3. Suppose Clarence decides to triple the volume of the smaller box and keep the same length and height. What will be the width of the larger box? **12 cm**

EXERCISES

Find the missing measures.

1.

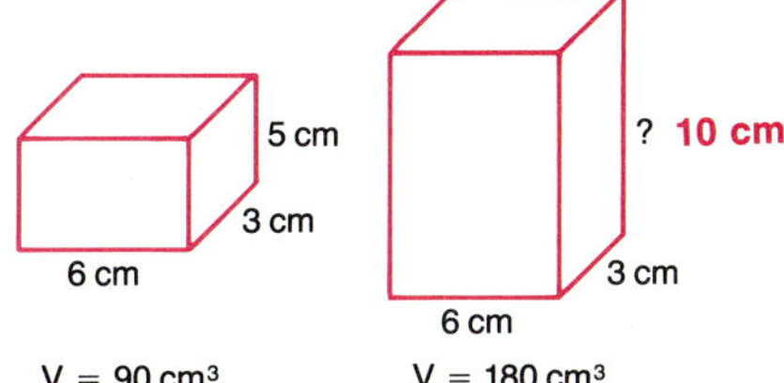

2.

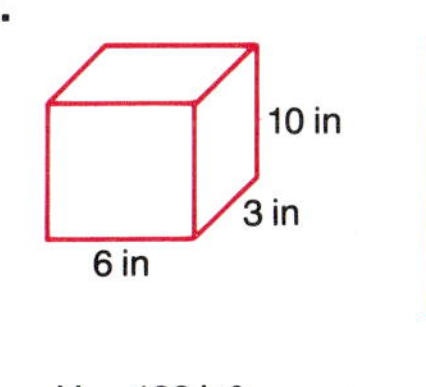

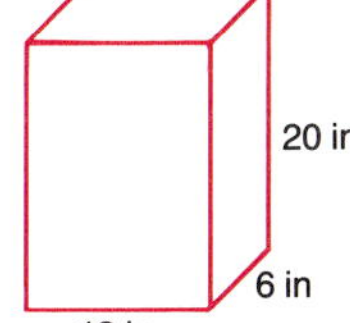

Objective

Student will apply the skill of finding the volume of a rectangular prism to problems involving the sizes of boxes.

Overview

This page is an extension of the skills and ideas presented in the previous lessons of this chapter. Since the content presented on this page is not included in the Chapter Review or Chapter Test, its use is optional.

Using the Pages

You may wish to have students work this lesson in small groups or you may wish to work with the class. Using it with the class, have a student read the first two paragraphs of the lesson. Then discuss the Example with the students. Have students answer questions 1–3 and Exercises 1 and 2.

Problem-Solving Skills

Using a diagram (Ex. 1, 2)

Critical Thinking

Questions 2 and 3 (in Lesson)

Lesson Resources

Maintenance: See below.
Reteaching/Alternate Teaching Strategy: p. M-36 (Visual 26)
Practice: p. M-36
Enrichment: p. M-36
Concrete Materials: Visual 26
Visual 26

Objectives

Student will

1. use a table to solve problems that involve computing the amount of food needed for a given number of servings.
2. use a table to solve problems that involve cost per serving.

Maintenance

1. Multiply: $2\frac{1}{3} \times 3$ ANS: 7
2. Divide: $1\frac{2}{3} \div 4$ ANS: $\frac{5}{12}$
3. Multiply: 320×0.25 ANS: 80
4. Add: \$350.65 + \$124.56 ANS: \$475.21
5. Liz earns a weekly salary of \$165 plus a 10% commission on sales. Find her total income for a week when her total sales were \$2700. ANS: \$435

1 Lesson Focus

Motivation: Have students discuss how they might determine how much it costs per person to eat a meal at home.

Purpose: This lesson will show students how to decide how much food to buy for a given number of servings and how to determine the cost of food per serving.

STRATEGY: USING "HIDDEN QUESTIONS" TO SOLVE A MULTI-STEP PROBLEM

Cost Per Serving

The Brady family saves money on food costs by not wasting food. Gina Brady uses this table to determine the number of pounds of meat to buy.

Meat	Servings Per Pound	Meat	Servings Per Pound	Meat	Servings Per Pound
Beef		**Lamb**		**Pork-Cured**	
Sirloin Steak	$2\frac{1}{2}$	Chops	3	Picnic ham	2
Porterhouse	2	Leg of lamb	3	Ham (cooked)	$3\frac{1}{2}$
Rib roast	$2\frac{1}{2}$	**Pork-Fresh**		**Poultry**	
Ground beef	4	Chops	4	Broiler	$1\frac{1}{2}$
Frankfurters	4	Roast	$2\frac{1}{2}$	Legs, thighs	3
Stew meat	5	Spareribs	$1\frac{1}{3}$	Breasts	4

1. How many servings are there in 1 pound of lamb chops? in 2 pounds? in 3 pounds? **3; 6; 9**
2. How many pounds of lamb chops are needed for 6 servings? for 9 servings? for 12 servings? **2; 3; 4**
3. *Complete:* To find the number of pounds of lamb chops needed for 12 servings, divide 12 by 3, the number of __?__. **servings per pound**

EXAMPLE 1 How many pounds of spareribs should Gina buy for 6 servings?

$6 \div 1\frac{1}{3} = 6 \div \frac{4}{3}$ ◀ Number of Servings ÷ Number of Servings Per Pound = Number of Pounds

$= \frac{\cancel{6}^{3}}{1} \times \frac{3}{\cancel{4}_{2}}$

$= \frac{9}{2}$, or $4\frac{1}{2}$

Gina should buy **$4\frac{1}{2}$ pounds.**

4. *Complete:* To find which of two meats costs less to serve, find the cost per __?__ for each meat. **serving**
5. The cost per serving equals the cost per pound divided by the number of __?__. **servings per pound**

EXAMPLE 2 Which costs less to serve?

Pork chops: $1.77 per pound Spareribs: $1.39 per pound

[1] Refer to the table to find the number of servings per pound.

Pork chops: **4** Spareribs: $\mathbf{1\frac{1}{3}}$

[2] Find the cost per serving for each meat. Round to the nearest cent.

Pork chops: $\$1.77 \div 4 = \$0.4425$, or **$0.44**

$$\text{Spareribs: } \$1.39 \div 1\tfrac{1}{3} = \$1.39 \div \tfrac{4}{3} = \$1.39 \times \tfrac{3}{4} = \$1.0425, \text{ or } \mathbf{\$1.04}$$

[3] Compare the costs.

Since $\$1.04 > \$0.44$, the **pork chops** cost less to serve.

6. The spareribs cost less per pound than the pork chops. Why do they cost more per serving? **Because there are more servings in one pound of pork chops than there are in one pound of spareribs.**

CHECK YOUR SKILLS

Write a fraction for each mixed number. **For additional practice, see pages 390 and 392.**

1. $1\frac{1}{2}$ $\frac{3}{2}$ **2.** $3\frac{1}{3}$ $\frac{10}{3}$ **3.** $1\frac{2}{3}$ $\frac{5}{3}$ **4.** $4\frac{1}{5}$ $\frac{21}{5}$ **5.** $2\frac{1}{4}$ $\frac{9}{4}$ **6.** $3\frac{1}{8}$ $\frac{25}{8}$

Divide.

7. $9 \div 1\frac{1}{4}$ $7\frac{1}{5}$ **8.** $8 \div 2\frac{1}{2}$ $3\frac{1}{5}$ **9.** $10 \div 3\frac{1}{2}$ $2\frac{6}{7}$ **10.** $7 \div 1\frac{1}{3}$ $5\frac{1}{4}$ **11.** $6 \div 2\frac{1}{4}$ $2\frac{2}{3}$

Divide. Round each answer to the nearest cent. **For additional practice, see page 391.**

12. $\$2.39 \div 1\frac{1}{2}$ **$1.59** **13.** $\$1.69 \div 1\frac{1}{3}$ **$1.27** **14.** $\$3.29 \div 2\frac{1}{2}$ **$1.32** **15.** $\$1.19 \div 1\frac{1}{4}$ **$0.95**

Compare. Use $<$, $=$, or $>$. **For additional practice, see page 373.**

16. 3.4 _?_ 3.04 **>** **17.** 0.8 _?_ 0.81 **<** **18.** 6.53 _?_ 6.5 **>** **19.** 3.4 _?_ 3.40 **=**

Multiply. Round each answer to the nearest cent when necessary. **For additional practice, see page 390.**

20. $\$1.60 \times 2\frac{3}{4}$ **$4.40** **21.** $\$1.65 \times 2\frac{2}{5}$ **$3.96** **22.** $\$2.39 \times 1\frac{1}{2}$ **$3.59** **23.** $\$3.62 \times 1\frac{1}{5}$ **$4.34**

[2] Teaching the Lesson

Focus students' attention on the table. Ask these questions.

1. What meat serves the most people per pound? (Stew meat)
2. Why might it serve the largest number of people? (No waste, and it is combined with other ingredients)
3. What meat serves the least number of people per pound? (Spare ribs)
4. Why might it serve the least number of people? (It is mostly bones.)
5. What else would you need to know to determine which is the best buy? (Answers will vary.)

Work through questions 1–6 and Examples 1 and 2.

[3] Close

Summary: Ask selected students to explain how knowing the number of servings per pound and the cost per serving will help when planning meals and buying food.

Evaluation

Guided Practice Ex. 1–3, 4–12 even
Independent Practice: Ex. 5–13 odd 14–16

Extension

Have students go to a local grocery store and make a list of the current prices per pound for the items shown in the table on page 210. Then have students compare the prices from different stores and discuss why there may be a difference in price.

Problem-Solving Skills

Using a table (Ex. 4–16)
Solving a multi-step problem (Ex. 15, 16)
Making a comparison (Ex. 15, 16)

EXERCISES

Complete. Choose your answers from the box at the right.

divide
multiply
servings per pound
cost per serving
cost per pound

1. To find the number of pounds of picnic hams to buy for a family of 4, __?__ 4 by 2. **divide**
2. Number of pounds to buy = Servings needed ÷ __?__. **servings per pound**
3. To find which of two meats is less expensive to serve, compare the __?__. **cost per serving**

Complete to find the number of pounds of each kind of meat needed. Refer to the table on page 210.

	Meat	Number of Servings	Pounds
4.	Stew meat	10	__?__ **2**
5.	Broiler	8	__?__ **$5\frac{1}{3}$**
6.	Chicken legs	25	__?__ **$8\frac{1}{3}$**

	Meat	Number of Servings	Pounds
7.	Sirloin steak	4	__?__ **$1\frac{3}{5}$**
8.	Pork roast	12	__?__ **$4\frac{4}{5}$**
9.	Lamb chops	7	__?__ **$2\frac{1}{3}$**

For Exercises 10–16, refer to the table on page 210.

For Exercises 10–13, find the cost per serving to the nearest cent.

	Meat	Price per Pound	Cost per Serving
10.	Picnic ham	\$1.05	__?__ **\$0.53**
11.	Ground Beef	\$1.84	__?__ **\$0.46**
12.	Frankfurters	\$1.38	__?__ **\$0.35**
13.	Rib roast	\$1.68	__?__ **\$0.67**

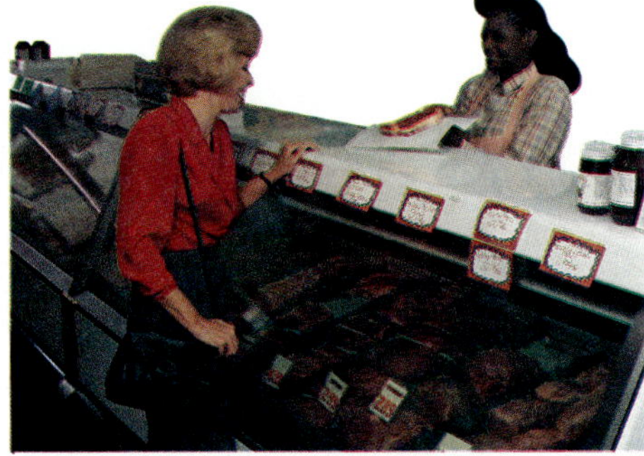

14. How many pounds of ground beef should Gina buy to make 9 servings for dinner? **$2\frac{1}{4}$ pounds**

15. At the butcher shop, chicken breasts are \$1.99 per pound. Pork roast is \$1.99 per pound. Which costs less per serving? **Chicken breasts**

16. Gina Brady's dinner menu for five days includes the meat shown in the list at the right. Her meat budget for the five days is \$15. Gina must have 6 servings of each meat for every meal. Will the meat cost more or less than her budget? How much more or less? **More than her budget; \$0.73**

Meat	Cost per pound
Chicken Breasts	\$1.89
Stew meat	\$1.89
Ham, Cooked	\$2.80
Pork roast	\$1.65
Ground beef	\$1.25

STRATEGY: USING "HIDDEN QUESTIONS" TO SOLVE A MULTI-STEP PROBLEM

Dining Out

Phil and Gina Brady like to dine out with their family at least once a week. This week, they decide they will try Green Gardens, a restaurant near their home.

1. What other costs besides food will the Brady's pay when eating at a restaurant? **sales tax and tip**

2. *Complete:* Cost of meal × sales tax rate = amount of _?_. **sales tax**

3. *Complete:* Cost of meal × percent for tip = amount of _?_. **tip**

The cost of the meal for Phil, Gina, their two children, and their children's two guests is \$48.90. The state sales tax rate is 6%. Phil Brady left a tip of 15%.

EXAMPLE Find the total cost of the meal.

[1] Find the amount of tax.

\$48.90 × 6% = \$48.90 × 0.06

= \$2.934, or **\$2.93** ◀ *Round to the nearest cent.*

[2] Find the amount of the tip. Use mental computation.

Think: 15% = 10% + 5%

10% of \$48.90 = \$4.890, or \$5.00. ◀ *Round up to a convenient number.*

Since a 5% tip is $\frac{1}{2}$ of a 10% tip,

$\frac{1}{2}$ × \$5.00 = \$2.50. ⟶ Tip: \$5.00 + \$2.50 = **\$7.50**

[3] Find the sum:

Cost of Meals	+	Sales Tax	+	Tip	=	Total
\$48.90	+	\$2.94	+	\$7.50	=	**\$59.34**

The total cost of the meal is **\$59.34.**

4. In step [2], why is \$5.00 a convenient number? **It is easier to mentally compute $\frac{1}{2}$ of \$5 than $\frac{1}{2}$ of \$4.89.**

Lesson Resources

Maintenance: See below.
Reteaching/Alternate Teaching Strategy: p. M-37 (Visual 27)
Practice: p. M-37
Enrichment: p. M-37
Concrete Materials: Visual 27
Visual 27

Objectives

Student will

1. solve multi-step problems that involve the amount of tax and the amount of a tip for a restaurant bill.
2. read a bar graph to solve problems that involve the number of meals served and the cost of a meal.

Maintenance

1. Add: \$860.07 + \$11.80 + \$43.98 ANS: \$915.85
2. Add: \$56.90 + \$3.41 + \$8.00 ANS: \$68.31
3. Divide: 1470 ÷ 30 ANS: 49
4. Multiply: \$2.15 × 30 ANS: \$64.50
5. Jane's car averages 25 miles per gallon of gasoline. She traveled 11,000 miles and spent an average of \$1.05 per gallon for gasoline. What is her total cost for gasoline? ANS: \$462

[1] Lesson Focus

Motivation: Ask students to name restaurant costs other than the cost of the food.

Purpose: Students need to realize that tax and tip must be added to the meal cost listed in the menu. This lesson shows students how to determine the amount of tax and the amount of a tip.

2 *Teaching the Lesson*

Have a student volunteer read the introductory paragraph. Discuss and have students answer questions 1–3 in the lesson. Then ask these questions. Suppose the cost of the food at a restaurant was $20.

1. What would you expect to pay in tax at a rate of 6%? ($1.20)
2. What would you pay if you figured a 15% tip? ($3)
3. How would you find the total cost of the meal? (Add the cost of the food, the tax, and the amount of the tip.) Work through the Example given in the lesson. Then have students answer question 4.

3 *Close*

Summary: Have students discuss why the cost of eating a meal in a restaurant would be more than preparing the same meal at home.

Evaluation
Guided Practice: Ex. 1–6
Independent Practice: Ex. 7–18

Problem-Solving Skills

Completing a table (Ex. 5–9)
Reading a graph (Ex. 10–18)
Interpreting information (Ex. 10, 11, 14)
Solving a multi-step problem (Ex. 15–18)

CHECK YOUR SKILLS

ESTIMATION/MENTAL MATH: Ex. 1–2, 15–18

Estimate to the nearest dollar. **For additional practice, see page 380.**

1. $7.32 + $8.03 + $0.95 **$16**
2. $6.92 + $0.72 + $1.68 + $2.00 **$12**

Write a decimal for each percent. **For additional practice, see page 403.**

3. 5% **0.05**
4. 6% **0.06**
5. 4% **0.04**
6. 7% **0.07**
7. 12% **0.12**
8. 15% **0.15**

Multiply. Round each answer to the nearest cent. **For additional practice, see page 372.**

9. $6.03 × 0.04 **$0.24**
10. $8.15 × 0.08 **$0.65**
11. $12.59 × 0.15 **$1.89**
12. $15.06 × 0.12 **$1.81**

For Exercises 13–14, find the mean, the median, and the mode. **For additional practice, see pages 10–13.**

13. Scores on seven math tests:
79, 92, 86, 92, 87, 85, 90
Mean: 87.3; Median: 87; Mode: 92
14. Enrollment at five schools:
387, 650, 821, 650, 503
Mean: 602.2; Median: 650; Mode: 650

Estimate to the nearest dollar. **For additional practice, see page 380.**

15. $8.72 − $2.13 **$7**
16. $7.56 − $0.89 **$7**
17. $2.31 − $0.65 **$1**
18. $5.86 − $1.47 **$5**

EXERCISES

Complete each statement.

1. The sales tax at a restaurant is based on the __?__ of the meal. **cost**
2. The tip at a restaurant is based on the __?__ of the meal. **cost**
3. Cost of a meal × percent for tip = __?__ **amount of the tip**
4. Total cost of a restaurant meal = cost of the meal + __?__ + __?__ **amount of tip; amount of the tax**

Complete the table. Find the total cost of each meal.

	Appetizer	*Dinner*	*Dessert*	*Beverage*	*Cost of Meal*	*6% Sales Tax*	*15% Tip*	*Total Cost*
5.	$1.50	$6.25	$1.80	65¢	? **$10.20**	? **$0.61**	? **$1.50**	? **$12.31**
6.	$2.25	$5.75	$2.00	90¢	? **$10.90**	? **$0.65**	? **$1.65**	? **$13.20**
7.	$5.75	$14.90	$3.50	$1.20	? **$25.35**	? **$1.52**	? **$3.75**	? **$30.62**
8.	—	$8.30	$1.75	95¢	? **$11.00**	? **$0.66**	? **$1.65**	? **$13.31**
9.	$1.35	$4.50	—	$1.10	? **$6.95**	? **$0.42**	? **$1.05**	? **$8.42**

This bar graph shows the number of dinners served at Green Gardens each night of one week in 1989. Use this graph for Exercises 10–12.

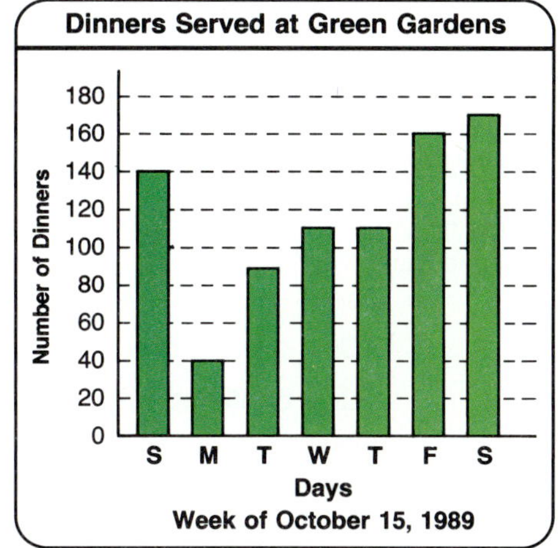

10. On which two nights would Green Gardens need the most food servers? **Friday and Saturday**

11. Which is the slowest night at Green Gardens? **Monday**

12. What is the mean, median, and mode of the number of dinners served at Green Gardens during the week? **Mean: 117.1; Median: 110; Mode: 110**

The line graph shows the average cost of dinner (without tax or tip) for five consecutive years at Green Gardens Restaurant.

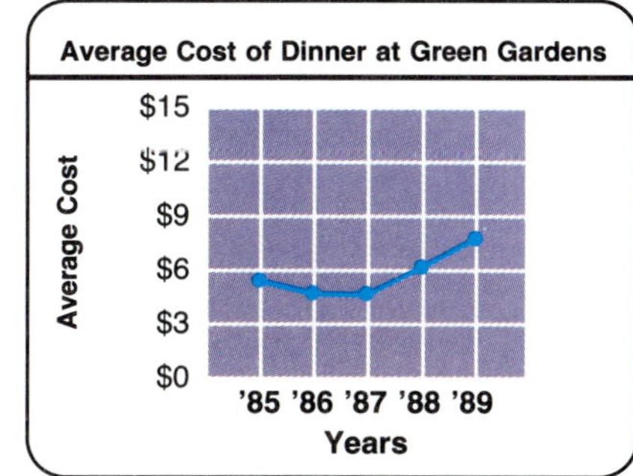

13. What was the average cost in 1985? in 1988? **About $5; $6**

14. Over what period did the average cost increase? decrease? **1987–1989; 1985–1986**

15. If the food tax rate in 1985 was 5% and a person gave a 15% tip, what was the approximate total average cost of a meal at Green Gardens that year? **About $6**

16. If the food tax rate in 1987 was 6% and a person gave a 15% tip, what was the approximate total average cost of a meal at Green Gardens that year? **About $5.50**

For Exercises 17–18, refer to both graphs. Assume the sales tax rate is 7% and that the average tip is 15%.

17. Find the approximate total amount spent on meals on Saturday night at Green Gardens restaurant. **About $1600**

18. Find the approximate total amount spent on tips on Thursday night at Green Gardens restaurant. **About $124**

19. As a class or in groups, discuss all the things you must consider when you plan to eat in a restaurant. For example, will you pay cash or use a credit card? Compare the costs of eating at a restaurant with eating at a "fast food" chain or eating at home. Make a list of the advantages and disadvantages of each. **Answers will vary.**

Critical Thinking

You may wish to have students work in small groups to solve these problems or you may wish to work with the class.

Question 4 (in Lesson), Ex. 19

Lesson Resources

Maintenance: See below.
Reteaching/Alternate Teaching Strategy: See the margin on page 217.
Practice: Activity Worksheet 52
Enrichment: See the enrichment topic "Consumer Price Index" on page 222.

Objectives

Student will

1. solve multi-step problems that involve the cost of commercials.
2. choose and apply an appropriate strategy to solve a problem.

Maintenance

Perform the indicated operations.

1. 5200 × 4 ANS: 20,800
2. 19,850 × 6 ANS: 119,100
3. 61,700 + 8500 + 101,967 ANS: 172,167

Find the numbers.

4. The sum of two numbers if 18. Their product is 72. ANS: 6 and 12
5. The sum of two numbers is 72. One number is three times the other. ANS: 18 and 54

1 Lesson Focus

Motivation: Ask students to estimate the number of minutes they spend watching television each day. Then ask them to estimate how much of their time is spent watching commercials.

Purpose: This lesson requires students to solve multi-step problems in a variety of situations related to television commercials.

2 Teaching the Lesson

After presenting the Example, choose a problem to show how the strategy can be applied to other situations, such as in Exercise 8.

Strategy: INTERPRETING INFORMATION

Food manufacturers often introduce new products on television commercials. Time for television commercials is usually sold in 10-second, 30-second, and 60-second intervals as follows.

Cost of 10-second commercial = $\frac{1}{2}$ × Cost of 30-second commercial
Cost of 60-second commercial = 2 × Cost of 30-second commercial

EXAMPLE The marketing manager of Ings Foods, Inc. plans to use television commercials to advertise three new soft drinks. The list at the right shows the number and length of the commercials, the showing times, and the rates for day and prime time advertising. What is the total cost?

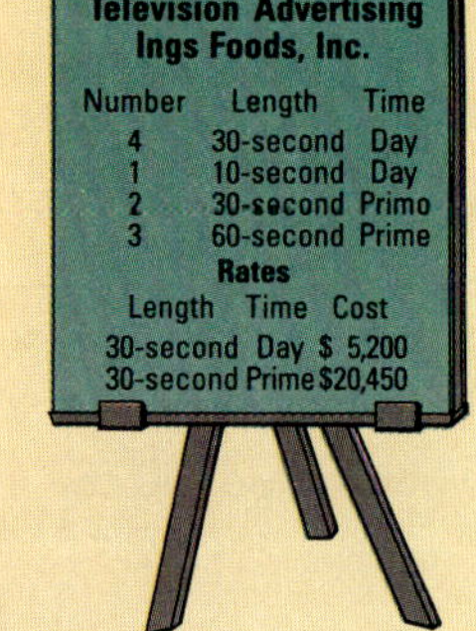

Television Advertising Ings Foods, Inc.

Number	Length	Time
4	30-second	Day
1	10-second	Day
2	30-second	Prime
3	60-second	Prime

Rates

Length	Time	Cost
30-second	Day	$ 5,200
30-second	Prime	$20,450

READ What are the facts? Refer to the table.

PLAN To find the total cost, first answer these "hidden questions."

What is the cost of the 30-second commercials?
What is the cost of the 10-second commercials?
What is the cost of the 60-second commercials?

SOLVE

1 Find the cost of the 30-second commercials.

Day: $5,200 × 4 = $20,800
Prime: $20,450 × 2 = $40,900
$61,700 ◀ *Cost for 30-second commercials*

2 Find the cost of the 10-second commercial.

($\frac{1}{2}$ × $5200) × 1 = **$2600** ◀ *$\frac{1}{2}$ × Cost of 30-second commercial = Cost of 10-second commercial*

3 Find the cost of the 60-second commercials.

(2 × $20,450) × 3 = $40,900 × 3 ◀ *2 × Cost of 30-second commercial = Cost of 60-second commercial*
= **$122,700**

4 Add to find the total cost.

$$\begin{array}{r} \$\ 61{,}700 \\ 2{,}600 \\ +\ 122{,}700 \\ \hline \$\ \mathbf{187{,}000} \end{array}$$ ◀ *Total Cost*

CHECK Check your answer with the facts of the problem. Is the answer reasonable?

1. Why did the marketing manager choose to run the 60-second commercials in prime time? **Because they would be seen by more people, since more people watch television during prime time.**
2. Why did the marketing manager choose to run the 10-second commercial during the day? **Because fewer people watch television during the day.**

EXERCISES

For Exercises 1–4, find the total cost for each advertising campaign. Costs are based on the rates for the 30-second commercials.

	Cost for 30 Seconds	Number of 10-second Commercials	Number of 30-second Commercials	Number of 60-second Commercials	Total Advertising Cost
1.	$ 30,000	1	2	0	? **$75,000**
2.	$ 25,000	0	2	1	? **$100,000**
3.	$ 80,000	0	3	2	? **$560,000**
4.	$100,000	0	4	3	? **$1,000,000**

5. A dog food manufacturer runs a 60-second ad on daytime television. A 30-second daytime ad costs $8600. What is the cost of the 60-second ad? **$17,200**

6. A 30-second ad on prime time television costs $45,000. What is the total cost for five 30-second ads and two 10-second ads? **$270,000**

7. The Suds Detergent Corporation plans to purchase television commercial time as shown in the table at the right. The rates are $5600 for 30-second daytime commercials and $26,500 for 30-second prime time commercials. Find the total cost. **$237,200**

Number	Length	Time
3	30-second	Day
3	10-second	Day
4	30-second	Prime
2	60-second	Prime

1. **Ask:** What is the problem about? (How many 10-second commercials were purchased?)
2. **Read** the problem to determine the FACTS. **Ask:** What is the cost of a 30-second commercial ($24,000) **Ask:** How much was paid in all for the commercials? ($576,000)
3. **Plan** the solution. **Ask:** What are the hidden questions in the problem? (The cost of a 10-second commercial) **Ask:** What operation will you use to find the number of 10-second commercials? (Division)
4. **Solve** the problem. **Ask:** What is the cost of a 10-second commercial? ($12,000)
5. **Check** the answer by having students check the facts in the problem with the solution.

3 Close

Summary: Have students discuss how the cost of television commercials could effect the price consumers pay for a product.

Evaluation
Guided Practice: Ex. 2–4 even, 5
Independent Practice: Ex. 1–3 odd, 6–13

Problem-Solving Skills

Using a table (Ex. 7)
Looking for a pattern (Ex. 11)
Making a table (Ex. 11–13)
Using guess and check (Ex. 12, 13)

Alternate Teaching Strategy

You may wish to have students work in small groups to complete the exercises. Have each group discuss their ideas for each exercise and record the group consensus.

8. The cost for a 30-second television commercial is $24,000. A fast-food restaurant purchases a block of 10-second commercials for a total cost of $576,000. How many 10-second commercials did the restaurant purchase? **48**

9. A food manufacturer purchased one 60-second television commercial and one 30-second television commercial for a total cost of $35,400. How much did the 30-second commercial cost? **$11,800**

10. A 30-second television commercial costs $32,000. Which costs less, one 30-second television commercial or three 10-second television commercials? How much less? **One 30-second commercial; $16,000 less**

For Exercises 11–13, choose a strategy from the box at the right that you can use to solve each problem.

a. Name the strategy.

b. Solve the problem.

Looking for a pattern
Making a table
Using guess and check
Making a List

11. Starting on a Monday, a television station will run 10-second, 30-second, and 60-second commercials for Rock Paper, Inc. according to the pattern in the table below. On what day after this will three commercials of each time length occur again on the same day? **a. Answers will vary. b. Saturday**

Time	*Mon.*	*Tues.*	*Wed.*	*Thurs.*	*Fri.*	*Sat.*	*Sun.*	*Mon.*	*Tues.*
10-sec	✓		✓		✓		✓		✓ . . .
30-sec	✓			✓			✓		. . .
60-sec	✓				✓				✓ . . .

12. Main Supermarket paid $65,000 for 8 television commercials. Some lasted for 30-seconds and some lasted for 60-seconds. A 30-second commercial costs $5000. How many 60-second commercials were there? **a. Answers will vary. b. 5**

13. Tilson Manufacturers budgeted $155,000 for television prime-time 10-second and 30-second commercials. A 30-second prime-time commercial costs $5500. The company wants to run three times as many 30-second as 10-second commercials. How many 30-second commercials can they buy? **a. Answers will vary. b. 24**

14. Why might a company prefer to purchase three 10-second commercials rather than one 30-second commercial? **Because 3 separate commercials can be broadcast at 3 separate times rather than just once.**

NOTE: A quiz covering the second half of the chapter is provided in the *Teacher's ResourceBank™*.

Critical Thinking

Ex. 14

Math and Recipes

Barbara Voorhis is a dietician for the Greenboro Community Hospital. She is planning a lunch menu for 300 people. The recipe for chicken salad at the right will serve 24 people.

CHICKEN SALAD

10 cups chicken
3 cups chopped celery
1 cup pickle relish
$2\frac{1}{2}$ cups mayonnaise
2 teaspoons salt

Serves 24.

EXAMPLE How many cups of chicken are needed to make 300 servings of chicken salad?

1 Use a proportion.

Chicken → $\frac{10}{24} = \frac{n}{300}$ ← Chicken
Servings → ← Servings

2 Solve the proportion.

$24n = 10(300)$

$24n = 3000$

$\frac{24n}{24} = \frac{3000}{24}$

$n = 125$

She will need **125 cups** of chicken.

EXERCISES

For Exercises 1–4, use the recipe for chicken salad above to find how much of each ingredient is needed for the number of servings.

1. Salt for 60 servings 5 tsp
2. Celery for 100 servings $12\frac{1}{2}$ c
3. Mayonnaise for 48 servings 5 c
4. Pickle relish for 150 servings $6\frac{1}{4}$ c
5. To make 24 muffins, you need 5 teaspoons of baking powder. How many teaspoons would you need to make 180 muffins? $37\frac{1}{2}$ tsp
6. A recipe for 6 servings of vegetable soup uses $\frac{1}{2}$ cup of green peas. How many cups of peas would you need for 80 servings? $6\frac{2}{3}$ c

PROJECT Find a recipe for one of your favorite foods. Then determine how much of each ingredient in the recipe would have to be used to make enough to serve 50 people, to serve 100 people, and to serve 200 people.

Objective

Student will apply the skill of solving a proportion to problems involving recipes.

Overview

This page is an extension of the skills and ideas presented in the previous lessons of this chapter. Since the content presented on this page is not included in the Chapter Review or Chapter Test, its use is optional.

Using the Pages

You may wish to have students work this lesson in small groups or you may wish to work with the class. Using it with the class, have a student read the first paragraph. Then work through the Example with the students. Use Exercises 1 and 2 as guided practice and have the students do Exercises 3–6 as independent practice.

Problem-Solving Skills

Using a table (Ex. 1–6)

Objectives

Students will

1. explore solutions to a variety of problems that emerge from this situational lesson.
2. explore solutions to food choice problems having more than one solution.
3. make consumer decisions relevant to their teen-age world.

Situational Lesson

These two pages present a situational lesson as the framework from which a variety of problem situations emerge.

Teaching Strategies

This lesson lends itself to cooperative learning groups for the problem solving activities of comparing choices and exploring decisions. (See page M-13.)

However, these activities can also be carried out by the class as a whole or by individual students.

1 Lesson Focus

Motivation: Ask students to name the different kinds of foods available in the school cafeteria. Ask them to estimate the average amount spent for lunch each day by each student.

Purpose: This lesson asks students to consider the nutritional value of food as well as the cost when making choices at lunch.

2 Teaching the Lesson

Focus students' attention on the cafeteria lunch menu. Ask these questions.

1. Which sandwich costs the most? (Ham)
2. Which sandwich has the fewest calories? (Tuna)
3. How much would two slices of pizza cost? ($1.10)

Consumer's Choice

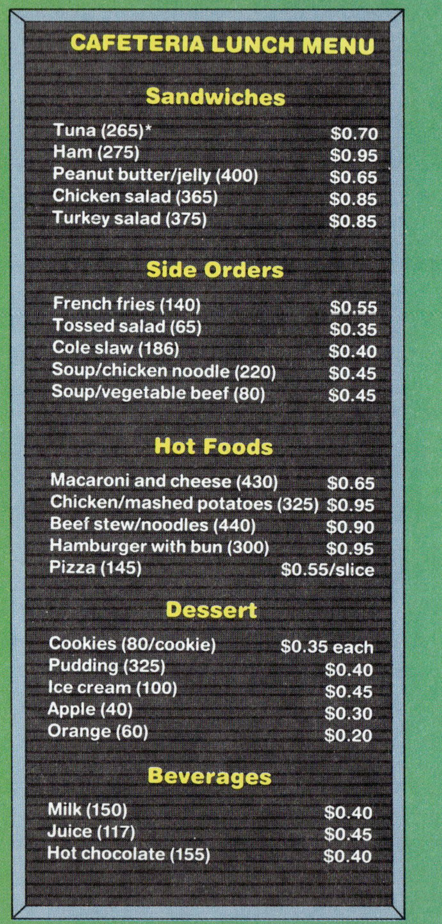

CAFETERIA LUNCH MENU

Sandwiches

Item	Price
Tuna (265)*	$0.70
Ham (275)	$0.95
Peanut butter/jelly (400)	$0.65
Chicken salad (365)	$0.85
Turkey salad (375)	$0.85

Side Orders

Item	Price
French fries (140)	$0.55
Tossed salad (65)	$0.35
Cole slaw (186)	$0.40
Soup/chicken noodle (220)	$0.45
Soup/vegetable beef (80)	$0.45

Hot Foods

Item	Price
Macaroni and cheese (430)	$0.65
Chicken/mashed potatoes (325)	$0.95
Beef stew/noodles (440)	$0.90
Hamburger with bun (300)	$0.95
Pizza (145)	$0.55/slice

Dessert

Item	Price
Cookies (80/cookie)	$0.35 each
Pudding (325)	$0.40
Ice cream (100)	$0.45
Apple (40)	$0.30
Orange (60)	$0.20

Beverages

Item	Price
Milk (150)	$0.40
Juice (117)	$0.45
Hot chocolate (155)	$0.40

On Tuesday, Sam Brady considered three possible choices from the school cafeteria menu. Sam can spend up to $2.50 per day for lunch and he must select at least one food from each of the four basic food groups. (See page 221.)

Choice 1	Choice 2
Ham sandwich	Beef stew/noodles
Two cookies	Tossed salad
Orange	Apple
	Milk

Choice 3

Hamburger with bun
French fries
Cole slaw
Pudding
Milk

Comparing the Choices

1. Does each choice cost $2.50 or less? Explain. No; Choice 3: $2.70
2. Does each choice represent a balanced meal? Explain. No; choice 1 has no item from the Milk Group.

Four Basic Food Groups

Milk Group

Fruit and Vegetable Group

Bread and Cereal Group

Meat Group

EXPLORING DECISIONS

Refer to Sam's choices and to the cafeteria menu.

3. What food or foods could Sam add to Choice 1 to make it a balanced meal? Will the cost be $2.50 or less?

4. What food or foods could Sam take away from Choice 3 and still have a balanced meal? Will the meal cost $2.50 or less?

5. Use the cafeteria menu to list four different balanced meals Sam might choose. Remember that each meal can cost no more than $2.50. **Answers will vary.**

For Exercises 6–9, suppose that Sam is watching his weight and is trying not to exceed 800 calories for lunch.

6. Find the number of calories for each of Sam's three choices. Use the number in parentheses after each food in the cafeteria menu.

7. Which of the three lunch choices will satisfy Sam's requirement of not exceeding 800 calories for lunch? **Choices 1 and 2**

8. What food or foods could Sam take away from Choice 3 in order to have 800 or fewer calories for lunch? Be sure that the meal costs $2.50 or less and remains balanced.

9. Which meals you listed in Exercise 5 exceed 800 calories? If there are any, change as few food items as possible in each meal in order to keep it balanced with an 800-calorie limit that costs $2.50 or less.

10. If Sam can spend an average of $2.50 per day for lunch, is it possible for him to spend $3.10 for lunch on one day? Explain your answer.

4. How many more calories are there in one serving of coleslaw than in one serving of tossed salad? (121)

Have students read the situations on page 221 and the three choices and answer Exercises 1–4. Then discuss Exercises 5–10 with the class.

3 Close

Summary: Have students discuss choices relating to food and food costs that they make in their own school cafeteria.

Extension

Have students use the lunch menu from their school cafeteria to complete Exercises 1–9. If there is no printed menu, have students construct one using daily cafeteria offerings.

Problem-Solving Skills

Using logical reasoning (Ex. 3–5, 8–10)
Solving a multi-step problem (Ex. 1–6, 8–10)
Making a comparison (Ex. 1–5, 7–10)
Using guess and check (Ex. 3–5, 8–10)
Making a list (Ex. 3–5, 8, 9)
Interpreting information (Ex. 1–9)
Reading a chart (Ex. 1–6, 8, 9)

Critical Thinking

Ex. 9, 10

Additional Answers

3. Pudding, ice cream, or hot chocolate; Yes, if only one of the items is chosen.
4. French fries or cole slaw, and pudding or milk; Yes
6. Choice 1: 495 calories; Choice 2: 695 calories; Choice 3: 1101 calories
8. Cole slaw and pudding, or just pudding
9. Answers will vary.
10. Yes; He would have to balance this out by spending 60¢ below the $2.50 average on the remaining days.

Objective

Student will use the information on a graph to solve problems that involve the consumer price index.

Overview

This topic is optional. The word "Enrichment" that appears to the right of the title in this Teacher's Edition does not appear in the student textbook. Therefore, this material is not included in the Chapter Review and Chapter Test.

Using the Page

You may wish to have students work this Enrichment in small groups or you may wish to work with the class.

Problem-Solving Skills

Using a graph (Ex. 1–7)

Estimation

Ex. 6 and 7

Consumer Price Index ENRICHMENT

A **price index** is a number that compares prices in a given year to those of a base year. The base year is assigned a number of 100.

EXERCISES

This bar graph shows price index numbers for a certain brand of rice. Use the bar graph for Exercises 1–6.

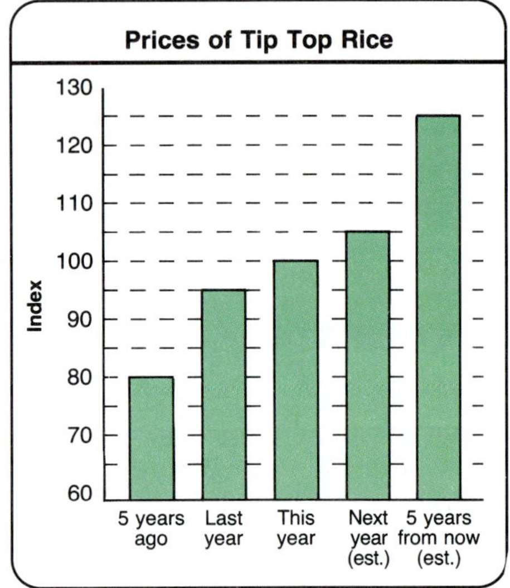

1. What is the base year? **This year**
2. The price index increased from 80 to 100 in the last 5 years. What is the price index expected to be 5 years from now? **125**
3. Is the increase in the price of Tip Top Rice expected to be less or greater in the next 5 years than in the past 5 years? **Greater**
4. A large box of Tip Top Rice sells for \$1.20 this year. How much would it have cost 5 years ago?

Think: $\frac{\text{Today's price}}{\text{Today's index}} = \frac{\text{Price 5 years ago}}{\text{Index 5 years ago}}$

Today's price: \$1.20
Today's index: 100
Price 5 years ago: n
Index 5 years ago: 80

$$\frac{1.20}{100} = \frac{n}{80}$$

\$0.96 $\underline{\ ?\ } = n$

5. How much would a large box of Tip Top Rice have cost one year ago? **\$1.14**
6. What is the estimated price of a large box of Tip Top Rice next year? **\$1.26**
7. What percent of this year's price is \$1.26? Is this percent the same as the estimated price index for next year? **105%; Yes**

Chapter Summary

IMPORTANT IDEAS

1. Consumers can use the nutrition labels on food packages to select foods that are good "nutrition buys."
2. **Unit Price = Cost of Item ÷ Number of Units**
3. **Amount Paid for an Item = Regular Price − Coupon Savings**
4. **Amount of Meat Needed = Number of Servings ÷ Servings Per Pound**
5. **Cost Per Serving of Meat = Cost Per Pound ÷ Servings Per Pound**
6. **Total Cost of Restaurant Meal = Cost of Meal + Sales Tax + Tip**

Chapter Review

Part 1: VOCABULARY

For Exercises 1–5, choose from the box at the right the word(s) that complete(s) each statement.

unit price
serving
sales tax
quality
servings per pound
cost per serving
tip

1. The cost of an item per gram, per pound, per liter and so on, is called the ___?___. (Pages 203–205) unit price
2. When using unit prices to determine the better buy, be sure that the ___?___ of the products compared is the same. (Pages 203–205) quality
3. A shopper can find the amount of meat needed for a meal by knowing the number of servings needed and the number of ___?___. (Pages 210–212) servings per pound
4. To find which of two meats costs less to serve, compare the ___?___ for each meat. (Pages 210–212) cost per serving
5. The total cost of a restaurant meal includes the cost of a meal, the ___?___, and the ___?___. (Pages 213–215) sales tax tip

Chapter Summary

The Chapter Summary contains a listing of the important ideas that were presented in the chapter. This listing is intended to assist the student with the Chapter Review that follows.

Objective

To review the important terms, skills, problem solving, and applications presented in Chapter 9.

Overview

The Chapter Review is structured in three parts. Part 1 is a review of the important terms that were introduced in the chapter. Part 2 reviews the skills that were presented in the chapter. Part 3 reviews the problem-solving strategies and applications that were presented in the chapter. Each item in the Chapter Review is referenced to the related pages where the concept, skill, or application was presented.

Using the Pages

You may wish to assign this Chapter Review for homework or treat it as a class review prior to administering the formal Chapter Test. In doing this, it is suggested that you only use the even- or odd-numbered exercises. You can then use the remaining exercises as a bank for use later.

Part 2: SKILLS

Find the better buy. (Pages 203–205)

6. Three oranges for 35¢, or ten oranges for $1.19 **3 for 35¢**

7. A 2-pound bag of sugar for 79¢, or a 5-pound bag of sugar for $1.53 **5-pound bag**

For Exercises 8–11, first double the coupon savings. Then find the actual price. (Pages 206–207)

	Item	Regular Price	Coupon Savings
8.	Eggs	$0.89	$0.06 **$0.77**
9.	Lettuce	$0.79	$0.15 **$0.49**

	Item	Regular Price	Coupon Savings
10.	Cereal	$2.24	$0.35 **$1.54**
11.	Flour	$1.69	$0.20 **$1.29**

Complete each table. Refer to the table on page 210. (Pages 210–212)

	Meat	Number of Servings	Pounds of Meat Needed
12.	Stew meat	7	? **$1\frac{2}{5}$**
13.	Spareribs	8	? **6**

	Meat	Price Per Pound	Cost Per Serving
14.	Ham (cooked)	$1.82	? **$0.52**
15.	Lamb chops	$5.49	? **$1.83**

Complete the table. (Pages 213–215)

	Appetizer	Dinner	Dessert	Beverage	Cost of Meal	5% Sales Tax	15% Tip	Total Cost
16.	$2.25	$8.90	$1.60	75¢	? **$13.50**	? **$0.68**	? **$2.10**	? **$16.28**
17.	$1.80	$7.20	$1.40	95¢	? **$11.35**	? **$0.57**	? **$1.65**	? **$13.57**

Part 3: APPLICATIONS

For Exercises 18–20, use the nutrition label. (Pages 200–202)

18. How many calories are there in a serving of crushed pineapple? **90 calories**

19. A diet low in sodium (salt) requires no more than 500 milligrams of sodium per day. What percent of this daily requirement is contained in one serving of crushed pineapple? **2%**

20. There are 3.6 milligrams of Vitamin C in one serving of crushed pineapple. What is the approximate U.S. RDA for Vitamin C? **60 milligrams**

CRUSHED PINEAPPLE

SERVING SIZE .... ½ cup

NUTRITIONAL INFORMATION PER SERVING

CALORIES 90
CARBOHYDRATES .... 23 g
SODIUM .... 10 mg

% U.S. RDA PER SERVING

VITAMIN C 6%
THIAMIN 6%

21. A 16-ounce package of crackers cost $1.39. Find the unit price. Round your answer to the nearest tenth of a cent. (Pages 203–205) **8.7¢**

22. Which is the better buy?
  a. 16-ounce bag of rice for 29¢
  b. 24-ounce bag of rice for 36¢
  (Pages 203–205) **b**

For Exercises 23–25, refer to these coupons. (Pages 206–207)

23. Find the price Gina paid for 3 cans of coffee and a loaf of bread when she used discount coupons. **$10.39**

24. How much would Gina have paid at a store offering double discount savings? **$6.09**

25. Stuart has $5.00 in his pocket. Does he have enough money to buy three loaves of bread and one can of coffee if he uses discount coupons? **No; the total cost would be $5.97.**

For Exercises 26–27, use the table on page 210. (Pages 210–212)

26. Ground beef costs $1.59 per pound. Spareribs cost $1.30 per pound. Which meat costs less to serve? **Ground beef**

27. How many pounds of pork chops should Gina buy to serve 7 people? **$1\frac{3}{4}$ pounds**

28. A dinner at Big Burger Restaurant costs $4.59. The sales tax rate is 6%. Find the amount of sales tax due. (Pages 213–215) **$0.28**

29. Craig's restaurant meal cost $6.20. The sales tax rate was 5%. Craig left a tip of 15%. Find the total cost. (Pages 213–215) **$7.44**

Use this information for Exercises 30–31. (Pages 216–218)

The cost of a 10-second commercial is one half the cost of a 30-second commercial.
The cost of a 60-second commercial is twice the cost of a 30-second commercial.
The cost for a 30-second commercial is $9800.

30. Find the total cost of three 10-second commercials and one 30-second commercial. **$24,500**

31. Find the total cost of two 30-second commercials and three 60-second commercials. **$78,400**

Objective

To informally assess students' mastering of the major skills, concepts, problem solving, and applications presented in Chapter 9

Using the Page

After completing the Chapter Review with the class, you may wish to use this Chapter Test as an informal assessment. This Chapter Test parallels the formal chapter tests (Form A and Form B) provided in the *Teacher's ResourceBank.*™

Chapter Test

LOWFAT YOGURT

NUTRITIONAL INFORMATION PER 1-CUP SERVING

CARBOHYDRATE	43 g
SODIUM	120 mg

% U.S. RDA PER SERVING

PROTEIN	20
RIBOFLAVIN	30
CALCIUM	35
VITAMIN B_{12}	15

1. How many milligrams of sodium are in each serving of lowfat yogurt? **120 milligrams**
2. A diet low in sodium requires no more than 500 milligrams of sodium per day. What percent of this 500 milligrams is contained in one serving of lowfat yogurt? **24%**
3. There are 350 milligrams of calcium in one serving of lowfat yogurt. What is the U.S. RDA for calcium? **1000 milligrams**

For Exercises 4–7, find the better buy.

	Item	Smaller Quantity	Larger Quantity
4.	Taco Shells	12/\$1.35	18/\$1.86 **Larger**
5.	Cucumbers	3/69¢ **Smaller**	4/99¢

	Item	Smaller Quantity	Larger Quantity
6.	Honey	2 lb/\$2.49 **Smaller**	3 lb/\$3.79
7.	Nuts	$2\frac{1}{2}$ oz/89¢	6 oz/\$1.65 **Larger**

8. On double-discount savings day, Phil used coupons worth 79¢ on food that regularly cost \$5.61. Find the amount Phil paid. **\$4.03**
9. There are $2\frac{1}{2}$ servings in one pound of pork roast. A pound of pork roast costs \$2.59. Find the cost per serving to the nearest cent. **\$1.04**

Complete the table. Find the total cost of the meal.

	Appetizer	Dinner	Dessert	Beverage	Cost of Meal	6% Sales Tax	15% Tip	Total Cost
10.	\$2.35	\$7.10	\$1.80	90¢	? **\$12.15**	? **\$0.73**	? **\$1.80**	? **\$14.68**
11.	\$1.40	\$5.20	\$1.75	65¢	? **\$9.00**	? **\$0.54**	? **\$1.35**	? **\$10.89**

12. The cost of a 10-second commercial is one half the cost of a 30-second commercial. The cost of a 60-second commercial is twice the cost of a 30-second commercial. The cost of a 30-second commercial is \$18,600. Find the total cost of three 10-second commercials and two 60-second commercials. **\$102,300**

Cumulative Maintenance: Chapters 1–9

Choose the correct answer. Choose **a, b, c,** *or* **d.**

1. Ken Hill drove 550 miles from Nashville to Indianapolis. He traveled at an average speed of 50 miles per hour. Find the total number of hours he traveled. b

a. 10 **b.** 11
c. 9.5 **d.** 10.5

2. Find the net deposit. b

		Dollars	Cents
CASH			
CHECKS	1	41	25
List	2	208	13
Each	3		
Check	4		
SUBTOTAL		?	
▸ *Less Cash Rec'd.*		81	20
NET DEPOSIT		?	

a. $330.58 **b.** $168.18
c. $167.93 **d.** $249.38

3. Divide. Round the answer to the nearest cent. b

$$\$2.78 \div 2\frac{1}{3}$$

a. $6.49 **b.** $1.19
c. $0.45 **d.** $5.11

4. Find the total cost of the car repair bill below. Include 5% sales tax on all but labor costs. a

REPAIR BILL	
Tires:	$146.95
Oil Filter and Oil:	9.85
Labor:	42.50

a. $207.14 **b.** $199.30
c. $164.60 **d.** $209.27

5. One year Brian King recorded the following operating costs for his car. b

Variable Costs	$2229.70
Fixed Costs	3410.00
Other Costs	350.00

He drove 25,000 miles. Find Brian's yearly driving cost per mile to the nearest tenth of a cent.

a. 24¢ **b.** 23.9¢
c. 25¢ **d.** 0.239¢

6. Patty Leahy drove 1356 kilometers from Dallas to Memphis. Her car's fuel economy was 12 kilometers per liter, and she paid 30¢ per liter for gasoline. Find the total cost of gasoline. c

a. 33.9¢ **b.** $113.00
c. $33.90 **d.** $3.60

7. On what day were about 175 gallons of gasoline sold? a

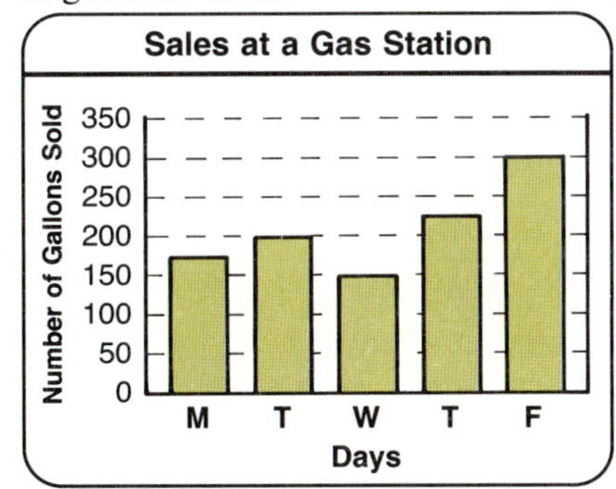

a. Monday **b.** Thursday
c. Tuesday **c.** Wednesday

Objective

To review the content presented in Chapters 1–9

Using the Pages

You may wish to use this Cumulative Maintenance as an informal assessment tool. These pages can be assigned for homework or they may be used as review in class.

8. The manager of a sporting goods store wants to arrange a bowling ball, a basketball, and a soccer ball in a window display. In how many different ways can the three objects be arranged in a row? d

a. 3 **b.** 9 **c.** 5 **d.** 6

9. A 5-ounce jar of mustard costs 59¢. Find the unit price. b

a. 12¢ **b.** 11.8¢
c. $1.18 **d.** $1.20

10. Carlos bought a box of spaghetti marked 95¢ at a store giving double coupon savings. He used the coupon below. How much did Carlos pay? c

a. $1.05
b. 80¢
c. 65¢
d. 30¢

11. Bell peppers are priced at 3 for 89¢. How much will 7 bell peppers cost? a

a. $2.08 **b.** $0.30
c. $2.07 **d.** $1.78

12. Michael Salmon has $1000 in an account that pays a yearly interest rate of 6%. How much simple interest will the account earn in six months? a

a. $30 **b.** $1030
c. $300 **d.** $60

13. Find the total cost of the car advertised below. d

TURBO EXC
$500 down
$230/month
48 months

a. $11,040 **b.** $10,540
c. $24,230 **d.** $11,540

14. Hector earns a weekly salary of $150 plus a 20% commission on all sales. Find Hector's total weekly income for a week in which his sales total $2500. a

a. $650 **b.** $2650
c. $530 **d.** $500

15. Roberta intends to buy a car that has a base price of $8700. The options that she wants cost $957. The dealer pays 80% of the base price, and 75% of the options price. Destination charges are $175. Find the dealer's cost. a

a. $7852.75 **b.** $7865.60
c. $7477.75 **d.** $9832.00

16. Round 29.666¢ to the nearest tenth of a cent. d

a. 31¢ **b.** 29.6¢ **c.** 30¢ **d.** 29.7¢

17. George Heubert earned $21,674.00 as a computer programmer last year. He also received a bonus of $500. What was his adjusted gross income? b

a. $21,174 **b.** $22,174
c. $21,674 **d.** $23,674

Housing

Sue Lee Chung is being relocated by her employer to another city. Sue Lee needs to find adequate housing for herself and her elderly mother, Lian Chung. Sue Lee wants to gather as much information as possible before she makes her decision.

- How much can Sue Lee afford to spend on housing?
- If Sue Lee decides to buy a house, how large a down payment should she make?
- How is the monthly payment for a mortgage loan calculated?
- How much will Sue Lee have to pay for homeowner's insurance?
- How much will Sue Lee have to pay in property taxes?

Chapter 10: Housing

Overview

The focus of Chapter 10 is on housing. The lessons of this chapter explore mortgage loans, monthly mortgage payments, homeowner's insurance, and property taxes. Since costs associated with home ownership vary according to location, you may wish to have your students collect currect local information on the various topics studied.

Although all lessons in this chapter involve problem solving, the strategy lesson on pages 243–244 applies the skill of solving proportions to problems involving scale drawings. The *Consumer's Choice* on pages 248–249 presents a **situational lesson** in which students make housing decisions in a real-life situation. Finally, the *Enrichment* lesson on page 250 deals with closing costs and mortgage points.

Using This Page

Have students read the introductory paragraph and questions. Have them list possible solutions to the problems presented. After completing the chapter, have students review their suggested solutions, comparing them with those presented in the lessons. You may wish to have students suggest other possible problems resulting from the situation described on this page and to discuss possible solutions.

You may wish to organize the class into small groups to complete the situational activity described on this *Using the Page*.

Lesson Resources

Maintenance: See below.
Reteaching/Alternate Teaching Strategy: p. M-37 (Visual 28)
Practice: p. M-37
Enrichment: p. M-37
Concrete Materials: Activity Worksheet 53C
Visual 28

Objective

Student will solve problems that involve renting costs.

Maintenance

1. Multiply: 130×8 ANS: 1040
2. Divide: $384 \div 12$ ANS: 32
3. Solve for x: $6x = 108$ ANS: $x = 18$
4. Solve the proportion. $\frac{3}{5} = \frac{x}{20}$ ANS: $x = 12$
5. Two pounds of hamburger are needed to make pizza for 15 people. How many pounds are needed to make pizza for 60 people? ANS: 8 pounds

1 Lesson Focus

Motivation: As a class or in small groups, have students list some of the advantages of renting a house or an apartment, as opposed to buying.

Purpose: In this lesson, students learn to apply a guideline for affordable housing. Since many students will be renters in the future, the ability to determine if the amount of rent is affordable is an important consumer skill.

STRATEGY: USING A "HIDDEN QUESTION" TO SOLVE A MULTI-STEP PROBLEM

Renting

Sue Lee Chung is moving to a new city. She needs to find adequate housing for herself and her mother, Lian Chung. One option Sue Lee is considering is renting an apartment. A real estate agent gave her this guideline.

> An average affordable amount to spend on housing is one-fourth to one-third of the net household income.

1. What does "net household income" mean? The take-home pay of all of the working members of the household.
2. Would an apartment which costs $\frac{1}{5}$ of the net monthly income be affordable? Why? Yes; one-fifth is less than one-fourth.

Park Slope Area
2 Bedroom
2 Bath
$469 per month

EXAMPLE Sue Lee and her mother have a net income of $1490 per month. Can they afford the apartment in the advertisement?

[1] What are $\frac{1}{4}$ and $\frac{1}{3}$ of their net household income? Round to the nearest cent.

$\frac{1}{4}$ of \$1490 $= \$1490 \times \frac{1}{4}$ $= \mathbf{\$372.50}$

$\frac{1}{3}$ of \$1490 $= \$1490 \times \frac{1}{3}$ $= \mathbf{\$496.67}$

[2] Compare the amount in the advertisement to the amounts in Step 1.

Is $469 between $372.50 and $496.67? Yes.

Sue Lee and her mother **can afford** the apartment.

3. Is the price of the apartment closer to $\frac{1}{3}$ or $\frac{1}{4}$ of the Chung's net household income? $\frac{1}{3}$
4. Why might Sue Lee and Lian look for a less expensive apartment? See below.

CHECK YOUR SKILLS

Multiply. For additional practice, see page 389.

1. $\$1580 \times \frac{1}{4}$ $395
2. $\$1155 \times \frac{1}{3}$ $385
3. $\$1750 \times \frac{1}{4}$ $437.50
4. $\$1263 \times \frac{1}{3}$ $421
5. $\$1479 \times \frac{1}{3}$ $493

Round to the nearest cent. For additional practice, see page 378.

6. $548.333 $548.33
7. $546.666 $546.67
8. $326.125 $326.13
9. $348.812 $348.81
10. $691.799 $691.80

4. It would be easier to pay a rent closer to $\frac{1}{4}$ of their household income if some unexpected expenses arose.

EXERCISES

1. *Complete:* As a general guideline, people can afford to spend between _?_ and _?_ of their net household income on housing. $\frac{1}{4}$; $\frac{1}{3}$

For Exercises 2–5, complete the table.

	Proposed Rent	Net Income	$\frac{1}{4}$ of Income	$\frac{1}{3}$ of Income	Between $\frac{1}{3}$ and $\frac{1}{4}$?
2.	$525	$1750	? $437.50	? $583.33	? Yes
3.	$550	$1600	? $400	? $533.33	? No
4.	$700	$2245	? $561.25	? $748.33	? Yes
5.	$445	$1784	? $446	? $594.67	? No

For Exercises 6–7, decide if Sue Lee and Lian can afford the apartment advertised.

6. **Carlton Arms**
Affordable Luxury
2 bedrooms — $370 per month
Yes

7. **Monterey Terrace**
Spacious Living Area
2 bedrooms — $500 per month
No

8. Marilyn Smith's monthly net income is $1645. Can she afford to rent an apartment which costs $525 per month? Yes

9. Jake Walters has an *annual* net income of $15,300. According to the guideline, what is the most he should budget per month for rent? $425

Pete is a college student. He usually spends $2700 for dorm housing for the school year (9 months). A friend of Pete's asks him to share an apartment and pay half the monthly rent of $440.

10. How much does Pete usually pay for dorm housing for a school year? $2700

11. How much would Pete pay for living in the apartment for the school year? $1980

12. Pete is considering taking summer courses this year. Would the cost of renting the apartment for 12 months be less than the cost of dorm housing for 9 months? Yes; $60 less

2 Teaching the Lesson

Discuss the affordable housing guideline with the students. Emphasize that it is just a guideline and that individual considerations may result in spending less than one-fourth or more than one-third of income on housing. Be sure that students understand that $\frac{1}{4}$ of the income is less than $\frac{1}{3}$ of the income. Then have students answer questions 1 and 2. After presenting the Example, have students answer question 3. You may wish to have the students discuss question 4 in small groups first and then as a class.

3 Close

Summary: Ask a student to explain the guideline used to determine affordable housing.

Evaluation
Guided Practice: Ex. 1, 2–6 even
Independent Practice: Ex. 3–7 odd, 8–12

Extension

Have students look in a local newspaper and find the range of rental prices for houses and apartments advertised. Have them find the income needed to afford the lowest rent and the income needed to afford the highest rent.

Problem-Solving Skills

Making a comparison (Ex. 2–8, 12)
Solving a multi-step problem (Ex. 6–9, 12)
Interpreting information (Ex. 8–12)
Choosing the operation (Ex. 9, 11, 12)

Critical Thinking

You may wish to have students work in small groups to solve this problem or you may wish to work with the class.

Question 4 (in Lesson)

Lesson Resources

Maintenance: See below.
Reteaching/Alternate Teaching
Strategy: p. M-38 (Visual 29)
Practice: p. M-38
Enrichment: p. M-38
Visual 29

Objectives

Student will

1. find the amount of down payment and the amount of mortgage.
2. solve multi-step problems that involve the amount of interest charged on a mortgage.

Maintenance

Complete.

1. 1 foot = __?__ inches ANS: 12
2. 1 gallon = __?__ quarts ANS: 4
3. 35 inches = 2 feet __?__ inches ANS: 11
4. 15 quarts = __?__ gallons 3 quarts ANS: 3
5. A caterer used a recipe which requires 1 quart of orange juice for each bowl of punch. How much orange juice should the caterer use for 25 bowls of punch? Give the answer in gallons and quarts. ANS: 6 gallons 1 quart

1 Lesson Focus

Motivation: As a class or in small groups, have the students list some of the advantages of buying a house, as opposed to renting.

Purpose: As adult consumers, many students will obtain a mortgage for a house. This lesson shows students how to find the amount of the down payment, the amount of the mortgage loan, and the amount of interest charged for a mortgage loan.

STRATEGY: USING "HIDDEN QUESTIONS" TO SOLVE A MULTI-STEP PROBLEM

Mortgage Loans

Sue Lee Chung and her mother want to explore the cost of buying a house. Sue Lee knows that most people who buy a home pay part of the purchase price of the house with a down payment. The remainder of the purchase price is borrowed by obtaining a mortgage loan from a bank or other lending institution.

1. Why do most people need a mortgage loan?
   They cannot save the total cost of a house.

EXAMPLE 1 Sue Lee and her mother look at a house which costs $74,000. The down payment is 20% of the purchase price.

a. What is the amount of down payment?

20% of $74,000 = $74,000 × 0.20

= **$14,800**

b. What is the amount of the mortgage loan?

$74,000 − $14,800 = **$59,200** ◀ *Purchase Price − Down Payment = Amount of Mortgage*

Mortgage loans are repaid with interest in equal monthly payments over a specified number of years.

EXAMPLE 2 A bank loan officer tells Sue Lee Chung that she could take out a 30-year mortgage loan for $59,200. The monthly mortgage payment would be $476.90. Find the total interest charged.

1 Find the total number of monthly payments.

12 × 30 = **360** ◀ *12 months per year × Number of Years = Total Number of Monthly Payments*

2 Find the total of the monthly payments.

$476.90 × 360 = **$171,684** ◀ *Monthly Payment × Number of Months = Total of Monthly Payments*

3 Find the amount of interest.

$171,684 − $59,200 = **$112,484** ◀ *Total of Monthly Payments − Amount of Mortgage = Amount of Interest*

Banks and other lending institutions usually offer 15-year, 20-year, and 30-year mortgage loans.

2. Explain why the monthly payment on a 30-year mortgage for $70,000 would be less than the monthly payment on a 15-year mortgage for $70,000. **Because the amount of interest on the loan would be less since the money would be paid back in less time.**

3. Explain why the interest charged on a 30-year mortgage for $90,000 would be greater than the interest charged on a 15-year mortgage for $90,000. **Since the amount of interest is dependent on the length of time the money is borrowed, the longer loan builds up more interest.**

CHECK YOUR SKILLS

Write a decimal for each percent. For additional practice, see page 405.

1. 20% **0.20 or 0.2**
2. 5% **0.05**
3. 7% **0.07**
4. 10% **0.10 or 0.1**
5. 25% **0.25**
6. 15% **0.15**

Find each answer. For additional practice, see pages 407 and 408.

7. 15% of $82,500 **$12,375**
8. 20% of $68,700 **$13,740**
9. 15% of $76,000 **$11,400**
10. 10% of $110,000 **$11,000**

Multiply. For additional practice, see page 372.

11. $568.60 × 180 **$102,348**
12. $398.50 × 360 **$143,460**
13. $618.50 × 300 **$185,550**
14. $79,000 × 0.20 **$15,800**

Complete. For additional practice, see page 367.

15. $65,000 − ? = $52,000 **$13,000**
16. $79,800 − ? = $59,850 **$19,950**
17. $216,996 − ? = $151,996 **$65,000**
18. $171,651 − ? = $120,451 **$51,200**

EXERCISES

Complete. Choose your answers from the box at the right below.

1. Most people who buy a home pay part of the purchase price with a ? and obtain a ? to pay for the remainder of the purchase price. **down payment; mortgage loan**

2. The amount of down payment is usually a ? of the purchase price. **percent**

3. Purchase Price − Down Payment = ? **amount of mortgage**

4. Monthly Payment × Number of Months = ? **total of monthly payments**

5. Total of Monthly Payments − Amount of Mortgage = ? **amount of interest**

amount of interest
mortgage loan
total of monthly payments
percent
down payment
amount of mortgage

2 Teaching the Lesson

Have a volunteer read the opening paragraph. Ask these questions to be sure students understand the terms which will be used in the lesson.

1. What is a "down payment"? (The amount paid on a house before obtaining a mortgage)
2. What is a "mortgage loan"? (A loan obtained from a bank or other lending institution to pay for a house)
3. What is "interest" on a loan? (The amount paid for use of the money)

Have the students answer question 1. Then discuss Example 1. Point out the relationship between the down payment and the mortgage loan. Show students that a larger down payment will result in a smaller mortgage amount.

Then discuss Example 2. Point out that the amount of interest on a mortgage loan is usually greater than the amount of the mortgage. Then discuss questions 2 and 3.

3 Close

Summary: Ask selected students to explain how to find the amount of a down payment, the amount of a mortgage, the total of the monthly payments, and the amount of interest charged on a mortgage.

Evaluation

Guided Practice: Ex. 1–5, 6–10 even, 14, 16

Independent Practice: Ex. 7–11 odd, 12, 13, 15, 17–21

Critical Thinking

You may wish to have students work in small groups to solve these problems or you may wish to work with the class. Questions 2 and 3 (in Lesson)

Problem-Solving Skills

Interpreting information (Ex. 12, 13, 18–21)
Using estimation (Ex. 13)
Choosing the operation (Ex. 18–20)
Solving a multi-step problem (Ex. 18–21)
Making a comparison (Ex. 18–21)

Estimation Ex. 13

For Exercises 6–11, find the amount of down payment and the amount of mortgage.

	Purchase Price	Rate of Down Payment
6.	$40,000	10% $4,000; $36,000
7.	$76,000	25% $19,000; $57,000
8.	$92,000	20% $18,400; $73,600

	Purchase Price	Rate of Down Payment
9.	$160,000	10% $16,000; $144,000
10.	$88,000	25% $22,000; $66,000
11.	$69,000	10% $6,900; $62,100

12. Sam Lange wants to buy a house which costs $65,000. He must make a down payment of 25% of the purchase price. What is the amount of the down payment? **$16,250**

13. Evelyn Haskins wants to buy a house which costs $88,900. She must make a down payment of 33% of the purchase price. Estimate the amount of the down payment. **About $30,000**

For Exercises 14–17, complete the table.

	Amount of Mortgage	Length of Mortgage (Years)	Number of Monthly Payments	Monthly Payment	Total of Monthly Payments	Amount of Interest
14.	$60,000	20	? 240	$579.60	? $139,104	? $79,104
15.	$49,000	30	? 360	$466.97	? $168,109.20	? $119,109.20
16.	$72,000	15	? 180	$795.60	? $143,208	? $71,208
17.	$85,000	30	? 360	$777.75	? $279,990	? $194,990

Sue Lee and Lian Chung like a house which costs $67,000. They go to two different lending institutions to shop for a mortgage loan.

Sunrise Federal Savings
Down Payment: 15%
Length of Mortgage: 30 years
Monthly Payment: $542.75

First National Bank of Sparta
Down Payment: 10%
Length of Mortgage: 30 years
Monthly Payment: $551.75

18. Which mortgage loan plan has the greater down payment? How much greater? **Sunrise Federal Savings; $3350**

19. Which mortgage loan has the greater total of monthly payments? How much greater? **First National Bank of Sparta; $3240**

20. With which mortgage loan will Sue Lee and Lian have to pay the greater amount of interest? How much greater? **Sunrise Federal Savings; $110**

21. Which mortgage has the greater total cost (down payment + mortgage + amount of interest)? How much greater? **Sunrise Federal Savings; $110**

STRATEGY: USING "HIDDEN QUESTIONS" TO SOLVE A MULTI-STEP PROBLEM

Monthly Mortgage Payments

Each time Sue Lee and Lian Chung find a house that they consider buying they want to know the amount of the monthly mortgage payment. They want to be sure that the payment is affordable for them.

The amount of the monthly mortgage payment depends on:

a. The amount of the mortgage
b. The time taken to pay off the mortgage
c. The interest rate

You can use a table to find the monthly payment.

Mortgage Loan Schedule
Monthly Cost per $1000

Years	9%	9.5%	10%	10.5%	11%	11.5%	12%	12.5%	13%
15	$10.14	$10.44	$10.75	$11.05	$11.37	$11.68	$12.00	$12.33	$12.65
20	9.00	9.32	9.65	9.98	10.32	10.66	11.01	11.36	11.72
25	8.39	8.74	9.09	9.44	9.80	10.17	10.53	10.90	11.28
30	8.05	8.41	8.78	9.15	9.52	9.90	10.29	10.67	11.06

1. *Complete:* The table shows monthly cost per __?__. $1000
2. How many $1000's are there in $72,000? 72

EXAMPLE

Sue Lee and Lian consider a mortgage loan of $65,000. If they agree to pay 10% interest and to repay the loan in 30 years, what will the monthly mortgage payment be?

[1] Find 30 under Years in the table.
Look to the right under 10%. → **$8.78** ◀ *Monthly Cost per $1000*

[2] Find the number of thousands borrowed.
65,000 ÷ 1000 = **65**

[3] Find the monthly payment.
$8.78 × 65 = **$570.70** ◀ *Monthly Cost Per $1000* × *Number of 1000's* = *Monthly Payment*

Lesson Resources

Maintenance: See below.
Reteaching/Alternate Teaching Strategy: p. M-38 (Visual 30)
Practice: p. M-38
Enrichment: p. M-38
Concrete Materials: Activity Worksheet 55C, and Visual 30
Visual 30

Objective

Student will use a table to solve multi-step problems that involve monthly mortgage payments.

Maintenance

1. Write $4\frac{2}{5}$ as a fraction. ANS: $\frac{22}{5}$
2. Multiply: $3 \times 5\frac{1}{3}$ ANS: 16
3. Multiply: $4 \times 6 \times 15$ ANS: 360
4. A rectangle has a length of 12 feet and a width of $6\frac{1}{2}$ feet. Find the area. ANS: 78 ft^2
5. Find the volume. ANS: 480 cm^3

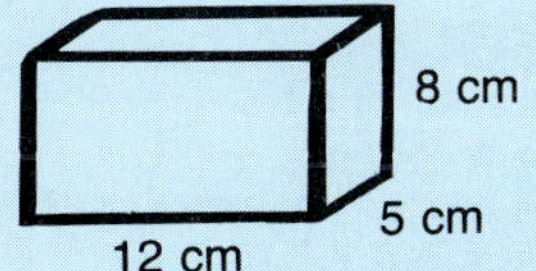

[1] Lesson Focus

Motivation: Ask students to name items that consumers might purchase using monthly payments.

Purpose: This lesson shows students how to use a mortgage loan schedule to find the amount of a monthly payment. The table is also an effective tool for showing how the monthly payments change with the amount of interest charged.

2 Teaching the Lesson

Have a student read the introductory material above the table. Then direct the students' attention to the table. Point out that the monthly cost depends on the amount of interest and the number of years of the mortgage. Emphasize that the monthly costs shown in the table are for each $1000 of the loan. Then have students answer questions 1 and 2.

Work through the Example, making sure each student understands steps 2 and 3. Then discuss questions 3 and 4.

Note that Exercise 14 reviews the affordable housing guideline from page 230.

3 Close

Summary: Ask a student to explain how to use the mortgage loan schedule to find the amount of a monthly payment.

Evaluation
Guided Practice: Ex. 1–4, 6–10 even
Independent Practice: Ex. 5–9 odd, 11–14

Extension

Have students look at a local newspaper to find the price of a house which is for sale. Have them find:

1. the amount of a 10% down payment.
2. the amount of the mortgage.
3. the amount of the monthly payment at 10.5% for 30 years.
4. the total monthly payments.
5. the total interest paid.
6. how much income would be required to afford the house.

You may wish to adapt the amount of the down payment and the interest rate to reflect current local conditions.

Critical Thinking

You may wish to have students work in small groups to solve these problems or you may wish to work with the class. Questions 3 and 4 (in Lesson)

3. It would decrease the monthly payment. Note that in the table as the number of years increases for each interest rate, the monthly cost per $1000 decreases.

3. Suppose the Chungs took the mortgage loan for 35 years rather than 30 years. How would this affect the monthly mortgage payment?

4. Suppose the Chungs obtained the above mortgage at an 11% interest rate rather than a 10% interest rate. How would this affect the monthly mortgage payment?
It would increase the monthly payment. Note that in the table as the interest rate increases for each number of years, the monthly cost per $1000 increases.

CHECK YOUR SKILLS

Divide without using paper and pencil. For additional practice, see page 375.

1. 125,000 ÷ 1000 125 **2.** 80,000 ÷ 1000 80 **3.** 65,000 ÷ 1000 65 **4.** 81,000 ÷ 1000 81

Multiply For additional practice, see pages 370, 372, and 389.

5. $9.99 × 55 $549.45 **6.** $623.38 × 360 $224,416.80 **7.** $10.32 × 71 $732.72 **8.** 20 × 12 240

9. $10.29 × 93 $956.97 **10.** $1800 × $\frac{1}{4}$ $450 **11.** $9.91 × 40 $396.40 **12.** $549.45 × 240 $131,868

13. 30 × 12 $360 **14.** $8.05 × 60 $483 **15.** $1800 × $\frac{1}{3}$ $600 **16.** $9.32 × 131 $1220.92

Subtract. For additional practice, see page 369.

17. $505.41 − $485.52 $19.89 **18.** $284,457.60 − $192,228.85 $92,228.75 **19.** $800.95 − $790.16 $10.79

EXERCISES

2. Larger down payment; borrowing less money results in a lower monthly payment.

For each of Exercises 1–4, select the option that could result in a lower monthly mortgage payment. Give a reason for each choice.

1. Purchase a house that is more expensive or a house which is less expensive Less expensive; a lower loan amount results in a lower monthly payment.

2. Make a larger down payment or a smaller down payment See above.

3. Obtain a mortgage loan with a higher interest rate or with a lower interest rate Lower interest rate; paying a lower rate results in a lower monthly payment.

4. Obtain a mortgage loan payable over a greater number of years or over a fewer number of years. Greater number of years; repaying the loan over a greater number of years results in a lower monthly payment.

For Exercise 5–10, find the amount of the monthly mortgage payment. Use the table on page 235.

	Amount of Mortgage	Interest Rate	Length of Mortgage (Years)
5.	$83,000	10%	20 **$800.95**
6.	$69,000	11.5%	15 **$805.92**
7.	$115,000	9%	30 **$925.75**

	Amount of Mortgage	Interest Rate	Length of Mortgage (Years)
8.	$92,000	12%	30 **$946.68**
9.	$71,000	13%	15 **$898.15**
10.	$79,000	10.5%	30 **$722.85**

Problem-Solving Skills

Solving a multi-step problem (Ex. 5–14)
Using a table (Ex. 5–14)
Choosing the operation (Ex. 12–14)
Interpreting information (Ex. 11–14)
Making a comparison (Ex. 13, 14)

For Exercises 11–14, use the table on page 235.

11. The Burhenn family obtains a $60,000 mortgage at 12%. The mortgage is to be repaid over 30 years. How much will their monthly mortgage payment be? **$617.40**

12. Find the difference in the amount of the monthly payment for a $72,000 mortgage at 10% for 30 years, and a $72,000 mortgage at 10.5% for 30 years. **$26.64**

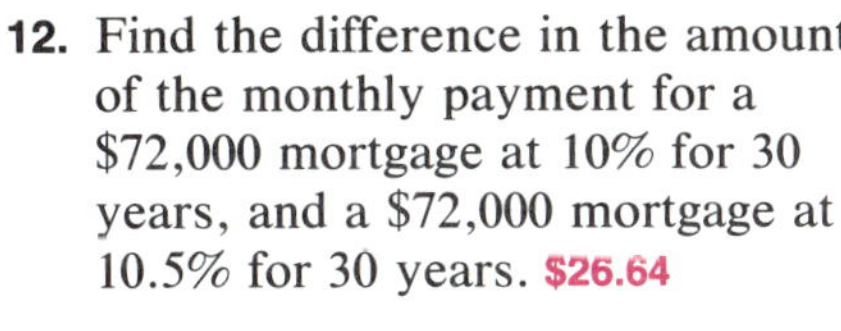

13. One bank offers a $64,000 mortgage at 10.5% payable over 20 years. Another bank offers a $64,000 mortgage at 11.5% payable over 30 years.

a. Which mortgage has the lower monthly payment? How much lower is it? **11.5% over 30 years; $5.12**

b. With which mortgage would you pay more interest? How much more? **11.5% over 30 years; $74,803.20**

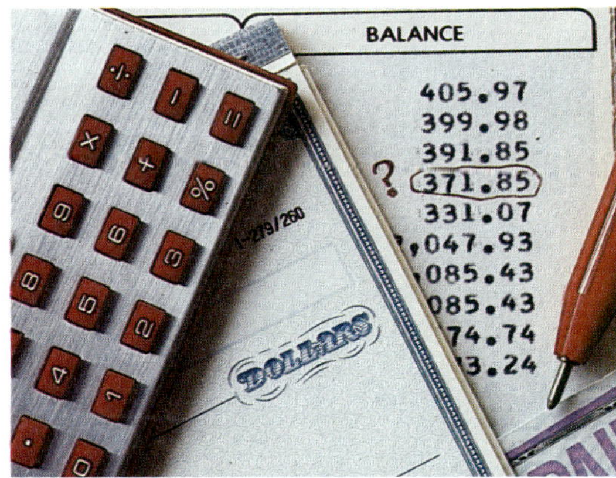

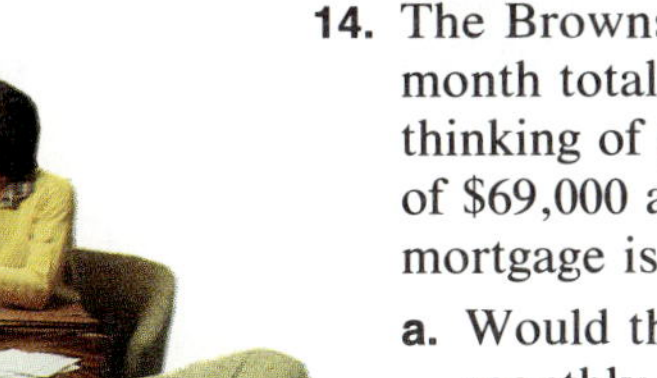

14. The Browns' net earnings each month total $2100. They are thinking of getting a mortgage loan of $69,000 at 12% interest. The mortgage is payable over 30 years.

a. Would the amount of the monthly mortgage payment be between $\frac{1}{3}$ and $\frac{1}{4}$ of their monthly net income? Explain.

No. The monthly mortgage payment would be $710.01, which is more than $\frac{1}{3}$ of their net monthly income ($700).

Objective

Student will

1. review the skills, concepts, and applications in the first part of Chapter 10.
2. maintain key skills and concepts taught in Chapters 1 and 9.

Using the Page

Exercises 1–8 provide an informal assessment of the student's mastery of the major skills and concepts presented in the first half of Chapter 10. Each item is referenced to the related pages where the particular item was presented. These exercises parallel the quiz provided in the *Teacher's ResourceBank.*™

A quiz covering the second half of the chapter is also provided in the *Teacher's ResourceBank.*™

Exercises 9–10 maintain skills and concepts taught in Chapters 1 and 9.

Mid-Chapter Review

1. The Waters family wants to move into an apartment that rents for $625. To afford the apartment, the rent should be between $\frac{1}{4}$ and $\frac{1}{3}$ of the family's monthly net household income of $1863. Can they afford it? (Pages 230–231) **No; $\frac{1}{3}$ of their net monthly income is $621.**

2. Louise Anatro wants to move into an apartment that rents for $435. To afford the apartment, the rent should be between $\frac{1}{4}$ and $\frac{1}{3}$ of her net yearly household income of $15,000. Can she afford it? (Pages 230–231) **No; $\frac{1}{3}$ of her net monthly income is $416.67.**

3. Susie Barrochas wants to buy a house which costs $72,000. She must make a down payment of 15% of the purchase price. What is the amount of the down payment? (Pages 232–234) **$10,800**

4. Tom Sneech wants to buy a house which costs $69,000. He must make a down payment of 20% of the purchase price. What is the amount of the mortgage loan? (Pages 232–234) **$55,200**

Complete the table. (Pages 232–234)

	Amount of Mortgage	Length of Mortgage (Years)	Number of Monthly Payments	Monthly Payment	Total of Monthly Payments	Amount of Interest
5.	$65,000	15	? **180**	$718.25	? **$129,285**	? **$64,285**
6.	$130,000	30	? **360**	$1287.00	? **$463,320**	? **$333,320**

For Exercises 7–8, find the monthly mortgage payment. Use the table on page 235. (Pages 235–237)

7. The Fossums get a mortgage loan of $80,000. They will pay 11.5% interest over 25 years. **$813.60**

8. The Van Dykes get a mortgage loan of $62,000. They will pay 11% interest over 30 years. **$590.24**

MAINTENANCE

9. Find the total cost of the meal below. Include 6% sales tax and a 15% tip. (Pages 213–215) **$24.20**

Salad:	$2.75	Dessert:	$3.50
Dinner:	$12.25	Beverage:	$1.50

10. The graph at the right shows bicycle sales over several months. Find the mean, median, and mode. (Pages 10–13)
Mean: 42.9; Median: 45; Mode: 60

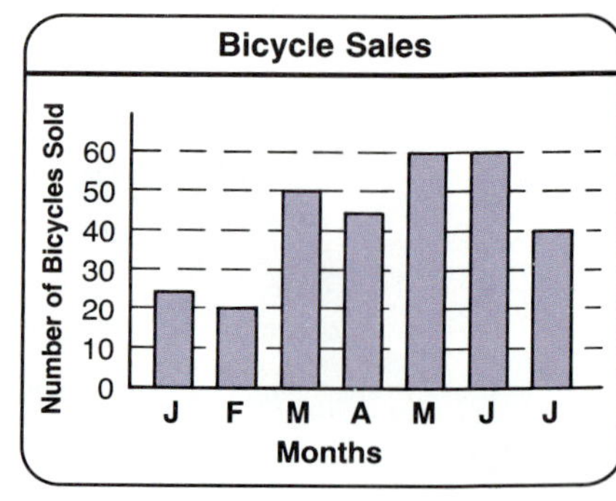

Math and Property Management

Leon Endicott is the property manager for an office building that contains 30,000 square meters of space. He has to determine the yearly operating expenses, such as utilities, for the entire building.

EXAMPLE Leon estimates that the yearly cost for utilities is $1.60 per square meter. Find the estimated yearly cost for utilities for the building.

READ What are the facts?

Number of square meters: 30,000 Cost per square meter: $1.60

PLAN Number of Square Meters × Cost per Square Meter = Utilities Cost

SOLVE 30,000 × $1.60 = **$48,000**

CHECK Did you use all the facts correctly in the solution?

The yearly utilities cost is about **$48,000.**

EXERCISES

For Exercises 1–4, complete the table.

	Operating Expense	Number of Square Meters	Estimated Cost per Square Meter	Estimated Yearly Cost
1.	Advertising	30,000	$0.40	? $12,000
2.	Insurance	30,000	$0.70	? $21,000
3.	Maintenance	30,000	$2.90	? $87,000
4.	Real estate taxes	30,000	$4.50	? $135,000

5. Find the total of the estimated yearly costs for the building, including utilities. $303,000

6. The yearly rental income for the building is $420,000. Which is greater, costs or income? How much greater? Income; $117,000

PROJECT Determine how many square meters of space your home or apartment contains. Then, using the cost of utilities for one month, determine the utility expense per square meter.

Objective

Student will use a formula to find the estimated cost of expenses.

Overview

This page is an extension of the skills and ideas presented in the previous lessons of this chapter. Since the content presented on this page is not included in the Chapter Review or Chapter Test, its use is optional.

Using the Pages

You may wish to have students work this lesson in small groups or you may wish to work with the class. Using it with the class, have a student read the opening paragraph. Then discuss the Example. Use Exercise 1 as guided practice and assign Exercises 2–6 as independent practice.

Problem-Solving Skills

Completing a table (Ex. 1–4)
Making a comparison (Ex. 6)

Lesson Resources

Maintenance: See below.
Reteaching/Alternate Teaching Strategy: p. M-39 (Visuals 31 and 32)
Practice: p. M-39
Enrichment: p. M-39
Concrete Materials: Activity Worksheet 56C, and Visuals 31 and 32
Visuals 31 and 32

Objectives

Student will

1. use a table to solve problems that involve homeowner's insurance coverage.
2. use a table to solve problems that involve monthly premiums for homeowner's insurance.

Maintenance

1. Complete: $\frac{15}{20} = \frac{?}{100}$ ANS: 75
2. Express $\frac{9}{10}$ as a percent. ANS: 90%
3. Divide: 60 ÷ 80 ANS: $\frac{3}{4}$, or 0.75
4. What percent of 15 is 6? ANS: 40%
5. Out of 50 people surveyed, 30 prefer Brand Z. What percent of those surveyed prefer Brand Z? ANS: 60%

1 Lesson Focus

Motivation: As a class or in small groups, have students make a list of ways in which their home or its contents could be damaged.

Purpose: This lesson shows students the kinds of protection and the coverage provided by homeowner's insurance. The lesson also shows the factors that determine the cost of homeowner's insurance.

Homeowner's Insurance

When Sue Lee Chung applied at her bank for a mortgage, she learned that she must purchase **homeowner's insurance** to protect herself and the bank from loss. The kinds of protection and the coverage provided by many homeowner's insurance policies are shown in the table.

Category	Coverage
Home	100% of policy
Additional Structures	10% of policy
Personal Property on or off the Premises	50% of policy
Additional Living Expenses	20% of policy
*Liability	$100,000

*Liability protects homeowners from loss if someone is injured on their property.

Under which category would each of these claims be covered?

1. Lightning striking a fence
   Additional structures
2. Cost of a night spent in a motel because of a house fire
   Additional living expenses

EXAMPLE 1 Use the table to find these coverages for a $60,000 policy.

a. A storage shed on the property

10% of $60,000 = $60,000 × 0.1 = **$6,000**

b. Personal property (furniture, clothing, etc.)

50% of $60,000 = $60,000 × 0.5 = **$30,000**

The amount of money you pay for homeowner's insurance is called the **premium.** The amount of the premium depends on the amount of coverage, the material from which the house is built, and the quality of the fire protection (fire protection class).

Yearly Premiums								
Amount of Insurance Coverage	Brick/Masonry Veneer				Wood Frame			
	Fire Protection Class				Fire Protecion Class			
	1–6	7–8	9	10	1–6	7–8	9	10
40,000	133	143	172	180	143	150	180	190
50,000	153	165	197	207	165	173	207	210
60,000	178	191	230	240	191	201	240	254
70,000	203	218	263	275	218	229	275	291
80,000	233	251	302	316	251	264	316	335
90,000	263	284	341	358	284	297	358	379
100,000	294	317	382	400	317	333	400	424
150,000	446	482	582	610	482	506	610	646

EXAMPLE 2 The house that Sue Lee wants to insure is a brick structure. It is rated in fire protection class 3. Find the monthly premium for homeowner's coverage of $60,000.

[1] In the table, find $60,000 under "Amount of Insurance Coverage." Look to the right under "Brick/Masonry Veneer: Fire Protection Class 1–6."

[2] Divide the yearly premium by 12. Round to the nearest cent.

$178 ÷ 12 = **$14.83** ◀ *Monthly Premium*

3. For each fire class given, which type of construction has the less expensive yearly premium? Why? **Brick/Masonry Veneer; there is less of a fire hazard than wood.**

CHECK YOUR SKILLS

Write a fraction for each percent. **For additional practice, see page 404.**

1. 50% $\frac{1}{2}$
2. 75% $\frac{3}{4}$
3. 10% $\frac{1}{10}$
4. 25% $\frac{1}{4}$
5. 20% $\frac{1}{5}$
6. 40% $\frac{2}{5}$

Find each answer. **For additional practice, see pages 407 and 408.**

7. 2% of $125,000 **$2500**
8. 100% of $80,000 **$80,000**
9. 20% of $60,000 **$12,000**
10. 10% of $150,000 **$15,000**

Divide. Round each answer to the nearest cent. **For additional practice, see page 379.**

11. $50,000 ÷ 12 **$4166.67**
12. $90,000 ÷ 12 **$7500**
13. $70,000 ÷ 12 **$5833.33**
14. $100,000 ÷ 12 **$8333.33**
15. $40,000 ÷ 12 **$3333.33**
16. $75,000 ÷ 12 **$6250**
17. $95,000 ÷ 12 **$7916.67**
18. $150,000 ÷ 12 **$12,500**

EXERCISES

Complete. Choose your answers from the box at the right.

premium
personal property
liability
additional living expenses
additional structures
homeowner's insurance

1. The type of insurance which protects both the homeowner and the mortgage lender from loss is called __?__. **homeowner's insurance**
2. The contents of your house such as furniture, clothing, etc, would be covered under the __?__ category of an insurance policy. **personal property**
3. The category on an insurance policy which protects homeowners from loss if someone is injured on their property is known as __?__. **liability**
4. The amount paid for homeowner's insurance is known as the __?__. **premium**

[2] *Teaching the Lesson*

Have a volunteer read the introduction and the table of coverages. Discuss the table and then have students answer questions 1 and 2. After presenting Example 1, have a student read the paragraph above the Yearly Premiums table. Discuss the table and ask students to find the yearly premium for each of the following.

1. Wood Frame House
   Fire Protection Class 3
   Insurance Coverage: $50,000 ($165)
2. Brick Veneer House
   Fire Protection Class 8
   Insurance Coverage: $80,000 ($251)

Discuss Example 2 and have students answer question 3.

[3] *Close*

Summary: Ask selected students to name the losses that are covered by homeowner's insurance and the three factors that determine the insurance premium.

Evaluation
Guided Practice: Ex. 1–4, 6–14 even
Independent Practice: Ex. 5–13 odd, 15–20

Extension

Tell students that if everything in their rooms at home were destroyed or stolen, they would need to be able to state what was in the rooms and how much it would cost to replace the contents. Have students inventory their rooms, making a list of the contents and an estimate of the replacement costs.

Problem-Solving Skills

Using a table (Ex. 5–20)
Interpreting information (Ex. 15–20)
Using estimation (Ex. 15, 16)
Choosing the operation (Ex. 19, 20)
Solving multi-step problems (Ex. 19, 20)

Estimation Ex. 15 and 16

For Exercises 5–8, find the amount of coverage for each item. Use the insurance schedule on page 240.

	Amount of Policy	Home	Additional Structures	Personal Property	Additional Living Expenses
5.	\$80,000	? \$80,000	? \$8000	? \$40,000	? \$16,000
6.	\$50,000	? \$50,000	? \$5000	? \$25,000	? \$10,000
7.	\$150,000	? \$150,000	? \$15,000	? \$75,000	? \$30,000
8.	\$70,000	? \$70,000	? \$7000	? \$35,000	? \$14,000

For Exercises 9–14, find the amount of the monthly premium. Use the table on page 240.

	Amount of Policy	Type of Construction	Fire Protection Class
9.	\$60,000	Brick	5 \$14.83
10.	\$90,000	Brick	10 \$29.83
11.	\$50,000	Wood-frame	9 \$17.25
12.	\$150,000	Wood-frame	3 \$40.17
13.	\$80,000	Brick	8 \$20.92
14.	\$100,000	Wood-frame	7 \$27.75

For Exercises 15–20, use the table on page 240.

15. Andrew Hill insures his house for \$99,500. Estimate the amount of coverage for the fence in his yard. **About \$10,000**

16. Tanya Smith buys a \$90,000 homeowner's insurance policy. Her yearly premium is \$359. Estimate the amount of the monthly premium. **About \$30**

Dorothy Leon insures her wood-frame house for \$90,000. The house is in fire protection class 9.

17. What is the annual premium? **\$358**

18. What is the monthly premium? **\$29.83**

19. What is the total amount of insurance coverage on the house and the contents? **\$135,000**

20. Suppose that Dorothy has paid the same yearly premium for the last 15 years. What is the difference in the total amount she has paid in annual premiums and the amount of insurance coverage she has for the house and the contents? **\$129,630**

Strategy: USING A DRAWING

Sue Lee also considered having a home built. This is a scale drawing of the floor plan of the house she might want.

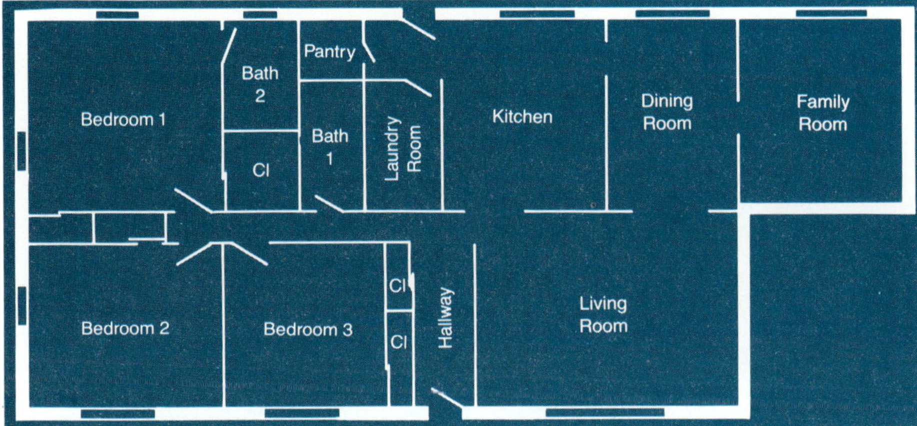

Scale: 2 cm represents 3 m.

The scale "2 cm represents 3 m" means that 2 centimeters of the drawing represents 3 meters of actual length.

1. What length does each of the following represent?
   a. 4 cm 6 m **b.** 1 cm 1.5 m **c.** 3 cm 4.5 m

To find how much carpet she will need for the living room, Sue uses the drawing to find its length and width.

EXAMPLE What is the length and width of the living room?

READ What are the facts?
The scale is: "2 cm represents 3 m.

PLAN Measure the length and width on the drawing.
Use these to find the actual measures.

SOLVE Length on drawing: **4 cm** Width on drawing: **3 cm**

Write a proportion to find the actual measures.

Length on drawing (cm) → $\frac{2}{3} = \frac{4}{\ell}$ ← *Length on drawing (cm)*
Actual length (m) → ← *Actual length (m)*

$2\ell = \mathbf{12}$ ← $2 \times \ell = 4 \times 3$

$\ell = \mathbf{6\ meters}$

Lesson Resources

Maintenance: See below.
Reteaching/Alternate Teaching Strategy: See the margin on page 244.
Practice: Activity Worksheet 57
Enrichment: You may wish to use the Project on page 244 or the enrichment topic "Closing Costs" on page 250.

Objectives

Student will

1. use a scale drawing to find the actual dimensions.
2. find the scale drawing dimensions.

Maintenance

Solve each proportion.

1. $\frac{1}{2} = \frac{x}{6}$ ANS: x = 3
2. $\frac{2}{5} = \frac{6}{x}$ ANS: x = 15
3. $\frac{x}{4} = \frac{5}{20}$ ANS: x = 1
4. $\frac{3}{x} = \frac{18}{36}$ ANS: 6
5. Joan's room is $9\frac{1}{2}$ feet wide and 10 feet long. How many square feet of carpet should she buy for the room? ANS: 95

1 Lesson Focus

Motivation: Have students discuss the different scale drawings they have seen and how a scale drawing might be used.

Purpose: Students need to learn to read scale drawing so that they can estimate dimensions for consumer purchases.

2 Teaching the Lesson

After presenting the Example, choose a problem to show how the strategy can be applied to other situations, such as in Exercise 5.

1. **Ask:** What is the problem about? (Finding the actual dimensions of a school office)

2. **Read** the problem to determine the FACTS. **Ask:** What is the scale for this drawing? (1 cm : 4.5 m) **Ask:** What are the scale drawing dimensions? (2 cm × 1 cm)
3. **Plan** the solution. **Ask:** What is the proportion for the length? ($\frac{1}{4.5} = \frac{2}{l}$) **Ask:** What is the proportion for the width? ($\frac{1}{4.5} = \frac{1}{w}$)
4. **Solve** the problem. **Ask:** What is the office's length? (9 m) What is the office's width? (4.5 m)
5. **Check** the answer by having students check the facts in the problem with the solution.

3 Close

Summary: Have students discuss why it is difficult to compare the size of the house and the school by looking at the drawings. Ask them how they would compare the size of the two buildings.

Evaluation
Guided Practice: Ex. 1–4
Independent Practice: Ex. 5–13

Problem-Solving Skills

Reading a diagram (Ex. 1–10)
Drawing a diagram (Project)
Solving an equation (Ex. 1–13)

Alternate Teaching Strategy

You may choose to have the students work in small groups to make a scale drawing of the classroom. Make sure each member of the group is assigned a job. Make sure to have measuring equipment on hand.

Width on drawing (cm) → / *Actual width (m)* →

$$\frac{2}{3} = \frac{3}{w}$$

← *Width on drawing (cm)* / ← *Actual width (m)*

$$2w = 9$$
$$w = \textbf{4.5 meters}$$

CHECK Did you measure the drawing correctly?
Did you use these measures correctly to find the actual measures?
Did you use the actual measures correctly in the formula?

EXERCISES

Find the actual dimensions of these rooms. Use the scale drawing on page 243.

1. Bedroom 2 — 4.5 m × 3.75 m
2. Pantry — 1.5 m by 1.5 m
3. Bedroom 3 — 3.75 m by 3.75 m
4. Bath 1 — 3 m × 1.5 m

This is a scale drawing of the first floor of a school.

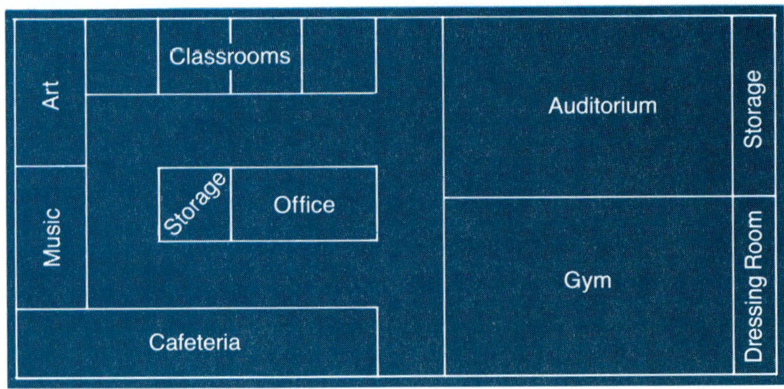

Scale: 1 cm represents 4.5 m.

Find the actual dimensions of these rooms.

5. Office — 9 m × 4.5 m
6. Cafeteria — 22.5 m × 4.5 m
7. Auditorium — 18 m × 11.25 m
8. Music room — 9 m × 4.5 m
9. Find the school's actual length. 47.25 m
10. Find the actual width of the school. 22.5 m

The actual dimensions of four rectangular rooms are given in Exercises 11–13. What would be their dimensions on a scale drawing if the scale is 1 cm represents 2.5 m?

11. $\ell = 5$ m; w = 5 m — 2 cm; 2 cm
12. $\ell = 10$ m; $w = 7.5$ m — 4 cm; 3 cm
13. $\ell = 6.25$ m; $w = 3.75$ m — 2.5 cm; 1.5 cm

PROJECT Make a scale drawing of a room in your home. Be sure to indicate the scale that you used.

Property Taxes

Sue Lee and Lian Chung know that homeowners are responsible for property taxes. City and county property taxes help pay for public schools, hospitals, streets, fire and police protection, and other public services.

The amount of tax that the Chungs will pay yearly depends on:

a. The assessed value of the property

b. The tax rate

> The **assessed value** of property is found by multiplying the **market value** (the amount for which the property would likely sell) by the **rate of assessment.**

The rate of assessment is determined by a tax assessor.

1. One house has a market value of \$70,000 and a 30% rate of assessment. Another house has a market value of \$70,000 and a 65% rate of assessment. Which house will have the greater assessed value? Why? **The second house, because the rate of assessment is higher.**

EXAMPLE 1 The market value of the house that the Chungs want is \$60,000. The rate of assessment is 65%. What is the assessed value?

$$65\% \text{ of } \$60{,}000 = \$60{,}000 \times 0.65$$
$$= \mathbf{\$39{,}000}$$

The assessed value of the house is **\$39,000.**

2. Will a house with a 45% rate of assessment have an assessed value that is more than $\frac{1}{2}$ of its market value? Explain. **No, because 45% of the assessed value will be less than 50% of the assessed value.**

3. Two houses have the same market value. One house has a 40% rate of assessment; the other house has a 35% rate of assessment. For which house do you think the taxes would be higher? Explain.
The first house, because the rate of assessment is higher.

The tax rate is often set as an amount per \$100 of assessed value.

Lesson Resources

Maintenance: See below.
Reteaching/Alternate Teaching Strategy: p. M-39
Practice: p. M-39
Enrichment: p. M-39

Objectives

Student will

1. find the assessed value of a house.
2. use the assessed value to find the yearly property tax.

Maintenance

1. Divide: 63,000 ÷ 100 ANS: 630
2. Divide: 1134 ÷ 45 ANS: 25.2
3. Multiply: \$2.03 × 12.5 ANS: \$25.375
4. Round 27.052 to the nearest hundredth. ANS; 27.05
5. A salesperson's car has a fuel economy of 35 miles per gallon. The salesperson drove 539 miles on one trip and paid an average of \$1.14 per gallon of gasoline. Find the total cost of gasoline for the trip. Round the answer to the nearest cent. ANS: \$17.56

1 Lesson Focus

Motivation: Taxes are decided on by citizens or their representatives. Ask students to tell why they think citizens decide to pay taxes.

Purpose: Many students will be responsible for paying property taxes in the future. This lesson shows students how to find the assessed value of property and how to use the tax rate to compute property taxes.

2 Teaching the Lesson

Have students read the first three paragraphs of the lesson. Discuss question 1. Then ask the following question.

For a house with a market value of \$70,000 and a 65% rate of assessment, which would be greater, the market value or the assessed value? (Market value)

Work through Example 1 and have students answer questions 2 and 3. Discuss Example 2, making sure that students understand that they must find the number of 100's in the assessed value before they can find the amount of property tax. Then have students answer question 4.

3 Close

Summary: Ask a student to explain the procedure for finding the assessed value of property and for finding the amount of property tax.

Evaluation

Guided Practice: Ex. 1–5, 6–10 even
Independent Practice: Ex. 7, 9, 11–19

Extension

Property taxes are often expressed in mills. One mill is one-thousandth of a dollar. Have students find the property tax for each of the following assessed values when the rate is 20 mills.

1. \$50,000 (\$1000.00)
2. \$85,000 (\$1700.00)
3. \$100,000 (\$2000.00)
4. \$72,500 (\$1450.00)

EXAMPLE 2 The tax rate for the city where the Chungs live is \$8.60 per \$100. Use the assessed value in Example 1 to find the amount of property tax that the Chungs would pay.

1 Find the number of 100's in the assessed value.

39,000 ÷ 100 = **390**

2 Find the amount of property tax.

\$8.60 × 390 = **\$3354.00**

The yearly property tax for the house is **\$3354.00.**

CHECK YOUR SKILLS

Write a decimal for each percent. For additional practice, see pages 403.

1. 65% 0.65
2. 45% 0.45
3. 30% 0.30 or 0.3
4. 50% 0.50 or 0.5
5. 55% 0.55
6. 40% 0.40 or 0.4

Find each answer. For additional practice, see page 407.

7. 60% of \$73,000 \$43,800
8. 45% of \$112,000 \$50,400
9. 3% of \$980 \$29.40
10. 40% of \$97,000 \$38,800

Estimate to determine whether the answer is reasonable. Answer Yes and No. For additional practice, see pages 52–53.

11. \$8.90 × 395 = \$3315.50 No
12. 505 × \$7.95 = \$4014.75 Yes
13. \$9.10 × 102 = \$928.20 Yes
14. 690 × \$8.85 = \$5106.50 No
15. \$69,000 × 0.51 = \$35,190 Yes
16. \$48,000 × 0.33 = \$18,840 No

EXERCISES

Match each term on the left with its meaning on the right.

1. Property taxes e
2. Market value c
3. Rate of assessment a
4. Assessed value b
5. Tax rate d

a. A percent of the market value of a house that a tax assessor assigns
b. Market value × rate of assessment
c. The amount for which a property would likely sell
d. A certain amount per \$100
e. Taxes paid on property to pay for public services.

For Exercise 6–10, complete the table.

	Market Value	Rate of Assessment	Assessed Value	Tax Rate (Per $100)	Property Tax
6.	$75,000	45%	? $33,750	$7.10	? $2396.25
7.	$90,000	30%	? $27,000	$6.95	? $1876.50
8.	$120,000	65%	? $78,000	$8.55	? $6669.00
9.	$69,000	50%	? $34,500	$9.75	? $3363.75
10.	$88,000	40%	? $35,200	$10.15	? $3572.80

11. The property assessment rate of the Snide family's home is 50% of its market value of $95,000. Find the assessed value of the house. **$47,500**

12. Find the amount of property tax for a house with an assessed value of $57,500 in a city with a tax rate of $10.45 per $100 of assessed value. **$6008.75**

13. The assessment rate of the Brenner's home is 48% of its market value of $81,000. Which is the best estimate of the assessed value of the house? **c**

a. $\frac{1}{2} \times \$90{,}000$ **b.** $\frac{1}{4} \times \$90{,}000$
c. $\frac{1}{2} \times \$80{,}000$ **d.** $\frac{1}{4} \times \$80{,}000$

14. Sam Spock's mortgage lender requires Sam to pay his yearly property taxes in equal monthly payments as part of his monthly mortgage payment. Sam's home is assessed at $45,600. The property tax rate is $6.40 per $100. How much is added per month to Sam's monthly mortgage payment for property taxes? **$243.20**

15. What is the actual assessed value of the house in Exercise 13? **$38,880**

Arlene Colbert's yearly property taxes are $1520.00 The taxes are due by January 31. If she pays her taxes early, Arlene receives these discounts.

Pay in October: Deduct 3%
Pay in November: Deduct 2%
Pay in December: Deduct 1%

16. What are Arlene's property taxes if she pays in October? **$1474.40**

17. What are her property taxes if she pays in November? **$1489.60**

Property taxes vary depending on where you live.

18. What are some possible advantages of living in a county with lower property taxes? **Answers will vary.**

19. What are some possible advantages of living in a county with higher property taxes? **Answers will vary.**

Problem-Solving Skills

Interpreting information (Ex. 11–17)
Solving a multi-step problem (Ex. 12, 14, 16, 17)
Choosing the operation (Ex. 14, 16, 17)
Reading a table (Ex. 16, 17)

NOTE: A quiz covering the second half of the chapter is provided in the *Teacher's ResourceBank™*.

Critical Thinking

You may wish to have students work in small groups to solve these problems or you may wish to work with the class.

Ex. 18 and 19

Estimation

Ex. 13

Objectives

Students will

1. explore solutions to a variety of problems that emerge from this situational lesson.
2. explore solutions to housing problems having more than one solution.

Situational Lesson

These two pages present a situational lesson as the framework from which a variety of problem situations emerge.

Teaching Strategies

This lesson lends itself to cooperative learning groups for the problem solving activities of comparing choices and exploring decisions. (See page M-13.)

However, these activities can also be carried out by the class as a whole or by individual students.

1 Lesson Focus

Motivation: Have students discuss and list all of the expenses associated with home ownership.

Purpose: Consumers need to be aware of all the expenses that go into the cost of owning a home so that they can make educated decisions.

2 Teaching the Lesson

Have a volunteer read the introductory paragraphs. Focus students' attention on the advertisements and Choices 1–3. Ask these questions.

1. Which house has the highest down payment? (Choice 1)
2. Which house has the lowest monthly mortgage payment? (Choice 2)
3. Which house has the lowest property taxes? (Choice 1)
4. Which house has the lowest insurance costs? (Choice 1)

Consumer's Choice

After living in an apartment complex for 5 years, the Robinsons decided to buy a house. They narrowed their choices to three places.

Choice 1

A 20-year old house advertised for $64,500.
Down payment: $6450
Monthly mortgage payment: $531
Property taxes: $600/year
Homeowner's insurance: $360/year

Choice 2

A suburban townhome advertised for $63,900.
Down payment: $6390
Monthly mortgage payment: $526
Property taxes: $828/year
Homeowner's insurance: $456/year

Choice 3

A 5-year old house priced at $71,900.
Down payment: $3600
Monthly mortgage payment: $599
Property taxes: $792/year
Homeowner's insurance: $432/year

COMPARING THE CHOICES

1. Which of the choices has the lowest down payment? Choice 3
2. Which of the choices would require using the most money from savings to make the down payment? Choice 1

Find the total monthly cost, including the mortgage payment, property taxes, and homeowner's insurance, for each choice.

3. Choice 1 $611

4. Choice 2 $633

5. Choice 3 $701

6. What is the difference between the highest monthly cost and the lowest monthly cost? $90

7. How much will the difference in Exercise 6 amount to in one year? In 15 years? $1080; $16,200

EXPLORING DECISIONS

8. Suppose that the Robinsons do not wish to spend more than $535 for monthly mortgage payments. What choice does this eliminate? Choice 3

9. Suppose that the Robinsons do not wish to spend more than a total of $625 a month for housing. Which choices does this eliminate? Choices 2 and 3

10. The Robinsons have two children of school age. How might this influence their decision?

11. Suppose that property values are expected to rise steadily over the next 10 years. How might this influence the Robinsons' decision?

12. State one advantage and one disadvantage of Choice 1.

13. State one advantage and one disadvantage of Choice 2.

14. State one advantage and one disadvantage of Choice 3.

15. Which house would you choose? Give reasons for your answer.

Have students work on Exercises 1–9. Do not go on until all the students understand how to get the answers. Discuss Exercises 10–15 with the class.

3 Close

Summary: Have students discuss the things they should consider when making a decision on buying a house.

Problem-Solving Skills

Making a comparison (Ex. 1, 2, 8, 9)
Choosing the operation (Ex. 6, 7)

Critical Thinking

Ex. 10-15

Project

Have students find a house they like in a real estate ad in the newspaper. Have them call the agency to find the same information given for the houses in the text. Have students write a summary telling why they chose the house and how much they estimate the monthly and yearly expenses for the house would be.

Additional Answers

10. They might wish to purchase the house in choice 1 or choice 3 because of the schools.

11. They might want to purchase the house in choice 3 because the value would increase the most.

12. One advantage: lowest property taxes; one disadvantage: 20 years old; Answers will vary.

13. One advantage: lowest mortgage payment; one disadvantage: highest property taxes; Answers will vary.

14. One advantage: lowest down payment; one disadvantage: highest mortgage payment; Answers will vary.

15. Answers will vary.

Objective

Student will find the total closing costs.

Overview

This topic is optional. The word "Enrichment" that appears to the right of the title in this Teacher's Edition does not appear in the student textbook. Therefore, this material is not included in the Chapter Review and Chapter Test.

Using the Page

You may wish to have students work this Enrichment in small groups or you may wish to work with the class.

Problem-Solving Skills

Solving a multi-step problem (Ex. 1–3)

Closing Costs ENRICHMENT

Closing costs, such as those shown below, are an expense that a home buyer pays before the sale of the house is final.

Lawyer's Fees	Appraisal Fee	Insurance Premium
Land Survey	Documentation Stamps	Property Taxes
Title Search	Credit Report	Processing Fee

EXAMPLE Esther and Andrew Franklin obtained a $50,000 mortgage. At the time the sale of the house is closed, they also have to pay the closing costs at the right. Find the total of the closing costs.

Lawyer's Fees:	$200
Credit Report:	$ 35
Title Search and Insurance:	$160
Documentation Stamp:	0.2% of mortgage
Property Taxes:	$115

1. Find the cost of the documentation stamps.
   0.2% of $50,000 = 0.002 × $50,000
   = **$100**

2. Find the total of the closing costs.
   $200 + $35 + $160 + $100 + $115 = **$610.**

EXERCISES

1. The Martin family obtained a $60,000 mortgage. Find the total of these closing costs.
   Title Search: $30
   Processing Fee: 1% of mortgage
   Lawyer's Fees: $325
   Credit Report: $35
   Insurance: $150 $1140

2. The Horton family is financing $85,000 for a new house. Find the total of these closing costs.
   Land Survey: $125
   Documentation Stamps: 0.3% of mortgage
   Lawyer's Fees: $210
   Property Taxes: $350
   Appraisal Fee: $45 $985

Many banks and lending institutions add points to the mortgage closing charges. A ***point*** *is 1% of the mortgage.*

3. The Brannon family is financing $72,000 at 9% for 30 years plus 3 points. They also have to pay the closing costs at the right. Find the total of the closing costs, including points.
   $2999

Title Search:	$70
Appraisal Fee:	$35
Lawyer's Fees:	$190
Documentation Stamp:	0.2% of mortgage
Property Taxes:	$400

Chapter Summary

IMPORTANT IDEAS

1. An average affordable amount to spend on housing is one fourth to one third of net household income.
2. **Purchase Price − Down Payment = Amount of Mortgage**
3. **Total of Monthly Payments − Amount of Mortgage = Amount of Interest**
4. The amount of a monthly mortgage loan payment depends on the amount of the mortgage, the time taken to pay off the mortgage, and the interest rate.
5. Homeowner's insurance protects you and your lending institution against losses due to theft or damage from fire, lightning, and other disasters.
6. The amount of property tax paid is based on the assessed value of the property and the local tax rate.

Chapter Review

Part 1: VOCABULARY

For Exercises 1–5, choose from the box at the right the word(s) that complete(s) each statement.

liability
homeowner's insurance
monthly payments
premium
down payment
market value
mortgage loan
assessed value

1. Most people pay part of the purchase price of a new home by making a __?__, and obtaining a __?__ to pay the remainder. (Pages 232–234) **down payment; mortgage loan**
2. The type of insurance which protects both the homeowner and the mortgage lender from loss is known as __?__. (Pages 240–242) **homeowner's insurance**
3. The amount you pay for homeowner's insurance is known as the __?__. (Pages 240–242) **premium**
4. The amount a property would likely sell for is known as its __?__. (Pages 245–247) **market value**
5. The amount of property tax is based on the tax rate and the __?__ of the property. (Pages 245–247) **assessed value**

Chapter Summary

The Chapter Summary contains a listing of the important ideas that were presented in the chapter. This listing is intended to assist the student with the Chapter Review that follows.

Objective

To review the important terms, skills, problem solving, and applications presented in Chapter 10.

Overview

The Chapter Review is structured in three parts. Part 1 is a review of the important terms that were introduced in the chapter. Part 2 reviews the skills that were presented in the chapter. Part 3 reviews the problem-solving strategies and applications that were presented in the chapter. Each item in the Chapter Review is referenced to the related pages where the concept, skill, or application was presented.

Using the Pages

You may wish to assign this Chapter Review for homework or treat it as a class review prior to administering the formal Chapter Test. In doing this, it is suggested that you only use the even- or odd-numbered exercises. You can then use the remaining exercises as a bank for use later.

Part 2: SKILLS

For Exercises 6–9, complete the table. (Pages 230–231)

	Proposed Rent	Net Income	$\frac{1}{4}$ of Income	$\frac{1}{3}$ of Income	Between $\frac{1}{4}$ and $\frac{1}{3}$?
6.	$575	$1750	? $437.50	? $583.33	? Yes
7.	$400	$1506	? $376.50	? $502	? Yes
8.	$775	$1775	? $443.75	? $591.67	? No
9.	$500	$1800	? $450	? $600	? Yes

For Exercises 10–13, complete the table. (Pages 232–234)

	Amount of Mortgage	Length of Mortgage (Years)	Number of Monthly Payments	Monthly Payment	Total of Monthly Payments	Amount of Interest
10.	$80,000	30	? 360	$761.60	? $274,176	? $194,176
11.	$90,000	20	? 240	$868.50	? $208,440	? $118,440
12.	$45,000	15	? 180	$497.25	? $89,505	? $44,505
13.	$55,000	30	? 360	$565.95	? $203,742	? $148,742

For Exercises 14–21, find the monthly mortgage payment. Use the table on page 235. (Pages 235–237)

	Amount of Mortgage	Interest Rate	Length of Mortgage (Years)		Amount of Mortgage	Interest Rate	Length of Mortgage (Years)
14.	$65,000	10%	30 $570.70	**18.**	$60,000	12%	15 $720
15.	$80,000	11.5%	25 $813.60	**19.**	$140,000	11%	20 $1444.80
16.	$95,000	9.5%	20 $885.40	**20.**	$84,000	12.5%	30 $896.28
17.	$70,000	10.5%	30 $640.50	**21.**	$94,000	13%	25 $1060.32

For Exercises 22–24, complete the table. (Pages 245–247)

	Market Value	Rate of Assessment	Assessed Value	Tax Rate (Per $100)	Property Tax
22.	$95,000	50%	? $47,500	$9.20	? $4370
23.	$110,000	40%	? $44,000	$7.90	? $3476
24.	$75,000	55%	? $41,250	$8.50	? $3506.25

25. The Greiners have a net household income of \$1975 per month. They can afford to spend between $\frac{1}{4}$ and $\frac{1}{3}$ of the net household income for rent. Can they afford to rent the apartment in the ad? (Pages 230–231) **Yes**

Palm Coast West
3 bedroom, 2 Bath
Children allowed
New appliances
Only \$625 per month

26. Gertrude Bishop wants to buy a house which costs \$82,500. She must make a down payment of 15% of the purchase price. What is the amount of the mortage loan? (Pages 232–234) **\$70,125**

27. The Cox family obtains a \$80,000 mortgage at 12%. The mortgage is to be repaid over 30 years. Use the table on page 235 to find out the amount of the monthly mortgage payment. (Pages 235–237) **\$823.20**

For Exercises 28–29, use the tables on page 240. (Pages 240–242)

28. Suzanne Gallant insures her house for \$110,000. What is the amount of coverage for additional living expenses? **\$22,000**

29. Richard Strobel buys a \$70,000 homeowner's insurance policy. His house is wood-frame, fire protection class 4. What is his monthly premium? **\$18.17**

30. Find the amount of property tax for a house with a market value of \$130,000. The property assessment rate is 45%. The tax rate is \$9.40 per \$100. (Pages 245–247) **\$5499**

31. Susan Coyne is a handicapped homeowner. Her house has an assessed value of \$70,000. The tax rate where she lives is \$8.80 per \$100. Susan receives a 5% property tax deduction because she is handicapped. What is her annual property tax? (Pages 245–247) **\$5852**

32. Interior decorators often use this scale.

$\frac{1}{4}$ inch represents 1 foot.

a. Using this scale, what length would represent 20 feet? **5 in**

b. On a drawing using this scale, the length of a kitchen is $3\frac{3}{4}$ inches. What is the actual width? (Pages 243–244) **15 ft**

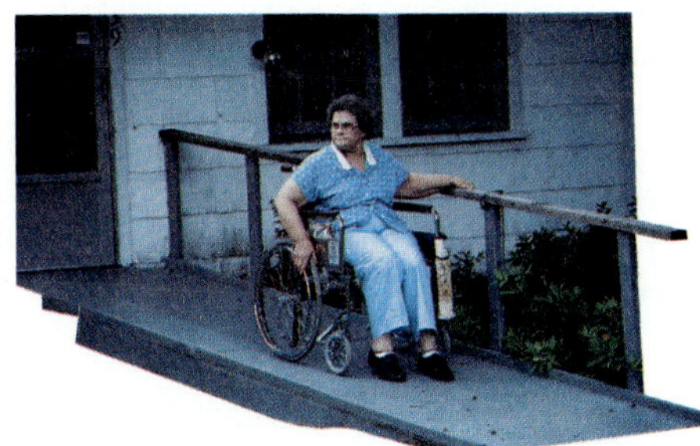

Objective

To informally assess students' mastering of the major skills, concepts, problem solving, and applications presented in Chapter 10.

Using the Page

After completing the Chapter Review with the class, you may wish to use this Chapter Test as an informal assessment. This Chapter Test parallels the formal chapter tests (Form A and Form B) provided in the *Teacher's ResourceBank.*™

Chapter Test

1. The Seels have a net household income of $2700 per month. They can afford to spend between $\frac{1}{4}$ and $\frac{1}{3}$ of the household income for rent. Can they afford to rent the apartment in the ad? **No**

Affordable Luxury
Executive Townhouses
Pool and Racquetball Courts
1 bedroom, 1 bathroom
Starting at $925 per month

2. Art Weisman buys a house for $51,300. He makes a 25% down payment. What is the amount of down payment? **$12,825**

3. What is the amount of the mortgage loan in Exercise 2? **$38,475**

4. The Morrison family took out an $85,000 mortgage loan which is payable over 30 years. Their monthly mortgage payment is $1143.25. Find the total amount of interest charged. **$326,570**

5. The Todds obtained a $55,000 mortgage loan at 11% which is payable over 30 years. Use the table at the right to find the amount of the monthly mortgage payment. **$523.60**

6. In Exercise 5, what would the monthly mortgage payment be if the loan were at 10%? **$482.90**

Mortgage Loan Schedule
Monthly Cost per $1000

Years	10%	10.5%	11%
15	$10.75	$11.05	$11.37
20	$9.65	$9.98	$10.32
25	$9.09	$9.44	$9.80
30	$8.78	$9.15	$9.52

7. Richard Ings has a $65,000 homeowner's insurance policy. Additional structures on his property are covered for 10% of the policy. What is the amount of coverage for additional structures? **$6500**

8. The property assessment rate of the Brown family's home is 45% of its market value of $105,000. The tax rate is $9.10 per $100. Find the yearly property tax. **$4299.75**

9. A certain house has a yearly homeowner's insurance premium of $333. How much is the monthly premium? **$27.75**

10. A basement recreation room is 9 meters long. Find the length of the room on a drawing that uses this scale.

    2 cm represents 3 m
    6 cm

Cumulative Maintenance: Chapters 1–10

*Choose the correct answer. Choose **a, b, c,** or **d.***

1. The round-trip plane fare from Orlando to New York is $199 per person plus an 8% tax. What is the total of the plane fares for a family of four? c

a. $796 **b.** $636.80
c. $859.68 **d.** $214.92

2. The circle graph below shows how a family spent its $900–vacation budget. How much was spent on meals? b

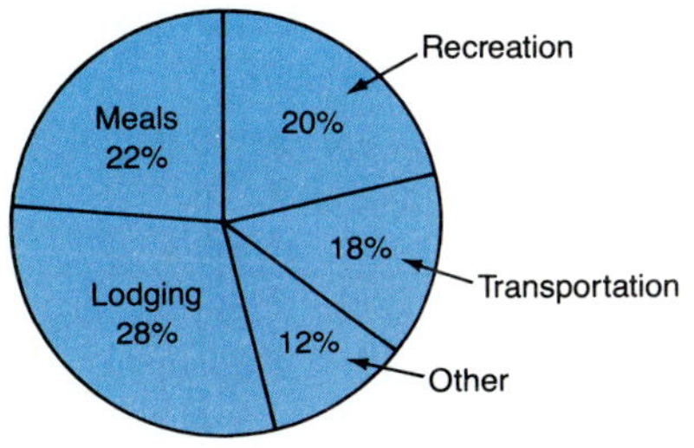

a. $180 **b.** $198
c. $108 **d.** $252

3. Write a decimal for 36%. a

a. 0.36 **b.** 0.0036
c. 3.6 **d.** 36.0

4. The Jacob's home is assessed at $54,500. The property tax rate is $7.20 per $100 of assessed value. Find the amount of property tax. a

a. $3924 **b.** $39,240
c. $39.24 **d.** $392.40

5. Gretchen Hale's monthly gross income last year was $965. She also received $145.60 and $87.39 in interest from two savings accounts last year. Find her adjusted gross income for the year. d

a. $1197.99 **b.** $14,375.88
c. $11,347.01 **d.** $11,812.99

6. Sue Loring's home is assessed at 45% of its market value of $92,000. What is the assessed value? b

a. $50,000 **b.** $41,400
c. $204,444 **d.** $44,100

7. Mary saw the same kind of juice in 5 different stores with prices of 73¢, 78¢, 78¢, 79¢, and 82¢. What was the median price? b

a. 82¢ **b.** 78¢ **c.** 79¢ **d.** 73¢

8. What is the new balance forward (Bal. For'd.) on the check stub below? a

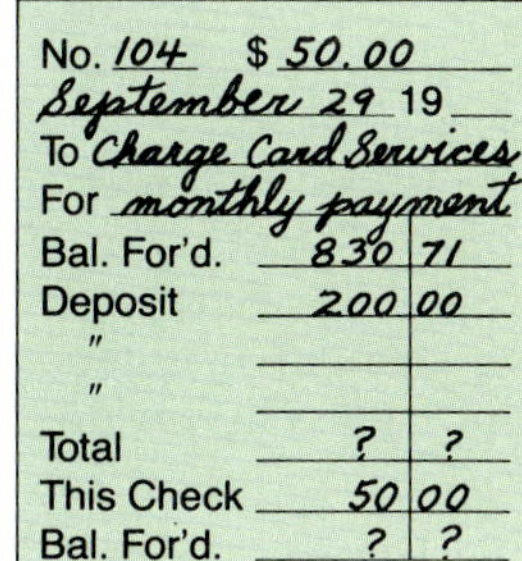
No. 104 $ 50.00
September 29 19
To Charge Card Services
For monthly payment

Bal. For'd.	830	71
Deposit	200	00
"		
"		
Total	?	?
This Check	50	00
Bal. For'd.	?	?

a. $980.71
b. $1080.71
c. $1030.71
d. $580.71

Objective

To review the content presented in Chapters 1–10

Using the Pages

You may wish to use this Cumulative Maintenance as an informal assessment tool. These pages can be assigned for homework or they may be used as review in class.

9. Use the graph below to determine the approximate resale value of a car after 2 years of depreciation. The new car cost was $10,200. a

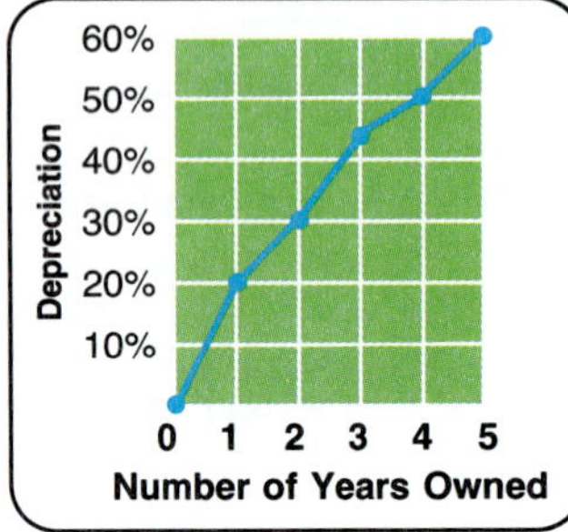

a. $7140 **b.** $3060
c. $4590 **d.** $2040

10. Nancy Brown's net monthly income is $960. She can spend between $\frac{1}{4}$ and $\frac{1}{3}$ of this for rent. What is the most she can spend? d

a. $2880 **b.** $480
c. $360 **d.** $320

11. Write a fraction for 20%. c

a. $\frac{1}{10}$ **b.** $\frac{2}{5}$
c. $\frac{1}{5}$ **d.** $\frac{2}{10}$

12. Tom Turner is ordering personalized checks from his bank. There are four different styles of checks he can order. Each style of check is available in five colors. How many possible choices does Tom have? c

a. 4 **b.** 5 **c.** 20 **d.** $\frac{4}{5}$

13. Bonnie Bishop wants to buy a house which costs $91,000. She must make a down payment of 15% of the purchase price. What is the amount of the mortgage loan? d

a. $13,650 **b.** $104,650
c. $136,500 **d.** $77,350

14. Carol Sywetz, a real estate agent, sold a house for $102,500. Her commission was 5% of the selling price. How much did she earn? c

a. $51,250 **b.** $2500
c. $5125 **d.** $512.50

15. A pound of lamb costs $2.79. Each pound provides 3 servings. What is the cost per serving? a

a. $0.93 **b.** $0.84
c. $0.91 **d.** $8.37

16. The assessed value of the Sorvell family's home is 49% of its market value of $104,000. Estimate the assessed value. b

a. $40,000 **b.** $50,000
c. $45,000 **d.** $60,000

17. Find the finance charge for the car in the advertisement below. c

780 VT
$7800 Cash or
20% Down and
$142/month for
60 months

a. $8520 **b.** $6240
c. $2280 **d.** $1560

Housing Costs

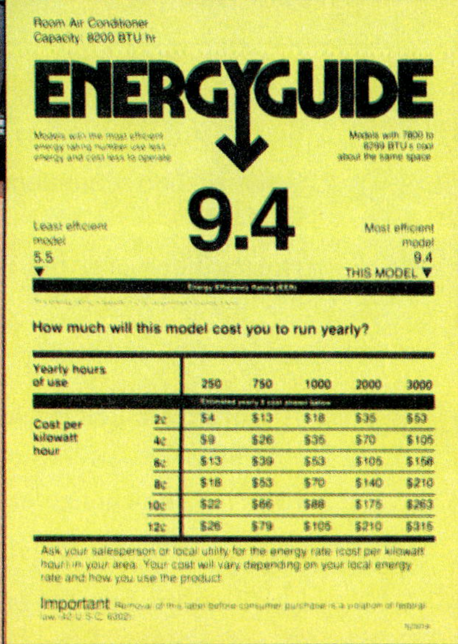
Room Air Conditioner
Capacity: 8200 BTU hr

ENERGYGUIDE

Models with the most efficient energy rating number use less energy and cost less to operate

Models with 7800 to 8299 BTU's cool about the same space

9.4

Least efficient model 5.5

Most efficient model 9.4

THIS MODEL

Energy Efficiency Rating (EER)

How much will this model cost you to run yearly?

Yearly hours of use		250	750	1000	2000	3000
		Estimated yearly $ cost shown below				
Cost per kilowatt hour	2¢	$4	$13	$18	$35	$53
	4¢	$9	$26	$35	$70	$105
	6¢	$13	$39	$53	$105	$158
	8¢	$18	$53	$70	$140	$210
	10¢	$22	$66	$88	$175	$263
	12¢	$26	$79	$105	$210	$315

Ask your salesperson or local utility for the energy rate (cost per kilowatt hour) in your area. Your cost will vary depending on your local energy rate and how you use the product.

Important Removal of this label before consumer purchase is a violation of federal law (42 U.S.C. 6302)

Nina and Sam Benally decide to save money by reducing utility costs. They hope to save enough money to redecorate their home.

- How can they save on heating and cooling costs?
- How much does it cost to operate appliances such as washing machines and dryers?
- How can they find just how much electricity and gas they are using?
- How much wallpaper and paint will they need to redecorate their home?

Chapter 11: Housing Costs

Overview

The focus of Chapter 11 is on housing costs and on saving on energy costs. As in Chapter 10, you may wish to have students collect current local information on the various topics studied, since housing and energy costs vary widely from locality to locality.

Although all lessons in this chapter involve problem-solving, the strategy lesson on pages 272–273 presents four strategies from which students are asked to select the most appropriate to apply in a given problem-solving situation. The *Consumer's Choice* on pages 274–275 presents a **situational lesson** in which students make consumer choices in a familiar, real-life situation. Finally, the *Enrichment* lesson on page 276 applies the strategy of Interpreting information to solving problems that involve long-distance telephone costs.

Using This Page

Have students read the introductory paragraph and questions. Have them list possible solutions to the problems presented. After completing the chapter, have students review their suggested solutions, comparing them with those presented in the lessons. You may wish to have students suggest other possible problems resulting from the situation described on this page and to discuss possible solutions.

You may wish to organize the class into small groups to complete the situational activity described on this *Using the Page.*

Lesson Resources

Maintenance: See below.
Reteaching/Alternate Teaching Strategy: p. M-40
Practice: p. M-40
Enrichment: p. M-40
Concrete Materials: Activity Worksheet 59B

Objectives

Student will

1. solve multi-step problems that involve savings on home heating costs.
2. use a table to solve problems that involve savings on home cooling costs.

Maintenance

1. Write a decimal for 8%. ANS: 0.08
2. Multiply: $432 × 0.16 ANS: $69.12
3. What is 25% of 60? ANS: 15
4. Add: $325.50 + $124.32 ANS: $449.82
5. Mr. Vesco receives a salary of $220.50 per week plus a commission of 3% of sales. Find his total pay for a week when his sales were $4225. ANS: $347.25

1 Lesson Focus

Motivation: Ask students to estimate how much they think their family would save a year in heating costs if they lowered their thermostat 2 degrees.

Purpose: This lesson shows students how to calculate their savings on heating and cooling costs by adjusting the thermostat. This skill will encourage them to conserve energy, so they will save money.

STRATEGY: USING "HIDDEN QUESTIONS" TO SOLVE A MULTI-STEP PROBLEM

Heating and Cooling Costs

Sam and Nina Benally received this notice with their February utility bill.

SAVE ON UTILITIES

LOWER THE THERMOSTAT AND LOWER YOUR HEATING BILL

For each degree Fahrenheit that the thermostat is lowered, heating costs are lowered by about 3%.

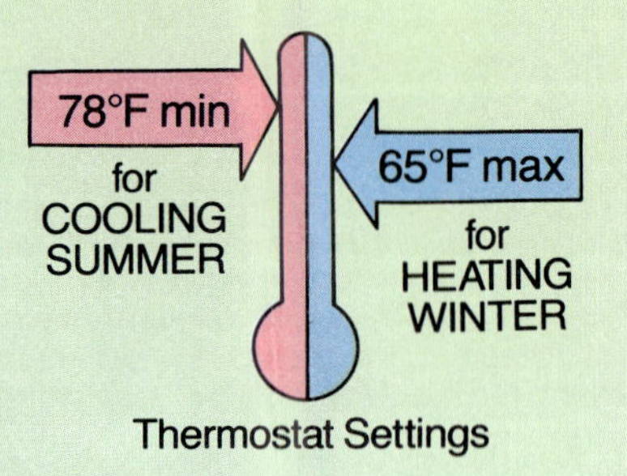

Thermostat Settings

1. What percent can you save on heating costs by lowering the thermostat two degrees? 6%
2. What is the recommended thermostat setting for heating your home? 65°F

During February, the Benallys kept the thermostat at 72°F. Their heating bill was $85.

EXAMPLE 1 About how much could the Benallys have saved by keeping the thermostat at 70°F?

1 Find the change in thermostat settings.

72° − 70° = **2° lower**

2 Find the percent of savings.

2 × 3% = **6%** ◀ *Each degree lowers heating costs by about 3%.*

3 Find the amount of savings.

6% of $85 = 0.06 = $85

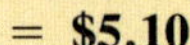

= **$5.10**

The Benallys could have saved about **$5.10.**

In May, the Benallys received this notice with their utility bill.

Thermo-stat Setting	Saving(S) or Loss(L)
80°F	16%(S)
79	8%(S)
78	0
77	8%(L)
76	18%(L)
75	28%(L)
74	39%(L)
73	50%(L)
72	63%(L)

RAISE THE THERMOSTAT AND RAISE YOUR SAVINGS

The recommended thermostat setting for air conditioning is 78° Fahrenheit. Setting the thermostat 1° higher will save you about 8% of your cooling costs.

3. According to the notice, what percent can you save on cooling costs by raising the thermostat from 78°F to 80°F? 16%

EXAMPLE 2 In July, Sam and Nina Benally spent $83 cooling their home with the thermostat set at 78°F. About how much would they have saved by setting the thermostat at 80°F?

16% of $83 = 0.16 × $83 ◀ *Percent of Savings × Amount Bill = Amount of Savings*

= **$13.28**

Sam and Nina would have saved about **$13.28.**

4. If the Benallys had set the thermostat at 80°F in July, how much would they have spent for cooling costs? About $69.72

CHECK YOUR SKILLS

Write a percent for each decimal. For additional practice, see page 405.

1. 0.63 63% **2.** 0.08 8% **3.** 0.25 25% **4.** 0.5 50% **5.** 0.375 37.5% **6.** 0.015 1.5%

Solve. For additional practice, see pages 407 and 409.

7. Find 6% of $94. $5.64

8. Find 12% of $1356. $162.72

9. What percent of 900 is 135? 15%

10. What percent of 800 is 192? 24%

2 Teaching the Lesson

Focus students' attention on the notice at the top of the page. Ask these questions.

1. How can you save money on your heating bill? (Lower the setting of the thermostat.)
2. How much do you save on your heating bill for each degree you lower the thermostat? (3%)

Then ask questions 1 and 2 in the lesson and discuss Example 1. Focus students' attention on the notice on page 259. Have students answer question 3. Then discuss Example 2 and question 4.

3 Close

Summary: Have students discuss how they can save money on heating and cooling costs.

Evaluation

Guided Practice: Ex. 1–4, 6, 8

Independent Practice: Ex. 5, 7, 9–14

Extension

Have students survey thermostat settings of their homes to see if the guidelines shown in the notices are being followed. Have students find the heating and cooling costs of their homes and calculate the savings if the thermostats are brought into agreement with the guidelines.

EXERCISES

Complete. Choose your answers from the box at the right.

1. Changing the thermostat from 74°F to 76°F will __?__ cooling costs. **lower**
2. The recommended thermostat setting for air conditioning is __?__. **78°**
3. Changing the thermostat from 70°F to 72°F will __?__ heating costs. **raise**
4. Changing the thermostat from 74°F to 68°F will lower heating costs by __?__%. **18**

For Exercises 5–8, find how much each family will save on heating costs this year.

	Last Year's Heating Costs	Last Year's Thermostat Setting	This Year's Thermostat Setting
5.	$1350	72°F	69°F **$121.50**
6.	$1125	70°F	65°F **$168.75**

	Last Year's Heating Costs	Last Year's Thermostat Setting	This Year's Thermostat Setting
7.	$975	69°F	67°F **$58.50**
8.	$800	69°F	65°F **$96**

9. Last year the Delano family spent $1050 on heating their home with the thermostat set at 71°F. About how much can they save by setting the thermostat at 68°F this year? **About $94.50**

10. The Huffaker family spent $890 to heat their home last year. They kept the thermostat at 69°F. About how much would they have spent if they had kept the thermostat at 65°F? **About $106.80**

For Exercises 11–13, use the table on page 259.

11. Last year the Cantrell family spent $560 on cooling their home with the thermostat set at 78°F. About how much can they save by setting the thermostat at 80°F this year? **About $89.60**

12. The Wong family spent $650 on cooling costs last year. They kept the thermostat at 78°F. About how much more would they have spent if they had kept the thermostat at 74°F? **About $253.50**

13. The Johnson family spent $710 on cooling costs last year. They kept their thermostat at 78°F. About how much would they have spent if they had kept the thermostat at 76°F? **About $837.80**

14. Last year the Young family spent $900 heating their home. They kept the thermostat at 72°F. This year they want to reduce their heating costs by $108. At what temperature should they set the thermostat? **68°F**

Problem-Solving Skills

Solving a multi-step problem (Ex. 5–10, 14)
Using a table (Ex. 11–14)
Choosing the operation (Ex. 14)

Math and Cooling Costs

The size or cooling capacity of an air conditioner is measured in **British Thermal Units (Btu's).** One Btu is the energy needed to raise the temperature of one pound of water one degree Farhenheit. The formula below gives an estimate for the correct size of an air conditioner.

$$c = 12.5a + 2000$$

***c* = cooling capacity in Btu's**
***a* = area of the space in square feet**

Julia Wilson is a building contractor. She uses the formula above to estimate the size of air conditioners that she will need to use in new houses.

EXAMPLE Estimate the size air conditioner Julia will need for a house with 1400 square feet of living space. Write the answer to the nearest thousand.

Use the formula.

$c = 12.5a + 2000$ ◀ $a = 1400$

$c = 12.5(1400) + 2000$
$c = 17{,}500 + 2000$
$c = 19{,}500$, or about **20,000 Btu's**

EXERCISES

For Exercises 1–6, estimate the size of an air conditioner needed to cool each space. Write your answers to the nearest thousand.

1. 500 square feet 8000 Btu's
2. 1100 square feet 16,000 Btu's
3. 800 square feet 12,000 Btu's
4. 1600 square feet 22,000 Btu's
5. 1220 square feet 17,000 Btu's
6. 960 square feet 14,000 Btu's
7. The cooling capacity of a room air conditioner is 10,000 Btu's. The room has an area of 600 square feet. Is the air conditioner the right size for the room? Yes
8. A room is 20 feet long and 15 feet wide. Estimate the size of air conditioner needed to cool the room. 6000 Btu's

Objective

Student will apply the skill of using a formula to solving problems that involve cooling capacity.

Overview

This page is an extension of the skills and ideas presented in the previous lessons of this chapter. Since the content presented on this page is not included in the Chapter Review or Chapter Test, its use is optional.

Using the Pages

You may wish to have students work this lesson in small groups or you may wish to work with the class. Using it with the class, have a student read the two introductory paragraphs. Point out that to use the formula, students need to know the area of the space to be cooled or the cooling capacity. Work Exercises 2 and 4 with the class and assign Exercises 1, 3, and 5–8 as independent practice.

Problem-Solving Skills

Using a formula (Ex. 1–8)
Making a Comparison (Ex. 7)

Estimation

Ex. 1–6 and 8

Lesson Resources

Maintenance: See below.
Reteaching/Alternate Teaching Strategy: p. M-40 (Visual 33)
Practice: p. M-40
Enrichment: p. M-40
Concrete Materials: Activity Worksheet 60B, and Visual 33
Visual 33

Objective

Student will use a table to solve problems that involve the costs for operating appliances.

Maintenance

1. Add: \$14.50 + \$13.35 + \$4.95 ANS: \$32.80
2. Subtract: 3586 − 421 ANS: 3165
3. Multiply: 30 × 4.15 × 38 ANS: 4731
4. Bill earns \$1985 a month and has \$535.95 in deductions. What is his take-home pay? ANS: \$1449.05
5. Gina earns \$5.90 per hour and works 40 hours per week. What are her yearly earnings? ANS: \$12,272

1 Lesson Focus

Motivation: Ask students to estimate how much it costs for them to watch television for one week.

Purpose: This lesson describes how to determine the cost of operating different appliances. This information will help students conserve energy by making wise use of electricity.

STRATEGY: USING "HIDDEN QUESTIONS" TO SOLVE A MULTI-STEP PROBLEM

Cost of Operating Appliances

In the area in which the Benallys live, electricity costs 14¢ per *kilowatt-hour*. One **kilowatt-hour (kwh)** is 1000 watts of electricity used for one hour.

This table shows estimated costs of operating some appliances.

Appliance	Cost	Appliance	Cost
Refrigerator/Freezer (18 cu ft, frost-free)	30¢ per day	Vacuum Cleaner	9¢ per hour
Television (color)	5¢ per hour	Iron	8¢ per hour
Television (black and white)	$3\frac{1}{2}$¢ per hour	Coffee Maker	2¢ per pot
Light Bulb (60 watt)	1¢ per hour	Dishwasher	8¢ per load
		Washing Machine	$2\frac{1}{2}$¢ per load
		Dryer	43¢ per load

1. About how much more does it cost to dry a load of laundry than to wash a load of laundry? $40\frac{1}{2}$¢ more

EXAMPLE The Benallys average four loads of laundry per week. Find the total estimated cost of electricity for operating the washer and the dryer each week.

1 Find the estimated cost of operating the washer.

$$4 \times 2\tfrac{1}{2}¢ = 4 \times \$0.025 \quad \text{(} 2\tfrac{1}{2}¢ = \$0.025 \text{)}$$
$$= \mathbf{\$0.10}$$

2 Find the estimated cost of operating the dryer.

$$4 \times 43¢ = 4 \times \$0.43 = \mathbf{\$1.72}$$

3 Find the total estimated cost.

$$\$0.10 + \$1.72 = \mathbf{\$1.82}$$

The weekly cost of operating the washer and dryer is about **\$1.82.**

CHECK YOUR SKILLS

Complete. For additional practice, see pages 368 and 369.

1. \$1.34 + ? = \$2.09 (\$0.75)
2. \$1.26 + ? = \$1.95 (\$0.69)
3. \$1.95 + ? = \$2.43 (\$0.48)
4. \$1.00 − ? = \$0.65 (\$0.35)
5. \$3.00 − ? = \$0.57 (\$2.43)
6. \$2.00 − ? = \$0.93 (\$1.07)

Write a percent for each fraction. **For additional practice, see page 406.**

7. $\frac{1}{10}$ **10%** **8.** $\frac{1}{5}$ **20%** **9.** $\frac{21}{25}$ **84%** **10.** $\frac{2}{3}$ **$66\frac{2}{3}$%** **11.** $\frac{1}{8}$ **$12\frac{1}{2}$%** **12.** $\frac{17}{20}$ **85%**

Solve. **For additional practice, see page 409.**

13. What percent of 80 is 8? **10%**

14. What percent of 60 is 12? **20%**

EXERCISES

For Exercises 1–17, use the table on page 262 to find the cost of operating each appliance.

	Appliance	Amount of Use
1.	Iron	5 hours **$0.40**
2.	Dishwasher	17 loads **$1.36**
3.	Light Bulb	65 hours **$0.65**
4.	Television (black and white)	36 hours **$1.26**

	Appliance	Amount of Use
5.	Coffee Maker	24 pots **$0.48**
6.	Dryer	16 loads **$6.88**
7.	Vacuum Cleaner	8 hours **$0.72**
8.	Refrigerator/ Freezer	45 days **$13.50**

9. Norm Smith ironed for 6 hours last month. Find the estimated cost of electricity. **About $0.48**

10. Peg Kelly made 45 pots of coffee last month. About how much did this add to her electric bill? **About $0.90**

11. Paul Kopatz estimated that a 60-watt light bulb works for 400 hours. Find the cost of electricity for the lifetime of the bulb. **$4.00**

12. About how much more does it cost to watch a color television set for 20 hours than a black and white television set for 20 hours? **About $0.30 more**

13. The Mendoza family had 20 loads of laundry last month. Find the total estimated cost of elcctricity for operating both the washer and the dryer. **About $9.10**

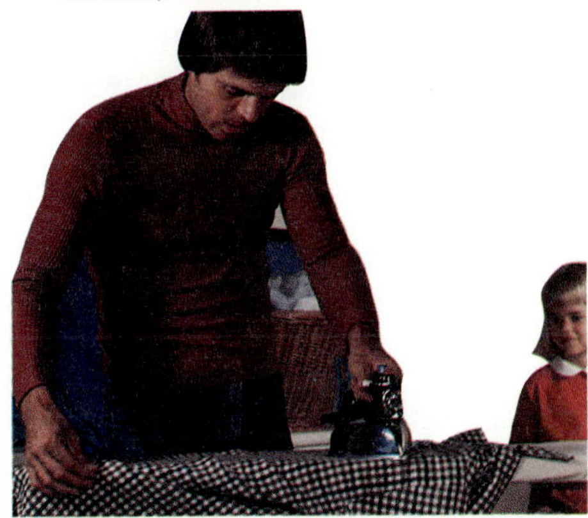

14. The Chung family's electric bill for a 30-day period was $90.00. What percent of the total electric bill was the estimated cost of running the refrigerator/freezer during this period? **10%**

15. Isaac Neff watches an average of 35 hours of color television each week. About how much can he save in yearly electricity costs by limiting his television time to 15 hours per week? **About $52**

2 Teaching the Lesson

Focus students' attention on the table. Ask these questions.

1. How is electricity measured? (Kilowatt-hours)
2. How much does it cost to watch a color television for one hour? (5¢)
3. How much would it cost you to watch 20 hours of color television? ($1.00)

Have students answer question 1 in the lesson. Then discuss the Example.

2 Close

Summary: Have students discuss different ways they use electricity and how they might conserve electricity by using it more wisely.

Evaluation
Guided Practice: Ex. 2–8 even
Independent Practice: Ex. 1–7 odd, 9–15

Extension

Have students do an energy usage survey of appliances in their homes. They should keep track of how much each appliance is used. Then calculate how much it costs to run each appliance.

Problem-Solving Skills

Using a table (Ex. 1–15)
Solving a multi-step problem (Ex. 12–15)
Choosing the operation (Ex. 14, 15)

Estimation
Ex. 9, 11, 13 and 14

Lesson Resources

Maintenance: See below.
Reteaching/Alternate Teaching Strategy: p. M-41 (Visual 34)
Practice: p. M-41
Enrichment: p. M-41
Concrete Materials: Activity Worksheets 61A and 61B, and Visual 34
Visual 34

Objectives

Student will

1. read an electric meter to compute the number of kilowatt-hours of electricity used.
2. read a gas meter to compute the number of cubic feet of gas used.

Maintenance

1. Divide: 18 ÷ 25 ANS: 0.72
2. Write 0.32 as a percent. ANS: 32%
3. 16 is what percent of 64? ANS: 25%
4. What is 40% of 30? ANS: 12
5. In last week's basketball game, Chris made 12 of the 16 shots he took. What percent of his shots did he make? ANS: 75%

[1] Lesson Focus

Motivation: Ask students how the utility company keeps track of how much energy its customers are using.

Purpose: This lesson will demonstrate to students how they can read utility meters. This will allow them to monitor their own usage and check the utility company.

Reading Meters

Use these rules to read an electric meter.

Rules

1. Read the dials from left to right.
2. When the hand is between the numbers, read the smaller number.
3. When the hand is between 0 and 9, read 9.

Previous Reading

KILOWATT-HOURS

Present Reading

KILOWATT-HOURS

1. Do you read the first dial of the previous reading as 5 or 6? Why?
5; when the hand is between numbers, you read the smaller number.
2. Do you read the second dial of the previous reading as 9 or 0? Why?
9; when the hand is between 0 and 9, you read 9.

EXAMPLE 1 Read the meters above to find the number of killowatt–hours used.

[1] Previous reading: **5902** Present reading: **7019**

[2] Subtract: 7019 − 5902 = **1117 kilowatt–hours**

Meters measure the amount of gas used in hundreds of cubic feet.

Previous Reading

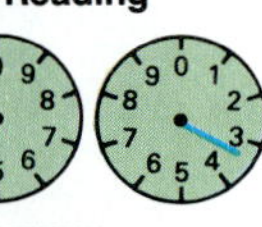

CUBIC FEET

Present Reading

CUBIC FEET

EXAMPLE 2 Read the meters above to find the number of cubic feet of gas used.

[1] Previous reading: **143** Present reading: **152**

[2] Subtract: 152 − 143 = **9**

[3] Since gas is measured in units of 100 cubic feet, multiply the difference by 100. → 9 × 100 = **900 cubic feet**

CHECK YOUR SKILLS

Complete. For additional practice, see pages 366 and 367.

1. 4819 − ? = 3795 1024
2. 8001 − ? = 7453 548
3. 4886 + ? = 5794 908
4. 3860 + ? = 4205 345
5. 396 − ? = 289 107
6. 7003 − ? = 6257 746

EXERCISES

For Exercises 1–2, find the meter reading.

1. 2.

1. 4294
2. 8193

For Exercises 3–5, find how many kilowatt-hours were used.

3. Present Reading: 5794
   Previous Reading: 4886
   908
4. Present Reading: 7593
   Previous Reading: 6187
   1406
5. Present Reading: 3850
   Previous Reading: 3078
   772
6. Last month, Vicki Frost's electric meter read 5689. It now reads 7153. How many kilowatt-hours of electricity were used?
   1464 kilowatt-hours
7. Thomas Pittman's gas meter has a reading of 314. One month ago the meter read 298. Find how many cubic feet of gas Thomas used.
   1600 cubic feet

For Exercises 8–10, read the meters to find how many cubic feet of gas were used.

8. 9. 10.

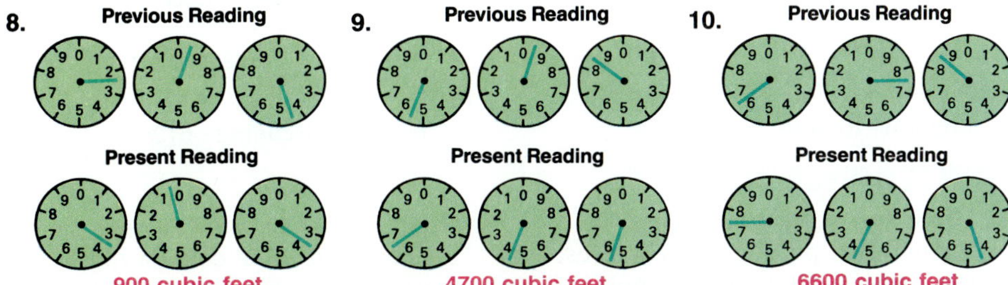

8. 900 cubic feet
9. 4700 cubic feet
10. 6600 cubic feet

11. On August 31, the Jackson family's gas meter read 645. A representative from the gas company mistakenly recorded the reading as 654. a. Higher; the mistaken reading is 9 hundred, or 900 cubic feet, higher than the actual reading.
    a. Will the Jackson family's gas bill for the period ending August 31 be higher or lower than it should be? Explain.
    b. Will the gas bill for the period beginning August 31 be higher or lower than it should be? Explain. Lower; they already paid for the first 900 cubic feet they use on last month's bill.

2 Teaching the Lesson

Have students read the instructions in the box at the top of the page. Then direct students' attention to the two sets of electric meter dials. Have students answer questions 1 and 2. Discuss Example 1. Then direct students' attention to the 2 sets of gas meter dials. Inform students that gas meters are read the same way as electric meters. Discuss Example 2.

3 Close

Summary: Draw a set of electric meter dials on the chalkboard. Have a student come to the chalkboard and explain how to read the dials.

Evaluation
Guided Practice: Ex. 2, 4, 8, 10
Independent Practice: Ex. 1–5 odd, 6, 7, 9, 11

Extension

Have students read their electric meters at home daily for a week. Have them make a bar graph showing their daily electricity usage. Then have them analyze the difference in daily usages.

Problem-Solving Skills

Using logical reasoning (Ex. 11)

Critical Thinking

You may wish to have students work in small groups to solve this problem or you may wish to work with the class.

Ex. 11

Objective

Student will

1. review the skills, concepts, and applications in the first part of Chapter 11.
2. maintain key skills and concepts taught in Chapters 5, 7, 9, and 10.

Using the Page

Exercises 1–10 provide an informal assessment of the student's mastery of the major skills and concepts presented in the first half of Chapter 11. Each item is referenced to the related pages where the particular item was presented. These exercises parallel the quiz provided in the *Teacher's ResourceBank.*™

A quiz covering the second half of the chapter is also provided in the *Teacher's ResourceBank.*™

Exercises 11–14 maintain skills and concepts taught in Chapters 5, 7, 9, and 10.

Mid-Chapter Review

1. Last year, the Calderon family spent $870 heating their home with the thermostat set at 69°F. About how much would they have spent if they had kept the thermostat at 67°F? (Pages 258–260) About $52.20

2. The Marney family spent $580 on cooling costs last year. They kept their thermostat at 78°F. Use the table on page 259 to find how much more they would have spent if they had kept the thermostat at 75°F. (Pages 258–260) About $742.40

For Exercises 3–6, use the table on page 262 to find the cost of operating each appliance. (Pages 262–263)

	Appliance	*Amount of Use*
3.	Vacuum Cleaner	12 hours $1.08
4.	Dishwasher	28 loads $2.24
5.	Iron	18 hours $1.44
6.	Television (color)	35 hours $1.75

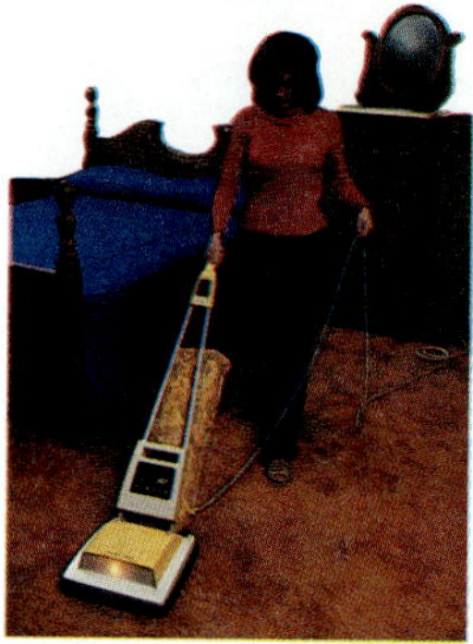

For Exercises 7–8, find the meter reading. (Pages 264–265)

7.  3470

8. 4294

Find how many cubic feet of gas were used. (Pages 264–265)

9. Present Reading: 516
Previous Reading: 497 1900 cubic feet

10. Present Reading: 630
Previous Reading: 612 1800 cubic feet

MAINTENANCE

11. Mitch has $1500 in a savings account that pays a yearly interest rate of $6\frac{1}{2}$%. How much simple interest will the account earn in six months? (Pages 110–111) $48.75

12. On double discount savings day, Gina used a 15¢ coupon to buy a can of corn regularly priced at 59¢. Find the price Gina paid for the corn. (Pages 206–207) $0.29

13. Martin drove 203 miles. His car's fuel economy was 29 miles per gallon, and he paid $1.12 per gallon of gasoline. Find the total gasoline cost. (Pages 160–162) $7.84

14. Cathy Small lives in a city where the property tax is $7.60 per $100 of assessed value. Her property is assessed at $47,500. Find the tax amount. (Pages 245–247) $3610

Math and Solar Energy

Eric Connors gives the Benallys the chart below to show how much they can save in one year by using solar energy.

Climate Zone	Electricity: Kilowatt-hours Saved (kwh)	Oil: Gallons Saved
1	19,900	757
2	16,000	612
3	24,000	914
4	12,200	466
5	9,900	377
6	29,000	1,103

EXAMPLE The Benallys live in Climate Zone 2. Their cost for electricity is \$0.05 per kilowatt-hour. How much will they save in one year if they install a solar heating and hot water system?

1. Find the number of kilowatt-hours saved. → **16,000**
2. Multiply the number of kilowatt-hours by the cost per kilowatt-hour. → $16{,}000 \times 0.05 = \mathbf{800}$

They will save about **\$800** on electricity costs.

EXERCISES

For Exercises 1–2, complete the table.

	Climate Zone	Electricity			Oil		
		Cost per Kwh	Kwh Saved	Dollars Saved	Cost per Gallon	Gallons Saved	Dollars Saved
1.	1	\$0.05	19,900 ?	\$995 ?	\$0.90	? 757	\$681.30 ?
2.	3	\$0.045	24,000 ?	\$1080 ?	\$1.10	? 914	\$1005.40 ?

\$1015

3. The Mitchell family lives in Zone 6. Their cost for electricity is \$0.035 per kilowatt-hour. How much could they save in one year if they used a solar heating and hot water system?

12 years

4. The solar system that the Benallys want to buy will cost about \$9200. Estimate how many years they will have to use the system before the savings are greater than the cost.

Objective

Student will use a table to solve problems that involve solar energy.

Overview

This page is an extension of the skills and ideas presented in the previous lessons of this chapter. Since the content presented on this page is not included in the Chapter Review or Chapter Test, its use is optional.

Using the Pages

You may wish to have students work this lesson in small groups or you may wish to work with the class. Using it with the class, have a student read the first paragraph. Then focus students' attention on the table. Explain that the climate zone is dependent on the average temperature of an area. Work through the Example and assign Exercises 1–4 as independent practice.

Problem-Solving Skills

Using a table (Ex. 1–3)
Using estimation (Ex. 4)

Estimation Ex. 4

Lesson Resources

Maintenance: See below.
Reteaching/Alternate Teaching Strategy: p. M-41 (Visual 35)
Practice: p. M-41
Enrichment: p. M-41
Concrete Materials: Visual 35
Visual 35

Objective

Student will use a table and estimation to solve multi-step problems that involve wallpapering.

Maintenance

1. Complete: 2 years = __?__ months ANS: 24
2. Multiply: 12 × 25 ANS: 300
3. Multiply: $12.96 × 16 ANS: $207.36
4. Add: 932 + 6853 ANS: 7785
5. Julie made a down payment of $400 on a new car and will pay $180 each month for 4 years. Find the total amount she will pay for the car. ANS: $9040

1 Lesson Focus

Motivation: Ask students what information they think they would need to know before they could purchase wallpaper for a room.

Purpose: This lesson describes how to determine how many rolls of wallpaper to buy when you know the dimensions of a room and are using a manufacturer's table. This skill will be useful when students decorate their homes and apartments in the future.

STRATEGY: USING "HIDDEN QUESTIONS" TO SOLVE A MULTI-STEP PROBLEM

Wallpapering and Estimation

Sam and Nina Benally want to wallpaper the den in their home. They use this table to estimate how much wallpaper they need.

CEILING HEIGHT	2.4 Meters	2.7 Meters	3 Meters	3.3 Meters	3.6 Meters
Size of Room in Meters	NUMBER OF SINGLE ROLLS				
2.4 × 3.0	9	10	11	12	13
3.0 × 3.0	10	11	13	14	15
3.0 × 4.3	12	14	15	15	16
3.6 × 3.6	12	14	15	16	18
3.6 × 4.3	13	15	16	18	18
3.6 × 4.9	14	16	17	18	18

NOTE: Subtract 1 roll for each door.
Subtract 1 roll for every two windows.

1. How many rolls of wallpaper should you subtract for 4 windows? for 5 windows? 2 rolls; $2\frac{1}{2}$ rolls

EXAMPLE

The Benallys' den is 3.5 meters long, 4.1 meters wide, and 3 meters high. There are 2 doors and 5 windows. Estimate how many single rolls of wallpaper Nina and Sam should buy.

1 Round 3.5 × 4.1 up to the nearest measure in the table. → **3.6 × 4.3**

2 Find the number of rolls. Refer to the table . → **16**

3 Compute the allowance for doors and windows.

2 Doors:	2 rolls	From the table
5 Windows:	$2\frac{1}{2}$ rolls	
Total allowance:	$4\frac{1}{2}$ rolls	

4 Subtract: $16 - 4\frac{1}{2} = 11\frac{1}{2}$, or **12** — Rounded up to the next whole number

The Benallys will need about **12 single rolls of wallpaper.**

2. Why do you round up when estimating how much wallpaper to buy? You do not want to run short of wallpaper.

CHECK YOUR SKILLS

ESTIMATION/MENTAL MATH: Ex. 1–8

Estimate each answer.
pages 380 and 393.

1. \$10.52 × 19 **\$200**
2. \$12.96 × 31 **\$390**
3. \$19.75 × 21 **\$400**
4. \$40.03 × 31 **\$1200**
5. $4\frac{7}{8} + 9\frac{5}{6}$ **15**
6. $8 - 1\frac{4}{5}$ **6**
7. $11\frac{1}{8} - 7\frac{11}{12}$ **3**
8. $6\frac{1}{10} + 21\frac{1}{5}$ **27**

EXERCISES

For Exercises 1–9, use the table on page 268 to estimate the number of single rolls of wallpaper needed for each room.

1. Dining Room

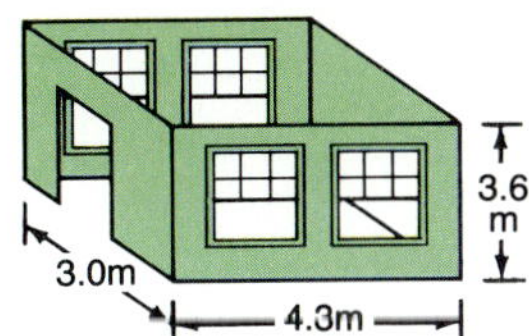

Number of Doors: 2
Number of Windows: 4
About 12 rolls

2. Den

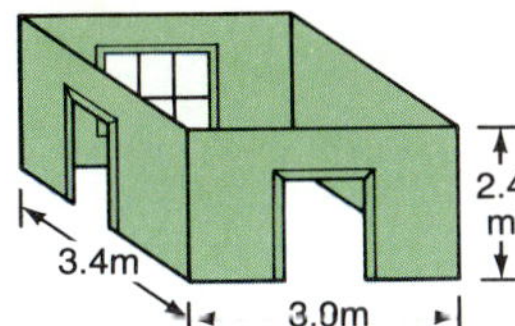

Number of Doors: 2
Number of Windows: 1
About 11 rolls

3. Kitchen

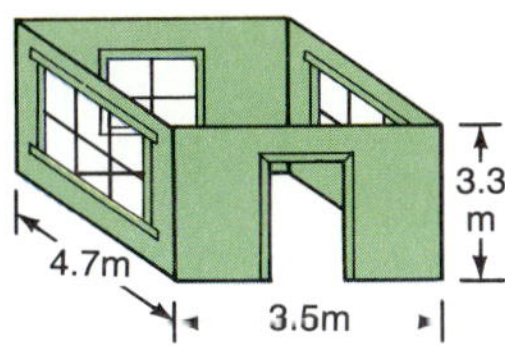

Number of Doors: 1
Number of Windows: 3
About 16 rolls

	Room	Length	Width	Height	Doors	Windows
4.	Kitchen	3.6 m	3.6 m	2.7 m	2	4 **About 10 rolls**
5.	Living Room	4.3 m	3.6 m	3.0 m	3	5 **About 11 rolls**
6.	Hall	2.8 m	2.3 m	2.4 m	2	0 **About 7 rolls**

7. Laura Yancey wants to paper the walls of her living room. The room is 4.3 meters long, 3 meters wide, and 2.4 meters high. There are four windows and three doors. Estimate how many single rolls of wallpaper Laura will need. **About 7 rolls**

8. Tim Indo's den is 3.6 meters long and 3.6 meters wide. It has a ceiling height of 3 meters. Tim plans to paper just one wall of his den. The wall has two windows on it. How many single rolls of wallpaper Tim should buy. **3 rolls**

9. Chen Wong plans to wallpaper his bedroom. The room is 2.9 meters long, 4.1 meters wide, and 2.7 meters high. There are three windows and a door. The wallpaper that Chen wants costs \$9.95 per roll. Estimate the total cost. **About \$120**

2 Teaching the Lesson

Focus students' attention on the table. Ask questions such as:

1. What two things do you need to know to use this table? (Size of room, ceiling height)
2. If you wanted to wallpaper a room 2.7 m wide by 3.0 m long, which row would you use in the table? (3.0 × 3.0)
3. If you used the 2.4 × 3.0 row with this room, what might happen? (You might not have enough paper.)
4. If the ceiling is 2.5 m high, what column should you use? (2.7 m)

Have students answer question 1 in the lesson. Then work through the Example and have students answer question 2.

3 Close

Summary: Have the students list the things they have to know before they can estimate the amount of wallpaper to buy.

Evaluation
Guided Practice: Ex. 2–6 even
Independent Practice: Ex. 1–5 odd, 7–9

Extension

Have students measure the dimensions of their rooms at home. Then have them go to a wallpaper store and use a commercial table to determine how many rolls to buy.

Problem-Solving Skills

Using estimation (Ex. 1–9)
Using a table (Ex. 1–9)
Solving a multi-step problem (Ex. 1–9)
Using a diagram (Ex. 1–3)

Lesson Resources

Maintenance: See below.
Reteaching/Alternate Teaching Strategy: p. M-42 (Visual 36)
Practice: p. M-42
Enrichment: p. M-42
Visual 36

Objective

Student will solve multi-step problems to estimate the amount of paint needed to paint a room.

Maintenance

1. Multiply: 3.6 × 2.7 ANS: 9.72
2. Round 37.85 to the nearest whole number. ANS: 38
3. Add: 178 + 124 + 134 + 53 ANS: 489
4. Evaluate: (3 × 24) + (2 × 16) ANS: 104
5. The adult train fare to Columbus is $150. The fare for a child is $85. Find the total train fare for 2 adults and 3 children. ANS: $555

1 Lesson Focus

Motivation: Ask the students what they would need to know to determine how much paint to buy for a room.

Purpose: This lesson will inform students how to use the surface area of a room to estimate how much paint to buy. This will help students in their future roles as consumers in decorating their homes and apartments.

2 Teaching the Lesson

Have students read the first 3 sentences of the lesson and answer question 1. Discuss question 2 with the class. Then draw this diagram on the chalkboard.

Front	Side	Back	Side	3 m
5 m	4 m	5 m	4 m	

STRATEGY: USING "HIDDEN QUESTIONS" TO SOLVE A MULTI-STEP PROBLEM

Painting and Estimation

The Benallys are painting the living room in their house. Nina finds this information on the back of a paint can.

One liter of paint covers an area of 9 square meters.

1. About how much paint is needed to cover an area of 36 square meters? About 4 liters
2. To cover an area of 39 square meters, should you buy 4 liters of paint or 5 liters of paint? Why? 5 liters, because 39 ÷ 9 is greater than 4.

EXAMPLE Nina and Sam's living room is 4.3 meters long, 3.6 meters wide, and 2.8 meters high. About how many liters of paint are needed?

FRONT	SIDE	BACK	SIDE	2.8 m
4.3 m	3.6 m	4.3 m	3.6 m	

1 To find the area of the walls, multiply the perimeter and the height of the room.
Perimeter → 4.3 m + 3.6 m + 4.3 m + 3.6 m = **15.8 m**
Area of Walls → 15.8 m × 2.8 m = **44.24 m²**

2 Find the area of the ceiling.
4.3 m × 3.6 m = **15.48 m²** ◀ *Length × Width = Area*

3 Find the total area of the walls and the ceiling.
44.24 m² + 15.48 m² = 59.72, or **60 m²** ◀ *Rounded up to the next whole number*

4 Find how much paint is needed.
60 ÷ 9 = 6.66 or **7 liters** ◀ *Rounded up to the next whole number*

CHECK YOUR SKILLS

ESTIMATION/MENTAL MATH: Ex. 1–6

Estimate to determine whether the answer is reasonable. Answer Yes or No. For additional practice, see pages 52–53.

1. 4.3 + 3.4 + 2.7 + 3.2 = 18.6 No
2. 9.7 + 3.4 + 2.7 + 5.8 = 19.6 No
3. 44.78 + 15.25 = 50.04 No
4. 63.27 + 26.53 = 89.8 Yes
5. 4.9 × 3.4 = 16.66 Yes
6. 3.1 × 2.9 = 8.99 Yes

EXERCISES

Complete. Choose your answers from the box at the right.

width of room
area of ceiling
4
height of room
area of walls
5

1. Perimeter of Room × Height of Room = __?__ area of walls

2. Area of Ceiling = Length of Room × __?__ width of room

3. If 1 liter of paint covers an area of 9 square meters, then you will need __?__ liters of paint to cover 40 square meters. 5

For Exercises 4–13, estimate the number of liters of paint needed to paint the walls and ceiling of each room. (NOTE: One liter of paint covers 9 square meters.)

	Room	Perimeter	Height	Area of Walls	Area of Ceiling	Area of Walls and Ceiling	Liters of Paint
4.	Hall	10 m	2.9 m	? $29\ m^2$	$6.16\ m^2$	? $36\ m^2$	? 4
5.	Den	14.8 m	3 m	? $44.4\ m^2$	$13.33\ m^2$	? $58\ m^2$	? 7
6.	Bedroom	14.2 m	3.2 m	? $45.44\ m^2$	$12.58\ m^2$	? $58\ m^2$	? 7

7. Dining Room 8 liters

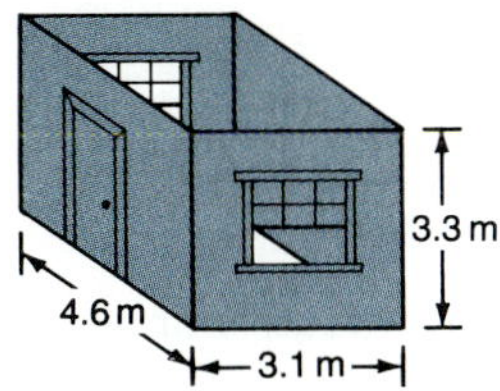

8. Hallway 7 liters

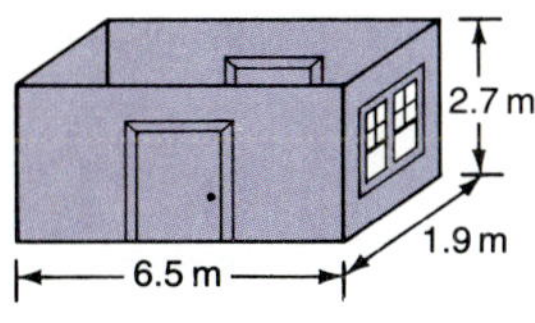

9. Living Room 7 liters

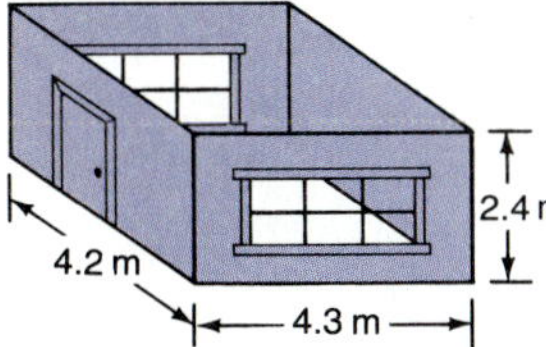

10. The living room in Robert's house is 5.2 meters long and 4.5 meters wide. The walls are 2.4 meters high. About how many liters of paint does Robert need to paint this room? About 8 liters

11. Sarah's bedroom is 5 meters long, 3.4 meters wide, and 2.7 meters high. Sarah wants to paint the walls blue and the ceiling white. How many liters of each color of paint should she buy? 6 liters of blue and 2 liters of white

12. Gretchen's family room is 6 meters long, 4.2 meters wide, and 2.8 meters high. The paint she bought for the walls cost $5.49 per liter. The paint for the ceiling cost $6.99 per liter. Find the total cost of the paint. $59.40

13. The Fifers are painting a room that is 6.5 meters long, 5.5 meters wide, and 3 meters high. One-liter cans of paint cost $3.99 each and four-liter cans cost $10.80 each. Estimate how much the Fifers will save by buying the four-liter cans. $15

Explain that the diagram shows the lengths and height of the four walls of a room. To find the area of all four walls, they could find the area of each wall and then add. Another way would be to find the perimeter of the room and multiply the perimeter by the height. Ask these questions.

1. What is the perimeter of the room? (18 m)
2. What is the total area of the four walls? (18 × 3, or 54 m^2)
3. What are the dimensions of the ceiling? (5 m × 4 m)
4. What is the area of the ceiling? (20 m^2)

Make sure students understand that they are finding both the area of the walls and of the ceiling for the exercises. Discuss the Example.

3 Close

Summary: Have students list what they need to know before they can estimate the amount of paint to buy for a room.

Evaluation

Guided Practice: Ex. 1–3, 4–8 even
Independent Practice: Ex. 5–9 odd, 10–13

Extension

Have students measure the dimensions of their own rooms at home and calculate the amount of paint they would need to paint the entire room.

Problem-Solving Skills

Using estimation (Ex. 4–13)
Solving a multi-step problem (Ex. 4–13)
Using a diagram (Ex. 7–9)

Lesson Resources

Maintenance: See below.
Reteaching/Alternate Teaching Strategy: See the margin on page 273.
Practice: Activity Worksheet 64
Enrichment: See the enrichment topic "Telephone Costs" on page 276.

Objectives

Student will

1. make a model to solve problems that involve area and perimeter.
2. choose and apply an appropriate strategy to solve a problem.

Maintenance

Find the perimeter of each rectangle.

1. Length: 5 inches Width: 3 inches
   ANS: 16 inches
2. Length: 10 cm Width: 6 cm
   ANS: 32 cm

Find the area of each rectangle.

3. Length: 4 feet Width: 3 feet
   ANS: 12 square feet
4. Length: 8 meters Width: 7 meters
   ANS: 56 square meters
5. A rectangle has a length of 12 inches and a width of 8 inches. Which is greater, the perimeter or the area?
   ANS: Area

1 Lesson Focus

Motivation: Draw a rectangle on the chalkboard. Ask students to tell what the length and width would have to be for the area to be 40 square feet. Discuss the different answers.

Purpose: Students need to see that there are a variety of strategies to solve a problem. This lesson will make them more aware of making a model to solve a problem.

Strategy: MAKING A MODEL

Tony wants to fence in as large a rectangular pen as possible for his dog. His father told him to use the thirty feet of fencing stored in the garage.

1. Will Tony find the perimeter or the area of the pen? **Both**
2. What must Tony find before he can determine the area of the pen? **length and width**

EXAMPLE What will be the dimensions of the pen?

READ What are the facts?
The pen will be a rectangle.
The perimeter of the pen will be 30 feet.

PLAN Use graph paper to draw possible rectangles having a perimeter of 30.

Think: $2\ell + 2w = 30$
$\ell + w = 15$ ◀ *One length + one width equals half the perimeter.*

SOLVE Complete the table to find the rectangle with the greatest area.

Width (ft)	Length (ft)	Perimeter (ft) $2\ell + 2w = P$	Area (ft^2) $\ell \times w = A$
1	14	2 + 28 = 30	1 × 14 = 14
2	? 13	4 + 26 = 30	2 × 13 = 26
3	12	? 6 + 24 = 30	3 × ? = 36 12
4	? 11	8 + 22 = 30	? 4 × 11 = 44
5 ?	10	? 10 + 20 = 30	5 × 10 = 50
6	9	12 + 18 = 30	? 6 × 9 = 54
? 7	8	? 14 + 16 = 30	7 × 8 = 56 ◀ *Greatest area: 56 ft^2*

The pen with the greatest area is 7 feet wide and 8 feet long.

CHECK Did you use the facts correctly in the problem?
Is the answer reasonable?

EXERCISES

1. Draw three different rectangles having a perimeter of 12 units.
   a. Find the area of each rectangle. **5, 8, and 9 square units**
   b. Which rectangle has the greatest area? **3 units × 3 units**

2. Draw 3 different rectangles having an area of 16 square units.
   a. Find the perimeter of each rectangle. **34, 20, and 16 units**
   b. Which rectangle has the smallest perimeter? **4 units × 4 units**

3. Sarah plans to buy edging for the perimeter of a rectangular flower garden. The garden will have an area of 12 square yards. What are the width and length of the garden that will need the least amount of edging? ***w*: 3 yds; *l*: 4 yds**

4. A vacant lot has an area of 100 square meters. It will cost the owner $15 per meter to fence in the lot. What is the least amount the owner can expect to pay for the fencing? **$600**

5. The Chung family plans to enclose 60 square feet of their back yard with a fence. What should be the length and width of the enclosed area if they want the shape to be as close to a square as possible? ***w*: 6 ft; *l*: 10 ft**

For Exercises 6–9, choose a strategy from the box at the right that you can use to solve each problem.
a. Name the strategy. **One strategy is given.**
b. Solve the problem. **Answers may vary.**

Solving a simpler problem
Guess and check
Using estimation
More than one step

6. John is buying wallpaper and paint for his den. The total cost of both is $150. The paper costs four times as much as the paint. Find the cost of the wallpaper. **Guess and check; $120**

7. The perimeter of a storage room is 15.4 meters. The walls are 2.9 meters high. You compute the total area of the four walls to be 33.6 square meters. Is your answer reasonable? **Using estimation; No**

8. For the first five months of the year, Alma's average electric bill was $87.40. For the next seven months, her average electric bill was $73.00. Find her average monthly electric bill for the year. **More than one step; $79**

9. Roy spent $13,000 remodeling three rooms in his home. The cost of remodeling the living room was half the cost of remodeling the kitchen. The cost of remodeling the den was one-fourth the cost of remodeling the living room. How much did it cost to remodel the living room? **Solving a simpler problem; $4000**

2 Teaching the Lesson

After presenting the Example, choose a problem to show how the strategy can be applied in other situations, such as in Exercise 3.

1. **Ask:** What is the problem about? (Finding the length and width of a garden that will use the least amount of edging)
2. **Read** the problem to determine the FACTS. **Ask:** What is the shape of the garden? (Rectangle) **Ask:** What is the area of the garden? (12 square yards)
3. **Plan** the solution. Have students draw all the possible rectangles on a piece of graph paper.
4. **Solve** the problem. Determine the perimeter of each rectangle.
   1 × 12: 26 yards
   2 × 6: 16 yards
   3 × 4: 14 yards
5. **Check** the answer by having students check the facts in the problem with the solution.

3 Close

Summary: Have students discuss what shape is best for containing the most area with the least amount of fencing.

Evaluation:
Guided Practice: Ex. 1–3
Independent Practice: Ex. 4–9

Problem-Solving Skills

Guess and check (Ex. 6)
Using estimation (Ex. 7)
More than one step (Ex. 8)
Solving a simpler problem (Ex. 9)

Alternate Teaching Strategy

You may wish to have students work in small groups to complete the exercises. Have them discuss their ideas for each problem and record the group consensus.

Estimation Ex. 7

NOTE: A quiz covering the second half of the chapter is provided in the *Teacher's ResourceBank™*.

Objectives

Students will

1. explore solutions to a variety of problems that emerge from this situational lesson.
2. explore solutions to problems involving terms of payment that have more than one solution.

Situational Lesson

These two pages present a situational lesson as the framework from which a variety of problem situations emerge.

Teaching Strategies

This lesson lends itself to cooperative learning groups for the problem solving activities of comparing choices and exploring decisions. (See page M-13.)

However, these activities can also be carried out by the class as a whole or by individual students.

1 Lesson Focus

Motivation: Have students discuss different ways they might be able to finance the cost of an addition on a house.

Purpose: As future adult consumers, students should understand that a lower monthly payment will also mean a higher total cost. However, by deferring the payment, they may also be able to invest the money and gain interest.

Consumer's Choice

Because Sam Benally's mother will come to live with them next year, the Benally family has decided to add an extra room to the house.

They asked three different builders to prepare an estimate of the total cost. The builders also indicated how they wished to be paid.

Choice 1 Elgin Builders

Estimate: $19,000

Terms of Payment: $1,000 on signing the construction contract.
$18,000 to be paid one month after the construction is completed.

Choice 2 Togo Construction

Estimate: $21,000

Terms of Payment: $3,000 on signing the construction contract. Thirty-six equal monthly payments plus a monthly interest charge of $110.83.

Choice 3 Baldwin, Inc.

Estimate: $20,000

Terms of Payment: $2,000 on signing the construction contract. Sixty equal monthly payments plus a monthly interest charge of $118.82

Comparing the Choices

1. In Choice 2, how much will the Benallys pay in interest over the 3 years? $3,989.88
2. In Choice 2, how much will the Benallys pay in all for the construction? $24,989.88
3. In Choice 3, how much will the Benallys pay in interest over the 5 years? $7,129.20
4. In Choice 3, how much will the Benallys pay in all for the construction? $27,129.20
5. The Benallys have an investment of $18,000 that will pay $6,267.27 in interest over 3 years. If they select Choice 1 and use the $18,000 to pay the builder, how much will the construction actually cost over 3 years? $25,267.27
6. The Benally's investment of $18,000 will earn $11,615.56 in interest over 5 years. If they select Choice 1 and use the $18,000 they invested to pay the builder, how much will the construction actually cost over 5 years? $30,615.56

EXPLORING DECISIONS

7. Suppose that the Benallys have only $15,000 in savings. What choice does this eliminate? Choice 1
8. Suppose that the Benallys wish to have finished paying for the construction by the time their oldest son is ready for college in 3 years. What choice does this eliminate? Choice 3
9. Name one advantage of Choice 2 over Choice 3. Answers will vary.
10. Name one advantage of Choice 3 over Choice 1. Answers will vary.
11. Suppose that you were a member of the Benally family. Which choice would you make? Give at least 2 reasons for your choice. Answers will vary.

2 Teaching the Lesson

Focus students' attention on the Choices and ask these questions.

1. Why might the Bekally's not be able to consider Choice 1 as an option? (They don't have enough cash.)
2. What would the monthly payment be if they choose Choice 2? ($610.83)
3. What would the monthly payment be if they choose Choice 3? ($418.82)
4. In Choices 2 and 3, what cost must also be included in the cost of the addition? (Interest)

Have the students complete Exercises 1–8. Discuss Exercises 9–11 with the class.

3 Close

Summary: Ask students to name the main advantage of Choice 1 over Choices 2 and 3. (The Benallys will only pay $19,000 for the addition.)

Critical Thinking

Ex. 9–11

Project

Have students go to a financial institution to find out how to take out a home improvement load or home equity loan. Have them find out the different possible payment plans. Have them report their findings to the class.

Objective

Student will use a table to find the cost of a telephone call.

Overview

This topic is optional. The word "Enrichment" that appears to the right of the title in this Teacher's Edition does not appear in the student textbook. Therefore, this material is not included in the Chapter Review and Chapter Test.

Using the Page

You may wish to have students work this Enrichment in small groups or you may wish to work with the class.

Problem-Solving Skills

Using a table (Ex. 1–4)

Telephone Costs ENRICHMENT

Many phone companies give a discount on long distance calls if the calls are made at night or on weekends. The table and key below show how one company determines its rates.

Rates from Houston to	■ Full Rate		▨ 35% Discount		▩ 60% Discount	
	1st Min.	*Each Add'l Min.*	*1st Min.*	*Each Add'l Min.*	*1st Min.*	*Each Add'l Min.*
Galveston	0.40	0.28	0.26	0.18	0.16	0.11
Beaumont	0.51	0.37	0.33	0.24	0.20	0.15
Austin	0.59	0.43	0.38	0.28	0.24	0.17

	M	T	W	T	F	S	S
8 A.M.–5 P.M.	■	■	■	■	■	▩	▩
5 P.M.–11 P.M.	▨	▨	▨	▨	▨	▩	▨
11 P.M.–8 A.M.	▩	▩	▩	▩	▩	▩	▩

Key: ■ represents full rate.
▨ represents 35% discount.
▩ represents 60% discount.

EXAMPLE Find the cost of a 30-minute phone call from Houston to Galveston on Wednesday at 9:00 P.M.

[1] Since 9:00 P.M. is between 5 P.M. and 11 P.M., there is a 35% discount on the rate.

[2] First minute: $0.26 Each additional minute: $0.18
Number of additional minutes: 29
$\$0.26 + (29 \times \$0.18) = \$0.26 + \$5.22$
$= \mathbf{\$5.48}$

The phone call will cost **$5.48.**

EXERCISES

Find the cost of a phone call from Houston to each city.

1. Beaumont
9:00 P.M. Tues.
40 minutes **$9.69**

2. Austin
11:30 P.M. Mon.
50 minutes **$8.57**

3. Galveston
10:00 A.M. Fri.
1 hour 5 minutes
$18.32

4. Austin
10:30 P.M. Sat.
12 minutes
$2.11

PROJECT Find information on the rates and discounts used for long distance phone calls by the phone companies in your area. Then use the information to determine the cost of a 30-minute long distance call at the full rate and at the discount rate(s).

Chapter Summary

IMPORTANT IDEAS

1. Lowering the thermostat setting in cool weather and raising the thermostat setting in warm weather will save on heating and cooling costs.
2. Electricity is measured in **kilowatt-hours.**
3. The amount of wallpaper needed to paper a room depends on the size of the room and the number of doors and windows.
4. **Perimeter of Room × Height of Room = Area of Walls**
5. **Length of Room × Width of Room = Area of Ceiling**

Chapter Review

Part 1: VOCABULARY

For Exercises 1–5, choose from the box at the right the word(s) that complete(s) each statement.

area
present meter reading
cubic feet
meter
thermostat setting
kilowatt-hour
width
previous meter reading

1. Heating costs are lowered by 3% for each degree Fahrenheit that the _?_ is lowered. (Pages 000–000) thermostat setting
2. One thousand watts of electricity used for one hour is one _?_ of electricity. (Pages 000–000) kilowatt-hour
3. To find the number of kilowatt-hours of electricity used, subtract the _?_ from the _?_. (Pages 000–000) previous meter reading; present meter reading
4. Gas bills are based on the number of _?_ of gas used. (Pages 000–000) cubic feet
5. The amount of paint needed for a room depends on the combined _?_ of the walls and ceiling. (Pages 000–000) area

Chapter Summary

The Chapter Summary contains a listing of the important ideas that were presented in the chapter. This listing is intended to assist the student with the Chapter Review that follows.

Objective

To review the important terms, skills, problem solving, and applications presented in Chapter 11.

Overview

The Chapter Review is structured in three parts. Part 1 is a review of the important terms that were introduced in the chapter. Part 2 reviews the skills that were presented in the chapter. Part 3 reviews the problem-solving strategies and applications that were presented in the chapter. Each item in the Chapter Review is referenced to the related pages where the concept, skill, or application was presented.

Using the Pages

You may wish to assign this Chapter Review for homework or treat it as a class review prior to administering the formal Chapter Test. In doing this, it is suggested that you only use the even- or odd-numbered exercises. You can then use the remaining exercises as a bank for use later.

Part 2: SKILLS

For Exercises 6–7, find how much each family could save on last year's heating costs. (Pages 258–260)

	Last Year's Heating Costs	Last Year's Thermostat Setting	This Year's Thermostat Setting
6.	$875	68°F	65°F $78.75
7.	$1250	69°F	65°F $150

For Exercises 8–9, use the table on page 262 to find the estimated cost of operating each appliance. (Pages 262–263)

	Appliance	Amount of Use
8.	Dryer	27 loads $11.61
9.	Iron	9 hours $0.72

For Exercises 10–12, find the meter reading. (Pages 264–265)

10. 409 **11.** 710 **12.** 392

For Exercises 13–15, find how many kilowatt-hours of electricity were used. (Pages 264–265)

13. Present reading: 4567
Previous reading: 3295
1272

14. Present Reading: 6785
Previous Reading: 5849
936

15. Present Reading: 5402
Previous Reading: 4263
1139

For Exercises 16–17, use the table on page 268 to estimate the amount of wallpaper needed for each room. (Pages 268–269)

	Room	Length	Width	Height	Doors	Windows
16.	Den	4.3 m	3.6 m	2.7 m	2	4 About 11 rolls
17.	Kitchen	2.7 m	3.5 m	2.4 m	1	5 About 9 rolls

For Exercises 18–19, estimate the number of liters of paint needed to paint the walls and ceiling of each room. (NOTE: One liter of paint covers 9 square meters.) (Pages 270–271)

	Room	Length	Width	Height	Area of Walls	Area of Ceiling	Area of Walls and Ceiling	Liters of Paint
18.	Bedroom	5 m	4.3 m	2.7 m	? 50.22 m²	? 21.5 m²	? 72 m²	? 8
19.	Hall	4.2 m	3.6 m	3.1 m	? 48.36 m²	? 15.12 m²	? 64 m²	? 8

278 CHAPTER 11

Part 3: APPLICATIONS

20. The Shaws spent $980 to heat their home last year. They kept the thermostat at 70°F. Use the table on page 258 to find how much can they save by setting the thermostat at 68°F this year? (Pages 258–260) **About $58.80**

21. The Osaka family spent $650 on cooling costs last year. They kept their thermostat at 78°F. Use the table on page 259 to find how much they would have spent if they had kept the thermostat at 76°F. (Pages 258–260) **About $767**

For Exercises 22–23, use the table on page 262 to find the cost of operating each appliance. (Pages 262–263)

22. Rick Willey used his vacuum cleaner for 8 hours last month. About how much did this add to his electric bill? **About $0.72**

23. Kim Lanterman averages five loads of laundry per week. Find the total estimated cost of electricity for operating the washer and dryer each week. **About $2.28**

24. An electric meter reads 6472. Last month, the meter read 5159. How many kwh's were used? (Pages 264–265) **1313 kilowatt-hours**

25. Last month, Tom Rothrock's gas meter read 417. It now reads 431. Find the number of cubic feet of gas Tom used. (Pages 264–265) **1400 cubic feet**

For Exercises 26–27, use the table on page 268 to estimate the number of single rolls of wallpaper needed for each room. (Pages 268–269)

26. Dave's kitchen is 4.3 meters long and 3 meters wide. It has a ceiling height of 3.3 meters. There are two doors and four windows. About how many single rolls will he need? **About 11 rolls**

27. Carol plans to wallpaper her dining room. The room is 3.4 meters long, 3.9 meters wide, and 2.7 meters high. There are three windows and a door. How many single rolls should Carol buy? **13 rolls**

28. The family room in Anna's house is 4.5 meters long and 3.2 meters wide. The walls are 2.7 meters high. About how many liters of paint does Anna need to paint this room? (Pages 270–271) **About 7 liters**

29. A garden has an area of 36 square yards. If fencing costs $18 per square yard, what is the least amount the owner can expect to pay to fence in the garden? Pages 272–273) **$432**

Objective

To informally assess students' mastering of the major skills, concepts, problem solving, and applications presented in Chapter 11.

Using the Page

After completing the Chapter Review with the class, you may wish to use this Chapter Test as an informal assessment. This Chapter Test parallels the formal chapter tests (Form A and Form B) provided in the *Teacher's ResourceBank.*™

Chapter Test

1. Last year, the Sheng family spent $1250 on heating their home with the thermostat set at 72°F. About how much would they have spent if they had kept the thermostat at 69°F? **About $1137.50**

2. The Taylors spent $720 on cooling costs. If they had set their thermostat 2° higher, they would have saved about 16%. About how much would they have saved? **About $115.20**

For Exercises 3–4, find the estimated cost of operating each appliance.

	Appliance	Cost of Electricity	Amount of Use
3.	Iron	8¢ per hour	12 hours **$0.96**
4.	Dryer	43¢ per load	25 loads **$10.75**

5. Last month, Dora's gas meter read 562. It now reads 579. How many cubic feet of gas were used? **17 cubic feet**

For Exercises 6–7, find the meter reading.

6. **2803**

7. **8695**

8. Karen and Dale Coleman plan to wallpaper their family room. The room is 4.3 meters long, 3.6 meters wide, and 3 meters high. There are three windows and two doors. Use the table at the right to find the number of single rolls of wallpaper the Colemans need to buy. **13 rolls**

SIZE OF ROOM (METERS): 3.6 × 4.3				
Ceiling height (meters)	2.7	3.0	3.3	3.6
Number of Single Rolls	15	16	18	18
NOTE: Subtract 1 roll for each door and 1 roll for every two windows.				

9. Jill wants to paint her living room. The room is 4.6 meters long and 3.4 meters wide. The walls are 2.5 meters high. One liter will cover 9 square meters. About how many liters of paint does Jill need? **About 7 liters**

10. Abe plans to enclose 72 square yards of a lot with fencing. What should be the length and width of the enclosed area if he wants the shape to be as close to a square as possible? **l: 9 yd; w: 8 yd**

Cumulative Maintenance Chapters 1–11

Choose the correct answer. Choose a, b, c, or d.

1. Divide: 2.46 ÷ 1.2 a

   a. 2.05 b. 2.5
   c. 0.205 d. 20.5

2. The graph below shows the number of cars sold at a car dealership over a five-month period. Find the average number sold each month. c

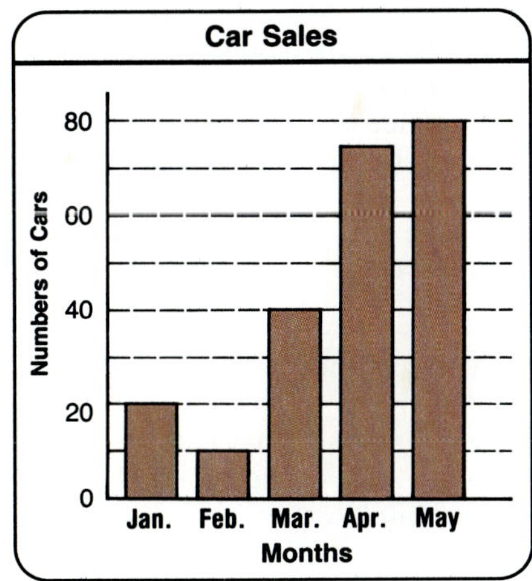

   a. 40 b. 47 c. 46 d. 55

3. The assessed value of the Davis family's home is 48% of its market value. The market value of their home is \$86,000. Find the assessed value. b

   a. \$41,360 b. \$41,280
   c. \$40,880 d. \$44,720

4. What percent of 80 is 16? c

   a. 5% b. 2%
   c. 20% d. 50%

5. Michael rented a car for 5 days and had 126 miles of excess mileage. The rental rate was \$21.99 per day plus 25¢ per mile for excess mileage. Find the total rental cost. d

   a. \$53.49 b. \$140.45
   c. \$109.95 d. \$141.45

6. When Mario Ortega had his car repaired, the parts cost \$213.70 and the labor cost \$105.00. Mario paid a sales tax of 4% on the parts. Find the total repair bill. a

   a. \$327.25 b. \$331.45
   c. \$318.70 d. \$222.25

7. Subtract:

$$12 - 4\frac{1}{2}$$ c

   a. $8\frac{1}{2}$ b. $16\frac{1}{2}$ c. $7\frac{1}{2}$ d. 8

8. Find the number of liters of paint needed to paint the walls and ceiling of the room below. (NOTE: One liter of paint covers 9 square meters.) c

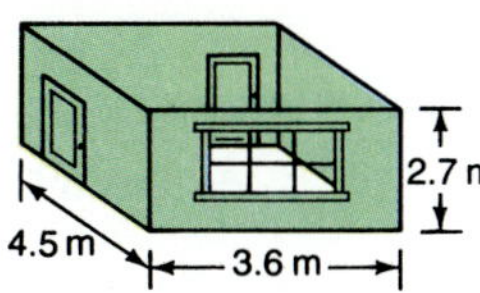

   a. 5 b. 60 c. 7 d. 6

Objective

To review the content presented in Chapters 1–11

Using the Pages

You may wish to use this Cumulative Maintenance as an informal assessment tool. These pages can be assigned for homework or they may be used as review in class.

9. Virginia Vafakos receives a salary of \$16,500 per year plus a commission of 3% on sales. What are her total earnings for a year in which her total sales amount to \$240,000? d

a. \$7200　**b.** \$240,495
c. \$23,600　**d.** \$23,700

10. Write 40% as a fraction. b

a. $\frac{1}{40}$　**b.** $\frac{2}{5}$　**c.** $\frac{1}{4}$　**d.** $\frac{3}{5}$

11. Debbie Graff must pay \$3419 in federal income tax this year. The amount of tax withheld from her pay was \$3523. Find the amount of the refund or the balance due. a

a. Refund: \$104
b. Refund: \$114
c. Balance due: \$104
d. Balance due: \$114

12. Find the total cost of the car below. a

Base Price:	\$8940.00
Optional Equipment:	\$1457.10
Destination Charge:	\$295.30
Sales Tax Rate:	5%

a. \$11,227.02　**b.** \$10,692.45
c. \$11,216.52　**d.** \$10,692.40

13. Add: \$8961 + \$37.46 + \$121.50 d

a. \$248.57　**b.** \$9129.96
c. \$9019.96　**d.** \$9119.96

14. Robert bought a can of corn marked 59¢ at a store giving double coupon savings. He used the coupon below. How much did he pay? c

a. 74¢
b. 44¢
c. 29¢
d. 59¢

15. Jessie Curtis buys an 18-ounce box of cereal for \$2.59 instead of a 12-ounce box for \$1.98. How much does she save per ounce? d

a. 61¢　**b.** 16.5¢
c. 14.4¢　**d.** 2.1¢

16. A box of men's shirts contains 12 blue shirts, 9 pink shirts, and 15 white shirts. What is the probability that a shirt chosen at random will be white? b

a. $\frac{1}{15}$　**b.** $\frac{5}{12}$　**c.** $\frac{5}{7}$　**d.** $\frac{1}{3}$

17. Find the balance forward (Bal. For'd.). c

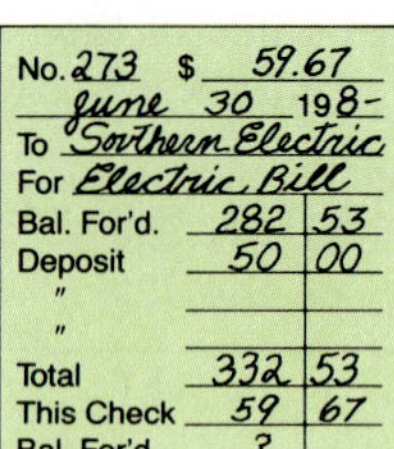

No. 273 \$ 59.67
June 30 198-
To Southern Electric
For Electric Bill

Bal. For'd.	282	53
Deposit	50	00
"		
"		
Total	332	53
This Check	59	67
Bal. For'd.	?	

a. \$283.96
b. \$392.20
c. \$272.86
d. \$327.14

Buying Goods

Joel Santos has been working after school to earn money to buy a stereo. Joel has gathered information about stereos by reading magazine articles, and by talking to his friends that have stereos. Now Joel needs to decide where he should buy his stereo and how he should pay for it.

- Should Joel buy his stereo at a local store or order it through the mail?
- Where can he get the best price?
- Should Joel pay for the stereo with cash, a credit card, or use an installment loan?

Chapter 12: Buying Goods

Overview

The focus of Chapter 12 is on consumer credit, credit cards, and installment loans. As your students progress through this chapter, you may wish to have them bring to class copies of the credit terms of several discount stores, mail order stores, and department stores for comparison and discussion.

Although all lessons in this chapter involve problem solving, the strategy lesson on pages 300–301 presents four strategies from which students are asked to select the most appropriate to apply in a given problem-solving situation. The *Consumer's Choice* on pages 302–303 presents a **situational lesson** in which students must consider various options and choose whether to purchase goods by mail or at a local store. The *Enrichment* lesson on page 304 introduces the topic of annual percentage rate and provides a table which can be used to compare credit costs.

Using This Page

Have students read the introductory paragraph and questions. Have them list possible solutions to the problems presented. After completing the chapter, have students review their suggested solutions, comparing them with those presented in the lessons. You may wish to have students suggest other possible problems resulting from the situation described on this page and to discuss possible solutions.

You may wish to organize the class into small groups to complete the situational activity described on this *Using the Page.*

Lesson Resources

Maintenance: See below.
Reteaching/Alternate Teaching Strategy: p. M-42 (Visual 37)
Practice: p. M-42
Enrichment: p. M-42
Visual 37

Objective

Student will solve multi-step problems that involve the discount and the selling price.

Maintenance

1. Subtract: $37.02 − $5.28 ANS: $31.74
2. Write 17% as a decimal. ANS: 0.17
3. Multiply: $6510 × 0.18 ANS: $1171.80
4. Add: $3752 + $1804 ANS: $5556
5. Albert's taxable income one year was $35,400. From a tax rate schedule he finds the amount of state income tax he owes is $750 + 6% of the excess over $25,000. Find the amount of state income tax. ANS: $1374

1 Lesson Focus

Motivation: Ask students to discuss which they think is a better buy.

1. An item with a regular price of $10 and discounted 30%.
2. The same item with a regular price of $9 with a discount of $2 off.

Purpose: Students will often need to compare prices of identical items which are represented in different ways. Although price is not the only concern of a consumer, it is a major factor in choices of purchase.

Discount

Strategy: Using a "hidden question" to solve a multi-step problem

Joel Santos wants to buy an "Allied Super System" stereo. He sees two advertisements in the newspaper for the stereo.

SUPER SPRING SALE!!!
DECIBEL SOUNDS
25% off all stereos
includes
"ALLIED SUPER SYSTEM" STEREO
regularly $499.00

VOLTS
ELECTRONICS
1/3 off "Allied Super System"
~~Regularly $549~~
PRICE BUSTER SALE

1. What is the regular price of the stereo at Decibel Sounds? **$499.00**
2. What is the regular price of the stereo at Volts Electronics? **$549.00**
3. What is the rate of discount at Decibel Sounds? **25%**
4. What is the rate of discount at Volts Electronics? **$\frac{1}{3}$ off, or $33\frac{1}{3}$%**

To find the sale price at each store, you must first answer the **hidden question.**

What is the amount of discount?

EXAMPLE 1 Find the sale price of the stereo At Decibel Sounds.

1 Find the amount of discount (hidden question).

0.25 × $499.00 = **$124.75** ◀ *Rate of Discount* × *Regular Price* = *Amount of Discount*

2 Now you can find the sale price of the stereo.

$499.00 − $124.75 = **$374.25** ◀ *Regular Price* − *Amount of Discount* = *Sale Price*

Sometimes the rate of discount is written as a fraction.

EXAMPLE 2 Find the sale price of the stereo at Volts Electronics.

1 Amount of Discount: $549.00 × $\frac{1}{3}$ = **$183**

2 Selling Price: $549.00 − $183.00 = **$366**

5. In which store does the stereo cost less? **Volts Electronics**
6. How much less does it cost? **$8.25**

CHECK YOUR SKILLS

Write a decimal for each percent. For additional practice, see page 405.

1. 33% 0.33
2. 25% 0.25
3. 30% 0.30 or 0.3
4. 10% 0.10 or 0.1
5. 5% 0.05
6. 7% 0.07

Find each answer. For additional practice, see page 407.

7. 25% of 52.60 \$13.15
8. 30% of 18.90 \$5.67
9. 20% of 42 \$8.40
10. 10% of 102.50 \$10.25
11. $\frac{1}{4} \times 51.96$ \$12.99
12. $\frac{1}{3} \times 37.80$ \$12.60
13. $\frac{1}{5} \times 113.75$ \$22.75
14. $\frac{1}{2} \times 123.84$ \$61.92

EXERCISES

Complete. Choose your answers from the box at the right.

sale price
fraction
discount
sale
amount of discount
percent

1. The amount of money you save by purchasing an item at the sale price is the __?__. discount
2. Rate of Discount × Regular Price = __?__ amount of discount
3. Regular Price − Amount of Discount = __?__ sale price
4. In an advertisement, the rate of discount may be shown as a __?__ or a __?__. percent; fraction

For Exercises 5–7, find the discount.

	Regular Price	Rate of Discount	Amount of Discount
5.	\$29.80	20%	? \$5.96
6.	\$48.69	$\frac{1}{3}$	? \$16.23
7.	\$105.00	25%	? \$26.25

For Exercises 8–10, find the sale price.

	Regular Price	Rate of Discount	Sale Price
8.	\$68.72	$\frac{1}{4}$	? \$17.18
9.	\$64.00	15%	? \$9.60
10.	\$18.50	30%	? \$5.55

11. Chris buys a telephone for $\frac{1}{3}$-off the regular price of \$51.99. She completed the manufacturer's **rebate** (refund) form and the proof of purchase to receive a rebate of \$5.00. How much did she actually pay for the telephone? \$29.66

12. Lori needs 5 quarts of oil for her car. The regular price is \$1.20 per quart. Oil is on sale for 25% off. How much will Lori pay for the 5 quarts of oil? \$4.50

13. A 1-liter bottle of soda sells for \$0.89. A 2-liter bottle of soda regularly sells for \$2.00, but is now 15% off. Which is the better buy? The 2-liter bottle

14. Joel can buy the same stereo at different prices. What reasons might Joel have for buying it at a store where it costs more? Answers will vary.

2 Teaching the Lesson

Focus the students' attention on the ads. Have students answer questions 1–4 under the ads. Then ask these questions.

1. What do you need to do to compare the discounts? (Change 25% to a fraction or change $\frac{1}{3}$ to a percent.)
2. How do you write 25% as a fraction? ($\frac{1}{4}$)
3. How do you write $\frac{1}{3}$ as a percent? (33$\frac{1}{3}$%)

Then discuss Examples 1 and 2 and have students answer questions 5 and 6. Emphasize that students must first find the amount of discount before they can find the selling price.

3 Close

Summary: Have students discuss what things need to be considered when comparing sale prices.

Evaluation
Guided Practice: Ex. 1–4, 6–10 even
Independent Practice: Ex. 5–9 odd, 11–14

Extension

Have students write consumer problems on discounts using ads from current newspapers.

Problem-Solving Skills

Solving a multi-step problem (Ex. 8–10, 12, 13)
Making a comparison (Ex. 13)

Critical Thinking

You may wish to have students work in small groups to solve this problem or you may wish to work with the class.

Ex. 14

Lesson Resources

Maintenance: See below.
Reteaching/Alternate Teaching Strategy: p. M-43
Practice: p. M-43
Enrichment: p. M-43
Concrete Materials: Activity Worksheet 66A (pages W-126 and W-127)

Objectives

Student will

1. use a table to solve problems involving shipping charges.
2. solve multi-step problems that involve the total cost of ordering by mail.

Maintenance

1. Complete: 30 oz = 1 lb __?__ oz ANS: 14
2. Round $16.486 to the nearest cent. ANS: $16.49
3. Add: 36.24 + 18.15 + 22.26 ANS: 76.65
4. Multiply: 6 × 14 × 10 ANS: 840
5. The distance from Susan's house to work is 22 miles. She makes a round trip 5 days each week. How many miles does she travel in 4 weeks going to and from work? ANS: 880 miles

1 Lesson Focus

Motivation: Ask the students to discuss why they might consider buying an item by mail or phone.

Purpose: This lesson allows students to determine the cost of items bought by mail. Direct purchasing by mail and phone is becoming more and more common. Direct purchasing may become even more prevalent as transactions begin to be handled by computer terminals at home.

Buying by Mail

Strategy: Using a "hidden question" to solve a multi-step problem

Joel saw the stereo he wanted in a mail order catalog. There was a note next to the stereo price.

Prices do not include shipping charges.
See the shipping charges table below.

1. What is a "hidden cost" when ordering by mail? The shipping charges

Joel will use this table to compute the shipping charges.

Column ↓ / Row 1 →

Weight Not to Exceed	Local zones 1, 2, and 3	Postal Zone 4	Postal Zone 5	Postal Zone 6	Postal Zone 7	Postal Zone 8
16 lb	8.39	10.86	12.54	14.14	15.75	17.75
17 lb	8.82	11.44	13.22	14.92	16.64	18.76
18 lb	9.24	12.01	13.90	15.70	17.52	19.77
19 lb	9.67	12.59	14.59	16.49	18.41	20.78
20 lb	10.09	13.17	15.27	17.27	19.29	21.79
21 lb	10.51	13.75	15.95	18.05	20.17	22.80
22 lb	10.94	14.33	16.64	18.84	21.06	23.81
23 lb	11.36	14.90	17.32	19.62	21.94	24.82
24 lb	11.79	15.48	18.00	20.40	22.83	25.83
25 lb	12.21	16.06	18.69	21.19	23.71	26.84

2. What information is needed to know which row of the table to use? The weight of the stereo

EXAMPLE 1 Find the total shipping charges for the stereo (2 speakers, 1 receiver, 1 turntable). Joel's home is in zone 4.

Item	Shipping Weight lb	oz
1 speaker	3	3
1 receiver	9	12
1 turntable	4	4

1 Find the total weight.

Speakers: (3 lb 3 oz) × 2 = 6 lb 6 oz
Receiver: 9 lb 12 oz
Turntable: + 4 lb 4 oz
19 lb 22 oz = **20 lb 6 oz** (22 oz = 1 lb 6 oz)

2 Use the table to find the shipping charges

	Zone 4
21 lb	13.75

The shipping charges are **$13.75.**

To find the total cost of the stereo, Joel filled out this order form.

CATALOG NUMBER	QTY	DESCRIPTION	PRICE EACH	SHIPPING WT. EACH lb	oz	TOTAL PRICE
AL 695 305SP	2	Speaker	$54.25	3	3	?
AL 431 250RC	1	Receiver	$125.64	9	12	?
AL 352 015TT	1	Turntable	$75.45	4	4	?
			Total for Goods			?
			Sales Tax			?
		From Example 1	Shipping Charges			$13.75
			TOTAL COST			?

The sales tax in Joel's state is 5%.

EXAMPLE 2 Find the total cost of the stereo order.

1 Find the total price for each item and the total for goods.

Speakers: $108.50 ◀ *$54.25 × 2 = $108.50*
Receiver: 125.64
Turntable: + 75.45
$309.59

2 Find the amount of sales tax.

5% of $309.59 = $309.59 × 0.05
= **$15.48** ◀ *Rounded to the nearest cent*

3 Total Cost = Total for Goods + Sales Tax + Shipping Charges
= $309.59 + $15.48 + $13.75
= $338.82 The total cost is **$338.82.**

CHECK YOUR SKILLS

Find the total weight. For additional practice, see page 414.

1. 1 lb 11 oz + 2 lb 10 oz 4 lb 5 oz
2. 3 lb 12 oz + 6 lb 8 oz 10 lb 4 oz
3. 3 × 4 lb 8 oz 13 lb 8 oz
4. 5 × 7 lb 4 oz 36 lb 4 oz

2 Teaching the Lesson

Have students read the first part of the lesson and answer question 1. Focus students' attention on the delivery rate table. Ask question 2 under the table. Then ask these questions.

1. What do you need to know to determine how much it will cost to ship something? (Weight, where it is to be delivered)
2. How much would it cost to ship something that weighs 20.5 pounds to zone 2? ($10.51)
3. You have 4 items that weigh 4 pounds each. How much will it cost to ship these items to zone 4? ($10.86)

Discuss Example 1. Then direct students' attention to the order form. Ask students where they would find the information they need to complete the form. (In the catalog) Discuss Example 2. Point out that the sales tax is computed before the shipping charges are added.

3 Close

Summary: Have students discuss what things they would have to consider when purchasing by mail.

Evaluation
Guided Practice: Ex. 1–4, 6–12 even
Independent Practice: Ex. 5–11 odd, 13–20

Extension

Have students bring in a mail order catalog. Instruct them that they have a total of $100 to spend. The $100 must cover taxes and shipping charges as well as the cost of the items. Have them fill out the appropriate form.

EXERCISES

Complete. Choose your answers from the box at the right.

weight
total for goods
shipping charges
sales tax
postal zone
total cost

1. Two additional expenses which must be considered when ordering by mail are _?_ and _?_. **sales tax; shipping charges**
2. In order to determine shipping charges, you must know the _?_ of an order, as well as the _?_ of the destination. **weight; postal zone**
3. The sales tax for an order is based on the _?_. **total for goods**
4. The _?_ are a "hidden expense" when ordering by mail. **shipping charges**

For Exercises 5–10, use the table on page 286 to determine the missing information.

	Weight	Zone	Shipping Charge
5.	16 lb 3 oz	5	? **$13.22**
6.	18 lb 1 oz	3	? **$9.67**
7.	23 lb 7 oz	8	? **$25.83**

	Weight	Zone	Shipping Charge
8.	24 lb 14 oz	? **1, 2, or 3**	12.21
9.	22 lb 1 oz	? **5**	17.32
10.	20 lb 5 oz	? **6**	18.05

Find the total cost of each order. The tax rate is 6%. Use the table on page 286 to find the shipping charges to zone 5.

11.

How Many	Name of Item	Price Each	Shipping Wt. Each lb	oz
1	headphone	$21.50	—	14
2	records	$8.68	2	1
2	cassette deck	$136.17	6	3

$343.77

12.

How Many	Name of Item	Price Each	Shipping Wt. Each lb	oz
5	record crates	$7.99	2	6
6	tapes	$1.89	—	5
3	antenna	$17.95	1	11

$126.04

Problem-Solving Skills

Reading a table (Ex. 5–14, 17, 18)
Solving a multi-step problem (Ex. 11–18)
Using guess and check (Ex. 15, 18)
Using logical reasoning (Ex. 15)
Choosing the operation (Ex. 15, 16)

13. Suppose the order in Exercise 11 is being shipped to zone 8. Find the total cost of the order. **$349.64**

14. Suppose the order in Exercise 12 is being shipped to zone 1. Find the total cost of the order. **$121.12**

For Exercises 15–16, refer to Example 2 on page 287.

15. At first, Joel computed that the total order would cost $325.07. What cost did he forget to add to the order? **The shipping charges**

16. How much money would Joel save on the order if there was a discount of 25% on the stereo equipment? **$81.27**

17. Some mail order companies use a table like the one below to determine shipping costs. (Subtotal = goods + sales tax)

Shipping Charges

If subtotal is	Add
$0.00–$25.00	$2.50
$25.01–$50.00	$4.50
$50.01–$100.00	$6.50
$100.01–$200.00	$8.50
$200.01 and over	$10.50

a. Find the subtotal for goods that cost $145.00. The sales tax is 5%. **$152.25**

b. Find the total cost of the order. **$160.75**

18. Copy the order form on page 287. Make an order of four things from the list at the right that have a total cost of less than $70.00. The total cost should include shipping charges to zone 2 and 5% sales tax. **Answers will vary.**

19. What are some advantages of ordering by mail? **Answers will vary.**

20. What are some disadvantages of ordering by mail? **Answers will vary.**

Item	*Cost*	*Shipping Weight* lb	oz
alarm clock	$13.99	3	13
am/fm radio	$12.59	4	3
desk top calculator	$14.50	4	10
reading lamp	$10.99	5	4
battery recharger	$ 9.95	3	6
rechargable batteries	$11.95	4	12

Critical Thinking

You may wish to have students work in small groups to solve these problems or you may wish to work with the class.

Ex. 19 and 20

Lesson Resources

Maintenance: See below.
Reteaching/Alternate Teaching Strategy: p. M-43 (Visuals 38 and 39)
Practice: p. M-43
Enrichment: p. M-43
Concrete Materials: Activity Worksheets 67A and 67B, Visuals 38 and 39
Visuals 38 and 39

Objective

Student will use formulas to solve multi-step problems that involve credit card statements.

Maintenance

1. Add: $3\frac{1}{2} + 2\frac{1}{4}$ ANS: $5\frac{3}{4}$
2. Divide: $7\frac{1}{3} \div \frac{5}{6}$ ANS: $8\frac{4}{5}$
3. Multiply: 0.15×356 ANS: 53.4
4. Add: $135.17 + $182.55 ANS: $317.22
5. A car rental agency charges $25 per day for a car plus $0.12 per mile. How much would be charged for a car rented for 5 days and driven 420 miles? ANS: $175.40

1 Lesson Focus

Motivation: Have students discuss the advantages and disadvantages of credit cards.

Purpose: In this lesson, students will calculate the finance charge for purchases with credit cards. Consumers must always weigh the convenience and immediacy of a credit card with its cost. A consumer should be aware of this cost when making a purchase.

STRATEGY: USING "HIDDEN QUESTIONS" TO SOLVE A MULTI-STEP PROBLEM

Credit Card Statement

Joel can use the family credit card to buy the stereo, and he is responsible for paying the bill. Joel knows that it is important to check these items on each monthly statement.

Finance Charge Balance **Finance Charge** **New Balance**

Last date on which purchases are added to bill (→ Billing Date)

Last date for payments (→ Due Date)

ACCOUNT NUMBER	BILLING DATE	DUE DATE	For bill inquiry, call (816) 430-9724
594 89 157	7 – 7 – 88	8 – 3 – 88	

DATE	STORE	REFERENCE NO.	DESCRIPTION	AMOUNT OF PURCHASE	PAYMENTS, AND CREDITS
6/19	841	468921	AUTOMOTIVE	29.95	
6/30		619773	PAYMENT, THANK YOU		50.00

PREVIOUS BALANCE	PAYMENTS AND CREDITS	FINANCE CHARGE BALANCE	FINANCE CHARGE	NEW BALANCE	MINIMUM PAYMENT DUE
99.89	50.00	49.89	0.75	80.59	20.00

FINANCE CHARGE IS COMPUTED AT A MONTHLY RATE (PERIOD RATE) OF 1.5%
Annual percentage rate: 18%

To avoid FINANCE CHARGE next month, payment of New Balance must reach us by Due Date shown above.

Amount subject to finance charge this month (→ Finance Charge Balance)

1. How much was paid towards the previous bill? $50
2. What is the minimum payment due? $20

EXAMPLE On the statement how were each of the following computed?

a. Finance Charge Balance **b.** Finance Charge **c.** New Balance

a. Finance Charge Balance = Previous Balance − Payments

$= \$99.89 - \$50.00 = \mathbf{\$49.89}$

b. Finance Charge = Finance Charge Balance × Monthly Rate

$= \$49.89 \times 0.015$

$= \mathbf{\$0.75}$ ◀ *Rounded to the nearest cent*

c. New Balance = Finance Charge Balance + Finance Charge + Purchases

$= \$49.89 + \$0.75 + \$29.95 = \mathbf{\$80.59}$

CHECK YOUR SKILLS

Write a decimal for each percent. For additional practice, see page 403.

1. 1.5% 0.015
2. 2.5% 0.025
3. 1.25% 0.0125
4. 18% 0.18
5. 15% 0.15
6. 5% 0.05

Round to the nearest hundredth. For additional practice, see page 378.

7. 52.385 52.39
8. 95.361 95.36
9. 7.792 7.79
10. 81.096 81.10
11. 8.112 8.11
12. 0.777 0.78

Multiply. Round each answer to the nearest cent. For additional practice, see page 372.

13. $289.76 × 0.015 $4.35
14. $424.50 × 0.015 $6.37
15. $385.16 × 0.015 $5.78

EXERCISES

Complete. Choose your answers from the box at the right.

new balance
billing date
due date
finance charge balance
finance charge
previous balance

1. The amount owed on the previous statement is called the __?__. previous balance
2. The amount subject to a finance charge is called the __?__. finance charge balance
3. The last date on which purchases are added to the bill is the __?__. billing date
4. To avoid a finance charge, payment of the new balance must be paid by the __?__, the last date for payments. due date
5. New Balance = __?__ + __?__ + Purchases finance charge balance; finance charge

For Exercises 6–11, find each of the following. The monthly finance charge rate is 1.5%.

a. Finance Charge Balance **b.** Finance Charge

	Previous Balance	Payments
6.	$78.56	$20.00 a. $58.56 b. $0.88
7.	$149.18	$28.00 a. $121.18 b. $1.82
8.	$289.70	$35.00 a. $254.70 b. $3.82

	Previous Balance	Payments
9.	$255.41	$31.00 a. $224.41 b. $3.37
10.	$376.41	$48.00 a. $328.41 b. $4.93
11.	$298.06	$50.00 a. $248.06 b. $3.72

12. In January, the Santos' credit card statement showed a previous balance of $100.38 and a payment of $40.00. Find the finance charge balance. $60.38

13. The Santos' credit card statement for February showed a previous balance of $61.29 and a payment of $35.00. Find the finance charge. $0.39

2 Teaching the Lesson

Focus students' attention on the monthly statement. Explain the meaning of the billing date and the payment date. Have student volunteers answer questions 1 and 2. Work through the Example. Make sure each student understands how each amount is determined. Then have students consider the situation if Joel's father had paid only the minimum payment of $20 instead of $50. Ask the following questions.

1. What would the finance charge balance be? ($79.89)
2. What would the finance charge on $79.89 be? ($1.20)
3. What would the new balance be? ($79.89 + $1.20 + $29.95 = $111.04)

3 Close

Summary: Have students discuss when they think it is wise to make credit card purchases.

Evaluation

Guided Practice: Ex. 1–5, 6–10 even, 14
Independent Practice: Ex. 7–11 odd, 12, 13, 15–19

Extension

Have students contact local banks and businesses that offer credit cards. Have them find the annual percentage rate for each card.

Problem-Solving Skills

Solving a multi-step problem (Ex. 13–18)
Choosing the operation (Ex. 18)

For Exercises 14–18, the finance charge rate is 1.5%.

14. New purchase: $89.75

Previous Balance	Payments and Credits	Finance Charge Balance	Finance Charge	New Balance	Minimum Payment Due
416.79	45.00	? **$371.79**	? **$5.58**	? **$467.12**	50.00

15. New purchases: $25.00 and $84.50

Previous Balance	Payments and Credits	Finance Charge Balance	Finance Charge	New Balance	Minimum Payment Due
264.08	35.00	? **$229.08**	? **$3.44**	? **$342.02**	50.00

16. New purchases: $50.24, $30.20, and $21.42

Previous Balance	Payments and Credits	Finance Charge Balance	Finance Charge	New Balance	Minimum Payment Due
145.20	20.00	? **$125.20**	? **$1.88**	? **$228.94**	35.00

19. a. The payments and credits are more than the previous balance.

17. The Santos' credit card statement for May showed a previous balance of $254.35. A payment of $30.00, as well as purchases for $29.95 and $108.90, were made. What is the new balance? **$366.57**

18. In July, the Santos' credit card statement showed a balance of $178.53. A payment of $45.00 was made. The new balance was shown as $168.67. What was the total amount of purchases that month? **$33.14**

Critical Thinking

You may wish to have students work in small groups to solve this problem or you may wish to work with the class.

Ex. 19

19. During September, Mr. Santos returned an item he had purchased with his credit card. He received a credit of $72.40. The credit statement for October showed a previous balance of $94.52, a payment of $40.00, and a credit of $72.40. There is no finance charge.

a. What is unusual about the credit card statement? **See above.**

b. What is the new balance? **See below.**

c. Explain why there is no finance charge. **Mr. Santos does not owe any money.**

19. b. A credit (overpayment) of $17.88

Mid-Chapter Review

1. Atlantic Airlines is offering a 25% discount on all flights. What is the amount of discount on a flight that regularly costs $310.60? (Pages 284–285) **$77.65**

2. A health club is having a sale of $\frac{1}{3}$ off on all new memberships. The regular price for a membership is $426. Find the sale price. (Pages 284–285) **$284**

Find the total cost of each order. The tax rate is 7%. Use the table on page 286 to find the postage for zone 7. (Pages 286–289)

3.

How Many	Name of Item	Price Each	Shipping Wt. Each lb	oz
2	Books	$14.95	5	4
1	Ham	$9.95	6	6

$59.28

4.

How Many	Name of Item	Price Each	Shipping Wt. Each lb	oz
1	Boots	$54.90	6	12
2	Cheeses	$39.75	5	3

$161.33

5. Randy's monthly credit card statement showed a previous balance of $329.87, and a payment of $40.00. The finance charge rate is 1.5%. Find the finance charge balance and the finance charge. (Pages 290–292) **$289.87; $4.35**

6. Geraldine's latest monthly credit card statement lists a previous balance of $149.83, a payment of $30.00, and a purchase of $79.85. The finance charge rate is 1.5%. Find the new balance. (Pages 290–292) **$201.48**

MAINTENANCE

The circle graph at the right shows how Pierre spends his $1400 monthly income. Refer to this graph for Exercises 7–9. (Pages 6–7)

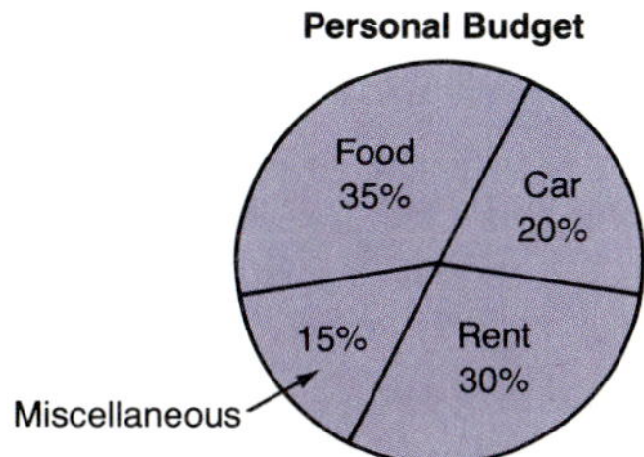

7. How much does Pierre spend on rent per month? **$420**

8. How much are Pierre's miscellaneous expenses per month? **$210**

9. How much more does he spend for food than for his car per month? **$210**

10. An 11-ounce can of soup costs 91¢. A 19-ounce can of the same soup costs $1.49. Which is the better buy? (Pages 203–205) **19-ounce can for $1.49**

11. Mitch's monthly gross income last year was $1620. He also received two bonuses of $2964 each. Find his yearly adjusted gross income. (Pages 72–73) **$25,368**

Objective

Student will

1. review the skills, concepts, and applications in the first part of Chapter 12.
2. maintain key skills and concepts taught in Chapters 1, 4, and 9.

Using the Page

Exercises 1–6 provide an informal assessment of the student's mastery of the major skills and concepts presented in the first half of Chapter 12. Each item is referenced to the related pages where the particular item was presented. These exercises parallel the quiz provided in the *Teacher's ResourceBank.*™

A quiz covering the second half of the chapter is also provided in the *Teacher's ResourceBank.*™

Exercises 7–11 maintain skills and concepts taught in Chapters 1, 4, and 9.

Objective

Student will apply addition skills and the skill of making a comparison to solving problems that involve credit limit.

Overview

This page is an extension of the skills and ideas presented in the previous lessons of this chapter. Since the content presented on this page is not included in the Chapter Review or Chapter Test, its use is optional.

Using the Pages

You may wish to have students work this lesson in small groups or you may wish to work with the class. Using it with the class, have a student read the first paragraph, the rule, and the definition of credit limit. Then work through the Example with the class. Have students do Exercises 1–5 as independent practice.

Problem-Solving Skills

Making a comparison (Ex. 1–3)
Solving a multi-step problem (Ex. 4, 5)

Math and Credit

Roberta Vega works in the credit department of a store. She uses this rule to determine whether a charge purchase can be approved.

Rule The sum of the amount of the charge purchase and the account balance must be less than or equal to the credit limit.

The **credit limit** is the greatest total amount that a customer can charge on a charge account.

EXAMPLE A customer wants to charge an item that costs $125.35. The customer's account balance is $945.20 and the credit limit is $1000.00. Can Roberta approve the purchase?

Account Balance	+	Amount of Purchase	=	New Balance
$948.20	+	$125.35	=	**$1073.55**

Since the sum of the account balance and the purchase amount is greater than the credit limit, Roberta **cannot approve** the purchase.

EXERCISES

For Exercises 1–3, find the sum of the account balance and the amount of purchase. Then determine if the purchase can be approved.

1. Balance: $450.80
   Purchase: $35.65
   Limit: $500.00
   $486.45; Yes
2. Balance: $1140.32
   Purchase: $252.30
   Limit:$1500.00
   $1392.62; Yes
3. Balance: $1435.06
   Purchase: $680.24
   Limit: $2000.00
   $2115.30; No
4. When a customer has a good credit record, Roberta can raise the amount of the credit limit. By how much would a customer's limit have to be raised if the account balance is $632.70, the amount of the charge purchase is $197.30, and the current limit is $800? $30
5. Albert Wilson wants to pay part of the amount of a purchase in cash and charge the rest so that he doesn't go over his credit limit of $500. His account balance is $382.90 and the item he wants to buy costs $154.35. What is the least amount he will have to pay in cash? $37.25

Strategy: Using "hidden questions" to solve a multi-step problem

Credit Card: MINIMUM PAYMENTS

Joel realized that charging his stereo on the family credit card would affect the minimum payment due. He used this table to determine the minimum payment on his next month's bill.

New Balance	Minimum Payment
.01–20.00	Full Balance
20.01–200.00	20.00
200.01–250.00	25.00
250.01–300.00	30.00
300.01–350.00	35.00
350.01–400.00	40.00
400.01–450.00	45.00
450.01–500.00	50.00
500.00 or more	$\frac{1}{5}$ of Balance

1. What will be the minimum payment for a new balance of $279.99? $30.00
2. What will be the minimum payment for a new balance of $441.31? $45.00

This was the family's statement for July. It is incomplete.

ACCOUNT NUMBER	BILLING DATE	DUE DATE	For bill inquiry, call (816) 430-9724
594 89 157	8 – 7 – 88	9 – 3 – 88	

DATE	STORE	REFERENCE NO.	DESCRIPTION	AMOUNT OF PURCHASE	PAYMENTS, AND CREDITS
7/21	369	591880	STEREO EQUIPMENT	338.82	20.00
7/29		619336	PAYMENT, THANK YOU		

PREVIOUS BALANCE	PAYMENTS AND CREDITS	FINANCE CHARGE BALANCE	FINANCE CHARGE	NEW BALANCE	MINIMUM PAYMENT DUE
80.59	20.00	?	?	?	?

FINANCE CHARGE IS COMPUTED AT A MONTHLY RATE (PERIOD RATE) OF 1.5%
Annual percentage rate: 18%

To avoid FINANCE CHARGE next month, payment of New Balance must reach us by Due Date shown above.

3. What is the last date on which purchases are added to the bill? 8-7-88 (the billing date)
4. What is the last date for payments? 9-3-88

EXAMPLE Find the new balance and the minimum payment due for the July monthly statement.

[1] Find the Finance Charge Balance: $80.59 − $20.00 = **$60.59**

[2] Find the Finance Charge: $60.59 × 0.015 = **$0.91**

[3] Find the New Balance: $60.59 + $0.91 + $338.82 = **$400.32**

[4] Read the minimum payment from the table. ⟶ **$45.00**

Lesson Resources

Maintenance: See below.
Reteaching/Alternate Teaching Strategy: p. M-44
Practice: p. M-44
Enrichment: p. M-44
Concrete Materials: Activity Worksheets 68A and 68B

Objectives

Student will

1. read a table to find the minimum payments due on credit card balances.
2. solve multi-step problems that involve minimum payments on credit card balances.

Maintenance

1. Subtract: $464.75 − $50.00 ANS: $414.75
2. Add: 48 + 95 + 136 + 24 ANS: 303
3. Divide: 396 ÷ 6 ANS: 66
4. Divide: 425.25 ÷ 1.5 ANS: 283.5
5. A student had test scores of 75, 86, 92, 83, and 76. Find the average test score. ANS: 82.4

[1] Lesson Focus

Motivation: Explain to students that with credit card purchases, they can choose to pay off the whole amount. They are required to pay only a part of the balance or a minimum payment. Have the students discuss if they think they should pay off the whole amount or make only the minimum payment.

Purpose: Issuers of credit cards would hope that only the minimum payment would be made so that they could collect interest on the outstanding amount. Students should be aware that if they choose the convenience of putting off payment, they will be paying an extra amount in interest.

2 Teaching the Lesson

Focus students' attention on the table. Ask questions 1 and 2 in the lesson. Then ask these questions.

1. What is the minimum payment on $350? ($35)
2. What is the minimum payment on $192.50? ($20)
3. What is the minimum payment on $750? ($\frac{1}{5} \times \$750 = \$150$)

Focus students' attention on the monthly statement and ask questions 3 and 4. Then discuss the Example. Point out that the calculations in steps 1, 2, and 3 are the same as in the lesson on page 290.

3 Close

Summary: Have students discuss why many people make only the minimum payment on a credit card.

Evaluation
Guided Practice: Ex. 1–3, 4, 6
Independent Practice: Ex. 5, 7, 8–10

Extension

Have students go to a bank or a department store and get information for applying for a credit card. Have them report back on the different ways the minimum payment is determined.

Problem-Solving Skills

Reading a table (Ex. 4–9)
Solving a multi-step problem (Ex. 9–10)
Completing a table (Ex. 10)

CHECK YOUR SKILLS

Multiply. Round each answer to the nearest cent. For additional practice, see pages 372 and 379.

1. $378.52 × $0.015 $5.68
2. $456.04 × 0.015 $6.84
3. $256.90 × 0.015 $3.85

EXERCISES

Complete. Choose your answers from the box at the right.

previous balance
finance charge
finance charge balance
new balance
minimum payment

1. Add the finance charge balance, the finance charge, and the purchases together to find the __?__. new balance
2. Multiply the finance charge balance and the finance charge monthly rate to find the __?__. finance charge
3. Use the new balance to read the __?__ from the table. minimum payment

Find the minimum payment. Use the table on page 295.

	Balance	Minimum Payment
4.	$30.95	? $20.00
5.	$309.50	? $35.00
6.	$469.09	? $50.00
7.	$19.95	? $19.95

8. A credit card statement showed a previous balance of $109.80, a payment of $25.00, and new purchases of $201.75 and $33.65. The finance charge rate is 1.5%. Find the following.
   a. Finance charge $1.27
   b. New balance $321.47
   c. Minimum payment $35.00

9. Joel wants to pay for the stereo in four payments. Since the stereo costs $338.82, he decides on a monthly payment of $85. There is a finance charge of 1.5% per month. No new purchases will be made. Complete the table to find his payment for the fourth month.

New Balance: $91.57 Previous Balance: $91.57 Payments and Credits $91.57

Month	Previous Balance	Payments and Credits	Finance Charge Balance	Finance Charge	New Balance
1	$338.82	$85.00	$253.82	$3.81	$257.63
2	$257.63	$85.00	$172.63	$2.59	$175.22
3	$175.22	$85.00	? $90.22	? $1.35	?
4	?	?	$0.00	—	—

His payment for the fourth month will be $91.57

10. In Exercise 9, what will be Joel's total cost for the stereo? $346.57

Strategy: Using "hidden questions" to solve a multi-step problem

Installment Loans

Joel discovered that there was another way to purchase his new stereo besides paying cash or charging it on a credit card. Stereo World offered him an installment loan with a 10% down payment.

An **installment loan** is a loan that you repay in equal payments over a specified amount of time. The payments include the interest, or **finance charge,** on the loan.

1. Do you pay more or less for an item when you buy it with an installment loan than when you buy it with cash? Explain. More; payments also include a finance charge.
2. What is the "hidden cost" in an installment loan? The finance charge
3. When do you actually own an item that you purchase with an installment loan? After you make the final payment

EXAMPLE The cost of the stereo Joel wants is $350.50. The installment loan offered by Stereo World requires a 10% down payment, and equal payments of $61.99 for the next 6 months. Find the finance charge.

[1] Find the amount of the down payment.

$350.50 × 0.10 = **$35.05** ◀ *Amount of Purchase* × *Rate* = *Down Payment*

[2] Find the amount financed.

$350.50 − $35.05 = **$315.45** ◀ *Original Amount* − *Down Payment* = *Amount Financed*

[3] Find the total of the monthly payments.

$61.99 × 6 = **$371.94** ◀ *Monthly Payment* × *Number of Months* = *Total of Monthly Payments*

[4] Find the finance charge.

$371.94 − $315.45 = **$56.49** ◀ *Total of Monthly Payments* − *Amount Financed* = *Finance Charge*

The finance charge is **$56.49.**

4. Why do you think some stores require a down payment for an installment loan? It is used as a guarantee of the customer's good intentions to repay the loan.

Lesson Resources

Maintenance: See below.
Reteaching/Alternate Teaching Strategy: p. M-44 (Visuals 40 and 41)
Practice: p. M-44
Enrichment: p. M-44
Concrete Materials: Activity Worksheet 69C
Visuals 40 and 41

Objective

Student will solve multi-step problems that involve installment loans.

Maintenance

1. Multiply: $78.25 × 0.04 ANS: $3.13
2. Find 6% of 85. ANS: 5.1
3. Round $3.125 to the nearest cent. ANS: $3.13
4. Add: $73.14 + $1.07 ANS: $74.21
5. Harold bought 2 shirts at $14.50 each, 1 pair of pants for $25.12, and a sweater for $32.72. He paid a 5% sales tax. What was the total amount he paid (nearest cent)? ANS: $91.18

[1] Lesson Focus

Motivation: Present the following ad to the students.

"Color Television
Just $20 per month"

Ask the students if this is a good deal and what other information they would like to know to make a better decision.

Purpose: In this lesson, students will be learning the true cost of a purchase made with an installment loan. Consumers need to be aware that merchandisers make installment loans look attractive by quoting only the monthly payments.

2 Teaching the Lesson

After discussing the Lesson Focus, give students this information.

Television Cost: $300
Down Payment: 10%
Number of Payments: 15
Monthly Payment: $20

Ask questions such as these.

1. How much is 10% of $300? ($30)
2. How much is owed after the $30 down payment is paid? ($270)
3. How much will be paid in total monthly payments? ($300)
4. What is the total of the down payment and the monthly payments? ($330)
5. What is the difference in the cost of the television and the amount that will be paid? ($30)

Then have students read the first two paragraphs of the lesson. Discuss questions 1, 2, and 3. Work through the steps of the Example with the students. Then discuss question 4.

3 Close

Summary: Have students discuss when it would be worthwhile to buy something with an installment loan.

Evaluation
Guided Practice: Ex. 1–4, 6–16 even
Independent Practice: Ex. 5–15 odd, 17–21

Extension

Have students look for and bring in ads from local newspapers showing items that can be bought for a down payment and then monthly payments. Then have students calculate the total cost of the items.

CHECK YOUR SKILLS

Write a decimal for each percent. For additional practice, see page 403.

1. 20% 0.20 or 0.2
2. 30% 0.30 or 0.3
3. 15% 0.15
4. 25% 0.25
5. 10% 0.10 or 0.1
6. 5% 0.05

Write a fraction for each percent. For additional practice, see page 404.

7. 20% $\frac{1}{5}$
8. 30% $\frac{3}{10}$
9. 15% $\frac{3}{20}$
10. 25% $\frac{1}{4}$
11. $12\frac{1}{2}$% $\frac{1}{8}$
12. 5% $\frac{1}{20}$

Choose the best estimate. Choose a or b. For additional practice, see page 412.

13. 20% of $998 b
    a. $\frac{1}{5} \times \$900$
    b. $\frac{1}{5} \times \$1000$
14. 25% of $1245 a
    a. $\frac{1}{4} \times \$1248$
    b. $\frac{1}{4} \times \$1200$
15. 15% of $775 b
    a. $\frac{1}{10} \times \$780$
    b. $\frac{3}{20} \times \$800$
16. 12% of $795 b
    a. $\frac{1}{10} \times \$800$
    b. $\frac{1}{8} \times \$800$
17. 35% of $1198 a
    a. $\frac{1}{3} \times \$1200$
    b. $\frac{2}{5} \times \$1200$
18. 30% of $910 a
    a. $\frac{3}{10} \times \$900$
    b. $\frac{1}{3} \times \$900$

Round to the nearest whole number. For additional practice, see page 378.

19. 33.9 34
20. 20.75 21
21. 11.65 12
22. 19.25 19

EXERCISES

Complete. Choose your answers from the box at the right.

finance charge
original amount
down payment
equal payments
amount financed

1. The "hidden cost" in an installment loan is the ___?___. finance charge
2. Installment loans are usually repaid in ___?___ over a specified amount of time. equal payments
3. With an installment loan the interest, or ___?___ is included in the payments. finance charge
4. The amount of money actually being financed in an installment loan that requires a down payment equals the ___?___ of the purchase less the ___?___. original amount; down payment

Complete the tables.

	Amount of Purchase	Rate of Down Payment	Down Payment	Amount Financed
5.	$998	20%	? $199.60	? $798.40
6.	$660	10%	? $66.00	? $594.00
7.	$1245	25%	? $311.25	? $933.75

	Amount of Purchase	Rate of Down Payment	Down Payment	Amount Financed
8.	$1576	20%	? $315.20	? $1260.80
9.	$800	30%	? $240.00	? $560.00
10.	$775	15%	? $116.25	? $658.75

	Amount Financed	Monthly Payment	Number of Months	Finance Charge
11.	$500	$87.76	6	? $26.56
12.	$875	$81.90	12	? $107.80
13.	$1350	$88.73	18	? $247.14

	Amount Financed	Monthly Payment	Number of Months	Finance Charge
14.	$759	$140.42	6	? $83.52
15.	$900	$82.51	12	? $90.12
16.	$2000	$92.28	24	? $214.72

17. Janice bought a new microwave oven on an installment plan. She made a 15% down payment on the purchase price of $490. Find the amount financed. $416.50

18. Denton bought a new computer with an 18-month installment loan. The total finance charges were $162.46. He will receive a **rebate** (refund) of 38% of the total finance charges if he repays the loan in 7 months. What is the amount of rebate? $61.73

19. Phil Louderback purchased a color television on an installment plan. He agreed to make 21 monthly payments of $19.75. Choose the expression below that would best help Phil estimate the total of his monthly payments. c

a. 30 × $20 **b.** 30 × $10

c. 20 × $20 **d.** 20 × $10

20. To pay for new kitchen appliances, Cecilia used an installment loan which required a 20% down payment. The down payment amounted to $480. She then made 30 monthly payments of $75.31 each. Find the finance charge. $339.30

21. In the Example on page 297 you computed the finance charge Joel would pay if he bought a stereo on a 6 month installment plan.

a. What would the finance charge be for the same stereo on an installment plan that required a 20% down payment and equal monthly payments of $31.25 for 12 months? $94.60

b. Which installment loan do you think is a better deal? Why? Answers will vary.

c. Why might you choose the installment loan with the higher finance charge? Because monthly payments are less.

Problem-Solving Skills

Solving a multi-step problem (Ex. 11–18, 20, 21a)
Using estimation (Ex. 19)

Critical Thinking

You may wish to have students work in small groups to solve these problems or you may wish to work with the class.

Question 4 (in Lesson), Ex. 21b, 21c

Estimation

Ex. 19

Lesson Resources

Maintenance: See below.
Reteaching/Alternate Teaching Strategy: See the margin on page 301.
Practice: Activity Worksheet 70
Enrichment: See the enrichment topic "Annual Percentage Rate" on page 304.

Objectives

Student will

1. use formulas to solve problems that involve markup, retail price, wholesale price, overhead, and profit.
2. choose and apply an appropriate strategy to solve a problem.

Maintenance

1. 10 is what percent of 50? ANS: 20%
2. 15% of 60 is what number? ANS: 9
3. 12 is 40% of what number? ANS: 30
4. 21 is what percent of 56? ANS: 37.5%
5. Harvey got 20 out of 24 problems correct. What percent of the problems did he get correct? ANS: $83\frac{1}{3}\%$

1 Lesson Focus

Motivation: Have students discuss how much they think a retailer makes in profit on different items.

Purpose: This lesson shows how formulas are used to determine markup, profit, and overhead. If the students have difficulty with the variables used for the rates, have them replace the letters with the corresponding words to give them more meaning.

2 Teaching the Lesson

Work through the Example, making sure each student understands how each of the formulas is used. Then choose a problem to show how the strategy can be applied in other situations, such as in Exercise 5.

Strategy: Using Formulas

The price that a consumer pays for a product is called **retail price.** The price that a dealer pays for a product is called **wholesale price.** The difference between these prices is the store's **markup.**

Markup = Retail Price − Wholesale Price

$$M = R - W$$

The markup consists of the overhead and profit.

Markup = Overhead + Profit

$$M = O + P$$

Overhead is the cost of doing business, such as paying salaries.

1. What are some other costs of doing business? Rent, utility charges, taxes, and so on

Markup is often expressed as a percent of the wholesale price.

$$MR = \frac{M}{W}$$ MR = Markup Rate

The markup rate for a product like milk may only be 5%. The markup rate for jewelry may be 100% or more.

2. Why do you think the markup rate is so low for milk and so high for jewelry? Milk is a basic food item; jewelry is a luxury item.

Profit is sometimes expressed as a percent of the wholesale price.

$$PR = \frac{P}{W}$$ PR = Profit Rate

Overhead is often expressed as a percent of the wholesale price.

3. Write a formula for the overhead rate. $OR = \frac{O}{W}$

EXAMPLE A dealer paid $30 for a radio and sold it for $40. This gave the dealer a profit of $6. What is the markup rate?

READ What are the facts?

Wholesale price: $30 Retail price: $40 Profit: $6

PLAN To find the markup rate, first answer this hidden question.

What is the markup?

Then use the formula for markup rate.

SOLVE 1 $M = R - W$

$M = \$40 - \$30 = \mathbf{\$10}$ Markup

2

$MR = \frac{M}{W}$

$MR = \frac{10}{30} = \frac{1}{3}$ Write a percent for $\frac{1}{3}$.

$MR = 33\frac{1}{3}\%$

CHECK Did you use the correct formulas?

EXERCISES

Complete the following table.

	Retail Price	Wholesale Price	Markup	Overhead	Profit	Markup Rate	Profit Rate
1.	$80.00	? $30	$50.00	$34.00	? $16	? $166\frac{2}{3}\%$	? $53\frac{1}{3}\%$
2.	? $30	$15.00	$15.00	? $9	$6.00	? 100%	? 40%
3.	? $42	$30.00	? $12	$9.00	$3.00	? 40%	? 10%
4.	? $70	$50.00	? $20	? $12.50	? $7.50	40%	15%

5. Top Tapes manufactures cassette tapes. It costs them $17.78 to produce one dozen. They sell them to stores for $33.48 a dozen.
   a. What is the markup on a dozen tapes? $15.70
   b. Find the markup on one tape to the nearest cent. $1.31

6. Golden Groves sells orange juice to stores in boxes of 24 quarts. It costs Golden Groves $12.48 to produce a box of 24 quarts. They sell it to stores for $0.69 per quart.
   a. What is the markup per quart of juice? $0.17
   b. What is the markup per box? $4.08

7. Holmes Home Appliances pays $380 for each washing machine they buy from Blue Dot Washers. The markup rate is 40% and the profit rate is 2.5%. What is the retail price of the washer? $532

Choose a strategy from the box at the right that you can use to solve each problem.
a. *Name the strategy.*
b. *Solve the problem.*

Making a Model
Guess and Check
Solving a Simpler Problem
Predicting

8. Top Tapes manufactures 10,000 tapes a day. Of these, they test 200. If 10 tapes are found to be defective, how many defective tapes could there be each day? 500

9. Holmes Home Appliances bought two types of toasters. The cost of the two is $40. The deluxe model costs three times as much as the cheaper model. What did each cost? $30; $10

1. **Ask:** What is the problem about? (Finding the markup on cassette tapes)
2. **Read** the problem to determine the FACTS. **Ask:** What does it cost the manufacturer to produce one dozen tapes? ($17.78) **Ask:** How much do stores pay for the tapes? ($33.48)
3. **Plan** the solution. **Ask:** What formula will you use to solve part a? ($M = R - W$) **Ask:** What must you do to solve part b? (Divide the markup by 12.)
4. **Solve** the problem. **Ask:** What is the markup on a dozen tapes? ($15.70) What is the markup on 1 tape? ($1.31)
5. **Check** the answer by having students check that they used the correct formula and used the facts correctly in the formula.

3 *Close*

Summary: Have students discuss why they think different retail businesses have different markups on the same products.

Evaluation

Guided Practice: Ex. 2, 4, 5
Independent Practice Ex. 1, 3, 6–9

Problem-Solving Skills

Solving a multi-step problem (Ex. 7)
Predicting (Ex. 8)
Guess and check (Ex. 9)

Critical Thinking

Questions 1 and 2 (in Lesson)

Alternate Teaching Strategy

As you go over the formulas, you may wish to use the following amounts to show students how to use each formula.
Retail Price: $100
Wholesale Price: $60 Profit: $30
Show these examples.

1. $M = R - W$; $M = \$100 - \$60$; $M = \$40$
2. $M = O + P$; $\$40 = O + \$30$; $\$10 = O$
3. $MR = \frac{M}{W}$; $MR = \frac{\$40}{\$60}$; $MR = \frac{2}{3}$, or $66\frac{2}{3}\%$
4. $PR = \frac{P}{W}$; $PR = \frac{\$30}{\$60}$; $PR = \frac{1}{2}$, or 50%

NOTE: A quiz covering the second half of the chapter is provided in the *Teacher's ResourceBank™*.

Objectives

Students will

1. explore solutions to a variety of problems that emerge from this situational lesson.
2. explore solutions to consumer problems having more than one solution.
3. make consumer decisions relevant to their teen-age world.

Situational Lesson

These two pages present a situational lesson as the framework from which a variety of problem situations emerge.

Teaching Strategies

This lesson lends itself to cooperative learning groups for the problem solving activities of comparing choices and exploring decisions. (See page M-13.)

However, these activities can also be carried out by the class as a whole or by individual students.

1 Lesson Focus

Motivation: Have students discuss any experience they have had with a book or record club. Have them discuss if they think they are a good idea.

Purpose: Students need to understand that buying clubs often offer cost advantages, but that they often encourage unwanted purchases. Students need to read the contracts carefully if they are going to be wise consumers.

Consumer's Choice

Joel Santos would like to get some cassettes to play on his new stereo. He saw the advertisement below in a magazine.

UNITED MUSIC CLUB
START SAVING NOW!

YES, PICK ANY 8 cassettes, records or compact discs (CD's). You agree to buy only 8 more at regular club prices ($9.98) . . . and take up to two full years to do it.

EXCITING "MEMBERS-ONLY" BENEFITS. Approximately every four weeks, you will receive the Club's exclusive magazine featuring the Main Selection in your music category. As a member in good standing, send no money when you order, we'll bill you later. A shipping and handling charge is added to each shipment.

CHOOSE FROM HUNDREDS OF HITS. As a member, you'll always have a wide range of choices. If you want the main selection, don't do a thing. It will arrive automatically. If you prefer an alternate, or none at all, just return the card provided by the date specified.

FREE 10-DAY NO-RISK OFFER! Listen to your 8 hits for a full 10 days. If not satisfied, return them with no further obligation. You risk nothing! So don't delay. Pick your hits, write their numbers on the coupon, and mail today!

• TAPE PENNY HERE

Mail to:

United Music Club
P.O. Box 89701
Typical TX

I enclosed 1¢. Please accept my trial membership in the Music Club and send me the 8 hits I've indicated here under the terms outlined in this ad. I agree to buy just 8 more hits at regular club prices in 2 years time. (A shipping and handling charge is added to each shipment.)

• SEND BY SELECTING ONE (check one only):
☐ CASSETTES ☐ RECORDS ☐ CD's

• I am most interested in the following type of music—but I am always free to choose from any category (check one only)
EASY LISTENING ☐1 COUNTRY ☐2
HARD ROCK ☐3 | POP/SOFT ROCK ☐4 | CLASSICAL ☐5

• SEND ME THESE SELECTIONS NOW (Indicate by number)

• ☐ Mr. ☐ Mrs. ☐ Miss ______ Full Name Middle Last Name (PLEASE PRINT)

Address ______ Apt. ______

City ______ State ______ Zip ______

Telephone [Area Code] ______

• Have you bought anything else by mail in:
☐ last 6 months ☐ year ☐ never

Joel must decide whether to buy his cassettes through the United Music Club or at a local music store. The local store offers a discount of 30% off on all cassettes with a $9.90 list price.

Choice 1	**Choice 2**
Join the United Music Club as advertised.	Buy the cassettes on sale at the local music store.

Comparing the Choices

Choice 1: Suppose that Joel joins the United Music Club.

1. How many cassettes must Joel buy over the two-year period? 8
2. How much will Joel pay in all for the first eight cassettes? 1¢
3. How much will Joel pay in all for the second eight cassettes? $79.84
4. If the club charges $1.50 per cassette for shipping and handling charges, how much will Joel pay for 16 cassettes? $24.00
5. What is the total cost for the 16 cassettes with shipping and handling costs of $1.50 per cassette? $103.85

Choice 2: Suppose that Joel buys the cassettes at the local store.

6. What is the price of one cassette with the 30% discount? $6.93
7. How much would 16 cassettes with the 30% discount cost? $110.88
8. How much would Joel save by buying the 16 cassettes through the music club rather than at the store? $7.03

EXPLORING DECISIONS

9. Suppose that Joel joins the United Music Club. Is it possible that cassettes will be sent to him even if he did not order them? (Read the advertisement carefully.)
10. What does Joel have to do to make sure he doesn't get a cassette he did not order? Send in the order card.
11. Make a list of the advantages and disadvantages of Choice 1. Answers will vary.
12. Make a list of the advantages and disadvantages of Choice 2. Answers will vary.
13. Which choice would you make? Give reasons for your choice. Answers will vary.

2 Teaching the Lesson

Focus students' attention on the ad and ask these questions.

1. How does the ad encourage you to join? (8 tapes for 1¢)
2. What are the benefits of being a member? (Answers will vary.)
3. How often will you have to make a choice about buying a record? (Once a month)

Have a volunteer read Joel's two choices before having students work on the exercises. Have students do Exercises 1–10 independently. Then discuss Exercises 11–13 with the class.

3 Close

Summary: Ask students to summarize what Joel will receive and what he will be required to do if he joins the record club.

Critical Thinking

Ex. 11–13

Project

You may want your students to make a collection of different buying club ads. Have them consider the advantages and disadvantages of each.

Additional Answers

9. Yes, the main selection is sent automatically if the order card is not returned.

Objective

Student will use a table to solve problems that involve the annual percentage rate.

Overview

This topic is optional. The word "Enrichment" that appears to the right of the title in this Teacher's Edition does not appear in the student textbook. Therefore, this material is not included in the Chapter Review and Chapter Test.

Using the Page

You may wish to have students work this Enrichment in small groups or you may wish to work with the class.

Problem-Solving Skills

Reading a table (Ex. 1, 2)

Annual Percentage Rate ENRICHMENT

Consumers can use *annual percentage rates* to compare credit costs. The **annual percentage rate (APR)** is the percent that shows the ratio of the finance charge to the amount financed.

ANNUAL PERCENTAGE RATES											
APR	17.00%	17.25%	17.50%	17.75%	18.00%	18.25%	18.50%	18.75%	19.00%	19.25%	19.50%
Number of Months	FINANCE CHARGE PER $100 OF AMOUNT FINANCED										
6	5.02	5.09	5.17	5.24	5.32	5.39	5.46	5.54	5.61	5.69	5.76
12	9.45	9.59	9.73	9.87	10.02	10.16	10.30	10.44	10.59	10.73	10.87
18	13.99	14.21	14.42	14.64	14.85	15.06	15.28	15.49	15.71	15.93	16.14
24	18.66	18.95	19.24	19.53	19.82	20.11	20.40	20.69	20.98	21.27	21.56

1. What is the APR of a 12-month loan which has a finance charge of $10.02 per $100? 18.00%

EXAMPLE Rosa Garcia obtained an $800 installment loan to buy a new refrigerator. Rosa agreed to repay the loan in 18 monthly payments. The finance charge was $122. Find the annual percentage rate.

[1] Find the finance charge per $100 of the amount financed.

(Finance Charge ÷ Amount Financed) × 100
($122 ÷ $800) × 100

122 [÷] 800 [×] 100 = [15.25] ◀ **Finance charge per $100 of amount financed**

[2] Use the table to find the number closest to 15.25 in the row for 18 months. ⟶ **15.28**

Look up to find the APR. ⟶ **[18.50%]**

The annual percentage rate for Rosa's loan is **18.50%.**

EXERCISES

For Exercises 1–2, refer to the table above.

1. Phil Louderback obtained a $400 loan to buy a microwave oven. The finance charge is $20. Phil agreed to repay the loan in 6 monthly payments. What is the APR? 17.00%

2. Kim Wu borrowed $800 to buy a new lawn mower. The finance charge is $82. Kim agreed to repay the loan in 12 monthly payments. What is the APR? 18.50%

The Chapter Summary contains a listing of the important ideas that were presented in the chapter. This listing is intended to assist the student with the Chapter Review that follows.

Chapter Summary

IMPORTANT IDEAS

1. **Discount** is an amount subtracted from the regular price of an item to obtain the sale price.

2. **Regular Price − Amount of Discount = Sale Price**

3. The shipping charges are a hidden cost when buying by mail.

4. When buying by mail,
Total Cost = Total for Goods + Sales Tax + Shipping Charges

5. The following computations are used on monthly credit card statements.
   - a. **Finance Charge Balance = Previous Balance − Payments**
   - b. **Finance Charge = Finance Charge Balance × Monthly Rate**
   - c. **New Balance = Finance Charge Balance + Finance Charge + Purchases**

6. An **installment** loan is a loan repaid in several equal payments over a specified amount of time. The payments include the interest, or finance charge on the loan.

7. The following computations are used for an installment loan with a down payment.
   - a. **Amount of Purchase × Rate = Down Payment**
   - b. **Original Amount − Down Payment = Amount Financed**
   - c. **Monthly Payment × Number of Months = Total of Monthly Payments**
   - d. **Total of Monthly Payments − Amount Financed = Finance Charge**

Objective

To review the important terms, skills, problem solving, and applications presented in Chapter 12.

Overview

The Chapter Review is structured in three parts. Part 1 is a review of the important terms that were introduced in the chapter. Part 2 reviews the skills that were presented in the chapter. Part 3 reviews the problem-solving strategies and applications that were presented in the chapter. Each item in the Chapter Review is referenced to the related pages where the concept, skill, or application was presented.

Using the pages

You may wish to assign this Chapter Review for homework or treat it as a class review prior to administering the formal Chapter Test. In doing this, it is suggested that you only use the even- or odd-numbered exercises. You can then use the remaining exercises as a bank for use later.

Chapter Review

Part 1: VOCABULARY

For Exercises 1–6, choose from the box at the right the word(s) that complete(s) each statement.

finance charge balance
down payment
sale price
previous balance
discount
shipping charges
installment loan
minimum payment

1. The difference between the regular price of an item and its sale price is the __?__. (Pages 284–285) **discount**
2. The price of an item after the discount has been subtracted from the regular price is called the __?__. (Pages 284–285) **sale price**
3. When buying by mail, a hidden cost is the amount you pay for __?__. (Pages 286–289) **shipping charges**
4. Your monthly credit card statement always tells you the __?__ that you must make. (Pages 290–292) **minimum payment**
5. On a monthly credit card statement, the finance charge is based on the __?__. (Pages 290–292) **finance charge balance**
6. A loan which requires several equal payments over a specified amount of time is called an __?__. (Pages 297–299) **installment loan**

Part 2: SKILLS

Find the discount. (Pages 284–285)

	Regular Price	Rate of Discount	Amount of Discount
7.	\$95	15%	? **\$14.25**
8.	\$208	20%	? **\$41.60**

Find the sale price. (Pages 284–285)

	Regular Price	Rate of Discount	Sale Price
9.	\$386.90	20%	? **\$309.52**
10.	\$147.60	$\frac{1}{3}$	? **\$98.40**

For Exercises 11–12, find the total cost of each order. The tax rate is 6%. Use the table on page 286 to find the shipping charges to zone 6. (Pages 286–289)

11.

How Many	Name of Item	Price Each	Shipping Wt. Each lb	oz
2	skillets	11.55	5	8
1	griddle	21.50	8	7

\$64.55

12.

How Many	Name of Item	Price Each	Shipping Wt. Each lb	oz
3	Dictionaries	13.95	4	2
3	Atlases	15.75	3	6

\$114.07

Complete. The finance charge rate is 1.5%. (Pages 290–292)

13. New purchases: $38.85

Previous Balance	Payments and Credits	Finance Charge Balance	Finance Charge	New Balance	Minimum Payment Due
201.81	50.00	? $151.81	? $2.28	? $192.94	25.00

For Exercises 14–19, find the minimum payment. Use the table on page 295. (Pages 295–296)

	Balance	Minimum Payment
14.	$200.59	? $25.00
15.	$369.00	? $40.00

	Balance	Minimum Payment
16.	$19.75	? $19.75
17.	$110.10	? $20.00

	Balance	Minimum Payment
18.	$401.75	? $45.00
19.	$499.99	? $50.00

For Exercises 20–23, complete the tables. (Pages 297–299)

	Amount of Purchase	Rate of Down Payment	Down Payment	Amount Borrowed
20.	$645.90	10%	? $64.59	? $581.31
21.	$220.80	20%	? $44.16	? $176.64

	Amount Borrowed	Monthly Payment	Number of Months	Finance Charge
22.	$371.60	6	$71.50	? $57.40
23.	$839.61	12	$81.16	? $134.31

Part 3: APPLICATIONS

24. Pete wants to buy a video tape that usually costs $49.95. The tape is on sale for 20% off.

a. Estimate the amount of the discount. D

A. $8 **B.** $15 **C.** $9 **D.** $10

b. Find the actual amount of discount. (Pages 284–285) $9.99

25. Sheila is ordering from a catalog. The total for goods is $71.70 and the total weight is 19 lb 9 oz. The sales tax rate in her state is 8%. Find the total cost of the order including shipping charges to zone 6. Use the table on page 286. (Pages 286–289) $94.71

26. Mike's credit card statement for May showed a previous balance of $336.91, a payment of $35.00, and a purchase of $55.91. The finance rate is 1.5%.

a. Find the new balance. $362.65

b. Use the table on page 295 to find the minimum payment due. (Pages 290–292, 295–296) $40.00

27. Acme Appliances buys Laundry Great washers from a distributor for $259.90 each. The washers are marked to sell for $395.08. What is the markup rate? (Pages 300–301) 52%

Objective

To informally assess students' mastering of the major skills, concepts, problem solving, and applications presented in Chapter 12.

Using the Page

After completing the Chapter Review with the class, you may wish to use this Chapter Test as an informal assessment. This Chapter Test parallels the formal chapter tests (Form A and Form B) provided in the *Teacher's ResourceBank.*™

Chapter Test

1. Jason bought a radio on sale at 15% off. The regular price was $49.60. Find the amount of discount. **$7.44**

2. A sweater that regularly sells for $36.69 is on sale for $\frac{1}{3}$ off. What is the sale price? **$24.46**

For Exercises 3–4, use the order shown below. The sales tax rate is 7%. The table at the right shows the shipping charges to zone 5.

How Many	Name of Item	Price Each	Shipping Wt. Each lb	oz.
1	receiver	$125.64	9	12
2	speakers	$54.25	4	3

Weight Not To Exceed	Postal Zone 5
16 lb	12.54
17 lb	13.22
18 lb	13.90
19 lb	14.59

3. Find the shipping charge to zone 5. **$14.59**

4. What is the total cost of the order? **$265.12**

For Exercises 5–6, the finance charge rate is 1.5%.
a. *Find the finance charge balance.*
b. *Find the finance charge.*

5. Previous balance: $364.80
Payment: $40.00 **a. $324.80 b. $4.87**

6. Previous balance: $150.15
Payment: $30.00 **a. $120.15 b. $1.80**

7. Complete the form for new purchases of $116.70 and $27.50. The finance charge is 1.5%.

Previous Balance	Payments and Credits	Finance Charge Balance	Finance Charge	New Balance	Minimum Payment Due
217.75	40.00	?	?	?	35.00

Finance Charge Balance: $177.75 Finance Charge $2.67 New Balance: $324.62

8. A monthly credit card statement shows a previous balance of $321.65, a payment of $35.00, and a purchase of $63.75. The finance charge rate is 1.5%. Use this table to find the minimum payment due. **$40.00**

New Balance	Minimum Payment
200.01–250.00	25.00
250.01–300.00	30.00
300.01–350.00	35.00
350.01–400.00	40.00

9. Susan bought patio furniture with an installment loan. She made a 25% down payment on a purchase price of $1300 and agreed to make 18 monthly payments of $65.27. Find the finance charge. **$199.86**

10. Claude Perez is a buyer for a department store. He bought an assortment of sweaters for $32.50 each. The store sold the sweaters for $68.25 each. Find the markup rate. **110%**

Cumulative Maintenance Chapters 1–12

Choose the correct answer. Choose a, b, c, *or* d.

1. All percents may be written as a fraction with a denominator of __?__. c

a. 1 **b.** 10
c. 100 **d.** 1000

2. What percent of 90 is 27? a

a. 30% **b.** 3%
c. 33% **d.** 300%

3. Find the NET DEPOSIT. b

	Dollars	Cents
CASH		
CHECKS 1	51	15
List 2	481	29
Each 3		
Check 4		
TOTAL	532	44
▶ Less Cash Rec'd	25	00
NET DEPOSIT	?	

a. $532.44 **b.** $507.44
c. $481.29 **d.** $557.44

4. At his job in a fast food restaurant, Denton is paid $3.60 per hour. For all hours worked over 40, he is paid $1\frac{1}{2}$ times his regular hourly rate. One week Denton works 49 hours. What is Denton's total income for the week? d

a. $144 **b.** $176.40
c. $264.60 **d.** $192.60

5. The table below shows the number of hours worked by 5 mechanics. Find the mean. b

Mechanic	*Hours Worked*
Juan	49
Steve	33
Kim	32
Russ	33
Jan	38

a. 33 **b.** 37
c. 185 **d.** 5

6. Add.

$2975 + $713.29 + $859.33 a

a. $4547.62 **b.** $160,237
c. $3547.52 **d.** $4757.52

7. Jim paid $9250 for his car. It has depreciated 45% over the last three years. Find the amount of depreciation. a

a. $4162.50 **b.** $13,412.50
c. $416.25 **d.** $4062.50

8. The finance charge balance on Noah's credit card statement is $289.65. He made new purchases totaling $61.28. Estimate the new balance. a

a. $290 + $60 **b.** $300 + $100
c. $280 + $60 **d.** $290 + $70

Objective

To review the content presented in Chapters 1–12

Using the Pages

You may wish to use this Cumulative Maintenance as an informal assessment tool. These pages can be assigned for homework or they may be used as review in class.

NOTE: The *Teacher's ResourceBank™* contains a Cumulative Test for Chapters 9–12. The Cumulative Test is presented in a standardized-test format.

9. Mario is a translator. One year he has a taxable income of $20,500. From a tax rate schedule he finds the amount of state income tax he owes is $1280 plus 12% of excess over $19,000. Find the amount of his state income tax. c

a. $1500 **b.** $2280
c. $1460 **d.** $3740

10. Find 36% of $2800. c

a. $1000 **b.** $1080
c. $1008 **d.** $100.80

11. Write a decimal for 15%. d

a. 0.0015 **b.** 1.5
c. 0.015 **d.** 0.15

12. Pam bought a can of coffee marked $3.79 at a store giving double coupon savings. She used the coupon below. How much did Pam pay for the coffee? c

a. 50¢
b. $3.04
c. $3.29
d. $3.54

13. Find the total cost of the car below. c

Base Price: $8360
Options: $1875
Destination charge: $275
Sales tax rate: 7%

a. $10,510.00 **b.** $9,095.20
c. $11,245.70 **d.** $11,095.20

14. Find the finance charge. a

Finance Charge Balance	Finance Charge Rate
$275.60	1.5%

a. $4.13 **b.** $41.30
c. $279.73 **d.** $0.41

15. A liter of paint covers 8 square meters. Ray wants to paint the walls of a room that is 6 meters long, 5 meters wide, and 2.5 meters high. How many liters of paint should he buy? d

a. 6 **b.** 55
c. 8 **d.** 7

16. On a certain flight, the adult fare is $175. The children's fare is $\frac{1}{2}$ the adult fare. Find the fare for two adults and two children. d

a. $175 **b.** $350
c. $87.50 **d.** $525

17. The Schrader family took out an $85,000 mortgage for 30 years. Their monthly payment is $1143.25. Find the total interest charged. d

a. $41,570 **b.** $34,297
c. $25,000 **d.** $326,570

Chapter 13: Investing

Overview

The focus of Chapter 13 is on making money with money. Topics studied in this chapter include various types of life insurance, certificates of deposit, stocks and bonds. You may wish to have students look through the financial sections of newspapers and bring to class current information on these topics. Such information can serve as a source of discussion, special projects, and homework assignments.

The strategy lesson on pages 330–331 involves using patterns to formulate the "Rule of 72" and applying the rule to solving problems that involve investments. The *Consumer's Choice* on pages 332–333 presents a **situational lesson** in which students consider the costs and benefits of three different types of insurance protection and explore decisions in a real-life situation. The *Enrichment* lesson on page 334 introduces Individual Retirement accounts and the new Federal regulations concerning them.

Investing Money

Kyle and Marita Osuna have been married for five years. Now that the Osunas are expecting their first child, they want to explore the different types of financial protection and investment opportunities available to them.

- What are the major types of life insurance available?
- How much will life insurance cost?
- How can investments in stocks and bonds help the Osunas to plan for the future?
- How is current yield used to compare the value of stocks and bonds?

Using This Page

Have students read the introductory paragraph and questions. Have them list possible solutions to the problems presented. After completing the chapter, have students review their suggested solutions, comparing them with those presented in the lessons. You may wish to have students suggest other possible problems resulting from the situation described on this page and to discuss possible solutions.

You may wish to organize the class into small groups to complete the situational activity described on this *Using the Page.*

Lesson Resources

Maintenance: See below.
Reteaching/Alternate Teaching Strategy: p. M-45
Practice: p. M-45
Enrichment: p. M-45
Concrete Materials: Activity Worksheet 71C

Objectives

Student will

1. use a table to solve multi-step problems that involve the premiums for term insurance.
2. use a table to solve multi-step problems that involve the cash value of whole life insurance.

Maintenance

1. Multiply: $\frac{3}{5} \times \frac{1}{2}$ ANS: $\frac{3}{10}$
2. Multiply: $5\frac{1}{3} \times 2\frac{1}{4}$ ANS: 12
3. Divide: $\frac{32}{3} \div 8$ ANS: $\frac{4}{3}$, or $1\frac{1}{3}$
4. Round $32\frac{3}{5}$ to the nearest whole number. ANS: 33
5. One square yard of carpet covers 9 square feet. How many square yards of carpet are needed to cover a floor that is $15\frac{1}{3}$ feet long and $10\frac{1}{2}$ feet wide? Round your answer to the nearest whole number.
ANS: 18 square yards

1 Lesson Focus

Motivation: Ask students to discuss what reasons people might have for buying life insurance.

Purpose: Life insurance is bought for financial protection in the case of death and as an investment. Students should know how different types of insurance may satisfy these goals.

Strategy: Using "hidden questions" to solve a multi-step problem

Life Insurance: TERM AND WHOLE LIFE

Kyle and Marita Osuna are expecting their first child. Since they feel that this is an important time to plan for their future, they consulted a financial planner. Phoebe Davis, the financial planner, suggested that the Osunas consider some form of life insurance, such as **term insurance.**

TERM INSURANCE

1. Gives financial protection for a specific term, such as 5 years, 10 years, or until a certain age.
2. Can be renewed after each term. However, the premium will be higher.
3. The **face value** (amount of insurance) will be paid to the policy holder's beneficiary (wife or husband, etc.) in case of death.

1. What happens to your insurance coverage if you do not renew your term insurance policy at the end of the term? The coverage stops.

EXAMPLE 1 Suppose that the Osuna's buy a $110,000 five-year term insurance policy for Kyle who is 25.

a. What will their yearly premium cost?

[1] Find the number of 1000's in $110,000.

110,000 ÷ 1000 = **110**

[2] Read the table to find the yearly premium per $1000 for a 25-year old man.

5-Year Term Insurance Premium per $1000 for One Year					
Age	Men	Women	Age	Men	Women
20	$1.62	$1.69	35	$1.87	$1.78
25	$1.69	$1.63	40	$2.34	$1.94
30	$1.77	$1.70	45	$3.26	$2.49

[3] **Number of $1000-units** × **Premium per $1000** = **Yearly Premium**
110 × $1.69 = **$185.90**

b. Find the total premium for five years: $185.90 × 5 = **$929.50**

Phoebe suggested that the Osunas might also want to consider **whole life insurance.**

WHOLE LIFE

1. Gives financial protection over entire life of policy holder.
2. The policy holder always pays the same premium.
3. The policy has a cash value and a loan value.

The Osunas like whole life insurance for two reasons.

a. They can collect the cash value of the policy at any time by canceling the policy.

b. They can borrow all, or part, of the cash value at a low interest rate. This amount is called the **loan value** of the policy.

Sample Cash Value				
Whole Life Paid up at 65				
Number of Years	5	10	15	20
Cash Value per $1000	39.20	113.43	198.62	294.08

EXAMPLE 2 Suppose that the Osunas purchase $50,000 worth of whole life insurance. Find the cash value after 10 years.

[1] Find the number of 1000's in $50,000.

50,000 ÷ 1000 = **50**

[2] Read the table to find the cash value per $1000 of insurance after 10 years. **113.43**

[3] Multiply: $113.43 × 50 = **$5,671.50**

The cash value of the policy after 10 years is **$5,671.50.**

CHECK YOUR SKILLS

Divide. For additional practice, see page 375.

1. 110,000 ÷ 1000 110
2. $130,000 ÷ 1000 130
3. $190,000 ÷ 1000 190
4. $100,000 ÷ 1000 100

Multiply. For additional practice, see page 372.

5. 110 × $1.65 $181.50
6. 180 × $1.87 $336.60
7. 160 × $1.93 $308.80
8. 170 × $1.77 $300.90
9. 40 × $38.30 $1532
10. 70 × $293.18 $20,522.60
11. 50 × $195.72 $9786
12. 30 × $40.10 $1203

[2] Teaching the Lesson

Discuss with students the conditions of term insurance given in the box. Then have students answer question 1. Focus students' attention on the premium table in Example 1. Ask questions like these.

1. The premiums listed are for how much insurance? ($1000)
2. What two things do you need to know to determine the yearly premium per $1000? (Age and whether male or female)
3. Why do you pay more for insurance as you grow older? (Risk of death increases as age increases)

Then discuss Example 1. Focus students' attention on the box for whole life insurance and the sample cash value table on page 313. Discuss the conditions shown in the box. Then ask these questions about the table.

1. The cash values listed are for how much life insurance? ($1000)
2. What happens to the cash value as you invest in whole life over the years? (It gets larger.)

Then go over Example 2 with the class.

[3] Close

Summary: Have students discuss which type of insurance they think would be the better investment. Have them give reasons for their answers.

Evaluation

Guided Practice: Ex. 1–4, 6–10 even, 14–18 even

Independent Practice: Ex. 5–9 odd, 11, 12, 13–17 odd, 19, 20

Extension

Have students work this problem. Wayne's yearly life insurance premium is $242. He pays the premium in 4 equal payments during the year. In addition to his premium, he must also pay a service charge of $1.25 with each payment. Find the amount of each payment, including the service charge. ($61.75)

Problem-Solving Skills

Reading a table (Ex. 5–20)
Solving a multi-step problem (Ex. 5–20)
Choosing the operation (Ex. 12, 20)

EXERCISES

Complete. Choose your answers from the box at the right.

whole life
cash value
face value
beneficiary
term
loan value

1. Insurance which gives financial protection for a specific amount of time is called __?__ insurance. term
2. The amount of an insurance policy's coverage is called its __?__. face value
3. Unlike term insurance policies, a whole life insurance policy has a __?__ and a __?__. cash value; loan value
4. The amount of money you will receive if you cancel your whole life policy is called its __?__. cash value

Find the yearly premium and the total amount paid for premiums over the term of the insurance policy. Use the table on page 312.

	Male/ Female	Age	Face Value	Term
5.	Female	20	$100,000	5 years
6.	Male	30	$150,000	5 years
7.	Female	40	$130,000	5 years

	Male/ Female	Age	Face Value	Term
8.	Male	35	$170,000	5 years
9.	Female	25	$160,000	5 years
10.	Male	20	$120,000	5 years

Term: 5. $169; $845 6. $265.50; $1327.50 7. $252.20; $1261 8. $317.90; $1589.50 9. $260.80; $1304 10. $194.40; $972

For Exercises 11–12, use the table on page 312.

11. Robert McCormick is 30 years old. Robert wants to buy a $150,000 5-year term insurance policy. What would be the total premium for the term of the policy? $1327.50

12. As a non-smoker, Sheila receives 5% off on her life insurance premium. She buys $80,000 worth of 5-year term insurance. If Sheila is 30 years old, what will be her yearly premium? $129.20

For Exercises 13–18, find the cash value of each whole life insurance policy. Use the table on page 313.

	Face Value	Term	Cash Value
13.	$50,000	5	__?__ $1960
14.	$100,000	10	__?__ $11,343
15.	$80,000	20	__?__ $23,526.40

	Face Value	Term	Cash Value
16.	$30,000	15	__?__ $5958.60
17.	$60,000	10	__?__ $6805.80
18.	$40,000	15	__?__ $7944.80

For Exercises 19–20, use the table on page 313.

19. Diana Gonzales purchased a $60,000 whole life insurance policy. What is the cash value of the policy after 15 years? $11,917.20

20. Mark Ebner has $90,000 worth of whole life insurance. After five years, he borrows 75% of the cash value. How much is Mark's loan? $2646

Strategy: Using "hidden questions" to solve a multi-step problem

Universal Life Insurance

The financial planner also discussed **universal life** insurance.

UNIVERSAL LIFE

1. Most of the time, the policy holder can choose the amount of the premium as long as it stays above a specified minimum.
2. The cash value of the policy earns interest, and is tax free until the money is withdrawn.
3. The policy holder is allowed to make partial withdrawals of the cash value and still keep the policy in effect.

With universal life insurance, the amount paid in premiums is added to the policy's cash value account. The insurance company then deducts monthly charges for insurance coverage and operating costs. What is left is the actual cash value which earns interest.

This table shows sample monthly deductions for insurance coverage and operating costs.

Sample Universal Life Insurance Deductions Per $1000 for One Year

Age	Men	Women	Age	Men	Women
20	$1.68	$1.56	**35**	$2.04	$1.56
25	1.56	1.68	**40**	3.00	2.04
30	1.56	1.56	**45**	4.44	3.00

EXAMPLE 1 The Osunas can afford a $50.00 premium each month. They would like to get a $60,000 policy for Marita who is 25 years old. What will be the cash value of the policy at the end of one year?

[1] Find the premiums for one year: $50.00 × 12 = **$600**

[2] Read the table to find out how much the insurance company deducts per year for each thousand. Multiply this by the number of 1000's in the policy.

$1.68 × 60 = **$100.80**

[3] **Amount Paid in Premiums** − **Insurance Company Deductions** = **Cash Value**

$600 − $100.80 = **$499.20**

Lesson Resources

Maintenance: See below.
Reteaching/Alternate Teaching Strategy: p. M-45
Practice: p. M-45
Enrichment: p. M-45
Concrete Materials: Activity Worksheet 72C

Objective

Student will use a table to solve multi-step problems that involve universal life insurance.

Maintenance

1. Divide: 50,000 ÷ 1000 ANS: 50
2. Multiply: 2.42 × 60 ANS: 145.2
3. Add: 42.5 + 18.75 + 37.22 ANS: 98.47
4. Subtract: $585.20 − $186.29 ANS: $398.91
5. Julia has the following deductions from her paycheck each week.

   Health insurance: $5.75
   Savings plan: $25
   Income tax: $51.50
   FICA: $24.40

   Her gross pay is $325.80. Find her net pay. ANS: $219.15

[1] Lesson Focus

Motivation: Have students discuss what advantages of term and whole life insurance they would like to combine if they could write their own policy.

Purpose: Universal life is the most popular form of life insurance. It combines a low term insurance with a very competitive cash value investment. Students need to be aware of this recently developed form of insurance.

2 Teaching the Lesson

Discuss with students the conditions of universal life insurance given in the box. Have a student volunteer read the paragraph. Focus students' attention on the premium table. Ask these questions.

1. What would the deduction be per $1000 for one year for a 25-year-old male? ($1.56)
2. What would the deduction be per $1000 for one year for a 40-year-old female? ($2.04)

Then discuss Example 1. Focus students' attention on the investment multiple table. Ask these questions.

1. A dollar invested every year for 5 years would grow to what amount if the interest is 7.5%? ($6.26)
2. $500 invested every year for 10 years would multiply by what factor at 10% interest? (17.52)
3. $500 multiplied by 17.52 would give what cash value? ($8760)

Make sure each student can answer these types of questions before going to Example 2.

3 Close

Summary: Have students discuss the advantages of universal life insurance over term or whole life insurance.

Evaluation
Guided Practice: Ex. 1–4, 6, 8
Independent Practice: Ex. 5, 7, 9–14

Extension

Divide the class into small groups. Have each group obtain pamphlets about different types of life insurance from local insurance agencies. Then have each group share its information with the class.

1. Suppose that the Osunas kept the same $60,000 policy as in Example 1, and increased their monthly premium by $20. What would the cash value be at the end of one year? $739.20

To give the Osunas an idea of how the cash value of a universal life insurance policy can accumulate over a certain time period, Phoebe showed them the table below.

Number of Years	Investment Multiple Table		
	5%	7.5%	10%
1	1.05	1.08	1.10
4	4.53	4.82	5.10
5	5.81	6.26	6.71
10	13.22	15.22	17.52

EXAMPLE 2 What is the approximate cash value of the Osunas policy after 10 years? The average interest rate for the 10 years is 7.5%. The Osunas continued to make monthly payments of $50.

1 Use the table to find the multiple for 10 years at 7.5% interest. **15.22**

2 Find the product of the multiple and the yearly cash value from Example 1.

Multiple × Yearly Cash Value = Total Cash Value

15.22 × $499.20 = **$7597.82** ◀ *Rounded to the nearest cent*

After 10 years, the policy would have an approximate cash value of **$7597.82.**

CHECK YOUR SKILLS

ESTIMATION/MENTAL MATH: Ex. 1–8

Estimate to determine whether the answer is reasonable. Answer Yes or No. For additional practice, see pages 52–53.

1. 4.82 × $317.33 = $1529.53 Yes
2. 4.44 × $80 = 455.22 No
3. 13.22 × $410.36 = $4424.96 No
4. 6.26 × $185.40 = $1160.60 Yes
5. 17.52 × $499.20 = $8745.98 Yes
6. 5.81 × $476.10 = $3766.14 No
7. $360 − $142.80 = $217.20 Yes
8. $720 − $399.60 = $320.40 Yes

EXERCISES

Complete. Choose your answers from the box at the right.

added
cash value
face value
withdrawal
deducted

1. With most universal life insurance policies, insurance coverage and operating costs are ___?___ from the cash value. **deducted**
2. With most universal life insurance policies, interest is ___?___ to the cash value. **added**
3. With most universal life insurance policies, the policy holder is allowed to make a partial ___?___ of the cash value. **withdrawal**
4. Amount Paid in Premiums − Insurance Company Deductions = ___?___ **cash value**

For Exercises 5–8, find the yearly insurance company deductions, and the yearly cash value. Use the table on page 315.

	Male/Female	Age	Face Value	Monthly Premium	
5.	Male	20	$50,000	$25.00	**$84; $216**
6.	Female	35	$70,000	$45.00	**$109.20; $430.80**
7.	Female	25	$70,000	$15.00	**$117.60; $62.40**
8.	Male	42	$60,000	$15.00	**$180; $0**

For Exercises 9–10, use the table on page 316.

9. Yearly Cash Value: $349.90
Number of Years: 4
Average Interest Rate: 5%
Approximate Cash Value: ___?___ **$1585.05**

10. Yearly Cash Value: $200.00
Number of Years: 5
Average Interest Rate: 7.5%
Approximate Cash Value: ___?___ **$1252**

For Exercises 11–14, use the tables on pages 315 and 316.

11. John Packel's insurance company deductions for one year totaled $53.28. John pays a monthly premium of $25.00. What will be the cash value of John's policy after one year? **$246.72**

12. Carol Sywetz is 25 years old and pays $95 a month for $80,000 worth of universal life insurance. What will be the cash value of her policy after one year? **$1005.60**

13. Ken McNeil's universal life insurance policy has a yearly cash value of $444. If the interest rate averages 10%, how much will the total cash value of the policy be in 10 years? **$7778.88**

14. Andreá Mele is 35 years old. She wants to get an $80,000 universal life insurance policy, and can afford to pay $40 per month. How much cash value will the policy have after 10 years if the interest rate averages 7.5%? **$5406.14**

Problem-Solving Skills

Reading a table (Ex. 5–14)
Solving a multi-step problem (Ex. 5–14)

Lesson Resources

Maintenance: See below.
Reteaching/Alternate Teaching Strategy: p. M-46 (Visual 42)
Practice: p. M-46
Enrichment: p. M-46
Concrete Materials: Visual 42
Visual 42

Objective

Student will use a table to solve multi-step problems involving certificates of deposit.

Maintenance

1. Multiply: 450 × 0.16 × 3 ANS: 216
2. Multiply: 278.5 × 8 ANS 2228
3. Add: $1475.24 + $386.56 ANS: $1861.80
4. Subtract: $485 − $256.20 ANS: $228.80
5. At the beginning of March, James had a balance of $325.62 in his checking account. During the month, he made 3 deposits of $222.50 each and wrote checks totaling $529.50. What was his balance at the end of the month? ANS: $463.62

1 Lesson Focus

Motivation: Have students list all the ways they know of saving money.

Purpose: Many students need to become aware that there are many ways to save money, such as personal cash or a passbook account. This lesson will introduce them to a certificate of deposit.

Certificates of Deposit

Strategy: Using "hidden questions" to solve a multi-step problem

The Osunas are also thinking of investing $10,000 in a **certificate of deposit.** They know that these certificates earn interest at a higher rate than savings accounts.

Certificates of deposit must be left on deposit for a specified period of time, such as 6 months.

Yearly Rate	Growth of $1.00 at Interest Compounded Quarterly		
	6 months	1 year	18 months
7%	1.0353	1.0719	1.1097
7.5%	1.0378	1.0771	1.1179
8%	1.0404	1.0824	1.1262
8.5%	1.0429	1.0877	1.1345
9%	1.0455	1.0930	1.1428
9.5%	1.0480	1.0984	1.1512
10%	1.0506	1.1038	1.1597

EXAMPLE The Osunas invested $10,000 in a one-year certificate that pays 8% interest compounded quarterly. How much interest will the certificate earn?

1. Use the table to find how much $1.00 will pay at 8% interest at the end of one year. **1.0824**
2. Find the amount $10,000 will pay at maturity.

   $10,000 × 1.0824 = **$10,824** ◀ *Amount Invested* × *Amount $1 will pay* = *Amount Paid*
3. Find the amount of interest.

   Amount paid at Maturity − **Amount Invested** = **Interest**

   $10,824 − **$10,000** = **$824**

Unlike savings accounts, there is usually a **penalty** (loss of interest) for withdrawing part or all of the money in a certificate of deposit before **maturity** (the specified period of deposit).

CHECK YOUR SKILLS

Multiply. For additional practice, see page 372.

1. $6000 × 1.1262 $6757.20
2. $15,000 × 1.0353 $15,529.50
3. $8000 × 1.0521 $8416.80
4. $5000 × 1.0671 $5335.50

Use the formula $i = p \times r \times t$ to find the amount of simple interest earned in one year at an interest rate of 8%. For additional practice, see page 110–111.

5. $2000 $160
6. $800 $64
7. $1500 $120
8. $7000 $560
9. $500 $40

EXERCISES

Complete. Choose your answers from the box at the right below.

matured
higher
bonus
amount of deposit
lower
interest
penalty

1. Usually, certificates of deposit earn interest at a _?_ rate than regular savings accounts. **higher**
2. There is usually a _?_ if money is withdrawn early from a certificate of deposit. **penalty**
3. When a certificate of deposit has been left for a specified period of deposit, it is said to have _?_. **matured**
4. Amount Paid at Maturity − Amount Invested = _?_ **interest**

For Exercises 5–10, use the table on page 318.

a. *Find the amount paid at maturity for each certificate.*

b. *Find how much interest each certificate earns.*

	Face Value	Yearly Rate	Interest Period
5.	$9000	7%	6 months **$9317.70; $317.70**
6.	$ 500	9%	6 months **$522.75; $22.75**
7.	$2000	7.5%	18 months **$2235.80; $235.80**
8.	$3000	7%	1 year **$3215.70; $215.70**
9.	$6000	8.5%	6 months **$6257.40; $257.40**
10.	$1500	8%	18 months **$1689.30; $189.30**

For Exercises 11–14, use the table on page 318.

11. George Heurbert invested $5000 in a one-year certificate of deposit paying 8.5% interest compounded quarterly. How much will the certificate be worth at maturity? **$5438.50**

12. Pauline Moore invested $1000 in an 18-month certificate of deposit paying 7% interest compounded quarterly. How much interest will the certificate earn at maturity? **$109.70**

Michael Salmon has $2000 in a savings account which pays 5% simple interest. Michael also has a $1500 one-year certificate of deposit paying 7% interest compounded quarterly.

13. Which will have the greater total value at the end of one year, the certificate of deposit or the savings account? **the savings account**

14. What is one advantage of a savings account over a certificate of deposit?
Answers will vary. One advantage is that money can be withdrawn from a savings account without paying a penalty.

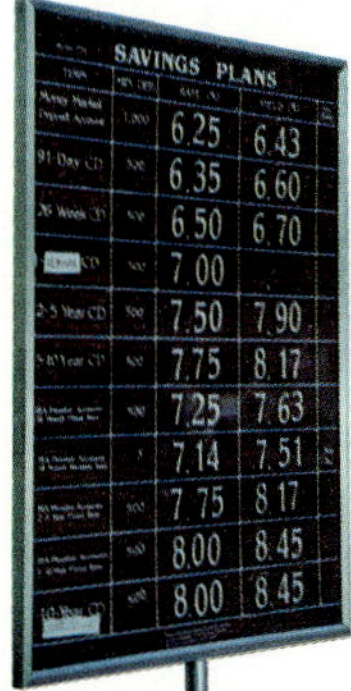

2 Teaching the Lesson

Focus students' attention on the table. Ask questions such as these.

1. What two things do you need to know to use this table? (Interest period and yearly rate)
2. How much money will you have for each dollar invested for 6 months at 10%? ($1.0506)
3. If you invested $1000 in a certificate for 12 months at 8%, how much money would you have in 1 year? ($1082.20)

Then discuss the Example.

3 Close

Summary: Have students discuss the benefits and drawbacks of investing in certificates of deposit.

Evaluation
Guided Practice: Ex. 1–4, 6–10 even
Independent Practice: Ex. 5–9 odd, 11–14

Extension

Have students find the interest rates for certificates of deposit at different banks in the area. Also have them find out the least amount that can be invested.

Problem-Solving Skills

Reading a table (Ex. 5–13)
Solving a multi-step problem (Ex. 5–13)

Critical Thinking

You may wish to have students work in small groups to solve this problem or you may wish to work with the class.
Ex. 14

Objective

Student will

1. review the skills, concepts, and applications in the first part of Chapter 13.
2. maintain key skills and concepts taught in Chapters 6, 11, and 12.

Using the Page

Exercises 1–10 provide an informal assessment of the student's mastery of the major skills and concepts presented in the first half of Chapter 13. Each item is referenced to the related pages where the particular item was presented. These exercises parallel the quiz provided in the *Teacher's ResourceBank.*™

A quiz covering the second half of the chapter is also provided in the *Teacher's ResourceBank.*™

Exercises 11–14 maintain skills and concepts taught in Chapters 6, 11, and 12.

Mid-Chapter Review

For Exercises 1–2, use the tables on pages 312 and 313. (Pages 312–314)

1. Jason Spodek is 45 years old. Jason wants to buy a $140,000 5-year term insurance policy. What would be the total premium for the term of the policy? **$2282**

2. Kim Murdoch purchased a $80,000 whole life insurance policy. What is the cash value of the policy after 10 years? **$9074.40**

For Exercises 3–4, use the tables on pages 315 and 316. (Pages 315–317)

3. Mary Ings is 35 years old and pays $60.00 per month for $70,000 worth of universal life insurance. What will the cash value of her policy be after one year? **$610.80**

4. Yearly Cash Value: $601.10
Number of Years: 4
Average Interest Rate: 5%
Approximate Cash Value: __?__ **$2722.98**

For Exercise 5–10, use the table on page 318.
a. *Find the amount paid at maturity for each certificate.*
b. *Find how much interest each certificate earns.* (Pages 318–319)

	Face Value	Yearly Rate	Interest Period
5.	$15,000	9%	1 year **$16,395; $1395**
6.	$ 5,000	7.5%	6 months **$5189; $189**
7.	$ 8,000	8%	18 months

7. Interest Period: $9009.60; $1009.60

	Face Value	Yearly Rate	Interest Paid
8.	$10,000	10%	18 months **$11,597; $1597**
9.	$12,000	9.5%	6 months **$12,576; $576**
10.	$ 4,000	7%	1 year

10. Interest Paid: $4287.60; $287.60

MAINTENANCE

For Exercises 11–12, find the indicated amount.

11. Cost of Car: $9540
Down Payment (%): 15%
Down Payment: __?__ **$1431**
(Pages 132–133)

12. Regular Price: $246.50
Rate of Discount: 30%
Selling Price: __?__ **$172.55**
(Pages 284–285)

13. Denton bought a refrigerator for $964.80. He made a 20% down payment and agreed to make 18 monthly payments of $51.00. Find the finance charge. (Pages 297–299) **$146.16**

14. Last month, Maureen McCleod's electric meter read 6790. It now reads 8264. How many kilowatt-hours of electricity were used? (Pages 264–265) **1474 kilowatt-hours**

Strategy: Using "hidden questions" to solve a multi-step problem.

Buying and Selling Stock

The Osunas are also thinking about investing in **stocks.** By buying shares of stock in a company you become a part owner of that company. Stock prices are usually quoted (listed) in **eighths of a dollar** in the business sections of daily newspapers.

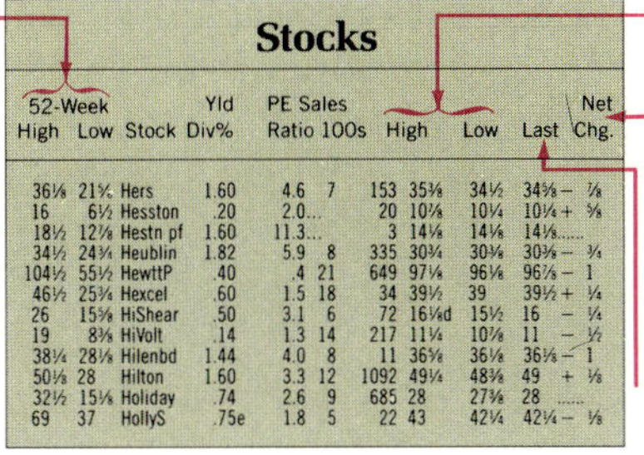

Stocks

52-Week High	52-Week Low	Stock	Yld Div%	PE Ratio	Sales 100s	High	Low	Last	Net Chg.
$36\frac{1}{8}$	$21\frac{3}{4}$	Hers	1.60	4.6	7	153	$35\frac{3}{8}$	$34\frac{1}{2}$	$34\frac{5}{8} - \frac{1}{8}$
16	$6\frac{1}{2}$	Hesston	.20	2.0	...	20	$10\frac{7}{8}$	$10\frac{1}{4}$	$10\frac{1}{4} + \frac{5}{8}$
$18\frac{1}{2}$	$12\frac{7}{8}$	Hestn pf	1.60	11.3	...	3	$14\frac{1}{8}$	$14\frac{1}{8}$	$14\frac{1}{8}$ .....
$34\frac{1}{2}$	$24\frac{3}{4}$	Heublin	1.82	5.9	8	335	$30\frac{3}{4}$	$30\frac{3}{8}$	$30\frac{3}{8} - \frac{3}{4}$
$104\frac{1}{2}$	$55\frac{1}{2}$	HewttP	.40	.4	21	649	$97\frac{1}{8}$	$96\frac{1}{8}$	$96\frac{7}{8} - 1$
$46\frac{1}{2}$	$25\frac{3}{4}$	Hexcel	.60	1.5	18	34	$39\frac{1}{2}$	39	$39\frac{1}{2} + \frac{1}{4}$
26	$15\frac{5}{8}$	HiShear	.50	3.1	6	72	$16\frac{1}{8}$d	$15\frac{1}{2}$	$16 - \frac{1}{4}$
19	$8\frac{3}{8}$	HiVolt	.14	1.3	14	217	$11\frac{1}{4}$	$10\frac{7}{8}$	$11 - \frac{1}{2}$
$38\frac{1}{4}$	$28\frac{1}{8}$	Hilenbd	1.44	4.0	8	11	$36\frac{5}{8}$	$36\frac{1}{8}$	$36\frac{1}{8} - 1$
$50\frac{1}{8}$	28	Hilton	1.60	3.3	12	1092	$49\frac{1}{4}$	$48\frac{3}{8}$	$49 + \frac{1}{8}$
$32\frac{1}{2}$	$15\frac{1}{8}$	Holiday	.74	2.6	9	685	28	$27\frac{3}{8}$	28 .....
69	37	HollyS	.75e	1.8	5	22	43	$42\frac{1}{4}$	$42\frac{1}{4} - \frac{1}{8}$

Find each of the following for a share of Hilton stock.

1. Low of the day: ___?___ $48\frac{3}{8}$

2. Net Change: ___?___ $1\frac{1}{8}$

3. Last price paid today: ___?___ 49

4. High of the day: ___?___ $49\frac{1}{4}$

> The total amount paid for a stock depends on three factors.
> **a.** The cost per share
> **b.** The number of shares purchased
> **c.** The stockbrokers' commission

EXAMPLE 1 The Osunas bought 70 shares of Advance Electronics stock which sells for $40\frac{5}{8}$ per share. The stockbroker's commission is \$32.75. Find the total cost.

[1] Write a decimal for $\$40\frac{5}{8}$.

$$\$40\frac{5}{8} = \mathbf{\$40.625} \qquad 8\overline{)5.000} = 0.625$$

[2] Number of Shares × Cost per Share = Cost of Stock

70 × 40.625 = **\$2843.75**

[3] Cost of Stock + Commision = Total Cost

\$2843.75 + \$32.75 = **\$2876.50**

The Osunas' total cost for the stock was **\$2876.50.**

Lesson Resources

Maintenance: See below.
Reteaching/Alternate Teaching Strategy: p. M-46 (Visuals 43 and 44)
Practice: p. M-46
Enrichment: p. M-46
Concrete Materials: Activity Worksheet 74 (page W-150), Visuals 43 and 44
Visuals 43 and 44

Objectives

Student will

1. use a formula to solve multi-step problems that involve buying shares of stock.
2. use a formula to solve multi-step problems that involve selling shares of stock.

Maintenance

1. Write $3\frac{1}{4}$ as a decimal. ANS: 3.25
2. Write $8\frac{3}{8}$ as a decimal. ANS: 8.375
3. Add: $2\frac{1}{2} + 3\frac{2}{3}$ ANS: $6\frac{1}{6}$
4. Multiply: $4 \times 5\frac{1}{3}$ ANS: $21\frac{1}{3}$
5. The length of a garden is $16\frac{1}{2}$ feet. The width is $10\frac{3}{4}$ feet. Find the perimeter of the garden. ANS: $54\frac{1}{2}$ feet.

[1] Lesson Focus

Motivation: Ask students to discuss how they would raise a large sum of money if they wanted to start a business.

Purpose: Students should be aware of stocks as an investment possibility. This lesson will explain that a stock is a share of a corporation.

2 *Teaching the Lesson*

Focus students' attention on the stock listing. Have students answer questions 1–4 in the lesson. Then discuss Example 1. Emphasize that the broker's commission must be included in the total cost of the stock. Then discuss Example 2. Point out that when stock is sold, the broker's commission is subtracted from the amount received.

3 *Close*

Summary: Have students discuss what they think are the advantages and disadvantages of investing in stocks.

Evaluation
Guided Practice: Ex. 1–4, 6, 10, 12
Independent Practice: Ex. 5, 7–9, 11, 13, 14–17

Extension

Have students use the newspaper stock listings to determine the values and gains and losses of different stocks. Have them watch the stocks they choose for a week to see how their values change. Have them graph the change.

When the Osunas sell their stock, they must also pay a broker's commission.

EXAMPLE 2 One year later, the Osunas decide to sell the stock they bought in Example 1. The price per share is now $\$48\frac{1}{4}$. The broker charges a commission of $38.25.

a. Find how much was received for the sale of the stock.

1 $\$48\frac{1}{4} = \$48.25$ ◀ $\frac{1}{4} = 0.25$

2 **Number of Shares × Selling Price = Amount of Sale**
70 × $48.25 = **$3377.50**

3 **Amount of Sale − Commission = Amount Received**
$3377.50 − $38.25 = **$3339.25**

b. Find the amount of profit or loss.

Since the amount received for selling the stock is greater than the amount spent on buying the stock, they made a profit.

Amount Received − Total Cost = Profit
$3339.25 − $2876.50 = **$462.75**

CHECK YOUR SKILLS

Write a decimal for each fraction. For additional practice, see page 373.

1. $\frac{1}{8}$ 0.125 **2.** $\frac{1}{2}$ 0.5 **3.** $\frac{3}{8}$ 0.375 **4.** $\frac{7}{8}$ 0.875 **5.** $\frac{5}{8}$ 0.625 **6.** $\frac{3}{4}$ 0.75

Multiply. For additional practice, see page 372.

7. 50 × $42.625 $2131.25 **8.** 100 × $36.75 $3675 **9.** 150 × $21.875 $3281.25 **10.** 200 × $61.375 $12,275

EXERCISES

Complete. Choose your answers from the box at the right.

profit
commission
cost per share
cost of stock
loss
stock

1. By buying shares of a company's __?__ you become a part owner of the company. stock

2. Stockbrokers receive a __?__ for buying and selling stocks for other people. commission

3. Total cost = __?__ + Commission cost of stock

4. If the amount received for selling a stock is greater than the amount spent on buying the stock, the stockholder makes a __?__. profit

For Exercises 5–7, complete the table.

	Stock	Cost Per Share	Number of Shares	Commission	Total Cost
5.	Bradley, Inc.	$\$27\frac{1}{2}$	50	$ 28.60	? $1403.60
6.	American Consulting	$\$69\frac{1}{8}$	200	$175.60	? $14,000.60
7.	Custom Service	$\$47\frac{3}{8}$	80	? $62.85	$3852.85

8. Virgil bought 150 shares of Quaker Ltd. at $\$14\frac{5}{8}$ per share. The commission charge was $73.95. Find the total cost of the purchase. **$2267.70**

9. Janine bought 200 shares of Acme Press stock at $\$24\frac{1}{4}$ per share. The commission charge was $80.25. Find the total cost of the purchase. **$4930.25**

For Exercises 10–13, find each of the following.

a. *The amount received for the sale of the stock.*

b. *The amount of profit or loss.*

10. $3849.10; $49.50 loss
11. $2658.70; $207.85 profit
12. $6255.40; $2804.55 loss
13. $6414.10; $248.20 profit

	Stock	Number of Shares	Buying Cost Per Share	Commission	Selling Cost Per Share	Commission
10.	Sun Power	100	$\$38\frac{3}{8}$	$61.10	$\$39\frac{1}{8}$	See above. $63.40
11.	Fenton Foods	150	$\$16\frac{1}{8}$	$32.10	$18	$41.30
12.	Alston, Ltd.	300	$\$29\frac{7}{8}$	$97.45	$\$21\frac{1}{8}$	$82.10
13.	Ings Foods	200	$\$30\frac{1}{2}$	$65.90	$\$32\frac{1}{2}$	$85.90

For Exercises 14–17, use the graph of Best Foods' stock prices at the right.

14. In what months did the stock increase in value the most? **March and April**

15. How much did 100 shares of Best Foods' stock cost in March? The stockbroker's commission was $75.40. **$5275.40**

16. How much was recieved from the sale of 100 shares of Best Foods' stock in May? The stockbroker's commission was $91.40. **$5208.60**

17. How much profit or loss would be made if the stocks were bought as described in Exercise 15 and then sold as described in Exercise 16? **A $66.80 loss**

Problem-Solving Skills

Solving a multi-step problem (Ex. 5–13, 15, 16)
Reading a graph (Ex. 14–16)

Lesson Resources

Maintenance: See below.
Reteaching/Alternate Teaching Strategy: p. M-47
Practice: p. M-47
Enrichment: p. M-47

Objectives

Student will

1. solve multi-step problems that involve yearly dividends.
2. use a formula to solve multi-step problems that involve annual yield.

Maintenance

1. Write $\frac{1}{8}$ as a decimal. ANS: 0.125
2. Multiply: 36 × \$6.20 ANS: \$223.20
3. Multiply: 1.5 × 9.4 ANS: 14.1
4. Add: \$138.70 + \$24.50 ANS: \$163.20
5. Lucinda earns \$5.60 per hour. She gets time and a half for any hours she works over 40 hours. Find her earnings for 46 hours. ANS: \$274.40

1 Lesson Focus

Motivation: Have students discuss why they think different stocks have different prices, and how they might be able to compare the value of stocks.

Purpose: Some students may invest in stocks in the future. They should know that different stocks have different values. The value of a stock is based on the stability of the company and the anticipated return on the investment through dividends.

Strategy" Using a "hidden question" to solve a multi-step problem

Dividends/Annual Yield

For the one year that they owned their Advance Electronics stocks, the Osunas received dividends. **Dividends** are a portion of a company's profits which the company pays to its stockholders. Dividends are usually distributed quarterly (every 3 months).

EXAMPLE 1 Advance Electronics paid a quarterly dividend of \$1.40 per share. Find the Osunas' total yearly dividends for their 70 shares of stock.

1 Find the total dividends for 1 quarter: 70 × \$1.40 = **\$98**

2 Find the total yearly dividends: \$98 × 4 = **\$392**

The percent of your investment that you receive as income each year is called the **annual yield.**

Annual Yield = Annual Dividend ÷ Price per Share

EXAMPLE 2 Find the annual yield of Advance Electronics' stocks when the quarterly dividend is \$1.40 per share and the price per stock is $\$40\frac{5}{8}$.

1 Find the annual dividend: \$1.40 × 4 = **\$5.60**

2 **Annual Yield = Annual Dividend ÷ Price Per Share**
= \$5.60 ÷ \$40.625 — $\$40\frac{5}{8} = \$40.625$
= 0.1378 — Round to the nearest thousandth
= **13.8%**

CHECK YOUR SKILLS

For additional practice, see page 379.

Divide. Round each answer to the nearest thousandth.

1. \$5.20 ÷ \$35.625 0.146
2. \$3.50 ÷ \$27.50 0.127
3. \$1.80 ÷ \$32.25 0.056
4. \$4.16 ÷ \$42.125 0.099

Find the mean of each group of numbers. For additional practice, see pages 10–11.

5. \$0.85, \$0.95, \$1.05, \$1.00, \$0.65 \$0.90
6. \$1.90, \$2.50, \$2.80, \$3.05, \$1.75 \$2.40

EXERCISES

Complete. Choose your answers from the box at the right.

three
annual yield
yearly
quarterly
four
dividends

1. That portion of a company's profits which the company pays to its stockholders is called _?_. dividends
2. Companies usually pay dividends _?_ times each year. four
3. The quarterly dividend multiplied by 4 equals the total _?_ dividend. yearly
4. Annual Dividend ÷ Price Per Share = _?_. annual yield

For Exercises 5–10, find the total yearly dividend.

	Stock	Number of Shares	Quarterly Dividend Per Share
5.	Bliss, Inc.	120	$1.15 $552
6.	Avco Ltd.	150	$2.05 $1230
7.	DC Energy	200	$1.75 $1400

	Stock	Number of Shares	Quarterly Dividend Per Share
8.	Surf Ltd.	50	$0.85 $170
9.	Linch	150	$1.42 $852
10.	Computex	100	$1.45 $580

11. American Consulting Corporation pays a quarterly dividend of $1.75 per share. James Francis owns 200 shares of this stock. Find James' total yearly dividend. $1400

12. For the past five years Custom Software, Inc. has paid quarterly dividends of $0.65, $0.85, $0.95, $1.05, and $1.00. What is the mean yearly dividend? $3.60

For Exercises 13–18, find the annual yield of each stock. Round your answer to the nearest tenth of a percent.

	Stock	Price Per Share	Quarterly Dividend Per Share
13.	AC Books	$27\frac{1}{4}$	$0.65 9.5%
14.	Finch	$43\frac{3}{8}$	$1.05 9.7%
15.	Bliss, Inc.	$36\frac{1}{2}$	$0.82 9%

	Stock	Price Per Share	Quarterly Dividend Per Share
16.	Woods, Ltd.	$60	$1.18 7.9%
17.	Tamber	$22\frac{5}{8}$	$0.60 10.6%
18.	Hart	$51\frac{3}{4}$	$1.05 8.1%

19. Pauline Moore owns Tivoli stock which pays a quarterly dividend of $0.75. She paid $39\frac{3}{4}$ for each share. Find the annual yield to the nearest tenth of a percent. 7.5%

20. Vincent Varga owns shares of Hotalings stock which he bought at $39\frac{7}{8}$ per share. The company pays a quarterly dividend of $1.99 per share. Estimate the annual yield. About 20%

2 Teaching the Lesson

Have a student volunteer read the first paragraph. Then discuss Example 1. Before discussing Example 2, emphasize that students must find the annual dividend before they can find the annual yield. You may want to ask these questions after discussing Example 2.

1. If you buy stock for $20 a share and you get a $1 dividend quarterly, how much will you receive in dividends for the year? ($4)
2. What is the annual yield for the investment in question 1? (20%)
3. If you buy stock for $36 a share and you get a $1 dividend quarterly, how much will you receive in dividends for the year? ($4)
4. What is the annual yield for the investment in question 3? (11%)
5. Which stock, the $20 or the $36, has a higher annual yield? ($20)

3 Close

Summary: Have students discuss all the things they need to consider in making an investment in stocks.

Evaluation
Guided Practice: Ex. 1–4, 6–10 even, 14–18 even
Independent Practice: Ex. 5–9 odd, 11, 12, 13–17 odd, 19, 20

Extension

Have students write a report on the stock exchanges in the United States. Their report should include information on the history of the exchanges, the purpose, the types of transactions, and the number of daily transactions.

Problem-Solving Skills

Solving multi-step problems (Ex. 5–20)
Choosing the operation (Ex. 12)
Using Estimation (Ex. 20)

Estimation Ex. 20

Lesson Resources

Maintenance: See below.
Reteaching/Alternate Teaching Strategy: p. M-47
Practice: p. M-47
Enrichment: p. M-47

Objectives

Student will

1. solve problems that involve bond prices.
2. use a formula to solve multi-step problems that involve current yield.

Maintenance

1. Round 0.3562 to the nearest hundredth. ANS: 0.36
2. Round 6.54218 to nearest thousandth ANS: 6.542
3. Divide: 1.32 ÷ 8 ANS: 0.165
4. Which is less, 0.375 or 0.382? ANS: 0.375
5. An 8-ounce can of soup sells for 79¢. A 14-ounce can of the same soup sells for $1.39. Which is the better buy? ANS: 8-ounce can

1 *Lesson Focus*

Motivation: Have students discuss how they could get money to start a business without selling shares in the business.

Purpose: Students need to see how bonds differ from stocks. This lesson will show them how to find costs and current yields of bonds so they can compare them to other investments.

Bonds

Strategy: Using a "hidden question" to solve a multi-step problem

When the Osunas were purchasing stock the broker told them they might also want to consider investing in **bonds.** Many corporations and governments raise money by selling bonds. When you purchase a bond you are lending money to the corporation or government that is selling the bonds. The price you pay for buying a bond is a percent of the face value of the bond. The **face value** is the amount printed on the bond.

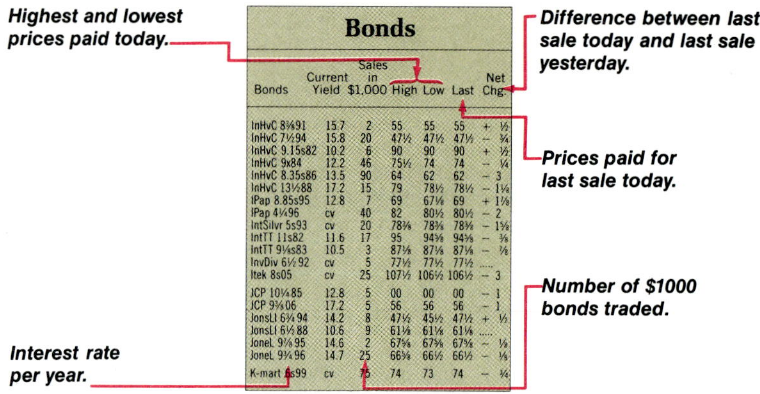

Bonds

Bonds	Current Yield	Sales in $1,000	High	Low	Last	Net Chg.
InHvC 8⅜91	15.7	2	55	55	55	+ ½
InHvC 7½94	15.8	20	47½	47½	47½	− ¾
InHvC 9.15s82	10.2	6	90	90	90	+ ½
InHvC 9x84	12.2	46	75½	74	74	− ¼
InHvC 8.35s86	13.5	90	64	62	62	− 3
InHvC 13½88	17.2	15	79	78½	78½	− 1⅛
IPap 8.85s95	12.8	7	69	67⅛	69	+ 1⅞
IPap 4¼96	cv	40	82	80½	80½	− 2
IntSilvr 5s93	cv	20	78⅜	78⅜	78⅜	− 1⅝
IntTT 11s82	11.6	17	95	94⅜	94⅜	− ⅜
IntTT 9⅛s83	10.5	3	87⅛	87⅛	87⅛	− ⅛
InvDiv 6½92	cv	5	77½	77½	77½	.....
Itek 8s05	cv	25	107½	106½	106½	− 3
JCP 10¼85	12.8	5	00	00	00	− 1
JCP 9⅜06	17.2	5	56	56	56	− 1
JonsLI 6¾94	14.2	8	47½	45½	47½	+ ½
JonsLI 6½88	10.6	9	61⅛	61⅛	61⅛	.....
JoneL 9⅞95	14.6	2	67⅝	67⅝	67⅝	− ⅛
JoneL 9¾96	14.7	25	66⅝	66½	66½	− ⅛
K-mart 6s99	cv	75	74	73	74	− ¾

1. What is the selling price of a $1000-bond selling at 50% of its face value? $500

EXAMPLE 1 Use the bond report above to find the last price of the day for a $1000-InvDiv bond.

1 Find the "InvDiv" bond in the bond report.
Look right to find the reading in the "Last" column. $77\frac{1}{2}$
$77\frac{1}{2}$ means $77\frac{1}{2}\%$.

2 $\$1000 \times 0.775 = \mathbf{\$775}$ ◀ $77\frac{1}{2}\% = 0.775$

Bondholders receive interest on their bonds. The interest is usually paid twice a year. The percent of a bondholder's investment received as income each year is called the *current yield*.

To find the current yield of a bond, you divide the yearly interest by the market price. The **market price** is the price at which the bond is currently selling.

EXAMPLE 2 A \$1000-InvDiv bond pays \$60 interest every six months. The current market price is \$775. Find the current yield.

[1] Find the yearly interest: $\$60 \times 2 = \mathbf{\$120}$

[2] **Current Yield = Yearly Interest ÷ Market Price**
= \$120 ÷ \$775
= 0.1548 ◀ *Round to the nearest thousandth*
= **15.5%**

CHECK YOUR SKILLS

Write a decimal for each mixed number. For additional practice, see step [1] of the Example and Exercises 43–60 on page 406.

1. $38\frac{3}{8}$ 38.375
2. $91\frac{7}{8}$ 91.875
3. $32\frac{1}{2}$ 32.5
4. $41\frac{3}{4}$ 41.75
5. $63\frac{5}{8}$ 63.625

Multiply. For additional practice, see page 372.

6. \$1000 × 0.56 \$560
7. \$1000 × 0.775 \$775
8. \$1000 × 0.61375 \$613.75
9. \$1000 × 0.81125 \$811.25

Divide. Round each answer to the nearest thousandth. For additional practice, see page 379.

10. \$90 ÷ \$725 0.124
11. \$160 ÷ \$985 0.162
12. \$190 ÷ \$940 0.202
13. \$110 ÷ \$840 0.131

EXERCISES

Complete. Choose your answers from the box at the right.

1. The price printed on a bond is its _?_ value. face
2. The price a bond is currently selling for is its _?_. market price
3. With bonds you usually receive interest _?_ times a year. two
4. Current Yield = Yearly Interest ÷ _?_ market price

selling price
two
market price
face
four

For Exercises 5–10, find the day's high and low prices for each \$1000 bond.

	Bond	Listed High	Listed Low
5.	Indo	$85\frac{1}{4}$ \$852.50	$84\frac{1}{4}$ \$842.50
6.	IBC	$99\frac{7}{8}$ \$998.75	$99\frac{1}{2}$ \$995
7.	GiGi	$94\frac{1}{2}$ \$945	$94\frac{1}{2}$ \$945
8.	IndRel	$88\frac{5}{8}$ \$886.25	$88\frac{1}{4}$ \$882.50
9.	YMart	90 \$900	$89\frac{1}{2}$ \$895
10.	AmCi	$45\frac{1}{2}$ \$455	40 \$400

[2] Teaching the Lesson

Have a volunteer read the first paragraph. Then focus students' attention on the bond report. Ask these questions.

1. What number is given in the "High" column for Itek? ($107\frac{1}{2}$)
2. What number is given in the "Last" column for Itek? ($106\frac{1}{2}$)
3. How many Itek \$1000 bonds were traded? (25)

Then have students answer question 1 in the lesson. Discuss Example 1 and Example 2.

[3] Close

Summary: Have a student explain how to find the price of a bond and how to determine the current yield.

Evaluation

Guided Practice: Ex. 1–4, 6–10 even, 14–20 even

Independent Practice: Ex. 5–9 odd, 11, 12, 13–19 odd, 21–24

Extension

Have students use the bond listings in the newspaper to write story problems about costs and annual yields. Have students exchange problems and solve.

Problem-Solving Skills

Using Estimation (Ex. 12)
Solving a multi-step problem (Ex. 13–24)

Estimation Ex. 12

11. RevCo issued a bond with a \$5000-face value. The newspaper gives $62\frac{3}{4}$ as the high for today. Find the high price for today. **\$3137.50**

12. The listed high of the day for a \$1000 Telex bond is $74\frac{5}{8}$. Estimate the high price of the day. **About \$750**

For Exercises 13–20, find the current yield for each bond. Round your answer to the nearest tenth of a percent.

	6-Month Interest	Market Price	Current Yield
13.	\$30	\$475	? 12.6%
14.	\$47	\$625	? 15.0%
15.	\$80	\$825	? 19.4%
16.	\$60	\$675	? 17.8%

	6-Month Interest	Market Price	Current Yield
17.	\$76	\$900	? 16.9%
18.	\$55	\$810	? 13.6%
19.	\$125	\$1700	? 14.7%
20.	\$220	\$4850	? 9.1%

21. Sabrina Marston bought a \$1000 bond that pays \$40 in interest every six months. The market price of the bond is \$690. Find the current yield to the nearest tenth of a percent. **11.6%**

22. Ronald Wilson has a \$5000–bond that pays \$320 in interest every six months. The market price of the bond is \$4350. Find the current yield to the nearest tenth of a percent. **14.7%**

Sometimes bonds are worth more than their face value. The current market value of a \$1000-BVV Communications bond is $112\frac{3}{4}$.

23. What is the selling price of the \$1000 bond? (HINT: First find 100% of the bond price. Then find $12\frac{3}{4}$% of the bond price. Add the two together.) **\$1127.50**

24. The bond pays \$130 in interest every six months. Find the annual yield to the nearest tenth of a percent. **23.1%**

Math and Savings Bonds

One of Tammy Chernak's jobs as a **securities teller** is selling U.S. Savings Bonds. Purchasers of these bonds are supporting the Federal Government by lending it money.

Most of the bonds Tammy sells are Series EE bonds. These bonds can be purchased for 50% of their face value. The bonds can be held until they reach **maturity** (full face value) or they may be **redeemed** (cashed in) anytime after the first six months. The amount received when a bond is redeemed depends on the interest rate and how long the bond is held.

EXAMPLE A Series EE bond with a face value of $1000 is held until maturity and cashed in for $1046.90. Find the interest on the investment.

1. Find the purchase price.

   50% of $1000 = $\frac{1}{2}$ × $1000 = **$500**

2. Find the interest.

   $1046.90 − $500.00 = **$546.90** ◀ *Value When Redeemed − Purchase Price = Interest*

EXERCISES

Find the interest paid on each Series EE bond.

	Face Value	Purchase Price	Value When Redeemed
1.	$50	? $25	$53.28 $28.28
2.	$100	? $50	$106.58 $56.58
3.	$500	? $250	$404.67 $154.67
4.	$1000	? $500	$705.30 $205.30

5. A Series EE bond with a face value of $50 is cashed in after 12 years for $57.08. Find the interest earned. $32.08

6. A Series EE bond with a face value of $500 is cashed in after 6 years for $377.77. Find the interest earned. $127.77

7. Edward Lawson bought a Series EE bond with a face value of $100. He cashed it in after 4 years for $62.
   a. Find the amount of interest earned in 4 years. $12
   b. Find the yearly rate of interest. (HINT: Yearly Interest ÷ $50 = Yearly Rate) 6%

Objective

Student will apply multiplication and subtraction skills to solving multi-step problems that involve series EE savings bonds.

Overview

This page is an extension of the skills and ideas presented in the previous lessons of this chapter. Since the content presented on this page is not included in the Chapter Review or Chapter Test, its use is optional.

Using the Pages

You may wish to have students work this lesson in small groups or you may wish to work with the class. Using it with the class, have a student read the first paragraph. Then discuss the Example with the class. Work Exercise 1 with the class and assign Exercises 2–7 and independent practice.

Problem-Solving Skills

Solving a multi-step problem (Ex. 1–6, 7a)

Lesson Resources

Maintenance: See below.
Reteaching/Alternate Teaching Strategy: See the margin on page 331.
Practice: Activity Worksheet 77
Enrichment: See the enrichment topic "Individual Retirement Account" on page 334.

Objectives

Student will

1. use a chart to find a pattern.
2. use the pattern to solve problems that involve annual yield.

Maintenance

1. Find 8% of $9500. ANS: $760
2. Find 36% of $2800. ANS: $1008
3. $763.20 − $475.81 ANS: $287.39
4. Divide: 72 ÷ 16 ANS: 4.5
5. A car is driven 15,000 miles in a year. The cost of gasoline for the year is $750. What is the cost of gasoline per mile. ANS: $0.05

1 *Lesson Focus*

Motivation: Have students discuss how long they think it would take $100 to double if it grew at a 10% annual rate. Have them discuss their reasoning.

Purpose: This lesson will allow students to discover the "Rule of 72" through patterns and use the rule to solve problems.

2 *Teaching the Lesson*

Focus students' attention on the chart. Have volunteers answer the questions. Have students observe that there is an overload of information in the chart.

Ask: Can you see a pattern that could help you condense the information in the chart? (No pattern is easily found.)

Then work through the Example.

Strategy: FINDING A PATTERN

The chart below shows the growth of $1.00 after 1 year, 2 years, and so on through 18 years for annual yields from 4% through 12%.

YEAR	4%	5%	6%	7%	8%	9%	10%	11%	12%
1	1.04	1.05	1.06	1.07	1.08	1.09	1.10	1.11	1.12
2	1.08	1.10	1.12	1.14	1.17	1.19	1.21	1.23	1.25
3	1.12	1.16	1.19	1.23	1.26	1.30	1.33	1.37	1.40
4	1.17	1.22	1.26	1.31	1.36	1.41	1.46	1.52	1.57
5	1.22	1.28	1.34	1.40	1.47	1.54	1.61	1.69	1.76
6	1.27	1.34	1.42	1.50	1.59	1.68	1.77	1.87	1.97
7	1.32	1.41	1.50	1.61	1.71	1.83	1.95	2.08	2.21
8	1.37	1.48	1.59	1.72	1.85	1.99	2.14	2.30	2.48
9	1.42	1.55	1.69	1.84	2.00	2.17	2.36	2.56	2.77
10	1.48	1.63	1.79	1.97	2.16	2.37	2.59	2.84	3.11
11	1.54	1.71	1.90	2.10	2.33	2.58	2.85	3.15	3.48
12	1.60	1.80	2.01	2.25	2.52	2.81	3.14	3.50	3.90
13	1.67	1.89	2.13	2.41	2.72	3.07	3.45	3.88	4.36
14	1.73	1.98	2.26	2.58	2.94	3.34	3.80	4.31	4.89
15	1.80	2.08	2.40	2.76	3.17	3.64	4.18	4.78	5.47
16	1.87	2.18	2.54	2.95	3.43	3.97	4.59	5.31	6.13
17	1.95	2.29	2.69	3.16	3.70	4.33	5.05	5.90	6.87
18	2.03	2.41	2.85	3.38	4.00	4.72	5.56	6.54	7.69

1. At a 4% yield, how much will $1.00 grow to at the end of 1 year? **$1.04**
2. At a 4% yield, how much will $100 grow to at the end of 18 years? **$203**

Investors are often interested in knowing how many years it takes for an investment to double.

3. About how many years does it take for $1.00 to grow to $2.00 at an annual yield of 12%? **about 6 years**

The problem is that the table does not include every yield.

EXAMPLE How long will it take for an investment of $1.00 to double at an annual yield of 14%?

READ What are the facts?
The table contains the facts.

PLAN Make a table for the yields given and the number of years it takes for $1.00 to double.

SOLVE Complete this table.

Yield	4%	5%	6%	7%	8%	9%	10%	11%	12%
Years to Double	18	?	?	?	?	?	?	?	6

Note that $4 \times 18 = 72$ and that $12 \times 6 = 72$. This suggests this rule.

Yield × Years to Double = 72

or

Years to Double = 72 ÷ Yield ← *Rule of 72*

For 14%,

Years to Double = 72 ÷ 14, or about **5 years.**

CHECK Is the product of the yield and the years to double for 5% through 11% approximately equal to 72?

EXERCISES

Complete the tables by using the "Rule of 72".

	Yield	Years to Double
1.	3%	? 24
2.	14%	? 5
3.	20%	? 3.6

	Yield	Years to Double
4.	? 4.5%	16
5.	? 18%	4
6.	? 36%	2

Solve.

7. Kathy Hardman can get a 15% yield on her investment. How long will it take to double? **About 4.8 years**

8. Ann Sundstrom would like to double her money in 5 years. What annual yield will an investment need to do this? **About 14.4%**

9. The rate of inflation averages 6% a year. At that rate, when will a hamburger that costs $1.50 today cost $3.00? **About 12 years**

10. If inflation rose to a rate of 12%, how long would it take prices to double? **About 6 years**

11. James Flores invested $1,000 in an account that yields 8% annually. What will he have in that account in 18 years? **About $4,000**

12. Ira Cohen invests in certificates that yield 9% annually. How much will the $10,000 be worth when he wants to retire in 40 years? **About $320,000**

3 Close

Summary: Have students write the "Rule of 72" in their own words.

Evaluation
Guided Practice Ex. 2–6 even
Independent Practice: Ex. 1–5 odd, 7–10

Problem-Solving Skills

Completing a table (Ex. 1–6)
Reading a chart (Ex. 11)

Alternate Teaching Strategy

After students know how to use the chart on page 330, you may wish to have them work in groups to complete the table below and answer the given questions. Then have them read the Example in the lesson.

Let A = yield and B = number of years to double

A	4%	5%	6%	7%	8%	9%	10%	11%	12%
B	18	14	12	?	?	?	?	?	?
A × B	72	70	72	?	?	?	?	?	?

1. What pattern do you see in the table? (A × B is about 72)
2. How could you use this pattern to determine how long it would take $100 to double at 10%? (72 ÷ 10 is about 7 years)

NOTE: A quiz covering the second half of the chapter is provided in the *Teacher's ResourceBank™*.

Objectives

Students will

1. explore solutions to a variety of problems that emerge from this situational lesson.
2. explore solutions to life insurance problems having more than one solution.

Situational Lesson

These two pages present a situational lesson as the framework from which a variety of problem situations emerge.

Teaching Strategies

This lesson lends itself to cooperative learning groups for the problem solving activities of comparing choices and exploring decisions. (See page M-13.) However, these activities can also be carried out by the class as a whole or by individual students.

1 Lesson Focus

Motivation: Have students discuss and list the advantages and disadvantages of term, whole, and universal life insurances.

Purpose: As future adult consumers, students need to understand the advantages and disadvantages of different types of life insurance.

Consumer's Choice

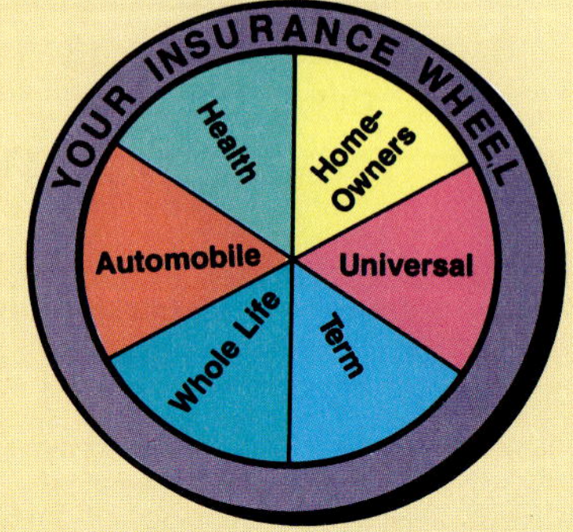

Marita Daley has decided to purchase life insurance in order to give her family more protection. She compares the costs and benefits of three different types of insurance protection.

Choice 1

Buy **term insurance.** A $50,000 five-year renewable term policy would cost Marita $58 a year.

Choice 2

Buy **whole life insurance.** Coverage continues as long as the premiums are paid. The yearly premium for a $50,000 policy for Marita would be $312.

Choice 3

Buy $50,000 worth of coverage through a **universal life policy.** The cash value would not be taxable as it accumulates. Marita could decide on the amount of the monthly premium. She considers $50 to be about what she can afford. The insurance company would deduct $84 per year from the account for insurance coverage and operating expenses.

Comparing the Choices

1. For which choice will Marita pay the lowest premium? **Choice 1**
2. For each of the three choices, find the total cost of the premiums for a total of five years. **Choice 1: $290; Choice 2: $1560; Choice 3: $3000**
3. Find the total amount paid in premiums over a 20-year period for Choice 2. **$6240**
4. Find the cash value of the policy in Choice 3 after 1 year. **$516**

EXPLORING DECISIONS

5. Suppose that Marita looks on insurance as an investment in which she can build-up cash value. Which choices might she prefer? Why? **Choices 2 and 3; reasons will vary.**
6. Suppose that Marita is concerned about low cost insurance coverage for the next 5 to 10 years. Which choice is she most likely to prefer? Why? **Choice 1; it has the lowest yearly premium.**
7. Choice 2 is sometimes considered a type of "fixed savings." What is one disadvantage to this method of saving money? **The money does not earn any interest.**
8. State a disadvantage to Choice 1. **Term insurance has no cash value.**
9. State one advantage of Choice 2 over Choice 1. **Whole life insurance has a cash value and a loan value.**
10. State one advantage of Choice 3 over Choice 2. **The policyholder can choose the amount of the premium under specified conditions.**
11. State one advantage of Choice 3 over Choices 1 and 2. **See above.**

11. The cash value earns interest which is tax free until the money is withdrawn.

2 *Teaching the Lesson*

Have volunteers read the introductory paragraph and the three choices. Ask these questions.

1. How much more per year would Marita pay for whole life than for term insurance? ($254)
2. Why might she be willing to pay this extra amount? (Whole life has cash value.)
3. How much would she pay per year for universal life insurance? ($600)
4. Why might she be willing to pay the extra amount? (Universal has cash value and pays interest.)

Have students work individually through Exercises 1–6. Make sure all students understand the answers to those questions before going on. Then discuss Exercises 7–11 with the class.

3 *Close*

Summary: Have a student explain the major difference in term, whole life, and universal life insurance.

Critical Thinking

Ex. 7–11

Objective

Student will read a table to solve problems that involve deductions for individual retirement accounts.

Overview

This topic is optional. The word "Enrichment" that appears to the right of the title in this Teacher's Edition does not appear in the student textbook. Therefore, this material is not included in the Chapter Review and Chapter Test.

Using the Page

You may wish to have students work this Enrichment in small groups or you may wish to work with the class.

Problem-Solving Skills

Reading a table (Ex. 1–4)
Using a formula (Ex. 5)

Individual Retirement Account ENRICHMENT

Many people invest money for their retirement in **Individual Retirement Accounts (IRA).** One of the advantages of an IRA is that the amount of money invested can often be deducted when filing an income tax return. Another advantage is that the interest earned is not taxed until the money is withdrawn.

This table shows whether a person can take an IRA deduction.

If Your Adjusted Gross Income Is		If You Are Covered by a Retirement Plan at Work and Your Filing Status is			If You Are Not Covered by a Retirement Plan at Work and Your Filing Status is			
At Least	But Less Than	*Single, or Head of Household* Deduction	*Married Filing Jointly* Deduction	*Married Filing Separately* Deduction	*Married Filing Jointly (Spouse covered by plan)* Deduction	*Single, or Head of Household* Deduction	*Married Filing Jointly (Spouse not covered by plan)* Deduction	*Married Filing Separetely* Deduction
$0	$10,000	Full	Full	Partial	Full	Full	Full	Full
$10,000	$25,001	Full	Full	None	Full	Full	Full	Full
$25,001	$35,000	Partial	Full	None	Full	Full	Full	Full
$35,000	$40,001	None	Full	None	Full	Full	Full	Full
$40,001	$50,000	None	Partial	None	Partial	Full	Full	Full
$50,000 or over		None	None	None	None	Full	Full	Full

EXERCISES

Write Full, Partial, or None to tell the deduction that can be taken.

1. Status: Single
Adjusted Gross Income: $26,000
Retirement Plan: Yes **Partial**

2. Status: Married Filing Jointly
Adjusted Gross Income: $43,000
Retirement Plan: Both No **Full**

3. Status: Married Filing Separately
Adjusted Gross Income: $27,500
Retirement Plan: Yes **None**

4. Status: Head of Household
Adjusted Gross Income: $35,000
Retirement Plan: No **Full**

5. The formula 20% × ($35,000 − adjusted gross income) can be used to determine the partial deduction that a single person with a retirement plan can take. Find the deduction if the adjusted gross income is $28,500. **$1300**

The Chapter Summary contains a listing of the important ideas that were presented in the chapter. This listing is intended to assist the student with the Chapter Review that follows.

Chapter Summary

IMPORTANT IDEAS

1. **Term insurance** gives financial protection for a specific period of time.

2. **Whole life insurance** gives financial protection over the entire life of the policyholder. Unlike term insurance, whole life insurance has a cash value and a loan value.

3. Unlike other types of life insurance, **universal life insurance** policyholders may often choose the amount of the premium as long as it stays above a specified amount. The cash value of a universal life insurance policy earns interest.

4. **Certificates of deposit** earn interest at a higher rate than regular savings accounts, but they must be left on deposit for a specific time period.

5. **Total Cost for Buying Stock = Cost of Stock + Stockbroker's Commission**

6. If the amount received for selling a stock is greater than the amount spent on buying the stock, the stockholder makes a profit.

7. **Annual Yield = Annual Dividend ÷ Price Per Share.**

8. The price you pay for buying a bond is a percent of the face value of the bond.

9. The **face value** of a bond is the amount printed on the bond.

10. **72 ÷ Annual Yield = Number of Years to Double in Value**

Objective

To review the important terms, skills, problem solving, and applications presented in Chapter 13.

Overview

The Chapter Review is structured in three parts. Part 1 is a review of the important terms that were introduced in the chapter. Part 2 reviews the skills that were presented in the chapter. Part 3 reviews the problem-solving strategies and applications that were presented in the chapter. Each item in the Chapter Review is referenced to the related pages where the concept, skill, or application was presented.

Using the Pages

You may wish to assign this Chapter Review for homework or treat it as a class review prior to administering the formal Chapter Test. In doing this, it is suggested that you only use the even- or odd-numbered exercises. You can then use the remaining exercises as a bank for use later.

Chapter Review

Part 1: VOCABULARY

Complete. Choose from the box at the right the word(s) that complete(s) each statement.

annual yield
term
market price
maturity
universal life
dividends
face value
whole life
cash value

1. The three major types of life insurance are _?_, _?_, and _?_. (Pages 312–317) **term; whole life; universal life**
2. When a certificate of deposit has been left for the specified period of deposit, it is said to have _?_. (Pages 318–319) **matured**
3. A portion of a company's profits that it pays to its stockholders is called _?_. (Pages 324–325) **dividends**
4. The percent of a stock investment that you receive as income each year is called _?_. (Pages 324–325) **annual yield**
5. The price that is printed on a bond is its _?_. (Pages 326–328) **face value**
6. The current selling price of a bond is its _?_. (Pages 326–328) **market price**

Part 2: SKILLS

For Exercises 7–10, find the cash value of each whole life insurance policy for the given number of years. Use the table on page 313. (Pages 312–314)

	Face Value	Term	Cash Value
7.	$ 80,000	5	_?_ **$3136**
8.	$100,000	10	_?_ **$11,343**

	Face Value	Term	Cash Value
9.	$30,000	15	_?_ **$5958.60**
10.	$70,000	5	_?_ **$2744**

For Exercises 11–12, find the approximate cash value of each universal life insurance policy. Use the table on page 316. (Pages 315–317)

11. Yearly Cash Value: $317.80
Number of Years: 5
Average Interest Rate: 7.5%
Approximate Cash Value: _?_ **$1989.43**

12. Yearly Cash Value: $184.60
Number of Years: 10
Average Interest Rate: 10%
Approximate Cash Value: _?_ **$3234.19**

For Exercises 13–14, find the amount of interest. Use the table on page 318. (Pages 318–319)

13. Face Value: $10,000
Yearly Rate: 9%
Interest Period: 18 months **$1428**

14. Face Value: $7000
Yearly Rate: 7.5%
Interest Period: 1 year **$539.70**

Find the amount of profit or loss for each stock. (Pages 321–323)

	Stock	Number of Shares	Buying Cost Per Share	Commission	Selling Price Per Share	Commission
15.	Harvest	100	$38\frac{1}{2}$	$67.78	$43	$ 72.95 **$309.27 profit**
16.	Kent Ind	200	$49	$136.86	$61\frac{1}{2}$	$164.80 **$2198.34 profit**
17.	AB Housing	500	$72\frac{3}{8}$	$592.79	$71\frac{1}{4}$	$584.36 **$1739.65 loss**

Find the annual yield on each stock. (Pages 324–325)

	Stock	Price Per Share	Quarterly Dividend Per Share
18.	Cribb Co	$71\frac{1}{4}$	$1.00 **5.6%**
19.	Dimex	$91\frac{7}{8}$	$1.25 **5.4%**

	Stock	Price Per Share	Quarterly Dividend Per Share
20.	Bard Trust	$50\frac{3}{8}$	$1.80 **14.3%**
21.	Sipho	$43	$0.80 **7.4%**

Part 3: APPLICATIONS

22. Susan Weeble is 35 years old. Susan wants to buy a $190,000 5-year term insurance policy. Use the table on page 312 to find the total premium for the term of the policy. (Pages 312–314) **$1691**

23. Ken Drew is 40 years old and pays $75 a month for $90,000 worth of universal life insurance. Use the table on page 315 to find out what the cash value of his policy will be after one year. (Pages 315–317) **$630**

24. Cathy Whitehead invested $7000 in a one-year certificate of deposit paying 8.5% interest compounded quarterly. Use the table on page 318 to find out how much it will be worth at maturity. (Pages 318–319) **$7613.90**

25. Tom Turner bought 200 shares of Haberle, Inc. stock at $38\frac{3}{8}$ per share. The commission charge was $75.75. Find the total cost of the purchase. (Pages 321–323) **$7750.75**

26. Sellmor stock pays a quarterly dividend of $1.25 per share. Roberta Madden owns 200 shares of this stock. Find Roberta's total yearly dividend. (Pages 324–325) **$1000**

27. A Comtek bond pays $85 interest every 6 months. The current market price of the bond is $895. Find the current yield. (Pages 326–328) **19.0%**

28. Karl can get a 9% annual yield on an investment of $25,000. About how long will it take for the investment to double in value? (Pages 330–331) **8 years**

29. Agatha invested $15,000 in an account that yields 8% annually. About how much will she have in the account after 27 years? (Pages 330–331) **$120,000**

Objective

To informally assess students' mastering of the major skills, concepts, problem solving, and applications presented in Chapter 13.

Using the Page

After completing the Chapter Review with the class, you may wish to use this Chapter Test as an informal assessment. This Chapter Test parallels the formal chapter tests (Form A and Form B) provided in the *Teacher's ResourceBank.*™

Chapter Test

1. Susan buys a 5-year term insurance policy worth \$170,000. The yearly premium per \$1000 is \$2.49. Find the total premium for the term of the policy. **\$2116.50**

2. Bill's insurance company deductions for one year totaled \$53.28. Bill pays a monthly premium of \$40.00. What will be the cash value of Bill's universal life policy after one year? **\$426.72**

3. James invested \$5000 in a certificate of deposit that pays 9.5% interest compounded quarterly. At this rate, \$1 grows to \$1.0984 in one year. How much interest will the certificate earn in one year? **\$492**

4. Find the total cost of the stock purchase.

Cost Per Share: $\$39\frac{1}{8}$
Number of Shares: 200
Commission: \$105.45
Total Cost: ___?___ **\$7930.45**

For Exercises 5–9, find the amount of profit or loss.

	Stock	Number of Shares	Buying Cost Per Share	Commission	Selling Price Per Share	Commission
5.	Tamber	200	$\$89\frac{3}{4}$	\$108.60	$\$91\frac{1}{2}$	\$123.15 **\$118.25 profit**
6.	Cosgrove	400	$\$52\frac{5}{8}$	\$ 99.30	$\$36\frac{7}{8}$	\$ 76.40 **\$6475.70 loss**
7.	Knectel	50	$\$71\frac{1}{2}$	\$137.80	\$74	\$155.60 **\$168.40 loss**
8.	FCS	100	$\$62\frac{3}{8}$	\$121.30	$\$98\frac{1}{4}$	\$171.90 **\$3294.30 profit**
9.	Virgil Ent	150	$\$83\frac{1}{2}$	\$109.15	$\$81\frac{5}{8}$	\$ 97.30 **\$487.70 loss**

10. Greg owns Chemco stock which pays a quarterly dividend of \$1.10 per share. Greg paid $\$64\frac{1}{4}$ per share for the stock. Find the annual yield. **6.8%**

11. NuLife issued a \$1000-bond. The newspaper lists $79\frac{3}{4}$ as the high for the day. Find the high price for the day. **\$797.50**

12. Clarissa invested \$5000 in an account that yields 10% annually. Refer to the table on page 330 to find about how long will it take for the investment to be worth \$20,000? **About 14 years**

Cumulative Maintenance Chapters 1–13

Choose the correct answer. Choose a, b, c, or d.

1. Find the finance charge for the car advertised. d

Destiny
$12,500 Cash or
$4500 down and $195/month
for 60 months

a. $8000 **b.** $9000
c. $11,700 **d.** $3700

2. As a secretary, Suzanne earns $5.50 per hour for a 40-hour week. Time and a half is paid for all hours worked over 40. Find her gross pay for a 48-hour week. c

a. $220 **b.** $154
c. $286 **d.** $264

3. The round-trip plane fare from Orlando to Great Bend is $369.50 per person plus a 6% tax. How much are plane fares for a family of four? b

a. $2364.80 **b.** $1566.68
c. $391.67 **d.** $1478.00

4. Andrew Smith insures his house for $70,000. Additional structures on his property are covered for 10% of the total policy amount. What is the maximum amount of coverage for additional structures? c

a. $700 **b.** $70
c. $7000 **d.** $1400

5. Kim Murdoch earned $18,502 last year. She also received $493 in interest and a bonus of $2010. Estimate her adjusted gross income. d

a. $20,500 **b.** $21,500
c. $21,400 **d.** $21,000

6. Karen is buying a $200,000 whole life insurance policy. The yearly premium per $1000 of insurance is $2.32. Find the total yearly premium. c

a. $46.40 **b.** $2320
c. $464 **d.** $232

7. A local grocery store is having a raffle for a turkey. A total of 185 tickets are sold. Mary bought 8 tickets. What is the probability that Mary will win the turkey? d

a. $\frac{8}{8}$ **b.** $\frac{1}{8}$
c. $\frac{1}{185}$ **d.** $\frac{8}{185}$

8. In Gotham, it costs 30¢ to dry one load of laundry. Find the cost of drying 2 loads of laundry 3 times a week for 4 weeks. b

a. $1.80 **b.** $7.20
c. $3.60 **d.** $2.40

9. Estimate the sale price. a

REGULAR PRICE
$98.75
NOW! 25% OFF

a. $75
b. $25
c. $33
d. $50

Objective

To review the content presented in Chapters 1–13

Using the Pages

You may wish to use this Cumulative Maintenance as an informal assessment tool. These pages can be assigned for homework or they may be used as review in class.

10. The listed high of the day for a Hi Volt-\$1000 bond is $84\frac{1}{4}$. What is the high price for the day? d

a. \$1842.50 **b.** \$840.00
c. \$157.50 **d.** \$842.50

11. Elizabeth has an investment account which pays a yearly interest rate of 12%. She has \$5000 in the account. Find the simple interest after 6 months. a

a. \$300 **b.** \$5600
c. \$600 **d.** \$5200

12. Use the line graph below to tell which month the stock was worth \$2 more than it was worth in June. b

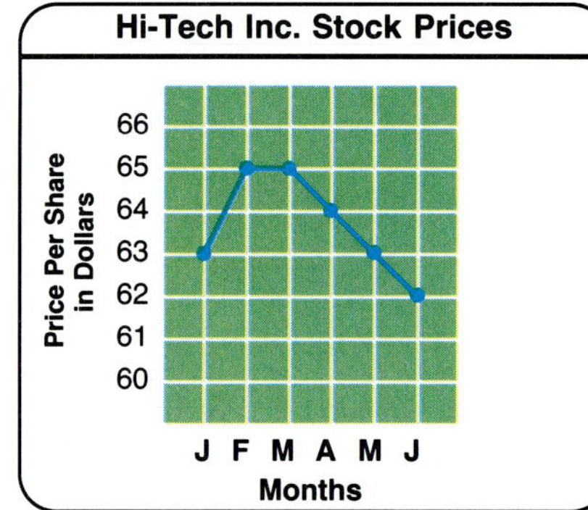

a. May **b.** April
c. January **d.** March

13. Jerry bought 150 shares of AMNH stock at \$25 per share. The commission charge was \$54.90. Find the total cost of the purchase. c

a. \$3750 **b.** \$3695.90
c. \$3804.90 **d.** \$11,985

14. Write a fraction for 36%. a

a. $\frac{9}{25}$ **b.** $\frac{18}{100}$ **c.** $\frac{36}{50}$ **d.** $\frac{6}{25}$

15. Find the unit price to the nearest tenth of a cent. a

BLUE CHEESE
\$5.69 for 16 ounces

a. 35.6¢ **b.** 36¢
c. 35.5¢ **d.** 35¢

16. Phil paid \$150 for new tires and \$89.50 to have the car's timing adjusted. The labor charge was \$32.75. The sales tax rate is 6%. Find the total repair bill. d

a. \$272.25 **b.** \$288.59
c. \$253.87 **d.** \$286.62

17. John's monthly credit card statement showed a previous balance of \$394.76, a payment of \$40, and a purchase of \$18.24. Find the new balance before the finance charge. c

a. \$453.00 **b.** \$336.52
c. \$373.00 **d.** \$354.76

18. Karen invested \$10,000 in a one year certificate of deposit that pays 8.5% interest compounded quarterly. After one year, \$1 is worth \$1.0877. How much will the certificate be worth at maturity? c

a. \$8500 **b.** \$18,500
c. \$10,877 **d.** \$85,000

19. What is the meter reading shown on the dials below? b

a. 408 **b.** 498
c. 509 **d.** 599

Budgeting Money

Every year, John and Sonia Jackson and their 19-year old son Willie plan a budget to help them manage their money. Preparing a budget raises many questions.

- Which of the Jacksons' expenses are fixed and which are variable?
- How do the Jacksons find an average for expenses which vary each month?
- How does the Jacksons' budget compare with standard budgets?
- What health insurance expenses should the Jacksons include in their budget?
- How can the Jacksons adjust their budget when income or expenses change?

Chapter 14: Budgeting Money

Overview

The focus of Chapter 14 is on budgets, average spending, and health insurance. You may wish to emphasize the importance of personal and family finances, pointing out that a budget is a plan, not a prescription.

Although all lessons in this chapter involve problem-solving, the strategy lesson on pages 354–355 presents four strategies from which students are asked to select the most appropriate to apply in a given problem-solving situation. The *Consumer's Choice* on pages 356–357 presents a **situational lesson** in which students make consumer choices in a familiar, real-life situation related to family budgeting. The *Enrichment* lesson on page 358 contrasts two health insurance plans.

Using This Page

Have students read the introductory paragraph and questions. Have them list possible solutions to the problems presented. After completing the chapter, having students review their suggested solutions, comparing them with those presented in the lessons. You may wish to have students suggest other possible problems resulting from the situation described on this page and to discuss possible solutions.

You may wish to organize the class into small groups to complete the situational activity described on this *Using the Page*.

Lesson Resources

Maintenance: See below.
Reteaching/Alternate Teaching Strategy: p. M-48
Practice: p. M-48
Enrichment: p. M-48

Objectives

Student will

1. understand the difference between fixed and variable expenses.
2. solve multi-step problems that involve the average monthly amount to be budgeted for items in the budget.

Maintenance

1. Divide: 4386 ÷ 6 ANS: 731
2. Round $146.49 to the nearest dollar. ANS: $146
3. Add: 9.65 + 9.65 ANS: 19.3
4. Multiply: 3.2 × 8 ANS: 25.6
5. Russell lives 1.8 miles from his school. He walks to school and back home three times each week. How many miles does he walk to and from school in 6 weeks? ANS: 64.8 miles

1 Lesson Focus

Motivation: Ask students to name the things they spend most of their money on and how much they spend on each item.

Purpose: Students need to see budgets as a tool and not an enemy. As consumers, they should see that budgets can help them plan their spending so they can make the most of their money.

Preparing a Budget

John and Sonia Jackson want to make a **budget** to better manage their money. To prepare the budget, the Jacksons used their computer to keep a record of their expenses over the past four months.

	JANUARY	FEBRUARY	MARCH	APRIL
MORTGAGE PAYMENT	$789.00	$789.00	$789.00	$789.00
FOOD	371.80	339.30	369.60	357.90
UTILITIES	156.65	153.35	136.75	132.10
CAR PAYMENT	185.00	185.00	185.00	185.00
INSURANCE	132.00	132.00	132.00	132.00
CLOTHING	140.50	143.50	241.30	191.45
RECREATION	122.80	92.35	70.30	75.20
MISCELLANEOUS	137.95	208.50	131.00	108.75
SAVINGS	265.30	258.00	246.05	329.60

Some of the Jacksons' expenses remain the same from month to month. These are called **fixed expenses.** Those that change from one month to the next are called **variable expenses.**

1. How do you find the average amount that the Jackson's spend on food each month? Find the total cost for the four months and divide by 4.

EXAMPLE How much should the Jacksons budget for food each month?

$$\text{Average} = \frac{\textbf{Sum of Food Costs for Four Months}}{\textbf{Number of Months}}$$

$$= \frac{\$371.80 + \$339.30 + \$369.60 + \$357.90}{4}$$

$$= \frac{\$1438.60}{4}$$

$$= \textbf{\$359.65}\text{, or } \textbf{\$360}$$ ◀ *Rounded to the nearest dollar*

The Jackson's should budget **$360** per month for food.

CHECK YOUR SKILLS

Find the average, or mean. For additional practice, see page 10–11.

1. *Earnings For Eight Months*

$720	$842	$1212	$1675
$2900	$3757	$2050	$1650

$1850.75

2. *Commissions for Ten Weeks*

$410	$580	$640	$530	$490
$755	$620	$650	$500	$575

$575

Round to the nearest dollar. For additional practice, see page 380.

3. \$319.47 \$319 **4.** \$426.83 \$427 **5.** \$557.56 \$558 **6.** \$124.09 \$124

Solve. For additional practice, see page 409.

7. What percent of 1200 is 96? 8% **8.** What percent of 1500 is 135? 9%

EXERCISES

Complete. Choose the answers from the box at the right.

variable
fixed
budget
savings

1. A __?__ is a plan for managing money. budget
2. Expenses that remain the same from month to month are called __?__ expenses. fixed
3. Food costs and utility bills are examples of __?__ expenses. variable

For Exercises 4–7, use the table on page 342 to find the amount the Jacksons should budget for each expense. Round each answer to the nearest dollar.

	Expense	Monthly Budget		Expense	Monthly Budget
4.	Utilities	? \$145	**6.**	Recreation	? \$90
5.	Clothing	? \$179	**7.**	Miscellaneous	? \$147

For Exercises 8–10, round each answer to the nearest dollar.

8. Over the last five months, Becky Cox has spent \$37.19, \$36.79, \$54.08, \$47.63, and \$36.92 on recreation. How much should she budget each month for recreation? \$43
9. Rodney Abshier's four most recent electric bills have been \$68.19, \$59.24, \$61.79, and \$52.38. Find how much Rodney should budget for the monthly electric bill. \$60
10. Amy Allen spent \$180.63, \$192.87, \$163.75, and \$184.54 on groceries during the past four months. How much should her monthly budget be? \$180
11. The Cole family has a total monthly income of \$1200. Their utility bills for the past five months have been \$114.19, \$105.35, \$101.80, \$102.32, and \$116.34. What percent of the Jackson family's monthly income should be budgeted for utilities? 9%

2 Teaching the Lesson

Focus students' attention on the table. Ask questions such as these.

1. What item was the greatest expense for the 4 months? (Mortgage payment)
2. What item was the smallest expense for the 4 months? (Recreation)
3. What items remained the same each month? (Mortgage, car payment, insurance)
4. What items changed from month to month? (Food, utilities, clothing, recreation, miscellaneous, savings)

Have students read the paragraph that is under the table. Then ask a student to answer question 1 in the lesson. Discuss the Example.

3 Close

Summary: Have students discuss which expenses the Jacksons could decrease if they needed to adjust their budget.

Evaluation
Guided practice: Ex. 1–3, 4, 6
Independent practice: Ex. 5, 7, 8–11

Extension

Have students use the table on page 342 to find the total of the fixed expenses and of the variable expenses for January. Then have students find what percent the fixed expenses and the variable expenses are of the total expenses for January. (Fixed expenses: \$1106; variable expenses: \$1195; total expenses: \$2301; % fixed: about 48%; % variable: about 52%)

Problem-Solving Skills

Using a table (Ex. 4–7)
Solving a multi-step problem (Ex. 4–11)
Choosing the operation (Ex. 11)

Lesson Resources

Maintenance: See below.
Reteaching/Alternate Teaching Strategy: p. M-48 (Visuals 45 and 46)
Practice: p. M-48
Enrichment: p. M-48
Visuals 45 and 46

Objectives

Student will

1. use a circle graph to solve problems that involve average spending.
2. use estimation and comparison to solve problems that involve average spending.

Maintenance

1. Write 45% as a decimal. ANS: 0.45
2. Multiply: 24,000 × 0.15 ANS: 3600
3. Divide: 18,630 ÷ 15 ANS: 1242
4. Subtract: 13,256 − 4215 ANS: 9041
5. The ticket sales for a concert totaled $14,400. Each ticket cost $12. Records showed that 1085 people actually attended the concert. How many people bought tickets but did not attend the concert? ANS: 115 people

1 Lesson Focus

Motivation: Ask students to name the expenses on which many families spend the most money.

Purpose: As students finish school, they will be facing decisions on how to spend their money. They may find it useful to compare their budget estimates with average figures.

2 Teaching the Lesson

Focus students' attention on the circle graphs. Ask these questions.

1. On what items did families spend the most? (Food and housing)

Strategy: Using a "hidden question" to solve a multi-step problem

Average Spending

The Jacksons thought it might be helpful to compare their family budget with standard budgets suggested by family planners. They know that standard budgets usually have to be adapted to fit family or personal needs.

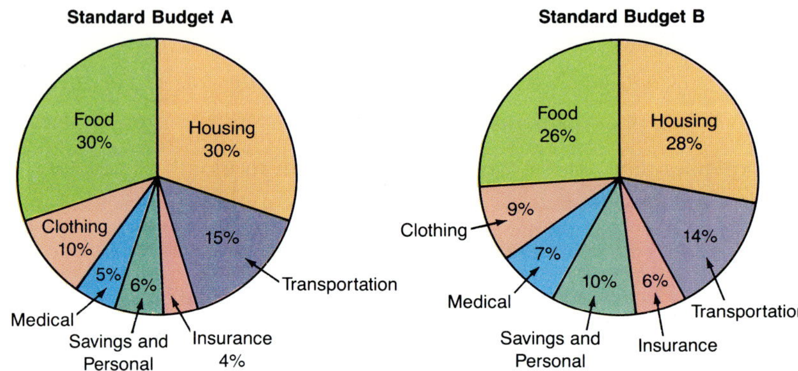

1. *Complete:* On the graph for Budget A, __?__ is budgeted for food. 30%

EXAMPLE 1 The Jacksons net pay per month is $2400. How much will they budget for food each month if they follow Budget A?

$\$2400 \times 0.30 = \mathbf{\$720}$ ◀ ***Monthly budget for food***

The Jacksons use estimation to determine whether their spending rate for an item is above or below the rate of standard budgets.

EXAMPLE 2 The Jacksons pay an average of $789 per month for housing. Is this above or below the percent budgeted for housing in Budget B?

1 Jackson family rate: $\frac{789}{2400}$ is about $\frac{800}{2400}$.

$\frac{800}{2400} = \frac{1}{3} = \mathbf{33\frac{1}{3}\%}$

Budget B rate: **28%**

2 Compare the rates: $33\frac{1}{3}\% > 28\%$

The Jacksons rate of spending is **higher** than that of Budget B.

CHECK YOUR SKILLS

Make a circle graph to show the data. For additional practice, see pages 6–7.

1.

Monthly Budget of a Recreation Center		
Salaries	40%	144°
Utilities	15%	54°
Repairs	10%	36°
Lease	20%	72°
Other	15%	54°

The measure of each angle is given above.

2.

Body Tissue of the Human Body		
Muscle	47%	≈169°
Supporting	33%	≈119°
Blood	7%	≈25°
Surface	13%	≈47°

The measure of each angle is given above.

Write a percent for each fraction. For additional practice, see page 406.

3. $\frac{1}{4}$ 25% **4.** $\frac{3}{4}$ 75% **5.** $\frac{3}{8}$ $37\frac{1}{2}$% **6.** $\frac{2}{3}$ $66\frac{2}{3}$% **7.** $\frac{1}{5}$ 20% **8.** $\frac{3}{10}$ 30%

Solve. For additional pracitce, see page 409.

9. What percent of 1600 is 1200? 75%

10. What percent of 1800 is 630? 35%

11. What percent of 2100 is 700? $33\frac{1}{3}$%

12. What percent of 900 is 112.5? $12\frac{1}{2}$%

13. What percent of 1050 is 315? 30%

14. What percent of 1400 is 84? 6%

EXERCISES

For Exercises 1–6, determine the amount the Jacksons should budget for each expense. Use Budget A on page 344 as a guide. The Jacksons monthly net pay is $2400.

1. Food: ? $720

2. Housing: ? $720

3. Transportation: ? $360

4. Savings and Personal: ? $144

5. Medical: ? $120

6. Insurance: ? $96

For Exercises 7–14, find the amount to be budgeted for each expense. Use Budget A on page 344 as a guide.

	Expense	Net Pay Per Month	Monthly Budget
7.	Food	$2100	? $630
8.	Medical	$3600	? $180
9.	Housing	$1050	? $315
10.	Transportation	$ 880	? $132

	Expense	Net Pay Per Month	Monthly Budget
11.	Clothing	$1100	? $110
12.	Insurance	$2700	? $108
13.	Savings	$1400	? $84
14.	Housing	$1250	? $375

2. On what items did families spend the least? (Insurance and medical)

3. In Budget B, what percent was budgeted for savings? (10%)

4. What is 10% of $1550? ($155)

Then work through Examples 1 and 2 with the students. Make sure they understand the estimation in step 1 of Example 2. You may wish to discuss the "Rate of Spending" column in Exercises 17–21 as additional examples.

3 Close

Summary: Have students discuss the differences in Budgets A and B on page 344. Have students give reasons why families might choose one budget over the other.

Evaluation

Guided Practice: Ex. 2–14 even, 18, 20

Independent Practice: Ex. 1–13 odd, 15, 16, 17–21 odd, 22–25

Extension

Have students do the following problem.

The Wilson's monthly net pay is $3000. Use Budget B on page 344 to determine the amount they should budget for each expense. (Food: $780; housing: $840; transportation: $420; insurance: $180; savings: $300; medical: $210; clothing: $270)

Then have students make a bar graph of their information.

Problem-Solving Skills

Using a graph (Ex. 1–23)
Solving a multi-step problem (Ex. 15)
Making a comparison (Ex. 16–23)
Using estimation (Ex. 17–23)
Making a graph (Ex. 25)

Additional Answers

2.

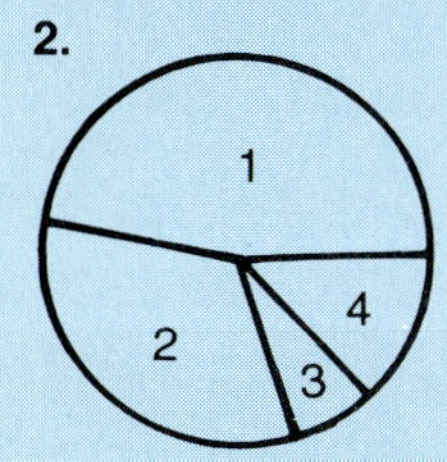

1. Muscle
2. Supporting
3. Blood
4. Surface

15. Mr. and Mrs. Lowry have a net monthly pay of $1900. How much should they budget for the three major expenses of food, housing, and transportation? **$1425**

16. A real estate agent told the Jacksons to expect to spend between $\frac{1}{4}$ and $\frac{1}{3}$ of their net monthly income on rent. Does this agree with the amount budgeted for housing in Budget A on page 344? **Yes**

For Exercises 17–21, refer to Budget B on page 344 to find how each family's expenses compare with the budget.

	Family	Net Pay Per Month	Expense	Amount Spent Per Month	Rate of Spending	Above/Below Budget B
17.	McDonald	$1570	Food	$412	$\frac{412}{1570} \approx \frac{400}{1600} = \frac{?}{}$ **25%**	? **Below**
18.	Green	$1200	Housing	$285	$\frac{285}{1200} \approx \frac{300}{1200} = \frac{?}{}$ **25%**	? **Below**
19.	Echandia	$1640	Clothing	$162	$\frac{162}{1640} \approx \frac{160}{1600} = \frac{?}{}$ **10%**	? **Above**
20.	Walter	$2480	Transportation	$480	$\frac{480}{2480} \approx \frac{500}{2500} = \frac{?}{}$ **20%**	? **Above**
21.	DeVito	$1590	Insurance	$82	$\frac{82}{1590} \approx \frac{80}{1600} = \frac{?}{}$ **5%**	? **Below**

22. Karen Brenner's net pay per month is $1850. She spends $195 each month on transportation. Is this above or below the percent budgeted in Budget B? **Below She spends about 10.5%.**

23. The DuPont family has a monthly net pay of $2130. They paid $640 last month for medical expenses. Is this above or below the percent budgeted in budget B? **Above They spent about 30%.**

The table below shows a typical budget for girls who are 16 to 19 years old. Use the table for Exercises 24–25.

Typical Budget Girls, Ages 16 to 19		
Clothes	**108°**	30%
Cosmetics	**72°**	20%
Food	**54°**	15%
Movies & Entertainment	**36°**	10%
Jewelry	**≈32°**	9%
Records and Tapes	**≈29°**	8%
Fragrances	**≈29°**	8%

24. Leona has a part-time job which pays $60.00 per week. According to the table, how much money will be spent on clothing? **$18**

25. Make a circle graph to show the data in the table. **The measure of each angle is given in the budget above.**

Math and Spending Patterns

Charles Townsend is a statistical clerk. He studies the national and regional spending patterns of consumers. Then he compiles the data in the form of tables and graphs to make it easier to read.

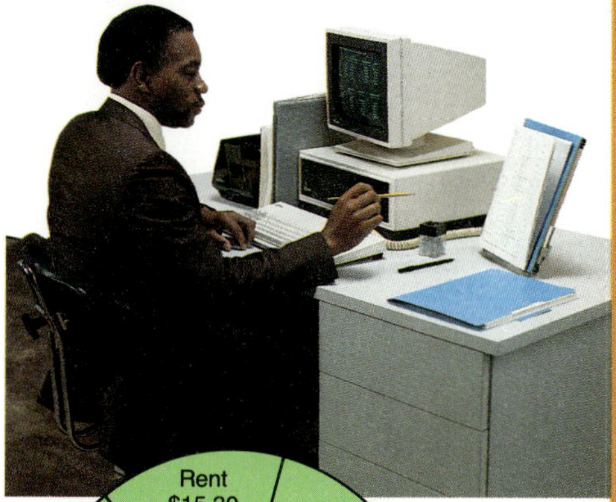

Charles used the circle graph at the right to show how four-member families in one section of the country spend each $100 of take-home pay.

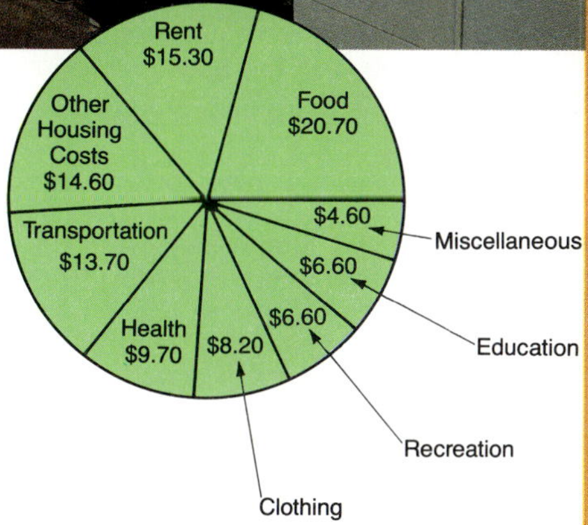

EXERCISES

Use the graph for Exercises 1–7.

1. Out of every $100, how much is spent on rent? $15.30

2. Out of every $100, how much is spent on transportation? $13.70

3. For which item is the largest portion of each $100 of take-home pay spent? Food

4. For which items is the same portion of each $100 of take-home pay spent? Education and Recreation

5. The graph shows that $9.70 of every $100 is spent on health. What percent is this? Round your answer to the nearest whole percent. 10%

6. Victor Tipton spends 35% of his take-home pay on rent and food. Is this more or less than the average amount shown in the graph? Less

7. The graph shows that $8.20 of every $100 is spent on clothing. How much of $30,000 in annual take-home pay would be spent on clothing? $2460

PROJECT Use the data that is shown in the circle graph above to make a bar graph. Have the horizontal axis show the items such as rent and food. Have the vertical axis show the dollars spent.

Objective

Student will apply percent skills and the skill of reading a circle graph to solving problems that involve statistical data.

Overview

This page is an extension of the skills and ideas presented in the previous lessons of this chapter. Since the content presented on this page is not included in the Chapter Review or Chapter Test, its use is optional.

Using the Pages

You may wish to have students work this lesson in small groups or you may wish to work with the class. Using it with the class, you may wish to have a student read the first two paragraphs of the lesson. Then focus students' attention on the circle graph. Ask student volunteers to answer Exercises 1–4. Then have all students write their answers to Exercises 5–7 and do the Project.

Problem-Solving Skills

Using a graph (Ex. 1–7)
Making a comparison (Ex 6)
Making a graph (Project)

Lesson Resources

Maintenance: See below.
Reteaching/Alternate Teaching Strategy: p. M-49
Practice: p. M-49
Enrichment: p. M-49
Concrete Materials: Activity Worksheet 80B

Objective

Student will solve multi-step problems that involve health insurance.

Maintenance

1. Solve the proportion: $\frac{x}{3} = \frac{7}{10}$ ANS: $x = 2.1$
2. Find 20% of 65. ANS: 13
3. Subtract: 68,142 − 1326 ANS: 66,816
4. Add: 24,136 + 16,354 ANS: 40,490
5. On Saturday, 32,040 people were at the stadium watching a baseball game. For Sunday's game, there were 3,150 fewer people at the stadium than on Saturday. Find the total number of people at the stadium on Saturday and Sunday. ANS: 60,930

1 Lesson Focus

Motivation: Have students tell how many times a member of their family has gone to see the doctor or dentist in the past year.

Purpose: Students need to see that medical costs are a very important item in a budget. They will need to be concerned with these costs as an adult consumer.

Strategy: Using a "hidden question" to solve a multi-step problem

Health Insurance

Included in the Jacksons' monthly budget is their health insurance premium. Many people receive health insurance as a benefit from their employer.

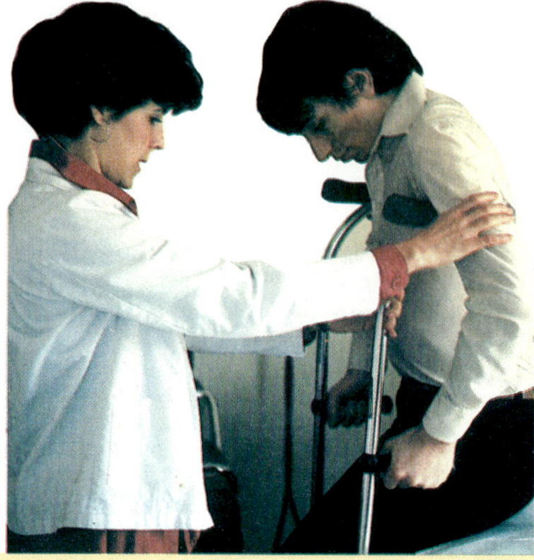

Health insurance helps pay doctor's and dentist's bills, hospital costs, and the cost of medicine.

Most health insurance policies have a **deductible** amount. Usually, insurance companies pay a percent of the total expenses after the deductible is subtracted.

EXAMPLE Sonia Jackson has a medical health insurance policy that has a deductible of $150. The plan pays 80% of the remaining expenses up to $40,000. Sonia's recent medical expenses total $1450.00.

a. How much will the insurance company pay?

1 Subtract the deductible amount from the total expenses.

$1450 − $150 = **$1300**

2 Find 80% of $1300: $1300 × 0.80 = **$1040**

The insurance company will pay **$1040.**

b. How much will the Jacksons have to pay?
Subtract the amount paid by the insurance company from the total expenses.
$1450 − $1040 = **$410** The Jacksons will have to pay **$410.**

CHECK YOUR SKILLS

Subtract. For additional practice, see page 367.

1. $1100 − $200 $900
2. $2500 − $175 $2325
3. $2850 − $2080 $770
4. $375 − $175 $200
5. $1750 − $450 $1300

Multiply. For additional practice, see page 372.

6. $1150 × 0.75 $862.50
7. $1000 × 0.80 $800
8. $900 × 0.85 $765
9. $960 × 0.90 $864
10. $3100 × 0.80 $2480

EXERCISES

1. For health benefits, the policy holder must first pay a __?__ before the insurance company will pay anything. **deductible**
2. The insurance company will pay a __?__ of the total expenses after the deductible is subtracted. **percent**
3. Usually, health insurance policies have a __?__ amount that they will pay. **maximum**

maximum
deductible
minimum
percent

5. $4666.50; $973.50 6. $168.75; $231.25

For Exercises 4–13, find each of the following.
a. *How much the insurance company will pay.*
b. *How much the policy holder will pay*

10. $382.50; $217.50
12. $1743.75; $756.25

	Medical Expenses	Insurance Coverage	Deductible
4.	$1100	80%	$100 **$800; $300**
5.	$5640	85%	$150 **See above.**
6.	$ 400	75%	$175 **See above.**
7.	$ 900	90%	$200 **$630; $270**
8.	$ 200	80%	$200 **$0; $200**

	Medical Expenses	Insurance Coverage	Deductible
9.	$ 200	80%	$100 **$80; $120**
10.	$ 600	85%	$150 **See above.**
11.	$3100	80%	$200 **$2320; $780**
12.	$2500	75%	$175 **See above**
13.	$8000	80%	$200 **$6240; $1760**

14. Bob Didsbury has a medical insurance policy that has a deductible of $150. It pays 75% of the remaining expenses. How much will the insurance company pay on expenses totaling $890? **$555**
15. Courtney Adams has a dental plan that pays 80% of the expenses after the deductible is subtracted. Her expenses after the deductible total $503.25. Estimate the amount the insurance company will pay. **About $400.**
16. The deductible for a certain medical plan is $250. After this, 80% of all remaining medical costs for an entire year are paid by the insurance company. How much will the insured person pay for a year in which there were medical bills of $185.00, $1000.00, and $610.00? **$559**

2 Teaching the Lesson

Have students read the first three paragraphs. Make sure students understand the term deductible. Ask these questions.

1. Would you prefer a low or a high deductible? (Answers will vary.)
2. Why would an insurance company prefer a high deductible? (The amount they pay would be less.)
3. With a $50 deductible and a bill of $450, how much would be left after the deductible is paid? ($400)
4. What is 80% of $400? ($320)
5. If the remaining bill is $400 and the insurance pays $320, how much is left to pay? ($80)

Then discuss the Example.

3 Close

Summary: Have students discuss whether they think high or low deductibles are good, and how much partial payment is good. Remind them that better coverage will cost more.

Evaluation
Guided Practice: Ex. 1–3, 4–12 even
Independent Practice: Ex. 5–13 odd, 14–16

Extension

Have students visit or call the local hospital to find the cost of common emergencies. Have them find what is required from the patient at the emergency room in order to be treated.

Problem-Solving Skills

Solving a multi-step problem (Ex. 4–16)
Using estimation (Ex. 15)

Estimation Ex. 15

Objective

Student will

1. review the skills, concepts, and applications in the first part of Chapter 14.
2. maintain key skills and concepts taught in Chapters 7, 9, 12, and 13.

Using the Page

Exercises 1–8 provide an informal assessment of the student's mastery of the major skills and concepts presented in the first half of Chapter 14. Each item is referenced to the related pages where the particular item was presented. These exercises parallel the quiz provided in the *Teacher's ResourceBank.*™

A quiz covering the second half of the chapter is also provided in the *Teacher's ResourceBank.*™

Exercises 9–12 maintain skills and concepts taught in Chapters 7, 9, 12, and 13.

Mid-Chapter Review

For Exercises 1–4, find how much to budget each month for each variable expense. Round each answer to the nearest dollar. (Pages 342–343)

	Item	Amount Spent Last 4 Months
1.	Savings	\$110.00; \$85.50; \$125.00; \$50.00 **\$93**
2.	Food	\$108.60; \$156.70; \$123.85; \$133.90 **\$131**
3.	Telephone	\$64.20; \$86.40; \$73.90; \$94.10 **\$80**
4.	Gasoline	\$40.00; \$59.30; \$53.60; \$72.10 **\$56**

For Exercises 5–6, use the sample standard budget at the right. Determine if the amount the Wilsons spend for each item is above or below the standard budget. The Wilson's monthly net income is \$1200. (Pages 344–346)

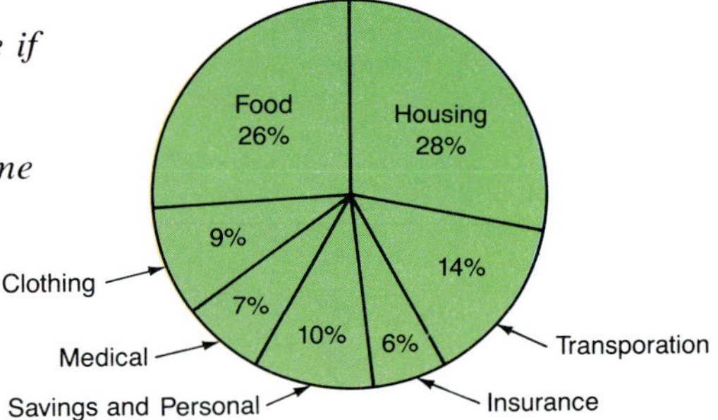

5. Expense: Clothing
   Amount Spent: \$119 **Above**

6. Expense: Housing
   Amount spent: \$289 **Below**

7. Karen Cook has a doctor's bill for \$360. Her health insurance policy has a \$175 deductible. The plan pays 80% of the remaining expenses. How much will Karen have to pay? (Pages 348–349) **\$212**

8. Michael Salmon has a health insurance plan with a \$200 deductible. The plan pays 85% of the remaining expenses. How much will the insurance company pay for medical expenses totaling \$980? (Pages 348–349) **\$663**

MAINTENANCE

9. Greg bought an umbrella on sale at 15% off. The regular price was \$12.00. Find the amount of the discount. (Pages 284–285) **\$1.80**

10. Suzanne bought 100 shares of Zebra Oil at $\$62\frac{3}{4}$ per share. The commission charge was \$97.46. Find the total cost of the purchase. (Pages 321–323) **\$6372.46**

11. A pound of cooked ham will serve $3\frac{1}{2}$ people. How many pounds are needed to serve 14 people? (Pages 210–212) **4 pounds**

12. A certain sports car travels 302 kilometers on 25.1 liters of gasoline. Estimate the fuel economy of the car. (Pages 160–162) **About 12 kilometers per liter**

Math and Budgets

As a **financial counselor,** Loretta Crawford gives George and Patrice Albertson advice about handling their budget. The Albertson's monthly take-home pay is $2050. They budget $400 each month for credit payments. Loretta tells them that they should budget no more than 20% of their monthly take-home pay for credit payments.

EXAMPLE Have the Albertsons budgeted more than 20% of their take-home pay for credit payments?

READ What are the facts?
Take-home pay: $2050
Credit payments: $400

PLAN Determine if $400 is more than 20% of $2050.

SOLVE 20% of $2050 = 0.20 × $2050
= **$410**

CHECK Did you use all the facts correctly in the solution?
The Albertsons **have not** budgeted more than 20% for credit payments.

EXERCISES *Complete the table.*

	Take-home Pay	Budgeted for Credit Payments	20% of Take-home Pay	Is the Amount Budgeted for Credit Payments over 20%?
1.	$1800	$300	? $360	? No
2.	$2400	$510	? $480	? Yes
3.	$1960	$420	? $392	? Yes
4.	$1500	$230	? $300	? No

5. The Hunt's monthly take-home pay is $2500. They budget $250 each month for credit payments. If they buy a car with monthly payments of $200, will they be over the 20% limit? No

6. Ron Martin's monthly take-home pay is $1600. He budgets $415 each month for credit payments.

a. Is he over the 20% limit? Yes

b. If so, how much over? $95

Objective

Student will apply the skill of finding a percent of a number to solving problems that involve budgets and credit payments.

Overview

This page is an extension of the skills and ideas presented in the previous lessons of this chapter. Since the content presented on this page is not included in the Chapter Review or Chapter Test, its use is optional.

Using the Pages

You may wish to have students work this lesson in small groups or you may wish to work with the class. Using it with the class, have a volunteer read the first paragraph of the lesson. Then work through the Example with the class. Do Exercises 1 and 2 as guided practice. Then assign Exercises 3–6 as independent practice.

Problem-Solving Skills

Making a comparison (Ex. 1–6)
Completing a table (Ex. 1–4)
Choosing the operation (Ex. 5, 6)

Lesson Resources

Maintenance: See below.
Reteaching/Alternate Teaching Strategy: p. M-49
Practice: p. M-49
Enrichment: p. M-49

Objective

Student will use a table to solve problems that involve adjusting a budget.

Maintenance

1. Round 1386 to the nearest 10. ANS: 1390
2. Divide: 384 ÷ 16 ANS: 24
3. Find 5% of 350. ANS: 17.5
4. Add: $456.35 + $182.92 ANS: $639.27
5. Maria bought a television that cost $352 and a VCR that cost $285. The sales tax rate was 6%. Find the total amount she paid for both items, including sales tax. ANS: $675.22

1 Lesson Focus

Motivation: Have students discuss how they decide to adjust their spending when they are short of money.

Purpose: Students must learn that there are no simple solutions to making budget adjustments. People make judgements according to their own goals. However, they need to see that deliberate choices usually lead to meeting expected goals.

Adjusting A Budget

The Jacksons present monthly net income is $2400. John Jackson wants to stop working for one year to finish his college education. This would mean that the Jacksons net monthly income would drop to $1800. The Jacksons now have to see how they can adjust their budget.

1. Which type of expenses do you think would be easier to adjust, fixed or variable? Why? Variable; fixed expenses are always the same.

Present Monthly Net Income **$2400** **Adjusted Monthly Net Income** ___?___

Item	Present Monthly Budget	Adjusted Monthly Budget	
Mortgage Payment	$ 790.00	$ 790.00	
Food	$ 375.00	$___?___	$300
Utilities	$ 160.00	$___?___	$160
Car Payment	$ 185.00	$ 185.00	
Insurance	$ 120.00	$ 120.00	
Clothing	$ 140.00	$___?___	$91
Recreation	$ 125.00	$___?___	$100
Savings	$ 265.00	$___?___	$200
Miscellaneous	$ 140.00	$___?___	$190
TOTAL:	**$2300.00**	TOTAL: ___?___	$2136

2. What is the difference between the present monthly net income and the present monthly budget total? $100
3. Is the present monthly net income enough money to cover the present monthly budget total? Explain. Yes; $2400 > $2300

CHECK YOUR SKILLS

Find each answer. For additional practice, see pages 407 and 408.

1. 25% of 375 $93.75
2. 20% of 2800 $560
3. 40% of 800 $320
4. 15% of 90 $13.50

Multiply. For additional practice, see page 372.

5. $350 × 0.25 $87.50
6. $250 × $\frac{1}{5}$ $50
7. $460 × 0.40 $184
8. $600 × $\frac{1}{12}$ $50

EXERCISES

Complete. Choose your answers from the box at the right.

increased
reduced

1. To balance a budget when the amount of income is reduced, the amount of expense must be __?__. **reduced**
2. To balance a budget when the amount of expenses is increased, the amount of income must be __?__. **increased**
3. How much is the Jacksons monthly net income reduced by John's not working? **$600**
4. By how much must the Jacksons reduce their monthly expenses to meet the adjusted monthly income? **$500**

For Exercises 5–12, use the present monthly budget on page 352.

a. *Which will be affected by the change described, the monthly budget or the monthly net income?*

b. *Find the amount to be added or subtracted to the monthly budget or the monthly net income.*

5. Reducing the monthly food expense by 20% through careful shopping **Affects monthly budget; subtracts $75**
6. A rent payment of $50 per week (4 weeks = 1 month) from their working 19-year-old son **Affects monthly net income; adds $200**
7. Continuing to budget the same amount each month for utilities **Affects neither; no change**
8. Reducing the monthly clothing budget by 35% **Affects budget; subtracts $49**
9. Reducing the monthly recreation budget by $\frac{1}{5}$ **Affects budget; subtracts $25**
10. Reducing the amount saved to $50 each week **Affects budget; subtracts $65**
11. Adding John's $600-tuition expense to the "miscellaneous" category in equal amounts throughout the year **Affects budget; adds $50**
12. Borrowing $1800 from the cash value on John's life insurance policy and using an equal amount each month **Affects income; adds $150**
13. Copy and complete the adjusted monthly budget column from the table on page 352. Use the answers to Exercises 5–12 above. **See table on page 352.**
14. What is the Jacksons' adjusted monthly net income? **$2150**
15. What is the Jacksons' adjusted monthly budget total? **$2136**
16. Is the adjusted monthly income enough money to cover the adjusted monthly budget? Explain. **Yes; $2150 > $2136**

2 Teaching the Lesson

Have a student read the first paragraph and answer question 1. Focus students' attention on the budget table. Ask questions such as these.

1. What are the fixed expenses? (Mortgage payment, car payment, and insurance)
2. How much are the Johnsons presently budgeting for food? ($375)
3. By how much will the Johnsons be reducing their income? ($600)

Then have students answer questions 2 and 3 in the lesson.

3 Close

Summary: Have students discuss how they would suggest their families adjust their budgets if they lost $400 of income each month.

Evaluation
Guided Practice: Ex. 1–4, 6, 8
Independent Practice: Ex. 5, 7, 9–16

Problem-Solving Skills

Using a table (Ex. 5–12)
Completing a table (Ex. 13)
Reading a table (Ex. 14, 15)
Making a comparison (Ex. 16)

Lesson Resources

Maintenance: See below.
Reteaching/Alternate Teaching Strategy: See the margin on page 355.
Practice: Activity Worksheet 82
Enrichment: You may wish to use the Project on page 355 or the enrichment topic "Two Health Insurance Plans" on page 358.

Objectives

Student will

1. use the model of a number line to solve problems involving stock.
2. identify a negative number as the amount of money lost and a positive number as the amount of money made.
3. choose and apply an appropriate strategy to solve a problem.

Maintenance

1. Divide: 84.36 ÷ 12 ANS: 7.03
2. Write $35\frac{1}{4}$ as a decimal. ANS: 35.25
3. Multiply: 200 × $22.75 ANS: $4550
4. Add: $462.50 + $135.12 ANS: $597.62
5. Jeanne bought 300 shares of stock at $\$49\frac{1}{2}$ per share. The stockbroker's commission was $120.16. Find the total cost. ANS: $14,970.16

1 Lesson Focus

Motivation: Draw a number line on the chalkboard. The number line should go from −20 to 20 and be marked in units of 1. Put a point at −10 and at 10. Ask a student to tell how many units it is from −10 to 10. You may want to repeat the exercise with different numbers.

Purpose: Students need to understand that there are many strategies to solving a problem. In this lesson they will see how making a model can be used to solve problems.

Strategy: MAKING A MODEL

Mark budgets a certain amount for investing.

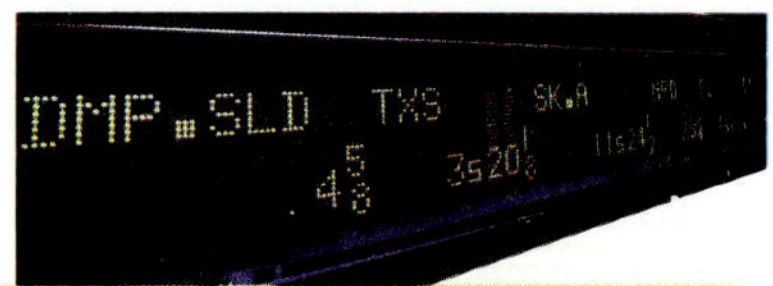

EXAMPLE He bought a share of stock for $30. He sold the stock when it reached $40 a share. He bought the stock later for $50 a share. He then sold it at $60 a share. How much did he make or lose (not including the broker's commissions)?

READ What are the facts?

1 Bought at $30.	2 Sold at $40.
3 Bought at $50.	4 Sold at $60.

PLAN Use a number line. When Mark buys stock, represent this as a negative number. When he sells stock, use a positive number.

SOLVE Draw a number line.

1 He bought at $30. Start at 0. Draw an arrow to the left for −30.

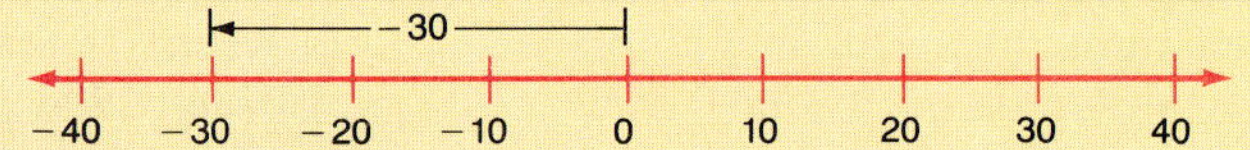

2 He sold at $40. Start at −30. Draw an arrow to the right for 40.

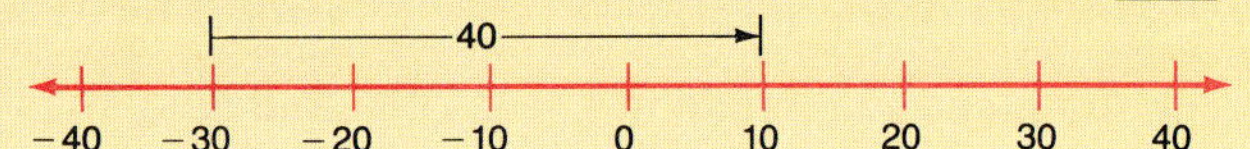

3 He bought at $50. Start at 10. Draw an arrow to the left for −50.

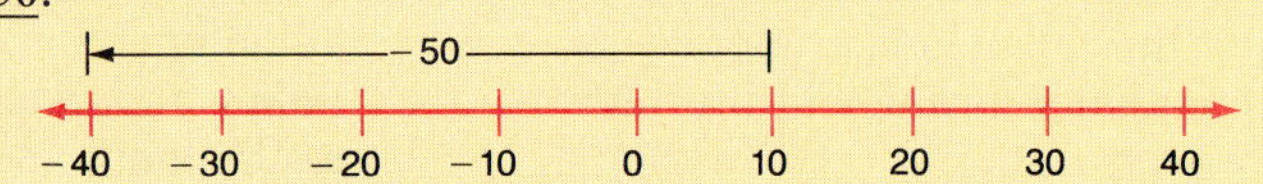

4 He sold at $60. Start at −40. Draw an arrow to the right for 60.

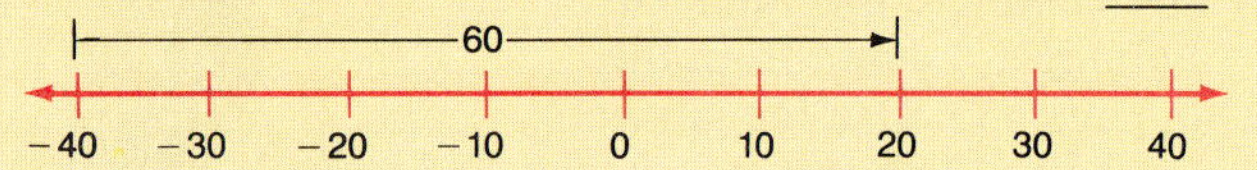

Mark **made $20.**

CHECK Did you use the facts correctly in the solution?

EXERCISES

Tell what positive or negative number each arrow represents.

1. 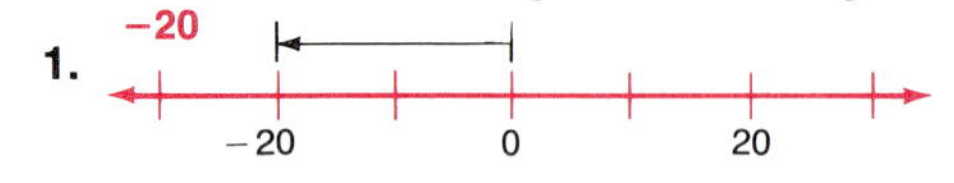

2. 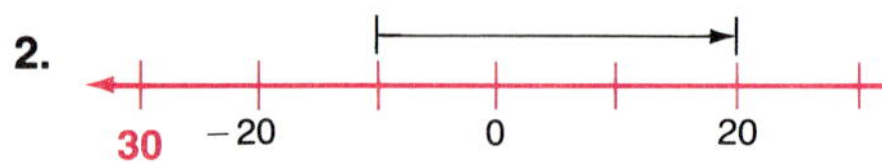

3.

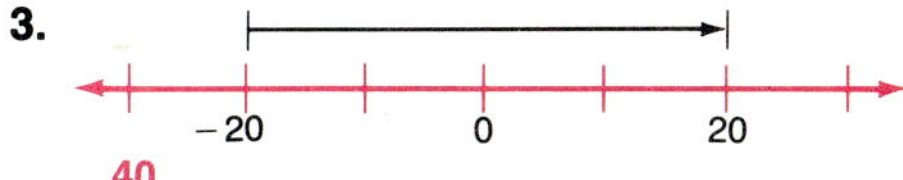

40

4.

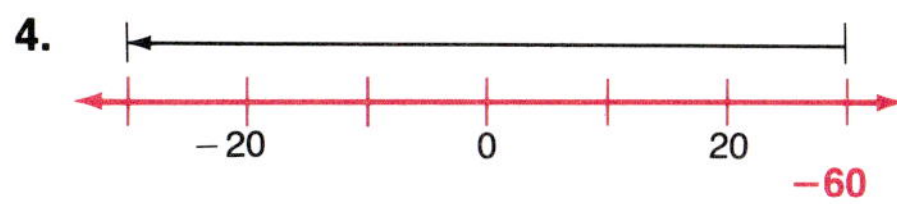

–60

How much was made or lost in each of Exercises 5–10.

5. Bought at $45.
Sold at $50.
Bought at $55. **Lost $50.**

6. Bought at $35.
Sold at $40.
Bought at $35.
Sold at $40. **Made $10.**

7. Bought at $10.
Sold at $20.
Bought at $20.
Sold at $15. **Made $5.**

8. Bought at $20.
Sold at $35.
Bought at $20.
Sold at $25.
Bought at $15. **Made $5.**

9. Bought at $40.
Sold at $35.
Bought at $45.
Sold at $40.
Bought at $10. **Lost $20.**

10. Bought at $10.
Sold at $12.
Bought at $15.
Sold at $14.
Bought at $15. **Lost $14.**

For Exercises 11–14, choose a strategy from the box at the right that you can use to solve the problem.

a. *Name the strategy.* **One strategy is given.**

b. *Solve the problem.* **Answers may vary.**

> **Guess and check**
> **Solving a simpler problem**
> **Using a pattern**
> **Using estimation**

11. Nick's health plan pays 80% of expenses after the deductible is subtracted. Nick has $962.50 in expenses (after the deductible). He computes the amount he will pay as $92.40. Is his answer reasonable? **Using estimation; no, he will pay $192.50.**

12. The winners of a health essay contest will share $1800. The second prize is one-half the first prize. The third prize is one-third the second prize. There will be six consolation prizes of $50 each. What is the first prize? **Solving a simpler problem; $900**

13. You budget $1620 a month for food and housing. The amount budgeted for food is four-fifths the amount budgeted for housing. How much do you budget for food? **Guess and check; $720**

14. About how many years will it take an investment of $15,000 with an annual yield of 10% to grow to $30,000? **Using a pattern; about 7 years**

PROJECT

a. Select a company from the stock market page of a newspaper. Pretend that you will buy one share at the price indicated.

b. Follow the stock for two weeks and then sell it at the price of the day. After another two weeks, purchase the same stock. Sell again after two weeks. Keep records of your transactions to see how much money you made or lost.

2 *Teaching the Lesson*

After presenting the Example, select a problem to show how the strategy can be applied to other situations, such as in Exercise 5.

1. **Ask:** What is the problem about? (How much money was made or lost)
2. **Read** the problem to determine the FACTS. **Ask:** What are the facts of this problem? (Bought at $45, sold at $50, bought at $55)
3. **Plan** the solution. Have the students make a number line. **Ask:** At what point on the number line will you start? (0) **Ask:** In which direction will you draw the first arrow? (Left)
4. **Solve.** Have students complete the steps using the number line. **Ask:** How much money was made or lost in all? (Lost $50)
5. **Check** the answer by having students read the problem again to check the facts with their solution.

3 *Close*

Summary: Have students discuss how they might use integers (positive and negative numbers) to represent what was happening on the model.

Evaluation
Guided Practice: Ex. 2–10 even
Independent Practice: Ex. 1–9 odd, 11–14

Problem-Solving Skills

Using estimation (Ex. 12)
Solving a simpler problem (Ex. 13)
Guess and check (Ex. 14)
Using a pattern (Ex. 15)

Alternate Teaching Strategy

You may wish to have selected students work Exercises 5–10 on the chalkboard or on an overhead projector. As the student works the problem at the chalkboard or on the overhead, have the remaining students work the problem at their desks. Then have students compare their answers.

Estimation Ex. 11

NOTE: A quiz covering the second half of the chapter is provided in the *Teacher's ResourceBank™*.

Objectives

Students will

1. explore solutions to a variety of problems that emerge from this situational lesson.
2. explore solutions to budget problems that have more than one solution.

Situational Lesson

These two pages present a situational lesson as the framework from which a variety of problem situations emerge.

Teaching Strategies

This lesson lends itself to cooperative learning groups for the problem solving activites of comparing choices and exploring decisions. (See page M-13.)

However, these activities can also be carried out by the class as a whole or by individual students.

1 Lesson Focus

Motivation: Have students discuss how they might go about paying for an appliance they wanted to buy.

Purpose: This lesson will help students understand the advantages and disadvantages of different types of payment plans.

Consumer's Choice

Since the "miscellaneous" category in their budget allows the Jackson family to save for special items not included as fixed or variable expenses, they have decided to buy a new color TV. The model they want costs $525. The Jacksons are considering these ways of paying for the TV.

Choice 1

Withdraw $525 from their savings account and pay cash. Then deposit $25 a month in the savings account until all the money withdrawn is replaced.

Choice 2

Use the Easy Pay Plan at the store where they will buy the TV. They will pay $31.27 a month for 2 years.

Choice 3

Charge the purchase on a credit card. Then make the minimum payment of $20 a month. They will pay a **finance charge** (interest on the loan) of 1.5% per month on the amount not yet paid.

Comparing the Choices

1. Suppose that the Jackson family selects Choice 1. How many months will it take them to replace the money withdrawn from the savings account? 21 months

2. Suppose that the Jackson family selects Choice 2.
   a. How much will they pay in all for the TV? $750.48
   b. How much will they pay in all in interest? $255.48

3. If the Jacksons select Choice 3, they will pay about $107.46 in finance (interest) charges. How much will they pay in all? $632.46

4. Suppose that the Jacksons select Choice 3. How many months will it take them to pay for the TV? 32

5. Give one advantage and one disadvantage of Choice 1. Answers will vary.

6. Why might the Jacksons prefer Choice 3 over Choice 2? Answers will vary.

7. Give one disadvantage to Choice 3. It takes the longest time to pay off.

8. Suppose that the Jacksons do not wish to withdraw money from their savings. Which choice does this eliminate? Choice 1

9. The Jacksons will need to purchase a new car in one year. How may this affect their choices? Answers will vary.

10. Suppose you were one of the Jackson family. Which choice would you make? Give a reason for your answer. Answers will vary.

2 Teaching the Lesson

After having students discuss the motivation topic, have volunteers read the introductory paragraph and the three Choices. Ask questions such as these.

1. What choices have hidden costs? (Choices 2 and 3)
2. Why would someone be willing to pay this extra cost? (Answers will vary.)
3. About how much interest would the $525 in savings earn in one year if the annual rate is 5.25%? ($27.56)

Have students work Exercises 1–4. Then discuss Exercises 5–10 with the class.

3 Close

Summary: Have a volunteer give two reasons to pay for a purchase with cash. Have a second volunteer give two reasons for using an installment plan or a credit card for a purchase.

Critical Thinking

Ex. 5–10

Objective

Student will solve multi-step problems that involve the cost of health care.

Overview

This topic is optional. The word "Enrichment" that appears to the right of the title in this Teacher's Edition does not appear in the student textbook. Therefore, this material is not included in the Chapter Review and Chapter Test.

Using the Page

You may wish to have students work this Enrichment in small groups or you may wish to work with the class.

Problem-Solving Skills

Using a table (Ex. 1–3)
Solving a multi-step problem (Ex. 1–4)

Two Health Insurance Plans ENRICHMENT

Many employers offer their employees a choice of two types of health insurance. One type was described on page 348. The other type is called a **Health Maintenance Organization,** or **HMO.** Sample costs for each type are shown below.

Metro Inc. Health Plan
Monthly Premium: $0
Deductible: $175
% of Expenses Paid: 80%

All-Life HMO
Monthly Premium: $21.32
Deductible: $0
% of Expenses Paid: $100%

EXERCISES

1. Robert Hobson chose the Metro Inc. Health Plan. He had $2000 in medical expenses last year. How much did he pay for health care last year? $540

2. Lucille Simmons chose the All-Life HMO. She had $2000 in medical expenses one year. How much did she pay for health care, including premiums, for the year? $255.84

3. Stephanie Jones chose the Metro Inc. Health Plan. She pays a premium of $10.00 per month for each of her two children. Her family had $1525 in medical expenses last year. How much did she pay for health care, including premiums, last year? $685

4. George Tyson belongs to an HMO that pays 100% of his expenses. He pays a premium of $15.30 each month and pays $2.00 for each doctor's office visit. In one year he had medical expenses of $150, $215, and $52. He visited the doctor's office 5 times. Find how much he paid for health care that year. $193.60

PROJECT Work in small groups or as your teacher directs. Find information on at least two different HMO health plans in your area. The information should include the premiums, the benefits, any additional costs, and how many people are enrolled in each plan.

Chapter Summary

IMPORTANT IDEAS

1. Expenses which remain the same from month to month are fixed expenses.
2. Expenses which change from month to month are variable expenses.
3. To find the amount to budget for variable expenses find the average amount spent over several months.
4. When planning a budget, it is sometimes helpful to compare it to standard budgets suggested by consumer agencies and other sources.
5. Health insurance helps pay doctors' and dentists' bills, hospital costs, and the cost of medicine.
6. Most health insurance policies have a deductible amount. Usually, insurance companies pay a percent of total expenses after the deductible is subtracted.

Chapter Review

Part 1: VOCABULARY

For Exercises 1–4, choose from the box at the right the word(s) that complete(s) each statement.

variable deductible fixed budget

1. A plan for balancing income and expenses is a __?__. (Pages 342–343) **budget**
2. Utility bills and food costs are examples of __?__ expenses. (Pages 342–343) **variable**
3. Mortgage and car payments are examples of __?__ expenses. (Pages 342–343) **fixed**
4. The amount of medical expenses that must be subtracted before an insurance company pays health insurance is the __?__ amount. (Pages 348–349) **deductible**

Chapter Summary

The Chapter Summary contains a listing of the important ideas that were presented in the chapter. This listing is intended to assist the student with the Chapter Review that follows.

Objective

To review the important terms, skills, problem solving, and applications presented in Chapter 14.

Overview

The Chapter Review is structured in three parts. Part 1 is a review of the important terms that were introduced in the chapter. Part 2 reviews the skills that were presented in the chapter. Part 3 reviews the problem-solving strategies and applications that were presented in the chapter. Each item in the Chapter Review is referenced to the related pages where the concept, skill, or application was presented.

Using the Pages

You may wish to assign this Chapter Review for homework or treat it as a class review prior to administering the formal Chapter Test. In doing this, it is suggested that you only use the even- or odd-numbered exercises. You can then use the remaining exercises as a bank for use later.

Part 2: SKILLS

For Exercises 5–8, find how much to budget each month for each variable expense. Round each answer to the nearest dollar. (Pages 342–343)

	Expense	Amount Spent Last 4 Months		Expense	Amount Spent Last 4 Months
5.	Food	\$236.90; \$256.40 \$209.45; \$240.75 \$236	**7.**	Gasoline	\$40.00; \$35.00 \$38.00; \$42.00 \$39
6.	Clothing	\$106.46; \$139.80 \$ 74.65; \$122.50 \$111	**8.**	Savings	\$168.00; \$248.75 \$199.00; \$182.50 \$200

For Exercises 9–16, find the amount to be budgeted for each expense. (Pages 344–346)

	Expense	Net Pay Per Month	Percent to Be Budgeted		Expense	Net Pay Per Month	Percent to Be Budgeted
9.	Food	\$3000	30% \$900	**13.**	Medical	\$2600	7% \$182
10.	Clothing	\$2100	10% \$210	**14.**	Food	\$3400	26% \$884
11.	Medical	\$1400	5% \$70	**15.**	Housing	\$1800	30% \$540
12.	Transportation	\$ 900	15% \$135	**16.**	Insurance	\$1200	6% \$72

For Exercise 17–24, find each of the following.

a. *How much the insurance company will pay*

b. *How much the policy holder will pay*

(Pages 348–349)

18. a. \$875.50 b. \$354.50

22. a. \$393.75 b. \$181.25

	Medical Expenses	Insurance Coverage	Deductible		Medical Expenses	Insurance Coverage	Deductible
17.	\$ 950	80%	\$ 150 \$640; \$310	**21.**	\$1300	80%	\$ 100 \$960; \$340
18.	\$1230	85%	\$ 200 See above.	**22.**	\$ 575	75%	\$ 50 See above.
19.	\$1065	90%	\$ 300 See below.	**23.**	\$ 210	80%	\$ 175 \$28; \$182
20.	\$ 700	80%	\$ 175 \$420; \$280	**24.**	\$ 165	80%	\$ 200 \$0; \$165

19. a. \$688.50 b. \$376.50

Part 3: APPLICATIONS

25. Over the last three months Colin Hale has spent \$48.50, \$35.16, and \$42.12 on gas. How much should he budget each month for gas? (Pages 342–343) \$42

26. Beverly Burbeen's last five telephone bills were for \$101.75, \$86.75, \$99.40, \$75.60, and \$68.45. How much should she budget per month for her telephone bills? (Pages 342–343) \$86

27. George Harrah has a monthly net income of $1300. Last month he spent $250 on food. Is this more or less than 20% of his monthly net income? (Pages 344–346) $10 less

28. Mr. and Mrs. McGuiness have a net monthly pay of $2250. They budget 24% of this for housing. Find the amount they budget per month for housing. (Pages 344–346) $540

29. Carol Sywetz has a doctor's bill of $1600. Her health insurance policy has a $200 deductible. The plan pays 80% of the remaining expenses. How much will the insurance company pay? (Pages 348–349) $1120

30. Patrick Brady has a dental bill of $395. The insurance company will pay 80% of expenses after a $75 deductible. How much will Patrick have to pay? (Pages 348–349) $139

31. To reduce their expenses the Wagners plan to reduce their monthly food budget by 15%. Their present monthly food budget is $305.00. How much will the Wagners' adjusted food budget be? (Pages 352–353) $259

32. The Maddens have a monthly net income of $1430. Roberta Madden plans to get a second job which pays $70 per week. How will this affect the Maddens monthly net income? (Pages 352–353) It will increase their monthly net income to $1710.

For Exercises 33–35, find the amount made or lost. (Pages 354–355)

33. Bought at $38.
Sold at $45.
Bought at $40.
Sold at $52. Made $19.

34. Bought at $21.
Sold at $30.
Bought at $25.
Sold at $39.
Bought at $27. Lost $4.

35. Bought at $16.
Sold at $28.
Bought at $19.
Sold at $16.
Bought at $10.
Lost $1.

Objective

To informally assess students' mastering of the major skills, concepts, problem solving, and applications presented in Chapter 14

Using the Page

After completing the Chapter Review with the class, you may wish to use this Chapter Test as an informal assessment. This Chapter Test parallels the formal chapter tests (Form A and Form B) provided in the *Teacher's ResourceBank.*™

Chapter Test

For Exercises 1–4, use the sample standard budget at the right to determine how much a family with a net income of $1700 should budget for each expense.

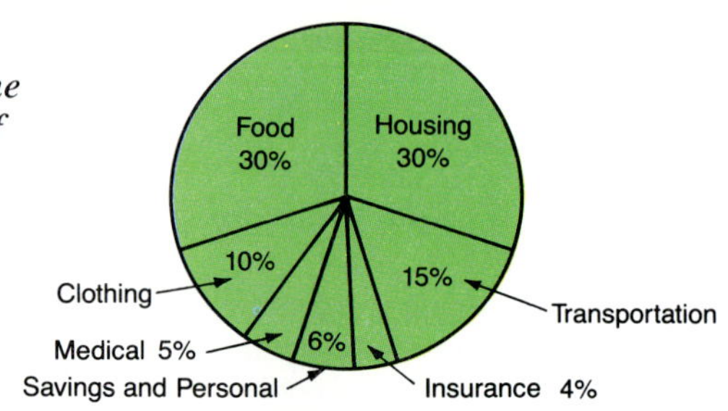

1. Food: ? $510
2. Transportation: ? $255
3. Insurance: ? $68
4. Clothing: ? $170
5. The Columbus family's four most recent phone bills were $89.75, $102.65, $59.75, and $76.49. To the nearest dollar, how much should they budget for their telephone bill each month. $82

For Exercises 6–7, find the amount the insurance company will pay.

	Medical Expenses	Insurance Coverage	Deductible
6.	$2780	80%	$175 $2084
7.	$ 390	80%	$150 $192

8. Phil Lauderback has a monthly net income of $1800. Last month he spent $306 on transportation. Is this more or less than 14% of his monthly net income? More than

9. The Lees plan to reduce their monthly transportation budget by 30%. Their present monthly transportation budget is $230. How much will their adjusted transportation budget be? $161

10. Find the amount gained or lost.

    Bought at $8.
    Sold at $10.
    Bought at $13.
    Sold at $15. Made $4.

Cumulative Maintenance Chapters 1–14

Choose the correct answer. Choose **a, b, c,** *or* **d.**

1. Find the average of this group of numbers. a

$15.63; $22.41; $18.97

a. $19.01 **b.** $18.97
c. $57.03 **d.** $19.00

2. Ramone rented a car and drove 502 kilometers. The cost per kilometer is $0.19. Estimate the total cost. d

a. $70 **b.** $80 **c.** $90 **d.** $100

3. Which sport received about 30 votes? a

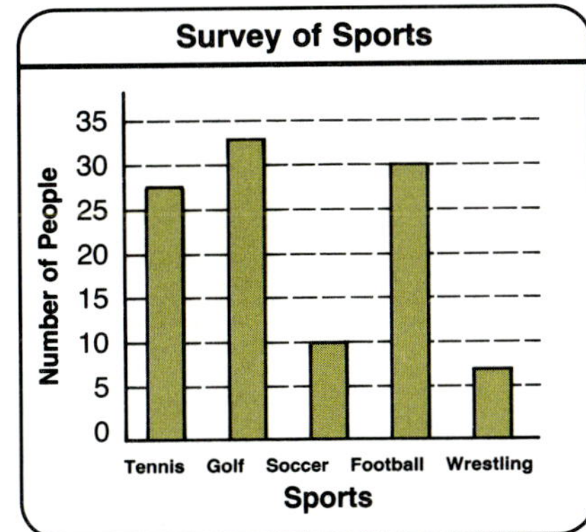

a. Football **b.** Wrestling
c. Soccer **d.** Tennis

4. Ceiling paint costs $2.70 per liter. A liter covers 9 square meters. What is the cost of painting a ceiling that measures 4 meters by 4.5 meters? c

a. $2.00 **b.** $8.10
c. $5.40 **d.** $10.10

5. Write 26% as a decimal. c

a. 2.6 **b.** 0.026
c. 0.26 **d.** 0.0026

6. A King Electronics bond with a face value of $5000 has a listed high today of $85\frac{1}{4}$. Find the high price. a

a. $4262.50 **b.** $4250
c. $852.50 **d.** $1250

7. Pam purchased cream cheese with the coupon below on double coupon day. How much did she pay for the cream cheese? b

25¢ savings on Mrs Barton's cream cheese with this coupon. **Regular price $1.10.**

a. $1.60 **b.** 60¢
c. 70¢ **d.** 85¢

8. The circle graph below shows how Joe spends his income. Joe's net monthly income is $1430. To the nearest dollar, how much money does Joe spend on food each month? c

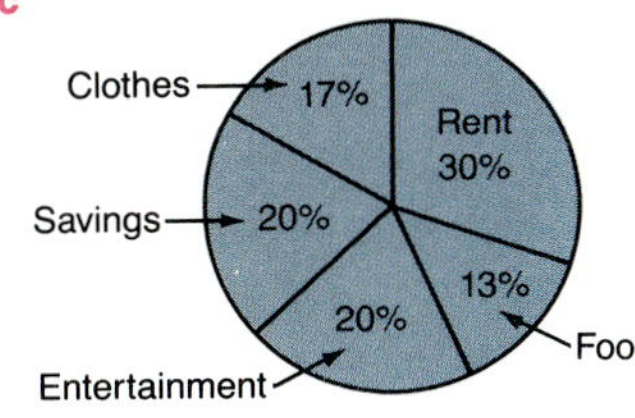

a. $286 **b.** $243
c. $186 **d.** $429

Objective

To review the content presented in Chapters 1–14

Using the Pages

You may wish to use this Cumulative Maintenance as an informal assessment tool. These pages can be assigned for homework or they may be used as review in class.

NOTE: The *Teacher's ResourceBank™* contains a Cumulative Test for Chapters 13 and 14. The Cumulative Test is presented in a standardized-test format. The *Teacher's ResourceBank™* also contains a Consumer Competency Test covering Chapters 1–14.

9. Dan had $2917 withheld from his pay for federal income tax. He owes $2309. Estimate the amount of his refund. b

a. $500 **b.** $600
c. $400 **d.** $700

10. The graph below shows the percent of depreciation for a certain car over 4 years. The car cost $10,200 when new. Find the approximate resale value after the first year. c

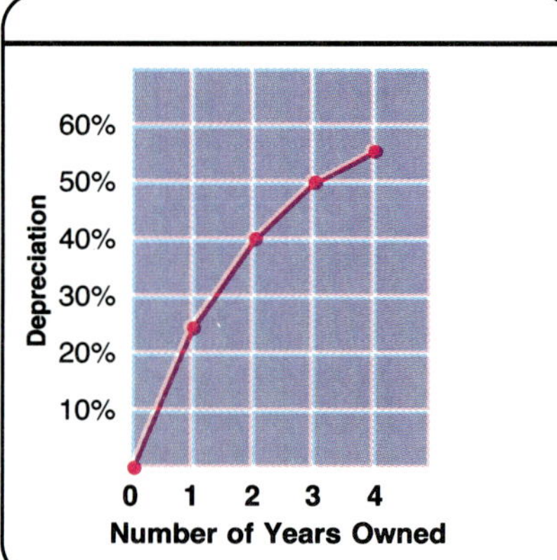

a. $2550 **b.** $6120
c. $7650 **d.** $4080

11. Maureen bought a bedroom set for $1875. She put 20% down. How much does she still owe? d

a. $1875.20 **b.** $375
c. $1600 **d.** $1500

12. The sticker price for a certain car is $11,950. The tax rate is 7%. Find the total cost. c

a. $836.50 **b.** $11,975
c. $12,786.50 **d.** $11,950.07

13. Tim Higgins deposited $2000 in an account that pays 8% interest compounded quarterly. Use the compound interest table below to find the new balance after 1 year. b

Total Interest Periods	Interest Rate Per Period		
	1.5%	2%	2.5%
1	1.0150	1.0200	1.0250
2	1.0302	1.0404	1.0506
3	1.0457	1.0612	1.0769
4	1.0614	1.0824	1.1038

a. $160 **b.** $2164.80
c. $2080 **d.** $2160.00

14. Kim Murdoch is a travel agent. She receives a salary of $500 per month plus a commission of $1\frac{1}{2}$% on total sales. Find Kim's total earnings for a month in which her sales total $45,000. d

a. $6750 **b.** $675
c. $567.50 **d.** $1175

15. Kim Bond has a medical bill of $825. The insurance company will pay 80% of expenses after a $100 deductible. How much will the insurance comapny pay? d

a. $660 **b.** $725
c. $825 **d.** $580

16. The Hughes' home is assessed at $54,500. The property tax rate is $7.20 per $100 of assessed value. Find the amount of property tax. a

a. $3924 **b.** $29,240
c. $39.24 **d.** $392.40

APPENDIX A

ADDITIONAL PRACTICE

These pages of *Additional Practice* contain a review of whole numbers, decimals, fractions, ratio, proportion, percent, and estimation. Also included is a review of customary and metric measures as well as their application to perimeter, area, and volume.

Each skill covered in the *Additional Practice* uses an *Example* to serve as a model for students who may need additional help. The *Example* is followed by a related set of Practice *exercises.*

Each of the *Check Your Skills* exercises that reviews a given arithmetic skill is referenced to the corresponding pages either in the student text where the skill was taught or in the *Additional Practice.* Thus, students who need help will know where to look for the models and practice they need.

Addition: WHOLE NUMBERS

EXAMPLE Add: 74 + 352 + 721 + 5

Solution:

1 Add the ones. Carry the "ten" to the tens column.

$4 + 2 + 1 + 5 = 12$

```
   1
   74
  352
  721
+   5
    2
```

2 Add the tens. Carry the "hundred" to the hundreds column.

$10 + 70 + 50 + 20 = 150$

```
  11
   74
  352
  721
+   5
   52
```

3 Add the hundreds.

$100 + 300 + 700 = 1100$

```
  11
   74
  352
  721
+  05
 1152
```

PRACTICE

1. 65 + 47 **112**
2. 87 + 9 **96**
3. 75 + 96 **171**
4. 207 + 99 **306**
5. 325 + 188 **513**
6. 367 + 292 + 245 **904**
7. 439 + 803 + 287 **1529**
8. 175 + 622 + 437 **1234**
9. 299 + 370 + 808 **1477**
10. 816 + 993 + 201 **2010**
11. 4317 + 2675 + 1817 + 2923 **11,732**
12. 3162 + 139 + 7144 + 284 **10,729**
13. 83 + 297 + 4415 + 67 **4862**
14. 803 + 2925 + 47 + 33 **3808**
15. 1008 + 235 + 47 + 8179 **9469**
16. 6822 + 137 + 192 + 14 **7165**
17. 1403 + 62 + 79 + 873 **2417**
18. 2934 + 182 + 19 + 11 **3146**
19. 603 + 1728 + 23 + 2921 **5275**
20. 807 + 8622 + 435 + 176 **10,040**

21. 92 + 68 **160**
22. 157 + 79 **236**
23. 516 + 42 + 178 **736**
24. 37 + 120 + 563 **720**
25. 97 + 243 + 3135 + 27 **3502**
26. 4325 + 188 + 11 + 225 **4749**
27. 193 + 27 + 481 + 22 **723**
28. 113 + 22 + 976 + 80 **1191**

Subtraction: WHOLE NUMBERS

Be careful when renaming with zeros.

EXAMPLE

Subtract: **a.** 902 − 775 **b.** 5000 − 327

Solutions:

a.

$$\begin{array}{r} \scriptstyle 8\ 9\ 12 \\ 902 \\ -775 \\ \hline \mathbf{127} \end{array}$$

902 = 8 hundreds + 9 tens + 12 ones

b.

$$\begin{array}{r} \scriptstyle 4\ 9\ 9\ 10 \\ 5000 \\ -\ \ 327 \\ \hline \mathbf{4673} \end{array}$$

5000 = 4 thousands + 9 hundreds + 9 tens + 10 ones

PRACTICE

Subtract.

1. 70 − 48 = 22	**2.** 80 − 25 = 55	**3.** 60 − 7 = 53	**4.** 90 − 36 = 54	**5.** 40 − 13 = 27
6. 400 − 85 = 315	**7.** 500 − 124 = 376	**8.** 702 − 359 = 343	**9.** 804 − 45 = 759	**10.** 900 − 332 = 568
11. 225 − 176 = 49	**12.** 600 − 286 = 314	**13.** 8092 − 1397 = 6695	**14.** 6688 − 1839 = 4849	**15.** 4175 − 2086 = 2089
16. 492 − 96 = 396	**17.** 2311 − 129 = 2182	**18.** 2000 − 1629 = 371	**19.** 8000 − 366 = 7634	**20.** 397 − 28 = 369
21. 3000 − 1267 = 1733	**22.** 5203 − 2318 = 2885	**23.** 6007 − 3508 = 2499	**24.** 2235 − 1974 = 261	**25.** 4072 − 1614 = 2458
26. 7065 − 2409 = 4656	**27.** 7605 − 3007 = 4598	**28.** 7650 − 1983 = 5667	**29.** 5555 − 3666 = 1889	**30.** 6186 − 3097 = 3089
31. 882 − 93 = 789	**32.** 9071 − 4207 = 4864	**33.** 4107 − 3808 = 299	**34.** 4107 − 3088 = 1019	**35.** 9876 − 4987 = 4889

36. 50 − 24 26 **37.** 30 − 7 23 **38.** 80 − 38 42

39. 400 − 56 344 **40.** 503 − 209 294 **41.** 137 − 108 29

42. 8034 − 247 7787 **43.** 6315 − 1876 4439 **44.** 2106 − 1529 577

45. 9045 − 358 8687 **46.** 7426 − 2987 4439 **47.** 3207 − 2639 568

367

Addition: DECIMALS

EXAMPLE Add: **a.** 12.067 + 234.06 + 9.32 + 26.7
b. 147.034 + 36 + 9.5 + 16.1

Solutions:

Line up the decimal points.

a.		b.
12.067 234.06 9.32 + 26.7 **282.147**	*Annex a zero to help line up the decimal points.*	147.034 36. 9.5 + 16.1 **208.634**

PRACTICE

Add.

1. 25.86 + 12.3 **38.16**	**2.** 427.6 + 89.74 **517.34**	**3.** 61.27 + 7.09 **68.36**	**4.** 39.4 + 86.738 **126.138**	**5.** 506.825 + 19.5 **526.325**
6. 36.93 2.07 + 14.4 **53.40**	**7.** 235.07 11.914 + 18.2 **265.184**	**8.** 67.335 211.8 + 6.42 **285.555**	**9.** 61.18 2.09 + 127.375 **190.645**	**10.** 864.27 43.998 + 2.407 **910.675**
11. 31.974 2.08 163.48 + 109.335 **306.869**	**12.** 172.431 6.87 14.881 + 2.9 **197.082**	**13.** 83.884 2.93 17.623 + 4.093 **108.530**	**14.** 16.027 8.1 170.33 + 42.91 **237.367**	**15.** 6.03 111.97 6.18 + 2.937 **127.117**
16. 41.085 3.19 274.59 + 210.446 **529.311**	**17.** 283.542 7.98 25.992 + 3.06 **320.574**	**18.** 94.995 3.04 28.734 + 5.104 **131.873**	**19.** 27.138 9.2 281.44 + 53.02 **370.798**	**20.** 7.14 222.08 7.29 + 3.048 **239.558**

21. 4.81 + 86.7 **91.51**

22. 154.3 + 86.753 **241.053**

23. 93.2 + 18.75 + 17.811 **129.761**

24. 93.18 + 8.231 + 121 **222.411**

25. 46.4 + 3.9 + 6.081 + 2.9 **59.281**

26. 34.75 + 13.2 + 814.76 + 2.035 **864.745**

27. 18.16 + 7.391 + 2.07 + 200.1 **227.721**

28. 6.88 + 7.9 + 48.26 + 8.003 **71.043**

29. 311.27 + 9.48 + 2.44 + 80.1 **403.29**

30. 272.01 + 18.37 + 224 + 4.009 **518.389**

Subtraction: DECIMALS

EXAMPLE Subtract.

a. 87.3 − 55.42 **b.** 7 − 3.263

Solutions:

Line up the decimal points.

a.
```
   6 12
    2 10
  8 7 . 3 0
− 5 5 . 4 2
  3 1 . 8 8
```
Annex one zero.

b.
```
   6  9 9 10
   7 . 0 0 0
 − 3 . 2 6 3
   3 . 7 3 7
```
Insert the decimal point. Annex three zeros.

Remember: You can use addition to check subtraction.

Check:

a. 31.88 + 55.42 = 87.30 *87.30 = 87.3*

b. 3.737 + 3.263 = 7.000 *7.000 = 7*

PRACTICE

Subtract.

1. 6.42 − 1.19 **5.23**
2. 17.08 − 9.79 **7.29**
3. 6.431 − 1.902 **4.529**
4. 5.812 − 2.497 **3.315**
5. 8.02 − 4.76 **3.26**
6. 21.9 − 6.75 **15.15**
7. 37.46 − 9.85 **27.61**
8. 16.14 − 7.267 **8.873**
9. 99.1 − 6.84 **92.26**
10. 50.75 − 13.999 **36.751**
11. 21.93 − 8.42 **13.51**
12. 94.8 − 13.66 **81.14**
13. 7.291 − 3.407 **3.884**
14. 6.31 − 2.196 **4.114**
15. 9.08 − 3.19 **5.89**
16. 6.277 − 0.2431 **6.0339**
17. 4.81 − 2.307 **2.503**
18. 16.18 − 2.113 **14.067**
19. 3.8 − 0.91 **2.89**
20. 62.89 − 1.476 **61.414**
21. 11 − 2.613 **8.387**
22. 14 − 8.071 **5.929**
23. 39 − 4.821 **34.179**
24. 67 − 7.335 **59.665**
25. 20 − 1.27 **18.73**
26. 1000 − 91.25 **908.75**
27. 62.18 − 41.19 **20.99**
28. 16.219 − 12.403 **3.816**
29. 82.19 − 4.236 **77.954**
30. 6.208 − 2.35 **3.858**
31. 49.217 − 1.75 **47.467**
32. 17.06 − 2.954 **14.106**
33. 31 − 2.38 **28.62**
34. 2111 − 82.36 **2028.64**
35. 83.29 − 82.28 **1.01**
36. 27.32 − 23.514 **3.806**
37. 93.27 − 5.347 **87.923**
38. 7.319 − 3.46 **3.859**
39. 50.328 − 2.86 **47.468**
40. 28.17 − 2.065 **26.105**

Multiplication: WHOLE NUMBERS

When you multiply two numbers, the numbers are called **factors.** The answer is the **product.**

$$\begin{array}{r} 23 \\ \times\ 3 \\ \hline \mathbf{69} \end{array}$$

23, 3 ← *Factors*
69 ← *Product*

EXAMPLE

Multiply: **a.** 32 × 67 **b.** 256 × 85

Solutions:

a.

$$\begin{array}{r} 32 \\ \times 67 \\ \hline 224 \\ 1920 \\ \hline \mathbf{2144} \end{array}$$

224 ← *7 × 32*
1920 ← *60 × 32*
2144 ← *224 + 1920*

b.

$$\begin{array}{r} 256 \\ \times\ 85 \\ \hline 1280 \\ 20480 \\ \hline \mathbf{21{,}760} \end{array}$$

1280 ← *5 × 256*
20480 ← *80 × 256*
21,760 ← *1280 + 20,480*

When multiplying, you can leave out the zeros as shown at the right. Be sure to line up the products under the corresponding multipliers.

$$\begin{array}{r} 32 \\ \times 67 \\ \hline 224 \\ 192 \\ \hline 2144 \end{array}$$

224 ← *7 × 32*
192 ← *6 × 32*

PRACTICE

Multiply.

1. 31 × 3 93
2. 46 × 4 184
3. 57 × 6 342
4. 83 × 5 415
5. 28 × 9 252
6. 77 × 5 385
7. 46 × 82 3772
8. 97 × 83 8051
9. 213 × 74 15762
10. 518 × 63 32634
11. 63 × 29 1827
12. 652 × 75 48900
13. 686 × 143 98098
14. 775 × 214 165850
15. 871 × 29 25259
16. 844 × 47 39668
17. 69 × 27 1863
18. 35 × 83 2905
19. 217 × 87 18879
20. 395 × 84 33180
21. 71 × 63 4473
22. 27 × 48 1296
23. 293 × 723 211839
24. 173 × 294 50862
25. 328 × 98 32144
26. 486 × 95 46170
27. 82 × 74 6068
28. 38 × 59 2242
29. 384 × 834 320256
30. 284 × 375 106500

31. 32 × 68 2176
32. 94 × 45 4230
33. 574 × 38 21812
34. 932 × 76 70832
35. 735 × 98 72030
36. 21 × 79 1659
37. 83 × 34 2822
38. 463 × 27 12501
39. 821 × 65 53365
40. 624 × 87 54288
41. 129 × 73 9417
42. 616 × 243 149688
43. 817 × 324 264708
44. 16 × 28 448
45. 84 × 27 2268

Multiplication: ZEROS IN FACTORS

Sometimes there are zeros in <u>one</u> or <u>both factors</u> of a multiplication problem.

Remember: *Zero times any number is zero.*

EXAMPLE Multiply: **a.** 432 × 703 **b.** 304 × 605

Solutions:

a.

```
     432
   × 703
    1296  ← 3 × 432
    0000  ← 0 tens × 432
  302400  ← 700 × 432
 303,696
```

b.

```
     304
   × 605
    1520
    0000  ← 0 tens × 304
  182400
 183,920
```

Another way to multiply 304 by 605 is shown at the right. Use the method that is easier for you.

```
     304
   × 605
    1520
   18240
 183,920
```

Replace the row of zeros with one zero.

PRACTICE

Multiply.

1. 76 × 20 = 1520	**2.** 904 × 50 = 45200	**3.** 764 × 109 = 83276	**4.** 615 × 706 = 434190	**5.** 803 × 359 = 288277	**6.** 304 × 589 = 179056
7. 84 × 30 = 2520	**8.** 801 × 60 = 48060	**9.** 883 × 207 = 182781	**10.** 419 × 807 = 338133	**11.** 804 × 236 = 189744	**12.** 509 × 234 = 119106
13. 404 × 309 = 124836	**14.** 209 × 503 = 105127	**15.** 240 × 87 = 20880	**16.** 208 × 435 = 90480	**17.** 607 × 26 = 15782	**18.** 405 × 34 = 13770
19. 503 × 29 = 14587	**20.** 709 × 36 = 25524	**21.** 810 × 67 = 54270	**22.** 750 × 42 = 31500	**23.** 803 × 207 = 166221	**24.** 901 × 308 = 277508

25. 801 × 27 (21627)	**26.** 403 × 43 (17329)	**27.** 702 × 209 (146718)	**28.** 608 × 405 (246240)	**29.** 709 × 21 (14889)
30. 503 × 63 (31689)	**31.** 808 × 292 (235936)	**32.** 903 × 481 (434343)	**33.** 606 × 27 (16362)	**34.** 204 × 43 (8772)
35. 400 × 35 (14000)	**36.** 206 × 28 (5768)	**37.** 502 × 572 (287144)	**38.** 490 × 58 (28420)	**29.** 505 × 37 (18685)

Multiplication: DECIMALS

Rules for Multiplying With Decimals

1. Multiply as with whole numbers.
2. Count the number of digits to the right of the decimal point in each factor. This is called the number of decimal places.
3. Add the number of decimal places in the factors to place the decimal point in the product. Insert zeros when necessary.

EXAMPLE Multiply: **a.** 636 × 0.12 **b.** 0.31 × 0.0024

a.	**Decimal Places**
636	0
× 0.12	2
1272	
6360	
76.32	0 + 2 = 2

b.	**Decimal Places**
0.31	2
× 0.0024	4
124	
620	
0.000744	2 + 4 = 6

Insert 3 zeros.

PRACTICE

Multiply.

1. 28 × 0.6 = **16.8**	**2.** 73 × 0.8 = **58.4**	**3.** 62 × 1.7 = **105.4**	**4.** 29 × 2.9 = **84.1**	**5.** 6 × 0.09 = **0.54**
6. 8 × 0.08 = **0.64**	**7.** 723 × 0.02 = **14.46**	**8.** 197 × 0.07 = **13.79**	**9.** 4321 × 0.09 = **388.89**	**10.** 8647 × 0.06 = **518.82**
11. 1.83 × 4.87 = **8.9121**	**12.** 12.08 × 4.07 = **49.1656**	**13.** 6.97 × 0.73 = **5.0881**	**14.** 7.28 × 0.16 = **1.1648**	**15.** 9.04 × 2.5 = **22.600**
16. 2.7 × 0.002 = **0.0054**	**17.** 3.5 × 0.005 = **0.0175**	**18.** 1.6 × 0.04 = **0.064**	**19.** 1.7 × 0.007 = **0.0119**	**20.** 8.1 × 0.0008 = **0.00648**
21. 0.73 × 0.075 = **0.05475**	**22.** 2.07 × 0.0066 = **0.013662**	**23.** 98.72 × 0.0002 = **0.019744**	**24.** 39.17 × 0.0004 = **0.015668**	**25.** 8.43 × 0.0029 = **0.024447**

Comparing Decimals/Fractions

To compare numbers, compare digits that are in the same place. Start at the left. Use the symbols $<$ (**is less than**) and $>$ (**is greater than**).

EXAMPLE 1 Which number is greater?

a. 83.5 or 83.05

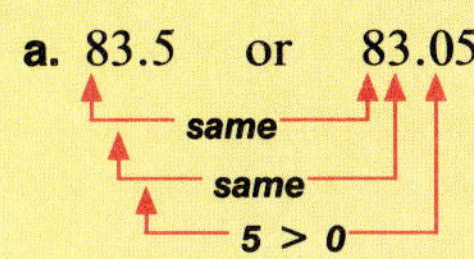

So **8.35 > 83.05.**

b. 7.021 or 7.022

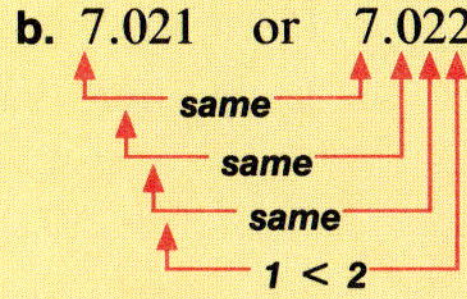

So **7.021 < 7.022.**

You can use decimal equivalents to compare fractions.

EXAMPLE 2 Compare the fractions. Write $<$, $=$, or $>$: $\frac{3}{4} \bullet \frac{7}{8}$

Plan: Write a decimal for each fraction.

$\frac{3}{4} \rightarrow 4\overline{)3.00}$ = **0.75** $\quad \frac{7}{8} \rightarrow 8\overline{)7.000}$ = **0.875**

Since $0.75 < 0.875$, $\mathbf{\frac{3}{4} < \frac{7}{8}}$.

PRACTICE

Compare. Replace the ● with $<$, $>$, or $=$.

1. 7.01 ● 7.89 $<$ **2.** 0.450 ● 0.45 $=$ **3.** 14,682 ● 14,689 $<$

4. 1.09 ● 1.9 $<$ **5.** 8.421 ● 8.422 $<$ **6.** 569,998 ● 569,909 $>$

7. 0.1005 ● 1.0036 $<$ **8.** 18.72 ● 18.7 $>$ **9.** 48.07 ● 48.7 $<$

10. 0.941 ● 92 $<$ **11.** 1.1 ● 1.01 $>$ **12.** 896.3 ● 897 $<$

13. $\frac{1}{5} \bullet \frac{1}{4}$ $<$ **14.** $\frac{1}{8} \bullet \frac{1}{9}$ $>$ **15.** $\frac{1}{5} \bullet \frac{1}{6}$ $>$ **16.** $\frac{1}{3} \bullet \frac{1}{2}$ $<$ **17.** $\frac{1}{7} \bullet \frac{1}{10}$ $>$

19. $\frac{3}{4} \bullet \frac{7}{8}$ $<$ **19.** $\frac{2}{5} \bullet \frac{1}{2}$ $<$ **20.** $\frac{5}{8} \bullet \frac{2}{5}$ $>$ **21.** $\frac{7}{20} \bullet \frac{3}{10}$ $>$ **22.** $\frac{1}{2} \bullet \frac{5}{10}$ $=$

23. $\frac{3}{10} \bullet \frac{2}{5}$ $<$ **24.** $\frac{1}{4} \bullet \frac{3}{10}$ $<$ **25.** $\frac{3}{5} \bullet \frac{7}{10}$ $<$ **26.** $\frac{3}{5} \bullet \frac{3}{8}$ $>$ **27.** $\frac{3}{4} \bullet \frac{7}{8}$ $<$

Write in order from least to greatest.

28. 18.047, 18.450, 18.046 — 18.046, 18.047, 18.450

29. 8.063, 80.002, 8.603, 80.01, 80.009 — 8.063, 8.603, 80.002, 80.009, 80.01

30. $\frac{2}{3}, \frac{5}{6}, \frac{5}{7}$ — $\frac{2}{3}, \frac{5}{7}, \frac{5}{6}, \frac{7}{8}$

31. $\frac{7}{12}, \frac{3}{4}, \frac{8}{9}, \frac{5}{6}$ — $\frac{7}{12}, \frac{3}{4}, \frac{5}{6}, \frac{8}{9}$

32. $\frac{11}{12}, \frac{9}{10}, \frac{7}{8}, \frac{5}{6}$ — $\frac{5}{6}, \frac{7}{8}, \frac{9}{10}, \frac{11}{12}$

Rounding Whole Numbers

Rules for Rounding Whole Numbers

1 Look at the digit to the right of the place to which you are rounding.

2 **a.** If the digit is 5 or greater than 5, round up.
b. If the digit is less than 5, round down.

EXAMPLE

a. 46 rounded to the nearest **ten** is 50.
b. 322 rounded to the nearest **ten** is 320.
c. 678 rounded to the nearest **hundred** is 700.
d. 25,413 rounded to the nearest **hundred** is 25,400.
e. 14,329 rounded to the nearest **thousand** is 14,000.
f. 36,540 rounded to the nearest **thousand** is 37,000.

PRACTICE

Round to the nearest ten.

1. 43 40	**2.** 57 60	**3.** 86 90	**4.** 25 30	**5.** 62 60	**6.** 79 80
7. 263 260	**8.** 872 870	**9.** 439 440	**10.** 598 600	**11.** 774 770	**12.** 813 810
13. 2613 2610	**14.** 7085 7090	**15.** 1917 1920	**16.** 9376 9380	**17.** 5271 5270	**18.** 4823 4820

Round to the nearest hundred

19. 763 800	**20.** 871 900	**21.** 408 400	**22.** 579 600	**23.** 628 600	**24.** 350 400
25. 4935 4900	**26.** 2817 2800	**27.** 7449 7400	**28.** 2193 2200	**29.** 8109 8100	**30.** 4450 4500
31. 16,066 16,100	**32.** 27,029 27,000	**33.** 15,425 15,400	**34.** 38,802 38,800	**35.** 56,918 56,900	**36.** 30,227 30,200

Round to the nearest thousand.

37. 8700 9000	**38.** 4315 4000	**39.** 2499 2000	**40.** 8615 9000	**41.** 6329 6000	**42.** 3468 3000
43. 11,269 11,000	**44.** 18,436 18,000	**45.** 14,781 15,000	**46.** 29,585 30,000	**47.** 37,998 38,000	**48.** 23,251 23,000
49. 7800 8000	**50.** 88,437 88,000	**51.** 7145 7000	**52.** 39,504 40,000	**53.** 49,499 49,000	**54.** 5098 5000

Division: WHOLE NUMBERS

EXAMPLE Divide: 1121 ÷ 36 (The **divisor** is 36. The **dividend** is 1121.)

Solution:

1 Determine where to place the first digit in the quotient.

36) 1121 — *11 is less than 36. Draw a new line.* → 36) 1121 (X over the second 1)

2 Round to find a trial divisor.

36 rounded to the nearest ten is 40. — *Trial Divisor*

Think: 40) 112, quotient 2. Try 2 for the first digit.

3 Divide.

```
     2
36) 1121
     72
     40
```

Since 40 is greater than 36, 2 is not enough. Try 3.

```
     31
36) 1121
    108
     41
     36
      5
```

40) 41, quotient 1

Answer: **31 r 5**

Remember: You can use multiplication to check division.

Check: Multiply the quotient and the divisor.

```
   31   ← Quotient
 × 36   ← Divisor
  186
  93
 1116
```

Then add the remainder. This should equal the dividend.

```
  1116
 +   5  ← Remainder
  1121
```

PRACTICE

1. 5) 435 — 87	**2.** 7) 294 — 42	**3.** 3) 228 — 76	**4.** 4) 3604 — 901	**5.** 6) 4218 — 703
6. 24) 504 — 21	**7.** 32) 416 — 13	**8.** 22) 635 — 28R19	**9.** 43) 498 — 11R25	**10.** 18) 644 — 35R14
11. 13) 942 — 72R6	**12.** 26) 2669 — 102R17	**13.** 34) 3726 — 109R20	**14.** 43) 2513 — 58R19	**15.** 67) 1683 — 25R8
16. 325) 3900 — 12	**17.** 143) 9295 — 65	**18.** 549) 7447 — 13R310	**19.** 223) 8451 — 37R200	**20.** 357) 1393 — 3R322
21. 426) 2768 — 6R212	**22.** 292) 16936 — 58	**23.** 662) 12578 — 19	**24.** 283) 14189 — 50R39	**25.** 662) 20304 — 30R444

Division: DECIMALS BY A WHOLE NUMBER

Dividing a decimal by a whole number is similar to dividing with whole numbers.

EXAMPLE Divide 5.292 by 63. Check your answer.

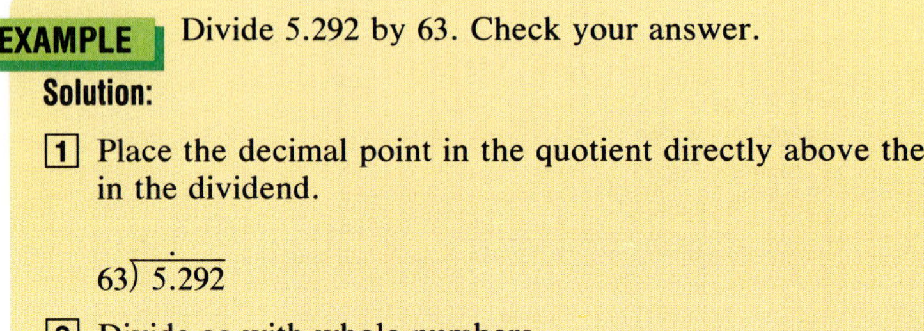

Solution:

[1] Place the decimal point in the quotient directly above the decimal point in the dividend.

$$63\overline{)\,5.292}$$ (with the decimal point placed above the decimal point)

[2] Divide as with whole numbers.

$$\begin{array}{r} 0. \\ 63\overline{)\,5.292} \end{array}$$

Since 5 is not divisible by 63, write a 0 above the 5.

$$\begin{array}{r} 0.0 \\ 63\overline{)\,5.292} \end{array}$$

Since 52 is not divisible by 63, write a 0 above the 2.

$$\begin{array}{r} \mathbf{0.084} \\ 63\overline{)\,5.292} \\ \underline{5\ 04} \\ 252 \\ \underline{252} \end{array}$$

Check:

$$\begin{array}{r} 0.084 \\ \times\ \ 63 \\ \hline 252 \\ \underline{504\ } \\ 5.292 \end{array}$$

These should be the same.

PRACTICE

Divide.

1. $4\overline{)\,18.72}$ **4.68**	**2.** $6\overline{)\,38.76}$ **6.46**	**3.** $7\overline{)\,8.869}$ **1.267**	**4.** $8\overline{)\,9.976}$ **1.247**
5. $7\overline{)\,0.966}$ **0.138**	**6.** $4\overline{)\,0.732}$ **0.183**	**7.** $6\overline{)\,0.564}$ **0.094**	**8.** $9\overline{)\,0.486}$ **0.054**
9. $4\overline{)\,24.36}$ **6.09**	**10.** $5\overline{)\,10.45}$ **2.09**	**11.** $7\overline{)\,1.428}$ **0.204**	**12.** $8\overline{)\,1.632}$ **0.204**
13. $21\overline{)\,68.46}$ **3.26**	**14.** $32\overline{)\,88.96}$ **2.78**	**15.** $18\overline{)\,46.098}$ **2.561**	**16.** $14\overline{)\,51.408}$ **3.672**
17. $97\overline{)\,54.32}$ **0.56**	**18.** $42\overline{)\,28.14}$ **0.67**	**19.** $83\overline{)\,1.743}$ **0.021**	**20.** $24\overline{)\,1.344}$ **0.056**
21. $14\overline{)\,0.406}$ **0.029**	**22.** $54\overline{)\,28.89}$ **0.535**	**23.** $39\overline{)\,15.405}$ **0.395**	**24.** $19\overline{)\,50.692}$ **2.668**
25. $122\overline{)\,434.32}$ **3.56**	**26.** $163\overline{)\,402.61}$ **2.47**	**27.** $211\overline{)\,66.887}$ **0.317**	**28.** $123\overline{)\,39.975}$ **0.325**
29. $162\overline{)\,5.508}$ **0.034**	**30.** $247\overline{)\,9.386}$ **0.038**	**31.** $397\overline{)\,42.082}$ **0.106**	**32.** $261\overline{)\,53.244}$ **0.204**

Division: DECIMALS BY A DECIMAL

When dividing by a decimal, the first step is to multiply both the divisor and dividend by 10, or by 100, or by 1000, and so on, in order to obtain a whole-number divisor.

EXAMPLE

Divide: $0.224\overline{)5.6}$

Solution:

[1] Since the divisor is 224 <u>thousandths</u>, multiply the divisor and the dividend by <u>1000</u>.

$0.224\overline{)5.600}$ ◀ ***Annex two zeros.***

[2] Divide.

$$\begin{array}{r} \mathbf{25} \\ 224\overline{)5600.} \\ \underline{448} \\ 1120 \\ \underline{1120} \end{array}$$

Check:

$$\begin{array}{r} 0.224 \\ \underline{\times \quad 25} \\ 1120 \\ \underline{448} \\ 5.600 \end{array}$$

PRACTICE

Divide.

1. $0.7\overline{)4.34}$ **6.2**	**2.** $0.4\overline{)3.88}$ **9.7**	**3.** $0.5\overline{)46.5}$ **93**	**4.** $0.8\overline{)52.8}$ **66**
5. $0.08\overline{)1.84}$ **23**	**6.** $0.09\overline{)2.16}$ **24**	**7.** $0.006\overline{)3.456}$ **576**	**8.** $0.004\overline{)2.744}$ **686**
9. $0.04\overline{)2.6}$ **65**	**10.** $0.05\overline{)3.4}$ **68**	**11.** $0.008\overline{)6.28}$ **785**	**12.** $0.006\overline{)5.25}$ **875**
13. $1.4\overline{)3.64}$ **2.6**	**14.** $2.8\overline{)4.76}$ **1.7**	**15.** $4.9\overline{)5.145}$ **1.05**	**16.** $2.2\overline{)6.732}$ **3.06**
17. $0.48\overline{)0.576}$ **1.2**	**18.** $0.36\overline{)0.864}$ **2.4**	**19.** $0.29\overline{)1.102}$ **3.8**	**20.** $0.51\overline{)2.448}$ **4.8**
21. $0.46\overline{)39.1}$ **85**	**22.** $0.74\overline{)25.9}$ **35**	**23.** $4.6\overline{)115}$ **25**	**24.** $3.2\overline{)144}$ **45**
25. $2.17\overline{)11.935}$ **5.5**	**26.** $4.01\overline{)10.025}$ **2.5**	**27.** $4.56\overline{)12.312}$ **2.7**	**28.** $2.43\overline{)17.253}$ **7.1**
29. $1.54\overline{)92.4}$ **60**	**30.** $3.19\overline{)63.8}$ **20**	**31.** $0.582\overline{)75.66}$ **130**	**32.** $0.199\overline{)63.68}$ **320**

377

Rounding Decimals

Rules for Rounding Decimals

1. Look at the digit to the right of the place to which you are rounding.
2. **a.** If the digit is 5 or greater, round up.
   b. If the digit is less than 5, round down.

EXAMPLE

a. 23.7453 rounded to the nearest whole number is **24**.
b. 23.7453 rounded to the nearest tenth is 23.**7**
c. 23.7453 rounded to the nearest hundredth is 23.7**5**
d. 23.7453 rounded to the nearest thousandth is 23.74**5**

Round to the nearest whole number.

1. 29.7 30 **2.** 4.3 4 **3.** 25.9 26 **4.** 8.7 9 **5.** 9.9 10 **6.** 5.8 6

7. 16.82 17 **8.** 14.49 14 **9.** 11.38 11 **10.** 19.95 20 **11.** 6.27 6 **12.** 13.15 13

Round to the nearest tenth.

13. 31.27 31.3 **14.** 14.49 14.5 **15.** 17.84 17.8 **16.** 83.35 83.4 **17.** 76.13 76.1 **18.** 11.29 11.3

19. 62.294 62.3 **20.** 81.349 81.3 **21.** 11.409 11.4 **22.** 67.98 68.0 **23.** 124.649 124.6 **24.** 18.551 18.6

Round to the nearest hundredth.

25. 37.285 37.29 **26.** 43.634 43.63 **27.** 59.136 59.14 **28.** 14.188 14.19 **29.** 77.114 77.11 **30.** 264.818 264.82

31. 47.297 47.30 **32.** 11.276 11.28 **33.** 88.225 88.23 **34.** 19.349 19.35 **35.** 62.194 62.19 **36.** 18.399 18.40

Round to the nearest thousandth.

37. 8.2941 8.294 **38.** 7.3939 7.394 **39.** 0.29247 0.292 **40.** 1.1777 1.178 **41.** 2.6455 2.646 **42.** 2.0058 2.006

43. 1.3297 1.330 **44.** 0.4846 0.485 **45.** 2.1121 2.112 **46.** 12.3998 12.400 **47.** 1.1944 1.194 **48.** 6.6666 6.667

378

Rounding the Quotient

EXAMPLE 2 Divide 57.5 by 6.6. Round the quotient to the nearest tenth.

Solution:

1. Carry the division to one additional place, hundredths.

```
        8.71
6.6)57.500     ◄ Annex two zeros.
    528
     470
     462
       80
       66
       14
```

2. Round the quotient to the given decimal place.
8.71 rounded to the nearest tenth is **8.7.**

PRACTICE

Divide. Round each answer to the nearest tenth.

1. 3.2)59.73 **18.7** **2.** 7.4)11.7 **1.6** **3.** 18.1)27.2 **1.5** **4.** 14.9)18.1 **1.2**

5. 6.89)21.03 **3.1** **6.** 7.22)18.331 **2.5** **7.** 11.9)35.88 **3.0** **8.** 1.03)4.233 **4.1**

9. 11.1)54.83 **4.9** **10.** 6.83)12.94 **1.9** **11.** 1.9)18.37 **9.7** **12.** 4.05)11 **2.7**

13. 14.62 ÷ 0.4 **36.6** **14.** 22.39 ÷ 0.7 **32.0** **15.** 15.78 ÷ 2.1 **7.5** **16.** 28.94 ÷ 9.7 **3.0**

17. 12.976 ÷ 8.7 **1.5** **18.** 16.93 ÷ 1.4 **12.1** **19.** 8.89 ÷ 7.22 **1.2** **20.** 28.1 ÷ 7.3 **3.8**

Divide. Round each answer to the nearest hundredth.

21. 8.72)11.84 **1.36** **22.** 2.38)16.96 **7.13** **23.** 4.18)7.3 **1.75** **24.** 18.3)19.7 **1.08**

25. 1.93)14.887 **7.71** **26.** 7.72)18.11 **2.35** **27.** 3.9)11.71 **3.00** **28.** 4.9)18.61 **3.80**

29. 12.7)7.83 **0.62** **30.** 8.8)6.5 **0.74** **31.** 1.5)60.1 **40.07** **32.** 2.9)5.77 **1.99**

33. 1.249 ÷ 0.5 **2.50** **34.** 3.631 ÷ 0.8 **4.54** **35.** 24.72 ÷ 3.8 **6.51** **36.** 15.32 ÷ 2.2 **6.96**

37. 9.941 ÷ 9.7 **1.02** **38.** 292.4 ÷ 68.3 **4.28** **39.** 9.807 ÷ 5.85 **1.68** **40.** 2.9 ÷ 3.92 **0.74**

Estimation Ex. 1–12

Rounding and Estimation

Recall the symbol ≈ means "is approximately equal to."

EXAMPLE Estimate each answer.

a. $5.89 + 3.12$ **b.** $794 - 418$ **c.** 59×71 **d.** $207.5 \div 28.4$

Solutions:

a. Round each number to the nearest whole number.
Think: $5.89 + 3.12 \approx 6 + 3 = \mathbf{9}$

b. Round each number to the nearest hundred.
Think: $794 - 418 \approx 800 - 400 = \mathbf{400}$

c. Round each number to the nearest ten.
Think: $59 \times 71 \approx 60 \times 70 = \mathbf{4200}$

d. Round each number to the nearest ten.
Think: $207.5 \div 28.4 \approx 210 \div 30 = \mathbf{7}$

PRACTICE

Choose the best estimate. Choose a, b, or c.

		a.	b.	c.
1.	$438 + 21$	$430 + 20$	(b.) $440 + 20$	$440 + 30$
2.	$10.2 - 7.8$	(a.) $10 - 8$	$11 - 8$	$10 - 7$
3.	22×49	30×40	30×50	(c.) 20×50
4.	3.8×10.1	(a.) 4×10	4×11	3×10
5.	$321 \div 83$	$330 \div 80$	(b.) $320 \div 80$	$330 \div 90$
6.	$60.3 \div 29.8$	$61 \div 20$	$70 \div 30$	(c.) $60 \div 30$

Choose the best estimate. Choose a, b, c, or d.

		a.	b.	c.	d.
7.	$39 + 572$	640	620	(c.) 610	600
8.	$14.8 + 6.75$	25	(b.) 22	20	18
9.	$397 - 241$	180	170	150	(d.) 160
10.	10.3×28.9	500	400	(c.) 300	200
11.	$78 \div 19$	2	3	5	(d.) 4
12.	$19.9 \div 1.8$	15	(b.) 10	5	20

Fractions: MIXED NUMBERS

A fraction greater than 1 can be written as a **mixed number.**

EXAMPLE Write a mixed number for $\frac{17}{3}$.

Solution:

[1] Divide the numerator by the denominator.

$\frac{17}{3}$ means 17 ÷ 3. → $3\overline{)17}$ quotient 5; 15; remainder 2

[2] Write a fraction for the remainder.

Quotient: **5 r 2**, or $5\frac{2}{3}$ ← *Remainder* ← *Divisor*

Thus, $\frac{17}{3} = 5\frac{2}{3}$ ◀ *Mixed number*

PRACTICE

Write a mixed number for each fraction.

1. $\frac{9}{5}$ $1\frac{4}{5}$ **2.** $\frac{12}{7}$ $1\frac{5}{7}$ **3.** $\frac{7}{3}$ $2\frac{1}{3}$ **4.** $\frac{16}{9}$ $1\frac{7}{9}$ **5.** $\frac{12}{5}$ $2\frac{2}{5}$ **6.** $\frac{19}{6}$ $3\frac{1}{6}$ **7.** $\frac{21}{8}$ $2\frac{5}{8}$

8. $\frac{18}{7}$ $2\frac{4}{7}$ **9.** $\frac{13}{4}$ $3\frac{1}{4}$ **10.** $\frac{15}{8}$ $1\frac{7}{8}$ **11.** $\frac{20}{11}$ $1\frac{9}{11}$ **12.** $\frac{17}{7}$ $2\frac{3}{7}$ **13.** $\frac{19}{11}$ $1\frac{8}{11}$ **14.** $\frac{25}{3}$ $8\frac{1}{3}$

15. $\frac{37}{12}$ $3\frac{1}{12}$ **16.** $\frac{43}{12}$ $3\frac{7}{12}$ **17.** $\frac{97}{21}$ $4\frac{13}{21}$ **18.** $\frac{64}{3}$ $21\frac{1}{3}$ **19.** $\frac{38}{13}$ $2\frac{12}{13}$ **20.** $\frac{27}{19}$ $1\frac{8}{19}$ **21.** $\frac{43}{9}$ $4\frac{7}{9}$

22. $\frac{89}{12}$ $7\frac{5}{12}$ **23.** $\frac{11}{6}$ $1\frac{5}{6}$ **24.** $\frac{47}{15}$ $3\frac{2}{15}$ **25.** $\frac{8}{5}$ $1\frac{3}{5}$ **26.** $\frac{17}{6}$ $2\frac{5}{6}$ **27.** $\frac{13}{8}$ $1\frac{5}{8}$ **28.** $\frac{51}{14}$ $3\frac{9}{14}$

29. $\frac{64}{15}$ $4\frac{4}{15}$ **30.** $\frac{29}{17}$ $1\frac{12}{17}$ **31.** $\frac{81}{11}$ $7\frac{4}{11}$ **32.** $\frac{16}{5}$ $3\frac{1}{5}$ **33.** $\frac{17}{3}$ $5\frac{2}{3}$ **34.** $\frac{19}{2}$ $9\frac{1}{2}$ **35.** $\frac{21}{4}$ $5\frac{1}{4}$

36. $\frac{37}{3}$ $12\frac{1}{3}$ **37.** $\frac{64}{13}$ $4\frac{12}{13}$ **38.** $\frac{83}{22}$ $3\frac{17}{22}$ **39.** $\frac{88}{15}$ $5\frac{13}{15}$ **40.** $\frac{13}{3}$ $4\frac{1}{3}$ **41.** $\frac{29}{11}$ $2\frac{7}{11}$ **42.** $\frac{85}{16}$ $5\frac{5}{16}$

43. $\frac{74}{23}$ $3\frac{5}{23}$ **44.** $\frac{92}{13}$ $7\frac{1}{13}$ **45.** $\frac{67}{11}$ $6\frac{1}{11}$ **46.** $\frac{77}{24}$ $3\frac{5}{24}$ **47.** $\frac{62}{17}$ $3\frac{11}{17}$ **48.** $\frac{91}{12}$ $7\frac{7}{12}$ **49.** $\frac{63}{19}$ $3\frac{6}{19}$

50. $\frac{67}{13}$ $5\frac{2}{13}$ **51.** $\frac{57}{14}$ $4\frac{1}{14}$ **52.** $\frac{79}{21}$ $3\frac{16}{21}$ **53.** $\frac{83}{31}$ $2\frac{21}{31}$ **54.** $\frac{27}{7}$ $3\frac{6}{7}$ **55.** $\frac{94}{27}$ $3\frac{13}{27}$ **56.** $\frac{55}{12}$ $4\frac{7}{12}$

57. $\frac{16}{7}$ $2\frac{2}{7}$ **58.** $\frac{47}{11}$ $4\frac{3}{11}$ **59.** $\frac{34}{9}$ $3\frac{7}{9}$ **60.** $\frac{85}{18}$ $4\frac{13}{18}$ **61.** $\frac{95}{14}$ $6\frac{11}{14}$ **62.** $\frac{10}{3}$ $3\frac{1}{3}$ **63.** $\frac{68}{13}$ $5\frac{3}{13}$

Fractions: LOWEST TERMS

A fraction is in **lowest terms** when the numerator and the denominator cannot be divided by the same number except one.

EXAMPLE

Write in lowest terms. Then write a mixed number for any fraction greater than 1.

a. $\frac{42}{48}$ **b.** $\frac{54}{36}$

Divide the numerator and the denominator by a number that will divide evenly into both. Repeat until the numerator and denominator cannot be divided evenly by the same number except 1.

a. $\frac{42}{48} = \frac{42 \div 2}{48 \div 2}$

$= \frac{21}{24}$ ◀ *Not in lowest terms*

$= \frac{21 \div 3}{24 \div 3}$

$= \frac{7}{8}$ ◀ *Lowest terms*

b. $\frac{54}{36} = \frac{54 \div 9}{36 \div 9}$

$= \frac{6}{4}$ ◀ *Not in lowest terms*

$= \frac{6 \div 2}{4 \div 2}$

$= \frac{3}{2}$ ◀ *Write as a mixed number.*

$= 1\frac{1}{2}$

PRACTICE

Write in lowest terms. Then write a whole number or a mixed number for any fraction greater than one.

1. $\frac{8}{24}$ $\frac{1}{3}$	**2.** $\frac{9}{27}$ $\frac{1}{3}$	**3.** $\frac{3}{27}$ $\frac{1}{9}$	**4.** $\frac{6}{30}$ $\frac{1}{5}$	**5.** $\frac{17}{68}$ $\frac{1}{4}$	**6.** $\frac{12}{48}$ $\frac{1}{4}$	**7.** $\frac{16}{60}$ $\frac{4}{15}$
8. $\frac{18}{45}$ $\frac{2}{5}$	**9.** $\frac{60}{90}$ $\frac{2}{3}$	**10.** $\frac{11}{33}$ $\frac{1}{3}$	**11.** $\frac{50}{12}$ $4\frac{1}{6}$	**12.** $\frac{68}{24}$ $2\frac{5}{6}$	**13.** $\frac{16}{32}$ $\frac{1}{2}$	**14.** $\frac{15}{40}$ $\frac{3}{8}$
15. $\frac{6}{36}$ $\frac{1}{6}$	**16.** $\frac{24}{16}$ $1\frac{1}{2}$	**17.** $\frac{50}{75}$ $\frac{2}{3}$	**18.** $\frac{81}{27}$ 3	**19.** $\frac{66}{30}$ $2\frac{1}{5}$	**20.** $\frac{11}{44}$ $\frac{1}{4}$	**21.** $\frac{17}{51}$ $\frac{1}{3}$
22. $\frac{7}{35}$ $\frac{1}{5}$	**23.** $\frac{28}{16}$ $1\frac{3}{4}$	**24.** $\frac{25}{15}$ $1\frac{2}{3}$	**25.** $\frac{40}{12}$ $3\frac{1}{3}$	**26.** $\frac{65}{13}$ 5	**27.** $\frac{38}{18}$ $2\frac{1}{9}$	**28.** $\frac{16}{54}$ $\frac{8}{27}$
29. $\frac{28}{32}$ $\frac{7}{8}$	**30.** $\frac{9}{30}$ $\frac{3}{10}$	**31.** $\frac{24}{18}$ $1\frac{1}{3}$	**32.** $\frac{9}{57}$ $\frac{3}{19}$	**33.** $\frac{200}{40}$ 5	**34.** $\frac{80}{24}$ $3\frac{1}{3}$	**35.** $\frac{95}{38}$ $2\frac{1}{2}$
36. $\frac{27}{60}$ $\frac{9}{20}$	**37.** $\frac{400}{1200}$ $\frac{1}{3}$	**38.** $\frac{49}{63}$ $\frac{7}{9}$	**39.** $\frac{98}{144}$ $\frac{49}{72}$	**40.** $\frac{180}{600}$ $\frac{3}{10}$	**41.** $\frac{13}{78}$ $\frac{1}{6}$	**42.** $\frac{29}{58}$ $\frac{1}{2}$
43. $\frac{65}{130}$ $\frac{1}{2}$	**44.** $\frac{81}{18}$ $4\frac{1}{2}$	**45.** $\frac{63}{27}$ $2\frac{1}{3}$	**46.** $\frac{54}{42}$ $1\frac{2}{7}$	**47.** $\frac{88}{44}$ 2	**48.** $\frac{90}{15}$ 6	**49.** $\frac{21}{63}$ $\frac{1}{3}$
50. $\frac{76}{125}$ $\frac{76}{125}$	**51.** $\frac{4}{76}$ $\frac{1}{19}$	**52.** $\frac{27}{72}$ $\frac{3}{8}$	**53.** $\frac{84}{30}$ $2\frac{4}{5}$	**54.** $\frac{9}{39}$ $\frac{3}{13}$	**55.** $\frac{38}{24}$ $1\frac{7}{12}$	**56.** $\frac{360}{150}$ $2\frac{2}{5}$
57. $\frac{64}{60}$ $1\frac{1}{15}$	**58.** $\frac{6}{42}$ $\frac{1}{7}$	**59.** $\frac{33}{30}$ $1\frac{1}{10}$	**60.** $\frac{8}{56}$ $\frac{1}{7}$	**61.** $\frac{27}{45}$ $\frac{3}{5}$	**62.** $\frac{16}{56}$ $\frac{2}{7}$	**63.** $\frac{8}{99}$ $\frac{8}{99}$

Like Fractions: ADDITION AND SUBTRACTION

Fractions such as $\frac{7}{9}$ and $\frac{8}{9}$ are **like fractions** because they have a **common denominator**, 9.

EXAMPLE

a. $\frac{1}{8} + \frac{3}{8} = \underline{\ ?\ }$

b. $\frac{5}{9} - \frac{2}{9} = \underline{\ ?\ }$

Solutions:

Add the numerators. Write the sum over the common denominator.

a. $\begin{array}{r} \frac{1}{8} \\ +\frac{3}{8} \\ \hline \frac{4}{8} \end{array} = \frac{1}{2}$ ◀ *Lowest Terms*

Subtract the numerators. Write the difference over the common denominator.

b. $\begin{array}{r} \frac{5}{9} \\ -\frac{2}{9} \\ \hline \frac{3}{9} \end{array} = \frac{1}{3}$ ◀ *Lowest Terms*

PRACTICE

Add or subtract. Write each answer in lowest terms.

1. $\frac{2}{4} + \frac{1}{4}$ $\frac{3}{4}$
2. $\frac{5}{8} - \frac{1}{8}$ $\frac{1}{2}$
3. $\frac{3}{7} + \frac{1}{7}$ $\frac{4}{7}$
4. $\frac{8}{9} - \frac{3}{9}$ $\frac{5}{9}$
5. $\frac{2}{13} + \frac{5}{13}$ $\frac{7}{13}$
6. $\frac{7}{12} + \frac{3}{12}$ $\frac{5}{6}$
7. $\frac{3}{5} + \frac{2}{5}$ 1
8. $\frac{5}{6} - \frac{3}{6}$ $\frac{1}{3}$
9. $\frac{11}{15} - \frac{8}{15}$ $\frac{1}{5}$
10. $\frac{13}{21} + \frac{1}{21}$ $\frac{2}{3}$
11. $\frac{8}{35} - \frac{3}{35}$ $\frac{1}{7}$
12. $\frac{6}{19} + \frac{1}{19}$ $\frac{7}{19}$
13. $\frac{11}{12} - \frac{5}{12}$ $\frac{1}{2}$
14. $\frac{7}{10} - \frac{5}{10}$ $\frac{1}{5}$
15. $\frac{11}{14} - \frac{4}{14}$ $\frac{1}{2}$
16. $\frac{29}{30} - \frac{15}{30}$ $\frac{7}{15}$
17. $\frac{6}{25} + \frac{9}{25}$ $\frac{3}{5}$
18. $\frac{8}{27} + \frac{10}{27}$ $\frac{2}{3}$
19. $\frac{4}{5} - \frac{3}{5}$ $\frac{1}{5}$
20. $\frac{7}{9} - \frac{4}{9}$ $\frac{1}{3}$
21. $\frac{5}{12} + \frac{1}{12}$ $\frac{1}{2}$
22. $\frac{3}{13} + \frac{1}{13}$ $\frac{4}{13}$
23. $\frac{7}{8} - \frac{1}{8}$ $\frac{3}{4}$
24. $\frac{17}{20} + \frac{1}{20}$ $\frac{9}{10}$
25. $\frac{18}{35} + \frac{7}{35}$ $\frac{5}{7}$
26. $\frac{24}{42} - \frac{3}{42}$ $\frac{1}{2}$
27. $\frac{16}{50} + \frac{4}{50}$ $\frac{2}{5}$
28. $\frac{13}{18} - \frac{5}{18}$ $\frac{4}{9}$
29. $\frac{5}{12} - \frac{1}{12}$ $\frac{1}{3}$
30. $\frac{7}{8} - \frac{3}{8}$ $\frac{1}{2}$
31. $\frac{13}{21} + \frac{5}{21}$ $\frac{6}{7}$
32. $\frac{8}{33} + \frac{14}{33}$ $\frac{2}{3}$
33. $\frac{21}{40} - \frac{6}{40}$ $\frac{3}{8}$

Least Common Denominator

Fractions such as $\frac{7}{8}$ and $\frac{5}{6}$ are **unlike fractions** because their denominators are not the same. To write like fractions for unlike fractions, you first find the **least common denominator** (LCD).

EXAMPLE

Write like fractions for $\frac{7}{8}$ and $\frac{5}{6}$.

[1] Find the LCD of the denominators.

Write multiples of 8 until you reach a number that is also a multiple of 6.

$8 \times 1 = 8 \quad 8 \times 2 = 16 \quad 8 \times 3 = 24$ ◀ ***Stop! 24 is also a multiple of 6.***

LCD: 24

[2] Multiply both the numerator and denominator of each fraction by a number that will make the denominator equal to the LCD.

$\frac{7}{8} = \frac{7 \times 3}{8 \times 3}$ $\qquad$ $\frac{5}{6} = \frac{5 \times 4}{6 \times 4}$

$\frac{7}{8} = \mathbf{\frac{21}{24}}$ $\qquad$ $\frac{5}{6} = \mathbf{\frac{20}{24}}$

Like fractions

PRACTICE

Find the LCD for each pair of fractions.

1. $\frac{1}{2}$ and $\frac{1}{3}$ **6** **2.** $\frac{1}{3}$ and $\frac{5}{6}$ **6** **3.** $\frac{3}{4}$ and $\frac{7}{8}$ **8** **4.** $\frac{1}{5}$ and $\frac{3}{4}$ **20** **5.** $\frac{5}{6}$ and $\frac{1}{4}$ **12**

6. $\frac{3}{8}$ and $\frac{2}{5}$ **40** **7.** $\frac{3}{4}$ and $\frac{2}{3}$ **12** **8.** $\frac{5}{6}$ and $\frac{3}{5}$ **30** **9.** $\frac{3}{8}$ and $\frac{1}{2}$ **16** **10.** $\frac{7}{8}$ and $\frac{5}{9}$ **72**

11. $\frac{1}{4}$ and $\frac{2}{7}$ **28** **12.** $\frac{3}{5}$ and $\frac{2}{3}$ **15** **13.** $\frac{3}{7}$ and $\frac{1}{2}$ **14** **14.** $\frac{5}{8}$ and $\frac{2}{3}$ **24** **15.** $\frac{7}{9}$ and $\frac{1}{4}$ **36**

16. $\frac{5}{12}$ and $\frac{5}{6}$ **12** **17.** $\frac{3}{7}$ and $\frac{2}{4}$ **28** **18.** $\frac{5}{9}$ and $\frac{2}{3}$ **9** **19.** $\frac{1}{6}$ and $\frac{4}{7}$ **42** **20.** $\frac{5}{8}$ and $\frac{2}{7}$ **56**

Write like fractions for each pair of fractions.

21. $\frac{1}{2}$ and $\frac{2}{3}$ $\frac{3}{6}$; $\frac{4}{6}$ **22.** $\frac{4}{9}$ and $\frac{3}{6}$ $\frac{8}{18}$; $\frac{9}{18}$ **23.** $\frac{3}{4}$ and $\frac{2}{3}$ $\frac{9}{12}$; $\frac{8}{12}$ **24.** $\frac{1}{5}$ and $\frac{3}{10}$ $\frac{2}{10}$; $\frac{3}{10}$ **25.** $\frac{7}{16}$ and $\frac{3}{12}$ $\frac{21}{48}$; $\frac{12}{48}$

26. $\frac{5}{8}$ and $\frac{2}{3}$ $\frac{15}{24}$; $\frac{16}{24}$ **27.** $\frac{5}{12}$ and $\frac{3}{4}$ $\frac{5}{12}$; $\frac{9}{12}$ **28.** $\frac{9}{16}$ and $\frac{1}{2}$ $\frac{9}{16}$; $\frac{8}{16}$ **29.** $\frac{2}{3}$ and $\frac{4}{7}$ $\frac{14}{21}$; $\frac{12}{21}$ **30.** $\frac{5}{8}$ and $\frac{1}{9}$ $\frac{45}{72}$; $\frac{8}{72}$

31. $\frac{2}{5}$ and $\frac{3}{4}$ $\frac{8}{20}$; $\frac{15}{20}$ **32.** $\frac{1}{22}$ and $\frac{3}{4}$ $\frac{2}{44}$; $\frac{33}{44}$ **33.** $\frac{8}{9}$ and $\frac{5}{12}$ $\frac{32}{36}$; $\frac{15}{36}$ **34.** $\frac{1}{14}$ and $\frac{2}{3}$ $\frac{3}{52}$; $\frac{28}{52}$ **35.** $\frac{17}{25}$ and $\frac{3}{10}$ $\frac{34}{50}$; $\frac{15}{50}$

Addition: UNLIKE FRACTIONS

EXAMPLE

a. $\frac{5}{6} + \frac{1}{10} = \underline{\ ?\ }$

b. $\frac{3}{4} + \frac{1}{3} = \underline{\ ?\ }$

Solutions:

Use the LCD to write like fractions. Then add.

a. LCD: 30

$$\frac{5}{6} = \frac{25}{30} \quad \frac{5 \times 5}{6 \times 5}$$
$$+\frac{1}{10} = +\frac{3}{30} \quad \frac{1 \times 3}{10 \times 3}$$
$$\frac{28}{30} = \frac{14}{15} \quad \text{Lowest terms}$$

b. LCD: 12

$$\frac{3}{4} = \frac{9}{12} \quad \frac{3 \times 3}{4 \times 3}$$
$$+\frac{1}{3} = +\frac{4}{12} \quad \frac{1 \times 4}{3 \times 4}$$
$$\frac{13}{12} = 1\frac{1}{12}$$

PRACTICE

Add. Write each answer in lowest terms.

1. $\frac{5}{8} + \frac{1}{4}$ $\frac{7}{8}$
2. $\frac{5}{6} + \frac{1}{3}$ $1\frac{1}{6}$
3. $\frac{11}{15} + \frac{2}{3}$ $1\frac{2}{5}$
4. $\frac{3}{5} + \frac{1}{3}$ $\frac{14}{15}$
5. $\frac{2}{9} + \frac{1}{6}$ $\frac{7}{18}$
6. $\frac{13}{16} + \frac{1}{12}$ $\frac{43}{48}$
7. $\frac{5}{8} + \frac{1}{3}$ $\frac{23}{24}$
8. $\frac{3}{20} + \frac{2}{5}$ $\frac{11}{20}$
9. $\frac{5}{12} + \frac{3}{8}$ $\frac{19}{24}$
10. $\frac{2}{7} + \frac{1}{5}$ $\frac{17}{35}$
11. $\frac{2}{3} + \frac{1}{10}$ $\frac{23}{30}$
12. $\frac{7}{8} + \frac{2}{5}$ $1\frac{11}{40}$
13. $\frac{3}{4} + \frac{1}{8}$ $\frac{7}{8}$
14. $\frac{4}{5} + \frac{2}{3}$ $1\frac{7}{15}$
15. $\frac{5}{9} + \frac{1}{2}$ $1\frac{1}{18}$
16. $\frac{2}{3} + \frac{5}{6}$ $1\frac{1}{2}$
17. $\frac{8}{15} + \frac{3}{5}$ $1\frac{2}{15}$
18. $\frac{5}{12} + \frac{1}{3}$ $\frac{3}{4}$
19. $\frac{7}{5} + \frac{1}{4}$ $1\frac{13}{20}$
20. $\frac{2}{9} + \frac{4}{15}$ $\frac{22}{45}$
21. $\frac{5}{7} + \frac{2}{3}$ $1\frac{8}{21}$
22. $\frac{1}{8} + \frac{1}{6}$ $\frac{7}{24}$
23. $\frac{1}{12} + \frac{3}{4}$ $\frac{5}{6}$
24. $\frac{5}{6} + \frac{1}{4}$ $1\frac{1}{12}$
25. $\frac{2}{3} + \frac{1}{2}$ $1\frac{1}{6}$
26. $\frac{1}{16} + \frac{3}{5}$ $\frac{53}{80}$
27. $\frac{2}{9} + \frac{1}{5}$ $\frac{19}{45}$
28. $\frac{11}{14} + \frac{5}{21}$ $1\frac{1}{42}$
29. $\frac{1}{4} + \frac{3}{8}$ $\frac{5}{8}$
30. $\frac{1}{2} + \frac{5}{7}$ $1\frac{3}{14}$
31. $\frac{7}{15} + \frac{4}{5}$ $1\frac{4}{15}$
32. $\frac{2}{3} + \frac{2}{9}$ $\frac{8}{9}$
33. $\frac{5}{6} + \frac{3}{8}$ $1\frac{5}{24}$
34. $\frac{3}{5} + \frac{3}{4}$ $1\frac{7}{20}$
35. $\frac{4}{9} + \frac{3}{18}$ $\frac{11}{18}$
36. $\frac{3}{4} + \frac{2}{3}$ $1\frac{5}{12}$
37. $\frac{1}{5} + \frac{1}{2}$ $\frac{7}{10}$
38. $\frac{7}{12} + \frac{3}{4}$ $1\frac{1}{3}$
39. $\frac{3}{5} + \frac{3}{10}$ $\frac{9}{10}$
40. $\frac{2}{7} + \frac{2}{3}$ $\frac{20}{21}$
41. $\frac{3}{8} + \frac{5}{6}$ $1\frac{5}{24}$
42. $\frac{2}{9} + \frac{1}{4}$ $\frac{17}{36}$
43. $\frac{3}{5} + \frac{3}{20}$ $\frac{3}{4}$
44. $\frac{1}{2} + \frac{1}{10}$ $\frac{3}{5}$
45. $\frac{3}{4} + \frac{3}{8}$ $1\frac{1}{8}$
46. $\frac{3}{7} + \frac{9}{28}$ $\frac{3}{4}$
47. $\frac{5}{16} + \frac{3}{8}$ $\frac{11}{16}$
48. $\frac{5}{7} + \frac{7}{9}$ $1\frac{31}{63}$

Addition: MIXED NUMBERS

EXAMPLE

a. $3\frac{1}{2} + 7\frac{2}{3} = \underline{\ ?\ }$ **b.** $2\frac{3}{8} + 4\frac{2}{5} = \underline{\ ?\ }$

Solutions:

Use the LCD to write like mixed numbers. Then add.

a. LCD: 6

$$\begin{array}{rcr} 3\frac{1}{2} & = & 3\frac{3}{6} \\ +7\frac{2}{3} & = & +7\frac{4}{6} \\ \hline & & 10\frac{7}{6} \end{array} = 10 + 1\frac{1}{6} = \mathbf{11\frac{1}{6}}$$

$\frac{7}{6} = 1\frac{1}{6}$

b. LCD: 40

$$\begin{array}{rcr} 2\frac{3}{8} & = & 2\frac{15}{40} \\ +4\frac{2}{5} & = & +4\frac{16}{40} \\ \hline & & 6\frac{31}{40} \end{array}$$

Lowest terms

PRACTICE

Add. Write each answer in lowest terms.

1. $4\frac{1}{3} + 2\frac{4}{5}$ → $7\frac{2}{15}$
2. $8\frac{1}{3} + 7\frac{7}{9}$ → $16\frac{1}{9}$
3. $3\frac{1}{5} + 6\frac{1}{4}$ → $9\frac{9}{20}$
4. $2\frac{2}{3} + 5\frac{1}{2}$ → $8\frac{1}{6}$
5. $6\frac{1}{2} + 2\frac{7}{9}$ → $9\frac{5}{18}$
6. $2\frac{1}{2} + 4\frac{2}{5}$ → $6\frac{9}{10}$
7. $3\frac{1}{4} + 2\frac{1}{2}$ → $5\frac{3}{4}$
8. $6\frac{3}{10} + 2\frac{2}{5}$ → $8\frac{7}{10}$
9. $3\frac{5}{8} + 2\frac{5}{6}$ → $6\frac{11}{24}$
10. $4\frac{2}{3} + 5\frac{1}{5}$ → $9\frac{13}{15}$
11. $3\frac{1}{7} + 2\frac{2}{3}$ → $5\frac{17}{21}$
12. $1\frac{5}{6} + 2\frac{1}{4}$ → $4\frac{1}{12}$
13. $7\frac{1}{2} + \frac{2}{3}$ → $8\frac{1}{6}$
14. $3\frac{1}{4} + \frac{2}{9}$ → $3\frac{17}{36}$
15. $2\frac{11}{12} + 3\frac{1}{8}$ → $6\frac{1}{24}$
16. $4\frac{2}{15} + 3\frac{4}{5}$ → $7\frac{14}{15}$
17. $6\frac{2}{5} + \frac{1}{4}$ → $6\frac{13}{20}$
18. $3\frac{4}{9} + \frac{1}{5}$ → $3\frac{29}{45}$
19. $1\frac{1}{2} + 2\frac{1}{8}$ → $3\frac{5}{8}$
20. $3\frac{4}{5} + 5\frac{7}{10}$ → $9\frac{1}{2}$
21. $1\frac{3}{10} + \frac{5}{8}$ → $1\frac{37}{40}$
22. $2\frac{1}{3} + 3\frac{1}{4}$ → $5\frac{7}{12}$
23. $3\frac{1}{6} + 4\frac{1}{5}$ → $7\frac{11}{30}$
24. $4\frac{2}{3} + 3\frac{3}{4}$ → $8\frac{5}{12}$
25. $2\frac{1}{2} + 5\frac{5}{8}$ → $8\frac{1}{8}$
26. $6\frac{2}{3} + 3\frac{5}{6}$ → $10\frac{1}{2}$
27. $2\frac{1}{16} + 7\frac{5}{6}$ → $9\frac{43}{48}$
28. $9\frac{1}{2} + 1\frac{1}{6}$ → $10\frac{2}{3}$
29. $3\frac{1}{6} + 2\frac{1}{3}$ → $5\frac{1}{2}$
30. $3\frac{1}{4} + 5\frac{5}{6}$ → $9\frac{1}{12}$
31. $\frac{1}{3} + 2\frac{1}{8}$ → $2\frac{11}{24}$
32. $4\frac{1}{12} + 2\frac{3}{4}$ → $6\frac{5}{6}$
33. $15\frac{1}{2} + 6\frac{3}{5}$ → $22\frac{1}{10}$
34. $9\frac{2}{7} + 3\frac{1}{14}$ → $12\frac{5}{14}$
35. $51\frac{3}{8} + 2\frac{1}{5}$ → $53\frac{23}{40}$
36. $16\frac{4}{9} + 2\frac{1}{6}$ → $18\frac{11}{18}$
37. $1\frac{4}{11} + 2\frac{1}{2}$ → $3\frac{19}{22}$
38. $11\frac{1}{3} + 3\frac{5}{16}$ → $14\frac{31}{48}$
39. $2\frac{1}{2} + 4\frac{3}{5}$ → $7\frac{1}{10}$
40. $\frac{1}{4} + 6\frac{2}{3}$ → $6\frac{11}{12}$
41. $14\frac{1}{4} + 8\frac{3}{8}$ → $22\frac{5}{8}$
42. $5\frac{5}{6} + 6\frac{2}{3}$ → $12\frac{1}{2}$

Subtraction: UNLIKE FRACTIONS/MIXED NUMBERS

EXAMPLE

a. $\frac{7}{8} - \frac{1}{5} = \underline{\ ?\ }$ **b.** $3\frac{8}{9} - 1\frac{3}{4} = \underline{\ ?\ }$

Solutions:

Use the LCD to write like fractions. Then subtract.

a. LCD: 40

$$\begin{array}{rcr} \frac{7}{8} & = & \frac{35}{40} \\ -\frac{1}{5} & = & -\frac{8}{40} \\ \hline & & \frac{27}{40} \end{array}$$

b. LCD: 36

$$\begin{array}{rcr} 3\frac{8}{9} & = & 3\frac{32}{36} \\ -1\frac{3}{4} & = & -1\frac{27}{36} \\ \hline & & 2\frac{5}{36} \end{array}$$

PRACTICE

Subtract. Write each answer in lowest terms.

1. $\frac{3}{5} - \frac{1}{3}$ $\frac{4}{15}$
2. $\frac{7}{12} - \frac{1}{2}$ $\frac{1}{12}$
3. $\frac{5}{9} - \frac{2}{5}$ $\frac{7}{45}$
4. $\frac{6}{7} - \frac{1}{4}$ $\frac{17}{28}$
5. $\frac{11}{13} - \frac{2}{3}$ $\frac{7}{39}$
6. $\frac{5}{8} - \frac{2}{5}$ $\frac{9}{40}$

7. $\frac{4}{5} - \frac{3}{10}$ $\frac{1}{2}$
8. $\frac{7}{9} - \frac{1}{5}$ $\frac{26}{45}$
9. $\frac{6}{7} - \frac{2}{5}$ $\frac{16}{35}$
10. $\frac{7}{12} - \frac{1}{4}$ $\frac{1}{3}$
11. $\frac{9}{14} - \frac{1}{4}$ $\frac{11}{28}$
12. $\frac{8}{9} - \frac{4}{5}$ $\frac{4}{45}$

13. $3\frac{5}{9} - 1\frac{3}{8}$ $2\frac{13}{72}$
14. $2\frac{11}{15} - 1\frac{2}{3}$ $1\frac{1}{15}$
15. $7\frac{4}{7} - 3\frac{1}{3}$ $4\frac{5}{21}$
16. $6\frac{9}{10} - 2\frac{1}{4}$ $4\frac{13}{20}$
17. $5\frac{2}{3} - 1\frac{1}{4}$ $4\frac{5}{12}$
18. $6\frac{4}{5} - 2\frac{1}{4}$ $4\frac{11}{20}$

19. $21\frac{3}{5} - 13\frac{1}{10}$ $8\frac{1}{2}$
20. $6\frac{7}{9} - 3\frac{1}{2}$ $3\frac{5}{18}$
21. $17\frac{3}{5} - 9\frac{1}{4}$ $8\frac{7}{20}$
22. $11\frac{7}{8} - 6\frac{5}{16}$ $5\frac{9}{16}$
23. $10\frac{5}{6} - 5\frac{2}{3}$ $5\frac{1}{6}$
24. $10\frac{1}{2} - 6\frac{3}{10}$ $4\frac{1}{5}$

25. $7\frac{1}{2} - 4\frac{1}{3}$ $3\frac{1}{6}$
26. $\frac{5}{8} - \frac{1}{3}$ $\frac{7}{24}$
27. $5\frac{7}{12} - 3\frac{1}{4}$ $2\frac{1}{3}$
28. $\frac{7}{10} - \frac{2}{5}$ $\frac{3}{10}$

29. $12\frac{7}{15} - 8\frac{1}{3}$ $4\frac{2}{15}$
30. $3\frac{7}{8} - 2\frac{2}{3}$ $1\frac{5}{24}$
31. $\frac{1}{2} - \frac{1}{9}$ $\frac{7}{18}$
32. $11\frac{5}{7} - 2\frac{1}{6}$ $9\frac{23}{42}$

33. $3\frac{7}{12} - 2\frac{1}{9}$ $1\frac{17}{36}$
34. $\frac{3}{4} - \frac{1}{3}$ $\frac{5}{12}$
35. $\frac{11}{12} - \frac{2}{3}$ $\frac{1}{4}$
36. $12\frac{9}{16} - 3\frac{5}{12}$ $9\frac{7}{48}$

37. $8\frac{1}{3} - 5\frac{1}{4}$ $3\frac{1}{12}$
38. $\frac{7}{8} - \frac{2}{3}$ $\frac{5}{24}$
39. $6\frac{11}{12} - 4\frac{3}{4}$ $2\frac{1}{6}$
40. $\frac{9}{10} - \frac{3}{5}$ $\frac{3}{10}$

41. $13\frac{4}{15} - 7\frac{1}{5}$ $6\frac{1}{15}$
42. $5\frac{7}{9} - 3\frac{1}{3}$ $2\frac{4}{9}$
43. $\frac{1}{2} - \frac{1}{10}$ $\frac{2}{5}$
44. $10\frac{6}{7} - 4\frac{5}{6}$ $6\frac{1}{42}$

Subtraction: MIXED NUMBERS

When subtracting with mixed numbers, it is sometimes necessary to "borrow" from the whole number.

EXAMPLE $3\frac{1}{4} - 1\frac{5}{8} = \underline{\ ?\ }$

Solution:

Use the LCD to write like fractions. "Borrow" from the whole number when necessary. Then subtract.

LCD: 8

$$\begin{array}{rcr} 3\frac{1}{4} & = & 3\frac{2}{8} \\ -1\frac{5}{8} & = & -1\frac{5}{8} \\ \hline \end{array}$$

Since $\frac{2}{8}$ is less than $\frac{5}{8}$, borrow 1, or $\frac{8}{8}$, from 3. →

$$\begin{array}{rcr} 3\frac{1}{4} & = & 2\frac{10}{8} \\ -1\frac{5}{8} & = & -1\frac{5}{8} \\ \hline & & 1\frac{5}{8} \end{array}$$

$\frac{2}{8} + \frac{8}{8} = \frac{10}{8}$

PRACTICE

Subtract. Write each answer in lowest terms.

1. $3\frac{1}{4} - 1\frac{3}{8}$ **$1\frac{7}{8}$**
2. $6\frac{1}{4} - \frac{1}{2}$ **$5\frac{3}{4}$**
3. $11 - 8\frac{1}{4}$ **$2\frac{3}{4}$**
4. $5 - \frac{1}{2}$ **$4\frac{1}{2}$**
5. $1\frac{2}{3} - \frac{3}{4}$ **$\frac{11}{12}$**
6. $11\frac{1}{5} - 3\frac{1}{2}$ **$7\frac{7}{10}$**
7. $3\frac{1}{9} - 2\frac{3}{4}$ **$\frac{13}{36}$**
8. $7\frac{1}{6} - 2\frac{2}{3}$ **$4\frac{1}{2}$**
9. $8\frac{3}{5} - 5\frac{3}{4}$ **$2\frac{17}{20}$**
10. $7\frac{3}{8} - 5\frac{7}{12}$ **$1\frac{19}{24}$**
11. $8\frac{1}{7} - 4\frac{2}{3}$ **$3\frac{10}{21}$**
12. $11\frac{1}{2} - 2\frac{5}{8}$ **$8\frac{7}{8}$**
13. $6\frac{1}{12} - 3\frac{1}{4}$ **$2\frac{5}{6}$**
14. $2\frac{1}{15} - 1\frac{1}{10}$ **$\frac{29}{30}$**
15. $6 - 3\frac{1}{12}$ **$2\frac{11}{12}$**
16. $18\frac{3}{16} - 4\frac{5}{8}$ **$13\frac{9}{16}$**
17. $13\frac{3}{10} - \frac{3}{4}$ **$12\frac{11}{20}$**
18. $41\frac{2}{11} - 3\frac{1}{3}$ **$37\frac{28}{33}$**
19. $14 - 9\frac{2}{3}$ **$4\frac{1}{3}$**
20. $19\frac{2}{5} - 4\frac{3}{4}$ **$14\frac{13}{20}$**
21. $7\frac{1}{3} - 3\frac{5}{9}$ **$3\frac{7}{9}$**
22. $28 - 14\frac{3}{4}$ **$13\frac{1}{4}$**
23. $10 - 2\frac{1}{8}$ **$7\frac{7}{8}$**
24. $36 - 5\frac{4}{5}$ **$30\frac{1}{5}$**
25. $6\frac{5}{9} - 4\frac{7}{12}$ **$1\frac{35}{36}$**
26. $11\frac{3}{8} - 2\frac{2}{3}$ **$8\frac{17}{24}$**
27. $17\frac{1}{12} - 3\frac{3}{10}$ **$13\frac{47}{60}$**
28. $9\frac{2}{7} - 3\frac{2}{3}$ **$5\frac{13}{21}$**
29. $8\frac{1}{3} - 4\frac{7}{12}$ **$3\frac{3}{4}$**
30. $13\frac{3}{16} - 7\frac{2}{3}$ **$5\frac{25}{48}$**
31. $4\frac{3}{8} - 1\frac{5}{9}$ **$2\frac{59}{72}$**
32. $16\frac{2}{5} - 11\frac{5}{6}$ **$4\frac{17}{30}$**
33. $5 - 3\frac{2}{5}$ **$1\frac{3}{5}$**
34. $6\frac{1}{4} - 2\frac{3}{4}$ **$3\frac{1}{2}$**
35. $7\frac{1}{6} - 4\frac{2}{3}$ **$2\frac{1}{2}$**
36. $9\frac{2}{3} - 4\frac{6}{7}$ **$4\frac{17}{21}$**

Multiplication: FRACTIONS

When multiplying with fractions, you multiply the numerators and then multiply the denominators.

Sometimes you can divide a numerator and denominator by the same number before you multiply. (See Example 1b.)

EXAMPLE

a. $\frac{3}{5} \times \frac{11}{15} = \underline{\ ?\ }$

b. $\frac{5}{6} \times \frac{12}{13} = \underline{\ ?\ }$

Solutions:

a. $\frac{3}{5} \times \frac{11}{15} = \frac{3 \times 11}{5 \times 15}$

$= \frac{33}{75}$ *Write in lowest terms.*

$= \mathbf{\frac{11}{25}}$

b. $\frac{5}{6} \times \frac{12}{13} = \frac{5}{\cancel{6}_1} \times \frac{\cancel{12}^2}{13}$ $6 \div 6 = 1$; $12 \div 6 = 2$

$= \frac{5 \times 2}{1 \times 13}$

$= \mathbf{\frac{10}{13}}$

PRACTICE

Multiply. Write each answer in lowest terms.

1. $\frac{1}{5} \times \frac{1}{3}$ $\frac{1}{15}$ **2.** $\frac{3}{5} \times \frac{3}{8}$ $\frac{9}{40}$ **3.** $\frac{2}{3} \times \frac{5}{7}$ $\frac{10}{21}$ **4.** $\frac{3}{8} \times \frac{1}{5}$ $\frac{3}{40}$ **5.** $\frac{7}{15} \times \frac{1}{2}$ $\frac{7}{30}$

6. $\frac{3}{4} \times \frac{5}{7}$ $\frac{15}{28}$ **7.** $\frac{1}{12} \times \frac{3}{4}$ $\frac{1}{16}$ **8.** $\frac{3}{8} \times \frac{1}{7}$ $\frac{3}{56}$ **9.** $\frac{6}{13} \times \frac{3}{5}$ $\frac{18}{65}$ **10.** $\frac{3}{11} \times \frac{8}{10}$ $\frac{12}{55}$

11. $\frac{3}{8} \times \frac{11}{20}$ $\frac{33}{160}$ **12.** $\frac{8}{15} \times \frac{4}{9}$ $\frac{32}{135}$ **13.** $\frac{4}{5} \times \frac{3}{7}$ $\frac{12}{35}$ **14.** $\frac{2}{9} \times \frac{4}{5}$ $\frac{8}{45}$ **15.** $\frac{3}{4} \times \frac{3}{5}$ $\frac{9}{20}$

16. $\frac{1}{2} \times \frac{3}{5}$ $\frac{3}{10}$ **17.** $\frac{2}{7} \times \frac{1}{6}$ $\frac{1}{21}$ **18.** $\frac{3}{5} \times \frac{1}{8}$ $\frac{3}{40}$ **19.** $\frac{4}{7} \times \frac{3}{8}$ $\frac{3}{14}$ **20.** $\frac{3}{5} \times \frac{5}{7}$ $\frac{3}{7}$

21. $\frac{1}{12} \times \frac{2}{7}$ $\frac{1}{42}$ **22.** $\frac{8}{9} \times \frac{15}{32}$ $\frac{5}{12}$ **23.** $\frac{5}{21} \times \frac{3}{8}$ $\frac{5}{56}$ **24.** $\frac{2}{9} \times \frac{18}{25}$ $\frac{4}{25}$ **25.** $\frac{3}{11} \times \frac{22}{39}$ $\frac{2}{13}$

26. $\frac{6}{7} \times \frac{21}{23}$ $\frac{18}{23}$ **27.** $\frac{8}{17} \times \frac{34}{45}$ $\frac{16}{45}$ **28.** $\frac{4}{5} \times \frac{10}{16}$ $\frac{1}{2}$ **29.** $\frac{7}{50} \times \frac{25}{49}$ $\frac{1}{14}$ **30.** $\frac{8}{15} \times \frac{45}{56}$ $\frac{3}{7}$

31. $\frac{4}{5} \times \frac{5}{7}$ $\frac{4}{7}$ **32.** $\frac{3}{5} \times \frac{2}{3}$ $\frac{2}{5}$ **33.** $\frac{4}{5} \times \frac{7}{12}$ $\frac{7}{15}$ **34.** $\frac{2}{9} \times \frac{3}{4}$ $\frac{1}{6}$ **35.** $\frac{7}{16} \times \frac{4}{21}$ $\frac{1}{12}$

36. $\frac{7}{8} \times \frac{8}{9}$ $\frac{7}{9}$ **37.** $\frac{5}{8} \times \frac{4}{9}$ $\frac{5}{18}$ **38.** $\frac{4}{5} \times \frac{5}{12}$ $\frac{1}{3}$ **39.** $\frac{1}{6} \times \frac{3}{7}$ $\frac{1}{14}$ **40.** $\frac{4}{11} \times \frac{33}{40}$ $\frac{3}{10}$

41. $\frac{3}{5} \times \frac{15}{24}$ $\frac{3}{8}$ **42.** $\frac{7}{12} \times \frac{24}{25}$ $\frac{14}{25}$ **43.** $\frac{6}{13} \times \frac{13}{18}$ $\frac{1}{3}$ **44.** $\frac{3}{4} \times \frac{16}{33}$ $\frac{4}{11}$ **45.** $\frac{2}{3} \times \frac{18}{21}$ $\frac{4}{7}$

46. $\frac{5}{8} \times \frac{3}{20}$ $\frac{3}{32}$ **47.** $\frac{4}{7} \times \frac{5}{16}$ $\frac{5}{28}$ **48.** $\frac{5}{9} \times \frac{3}{20}$ $\frac{1}{12}$ **49.** $\frac{2}{5} \times \frac{3}{8}$ $\frac{3}{20}$ **50.** $\frac{8}{13} \times \frac{39}{40}$ $\frac{3}{5}$

Multiplication: MIXED NUMBERS

Writing a fraction for each mixed number is the first step in multiplying with mixed numbers.

Mixed Number	1 Multiply the denominator and the whole number.	2 Add this product to the numerator.	3 Write this sum over the denominator.
$5\frac{3}{4}$	$4 \times 5 = 20$	$20 + 3 = 23$	$\frac{23}{4}$ ◀ $5\frac{3}{4} = \frac{23}{4}$

EXAMPLE

a. $5 \times 3\frac{7}{10} = \underline{?}$ **b.** $2\frac{2}{5} \times 3\frac{1}{8} = \underline{?}$

Write a fraction for each mixed number, then multiply.

a. $5 \times 3\frac{7}{10} = \frac{5}{1} \times \frac{37}{10}$

$= \frac{\overset{1}{\cancel{5}}}{1} \times \frac{37}{\underset{2}{\cancel{10}}}$

$= \frac{37}{2}$ ◀ $\frac{1 \times 37}{1 \times 2}$

$= \mathbf{18\frac{1}{2}}$

b. $2\frac{2}{5} \times 3\frac{1}{8} = \frac{12}{5} \times \frac{25}{8}$

$= \frac{\overset{3}{\cancel{12}}}{\underset{1}{\cancel{5}}} \times \frac{\overset{5}{\cancel{25}}}{\underset{2}{\cancel{8}}}$

$= \frac{15}{2}$ ◀ $\frac{3 \times 5}{1 \times 2}$

$= \mathbf{7\frac{1}{2}}$

PRACTICE

Write a fraction for each mixed number.

1. $4\frac{7}{8}$ $\frac{39}{8}$ **2.** $3\frac{2}{3}$ $\frac{11}{3}$ **3.** $5\frac{1}{8}$ $\frac{41}{8}$ **4.** $7\frac{2}{5}$ $\frac{37}{5}$ **5.** $6\frac{5}{7}$ $\frac{47}{7}$ **6.** $3\frac{4}{9}$ $\frac{31}{9}$ **7.** $2\frac{1}{4}$ $\frac{9}{4}$

8. $3\frac{7}{9}$ $\frac{34}{9}$ **9.** $4\frac{1}{7}$ $\frac{29}{7}$ **10.** $8\frac{1}{3}$ $\frac{25}{3}$ **11.** $2\frac{5}{8}$ $\frac{21}{8}$ **12.** $11\frac{1}{2}$ $\frac{23}{2}$ **13.** $4\frac{3}{4}$ $\frac{19}{4}$ **14.** $3\frac{7}{10}$ $\frac{37}{10}$

Multiply. Write each answer in lowest terms. (Example 2)

15. $7 \times 2\frac{1}{2}$ $17\frac{1}{2}$ **16.** $8 \times 6\frac{1}{3}$ $50\frac{2}{3}$ **17.** $12\frac{1}{3} \times 1\frac{4}{5}$ $22\frac{1}{5}$ **18.** $2\frac{2}{3} \times 4\frac{1}{2}$ 12 **19.** $12\frac{1}{3} \times 1\frac{1}{8}$ $13\frac{7}{8}$

20. $16\frac{1}{2} \times 2\frac{1}{3}$ $38\frac{1}{2}$ **21.** $6\frac{3}{5} \times \frac{10}{11}$ 6 **22.** $5\frac{1}{8} \times \frac{1}{41}$ $\frac{1}{8}$ **23.** $\frac{2}{5} \times 3\frac{1}{3}$ $1\frac{1}{3}$ **24.** $4\frac{2}{7} \times 49$ 210

25. $7\frac{1}{3} \times 12$ 88 **26.** $\frac{1}{8} \times 4\frac{3}{4}$ $\frac{19}{32}$ **27.** $1\frac{3}{7} \times 2\frac{1}{5}$ $3\frac{1}{7}$ **28.** $6\frac{1}{2} \times 2\frac{1}{3}$ $15\frac{1}{6}$ **29.** $1\frac{5}{8} \times 3\frac{1}{2}$ $5\frac{11}{16}$

30. $\frac{7}{8} \times 4\frac{1}{2}$ $3\frac{15}{16}$ **31.** $7\frac{1}{3} \times 8\frac{1}{2}$ $62\frac{1}{3}$ **32.** $1\frac{1}{2} \times 2\frac{3}{4}$ $4\frac{1}{8}$ **33.** $4\frac{1}{2} \times \frac{2}{9}$ 1 **34.** $4\frac{2}{3} \times 5\frac{1}{6}$ $24\frac{1}{9}$

Division: FRACTIONS

Two numbers whose product is one are **reciprocals** of each other.

$\frac{4}{9} \times \frac{9}{4} = 1$ **Reciprocals:** $\frac{4}{9}$ and $\frac{9}{4}$

$7 \times \frac{1}{7} = 1$ **Reciprocals:** 7 and $\frac{1}{7}$

Dividing by a number is <u>the same</u> as multiplying by its reciprocal.

EXAMPLE **a.** $\frac{3}{7} \div \frac{9}{14} = \underline{\ ?\ }$ **b.** $\frac{5}{9} \div 15 = \underline{\ ?\ }$

Solutions: Use the reciprocal of the divisor to write the corresponding multiplication problem, then multiply.

a. $\frac{3}{7} \div \frac{9}{14} = \frac{3}{7} \times \frac{14}{9}$ ◀ *The reciprocal of $\frac{9}{14}$ is $\frac{14}{9}$.*

$= \frac{\overset{1}{\cancel{3}}}{\underset{1}{\cancel{7}}} \times \frac{\overset{2}{\cancel{14}}}{\underset{3}{\cancel{9}}}$

$= \frac{2}{3}$

b. $\frac{5}{9} \div 15 = \frac{5}{9} \times \frac{1}{15}$ ◀ *The reciprocal of 15 is $\frac{1}{15}$.*

$= \frac{\overset{1}{\cancel{5}}}{9} \times \frac{1}{\underset{3}{\cancel{15}}}$

$= \frac{1}{27}$

PRACTICE

Write the reciprocal of each number.

1. $\frac{2}{3}$ $\frac{3}{2}$ **2.** $\frac{3}{5}$ $\frac{5}{3}$ **3.** $\frac{9}{7}$ $\frac{7}{9}$ **4.** 2 $\frac{1}{2}$ **5.** 4 $\frac{1}{4}$ **6.** $\frac{5}{8}$ $\frac{8}{5}$ **7.** $\frac{6}{7}$ $\frac{7}{6}$ **8.** $\frac{5}{3}$ $\frac{3}{5}$

9. 15 $\frac{1}{15}$ **10.** 8 $\frac{1}{8}$ **11.** $\frac{3}{2}$ $\frac{2}{3}$ **12.** $\frac{7}{12}$ $\frac{12}{7}$ **13.** $\frac{8}{13}$ $\frac{13}{8}$ **14.** $\frac{2}{11}$ $\frac{11}{2}$ **15.** $\frac{6}{13}$ $\frac{13}{6}$ **16.** 18 $\frac{1}{18}$

Divide.

17. $\frac{1}{4} \div \frac{1}{3}$ $\frac{3}{4}$ **18.** $\frac{3}{8} \div 3$ $\frac{1}{8}$ **19.** $\frac{2}{7} \div \frac{1}{8}$ $2\frac{2}{7}$ **20.** $\frac{4}{5} \div \frac{16}{25}$ $1\frac{1}{4}$ **21.** $\frac{7}{10} \div 14$ $\frac{1}{20}$

22. $\frac{4}{9} \div 16$ $\frac{1}{36}$ **23.** $6 \div \frac{1}{4}$ 24 **24.** $12 \div \frac{3}{5}$ 20 **25.** $\frac{1}{18} \div \frac{2}{45}$ $1\frac{1}{4}$ **26.** $\frac{1}{2} \div 6$ $\frac{1}{12}$

27. $6 \div \frac{3}{7}$ 14 **28.** $\frac{4}{7} \div \frac{2}{3}$ $\frac{6}{7}$ **29.** $\frac{9}{10} \div \frac{3}{5}$ $1\frac{1}{2}$ **30.** $81 \div \frac{9}{11}$ 99 **31.** $\frac{7}{6} \div \frac{5}{3}$ $\frac{7}{10}$

32. $\frac{2}{9} \div \frac{1}{3}$ $\frac{2}{3}$ **33.** $7 \div \frac{7}{12}$ 12 **34.** $16 \div \frac{8}{13}$ 26 **35.** $\frac{7}{22} \div 14$ $\frac{1}{44}$ **36.** $\frac{9}{10} \div 15$ $\frac{3}{50}$

37. $\frac{1}{5} \div \frac{1}{10}$ 2 **38.** $4 \div \frac{1}{4}$ 16 **39.** $18 \div \frac{2}{9}$ 81 **40.** $8 \div \frac{1}{2}$ 16 **41.** $\frac{3}{5} \div \frac{15}{20}$ $\frac{4}{5}$

42. $\frac{2}{9} \div \frac{20}{27}$ $\frac{3}{10}$ **43.** $18 \div \frac{1}{3}$ 54 **44.** $\frac{2}{5} \div \frac{1}{25}$ 10 **45.** $\frac{3}{8} \div \frac{6}{16}$ 1 **46.** $\frac{1}{7} \div 21$ $\frac{1}{147}$

47. $\frac{4}{11} \div \frac{2}{5}$ $\frac{10}{11}$ **48.** $\frac{11}{12} \div 22$ $\frac{1}{24}$ **49.** $\frac{1}{5} \div \frac{3}{10}$ $\frac{2}{3}$ **50.** $5 \div \frac{1}{5}$ 25 **51.** $14 \div \frac{7}{8}$ 16

52. $\frac{4}{5} \div \frac{28}{30}$ $\frac{6}{7}$ **53.** $\frac{3}{10} \div \frac{9}{20}$ $\frac{2}{3}$ **54.** $16 \div \frac{1}{4}$ 64 **55.** $\frac{3}{5} \div \frac{3}{25}$ 5 **56.** $\frac{3}{4} \div \frac{9}{12}$ 1

Division: MIXED NUMBERS

EXAMPLE 2 **a.** $7\frac{3}{4} \div 7\frac{1}{2} = \underline{\ ?\ }$ **b.** $12 \div 2\frac{4}{7} = \underline{\ ?\ }$

Solutions: Write a fraction for each mixed number, then divide.

a. $7\frac{3}{4} \div 7\frac{1}{2} = \frac{31}{4} \div \frac{15}{2}$

$= \frac{31}{4} \times \frac{2}{15}$ ◀ *The reciprocal of $\frac{15}{2}$ is $\frac{2}{15}$.*

$= \frac{31}{\cancel{4}_{2}} \times \frac{\cancel{2}^{1}}{15}$

$= \frac{31}{30}$ ◀ *Write a mixed number for $\frac{31}{30}$.*

$= \mathbf{1\frac{1}{30}}$

b. $12 \div 2\frac{4}{7} = \frac{12}{1} \div \frac{18}{7}$

$= \frac{12}{1} \times \frac{7}{18}$ ◀ *The reciprocal of $\frac{18}{7}$ is $\frac{7}{18}$.*

$= \frac{\cancel{12}^{2}}{1} \times \frac{7}{\cancel{18}_{3}}$

$= \frac{14}{3}$

$= \mathbf{4\frac{2}{3}}$

PRACTICE

Write the reciprocal of each mixed number.

1. $2\frac{5}{16}$ $\frac{16}{37}$ **2.** $3\frac{5}{7}$ $\frac{7}{26}$ **3.** $4\frac{1}{10}$ $\frac{10}{41}$ **4.** $2\frac{1}{2}$ $\frac{2}{5}$ **5.** $1\frac{5}{8}$ $\frac{8}{13}$ **6.** $3\frac{1}{12}$ $\frac{12}{37}$ **7.** $1\frac{2}{3}$ $\frac{3}{5}$ **8.** $4\frac{1}{3}$ $\frac{3}{13}$

9. $1\frac{1}{2}$ $\frac{2}{3}$ **10.** $7\frac{1}{8}$ $\frac{8}{57}$ **11.** $3\frac{3}{4}$ $\frac{4}{15}$ **12.** $7\frac{7}{10}$ $\frac{10}{77}$ **13.** $5\frac{1}{8}$ $\frac{8}{41}$ **14.** $3\frac{1}{6}$ $\frac{6}{19}$ **15.** $1\frac{5}{8}$ $\frac{8}{13}$ **16.** $6\frac{3}{8}$ $\frac{8}{51}$

Divide.

17. $7\frac{1}{2} \div 15$ $\frac{1}{2}$ **18.** $2\frac{1}{2} \div 3\frac{1}{3}$ $\frac{3}{4}$ **19.** $8\frac{2}{5} \div 4\frac{1}{5}$ 2 **20.** $9\frac{3}{4} \div 13$ $\frac{3}{4}$ **21.** $2\frac{4}{5} \div 7$ $\frac{2}{5}$

22. $9\frac{2}{3} \div 4\frac{1}{6}$ $2\frac{8}{25}$ **23.** $8\frac{1}{2} \div 3\frac{2}{5}$ $2\frac{1}{2}$ **24.** $12 \div 1\frac{1}{2}$ 8 **25.** $4 \div 1\frac{1}{3}$ 3 **26.** $7\frac{1}{5} \div 2\frac{2}{5}$ 3

27. $4\frac{5}{9} \div \frac{5}{18}$ $16\frac{2}{5}$ **28.** $3 \div 7\frac{1}{2}$ $\frac{2}{5}$ **29.** $33 \div 4\frac{1}{8}$ 8 **30.** $2\frac{1}{2} \div 2\frac{1}{2}$ 1 **31.** $4\frac{3}{4} \div 3\frac{1}{4}$ $1\frac{6}{13}$

32. $8\frac{4}{5} \div \frac{11}{15}$ 12 **33.** $12\frac{3}{8} \div 1\frac{3}{8}$ 9 **34.** $2\frac{1}{12} \div \frac{5}{6}$ $2\frac{1}{2}$ **35.** $4\frac{8}{9} \div 2\frac{2}{3}$ $1\frac{5}{6}$ **36.** $10\frac{2}{5} \div 3\frac{1}{5}$ $3\frac{1}{4}$

37. $14 \div 1\frac{2}{5}$ 10 **38.** $21 \div 3\frac{3}{7}$ $6\frac{1}{8}$ **39.** $5\frac{1}{3} \div 8$ $\frac{2}{3}$ **40.** $1\frac{1}{3} \div 2$ $\frac{2}{3}$ **41.** $4\frac{1}{6} \div 6\frac{1}{4}$ $\frac{2}{3}$

42. $2\frac{1}{4} \div 3\frac{3}{8}$ $\frac{2}{3}$ **43.** $7\frac{1}{2} \div 1\frac{1}{4}$ 6 **44.** $\frac{3}{4} \div 4\frac{1}{12}$ $\frac{9}{49}$ **45.** $4\frac{6}{7} \div 8\frac{1}{2}$ $\frac{4}{7}$ **46.** $\frac{5}{12} \div 60$ $\frac{1}{144}$

47. $3\frac{4}{9} \div \frac{12}{27}$ $7\frac{3}{4}$ **48.** $10 \div 2\frac{1}{2}$ 4 **49.** $26 \div 3\frac{1}{4}$ 8 **50.** $7\frac{1}{8} \div 7\frac{1}{8}$ 1 **51.** $5\frac{1}{4} \div 2\frac{3}{4}$ $1\frac{10}{11}$

52. $6\frac{3}{5} \div 1\frac{1}{2}$ $4\frac{2}{5}$ **53.** $9\frac{5}{8} \div 2\frac{5}{8}$ $3\frac{2}{3}$ **54.** $4\frac{1}{6} \div \frac{5}{6}$ 5 **55.** $3\frac{7}{9} \div 1\frac{2}{3}$ $2\frac{4}{15}$ **56.** $7\frac{2}{3} \div 5\frac{3}{4}$ $1\frac{1}{3}$

57. $12 \div 1\frac{3}{5}$ $7\frac{1}{2}$ **58.** $18 \div 4\frac{1}{2}$ 4 **59.** $6\frac{1}{3} \div 19$ $\frac{1}{3}$ **60.** $5\frac{4}{7} \div 10\frac{1}{7}$ $\frac{39}{71}$ **61.** $9\frac{2}{3} \div 145$ $\frac{1}{15}$

Rounding and Estimation

The rules for rounding mixed numbers can help you to estimate answers.

Rules for Rounding Mixed Numbers

1. Look at the fractional part of the mixed number.
2. **a.** If the fraction is less than $\frac{1}{2}$, round <u>down</u> to the nearest whole number.
   b. If the fraction is greater than or equal to $\frac{1}{2}$, round <u>up</u> to the next whole number.

EXAMPLE

a. $4\frac{1}{3}$ rounded to the nearest whole number is **4.**

b. $8\frac{1}{2}$ rounded to the nearest whole number is **9.**

c. $12\frac{7}{8}$ rounded to the nearest whole number is **13.**

PRACTICE

Round to the nearest whole number.

1. $3\frac{1}{3}$ 3 **2.** $7\frac{7}{8}$ 8 **3.** $2\frac{2}{9}$ 2 **4.** $4\frac{11}{12}$ 5 **5.** $15\frac{1}{2}$ 16 **6.** $6\frac{3}{5}$ 7 **7.** $11\frac{13}{25}$ 12

8. $2\frac{9}{16}$ 3 **9.** $3\frac{3}{4}$ 4 **10.** $4\frac{5}{7}$ 5 **11.** $6\frac{3}{13}$ 6 **12.** $1\frac{1}{7}$ 1 **13.** $5\frac{4}{9}$ 5 **14.** $8\frac{3}{8}$ 8

15. $4\frac{2}{11}$ 4 **16.** $6\frac{13}{18}$ 7 **17.** $6\frac{5}{11}$ 6 **18.** $8\frac{6}{12}$ 9 **19.** $3\frac{9}{17}$ 4 **20.** $18\frac{3}{10}$ 18 **21.** $2\frac{4}{7}$ 3

Choose the best estimate. Choose a, b, c, or d.

22. $2\frac{8}{9} + 3\frac{1}{10}$ a	**a.** $3 + 3$	**b.** $2 + 3$	**c.** $3 + 4$	**d.** $2 + 2$
23. $112\frac{1}{8} + 5\frac{4}{5}$ c	**a.** $113 + 6$	**b.** $111 + 5$	**c.** $112 + 6$	**d.** $112 + 5$
24. $21\frac{7}{8} - 17\frac{1}{8}$ c	**a.** $21 - 17$	**b.** $21 - 18$	**c.** $22 - 17$	**d.** $20 - 18$
25. $7\frac{1}{5} \div 6\frac{1}{8}$ c	**a.** $7 \div 7$	**b.** $8 \div 5$	**c.** $7 \div 6$	**d.** $8 \div 6$
26. $14\frac{8}{9} \div 5\frac{1}{12}$ a	**a.** $15 \div 5$	**b.** $14 \div 5$	**c.** $14 \div 6$	**d.** $15 \div 6$
27. $21\frac{1}{8} \times 14\frac{9}{10}$ d	**a.** 22×15	**b.** 21×14	**c.** 22×14	**d.** 21×15
28. $\frac{9}{10} \times 10\frac{2}{11}$ a	**a.** 10	**b.** 12	**c.** 13	**d.** 14
29. $6\frac{1}{5} \div 1\frac{1}{10}$ b	**a.** 4	**b.** 6	**c.** 8	**d.** 10

Estimation Ex. 22–29

Equations: ADDITION

An **equation** is a sentence that uses "=". Here are some examples of equations.

$n + 17 = 21$ $\qquad$ $n - 2.3 = 6.5$ $\qquad$ $14 + n = 25$

The letter n is called a **variable.** To solve an equation for n, you have to get **n alone on one side of the equation.**

EXAMPLE Solve and check: **a.** $n + 7 = 15$ $\qquad$ **b.** $16 + n = 25$

Solutions:

Use subtraction to solve an **addition equation.**

a. $n + 7 = 15$ — *Subtract 7 from each side.*

$n + 7 - \mathbf{7} = 15 - \mathbf{7}$

$n = \mathbf{8}$

Check: $n + 7 = 15$ — *Replace n with 8.*

$8 + 7 \stackrel{?}{=} 15$

$15 \stackrel{?}{=} 15$ Yes ✓

b. $16 + n = 25$ — *Subtract 16 from each side.*

$16 - \mathbf{16} + n = 25 - \mathbf{16}$

$n = \mathbf{9}$

Check: $16 + n = 25$ — *Replace n with 9.*

$16 + 9 \stackrel{?}{=} 25$

$25 \stackrel{?}{=} 25$ Yes ✓

PRACTICE

Solve and check.

1. $n + 8 = 13$ 5	**2.** $n + 5 = 9$ 4	**3.** $n + 11 = 20$ 9	**4.** $n + 4 = 6$ 2
5. $n + 18 = 37$ 19	**6.** $n + 34 = 38$ 4	**7.** $n + 55 = 62$ 7	**8.** $n + 29 = 38$ 9
9. $n + 11 = 23$ 12	**10.** $n + 29 = 34$ 5	**11.** $n + 18 = 23$ 5	**12.** $n + 15 = 30$ 15
13. $n + 6 = 21$ 15	**14.** $n + 8 = 46$ 38	**15.** $n + 39 = 74$ 35	**16.** $n + 64 = 120$ 56
17. $n + 48 = 63$ 15	**18.** $n + 53 = 81$ 28	**19.** $n + 75 = 110$ 35	**20.** $n + 57 = 96$ 39
21. $14 + n = 27$ 13	**22.** $38 + n = 51$ 13	**23.** $42 + n = 80$ 38	**24.** $18 + n = 95$ 77
25. $26 + n = 32$ 6	**26.** $51 + n = 68$ 17	**27.** $26 + n = 43$ 17	**28.** $35 + n = 54$ 19
29. $84 + n = 108$ 24	**30.** $57 + n = 100$ 43	**31.** $55 + n = 121$ 66	**32.** $79 + n = 117$ 38
33. $81 + n = 126$ 45	**34.** $14 + n = 23$ 9	**35.** $60 + n = 122$ 62	**36.** $32 + n = 140$ 108
37. $17 + n = 26$ 9	**38.** $65 + n = 92$ 27	**39.** $72 + n = 151$ 79	**40.** $37 + n = 165$ 128
41. $n + 1.2 = 3.4$ 2.2	**42.** $n + 3.7 = 11.2$ 7.5	**43.** $4.6 + n = 8.4$ 3.8	**44.** $6.5 + n = 12.3$ 5.8
45. $n + 3.4 = 7$ 3.6	**46.** $n + 1.9 = 5.3$ 3.4	**47.** $5.9 + n = 10$ 4.1	**48.** $9.1 + n = 15.2$ 6.1

Equations: SUBTRACTION

To solve a **subtraction equation** such as $n - 13 = 21$, *add* 13 to each side of the equation.

EXAMPLE Solve and check: $n - 36 = 25$

Solution:

Use addition to solve a subtraction equation.

$$n - 36 = 25$$

Add 36 to each side.

$$n - 36 + \mathbf{36} = 25 + \mathbf{36}$$

$$n = 61$$

Check: $n - 36 = 25$

Replace n with 61.

$$61 - 36 \stackrel{?}{=} 25$$

$$25 = 25 \quad \text{Yes} ✓$$

PRACTICE

Solve and check.

1. $n - 6 = 11$ 17	**2.** $n - 5 = 4$ 9	**3.** $n - 3 = 8$ 11	**4.** $n - 16 = 20$ 36
5. $n - 29 = 8$ 37	**6.** $n - 7 = 49$ 56	**7.** $n - 8 = 31$ 39	**8.** $n - 27 = 5$ 32
9. $n - 14 = 74$ 88	**10.** $n - 24 = 36$ 60	**11.** $n - 16 = 12$ 28	**12.** $n - 26 = 37$ 63
13. $n - 13 = 42$ 55	**14.** $n - 84 = 93$ 177	**15.** $n - 64 = 27$ 91	**16.** $n - 29 = 18$ 47
17. $n - 24 = 63$ 87	**18.** $n - 42 = 37$ 79	**19.** $n - 45 = 57$ 102	**20.** $n - 18 = 38$ 56
21. $n - 87 = 22$ 109	**22.** $n - 34 = 69$ 103	**23.** $n - 63 = 27$ 90	**24.** $n - 14 = 98$ 112
25. $n - 5 = 19$ 24	**26.** $n - 6 = 12$ 18	**27.** $n - 14 = 16$ 30	**28.** $n - 25 = 16$ 41
29. $n - 72 = 12$ 84	**30.** $n - 46 = 18$ 64	**31.** $n - 78 = 12$ 90	**32.** $n - 27 = 46$ 73
33. $n - 38 = 14$ 52	**34.** $n - 14 = 39$ 53	**35.** $n - 58 = 96$ 154	**36.** $n - 64 = 88$ 152
37. $n - 3.2 = 6.1$ 9.3	**38.** $n - 7.5 = 8.4$ 15.9	**39.** $n - 1.6 = 8$ 9.6	**40.** $n - 5 = 7.3$ 12.3
41. $n - 6.3 = 8$ 14.3	**42.** $n - 4.7 = 10$ 14.7	**43.** $n - 3.7 = 9.3$ 13.0	**44.** $n - 3 = 6.2$ 9.2
45. $n - 8 = 9.1$ 17.1	**46.** $n - 3.2 = 7$ 10.2	**47.** $n - 2.9 = 6.1$ 9.0	**48.** $n - 4 = 16.5$ 20.5

Equations: MULTIPLICATION

An equation such as $3n = 81$ is a **multiplication equation.** Note that $3n$ means $3 \times n$.

EXAMPLE

Solve and check: **a.** $5n = 20$ **b.** $36 = 4n$

Solutions:

Use division to solve a multiplication equation.

a. $5n = 20$ ◀ *Divide each side by 5.*

$\frac{5n}{5} = \frac{20}{5}$

$n = 4$

Check: $5n = 20$ ◀ *Replace n with 4.*

$5 \times 4 \stackrel{?}{=} 20$

$20 \stackrel{?}{=} 20$ Yes ✓

b. $36 = 4n$ ◀ *Divide each side by 4.*

$\frac{36}{4} = \frac{4n}{4}$

$9 = n$

Check: $36 = 4n$ ◀ *Replace n with 9.*

$36 \stackrel{?}{=} 4 \times 9$

$36 \stackrel{?}{=} 36$ Yes ✓

PRACTICE

Solve and check.

1. $7n = 42$ 6 **2.** $8n = 32$ 4 **3.** $11n = 88$ 8 **4.** $25n = 100$ 4

5. $6n = 30$ 5 **6.** $6n = 156$ 26 **7.** $5n = 820$ 164 **8.** $12n = 288$ 24

9. $7n = 98$ 14 **10.** $13n = 104$ 8 **11.** $37n = 74$ 2 **12.** $41n = 123$ 3

13. $71n = 284$ 4 **14.** $21n = 105$ 5 **15.** $19n = 95$ 5 **16.** $25n = 375$ 15

17. $21n = 42$ 2 **18.** $18n = 270$ 15 **19.** $35n = 140$ 4 **20.** $27n = 108$ 4

21. $63 = 7n$ 9 **22.** $84 = 7n$ 12 **23.** $300 = 15n$ 20 **24.** $120 = 24n$ 5

25. $144 = 72n$ 2 **26.** $38 = 19n$ 2 **27.** $115 = 5n$ 23 **28.** $96 = 16n$ 6

29. $112 = 28n$ 4 **30.** $350 = 14n$ 25 **31.** $340 = 17n$ 20 **32.** $221 = 13n$ 17

33. $130 = 26n$ 5 **34.** $120 = 15n$ 8 **35.** $144 = 24n$ 6 **36.** $756 = 21n$ 36

37. $104 = 13n$ 8 **38.** $216 = 24n$ 9 **39.** $126 = 18n$ 7 **40.** $126 = 14n$ 9

41. $0.8n = 9.6$ 12 **42.** $0.5n = 2.5$ 5 **43.** $0.2n = 1.8$ 9 **44.** $57.6 = 2.4n$ 24

45. $39.6 = 3.3n$ 12 **46.** $5n = 27.5$ 5.5 **47.** $8n = 64.8$ 8.1 **48.** $6.4 = 3.2n$ 2

Equations: DIVISION

To solve a **division equation** such as $\frac{n}{4} = 21$, *multiply* each side by 4.
Remember: You can think of $\frac{n}{4}$ as $n \div 4$.

EXAMPLE Solve and check: **a.** $\frac{n}{3} = 75$ **b.** $8 = \frac{n}{7}$

Solution:

Use multiplication to solve a division equation.

a. $\frac{n}{3} = 75$ *Multiply each side by 3.*

$\frac{n}{3} \times \mathbf{3} = 75 \times \mathbf{3}$

$n = \mathbf{225}$

Check: $\frac{n}{3} = 75$ *Replace n with 225.*

$\frac{225}{3} \stackrel{?}{=} 75$

$75 \stackrel{?}{=} 75$ Yes ✓

b. $8 = \frac{n}{7}$ *Multiply each side by 7.*

$8 \times \mathbf{7} = \frac{n}{7} \times \mathbf{7}$

$\mathbf{56} = n$

Check: $8 = \frac{n}{7}$ *Replace n with 56.*

$8 \stackrel{?}{=} \frac{56}{7}$

$8 \stackrel{?}{=} 8$ Yes ✓

PRACTICE

Solve and check.

1. $\frac{n}{7} = 2$ **14**	**2.** $\frac{n}{3} = 18$ **54**	**3.** $\frac{n}{5} = 20$ **100**	**4.** $\frac{n}{3} = 11$ **33**
5. $\frac{n}{10} = 16$ **160**	**6.** $\frac{n}{8} = 8$ **64**	**7.** $\frac{n}{15} = 10$ **150**	**8.** $\frac{n}{4} = 2$ **8**
9. $\frac{n}{11} = 5$ **55**	**10.** $\frac{n}{2} = 27$ **54**	**11.** $\frac{n}{4} = 20$ **80**	**12.** $\frac{n}{18} = 9$ **162**
13. $\frac{n}{9} = 8$ **72**	**14.** $\frac{n}{12} = 4$ **48**	**15.** $\frac{n}{8} = 5$ **40**	**16.** $\frac{n}{8} = 25$ **200**
17. $\frac{n}{3} = 29$ **87**	**18.** $\frac{n}{27} = 15$ **405**	**19.** $\frac{n}{16} = 34$ **544**	**20.** $\frac{n}{7} = 31$ **217**
21. $14 = \frac{n}{6}$ **84**	**22.** $24 = \frac{n}{4}$ **96**	**23.** $13 = \frac{n}{7}$ **91**	**24.** $41 = \frac{n}{6}$ **246**
25. $25 = \frac{n}{7}$ **175**	**26.** $13 = \frac{n}{9}$ **117**	**27.** $8 = \frac{n}{11}$ **88**	**28.** $12 = \frac{n}{20}$ **240**
29. $18 = \frac{n}{13}$ **234**	**30.** $24 = \frac{n}{12}$ **288**	**31.** $16 = \frac{n}{18}$ **288**	**32.** $10 = \frac{n}{24}$ **240**
33. $21 = \frac{n}{20}$ **420**	**34.** $25 = \frac{n}{14}$ **350**	**35.** $19 = \frac{n}{10}$ **190**	**36.** $6 = \frac{n}{22}$ **132**
37. $13 = \frac{n}{8}$ **104**	**38.** $87 = \frac{n}{10}$ **870**	**39.** $11 = \frac{n}{11}$ **121**	**40.** $28 = \frac{n}{19}$ **532**
41. $\frac{n}{2} = 1.3$ **2.6**	**42.** $\frac{n}{6} = 9.7$ **58.2**	**43.** $10 = \frac{n}{3.7}$ **37**	**44.** $5.8 = \frac{n}{13}$ **75.4**
45. $4.2 = \frac{n}{5.5}$ **23.1**	**46.** $\frac{n}{4} = 1.2$ **4.8**	**47.** $\frac{n}{3} = 18.7$ **56.1**	**48.** $\frac{n}{5.5} = 5$ **27.5**

Solving Equations

Sometimes you use more than one operation to solve an equation.

EXAMPLE Solve and check: $24n + 7 = 55$

Solution:

[1] Subtract the same number from each side of the equation.

$24n + 7 = 55$ ◀ ***Subtract 7 from each side.***

[2] Divide each side of the equation by the same number (except zero).

$$24n + 7 - \mathbf{7} = 55 - \mathbf{7}$$

$$24n = 48$$ ◀ ***Divide each side by 24.***

$$\frac{24n}{\mathbf{24}} = \frac{48}{\mathbf{24}}$$

$$n = \mathbf{2}$$

Check:

$$24n + 7 = 55$$ ◀ ***Replace n by 2.***

$$24 \times 2 + 7 \stackrel{?}{=} 55$$

$$48 + 7 \stackrel{?}{=} 55$$

$$55 \stackrel{?}{=} 55 \quad \text{Yes}✓$$

PRACTICE

Solve and check.

1. $13n + 6 = 32$ **2**
2. $5n + 11 = 36$ **5**
3. $11n + 5 = 115$ **10**
4. $8n - 5 = 59$ **8**
5. $7n - 9 = 40$ **7**
6. $12n - 10 = 122$ **11**
7. $5n + 16 = 96$ **16**
8. $4n + 28 = 68$ **10**
9. $21n + 6 = 111$ **5**
10. $18n - 7 = 83$ **5**
11. $13n - 5 = 60$ **5**
12. $12n - 3 = 33$ **3**
13. $18n + 12 = 102$ **5**
14. $7n - 8 = 62$ **10**
15. $2n + 50 = 100$ **25**
16. $4n + 0.6 = 5.4$ **1.2**
17. $2n + 0.3 = 2.9$ **1.3**
18. $12n + 1.7 = 4.1$ **0.2**
19. $3n - 2.4 = 2.4$ **1.6**
20. $7n + 0.7 = 29.4$ **4.1**
21. $16n + 2.9 = 52.5$ **3.1**
22. $0.3n + 4 = 5.5$ **5**
23. $3.2n - 4 = 12$ **5**
24. $1.9n + 6 = 17.4$ **6**

More on Solving Equations

EXAMPLE Solve and check: $\frac{n}{3} - 4 = 12$

Solution:

1 Add the same number to each side of the equation.

$$\frac{n}{3} - 4 = 12$$ *Add 4 to each side.*

$$\frac{n}{3} - 4 + \mathbf{4} = 12 + \mathbf{4}$$

2 Multiply each side of the equation by the same number.

$$\frac{n}{3} = 16$$ *Multiply each side by 3.*

$$\frac{n}{3} \times \mathbf{3} = 16 \times \mathbf{3}$$

$$n = \mathbf{48}$$

Check: $\frac{n}{3} - 4 = 12$ *Replace n with 48.*

$$\frac{48}{3} - 4 \stackrel{?}{=} 12$$

$$16 - 4 \stackrel{?}{=} 12$$

$$12 \stackrel{?}{=} 12 \quad \text{Yes}\checkmark$$

PRACTICE

Solve and check.

1. $\frac{n}{2} + 9 = 18$ **18**
2. $\frac{n}{3} + 5 = 12$ **21**
3. $\frac{n}{8} - 5 = 5$ **80**
4. $\frac{n}{6} - 5 = 0$ **30**
5. $\frac{n}{2} + 8 = 11$ **6**
6. $\frac{n}{7} + 14 = 20$ **42**
7. $\frac{n}{8} - 4 = 6$ **80**
8. $\frac{n}{3} - 6 = 2$ **24**
9. $\frac{n}{4} - 3 = 3$ **24**
10. $\frac{n}{8} + 5 = 10$ **40**
11. $\frac{n}{3} - 7 = 7$ **42**
12. $\frac{n}{13} - 5 = 8$ **169**
13. $\frac{n}{8} + 1 = 3$ **16**
14. $\frac{n}{11} - 16 = 1$ **187**
15. $\frac{n}{8} + 7 = 32$ **200**
16. $\frac{n}{4} - 5 = 100$ **420**
17. $\frac{n}{9} - 3 = 46$ **441**
18. $\frac{n}{3} + 4 = 28$ **72**
19. $\frac{n}{2} + \frac{1}{12} = \frac{7}{12}$ **1**
20. $\frac{n}{9} + \frac{5}{9} = \frac{7}{9}$ **2**
21. $\frac{n}{10} - \frac{1}{5} = \frac{3}{5}$ **8**
22. $\frac{n}{6} - \frac{1}{4} = \frac{7}{12}$ **5**
23. $\frac{n}{9} + \frac{1}{6} = \frac{11}{18}$ **4**
24. $\frac{n}{25} + \frac{1}{5} = \frac{2}{5}$ **5**

Ratio

A **ratio** is a way to compare numbers. You can write a ratio as a fraction.

EXAMPLE Write each ratio as a fraction.

a. 5 to 17 **b.** 27 to 45

Solutions:

Write fractions in lowest terms.

a. $\frac{5}{17}$

b. $\frac{27}{45} = \frac{27 \div 9}{45 \div 9}$

$= \frac{3}{5}$ ◀ *Lowest Terms*

PRACTICE

Write a fraction in lowest terms for each ratio.

1. 5 to 9 $\frac{5}{9}$	**2.** 4 to 11 $\frac{4}{11}$	**3.** 6 to 15 $\frac{2}{5}$	**4.** 8 to 18 $\frac{4}{9}$
5. 20 to 50 $\frac{2}{5}$	**6.** 30 to 25 $\frac{6}{5}$	**7.** 8 to 6 $\frac{4}{3}$	**8.** 3 to 12 $\frac{1}{4}$
9. 4 to 14 $\frac{2}{7}$	**10.** 7 to 21 $\frac{1}{3}$	**11.** 5 to 15 $\frac{1}{3}$	**12.** 10 to 15 $\frac{2}{3}$
13. 6 to 19 $\frac{6}{19}$	**14.** 18 to 27 $\frac{2}{3}$	**15.** 4 to 3 $\frac{4}{3}$	**16.** 11 to 22 $\frac{1}{2}$
17. 3 to 27 $\frac{1}{9}$	**18.** 5 to 40 $\frac{1}{8}$	**19.** 1 to 11 $\frac{1}{11}$	**20.** 81 to 162 $\frac{1}{2}$
21. 6 to 54 $\frac{1}{9}$	**22.** 9 to 81 $\frac{1}{9}$	**23.** 7 to 56 $\frac{1}{8}$	**24.** 3 to 48 $\frac{1}{16}$
25. 12 to 60 $\frac{1}{5}$	**26.** 5 to 25 $\frac{1}{5}$	**27.** 3 to 3 $\frac{1}{1}$	**28.** 9 to 54 $\frac{1}{6}$
29. 6 to 84 $\frac{1}{14}$	**30.** 3 to 1 $\frac{3}{1}$	**31.** 12 to 3 $\frac{4}{1}$	**32.** 18 to 9 $\frac{2}{1}$
33. 14 to 28 $\frac{1}{2}$	**34.** 4 to 6 $\frac{2}{3}$	**35.** 8 to 32 $\frac{1}{4}$	**36.** 81 to 27 $\frac{3}{1}$
37. 9 to 36 $\frac{1}{4}$	**38.** 4 to 40 $\frac{1}{10}$	**39.** 60 to 12 $\frac{5}{1}$	**40.** 14 to 40 $\frac{7}{20}$
41. 13 to 39 $\frac{1}{3}$	**42.** 7 to 16 $\frac{7}{16}$	**43.** 5 to 35 $\frac{1}{7}$	**44.** 15 to 45 $\frac{1}{3}$
45. 17 to 68 $\frac{1}{4}$	**46.** 60 to 15 $\frac{4}{1}$	**47.** 9 to 30 $\frac{3}{10}$	**48.** 54 to 18 $\frac{3}{1}$
49. 14 to 2 $\frac{7}{1}$	**50.** 36 to 72 $\frac{1}{2}$	**51.** 12 to 88 $\frac{3}{22}$	**52.** 50 to 10 $\frac{5}{1}$
53. 11 to 55 $\frac{1}{5}$	**54.** 26 to 39 $\frac{1}{3}$	**55.** 42 to 12 $\frac{7}{2}$	**56.** 35 to 25 $\frac{7}{5}$
57. 30 to 50 $\frac{3}{5}$	**58.** 35 to 55 $\frac{7}{11}$	**59.** 46 to 23 $\frac{2}{1}$	**60.** 21 to 39 $\frac{7}{13}$

Equivalent Ratios

Ratios such as $\frac{27}{45}$ and $\frac{3}{5}$ are **equivalent ratios.** They are equal. Equivalent ratios have equal cross-products.

EXAMPLE Determine whether the ratios are equivalent.

a. $\frac{3}{7}$ and $\frac{12}{28}$ **b.** $\frac{5}{12}$ and $\frac{4}{11}$

Solutions:

1 Find the cross-products.

a. $\frac{3}{7} \stackrel{?}{=} \frac{12}{28}$ ◀ *The loop shows the cross-product.* **b.** $\frac{5}{12} \stackrel{?}{=} \frac{4}{11}$

2 Compare the cross-products. Equivalent ratios have equal cross-products.

a. $3 \times 28 \stackrel{?}{=} 7 \times 12$

$84 \stackrel{?}{=} 84$ Yes ✓

The cross-products are equal. So the ratios are **equivalent.**

b. $5 \times 11 \stackrel{?}{=} 12 \times 4$

$55 \stackrel{?}{=} 48$ No

The cross-products are not equal. So the ratios are **not equivalent.**

PRACTICE

Determine whether the ratios are equivalent. Answer Yes or No.

1. $\frac{3}{5}$ and $\frac{9}{15}$ **Yes**
2. $\frac{2}{3}$ and $\frac{3}{4}$ **No**
3. $\frac{8}{12}$ and $\frac{10}{15}$ **Yes**
4. $\frac{18}{3}$ and $\frac{12}{2}$ **Yes**
5. $\frac{7}{8}$ and $\frac{12}{16}$ **No**
6. $\frac{1}{5}$ and $\frac{7}{49}$ **No**
7. $\frac{2}{7}$ and $\frac{6}{21}$ **Yes**
8. $\frac{1}{3}$ and $\frac{17}{61}$ **No**
9. $\frac{9}{12}$ and $\frac{18}{25}$ **No**
10. $\frac{7}{13}$ and $\frac{21}{39}$ **Yes**
11. $\frac{6}{7}$ and $\frac{24}{21}$ **No**
12. $\frac{3}{5}$ and $\frac{21}{35}$ **Yes**
13. $\frac{3}{5}$ and $\frac{36}{60}$ **Yes**
14. $\frac{4}{6}$ and $\frac{20}{24}$ **No**
15. $\frac{9}{8}$ and $\frac{36}{32}$ **Yes**
16. $\frac{3}{10}$ and $\frac{22}{80}$ **No**
17. $\frac{4}{1}$ and $\frac{28}{7}$ **Yes**
18. $\frac{2}{5}$ and $\frac{18}{45}$ **Yes**
19. $\frac{39}{26}$ and $\frac{3}{2}$ **Yes**
20. $\frac{1}{8}$ and $\frac{17}{136}$ **Yes**
21. $\frac{3}{4}$ and $\frac{15}{21}$ **No**
22. $\frac{5}{8}$ and $\frac{15}{25}$ **No**
23. $\frac{7}{6}$ and $\frac{42}{36}$ **Yes**
24. $\frac{5}{8}$ and $\frac{10}{16}$ **Yes**
25. $\frac{11}{13}$ and $\frac{44}{52}$ **Yes**
26. $\frac{3}{7}$ and $\frac{20}{49}$ **No**
27. $\frac{5}{9}$ and $\frac{30}{45}$ **No**
28. $\frac{8}{13}$ and $\frac{39}{24}$ **No**
29. $\frac{4}{5}$ and $\frac{64}{80}$ **Yes**
30. $\frac{2}{11}$ and $\frac{33}{6}$ **No**
31. $\frac{1}{8}$ and $\frac{5}{40}$ **Yes**
32. $\frac{3}{4}$ and $\frac{24}{32}$ **Yes**
33. $\frac{3}{4}$ and $\frac{9}{16}$ **No**
34. $\frac{7}{8}$ and $\frac{49}{56}$ **Yes**
35. $\frac{21}{25}$ and $\frac{3}{5}$ **No**
36. $\frac{18}{30}$ and $\frac{3}{5}$ **Yes**

Proportions

A **proportion** is an equation that shows equivalent ratios.

$\frac{n}{7} = \frac{4}{14}$ and $\frac{2}{n} = \frac{12}{24}$ are examples of proportions.

Solving a proportion is similar to solving a multiplication equation.

EXAMPLE Solve the proportion for n.

a. $\frac{n}{6} = \frac{20}{30}$ **b.** $\frac{7}{5} = \frac{21}{n}$

Solutions:

[1] Write the cross-products.

a. $n \times 30 = 6 \times 20$

$30n = 120$

b. $7 \times n = 5 \times 21$

$7n = 105$

[2] Solve the multiplication equation for n.

a. $\frac{30n}{30} = \frac{120}{30}$

$n = 4$

Check: $\frac{n}{6} = \frac{20}{30}$ *Replace n with 4.*

$\frac{4}{6} \stackrel{?}{=} \frac{20}{30}$

$4 \times 30 \stackrel{?}{=} 6 \times 20$

$120 \stackrel{?}{=} 120$ Yes ✓

b. [2] $\frac{7n}{7} = \frac{105}{7}$

$n = 15$

Check: $\frac{7}{5} = \frac{21}{n}$

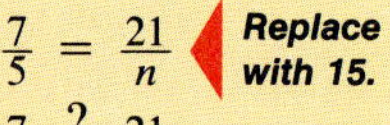

$\frac{7}{5} \stackrel{?}{=} \frac{21}{15}$

$7 \times 15 \stackrel{?}{=} 5 \times 21$

$105 \stackrel{?}{=} 105$ Yes ✓

PRACTICE

Solve each proportion for n.

1. $\frac{n}{8} = \frac{3}{24}$ 1	**2.** $\frac{n}{2} = \frac{5}{10}$ 1	**3.** $\frac{n}{7} = \frac{6}{42}$ 1	**4.** $\frac{n}{4} = \frac{9}{12}$ 3	**5.** $\frac{n}{5} = \frac{21}{35}$ 3
6. $\frac{n}{10} = \frac{35}{50}$ 7	**7.** $\frac{n}{16} = \frac{3}{8}$ 6	**8.** $\frac{n}{9} = \frac{24}{54}$ 4	**9.** $\frac{n}{18} = \frac{2}{3}$ 12	**10.** $\frac{n}{3} = \frac{10}{15}$ 2
11. $\frac{n}{27} = \frac{5}{9}$ 15	**12.** $\frac{n}{81} = \frac{2}{27}$ 6	**13.** $\frac{n}{4} = \frac{11}{44}$ 1	**14.** $\frac{n}{6} = \frac{60}{72}$ 5	**15.** $\frac{n}{18} = \frac{15}{90}$ 3
16. $\frac{n}{25} = \frac{96}{200}$ 12	**17.** $\frac{n}{3} = \frac{19}{57}$ 1	**18.** $\frac{n}{84} = \frac{3}{14}$ 18	**19.** $\frac{n}{20} = \frac{65}{100}$ 13	**20.** $\frac{n}{8} = \frac{9}{24}$ 3
21. $\frac{n}{15} = \frac{15}{75}$ 3	**22.** $\frac{n}{28} = \frac{2}{7}$ 8	**23.** $\frac{n}{60} = \frac{6}{20}$ 18	**24.** $\frac{n}{19} = \frac{3}{57}$ 1	**25.** $\frac{n}{92} = \frac{2}{23}$ 8
26. $\frac{6}{81} = \frac{2}{n}$ 27	**27.** $\frac{3}{12} = \frac{15}{n}$ 60	**28.** $\frac{7}{10} = \frac{28}{n}$ 40	**29.** $\frac{9}{7} = \frac{72}{n}$ 56	**30.** $\frac{3}{5} = \frac{21}{n}$ 35
31. $\frac{5}{8} = \frac{25}{n}$ 40	**32.** $\frac{7}{25} = \frac{28}{n}$ 100	**33.** $\frac{6}{13} = \frac{18}{n}$ 39	**34.** $\frac{30}{70} = \frac{6}{n}$ 14	**35.** $\frac{9}{10} = \frac{45}{n}$ 50

Percents and Decimals

Percent means **hundredths** or **per hundred.**

8% means 8 hundredths or 0.08.

You can write a decimal for a percent.

EXAMPLE

Write a decimal for each percent.

a. 28% **b.** 5% **c.** 148% **d.** $12\frac{1}{2}\%$

Solutions:

Move the decimal point two places to the left.

a. 28% = 0.28

b. 05% = 0.05 — *Insert one zero.*

c. 148% = 1.48

d. $12\frac{1}{2}\% = 0.12\frac{1}{2}$

PRACTICE

Write a decimal for each per cent.

1. 36% 0.36	**2.** 42% 0.42	**3.** 85% 0.85	**4.** 49% 0.49	**5.** 34% 0.34	**6.** 24% 0.24
7. 25% 0.25	**8.** 16% 0.16	**9.** 46% 0.46	**10.** 58% 0.58	**11.** 83% 0.83	**12.** 74% 0.74
13. 44% 0.44	**14.** 67% 0.67	**15.** 98% 0.98	**16.** 43% 0.43	**17.** 51% 0.51	**18.** 12% 0.12
19. 56% 0.56	**20.** 21% 0.21	**21.** 73% 0.73	**22.** 29% 0.29	**23.** 53% 0.53	**24.** 82% 0.82
25. 6% 0.06	**26.** 8% 0.08	**27.** 4% 0.04	**28.** 9% 0.09	**29.** 3% 0.03	**30.** 2% 0.02
31. 121% 1.21	**32.** 156% 1.56	**33.** 373% 3.73	**34.** 438% 4.38	**35.** 129% 1.29	**36.** 364% 3.64
37. 71% 0.71	**38.** 68% 0.68	**39.** 7% 0.07	**40.** 89% 0.89	**41.** 52% 0.52	**42.** 21% 0.21
43. 35% 0.35	**44.** 11% 0.11	**45.** 208% 2.08	**46.** 80% 0.80	**47.** 138% 1.38	**48.** 86% 0.86
49. $33\frac{1}{3}\%$ $0.33\frac{1}{3}$	**50.** $12\frac{1}{2}\%$ $0.12\frac{1}{2}$	**51.** $16\frac{2}{3}\%$ $0.16\frac{2}{3}$	**52.** $37\frac{1}{2}\%$ $0.37\frac{1}{2}$	**53.** $11\frac{1}{9}\%$ $0.11\frac{1}{9}$	**54.** $14\frac{2}{7}\%$ $0.14\frac{2}{7}$
55. $66\frac{2}{3}\%$ $0.66\frac{2}{3}$	**56.** $19\frac{3}{4}\%$ $0.19\frac{3}{4}$	**57.** $62\frac{1}{2}\%$ $0.62\frac{1}{2}$	**58.** $86\frac{2}{3}\%$ $0.86\frac{2}{3}$	**59.** $75\frac{1}{2}\%$ $0.75\frac{1}{2}$	**60.** $48\frac{1}{4}\%$ $0.48\frac{1}{4}$

Percents and Fractions

11% means 11 per hundred or $\frac{11}{100}$.

You can write a fraction for a percent.

EXAMPLE Write a fraction for each percent.

a. 17% **b.** 20% **c.** $\frac{1}{2}\%$ **d.** $33\frac{1}{3}\%$

Solutions:

Write a fraction with a denominator of 100 for the percent. Write the fraction in lowest terms.

a. $17\% = \mathbf{\frac{17}{100}}$ ◀ ***Lowest terms***

b. $20\% = \frac{20}{100}$ ◀ ***Write in lowest terms***

$= \mathbf{\frac{1}{5}}$

c. $\frac{1}{2}\% = \frac{\frac{1}{2}}{100}$ ◀ ***$\frac{1}{2}$% means $\frac{1}{2}$ per hundred.***

$= \frac{1}{2} \div 100$

$= \frac{1}{2} \times \frac{1}{100}$

$= \mathbf{\frac{1}{200}}$

d. $33\frac{1}{3}\% = \frac{33\frac{1}{3}}{100}$

$= 33\frac{1}{3} \div 100$

$= 33\frac{1}{3} \times \frac{1}{100}$

$= \frac{\overset{1}{\cancel{100}}}{3} \times \frac{1}{\underset{1}{\cancel{100}}}$

$= \mathbf{\frac{1}{3}}$

PRACTICE

Write a fraction for each percent.

1. 19% $\frac{19}{100}$	**2.** 21% $\frac{21}{100}$	**3.** 37% $\frac{37}{100}$	**4.** 53% $\frac{53}{100}$	**5.** 50% $\frac{1}{2}$	**6.** 20% $\frac{1}{5}$
7. 30% $\frac{3}{10}$	**8.** 45% $\frac{9}{20}$	**9.** 25% $\frac{1}{4}$	**10.** 80% $\frac{4}{5}$	**11.** 75% $\frac{3}{4}$	**12.** 60% $\frac{3}{5}$
13. 42% $\frac{21}{50}$	**14.** 85% $\frac{17}{20}$	**15.** 56% $\frac{14}{25}$	**16.** 38% $\frac{19}{50}$	**17.** 48% $\frac{12}{25}$	**18.** 15% $\frac{3}{20}$
19. 65% $\frac{13}{20}$	**20.** 22% $\frac{11}{50}$	**21.** 78% $\frac{39}{50}$	**22.** 95% $\frac{19}{20}$	**23.** 14% $\frac{7}{50}$	**24.** 34% $\frac{17}{50}$
25. 40% $\frac{2}{5}$	**26.** 24% $\frac{6}{25}$	**27.** 50% $\frac{1}{2}$	**28.** 37% $\frac{37}{100}$	**29.** 49% $\frac{49}{100}$	**30.** 62% $\frac{31}{50}$
31. 79% $\frac{79}{100}$	**32.** 90% $\frac{9}{10}$	**33.** 16% $\frac{4}{25}$	**34.** 10% $\frac{1}{10}$	**35.** 47% $\frac{47}{100}$	**36.** 81% $\frac{81}{100}$
37. 99% $\frac{99}{100}$	**38.** 32% $\frac{8}{25}$	**39.** 51% $\frac{51}{100}$	**40.** 13% $\frac{13}{100}$	**41.** 44% $\frac{11}{25}$	**42.** 96% $\frac{24}{25}$
43. $\frac{1}{3}\%$ $\frac{1}{300}$	**44.** $\frac{1}{4}\%$ $\frac{1}{400}$	**45.** $\frac{1}{8}\%$ $\frac{1}{800}$	**46.** $\frac{1}{5}\%$ $\frac{1}{500}$	**47.** $\frac{1}{10}\%$ $\frac{1}{1000}$	**48.** $\frac{1}{12}\%$ $\frac{1}{1200}$
49. $\frac{2}{3}\%$ $\frac{1}{150}$	**50.** $\frac{3}{4}\%$ $\frac{3}{400}$	**51.** $66\frac{2}{3}\%$ $\frac{2}{3}$	**52.** $37\frac{1}{2}\%$ $\frac{3}{8}$	**53.** $62\frac{1}{2}\%$ $\frac{5}{8}$	**54.** $87\frac{1}{2}\%$ $\frac{7}{8}$

Writing Percents for Decimals

You can write a percent for a decimal.

EXAMPLE Write a percent for each decimal.

a. 0.48 **b.** 0.225 **c.** 4.16 **d.** $0.12\frac{1}{2}$

Solutions:

Move the decimal point two places to the right.

a. 0.48 = **48%** **b.** 0.225 = **22.5%**

c. 4.16 = 416% **d.** $0.12\frac{1}{2}$ = **$12\frac{1}{2}$%**

PRACTICE

Write a percent for each decimal.

1. 0.37 37% **2.** 0.29 29% **3.** 0.32 32% **4.** 0.37 37% **5.** 0.41 41%

6. 0.25 25% **7.** 0.28 28% **8.** 0.39 39% **9.** 0.91 91% **10.** 0.99 99%

11. 0.33 33% **12.** 0.27 27% **13.** 0.04 4% **14.** 0.09 9% **15.** 0.03 3%

16. 0.02 2% **17.** 0.15 15% **18.** 0.62 62% **19.** 1.32 132% **20.** 4.65 465%

21. 11.02 1102% **22.** 9.03 903% **23.** 7.15 715% **24.** 1.54 154% **25.** 0.224 22.4%

26. 0.185 18.5% **27.** 0.575 57.5% **28.** 0.282 28.2% **29.** 0.443 44.3% **30.** 0.916 91.6%

31. 1.346 134.6% **32.** 5.428 542.8% **33.** 7.199 719.9% **34.** 2.048 204.8% **35.** 3.264 326.4%

36. 4.533 453.3% **37.** 0.002 0.2% **38.** 0.003 0.3% **39.** 0.005 0.5% **40.** 1.004 100.4%

41. 2.008 200.8% **42.** 0.007 0.7% **43.** $0.37\frac{1}{2}$ $37\frac{1}{2}$% **44.** $0.33\frac{1}{3}$ $33\frac{1}{3}$% **45.** $0.62\frac{1}{2}$ $62\frac{1}{2}$%

46. $0.11\frac{1}{9}$ $11\frac{1}{9}$% **47.** $0.66\frac{2}{3}$ $66\frac{2}{3}$% **48.** $0.86\frac{2}{3}$ $86\frac{2}{3}$% **49.** $0.28\frac{1}{4}$ $28\frac{1}{4}$% **50.** $0.37\frac{1}{3}$ $37\frac{1}{3}$%

51. $0.44\frac{5}{8}$ $44\frac{5}{8}$% **52.** $0.75\frac{1}{2}$ $75\frac{1}{2}$% **53.** $0.27\frac{1}{4}$ $27\frac{1}{4}$% **54.** $0.19\frac{3}{4}$ $19\frac{3}{4}$% **55.** $0.17\frac{1}{5}$ $17\frac{1}{5}$%

56. $0.23\frac{7}{10}$ $23\frac{7}{10}$% **57.** $0.45\frac{3}{8}$ $45\frac{3}{8}$% **58.** $0.12\frac{1}{2}$ $12\frac{1}{2}$% **59.** $0.19\frac{2}{3}$ $19\frac{2}{3}$% **60.** $0.08\frac{2}{5}$ $8\frac{2}{5}$%

61. $0.05\frac{4}{5}$ $5\frac{4}{5}$% **62.** $0.07\frac{1}{3}$ $7\frac{1}{3}$% **63.** $0.36\frac{3}{5}$ $36\frac{3}{5}$% **64.** $0.55\frac{3}{10}$ $55\frac{3}{10}$% **65.** $0.76\frac{1}{4}$ $76\frac{1}{4}$%

405

Writing Percents for Fractions

You can write a percent for a fraction or mixed number.

EXAMPLE Write a percent for each fraction or mixed number.

a. $\frac{3}{4}$ **b.** $\frac{3}{8}$ **c.** $1\frac{1}{5}$

Solutions:

1 Divide the numerator of the fraction by the denominator. Carry the division to two decimal places.

a. $\frac{3}{4}$ means $3 \div 4$.

$$4\overline{)3.00} = 0.75$$

b. $\frac{3}{8}$ means $3 \div 8$.

$$\begin{array}{r} 0.37\frac{4}{8} = 0.37\frac{1}{2} \\ 8\overline{)3.00} \\ \underline{2\,4} \\ 60 \\ \underline{56} \\ 4 \end{array}$$

Lowest terms

c. $1\frac{1}{5} = \frac{6}{5}$

$\frac{6}{5}$ means $6 \div 5$.

$$5\overline{)6.00} = 1.20$$

2 Write a percent for the decimal.

a. $0.75 = \mathbf{75\%}$ **b.** $0.37\frac{1}{2} = \mathbf{37\frac{1}{2}\%}$ **c.** $1\frac{1}{5} = \mathbf{120\%}$

PRACTICE

Write a percent for each fraction or mixed number.

1. $\frac{3}{10}$ **30%** **2.** $\frac{7}{10}$ **70%** **3.** $\frac{4}{50}$ **8%** **4.** $\frac{7}{25}$ **28%** **5.** $\frac{9}{25}$ **36%** **6.** $\frac{6}{40}$ **15%**

7. $\frac{3}{5}$ **60%** **8.** $\frac{1}{2}$ **50%** **9.** $\frac{2}{8}$ **25%** **10.** $\frac{1}{5}$ **20%** **11.** $\frac{1}{4}$ **25%** **12.** $\frac{4}{5}$ **80%**

13. $\frac{9}{10}$ **90%** **14.** $\frac{27}{50}$ **54%** **15.** $\frac{11}{20}$ **55%** **16.** $\frac{2}{5}$ **40%** **17.** $\frac{8}{40}$ **20%** **18.** $\frac{6}{12}$ **50%**

19. $\frac{13}{20}$ **65%** **20.** $\frac{17}{25}$ **68%** **21.** $\frac{33}{50}$ **66%** **22.** $\frac{18}{40}$ **45%** **23.** $\frac{6}{20}$ **30%** **24.** $\frac{23}{25}$ **92%**

25. $\frac{2}{3}$ $66\frac{2}{3}\%$ **26.** $\frac{5}{8}$ $62\frac{1}{2}\%$ **27.** $\frac{7}{12}$ $58\frac{1}{3}\%$ **28.** $\frac{3}{8}$ $37\frac{1}{2}\%$ **29.** $\frac{1}{40}$ $2\frac{1}{2}\%$ **30.** $\frac{15}{16}$ $93\frac{3}{4}\%$

31. $\frac{1}{12}$ $8\frac{1}{3}\%$ **32.** $\frac{7}{8}$ $87\frac{1}{2}\%$ **33.** $\frac{1}{7}$ $14\frac{2}{7}\%$ **34.** $\frac{5}{6}$ $83\frac{1}{3}\%$ **35.** $\frac{2}{9}$ $22\frac{2}{9}\%$ **36.** $\frac{4}{11}$ $36\frac{4}{11}\%$

37. $\frac{1}{3}$ $33\frac{1}{3}\%$ **38.** $\frac{3}{40}$ $7\frac{1}{2}\%$ **39.** $\frac{3}{16}$ $18\frac{3}{4}\%$ **40.** $\frac{1}{6}$ $16\frac{2}{3}\%$ **41.** $\frac{7}{16}$ $43\frac{3}{4}\%$ **42.** $\frac{4}{7}$ $57\frac{1}{7}\%$

43. $3\frac{9}{10}$ **390%** **44.** $5\frac{1}{10}$ **510%** **45.** $8\frac{3}{20}$ **815%** **46.** $7\frac{2}{5}$ **740%** **47.** $5\frac{4}{5}$ **580%** **48.** $10\frac{3}{4}$ **1075%**

49. $2\frac{5}{6}$ $283\frac{1}{3}\%$ **50.** $1\frac{11}{12}$ $191\frac{2}{3}\%$ **51.** $5\frac{5}{8}$ $562\frac{1}{2}\%$ **52.** $16\frac{1}{3}$ $1633\frac{1}{3}\%$ **53.** $12\frac{1}{8}$ $1212\frac{1}{2}\%$ **54.** $5\frac{1}{9}$ $511\frac{1}{9}\%$

55. $4\frac{1}{5}$ **420%** **56.** $6\frac{3}{4}$ **675%** **57.** $5\frac{7}{10}$ **570%** **58.** $4\frac{1}{4}$ **425%** **59.** $3\frac{4}{5}$ **380%** **60.** $8\frac{9}{20}$ **845%**

Finding a Percent of a Number Using a Decimal

EXAMPLE

a. What number is 12% of 750? **b.** What number is 62.5% of 80?

Solutions:

1 Write an equation.

a. What number is 12% of 750? **b.** What number is 62.5% of 80?

$n = 12\% \times 750$ $\quad$ $n = 62.5\% \times 80$

2 Write a decimal for the percent.

$n = 0.12 \times 750$ $\quad$ $n = 0.625 \times 80$

3 Solve the equation.

$n = \mathbf{90}$ $\quad$ $n = \mathbf{50}$

Thus, 12% of 750 = **90**. Thus, 62.5% of 80 = **50.**

PRACTICE

Find each answer. Write a decimal for the percent.

1. 70% of 63 44.1 **2.** 18% of 90 16.2 **3.** 25% of 16 4 **4.** 40% of 82 32.8

5. 28% of 60 16.8 **6.** 7% of 25 1.75 **7.** 11% of 50 5.5 **8.** 17% of 100 17

9. 95% of 20 19 **10.** 36% of 40 14.4 **11.** 4% of 83 3.32 **12.** 9% of 72 6.48

13. 63% of 80 50.4 **14.** 17% of 400 68 **15.** 30% of 28 8.4 **16.** 27% of 900 243

17. 5% of 20 1 **18.** 8% of 120 9.6 **19.** 6% of 50 3 **20.** 3% of 400 12

21. 12% of 36 4.32 **22.** 14% of 18 2.52 **23.** 21% of 42 8.82 **24.** 43% of 100 43

25. 85% of 50 42.5 **26.** 74% of 300 222 **27.** 28% of 500 140 **28.** 32% of 56 17.92

29. 10.1% of 16 1.616 **30.** 30.4% of 400 121.6 **31.** 19.5% of 60 11.7 **32.** 21.2% of 800 169.6

33. 14.5% of 600 87 **34.** 15.5% of 200 31 **35.** 87.5% of 120 105 **36.** 32.5% of 64 20.8

Finding a Percent of a Number Using a Fraction

Equivalent Fractions and Percents			
$\frac{1}{4} = 25\%$	$\frac{1}{2} = 50\%$	$\frac{3}{4} = 75\%$	
$\frac{1}{5} = 20\%$	$\frac{2}{5} = 40\%$	$\frac{3}{5} = 60\%$	$\frac{4}{5} = 80\%$
$\frac{1}{6} = 16\frac{2}{3}\%$	$\frac{1}{3} = 33\frac{1}{3}\%$	$\frac{2}{3} = 66\frac{2}{3}\%$	$\frac{5}{6} = 83\frac{1}{3}\%$
$\frac{1}{8} = 12\frac{1}{2}\%$	$\frac{3}{8} = 37\frac{1}{2}\%$	$\frac{5}{8} = 62\frac{1}{2}\%$	$\frac{7}{8} = 87\frac{1}{2}\%$

EXAMPLE

a. What number is 25% of 40? **b.** What number is $37\frac{1}{2}\%$ of 64?

[1] Write an equation.

a. What number is 25% of 40?

$n = 25\% \times 40$

b. What number is $37\frac{1}{2}\%$ of 64?

$n = 37\frac{1}{2}\% \times 64$

[2] Write a fraction for the percent.

$n = \frac{1}{4} \times 40$

$n = \frac{3}{\cancel{8}_1} \times \frac{\cancel{64}^{8}}{1}$

[3] Solve the equation.

$n = \mathbf{10}$

Thus, $37\frac{1}{2}\%$ of 64 = **24.**

Thus, 25% of 40 = **10.**

PRACTICE

Find each answer. Write a fraction for the percent.

1. 60% of 45 27
2. $83\frac{1}{3}\%$ of 66 55
3. $37\frac{1}{2}\%$ of 56 21
4. 50% of 90 45
5. $12\frac{1}{2}\%$ of 88 11
6. 75% of 44 33
7. $33\frac{1}{3}\%$ of 72 24
8. $16\frac{2}{3}\%$ of 84 14
9. $66\frac{2}{3}\%$ of 120 80
10. 20% of 65 13
11. 25% of 76 19
12. $87\frac{1}{2}\%$ of 96 84
13. 40% of 75 30
14. 50% of 86 43
15. 80% of 70 56
16. 75% of 400 300
17. $12\frac{1}{2}\%$ of 80 10
18. $87\frac{1}{2}\%$ of 48 42
19. $62\frac{1}{2}\%$ of 96 60
20. $33\frac{1}{3}\%$ of 51 17
21. 40% of 60 24
22. 80% of 25 20
23. 25% of 80 20
24. 50% of 110 55
25. $33\frac{1}{3}\%$ of 27 9
26. $87\frac{1}{2}\%$ of 64 56
27. $16\frac{2}{3}\%$ of 54 9
28. $37\frac{1}{2}\%$ of 96 36
29. 75% of 28 21
30. 60% of 120 72
31. 20% of 15 3
32. 35% of 40 14

Finding What Percent A Number is of Another

EXAMPLE **a.** What percent of 15 is 12? **b.** 30 is what percent of 48?

Solutions:

1 Write an equation.

a. What percent of 15 is 12?

$n \times 15 = 12$, or
$15n = 12$

b. 30 is what percent of 48?

$30 = n \times 48$
$30 = 48n$

2 Solve the equation for n.

a.

$15n = 12$

$\frac{15n}{15} = \frac{12}{15}$

$n = \frac{12}{15}$, or $\frac{4}{5}$

b.

$48n = 30$ ◀ *30 = 48n is the same as 48n = 30.*

$\frac{48n}{48} = \frac{30}{48}$

$n = \frac{30}{48}$, or $\frac{5}{8}$

3 Write a percent for n.

a. $\frac{4}{5} = $ **80%**

b. $\frac{5}{8} \longrightarrow 8\overline{)5.00}$ gives $0.62\frac{4}{8} = 0.62\frac{1}{2}$

$0.62\frac{1}{2} = $ **$62\frac{1}{2}$%**

PRACTICE

Write an equation for each exercise.

1. What percent of 20 is 14? $n \times 20 = 14$
2. What percent of 90 is 45? $n \times 90 = 45$
3. 20 is what percent of 80? $20 = n \times 80$
4. 75 is what percent of 225? $75 = n \times 225$

Solve.

5. What percent of 40 is 30? 75%
6. What percent of 90 is 15? $16\frac{2}{3}$%
7. What percent of 50 is 20? 40%
8. What percent of 75 is 25? $33\frac{1}{3}$%
9. What percent of 24 is 3? $12\frac{1}{2}$%
10. What percent of 65 is 26? 40%
11. What percent of 120 is 80? $66\frac{2}{3}$%
12. What percent of 240 is 180? 75%
13. 18 is what percent of 90? 20%
14. 16 is what percent of 64? 25%
15. 75 is what percent of 300? 25%
16. 36 is what percent of 108? $33\frac{1}{3}$%
17. 25 is what percent of 200? $12\frac{1}{2}$%
18. 70 is what percent of 420? $16\frac{2}{3}$%

Using a Decimal to Find a Number Given a Percent

EXAMPLE 30 is 60% of what number?

Solution:

1 Write an equation using a decimal.

30 is 60% of what number?

$30 = 0.60 \times n$

$0.60n = 30$ ◀ *30 = 0.60n is the same as 0.60n = 30.*

2 Solve the equation.

$\frac{0.60n}{0.60} = \frac{30}{0.60}$

$n = \mathbf{50}$ 30 is 60% of **50.**

PRACTICE

Write an equation for each exercise.

1. 60 is 25% of what number? $60 = 0.25 \times n$

2. 11 is 20% of what number? $11 = 0.20 \times n$

3. 5 is 10% of what number? $5 = 0.10 \times n$

4. 60 is 30% of what number? $60 = 0.30 \times n$

Solve. Use a decimal for the percent.

5. 9 is 20% of what number? 45

6. 24 is 50% of what number? 48

7. 6 is 40% of what number? 15

8. 21 is 35% of what number? 60

9. 16 is 80% of what number? 20

10. 9 is 5% of what number? 180

11. 81 is 27% of what number? 300

12. 45 is 30% of what number? 150

13. 99 is 18% of what number? 550

14. 90 is 15% of what number? 600

15. 14 is 25% of what number? 56

16. 195 is 65% of what number? 300

17. 55 is 22% of what number? 250

18. 70 is 28% of what number? 250

19. 234 is 52% of what number? 450

20. 204 is 85% of what number? 240

21. 54 is 45% of what number? 120

22. 18 is 24% of what number? 75

Using a Fraction to Find a Number Given a Percent

EXAMPLE 72 is $33\frac{1}{3}\%$ of what number?

Solution:

1 Write an equation using a fraction.

72 is $33\frac{1}{3}\%$ of what number ◀ $33\frac{1}{3}\% = \frac{1}{3}$

$72 = \frac{1}{3} \times n$, or $72 = \frac{1}{3}n$

$\frac{n}{3} = 72$ ◀ $\frac{1}{3}n = \frac{n}{3}$

2 Solve the equation.

$\frac{n}{3} \times \frac{3}{1} = 72 \times 3$

$n = \mathbf{216}$ 72 is $33\frac{1}{3}\%$ of **216.**

PRACTICE

Write an equation for each exercise.

1. 15 is $33\frac{1}{3}\%$ of what number? $15 = \frac{1}{3} \times n$
2. 7 is $16\frac{2}{3}\%$ of what number? $7 = \frac{1}{6} \times n$
3. 9 is $12\frac{1}{2}\%$ of what number? $9 = \frac{1}{8} \times n$
4. 12 is $33\frac{1}{3}\%$ of what number? $12 = \frac{1}{3} \times n$

Solve. Use a fraction for the per cent.

5. 9 is 50% of what number? 18
6. 14 is 25% of what number? 56
7. 73 is 10% of what number? 730
8. 14 is 40% of what number? 35
9. 24 is $37\frac{1}{2}\%$ of what number? 64
10. 8 is 25% of what number? 32
11. 17 is $16\frac{2}{3}\%$ of what number? 102
12. 42 is 60% of what number? 70
13. 60 is $83\frac{1}{3}\%$ of what number? 72
14. 30 is $62\frac{1}{2}\%$ of what number? 48
15. 4 is $12\frac{1}{2}\%$ of what number? 32
16. 45 is 25% of what number? 180
17. 14 is $33\frac{1}{3}\%$ of what number? 42
18. 56 is $12\frac{1}{2}\%$ of what number? 448
19. 5 is 30% of what number? $16\frac{2}{3}$
20. 28 is $33\frac{1}{3}\%$ of what number? 84
21. 60 is $62\frac{1}{2}\%$ of what number? 96
22. 30 is $83\frac{1}{3}\%$ of what number? 36

Percent and Estimation

EXAMPLE **a.** What number is 25% of 158? **b.** What number is 19% of 50?

Solution:

a.

[1] $25\% = \frac{1}{4}$

[2] Round to a **convenient number;** that is, to a number that is easy to multiply by $\frac{1}{4}$.

158 is about **160.**

[3] $\frac{1}{4} \times 160 = \mathbf{40}$

25% of $158 \approx \mathbf{40}$

b.

[1] Round to a **convenient number;** that is, to a percent close to 19% *and* easy to multiply by 50.

19% is about 20%, and $20\% = \frac{1}{5}$.

[2] $\frac{1}{5} \times 50 = \mathbf{10}$

19% of $50 \approx \mathbf{10}$

PRACTICE

Estimation Ex. 1–10

Choose the best estimate. Choose a, b, or c.

1. 60% of 63 a	**a.** 60% of 60	**b.** 60% of 65	**c.** 60% of 70
2. 25% of 410 b	**a.** 25% of 500	**b.** 25% of 400	**c.** 25% of 450
3. 29% of 400 c	**a.** 20% of 400	**b.** 25% of 400	**c.** 30% of 400
4. 10.4% of 90 a	**a.** 10% of 90	**b.** 15% of 90	**c.** 20% of 90
5. 50% of 89 b	**a.** 40	**b.** 45	**c.** 50
6. 80% of 403 b	**a.** 300	**b.** 320	**c.** 400
7. 20% of 31.98 b	**a.** 5	**b.** 6	**c.** 7
8. 16% of 30 b	**a.** 3	**b.** 5	**c.** 7
9. 74% of 20 a	**a.** 15	**b.** 14	**c.** 13
10. 9.7% of 1700 c	**a.** 160	**b.** 165	**c.** 170

Customary Measures

Length	Capacity
12 inches (in) = 1 foot (ft) 3 feet = 1 yard (yd) 36 inches = 1 yard 5280 feet = 1 mile (mi)	2 cups (c) = 1 pint (pt) 2 pints = 1 quart (q) 4 quarts = 1 gallon (gal)

Time	Weight
60 seconds (s) = 1 minute (min) 60 minutes = 1 hour (h) 24 hours = 1 day (d)	16 ounces (oz) = 1 pound (lb) 2000 pounds = 1 ton (T)

You can use the table to help change between units.

EXAMPLE

a. 8 ft = __?__ in **b.** 6 pt = __?__ qt

Solutions:

Larger to smaller

a. 8 ft = __?__ in
Since 1 ft = 12 in,
multiply 8 by 12.
8 × 12 = 96
8 ft = **96 in**

Smaller to larger

b. 6 pt = __?__ qt
Since 2 pt = 1 qt,
divide 6 by 2.
6 ÷ 2 = 3
6 pt = **3 qt**

PRACTICE

Complete.

1. 5 lb = __?__ oz **80**
2. 8 c = __?__ pt **4**
3. 30 in = __?__ ft **$2\frac{1}{2}$**
4. 9 feet = __?__ yd **3**
5. 144 in = __?__ yd **4**
6. $4\frac{1}{3}$ d = __?__ h **104**
7. 3 gal = __?__ qt **12**
8. $4\frac{1}{2}$ T = __?__ lb **9000**
9. 32 oz = __?__ lb **2**
10. 390 s = __?__ min **$6\frac{1}{2}$**
11. 2 mi = __?__ ft **10,560**
12. 4 qt = __?__ pt **8**
13. 8 qt = __?__ gal **2**
14. 420 min = __?__ h **7**
15. 4 mi = __?__ ft **21,120**
16. 5 yd = __?__ in **180**
17. 8 yd = __?__ ft **24**
18. $9\frac{1}{2}$ h = __?__ min **570**
19. 7,000 lb = __?__ T **$3\frac{1}{2}$**
20. 18 qt = __?__ gal **$4\frac{1}{2}$**
21. 15,840 ft = __?__ mi **3**
22. 8 ft = __?__ in **96**
23. 7 yd = __?__ ft **21**
24. 2 pt = __?__ c **4**

Operations with Measures

EXAMPLE

a. 2 ft 6 in + 1 ft 9 in

b. 4 h 25 min − 2 h 40 min

Solutions:

a.

```
  2 ft  6 in
+ 1 ft  9 in
  3 ft 15 in
```

15 in > 1 ft
15 in = 1 ft + 3 in.

3 ft + 1 ft + 3 in = 4 ft 3 in

Since 12 in = 1 ft,

3 in = $\frac{3}{12}$, or $\frac{1}{4}$ft *Lowest Terms*

Thus, 4 ft 3 in = **$4\frac{1}{4}$ ft.**

b.

```
  3    85
  4̸ h 2̸5̸ min
− 2 h 40 min
```

40 min > 25 min
1 h = 60 min
4 h 25 min = 3 h 85 min

```
  3 h 85 min
− 2 h 40 min
  1 h 45 min
```

Since 60 min = 1 h,

45 min = $\frac{45}{60}$, or $\frac{3}{4}$ h *Lowest Terms*

Thus, 1 h 45 min = **$1\frac{3}{4}$ h.**

PRACTICE

Add.

1. 3 ft 9 in + 2 ft 7 in — $6\frac{1}{3}$ ft
2. 6 h 14 min + 4 h 36 min — $10\frac{5}{6}$ h
3. 6 lb 12 oz + 3 lb 10 oz — $10\frac{3}{8}$ lb
4. 5 yd 2 ft + 3 yd 1 ft — 9 yd
5. 6 gal 3 qt + 7 gal 2 qt — $14\frac{1}{4}$ gal
6. 2 h 25 min + 5 h 35 min — 8 h
7. 8 yd 2 ft + 3 ft — $9\frac{2}{3}$ yd
8. 12 lb 10 oz + 6 lb 14 oz — $19\frac{1}{2}$ lb
9. 5 ft 4 in + 3 ft 2 in — $8\frac{1}{2}$ ft
10. 1 pt 1 c + 1 c — 2 pt
11. 3 gal 1 qt + 2 gal 5 qt — $6\frac{1}{2}$ gal
12. 5 min 20 s + 3 min 10 s — $8\frac{1}{2}$ min

Subtract.

13. 9 h 18 min − 4 h 33 min — $4\frac{3}{4}$ h
14. 3 gal 2 qt − 1 gal 3 qt — $1\frac{3}{4}$ gal
15. 6 yd 2 ft − 3 yd 1 ft — $3\frac{1}{3}$ yd
16. 8 lb 4 oz − 3 lb 6 oz — $4\frac{7}{8}$ lb
17. 12 ft 9 in − 4 ft 7 in — $8\frac{1}{6}$ ft
18. 5 yd − 2 yd 2 ft — $2\frac{1}{3}$ yd
19. 6 gal − 2 gal 3 qt — $3\frac{1}{4}$ gal
20. 5 h 20 min − 2 h 40 min — $2\frac{2}{3}$ h
21. 2 mi − 2,640 ft — $1\frac{1}{2}$ mi
22. 4 ft 9 in − 2 ft 6 in — $2\frac{1}{4}$ ft
23. 3 yd 2 ft − 5 ft — 2 yd
24. 7 h − 2 h 30 min — $4\frac{1}{2}$ h

414 APPENDIX A

Metric Units of Length

The following relationships are useful in changing units.

10 millimeters = 1 centimeter **100 centimeters = 1 meter**
1000 meters = 1 kilometer

Rules for Changing Between Metric Units

1. To change to a smaller metric unit, multiply by 10, by 100, or by 1000, and so on.
2. To change to a larger metric unit, multiply by 0.1, by 0.01, or by 0.001, and so on.

EXAMPLE

a. 5 km = ___?___ m **b.** 42 mm = ___?___ cm
c. 6 m = ___?___ cm **d.** 640 cm = ___?___ m

Solutions:

Larger to smaller

a. 5 km = (5 × 1000) m
= **5000 m**

c. 6 m = (6 × 100) cm
= **600 cm**

Smaller to larger

b. 42 mm = (42 × 0.1) cm
= **4.2 cm**

d. 640 cm = (640 × 0.01) m
= **6.4 m**

PRACTICE *Choose the equivalent measure. Choose a, b, c, or d.*

1. 15 meters a	**a.** 1500 cm	**b.** 150 cm	**c.** 1.5 cm	**d.** 0.15 cm
2. 20 kilometers c	**a.** 200 m	**b.** 2000 m	**c.** 20,000 m	**d.** 2 m
3. 54 centimeters b	**a.** 5.4 m	**b.** 0.54 m	**c.** 540 m	**d.** 5400 m
4. 6.8 centimeters d	**a.** 6800 mm	**b.** 680mm	**c.** 0.68 mm	**d.** 68 mm
5. 724 meters c	**a.** 72.4 km	**b.** 7.24 km	**c.** 0.724 km	**d.** 7240 km

Complete.

6. 65 m = ___?___ cm 6500 **7.** 346 mm = ___?___ m 0.346 **8.** 6.7 km = ___?___ m 6700

9. 5 m = ___?___ cm 500 **10.** 1.6 m = ___?___ mm 1600 **11.** 64 m = ___?___ km 0.064

12. 26 mm = ___?___ m 0.026 **13.** 28 m = ___?___ mm 28,000 **14.** 31 km = ___?___ m 31,000

Perimeter

The **perimeter** of a figure is the distance around it.

EXAMPLE Find the perimeter of each figure.

a. Triangle **b. Rectangle** **c. Octagon**

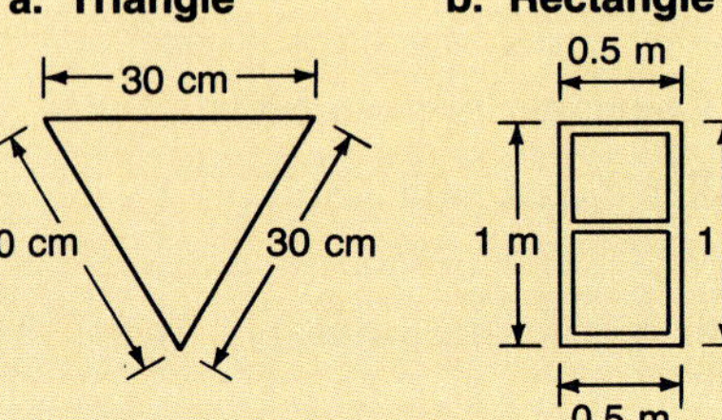

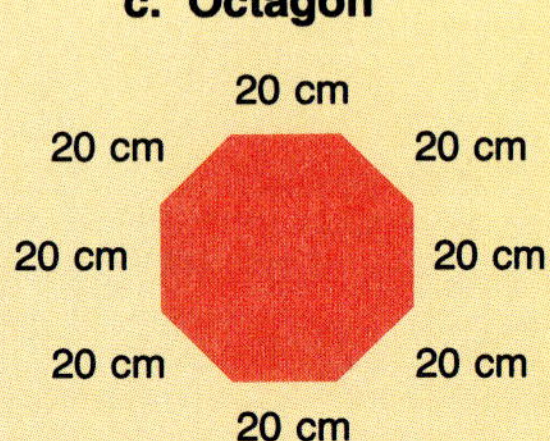

Solutions:

Add the lengths of the sides.

a. $P = 30 + 30 + 30$

$P =$ **90 centimeters**

b. $P = 0.5 + 1 + 0.5 + 1$

$P =$ **3 meters**

c. $P = 20 + 20 + 20 + 20 + 20 + 20 + 20 + 20$

$P =$ **160 centimeters**

PRACTICE

Find the perimeter of each figure.

1. Postage Stamp 8.8 cm

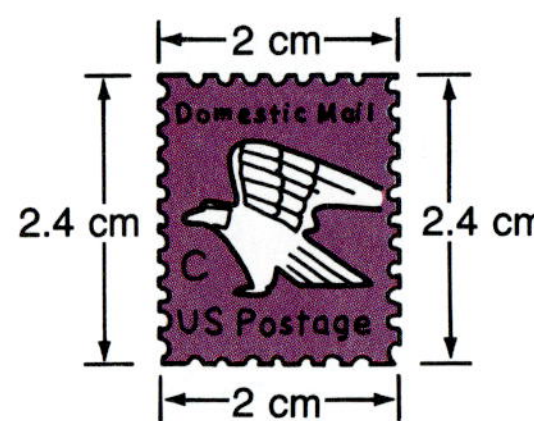

2. Garden 64.8 m

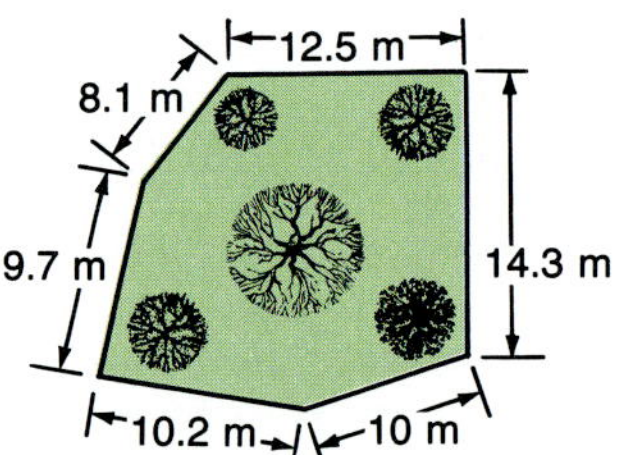

3. Pendant 95 mm

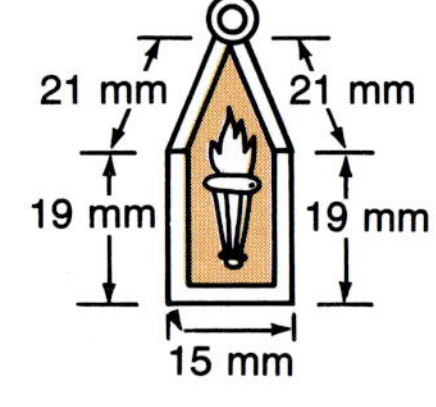

4.

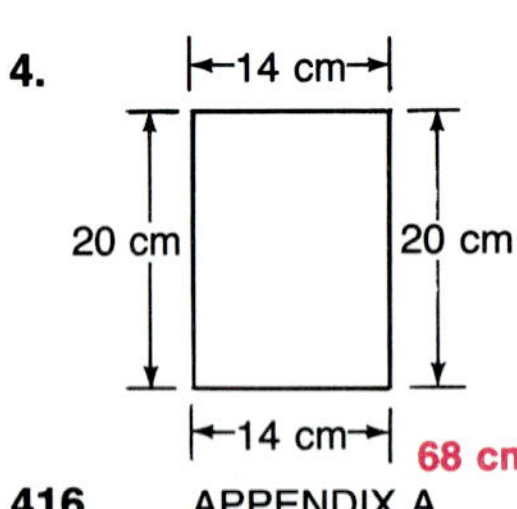

68 cm

5. Hexagon: 6 sides

39 cm
60 cm
60 cm

159 cm

6. Pentagon: 5 sides

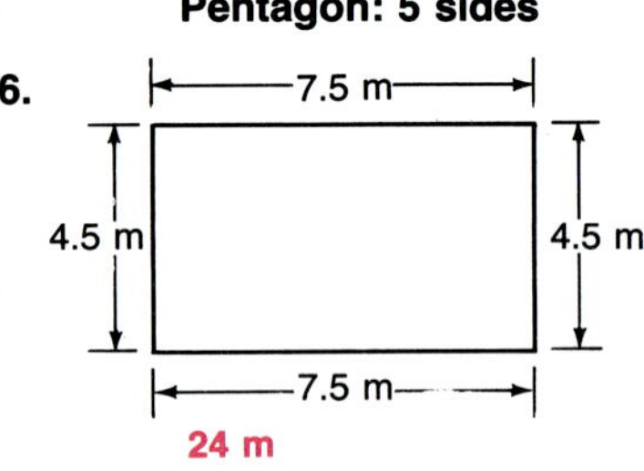

24 m

Perimeter Using Formulas

You can use a **formula** to find the perimeter of a rectangle.
The opposite sides of a **rectangle** *are equal in length.*

$$P = 2(l + w)$$ ◀ P = perimeter, l = length, w = width

EXAMPLE An envelope is 24 centimeters long and 10.5 centimeters wide. Find the perimeter.

Solution:

$P = 2(l + w)$ ◀ l = 24 cm, w = 10.5 cm

$P = 2(24 + 10.5)$

$P = 2(34.5)$

$P = \mathbf{69}$

The perimeter is **69 centimeters.**

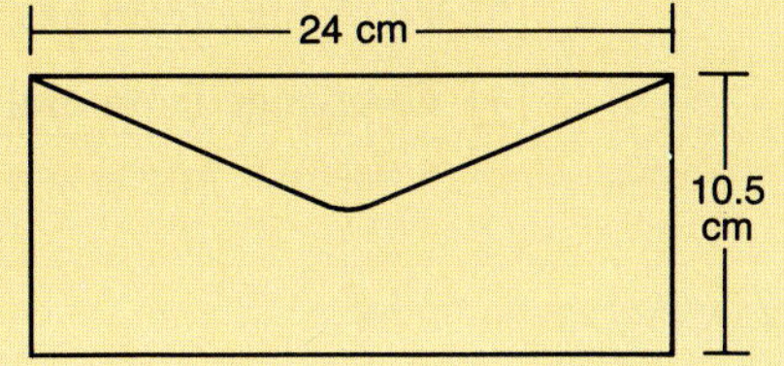

The sides of a **square** *have equal lengths.*

To find the perimeter of a square, you use the formula $P = 4 \times s$ where s represents the length of a side.

PRACTICE

Use the formula $P = 4 \times s$ or $P = 2(l + w)$ to find each perimeter.

1. Picture Frame 116 cm

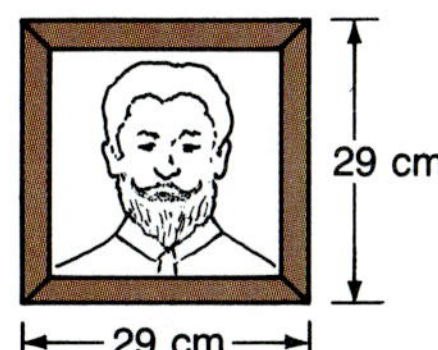

2. Desk Top 4.0 m

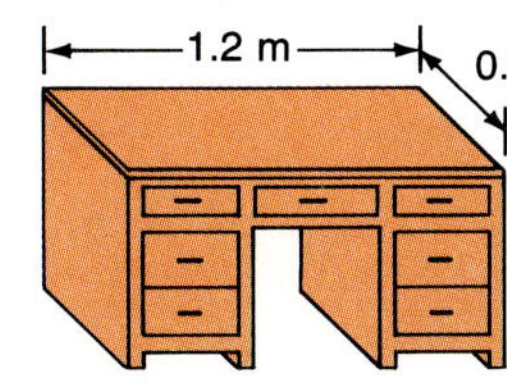

3. Sheet of Paper 50 cm

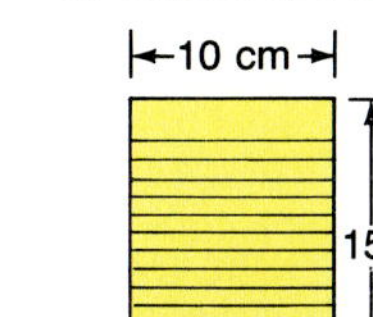

	Length	Width	Perimeter
4.	7 cm	4 cm	? 22 cm
5.	15 m	15 m	? 60 m
6.	0.8 m	0.3 m	? 2.2 m
7.	8.2 m	8.2 m	? 32.8 m

	Length	Width	Perimeter
8.	12.4 cm	8.9 cm	? 42.6 cm
9.	21 cm	21 cm	? 84 cm
10.	9.2 cm	7.6 cm	? 33.6 cm
11.	6.5 m	3.7 m	? 20.4 m

Metric Units of Mass

The **kilogram** is the base unit of mass in the metric system.

The following relationships are useful in changing units.

1 kilogram = 1000 grams **1 gram = 1000 milligrams**

Rules for Changing Between Metric Units

[1] To change from kilograms to grams, multiply by 1000.

[2] To change from grams to kilograms, multiply by 0.001.

[3] To change from grams to milligrams, multiply by 1000.

[4] To change from milligrams to grams, multiply by 0.001.

EXAMPLE

a. 62 kg = ? g **b.** 3700 g = ? kg

Solutions:

Larger to smaller

a. 62 kg = (62 × 1000) g
= **62,000 g**

Smaller to larger

b. 3700 g = (3700 × 0.001) kg
= **3.7 kg**

PRACTICE

Choose the equivalent measure. Choose a, b, or c.

1. 9 kilograms a — **a.** 9000 g **b.** 90 g **c.** 0.09 g
2. 14,000 grams c — **a.** 1400 kg **b.** 140 kg **c.** 14 kg
3. 5 grams b — **a.** 50,000 mg **b.** 5,000 mg **c.** 500 mg
4. 600 mg a — **a.** 0.6 g **b.** 0.06 g **c.** 0.006 g

Complete.

5. 25 kg = ? g 25,000
6. 363 kg = ? g 363,000
7. 4.2 kg = ? g 4200
8. 264 g = ? kg 0.264
9. 3.8 g = ? kg 0.0038
10. 0.4 g = ? kg 0.0004
11. 6 g = ? mg 6000
12. 21.8 g = ? mg 21,800
13. 7.6 g = ? mg 7600
14. 6421 mg = ? g 6.421
15. 4.81 mg = ? g 0.00481
16. 0.7 mg = ? g 0.0007
17. 28 kg = ? g 28,000
18. 67.5 mg = ? g 0.0675
19. 2.21 g = ? mg 2210
20. 35 g = ? mg 35,000
21. 25 g = ? kg 0.025
22. 2130 g = ? kg 2.130

Metric Units of Capacity

The amount a container will hold is called **capacity.** In the metric system, the most commonly used units of capacity are the **milliliter** (abbreviated: mL) and the **liter** (abbreviated: L).

1000 milliliters = 1 liter

Rules for Changing Between Metric Units

[1] To change from liters to milliliters, multiply by 1000.

[2] To change milliliters to liters, multiply by 0.001.

EXAMPLE

a. 5 L = ? mL

b. 13.7 mL = ? L

Solutions:

Larger to smaller

a. 5 L = (5 × 1000) mL
= **5000 mL**

Smaller to larger

b. 13.7 mL = (13.7 × 0.001) L
= **0.0137 L**

PRACTICE

Choose the most suitable measure. Choose a, b, or c.

1. Coffee pot

c

a. 25 mL
b. 2.5 mL
c. 2.5 L

2. Swimming Pool

a

a. 75,000 L
b. 75 L
c. 75 mL

3. Stew Pot

a

a. 6 L
b. 6 mL
c. 600 mL

4. Can of oil

b

a. 100 L
b. 1 L
c. 1 mL

Complete.

5. 37 L = ? mL 37,000

6. 321 L = ? mL 321,000

7. 229 L = ? mL 229,000

8. 3.4 L = ? mL 3400

9. 5.8 L = ? mL 5800

10. 22.3 L = ? mL 22,300

11. 386 mL = ? L 0.386

12. 792 mL = ? L 0.792

13. 2478 mL = ? L 2.478

14. 22 mL = ? L 0.022

15. 7.2 mL = ? L 0.0072

16. 0.8 L = ? mL 800

17. 0.04 L = ? mL 40

18. 0.005 L = ? mL 5

19. 21 mL = ? L 0.021

Area

Each side of this square is 1 centimeter long. Its area is 1×1, or 1 **square centimeter** (abbreviated: 1 cm^2).

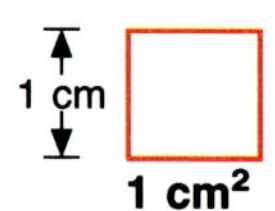

Area is measured in **square units.** You can use a formula to find the area of some figures.

To find the area of a rectangle multiply the length and the width.

$$A = lw$$

lw means l × w.
l = length
w = width

EXAMPLE A basketball court is 26 meters long and 15 meters wide. Find the area of the court.

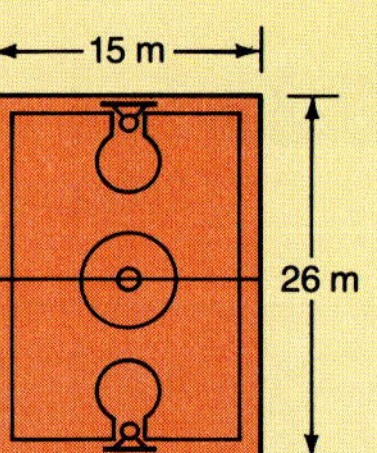

Solution:

$A = lw$ — *l = 26 m*, *w = 15 m*

$A = 26 \times 15$

$A = \mathbf{390}$ The area is **390 m²**.

PRACTICE

For Exercises 1–13, find the area of each rectangle.

1. Check 10,500 mm²

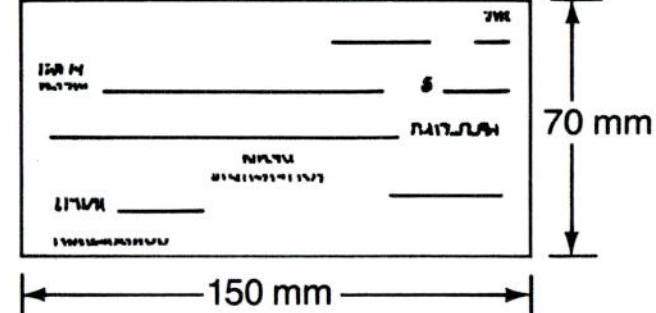

2. Photograph 500 cm²

3. Rug 17.64 m²

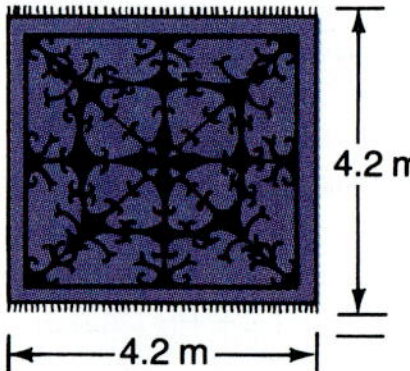

	Length	*Width*	*Area*		*Length*	*Width*	*Area*
4.	14 cm	8 cm	? 112 cm²	**9.**	25 mm	18 mm	?
5.	3 m	1.5 m	? 4.5 cm²	**10.**	1.2 m	1.2 m	?
6.	5 m	3 m	? 15 m²	**11.**	36 mm	18 mm	?
7.	10 cm	8 cm	? 80 cm²	**12.**	10 m	10 m	?
8.	6.7 m	2.4 m	? 16.08 m²	**13.**	22.3 cm	20.4 cm	?

9. 450 mm² 10. 1.44 m² 11. 648 mm² 12. 100 m² 13. 454.92 cm²

Volume

A **rectangular prism** is a solid such as the filing cabinet at the right. The **volume** of a rectangular prism is the amount of space it contains. Volume is measured in **cubic units.**

To find the volume of a rectangular prism, find the product of the length, width, and height.

$$V = lwh$$

EXAMPLE Find the volume of this box of cereal.

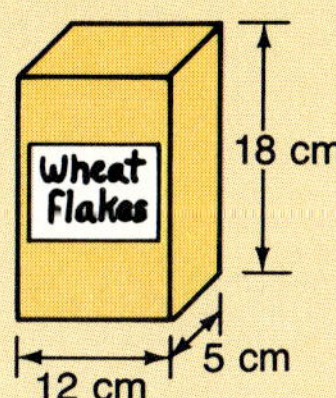

Solution:

$V = lwh$ ◀ l = 12 cm; w = 5 cm; h = 18 cm

$V = 12 \times 5 \times 18$

$V = \mathbf{1080}$ The volume is **1080 cm³**.

PRACTICE

For Exercises 1–13, find the volume of each rectangular prism.

1. Briefcase 11,020 cm³

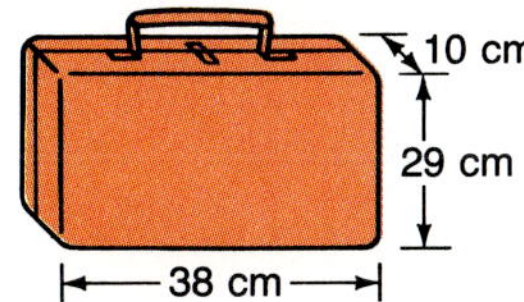

2. Trunk 0.63 m³

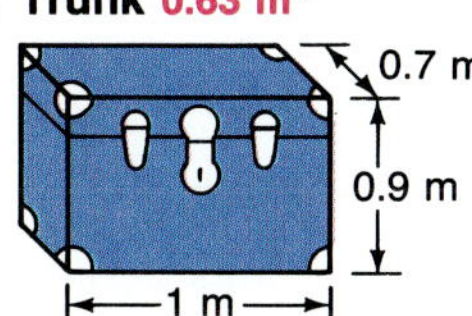

3. Shoe Box 6480 cm³

18 cm
12 cm
30 cm

	Length	Width	Height
4.	6 m	4 m	10 m 240 m³
5.	21 cm	15 cm	5 cm 1575 cm³
6.	4 m	3 m	6 m 72 m³
7.	8 m	8 m	8 m 512 m³
8.	21 cm	12 cm	10 cm 2520 cm³

	Length	Width	Height
9.	2.4 m	1.8 m	6.3 m 27.216 m³
10.	12 cm	12 cm	12 cm 1728 cm³
11.	4.6 m	3.2 m	5 m 73.6 m³
12.	25 cm	10 cm	30 cm 7500 cm³
13.	2.8 m	1.9 m	0.6 m 3.192 m³

Temperature

In the metric system, the **Celsius** thermometer is used to measure temperature.

It may be helpful to memorize the temperatures and the information in the following table.

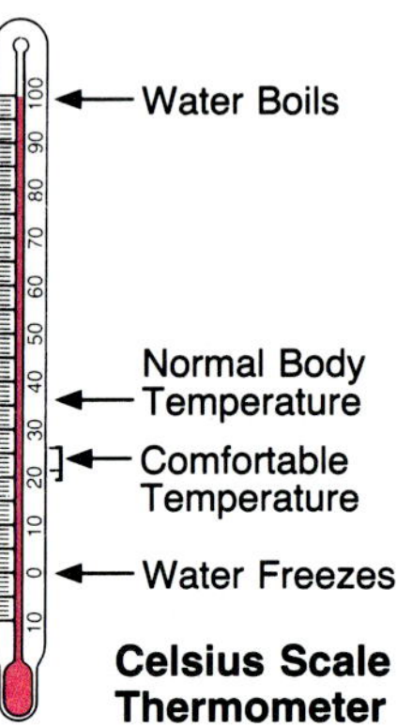

Celsius Scale Thermometer

Temperature	*Meaning*
100°C	Water boils
37°C	Normal body temperature
35°C	Hot summer days
22°C–26°C	Comfortable room temperature
0°C	Water freezes

PRACTICE

Choose the most suitable temperature. Choose a, b, or c.

		a.	b.	c.
1.	The temperature of a hot cup of soup **c**	**a.** 10°C	**b.** 25°C	**c.** 75°C
2.	The temperature of a cool fall day **b**	**a.** 0°C	**b.** 11°C	**c.** 40°C
3.	The temperature of a glass of ice water **a**	**a.** 0°C	**b.** 10°C	**c.** 20°C
4.	The temperature of a comfortable room **a**	**a.** 21°C	**b.** 31°C	**c.** 41°C
5.	The temperature of a person with a fever **b**	**a.** 25°C	**b.** 38°C	**c.** 45°C
6.	The temperature of a cold winter day **a**	**a.** 4°C	**b.** 14°C	**c.** 24°C
7.	The temperature of a warm summer day **b**	**a.** 5°C	**b.** 28°C	**c.** 43°C
8.	The temperature of a cold glass of milk **a**	**a.** 3°C	**b.** 10°C	**c.** 20°C
9.	The temperature for sunbathing **b**	**a.** 0°C	**b.** 30°C	**c.** 50°C
10.	The temperature of a snowball **a**	**a.** 1°C	**b.** 10°C	**c.** 20°C

11. The outdoor temperature is 2°C. Is this warm enough for you to go sunbathing? **No**

12. The outdoor temperature is 30°C. Would you go to the beach or to a ski resort? **beach**

13. The room temperature is 15°C. Would you turn the air conditioning on or turn the heat on? **the heat**

14. The room temperature is 30°C. Would you need to wear a woolen sweater? **No**

APPENDIX B

CALCULATOR MANUAL

Using the Calculator

A calculator is a tool that you must learn to use properly. Just as there are different kinds of tools, there are different calculators with different keys and different modes of operation. Here are some ideas for working with an unfamiliar calculator.

a. Carefully read the instruction booklet.

b. Estimate each answer to be sure the calculator's result makes sense.

c. Experiment with solving problems in different ways.

Don't be afraid to experiment with different sequences of keys.

If the calculator has these keys:	To clear the last number entered, press:	To clear the entire problem, press:
[C] and [CE]	[CE]	[C]
[CE/C]	[CE/C]	[CE/C] [CE/C]
[ON/C]	[ON/C]	[ON/C] [ON/C]

The following examples show how to correct entries.

A. Correcting a number that has been entered incorrectly.
Add: 235 + 168 = ?

235 [+] 167 [CE] 168 [=] 403.

B. Clearing all the entries
Add: 235 + 168 = ?

233 [+] 168 [C] 235 [+] 168 [=] 403.

C. Correcting an operation that has been entered incorrectly.
Add: 235 + 168 = ?

235 [×] [+] 168 [=] 403.

Addition/Subtraction: WHOLE NUMBERS

When adding on a calculator you may become careless and enter a wrong number. It is important to **estimate** the sum before you add.

EXAMPLE 1

8,417 + 9,205 + 1,875 = ?

Round to the nearest thousand.

8,417	→	8,000
9,205	→	9,000
+ 1,875	→	2,000

To estimate a sum, round each addend. Then add.

Estimated sum: 19,000

Press: 8417 [+] 9205 [+] 1875 [=] 19497.

Commas are not entered.

The sum is **19,497.** The answer is close to the estimate.

When subtracting you should always **check** your answer.

EXAMPLE 2

In 1970 the population of Pine Falls was 79,084. By 1980 the population had grown to 82,321. What was the increase?

Press: 82321 [−] 79084 [=] 3237.

To check your answer, add.

Check: 3237 [+] 79084 [=] 82321.

The population increased by **3,237.**

TRY THESE

First estimate the answer. Then find the exact answer. Compare the answer with the estimate to see if it is reasonable.

1. One year 436,725 personal computers were sold. The next year 1,217,841 were sold. How many computers were sold? 1,654,566
2. Carla says she is 6,307,200 minutes old. Todd is only 6,044,400 minutes old. How many minutes older is Carla? 262,800
3. One year a band sold 1,420,760 records. The next year the band sold 884,912 records. How many records were sold in the two years? 2,305,672

An Addition/Subtraction Shortcut

You can add or subtract a number repeatedly by entering that number into the calculator only once.

Problem: 45 + 15 + 15 + 15 + 15 = ?

45 [+] 15 [=] 60. [=] 75. [=] 90. [=] 105

Problem: 360 − 30 − 30 − 30 − 30 = ?

360 [−] 30 [=] 330. [=] 300. [=] 270. [=] 240

TRY THESE

1. Marva Johnson is a research scientist. She recently received a grant to help her finish a project. The terms of the grant entitle her to an initial payment of $5,000 and additional payments of $2,500 a year for 5 years. How much money will she receive under this grant? $17,500

2. The Oceangate Library has a collection of 36,489 books. The town council voted to increase the library's budget. The library will now be able to buy 725 new books each year. How many books will be in the library's collection after 6 years? 40,839

3. A neighborhood group of volunteers opened a soup kitchen to help feed needy people in their section of the city. When the soup kitchen opened, there were 2,800 cans of stew in the storeroom. The cooks estimated that about 220 cans will be used each week. About how many cans of stew will be in the storeroom after 8 weeks? 1,040

4. Yoshi Keto is a computer programmer. His employer offered him a 5-year contract. According to the contract, his salary during the first year will be $25,000. During the next four years, his salary will increase by $2,750 a year. If Yoshi accepts the contract, what will his annual salary be during the fifth year of the contract? $36,000

5. The AQ Comp Manufacturing Company announced that it was accepting advance orders for its new line of minicomputers. The company expects to produce 15,000 computers within the next three months. During the first week after the announcement, the company received orders for 1,685 computers. If orders are received at the same rate each week, how many computers will the company have left to sell after 7 weeks? 3,205

Using the Calculator Memory

Many calculators have a **memory.** The number in the memory is controlled by using either three or four keys, depending on the calculator.

If the calculator has this key:	the key:
M+ or M±	Adds the displayed number to the number in the memory.
M− or M∓	Subtracts the displayed number from the number in the memory.
RM or MR	Recalls the number in the memory for display or use.
CM or MC	Clears (erases) the number in the memory.
RM/CM or RCM or RMC	When you press this key once, it recalls the number from the memory. When you press it twice, it clears the number in the memory.

When a number is stored in the memory, a small M is displayed to remind you. Before starting a new problem, always press CM and C to clear the calculator.

EXAMPLE Mrs. Weiss bought 6 bars of soap at $0.39 each and 3 boxes of cereal at $1.19 each. How much money did she spend? How much change did she receive from a $20.00 bill?

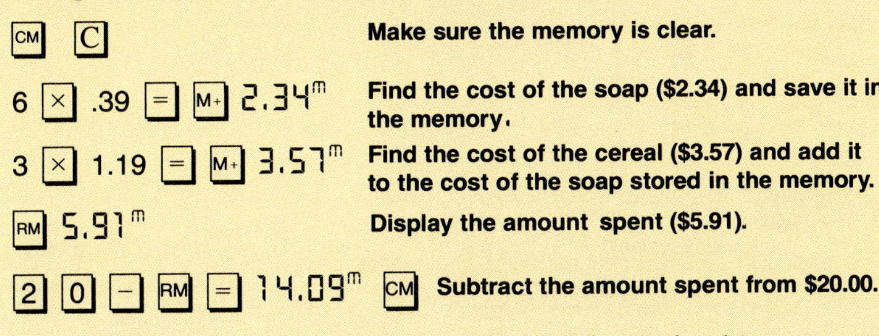

Make sure the memory is clear.

Find the cost of the soap ($2.34) and save it in the memory.

Find the cost of the cereal ($3.57) and add it to the cost of the soap stored in the memory.

Display the amount spent ($5.91).

Subtract the amount spent from $20.00.

Mrs. Weiss spent **$5.91** and received **$14.09** in change.

TRY THESE *Solve.*

1. Alfredo purchased 3 pads at $0.79 each, and 5 blank cassettes at $2.29 each. What did he spend? How much change did he receive from a $20 bill? $13.82; $6.18

2. A salesperson sold 2 typewriters at $189.95 each, 7 calculators at $9.99 each, and a camera for $139.49. What were the total sales? $589.32

Order of Operations/Powers

Different answers can be obtained for the same problem, especially when a calculator is used. Consider the problem 700 − 200 × 3.

On many calculators: 700 [−] 200 [×] 3 [=] 1500 ◀ *Which is correct?*

On some calculators: 700 [−] 200 [×] 3 [=] 100

Mathematicians have agreed upon the **order of operations:**

a. Perform operations within parentheses first.
b. Multiply and divide, in order from left to right.
c. Add and subtract, in order from left to right.

Therefore, 700 − 200 × 3 = 700 − 600, or **100.**

If you follow the rules for order of operations, you will get the correct answer no matter which type of calculator you use.

EXAMPLE 1 25 × 35 + (400 − 125) = ?

a. Within parentheses. 400 [−] 125 [=] 275. [M+]

b. Multiply. Then add. 25 [×] 35 [=] 875. [+] [RM] [=] 1150.

c. Press [CM]. The result is **1,150.**

EXAMPLE 2 9^3 = ?

a. Method 1
9 [×] 9 [×] 9 [=] 729.

b. Method 2 (Scientific Calculator)
9 [y^x] 3 [=] 729.

TRY THESE

Use your calculator. Remember to clear the memory after each problem.

1. 639 − 41 × 9 270
2. 123 + 18 × 23 537
3. (947 + 787) ÷ (120 − 86) 51
4. (82 − 58) × (96 + 47) 3,432
5. 15^4 50,625
6. 6^5 7,776
7. 5^6 15,625
8. 12^3 1,728

Addition/Subtraction: DECIMALS

The calculator automatically places the decimal point in the answer. It is easy to make an error in entering or reading a decimal point. It is important that you estimate first to see that the answer displayed makes sense.

EXAMPLE 1 6.875 + 3.25 + 4.1875 = ?

Estimate: Round to the nearest whole number: 7 + 3 + 4 = **14**

6.875 [+] 3.25 [+] 4.1875 = 14.3125

The answer, **14.3125,** is close to the estimate of 14.

EXAMPLE 2 215.4 − 92.625 = ?

Estimate: Round to the nearest ten: 220 − 90 = **130**

215.4 [−] 92.625 [=] 122.775

The answer, **122.775,** is close to the estimate of 130.

When a problem involving decimals has too many digits for the calculator, the digits farthest to the right are dropped or rounded off. There is no error signal to show that digits have been lost.

EXAMPLE 3 50,000,000 + 215.375 = ?

Think: The sum is 50,000,215.375.

50000000 [+] 215.375 [=] 50000215.

The calculator displays an answer that is only approximate.

TRY THESE

First estimate the answer. Then find the exact answer. Compare the answer with the estimate to see if it is reasonable.

1. 94.7 + 8.85 + 46.3 149.85
2. 113.7 − 49.85 63.85
3. 139.8 + 86.95 + 62.4 289.15
4. 72.3 − 38.675 33.625
5. 7.875 + 13.375 + 9.5 30.75
6. 400 − 129.63 270.37
7. \$426,723.19 + \$217,406.58 \$644,129.77
8. \$600,000 − \$139,416.27 \$460,583.73

Multiplication and Estimation:
WHOLE NUMBERS/DECIMALS

You can tell whether the answer displayed by the calculator makes sense by estimating the answer first.

EXAMPLE 1 539 × 78 = ?

Think: Round 539 to 500. Round 78 to 80. 500 × 80 = **40,000**

539 [×] 78 [=] 42042.

The estimate of 40,000 suggests that the product **42,042** is correct.

EXAMPLE 2 387 × 6.2 = ?

Think: Round 387 to 400. Round 6.2 to 6. 400 × 6 = **2,400**

387 [×] 6.2 [=] 2399.4

The estimate of 2,400 suggests that the product **2,399.4** is correct.

TRY THESE

First estimate the answer. Then find the exact answer. Compare the answer with the estimate to see if it is reasonable.

		Estimate	Product			Estimate	Product
1.	91 × 87	? 8,100	? 7,917	**13.**	83 × 7.9	? 640	? 655.7
2.	51 × 52	? 2,500	? 2,652	**14.**	62 × 6.1	? 360	? 378.2
3.	28 × 33	? 900	? 924	**15.**	34 × 8.9	? 270	? 302.6
4.	77 × 61	? 4,800	? 4,697	**16.**	71 × 5.2	? 350	? 369.2
5.	68 × 84	? 5,600	? 5,712	**17.**	58 × 3.8	? 240	? 220.4
6.	83 × 219	? 16,000	? 18,177	**18.**	82 × 41.5	? 3,280	? 3,403
7.	58 × 643	? 39,000	? 37,294	**19.**	91 × 63.3	? 5,400	? 5,760.3
8.	72 × 307	? 21,000	? 22,104	**20.**	21 × 30.8	? 600	? 646.8
9.	66 × 1,259	? 91,000	? 83,094	**21.**	1,126 × 6.7	? 7,700	? 7,544.2
10.	68 × 3,269	? 231,000	? 222,292	**22.**	5,231 × 5.7	? 31,200	? 29,816.7
11.	228 × 684	? 140,000	? 155,952	**23.**	318 × 68.4	? 21,000	? 21,751.2
12.	26 × 4,349	? 129,000	? 113,074	**24.**	709 × 42.6	? 28,000	? 30,203.4

Multiplying Large Numbers: OVERFLOW

When the answer to a problem has too many digits to be displayed, the calculator **overflows.**

EXAMPLE 1 52,645 × 7,983 = ?

52645 [×] 7983 [=] 4.2026503E

The E indicates that the entire answer has not been displayed. The decimal point helps to tell how many digits are missing. There is one digit before the decimal. So one digit is missing.

Look at the original problem. The first factor ends in 5. The second factor ends in 3. So 5 × 3 = 15. Therefore, the final digit of the answer must be a 5.

52,645 × 7,983 = **420,265,035**

Now press [C] to clear the calculator.

EXAMPLE 2 98,542 × 81,086 = ?

98542 [×] 81086 [=] 79.903766E.

There are two digits before the decimal. So two digits are missing.

Think: The last two digits of the product depend on the last two digits of each factor.

[C] 42 [×] 86 [=] 3612.

The last two digits of this product are 1 and 2.

98,542 × 81,086 = **7,990,376,612**

TRY THESE

1. 13,407 × 9,526 127,715,082
2. 37,512 × 3,589 134,630,568
3. 61,039 × 4,203 256,546,917
4. 53,826 × 7,816 420,704,016
5. 43,609 × 4,933 215,123,197
6. 92,125 × 6,515 600,194,375
7. 51,439 × 24,302 1,250,070,578
8. 82,065 × 46,127 3,785,412,255
9. 29,842 × 38,094 1,136,801,148
10. 43,663 × 63,693 2,781,027,459
11. 58,391 × 42,107 2,458,669,837
12. 64,089 × 29,312 1,878,576,768
13. 111,111 × 11,111 1,234,554,321
14. 412,205 × 16,519 6,809,214,395
15. 653,417 × 13,921 9,096,218,057

Multiplication: DECIMALS

A calculator multiplies decimals as easily as it multiplies whole numbers. The result displayed may be approximate, or the calculator may **underflow** and display a zero, without any indication or error signal.

EXAMPLE 1 To find when the calculator:

a. Displays an approximate product;

b. Underflows and displays a zero.

.025 [×] .035 [=] 0.000875

.0025 [×] .035 [=] 0.0000875

.0025 [×] .0035 [=] 0.0000087

.00025 [×] .0035 [=] 0.0000008

When the product requires more than eight digits, an approximate answer is displayed.

.00025 [×] .00035 [=] 0.

When the product is less than 0.0000001, a nonscientific calculator underflows and displays 0.

EXAMPLE 2 0.00025 × 0.00034

Think: The product will have 10 decimal places.

25 [×] 34 [=] 850.

When the calculator underflows, this method will often give the product.

Write: 0.0000000850 or 0.000000085

TRY THESE

First estimate the answer. Then find the exact answer. Compare the answer with the estimate to see if it is reasonable.

1. 46.4 × 36.25 1,682

2. 31.75 × 6.64 210.82

3. 78.35 × 11.8 924.53

4. 5.375 × 49.6 266.6

5. 631.4 × 916.3 578,551.82

6. 147.8 × 802.6 118,624.28

7. 925.73 × 412.9 382,233.917

8. 302.75 × 98.43 29,799.6825

9. 692 × 723.85 500,904.2

10. 47.88 × 531.25 25,436.25

11. 0.09 × 0.36 0.0324

12. 0.285 × 0.4 0.114

13. 0.0045 × 0.063 0.0002835

14. 0.175 × 0.0049 0.0008575

15. 2.0083 × 1.0092 2.02677636

16. 0.64175 × 0.55413 0.3556129275

17. 0.00017 × 0.00039 0.0000000663

18. 0.00023 × 0.00021 0.0000000483

Division: WHOLE NUMBERS/DECIMALS

When you are using a calculator to do a division problem, remember that the dividend must always be entered first.

EXAMPLE 1 Janine drove 255 miles in 4.25 hours. Find the speed of the automobile in miles per hour.

Think: 255 ÷ 4.25 **Estimate:** 260 ÷ 4 = 65

255 [÷] 4.25 [=] 60. Janine drove at a rate of 60 miles per hour.

Multiplication and division are **inverse operations.**
Use multiplication to **check** the answer to a division problem.

Think: 60 miles per hour for 4.25 hours

60 [×] 4.25 [=] 255. The answer checks.

Solving problems on a calculator sometimes involves difficulties.

EXAMPLE 2 Fred has 81 books to put in boxes. He puts one dozen books into each box. How many boxes does he fill? How many books are left over?

81 [÷] 12 [=] 6.75

Think: The display shows that Fred can fill 6 boxes. But the remainder has been expressed as a decimal. It does not tell how many books are left over.

Here are two ways to find the remainder.

12 [×] .75 [=] 9.

1. Multiply the decimal part of the answer, 0.75, by the divisor, 12.

12 [×] 6 [=] 72.
81 [−] 72 [=] 9.

2. Multiply the whole-number part of the answer, 6, by the divisor, 12. Then subtract the result from the dividend.

Both methods show that Fred has **9** books left over.

TRY THESE *First estimate the answer. Then find the exact answer. Compare the answer with the estimate to see if it is reasonable.*

1. 8.6) 51,944 6040 **2.** 24.68) 21,328,456 864,200 **3.** 39) 21,305 546 r11 **4.** 505,467 ÷ 758 666 r639

Fractions and Decimals

On most calculators fractions and mixed numbers must be expressed in decimal form.

To indicate a **repeating decimal,** draw a bar over the digit(s) that repeat.

EXAMPLE 1

a. Find the decimal for $\frac{5}{12}$.

5 [÷] 12 [=] 0.4166666

$\frac{5}{12}$ = **0.4166666** or **$0.41\overline{6}$**

A calculator that rounds may display 0.4166667.

b. Find the decimal for $9\frac{7}{16}$.

Think: $9\frac{7}{16} = \frac{7}{16} + 9$

7 [÷] 16 [+] 9 [=] 9.4375.

$9\frac{7}{16}$ = **9.4375**

EXAMPLE 2

a. Write the decimal for $\frac{11}{15}$.

11 [÷] 15 [=] 0.7333333

$\frac{11}{15}$ [=] **$0.7\overline{3}$**

b. Write the decimal for $5\frac{3}{11}$.

3 [÷] 11 [+] 5 [=]

5.2727272

A calculator that rounds may display 5.2727273

$5\frac{3}{11}$ = **$5.\overline{27}$**

TRY THESE

Find the decimal for each fraction.

1. $\frac{31}{80}$ 0.3875 **2.** $\frac{15}{16}$ 9.937 **3.** $\frac{113}{160}$ 0.70625 **4.** $21\frac{35}{56}$ 21.625 **5.** $\frac{23}{40}$ 0.575 **6.** $57\frac{5}{32}$ 57.15625

7. $\frac{157}{200}$ 0.785 **8.** $\frac{29}{116}$ 0.25 **9.** $4\frac{307}{500}$ 4.614 **10.** $48\frac{58}{87}$ $48.\overline{6}$ **11.** $\frac{101}{128}$ 0.7890625 **12.** $\frac{91}{143}$ $0.\overline{63}$

13. $\frac{59}{64}$ 0.921875 **14.** $17\frac{56}{111}$ $17.\overline{504}$ **15.** $\frac{14}{15}$ $0.9\overline{3}$ **16.** $31\frac{13}{64}$ 31.203125 **17.** $\frac{117}{143}$ $0.\overline{81}$ **18.** $92\frac{113}{200}$ 92.565

19. $\frac{19}{30}$ $0.6\overline{3}$ **20.** $11\frac{37}{40}$ 11.925 **21.** $\frac{196}{252}$ $0.\overline{7}$ **22.** $104\frac{13}{16}$ 104.8125 **23.** $\frac{119}{280}$ 0.425 **24.** $58\frac{313}{400}$ 58.7825

25. $\frac{148}{407}$ $0.\overline{36}$ **26.** $\frac{236}{649}$ $0.\overline{36}$ **27.** $\frac{468}{1,287}$ $0.\overline{36}$ **28.** $5\frac{35}{112}$ 5.3125 **29.** $5\frac{195}{624}$ 5.3125 **30.** $5\frac{1}{32}$ 5.03125

Proportions

Two **equivalent ratios** can be written to form a true **proportion.** When a proportion is true, its cross products are equal.

EXAMPLE 1 Does $\frac{39}{26} = \frac{51}{34}$?

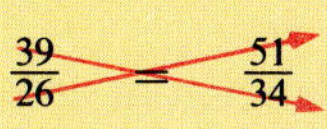

26 [×] 51 [=] 1326.

39 [×] 34 [=] 1326.

The ratios are equivalent.

A missing term of a proportion can be found if the other three terms are known.

EXAMPLE 2 Solve for n. $\frac{9}{n} = \frac{57}{152}$

Think: Find the cross products.

$$9 \times 152 = n \times 57$$

$$\frac{9 \times 152}{57} = \frac{n \times \overset{1}{\cancel{57}}}{\underset{1}{\cancel{57}}}$$

$$\frac{9 \times 152}{57} = n$$

9 [×] 152 [÷] 57 [=] 24.

Therefore n = **24.**

TRY THESE

Is it a true proportion? Write yes *or* no.

1. $\frac{28}{42} = \frac{38}{57}$ Yes **2.** $\frac{51}{68} = \frac{213}{284}$ Yes **3.** $\frac{52}{65} = \frac{92}{125}$ No **4.** $\frac{46}{73.6} = \frac{37.5}{60}$ Yes **5.** $\frac{22}{49.5} = \frac{26}{59.5}$ No

Solve each proportion for n. Use the cross products to check.

6. $\frac{52}{65} = \frac{92}{n}$ 115 **7.** $\frac{68}{153} = \frac{n}{135}$ 60 **8.** $\frac{n}{91} = \frac{152}{133}$ 104 **9.** $\frac{161}{n} = \frac{98}{112}$ 184 **10.** $\frac{84}{112} = \frac{n}{156}$ 117

11. $\frac{69}{n} = \frac{138}{276}$ 138 **12.** $\frac{57}{9} = \frac{n}{57}$ 361 **13.** $\frac{12}{n} = \frac{0.25}{12}$ 576 **14.** $\frac{n}{49.6} = \frac{42.5}{68}$ 31 **15.** $\frac{92.5}{222} = \frac{48}{n}$ 115.2

16. $\frac{208}{260} = \frac{n}{123}$ 98.4 **17.** $\frac{12.6}{33.6} = \frac{6.375}{n}$ 17 **18.** $\frac{48}{51.2} = \frac{n}{56}$ 52.5 **19.** $\frac{n}{22.3} = \frac{14.1}{60}$ 5.24 **20.** $\frac{35.6}{n} = \frac{88}{127.4}$ 51.54

435

Percent

Many calculators have a percent key, but they do not all work the same way. It is important to estimate the answer and then check to see that the display makes sense. Percent problems can be solved by using decimals instead of the percent key. (See Method 4.)

EXAMPLE 1 How much is 45% of 780?

Estimate: 45% is close to one half. One half of 800 is 400. The answer is less than 400.

Method 1 780 [×] 45 [%] 351.

Method 2 780 [×] 45 [%] [=] 351.

Method 3 45 [%] [×] 780 [=] 351.

Find which methods work on your calculator.

Method 4 Remember: 45% = 0.45

.45 [×] 780 [=] 351. Therefore, 45% of 780 is **351.**

EXAMPLE 2 A family with weekly take-home pay of $250 budgets these amounts.

Rent: $100	Carfare: $10	Food: $80
Clothes: $20	Savings: $15	Other: $25

What percent is budgeted for each?

Ignore the [=] if the calculator you are using does not need it.

100 [÷] 250 [%] [=] 40. 10 [÷] 250 [%] [=] 4. 80 [÷] 250 [%] [=] 32.

20 [÷] 250 [%] [=] 8. 15 [÷] 250 [%] [=] 6. 25 [÷] 250 [%] [=] 10.

The family budgets **40% for rent, 4% for carfare, 32% for food, 8% for clothes, 6% for savings,** and **10% for other items.**

Check: 40% + 4% + 32% + 8% + 6% + 10% = 100%

TRY THESE

1. 17% of 1,400 238 **2.** 49% of 6,400 3,136 **3.** 9.75% of 132 12.87

Compound Interest

When interest on a bank account is compounded, the interest earned is added to the principal at certain intervals during the year.

EXAMPLE Maria deposited $1,000 in a bank offering an annual interest rate of 15%, compounded monthly. What is the balance in her account at the end of the second month?

Step 1 Calculate the monthly rate.

.15 [÷] 12 [=] 0.0125

Step 2 Add 1.00 (or 100%) to represent the previous balance.

.0125 [+] 1 [=] 1.0125

Step 3 Use 1.0125 as the constant factor for each month.

1.0125 [×] 1000 [=] 1012.5

At the end of 1 month, Maria has a balance of $1,012.50.

Step 4 Continue to press [×] 1.0125 [=] for each of the remaining 11 months.

[×] 1.0125 [=] 1025.1562

If your calculator rounds, the display may be 1025.1563

At the end of the second month, Maria has a balance of **$1,025.16.**

TRY THESE

Calculate the balance. The interest is compounded monthly.

	Deposit	Annual Rate	Time	Balance		Deposit	Annual Rate	Time	Balance
1.	$5,000	12%	1 yr	? $5,634.13	**2.**	$2,000	18%	1 yr	? $2,391.24
3.	$3,000	15%	2 yr	? $4,042.05	**4.**	$1,200	9%	$2\frac{1}{2}$ yr	? $1,501.53
5.	$ 4,500	12%	15 mo	? $5,224.36	**6.**	$4,500	15%	10 mo	? $5,095.22
7.	$10,500	6%	9 mo	? $10,982.06	**8.**	$12,500	9%	8 mo	? $13,269.99

437

Powers and Roots

The second **power** of 5 is 25. 5 is a **square root** of 25.

$5^2 = 25$ $\sqrt{25} = 5$

Which of these methods works on your calculator?

EXAMPLE 1 Find the value of 7^4.

a. 7 [×] 7 [×] 7 [×] 7 [=] 2401. **b.** 7 [×] 7 [=] [=] [=] 2401.

On a scientific calculator, you find powers by using the [y^x] key.

EXAMPLE 2 Find the value of 2^3.

2 [×] 2 [×] 2 [=] 8. or 2 [y^x] 3 [=] 8.

If your calculator has a [√] key, you can easily find the square root of a number.

EXAMPLE 3 **a.** Find the square root of 1,369.

1,369 [√] 37.

Check: $37 \times 37 = 1,369$

b. $\sqrt{75} = \underline{\ ?\ }$

75 [√] 8.660254.

Check: 8.660254×8.660254

$= \mathbf{74.999999}$

The answer is approximate.

TRY THESE

Find the value of the following.

1. 15^3 3,375 **2.** 99^2 9,801 **3.** 8^6 262,144 **4.** 6^7 279,936 **5.** 114^3 1,481,544

6. 5^{11} 48,828,125 **7.** 347^3 41,781,923 **8.** 2^{24} 16,777,216 **9.** 37^5 69,343,957 **10.** 7.5^2 56.25

11. 3.25^3 34.328125 **12.** 0.3^5 0.00243 **13.** 8.35^2 69.7225 **14.** 0.09^2 0.0081 **15.** 9.8^3 941.192

16. $\sqrt{34,969}$ 187 **17.** $\sqrt{50}$ 7.0710678 **18.** $\sqrt{1.1}$ 1.0488088 **19.** $\sqrt{79}$ 8.8881944 **20.** $\sqrt{0.0144}$ 0.12

21. $\sqrt{113}$ 10.6301 **22.** $\sqrt{271}$ 16.4621 **23.** $\sqrt{317}$ 17.8045 **24.** $\sqrt{805}$ 28.3725 **25.** $\sqrt{31}$ 5.56777

26. $\sqrt{250}$ 15.8114 **27.** $\sqrt{1,000}$ 31.6228 **28.** $\sqrt{12.7}$ 3.56371 **29.** $\sqrt{50.41}$ 7.1 **30.** $\sqrt{61.83}$ 7.86321

438

Operations with Integers

Change-sign keys such as [+/−] or [CS] are usually used to enter negative numbers. When such a key is pressed, the sign of the displayed number changes.

EXAMPLE

a. $-24 + 31 = \underline{\ ?\ }$

24 [CS] [+] 31 [=] 7.

b. $-33 - (-19) = \underline{\ ?\ }$

33 [CS] [−] 19 [CS] [=] −14.

c. $-112 \div 7 = \underline{\ ?\ }$

112 [CS] [÷] 7 [=] −16

d. $-36 \times -14 = \underline{\ ?\ }$

36 [CS] [×] 14 [CS] [=] 504

TRY THESE

Use your calculator.

1. $36 + (-57)$ **−21**	**2.** $-56 + 83$ **27**	**3.** $-68 + (-21)$ **−89**	**4.** $29 + (-14)$ **15**
5. $72 + 38$ **110**	**6.** $-19 + (-54)$ **−73**	**7.** $-83 + 59$ **−24**	**8.** $-51 + 98$ **47**
9. $92 + (-92)$ **0**	**10.** $45 + 45$ **90**	**11.** $-78 + 78$ **0**	**12.** $33 + (-79)$ **−46**
13. $-34 - (-46)$ **12**	**14.** $28 - 59$ **−31**	**15.** $52 - 35$ **17**	**16.** $-47 - (-29)$ **−18**
17. $-85 - 51$ **−136**	**18.** $47 - (-80)$ **127**	**19.** $91 - (-43)$ **134**	**20.** $-70 - 87$ **−157**
21. $-63 - (-63)$ **0**	**22.** $19 - 19$ **0**	**23.** $29 - (-29)$ **58**	**24.** $-41 - 41$ **−82**
25. $215 + (-86)$ **129**	**26.** $-113 + (-78)$ **−191**	**27.** $59 - 131$ **−72**	**28.** $-71 - 129$ **−200**
29. $-10 \times (-16)$ **160**	**30.** $-100 \times (-21)$ **2,100**	**31.** $-100 \times (-46)$ **4,600**	**32.** $-10 \times (-92)$ **920**
33. $-21 \times (-21)$ **441**	**34.** $-36 \times (-12)$ **432**	**35.** $-46 \times (-25)$ **1,150**	**36.** $-72 \times (-81)$ **5,832**
37. -38×42 **−1596**	**38.** $24 \times (-27)$ **−648**	**39.** $53 \times (-16)$ **−848**	**40.** -87×29 **−2,523**
41. $-345 \div 23$ **−15**	**42.** $765 \div (-17)$ **−45**	**43.** $957 \div (-11)$ **87**	**44.** $-352 \div (-16)$ **22**
45. $-510 \div (-15)$ **34**	**46.** $-672 \div 16$ **−42**	**47.** $882 \div (-14)$ **−63**	**48.** $-860 \div (-43)$ **20**
49. $-714 \div 51$ **−14**	**50.** $-832 \div (-26)$ **32**	**51.** $-612 \div 18$ **−34**	**52.** $483 \div (-21)$ **−23**

TABLE OF MEASURES

METRIC SYSTEM OF MEASURES

Length

10 millimeters (mm) = 1 centimeter (cm)
10 centimeters = 1 decimeter (dm)
100 millimeters = 1 decimeter (dm)
10 decimeters = 1 meter (m)
100 centimeters = 1 meter (m)
1000 meters = 1 kilometer (km)

Area

100 sq millimeters (mm^2) = 1 sq centimeter (cm^2)
10,000 sq centimeters = 1 sq meter (m^2)
100 sq meters = 1 are (a)
10,000 sq meters = 1 hectare (ha)

Volume

1000 cu millimeters (mm^3) = 1 cu centimeter (cm^3)
1000 cu centimeters = 1 cu decimeter (dm^3)
1,000,000 cu centimeters = 1 cu meter (m^3)

Mass

1000 milligram (mg) = 1 gram (g)
1000 grams = 1 kilogram (kg)
1000 kilograms = 1 metric ton (t)

Capacity

1000 milliliters (mL) = 1 liter (L)
1000 liters = 1 kiloliter (kL)

Temperature

Water freezes at 0° Celsius (°C).
Water boils at 100° Celsius.
Normal body temperature is 37° Celsius.

CUSTOMARY SYSTEM OF MEASURES

Length

12 inches (in) = 1 foot (ft)
3 feet = 1 yard (yd)
36 inches = 1 yard (yd)
1760 yards = 1 mile (mi)
5280 feet = 1 mile (mi)
6076 feet = 1 nautical mile

Area

144 sq inches (in^2) = 1 sq foot (ft^2)
9 sq feet = 1 sq yard (yd^2)
4840 sq yards = 1 acre (A)

Volume

1728 cu inches (in^3) = 1 cu foot (ft^3)
27 cu feet = 1 cu yard (yd^3)

Weight

16 ounces (oz) = 1 pound (lb)
2000 pounds = 1 ton (T)

Capacity

8 fluid ounces (fl oz) = 1 cup (c)
2 cups = 1 pint (pt)
2 pints = 1 quart (qt)
4 quarts = 1 gallon (gal)

Temperature

Water freezes at 32° Fahrenheit (°F).
Water boils at 212° Fahrenheit.
Normal body temperature is 98.6° Fahrenheit.

GLOSSARY

The following definitions and statements reflect the usage of terms in this textbook.

Adjusted gross income The sum of all kinds of income a person may have which must be reported for figuring income tax. (Page 72)

Annual yield The percent of an investment received as income each year. (Page 324)

Area The measure in square units of the amount of surface inside a closed, plane figure. (Page 420)

Average, or **mean**

$$\textit{Average} = \frac{\text{Sum of Items}}{\text{Number of Items}} \quad \text{(Page 10)}$$

Axis (Plural: axes) A horizontal or vertical number line used to locate points. (Page 167)

Balance Amount left in a bank account after a withdrawal is made or a check is written. (Page 100)

Bar graph A *bar graph* uses horizontal or vertical bars to show data. (Page 2)

Bonds Sold by many governments and corporations to raise money. People who buy them are lending money to the corporation or government. In turn, bondholders receive interest (usually twice a year) on their bonds. (Page 326)

Budget A plan for balancing income and expenses. (Page 342)

Canceled checks Checks that the bank has paid. (Page 106)

Centimeter A unit of length in the metric system. *100 centimeters* equal 1 meter. (Page 415)

Certificate of deposit A way of investing money at a bank that allows the owner to earn interest at a higher rate than in a regular savings account. Certificates must be left on deposit for 6 months or longer and interest is lost if all or some of the money is withdrawn early. (Page 318)

Check A written order directing a bank to pay money as instructed. (Page 98)

Circle graph A graph in the shape of a circle used to show data. The graph uses per cents to show parts of a whole. (Page 6)

Collision insurance A type of car insurance that helps pay for repairs on a car if it is damaged in an accident. (Page 137)

Commission An amount, usually a per cent of goods sold, given to a salesperson, real estate agent, and so on, for services. (Page 45)

Compound interest Interest that is computed on the principal plus the interest previously earned. (Page 112)

Comprehensive car insurance Insurance that protects the owner from losses due to theft, fire, vandalism, and so on. (Page 137)

Cubic centimeter The capacity of this container is 1 *cubic centimeter* (abbreviated: 1 cm^3). (Page 209)

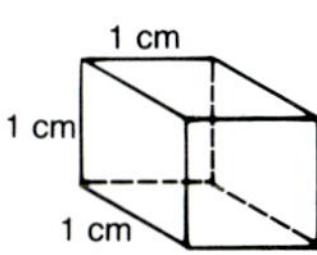

Deductible Any amount that the owner pays to cover damages before the insurance company pays the rest. (Page 137)

Deductions **For wages:** amounts subtracted from gross income for taxes and personal items such as insurance and pension. **For income tax:** amounts subtracted from adjusted gross income to determine taxable income. (Pages 48, 72)

Deposit Money put into a bank account. (Page 96)

Depreciation The decrease in value of a car because of its age and condition. (Page 156)

Discount An amount subtracted from the regular (list) price to obtain the sale price or a per cent of the regular price. (Page 284)

Dividends A portion of a company's profits which the company pays to its stockholders. (Page 324)

Down payment The amount of money paid before financing the purchase of a home or car. (Page 132)

Empirical data The information collected in a survey. (Page 31)

Empirical probability The *probability* you arrive at by using empirical data. (Page 31)

Estimation The process of calculating with rounded numbers. (Page 52)

Exemptions The number of people a worker claims to support. The number includes the worker. (Page 70)

Face value The amount printed on a bond. (Page 326)

Factorial The product of all the positive integers from one to a number. 5! (read: 5 factorial) equals $5 \times 4 \times 3 \times 2 \times 1$, or 120 (Page 25)

Finance charge The amount of interest paid for borrowing money or for buying on credit. (Page 132)

Formula A rule stated in words or in symbols that can be used in solving problems. (Page 300)

Frequency table A *table* that shows how many times items appear within given data. (Page 29)

Fundamental Principle of Counting If there are r choices for the way one thing can be done and s choices for the way another thing can be done, then together they may be done in $r \times s$ different ways. (Page 22)

Gross pay The total income before deductions are subtracted. (Page 48)

Histogram A bar graph that lists data by intervals. (Page 167)

Income tax A tax on the net income of an individual or a business. (Page 70)

Installment loan A loan that is repaid in several equal payments, with interest, over a specified amount of time. (Page 297)

Interest An amount paid for the use of money. *Interest* is usually a per cent of the amount invested, or lent, or borrowed. (Page 110)

Kilowatt-hour A measure of electricity used. *One kilowatt-hour* is 1000 watts of electricity used for 1 hour. (Page 262)

Liability insurance A type of car insurance, required by many states, that protects the owner from financial loss if others are injured by the car or if the car damages someone's property. (Page 135)

Line graph A graph that shows the amount of change over a period of time. (Page 4)

Maintenance costs The costs of upkeep and repair for a car. (Page 152)

Market price The current selling price of a bond. (Page 326)

Markup An amount added to the dealer's cost to cover profit and expenses. (Page 300)

Mean Another name for *average.* The *mean* of 2, 5, 6, and 7 is $(2 + 5 + 6 + 7) \div 4$, or 5. (Page 10)

Median In a list of numbers organized from least to greatest, the median is the middle number. The median of 1.6, 2.9, 3.4, 7.8, and 12.2 is 3.4. (Page 12)

Meter The base unit of length in the metric system. (Page 415)

Mode In a series, the item or number that occurs most often. (Page 10)

Mortgage loan A loan obtained from a bank or other lending institution used to pay for a home. (Page 232)

Net pay Take-home pay, found by subtracting deductions from gross pay. (Page 48)

Outstanding checks Checks that have been written but not paid by the bank. (Page 106)

Overtime Hours worked beyond the number of hours agreed upon for a regular week's pay. (Page 42)

Perimeter The sum of the lengths of the sides of a polygon, such as a rectangle. (Page 272)

Permutations The number of different ways in which the members of a group can be arranged. (Page 24)

Premium The amount paid each year or every six months for insurance. (Page 135)

Principal An amount of money deposited in a savings account to earn interest. (Page 110)

Probability A number from 0 to 1 which tells how likely it is that an event will happen. (Page 26)

Probability ratio The ratio of the number of successful ways to the number of possible ways. (Page 26)

Random numbers The digits 0, 1, 2, 3, 4, 5, 6, 7, 8, 9 arranged so that each digit occurs about the same number of times. (Page 34)

Range The difference between the greatest and smallest numbers in a list of numbers. (Page 10)

Rectangle A four-sided polygon whose opposite sides are equal and whose angles are right angles. (Page 129)

References Persons or documents that vouch for your character and ability. (Page 58)

Sample A group chosen to represent a larger group. (Page 9)

Sample space The possible ways in which an event can occur. (Page 26)

Service charge A fee banks charge for handling checking accounts. (Page 106)

Social security tax An amount deducted from the gross pay to provide benefits for retired and disabled workers. Also called FICA, or Federal Insurance Contributions Act. (Page 54)

Sticker Price The price of a new car that includes the base price, the cost of optional equipment, and the delivery charges. (Page 126)

Stock Shares of a corporation that people buy to become part owners of a corporation and to share in its profits. (Page 321)

Stock dividend The portion of a company's earnings that it pays (usually every 3 months) to its stockholders. (Page 324)

Whole life insurance A type of policy that gives financial protection over the entire life of the policy holder. It has both a cash value and a loan value. The premium is always the same. (Page 313)

Taxable income For purposes of income tax, the difference between adjusted gross income and the total of exemptions and deductions. (Page 80)

Term life insurance A type of policy that gives financial protection for a specific period of time or until a certain age. It can be renewed after each term, but at a higher premium. The amount of the insurance will be paid to the policy holder's beneficiary in case of death. (Page 312)

Triangle A polygon with three sides. (Page 129)

Unit price The cost per gram, per pound, per liter, and so on. The *unit price* of a 16-ounce container of cottage cheese that sells for $0.96 is 6¢ per ounce. (Page 203)

Universal life insurance A type of policy that allows the policy-holder to choose the amount of the premium without going below a specified minimum. The cash value of the policy earns interest, and is tax free until the money is withdrawn. The policy holder is allowed to make partial withdrawals of the cash value and still keep the policy in effect. (Page 315)

Volume The measure of the amount of space inside a space figure. (Page 209)

W-2 form A wage and tax statement given employees each year by the employer. (Page 75)

INDEX

Boldface numerals indicate the pages that contain formal or informal definitions.

ANSWERS TO ODD-NUMBERED EXERCISES

CHAPTER 1 CONSUMER AND STATISTICS

Pages 2–3 **Exercises** **1.** 160 calories **3.** About 30 more calories **5.** Answers will vary. **7.** $4.50 more **9.** 150% **11.** See the graph at the right.

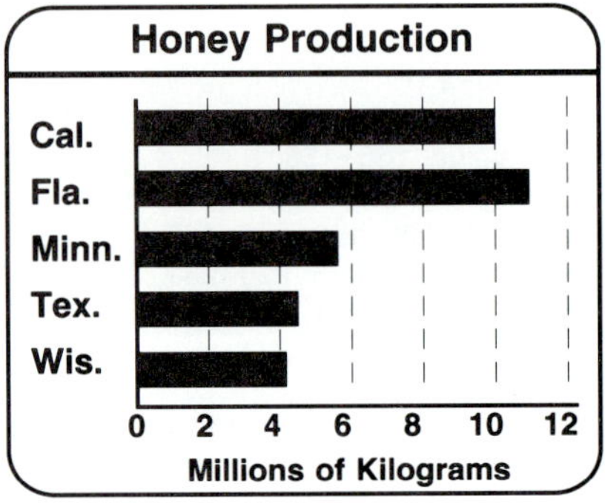

Pages 4–5 **Exercises** **1.** 1985 **3.** About 1,300,000 cassettes **5.** October **7.** $36,000 **9.** September and October **11.** See the graph at the right.

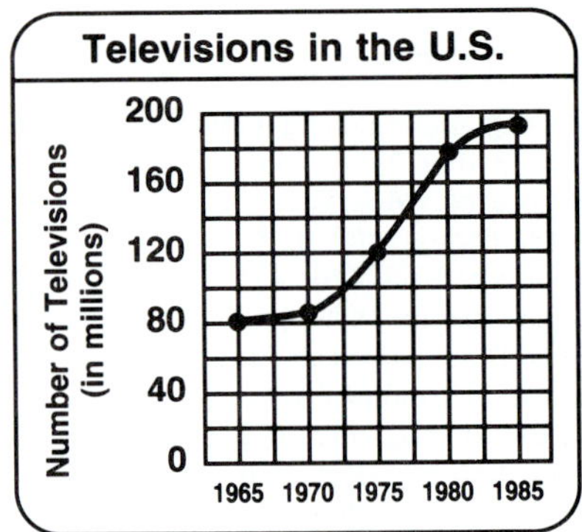

Page 7 **Exercises** **1.** 100% **3.** 36° **5.** 144° **7.** 234° **9.** Food **11.** Food and Movies **13.** $9

15. **A Disc Jockey's Hour**

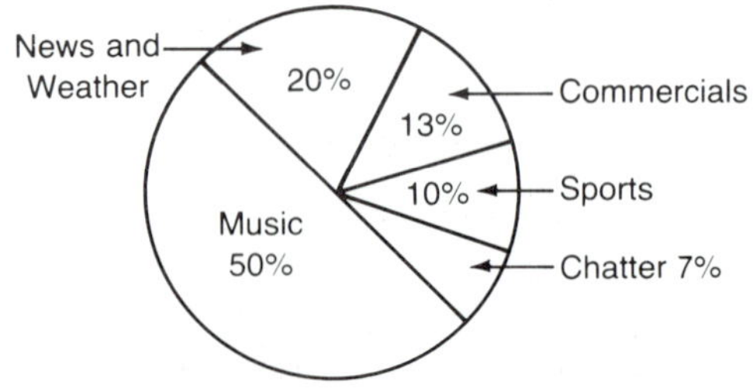

17. **Town Budget**

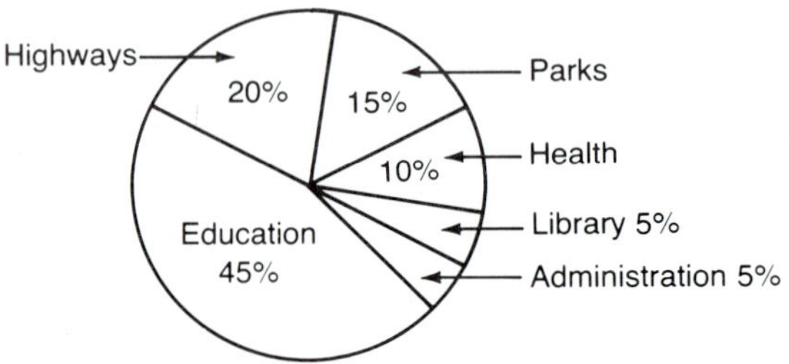

Page 8 **Mid–Chapter Review** **1.** About 290 pounds **3.**

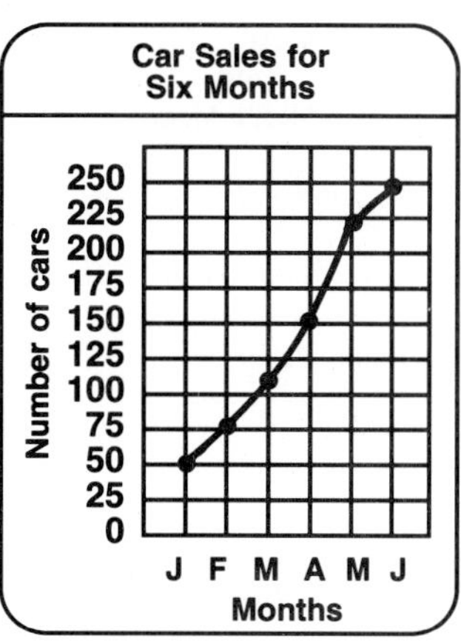

5. 6 billion dollars **7.** 4

Page 9 **Math in Advertising** **1.** No; sample is not sufficiently large. **3.** No; sample is not random.

Page 11 **Exercises** **1.** mode **3.** add, 5 **5.** 4 **7.** Mean: $21,900; Range: $9,800 **9.** Mean: $279.75; Range: $85 **11.** 4–6 P.M.

Page 13 **Exercises** **1.** middle **3.** one half; one half **5.** 43¢ **7.** $2,950 **9.** $479.50 **11.** $7,714.50

Pages 14–15 **Exercises** **1.** 1:00–6:00 **3.** The greatest number of customers are in the store during these hours. **5.** Yes; the number of customers is above the mean during these hours. **7.** The store had more than 20 customers. **9.** 2–6 **11.** $18,500 **13.** $12,250 **15.** Median yearly salary; it is closer to most of the salaries.

Page 16 **Histograms** **1.** 3 **3.** 8 **5.** $\frac{1}{6}$ **7.**

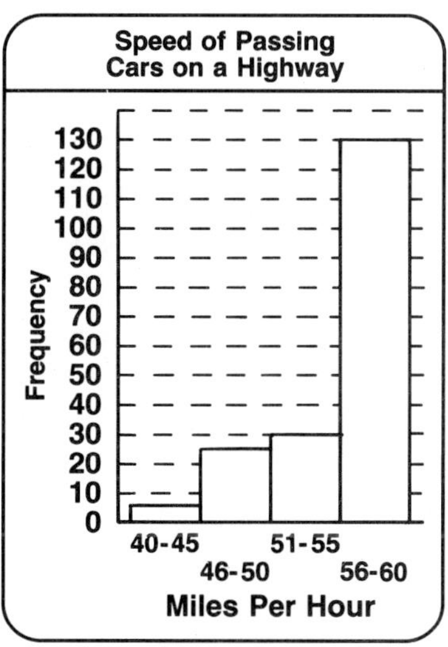

Pages 18–19 Chapter Review **1.** number **3.** 360 **5.** mode **7.** Iowa **9.** Indiana and Kansas **11.** 1981 **13.** About \$1 more **15.** See the graph at the right. **17.** Mean: \$236.25; Mode: None **19.** \$2.27

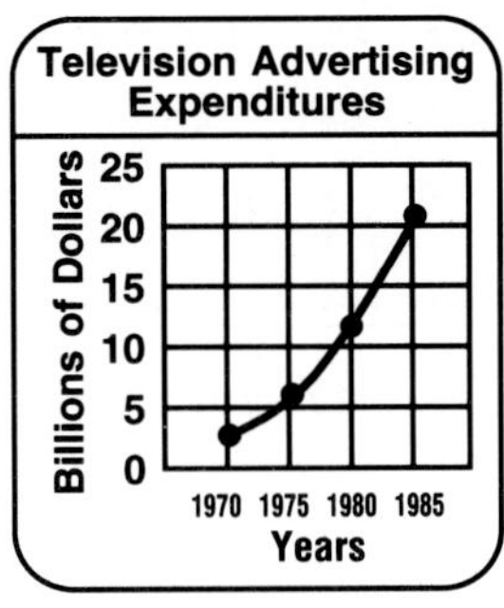

Page 20 Chapter Test **1.** Exeter and Blue Hollow **3.** \$30,000 **5.** February **7.** See the graph at the right. **9.** \$12,555

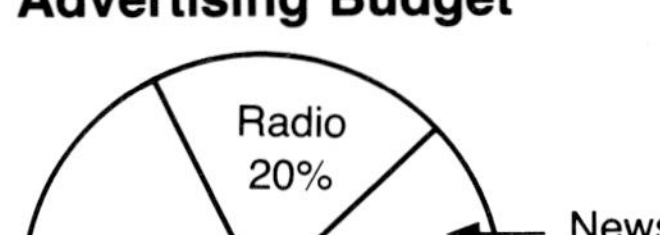

CHAPTER 2 PROBABILITY

Page 23 Exercises **1.** 6 choices **3.** 24 choices **5.** 12 choices **7.** 60 systems

Page 25 Exercises **1.** 6 ways **3.** 120 ways **5.** 3,628,800 **7.** 479,001,600 **9.** 24 numbers

Page 27 Exercises **1.** 0 **3.** 1 **5. a.** $\frac{1}{8}$ **b.** $12\frac{1}{2}\%$ **7. a.** $\frac{1}{2}$ **b.** 50% **9. a.** $\frac{3}{8}$ **b.** $37\frac{1}{2}\%$ **11. a.** $\frac{3}{10}$ **b.** 30% **13. a.** $\frac{1}{5}$ **b.** 20% **15. a.** $\frac{0}{10}$ **b.** 0% **17.** $\frac{8}{125}$, or $6\frac{2}{5}\%$ **19.** $\frac{2}{3}$, or $66\frac{2}{3}\%$ **21.** $\frac{1}{7}$, or $14\frac{2}{7}\%$

Page 28 Mid–Chapter Review **1.** 8 choices **3.** 72 choices **5.** 24 ways **7. a.** $\frac{1}{4}$ **b.** 25% **9. a.** $\frac{1}{12}$ **b.** $8\frac{1}{3}\%$ **11.** Mean: 5; Median: 4; Mode: 4 **13.** Mean: 99; Median: 98; Mode: None **15.** Mean: 12.5; Median: 14; Mode: None **17.** Mean: 7; Median: 7; Mode: 7 **19.** $\frac{3}{5}$ **21.** $\frac{5}{6}$ **23.** $\frac{2}{3}$

Page 31 Exercises **1.** Answers will vary. **3. a.** $\frac{7}{50}$ **b.** 14% **5. a.** $\frac{11}{100}$ **b.** 11% **7.** \$2,100,000 **9.** \$1,650,000

Page 33 Exercises **1.** 1 to 999,999 **3.** 23 to 249,977 **5.** 1 to 5; 5 to 1 **7.** 1 to 7; 7 to 1 **9.** 7 to 17; 17 to 7 **11.** 35 to 1 **13.** 11 to 1 **15.** 8 to 1 **17.** 25 to 11 **19.** 7 to 2

Page 34 Sampling and Random Numbers **1.** 213, 270, 205, 042, 264, 110, 054, 224, 055, 288, 048, 256, 079, 102, 034 **3.** Answers will vary.

Pages 36–37 Chapter Review **1.** tree diagram **3.** probability **5.** sample space **7.** 6 choices **9.** 56 choices **11.** 362,880 ways **13. a.** $\frac{1}{4}$ **b.** 25% **15. a.** $\frac{1}{2}$ **b.** 50% **17. a.** $\frac{0}{4}$ **b.** 0% **19.** $23\frac{1}{3}$% **21.** $3\frac{1}{3}$% **23.** About 280 students **25.** About 40 students **27.** 1 to 11 **29.** 5 to 13

Page 38 Chapter Test **1.** 6 choices **3.** 120 ways **5. a.** $\frac{1}{16}$ **b.** $6\frac{1}{4}$% **7. a.** $\frac{3}{8}$ **b.** $37\frac{1}{2}$% **9.** 40% **11.** 10% **13.** About 560 students **15.** 3 to 5

Pages 39–40 Cumulative Maintenance: Chapters 1–2 **1.** b **3.** d **5.** c **7.** c **9.** b **11.** d **13.** b **15.** d

CHAPTER 3 MAKING MONEY

Page 43 Check Your Skills **1.** $266 **3.** $42.30 **5.** $11.70 **7.** $12.15 **9.** $186.30 **11.** $233.45 **13.** 16 **15.** 9

Pages 43–44 Exercises **1.** Hours **3.** Base Pay **5.** Overtime Pay **7.** $214.60 **9.** $422.75 **11.** $232.05 **13.** $392.70 **15.** About 7 hours **17.** $358.80 **19.** $101.50 **21. a.** Advantages: Driver: highest hourly pay; Clerk: benefits; Hostess: no overtime; Disadvantages: Driver: must buy own uniforms; Clerk: farthest distance to drive; Hostess: lowest hourly pay **b.** Answers will vary.

Page 46 Check Your Skills **1.** 0.12 **3.** 0.04 **5.** 0.055 **7.** $1,200 **9.** $30 **11.** $1,000 **13.** $1,200 **15.** $8,100 **17.** $1,500

Pages 46–47 Exercises **1.** sales **3.** straight commission **5.** $450 **7.** $580 **9.** $1,540 **11.** $1,123 **13.** $2,610 **15.** $5,000 **17.** $2,900 **19.** $520,000

Page 49 Check Your Skills **1.** $221.83 **3.** $235.36 **5.** $88.36 **7.** $284.66 **9.** $360.94 **11.** $314 **13.** $64.89

Pages 49–50 Exercises **1.** social security **3.** subtract **5.** $53.24; $200.76 **7.** $62.93; $151.07 **9.** $57.60; $170.40 **11.** $780.82 **13.** $27.89 **15.** $530 **17.** $565 **19.** About $75

Page 51 Mid–Chapter Review **1.** $296.70 **3.** $342 **5.** $373 **7.** $125.79; $324.21 **9.** 1.875 million tons **11.** It will not rain.

Page 53 Exercises **1.** No; [$9.60] **3.** Yes; [$407,000] **5.** Yes; [$40.00] **7.** Yes; [$60.00]

Pages 54–55 Check Your Skills **1.** 0.089 **3.** 0.0925 **5.** 0.0765 **7.** $270 **9.** $65.64 **11.** $24.94 **13.** $2,500 **15.** $1,040

Page 55 Exercises **1.** F; federal government **3.** T **5.** T **7.** $44.69 **9.** $67.27 **11.** $1,945.40 **13.** $311.03; $21.44; $0; The maximum taxable amount was reached in November, so no tax was withheld in December. **15.** $5,859

Page 57 Exercises **1.** $563 **3.** $157 **5.** Retired worker: $659; Spouse: $329; Total: $988 **7.** $5,028 **9.** $48,720

Page 58 Exercises **1.** Draftsman **3.** Preparation of construction prints, plan layouts, and elevations **5. a.** Parkland Vocational School, Springfield, Illinois **b.** Architectural drafting **c.** August **d.** 1986 **e.** May **f.** 1988 **g.** Associate's degree **7.** The most recent job is listed first.

Pages 60–61 Consumer's Choice **1.** Delivery person, Food server **3.** Food server, Rental clerk; Tips and commissions will vary. **5.** \$91.67; \$18.33 **7.** \$689.60 **9.** Yes; she could exceed the amount needed in tips or commission. **11.** No **13.** \$20.40 **15.** Answers will vary.

Page 62 Fringe Benefits **1.** 21.9% **3.** 15.5%

Pages 63–65 Chapter Review **1.** overtime pay **3.** gross pay **5.** social security **7.** \$279.50 **9.** \$232.96 **11.** \$5,144.40 **13.** \$570 **15.** \$67.83; \$221.17 **17.** \$89.38 **19.** \$139.91 **21.** \$374 **23.** \$612.50 **25.** \$30,240 **27.** \$306.95 **29.** Estimate: 2.5 in.; No **31.** \$130.15

Page 66 Chapter Test **1.** \$338 **3.** \$363.60 **5.** \$2,975 **7.** \$1,142.38 **9.** \$3,131.70 **11.** Estimate: \$90; Reasonable

Pages 67–68 Cumulative Maintenance: Chapters 1–3 **1.** c **3.** c **5.** b **7.** d **9.** d **11.** a **13.** d **15.** c

CHAPTER 4 PAYING TAXES

Page 70 Check Your Skills **1.** \$344 **3.** \$374.30 **5.** \$31.50 **7.** \$29.80

Page 71 Exercises **1.** gross pay; exemptions **3.** increases **5.** \$42 **7.** \$33 **9.** \$274; \$38 **11.** \$345.60; \$38 **13.** \$47 **15.** Increase; as the number of exemptions increases, the amount of tax withheld decreases.

Page 72 Check Your Skills **1.** Yes **3.** No **5.** Yes

Page 73 Exercises **1.** wages; interest **3.** adjusted gross income **5.** \$16,876.46 **7.** \$12,651.59 **9.** \$13,219.60 **11.** \$11,758.72 **13.** Yes **15.** Yes **17.** Yes

Page 74 Math and Income Tax **1.** No **3.** Yes

Page 75 Check Your Skills **1.** 3485.71 **3.** 9268.03 **5.** 3018.37

Pages 76–77 Exercises **1.** Print **3.** \$274.00 **5.** \$2,540 **7.** \$1,900 **9.** \$1,627.00 **11.** \$17 **13.** Line 11 **15. a.** owe money **b.** \$207 **17. a.** refund **b.** \$378 **19. a.** owe money **b.** \$516 **21.** No; Form 1040EZ is only for single persons with no dependents.

Page 78 Mid–Chapter Review **1.** \$50 **3.** \$33 **5.** \$14,608.35 **7.** \$436 balance due **9.** 30 books **11.** $\frac{1}{25}$

Page 79 Math and Sales Tax **1.** \$0.46 **3.** \$0.62 **5.** \$0.90 **7.** \$0.77 **9.** \$6.28 **11.** \$11.93

Page 81 Check Your Skills **1.** \$457 **3.** \$23,560

Page 81 Exercises **1.** 1040 **3.** \$1,900 **5.** \$2,752; \$17,646 **7.** \$4,000; \$9,665 **9.** \$2,410 **11.** \$2,932 **13.** \$7

Page 83 Check Your Skills **1.** 24.80 **3.** 24.81 **5.** 6.20 **7.** \$43.80 **9.** \$69.62

Page 83 Exercises **1.** \$154.50 **3.** \$104.70 **5.** \$34.49 **7.** \$565.73 **9.** \$85 **11.** \$127.25 **13.** \$156.13 **15.** \$79.86 **17.** No; her city tax is \$104.50. Since her employer withheld \$8.50 × 12, or \$102, Lori owes \$2.50.

Page 85 **Exercises** **1.** Exact average; Batting averages need to be precise. **3.** Mental computation; It is faster. **5.** Frank, Clarence, Phil, Brian, Julio, Sam, Gregg, Steve, Fred **7.** No; Recipes require exact amounts. **9.** Flour, $11\frac{1}{4}$ c; Sugar, 6 c; Eggs, 6; Molasses, $1\frac{1}{2}$ c; Oleo, $2\frac{1}{4}$ c; Soda, 3 tsp; Cinnamon, $1\frac{1}{2}$ tsp; Cloves, $\frac{3}{4}$ tsp

Page 87 **Consumer's Choice** **1.** Choice 4 **3.** Choice 4 **5.** More than $80; the amount in his savings account will be $50 × 12, or $600, plus the interest it earns during the 12 months. **7.** One disadvantage: he must pay interest on the loan. Answers will vary. **9.** One advantage: he would not owe any additional taxes. Answers will vary.

Page 88 **Hidden Taxes** **1.** $1.14 **3.** $9.60 **5.** $11.28 **7. a.** $60.00 **b.** $460.00

Pages 89–91 **Chapter Review** **1.** adjusted gross income **3.** deduction **5.** taxable income **7.** $41 **9.** $19,963.45 **11.** $11,809.13 **13.** No **15.** No **17.** refund: $228 **19.** $2,834; $12,145 **21.** $2,932 **23.** $2,410 **25.** $251.67 **27.** $32.40 **29.** $29 **31.** $20,700 **33.** refund: $172 **35.** $18,532 **37. a.** The actual amount is needed on an income tax return. **b.** Answers will vary.

Page 92 **Chapter Test** **1.** $30 **3.** $14,538.27 **5.** refund: $239 **7.** $1,937 **9.** $1,536 **11.** $434.40 **13.** A; an exact answer is needed on income tax returns.

Pages 93–94 **Cumulative Maintenance: Chapters 1–4** **1.** c **3.** d **5.** c **7.** b **9.** b **11.** d **13.** c **15.** b **17.** b

CHAPTER 5 BANKING AND MONEY

Page 96 **Check Your Skills** **1.** 160 **3.** 95 **5.** 170 **7.** 60

Page 97 **Exercises** **1.** subtotal **3.** cash received **5.** Subtotal: $335.65; Net deposit: $285.66 **7.** Subtotal: $203.63; Net deposit: $203.63 **9.** Net deposit: $329.81 **11.** $421.92 **13.** $274.42

Page 99 **Exercises** **1.** Three and 47/100 **3.** Thirty–four and 21/100 **5.** Sixty–three and 00/100 **7.** One hundred twenty–one and 14/100 **9.** One thousand five hundred forty and 51/100 **11. a.** 116 **b.** November 28 **c.** Parks' Home Center **d.** $16.70 **e.** Sixteen and 70/100 **f.** curtain rods **g.** Lila Brown **13.** November 29, 1989 **15.** The signature **17.** b **19.** If the check is lost, anyone who finds it could fill in the amount.

Page 101 **Check Your Skills** **1.** Yes **3.** No **5.** No

Pages 101–102 **Exercises** **1.** balance **3.** check amount **5.** Total: $559.33; Bal. For'd.: $234.33 **7.** Bal. For'd.: $167.18; Total: $293.21; This Check: $57.81; Bal. For'd.: $236.03 **9.** Bal. For'd. is $511.75. **11.** $185.46; $270.62; $235.62 **13.** $305.09 **15.** $50.28

Page 103 **Mid–Chapter Review** **1.** $581.25; $506.25 **3.** $49.95 **5.** Riker's Automotive Shop **7.** $137,260 **9.** 90

Pages 104–105 **Math and Making Change** **1.** b **3.** c **7.** None; 1; 1; 2; 2; None; 3 **9.** $6.23; None; 1; 1; None; 2; None; 3 **11.** $11.91; 1; None; 1; 3; 1; 1; 1 **13. a.** $2.68 **b.** Two $1–bills, 2 quarters, 1 dime, 1 nickel, 3 pennies **15. a.** $14.87 **b.** One $10–bill, four $1–bills, 3 quarters, 1 dime, 2 pennies **17. a.** $2.46 **b.** Two $1–bills, 1 quarter, 2 dimes, 1 penny **19. a.** $13.00 **b.** One $10–bill, three $1–bills

Page 107 **Check Your Skills** **1.** $702.95 **3.** $650.79 **5.** $125.60 **7.** $1,323.18

Pages 107–109 Exercises **1.** outstanding **3.** subtracted from **5.** $608.69; $722.73; $608.69; Yes **7.** $349.86; $404.86; $349.86; Yes **9.** $341.02 **11.** $304.71 **13. a.** Newton Memorial Trust **b.** $1.80 **15.** 3 **17.** Yes; one **19.** The check did not arrive at the bank until two days after it was written.

Page 111 Check Your Skills **1.** 0.12 **3.** 0.085 **5.** 0.05 **7.** $50 **9.** $13.80

Page 111 Exercises **1.** $30 **3.** $42 **5.** $189 **7.** $19 **9.** $40; $4,040 **11.** $40.80; $4,121.20 **13.** $33.75; $2,733.75 **15.** $34.60; $2,802.52

Page 113 Check Your Skills **1.** 1060 **3.** 1573.76 **5.** 4174.92 **7.** 945

Page 113 Exercises **1.** $1\frac{1}{2}$ **3.** interest **5.** 2%; 4; 1.0824; $541.20 **7.** 2.5%; 10; 1.2801; $2,304.18 **9.** 3.5%; 6; 1.2293; $15,489.18 **11.** $551.88 **13.** $2\frac{1}{2}$ years

Page 115 Exercises **1.** $40,000 **3.** $5,000 **5.** $10,000 **7.** $1,250 **9.** $10,000; $5,000; $2,500; $2,000 **11.** $58,500 **13.** $20,000 **15.** $\frac{1}{10,000}$

Page 117 Consumer's Choice **1.** $4.70 **3.** $10.00 **5.** $44 more **7.** Choice 1 **9.** Choices 2 and 3 **11.** One disadvantage: the minimum balance must be maintained. Answers will vary. **13.** Answers will vary.

Pages 119–121 Chapter Review **1.** balance **3.** canceled **5.** Compound **7.** $543.25; $516.50 **9.** 313 **11.** To pay for a ceiling fan **13.** Twenty-one and 45/100 **15.** Three hundred seventy-two and 60/100 **17.** $12.50 **19.** $40 **21.** $55 **23.** $37.50; $3,037.50 **25.** $38.44; $3,113.91 **27.** $680.54 **29.** c **31.** $932.82 **33.** $35.75 **35.** $564.75 **37.** $500

Page 122 Chapter Test **1.** $503.78 **3.** To record the purpose of the check **5.** $12 **7.** $90 **9.** $106.40 **11.** $138.42

Pages 123–124 Cumulative Maintenance: Chapters 1–5 **1.** b **3.** c **5.** d **7.** b **9.** b **11.** c **13.** c **15.** a

CHAPTER 6 BUYING A CAR

Page 127 Check Your Skills **1.** No **3.** Yes **5.** No **7.** 0.06 **9.** 0.04 **11.** 0.09 **13.** $2,000 **15.** $3,500

Pages 127–128 Exercises **1.** optional equipment **3.** base price **5.** $7,957.50 **7.** $10,148.75 **9.** $13,860.80 **11.** $8,691.50 **13.** $471; $9,891 **15.** $810.40; $10,940.40 **17.** $485.94; $7,427.94 **19.** b **21.** $11,811.29 **23.** An AM/FM radio and power steering

Page 129 Math and Driving **1.** a **3.** a **5.** d **7.** a

Page 130 Check Your Skills **1.** $8,394.60 **3.** $415.75 **5.** $7,321.20 **7.** $8,303.75

Page 131 Exercises **1.** $8,674.00 **3.** $10,678.56 **5.** $8,880.50 **7.** $10,544.35 **9.** $8,130.89

Page 132 Check Your Skills **1.** $1,186.80 **3.** $805.05 **5.** Yes **7.** Yes **9.** No

Page 133 Exercises **1.** down payment **3.** finance charge **5.** $946.50 **7.** $1,017 **9.** $2,171 **11.** $2,280 **13.** $11,776 **15.** b **17.** $480

Page 134 Mid-Chapter Review **1.** $7,487.65 **3.** $9,755.72 **5.** $6,918.16 **7.** $3,120 **9.** $19,750 **11.** Balance due: $311

Page 136 **Exercises** **1.** bodily injury; property damage **3.** $100,000 **5.** $514.08 **7.** $498.30 **9.** $617.76 **11.** $652.32 **13.** $105.60

Page 138 **Check Your Skills** **1.** $201.60 **3.** 3.75 **5.** $1,086.80

Pages 138–139 **Exercises** **1.** collision **3.** comprehensive **5.** $647.92 **7.** $1,403.27 **9.** $714.25 **11.** $306 **13.** $108 **15.** $66 **17.** $268.40 **19.** $28.05

Page 141 **Exercises** **1.** 11 and 9 **3.** $8\frac{1}{2}$ and $5\frac{1}{2}$ **5.** Radial Star, $45; Radial Sun, $51 **7.** $40; $80 **9.** 26 miles **11. a.** Solving a simpler problem **b.** $30,000; $6,000; $1,000

Pages 142–143 **Consumer's Choice** **1.** $1,106.70 **3.** $522.24 more **5.** $10,594.56; $10,908.00; $11,227.68 **7.** The 48–month loan at the credit union **9.** Answers will vary.

Page 144 **Inflation** **1.** $113,520 **3. a.** More **b.** $15.40

Pages 145–147 **Chapter Review** **1.** down payment **3.** liability **5.** collision **7.** $10,832.80; $541.64; $11,374.44 **9.** $8,954.19 **11.** $10,836 **13.** $2,960 **15.** $2,835 **17.** $772.20 **19.** $453 **21.** $756.04 **23.** $163.59 **25.** $12,435.99 **27.** $3,760 **29.** $772.20 **31.** $13.20 **33.** $392.50

Page 148 **Chapter Test** **1.** $11,817.47 **3.** $7,119.09 **5.** $9,552 **7.** $514.08 **9.** $414.73

Pages 149–150 **Cumulative Maintenance: Chapters 1–6** **1.** b **3.** d **5.** c **7.** d **9.** a **11.** c **13.** b **15.** d **17.** a

CHAPTER 7 OWNING A CAR

Page 153 **Check Your Skills** **1.** 0.04 **3.** 0.06 **5.** 0.05 **7.** 12.40 **9.** 264.82 **11.** 2¢ **13.** 2¢ **15.** $48.90 **17.** $8.33

Page 154 **Exercises** **1.** parts; labor **3.** cost of the parts; sales tax **5.** $137.38 **7.** 2¢ **9.** 6¢ **11.** $197.04

Page 155 **Math and Braking Distance** **1.** 45 ft **3.** 25 ft **5.** 35 mph **7.** 51 mph

Page 157 **Check Your Skills** **1.** 0.45 **3.** 0.20 or 0.2 **5.** 0.65 **7.** 7344 **9.** 0.9 **11.** 2200 **13.** 80% of $900 **15.** They are equal. **17.** 75% of $2,000

Pages 157–158 **Exercises** **1.** depreciation **3.** resale value **5.** $6,987.50 **7.** $5,596 **9.** $4,048 **11.** $5,833.75 **13.** $2,320; $4,060; $5,220; $6,380; $5,220 **15.** $1,938; $3,391.50; $4,360.50; $5,329.50; $4,360.50 **17.** $1,390; $2,432.50; $3,127.50; $3,822.50; $3,127.50 **19.** About $6,000 **21.** $5,055

Page 159 **Mid–Chapter Review** **1.** $103.43 **3.** 3¢ **5.** $3,323.70 **7.** $15.40 **9.** 15

Page 161 **Check Your Skills** **1.** 28 **3.** 40 **5.** 13 **7.** 39 **9.** 33 **11.** 0.04 **13.** 0.09 **15.** 0.06 **17.** 9¢ **19.** 7¢

Pages 161–162 **Exercises** **1.** greater **3.** total yearly cost; total kilometers driven **5.** 27 **7.** 32 **9.** 11 **11.** 12 **13.** 4¢ **15.** 6¢ **17.** 6¢ **19.** 9¢ **21.** 7¢ **23.** About 10¢ **25.** The first car **27.** $157.50

Page 164 **Check Your Skills** **1.** 0.38 **3.** 0.06 **5.** 0.73 **7.** 0.300 **9.** 0.397 **11.** 0.389 **13.** 0.432 **15.** 39.2¢ **17.** 10.1¢ **19.** 6.9¢ **21.** 39.9¢

Pages 164–165 **Exercises** **1.** variable **3.** variable; fixed **5.** $5,822; 29.1¢ **7.** $5,050; 27.3¢ **9.** $6,555; 21.9¢ **11. a.** $6,300 **b.** $2,093 **c.** $8,793 **d.** 44.0¢ **13. a.** $3,230 **b.** $2,566 **c.** $5,976 **d.** 24.9¢ **15.** $3,652.50 **17.** $1,792.90

Page 167 **Exercises** **1.** See table and graph below. **3.** 56 **5.** $9,975

Interval	*Midpoint*	*Tally*	*Frequency*
190–199	194	III	3
200–209	204	I	1
210–219	214	IIII	4
220–229	224	卌	5
230–239	234	卌 I	6
240–249	244	III	3
250–259	254	III	3

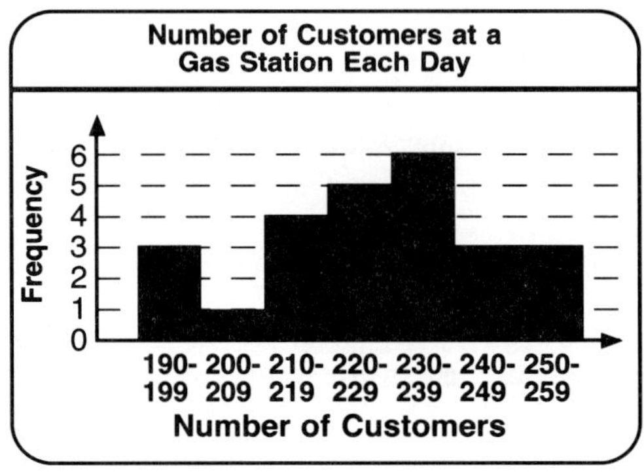

Page 169 **Consumer's Choice** **1.** $270 **3.** About $19.69 **5.** $6 **7.** He might not want to spend the additional 30 minutes traveling each way. **9.** One advantage: it is the least expensive choice. Answers will vary. **11.** It eliminates Choices 1 and 2.

Page 170 **Automobile Maintenance** **1.** 20W–40 **3.** 5W–30 **5.** 100°F

Pages 171–173 **Chapter Review** **1.** maintenance **3.** fuel economy **5.** variable **7.** $105.82 **9.** $7,572.50 **11.** $5,220 **13.** $3,528.45 **15.** 30 **17.** 19 **19.** 6¢ **21.** $6,912; 34.6¢ **23.** $6,112; 24.4¢ **25.** $127.47 **27.** $3,646.50 **29.** 8¢ **31.** See graph at right.

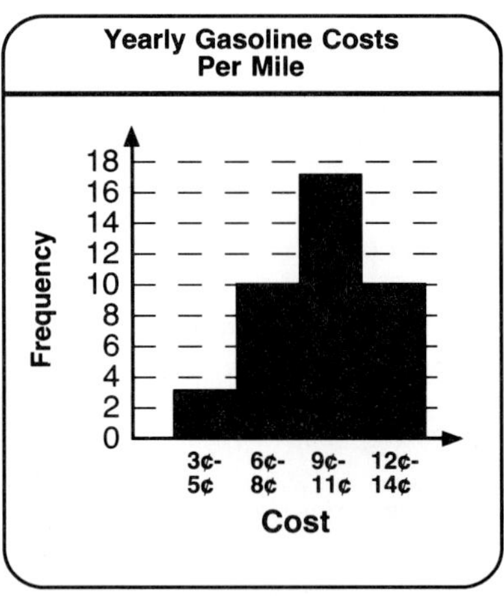

Page 174 **Chapter Test** **1.** $79.51 **3.** $3,744 **5.** $3,744 **7.** c **9.** $7,614; 42.3¢

11.

Interval	*Midpoint*	*Tally*	*Frequency*
26–30	28	卌 II	7
31–35	33	I	1
36–40	38	II	2
41–45	43	卌 II	7
46–50	48	卌 III	8

Pages 175–176 **Cumulative Maintenance: Chapters 1–7** **1.** d **3.** c **5.** b **7.** d **9.** c **11.** b **13.** c **15.** a **17.** d

CHAPTER 8 OTHER WAYS TO TRAVEL

Page 179 **Check Your Skills** **1.** \$460 **3.** \$168.48 **5.** \$57.50 **7.** \$35.50 **9.** 12 **11.** 120

Page 179 **Exercises** **1.** Yes **3.** About $1\frac{1}{2}$ days **5.** \$993 **7.** Answers will vary.

Page 181 **Check Your Skills** **1.** \$14.64 **3.** \$24.90 **5.** \$285 **7.** \$504 **9.** \$59.50 **11.** \$107 **13.** \$455.94 **15.** \$625.14

Page 181 **Exercises** **1.** \$23.20; \$313.20 **3.** \$20.48; \$276.48 **5.** \$200 **7.** $44\frac{1}{2}$ hours **9.** Answers will vary.

Page 182 **Mid–Chapter Review** **1.** \$418 **3.** \$140 **5.** \$60 **7.** $\frac{9}{14}$ **9.** \$24.75

Page 183 **Math and Time Zones** **1.** 4:00 P.M. **3.** 2:00 P.M. **5.** 7:30 A.M. **7.** 6:30 A.M. **9.** The plane leaving Dallas; 1 hr earlier

Page 185 **Check Your Skills** **1.** No **3.** Yes **5.** No **7.** Yes **9.** Yes

Pages 185–186 **Exercises** **1.** mileage allowance **3.** Total Rental Cost **5.** \$71.98 **7.** \$282.24 **9.** \$325.57 **11.** Columbia Car Rental; \$30.99 **13.** \$238.42 **15.** \$7.67; \$14.40; \$6.73 **17.** \$13.53; \$21.35; \$7.82 **19.** One consideration would be the convenience of the rental company's location.

Page 188 **Check Your Skills** **1.** \$45.36 **3.** \$26.78 **5.** \$4.55 **7.** 4.4

Pages 188–189 **Exercises** **1.** b **3.** a **5.** c **7.** B–6 **9.** C–4 **11.** B–7 **13.** 3.35 hours **15.** About \$5.20 **17.** Julesburg to Cheyenne Wells; it is 163 miles to Cheyenne Wells and 173 miles to Denver. **19.** 3 hours

Page 191 **Consumer's Choice** **1.–7.** Answers will vary.

Page 192 **Making a Map** **1.–9.** Answers will vary.

Pages 193–195 **Chapter Review** **1.** round trip **3.** mileage allowance **5.** \$14.56; \$196.56 **7.** \$25.92; \$349.92 **9.** \$52.22 **11.** \$218.37 **13.** \$60; $1500 \div 25 = 60$ and $60 \times \$1 = \$60$ **15.** \$414 **17.** \$176.07 **19.** Pueblo to Lamar; it is 152 miles to Gunnison, but only 121 miles to Lamar.

Page 196 **Chapter Test** **1.** \$297.50 **3.** \$1,490.40 **5.** \$57 **7.** \$204.91 **9.** South

Pages 197–198 **Cumulative Maintenance: Chapters 1–8** **1.** a **3.** c **5.** b **7.** b **9.** a **11.** a **13.** b **15.** d

CHAPTER 9 BUYING FOODS

Page 201 **Check Your Skills** **1.** 15 **3.** 100 **5.** 10 **7.** 40% **9.** 1.2 **11.** 0.18 **13.** 0.009

Pages 201–202 **Exercises** **1.** 110; 150 **3.** 20 g; 26 g **5.** 10%; 25% **7.** 6%; 8% **9.** 500 milligrams **11.** 20% **13.** 1.7 milligrams **15.** 3 milligrams **17.** 2.5% **19.** They help consumers compare the nutritional value of the products.

Page 204 **Check Your Skills** **1.** 3.5 **3.** 7.0 **5.** 23.5 **7.** 2.4 **9.** 17.8 **11.** 224 **13.** 31.3 **15.** 2.7 **17.** $>$ **19.** $=$ **21.** 8.4 **23.** 15.4 **25.** 1000

Pages 204–205 **Exercises** **1.** unit **3.** quality **5.** 4.1¢ **7.** 2.5¢ **9.** 3.0¢ **11.** 2.1¢ **13.** 32–oz size **15.** 4–qt size **17.** Larger **19.** Smaller **21.** Larger **23.** $3.56 **25.** a **27.** 17.28¢ **29.** 30¢ **31.** To sell larger quantities of the items

Page 206 **Check Your Skills** **1.** $0.70 **3.** $53.82 **5.** $0.77 **7.** $2.41 **9.** $2.30 **11.** 21.1 **13.** 9.7

Pages 206–207 **Exercises** **1.** coupons; less **3.** $0.45 **5.** $0.69 **7.** $0.70 **9.** $1.50 **11.** 72¢ **13.** $4.00 **15.** No; the cost would be $5.10. **17. a.** $364 **b.** Answers will vary.

Page 208 **Mid–Chapter Review** **1.** 310 milligrams **3.** 20 milligrams **5.** Smaller **7.** No, the total would be $3.11. **9.** $480 **11.** The car that travels 360 miles on 12.9 gallons

Page 209 **Math and Boxes** **1.** 10 cm

Page 211 **Check Your Skills** **1.** $\frac{3}{2}$ **3.** $\frac{5}{3}$ **5.** $\frac{9}{4}$ **7.** $7\frac{1}{5}$ **9.** $2\frac{6}{7}$ **11.** $2\frac{2}{3}$ **13.** $1.27 **15.** $0.95 **17.** $<$ **19.** $=$ **21.** $3.96 **23.** $4.34

Page 212 **Exercises** **1.** divide **3.** cost per serving **5.** $5\frac{1}{3}$ **7.** $1\frac{3}{5}$ **9.** $2\frac{1}{3}$ **11.** $0.46 **13.** $0.67 **15.** Chicken breasts

Page 214 **Check Your Skills** **1.** $16 **3.** 0.05 **5.** 0.04 **7.** 0.12 **9.** $0.24 **11.** $1.89 **13.** Mean: 87.3; Median: 87; Mode: 92 **15.** $7 **17.** $1

Pages 214–215 **Exercises** **1.** cost **3.** amount of the tip **5.** $10.20; $0.61; $1.50; $12.31 **7.** $25.35; $1.52; $3.75; $30.62 **9.** $6.95; $0.42; $1.05; $8.42 **11.** Monday **13.** About $5; $6 **15.** About $6 **17.** About $1,555.50 **19.** Answers will vary.

Pages 217–218 **Exercises** **1.** $75,000 **3.** $560,000 **5.** $17,200 **7.** $237,200 **9.** $11,800 **11. a.** Answers will vary. **b.** Saturday **13. a.** Answers will vary. **b.** 24

Page 219 **Math and Recipes** **1.** 5 tsp **3.** 5 c **5.** $37\frac{1}{2}$ tsp

Pages 220–221 **Consumer's Choice** **1.** No; Choice 3: $2.70 **3.** Pudding, ice cream, or hot chocolate; Yes; if only one of the items is chosen. **5.** Answers will vary. **7.** Choices 1 and 2 **9.** Answers will vary.

Page 222 **Consumer Price Index** **1.** This year **3.** Greater **5.** $1.14 **7.** 105%; Yes

Pages 223–225 **Chapter Review** **1.** unit price **3.** servings per pound **5.** sales tax; tip **7.** 5–pound bag **9.** $0.49 **11.** $1.29 **13.** 6 **15.** $1.83 **17.** $11.35; $0.57; $1.65; $13.57 **19.** 2% **21.** 8.7¢ **23.** $10.39 **25.** No; the total cost would be $5.97. **27.** $1\frac{3}{4}$ pounds **29.** $7.44 **31.** $78,400

Page 226 **Chapter Test** **1.** 120 milligrams **3.** 1000 milligrams **5.** Smaller **7.** Larger **9.** $1.04 **11.** $9.00; $0.54; $1.35; $10.89

Pages 227–228 **Cumulative Maintenance: Chapters 1–9** **1.** b **3.** b **5.** b **7.** a **9.** b **11.** a **13.** d **15.** a **17.** b

CHAPTER 10 HOUSING

Page 230 **Check Your Skills** **1.** $395 **3.** $437.50 **5.** $493 **7.** $546.67 **9.** $348.81

Page 231 **Exercises** **1.** $\frac{1}{4}$; $\frac{1}{3}$ **3.** $400; $533.33; No **5.** $446; $594.67; No **7.** No **9.** $425 **11.** $1,980

Page 233 **Check Your Skills** **1.** 0.20 or 0.2 **3.** 0.07 **5.** 0.25 **7.** $12,375 **9.** $11,400 **11.** $102,348 **13.** $185,550 **15.** $13,000 **17.** $65,000

Pages 233–234 **Exercises** **1.** down payment; mortgage loan **3.** amount of mortgage **5.** amount of interest **7.** $19,000; $57,000 **9.** $16,000; $144,000 **11.** $6,900; $62,100 **13.** About $30,000 **15.** 360; $168,109.20; $119,109.20 **17.** 360; $279,990; $194,990 **19.** First National Bank of Sparta; $3,240 **21.** Sunrise Federal Savings; $110

Page 236 **Check Your Skills** **1.** 125 **3.** 65 **5.** $549.45 **7.** $732.72 **9.** $956.97 **11.** $396.40 **13.** $360 **15.** $600 **17.** $19.89 **19.** $10.79

Pages 236–237 **Exercises** **1.** Less expensive; a lower loan amount results in a lower monthly payment. **3.** Lower interest rate; paying a lower rate results in a lower monthly payment. **5.** $800.95 **7.** $925.75 **9.** $898.15 **11.** $617.40 **13. a.** 11.5% over 30 years; $5.12 **b.** 11.5% over 30 years; $74,803.20

Page 238 **Mid–Chapter Review** **1.** No; $\frac{1}{3}$ of their net monthly income is $621. **3.** $10,800 **5.** 180; $129,285; $64,285 **7.** $813.60 **9.** $24.20

Page 239 **Math and Property Management** **1.** $12,000 **3.** $87,000 **5.** $303,000

Page 241 **Check Your Skills** **1.** $\frac{1}{2}$ **3.** $\frac{1}{10}$ **5.** $\frac{1}{5}$ **7.** $2,500 **9.** $12,000 **11.** $4,166.67 **13.** $5,833.33 **15.** $3,333.33 **17.** $7,916.67

Pages 241–242 **Exercises** **1.** homeowner's insurance **3.** liability **5.** $80,000; $8,000; $40,000; $16,000 **7.** $150,000; $15,000; $75,000; $30,000 **9.** $14.83 **11.** $17.25 **13.** $20.92 **15.** About $10,000 **17.** $358 **19.** $135,000

Page 244 **Exercises** **1.** 4.5 m × 3.75 m **3.** 3.75 m × 3.75 m **5.** 9 m × 4.5 m **7.** 18 m × 11.25 m **9.** 47.25 m **11.** 2 cm; 2 cm **13.** 2.5 cm; 1.5 cm

Page 246 **Check Your Skills** **1.** 0.65 **3.** 0.30 or 0.3 **5.** 0.55 **7.** $43,800 **9.** $29.40 **11.** No **13.** Yes **15.** Yes

Pages 246–247 **Exercises** **1.** e **3.** a **5.** d **7.** $27,000; $1,876.50 **9.** $34,500; $3,363.75 **11.** $47,500 **13.** c **15.** $38,880 **17.** $1,489.60 **19.** Answers will vary.

Pages 248–249 **Consumer's Choice** **1.** Choice 3 **3.** $611 **5.** $701 **7.** $1,080; $16,200 **9.** Choices 2 and 3 **11.** They might want to purchase the house in Choice 3 because its value would increase the most. **13.** One advantage: lowest mortgage payment; one disadvantage: highest property taxes; Answers will vary. **15.** Answers will vary.

Page 250 **Closing Costs** **1.** $1,140 **3.** $2,999

Pages 251–253 **Chapter Review** **1.** down payment; mortgage loan **3.** premium **5.** assessed value **7.** $376.50; $502; Yes **9.** $450; $600; Yes **11.** 240; $208,440; $118,440 **13.** 360; $203,742, $148,742 **15.** $813.60 **17.** $640.50 **19.** $1,444.80 **21.** $1,060.32 **23.** $44,000; $3,476 **25.** Yes **27.** $823.20 **29.** $18.17 **31.** $5,852

Page 254 **Chapter Test** **1.** No **3.** $38,475 **5.** $523.60 **7.** $6,500 **9.** $27.75

Pages 255–256 **Cumulative Maintenance: Chapters 1–10** **1.** c **3.** a **5.** d **7.** b **9.** a **11.** c **13.** d **15.** a **17.** c

CHAPTER 11 HOUSING COSTS

Page 259 **Check Your Skills** **1.** 63% **3.** 25% **5.** 37.5% **7.** $5.64 **9.** 15%

Page 260 **Exercises** **1.** lower **3.** raise **5.** $121.50 **7.** $58.50 **9.** About $94.50 **11.** About $89.60 **13.** About $837.80

Page 261 **Math and Cooling Costs** **1.** 8000 Btu's **3.** 12,000 Btu's **5.** 17,000 Btu's **7.** Yes

Pages 262–263 **Check Your Skills** **1.** $0.75 **3.** $0.48 **5.** $2.43 **7.** 10% **9.** 84% **11.** $12\frac{1}{2}$% **13.** 10%

Page 263 **Exercises** **1.** $0.40 **3.** $0.65 **5.** $0.48 **7.** $0.72 **9.** About $0.48 **11.** $4.00 **13.** About $9.10 **15.** About $52

Page 265 **Check Your Skills** **1.** 1024 **3.** 908 **5.** 107

Page 265 **Exercises** **1.** 4294 **3.** 908 **5.** 772 **7.** 1600 cubic feet **9.** 4700 cubic feet **11. a.** Higher; the mistaken reading is 9, or 900 cubic feet, higher than the actual reading. **b.** Lower; they already paid for the first 900 cubic feet they use on last month's bill.

Page 266 **Mid–Chapter Review** **1.** About $52.20 **3.** $1.08 **5.** $1.44 **7.** 3470 **9.** 1900 cubic feet **11.** $48.75 **13.** $7.84

Page 267 **Math and Solar Energy** **1.** 19,900; $995; 757; $681.30 **3.** $1,015

Page 269 **Check Your Skills** **1.** $200 **3.** $400 **5.** 15 **7.** 3

Page 269 **Exercises** **1.** About 12 rolls **3.** About 16 rolls **5.** About 11 rolls **7.** About 7 rolls **9.** About $120

Page 270 **Check Your Skills** **1.** No **3.** No **5.** Yes

Page 271 **Exercises** **1.** area of walls **3.** 5 **5.** 44.4 m^2; 58 m^2; 7 **7.** 8 liters **9.** 7 liters **11.** 6 liters of blue and 2 liters of white **13.** $15

Page 273 **Exercises** **1. a.** 5, 8, and 9 square units **b.** 3 units × 3 units **3.** w: 3 yds; ℓ: 4 yds **5.** w: 6 ft; ℓ: 10 ft For Exercises 7 and 9, one strategy is given. Answers may vary. **7. a.** Using estimation **b.** No **9. a.** Solving a simpler problem **b.** $4,000

Page 275 **Consumer's Choice** **1.** $3,989.88 **3.** $7,129.20 **5.** $25,267.27 **7.** Choice 1 **9.** Answers will vary. **11.** Answers will vary.

Page 276 **Telephone Costs** **1.** $9.69 **3.** $18.32

Pages 277–279 **Chapter Review** **1.** thermostat setting **3.** previous meter reading; present meter reading **5.** area **7.** $150 **9.** $0.72 **11.** 710 **13.** 1272 **15.** 1139 **17.** About 9 rolls **19.** 48.36 m^2; 15.12 m^2; 64 m^2; 8 **21.** About $767 **23.** About $2.28 **25.** 1400 cubic feet **27.** 13 rolls **29.** $432

Page 280 **Chapter Test** **1.** About $1,137.50 **3.** $0.96 **5.** 17 cubic feet **7.** 8695 **9.** About 7 liters

Pages 281–282 **Cumulative Maintenance: Chapters 1–11** **1.** a **3.** b **5.** d **7.** c **9.** d **11.** a **13.** d **15.** d **17.** c

CHAPTER 12 BUYING GOODS

Page 285 **Check Your Skills** **1.** 0.33 **3.** 0.30 or 0.3 **5.** 0.05 **7.** $13.15 **9.** $8.40 **11.** $12.99 **13.** $22.75

Page 285 **Exercises** **1.** discount **3.** sale price **5.** $5.96 **7.** $26.25 **9.** $9.60 **11.** $29.66 **13.** The 2–liter bottle

Page 287 **Check Your Skills** **1.** 4 lb 5 oz **3.** 13 lb 8 oz

Pages 288–289 **Exercises** **1.** sales tax; shipping charges **3.** total for goods **5.** $13.22 **7.** $25.83 **9.** 5 **11.** $343.77 **13.** $349.64 **15.** The shipping charges **17. a.** $152.25 **b.** $160.75 **19.** Answers will vary.

Page 291 **Check Your Skills** **1.** 0.015 **3.** 0.0125 **5.** 0.15 **7.** 52.39 **9.** 7.79 **11.** 8.11 **13.** $4.35 **15.** $5.78

Pages 291–292 **Exercises** **1.** previous balance **3.** billing date **5.** finance charge balance; finance charge **7. a.** $121.18 **b.** $1.82 **9. a.** $224.41 **b.** $3.37 **11. a.** $248.06 **b.** $3.72 **13.** $0.39 **15.** $229.08; $3.44; $342.02 **17.** $366.57 **19. a.** Their payments and credits are more than their previous balance. **b.** A credit (overpayment) of $17.88 **c.** Mr. Santos does not owe any money.

Page 293 **Mid–Chapter Review** **1.** $77.65 **3.** $59.28 **5.** $289.87; $4.35 **7.** $420 **9.** $210 **11.** $25,368

Page 294 **Math and Credit** **1.** $486.45; Yes **3.** $2,115.30; No **5.** $37.25

Page 296 **Check Your Skills** **1.** $5.68 **3.** $3.85

Page 296 **Exercises** **1.** new balance **3.** minimum payment **5.** $35.00 **7.** $19.95 **9.** Month 3: $90.22, $1.35, $91.57; Month 4: $91.57, $91.57; His payment for the fourth month will be $91.57.

Page 298 **Check Your Skills** **1.** 0.20 or 0.2 **3.** 0.15 **5.** 0.10 or 0.1 **7.** $\frac{1}{5}$ **9.** $\frac{3}{20}$ **11.** $\frac{1}{8}$ **13.** b **15.** b **17.** a

Pages 298–299 **Exercises** **1.** finance charge **3.** finance charge **5.** $199.60; $798.40 **7.** $311.25; $933.75 **9.** $240.00; $560.00 **11.** $26.56 **13.** $247.14 **15.** $90.12 **17.** $416.50 **19.** c **21. a.** $94.60 **b.** Answers will vary. **c.** Because the monthly payments are less.

Page 301 **Exercises** **1.** $30; $16; $166\frac{2}{3}\%$; $53\frac{1}{3}\%$ **3.** $42; $12; 40%; 10% **5. a.** $15.70 **b.** $1.31 **7.** $532 **9.** $30; $10

Page 303 **Consumer's Choice** **1.** 8 **3.** $79.84 **5.** $103.85 **7.** $110.88 **9.** Yes, the main selection is sent automatically if the order card is not returned. **11.** Answers will vary. **13.** Answers will vary.

Page 304 **Annual Percentage Rate** **1.** 17.00%

Pages 306–307 **Chapter Review** **1.** discount **3.** shipping charges **5.** finance charge balance **7.** $14.25 **9.** $309.52 **11.** $64.55 **13.** $151.81; $2.28; $192.94 **15.** $40.00 **17.** $20.00 **19.** $50.00 **21.** $44.16; $176.64 **23.** $134.31 **25.** $94.71 **27.** 52%

Page 308 **Chapter Test** **1.** $7.44 **3.** $14.59 **5. a.** $324.80 **b.** $4.87 **7.** $177.75; $2.67; $324.62 **9.** $199.86

Pages 309–310 **Cumulative Maintenance: Chapters 1–12** **1.** c **3.** b **5.** b **7.** a **9.** c **11.** d **13.** c **15.** d **17.** d

CHAPTER 13 INVESTING MONEY

Page 313 **Check Your Skills** **1.** 110 **3.** 190 **5.** $181.50 **7.** $308.80 **9.** $1,532 **11.** $9,786

Page 314 **Exercises** **1.** term **3.** cash value; loan value **5.** $169; $845 **7.** $252.20; $1,261 **9.** $260.80; $1,304 **11.** $1,327.50 **13.** $1,960 **15.** $23,526.40 **17.** $6,805.80 **19.** $11,917.20

Page 316 **Check Your Skills** **1.** Yes **3.** No **5.** Yes **7.** Yes

Page 317 **Exercises** **1.** deducted **3.** withdrawal **5.** $84; $216 **7.** $117.60; $62.40 **9.** $1,585.05 **11.** $246.72 **13.** $7,778.88

Page 318 **Check Your Skills** **1.** $6,757.20 **3.** $8,416.80 **5.** $160 **7.** $120 **9.** $40

Page 319 **Exercises** **1.** higher **3.** matured **5. a.** $9,317.70 **b.** $317.70 **7. a.** $2,235.80 **b.** $235.80 **9. a.** $6,257.40 **b.** $257.40 **11.** $5,438.50 **13.** The savings account

Page 320 **Mid–Chapter Review** **1.** $2,282 **3.** $610.80 **5. a.** $16,395 **b.** $1,395 **7. a.** $9,009.60 **b.** $1,009.60 **9. a.** $12,576 **b.** $576 **11.** $1,431 **13.** $146.16

Page 322 **Check Your Skills** **1.** 0.125 **3.** 0.375 **5.** 0.625 **7.** $2,131.25 **9.** $3,281.25

Pages 322–323 **Exercises** **1.** stock **3.** cost of stock **5.** $1,403.60 **7.** $62.85 **9.** $4,930.25 **11. a.** $2,658.70 **b.** $207.85 profit **13. a.** $6,414.10 **b.** $248.20 profit **15.** $5,275.40 **17.** A $66.80 loss

Page 324 **Check Your Skills** **1.** 0.146 **3.** 0.056 **5.** $0.90

Page 325 **Exercises** **1.** dividends **3.** yearly **5.** $552 **7.** $1,400 **9.** $852 **11.** $1,400 **13.** 9.5% **15.** 9.9% **17.** 10.6% **19.** 7.5%

Page 327 **Check Your Skills** **1.** 38.375 **3.** 32.5 **5.** 63.625 **7.** $775 **9.** $811.25 **11.** 0.162 **13.** 0.131

Pages 327–328 **Exercises** **1.** face **3.** two **5.** High: $852.50; Low: $842.50 **7.** High: $945.00; Low: $945.00 **9.** High: $900.00; Low: $895.00 **11.** $3,137.50 **13.** 12.6% **15.** 19.4% **17.** 16.9% **19.** 14.7% **21.** 11.6% **23.** $1,127.50

Page 329 **Math and Savings Bonds** **1.** $25; $28.28 **3.** $250; $154.67 **5.** $32.08 **7. a.** $12 **b.** 6%

Page 331 **Exercises** **1.** 24 **3.** 3.6 **5.** 18% **7.** About 4.8 years **9.** About 12 years **11.** About $4,000

Page 333 **Consumer's Choice** **1.** Choice 1 **3.** $6,240 **5.** Choices 2 and 3; reasons will vary. **7.** The money does not earn any interest. **9.** Whole life insurance has a cash value and a loan value. **11.** The cash value of the policy earns interest which is tax free until the money is withdrawn.

Page 334 **Individual Retirement Account** **1.** Partial **3.** None **5.** $1,300

Pages 336–337 **Chapter Review** **1.** term; whole life; universal life **3.** dividends **5.** face value **7.** \$3,136 **9.** \$5,958.60 **11.** \$1,989.43 **13.** \$1,428 **15.** \$309.27 profit **17.** \$1,739.65 loss **19.** 5.4% **21.** 7.4% **23.** \$630 **25.** \$7,750.75 **27.** 19.0% **29.** \$60,000

Page 338 **Chapter Test** **1.** \$2,116.50 **3.** \$492 **5.** \$118.25 profit **7.** \$168.40 loss **9.** \$487.70 loss **11.** \$797.50

Pages 339–340 **Cumulative Maintenance: Chapters 1–13** **1.** d **3.** b **5.** d **7.** d **9.** a **11.** a **13.** c **15.** a **17.** c **19.** b

CHAPTER 14 BUDGETING MONEY

Pages 342–343 **Check Your Skills** **1.** \$1,850.75 **3.** \$319 **5.** \$558 **7.** 8%

Page 343 **Exercises** **1.** budget **3.** variable **5.** \$179 **7.** \$147 **9.** \$60 **11.** 9%

Page 345 **Check Your Skills** **1.** See circle graph at right. **3.** 25% **5.** $37\frac{1}{2}$% **7.** 20% **9.** 75% **11.** $33\frac{1}{3}$% **13.** 30%

Monthly Budget of a Recreation Center

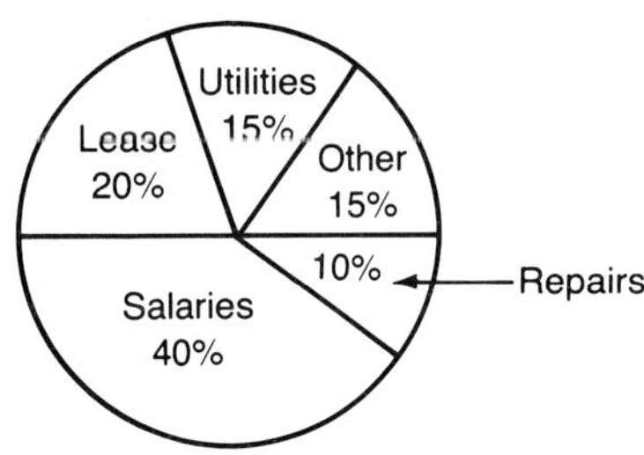

Pages 345–346 **Exercises** **1.** \$720 **3.** \$360 **5.** \$120 **7.** \$630 **9.** \$315 **11.** \$110 **13.** \$84 **15.** \$1,425 **17.** 25%; Below **19.** 10%; Above **21.** 5%; Below **23.** Above; They spent about 30%. **25.** See circle graph at right.

Typical Budget, Girls Ages 16 to 19

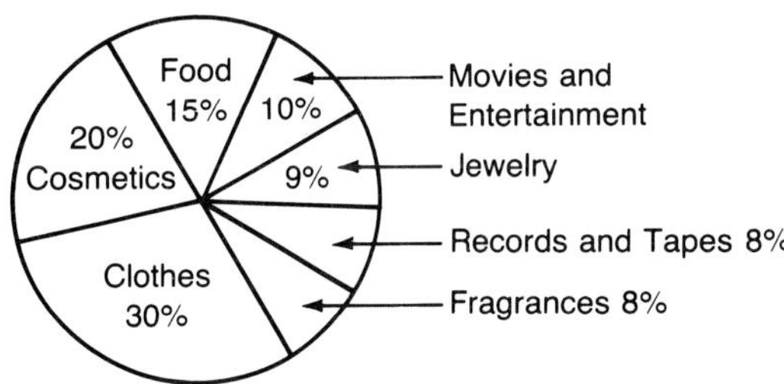

Page 347 **Math and Spending Patterns** **1.** \$15.30 **3.** Food **5.** 10% **7.** \$2,460

Page 348 **Check Your Skills** **1.** \$900 **3.** \$770 **5.** \$1,300 **7.** \$800 **9.** \$864

Page 349 **Exercises** **1.** deductible **3.** maximum **5. a.** \$4,666.50 **b.** \$973.50 **7. a.** \$630 **b.** \$270 **9. a.** \$80 **b.** \$120 **11. a.** \$2,320 **b.** \$780 **13. a.** \$6,240 **b.** \$1,760 **15.** About \$400

Page 350 **Mid-Chapter Review** **1.** \$93 **3.** \$80 **5.** Above **7.** \$212.00 **9.** \$1.80 **11.** 4 pounds

Page 351 **Math and Budgets** **1.** \$360; No **3.** \$392; Yes **5.** No

Page 352 **Check Your Skills** **1.** \$93.75 **3.** \$320 **5.** \$87.50 **7.** \$184

Page 353 Exercises **1.** reduced **3.** $600 **5. a.** Affects monthly budget **b.** Subtracts $75 **7. a.** Affects neither **b.** No change **9. a.** Affects budget **b.** Subtracts $25 **11. a.** Affects budget **b.** Adds $50 **13.** Food: $300; Utilities: $160; Clothing: $91; Recreation: $100; Savings: $190; Miscellaneous: $200; Total: $2,136 **15.** $2,136

Pages 354–355 Exercises **1.** −20 **3.** 40 **5.** Lost $50. **7.** Made $5. **9.** Lost $20. **11. a.** Using estimation **b.** No, he will pay $192.50. **13. a.** Guess and check **b.** $720

Page 357 Consumer's Choice **1.** 21 months **3.** $632.46 **5.** Advantage: No interest must be paid. Disadvantage: It will take 21 months to replace the money in the account. **7.** Choice 3 takes the longest to pay off. **9.** Answers will vary. One answer is that they may wish to keep money in their savings account to use for a down payment on the car.

Page 358 Two Health Insurance Plans **1.** $540 **3.** $685

Pages 359–361 Chapter Review **1.** budget **3.** fixed **5.** $236 **7.** $39 **9.** $900 **11.** $70 **13.** $182 **15.** $540 **17. a.** $640 **b.** $310 **19. a.** $688.50 **b.** $376.50 **21. a.** $960 **b.** $340 **23. a.** $28 **b.** $182 **25.** $42 **27.** $10 less **29.** $1,120 **31.** $259 **33.** Made $19.

Page 362 Chapter Test **1.** $510 **3.** $68 **5.** $82 **7.** $192 **9.** $161

Pages 363–364 Cumulative Maintenance: Chapters 1–14 **1.** a **3.** a **5.** c **7.** b **9.** b **11.** d **13.** b **15.** d

APPENDIX A ADDITIONAL PRACTICE

Page 366 Practice **1.** 112 **3.** 171 **5.** 513 **7.** 1529 **9.** 1477 **11.** 11,732 **13.** 4862 **15.** 9469 **17.** 2417 **19.** 5275 **21.** 160 **23.** 736 **25.** 3502 **27.** 723

Page 367 Practice **1.** 22 **3.** 53 **5.** 27 **7.** 376 **9.** 759 **11.** 49 **13.** 6695 **15.** 2089 **17.** 2182 **19.** 7634 **21.** 1733 **23.** 2499 **25.** 2458 **27.** 4598 **29.** 1889 **31.** 789 **33.** 299 **35.** 4889 **37.** 23 **39.** 344 **41.** 29 **43.** 4439 **45.** 8687 **47.** 568

Page 368 Practice **1.** 38.16 **3.** 68.36 **5.** 526.325 **7.** 265.184 **9.** 190.645 **11.** 306.869 **13.** 108.530 **15.** 127.117 **17.** 320.574 **19.** 370.798 **21.** 91.51 **23.** 129.761 **25.** 59.281 **27.** 227.721 **29.** 403.29

Page 369 Practice **1.** 5.23 **3.** 4.529 **5.** 3.26 **7.** 27.61 **9.** 92.26 **11.** 13.51 **13.** 3.884 **15.** 5.89 **17.** 2.503 **19.** 2.89 **21.** 8.387 **23.** 34.179 **25.** 18.73 **27.** 20.99 **29.** 77.954 **31.** 47.467 **33.** 28.62 **35.** 1.01 **37.** 87.923 **39.** 47.468

Page 370 Practice **1.** 93 **3.** 342 **5.** 252 **7.** 3772 **9.** 15,762 **11.** 1827 **13.** 98,098 **15.** 25,259 **17.** 1863 **19.** 18,879 **21.** 4473 **23.** 211,839 **25.** 32,144 **27.** 6068 **29.** 320,256 **31.** 2176 **33.** 21,812 **35.** 72,030 **37.** 2822 **39.** 53,365 **41.** 9417 **43.** 264,708 **45.** 2268

Page 371 Practice **1.** 1520 **3.** 83,276 **5.** 288,277 **7.** 2520 **9.** 182,781 **11.** 189,744 **13.** 124,836 **15.** 20,880 **17.** 15,782 **19.** 14,587 **21.** 54,270 **23.** 166,221 **25.** 21,627 **27.** 146,718 **29.** 14,889 **31.** 235,936 **33.** 16,362 **35.** 14,000 **37.** 287,144 **39.** 18,685

Page 372 Practice **1.** 16.8 **3.** 105.4 **5.** 0.54 **7.** 14.46 **9.** 388.89 **11.** 8.9121 **13.** 5.0881 **15.** 22.600 **17.** 0.0175 **19.** 0.0119 **21.** 0.05475 **23.** 0.019744 **25.** 0.024447

Page 373 Practice **1.** $<$ **3.** $<$ **5.** $<$ **7.** $<$ **9.** $<$ **11.** $>$ **13.** $<$ **15.** $>$ **17.** $>$ **19.** $<$ **21.** $>$ **23.** $<$ **25.** $<$ **27.** $<$ **29.** 8.063, 8.603, 80.002, 80.009, 80.01 **31.** $\frac{7}{12}, \frac{3}{4}, \frac{5}{6}, \frac{8}{9}$

Page 374 **Practice** **1.** 40 **3.** 90 **5.** 60 **7.** 260 **9.** 440 **11.** 770 **13.** 2610 **15.** 1920 **17.** 5270 **19.** 800 **21.** 400 **23.** 600 **25.** 4900 **27.** 7400 **29.** 8100 **31.** 16,100 **33.** 15,400 **35.** 56,900 **37.** 9000 **39.** 2000 **41.** 6000 **43.** 11,000 **45.** 15,000 **47.** 38,000 **49.** 8000 **51.** 7000 **53.** 49,000

Page 375 **Practice** **1.** 87 **3.** 76 **5.** 703 **7.** 13 **9.** 11 r25 **11.** 72 r6 **13.** 109 r20 **15.** 25 r8 **17.** 65 **19.** 37 r200 **21.** 6 r212 **23.** 19 **25.** 30 r444

Page 376 **Practice** **1.** 4.68 **3.** 1.267 **5.** 0.138 **7.** 0.094 **9.** 6.09 **11.** 0.204 **13.** 3.26 **15.** 2.561 **17.** 0.56 **19.** 0.021 **21.** 0.029 **23.** 0.395 **25.** 3.56 **27.** 0.317 **29.** 0.034 **31.** 0.106

Page 377 **Practice** **1.** 6.2 **3.** 93 **5.** 23 **7.** 576 **9.** 65 **11.** 785 **13.** 2.6 **15.** 1.05 **17.** 1.2 **19.** 3.8 **21.** 85 **23.** 25 **25.** 5.5 **27.** 2.7 **29.** 60 **31.** 130

Page 378 **Practice** **1.** 30 **3.** 26 **5.** 10 **7.** 17 **9.** 11 **11.** 6 **13.** 31.3 **15.** 17.8 **17.** 76.1 **19.** 62.3 **21.** 11.4 **23.** 124.6 **25.** 37.29 **27.** 59.14 **29.** 77.11 **31.** 47.30 **33.** 88.23 **35.** 62.19 **37.** 8.294 **39.** 0.292 **41.** 2.646 **43.** 1.330 **45.** 2.112 **47.** 1.194

Page 379 **Practice** **1.** 18.7 **3.** 1.5 **5.** 3.1 **7.** 3.0 **9.** 4.9 **11.** 9.7 **13.** 36.6 **15.** 7.5 **17.** 1.5 **19.** 1.2 **21.** 1.36 **23.** 1.75 **25.** 7.71 **27.** 3.00 **29.** 0.62 **31.** 40.07 **33.** 2.50 **35.** 6.51 **37.** 1.02 **39.** 1.68

Page 380 **Practice** **1.** b **3.** c **5.** b **7.** c **9.** d **11.** d

Page 381 **Practice** **1.** $1\frac{4}{5}$ **3.** $2\frac{1}{3}$ **5.** $2\frac{2}{5}$ **7.** $2\frac{5}{8}$ **9.** $3\frac{1}{4}$ **11.** $1\frac{9}{11}$ **13.** $1\frac{8}{11}$ **15.** $3\frac{1}{12}$ **17.** $4\frac{13}{21}$ **19.** $2\frac{12}{13}$ **21.** $4\frac{7}{9}$ **23.** $1\frac{5}{6}$ **25.** $1\frac{3}{5}$ **27.** $1\frac{5}{8}$ **29.** $4\frac{4}{15}$ **31.** $7\frac{4}{11}$ **33.** $5\frac{2}{3}$ **35.** $5\frac{1}{4}$ **37.** $4\frac{12}{13}$ **39.** $5\frac{13}{15}$ **41.** $2\frac{7}{11}$ **43.** $3\frac{5}{23}$ **45.** $6\frac{1}{11}$ **47.** $3\frac{11}{17}$ **49.** $3\frac{6}{19}$ **51.** $4\frac{1}{14}$ **53.** $2\frac{21}{31}$ **55.** $3\frac{13}{27}$ **57.** $2\frac{2}{7}$ **59.** $3\frac{7}{9}$ **61.** $6\frac{11}{14}$ **63.** $5\frac{3}{13}$

Page 382 **Practice** **1.** $\frac{1}{3}$ **3.** $\frac{1}{9}$ **5.** $\frac{1}{4}$ **7.** $\frac{4}{15}$ **9.** $\frac{2}{3}$ **11.** $4\frac{1}{6}$ **13.** $\frac{1}{2}$ **15.** $\frac{1}{6}$ **17.** $\frac{2}{3}$ **19.** $2\frac{1}{5}$ **21.** $\frac{1}{3}$ **23.** $1\frac{3}{4}$ **25.** $3\frac{1}{3}$ **27.** $2\frac{1}{9}$ **29.** $\frac{7}{8}$ **31.** $1\frac{1}{3}$ **33.** 5 **35.** $2\frac{1}{2}$ **37.** $\frac{1}{3}$ **39.** $\frac{49}{72}$ **41.** $\frac{1}{6}$ **43.** $\frac{1}{2}$ **45.** $2\frac{1}{3}$ **47.** 2 **49.** $\frac{1}{3}$ **51.** $\frac{1}{19}$ **53.** $2\frac{4}{5}$ **55.** $1\frac{7}{12}$ **57.** $1\frac{1}{15}$ **59.** $1\frac{1}{10}$ **61.** $\frac{3}{5}$ **63.** $\frac{8}{99}$

Page 383 **Practice** **1.** $\frac{3}{4}$ **3.** $\frac{4}{7}$ **5.** $\frac{7}{13}$ **7.** 1 **9.** $\frac{1}{5}$ **11.** $\frac{1}{7}$ **13.** $\frac{1}{2}$ **15.** $\frac{1}{2}$ **17.** $\frac{3}{5}$ **19.** $\frac{1}{5}$ **21.** $\frac{1}{2}$ **23.** $\frac{3}{4}$ **25.** $\frac{5}{7}$ **27.** $\frac{2}{3}$ **29.** $\frac{1}{3}$ **31.** $\frac{6}{7}$ **33.** $\frac{3}{8}$

Page 384 **Practice** **1.** 6 **3.** 8 **5.** 12 **7.** 12 **9.** 16 **11.** 28 **13.** 14 **15.** 36 **17.** 28 **19.** 42 **21.** $\frac{3}{6}; \frac{4}{6}$ **23.** $\frac{9}{12}; \frac{8}{12}$ **25.** $\frac{21}{48}; \frac{12}{48}$ **27.** $\frac{5}{12}; \frac{9}{12}$ **29.** $\frac{14}{21}; \frac{12}{21}$ **31.** $\frac{8}{20}; \frac{15}{20}$ **33.** $\frac{32}{36}; \frac{15}{36}$ **35.** $\frac{34}{50}; \frac{15}{50}$

Page 385 **Practice** **1.** $\frac{7}{8}$ **3.** $1\frac{2}{5}$ **5.** $\frac{7}{18}$ **7.** $\frac{23}{24}$ **9.** $\frac{19}{24}$ **11.** $\frac{23}{30}$ **13.** $\frac{7}{8}$ **15.** $1\frac{1}{18}$ **17.** $1\frac{2}{15}$ **19.** $1\frac{13}{20}$ **21.** $1\frac{8}{21}$ **23.** $\frac{5}{6}$ **25.** $1\frac{1}{6}$ **27.** $\frac{19}{45}$ **29.** $\frac{5}{8}$ **31.** $1\frac{4}{15}$ **33.** $1\frac{5}{24}$ **35.** $\frac{11}{18}$ **37.** $\frac{7}{10}$ **39.** $\frac{9}{10}$ **41.** $1\frac{5}{24}$ **43.** $\frac{3}{4}$ **45.** $1\frac{1}{8}$ **47.** $\frac{11}{16}$

Page 386 **Practice** **1.** $7\frac{2}{15}$ **3.** $9\frac{9}{20}$ **5.** $9\frac{5}{18}$ **7.** $5\frac{3}{4}$ **9.** $6\frac{11}{24}$ **11.** $5\frac{17}{21}$ **13.** $8\frac{1}{6}$ **15.** $6\frac{1}{24}$ **17.** $6\frac{13}{20}$ **19.** $3\frac{5}{8}$ **21.** $1\frac{37}{40}$ **23.** $7\frac{11}{30}$ **25.** $8\frac{1}{8}$ **27.** $9\frac{43}{48}$ **29.** $5\frac{1}{2}$ **31.** $2\frac{11}{24}$ **33.** $22\frac{1}{10}$ **35.** $53\frac{23}{40}$ **37.** $3\frac{19}{22}$ **39.** $7\frac{1}{10}$ **41.** $22\frac{5}{8}$

Page 387 **Practice** **1.** $\frac{4}{15}$ **3.** $\frac{7}{45}$ **5.** $\frac{7}{39}$ **7.** $\frac{1}{2}$ **9.** $\frac{16}{35}$ **11.** $\frac{11}{28}$ **13.** $2\frac{13}{72}$ **15.** $4\frac{5}{21}$ **17.** $4\frac{5}{12}$ **19.** $8\frac{1}{2}$ **21.** $8\frac{7}{20}$ **23.** $5\frac{1}{6}$ **25.** $3\frac{1}{6}$ **27.** $2\frac{1}{3}$ **29.** $4\frac{2}{15}$ **31.** $\frac{7}{18}$ **33.** $1\frac{17}{36}$ **35.** $\frac{1}{4}$ **37.** $3\frac{1}{12}$ **39.** $2\frac{1}{6}$ **41.** $6\frac{1}{15}$ **43.** $\frac{2}{5}$

Page 388 **Practice** **1.** $1\frac{7}{8}$ **3.** $2\frac{3}{4}$ **5.** $\frac{11}{12}$ **7.** $\frac{13}{36}$ **9.** $2\frac{17}{20}$ **11.** $3\frac{10}{21}$ **13.** $2\frac{5}{6}$ **15.** $2\frac{11}{12}$ **17.** $12\frac{11}{20}$ **19.** $4\frac{1}{3}$ **21.** $3\frac{7}{9}$ **23.** $7\frac{7}{8}$ **25.** $1\frac{35}{36}$ **27.** $13\frac{47}{60}$ **29.** $3\frac{3}{4}$ **31.** $2\frac{59}{72}$ **33.** $1\frac{3}{5}$ **35.** $2\frac{1}{2}$

Page 389 **Practice** **1.** $\frac{1}{15}$ **3.** $\frac{10}{21}$ **5.** $\frac{7}{30}$ **7.** $\frac{1}{16}$ **9.** $\frac{18}{65}$ **11.** $\frac{33}{160}$ **13.** $\frac{12}{35}$ **15.** $\frac{9}{20}$ **17.** $\frac{1}{21}$ **19.** $\frac{3}{14}$ **21.** $\frac{1}{42}$ **23.** $\frac{5}{56}$ **25.** $\frac{2}{13}$ **27.** $\frac{16}{45}$ **29.** $\frac{1}{14}$ **31.** $\frac{4}{7}$ **33.** $\frac{7}{15}$ **35.** $\frac{1}{12}$ **37.** $\frac{5}{18}$ **39.** $\frac{1}{14}$ **41.** $\frac{3}{8}$ **43.** $\frac{1}{3}$ **45.** $\frac{4}{7}$ **47.** $\frac{5}{28}$ **49.** $\frac{3}{20}$

Page 390 **Practice** **1.** $\frac{39}{8}$ **3.** $\frac{41}{8}$ **5.** $\frac{47}{7}$ **7.** $\frac{9}{4}$ **9.** $\frac{29}{7}$ **11.** $\frac{21}{8}$ **13.** $\frac{19}{4}$ **15.** $17\frac{1}{2}$ **17.** $22\frac{1}{5}$ **19.** $13\frac{7}{8}$ **21.** 6 **23.** $1\frac{1}{3}$ **25.** 88 **27.** $3\frac{1}{7}$ **29.** $5\frac{11}{16}$ **31.** $62\frac{1}{3}$ **33.** 1

Page 391 **Practice** **1.** $\frac{3}{2}$ **3.** $\frac{7}{9}$ **5.** $\frac{1}{4}$ **7.** $\frac{7}{6}$ **9.** $\frac{1}{15}$ **11.** $\frac{2}{3}$ **13.** $\frac{13}{8}$ **15.** $\frac{13}{6}$ **17.** $\frac{3}{4}$ **19.** $2\frac{2}{7}$ **21.** $\frac{1}{20}$ **23.** 24 **25.** $1\frac{1}{4}$ **27.** 14 **29.** $1\frac{1}{2}$ **31.** $\frac{7}{10}$ **33.** 12 **35.** $\frac{1}{44}$ **37.** 2 **39.** 81 **41.** $\frac{4}{5}$ **43.** 54 **45.** 1 **47.** $\frac{10}{11}$ **49.** $\frac{2}{3}$ **51.** 16 **53.** $\frac{2}{3}$ **55.** 5

Page 392 **Practice** **1.** $\frac{16}{37}$ **3.** $\frac{10}{41}$ **5.** $\frac{8}{13}$ **7.** $\frac{3}{5}$ **9.** $\frac{2}{3}$ **11.** $\frac{4}{15}$ **13.** $\frac{8}{41}$ **15.** $\frac{8}{13}$ **17.** $\frac{1}{2}$ **19.** 2 **21.** $\frac{2}{5}$ **23.** $2\frac{1}{2}$ **25.** 3 **27.** $16\frac{2}{5}$ **29.** 8 **31.** $1\frac{6}{13}$ **33.** 9 **35.** $1\frac{5}{6}$ **37.** 10 **39.** $\frac{2}{3}$ **41.** $\frac{2}{3}$ **43.** 6 **45.** $\frac{4}{7}$ **47.** $7\frac{3}{4}$ **49.** 8 **51.** $1\frac{10}{11}$ **53.** $3\frac{2}{3}$ **55.** $2\frac{4}{15}$ **57.** $7\frac{1}{2}$ **59.** $\frac{1}{3}$ **61.** $\frac{1}{15}$

Page 393 **Practice** **1.** 3 **3.** 2 **5.** 16 **7.** 12 **9.** 4 **11.** 6 **13.** 5 **15.** 4 **17.** 6 **19.** 4 **21.** 3 **23.** c **25.** c **27.** d **29.** b

Page 394 **Practice** **1.** 5 **3.** 9 **5.** 19 **7.** 7 **9.** 12 **11.** 5 **13.** 15 **15.** 35 **17.** 15 **19.** 35 **21.** 13 **23.** 38 **25.** 6 **27.** 17 **29.** 24 **31.** 66 **33.** 45 **35.** 62 **37.** 9 **39.** 79 **41.** 2.2 **43.** 3.8 **45.** 3.6 **47.** 4.1

Page 395 **Practice** **1.** 17 **3.** 11 **5.** 37 **7.** 39 **9.** 88 **11.** 28 **13.** 55 **15.** 91 **17.** 87 **19.** 102 **21.** 109 **23.** 90 **25.** 24 **27.** 30 **29.** 84 **31.** 90 **33.** 52 **35.** 154 **37.** 9.3 **39.** 9.6 **41.** 14.3 **43.** 13.0 **45.** 17.1 **47.** 9.0

Page 396 **Practice** **1.** 6 **3.** 8 **5.** 5 **7.** 164 **9.** 14 **11.** 2 **13.** 4 **15.** 5 **17.** 2 **19.** 4 **21.** 9 **23.** 20 **25.** 2 **27.** 23 **29.** 4 **31.** 20 **33.** 5 **35.** 6 **37.** 8 **39.** 7 **41.** 12 **43.** 9 **45.** 12 **47.** 8.1

Page 397 **Practice** **1.** 14 **3.** 100 **5.** 160 **7.** 150 **9.** 55 **11.** 80 **13.** 72 **15.** 40 **17.** 87 **19.** 544 **21.** 84 **23.** 91 **25.** 175 **27.** 88 **29.** 234 **31.** 288 **33.** 420 **35.** 190 **37.** 104 **39.** 121 **41.** 2.6 **43.** 37 **45.** 23.1 **47.** 56.1

Page 398 **Practice** **1.** 2 **3.** 10 **5.** 7 **7.** 16 **9.** 5 **11.** 5 **13.** 5 **15.** 25 **17.** 1.3 **19.** 1.6 **21.** 3.1 **23.** 5

Page 399 **Practice** **1.** 18 **3.** 80 **5.** 6 **7.** 80 **9.** 24 **11.** 42 **13.** 16 **15.** 200 **17.** 441 **19.** 1 **21.** 8 **23.** 4

Page 400 **Practice** **1.** $\frac{5}{9}$ **3.** $\frac{2}{5}$ **5.** $\frac{2}{5}$ **7.** $\frac{4}{3}$ **9.** $\frac{2}{7}$ **11.** $\frac{1}{3}$ **13.** $\frac{6}{19}$ **15.** $\frac{4}{3}$ **17.** $\frac{1}{9}$ **19.** $\frac{1}{11}$ **21.** $\frac{1}{9}$ **23.** $\frac{1}{8}$ **25.** $\frac{1}{5}$ **27.** $\frac{1}{1}$ **29.** $\frac{1}{14}$ **31.** $\frac{4}{1}$ **33.** $\frac{1}{2}$ **35.** $\frac{1}{4}$ **37.** $\frac{1}{4}$ **39.** $\frac{5}{1}$ **41.** $\frac{1}{3}$ **43.** $\frac{1}{7}$ **45.** $\frac{1}{4}$ **47.** $\frac{3}{10}$ **49.** $\frac{7}{1}$ **51.** $\frac{3}{22}$ **53.** $\frac{1}{5}$ **55.** $\frac{7}{2}$ **57.** $\frac{3}{5}$ **59.** $\frac{2}{1}$

Page 401 **Practice** **1.** Yes **3.** Yes **5.** No **7.** Yes **9.** No **11.** No **13.** Yes **15.** Yes **17.** Yes **19.** Yes **21.** No **23.** Yes **25.** Yes **27.** No **29.** Yes **31.** Yes **33.** No **35.** No

Page 402 **Practice** **1.** 1 **3.** 1 **5.** 3 **7.** 6 **9.** 12 **11.** 15 **13.** 1 **15.** 3 **17.** 1 **19.** 13 **21.** 3 **23.** 18 **25.** 8 **27.** 60 **29.** 56 **31.** 40 **33.** 39 **35.** 50

Page 403 **Practice** **1.** 0.36 **3.** 0.85 **5.** 0.34 **7.** 0.25 **9.** 0.46 **11.** 0.83 **13.** 0.44 **15.** 0.98 **17.** 0.51 **19.** 0.56 **21.** 0.73 **23.** 0.53 **25.** 0.06 **27.** 0.04 **29.** 0.03 **31.** 1.21 **33.** 3.73 **35.** 1.29 **37.** 0.71 **39.** 0.07 **41.** 0.52 **43.** 0.35 **45.** 2.08 **47.** 1.38 **49.** $0.33\frac{1}{3}$ **51.** $0.16\frac{2}{3}$ **53.** $0.11\frac{1}{9}$ **55.** $0.66\frac{2}{3}$ **57.** $0.62\frac{1}{2}$ **59.** $0.75\frac{1}{2}$

Page 404 **Practice** **1.** $\frac{19}{100}$ **3.** $\frac{37}{100}$ **5.** $\frac{1}{2}$ **7.** $\frac{3}{10}$ **9.** $\frac{1}{4}$ **11.** $\frac{3}{4}$ **13.** $\frac{21}{50}$ **15.** $\frac{14}{25}$ **17.** $\frac{12}{25}$ **19.** $\frac{13}{20}$ **21.** $\frac{39}{50}$ **23.** $\frac{7}{50}$ **25.** $\frac{2}{5}$ **27.** $\frac{1}{2}$ **29.** $\frac{49}{100}$ **31.** $\frac{79}{100}$ **33.** $\frac{4}{25}$ **35.** $\frac{47}{100}$ **37.** $\frac{99}{100}$ **39.** $\frac{51}{100}$ **41.** $\frac{11}{25}$ **43.** $\frac{1}{300}$ **45.** $\frac{1}{800}$ **47.** $\frac{1}{1000}$ **49.** $\frac{1}{150}$ **51.** $\frac{2}{3}$ **53.** $\frac{5}{8}$

Page 405 **Practice** **1.** 37% **3.** 32% **5.** 41% **7.** 28% **9.** 91% **11.** 33% **13.** 4% **15.** 3% **17.** 15% **19.** 132% **21.** 1102% **23.** 715% **25.** 22.4% **27.** 57.5% **29.** 44.3% **31.** 134.6% **33.** 719.9% **35.** 326.4% **37.** 0.2% **39.** 0.5% **41.** 200.8% **43.** $37\frac{1}{2}\%$ **45.** $62\frac{1}{2}\%$ **47.** $66\frac{2}{3}\%$ **49.** $28\frac{1}{4}\%$ **51.** $44\frac{5}{8}\%$ **53.** $27\frac{1}{4}\%$ **55.** $17\frac{1}{5}\%$ **57.** $45\frac{3}{8}\%$ **59.** $19\frac{2}{3}\%$ **61.** $5\frac{4}{5}\%$ **63.** $36\frac{3}{5}\%$ **65.** $76\frac{1}{4}\%$

Page 406 **Practice** **1.** 30% **3.** 8% **5.** 36% **7.** 60% **9.** 25% **11.** 25% **13.** 90% **15.** 55% **17.** 20% **19.** 65% **21.** 66% **23.** 30% **25.** $66\frac{2}{3}\%$ **27.** $58\frac{1}{3}\%$ **29.** $2\frac{1}{2}\%$ **31.** $8\frac{1}{3}\%$ **33.** $14\frac{2}{7}\%$ **35.** $22\frac{2}{9}\%$ **37.** $33\frac{1}{3}\%$ **39.** $18\frac{3}{4}\%$ **41.** $43\frac{3}{4}\%$ **43.** 390% **45.** 815% **47.** 580% **49.** $283\frac{1}{3}\%$ **51.** $562\frac{1}{2}\%$ **53.** $1212\frac{1}{2}\%$ **55.** 420% **57.** 570% **59.** 380%

Page 407 **Practice** **1.** 44.1 **3.** 4 **5.** 16.8 **7.** 5.5 **9.** 19 **11.** 3.32 **13.** 50.4 **15.** 8.4 **17.** 1 **19.** 3 **21.** 4.32 **23.** 8.82 **25.** 42.5 **27.** 140 **29.** 1.616 **31.** 11.7 **33.** 87 **35.** 105

Page 408 **Practice** **1.** 27 **3.** 21 **5.** 11 **7.** 24 **9.** 80 **11.** 19 **13.** 30 **15.** 56 **17.** 10 **19.** 60 **21.** 24 **23.** 20 **25.** 9 **27.** 9 **29.** 21 **31.** 3

Page 409 **Practice** **1.** $n \times 20 = 14$ **3.** $20 = n \times 80$ **5.** 75% **7.** 40% **9.** $12\frac{1}{2}\%$ **11.** $66\frac{2}{3}\%$ **13.** 20% **15.** 25% **17.** $12\frac{1}{2}\%$

Page 410 **Practice** **1.** $60 = 0.25 \times n$ **3.** $5 = 0.10 \times n$ **5.** 45 **7.** 15 **9.** 20 **11.** 300 **13.** 550 **15.** 56 **17.** 250 **19.** 450 **21.** 120

Page 411 **Practice** **1.** $15 = \frac{1}{3} \times n$ **3.** $9 = \frac{1}{8} \times n$ **5.** 18 **7.** 730 **9.** 64 **11.** 102 **13.** 72 **15.** 32 **17.** 42 **19.** $16\frac{2}{3}$ **21.** 96

Page 412 **Practice** **1.** a **3.** c **5.** b **7.** b **9.** a

Page 413 **Practice** **1.** 80 **3.** $2\frac{1}{2}$ **5.** 4 **7.** 12 **9.** 2 **11.** 10,560 **13.** 2 **15.** 21,120 **17.** 24 **19.** $3\frac{1}{2}$ **21.** 3 **23.** 21

Page 414 **Practice** **1.** $6\frac{1}{3}$ ft **3.** $10\frac{3}{8}$ lb **5.** $14\frac{1}{4}$ gal **7.** $9\frac{2}{3}$ yd **9.** $8\frac{1}{2}$ ft **11.** $6\frac{1}{2}$ gal **13.** $4\frac{3}{4}$ hr **15.** $3\frac{1}{3}$ yd **17.** $8\frac{1}{6}$ yd **19.** $3\frac{1}{4}$ gal **21.** $1\frac{1}{2}$ mi **23.** 2 yd

Page 415 **Practice** **1.** a **3.** b **5.** c **7.** 0.346 **9.** 500 **11.** 0.064 **13.** 28,000

Page 416 **Practice** **1.** 8.8 cm **3.** 95 mm **5.** 159 cm

Page 417 **Practice** **1.** 116 cm **3.** 50 cm **5.** 60 m **7.** 32.8 m **9.** 84 cm **11.** 20.4 m

Page 418 **Practice** **1.** a **3.** b **5.** 25,000 **7.** 4200 **9.** 0.0038 **11.** 6000 **13.** 7600 **15.** 0.00481 **17.** 28,000 **19.** 2210 **21.** 0.025

Page 419 **Practice** **1.** c **3.** a **5.** 37,000 **7.** 229,000 **9.** 5800 **11.** 0.386 **13.** 2.478 **15.** 0.0072 **17.** 40 **19.** 0.021

Page 420 **Practice** **1.** 10,500 mm^2 **3.** 17.64 m^2 **5.** 4.5 cm^2 **7.** 80 cm^2 **9.** 450 mm^2 **11.** 648 mm^2 **13.** 454.92 cm^2

Page 421 **Practice** **1.** 11,020 cm^3 **3.** 6480 cm^3 **5.** 1575 cm^3 **7.** 512 m^3 **9.** 27.216 m^3 **11.** 73.6 m^3 **13.** 3.192 m^3

Page 422 **Practice** **1.** c **3.** a **5.** b **7.** b **9.** b **11.** No **13.** The heat

APPENDIX B CALCULATOR MANUAL

Page 425 **Try These** **1.** 1,654,566 **3.** 2,305,672

Page 426 **Try These** **1.** $17,500 **3.** 1040 **5.** 3205

Page 427 **Try These** **1.** $13.82; $6.18

Page 428 **Try These** **1.** 270 **3.** 51 **5.** 50,625 **7.** 15,625

Page 429 **Try These** **1.** 149.85 **3.** 289.15 **5.** 30.75 **7.** $644,129.77

Page 430 **Try These** **1.** 8100; 7917 **3.** 900; 924 **5.** 5600; 5712 **7.** 39,000; 37,294 **9.** 91,000; 83,094 **11.** 140,000; 155,952 **13.** 640; 655.7 **15.** 270; 302.6 **17.** 240; 220.4 **19.** 5400; 5760.3 **21.** 7700; 7544.2 **23.** 21,000; 21,751.2

Page 431 **Try These** **1.** 127,715,082 **3.** 256,546,917 **5.** 215,123,197 **7.** 1,250,070,578 **9.** 1,136,801,148 **11.** 2,458,669,837 **13.** 1,234,554,321 **15.** 9,096,218,057

Page 432 **Try These** **1.** 1682 **3.** 924.53 **5.** 578,551.82 **7.** 382,233.917 **9.** 500,904.2 **11.** 0.0324 **13.** 0.0002835 **15.** 2.02677636 **17.** 0.0000000663

Page 433 **Try These** **1.** 6040 **3.** 546 r11

Page 434 **Try These** **1.** 0.3875 **3.** 0.70625 **5.** 0.575 **7.** 0.785 **9.** 4.614 **11.** 0.7890625 **13.** 0.921875 **15.** $0.9\overline{3}$ **17.** $0.\overline{81}$ **19.** $0.6\overline{3}$ **21.** $0.\overline{7}$ **23.** 0.425 **25.** $0.\overline{36}$ **27.** $0.\overline{36}$ **29.** 5.3125

Page 435 **Try These** **1.** Yes **3.** No **5.** No **7.** 60 **9.** 184 **11.** 138 **13.** 576 **15.** 115.2 **17.** 17 **19.** 5.24

Page 436 **Try These** **1.** 238 **3.** 12.87

Page 437 **Try These** **1.** \$5,634.13 **3.** \$4,042.05 **5.** \$5,224.36 **7.** \$10,982.06

Page 438 **Try These** **1.** 3375 **3.** 262,144 **5.** 1,481,544 **7.** 41,781,923 **9.** 69,343,957 **11.** 34.328125 **13.** 69.7225 **15.** 941.192 **17.** 7.0710678 **19.** 8.8881944 **21.** 10.6301 **23.** 17.8045 **25.** 5.56777 **27.** 31.6228 **29.** 7.1

Page 439 **Try These** **1.** −21 **3.** −89 **5.** 110 **7.** −24 **9.** 0 **11.** 0 **13.** 12 **15.** 17 **17.** −136 **19.** 134 **21.** 0 **23.** 58 **25.** 129 **27.** −72 **29.** 160 **31.** 4600 **33.** 441 **35.** 1150 **37.** −1596 **39.** −848 **41.** −15 **43.** 87 **45.** 34 **47.** −63 **49.** 14 **51.** −34

Key: (t) top, (c) center, (b) bottom, (l) left, (r) right.

COVER PHOTOS: (tl), Ann Rippy/The Image Bank; (tc), HBJ Photo/Blaise Zito Associates; (tr), HBJ Photo; (c), Cindy Lewis/The Stock Market; (cr), Cindy Lewis/The Stock Market; (bl), C. D. Luria/FPG; (bc), Murray Alcosser/The Image Bank; (br), Chris Jones/The Stock Market.

PICTURE CREDITS: pages 1 (l), Lou Jones/The Image Bank; (r), Steve Niedorf/The Image Bank; 4, Audrey Gottlieb/Monkmeyer Press Photo Service; 9, Lawrence Fried/The Image Bank; 11, Strix Pix (David S. Strickler)/Monkmeyer Press Photo Service; 12, Chuck Place/The Image Bank; 14 (t), Zao-Longfield/The Image Bank; (b), Peter C. Poulides/Manhattan Views; 15 (t), Rhoda Sidney/Monkmeyer Press Photo Service; (b), Tim Bieber/The Image Bank; 21 (t), John Lei/Stock, Boston; (b), Brian Brake/Photo Researchers; 25, HBJ Photo/Earl Kogler; 31, Hugh Rogers/Monkmeyer Press Photo Service; 41, HBJ Photo; 47, Tom Burnside/Photo Researchers; 52, HBJ Photo; 53, Gary Cralle/The Image Bank; 57, HBJ Photo; 58, HBJ Photo; 61 (l), HBJ Photo; (c), HBJ Photo; (r), HBJ Photo; 62, B. I. Ullmann/Taurus Photos; 65, HBJ Photo; 69, Murray Alcosser/The Image Bank; 73, Victoria Arlak/Merritt Productions; 74, HBJ Photo; 82, HBJ Photo/Blaise Zito Associates; 85, Mark Sherman/Manhattan Views; 86, HBJ Photo; 88, HBJ Photo; 91, HBJ Photo/Rodney Jones; 95, Gabe Palmer/The Stock Market; 102, HBJ Photo; 105 (t), HBJ Photo; (b), HBJ Photo; 108, Jeff Smith/The Image Bank; 109, HBJ Photo; 114, Bill Varie/The Image Bank; 116 (l), Murray Alcosser/The Image Bank; (r), Henri Dauman/Kay Reese & Associates; 117, HBJ Photo; 125 (t), David W. Hamilton/The Image Bank; (c), Butch Martin/The Image Bank; (b), National Automobile Transporters Association; 128, HBJ Photo; 129, H. Armstrong Roberts; 135, B. I. Ullmann/Taurus Photos; 137, Michael & Elvan Habicht/Taurus Photos; 139, HBJ Photo/Blaise Zito Associates; 140 (t), David W. Hamilton/The Image Bank; (bl), Grant V. Faint/The Image Bank; (br), Butch Martin/The Image Bank; 141, HBJ Photo; 142 (t), HBJ Photo; (c), HBJ Photo; (b), HBJ Photo/Beverly Brosius; 143, HBJ Photo/Beverly Brosius; 151, Ted Kawalerski/The Image Bank; 152, HBJ Photo; 154, J. McNee/FPG; 158, HBJ Photo; 161, HBJ Photo; 162, HBJ Photo/Blaise Zito Associates; 165, HBJ Photo; 168 (tl), Ken Biggs/The Stock Market; (tr), HBJ Photo/Earl Kogler; (b), Cindy Lewis/The Stock Market; 169, HBJ Photo/Earl Kogler; 170, HBJ Photo; 172, HBJ Photo/Blaise Zito Associates; 173, HBJ Photo; 177 (tl), Ron Glazer/Photo Researchers; (r), James R. Fisher/Photo Researchers; (bl), Gary Cralle/The Image Bank; 179, Peter Henschel/Shostal Associates; 180, HBJ Photo; 181 (t), Langley Research Center/NASA; (b), Lawrence V. Smith/DPI; 182, Jack Fields/Photo Researchers; 186, HBJ Photo/Earl Kogler; 188, HBJ Photo/Blaise Zito Associates; 189, H. Wendelr/The Image Bank; 190 (tr), HBJ Photo; 191 (l), HBJ Photo/Rodney Jones; (c), HBJ Photo/Gary Slack; (r), HBJ Photo; 192, Peter Beck/Manhattan Views; 194 (l), HBJ Photo; (r), Lowell Georgia/Photo Researchers; 195 (t), HBJ Photo; (b), HBJ Photo/Blaise Zito Associates; 196, HBJ Photo; 199, Al Hamden/The Image Bank; 200, Paul Conklin/Monkmeyer Press Photo Service; 202, HBJ Photo, 212, HBJ Photo; 213, HBJ Photo; 216, Lou Jones/The Image Bank; 218, Steve Niedorf/The Image Bank; 220, HBJ Photo/Rodney Jones; 221 (l), HBJ Photo; (lc), HBJ Photo; (rc), HBJ Photo; (r), HBJ Photo; 225, Dan Hummel/The Image Bank; 226, Al Satterwhite/The Image Bank; 229 (tl), Robert Kristofik/TThe Image Bank; (r), Eric Carle/Shostal Associates; (bl), George Haling/Photo Researchers; 231, HBJ Photo; 232, HBJ Photo; 235, Robert Kristofik/The Image Bank; 236 (l), Ellis Herwig/Stock, Boston; (r), Elaine Wicks/Taurus Photos; 237 (t), Murray Alcosser/The Image Bank; (b), Steve Niedorf/The Image Bank; 239, Mimi Forsysth/Monkmeyer Press Photo Service; 242, DPI; 245, Susan Van Etten/Taurus Photos; 249 (tl), HBJ Photo; (tc), HBJ Photo; (tr), HBJ Photo; (b), HBJ Photo; 253, Charles Gupton/Stock, Boston; 257 (t), Edward Lettau/Photo Researchers; (b), John V. A. F. Neal/Photo Researchers; 261 HBJ Photo/Rodney Jones; 263 Phoebe Dunn/DPI; 266, Jeff Smith/The Image Bank; 267, HBJ Photo; 269, Steve Niedorf/The Image Bank; 270, HBJ Photo/Earl Kogler; 272, HBJ Photo/Rodney Jones; 273, HBJ Photo/David & Linda Phillips; 274 (l), William Rivelli/The Image Bank; (r), HBJ Photo; 275, HBJ Photo/Beverly Brosius; 279, John Lei/Stock, Boston; 280, Coco McCoy/Rainbow; 283 (tl), Lily Solmssen/Photo Researchers; (r), William Rivelli/The Image Bank; (bl), Alvis Upitis/The Image Bank; 288, Gregory Heisler/The Image Bank; 289, HBJ Photo/Earl Kogler; 292, Paul Conklin/Monkmeyer Press Photo Service; 294, HBJ Photo/David Phillips; 297, Ben Rose/The Image Bank; 299 (l), Hank Morgan/Rainbow; (r), Gary Gladstone/The Image Bank; 300, HBJ Photo; 301, HBJ Photo; 302, HBJ Photo; 311, Murray Alcosser/The Image Bank; 319, Hugh Rogers/Monkmeyer Press Photo Service; 324, Robert Kristofik/The Image Bank; 328 (t), Charles Marden/Taurus Photos; (b), Wolf von dem Bussche/The Image Bank; 329, HBJ Photo/David Phillips; 332, Ken Biggs/The Stock Market; 333, Greg Mancuso/Stock, Boston; 341, Murray Alcosser/The Image Bank; 343, HBJ Photo; 346, Rick Kopstein/Monkmeyer Press Photo Service; 347, HBJ Photo/Rodney Jones; 348, John Lei/Stock, Boston; 349, H. Armstrong Roberts; 351, HBJ Photo/Rodney Jones; 353, Blair Seitz/Photo Researchers; 354, Michael Melford/The Image Bank; 356 (l), Ted Horowitz/The Stock Market; (r) HBJ Photo/Ron Kunzman; 357, HBJ Photo/Ron Kunzman; 358, HBJ Photo/Rodney Jones; 361, Robert Motzjin/The Stock Shop; 362 (l), Junebug Clark/Photo Researchers; (r), Richard Hutchings/Photo Researchers.

B 8
C 9
D 0
E 1
F 2
G 3
H 4
I 5
J 6